The Community of Sierpc - Memorial Book (Sierpc, Poland)

Translation of *Kehilat Sierpc; Sefer Zikaron*

Memorial Book in Yiddish and Hebrew

Published in Tel Aviv, 1959

Edited by: E. Talmi (Wloka)

English Edition Translation Coordinated and Edited by:
Sandra Krisch
Dorothy Kerzner Lipsky

Translated from the Yiddish by Jerrold Landau
Translated from the Hebrew by Alex Weingarten

Published by JewishGen

An Affiliate of the Museum of Jewish Heritage - A Living Memorial to the Holocaust
New York

Memorial (Yizkor) Book of the Community of Sierpc, Poland
Translation of *Kehilat Sierpc; Sefer Zikaron*

First Printing: November 2014, Heshvan 5775
Second Printing: March 2019, Adar II 5779

Translation Project Coordinators and Editors:
Sandra Krisch and Dorothy Kerzner Lipsky
Translators: Jerrold Landau (Yiddish) and Alex Weingarten (Hebrew)
Layout: Lynn Mercer and Joel Alpert
Cover Design: Jan R. Fine
Yiddish and Hebrew Consultant: Josef Rosin
Indexing: Jonathan Wind

Published by JewishGen, Inc.
An Affiliate of the Museum of Jewish Heritage
A Living Memorial to the Holocaust
36 Battery Place, New York, NY 10280

Printed in the United States of America by Lightning Source, Inc.

Library of Congress Control Number (LCCN): 2014951761
ISBN: 978-1-939561-24-4 (hard cover: 858 pages, alk. paper)

Front Cover: Artwork from the title page of the original Sierpc Yizkor book

JewishGen and the Yizkor-Books-in-Print Project

This book has been published by the **Yizkor-Books-in-Print Project,** as part of the **Yizkor Book Project** of **JewishGen, Inc**.

JewishGen, Inc. is a non-profit organization founded in 1987 as a resource for Jewish genealogy. Its website [www.jewishgen.org] serves as an international clearinghouse and resource center to assist individuals who are researching the history of their Jewish families and the places where they lived. JewishGen provides databases, facilitates discussion groups, and coordinates projects relating to Jewish genealogy and the history of the Jewish people. In 2003, JewishGen became an affiliate of the **Museum of Jewish Heritage - A Living Memorial to the Holocaust** in New York.

The **JewishGen Yizkor Book Project** was organized to make more widely known the existence of Yizkor (Memorial) Books written by survivors and former residents of various Jewish communities throughout the world. Later, volunteers connected to the different destroyed communities began cooperating to have these books translated from the original language—usually Hebrew or Yiddish—into English, thus enabling a wider audience to have access to the valuable information contained within them. As each chapter of these books was translated, it was posted on the JewishGen website and made available to the general public.

The **Yizkor-Books-in-Print Project** began in 2011 as an initiative to print and publish Yizkor Books that had been fully translated, so that hard copies would be available for purchase by the descendants of these communities and also by scholars, universities, synagogues, libraries, and museums.

These Yizkor books have been produced almost entirely through the volunteer effort of researchers from around the world, assisted by donations from private individuals. The books are printed and sold at near cost, so as to make them as affordable as possible. Our goal is to make this important genre of Jewish literature and history available in English in book form, so that people can have the personal histories of their ancestral towns on their bookshelves for themselves and for their children and grandchildren.

A list of all published translated Yizkor Books can be found at:
http://www.jewishgen.org/Yizkor/ybip.html

Lance Ackerfeld, Yizkor Book Project Manager

Joel Alpert, Yizkor-Book-in-Print Project Coordinator

This book is presented by the
Yizkor Books in Print Project
Project Coordinator: Joel Alpert

Part of the
Yizkor Books Project of JewishGen, Inc.
Project Manager: Lance Ackerfeld

These books have been produced solely through volunteer effort of individuals from around the world. The books are printed and sold at near cost, so as to make them as affordable as possible.

Our goal is to make this history and important genre of Jewish literature available in English in book form so that people can have the near-personal histories of their ancestral towns on their bookshelves for themselves and for their children and grandchildren.

Any donations to the Yizkor Books Project are appreciated.

Please send donations to:
Yizkor Book Project
JewishGen
36 Battery Place
New York, NY 10280

JewishGen, Inc. is an affiliate of the
Museum of Jewish Heritage
A Living Memorial to the Holocaust

Title Page of Original Yiddish and Hebrew Yizkor Book

English Title Page of the Original Yiddish and Hebrew Yizkor Book

The Community of Sierpc
Memorial Book

Dedication

We Remember Them

At the rising of the sun and at its going down
  We remember them.
At the blowing of the wind and the chill of winter
  We remember them.
At the opening of the buds and in the rebirth of spring
  We remember them.
At the blueness of the skies and in the warmth of summer
  We remember them
At the rustling of the leaves and in the beauty of autumn
  We remember them.
At the beginning of the year and when it ends
  We remember them.
As long as we live, they too will live; for they are now a part of us,
  as we remember them.

When we are weary and in need of strength
  We remember them.
When we are lost and sick at heart
  We remember them.
When we have joy we crave to share
  We remember them.
When we have decisions that are difficult to make
  We remember them.
When we have achievements that are based on theirs
  We remember them.
As long as we live, they too will live; for they are now a part of us,
  as we remember them.

Acknowledgements

We wish to acknowledge the Memorial pamphlet written by Y. Frankel, S. Lelonek, Y. Nemlich, M. Rajchgat and R. Yorish, published in the US Zone Germany in 1948 by the Sherpcer Jewish Committee, parts of which are included in this Sierpc Yiddish and Hebrew Memorial Book.

The Sierpc Memorial Translation was generously supported in part by Puffin Foundation Ltd.

Map of Poland with location of Sierpc indicated

Geopolitical Information:

Alternate names for the town are: Sierpc [Polish], Sheps [Yiddish], Sherpts [Yiddish], Serptz [Russian], Scherps, Serepets, Serpec, Shepsk, Sherptz

Region: Plock

Russian: Серпц. Yiddish: שערפּץ
23 miles North of Płock (Plotsk), 16 miles South East of Rypin.

Period	Town	District	Province	Country
Before WWI (c. 1900):	Sierpc	Sierpc	Płock	Russian Empire
Between the wars (c. 1930):	Sierpc	Sierpc	Warszawa	Poland
After WWII (c. 1950):	Sierpc			Poland
Today (c. 2000):	Sierpc			Poland

Nearby Jewish Communities:

Bieżuń 12 miles ENE
Skępe 13 miles W
Rypin 16 miles NW
Bielsk 16 miles SSE
Drobin 16 miles SE
Żuromin 16 miles NE
Radzanów 18 miles E
Lipno 20 miles W
Raciąż 20 miles ESE
Szreńsk 21 miles ENE
Zieluń 21 miles NNE
Kuczbork 21 miles NE
Dobrzyń nad Wisłą 21 miles SW
Kikół 23 miles W
Płock 23 miles S
Strzegowo 26 miles E
Glinojeck 27 miles E
Lidzbark 27 miles NNE
Brodnica 28 miles NNW

Our Town, Sierpc

There once was a Jewish community in the ancient Polish town of Sierpc. As hundreds of other Jewish communities in Poland, Jewish Sierpc is no more. On the eighth day of the Second World War, September 8, 1939, the Germans occupied Sierpc, burnt the synagogue, and remained until they were expelled by the Red Army in January, 1945.

Before the start of the Second World War and the Holocaust, Sierpc had a population of 10,051, more than 30% of which was Jewish. Sierpc was nestled in the valley and surrounded by mountains. Three rivers flowed within the boundaries of Sierpc; the river that was the namesake of the district, the Sierpianitza River, bisected the two parts of the town. The town was linked by four bridges; the bridge with the greatest traffic was on the Jewish Street. The surrounding countryside was known for its fertile fields and many orchards, as well as for its weaver establishments, breweries, tanneries, and vinegar factories.

In the Sierpc Memorial Book, the Jewish community is vividly brought to life by the first-hand social, historical and political accounts by its former residents and by the numerous photographs. The exemplary writing makes this book unique and a must for all descendants of its residents and researchers of the history of the Sierpc Jewish Community.

Notes to the Reader:

Within the text the reader will note "{34}" standing ahead of a paragraph. This indicates that the material translated below was on page 34 of the original book. However, when a paragraph was split between two pages in the original book, the marker is placed in this book after the end of the paragraph for ease of reading.

Also please note that all references within the text of the book to page numbers refer to the page numbers of the original Yizkor Book.

Family Notes:

TABLE OF CONTENTS OF THIS BOOK

Table of Contents of the 1959 Hebrew (H) and Yiddish (Y) Sierpc Yizkor Book

Footnotes:

1. *Poalei Zion*: Workers of Zion.
2. *Hashomer Hatzair*: The Young Guard - a left-wing youth movement.
3. *Hanoar Hatzioni*: Zionist Youth.
4. *HeHalutz HaMizrachi*: Religious Pioneers.
5. *Beitar*: Acronym for Brit Yosef Trumpeldor - Covenant of Joseph Trumpeldor.
6. *Agudat Yisrael*: Union of Israel - the Orthodox Jewish (anti-Zionist) political movement.
7. *Banot Agudat Yisrael*: Daughters of Agudat Israel.
8. *Yesodei HaTorah*: Foundations of the Torah.
9. WIZO: Women's International Zionist's Organization.

The Community of Sierpc Memorial Book

From the 1959 Hebrew and Yiddish Yizkor Book

Printed in the Year 5720 – 1959
Tel-Aviv, State of Israel
"Arazi" Printers, Tel-Aviv Yafo, Tel. 83331

From the 1959 Hebrew and Yiddish Yizkor Book

Editor: **Ephraim Talmi (Wluka)**
Collection of Information: **I.M. Sidroni (Sendrowicz)**
Proofreader and Print Supervision: **Yitzhak Bergson**
Material Written in Yiddish, Edited for Printing:
W. Yasni

Cover Artist: **Avraham Meiron (Marantz)**

We have succeeded in concluding this momentous undertaking – preparing a memorial book for the Community of Sierpc.

We knew that there were differences of opinion as to the most proper way to honor the Community of Sierpc. There were some that objected to the very idea of publishing a book. Some argued for other forms of memorial, such as the planting of trees, etc. But the few comrades that were in Israel, who vigorously supported a memorial book, felt there was no better way to honor our ancient community than a literary, historic, and documentary monument for the generations to come. When, in the future, a historian will write the chronicles of the Jewish communities of Europe, he will not do it by consulting forests or cenotaphs and so forth; he will use the material collected in the memorial books as his important references.

This has not been an ordinary task. By its very nature, the preparation of this type of book presents many difficulties. We had to make a book out of ashes... But thanks to the stubbornness of a few, and their perseverance, our remembrance has reached its climax after six years. Important material had to be collected bit by bit, with the utmost patience, with unceasing love and great respect for the community and its Jews, for all our loved ones who were there and are no longer.

We know that we have not managed to collect all of the bricks necessary to erect a monument that would be fully worthy of a great and important community like Sierpc. Many who could have made an important contribution are no longer among the living, and some did not reply to our requests.

A compilation such as this one cannot be approached as just another book, as scientific or historical literature. The ways of life described in these pages will not be weighed by the balances of literature or the scales of scholarship. The historian Nachman Blumenthal states that the importance of a memorial book, even for scholarship, is that its authors are not academics. Sometimes there is certain charm in the primitive form of the book, with a language and style that are not faultless, not without grammatical error, but is evidence of the innocence and directness of the descriptions. And most important, these books contain an abundance of material for getting to know the spirit of the people, something that may be missing in more scholarly tomes.

We, the remaining townspeople of Sierpc, who by the grace of the Creator have been left the few out of many, have been privileged to be part of the builders of the fatherland in the Land of Israel. We felt that we have to fulfill a sacred obligation, to leave a testament to our community. We could not rest or stop until we finished our labors, this holy work of sorrow and pain.

We would like to thank all those who helped in preparing this remembrance book, who supported us in searching for material, with advice and guidance. Especially the members of the organization committee in Israel: Avraham Yerushalmi (Fried), chairman; Z. Arpa, secretary; Yosef Appelbaum, treasurer; Ephraim Panfil, Rivkah Tzipris, I.M. Sidroni, and B-Z Kempner. The members of the book committee in America were: Rivkah Arpa, Golda Goldman, Rasha and Leib Mintz, Chayim Pindek, and Sarah and Mordecai Rzeszotka.

Let us also acknowledge our comrades: Y.A. Liebson, M. Tzina, and A. Ben-David (Mlawa) for their help in getting the book published.

To all, thank you and bless you.

Tel-Aviv, 5720 (1959) **The Editors**

In Memorium (*Yizkor*)

Let us, the people of Israel, remember the holy communities of the lands of the Diaspora, that were uprooted, destroyed, and obliterated; their members who were killed, the victims of the kingdom of evil, that were brutalized by physical and spiritual torture in the death camps, who were deported to the cruelest land and left no trace. The multitudes that were murdered in the marketplaces and streets; that were brought to slaughter in freight cars; that were buried alive and incinerated in the holy tabernacle on Torah parchment. Those that were crushed, drowned, and strangled, whose honor was desecrated and whose blood was spilled by polluted hands – martyrs of God.

Let us, the people of Israel, remember our innocent children, the purest of the pure, who were snatched from the bosoms of their parents by the most bestial of mankind and led to slaughter like sheep. That were decapitated and massacred by all means, and whose bodies were left exposed in the streets; toddlers and nurslings who were smashed against walls of stone. That were thrown from high ramparts and dropped alive into the depths of rivers; whose lives were cut off in the bud by the cruelest of hands – the martyrs of God. *Yizkor* - In Memorium.

There Once Was...

There once was the Community of Sierpc. It was a city among cities, a community among communities, and is no more. Just as hundreds of Jewish communities in Poland that are no more. Gone like the six million of our brothers and sisters who perished in the awful Holocaust.

There once was...

The open wound keeps bleeding. The fountainhead of tears boils. And the frozen eye stares into the pits of time and sees everything up to the deepest depths, until the soul trembles... It clearly sees the town that squats on an essential crossroad. A town that was half Jewish, and where there are no more Jews... It sees the houses that are no longer there, and the Jews who lived there and are not there... It sees the lives that were lived in those houses, the private and the public lives, the life of a holy community that is not there... The eye sees everything, and the hand chronicles it with twisted fingers so that it will become history. So that we can remember and not forget! So we can merge our boiling tears for the loss of our community with the great reservoir of tears of the nation, in that enormous house of pain, that is like no other for any nation or tongue.

There once was...

It ascended to heaven in blood and fire... But it was in our hearts and will be in our memories for the generations. We have not forgotten and we will not forget and it is impossible to forget! In the silence! And in the eternal silence!

"*Yit'gadal v'yit'kadash*" – may they be exalted and sanctified.

צענטראלע פון ריעטאליסטן אין קליינהענדלער פארבאנד
אין פוילן
אבטיילונג אין שערפץ

BANK LUDOWY w SIERPCU
Spółdzielnia z odpowiedzialnością ograniczona

Rubber Stamps of Sierpc Jewish Organizations

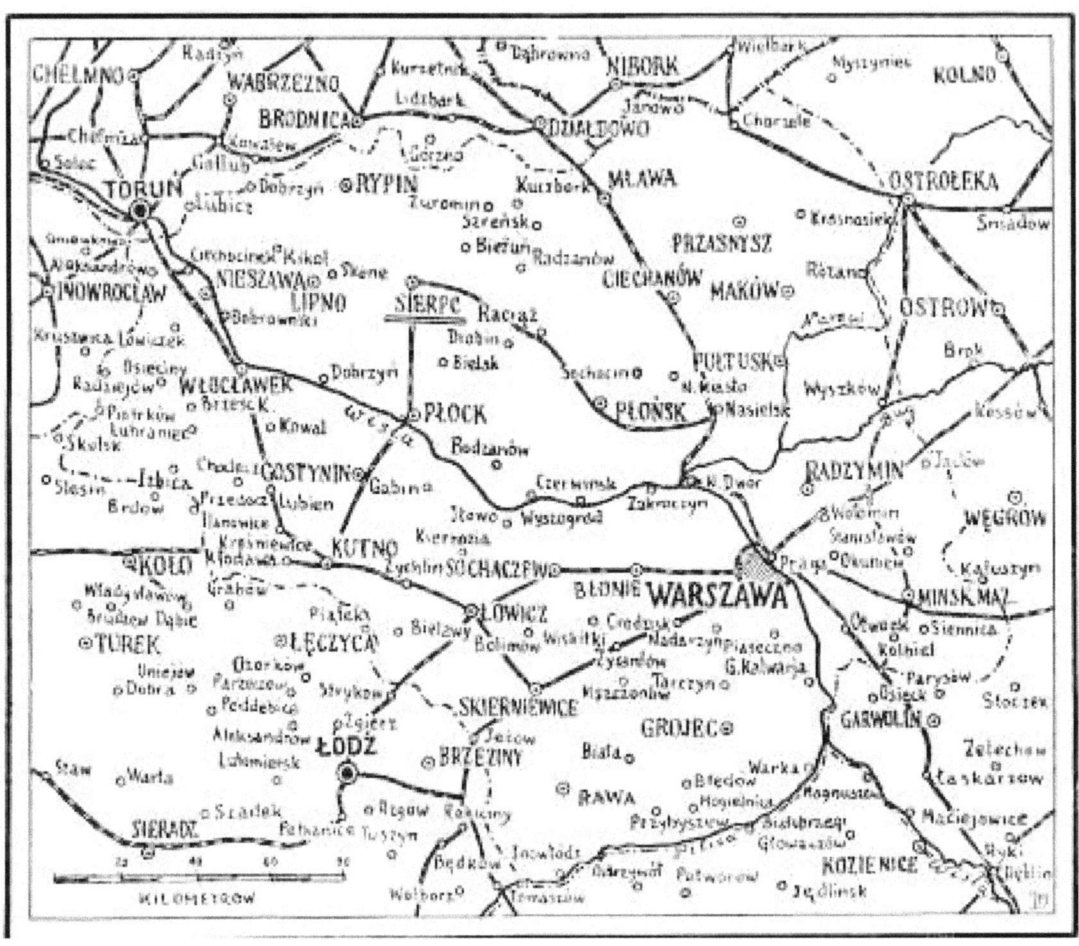

Map of Pre-World War II Poland

View of Sierpc

The Market

The Magistrat (Town Hall) and Shmiga's House

In Memory of my Father Eliezer Sendrowicz (5630-5668) [1869-1907]
In Memory of my Mother Yocheved Sendrowicz (5631-5698) [1870-1937]
In Memory of my Sister Gitel Billa Karpa (5650-5683) [1889-1922]

Of Sacred Memory...

For Sierpc, my town
My birthplace, my own
I bring my dirge, my grief
Of the Jews, their annihilation
Their destruction, obliteration
My mourning brings no relief

Heavens wail and the earth is furious
Of the Holocaust inglorious
By the polluted ones, the vicious
Our nation was decimated by their malice
Sierpc was also stricken
And brought to total extinction

To their sacred memory
I dedicate my chronicles
I will pray Kadish
And invoke my supplications
I.M. Sidroni

The History of Sierpc (Sheps)

By I.M. Sidroni

Since there is little information available on the history of Sierpc, and especially its Jewish community, we cannot claim to be writing the complete chronicles of our birthplace, or of its Jewish community. What year was the town founded, and when did Jews first settle in it? What was its population in various eras, and what was the number of Jews who lived there? What was the town like, culturally, commercially, and in general? And how secure was the position of the Jews there, both by law and in their relations with their neighbors? Who were the rabbis that served their worshippers, and who were the community leaders and benefactors? We have only a few answers to these questions and to similar ones. We never thought about these things in our youth, and we did not search for the answers. Even when we were older, and studied the ways of the world, we did not think to learn of the ways of Sierpc.

When we began preparing material for this "Yizkor" book for the martyrs of our town, we started to search and explore various sources, and look for relevant materials in books and newspapers. And we validated at least in part, the saying of our ancient sages: "you toiled and you found it, and then believe it". We toiled, and we found a little, and a little was found and discovered by our friends and acquaintances from the town. And so we present this for our townspeople and for all our readers.

This chapter was prepared using the following books:

"Staroztyna Polska" ("Ancient Poland") by Balinski and Lipinski, published in Warsaw in the year 1843.

"Slownik Geograficany Krolestwa Polskiego" ("Geographic Dictionary of the Kingdom of Poland") by Sulimarski, Chlabovsky, and Balavsky, published in Warsaw in ninth decade of the eighteenth century.

"Ibreisca Encyklopedia" ("The Jewish Encyclopedia"), Chief Editor: Dr. I.L. Katznelson Published in Petersburg (Leningrad) in the years 1910-1918.

"Registry of the Council of Four Nations" Chief Organizer and Interpreter Israel Halpern, published in Jerusalem in the year 5705 (1944).

A. The Chronicles of Sierpc

Sierpc is an ancient town. An old palace in Sierpc is mentioned in a document from King Boleslaw in the year 1155. Apparently, the palace was used by the governors of Mazovia[1], and this was the beginning of the settlement.

Our town was not always called by its present name – Sierpc. In different documents at various times, the town is mentioned with slight changes of name:

In a Document from the Year:	The Town was Called:
1165	Seprch
1322	Sieprz
1385	Sczeprcz
1389	Seprcz
1509	Syeprcz

We do not know when the town started being called by its present name, but we find the name Sierpc in a document from 1771.

The Russians, when they governed Poland, called it Serpec. The Germans, when they occupied Poland during World War 2, called it Sichelberg (according to the Hebrew newspaper "Davar", in Palestine, 16 November, 1941).

And as we know, the Jews called the town – Sheps.

*

Sierpc is a provincial town, and part of the Warsaw Region ("Wiabudotvo"). Until 1867, when it was declared to be the Sierpc District ("Poviat"), it was part of the Mlava District. From then to the First World War, it was part of the Plotzk Province ("Guvarnia"). Sierpc is 360 meters above sea level, and is situated in a wide valley on the Sierpienica River, not far from where it joins the Skrawa River. Sierpc is about 45 kilometers from Plotzk, 70 kilometers from Mlava, and 140 kilometers from Warsaw.

One of the above books states, "The town is composed of a number of sections, and each section has its own name: the Old Town, the New Town, Lorait, Chaplin (the Jewish Section), and "Ostrov". The first two names apparently refer to the old market and its neighborhood and the new market with its neighborhood[2]. Unfortunately, we do not know which parts of the town are referred to by the last three names.

Further on in the book, we read: "The city covers 2480 morgs (1 morg is about 5 dunams or 1.2 acres). There is an estate near the town called 'Vloki Mala' (Small Vloki), and 'Vloki Piaski' (Sandy Vloki) which is part of the village of Burkova. The estate covers 642 morgs, and has a water mill."

The town, during the eighteen-eighties, had 3 elementary schools, a district court, provincial offices, a post and telegraph office, a town hall, a (Polish) old peoples' home, and a (Jewish) guest house.

*

The land in Sierpc, over the years, belonged to different institutions and landlords:

- In 1322 Sierpc belonged, in part, to the Duke of Mazovia-Vatzlav, and in part to the Bishop of Plotzk (from Florian). In later years, various parts of the town were passed to other landlords:
- A document from the year 1385 contains the name "Filik of Sierpc".
- A document from the year 1389 mentions the name "Jacobus of Sierpc".
- During the first half of the sixteenth century, Sierpc belonged to two brothers named Sharfski. A document from King Zigmund I, in the year 1509, says "In the town of Syeprcz, that belongs to the brothers Sharfski".
- The brothers Sharfski divided the town into two equal parts in the middle of the sixteenth century. After the daughters of the two brothers were married, one half of the town passed into the hands of the Potolitzki family, and the other half, to the Fibo family. Zofia Potolitzki, who inherited half the town, built a convent for Benedictine nuns that were brought from Chelmno. In 1625 Zofia and her daughter Anna entered the convent, and she willed her inheritance to it.
- In 1771, Sierpc belonged to a man named Adam Bromirski. A document from 1771 by King Stanislaw August says: "We are responding to the request of the Khurunzhi (a military title) Mr. Adam Bromirski of Plotzk concerning a permit to move the fairs from his town Sierpc to the new town called 'Vloki'".
- Around the year 1800, during the Prussian regime, half the town belonged to a landlord named Braminski (or Draminski), and the other half was imperial property.

*

Until Sierpc became part of "Congressional Poland", it underwent a number of the conquests and transitions that affected the country. After the liquidation of independent Poland in 1795 and its division by its neighbors Russia, Prussia, and Austria, Sierpc found itself in the domain of Prussia. Sierpc was under the control of Prussia until 1807. In that year, Napoleon, after his European victories, established the Principality of Warsaw, and Sierpc was part of the Principality. After Napoleon's defeat in 1813, the Principality of Warsaw was nullified, and in accordance with the decision of the Congress of Vienna in 1815, central Poland ("Congressional Poland"), including Sierpc, was turned over to Russia. Sierpc remained part of the Russian Empire until the First World War.

On February 11, 1915, in the seventh month of World War 1, the Germans conquered Sierpc, and remained there until the end of the conflict, November 11, 1918. After that, Sierpc was part of an independent Poland.

During Poland's war with Bolshevik Russia, the Bolsheviks occupied Sierpc on August 12, 1920, and stayed there for 10 days.

On the eighth day of the Second World War, September 8, 1939, the Germans occupied Sierpc, and remained until they were pushed out by the Red Army in January, 1945.

*

The population statistics of Sierpc, from the books we mentioned previously, are as follows:

Year	Number of Houses	% Increase[3]	Population	% Increase[4]
1800	62	---	970	---
1827	272	67	2583	166
1856	---	---	4645	80
1858	320[5]	18	5015	8
1871	---	---	6389	27
1880	301[6]	6[7]	6726	5
1897	---	---	7000[8]	4
1921[9]	---	---	6722	4
1938	---	---	10051[10]	49

The customs and development of towns in Poland were influenced by two factors: the regional church and market days and fairs. A village or town where a regional church or fixed market days and fairs were established would quickly grow and develop. It would be settled by both Jews and non-Jews, businesses and workshops would open, commerce would increase, and more work would be available, and in a short time, the village would become a town, and the town would become a city.

These two factors were present in Sierpc. Sierpc had a regional church since medieval times, and had hosted market days and fairs for hundreds of years. We find the following information on these factors in the above the above books:

a. Churches *(the only ancient buildings in Sierpc were three churches and a convent.)*

The oldest church was the regional Church of Saints Vita, Modesta, and Kraschanchi, that was on Fara Street (Farska). According to tradition, it was built in the eleventh century, on a spot where there had previously been a pagan temple. In 1569, the church was repaired, and the spire was probably added. There were fires in the years 1630 and 1648. The repairs made after the fires, and repairs made in later years ruined not only the original building lines, but also the additions.

A second church, called "The Ascent to Heaven of the Mother of God" *("Wniebowziecie Matki Boskiej")* is on the Third of May Street, on the hill. This church was erected in 1453 to display the image of the mother of God that was discovered miraculously. The original building lines of the church have remained in place in spite of the changes made to the church in 1787 and 1801, and the fire that broke out there in 1794. A convent was built next to the church in 1620, and Benedictine nuns from Chelmno were brought there. When the wooden building burned down in 1703, a brick structure was erected in its place and remains there to this day. King Zigmund III visited the church and convent in 1624.

A third, small church called "Holy Spirit" *("Swiety Duch")* was built in 1519 at the entrance to the new market. This church burned down in 1614, and was rebuilt in 1850.

In addition to these three churches, Sierpc had three small churches that were destroyed over the years: the Church of Saint Vazhinietz that was demolished in 1813 when an army came through; the Church of the Holy Cross, with a cemetery, that was already a ruin in 1794; and the wooden Church of Saint Ducha, that burned down in 1794.

There was also a regional Evangelical Church in Sierpc. (A few years prior to World War I, a new church, large and graceful, was erected.)

At the beginning of the nineteenth century, there were 4084 Catholics in Sierpc. The Evangelical Church served about 2000 souls, who were German colonists.

b. Market Days and Fairs

The market days and fairs were, as we mentioned, important to the culture and development of the town, and we find accounts of them in the above mentioned books: "Pyotr Potolitzki, the regional minister from Plotzk, the heir of one of the Sharfski brothers, together with Anna Fibova, the heiress of the other brother, renewed, in 1577, the town ordinances that were lost during the fire, and declared that market days would be every Tuesday, and fairs would be held before the following holidays: Saint Lucia, Saint Vita, and the Holy Cross."

According to this, Sierpc had three fairs every year, but we see from the document quoted below that there were six annual fairs in later years, and each one of them lasted for three days. A "New Town" or new district was put up by the town, a suburb that is known as "Vloki" *("Vlikes")* where the fairs were held – an indication that over time the town and its surroundings developed, the population grew, and commerce increased.

An ordinance issued in 1771 by King Stanislaw August says: "We are responding to the request of the Khurunzhi (a military title) Mr. Adam Bromirski of Plotzk concerning a permit to move the fairs from his town Sierpc to the new town called 'Vloki', and declare that they will be held on January 17, the last day of February, the last day of April, May 27, August 21, and November 27. Each fair will last for three days."

As stated previously, these two factors – the regional church and the market days and fairs – brought about the town's development. Another factor in its development was the institution of the Sierpc District, and establishment of district offices in the town in 1867.

*

The commercial life in Sierpc is described by the above sources:

A permit was issued in 1389 by King Vladislav Yagello to settle weavers, apparently German, in Sierpc. Their industry developed in the fifteenth century.

King Zigmund I issued a permit in 1509 to the weavers of the town Syeprcz that belongs to the two Sharfski brothers, because of the weavers' diligence and meticulousness. They were allowed to place the letter "S" above the crown symbol, and a lion underneath it, and sell their goods throughout the kingdom.

The following industrial plants existed in Sierpc in the 1880's:

- Two breweries, whose annual revenues were about 6000 silver Rubles.
- Three tanneries, whose annual revenues were about 1710 silver Rubles.
- Four factories for making vinegar, whose annual revenues were about 1609 silver Rubles.

The "Encyklopedia Handlowa" *("Commercial Encyclopedia")* that was published in Warsaw in 1891, on page 652, contains the following details on industry in Sierpc: "Sierpc – a brewery, a vinegar plant, a tannery, and a vegetable oil press."

In 1858, the houses in Sierpc were insured for 72280 silver Rubles. In that same year, the income of the town treasury was 2204 silver Rubles and 74 Kopeks (100 Kopeks to the Ruble). In 1877, the town's income grew to 11732 silver Rubles, an increase of 432 per cent. Sierpc was a center of the grain trade for all of the surrounding area.

* * *

The above mentioned books also have some information and numbers on the District (Poviat) of Sierpc. The District of Sierpc was established in 1867 from half of the former District of Mlava. Until the First World War (during Russian control), the District of Sierpc was part of the Plotzk Province *("Guvarnia")*. Since Polish independence, Sierpc was part of the Warsaw Region *("Wiabudotvo")*.

The Sierpc District borders the Mlava District on the north. On the east, it borders both the Mlava District, and the Plonsk District. On the south, it borders the Plonsk and Plotzk Districts, and to the west – the Districts of Lipno, Ripin, and Mlava.

The area of the Sierpc District is 1977 square kilometers. The district is a plain, whose middle expanse reaches a height of 400 to 420 feet above sea level (around Zhoromin – 588 feet, around Biazhun – 420 feet, around Sierpc 360 feet, and around Rachonz – 302 feet).

Two rivers flow within the boundaries of the District of Sierpc – the Wkra and the Skrawa. They flow in almost a straight line, 14 to 18 kilometers from each other. Both rivers flow into the Visla River.

In addition to these two rivers, the river that is the namesake of the district also flows through it. The river bisects the district town, Sierpc, and is called *"Sierpianitza"* (or *"Sierptzuvka"*), and we called it *"Zhika"* from the Polish word for river, *"Zhaka"*. The source of the river is in the Plotzk district, east of Bilsk (Balsk). The river flows northward, behind Grazhini, from Ikami. It enters the Sierpc District, turns southwest, and flows behind Zharovo, Grumbiatz, and Burkova, passes through Sierpc, and between Studzianitch and Vimishlini it flows from the left into the Skrawa River. Its length is about 42 kilometers.

Administratively, the District of Sierpc was divided into one town, Sierpc, and 12 communities *("Gmini")*: Bialishavo, Biazhun, Burkova, Gradzanova, Gutkova, Kozabrodi, Kosamin, Lisivo, Rachonz, Rostchishovo, Stavishin, and Zhoromin. Among the communities *("Gmini"),* there were the three smaller towns: Biazhun, Rachonz, and Zhoromin.

*

Below are some population numbers for the Sierpc District over the years:

Year	Population	% Increase
1867	42073	---
1880	57024	21
1887	64000	12
1897	68000	6
1931[11]	83168	23

In 1897, the populations of the district town and of the three other towns of the district were as follows: Sierpc – about 7000; Rachonz – 4650; Zhoromin – 3119; Biazhun – 2892.

In 1931, the population of the District of Sierpc was divided among the town and villages as follows:

Population	In Towns	%	In Villages	%
83168	19019	21	64149	77

*

In 1883, there were three elementary schools in Sierpc, and 21 more schools in the rest of the district. There were 1638 students in these schools (including 675 girls).

There were four courts: one in Sierpc, for its residents, and three more, in Biazhun, Zhitov, and Rachonz for the residents of the other towns and villages. The district had three post offices: in Sierpc, Rachonz, and Biazhun.

The only credit and banking institutions in the district were the savings and loan funds. In 1886, there were 11 such funds in the 12 communities (Gmini) of the district, and their total capital amounted to 4782 Rubles.

*

A few more details on the commercial life of the District of Sierpc, on its agriculture and industry: The main agricultural products of the district were grain and potatoes. In terms of agricultural production, the District of Sierpc was in the next to last place in Plotzk Province (the last was the District of Mlava). The dearth of paved roads, and the distance to railroads and waterways hampered the development of agriculture and industry.

*

There were no large factories in the district. In 1880, the following types of industries existed in the District of Sierpc:

Type of Industry	Number of Plants	Number of Workers	Annual Revenue (in silver Rubles)
Breweries	4	10	13814
Vinegar	2	--	650
Tanneries	7	10	3540
Brickworks	5	20	15909
Glassworks	1	11	18000

In addition, there were about 50 windmills and a few water mills in the District of Sierpc.

B. The Chronicles of Sheps

We have already stated that we have very little information on the history of Sierpc in general, and Jewish Sheps in particular. The little knowledge that we have does not give us a clear picture of the lives of the first Jew of Sheps, but it is all we have.

The earliest information that we have on Jews in Sheps is from 1739, in the book "Slownik Geograficany Krolestwa Polskiego" ("Geographic Dictionary of the Kingdom of Poland"). The heading "Sierpc" (Volume 10, page 594) states, in part: "There is a brick pillar in the center of the town that was built by Jews, on the authority of a decision of Pyotrekov in the year 1739, because of sacrilege that they committed. The Jews were obliged to maintain this pillar until the year 1850."

This excerpt tells us that there were already Jews in Sierpc then, and that they suffered from the various slanders heaped upon them by their Polish neighbors, and were punished by them in various ways. Unfortunately, we have not been able to determine what "sacrilege" was committed by the Jews of Sheps. Similarly, we do know anything about the pillar mentioned in the excerpt, or where it was located.

The same volume of that book tells us that the town of Sheps consisted of a number of sections, and that each section had its own name. The phrase "Jewish Section" appears in parentheses next to the name of one of these sections, "Chaplin". Unfortunately, we do not know where this section of town was. However, there was a street in Sheps called "Chalpin" (the letters "p" and "l" are interchanged), but this was a small street, almost an alley, barely populated and at the edge of the town, far from the "Jewish Section", and near the church. It does not seem reasonable that this street was then the "Jewish Section" of the town. It is more likely that the "Jewish Street" of our time *("Ulica Warszawska")* was the "Jewish Section" of town in the old days, at the beginning of the Jewish settlement of the town. There are two pieces of evidence for this: a) the popular street name, called by both Jews and Gentiles *"Ulica Zydowska"* ("the Jewish street"), and b) the fact that all the Jewish institutions were on this street. And possibly the previous name of the street was "Chaplin"?

*

An important piece of information about the Jews of Sheps appears in 1766 in the book "Registry of the Council of Four Nations". Page 445, paragraph 840, of the "Registry" says "An announcement of the Debt Resolution Committee [12] – from April 22, 1766 (13 Iyar 5526) states that 3 gold coins per head must be collected from the Jews to settle the debts of the Councils, and the times and places of payment have been established. The creditors are mainly the fortresses of Cracow, Lwow, and Kalish, various institutions in Russia, Poland, and private citizens."

Page 449, Paragraph 843: "An announcement of the Debt Resolution Committee – from 21 March 1767 (20 Adar B 5527) on the instructions and demands that were made in the announcement of April 22, 1766 (13 Iyar 5526) and have not been met until now, and the debts of the Jews have increased because they have not been paid off, by the addition of interest and fines. "One variant of the announcement, a four page printed pamphlet, is in the National Library at the Hebrew University in Jerusalem, Collection of Miscellaneous Items No. 568, and I present it in full in the Section of Foreign Language Documents at the end of this book."

At the end of the book ["Registry of the Council of Four Nations"], Document No. 83 on page LXXIX (of Paragraph 843) is written in Polish, and lists the communities in various parts of Poland whose Jews must pay the debts of the councils, and the amount every "head" must pay. The community of Sheps is listed among the communities of Greater Poland, where Jews must pay 15 copper *"Grush"* per head.

This document tells us that in the year 5526 (1766) there was already a Jewish community in Sheps that participated in the public life of the Jews of Poland. It was affiliated to the Council of Greater Poland Communities through the "Council of Four Nations".

*

The Journal *"HaTkufa"* ("The Era") No. 14-15, that was published in Warsaw in the year 5682 (1922) has a research article by A. N. Frank "History of the Jews in Poland". Page 373 contains a discussion of the purchase of land and houses by Jews in the Principality of Poland and Congressional Poland. The following paragraphs paraphrase parts of this article:

According to the Order of the Day of March 16, 1809, only Jews who met the following requirements were permitted to purchase land and houses in towns: 1) Shaved their beards and sideburns; 2) Wore Gentile clothes; 3) Could read and write; 4) Sent their sons to school. Of course, very few Jews were found worthy of these permits.

During the years when disorder increased in the land, the years that Poland was at war with Russia (1812-1813) and in the years between the liquidation of the "Principality of Warsaw" and establishment of the "Kingdom of Poland" under Russian hegemony (1813-1815), Jews purchased houses from Christians in a few towns. The notaries registered the contracts of sale and purchase, despite the fact that the Jews did not have any special permits.

Before the fate of the "Kingdom of Poland" was known, and before the constitution of this Kingdom was written, the Polish authorities started to interfere with the sale of houses to Jews. They also started investigating the purchase of houses that Jews bought without permits in the years of disorder. It turned out that Jews in the Department of Plotzk purchased 373 houses without permits, of which five were in Sheps (page 383).

*

There is more information on the Jews of Sheps in the "Ibreisca Encyklopedia" ("Jewish Encyclopedia"). The entry on "Sarpach" (Volume 14, page 174) states: "Despite the fact that Sarpach had no special restrictions on the rights of Jews to settle, but because Jews in fact were not allowed to settle there, a government committee resolved in 1830 that only Jews who owned or leased their houses would remain there. The others would be expelled from the town. The ban was lifted in 1862."

It is apparent from this entry that it was once forbidden for Jews to settle in Sheps, even if this restriction was illegal. The restriction was forgotten over the years, or the authorities ignored it because of its illegality, and Jews settled in the town. In 1830, a government committee decided, in a compromise between the illegal restriction and reality, to banish those Jews who were not property owners from the town. The restriction was cancelled in 1862, and we apologize again how little knowledge we have about the history of Jew in our town. We do not know when the restriction on Jewish settlement in Sheps began; we also do not know if the government decision of 1830 for the partial expulsion of the Jews of Sheps was implemented.

*

The above mentioned books contain a few numbers on the Jews of Sheps over the years:

Year	Population	% Increase[13]	Number of Jews	% Increase[14]	% of Total Population
1800	970	---	649	---	67
1856	4645	379	2604	301	56
1858	5015[15]	8	2571	-1	51
1897	7000[16]	39	2935	14	42
1921[17]	6722	-4	2861[18]	-2.5	42.5
1938[19]	1051[20]	49	3077	8	30.5

This table shows that in 1800, the Jews were a large majority of the population of Sheps: two-thirds of the population was Jewish! Apparently Sheps was a center of industry and commerce; the inhabitants of the surrounding villages must have visited the town often, either because of market days, or because of the churches. Many Jews therefore settled in Sheps, opened stores and workshops, and developed the town. But this majority did not last very long. The majority diminished slowly and became a minority, and the same table indicates that the Jews were already a minority in the last quarter of the nineteenth century. In the year before the start of the Second World War and the Holocaust, the Jews were only 30 per cent of the population.

* * *

The above books present the following statistics on the Jews in the District of Sheps:

Year	Population	% Increase[21]	Number of Jews	% Decrease[22]	% of Total Population
1880	57024[23]	---	9936	---	17
1897	68000	19	7695	29	12
1931[24]	83168	22	7574	5	9

* * *

The previous table shows a continuing decrease in the Jewish population of the district of Sheps, both in percentages and in absolute numbers. The probable cause is emigration to various countries, especially the United States, which grew following the pogroms of the Jews in the 1880's.

The distribution of the Jewish population in the District of Sheps in 1931 between town dwellers and villagers was as follows:

1931	Total Number	In Towns	%	%	In Villages	%	%
Population	83168	19019	23	---	64149	77	---
Non-Jews	75594	12378	16	65[25]	63156	84	98.5[26]
Jews	7574	6641	87	35[27]	993	13	1.5[28]

The mother tongues of the Jewish population in that same year were as follows:

Total Number	Yiddish	%	Hebrew	%	Polish	%
7574	6513	86	1009	13.33	52	0.67

C. *"Kolhekot"*

An important incident in the lives of the Jews of Sheps was the *"Kolhekot"* affair. This year, the Jewish year 5719 (1958-1959) is the centennial of the start of the great controversy in the community of Sheps. This dispute caused a rift in the community, and a group of Mitnagdim-Maskilim[29] ("Enlightened Mitnagdim") founded a separate congregation, with its own Rabbi and Shochet (Kosher slaughterer), that was called *"Kolhekot"*.

We will relate here how this division developed, the reason for the rift, the significance of the term *"Kolhekot"*, and how long the congregation existed.

At the beginning of the nineteenth century, the Hasidic movement was still young, and it had little influence in Poland, so that the Mitnagdim had the upper hand in the community of Sheps. However, the Rabbi of Sheps at the time, Rabbi Meirel Dabash, was a Hasid. He was not only a Hasid, but he was also a Rebbe of Hasidim[30]. This is puzzling to us, and we cannot explain it. But later, conditions changed, and a Hasidic Rabbi was accepted as the Rabbi of Sierpc in the second decade of the nineteenth century. This was at the recommendation of a "well known scholar from the town of Makova" (the recommendation was required because "the town is a town of Mitnagdim"). The Rabbi, Rebbe Schrage Fivel Danziger, was forced to leave the town after a short time, because of the enmity of the Mitnagdim.

We do not have any clear knowledge about Rabbi Avrahamel Charif, who followed Reb Schrage Fivel as the Rabbi of Sheps in the next decade the nineteenth century, whether he was a Hasid or a Mitnaged. It stands to reason that if the community of Sierpc agreed to accept him as their Rabbi, and he agreed to serve (after the expulsion of the previous Hasidic Rabbi), he was a Mitnaged. The Rabbi who served in Sheps in the 1830's, Rabbi Moshe Yehuda Leib Zilberberg, was a Mitnaged as well. Rabbi Mordecai Greenbaum (the grandfather of Yitzhak Greenbaum, the outstanding Polish-Jewish activist prior to World War 2), who served as Rabbi of Sheps in the 1840's and 1850's was also a Mitnaged.

However, during those years, the power of the Hasidim increased, and Rabbi Mordecai Greenbaum suffered greatly because of the Hasidim. In the introduction to Part 1 of the book "The Ears of Yehoshua (Questions and Answers)" by Rabbi Yehoshua Segal (grandson of Rabbi Mordecai Greenbaum, and also a Rabbi of Sheps), that was published in Jerusalem in the year 5674 (1913)[31], he states:

"He[32] later was accepted as the Rabbi of the town of Sheps in the Province of Plotzk, and there were disputes and strife between him and the Hasidim of the town. But during that time, his student Rabbi Leibl[33] fled from his father and became a Hasid of the Great Rabbi in Lublin. When the Hasidim bothered Rabbi Mordecai too much, he informed his student Rabbi Leibl, who wrote to the Tzadik (Saintly Hasidic Rabbi) of Kotzk, of saintly blessed memory, and he ordered all his Hasidim to honor Rabbi Mordecai, so then they all calmed down, and respected Rabbi Mordecai."

Rabbi Mordecai Greenbaum passed away on the 16th of the month of Heshvon, 5619 (the latter part of October, 1858). Of course the Mitnagdim wanted his successor to be a Mitnaged, but they apparently realized that the times had changed, and their wishes would not be supported by the community. What they did was to try and create a fait accompli, and on the third day following the Rabbi's death appointed his son-in-law, Rabbi Moshe Yosef Segal, the Rabbi of Kidrobarg (Kodzhburg, a village in the Mlava District), who was a Mitnaged. They felt (so we understand their actions) that two factors would make the community accept the new Rabbi. a) The de facto appointment of a new Rabbi, and b) that the new Rabbi was the son-in-law of the late Rabbi. But the congregation refused to consent to the appointment of the Mitnagdim and appointed Rabbi Gedalia of Zhoromin as the official Rabbi of Sheps.

The appointment of Rabbi Moshe Yosef Segal caused a lot of disagreement, and a rift in the community. A new congregation of Mitnagdim was founded, and called "Kolhekot". Rabbi Moshe Yosef Segal was the Rabbi of the Kolhekot, and they also had a separate Shochet (Kosher Slaughterer).

The book "Ears of Yehoshua" mentioned above, states: "When Rabbi Mordecai died, his son-in-law, Rabbi Moshe Yosef Segal was accepted in his place by the group of Mitnagdim. But the Hasidim of Sheps[34] took Rabbi Gedalia of Zhoromin as their Rabbi. At first there was a dispute between them, but later the two Rabbis reconciled, and served together in peace."

When the Rabbi of the "Kolhekot", Rabbi Moshe Yosef Segal died, his son, Rabbi Yehoshua, succeeded him. Rabbi Yehoshua Segal[35] was also a Mitnaged, and suffered from persecution by the Hasidim and left Sheps for America.

The above mentioned book, "Ears of Yehoshua", also states: "When his father died, he[36] took his place as the Rabbi of Sheps. But since he was a Mitnaged, he also suffered from the ill-treatment by the Hasidim. In spite of the warnings of the Gaon Mahari of Kitna, of saintly blessed memory[37] not to show him any lack of respect, he at last could not take all the suffering any more, left Poland with his whole family, and came to New York in about the year 5644 (1884)." After Rabbi Yehoshua Segal left Sierpc, the separate congregation "Kolhekot" was disbanded and the community of Sheps became united again, a community to which all the Jews of the town belonged, and could find shelter in.

*

Now we would like to make some clarifications and comments to the *"Kolhekot"* affair.

What is the meaning of the word *"Kolhekot"*? When we were children we heard that *"Kolhekot"* meant *"Kahala K'tata"*, a divided community. Another interpretation of the word can be found in the book "David Ben-Gurion and His Generation" by Bracha Habas, that was published in Tel-Aviv in the year 5712 (1951). The following paragraph appears on page 18.

"Under the influence of an enlightened village, Kuchari, a society was established in Plonsk with the name *"Kahal Katan"* (Small Society). Its purpose was to propagate learning among the simple people. The members of the society, which had the characteristics of "going to the people", took it upon themselves to teach Torah in the *"Beit HaMidrash"* (House of Prayer and Learning) to the tailor and the shoemaker and the carter. The Hasidim, of course, would not support such Enlightenment ideas. They mocked it and dismissed it, and they called the society, in a derisive manner, *"Kolikotnikes"* ("members of a small society")." It is possible that the *"Kolikotnikes"* in Sheps were also a small group *("Kahal Kat – Kolhekot").*

*

Our definition above (in connection with the appointment of a new Rabbi, and the rift in the community) of *"Mitnagdim"* is not precise enough. Only some of the Mitnagdim, mainly the more learned and enlightened ones, who afterwards were worshippers in the new *"Beit HaMidrash"* (House of Prayer) were members of the *"Kolhekot"*. The worshippers in the old House of Prayer were from both sides, some were members of the greater community, and others were from the *"Kolhekot"*.

*

This is a summary of the *"Kolhekot"* affair:

The *"Kolhekot"*, a separate congregation of "Enlightened Mitnagdim", lasted for 26 years, from the year 5619 (1858-59) until the year 5644 (1884). The *"Kolhekot"* congregation was served by the Rabbi Moshe Yosef Segal, and after his death, his son Rabbi Yehoshua. The Shochatim (ritual slaughterers) were, initially someone whose name is not known, and after him, Avraham Shochet (Burgand).

The group of "Enlightened Mitnagdim" of the *"Kolhekot"* prayed as a special *"Minyan"* in the "Kamnitza" ("Great Walled House") on the Jewish Street. After the new Beit HaMidrash was built (in the year 5646 [1886], two years after the Rabbi of the *"Kolhekot"*, Rabbi Yehoshua Segal, left Sheps), the remaining members of the *"Kolhekot"* worshipped there.

The leaders of the group of "Enlightened Mitnagdim" were Yisrael Yitzhak Badan, Yakov Hirsh Kirsch (at the beginning of the rift), Eliezer Vasolak, Ephraim Yosel Valuka, and Haim Nahum Tunbol.

D. Dates and Numbers

1153	The first mention of Sierpc
1739	The first mention of Jews in Sierpc
1795	Sierpc comes under Prussian rule
1807	Sierpc becomes part of the Principality of Warsaw
1815	Sierpc comes under Russian rule
1867	The District of Sierpc is established (Sierpc is the main District town)
1859 to 1884	The years of the separate "Kolhekot" congregation
1886	The new Beit HaMidrash (House of Prayer) was built
1895	The synagogue was built
11 Feb 1915	The occupation of Sierpc by the Germans in World War I
11 Nov 1918	The Germans leave Sierpc (Armistice Day)
12 Aug 1820	The occupation of Sierpc by the Bolsheviks during the Russian-Polish war
1 Sep 1939	Start of World War II
4 Sep 1939	Sierpc is bombed from the air, and the first Jewish victim falls – Arie Zhitalni
8 Sep 1939	The Germans enter Sierpc
28 Sep 1939	The first day of Sukkoth in the year 5700 – the expulsion of more than fifty young men to the Russian zone
29 Sep 1939	The second night of Sukkoth in the year 5700 – the burning of the synagogue. The second Jewish victim falls – Pinchas (Pinia) Valtsman
8 Nov 1939	26 of Heshvon, 5700 – the expulsion of the Jews from Sierpc (the day each year that is the memorial day of the martyrs of Sierpc)
March or April 1940	A Ghetto was put up in Sierpc (for the Jews that remained or returned)
6 Jan 1942	17 of Tevet, 5702 – the expulsion of the residents of the Ghetto to the Ghetto of Stezhogovo
24 Nov 1942	15 Kislev, 5703 – The transport of the last residents of the Ghetto of Stezhogovo to Auschwitz

First and Last Population Numbers of Sierpc

1800	Population: 970; number of Jews: 649, 67% of the total population
1938	Population: 10051; number of Jews: 3077, 30.5% of the total population

---

Translator's Footnotes

1. Sierpc was in the region called "Mazovia"
2. Perhaps the intent is to the *"Vloki" ("Vlikes")* that were called "New Town" in a document from 1771.
3. From previous year
4. From previous year
5. Six of which were large buildings
6. Two of which were large buildings
7. It is possible that the decrease was caused by a fire
8. Approximate
9. According to the Polish population census of 30 September 1921
10. According to the report of the "Joint" (American Jewish Joint Distribution Committee) on the state

of the Jews in Sierpc

11. According to the Polish Census of that year
12. The Debt Resolution Committee of the Kingdom Treasury that dealt with the decision of the Polish *"Sejm"* (Parliament) on the dissolution of the "Council of Four Nations" and of the councils of each of the member countries.
13. Increase over previous year
14. Increase over previous year
15. Including 235 Germans
16. Approximate
17. From the Polish Census of September 30, 1921
18. 2766 Jews, 96.7% of the Jewish population, are of the Jewish religion and Jewish nationality; 95 Jews, 3.3% of the Jewish population, are of the Jewish religion and Polish nationality.
19. According to the "Joint" [American Jewish Joint Distribution Committee] report on the state of the Jews of Sheps.
20. This large increase in the population of Sheps, almost all of it in the Polish population, is an artificial increase. The increase is a result of the annexation the "Vloki" ("Vlikes") – a suburb with a large Polish population. The suburb was attached to the town, but administratively was part of the village of Burkova about three kilometers away. The authorities annexed the suburb between the first municipal council election (1919) and the second election (1923), to purposely limit the number of Jewish council members.
21. Increase over previous year
22. Decrease over previous year
23. Including 133 Russians and 1091 Germans
24. From the Polish Census of that year
25. Per cent of non-Jews in towns with respect to the total population of towns
26. Per cent of non-Jews in villages with respect to the total population of villages
27. Per cent of Jews in towns with respect to the total population of towns
28. Per cent of Jews in villages with respect to the total population of villages
29. [Translator's Note: *"Mitnagdim"* (literally in Hebrew – Opponents, singular "Mitnaged") were Jews opposed to the Hasidic movement that began in the late eighteenth century in Eastern Europe; Maskilim (literally in Hebrew – the Enlightened), a Jewish movement that called for more openness to outside influences, that started in Europe at about the same time.]
30. See more in the chapter in this Yizkor book, "The History of the Rabbinate in Sierpc"
31. The book was published after the death of its author, and the introduction was written by the "conveyer to the printer" Rabbi Israel Zev Halevy Izsh Horowitz.
32. Rabbi Mordecai Greenbaum
33. Rabbi Leibl Iger, the grandson of the Gaon Rabbi Akiva Iger, was a student of Rabbi Mordecai Greenbaum in his youth.
34. The intention is to the greater community. After the rift, the Hasidim were a large majority.
35. According to reliable sources, Rabbi Yehoshua was called "A Teacher of Meaning" in Sheps.
36. Rabbi Yehoshua Segal
37. Moreinu (Our Teacher) Rabbi Yehoshua of Kitna, of saintly blessed memory.

Chronicles of the Sheps Rabbinate

By I.M. Sidroni (Sendrowicz)

The words of the introductory paragraph of the previous chapter, "The History of Sierpc (Sheps)" are applicable as an introduction to this chapter as well. Here too we say that we cannot claim to be writing the complete chronicles of the Sheps rabbinate, because we know little about the rabbinate in our town in general, and about each rabbi in particular. Just as we did not pay attention to the history of our town in our youth, we never considered the chronicles of its rabbinate. However, it is our aspiration to perpetuate the memory of our town and its martyrs in this book. Therefore, we began to research and discover the accounts of the rabbinate of the community of Sheps. This is how we arrived, partially through our efforts and partially through the efforts of friends and acquaintances from our town, at the material presented here.

Unfortunately, we have not found all the rabbis that served in Sheps in the early days; nor do we have detailed information and exact dates for rabbis mentioned in this chapter. Nevertheless, we have ascertained important facts and found sources that will interest the ex-townspeople of Sierpc, and researchers of its history.

Rabbi Segal

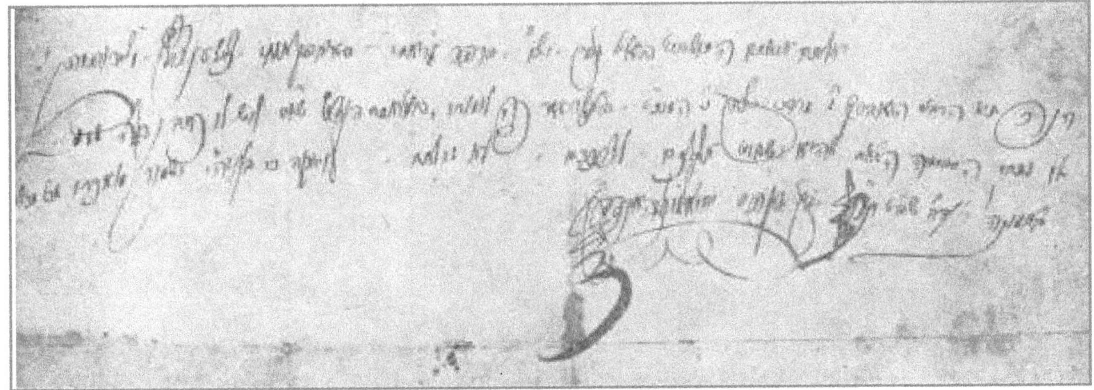

Handwriting of Rabbi Yechiel Michal Goldschlak – Written in the year 5630 (1870)

Among the first of the Enlightenment and Hovevei Tzion [Lovers of Zion] in the Town

Rabbi Eliezer Vasolak and his wife, Sheine
Among the first of the Enlightenment and Hovevei Tzion [Lovers of Zion] in the Town

A. Rabbi Meirel Dvash

The first rabbi about whom we have managed to find any information in our sources is Rabbi Meirel Dvash, the righteous of blessed memory. Rabbi Meirel was called "Dvash" because these were the initial letters of the three towns, Dobrzyń, Będzin, and Sheps [the sounds "b" and "v" use the same letter in Hebrew; "dvash" is the Hebrew word for "honey"], where he served simultaneously as rabbi. However, he became famous mainly as the rabbi of Sheps because he is mentioned in books as "Rabbi Meir of Sheps" or "Meir *Shepsir*". He also died in Sheps and was buried in the old cemetery. There is a "crypt" above the grave, and even during our times, the townspeople would come to visit his grave, spill their troubles to the rabbi, and drop little notes into the crypt. The notes would ask for complete recovery from all kinds of diseases, prosperity, good luck, and so forth.

Rabbi Meirel Dvash was both a Rabbi and a Rabi [leader of a Hasidic sect]. He had both followers that would travel to see him, and opponents who pursued him. Apparently, he had visions, so that his opponents called him " *meshuggeh* [crazy] scholar". According to our respected townsman Shmuel Itche Lanenter, Rabbi Meirel Dvash was called "*Baal Shem*" [miracle worker] because of the deeds and visions that he related to his followers, and his farsightedness. (They said that once, on a Sabbath eve, while sitting at his table surrounded by Hasidim, he saw a fire erupt in Dobrzyń...) Yisrael Karpa (now in Uruguay) wrote to us that his father, of blessed memory (my grandfather Mordechai Yitzhak, a ritual slaughterer and inspector in Żuromin) would tell him wonderful tales of the "Rabi"[1] Rabbi Meirel.

Apparently, Rabbi Meirel was a great and saintly rabbi, because he was a friend of Rabi Levi Yitzhak of Berdychiv, and Rabi Levi Yitzhak would come to Sheps to visit him.

*

When was Rabbi Meirel Dvash a rabbi in Sheps, and for how long did he serve?

We have not found exact answers to these questions. However, we know that he was a friend of Rabi Levi Yitzhak of Berdychiv (born in the year 5500 [1740] and died on the 25th of the month of Tishrei 5570 [1809]). In addition, the passage quoted below from the book "In Polish Forests" refers to the year 5573 (1812). In addition, there is the passage from the introduction to the "Passover Hagadah" quoted below. Using these sources, it seems that the period during which Rabbi Meirel Dvash was rabbi of Sheps was at the end of the 18th and beginning of the 19th centuries (approximately 1790 to 1812). This also appears in the book *"Mlawa Notebook"* [in Yiddish]: "It was at the end of the 18th century". Also in the book "A History of Hassidism" by Dubnow on page 458: "A list of giants of righteousness from the year 5558 (1798)".

The following are some excerpts from the books a) "In Polish Forests" by J. Opatoshu b) "Mlawa Notebook" c) "A History of Hassidism" by Dubnow d) Introduction to "Passover Hagadah" and e) "*In di Blihendeh Yahren*" by our townsman Yisrael Sapirsztajn. All refer to Rabbi Meirel Dvash.

The following passages about Rabbi Meirel Dvash appear in the book "In Polish Forests" by J. Opatoshu (translated [from Yiddish to Hebrew] by N. Lipson, Tel-Aviv, 5689 [1928]).

Page 50: "She had great affection for her old uncle, Rabbi Meirel "Dvash". Does this seem like a small thing? The friend of "Holy Levy"![2] Who had come to Sheps to see how he felt! However, father acts casually with the uncle. But to whom does father not act casually? He calls him 'Rabbi of women' because he would receive supplicating notes from Dobrzyń, Będzin, and Sheps. Nevertheless, who was she and what were her thoughts? Is it possible for a wretched and sinful woman to understand their ways? If Jews "travel", there must be a reason. After all, she travels every year, silently and secretly, to Sheps, to the celebration of the Rabi Meirel. She contributes 18 Zuzim [coins] for candles, and communes with the saint in his "crypt". The caretaker knows her, and knows not to let any strangers in when Dvorahle is talking to her uncle. Moreover, when she feels she has grievances, she does not hesitate to fling them at him. After all, he is her flesh and bone. And when she finishes she asks him again in the name of Rabi Gatzil, detailing her pedigree..."

Page 60: "Once, on a very cold day, according to the family, Rabbi Meirel Dvash came to grandfather's house in the forest on matters of charity. This was in the month of Tevet, in the year 5573.[3] Rabbi Meirel accepted Reb Mordechai's invitation to stay for the night. The two of them were together in the room, sitting by the hot stove, smoking their pipes, and discussing the news of the world. Rabbi Meir revealed to grandfather that the days of the Messiah have come, and evil edicts for all of Israel are expected. The "shoemaker's apprentice"[4] has already conquered most of the world. He is near Moscow, and he will pursue the "Greek"[5] to the Sea of Ice. But his end is near. The Kosienici[6] has struggled with his minister since the Musaf[7] prayer of Yom Kippur, and if not for the Berdychovi[8] of Blessed Memory, who in the year of his death united the Jews in his prayer for the victory of the "apprentice", the Kosienici would have had his way. Rabbi Meirel found a clue for this in "Midrash Talpiot"[9]. Under the letter zayin [7th letter of the Hebrew alphabet], the Midrash says:

'They say that there is a marble statue of a beautiful girl in Rome, and it was not created by human hands, but the Almighty Blessed He Be created it through his prowess. However, villains from the gentile nations, evil men, come and warm her, and sleep with her. And the Almighty preserves their droppings inside the stone and creates a living creature inside of her, and generates a fetus, and she splits open, and a man-like creature comes out of her. His name is Armilius the Devil, he who the gentiles call anti-Christ. His length was 12 *Amah*[10] and his width was 12 *Amah*. There was a pinkie between his eyes, which were red and deep, and the hair on his head was the color of gold. His feet are green, and he has two horns. He comes to the villains and tells them: I have given you the truth. I am the Messiah; I am your God. They believe in him immediately, and crown him their king, and all the sons of Esau[11] join him, and he conquers all the nations. He says to the sons of Esau: bring me my Torah that I have given you. So they bring him their rubbish, and he says to them: believe in me, for I am your Messiah. They immediately believe him. At the same time, he sends a message to Nehemiah son of Hushiel[12] and to all of Israel, and tells them: bring me your Torah and bear witness that I am your god. Within the hour Nehemiah son of Hushiel rises, together with thirty thousand champions from the champions of Ephraim[13], and they take the book of the Torah and read to him: I am the Lord thy God, Thou shalt have no other gods before me. So he tells them:

there is nothing in your Torah, come and come bear witness that I am god, as all the nations have done. Nehemiah immediately stands up to him and tells his servants: seize him and bind his hands and feet. Then Nehemiah son of Hushiel, who is the Messiah son of Joseph, rises together with his thirty thousand who will go to war and kill two hundred thousand. Then the evil Armilius becomes furious and brings all the nations of the world to the Valley of Haruz[14] and battles with Israel and kills piles of them and defeats them and the Messiah of God is killed. The angels come, take him, and inter him with the Patriarchs. Israel becomes disheartened and abandons the field, but Armilius does not know that the Messiah is dead, for if he knew he would not have left any remnants. At that time, all the nations of the world harass Israel inside their borders, and do not let Israel live with them, and Israel has prodigious troubles, such as it has never known before---.'

"While Rabbi Meirel was speaking, a winter coach stopped beneath the window of the house. Some people knocked on the door.

Rabbi Meirel jumped up: "---Mordechai, they are bringing him!" "---Who?" "---That same evil one!"

"His hands were shaking as Reb Mordecai opened the door. A few people entered the house. Their faces red with cold and a white frost covers their beards. They pushed Reb Mordecai aside and whispered a few words to him. Reb Mordecai immediately ordered Sarahle to open the drawing room and offered the bed. He was shaking all over as he waited breathlessly for them to bring in the evil Armilius with the two horns, twelve *Amah* tall and twelve *Amah* wide. The men came in carrying a pudgy man wrapped in robes. They say that he is French, a powerful minister, and he had caught a chill on the way.

"On seeing the pudgy man, Reb Mordecai became calmer. He was certain that the saintly one was not talking about this man, and he was not even sure that he was a minister. He is very obviously dying! He looked around, called to Rabbi Meirel, and the saint had already disappeared."

Page 71: "The notebook said that the 'Holy Levi' was on his way to Rabbi Meirel in Sheps, and went to their house for the midday prayer." Page 115: "One of them sighed 'He[15] went to war on Yom Kippur as well'. 'Let him!' The old man[16] lifted his cane as if to strike the Hasid over the head. 'Rabbi Meirel "Dvash" gave his permission. If you don't know that - put a muzzle on your mouth!'"

Page 116: "We did not leave the bushes[17] on Yom Kippur either. Rabbi Meirel allowed it."

We can read about the "Rabi" Rabbi Meirel Dvash in the book "Mlawa Notebook" (New York 1950), in a comment on Page 24 [in Yiddish]:

"There once lived, in a *shtetl* not far from Mlawa, in Makowa, the well-known opponent of Hasidism, the *Magid*[18] Rabbi David of Makowa. He was a pupil of the *Vilna Gaon*[19]. The battle against Hasidism became the life's mission of Rabbi David. However, he was not able to hold back the storm.

Hasidism even spread to the shtetls near Makowa. We know from a letter from Rabbi David of Makowa of a Hasidic shtibl in Ciechanów, and a Hasidic Rabi in Sheps, Rabbi Meir. This was at the end of the 18th century (see Dubnow, 'A History of Hassidism' Pages 458, 460: 'the *meshuggeh* man of letters of the community of Sheps'. Also on Page 462: 'Someone from this sect traveled to Ciechanów and with heretical speeches that attracted the wild ones established a Hasidic Minyan there')."

In Dubnow, "A History of Hassidism" (Tel-Aviv, 5691 [1931]), Pages 458 and 460, we find: Page 458: "A list of the greatest of the Righteous in the year 5558 [1978]: Rabbi Meir of Shebsh, Meir Shepser (Shepsir)." Page 460: "There were also crazy people with false visions and magic makers. Like the *meshuggeh* man of letters of the Sheps[20] community who shouted on Sabbath in a bitter voice that he saw Nahum Ish-Gamzu[21] and 'heard the secrets of the Torah from him, which our ancestors never achieved, and they are very embarrassed that they didn't understand them but I discovered it'."

An introduction to the Passover Hagadah called "The Glory of Sons and Fathers" appeared in Bilgoraj, Poland in the year 5689 [1928] with two exegeses. "The first exegesis is called the 'Delicacies of Yitzhak' by the righteous Rabbi, foundation of the world, a dear and holy light, the cabbalist, our teacher and Rabbi, Yitzhak Itzik of saintly memory in the next world Hurwitz Segal Chief Judge of the Rabbinical Court of the Community of Rypin. He served there in the years 5586 to 5583 [1796 to 1823] and there he rests in honorable peace.[22]". This exegesis includes the following:

"Once my lord my father my elder the holy Rabbi from Rypin of blessed memory went to visit the holy Rabbi Meirel Shepser. Rabbi Meirel of blessed memory asked him, 'Rypiner Rabbi, what have you brought me? ' The Rabbi from Rypin answered that he had brought a turkey. Rabbi Meirel ordered him to show the turkey. When they brought it inside, the holy Rabbi Meirel pointed to it and said, 'How good and fat this turkey is from all the fasting. ' They did not understand what he meant, so he explained his words. The rabbi from Rypin always fasted for a long time, and in order to hide this from his family, kept the turkey in his room and gave him all the food. Therefore, Rabbi Meirel said the foul is fat from all the fasting. It was well known that Rabbi Meirel of blessed memory was enveloped by the Holy Spirit and immediately understood. From then, the Rabbi of Rypin stopped fasting. He said that it was now public knowledge."

Another part of the life of Rabbi Meirel of Sheps is recounted in the form of a ballad, in the book of poems "*In di Blihendeh Yahren*" by our townsman Yisrael Sapirsztajn[23].

The Slain Pursuer

(A Ballad)
By I.M. Sidroni (Sendrowicz)

Elderly people gather together on occasion
In the old Sheps cemetery
That has such renowned association
With one of the greatest rabbis
With the finest, most noble of personalities,
Who is buried there.

Standing by the grave - surrounded by a wire fence --
Of the great Cabbalist Rabbi Meirel Dvash of blessed memory[24]
The rabbi and spiritual leader of the city
Who dedicated himself to the public,
He was a close Hassid of the *Kedushas Levi*[25]
Later - shackled with the bonds of the future.

They then start talking about in detail
Those curious youths of that time -
The awesome event - although it was already quite ancient
That took place during their grandfathers' childhood,
They listen with great interest
About the person who was suddenly found dead.

It was a short time after
Reb Meirel arrived as the rabbi
Of the Sheps Community - indeed though great effort,
And diligence - for one of the best creations,
Of the *Kedushas Levi*, his protector
That he required from the Kozienicer[26].

He who was regarded as the highest authority
For rabbinical questions of that time,
The Kozhnitzer Maggid, who, as for many cities
Requested that a man conform
If he was to be accepted as a rabbi.
Such a request also came regarding Sheps.

The following took place: He was going to travel
To the *Kedushas Levi* - Reb Meirel as a guest.
I want to hear an answer, a clarification.
"Are you happy?! Did you already become accustomed
To your new way of living of the present" -
He asked him immediately as a close friend.

"Yes!" He answered his rabbi immediately with joy

The Sheps Jews are very good people
However, it was destined for me to also suffer…
One of them does not let me have joy."
Reb Meirel thereby uttered sad words,
I am always summoned to court.

Oh-according to one case of such suffering
The *Kedushas Levi* called him up - he moved
My heart is broken from suffering,
Yes, it was not for nothing that I travelled to you…
You must not suffer for one alone.
No!… One cannot permit this,
No!!!

This lasted for several minutes
In the silence he said something with his mouth,
His face soured

And suddenly - he shouted out loud,
Loud, "Give the evil person according to his evil"!!!
He showed himself to everyone in this manner -- --

-- -- -- -- -- -- -- --

They also did not forget to mention,
Every Friday night, when in the synagogue
The *Kedushas Levi* stood for a long time
Reciting the *Shmone Esrei*[27] - with feelings of awe,
He squirmed at every thought…
The light - was already long extinguished.

And finally - it happened the next day:
When the congregation arrived earlier
Than usual to the synagogue in order to see
How the *Kedushas Levi* with his "fire"
From the beginning of the services, was completely burning
Shouting, running and jumping[28], moving through the turns.

That same pursuer opened the door suddenly
Seeing the enthusiasm, the dancing
He froze like a stone, he did not move,
Immediately, it dawned on him
The *Kedushas Levi* knows: that person[29]
Is indeed Reb Meirel's detractor.

He was already at the time of reciting *Yigdal*[30],
When he realized the truth
He looked at him for a long time. Oh! Perhaps it is a shame
The soul has become corrupted - he thought clearly
It is not a pity! He immediately noticed his glance,
Indeed, he cannot retract…

At the end of the story
They took him home after he fainted
The remedies of the physicians did not help
He lay unconscious like a lump of clay
The end of the protagonist was tragic,
He departed from the world within a few hours...

B. Rabbi Shraga Feibl Danziger

Rabbi Shraga Feibl[31] son of Rabbi Zvi Hirsch Danziger of blessed memory is the second rabbi of Sierpc about whom we have information in the literature. (Called Rabbi Fibili Gritzer, after the town Grójec, one of the places where he served as a Rabbi.) Rabbi Shraga Feibl was the father of Rabbi Yechiel, the first Rabi of Alexander. He served as the rabbi of Makowa during the last years of his life.

Reb Zvi Hirsch Danziger, the father of Rabbi Shraga Feibl was a rich and respected merchant, and an in-law of the "Holy Levi". Reb Zvi Hirsch would sometime travel to Danzig and Poznan on business. Every time he was in Poznan, he would make it a point to hear the words of the Torah from the *Gaon* [Genius] Rabbi Akiva Iger, who was the rabbi there.

Rabbi Shraga Feibl was a prodigy as a Yeshiva student. He was a pupil of the *Gaon* of Leszno, the author of "*Havat Daat*" ["An Opinion"], and the Gaon held him in great esteem because of his logical thinking and straightforward ideas.

His father, three brothers and sister were *Mitnagdim* [opponents of Hasidism]. What then brought Rabbi Shraga Feibl to Hasidism?

In those days, Lublin, the home of the "Visionary" of Lublin was at the center of Hasidism in Poland. The war of the Mitnagdim against the Hasidim was still going on, but because this was after the death of the Gaon of Vilnius, it was not as harsh, and there was a *rapprochement* between the two sides. There was even intermarriage. Hasidism became stronger then, as it won over more people, especially the younger ones. Rabbi Shraga Feibl was swayed by it, and he was attracted to Lublin, to the "Visionary". He looked for the opportunity to go to Lublin, and this came after his wedding, when he had to go there to receive his dowry from a trustee in that city. When he arrived there, Rabbi Shraga Feibl realized his strong desire, and visited the "Visionary". The "Visionary" recognized him as a prodigy, and made him part of his inner circle. After that, Rabbi Shraga Feibl became an enthusiastic follower of the "Visionary" of Lublin.

In order not to be dependent on his father-in-law, Rabbi Shraga Feibl studied to become a Torah scribe. When he was lettering a Torah scroll, he would the consult the book "*HaUrim veHaTummim*" ["The Oracle"] of Rabbi Yonatan. He maintained that reading the books of Rabbi Yonatan purified his thinking. The geniuses of the age said that he had two brains, and could write and learn simultaneously.

After the death of the "Visionary" in the year 5575 [1814], Rabbi Shraga Feibl traveled to see Rabbi Simchah Bunim of Piszczac. The Rabi from Piszczac had a very high opinion of Rabbi Shraga Feibl and they became bound by marriage ties when his daughter married the righteous son of Rabbi Shraga Feibl, Rabbi Levi Yitzhak, who was named after the "Holy Levi". Rabbi Simchah Bunim said, "Rabbi Shraga Feibl thinks he has received an honor [by the marriage], and I say that I have been honored".

Many tragedies struck Rabbi Shraga Feibl. Three of his four sons died while still young. The youngest son, the remaining survivor, was Rabbi Yechiel, the first Rabi of Alexander [a Hasidic sect].

Because of his hardships, Rabbi Shraga Feibl decided to accept the office of Rabbi of a town. First, he served in Sheps, later in Gombin, then to Grójec, and finally he was the Rabbi of Makowa.

After the death of Rabbi Simchah Bunim of Piszczac in the year 5587 [1826], Rabbi Shraga Feibl went to be with his son, Rabbi Avraham Moshe. Two years later, Rabbi Avraham Moshe also passed away. Rabbi Shraga Feibl then traveled to the Rabi of Warka, Rabbi Yitzhak Kalisz.

The Rabbi of Warka died in the year 5608 [1847]. On the Pentecost holiday of that year, the Hasidim of Warka went to Rabbi Shraga Feibl and crowned him as their Rabi. Rabbi Shraga Feibl was a Rabi of Hasidim for only a few months. He died on *Shmini Atzertet* [the last day of Sukkoth] in the year 5609 [1848] and was buried in Makowa.

*

We have read about Rabbi Shraga Feibl's time as rabbi of Sheps in the books "*Admorei Alexander*" ["The Rabis of Alexander"] and " *Kdoshat Yitzhak*" ["Holiness of Yitzhak"], as follows:

The book " *Admorei Alexander*" by Rabbi Avraham Yitzhak Bromberg that was published in Jerusalem in the year 5712 [1951], pages 21-22 states:

"The Rabi Rabbi Simchah Bunim told Rabbi Shraga Feibl to go to Sheps and accept the position when he heard that they were searching for a Rabbi. Because the town was a town of *Mitnagdim*, a well-known learned scholar from Makowa accompanied Rabbi Shraga Feibl, and recommended him to the community. However, Rabbi Shraga Feibl was not pleased with his situation in Sheps, where most of the people opposed him because he was a Hasid. He stayed there only four weeks. In spite of the fact that that Rabbi Simchah Bunim ordered him to stay, he had to leave, because it was not in his nature to tolerate conflicts. Years later, after he had suffered many misfortunes and most of his sons died young, he attributed it to the fact that he had not obeyed the Rabi's edict, and not stayed in Sheps."

The book "*Kdoshat Yitzhak*" ("The Lives of Our Holy Rabbis the *Admorim* of Alexander, their virtue will protect us") by Rabbi Yehuda Moshe Thiberg, the Rabi of Alexander in Jerusalem, published in the year 5712 [1951], page 21 states:

"When the Rabi Rabbi Feibli was the rabbi of Sheps there was much disagreement, and he was forced to leave. But his Rabi, Rabbi Bunim of Przedecz ordered him to return to Sheps[32]. However, the quarrels did not stop and he suffered a great deal. At that time, Rabi Meir Chayim, his brother-in-law's son, studied with Rabi Feibl. He requested permission from his Rabi and uncle to leave Sheps because he could not stand the suffering of his Rabi and uncle and said to him, 'You are commanded by the Rabi of Przedecz to be the Rabbi of Sheps, but I have not been ordered to see the suffering of my uncle and Rabi.' Rabbi Feibli answered him, 'You should be aware of the fact that all my suffering is caused by some negligence when I was Bar-Mitzvah because of your father Rabi Meir Chayim, and now you want to abandon me.'"

The same book, page 25, states: "When Sheps needed a Rabbi, the Sainted Rabbi Natkha Makower, the son-in-law of the holy Rabi, Rabbi Chayim Chayke of Amdur, recommended Rabi Feibli. He explained, 'It is written "Judges and officers shalt thou make thee in all thy gates, which the Lord thy God giveth thee" [Deuteronomy 16, 18] which means that the judges you are given should have the fear of heaven, and this is what the lord gives you.' The Rabi Feibli was a judge like that, who put the fear of heaven in everyone's heart. However, he was there for only a short time, because the town was full of *Mitnagdim*, and they hated Hasidim. His Rabi, Rabbi Bunim, felt he should not leave Sheps. Later, when he suffered the loss of his sons, something not to befall us, the merciful one will save us, he blamed that on his departure from the town of Sheps despite the wishes of the Rabi Bunim."

*

For how long and during which years did Rabbi Shraga Feibl serve as Rabbi of Sierpc? The answers to these questions do not appear in the books "*Admorei Alexander*" and "*Kdoshat Yitzhak*". But the answer to the first question can be determined, perhaps not exactly, but not too far from the correct answer.

Both sources tell us that Rabbi Shraga Feibl accepted the office of Rabbi of Sheps after the appointment of Rabbi Simchah Bunim of Przedecz as Rabi. This means after the year 5575 [1815]. We also know that Rabbi Shraga Feibl left Sheps when Rabbi Simchah Bunim was still alive, that is, before the year 5587 [1827], the year of his death. Therefore, Rabbi Shraga Feibl's period of service in Sierpc was sometime during the years 5575 to 5587 (1815 to 1827).

This is exactly how Rabbi Avraham Menachem Danziger, son of Rabbi Yehuda Moshe Thiburg, may he have a long life amen, the Rabi of Alexander in Jerusalem, answered our question:

"Unfortunately, I cannot tell you precisely. However, it was undoubtedly during the leadership of Rabbi Bunim of blessed memory of Przedecz. This was from the year 5574 [1814] or 5575 [1815], after the death of the saintly Jew, his virtue will protect us, and 'visionary', the Rabi of Lublin, his virtue will protect us, until the 12,th of the month of Elul, 5587 [1827], the date that Rabbi Bunim of blessed memory passed away."

We have not found an answer to the second question, how many years, not even an imprecise one. The second excerpt from the book "*Kdoshei Yitzhak*" states: "But he was there for only a short time". What is "a short time"? We do not know. The statement in the book "*Admorei Alexander*", "He stayed there only four weeks" is not reasonable. First, the community agreed to accept him as a Rabbi despite their knowledge that he was "of the Hasidim". What great harm could they find as soon as he settled in the town that would cause them to regret their decision enough to force him to leave town after four weeks, with all the problems and conflicts this would cause? Secondly, a faithful Hasid like Rabbi Shraga Feibl would not contravene the command of the Rabi after being in misery for only four weeks.

We can summarize this with two conclusions and an assumption.

Rabbi Shraga Feibl Danziger was the Rabbi of Sheps after Rabbi Meirel Dvash.

His period of service in Sheps was during the years 5575-5587 [1815-1827].

We can assume that Rabbi Shraga Feibl Danziger was rabbi of Sheps at the beginning of the above period. This means during the second half of the second decade of the 19th century (approximately 1815 to 1820).

C. Rabbi Avraham

We know very little about Rabbi Avraham, the righteous of blessed memory (who was called "Rabbi Avrahamel Charif" [Sharp]) and even less about his service in Sheps. We present below three excerpts from the pamphlet "*Tzemach Hasadeh*" ["Plant of the Field"] that mention "Rabbi Avraham the Chief Judge of the Court of the Community of Sheps".

The pamphlet "*Tzemach Hasadeh*" (about the Rabbis and great men of Plonsk) by Rabbi Zvi Yehezkel Michelson (Rabbi of Plonsk and later a member of the Rabbinical Committee of Warsaw, Warsaw 5695 [1934]), states on page 2[33].

"An orphan girl remained. Her brother-in-law, her sister's husband, the notary Yosef Frankel brought her up. He married her off to Rabbi Avraham who later became Rabbi and Chief Judge of the Court of the Community of Sheps, and was called Avrahamel Charif. He was the brother of the *Gaon* [Genius] Rabbi Itsheli Chief Judge of the Court of the Community of Plonsk."

Page 3 of the same pamphlet states: "My great uncle the *Gaon* Horvitz instilled the Torah in our town of Plonsk and studied with some charming lads in the great yeshiva. He also studied there with the *Gaon* Rabbi Avraham Chief Judge of the Court of the Community of Sheps. Many of the students left the lessons of Rabbi Eliezer and went to study with my great uncle the *Gaon* Horvitz because they preferred his teaching. Rabbi Eliezer stated clearly that there is no novelty here, because he is a 'master craftsman' since his brother-in-law, the head of the yeshiva, quotes to his pupils the innovations in the Torah of his father, the *Gaon* of Lipnic."

Page 8 of the same pamphlet states: "It is written in the book "Honor Thy Father", 'The Righteous Rabbi, the rich man Rabbi Yishai son of Rabbi Meir of the community of Plonsk built a large *Beit Midrash* [prayer and study house] in his town, with his own money. This was in the year 5562 [1802] and it is called to this day *Rav Yishai's Beit Midrash*'. During the great fire in the town of Plonsk, all the buildings burned down, and only the Beit Midrash was left standing. Rabbi Yishai supported ten scholars who constantly studied in shifts in the *Beit Midrash*, who were called the ten loafers. He also specifically sent the Gaon our teacher Avraham, Chief Judge of the Court of the Community of Sheps to Warsaw to buy a great number of books for the *Beit Midrash*."

*

We have here three pieces of information about Rabbi Avraham: about his marriage, that he would instill the Torah in young scholars, and that he was sent to Warsaw to buy books for the *Beit Midrash* of Rabbi Yishai. However all three of them are about Rabbi Avraham's time in Plonsk, before he became Rabbi of Sheps. The same commentary that appears in the first excerpt, "who later became Rabbi and Chief Judge of the Court of the Community of Sheps" should also apply to the other two.

We can also find two dates here: the third excerpt states that the Beit Midrash was built in the year 5562 (1802), and later in the same paragraph states that Rabbi Yishai passed away in the year 5576 (1816). However, these dates also tell us only about Rabbi Avraham's life in Plonsk. Therefore, we know that his mission to buy books for the *Beit Midrash* was between these two dates.

Consequently, we must speculate that Rabbi Avraham's service as Rabbi of Sheps was after the period of Rabbi Shraga Feibl Danziger. This means the third decade of the nineteenth century (approximately 1820-1830).

D. Rabbi Moshe Yehudah Leib Zilberberg

The Rabbi Moshe Yehudah Leib Zilberberg[34], son of Rabbi Binyamin Zilberberg the righteous of blessed memory was famous as a master of the

Torah, a genius and saint. Many of his pupils became masters of the Torah themselves, and great in teaching in the communities of Israel.

Rabbi Moshe Yehudah Leib corresponded with many of the Torah sages in Poland on questions of permission and prohibition. The rule "The power of permissiveness is preferable" was his guiding light. He tried to be as lenient as possible in most of his pronouncements and in all his searches for the hidden meaning of the Torah. This method is apparent in his book "*Zait Raanan*" ["The Fresh Olive"] (in two volumes, Questions and Answers in Accordance with the "*Shulchan Aruch*"[35]). There he displays his greatness and his depth of understanding of the Torah, both written and oral, and his knowledge and genius in the first and last books. The Rabbi used the above rule in many of his answers to Rabbis that asked him various questions, and he would rule leniently in problems of *Agunah*[36] and other matters. The Rabbi was a *Mitnaged* [opponent] of Hasidim, who questioned the rabbi, and called him insulting names.

The Rabbi Moshe Yehudah Leib was a rabbi in the towns of Kvuhal, Sheps, Dobre, Lask, and Kutno. At the end of his life, he went to the Land of Israel and lived in Jerusalem for eight years. During his time in Jerusalem, he studied Torah exclusively, learned, taught, and raised great Torah scholars and teachers. He was much respected in Jerusalem and was accepted by rabbis of Jerusalem of all the ethnic groups. He wrote the book " *Tifereth Yerushalaim*" ["Glory of Jerusalem"] about the Mishna, which demonstrates his outstanding knowledge of all the parts of the Torah.

Rabbi Moshe Yehudah Leib Zilberberg was born in the year 5554 (1794) in the town of łęczyca in Poland and died in Jerusalem in the year 5625 (1865).

*

During which years did Rabbi Moshe Yehudah Leib Zilberberg serve as Rabbi of Sierpc?

We know of two dates which give us a partial answer. In the book "*Zait Raanan*" ["The Fresh Olive"] (published in Warsaw in the year 5611 (1851), on page 162, Rabbi Moshe Yehuda Leib asks Rabbi Shlomo Zalman Lipchitz (" *Hemdat Shlomo*") about the problem of "a divorce decree in which both parties are from our community[37]". This decree, sent by the holy community of Prague contains a few "stutters"[38] concerning names. When he took the marriage vows, he was called "Mordechai Meshlem Zalman", but was called by everyone by the nickname "Matte", was also called "Mottel", and later "Mordechai Zalman". He was called to the Torah as "Mordechai Meshlem" and his signature is "Mordechai Meshulem (with a 'u') Zalman". "And there are additional stutters in this divorce decree. It contains 'Feril' with an 'i', but the authorization writes 'Ferul' with a 'u'." Therefore, it is the Rabbi's opinion that the divorce decree should state, "I, Mordechai Meshlem, called Zalman and also called Mordechai sometimes Mottel." "The name 'Matte' should not be mentioned at all, since it is a nickname for 'Mordechai'".

The beginning of the question states "Blessed be God, Friday, eve of the Holy Saturday, 24 of the month of Shevat, 5599". Therefore, we see that Rabbi Moshe Yehuda Leib Zilberberg was a rabbi in Sheps in the year 5599 (1839).

We also know that the replacement for Rabbi Moshe Yehuda Leib, Rabbi Mordechai Grinbaum, came to Sheps in the year 5601 [1841]. This means that Rabbi Moshe Yehuda Leib must have left Sierpc in about the year 5600 (1840).

Thus we have solved the second half of our question: the year that Rabbi Moshe Yehuda Leib stopped being Rabbi of Sheps. But the first part of the question, when he began his service, is still open. We can only state that Rabbi Moshe Yehuda Leib Zilberberg was the Rabbi of Sheps in the fourth decade of the 19th century (approximately 1830-1840).

The rabbi mentions that he was Rabbi of Sheps in a few other places in the above book. In the introduction to Part 1 of the book, the rabbi mentions the towns in which he listed the questions and answers and the Torah innovations that are printed in the book. He states, "Just some of the questions and answers and few of the innovations are still with me. What I taught in the holy communities of Dobre and Sheps, may our towns be blessed amen, and some from the holy community of Kvuhal, may our town be blessed amen. But I labored very hard over most of them in three years in the holy community of Lask, and here in the holy community of Kutno, may our town be blessed as I taught my exalted and bright sons and my superlative students."

In part 1 page 31, the second page about the " *Shulchan Aruch*", " *Orech Chayim*"[39], he makes a note about the problem "the non-Jew who is pledged the leavened items[40], and mainly, the question came up when I served the holy community of Sheps for about 15 years."

In Part 1, page 110, second column, "The famous Rabbi, the Great Genius and Saint, my relative and teacher Avraham the Rabbi of Ciechanów visited him when I was in the holy community of Shepsk[41]".

At the end of Part 1 of the book, in the list "Names of philanthropists who subscribed to this book", the following names from Sheps are mentioned: Reb Asher Zalman, Reb Eli Dov, Reb Eli Kaufman, Reb Avraham Hartbrot, Reb Aaron Yoseph, Reb Yisrael Yitzhak, Reb Reuven son of Reb Eli Dov, Reb Shmuel Tatze, Reb Shmuel Zvi HaCohen."

The book "An Encyclopedia of the Pioneers of the *Yishuv*[42] and its Builders" by David Tidhar[43] (Tel-Aviv, undated) contains a detailed biography of Rabbi Moshe Yehudah Leib Zilberberg.

Volume 3, Page 1102 states: "Born in the town of łęczyca, Kalisz District, Poland in the year 5554 (1794). His father was Reb Binyamin Beinisch and his mother was Basha daughter of Rabbi Zev Wolfe Aurbach (Rabbi of Vlodimiretz and later Blenchitz, replacing his father-in-law Rabbi Yosef Chayim Kara, who was, according to tradition, a descendant of Rabbi Yosef Karo, author of " *Beit Yosef*" and " *Shulchan Aruch*". He served as Rabbi there for 80 years, and died in 5560 [1800] at the age of 113. He was head and shoulders above everyone else, and the benevolence of his features threw a light of veneration on his surroundings).

"He studied in Heders and Yeshivot, and excelled in his diligence and knowledge of all the particulars of the Torah, and was ordained as a Rabbi.

"He was a Rabbi in the towns of Kvuhal, Shepsk[44], Dobre, Lask, and later in the city of Kutno. He was known in all the Diaspora of Israel as a genius and saint, and educated many pupils who were great in the Torah and teachers in Israel. He wrote the book "*Zait Raanan*" in two parts - questions and answers in the order of the "Shulchan Aruch. The book increased his fame and genius in the world of rabbis and students of the Torah.

"After he gave the Rabbinate of Kutno to his son, and his son agreed to send him sufficient means for his necessities, in order that he could be occupied with the Torah without having need of others, he ascended to the Land of Israel in 5617 (1857). He settled in Jerusalem in an apartment that he rented in the courtyard of the property of Rabbi David Yelin-Tavih of Lomza. It had a room at the end for a Beit Midrash for Torah study and prayer. Every day he would give two lessons of genius and logical thinking, in the Beit Midrash "Menachem Tzion" which was in the ruins of the courtyard of Rabbi Yehudah Hasid. One was in the morning on the Talmud, and the other in the evening on the adjudicators of Jewish law. Many pupils thronged his house, both young and old men great in the Torah. He would sit all day wearing a *tallit* and *tefilin* [prayer shawl and phylacteries] and teach the Torah without asking for any compensation. He would give lessons to outstanding scholars, together with Rabbi Shmuel Salant. In 5618 [1858] he became a leader of the Talmud Torah and Yeshiva "Etz Chaim" (together with Rabbi Yeshayahu Brodki, the Chief Rabbi Shmuel Salant, and Rabbi Shimon Zarchi of Taurage). In Jerusalem, he taught pupils who became great in the Torah. These include Rabbi Yehoshua Zvi Michal Shapiro (son-in-law of Rabbi Nachman Natan Korogal), Rabbi Yehoshua Orenstein, Rabbi Yehudah Bloomfield (Reb Yudel Blumzer), and Rabbi Nissim Sherlin.

"When in Jerusalem, he wrote the book "*Tifereth Yerushalaim*" ["Glory of Jerusalem"] about the *Mishna* (mainly to explain the questions and amazement of Rabbi Akiva Iger). He was the first to introduce public prayer at the Western Wall. A special *minyan* would gather there every day for the Morning Prayer, but this did not last very long.

"All the great men of Jerusalem, no matter what their ethnic group, respected him. He participated in all judicial events of great public interest. His signature remains at the head of all the Ashkenazi and Sephardic rabbis on the agreement between the rabbis of the two ethnic groups in the year 5619 [1859] on the problem of "titles to properties". He also signed, in 5624 [1864], the "bill of emissary" of Rabbi Yaakov Sapir (author of "*Even Sapir*"). He was fresh and alert until the end of his days. His eyes did not dim, nor did his memory weaken.

"He died on Jerusalem on the 3rd day of Shevat 5625 (1865). Hus descendants were Sarah Libe, wife of Rabbi Yisrael Yaakov Halevy (Rabbi of Plonsk, and later head of the rabbinical court in Jerusalem), Avraham Binyamin Beinisch (Rabbi of Kutno, and later Wieruszów, author of the book "*Alei Zait*" ['Leaves of the Olive"]).

The death of Rabbi Moshe Yehuda Leib Zilberberg is described in the book "One Hundred Years" by I. Troiaks, A. Shtigman, and I. Yaari-Polskin, published in Tel-Aviv in the year 5698 (1938). Page 256 contains a footnote:

"P. Grayevski (in "*Ginzei Yerushalaim*" ["Archives of Jerusalem"], Part 5, 5680 [1920]) quotes from the report of Dr. Binyamin Rata-Tsigal of the Rothschild Hospital in Jerusalem, from the month of Sivan in the year 5625 [1865]. 'There was a serious outbreak of rose disease [cellulitis] in the city and its surroundings, from the month of Elul to the middle of the month of Shevat which caused many fatalities....I will mention here the cases of two people who fell ill with this disease and died prematurely. One was the famous Rabbi and *Gaon* Rabbi Rabi Moshe Leib, of blessed memory, who had been Chief Judge of the Court of the Community of Kutno. The second was the wise and well-known Rabbi Rabi Yosef Schwartz of blessed memory.'"

E. Rabbi Mordechai Grinbaum

Rabbi Mordechai son of Rabbi Yehoshua the righteous of blessed memory Grinbaum[45] was appointed Rabbi of Sheps after Rabbi Moshe Yehuda Leib Zilberberg. He had an impressive pedigree, because he was thought to be a descendant of Rashi[46]. However, he did not just have the pedigree of his forefathers, but was himself a figure of importance. He was a scholar of such high rank that the well-known *Gaon* Rabbi Akiva Iger called him "*Gaon*".

Rabbi Mordechai Grinbaum was appointed Rabbi of Sheps in the year 5601 (1841). Previously, he had been Rabbi of Nieshtat. He was a *Mitnaged*, and the Hasidim of Sheps vexed him greatly. His suffering stopped only after lobbying with the Rabbi of Kotsk, and a warning from the Rabi to his followers[47].

Rabbi Mordechai Grinbaum was the Rabbi of Sheps for 18 years. He passed away on Saturday 16th of Heshvon 5619 (the end of October 1858), and he was buried on Sunday, the following day. The community of Sheps showed their great respect for him during the funeral. On Saturday night, they informed all the towns in the area, and six rabbis from neighboring towns came to the funeral. All the rabbis at the funeral eulogized him and described his mastery of the Torah, his great and good deeds, and the loss to Sheps and to all the communities in the area. The preparations and the funeral lasted all day, till the evening, and all the Jews of the town fasted that whole day. He was buried next to the grave of Rabbi Meirel Dabash.

We can find information on the life of Rabbi Mordechai Grinbaum in the introduction to the book "*Oznei Yehoshua* [Joshua's Ears] (Questions and Answers)" Part 1 by Rabbi Yehoshua Segal (grandson of Rabbi Mordechai Grinbaum and also a rabbi of Sheps), published in Jerusalem in the year 5674 [1913][48]. The following is an excerpt from the book:

"Two young men from the district of Piotrków in Poland became famous as great prodigies at the end of the passing century[49]. One was called Rabbi Mordechai Grinbaum (I believe that was his family name) who was descended from Rashi, and the other one was Rabbi Chayim Filipover. But while success came easily to the latter and he became the rabbi of his town Filipów, and was respected and almost serene there, the former was not as lucky. Because he was a forceful *Mitnaged*, he could not find a rabbinate then in Poland. The Hasidim had the upper hand then, and would persecute all who opposed them. Therefore he was forced to be a melamed in the house of the *Gaon* Rabbi Shlomo son of the Rabbi Akiva Iger, the righteous of blessed memory. He was the *melamed* of his two sons, one of whom was Reb Leibl. One day Rabbi Shlomo traveled from Warsaw to Poznan to meet his father the *Gaon*, the righteous of blessed memory, and brought along his two sons and their *melamed*, Reb Mordechai. When Rabbi Akiva Iger tested his Reb Leibl [on his knowledge of the Torah] he marveled at the teaching method, 'His teacher is a *Gaon* and not a simple *melamed*'. Then Rabbi Shlomo said, 'The *melamed* also came here'. When Reb Mordechai came and they split hairs over Torah meanings, Rabbi Akiva burst out excitedly, 'This Gaon is going to be a melamed? Never! Why shouldn't he be a rabbi? I will ordain you, and you will become a rabbi.'"

"He later became a rabbi in the town of Nieshtat in the Warsaw District, where there was also a rabbi for the Hasidic community. Of course, the two extremes met, but there was peace between them at all times. Then he became the rabbi of the town of Sheps in the district of Plotzk. There were constant quarrels and disputes between him and the Hasidim of the town. But at that time, his student Reb Leibl ran away from his father and became a Hasid of a great rabbi in Lublin. When the Hasidim bothered Rabbi Mordechai, he reported it to his student Reb Leibl. Reb Leibl wrote to the Saintly Rabbi of Kotsk of blessed memory, and he ordered all his Hasidim to beware and honor Rabbi Mordechai. Then everyone calmed down and was in awe of Rabbi Mordechai."

*

We can read about the death of Rabbi Mordechai in the weekly newspaper "HaMagid" that was published in the town of Ełk (Prussia), number 47, the 1st day of the month of Tevet 5619 (December 8, 1858). The article was written by Rabbi Mordechai's son, Rabbi Yehoshua (father of Yitzhak Grinbaum):

"Plonsk. I have just returned from the field of tears of the town Shepsk[50]. There, on the Holy Sabbath, on the 16th day of the month of Marheshvon, the chief Judge of this town, my glory and splendor was interred. That was my father, my master, my teacher, my Rabi, the great *Gaon*, a man of charm and lover of truth, a man of integrity and wisdom and perfection. He was tenfold above all others, our teacher Rabbi Mordecai HaCohen Grinbaum, the righteous of blessed memory. He first was crowned as the Rabbi of the small town of Nieshtat, near where he had settled. There he instilled the Torah in many pupils, some of whom have been ordained as Rabbis. Later he was appointed as Rabbi and Chief Judge of the Rabbinical Court of the town of Shepsk, and for eighteen years he wore the crown of Rabbi there. On this Holy Sabbath, in the afternoon, the light was extinguished, and the great priest was taken from his brothers, to serve at the secret inner sanctum on high. The sound of wailing was heard everywhere that the bad news spread. I also was bent when I heard that the tiara was taken from me. My soul, my soul, a house of winds has turned me into an instrument of mourning, and the sound of tears is my supplication. How great was the respect paid to him by his congregation at his death. On Holy Saturday evening, messengers were sent to the nearby towns to call the rabbis, his pupils, and also the brothers-in-law of the great Rabbi of the light, the strength of Israel, to wail with the multitude and to eulogize him. And all of them came. Six rabbis. Everyone mourned him, and their numbers grew on that day until the people didn't have the strength to cry more. The people stood, extolling and weeping. They did not eat bread or drink water from the end of the Sabbath until the light of day on Monday, the 18th of Marheshvon, when on the tenth hour, they returned to their homes. The lord will grant amnesty to his ashes and will wrap his soul with the bundle of life. On Monday morning, the congregation of Shepsk returned to do justice and charity for the living as they had done for the dead, and in the lead was the great philanthropist, our teacher the rabbi Yisrael Yitzhak Baden, followed in the doing of charity by my great friend and teacher Yaakov Hirsh Kirsch, the light of Israel, to strengthen my mother, the *Rabanit*, she of the great sorrow, with two orphans. They did this by taking my brother-in-law, the Rabbi and great light, versed in the Torah, my teacher and Rabbi, who had been Rabbi in a small town[51] to be the teacher and Rabbi of Shepsk, and he supports my mother, the *Rabanit*, may she live a long life, and her two orphaned sons. My feelings of gratitude come from heart to all the worthy people of the community of Shepsk for their charity and great deeds, your compensation will come from the master of rewards!

"These words are for seekers of god and servants of the truth.

"Yehoshua son of my master, my father, my teacher, my Rabbi, the *Gaon* our teacher and Rabbi Mordechai HaCohen, the righteous of blessed memory, Grinbaum."

F. Rabbi Moshe Yosef Segal

The excerpt from the newspaper " *HaMagid*" that we quoted above tells us that Rabbi Moshe Yosef Segal, of blessed memory, was appointed Rabbi of Sheps in place of his father-in-law Rabbi Mordechai Grinbaum, two days after his death and on the day following his burial, the 17th day of Heshvon in the year 5619 (1858). But this was not an appointment by the community, but by a small group of enlightened *Mitnagdim*, who did it on their own initiative.

The background for this act can be inferred from the way in which the affairs of the Sheps Rabbinate had developed. The last two Rabbis of Sheps, Rabbi Mordechai Grinbaum, and his predecessor, Rabbi Moshe Yehuda Leib Zilberberg, were *Mitnagdim*. It is also reasonable to assume that their predecessor, Rabbi Avrahamel Charif was a *Mitnaged* (after the Hasidic rabbi who preceded him, Rabbi Shraga Feibl Danziger, was forced to leave town because of the persecution of the *Mitnagdim*. The *Mitnagdim* wanted to continue the tradition and appoint their Rabbi, but they apparently knew that the community would not agree to this, because the Hasidim had become a majority (as we have shown above). Therefore, they took matters into their own hands and appointed Rabbi Moshe Yosef Segal, who was both a *Mitnaged* and the son-in-law of the previous rabbi. They apparently thought that establishing the fact on their part would force the community to agree. But the community did not agree, and appointed Rabbi Gedaliah of Żuromin as the official Rabbi of Sheps.

The act of the enlightened Mitnagdim caused the community of Sheps to split into two congregations: the community and the "Kolhekot".

*

The introduction to the book "*Oznei Yehoshua*" ["Joshua's Ears"] that we mentioned in a previous section states, "This Rabbi Mordechai[52] married off one of his daughters to a great scholar of the Torah called Rabbi Moshe Yosef of Plonsk who was appointed a Rabbi of the town of Kitzburg[53] on the border of Prussia, near Mlawa, a small town that could not give him more than 10 'Polish Guilder'[54] a week. Of course, this wage was sufficient only for[55] starvation, and in this desperate situation, he was forced to also be a Melamed.

"When Rabbi Mordechai died, his son-in-law, Rabbi Moshe Yosef was appointed in his place by the congregation of Mitnagdim. But the Hasidim of Sierpc[56] appointed Rabbi Gedaliah of Zrimin[57], so that at first there was a dispute between them, but later the two rabbis reconciled, and served peacefully."

G. Rabbi Gedaliah

The excerpt from the book "*Oznei Yehoshua*" ["Joshua's Ears"] that we quoted above states that when the group called "Kolhekot" appointed Rabbi Moshe Yosef Segal, the larger community appointed Rabbi Gedaliah of Żuromin, the righteous of blessed memory, as the Rabbi of Sheps.

We have very little information about Rabbi Gedaliah. From the fact that he was called "of Żuromin" we understand that before coming to Sheps, he served as Rabbi of Żuromin. The same excerpt tells us that Rabbi Gedaliah was appointed in the year 5619 (1859).

Since Rabbi Gedaliah's successor, Rabbi Yechiel Michal Goldschlak, was appointed Rabbi in Sierpc in the year 5625 (1865), we know that Rabbi Gedaliah's term of office ended during that year or the previous year. But we do not know if Rabbi Gedaliah moved to another town, or if he passed away in Sheps.

H. Rabbi Yehoshua Segal

When Rabbi Moshe Yosef Segal, who was the rabbi of the group of enlightened *Mitnagdim* called "Kolhekot", died, his son, Rabbi Yehoshua, was appointed as his successor.

Rabbi Yehoshua Segal, the righteous of blessed memory was born in Kuczbork on the 26th day of Av, 5606 (1846). He was outstandingly talented even as a child. At the age of 10 he was already famous as knowledgeable in the six tractates of the Mishna. Rabbi Yehoshua became great in the Torah and had noble attributes. He received certification as a teacher from the *Gaonim* Rabbi Leibush Charif of Plotzk and Rabbi Yehoshua of Kutno, and from other famous rabbis. As stated previously, he was accepted in Sheps[58] as the successor to his father as Rabbi of the "Kolhekot".

Rabbi Yehoshua Segal, like his father and grandfather, was a *Mitnaged*, and suffered persecution at the hands of the Hasidim. Quite like the Hasidic Rabbi Shraga Feibl Danziger left Sheps some sixty years earlier because of the harassment of the Mitnagdim, so this time the *Mitnaged* Rabbi Yehoshua left Sheps because of the provocations of the Hasidim.

Rabbi Yehoshua Segal left Sheps in approximately the year 5644 (1884). He emigrated to America, and settled in New York, where he was called "the Rabbi from Sheps". When he left, the affair of the "Kolhekot" ended, and the community of Sheps was once more united.

*

In New York[59], Rabbi Yehoshua Segal served for ten years as Rabbi of the synagogue " *Chevra Tehilim Anshel Vishkova*". In spite of the problems of supporting his family, Rabbi Joshua was busy day and night in America as well with Torah study and writing his books. In one book that he wrote and published there, the Rabbi said carrying an object on Sabbath was permitted in New York, because it was surrounded by water and is considered a single zone. He had a dispute about this with orthodox rabbis who disagreed with him.

Rabbi Yehoshua Segal decided to move to Palestine after the death of his wife. He came to Jerusalem in the month of Ellul, 5668 [1908] with his daughter, Bella. In Jerusalem, he contracted malaria. While taking care of her father, his daughter also contracted malaria, and on the advice of doctors left Palestine in the month of Tevet, 5668, and returned to New York.

His health improved in New York, and he returned to his main preoccupation, writing books on *Halacha* [Jewish Law], among them " *Halachot Tluyot BaAretz*" ["Laws Dependent on Country"] and " *Halachot Chala*" ["Laws of Illness"]. Rabbi Yehoshua died suddenly on the 13th of Adar A[60] in the year 5670 (1910) while sitting at his desk studying and writing.

*

The introduction to the book "*Oznei Yehoshua*" ["Joshua's Ears]" discusses the life of Rabbi Yehoshua Segal at length. The following are some excerpts from the book:

"...and the author in question became greater in Torah and good deeds. The Rabbi Leibush Charif who was called in his time the "iron brain" said about him with great feeling, 'He is the second *Gaon* of Vilnius', and he gave him the teaching certification, and was his advocate with the authorities to be appointed as 'deputy Rabbi'. The *Gaon* Rabbi Yehoshua of Kutno the righteous of blessed memory also ordained him, and so did the Gaon Rabbi Yosef Kara the righteous of blessed memory from Włocławek. When he was sixteen, he married the maiden Chanah, the daughter of a rich widow. She was a 'woman of valor', modest and god-fearing. She had pure and lofty attributes, very wise, and knew how to give her husband the respect that was due to him. She maintained the great man in a style that was suitable to him, so that he never knew any privation, and kept diligently studying the Torah day and night, in a way that was an example to everyone. When his father passed way, he was appointed as his successor as Rabbi of Sheps. However, since he was also a *Mitnaged*, he of course also suffered greatly because of the harassment of the Hasidim. In spite of all the warnings of the *Gaon*, our teacher Rabbi Yehoshua of Kutno, the righteous of blessed memory, that they not show him any disrespect, in the end he despaired of bearing all these troubles, since he was by nature a quiet man. He left Poland and came with all his family to Newark[61] in approximately the year 5644 (1884).

"Even in America, the land of commotion and pursuit of the dollar, he applied himself to the Torah day and night, with self-sacrifice that exceeded all others. As all his associates can testify, he never stopped studying the Talmud, and there he wrote most of his doctrines, that I am now publishing. And everyone who is acquainted with that land could only marvel at the generosity of the man, after all the trials he went through. He had to provide a living for his family, something more difficult than the parting of the Red Sea for a man exalted above the common horde, in a country like that. He succeeded in spending days and nights delving into the sea of the Talmud and the adjudicators, with great heroism and boundless energy. He should be an example to the rabbis who rest on their laurels in small towns without any worries or adversity.

"After the death of our teacher and Rabbi Rabi Yaakov Yosef the righteous of blessed memory, all the congregations of Newark looked to the Gaon and author and recognized him as one of the great rabbis of the city. But then he started to suffer from the harassment of well know people, who were jealous of the respect he was shown and that he did not pay enough attention to them. Thus they took livelihood after livelihood from him, until he had nothing left. After his saintly wife passed away in the year 5666 [1906], and he had to depend upon his sons for support, he decided to go to the Land of Israel. In the month of Elul, 5668 he came to Jerusalem accompanied by his daughter, the gentle and wise Bella, and his friend, Rabbi Avraham Yaakov Louis of blessed memory. His sons sent him what was necessary for him to live with honor.

"Here [Jerusalem], he was welcomed by the most respected figures of the city. Our teacher the *Gaon* the respected Rabbi and Rabi Shmuel Salant the righteous of blessed memory enjoyed debating at length with him on the Torah after they became acquainted. This is based on letters they exchanged containing questions and answers on various subjects. After a number of weeks, both he and his friend Rabbi Avraham Yaakov became very ill with malaria, to the point where they were ordered by their physicians to leave the country. His devoted daughter took wonderful and constant care of him. She labored so hard to relieve him of his pains that she too fell ill with the disease. Then they decided to leave the country in the month of Tevet 5669, and after many hardships during their journey, they reached America.

"In the meantime, I was successful in convincing him to publish the innovations of his Torah, and at the end of the winter of the year 5670 (1910), the first editions of this book were printed. But the shocking report reached us of the passing of the Gaon, which occurred suddenly on the 13th of the month of Adar A. His friend Rabbi Avraham Yaakov Louis passed away two days earlier, and on that day the *Gaon* eulogized him with a heavy heart, that he was his friend and soul-mate since their youth. During the funeral he felt nauseous, and his daughter took him home. When his sons returned home at twilight, the found him slumped over his desk. The immediately called a doctor, who declared that he was dead.

"According to the important New York newspapers '*Tagblatt*', Newark[62] Times, Newark World, and others, the report [of his death] spread like thunder and lightning among all the Jews of Newark. Immediately, hundreds of thousands of men gathered in the streets near his residence to pay their last respects, so that hundreds of policemen were sent to maintain order. Many rabbis eulogized him in the synagogue '*Chevra Tehilim Anshel Vishkova*'; he was their Rabbi and teacher there for the last ten years, and in the synagogue '*Anshei Makower*'. All the streets up to two Parsangs[63] away were filled with men standing shoulder to shoulder who participated in his funeral, and went to his final resting place. May his soul be wrapped with the bundle of life."

I. Rabbi Yechiel Michal Goldschlak

Rabbi Yechiel Michal son of Rabbi Avraham the righteous of blessed memory Goldschlak was born on the 12th of Tevet 5591 (1831) in Shrensk (Szreńsk, a town in the Mlawa district). Rabbi Yechiel was descended from lines of rabbis and learned scholars both on his father's and his mother's side. He was descended from "*Baal HaShach*"[64] on his father's side and on his mother's side he was a descendant of the saintly Rabbi Yechiel Michal of Niemirów, who was martyred during the "Decrees of 408"[65]. His grandfather on his mother's side was Rabbi Chayim Zelig of Shrensk, who was considered one of the righteous of his generation. Because of his great modesty, he rebuffed the many Hasidim that became devoted to him and wanted him to be their Rabi (after the death of Rabbi Shmuel of Kurów) and traveled by himself to the Rabbi of Przysucha, and after he died - to the Rabbi of Kotsk.

Even as a child, Rabbi Yechiel Michal was recognized for his great talents. He wrote of innovations to the Torah when he was a boy to the *Gaon* Rabbi Akiva Iger of blessed memory. The *Gaon* was amazed by this prodigy when he discovered his age. Other great sages of the Torah who spoke to him and read his phrases and innovations wondered at his wisdom and expertise in all parts of the Torah. He became well known in many towns and he became "the prodigy of Shrensk". The *Gaon* who was the author of "Innovations of *HaRim*"[66], of blessed memory said of him "Our Michal is a greater prodigy than all the prodigies of my time".

When he was seventeen years old, in the year 5608 (1848), Rabbi Yechiel Michal Goldschlak was appointed the Rabbi of Kikol, a town in the district of Lipno. He was ordained by the great rabbis, and the author of "Innovations of *HaRim*" also wrote, "In honor of my beloved friend who is the Rabbi that is incisive and expert, wise and complete in virtues and attributes, a patriarch in his wisdom and tender in his years...".

After Kikol, Rabbi Yechiel Michal Goldschlak became Rabbi of his birthplace, Shrensk, and the towns of Poddębice and Ostrołęka. In the year 5625 (1865), he was appointed Rabbi of Sheps.

Rabbi Yechiel Michal Goldschlak was the rabbi of Sheps for 53 years, and was a rabbi of various towns for seventy years. He passed away at the age of 88 on the 21st day of Shevat, 5678 (February 3, 1918).

The community of Sheps paid him great respect when he passed away. On the day of the funeral, the caretaker of the synagogue went throughout the town to call everyone to the funeral of the Rabbi. There were very many people at the funeral, and the eulogies were made at the old *Beit Hamidrash*, the new *Beit Hamidrash*, and at the synagogue. During the eulogies, all the prayer houses, including the women's sections, were full, with a great many people outside. The eulogizers were Rabbis from the area who came to the Rabbi's funeral. They talked about the greatness of the rabbi in the Torah and his wisdom and of the great loss to the town and the whole area. At the request of the *Chevra Kadisha* [Funeral Society], the *Mikve* [ritual bath house] was heated on the day of the funeral, and all the members of the society immersed themselves before the "purification". The funeral society ordered a new spade in honor of the deceased, which was burned immediately after the interment.

In later years, his grandson, Rabbi Yehudah Hashil David, the Rabbi of Sheps, erected a sepulcher above his grandfather's grave.

*

The Warsaw newspaper "*Heint*", in its edition at the end of the month of Shevat, 5678 (February 1918) published the following obituary [in Yiddish].

"The Gaon Rabbi Yechiel Michal Goldschlak the Righteous of Blessed Memory, Chief Judge of the Rabbinical Court of the Community of Sierpc"

"A few days ago the well-known Gaon Rabbi Yechiel Michal Goldschlak passed away. He had been the Rabbi of Sierpc (Plotzk District) for over fifty years.

"The deceased was the oldest rabbi in all of Poland, and was recognized all over the country for his knowledge of Torah and good deeds. He was born in Shrensk in the year 5591 (1841). As a child, he already carried on a scholarly correspondence with Rabbi Akiva Iger of blessed memory, who was amazed at the child prodigy and esteemed him highly.

"The deceased was already ordained Rabbi of Kikol at the age of seventeen and a half with the blessing of the great Warsaw rabbis and the author of 'Innovations of *HaRim*' of blessed memory. Later he became Rabbi of Shrensk, Poddębice and Ostrołęka. From there he went to Sierpc (in the year 5625). The deceased led great Yeshivot in all these towns, which instructed many great scholars and rabbis.

"In addition to his outstanding knowledge, the deceased was great in virtues and good deeds. He was also admired for his clear language, and among the many compositions that he left concerning law and myth, there are some Hebrew books about "*Bchinat Olam*" ["An Examination of the World"], "*Sefer Ben-Sira*" ["The Book of Ben-Sira"], and Lutzato's " *Layesharim Tehilla*" ["Praise to the Honest"].

"May his soul be wrapped with the bundle of life."

*

In addition to the praise heaped on Rabbi Yechiel Michal Goldschlak, it should be added that he was a lover of Zion. He also supported the Zionist movement, in its religious form, when it first appeared. It was only at the express command of the Rabi of Gur that he withdrew his support.

We present below an excerpt from an article titled "Talks with *Admorim* [Great Rabbis and Teachers] in Poland about Zionism" by Avraham Green (Ben-Gurion's brother) that appeared in the Tel-Aviv newspaper " *HaAretz*" on the 29th of Elul 5695 (September 27, 1935). He tells about Rabbi Yechiel Michal's desire to support the Zionist movement, and his refraining from doing so because of the command from Gur.

The author of the article tells of a delegation of Zionist rabbis that included Rabbi Yitzhak Yaakov Reines of Lida and Rabbi Rashi Rabinowicz of Sopotskin that went (on the 1st of the Month of 5660, 1900) to the *Admorim* of Gur and Sochaczew to try to influence them to stop their opposition to Zionism. In the rest of the article, he states:

"As stated above, the two Zionists from Plonsk, Eizik and Esterson, returned to their homes already on Tuesday, after the meeting at the home of Mr. Yasinowski. That same Tuesday, the elderly Rabbi Yechiel Michal Goldschlak of Sheps returned to his town from Gur. He was the author of many well-known books, and had rested there on the Sabbath in the court of the Rabi of Gur as one of his most respected followers. He did not know anything about the trip of our Rabbis there. On his way to Sheps, the Rabbi happened to meet the above Mr. Eizik, whom he had known for some time, on the train. The Rabbi turned to Mr. Eizik with great joy and welcomed him as a guardian angel. Mr. Eizik marveled at the Rabbi's words, and what was behind them. The Rabbi answered ingenuously that he had visited their Rabi in Gur the previous Saturday. On Monday, as they were taking leave of each other, the Rabi asked him if he had already signed the document at the house of one of their associates, whom he named. When he answered that he had not yet signed, the Rabi ordered him to go there and sign it. The Rabbi, who was accustomed to signing "A License of 100 Rabbis"[67], naively thought that this was the kind of document that the Rabi was referring to. When the Rabbi came to the appointed place, he asked about the man being divorced, and the divorce decree he wants to give. When the person there told him that nobody is being divorced there, and he does not have anything to do with a separation decree, the Rabbi returned to the Rabi and told him that no one asked him to sign "A License of 100 Rabbis" such as the Rabi had ordered. The Rabi told him that he had misspoken, and did not mean that he should sign such a license today. He had intended for him to sign the prohibition against Zionists and Zionism that had been prepared at the house of the man where he had been ordered to go. "Of course", added the Rabbi, "I was forced to return to the man's house and sign this prohibition". Twelve rabbis had already signed, among them Rabbi Ephraim Lubiner, a townsman of his (Eizik was born in Lubien). The Rabbi recounted the substance of the prohibition, which agreed with the contents relayed after the Shavuot holiday by one of the followers of the court, Mr. Elevski.

"The Rabbi continued that when he had received the public appeal from the Rabbi of Sopotskin in favor of Zionism, he sent him a long letter praising the idea. (The Rabbi of Sopotskin had already published hundreds of letters like that in the newspapers.) So when the Rabi of Gur's prohibition becomes public, and the Rabbi of Sopotskin will publish his letter in support of Zionism, the wild Hasidim in his town will throw rocks at him and make him out to be a heretic. At his age, he does not have the strength to oppose them and struggle with them. Because of this he asked that Mr. Eizik write to the Rabbi of Sopotskin and request that he not publish his letter until things quiet down."

*

Rabbi Yechiel Michal Goldschlak was not only a great scholar, but also the author of many books, a master of language and poetic phrasing. He wrote many books on Jewish law and literature, faith and thought, homiletics and commentaries, poetry and verse. But only a small part of his compositions ever saw the light of day. Most of them were lost with the loss of the community of Sheps.

*

A book called "*Imrai Emet*" ["Truthful Utterances"] was published in Piotrków in the year 5681 (1921). It contained the commentaries, new interpretations, and rulings that Rabbi Yechiel Michal Goldschlak would write on the blank pages at the beginning and the end and in the margins of the inner pages of the bound books in his library. These notes were collected by the Rabbi's son, Rabbi Yaakov Chayim Zelig. (He was the Rabbi in Tcheroinsk and Lubraniec, and later a teacher in Warsaw. He began collecting the notes when the Rabbi was still alive.) The editor, collector, and publisher presents a list of the books his father wrote in the introduction. These are:

- An exegesis of the Book of Psalms. Entitled "Zion" and "Jerusalem". (Printed in the year 5643 [1882])
- An exegesis of the Book of Ecclesiastes, entitled "Eyes to See" and "A Heart for Knowledge". (Printed in the year 5643 [1882])
- An exegesis of the Song of Songs, entitled "Eyes To See" and "Ears to Hear".
- An exegesis of the scroll of Micah, entitled "Bread of Tears".
- An exegesis of "*Tamni Api*"[68], entitled "Eight Garments".
- The Book of Illuminations, in seven parts:
- Called "Leave and Return", collects all the 613 commandments in one place,
- Called "The Major Illumination", collects all the positive commandments in one place.
- Called "The Minor Illumination", collects all the prohibitive commandments in one place.
- "The Light of Solomon", collects all the commandments pertaining to the "Tzitzit"[69].
- "The Light of Sabbath", as above for Sabbath commandments.
- "The Light from the Darkness", as above for commandments prohibiting superstitions.

- "The Light of Saints and the World", as above for commandments pertaining to circumcision.
- Exegesis of "*Midrash Rabbah*"[70], entitle "The Great Secrets of the Saints".
- An explanation of the " *Agadot HaShas*".[71]
- Innovations and casuistry and long opposing views on aspects of *HaShas*.
- Long commentaries on myths on the order of times of the year.
- Questions and answers on the order of the four parts of the *Shulchan Aruch*.
- "Pure Sayings". Notes on the holy book "Fragments of the Tablets". (Printed in the year 5671 [1910].
- This book "*Imrai Emet*" ["Truthful Utterances"] has two sections. The first is a collection of the various innovative pronouncements taken from the pages at the beginning and end of the bound books in his library. The second part is a group of commentaries and notes copied from the inside pages of these books.
- The book "Crown of the Torah". Verses of the 613 commandments *D'Aurita*[72] and the seven *D'Rabanan*[73] using the initials of the seven commandments, as in the book " *Oharot*" of Rabbi Sa'adia the *Gaon*, and the poetic commandments of *Rabeinu* Yonatan of blessed memory.
- The book "Precious Stone". "*Pirkei Avot*" ["Chapters of the Fathers"] transcribed into biblical language in verses such as in the Book of Proverbs, the book of Ben-Sira, and the book "Proverbs of the Sages" by Rabbi Shimon ben Gvirol and similar books.
- The book "Proverb of the Ancient". Pure poetry about Adam and Eve and the incitement of the serpent. It shows the glory of god with polemic, using verse and questions and answers laden with all the objects of homiletic interpretation, such as in the book "Praise to the Honest" by Rabbi Moshe Chayim Lutzato, the righteous of blessed memory.
- The pamphlet "The Prayer of the *Memin*" as in the *Memin*[74] requests at the end of the book "An Examination of the World", with the addition of poetic phrases, riddles, and songs.
- The pamphlet "A Sign for the Good". Keys to the Holy Zohar[75] with amendments from all the biblical verses it contains.

"He composed some of the works as a youth, such as the books "Crown of the Torah", "Proverb of the ancient", and "Precious Stone" Others he wrote as a young man, after having reached the age of eighteen, such as the books "Bread of Tears" and "Eight Garments" which is about the " *Tamni Api*". This also applies to his commentaries on homiletics and innovations on the six books of the *Mishna*, and his long sermons, which he wrote as a young man in Kikol, Shrensk, Poddębice, and Ostrołęka. This period did not last for eighteen years, and a few of these were written in his middle years, after he came to the town of Sheps at the end of the year 5625 [1865], when he was thirty-five. But the commentaries on the Psalms, Ecclesiastes, and the marginal notes were written when he was 46 or 47, and the questions and answers were written in the last years of his life."

*

This book, "*Imrai Emet*" ["Truthful Utterances"] contains two decrees that Rabbi Yechiel Michal Goldschlak issued on local matters.

The first decree (page 138) is on the matter of "*Ezrat Nashim*" [women's gallery in the synagogue] that was built larger (closer to the eastern wall) than allowed for in the sale of seats in the approved plan. The complaints and grievance came from both the men (that the added ceiling blocks the light and air) and the women (that the extra construction lessens their space and their view of the lower level). The Rabbi was asked if it is permissible to neutralize the extra construction that is part of the synagogue. After long negotiations, the Rabbi decided that to allow the demolition of part of balcony (" *Ezrat Nashim*") that was not built according to the plan, on condition that it does not weaken the whole building.

The second decree (last page) is about transporting the dead to the cemetery. It was the custom in Sheps to carry the deceased on a bed of ropes tied to two poles, with the poles being broken after the funeral and buried with the deceased. The Rabbi was asked if this could be changed to a permanent bed made specifically for this purpose and fitted with legs. And if it was permissible to transport the deceased in a carriage pulled by horses, as was customary in many communities? After long deliberation the Rabbi permitted transporting the deceased on a permanent bed, or transport by carriage, because there is no disrespect to the dead here, but just the opposite, it is a case of honoring both the dead and the living.

*

Rabbi Yechiel Michal Goldschlak wrote short paragraphs in the monthly journal devoted to the Torah, "*Shaarei Torah*" ["Gates of the Torah"] that was published in the years 5663-4 [1903-4]. In Pamphlet 4, page 117, paragraph 45, he comments on various matters of Jewish law found in various books. He agrees with some of them and adds some remarks, and he objects and contradicts others.

J. The Adjudicator Rabbi David Klinman

When Rabbi Yechiel Michal Goldschlak could not continue performing his duties because of his advanced age, Rabbi David Klinman the righteous of blessed memory (called "Friend David") took care of rabbinical matters. He would stay in the Rabbi's house, and issue decrees on what was kosher and not kosher, and permits and prohibitions. After the Rabbi's death, Rabbi Klinman became the official teacher and adjudicator[76] of the community of Sierpc.

Rabbi David Klinman was a very innocent man. He would be occupied day and night with matters of the Torah. He depended on his wife and daughters for a livelihood. They ran a store that sold notions in their house on the Jewish Street near the bridge.

Because Rabbi David Klinman was occupied with his studies all the time, and did not venture into the outside world, he was far from the realm of wheeling and dealing. Therefore, the Jews of Sheps did not come to him on problems of Torah law and arbitration that concerned money matters. Rabbi David Klinman remained an adjudicator in the town also after Rabbi

Yehoshua Heshel David Goldschlak, grandson of Rabbi Yechiel Michal took his grandfather's place as Rabbi of Sheps.

*

Rabbi David Klinman received a pension from the community in his old age. His son-in-law, Rabbi Yehoshua Popowski (from Neustadt) took over his duties. Rabbi Yehoshua Popowski however was not an official adjudicator of the community, and did not receive a salary. This was because the Rabbi (Rabbi Yehoshua Heshel David Goldschlak) vehemently opposed his appointment to this office. But the public paid no attention to the Rabbi's disapproval, since it knew that the Rabbi had an “interest” in the matter. He wanted his son-in-law, Rabbi Leibl Fleisher to be appointed as the adjudicator in the town. All the groups in town would turn to Rabbi Yehoshua Popowski on matters of kosher and not kosher, and permits and prohibitions whenever the Rabbi was out of town (and he travelled a lot, because of problems of illness in his family).

Rabbi Yehoshua Popowski was a great scholar, of noble character and sensitive, but he was also active in public affairs. He also taught Talmud, the interpretations of *Rashi*, and commentaries to young men, with no thought of compensation.

K. The Rabbi From Zelun

Rabbi Nehemcha, the righteous of blessed memory, came to live in Sheps in about the year 1915. He was called “the Rabbi from Zelun” since he had been the Rabbi in Zelun (a town in the Mlawa District). But because he was a difficult man to get along with, the community of Zelun removed him from office, and he moved to Zhoromin. After a few years (in the last years of Rabbi Yechiel Michal Goldschlak's life) he went to live in Sheps, thinking that he would find there the office he had lost in Zelun.

Whereas the adjudicator Rabbi David Klinman was innocent and ineffectual, the Rabbi from Zelun was clever and sharp. Because of this, anyone who needed judgments in Jewish law that concerned arbitration, money, or property would turn to him. He also had his Hasidim, who would come to him with questions of kosher and not kosher. But most of them did this not out of affection for him, but because of their opposition to Rabbi David Klinman. The Rabbi from Zelun lived in Sheps for about ten years, until he was appointed the rabbi of a village near Visla.

L. Rabbi Yehoshua Heshel David Goldschlak

Rabbi Yehoshua Heshel David Goldschlak, the righteous of blessed memory, was the son of Rabbi Yaakov Chayim Zelig (see below) and grandson of Rabbi Yechiel Michal, was a Rabbi in the village of Piszczac. When Rabbi

Yechiel Michal Goldschlak died, the Rabbi of Piszczac tried to use all possible means to obtain his grandfather's office as Rabbi of Sheps. He shouted out to the world, knocked on all doors, and sent warnings to all the newspapers and to all the rabbis that they should not dare to trespass on his property. Of course, he was aided in this by his father, and also by the "court" of "Gur", and by the "Aguda" (the Rabbi of Piszczac, like his father and grandfather, was a Hasid of Gur and a member of "Agudat Israel"). This widespread publicity campaign achieved its objective when the elections for rabbi were announced. Only two contenders submitted their candidacy: the Rabbi of Piszczac and another young rabbi from a village near Lodz, who was a candidate of "Mizrachi" [the religious Zionist party]. Many of the townspeople opposed the candidacy of the grandson of the deceased rabbi, so the election was postponed a number of times. When the elections were finally held (in 1922), the Rabbi of Piszczac won, but with a majority of only 14 votes.

Rabbi Yehoshua Heshel David Goldschlak came to Sheps in the month of Av, 5683 (1923). He was almost fifty years old. He was renowned as a great scholar and good preacher. His sermons were interesting, full of content, and spiced with the sayings of our sages of blessed memory that were appropriate to the theme of the speech. He had a large library of books on the Torah that filled the walls of his study. His behavior was a little eccentric. On the one hand, he conducted himself like a "Rabi", but on the other hand, he tried to display his "modernity". His praying, especially during the "Days of Awe" was very strange. His movements and tics were overdone, even for the religious fervor of the most pious. It was definitely hard work (as the saying of our sages of blessed memory goes "labor is prayer"). It is interesting to note that during the "Days of Awe" he ordered the cantor not to wait for him to finish " *Kriat Shma*" or "*Shmone Esrei*"[77]. Rabbi Yehoshua Heshel was very careful to maintain all the commandments of the *Sukkah* and lived in it for all eight days of the Sukkot [Tabernacles] holiday. For each prayer of grace after a meal in the Sukkah, he would invite a "*minyan*" of men whose names are those of the "ushpizin"[78] of that particular day (ten men named "Abraham" on the first day, ten with the name "Isaac" on the second, and so forth). He would also invite a "minyan" for the lighting of the Hanukkah candles. The Rabbi would eat with his sons in the dining room while his daughters ate in the kitchen.

On the other hand, as mentioned earlier, Rabbi Goldschlak would try to present himself as a modern rabbi. In his sermons he tried to display his wide ranging intelligence, his familiarity with world affairs, and his knowledge of internal and external politics. He spoke Polish fluently and read a Polish newspaper.

Rabbi Goldschlak did not have an easy life in Sheps. He received a sufficiently large salary, but he had many opponents, not only from the circles that initially resisted him, but also from those that elected him.

There was a universal, country-wide reason for the diminishment of the respect for rabbis in Poland. The Polish government had at that time promulgated a law concerning elections in Jewish communities. This was a very reactionary law (it had been tailored to meet the objectives of "*Aguda*"). One paragraph stated that the rabbi of the town will always be a member of the Community Council. Very few Polish rabbis did not take advantage of this undemocratic clause. Most exploited this reactionary paragraph, used the community [council] for their own purposes and provoked the anger of all the Jewish public in Poland on themselves and the institution of the Rabbinate.

It was the same in Sheps. Rabbi Goldschlak was a member of the community council. He interfered in all its affairs, both those that concerned him, and those that did not concern him. He quarreled with the representatives of other parties, and they quarreled with him. Because of this the general community was irritated with him, and their respect for him was diminished.

We have already mentioned the Rabbi's bitter opposition to the appointment of Rabbi Yehoshua Popowski, the son-in-law of Rabbi David Klinman, as adjudicator. In spite of this, many parts of the public turned to him on questions of kosher ant not kosher, prohibitions and permissions. Rabbi Goldschlak also opposed the appointment of Rabbi Shimon Petrikus, the son-in-law of Rabbi Avraham Shochet, as the ritual slaughterer. In spite of this, all parts of the public ate the meat of animals that he had slaughtered. The Rabbi's war on machine-made matzos is mentioned in another part of this book (in the chapter "My Town, Sierpc"). He decreed that they were absolutely leavened, but in spite of this, many of the townspeople ate them.

The above mentioned facts are only a small part of the constant disputes that took place between Rabbi Goldschlak and many different groups in the town (although an "open and public disagreement" in the accepted sense of the word never came to light).

*

Rabbi Yehoshua Heshel David Goldschlak ended the episode of the Rabbinate of Sheps, together with the episode of the Jewish community of Sheps when the hateful German enemy descended upon them and all the Jews of Poland and Europe. Rabbi Goldschlak was among the exiles of Sheps in Warsaw, and he struggled there greatly for the unfortunate refugees of his community. He tried at the "Joint" ["American Jewish Joint Distribution Committee"] and other aid institutions to obtain anything that might ease somewhat the terrible suffering of the Jews of Sheps who were rotting from hunger and disease.

Apparently, Rabbi Goldschlak held a much respected position in the rabbinical world. He is mentioned twice. In the book "Diary of the Warsaw Ghetto" by Hillel Zeidman, published in Tel-Aviv in the year 5706 [1946]. There is an entry on pages 239-241, from 13 April, 1943 (close to the time of the revolt of the Warsaw Ghetto):

"...public proclamations were declared [asking for] volunteers to go to Poniatowa and Trawniki[79] near Lublin...They will work there, under good conditions...The National Jewish Council met and decided: not to go...When the propaganda to go increased in the Ghetto...the rabbis met as a council to discuss this problem. The meeting was held on Kopitzka Street, where Rabbi Menachem Zamba lived, in the apartment of his brother Yitzhak Zamba. The rabbis who participated were Goldschlak from Sierpc...The rabbis decided not to counsel the Jews to go to Poniatowa and Trawniki."

Page 248 tells about the [Passover] *Seder* on the first day of the revolt of the Warsaw Ghetto: "A few rabbis gathered at the apartment of Rabbi Menachem Zamba, on 7 Kopitzka Street. Among them were the Rabbi Bar of Zduńska-Wola, Rabbi Goldschlak of Sierpc...conducting the Seder..."

M. Son and Father of Two Rabbis in Sheps

It is only fitting that we remember here Rabbi Yaakov Chayim Zelig Goldschlak, the righteous of blessed memory, son of Rabbi Yechiel Michal and father of Rabbi Yehoshua Heshel David. In the book "*Ohalei Shem*" ["God's Tabernacles"], there is an article on Rabbi Yechiel Michal, on page 55:

"Rabbi Yaakov Chayim Zelig son of the Rabbi the *Gaon* Yechiel Michal Goldschlak was born in the year 5613 (1853) to the above mentioned father, may he have a long life amen, the Chief Judge of the Rabbinical Court of the Community of Sheps. He is descended from Rabeinu HaShach of blessed memory and the Saintly *Gaon* Rabbi Yechiel Michal from Niemirów. On his mother's side he is the grandson of Rabeinu the *Turei Zahav*[80] the righteous of blessed memory and the *Gaon* Rabbi Heshel the righteous of blessed memory of Cracow. The above mentioned rabbi acquired most of his learning in the Torah from his father the *Gaon*, may he have a long life amen. He was ordained as a Rabbi by: the *Gaon* Our Teacher Rabbi Yaakov Gezundheit the righteous of blessed memory, Chief Judge of the Rabbinical Court of the Community of Warsaw, author of the books '*Tifereth Yaakov*' about '*Hushan Mishpat*'[81], and about Tractates of the *Mishna*; the *Gaon* Rabbi Eli Chayim Meisel, may he have a long life amen, the Chief Judge of the Rabbinical Court of the Community of Lodz; by the *Gaon* Rabbi Yechiel Meir the righteous of blessed memory, the *Admor* of the Holy Community of Gustinin; and by the *Gaon* Our Teacher Rabbi Yitzhak Zanwil Klepfish, the righteous of blessed memory, Chief Judge of the Rabbinical Court of the Community of Warsaw. He became Rabbi of the Holy Community of Shrensk in the year 5636 (1876), and then of the Holy Community of Lubrantz. Later he was appointed as head of a Yeshiva and adjudicator of the Holy Community of Warsaw.

"The following of his books appeared in print:

- '*Yerach LeMuadim*' ['Times of Month'] and '*Kochav MeYaakov*' ['A Star from Jacob'] on times and dates for the portions of the Torah readings.
- '*Emet LeYaakov*' ['Truth for Jacob'], a small anthology about the extent of truth.

- *'Marom Harim'* ['The Height of Mountains'], an eulogy on the Admor from Gustinin.
- *'Hesdai Yonatan'* ['Benevolence of Jonathan'], *'Gvurat Yonatan'* ['Courage of Jonathan'], 'Daat Yonatan' ['Wisdom of Jonathan'], and *'Birkat Yonatan'* ['Blessing of Jonathan']. These are four large books from the holy works of Rabeinu the Gaon Rabbi Yonatan Eibshitz of blessed memory from Prague with commentaries and new explanatory notes by the rabbi mentioned above.
- Questions and answers on the order of the four parts of *the Shulchan Aruch*
- A pamphlet 'Leadership of the Synagogue'

There are more writings and compositions on a part of the "'*Shulchan Aruch*' and an interpretation of '*Tana Divrei Eliahu*'[82]."

Translator's Footnotes

1. [A "Rabi" is the head of a Hasidic sect, considered infallible by his followers, who obey his every word and command.]
2. Rabi Levi Yitzhak of Berdychiv
3. December 1812
4. Napoleon
5. Russia
6. Rabbi of Kosienice
7. [The additional holiday prayer]
8. Rabbi Levi Yitzhak of Berdychiv
9. [A book of tales and teachings by Rabbi Eliyahu haCohen, a 17th century Jewish mystic.]
10. [An ancient Jewish measure of length - from the elbow to the tip of the forefinger.]
11. [The brother of Jacob (Israel)]
12. [Nehemiah ben (son of) Hushiel is a figure in mystical Jewish literature based on a historical 7th century Exilarch (Head of the Diaspora), also considered to be the Messiah son of Joseph who will come prior to the Messiah son of David, but will fail to redeem the Jews.]
13. [One of the tribes of Israel, descended from Ephraim, son of Joseph]
14. [In the central Negev desert of Israel]
15. Barak Yosileviz [An 18th century Jewish hero who was the head of a Polish cavalry battalion during a Polish uprising.]
16. Who fought in Barak's battalion and lost his leg there.
17. The encampment of the Jewish battalion.
18. [Famous preacher]
19. [*Vilna Gaon* - "The Genius of Vilnius" An 18th century Lithuanian rabbi and sage who was the chief opponent (*Mitnaged*) of the Hasidic movement.]
20. In a footnote: He is the same Meir Shepser mentioned above in the List of the Righteous in the ninth supplement and in the second "*Zamir Aritzim*" [an 18th century anti-Hasidic book] page 10: "About the army of the Hasidic Rabbi Rabi Meir of Sheps and all his satellites."
21. [One of the sages of the Mishna (about 2nd century)]
22. "The second exegesis is called 'The Hagadah of Jacob' by his son, the saintly and holy Rabbi, the lamp of light, the cabbalist our teacher and Rabbi Yaakov Uri Shraga, of saintly memory in the next world."
23. The author of the book of poems "*In di Blihendeh Yahren*," Yisrael Sapirsztajn, is the son of the lame bookbinder Reb Ziskind. The book was published in Lodz in the year 5695 (1935) by "Msora" and has an introduction by L. Schiff. The following dedication appears at the beginning of the book: "This work is dedicated to the creative Ms. Sarah Shenider of *Beit Yaakov Gedank*. The Author." The title poem takes up most of the book (132 out of 184 pages). It tells of a girl called Rachelke, who is quiet and delicate, serious and religious. She is a diligent student and talented artist who

becomes ill and dies young. The second part of the book is called "Songs and Ballads", with 18 songs, 2 ballads, and 2 lists. The ballad that is quoted here is on page 146. We can judge the poetic quality of the book by this ballad, but we are interested in its contents. The ballad is based on a legend that apparently was prevalent in town about the early days of Rabbi Meirel in Sheps.

24. [Mentioned here as Rabbi Meir Devash: http://www.jewishvirtuallibrary.org/jsource/judaica/ejud_0002_0018_0_18481.html]
25. [Rabbi Levi Yitzchak of Berditchev: http://en.wikipedia.org/wiki/Levi_Yitzchok_of_Berditchev]
26. [See http://en.wikipedia.org/wiki/Kozhnitz_%28Hasidic_dynasty%29 for the Kosienici Hassidic dynasty. The first Kozienici Rebbe was one of the forerunners in bringing Hassidism to Congress] Poland. See http://en.wikipedia.org/wiki/Yisroel_Hopsztajn]
27. [The Eighteen Benedictions - the main portion of the prayer service.]
28. [From religious fervor.]
29. [Referring to himself. The detractor realized that the Kedushas Levi has found out that he was the detractor, and that the game was up.]
30. [The hymn at the conclusion of the prayer service.]
31. This article is based on the book "*Admorei Alexander*" ["The Teachers and Rabis of Alexander"] by the Rabbi Avraham Yitzhak Bromberg, Jerusalem 5712 [1951].
32. Apparently, this wording "ordered him" is not exact, and the other version in the same book states "His Rabi, the Rabbi Bunim felt he should not leave Sheps" is correct.
33. The pamphlet ["Plant of the Field] is printed at the end of the volume "Plant for Avraham, a composition about "*Yalkut Shimoni*" ["The Anthology of Shimon"] that was written by the rabbinical biblical scholar, the elder, the great teacher, Rabi of my Rabi, Zvi Hirsch Halevi of the holy community of Plonsk.
34. The family name, Zilberberg, cannot be found in the Rabbi's books, or in the books written about him. However, we found out about this name from Rabbi Aaron Shlomo Ellberg, a learned scholar and enlightened man. He is a native of Kutno and author of a book on Rabbi Yehoshuale of Kutno (in manuscript). He learned of the family name of the Rabbi, who was also a Rabbi in Kutno according to Rabbi Yehoshuale, from members of the Rabbi's family.
35. ["The Set Table" - A book that codifies Jewish Law, by Yosef Karo, from the 16th century.]
36. [*Agunah* is a woman who is "chained" to her marriage because her husband is missing or will not give her a divorce.]
37. Sheps
38. Faults
39. 'Way of Life", Part 1 of the "*Shulchan Aruch*"
40. [Before Passover, the Jewish community has to (temporarily) sell any leavened food to a non-Jew.]
41. Also in "*HaMagid*" number 47 of the first day of the month of Tevet 5619 (December 8, 1859), in an article about the death of Rabbi Mordechai Grinbaum, our town is called "Shepsk". Apparently, during a certain time, this was the way that the name of our town was pronounced.
42. [Yishuv - the Jewish Settlement in Palestine]
43. Also in the book "Chronicles of the Sages of Jerusalem" by Arie Leib Fromkin with additions and comments by Eliezer Rivlin, Part 2, page 238
44. The author of the Encyclopedia apparently copied the name "Shepsk' from the book written by the Rabbi.
45. Rabbi Mordechai Grinbaum was the grandfather of Yitzhak Grinbaum, the leading political figure of the Jews of Poland, and the grandfather of our townsmen Shimshon Mordechai and Yehoshua Visroza.
46. [Rashi - acronym for Rabbi Shlomo Yitzhaki, an 11th century rabbinical scholar considered the "father" of biblical and Talmudic commentators. His commentaries, in his distinctive script, appear in almost all editions of the Pentateuch and Talmud.]
47. Apparently, the Hasidim had the upper hand in Sheps in those days. We have read previously that in the period that Rabbi Shraga Feibl Danziger was Rabbi in Sheps, Sheps was a "town of Mitnagdim",

and the troubles that that Hasidic Rabbi suffered at the hands of the Mitnagdim caused him to leave town. But now, the tide had turned and the town's Hasidim bothered the *Mitnaged* Rabbi.

48. The book was published after the author's death. The introduction was written by Rabbi Yisrael Zev Halevy Ish Horvitz.
49. The author's intention is apparently to the end of the sixth century [of the sixth millennium] according to the Hebrew calendar. The term "past" should have been used instead of "passing".
50. We have already commented in a previous excerpt "Apparently, during a certain time, this was the way that the name of our town was pronounced"
51. Kuczbork
52. Rabbi Mordechai Grinbaum
53. Kuczbork, a town in the Mlawa district
54. Polish silver coins
55. Apparently, the word "preventing" is missing here.
56. After the split, the community was almost completely Hasidim.
57. Żuromin
58. According to reliable sources, Rabbi Yehoshua Segal was called "adjudicator" in Sheps.
59. [The author states here that Rabbi Yehoshua settled in New York. However, in a later chapter of the Yizkor book ("Institutions and Activists"), the author mentions that Rabbi Yehoshua was Rabbi of a synagogue with the same name that was in Newark.]
60. [In the Jewish calendar, there are leap years where the month of Adar is repeated, so that there is Adar A and Adar B.]
61. [Again, here Newark appears instead of New York. It is possible that the author of this excerpt did not know there is a difference between the two cities, and this is the source of the confusion.]
62. [Again the confusion between "Newark" and "New York" in the source.]
63. [Another ancient measure of length, about 4 miles. Sounds a bit exaggerated.]
64. Author of the book "*Sfatei Cohen*" ["Lips of the Priest"]
65. [A series of pogroms in Poland and Ukraine during a Cossack uprising.]
66. Rabbi Yitzhak Meir, the first Rabi of Gur.
67. [A Rabbinical decree that can temporarily override a detail of Jewish law under particular circumstances, usually in matters of divorce]
68. [Aramaic for "Eight Faces", Psalm 119, this is the longest Psalm and the longest chapter in the bible, and an acrostic as well.]
69. [The fringes on the garments worn by Orthodox Jews]
70. [Aramaic for "The Great Interpretation". An exposition of the books of the bible.]
71. [More Rabbinical literature.]
72. [All sorts of ways of counting how many commandments there are]
73. [Ibid]
74. [Requests and prayers whose words all start with the Hebrew letter "mem"]
75. [The book of the Cabbala]
76. [The term in Hebrew is "*Moreh Hora'a*" (literally a "teacher of wisdom"), a title for an ordained rabbi who has been accepted by the community as an issuer of religious decrees and decisions.]
77. [Important parts of the prayer service.]
78. [From the Aramaic "Guests", a prayer recited by some in the Sukkah welcoming the seven shepherds of Israel: Abraham, Isaac, Jacob, Moses, Aaron, Joseph and David.]
79. [Sites of concentration camps]
80. "Turei Zahav" {"The Golden Columns"] is a commentary on the "*Shulchan Aruch*".
81. "*Hushan Mishpat*" ["A Breastplate of Judgment"] is one of four parts of the "Shulchan Aruch"
82. [A Midrash (interpretation of the Biblical narrative) by the *Tanaim* (Jewish Scholars of the first three centuries of the Common Era).]

The Holders of Religious Posts in Sierpc

By Rabbi Moshe Dov (Ber) Goldman

Rabbis and Cantors

Rabbi David Kleinman of blessed memory was the rabbinical decisor[1] of the community. He did not receive any salary. His primary livelihood was from his tailoring workshop that he ran near the bridge and from traveling to the fairs where he set up a stall. At times, he would earn a few rubles for an arbitration, or when the rabbi got him involved with koshering a mill or a matzo bakery for Passover.

Reb David was a Gerrer Hassid, a modest man, and a *tzadik*. He would study *Gemara* when he was in his store. When a customer, a farmer, would come to purchase merchandise on a "*spudnitze*,"[2] he would place his red kerchief over the page of *Gemara* as a testimony - a remedy[3] against forgetting - and conduct business with the gentile in a *Gemara* melody, thereby continuing to think about the Talmudic section that he had been studying. If a solution to a difficulty in *Tosafot* regarding "*Kofer HaKol*" or "*Modeh Bemiktzat*"[4] while he was measuring an *arshin*[5] or merchandise for the "*spudnitze*," he would forget about the gentile and run to the *Gemara* to write his idea down in the cover. Of course, he did not become a wealthy man from this type of business.

There was another rabbinical decisor in the city, who was never an officially recognized clergyman of the community. However, since he was knowledgeable in issuing rabbinical decisions, he would issue a decision on a question when one asked him. He was called Reb Efraim Yosel Wloka, a scholarly, intelligent Jew. He was a *Misnaged*[6] his entire life, and worshipped in the new *beis midrash* along with the *maskilim*. My father appreciated Reb Efraim Yosel very much, because he was one of the important scholars of the city.

The cantor, *shochet* [ritual slaughterer] and *mohel* [circumcisor] Reb Eliezerke Smolinski of blessed memory was a jewel of the community. He lived in Reb Yisraelik Lipson's house near the *zhika*. I recall from my childhood years how we used to fool around before the holidays, especially before Rosh Hashanah. Every evening, we would climb upon the railings of the bridge that was immediately opposite the cantor's open window and listen to him practice for the holidays with his choir.

The cantor, who was short, would usually wear a Polish-Hassidic tall pointed hat that made him a bit taller. He held his tuning fork in his right hand and a baton in his left hand, directing the choir like a choirmaster.

Aside from the bass and tenor professional singers who were preparing to be cantors, the rest of the choir members were children, artisans, or business "subjects" who had voices, but were very far from melodious and musical.

It was a pity to look at the elderly Reb Eliezerke as he toiled hard, with sweat running down his face, to bring a new "*umipne chataeinu*," "*kevakaras*," "*hayom harat olam*" or "*kedusha*"[7] to the choir. We youths, for the most part *Gemara* students with good heads, would catch on to the pieces from outside, and – one two three – sing with cantorial groans.

It was said that in his younger days, Reb Eliezerke was an exquisite musician with an exceptional voice. This was at the time he arrived in Sierpc from Lithuania. When he was older, he was often hoarse. Therefore, he wore a woolen scarf on his neck, even during the summer.

The Dispute Regarding a Cantor

After Reb Eliezerke's passing, they began to look for a replacement. Candidates came from various cities and towns to try out. Some of them wore short suits and had trimmed beards. They spoke a German style Yiddish. These were cantors, and not *shochtim* or *mohels*. They had studied in conservatories and had cultivated voices. They wore black capes with top hats, and would have been more appropriate for the opera or for a German choral synagogue than for the Sierpc synagogue. There were also cantorial candidates who were fine Jews, dressed in Hassidic garb, with beards and *peyos*, who were good *shochtim*, *mohels* or teachers, but dull in cantorial skills.

There were also fitting candidates for the cantorial position of Sierpc, whom the congregation did not want to hire for various reasons. For example, the cantor Reb Kalman came for a Sabbath from Nieszawa, a town near Wloclawec. Reb Kalman was a musician with a non-hard voice. He was also a good *shochet*, *bodek*[8], and *mohel*, with all fine traits, such as: a pious intelligent man, knowledgeable of the book -- was this not good? From the outset, apparently not. He had one major flaw, perhaps the greatest one. From his youth, he grew up in Reb Eliezerke's house, sang with him in the choir, studied *shechita*, *bedika*, and *mila* from him, and later became his son-in-law. Everyone in town knew him and would call him by his first name – Kalman. How can such a person be given appropriate honor by the community? Could they call him Cantor, *Shochet*, or Reb Kalman, given that they knew him from the time of his youth?

There was another one with all the appropriate requirements: the cantor of Lubraniec – a town near Wloclawec. He had everything: he was a good cantor, a fine Jew, a *shochet* and *mohel*, without exception. However, the rabbi, Rabbi Yechiel Michel of holy blessed memory, without whose approval, especially with regard to *shechita*, nobody could be hired, said: "No, never."

The reason for the rabbi's disapproval of the Lubrianer Cantor was as follows: the Siercper rabbi had a son, who was a *gaon* [rabbinic genius], Rabbi Yaakov Zelik Goldszlak, who was the author of many books. In his youth, he was the rabbi in Lubraniec. There had been a dispute against the rabbi, with slander to the authorities. There was a suspicion that the cantor had become involved in the slander. At the end, Rabbi Yaakov Chaim Zelik had to move away. He became a rabbinic decisor in Nalewkes in Warsaw, and remained there in great honor until the end of his life.

[Page 42]

Thus, the community of Sierpc was unable to choose a new cantor. The matter lasted several years. Various factions were formed with various ideas. The enlightened people claimed that Sierpc must be freed from the spoiled idea that the cantor must also be a *shochet.* They wanted a "cantor" a musician, a "La sirotta"[9].

The Hassidim shouted at the enlightened people, "You sinners, you want a 'cantor'? In truth, to quarrel[10] with our Father in Heaven. Troublers that you are, violators of the Sabbath, go to the theater with your girls if you want to hear singing. We need a representative of the congregation, someone G-d fearing, who will pray with proper intention. Who needs cantorialism?"

The average people, tradesmen, poor shopkeepers and market merchants would say, "We require both aspects. Both a good cantor, as well as a *shochet.* This is indeed our sole pleasure in life. A '*mimkomecha*'[11] that comes from the heart and evokes a tear. "

A Cantor for G-d and for People

One Sabbath eve, a rumor spread through the city that a cantor had arrived from Nowe Święciany, near Vilna -- exquisite, with a voice "roaring like a lion, " a "golden" person, a scholar, knowledgeable in Torah, pious, modern, a *shochet,* a *mohel,* a musician and a conductor. He lodged in Lent's guesthouse. He was examined by the pillars of cantorialism in the town: Noachek Fukacz, Rafaelka Kleinhaus, Noach Lobaszka, Aharon Rozenik, Wolfke Czornaczopki, and others. They determined that the cantor was appropriate, and began to work at convincing the common folk from their side.

People gathered at Lent's guesthouse, toasted a *lechaim,* and set out into the city to urge that the cantor be given a chance to try out. Noachke was already a bit tipsy, and spoke some harsh words, "Blood will flow if you do not accept the cantor!!" Indeed, he presented an "*Av Harachamim*"[12].

Noachke wept and sang, "Why, why, sweet Father, should they take revenge for our flowing blood... Why why, and aye, aye aye, should the gentiles say, a wind in their impure, piggish bowels: where is G-d? The singing of the new cantor goes through all the limbs."

They began to whisper that there might be strong opposition from the side of the Hassidim, for the cantor is a Lithuanian, and he came with a short coat and a hard kapelush hat, as was the custom of the Lithuanians.

Noachke did not accept this and declared, "We will dress him up. I am a master tailor, not second rate. We will make a long frock out of silk for our cantor. We will get a hat from Betzalel Lopatke. I will arrange to have a pair of chamois leather boots sewn for him at Baruch's, and we will turn him, in a single day, into a perfect Hassid."

He spoke and he acted. They hid his German style clothing, and dressed him up so well that even his own mother would not recognize him. He had a refined looking face, and a *yeshiva*-like appearance as if from his mother's womb. The Hassidim were also glace (what is the meaning of this word?) and said, "Seemingly this is from Heaven."

The cantor Reb Daniel Sheikes from Nowe Święciany near Vilna made such an impression Friday night with his service of Welcoming the Sabbath in the synagogue that all the worshipers in the packed synagogue enthusiastically talked about the new Sierpc cantor.

Immediately after *Havdala*[13] on Saturday night, the city notables, Noachke among them, gathered at a meeting in the Rabbi's courtroom. The rabbi inspected Reb Daniel's *shechita* knife, tested him on the laws, and nodded his head in assent.

"*Mazel Tov*," those gathered said, "Reb Daniel, you are the cantor of Sierpc."

The Sierpc community simply came to life and received a new soul with the arrival of the new cantor. The synagogue was packed every time that the cantor conducted services with his choir, on *Shabbat Mevorchim*[14], *Shabbat Rosh Chodesh*, the four special portions[15], the lighting of the Chanuka candles, and especially at festival services. The soda makers, businessmen, fishermen, butchers, tailors, furriers, shoemakers, blacksmiths, and locksmiths would first worship early in the morning in the old *beis midrash*, and, following, the *Kiddush* with the fish and fatty onions, would go to the large synagogue to enjoy the cantorial performance.

Shochtim and *Shamashim* [Ritual Slaughterers and Beadles]

When Reb Itche Yosel Canachowicz, the *shochet* of Sierpc for several years, left for Kalusz, they began to seek another *shochet*. A similar dispute took place, although on a smaller scale than the one regarding hiring a cantor. There were several candidates, and each one had his own side. This time, the sides were not *Misnagdim* and Hassidim, the common folk and the wealthier householders, but rather Hassidim against Hassidim. The dispute was between Ger and Alexander[16]. The Gerrers wanted the *shochet* to be a Gerrer Hassid, and the Alexanders wanted specifically an Alexander Hassid. In Sierpc, there was also a *shtibel* of the Plocker Hassidim, formerly Dobriner; however, they were so small and weak, and did not have their own power, so the Gerrers and Alexanders tried to win their Dobriners over to their own side.

Some time passed, and dozens of candidates came forward from near and far. They had differing skills, as well as letters of approbation from *rebbes*, but nobody moved from their place. If Ger said yes, Alexander said no.

A Jew once came to Sierpc from the small, nearby town of Sochocin, as a candidate for *shochet*. He was a young man, a "*tchotchke*"[17]: tall, head and shoulders taller than everyone, with a face as handsome as an angel, with a black beard and two black, fiery, hypnotic eyes. He always had a smile on his lips, and his joy and friendship were infectious. With the bat of an eye, he won over the Jews of Sierpc.

Before he was tested regarding *shechita* and *bedika* in the slaughterhouse, and before his *shechita* knife was checked, rumor had it in the city that the community would appoint him. The women simply fell in love with him, and wanted Reb Yankel Reitczyk to be the *shochet* of the Sierpc community.

Pious Hassidim were greatly unhappy with the new *shochet*. They smelled that everything was not entirely proper. That lovely, beloved, smiling young man who can tell a proper joke; who does not shut his eyes if a woman speaks to him, but rather looks directly at her face; who does not say "put it on the table" when she hands something to him, but rather takes it directly from her hand – the pious folk did not like that particular *shochet*. They felt that he was not so righteous because he wore a velvet hat during the week, and had *peyos* that were not so long.

The examination took place. The rabbi found him to be a sufficiently expert shochet. When the butchers saw how he slaughtered with nimbleness and dexterity, they immediately drank a few bottles of Akevit[18]. Reuven Zecharia's, Eliahu "Grepser," and all the other butchers were full of amazement, and wished the new *shochet* a *Mazel Tov*.

The *shochet* was loved greatly in the Sierpc community. Indeed, he was a Jew with all the fine traits: a fine prayer leader, an expert *shochet* and *mohel*, with a splendid appearance, wise and intelligent, getting along well with people, a good soul with a heart of gold, G-d fearing but not fanatic. He was a modern Orthodox Jew, who was loved by all classes of people: Hassidim, *Misnagdim*, observant and non-observant.

"Woe over those who are lost and will never be forgotten." He departed from the world tragically as a young man, in the second year of the First World War, during the typhus epidemic that spread through Sierpc and claimed many lives. A few months before his own death, he endured a great tragedy in his family, as his eldest daughter, Esther, died of typhus at the age of 15. Esther was the spitting image of her father. She was tall, well-grown, and beautiful, with the face of an angel, eyes like two lovely sapphires, and hair that covered her head like a crown.

After Reb Yankel's passing, Reb Yosel Eisenstat was hired as the *shochet.* Reb Yosel was a fine Hassidic musician, a *shochet*, *mohel*, and an honorable Jew. The community was content with him

*

Reb Moshe, the *shamash* of the old *beis midrash*, was a typical clergyman from his mother' womb. He was no scholar, but he carried out his holy work faithfully. On early winter mornings, he was the first person in the *beis midrash.* He heated the ovens, lit the lamps, and made the preparations for the first *minyan* [prayer quorum]. He was employed in this manner until 10:00. Then he was finished, and went home to eat something. He would also look in at the *beis midrash* at noontime.

"White friends" would play various tricks on Reb Moshe. The older he got, the weaker his eyesight became, and he had to wear dark eyeglasses. He would chase the children around the *bima* and would never catch them. His yelling and cursing out loud did not help. The more he shouted, the more the group laughed. It was a pity to see him while he was involved with the Jewish "*shkotzim*"[19] and unable to control them.

Reb Leibish, the *shamash* of the new *beis midrash*, was a great scholar who would sit and study day and night. He was formerly a merchant who owned a small leather shop.

Finally, I wish to mention one of the first *shochtim* of the Sierpc community. They called him Reb Avraham Shochet. This Jew was an exception in that he worked almost around the clock. He was only a *shochet* of fowl, and he lived all his life in his own small house behind the *beis midrash.* One could always find him in his house poring over a book. His *shechita* room was also there. Day or night, if someone needed a fowl slaughtered for a sick person, Reb Avraham was prepared. Reb Avraham's wife would remove the feathers on the spot so that they could sell it, thereby helping her husband with his livelihood.

Reb Avraham was an Alexander Hassid and a warm hearted Jew. Full of joy and faith, he greeted every Jew pleasantly. He was also a fine prayer leader. He would always lead the first *Selichot* service in the Alexander synagogue and "*Zechor Brit*"[20] in the old *beis midrash.* He would recite his prayers in a heartfelt manner, with Hassidic fervor. At times, he would lead the *Musaf* service on the High Holy Days in the old *beis midrash,* and at times in the new *beis midrash.*

Such were the clergymen in the former community of Sierpc.

Translator's Footnotes

1. Moreh Horaah – a rabbi who issues decisions on halachic questions. Such a person may be different than the community rabbi.
2. I am not completely sure what this word means, but "spodnie" is the Polish word for trousers.
3. Segula – a kabbalistic or mystical remedy.
4. Tosafot is a commentary on the page of Talmud. Kofer Hakol – a person who denies everything, and Modeh Bemiktzat – a person who partially admits, are concepts in Talmudic law.
5. An old Russian unit of measure, roughly 28 inches.
6. A non Hassid or opponent of Hassidism.
7. Various sections of the High Holy Day prayer service (although Kedusha is recited daily).
8. Bodek – someone who examines slaughtered animals to see if there are any blemishes or imperfections that might render the animal non-kosher.
9. I am not sure of the meaning of this term.
10. There is a play on words here, as the Hebrew is lekanter.
11. A section of the Sabbath and festival morning service.
12. A section of the Sabbath morning service – Noachke made a parody of it in the next paragraph.
13. The ceremony that marks the end of the Sabbath.
14. The Sabbath prior to Rosh Chodesh (the New Moon).
15. Four special Sabbaths in the vicinity of Purim, at which special prayers are recited.
16. See http://en.wikipedia.org/wiki/Aleksander_%28Hasidic_dynasty%29
17. This word does not translate well into English. It has the connotation of a fancy, superficial person. See http://en.wikipedia.org/wiki/Tchotchke
18. A Scandinavian liquor.
19. This is usually a derogatory term for gentiles, but here it has the connotation of a wild kid or an "urchin."
20. The Selichot service two days before Yom Kippur. Selichot are the penitential prayers recited during the period preceding Rosh Hashanah until Yom Kippur.

The Old *Beis Midrash*

by Moshe Dov (Ber) Goldman

Personalities and Characters of Scholars and Observant Jews

The old *beis midrash* was the living spirit of the Sierpc community. There, the heart, the soul of the town, beat. As a former Sierpc *beis midrash* lad, I remember well the appearance of the old holy place.

The old building was brown, with a red, greased roof. Through the high, old fashioned windows, one could see the blue sky and the sparkling rays of the sun.

Zelik Reichgot's small tavern was to the right of the *beis midrash*. After services, Jews would go there to recite a blessing, and to refresh their hearts with a glass of Akevit (a strong spirit) and a piece of herring with a *kichel*. The naïve Reb Naftali, with his "guitar" lived on the left.

Baruch Konenbrand's bakery was opposite the beis *midrash*. The aroma of freshly baked rolls and raisin bread would waft through the beis *midrash* windows every morning. We indeed worshipped and studied in a tasty manner...[1]

The aromas of Shlomo Chaya's spice shop and teahouse also captivated us yeshiva lads. The schmaltz herring of the casks, truly "Ulikes" [meaning of this word is unclear]and the hot tea with sugar and lemon teased our noses and palates as we were studying and worshipping. We usually thought, "Soon we will go home to eat a bit. It will be a pleasure. A fresh roll, a bit of herring, and a glass of hot, sweet tea with lemon."

The lovely, blue river flowed calmly and idyllically from behind the *beis midrash* past the yard. The water would recede around the month of May. Then, one would be able to walk easily across the river, dancing from stone to stone until one arrived at the other side. Maszerowske's orchard was there. We would quietly snatch and snack on fresh, supple, blood-red strawberries and indeed recite a "*Shehecheyanu*"[2].

What type of dreams did we *beis midrash* lads weave there by the river... In the winter nights on the ice, and in the summer nights on the sailing boats, we thought, strove, hoped and fantasized - at times even romanticized... However, very little of this remains in the memory. Only the old *beis midrash* is etched in my thoughts, for there was pure G-dliness and holiness there. The holiness continued for generations without interruption.

Anyone who visited the *beis midrash*, frequently or rarely, for a long time or a short time, whether for Torah, worship or charitable deeds, left with an inestimable spiritual treasure...

*

It was pitch dark outside. Doors and shutters were locked. At dawn, the hens crowed.

In a humid, dark room behind the bridge, right by the water, a Jew was snatching some sleep. He called out in terror, "It is already late! Soon the morning guardians will gather!"

He washed his hands with the *negl-vasser*[3] prepared by the bed, recited "*Mode Ani*"[4] with great devotion. He rubbed the sleep away from his eyes. He speedily put on his clothes and quickly ran to the *beis midrash*.

The Jew toils in his cellar for the entire day. He sews with his needle by the light of the dark kerosene "*Kopshtik* [*what is this?*] lamp." He plucks, rips, turns over, sews, and fixes farmers' clothes: trousers, parkas and caftans. With sweat, he toils for a morsel of bread for his family. Comes midnight and, as a "morning guardian," he is no longer a tailor and patcher. He is Yosefke Chaike's - a *tzadik*, a hidden righteous person, a *lamed-vovnik*[5]. His name was Reb Yosef. He takes his *tallis* and *tefillin* from the nail near the door. They hang there constantly in case the Messiah comes suddenly, and one must hasten to the land of Israel. His *tallis* and *tefillin* would be ready.

He kisses the mezuzah with great love and starts to run to the *beis midrash*. He opens the door of the *beis midrash* with a thrust. He enthusiastically states, "And I, with Your great mercy, come to Your house. I thank you G-d for the mercy with which you have restored my soul, and I am not late."

Nobody ever had to look for him. He was always the first in G-d's house. He bows toward the holy ark in the east: "And I bow down." The illuminated eternal light flickers toward him. He sees the Divine Presence smiling from between the cherubs over the ark.

It is still dark in the *beis midrash*. He lights the kerosene lamp. Out of habit, he puts a pot on the tile oven. They are cold, and there is no fire there. Soon, Moshe the *shamash* will come and throw in a few sticks of wood.

He takes out "*Shomer Laboker*" [Morning Guardian] from his pocket. He sings with devotion and wailing, "By the waters of Babylon, there we sat and wept as we remembered Zion..." His voice was sincerely sweet, and fills the entire space of the holy place.

Reb Yosef falls upon the flat, wooden table, as if he wants to kiss and embrace it. He breaks out in spasmodic weeping: "G-d, gentiles have come to Your inheritance and defiled Your holy sanctuary."

*

The clock strikes five.

Moshe the *shamash*, with his face smeared with soot, is out of breath. He had already lit a crackling, lively fire in both ovens of the *beis midrash*. Melechke, Shmuelke and Berishke, the town fools, have already descended from their beds atop the *shemos*[6] in the *beis midrash* attic. Now, they are warming themselves at the open oven doors. They push and shove each other for a better place near the fire. Soon, a fistfight will break out.

The fools fight and curse.

Moshe Shamash calms them with a burnt potato, left over from the previous night. They are already warm from the hot fire in the oven.

It is already light in all the corners of the *beis midrash*. All of the flashlights are already burning over all the tables. The Sterin candles[7] in the lamp at the prayer leader's podium are also burning. They light up the prayer leader's "Kol Bo" prayer book, and the "Know before Whom you are standing" sign.

The "*shiviti*"[8] was painted by David Noach Silberberg. He was a great scholar, as well as a reasonable artist. He expressed his talent in the designing of schools and houses of worship. David Noach Silberberg surrounded his painted "*shiviti*" with various verses, such as:

"A person worries about losing his money, and does not worry about losing his days. - His money does not help, and his days do not return."

His pictures were impressive: a lion, leopard, deer and eagle, with the inscription: "Brave as a lion, strong as a leopard, running like a deer, swift as an eagle."

A crowd of Jews come to the *beis midrash*: studiers, worshippers, reciters of Psalms, reciters of *Kaddish* and those observing *yahrzeits*, as well as guests who wish to receive donations.

Yehoshua Goldman sits at the small table near the oven and studies *Chulin* along with *Tosafot*[9] with his son.

Reb Yehoshua was a remarkable Jew with a sharp head and a phenomenal memory. He was an expert in all areas of Torah, and hard a sharp knowledge of other subjects.

He was a great scholar, expert in Talmud and halachic decisors, a true *Tzadik* and Hassid, as well as a *Maskil*, writer, and poet. He knew Bible, grammar, and was proficient in the "*Baal Akeida*," "*Alshich*,", and the "Guide of the Perplexed,"[10] and he would cite a world of poems by Naftali Hertz Wessely[11]. He was also familiar with the works of Yehuda Halevi and Shlomo Ibn Gabirol. He would read "*Hatzefira*," and look at modern Hebrew literature and poetry.

Reb Yehoshua was also a great innovator of Torah ideas. He would write Torah and didactics, answer a question in *Tosafot* with the help of grammar or a Biblical verse, and explain Hassidism with a philosophical approach of Maimonides. He loved all Jews with the same soulful love: the tradesman and the scholar, the common person and the well-pedigreed. In addition, he was a wise Jew, not a fanatic, with a practical approach to life. People would come to him for advice or to clarify their complexities.

Avraham Grinewicz and his brother Yosel also learned at the same table. They were two brothers, but each had his own character.

Avraham Chaim had the head of a genius, with a grasp like a *gaon*. Had he studied worldly subjects such as, for example, mathematics and physics, he would have certainly become an Einstein. He was terribly absentminded. He could not sit in one place for one minute. His *Gemara* always was open, but one never saw him learning. He would absorb entire pages, folios, chapters, and tractates of *Gemara* and Tosafot with the glance of an eye.

His manner of expression and diction were a wonder. He was able to piece together a didactic, and connect a wall to a wall. He knew the Russian classics: Tolstoy, Dostoyevsky, Gogol, and Pushkin. The old-fashioned scholar and the modern skeptic were blended together with [within?]him.

His brother Yosel was exactly the opposite. He had no special qualities. He was a quiet, modern, *beis midrash* youth. He was easygoing, polite, and had an understanding of business. In his free time, he would help his father Moshe a great deal in his small wholesale manufacturing business, located on the Jewish Street near the bridge.

Asher Glazer, the son of Avraham, also studied at the table at which those three students sat. He was dignified, and was a person of few words. He was not a great scholar, but quite pious and various diligent ['various diligent' is awkward]. He would always be studying.

*

At 6:00 a.m., the *beis midrash* was already almost full.

The first *minyan* [prayer quorum] began services. The tradesmen who must commence their work early, the people traveling to the villages who must be prepared to depart for the villages early so that they could return home before sunset, the merchants who must travel to Warsaw for merchandise, the market travelers who must go to the fairs to secure a good place for their stall all worshipped at this *minyan*. Those who were particular about reciting the prayers at the right time also worshipped at this early *minyan*.[12].

Now, the wall lamp over the copper "plate of honor" near the holy ark is also burning. The rabbi sits there. Today, he is coming to this *minyan*. It is *Rosh Chodesh* [the New Moon]. The old rabbi comes to that *minyan* only on Sabbaths and festivals. The entire week, he worships privately in his *beis din* [rabbinical court] room. His prayers last for at least three hours. "I cannot keep up with the prayer leader, who is running through the service like a speed train," he used to say. On *Rosh Chodesh* this was not relevant: there is *Hallel* and the reading of the Torah. "It would be superfluous if I worshipped at home."[13]

*

Youths and householders are already sitting around the tables. The youths are studying and the householders are peering into a book. Some are reciting Psalms or jumping ahead with the service.

The old *beis midrash*

The new *beis midrash.*

The synagogue (burnt by the Nazis)

Fixing the electricity in the synagogue in 1927 or 1929. One of the workers, standing next to the ladder, is Avrahamel Bergson. The electricians from Plock are standing on the ladder.

Let us mention in our Yizkor Book those householders, youths, and toilers who gave over their time to Torah.

Simcha Licht, a *Misnaged* and a scholar, always sat in the *beis midrash* and learned. He would have a habit of going to sleep right after *maariv* and taking a *Gemara* with him to bed. "An open *Gemara* is a great remedy for those who fall asleep," he used to say. He indeed fell asleep quickly and left the open *Gemara* atop the bed for the entire night.

Yosef Divan was an old learner in the *beis midrash* with a snow white, patriarchal beard, long eyebrows and tall, scholarly, wrinkled brow. He studied *Talmud* regularly with a musical melody somewhat like the tune of *Tal* and *Geshem*[14]. He would sing through his nose. Sometimes, a *beis midrash* youth would go to Reb Yosef to ask him to clarify a difficult piece of *Gemara* or a *Rashi*.

"So, what is the difficulty," Reb Yosef would say, "it is indeed very easy." He would immediately recite the *Gemara* in the original, not translating any word. Unfortunately, the youth would go away with the same question with which he had come.

Yosef Wessalek was the *gabbai* of the *beis midrash* for many years. He had the splendid appearance of a major rabbi, especially when he would wear his high, velvet yarmulke and smoke his long pipe. He always went through all the *minyanim* so that he could bang on the *pushke* [charity can] during the repetition of the *Shmone Esrei* at all the *minyanim*. The coins that the worshippers tossed in brought in a not-insignificant sum every week, which was used for various small expenditures of the *beis midrash*.

Reb Yosef never conducted an accounting of the*pushke* money. "This is my bookkeeping," he would say, as he opened his cloak with the velvet collar, "I have two large pickets in my bosom - the right for expenditures, and the left for income." Bold householders would then ask with suspicion, "One can sometimes make a mistake. It is possible to mix up expenditures with income and vice versa."

He wrinkled his brow, rolled up his scholarly, pious eyes and said, "I am careful and cautious, but... one is holy human... mistakes may happen..."

Pinchas Mlawa, a bit of a *Maskil* and a Zionist, loved to delve into Bible, especially the Latter Prophets. He would always discuss difficult chapters with the youths.

David Jawicki, a tailor used to come to the *beis midrash* evening, morning, and afternoon.

The studying youths were: Yosel Fukacz, a dear boy, a scholar with a pleasant personality. He would always disseminate his Torah and study a class with the younger youths. The brothers Berish and Leibka Krystal: Berish was pious and diligent, whereas Leibka was a bit of a modern *Maskil*. Moshe Yakir Waldenberg was a heartwarming, friendly youth. Leib Zelig Flatto was a Sochaczewer student, who knew how to learn well and to speak a fine Russian. David Burstyn, the son of Avraham Aharon the teacher, was an ideal, fine youth with a straightforward intellect. David Szarpharz was a student in the Gerrer Yeshiva, who had a beard and *peyos*. Later, he modernized. Efraim Weismel used to rise early to come early so that he could get the large "*Yoreh Deah*"[15], the Vilna edition, before Moshe Ber Goldman grabbed it. Weismel and Goldman studied rabbinics[16] simultaneously.

Baruch Lifschitz, Yonatan's son, was a studier and a friendly youth. His brother Mendel had a sharp head. He studied and spoke Hebrew. Yechiel Moshe Senderowicz, Yosel Goldman, and Motel Reitszyk were young lads who studied with the older students.

Baruch Konenbrand the baker was a pious Jew who observed Torah and the commandments. His sons Hirsch, Shmuel, Moshe and Baruch were brought up in the fashion of Torah. Shlomo Chaya's was a Torah youth, a prayer leader and a fine Torah reader. Akiva Lanienter, a *Misnaged*, was also a *gabbai* of the *beis midrash*. Avraham Zeev Lanienter was knowledgeable in Torah and very pious. Yitzchak Grobert was a modern Jew, and a *gabbai* of the *beis midrash*. Yosef Pundak was a warm Zionist who loved a good cantor. Davidl Czarnaczapka was a Torah scholar, a prayer leader, and Torah leader. He was related to the rabbi. Meir Cypris was a *beis midrash* student with a short cloak. Michel Smolinski was a modern, intelligent man, and a charitable man. He was the son of the old cantor. Yehoshua Czarnaczapka was a pious person who was diligent in his studies.

Hassidim from the *shtibels* also worshipped in the *beis midrash* during the week. Their names were Nachum Tatz of the city council; Yaakov Moshe Teitelbaum, a sharp, Gerrer Hassid; Yaakov Shlomo Neiszat; Izak Rozen, a scholar and a modern Jew, who was a traveler who spoke Russian like a native Russian; Yosel Blachman, who had rabbinical ordination and was a capable merchant; Chaim Shochet; Avraham Shochet; the cantor and *shochet* Daniel Sheikes; and Yankel Shochet.

Several Jews from the new *beis midrash* would come to worship here. One of them was Chaim Nachum Tonwel, a warm Zionist who could offer advice almost like a prophet. He was not afraid even when mentioning Zionism in our Hassidic town was considered non-kosher. Earlier than others, he felt that the future of the people of Israel lay only in the Land of Israel. He was a scholar, a *maskil*, observant of religion and the commandments, and a *mohel*. He was imbued with the love of his fellow Jew. Doing a favor for someone was never difficult for him.

The *minyanim* [prayer quorums] in the old *beis midrash* continued until 10:00 a.m. Each of the prayer leaders had his own manner of prayer and a different voice. In general, they conducted services with their hearts and souls. Davidl Czarnoczapke led the services almost like a cantor. This was no surprise, for his father was Yechezkel Ryweshes, who always led the *Musaf* service on the High Holy Days. Shlomo Chaike's had a boyish voice, between alto and soprano, and was always a bit nasal. However he led the services fluently, with a good style. Baruch Konenbrand had a thick, bass voice, but he was not a bad prayer leader. He had clear diction, and worshipped with his heart and with devotion. As is said, G-d wants the heart."

The Sierpc intelligentsia worshipped at the last *minyan*, around 10:00: former gymnasium students who had not yet been thrust into life, employees in businesses who were allowed by the business owners to go to services, and ordinary late-coming worshippers. I mention their names:

Heniek Ajnerowicz, Gorfinkel the lawyer's son, Heniek Lerer, Bluman, David, Gedalia and Yizchak Zwikelski, Yechiel Lidzborski, Moshe Cypris, David Bergzon, Zelik Rozen, Mordechai Rozen, Mendel Blum, Abba Koczalek, Chaim

Koczalek, Yaakov Bachrach, Baruch Lipson, the Schnitzer brothers: Hirsch, Chaim, Yehuda, Henech, Yaakov, Yitzchak, Chuna.

*

After 10:00 a.m., the *beis midrash* was almost empty. One of the last worshippers was always the small Itchele. He would come to the *beis midrash* around 8:00 a.m. He could not come earlier. Itchele had to open his dry good store in the market and had to remain there until his Dvora made the beds, cleaned the house, and cooked breakfast. His prayers lased at least four hours. He elongated the words, so that they became golden coins. In the middle, he had to go out a few times to prepare.

Itchele was a Hasid, a *tzadik*, and a great scholar. By nature, he would pray near the bookshelf. In that area, he would pace back and forth slowly and whisper, "Where are the appropriate places of the sacrifices?"[17]. In the middle, he would stop, glance at a book, and then begin again, "Where are the appropriate places of the sacrifices?"

He did not earn a great livelihood from his manufacturing shop. He was a poor man, in debt over his head. He would have to go around an entire day to borrow from his friends, so that he would be able to cover a promissory note that was being disputed. It could be that the *beis midrash* served as a refuge to him, a place where he could hide from his "thieving" creditors who wished to "kill" him.

There was also another who would come late to prayers. He prayed rapidly. He never had any time. Business was urgent for him exactly as soon as the *minyanim* concluded in the *beis midrash*. This was Zelik Reichgot, from the tavern near the *beis midrash*. First he had to deal with his customers who would come to the tavern right after services in order to refresh their hearts with a glass of whisky, tasty herring with onions and peppers, and oil cookies freshly baked by his Freidel. Reb Zelik would also sell homemade cigarettes, five for a kopeck. His cigarettes were very tasty, made from fresh, yellow Russian tobacco.

The excise officer often visited his shop. The street was then black with people. The excise officer Przybyszewski caught Zelik red-handed, serving a glass of spirits to Romba Jasza, 90 proof, from the flask with the green label, and selling cigarettes without a wrapper. Przybyszewski caught[might 'grabbed' or 'took' be better here? a flask of liquor and a packet of cigarettes in order to prove Zelik's infraction in court. He would put him in jail, for who knows how long. However, G-d did not let this happen.

Romba Jasza, the Jewish porter, whose drinking could bring misfortune upon a Jew, put two fingers in his mouth and let out a whistle that could be heard from one end of the Jewish street to the other. Immediately, his friends sprouted up, and placed Przybyszewski into a squeeze, as if in a vise.

"*Razem*!" (Together) - commanded Romba Jasza. Yuda pushed from the right, Yaakov from the left, Szustak from behind, and Romba Jasza from the front.

Przybyszewski's face turned as blue as a spleen to the point where he felt that death was approaching. From a rear door in Zelik's private room, where he kept his "merchandise," Reb David pushed forward with a closed eye. He calmly took the flask of liquor and the cigarettes from Przybyszewski. He put the cigarettes in his pocket, and with regard to the liquor, he made a "*Shehakol*"[18], and his friends the porters said Amen.

Reb David turned the flask over, one two three, and, like a trick, it flowed out of the flask to the last drop. In the middle of the drinking, Reb Dovidl gave a friendly *Lechaim* to the excise officer, and told him off with a sour look, "You should be ashamed. This you call liquor? It is pure water..."

Przybyszewski left in disgrace.

*

At 12:00, the *beis midrash* was already lively. Many lads had returned from their meal, and were sitting and learning. Older youths taught a class to the younger ones.

At that time, Efraim Weismel used to study *Ketubot*[19] with *Tosafot* with Noach's son. Leibish Zelik Flatto studied *Bava Kama* with Moshe Grosman's son and another student. Moshe Ber Goldman had four students: Aharon Reichgot the baker's son, his brother Nisan, Motel Rajtczyk, and Yechiel Moshe Senderowicz.

David Bursztajn had the ambition to study the entire Bible within one year. He succeeded. He indeed learned the entire Bible almost by heart. This helped him greatly in mastering Hebrew. He wrote a classic in Biblical Hebrew.

During the time that the *beis midrash* was half empty, it attracted lads who were the children of well-off families, or youths who were not occupied in business. They seldom studied and knew very little. For them, the open *beis midrash* was a type of club. They played chess and cards, or lay down in a corner to snatch a nap with a *tallis* as a blanket over their heads.

They would go home to eat at 3:00. Many lads would use the time before *Mincha* to study worldly subjects such as Russian, Polish, German, and arithmetic. They learned from Neidicz's "house teacher." Several youths had private lessons with Zainwil.

Zainwil was a known personality in Sierpc. His father Wolf, a teacher of young children, conducted his cheder in the office of the pharmacy. Zainwil was an expert in languages and science.

Zainwil wore his warm clothing for the entire year, summer and winter. He did not remove his winter coat, fur hat, woolen scarf and leather, fur-lined gloves even in the great heat of Tammuz.

He always went around with a rain umbrella. Children would bother him, and he threatened them with the umbrella. Some people considered him to be unstable. On the other hand, my father of blessed memory would always defend him: "He is highly educated and is a warm Jew. He is an individualist, who does not do things just because, and does not dress to please others."

Zainwil lived in a very poor manner. He earned his livelihood from giving lectures to children or youths who did not want to or were unable to go to the gentile school.

At *Mincha* time, the *beis midrash* was once again packed. Various groups of tradesmen and laborers studied after *Mincha*.

At one table, Yehoshua Goldman learned *Chayey Adam*[20] with a group. At another table, David Noach Silberberg studied *Chumash* and *Rashi*. Avraham Chaim Granowicz studied *Ein Yaakov*[21] with a group of youths, mainly tradesmen and employees.

The groups interrupted their learning if a *maggid* or a *meshulach*[22] would come and deliver a lecture between *Mincha* and *Maariv*.

The *maggidim* were of two types, "foot soldiers" and professionals. The "foot soldier" *maggidim* were for the most part poor folk and greatly unsuccessful people who had already tried various means of livelihood to earn a bit of bread, and did not succeed. They memorized a sermon by heart, or wrote it down on paper, and delivered the same sermon in every town, earned a few kopecks, and went on further. Since they went from town to town by foot, they were called "foot soldiers."

The *beis midrash* youths perpetrated various tricks on the *maggidim*. As soon as the *maggid* opened his mouth, the group standing next to the podium recited the sermon out loud, just as a *zogerke*[23] recited a petition for the women. With a *maggid* who had a written sermon, they would steal the paper from the table...

Once, an incident took place. A *maggid*, a small person from Bialystock who would come to the old *beis midrash* every year on the week of the Torah portion of *Korach* with a written sermon, had his sermon stolen from the table by Yosel the *beis midrash* lad. The *maggid* unfortunately began to drag on, "Korach, Korach, very wealthy like Korach..." He began to search through all his pockets, and then repeated, "Korach, very wealthy like Korach, would it be that they could say this about me... They should sink like Korach and his group," and he stood there, lost. He could not understand what had happened - the sermon is not here. With great anger, he shouted, "You should all sink, apostates!..." and descended from the podium.

Professional *maggidim* or preachers with talent would not come that often. When one did come, the *beis midrash* and the women's section were packed. Even the city notables and the wealthy people would come to hear him.

There were also a few talented speakers from amongst the *meshulachim*. I will mention only three: The Telzer, the Volozhiner, and the Novominsker.

The Telzer had the power to describe the exaggerations of the Rabba Bar Bar Chana's[24]. With a splendid tune, he was able to sing such a fantastic portrait with words, that it seemed that one saw with one's own eyes the portrait drawn by an artistic painter on a canvas. The Volozhiner was able to make the audience laugh heartily with his humor, or cry bitterly with his tragedy.

I will never forget how he eulogized the great *Gaon* who had died at that time. The entire audience wept as he described the loss suffered by Jewry with the passing of such a giant.

The Novominsker was a typical populist orator. The youth especially related to his speeches, which were very short, but nevertheless filled with logic and meaning.

*

In the evening, the *beis midrash* was filled with youths, especially older ones. What did they study until the late hours? The Thursday night study sessions [*Mishmar*][25] were especially interesting. A number of youths reviewed what they had learned for the entire week. Aside from the studiers, there were also those who came to just spend an evening in the *beis midrash.* They served the studiers roasted potatoes, prepared herring, and brought tea from Moshe Nathan's tea kettle. Before dawn, they would prepare fresh rolls for breakfast. At times, they tore out a piece of fence wood, brought in the boards, and heated the oven.

On *Mishmar* night, the *beis midrash* was very joyous, and the main thing was that people studied.

Translator's Footnotes

1. The translation is lost in English, but to "learn in a tasty manner" (*Lern geshmack*) is a Yiddish expression for enjoying one's studies.
2. A blessing recited upon eating a new fruit (i.e. a fruit that one has not eaten for a long time), as well as on other occasions.
3. Water for the ritual washing of hands upon arising.
4. The first prayer recited upon arising.
5. There is a legend that in every generation, there are 36 hidden, discreet especially righteous people in the world. These are called "*lamed-vovniks.*"
6. The place for storage of worn out holy books and objects in preparation for eventual burial.
7. Clear oil lamp.
8. A sign saying "I keep G-d before me at all times."
9. *Chulin* is the Talmudic tractate dealing with kashruth and ritual slaughter. *Tosafot* is a commentary on the Talmud.
10. Baal Akeida: http://en.wikipedia.org/wiki/Isaac_ben_Moses_Arama ; Alshich: http://en.wikipedia.org/wiki/Moshe_Alshich ; Guide for the Perplexed: http://en.wikipedia.org/wiki/The_Guide_for_the_Perplexed
11. See http://en.wikipedia.org/wiki/Naphtali_Hirz_Wessely
12. It is considered preferable, although not always possible, to recite the morning service near sunrise.
13. Additional Psalms of praise recited as part of the morning service on *Rosh Chodesh*, Chanukah, and festivals.

14. Tal is the prayer for dew recited on Passover, and *Geshem* is the prayer for rain recited on *Shemini Atzeret*. Both have the same unique melody.
15. A volume of the Code of Jewish Law.
16. *Horaah* - the skill of being able to issue rabbinical decrees on issues of Jewish law.
17. A section of the early part of the morning service.
18. The blessing before partaking of general food products, including liquor. This is a colloquial way of saying that he drank the liquor.
19. A Talmudic tractate relating to marriage contracts. In the next sentence, *Bava Kama* is a Talmudic tractate relating to civil law.
20. A detailed summary of Jewish Law.
21. An anthology of Talmudic lore.
22. A *maggid* is a preacher, often an itinerant preacher. A *meshulach* is an emissary of a charitable institution, who visits various communities to raise funds.
23. A woman who leads a group of woman in the recitation of petitions.
24. Rabba Bar Bar Chana was a Talmudic sage.
25. Especially intense study sessions, often lasting all night, would take place in *Yeshivas* on Thursday nights.

The Old *Beis Midrash* as I Remember it

by Ben Zion Kempner

I do not know how old the old *beis midrash* was. Perhaps 100 years, or perhaps less. Therefore, it was called the old *beis midrash*, for later, a new, taller, *beis midrash* was built on the same Jewish street, on the left. As a small child, I would go with my father of blessed memory to worship in the old *beis midrash* on the Sabbath. Later, as a child, when I already was able to worship alone, not a day passed when I did not spend long hours inside the walls of the old *beis midrash*.

Coming home from the Yesod Hatorah Cheder, we children felt it necessary to spend a bit of time in the old *beis midrash*, which was always open. There, one could play around a bit, run around the long tables or go out to the yard that led to the Zsika River. There, we floated in the river the paper boats that we made in *cheder*.

Later, when we were older, we would hasten to the old *beis midrash* for the *Mincha* and *Maariv* services and to hear a *maggid* who would often give a sermon between *Mincha* and *Maariv*.

Even later, when we were "*beis midrash* youths," we loved to go to the old *beis midrash*, take a *Gemara* from the bookcase, and sit down at a table to study it near the oven. We would study that way until late at night, oblivious to the passing of time. There was something attractive about the walls of the old *beis midrash*, and one could sense such a feeling of holiness when one crossed the threshold, that is hard to describe in words.

It seems as it was just yesterday that I was there in the house of worship. The old *beis midrash* stands before my eyes: on the left near the door was a large chest of books, *Ein Yaakovs*, various other books, *Siddurim* [prayer books], and very many Psalm books. From there, one moves trough the entire length until the eastern wall. The space was a long table with two long benches on both sides. The ordinary people sat there: fishermen, shoemakers, employees, and vegetable businessmen from the market.

There was a bench on the eastern wall that extended until the holy ark. There, sat the wealthy Jews, wheat merchants, and textile merchants who came to services in the winter wearing fine skunk furs with a gold watch in their vest pockets. Above stood the holy ark, with several steps to go up and two carved pillars on both sides. The rabbi of the city sat below the pillar, to the right on the holy ark on the east. Behind the rabbi, along the entire eastern wall, sat the well-off Jews, householders, large-scale merchants, and some of the *gabbaim*. Then, there was another long table that extended through the entire length until almost the door. There were two long benches on both sides, where the tailors, furriers, hat makers, small-scale merchants, and regular householders sat. Further on was a large bookcase. The small windows leading into the women's section were above the bookcase. Near the bookcase, close to the two ovens, stood a table. In the middle was the *bima*, with several steps leading up to it, and iron railings around it. The youth stood and prayed behind the *bima*, near the door from which one exits to the yard. This was the internal appearance of the *beis midrash*.

*

In the early mornings, both in the summer and the winter, when the sky was still dark, even when it was a cold of 20-30 degrees, or there was a severe snowfall, my father would arise from his warm bed and set out to the old *beis midrash*, wearing his *tallis* and *tefillin*, to be among the first ten to arrive for the first *minyan*. Since it was still dark outside, and it was still too early to recite the morning service, people would take the Psalms books from the shelves and recite the entire Book of Psalms with a *minyan*. How many tears did the simple Jews shed as they recited the chapters of Psalms?

Later, they began to conduct the service, word by word, without hurrying. After the service, they recited the entire *Maamadot*[1] of the day. Then, they went home, purified and in elevated spirits. They quickly ate breakfast and set out for work, some at the sewing machine and others by the shoemaker's table. One *minyan* followed another, until late in the day.

Among the Jews who worshipped in the old *beis midrash*, there were also scholars who would sit down to learn a page of *Gemara* after services.

Here comes Leibel Kramasz. He goes straight to the bookcase, takes out a heavy Vilna edition *Gemara*, and delves deeply into a difficult Talmudic section for several hours. Yehoshua Goldman and Mendel Lifschitz, both sharp scholars, debate a convoluted Rambam. At the second table, the rabbi's son-in-law Reb Yehoshua Papovski sits and teaches a class in *Gemara* and *Tosafot* to several students.

My beloved Rabbi Yehoshua Papovski, how calm and modest was your life, and how short was your lifespan. You were always prepared to disseminate Torah in public. You sat with and studied with youths during the day or late at night. Everything was so calm, without noise, and without a harsh word. You were the pure example of a human being and a Jew, until you were tortured by the Germans, along with many of your students. I am the only one of those who survived. Let the words of your dear student serve as the inscription upon your unknown grave.

*

In the evening, the old *beis midrash* was filled with hundreds of Jews. Tradesmen stopped their work; merchants closed their shops, and people ran to the *Mincha* and *Maariv* services. A *maggid* would often be present between *Mincha* and *Maariv*, and would expound with feeling about family purity[2], purity of character traits, and love of one's fellow Jew. Statements of our sages, and legends would be intermixed into his sermon. Jews listened with open mouths and absorbed every word. On the days when no *maggid* was present, the time between *Mincha* and *Maariv* was the appropriate time for conversations about the latest news in town, communal affairs, and politics. Often, one would find out that a child in town was very sick, or that a woman was having difficulties with a child. On such occasions, all those gathered in the *beis midrash* would recite Psalms with such anguish and weeping, that it tore the hearts.

After *Maariv*, those gathered went home, and some continued working until late at night. However, the *beis midrash* was not empty. Youths sat down to study until late at night, and the sweet *Gemara* melodies were carried through the stillness of the evening.

Poor people who spent the entire day making the rounds to the houses also came to the old *beis midrash* in the evening after a "hard day of work" to count the coins that they had collected. Late at night, they went to the guesthouse to spend the night.

On the Sabbath, the old *beis midrash* was set up specially in order to welcome the Sabbath Queen. The *shamash* [beadle] worked hard the entire Friday, turning things around, cleaning up, hanging a fresh canopy over the holy ark, and lighting all the candles. People started coming to services. They were completely different people than those who came throughout the week. "Jews of the Additional Soul"[3], washed up, having immersed in the ritual bath [mikva], wearing Sabbath garments - they felt as if they were reborn. They forgot, or tried to forget, the difficult work week, anti-Semitic "picketers" at the businesses, the loans that grew, and the unpaid promissory notes.

When the *shamash* banged the table and called out "*Lechu Nerenana Lashem, Naria Letzur Yisheinu*"[4], one could sense that the Jews were not only singing with their mouths, but they were also singing a love song with their eyes and hearts to the Creator who gave the Sabbath to the Jewish people, from which they could draw new strength.

The services ended. In the interim, a long line of poor people who were staying in town for the Sabbath formed at the door. How fortunate were the Jews when they had the opportunity to fulfill the commandment of tending to guests! Not one poor person was left in the *beis midrash*. Even Jews who had to borrow a few zlotys to prepare for the Sabbath were not willing to forgo the opportunity to bring a Sabbath guest home.

On the Sabbath morning, most of the Jews permitted themselves to sleep a bit longer. Aside from the "*Hashkama* Jews" who would come to the early service[5], people would walk with measured steps, as if a dance, holding their Sabbath *tallis* under their arms, as they went to the old *beis midrash*.

Young *cheder* students also went to services. The old *beis midrash* and the women's section were packed, and the services were completely different than during the week - more orderly and more respectful. Entire families of men, women, and children went home together after services in a joyous mood! After the Sabbath meal and a short nap, Jews once again set out for the old *beis midrash*, where one could study a chapter of *Mishna*, review the weekly Torah portion, or recite Psalms. Some people studied *Ein Yaakov*. This is what the Sabbath was like in the old *beis midrash*. This is what the festivals looked like, filled with holiness and sublime spirits that purified the Jew, gave a purpose to life, and imparted a belief in a better future.

The highest level of existence and holiness took place during the High Holy Days. In the month of Elul, when the first *shofar* blasts were blown in the old *beis midrash*, everything changed. These were seemingly not the same Jews as during the rest of the year. People went around with their heads lowered, for what are we, what is our life... When the days of *Selichot* arrived, people made their way like shadows to the old *beis midrash*. Even children were unable to remain at home, so they hurried to *Selichot* with sleepy eyes.

There was deathly silence in the old *beis midrash*. Every minute was like a year. The voice of the prayer leader could be heard, "*Yisgadal VeYiskadash Shemei Rabba*"[6]. The eyes were focused on the *Selichot* books, first silently, and then the voices were raised, "The soul is Yours and the body is Yours, have mercy on your handiwork." One would hear weeping voices that penetrated the deepest strands of the heart.

Thus passed the first days of Selichot. The *shofar* blowing during the services moved the hearts. In such a spirit, we moved on to the two days of Rosh Hashanah.

Dressed in *kittels* with white *yarmulkes* on the heads, enwrapped in *tallises*, the congregation worshipped for many hours. They did not even permit themselves to sit down. They worshipped with awe, and when they came to the recitation of the *Al Chet* confessional[7] in the *Shmone Esrei*, one could hear every bang on the heart, as tears fell from the eyes. Something felt lighter on the heart, as if a heavy stone was removed. The One Who Dwells On High certainly heard the warm prayers of the Jews and would inscribe a good verdict for them. However, one did not feel entirely certain of this. Jews made use of every free moment of the Ten Days of Penitence. They would run to the old *beis midrash* to snatch an additional chapter of Psalms. They would worship a bit longer, donate more charity, and go to the "good place" - the graves of righteous individuals.

On Shabbat Shuva[8], nobody took a nap. People recited Psalms, went to hear the rabbi's sermon, as the holy, awesome Day of Judgment was approaching.

People rushed the final meal before *Kol Nidre*, and Jews were already hastening to the old *beis midrash* for *Kol Nidre* while it was still daytime. Entire families, kith and kin, went, and nobody remained at home. It was crowded in the old *beis midrash*. The women's section was also packed, and hay was spread on the floor. Long boxes filled with sand were placed along the tables, and hundreds of memorial candles were placed therein. The hundreds of flames of the candles at twilight increased the poignancy of the moment. One could hear the quiet whisper of *Tefilla Zaka*[9], and then one could hear the bang on the *bima*.

A stout, tall Jew went up to the prayer leader's podium with slow steps, dressed in a long white *kittel* and a *tallis* with a large silver decorative band over the head. One could only see the black beard from the outside. Everybody knew that Reb Yosef Shochet was going to serve as cantor for the *Kol Nidre* service. Several youths stood near him, as the choir that would accompany him. Everyone held their breath. Reb Yosef began quietly, and then louder, with the choir even louder, as the splendid tones of *Kol Nidre* spread through the old *beis midrash*, penetrating all the limbs and stirring the soul.

Reb Yosef Shochet was a unique prayer leader in Sierpc. He had no equal. When he stood by the podium and led the services, it was if people were hypnotized and entered the highest existence. He awakened in the worshippers the deepest desire for repentance. Every word was sung, every verse was measured, and one did not[note the add 't'] feel the fast at all as the time passed. Thus I was the entire Yom Kippur.

It was *Neila*, and Yosel Shochet was again standing at the prayer leader's podium. The day was already nearing its end, and the people were tired. The candles had already begun to go out one at a time, as they cast shadows around. However, Yosel Shochet's tones did not get weaker, as he stood firmly by the podium. He addressed the Father in Heaven with a pleading voice, "Open for us the gate at the time of the closing of the gate, for the day has declined." And when one heard Yosel's shout "Next Year in Jerusalem," every

Jew felt at ease. Everyone believed that the warm prayers would certainly go before the Throne of Glory and a good year for the Jewish people would ensue.

*

All year long, the old *beis midrash* was a trusted companion for the Jews of Sierpc. It was a miniature temple that offered comfort, sweetness and strength in the darkest moments, and imparted a new belief in a better future, until a dark cloud settled over Poland.

The German beast rained fire and destruction on the Jewish cities and towns, and did not pass over Sierpc. The Jewish community of Sierpc was torn up from the roots. The old *beis midrash* was left standing forlorn.

Only a few Jews returned to Sierpc after the destruction. The old *beis midrash* remained standing, as if waiting for the Jews to return. However, they did not come. They were murdered with various unusual forms of death. The two last Jews of Sierpc, Moshe Grope and Yechezkel Leizerowicz, who attempted to establish their lives near the old *beis midrash*, found no peace there and made *aliya* to Israel. Jewish Sierpc ceased to exist.

Translator's Footnotes

1. Sections of various parts of the Bible, Mishna and Gemara, arranged by the day of the week, and meant to serve as a symbolic replacement for the sacrificial rite.
2. The laws of separation of spouses during the menstrual period.
3. Tradition claims that a Jew is granted an additional soul [Neshama yeteira] on the Sabbath.
4. The opening verse of the Sabbath evening service.
5. Hashkama means "getting up early". A Hashkama service is a Shacharit service that is timed to take place around sunrise.
6. The opening words of the kaddish prayer, recited with a special melody at the beginning of the Selichot service.
7. An error must have been made here, as the Al Chet confessional is recited on Yom Kippur, and not Rosh Hashanah.
8. Bodek – someone who examines slaughtered animals to see if there are any blemishes or imperfections that might render the animal non-kosher.
9. A personal prayer recited before Kol Nidre on Yom Kippur.

Parties and Institutions

Institutions and Activists

By I.M. Sidroni (Sendrowicz)

In this chapter, we want to recall the institutions, parties, organizations and societies that existed in our town - municipal, communal, educational, cultural, political, commercial, financial, charitable, and religious societies. Thus we will remember the founders and the public-spirited workers who toiled in the last sixty years (from the 1880s) before the destruction of the Jewish community of Sierpc by the brutal Germans.

We have received much of the information that is presented here from our townspeople. Partly from those who left many years ago, and partly from those who left the town at the beginning of the Holocaust. Not all the information is complete. Part of it is sadly inadequate, and for this we ask for forgiveness from the dead, and pardon from the living.

We would like to thank our honored townsman, Shmuel Ischia Lanter, for the information on the 1880s and 1890s. He very graciously answered our many bothersome questions, and shared with us his treasury of rich and refreshing memories.

A. The Town Council

During the period of Russian control (until the First World War), the town of Sierpc was governed by a *burmistrz* (mayor)[1], who was a government bureaucrat who had three *lavnikim* (advisors) who were citizens of the town, one of whom was Jewish. Both the mayor and his advisors were appointed by the central government authorities (elected town councils were non-existent in Russia then). In the last years before the war, the Jewish *lavnik* was Shmuel Graubart (one source mentions that he was known by his wife's family name - Lent).

At the beginning of the German occupation during World War I, the Germans appointed a mayor and a small town council, all town residents. The appointed mayor was Falka, a rich German landlord and brewery owner, popular in the town, and acceptable to both Jews and Poles. As Jewish council members, the Germans appointed Shmuel Graubart, Leib Malowanczyk, and Ahron Czarnaczapka. Leib Malowanczyk had been a *lavnik*.

Elections for the town council were held in Sierpc for the first time in 1916 or 1917, during the German occupation. The elections were not democratic -

they were held using the curia[2] system. The Jewish representatives that I can remember were Avraham Shlomo Glazer, Nathan Tatz, and Azrieltia Podskoc.

Sierpc had a democratically elected municipal council, like all Polish towns, only after Polish independence, following the First World War. Elections would take place every four years, and 24 members of the town council would be elected. One of them would be chosen to be the *burmistrz,* and three others, one of whom would be Jewish, were chosen as *lavnikim.*

The first municipal election in Sierpc, in an independent Poland, took place in 1919. All the Jews were on one electoral list that had representatives of all the parties. Thirteen Poles and eleven Jews were elected.

In order to reduce the number of Jewish representatives, a majority of the council decided to annex the *vloki* (*vlikes*) to the town. These had been part of the village of Burkova that was located about 4 kilometers from Sierpc, on the road to Drobin. As a result of this addition, in the next election to the town council, only 9 Jews were elected. In the third town council elections, in 1927, only 7 Jews were elected. The reduction in the number of Jewish representatives was a result of the splitting of the Jewish vote among a number of party lists. In all the elections, the tradesmen and the Zionists appeared on the same list.

These are the names of the council members that were elected one or more times:

- Shmualtia Zelig Rosen, Yeshayahu Frydman (Zionists)
- Azrieltia Podskoc (Mizrachi) [Religious Zionists]
- Yosef Blachman, Mendel Gurfinkel, Berish Poznanski, Ahron Czarnaczapka, Michal Kopolowicz (Agudat Yisrael) [Aguda - Religious, not Zionist]
- Moshe Gutsztat (Poale Zion, Left) [Labor Zionists]
- Leibush Usher, S. Green (Bund) [Yiddishists, not Zionists]
- Moshe Yehuda Karsh (Tradesmen's Society)
- Hershel Kopolowicz (Small Storeowners Society)
- Avraham Mlawa (Craftsmen's Association)

Moshe Yehuda Karsh was a Jewish *lavnik* (advisor) for many years. Ahron Czarnaczapka was a lavnik for a period of time.

The Jewish council members had to work hard, and suffer a lot of frustration in order to constantly forestall the plots of their anti-Semitic Polish "colleagues" against their civil rights and economic interests. The Jewish minority in the council - representing a large and important minority in the town, did not always succeed in preventing the passage of anti-Semitic edicts by the council majority.

B. The Community Council

During the time of Russian control of Sierpc (until World War I), there was a Community Council composed of five elected members (*parnasim* - elders).

Voting was limited to those who paid a Community tax of 85 kopeks (100 kopeks to the ruble).

The Elders of the Community of Sheps in the 1880s were Ischia Hartbrot (who was called Ischia Birchas, the father-in-law of Avouch Liberman), Hirsch David Kahana (father-in-law of Michal Kopolowicz), and others. At the beginning of the 1890s the Elders were Yisrael Bluman, Pravda (father-in-law of Kalman Lidzbarski), and others. In the middle of that decade, the elders were Eliyahu Glazer, Lipa Cahana, and others.

The Elders at the beginning of the twentieth century were Yukov (Yaakov) Gorlitz - the chairman, Zelig Bacharach, Eliyahu Glazer, Shmuel Graubart (Lent), and Isaac Rosen. The elders in the years before the World War I were Avraham Glazer, Moshe Grossman, Avigdor Greenberg (originally from Mlawa, lived in Sierpc for only a few years), Nahum Tatz (chairman), and Isaac Rosen.

During the German occupation of World War I, when only the chairman of the prewar Council remained (the others resigned, became ill, or left the town), the authorities set up an appointed Community Council, with two members from each party, institution, organization, and prayer house, This council could only advise. The decisions were made by the elected chairman, Nahum Tatz. I can remember six representatives: two from Agudat Zion - Avraham Fried (Yerushalmi, now in Israel) and Yeshayahu Frydman; two from the *shtibl* of Alexander - Yehuda Baruch Skornik and Yisrael Karpa (now in Uruguay); Avraham Glazer from the *shtibl* of Gur, and Avraham Shlomo Glazer from the Synagogue.

Between the two world wars, during Polish independence, Sierpc had a democratically elected Community Council. The voters did not have to be taxpayers, all were equal, and there was a secret ballot. Only the women were not allowed to vote, because according to law, the Community was a religious organization. Elections were held every four years for eight members of the council. The Chief Rabbi of the town was automatically a member of the council. The first elections were held in 1919.

In the Community Council elections, the *Aguda* almost always had the majority. This was because the average Jew thought of the Community as a religious institution, which should be controlled by religious Jews. Therefore the chairman of the council was almost always a member of the *Aguda* list. There was just one period of four years when the elected chairman was from a Zionist party.

The Zionists and tradesmen were always on the same electoral list. This unity is noteworthy, because we are familiar with the tendency of Jews to break into factions. As the saying goes, "Anywhere you have two Jews, you have three opinions."

Among the members of the council from *Agudat Israel* were Mendel Gurfinkel, Moshe Grossman (son-in-law of Hanach Czarnobroda), Shmuel Zanbal Dormbus, Nahum Tatz, and Yosef Karpa[3].

These are the Community Council members who were elected during the years 1919-1939 (some elected only once, others a number of times):

- Baruch Mendel Gotlibowski, Hanach Pepper, Yeshayahu Friedman Ber Charka (Zionists)
- Meir Cipris (*Mizrachi*)
- Eliyahu (Elia) Grossman, Itche Binem Rozenberg (*Poale Zion*, Left)
- Leibush Usher, Avraham Hirsch Yurkevitz (*Bund*)
- Hershel Kopolowicz (Small Shopkeepers Union)
- Avraham Shlomo Glazer, Avraham Mlawa (Ben David), Menachem Shapiro (Craftsmen's Association)
- Moshe Lidovski, Baruch Lipchitz[4] (independent list)

The chairman of the Community council for many years was Nahum Tatz. For one period of four years, the chairman was Yeshayahu Friedman. During its final years, until the destruction of the Jewish community of Sierpc, the chairman of the Community Council was Shmuel Zanbal Dormbus.

The Secretaries of the Council were: Yosef (Yossel) Farshnitzki, and later Ezriel Szampan and Herschel Valuka. The offices of the council were in Nahum Tatz's house, and in later years, in Avraham Groda's new house (in the market, formerly the house of Lent-Groubart).

C. Education

a. Religious Education

i. The Heder

The heder [literally "room" or "schoolroom"] in Sierpc was the basic and primary institution for the education of children, as it was in all the communities of Israel. When a Jewish boy reached the age of four, his father would take him to the heder and hand him over to the Rabi, to teach him Torah, and the mitzvahs [commandments] and good deeds. The child would be in the heder for many hours every day - from morning to evening, and in the winter, in the evening as well. The hours became days, the days became weeks, the weeks - months, and the months - years. The boy would study in the heder for many years, until he reached the age of bar-mitzvah.

We do not overlook the flaws of the *heder* from the standpoint of pedagogy, hygiene, and other defects. But we must admit that the child absorbed in the *heder* not only Torah, starting with the alphabet and up to the Talmud with commentaries, but also a deep and entrenched understanding of Judaism, a love and devotion to the people of Israel, the land of Israel. He also learned worthy attributes such as honesty and justice, mercy and help to the downtrodden. The child acquired this Judaic and humane heritage in the *heder*. These attributes equipped the Jewish child for his way in life and for his struggles in life. These qualities inoculated the child's gentle soul so that he could withstand and overcome his constant struggles in strange lands, among foreign peoples, with alien ideologies. These tools and qualities, that the Jewish child absorbed in the *heder* protected him as an adult, and the Jewish people in its long dark trek through the Diaspora, and saved it from the wandering and extinction.

*

The obligation to educate boys was widely accepted among Jews. The commandment to "Teach your sons" was carried out strictly and meticulously by Jews all over the world. There was no Jewish community that did not have a *heder*. Even a small country village, with very few Jewish families, would hire a *melamed* [*heder* teacher] for their sons, and every Jew, rich or poor sent his sons to the *heder*. Poor Jews would skimp on their meals to send their son to school. Even the sons of paupers, who did not have anything from which to save, were included in the *heder* framework. A special kind of *heder, Talmud Torah,* was maintained for the children of the poor who could not afford tuition. The children studied at a *Talmud Torah* that was supported by the local congregation and the contributions of community members. The instruction in the *Talmud Torah* however, was only for the lower grades of the *heder*. The children learned just to read and write, some Hebrew, the Pentateuch [first five books of the Bible], and a bit of the rest of the Bible. This was because the poorer children were removed from the *heder* at a young age, so they could learn a trade, and help support the family. However, a Jewish boy who did not study at all did not exist.

*

There were four levels of heder:

a) A *heder* for learning to read and write and for "Hebrew" (capable of reading the *siddur* - prayer book); approximately 25 children in the *heder*
b) *heder* for studying Pentateuch and Rashi [the Torah Commentary] to learn part of the weekly Torah Selection ["Portion," which would be read in the synagogue service], and the early prophets; about 18 children in the *heder*
c) The *heder* for Gemara [Talmud], Pentateuch and Rashi and the complete weekly Torah Selection, and the later prophets; about 12 children
d) *heder* for Gemara with Tosefot [Talmudic Annotations and Exegesis] to learn Pentateuch, and in addition to the weekly Torah Selection, the Talmudic commentaries on the weekly selection, and the rest of the Bible, including all the prophets and the Hagiographa; also about 12 children

The study of the Bible, except for the Pentateuch, was somewhat cursory at all levels, so that the students would have sufficient time to study Gemara, which was considered the main subject, because it instructed the Jew on how to behave in the world.

The *Rabi* was called both *Rabi* and *melamed.* The children called him *Rabi.* [He was not necessarily an ordained Rabbi, or *Rav* in Yiddish, but he called that out of respect.] A young children's *melamed* who had a large *heder* would have an assistant. This assistant would be called *belfer* (a corruption of the Yiddish word "*bahelfer* - helper). The *belfer* would bring the children who did not live near the school in the morning, and take them back home after school. He also helped the Rabi with the lessons.

I will try to note here the *melameds* who taught the Torah and the commandments to the children of Sierpc, at the various levels of *heder*, starting with the 1880s.

ii. Melameds of Reading and Writing

"Der Katzap" was a tall, strong, wide shouldered Jew with a long gray beard, who looked like a Russian peasant, which was why he was called "*Katzap.*" He taught the little children in the last two decades of the nineteenth century. He lived in the market, in the house of Shmuel David Mlawa (father of Pinchas and Avraham Mlawa). His wife sold notions and sewing items at a stall in the market. She was called "the Katzafte" and her son-in-law, Haskell Baszkes, was called the "Katzafte Eidem" (the son-in-law of the Katzafte).

Fishel Sander, also a *melamed* of little children in the last two decades of the nineteenth century, lived on Mikve Street, in the house of Kasazh.

Yisraeltia (family name - Efrati); he was the *melamed* of little children in the 1890s and the beginning of the twentieth century. He lived in the alley that led to the *lava* (the slum that was on the bank of the river, near the house of Dudia Czarnaczapka).

"Der Balsker Hoiker" (the Hunchback from Bielsk, a village 24 kilometers from Sierpc) lived near the new market, in Zalman (called Zalman Berias) Friedman's house.

"Eliyahu Meir Hoiker" (Eliyahu Meir the Hunchback) lived in Shimon David Szmiga's yard, and later on the Jewish Street, in the Litvinski house, opposite the synagogue.

"Pinchas Hoiker" (Pinchas the Hunchback) who lived on the Jewish Street, in one of the little houses near the synagogue (in a neighborhood called Horne's Giter - the Properties of Horn).

"Der Lemer Belfer" (the Lame Helper) was lame and had a twisted hand. Apparently, he was a *belfer* (helper) before he became a *melamed*, but the name stuck. He lived in Moshe Rozenek's house on the Jewish Street.

These last four *melameds* - all of them handicapped, were the teachers of very young children from the beginning of the twentieth century onwards.

A Group of Young Intellectuals in Sierpc in the Year 1904

Right to Left
First Row: Futel Garfinkel, Etta Graubart (Fax), Rivkah (Ika) Tatz, Wolf Tatz, Berta Garfinkel
Second Row: Wolf Glazer, Bronka Garfinkel, Nathan Tatz

A Group of Young Ladies Active Among Sierpc Youth at the Beginning of this (20th) Century

Right to Left
Row 1, Sitting: Burgand, M. Lanenter, Chazen, Fraidel Graubart, Heine Chazen
Row 2: Mania Chazen, Burgand, Mania Sznitzer, Etta Groubart (Fax), Karpa, S. M. Turkltaub
Standing: Rivka Karpa (Arpa), Esther Lanenter, Esther Podskoc, Fela Glazer, Rivkah (Ika) Tatz , Burgand, Czeshka Lubaszka (Asch)

Youth Activists in Sierpc in the First Years of this (20th) Century

Right to Left
Row 1: Yitzhak Sznitzer, Eliezer Szampan, Chayim Czarnaczapka, Leib Krufiash, Tinsky, Chayim Bluman
Second Row: Wolf Rozenek, Unknown, Wassermann
Third Row: Baruch Shvitzer, Lopatka, Landau, Yitzhak Yaakov Bode

A group of Young Lady Activists in the Library, About 1915

Right to Left
Sitting: Malkah Lidzbarski, Rasha Farkal (Mintz), Pesa Liebson, Bincha Tatz, Yaska Graubart
Standing: Mindel Liebson (Lipka), Baltcha Liebson, Gitel Vasolak, Chavah Bacharach, Mania Szerpherz, Hanna Lea Chazen

Yoventieh was a *melamed* of very young children during the same years as those mentioned above. He lived on one of the side streets near the Kamnitza (a large house on the Jewish street), in the basement of the house of Mordechai Hirsch Mintz.

Anshel (his family name was Mash) became a *melamed* of young children a little later than those mentioned previously. He lived on Fara (Farska) Street, in Nuchia Pukatcz's house.

"Pinhaia Glazer" ("Pinhaia the Glazier" - his name was Pinchas Mekler) was a glazier who became a teacher of very young children in the 1920s. He lived in an alley near the synagogue (the alley that led to the cemetery).

"Der Lemer Einbeinder" ("the Lame Bookbinder," Ziskind Sapirsztajn) was a bookbinder who also became a *melamed* of very young children in the 1920's. He lived in the market, near the start of Plotzki Street, in the house of Shimon David Szmiga.

iii. Melameds of Pentateuch and Rashi

The students in the heders of the *melameds* mentioned below would at first learn just the beginning of the weekly Torah selection (Portion) to be read in the synagogue, and later also the commentaries of Rashi and the weekly selection. In addition, they also learned *Pasuk* - the early prophets, and finally a bit of the Gemara (Talmud).

Shmuel Pepper lived on the Jewish Street, in the house of Moshe'ieh Sendrowicz.

"Der Bezoiner Melamed" (the *melamed* from Biezun, a town 21 kilometers from Sierpc), whose name was Avraham Yitzhak, was a glazier in his youth. He lived on the Jewish street, in the Kamnitza, and later in the Lusmar house.

Hershieh Zlociower was the only Jew in town who had a pale blue thread on one of his *tziztiot* [the ritual fringes that Jewish men wore on the corners of their garments], because he was a Radzin Hasid. In addition to being a *melamed*, he also made Kiddush wine from raisins, which he sold. He also sold matzo *shmura* [special matzo made to very strictest ritual requirements]. He lived on Mikve Street, in the house of the brothers Gunsher.

"Feibushieh mit D'Lilke" ("Fibush with the Pipe," called that because he smoked a long pipe), whose real name was Fibush Rosek, lived on Mikve Street, in the house of Shmuel Szampan (who was called Shmuel Nagid) [Shmuel the benefactor]. Later he lived in his own small house near the Kamnitza.

These last four *melameds* taught during the 1880s and 1890s, and in the first decade of the twentieth century.

Yeshaye Mordecaye (family name - Kaliski) lived in the Bursztajn house on Zhava Street, and later in the Shmigelski (Polani) house on Plotzki Street. He also sold lottery tickets.

Wolf Chazzan lived on the Jewish street, in his father-in-law's (Kalman Fenster) house. He also sold books for rabbis and *melameds* from his home.

Shmualtia Wilk lived on Fara Street in the house of Nuchia Pukacz. He also had a second income - a store that sold ready-made underwear. On market days, Tuesdays and Fridays, he had a stall in the market to sell the same merchandise that he sold in his store.

Moshe Soferis was called that because he was the son of a *sofer* [scribe]; his father was a *sofer stam* - the expert who did the calligraphy and handwriting for Torahs, *tefilin*, and *mezuzahs*. He lived on the Jewish Street, in an alley leading to the lava near the house of Dudia Czarnaczapka.

These last four *melameds* taught *heder* in the twentieth century (the first two also taught in the 1890s). The last three were different from the other practitioners of their profession; they were somewhat well educated with a broad knowledge of the Bible, and well versed in Hebrew grammar.

Hirsch Crystal (now in Israel, Zvi Algavish) ran a very special kind of *heder* in the 1920s. This was a Hebrew and Zionist *heder*. In addition to Pentateuch, Rashi, and the Bible, the students learned Hebrew as well. Hebrew was the language used in the classroom, not Yiddish. The *heder* was on the Jewish Street, in the yard of the house of Baruch Kanenbrand, his father-in-law. Hirsch Crystal had been the principal of the Yavne School (see the following section on "Modern Education"); after that shut down, he opened his *heder*.

iv. Melameds of the Gemara

The students in these *heders* studied only Gemara (the main part of the Talmud) and later, some *Tosefot* [commentaries]. In addition, they studied the weekly Torah portion every week, with interpretation by Rashi, and a few of the later prophets.

"Yitzhak Malkah's" (his name was Yitzhak Prager, and he was called by his wife's name, Malkah) owned a store, and his wife was the shopkeeper. After her death, he closed the store and became a Gemara *melamed*. He started as a *melamed* in the 1880s, and lived on the Jewish Street in a small house behind the *shlisharken* [A Jewish tavern in Sierpc, named after its owner].

Michalitia (his family name was Bendkowski) lived on Zhava (Zhavia) Street, in Binyamin Sobol's house, then in the house of Ezriel Yehuda Kotcholak, and later, on Fara (Farska) Street in the house of Nuchia Pukacz.

Chayim Yosef (family name Crystal) lived on the Jewish Street, in an alley leading to the *zhika* [river], near the house of Ahron Moshe Horvitz. Later he lived on Mikve Street, in the Kasazh house.

The last two *melameds* whom I mentioned above taught during the last decade of the nineteenth century, and kept teaching through the beginning of the twentieth century.

Leibush Rosenberg lived in his own house on the Jewish Street, between the market and the bridge. He started teaching in the year 5668 (1908), and taught there until he became the caretaker in the new *Beit Midrash*. He instituted an innovation in his *heder* - the pupils would spend an hour every day learning to write Yiddish using a lexicon (*brievenshteller*). He also had a store for shoelaces and other goods for shoes in his house.

Avraham Lipchitz started teaching between the year 5670 (1910) and the First World War. At the beginning of the war, he was expelled by the Russians to Siberia (he was suspected of spying for the Germans). He returned after the war, and immigrated to America. He lived near the market, in the house of Shimon David Szmiga.

Ischia Margel was a *melamed* for just one semester (6 months), in the summer of the year 5671 (1911). He lived on the Jewish Street near the bridge, in the house jointly owned by Feivel Boda and Leibush Liberman. He also had a small store that sold ready-made goods in the market run by his wife Devorah (called "Devorah Ischia's").

Binem Malach whose real name was Binem Galant. He was called *malach* [angel] after his father-in-law, Yosef Gorlitz, who was called "der Hoicher Malach" (the Tall Angel). He was from Mlawa. He started teaching after the

First World War, until he became a caretaker in the new *Beit Midrash.* He lived in the Bukat house in the new market.

v. Melameds of Gemara with Tosefot (Talmudic Annotations)

The *heders* of the *melameds* mentioned below were the highest levels of *heder* in Sierpc. The students studied *pushet Gemara* (simple Gemara, without annotations) and *sheiur* (Gemara with annotations), and considered other interpreters: Rabbi Shmuel Eliezer Bar Yehuda Edlish ("Maharsha"), Rabbi Shlomo Luria ("Maharshal"), and Rabbi Meir of Lublin ("Maharam"). They also studied Gemara by themselves, without the aid of their teacher (this was called *leinen*, apparently because they studied *alein* - alone).

Pesach Tatz (the uncle of Nahum Tatz) owned a store that sold mainly yeasts - he sold yeast to all the stores in town - at the beginning of the Jewish Street in the house of Bagner (later the house of Kalmanowicz). When business went bad, he became a *melamed* of young boys after bar mitzvah (he had just six pupils). He lived on the Jewish Street near the bridge, in the house of Israelite Liebson (the father of Meiria and Naftali Liebson, later it became the Minchin house).

Avraham Tatz (father of Shmuel Yitzhak Tatz) was a *shochet* [ritual slaughterer] in the villages in the Sierpc area. When he became old, he became a teacher of boys after their bar mitzvah. Avraham Tatz also taught his pupils some writing, and lived in the Mikve Street in the House of Shmuel Szampan (called "Shmuel Nagid").

Avraham Aharan (family name Bursztein) lived on Fara (Farska) Street in the Dikan house, and later, in the market, in a house he partially inherited from his father, Simchah Binem, called "Der Hoicher Binem" (the Tall Binem) or "Binem Esikmacher (Binem the Vinegar Maker). When his wife was alive, he had a grocery store that was run by his wife.

"Moshia Karmelkeies" (his name was Moshe Danziger) lived on the *vloki* (*vlikes*) in a small house near Yehuda Baruch Skornik, and later, on Fara Street in a house he and his brother-in-law, Avraham Dikan inherited from his father.

Moshia Karmelkeies had three innovations in his *heder*: only six pupils; the students came at nine in the morning, after finishing morning prayers and eating breakfast at home; and Bible study was an important part of the curriculum. Moshia Karmelkeies also had a second income - on market days, his wife would buy eggs, butter, and chickens to sell to traders. He was an invalid and sickly, he walked stooped and bent over, leaning on a cane. He died while still relatively young, in the year 5676 (1916).

The first two *melameds* mentioned above taught in the ninth and last decades of the nineteenth century. Avraham Aharan started teaching at the end of the nineteenth century, and continued in the twentieth century. Moshia Karmelkeies started teaching in the middle of the first decade of the twentieth century.

*

In the 1880s and 1890s there were in Sierpc two *melameds* who taught Gemara, annotations, and other interpreters to boys who were 15 and 16 years old. One was Yaakov Ahron Goldstein (the brother of Moshe Goldstein, the rich man of the town). He was lame in both legs, and lived in the Jewish Street in the house of Baruch Kanenbrand. The second was Moshe Ahron Sagi-Nahor (father-in-law of Chayim Mintz). He was blind in both eyes (according to his pupils, he knew from memory every subject they studied, both from the Gemara and the interpreters). He lived in the New Market, in the house of Itzhak Leib Podskoc (father-in-law of Itzik Neiman, who later inherited the house).

In spite of the fact that the studies took place in the apartments of the *melameds*, they were not called *heders*, because the age of the pupils and the level of learning were much higher than that in the *heders*.

vi. Talmud Torah

In addition to the *heders*, Sierpc had, like all the communities of Israel, an educational institution called Talmud Torah. This was a *heder* for poor children, whose parents couldn't afford to pay tuition. The expenses of the Talmud Torah were covered by the community and monthly payments of various supporters, and a committee would maintain the institution. Usually, the pupils of the Talmud Torah would finish their studies at a young age, because their parents would send them to work, or to learn a trade to help support the household. Therefore, the Talmud Torah taught just the subjects of the first two levels of *heder*: The alphabet, *ivri* (reading and writing), the Pentateuch, and the early prophets.

In the 1890s, there was no special building for the Talmud Torah. The poor children studied in the *heders* with all the other children, and the Talmud Torah Association would pay their tuition. Moshe Mintz (the father of Leib, Chayim, and Mordecai Hirsch Mintz), Shmuel David Mlawa (father of Pinchas and Avraham Mlawa) and others were managers of the association. A *minyan* of Talmud Torah would gather for prayer in the apartment of Moshe Mintz (in the house of Moshe Szalanowski in the market) on Saturdays and Holidays, and the contributions to the *minyan* would go to the association.

In the years just before World War I, the Talmud Torah had its own *heder*. This *heder* was in a house near the *mikve* (ritual bathhouse), in the house of Shmuel Szampan. The same building housed a *hachnasat orchim* [public guest house for traveling Jews].

During the German occupation of World War I, the *heder* - Yesodai HaTorah (see below) was founded. The poor children that previously learned in Talmud Torah were sent there, and the community paid for tuition to the new *heder*.

Avraham Fryd (Yerushalmi) who was then the representative of Agudat Zion in the local commuzity council contended that the community should not pay for Gemara studies for all poor children, since it was well known that they were not going to continue their studies. He maintained that only the most talented of the poor children should study Gemara, and these would continue in their studies. But the majority of the poor children should study only *Ivri*, Pentateuch and Rashi, Bible, writing and arithmetic, and the community should pay only for these studies.

In accord with Avraham Yerushalmi's demand, a special *heder* was reopened for the Talmud Torah. But the new *heder* was not in a dark and narrow room of a poor and invalid Rabi, but in a large and roomy apartment. At first it was at the start of Plotzki Street, in the yard of Moshe Elsztejn (in the building that previously housed the soup kitchen). In addition to studies of the holy books, the children learned writing and arithmetic. Their teacher was Bila Grossman, and Zvi Malowanczyk volunteered to train the children in athletics and exercise drills.

The community covered the expenses of the Talmud Torah. The committee of the institution included Avraham Fryd, Meir Cyprys, Yaakov Shimon Rozenfeld, and others. But the main supporter of the Talmud Torah was Agudat Zion, whose chairman was Avraham Fryd, who took care of the problems of the institution. The November 1920 report of the "Joint" [American Jewish Joint Distribution Committee] for the Plotzk District states that Sierpc has a Talmud Torah with 60 pupils.

After Yerushalmi (Fryd) made *aliyah* to Palestine in 1921, support for the Talmud Torah decreased, and it closed. For a while, the Talmud Torah was in the women's section of the old *Beit Midrash.* Later, the children of the Talmud Torah were placed in the *heder* - Yesodai HaTorah and the community paid their tuition.

A large house was built in approximately 1933, for *hachnasat orchim* (public guest house for traveling Jews) on Gurna Street, in back of the Kamnitza, with two rooms allocated for the Talmud Torah. Two "educators," who had finished the seminary of Agudat Israel in Grodno - Eliezer Shnipper and Kimchi - were brought in, and they were the teachers in the Talmud Torah. About seventy children attended the Talmud Torah at this time. The chairman of the Talmud Torah committee was Rabbi Yehoshua Heshel David Goldschlak, and later, it was Hershel Motil. One of the committee members was Itsha Ash.

vii. heder - Yesodai HaTorah

During the German occupation of Poland in the First World War, much changed in the day to day life of the Polish Jews. A progressive spirit that permeated the cities and towns of Poland did away with many practices and traditions of Jewish life, and replaced them with new ones. Among the changes that occurred was the decline of the traditional private *heder.* More modern and public educational institutions called Yesodai HaTorah [Elements of the Torah] were established in Polish towns, and such an institution was founded in Sierpc as well. This public educational establishment - *heder* - Yesodai HaTorah - absorbed almost all the private *heders*, as well as the *melameds*, who now taught in, and were employees of the institution. In addition to the sacred studies, the students studied Hebrew and secular subjects. The secular subjects were taught by certified teachers, and the children were exempted from attending government schools. *heder* - Yesodai HaTorah was managed by a committee, that looked after all the particulars - principal, teachers, pupils; enrollment of the pupils, collecting tuition, and paying salaries and the other details of running the institution.

Teachers and Pupils from the Jewish Pensia [School]

Right to Left
Row 1, Sitting: Sara Kline, *Yurkevitz*, Tovah Lelonek
Row 2: Teachers: Goldberg, Ika (Rivkah) Tatz, Clara Zichman
Row 3, Standing: Roza Lelonek, Mindel Podskoc

A Class from the Jewish "Pensia" [School]

Right to Left
Row 1, Sitting: Leah Konskowolski, Fraidel Goldsztajn, Tovah Koplowicz, Esther Valuka, Tzirel Bergson, Sara Smolinski, Hanna Gongola, Konitz
Row 2, Teachers: Yaakov Bacharach, Leatche Fogel (Koplowicz), Salk Garfinkel, Reich, Korzhan, Raizke Kratuszinska
Third Row, Standing: ---, ---, ---, Tzirel Czerka, Sara Devorah Skornik, Devorah Bluman, Zosha Bluman, Sochaczewski (not from Sierpc), Tovah Lanczner, ---, Sara Gotlibowski

The Jewish "Pensia," Class 4

Right to Left
Row 1, Sitting: Fela Motil, Rizal Lanenter, Moshe Futterman, Arche Yeshaievitch, Roza Lipszic, Esther Gitel Papierczyk
Row 2, Sitting, Teachers: Moniak Klinbert (Gustinin), Gocha Rosek (teacher of music and crafts) Malkah Luszinski (Plotzk), Roza Shivwits (Plotzk), Mania Klinbert (Moniak's Sister)
Row 3, Standing: Esther Motil, Rivkah Lasman, Andzha Bornsztajn, Helena Szerpherz (Teacher). Mania Tatz, Billa Lewita, Andzha Gurfinkel

The founders of Yesodai HaTorah were Nahum Tatz, Michael Koplowicz, Yudel Rabinowicz (originally from Sierpc, lived in Lodz, but lived in Sierpc during the war), and others. They were also members of the first committee. Michael Koplowicz was chairman and Yudel Rabinowicz was the treasurer. *heder* - Yesodai HaTorah was founded in about the year 1916.

Obviously, over the years, membership in the committee changed. In one of the last committees, during the 1930's, the members were: Shimon Zapel (son-in-law of Avraham Glazer), Ephraim Zilberberg (son-in-law of Hirsh Moshe Kanenbrand), Shimon Petrikus (son-in-law of Avraham Shochet), Leibl Piotrkowski (son-in-law of Nahum Tatz), and others. A principal was in charge of the teachers and pupils. Over time, a number of people served as principals. For a while, the principal was Yechiel Lazer Rizfader from Saransk. Following him, the principal was Eliyahu Meir Schleifer (son-in-law of Chayim Bergson).

Among the teachers of Yesodai HaTorah were the *melameds* of the *heders* mentioned above, and new teachers, such as Yekel (from Mlawa - Gemara),

Avraham Wolf Margel (from Plock - Pentateuch), Chayim Karpa (from the village of Tlochovka - Pentateuch), Yechiel Lazer Rizfader (from Saransk - Gemara), and Eliyahu Meir Schleifer (Bible and Gemara).

The first Hebrew teacher was Yerachmiel Weingarten (now in the United States). Following him as a Hebrew teacher was Asher Vatman, from the village of Skoilna (husband of Tzirel Bergson).

The first teacher of secular subjects was Yisrael Yaakov Cohen (from Plonsk), and after him, Hershel Turkltaub (from Nieshtat). They were, each during his tenure, the only teachers of all the subjects. After the founding of the Tarbuth school (in the early 1930's), when there was concern that certain parents (not the most pious ones) would take their children out of Yesodai HaTorah and register them in Tarbuth, a major reform was instituted in the school. Three graduates of the seminar of Agudat Israel in Grodno were brought in (they were called educators, dressed in the European style, and were clean shaven). We mentioned above that two of the educators taught in Talmud Torah, and one, Avraham Yaffe, taught in Yesodai HaTorah. They taught using modern methods, and also held exhibitions during school vacations.

In addition, certified teachers were brought in to teach secular subjects, which from then on were taught in the afternoon. The teachers who taught in Yesodai HaTorah were: Shmulik Valuka, David Maniamchevka, the sisters Carola, Mania, and Fela Tcharnotchepka, and Chayah Kanenbrand. For a while a teacher named Moshe Golomb (from Plonsk-Mlawa) also taught there.

The *heder* - Yesodai HaTorah was on the Jewish Street in the Litvinski house (across from the synagogue). In 1938, because of its poor financial situation, it moved to the *shtibl* of Gur, that was then in the yard of Ahron Lipke's house.

The *heder* - Yesodai HaTorah" was heavily influenced by Agudat Israel. In the report on educational institutions in Sierpc supported by the "Joint" [American Jewish Joint Distribution Committee] from 1938, the *heder* - Yesodai HaTorah is listed as having 185 pupils.

b. Beit Midrash

After the children had finished their years in the *heders*, they would continue their studies (at least those who wanted to continue or their parents wanted them to continue) in the *Beit Midrash*. The studies would be unrestricted, without any regimen, with no disciplining, and no supervision by anyone. The older students at the school would, supposedly, supervise the younger ones. But this supervision was voluntary, and didn't obligate the supervisor or the supervised. Only those that were really serious about learning would advance to the *Beit Midrash*.

This is the way it was in Sierpc as well. A boy who finished the *heder* of Avraham Ahron Burstein or Moshia Karmelkeies, and later Yesodai HaTorah, and wanted to continue only had the old *Beit Midrash*. (very few went to the new *beit*). Some would ask one of the scholars of the town who were immersed in the

Torah to help them. These included Yehoshua Goldman, Binem Wajsmel, David Noach Zilberberg, Leibl Kramarzh, Eliyahu Meir Schleifer and others. These would respond to the parents' requests to teach their sons, some for payment, and some who didn't want payment, and spend an hour or two a day teaching the Gemara and the interpreters. Some parents sent their sons to the famous yeshiva in Gur, or to another yeshiva. But there were few of either of these kinds of pupils. Most of the boys who wanted to continue studied in the old *Beit Midrash*, which resounded all day with the sounds of Torah and prayer.

The studies in the *Beit Midrash* lasted from dawn until late in the evening. The first pupils would come in the early hours of the morning (before morning during the winter). There would be youngsters who had just finished the *heder*, young men, and family men. The first worshippers would also arrive, who at this early hour would recite the Psalms. The pupils would start their studies, and the worshippers their prayers, and the *Beit Midrash* would begin to be crowded. The young men would study alone, or in pairs, and so did some of the youngsters. Possibly one of the young men or one of the older students would teach two or three youngsters. The subjects were Gemara, annotations, and other interpreters, each one according to his age, his knowledge, and the perceptions of the tutor. The students did not study almost any Pentateuch and Bible (only a few, the "enlightened" ones, studied Bible, and they would find a quiet time for this, when there were not many people in the *Beit Midrash*. The studies would last until just before ten in the morning. Then the students would pray, sometimes with the last Minyan, sometimes without a Minyan (of course, the blessings on the Torah and the Kriat Shma were recited earlier in the morning), and then they went home to eat breakfast.

At about noon, some of the boys and young men returned to the *Beit Midrash*. Those that helped their parents in their stores would study Torah only in the morning and evening, and spend the rest of their time working. During the hours when the more mature pupils were not in the *Beit Midrash*, discipline was not too strict. They would study a little, talk a little, and fool around a little. At three in the afternoon, they would go home for dinner.

At about five, they would return to the *Beit Midrash*. During the summer, they would study for a few hours until the evening prayer and most then finished their day. Only a few devoted souls would keep studying after evening prayer during the summer. However, during the winter, the hours after evening prayer were the best study times. During these hours, the two big ovens gave off pleasant warmth, and the "blitz" lamps (big oil lamps above the tables) lit the *Beit Midrash*. The boys, young men, family men and elders sat around the tables and studied the Torah aloud (the worshippers interfered with this in the mornings) and with appropriate melodies. Then, everyone had a desire to study, and willingly did so until late at night.

Some of the youngsters - and some of the young men - had studied secular subjects (Polish, Russian, Hebrew, and Arithmetic) with the teachers Leibl

Atlas and Shimon Gelbard in the afternoon. These came to the *Beit Midrash* a little later in the evening.

There was a practice in earlier years of studying all night on Thursday night (Friday eve). In the middle of these studies, they would stop and send the youngsters to bring hot rolls from the nearby bakery. They would brew tea, take out the herring they had brought with them earlier, and dine heartily. This would be a joyous, communal meal. For the youngsters, this "night vigil" was a special experience that was remembered for many years.

c. The Yeshiva

The Yeshiva was a higher religious education institution. Most towns did not have a Yeshiva, and young boys who wanted to, and whose parents wanted them to continue Torah studies after *heder*, would move to a town that had one. There they would continue the Torah studies - Gemara, and the annotations of Rabbi Shmuel Eliezer Bar Yehuda Edlish ("Maharsha"), Rabbi Shlomo Luria ("Maharshal"), and Rabbi Meir of Lublin ("Maharam") and others. They would usually sustain themselves according to the saying from the Mishnah: "Bread with salt you shall eat, water in small measure you shall drink, and upon the ground you shall sleep; live a life of deprivation and toil in Torah" (*Pirkei Avot* 6, 4). There was no Yeshiva in Sierpc. Very few parents could afford sending a son to a faraway town because of the great hardship and expense.

i. Yeshivat Beit Yosef

A Yeshiva called Beit Yosef was founded in Sierpc in the mid nineteen-thirties. It was founded by two young men from Yeshivat Novodruk, who came to Sierpc on their own, with stated purpose of enhancing and glorifying the Torah. They wore European clothes, like in all the Lithuanian Yeshivas and they were clean shaven and without sideburns. But the Hasidim of Sierpc, with all their admiration for the devotion of the two young men to spread the Torah, were astonished and amazed by their manners.

Many boys from Sierpc studied in *Yeshivat Beit Yosef*, as well as students from the surrounding towns. These would study in the Yeshiva, and get food (different days with different families) and lodging. The lessons took place in the old *Beit Midrash*, and the two young men were the headmasters, teachers, and *melameds*. The elders of the old *Beit Midrash* - Shmuel Yitzhak Tatz, Shmuel Moshe Kanenbrand, Leibl Kramarzh, and others, supported the Yeshiva. There was no tuition charged for studying at *Yeshivat Beit Yosef*.

ii. The "Small Yeshiva"

During the time that *Yeshivat Beit Yosef* existed in Sierpc, there was also a second Yeshiva, called the Small Yeshiva. As its name implies, it was smaller than *Yeshivat Beit Yosef*, with about thirty students. But though it was less in quantity than the first Yeshiva, it exceeded it in quality.

The Small Yeshiva was in the house of Yehoshua Popowski (son-in-law of David Klajnman, called Haver, an esteemed teacher in Sierpc, originally from Nieshtat, who lived in his father-in-law's house). Yehoshua, who was an outstanding scholar, a Hasid with noble qualities, was the head of the Small Yeshiva and a leader of the studies. The Small Yeshiva charged tuition.

The Small Yeshiva was also mentioned in the report on educational institutions in Sierpc supported by the "Joint" [American Jewish Joint Distribution Committee] from 1938, which stated that it had 77 pupils. However, because of the number of pupils, and from the text of the report, it seems that there was an error in the name of the institution, and they were actually referring to *Yeshivat Beit Yosef.*

B. Modern Education

a. Rivack's School

The first Jewish school in Sierpc was that of Rivack (who was not from Sierpc). The school was opened at the beginning of the 1880s, and was attended by both boys and girls (at different times of the day). The girls, of the usual school age, studied during regular school hours, in the mornings. The boys, who had already had bar mitzvah and had finished their *heder* studies learned in the afternoon. Some of them studied all day in the beit midrash, and only in the early evening, at a time which is neither day nor night, they would study secular subjects. Others would help their parents in their stores or in a trade, and would study for one or two hours in the afternoon. The subjects included Russian, Polish, German, and arithmetic. Rivack, the teacher, did not teach Yiddish, or talk to his pupils in Yiddish. He spoke in the language that he was then teaching, or in Russian.

The school was located in the market, in the house of Simchah Binem Burstyn (called "Binem Esikmacher" - the Vinegar Maker, or "der Hoicher Binem" - Tall Binem). Rivack's school lasted for a number of years, after which Rivack was accepted as a teacher in a government school, and sent to teach in another town.

b. Atlas's School

The school of Leibl Atlas opened after Rivack's school closed, in the mid-1880s. The school was in a room in Atlas's house which had special benches, and boys and girls learned with arrangements the same as in the previous school. The change was in the curriculum and language of study. In addition to the subjects studied in the previous school, Hebrew and Yiddish were also taught, and the lessons were in Yiddish.

The school lasted until nearly the start of the First World War. It began in the house of Bagner, which was later the house of Kalmanowicz.

c. Mintz's School

Mordecai Hirsch Mintz's school for boys had an important place in the education of Sierpc youth. The Mintz School taught Hebrew studies and general studies, but the emphasis was on Hebrew subjects: Bible, Jewish History, and Hebrew language, and later - a little Gemara. The parents of the children in this school were all modern and progressive. In its early years, the school was called the Improved *heder*, at least by its adherents, but its opponents called it Dangerous *heder* [in the Ashkenazi Hebrew dialect, the words "improved" and "dangerous" are practically homonyms]. The education at Mintz's school resulted in a group of young people who were nationalist, Zionist, and knew Hebrew; the Zionist movement in the town developed from their midst.

At the beginning, Mintz was the only teacher, and he had just 12 pupils. With time, the school expanded, more classes were added, as well as teachers to help the headmaster. The teachers (at different times) of Hebrew subjects were: Israel Yaakov Cohen (from Plonsk, taught in the school after he stopped being a partner in *skladap tatzhni*, a medical warehouse, then returned to Plonsk, where he was a teacher in the Jewish Gymnasium). Rozenblum (also from Plonsk and returned to Plonsk), and Richald (after the closing of his Improved *heder*, see below) also taught Hebrew. The Gemara teachers were David Noach Zilberberg, Binem Wajsmel, and later, Mintz himself. Teachers of general subjects were Mr. Dambski (a teacher in the Russian Government School), and Ms. Lichia (Leah) Fogel (Koplowicz's stepdaughter).

At first, the languages of instruction in the school were Yiddish for the Hebrew subjects and Russian for general subjects. Afterwards, except for foreign languages, all lessons were conducted in Hebrew. The school was located on the side street near the Kamnitza, in Mintz's house, which he had inherited from his wife's parents. Later, the school was located in the New Market, in the house of Ahron Tcharnotchepka. The school existed from the middle of the 1890s until 1922, when the Mintz family moved to America.

d. The Improved Heder

In about the year 1910, a teacher named Richald (not originally from Sierpc) opened a modern school called Improved *heder* (that the Haredim called Dangerous *Heder*). The school was on the Jewish Street, in the house of Litvinski. It lasted for only a short time. The Improved *heder* was more modern, and less traditional than Mintz's school. At that time in Sierpc, there were not enough supporters, and the school failed quickly. As stated above, Richald became a teacher in Mintz's school.

e. Yavne School

In the first half of the decade of the 1920's, there was a school in Sierpc called Yavne that was founded by *Mizrachi* (the religious Zionist organization). It was part of a nationwide network of fgZ*Mizrachi* schools that were called

Yavne. The school employed four teachers, two for Hebrew studies, and two for general studies. The teachers were: Hersh Crystal (now in Israel, Zvi Algavish) taught *ivri* (reading) and the Hebrew language; Meir Zev Glatman (from Warsaw) taught Bible and Jewish History; Yosef Przasnyszski taught arithmetic and the Polish language; and Ezriel Szampan taught geography and Polish history. The principal was Hersh Crystal. All the lessons, except for Polish language, were taught in Hebrew.

The school was in the *Mizrachi* center, in the New Market, in the house of Ms. Podskoc (in the yard of the Bukat house). The Yavne School existed for only a short time. It closed because of financial problems.

f. Tarbuth School

For ten years after Mintz's School closed, there was no educational institution in Sierpc (except for the Yavne School, which existed for only a short time) that offered combined Jewish and general studies. Although there were two schools for Jewish children, *heder - Yesodai HaTorah* and the Government School for Jewish Children, the former taught general studies very poorly, and the Jewish studies in the latter were of little value. So it was that parents who didn't want to forego a Jewish education and sent their children to Yesodai HaTorah lost out on general studies, and those that wouldn't give up a general education and sent their children to the government school, saw them grow up without a Jewish background, neither religious nor nationalist.

Therefore, the opening of the *Tarbuth* School was something whose time had come. This was a school that gave its pupils a Jewish modern-traditional education, in addition to a comprehensive general education. Many parents were expecting a school like this. They rejoiced at the news of the opening of their school, and sent their sons there to study Torah and knowledge.

The *Tarbuth* School was founded in 1931. That year, a kindergarten called *Tarbuth* opened on the Jewish street, in a house in the yard of Yosef Vasolak (later sold to Moshe Lasman and Israel Barco). With time, as more classes opened up, and the place became too small for all the pupils that wanted to enroll, and a more suitable location could not be found, the committee decided to construct a school building. A building committee was established, with the help of Sierpc emigrants in America. The committee was able to purchase a plot (on *Studolna* Street, later called *Lenarotovitzia*) and build a pleasant, two-story building that was suitable to the school's needs. Until the construction was finished, the school moved to a large apartment on Plotzki Street, behind the Kotcholak house. In 1935, the building was ready, and the school moved into its new, large and spacious home.

This enormous undertaking, a Hebrew school with a special edifice built for it, was unique in all the towns in the area. The establishment of the school and maintenance of the building cost the activists and volunteers a great deal of effort and no end of problems. However, in the end, they could be pleased that they established an institution that was the glory of the Jews of Sierpc, a project that was talked about in all the towns in the area.

The building committee of the *Tarbuth* School included: Yeshayahu Frydman, the chairman; Moshe Balt, secretary; Baruch Atlas, Hana Atlas, David Bergson, Avraham Groda, Yehuda Visroza, Avraham Zhabitsky, Yaska Konitz (Cohen), Zvi Malowanczyk, Israel Smolenski, Chayim Skorka, Shlomo Kutner, Yitzhak Klajnman, and Hershel Rotenberg (son-in-law of Esther Rachel Szampan).

The *Tarbuth* School had seven classes, with over two hundred students. If the kindergarten and the evening school are included, it had over three hundred students. Except for the Polish subjects, all lessons were taught in Hebrew. During lessons of sacred subjects, the children would wear hats. All students wore a dark blue uniform and hat, or beret for the girls. The hat or beret had a pale blue thread at the seam, with the school logo.

The report on educational institutions in Sierpc supported by the "Joint" [American Jewish Joint Distribution Committee] from 1938 states that the *Tarbuth* school had 195 pupils, and 52 children in the kindergarten. The evening school had 30 pupils.

A letter from the Building Committee and Management Committee of the *Tarbuth* School to the Committee of Sierpc Emigrants in America, from 13 September 1935 states "the school has about 200 pupils."

A letter from the aid committee in Sierpc to the Relief committee of Sierpc Emigrants in America that was written on 5 April 1939 mentions 220 pupils. It also states, "The school is supported by tuition fees paid by pupils' parents. Of the 220 pupils, 60 are poor, and are exempt from payment of tuition fees."

In addition to the educational activities, for which the school was established, the school and school building served as a center for all Zionist activities in Sierpc. The school building housed the Zionist Organization, the Zionist Library, and the Maccabee Sports Organization[5]. The halls of the school were hosts to Zionist meetings, lectures on Zionist, social or literary topics, and discussions of various subjects. The lecturers were the teachers, local residents, or from out of town. There was a clear Zionist spirit to the school that educated the children to be loyal Zionists, and also influenced their parents.

The school had a Parents' Committee, whose membership changed with time. The members were committed and faithful to their office. They tended to all the material and spiritual needs of the school, and cooperated with its management. The members of the first parents' committee were Yeshayahu Frydman, chairman; Yitzhak Meir Zilberberg (Simchoni), treasurer; David Bergson, Moshe Berman, Fibush Lipka, and Yitzhak Klajnman (the second and fourth are now in Israel). At a later time, the parents' committee consisted of Hana Atlas, David Bergson, Moshe Berman, Nasha Groda, Yaska Konitz

(Cohen), Yeshayahu Frydman, Yitzhak Klajnman, and Mendel Shtinhoz (Menachem Avni). (The third, fifth, and eighth are now in Israel.)

The members of the last Parents' Committee were: Yeshayahu Frydman, Chairman; Itche David Sznitzer, secretary; David Bergson, Moshe Gutsztat, Yaakov Yosef Visroza, Abba Licht, Israel Smolenski[6], Pesach Skornik, Moshe Ahron Flurman (from Lipno, son-in-law of Chayim David Arbiter), and Yitzhak Klajnman.

The following are the names of the teachers at the *Tarbuth* School (none of them were from Sierpc):

- Kindergarten: Hana Fleisher, Hadassah Goldberg.
- Female teachers: Zina Bacharach (Bialystok), Miriam Bloch (Bialystok), Goldberg, Malkah Gipman, Hana Dichter, Tapper (Kolomi), Fleishon, S. Kleinerman, S. Kellerman, and A. Shparko.
- Male teachers: M. Rubal (the first teacher in *Tarbuth*, died tragically in Israel), M. Handleman, Selvin, Ahron Skoropa (Zuromin), and others.
- Principals: Shaul Rozenblum, the first principal (Warsaw), Valkov, A.I. Dichter (now in Israel). The last principal, Dichter, served in the last two years until the destruction of the Community of Sierpc, and was deported by the Nazis (together with his wife, the teacher Hana Dichter, also in Israel) together with all the Jews of Sierpc, and all of his pupils.
- The caretaker of the *Tarbuth* School was Shlomo Gongola.

*

Translator's Footnotes

1. The word *Burmistazh* both in Russian and Polish, is a corruption of the German *Burgermeister* which means mayor. In Yiddish, we used to say *Burgmistazh* and also the expression *Roshiren* (used by the older people) which was a corruption of the Hebrew words for mayor.
2. *Curia* - a group of voters. The electorate was divided into six *Curia*: professionals, landlords, merchants, craftsmen, clerks, and workers. Each *Curia*, irrespective of the number of members, would elect the same number of representatives.
3. Yosef Karpa was an Alexander Hasid. The *Aguda* put a member of the Alexander Hasidim on their list in order to ensure their support.
4. Passed Away in Israel
5. The same institutions were housed in the previous two locations of the *Tarbuth* School.
6. A letter from the *Tarbuth* School to the Sierpc Emigrants Committee in America, from 13 September, 1935, is signed by Israel Smolinski as Chairman of the School Committee.

C. Business Organizations and Labor Unions

Business and professional affairs expanded during the German occupation of the First World War, as well as cultural and public life. Merchants, craftsmen, and workers all organized to protect their own interests and improve their living standards. Business associations of merchants, craftsmen's societies, and workers' and clerks' unions were founded. They promoted their members' interests and tried to improve their conditions.

Two business organizations and a labor union were founded in Sierpc during this period: The Merchants' Society, The Craftsmen's' Association, and a labor union.

D. The Merchants' Society

The founders of The Merchants' Society and its first committee members were Iskar Bergson, Shmualtia Tatz, Azrieltia Podskocz, and others. Shmuel Zanbal Dormbus, Zvi Malewanczyk and others joined in later periods. Shmualtia Tatz was the chairman for many years. The secretary during the 1920s was Ezriel Szampan.

The Merchants' Society at first used the apartment of Iskar Bergson for its meetings. Later it had an office on Fara Street in the house of Elia Ber Czarnoczapka. After that, it moved to the Bank *Mnoyot* (The Merchants' Bank) in the house of Ischia Shvitzer.

E. Small Merchants' Society

The Small Merchants' Society was founded in Sierpc in the 1920s. Small shopkeepers and owners of stalls joined the society to promote their causes. Their various interests in some cases, such as taxes, were at odds with those of the larger merchants. Some of the members of The Merchants' Society left to join the Small Merchants' Society, and were joined by other small shopkeepers who had not been organized till then.

The founder of the Small Merchants' Society was Hershel Koplowicz, who was its chairman for many years and its most active member. He was a member of both the town and district tax assessment committees, and worked diligently to obtain discounts and concessions for the members.

The other committee members were Moshe Burgand, Avrahamia Grossman, Baruch Lipszyc (passed away in Israel), and others. The Small Merchants Society did not have its own office. The committee meetings and other activities were held in the Alexander shtibl, at the start of the Jewish Street, in the house of Kalman Lidovarski.

F. Craftsmen's Association

The founders and active members of the Craftsmen's Association were: Baruch Atlas, Mordechai Lipa Atlas, Ziskind Arbiter, Moshe Gongola, Hersh Grina, Dudia Diogenes', Shmuel Hanach Dragon, Meir Zvirak, Ischia Meir Lelonek, (the last two are now in Israel), Avraham Mlawa, Yisraelik Smolinski,

Shmuel Fasa, Yossel Pukacz, Ezra Frankel, Shlomo Pszenica, Tzadok, Menachem Szpiro, and others.

Avraham Mlawa was the leader of the founders of the Craftsmen's Association, and its first chairman. After he immigrated to Palestine, Ezra Frankel became chairman. He was also the chairman of the shoemakers' cell of the association, and Hersh Graina was the chairman of the tailors' cell.

The office of the Craftsmen's Association was in the house of Lasman on the Jewish Street (later the house of Shvitzer). They held a *minyan* of craftsmen there for Saturday and holiday prayers. The reader of the Torah was Avraham Yitzhak Grodko.

The Craftsmen's Association in Sierpc had a Zionist orientation, and always collaborated with the Zionist organization in elections. The two organizations appeared on the same list for both the Community Council and Town Council elections.

G. Craftsmen's Organization

It was customary that a worker apprenticed to a craftsman would stay only until his wedding. After the worker was married, and had received a little money from the dowry, he would try to set himself up as an independent craftsman. He would take on a young boy as an apprentice, and when his situation improved a little, he would also hire a worker. The new craftsman was expected to be loyal to the same ideals he held as a worker, and he would remain a member of the same workers' party to which he had previously belonged. Over time, this presented a difficult problem for the workers' parties, especially in the small towns, since a sizable percentage of the members became employers and exploiters. The *Bund* came up with a solution: they ejected the independent craftsmen from the party, and made them part of a different organizational framework, the “Craftsmen's Organization” of the *Bund*.

A Craftsmen's Organization was founded in Sierpc as well, in the mid-1930s. It was led by Leibush Uszer and Hersh Yurkevitz.

H. Labor Union

All the Jewish workers in Sierpc belonged to the same labor union, no matter which party they belonged to, or their particular vocation. The union was divided into cells, one for each vocation.

A committee of five members was elected at the founding meeting of the union. The chairman was Avraham Gordon (*Bund*), and the secretary was the teacher Israel Yaakov Cohen (*Poalei Tzion*). The union headquarters was on Zhava (Zhavia) Street, in the yard of the house of Avraham Yitzhak Grodka.

I. Clerks' Union

The union of store assistants, clerks, and bookkeepers was founded in 1937. The committee members were: Zvi Arpa (now in Israel), Motel Lelonek, Michael Lipsker (from Lipno), Barak Feinberg, and David Frank (from Lipno). The union had over forty members.

***

The Economic Status of the Jews of Sierpc

The 1938 report of the "Joint" [American Jewish Joint Distribution Committee] contains the following statements about the economic conditions of the Jews of Sierpc:

"Sierpc has a population of 10,051, of which there are 3090 Jews, consisting of about 600 families. They earn their living mainly from petty trading and manual labor.

Number of shops owned by Jews	290
Number of stalls	65
Total tradesman	355

"There are 158 tradespeople who are members of the Small Merchants Society. The number of craftspeople is about 150 and most of them are tailors and seamstresses. There are about 100 members in the Craftsmen's Association.

"Of the industrial plants in the area, there are two factories that are owned by Jews: a lumberyard, and a tannery.

"The status of the Jewish shopkeepers has become worse because of competition from non-Jewish shopkeepers, who have recently opened stores in all branches of trade in the town itself and in the surrounding villages. The public boycotts are affecting the more established tradesmen as well."

According to the numbers in this report, there were 600 Jewish wage earners in Sierpc, divided as follows:

Merchants (storekeepers and stall owners)	59%
Craftsmen	25%
Miscellaneous occupations	16%
Total	**100%**

A. Financial Institutions

The possibility of establishing mutual credit companies to help the small tradesman and craftsman in their hard battle for existence was discussed in the Jewish neighborhoods even before the First World War. Financial institutions called Loan and Savings Funds were started in many cities, and were of great help to their members.

The economic status of the Jews in Poland became much worse in the years before the First World War. In the elections for the Fourth *duma* (Russian Parliament) in 1912, the candidate of the Polish Right Wing, Kochazhavski, suffered a major defeat. This defeat was due to the Jews, who supported the candidate of the Left, Yagalalo. As a result, a strong anti-Semitic movement arose, which declared an economic boycott of Jews. Poles opened stores in towns and villages, both private stores and cooperatives (*spolki*) and the economic conditions of the Jews, which were bad to begin with, became even worse. The Loan and Savings Funds were open then in various cities, and they aided the merchants and craftsman, and improved their economic conditions.

The capital of these funds was from the share assets of the members and the support of the J.C.A. (Jewish Colonization Association, a support group created by Baron Maurice de Hirsch).

a. Loan and Savings Fund

The first Jewish financial mutual aid institution was founded in Sierpc before the First World War, in about 1913. The founders of Loan and Savings Fund and its committee members were: Dr. Szpiro (a medical doctor who lived in Sierpc for a few years around the time of the First World War) chairman, Avraham Shlomo Glazer, Chayim Nachum Tunbol, Nahum Tatz, Shmualtia Tatz, Michal Smolinski, Yehuda Baruch Skornik, and others. Shmuel Glazer was the (volunteer) secretary of the fund. The fund's office was at first in the house of Nahum Tatz, and later, at the start of Fara (Farska) Street in the house of Grabovski (a Pole).

When the Russians left Poland during the First World War, the ruble (the Russian currency) lost its value, and the Loan and Savings Funds in all of Poland were wiped out, including the one in Sierpc.

b. People's Bank

A credit fund was established in Sierpc not long after the end of World War I, in 1919, to continue the work of the Loan and Savings Fund of before the war. The fund started with limited capital from the shares of the founders. The founders and committee members were; Shmualtia Tatz chairman, Yisachar Bergson treasurer, Avrahamia Grossman, Nachum Tatz, Meir Cipris, and others. The office was on Fara Street in the house of Elia Ber Czarnoczapka.

The moneys from the founders' shares obviously were not sufficient for wide-scale activity. The JCA (Jewish Colonization Association) that supported the Loan and Savings Funds before the war was not active in Poland after the war, so that the Fund's functioning was weak and unrecognized. This explains the sentence in the report of the representative of the “Joint” for the Plotzki

District from November, 1920: "There is no loan fund (or Beneficial Society) in Sierpc."

The managers of the "Joint" in Poland started to establish credit and financial institutions in 1920. A number of such institutions were founded or renewed in many towns. The fund in Sierpc also received support from the "Joint," and expanded its activities under a new name, Bank Ludowi or People's Bank, as such institutions were called in Poland. This bank was a cooperative, also called Craftsmen's Bank, and was a popular, general bank, as its name suggests. This bank helped all the classes in town by offering loans with easy terms to craftsmen, merchants, and other wage-earners. It was the largest Jewish financial institution in Sierpc.

A letter from the Aid Committee in Sierpc to the Relief Committee of Sierpc Townspeople in America of January 1939 contains some interesting details on the People's Bank:

"The capital of the bank consists of: a) Long term credit from the "Joint"; b) Money from members' shares; c) Savings accounts; d) Various deposits. The bank issues loans to most of the Jews of the town. It has more than 300 members. The maximum credit extended to a member (of course, a member in good financial condition) is 1200 zloty. Because of the crisis, there are unpaid debts. For this reason, the bank does not show a profit, but in spite of this, the bank is in good condition." The letter also mentions that ten years earlier the state of the bank was very bad, and it managed to cover its debts and survive the crisis then only because of the efforts of all its members.

The bank managers and board that were elected once, or a number of times, were: Leibush Uszer, Baruch Atlas, Mordechai Lipa Atlas, Ziskind Arbiter, Mendel Blum, Moshe Gongola, Avraham Groda, Avrahamia Grossman, Hersh Grina, David Diogenes', Shmuel Yitzhak Tatz, Avraham Mlawa (Ben-David), Yisraelik Smolinski, Shmuel Paso, Ezra Frankel, Shlomo Pszenica, Ber Charka, Ischia David Sznitzer, Menachem Szpiro, and others. The secretary of the People's Bank in the 1920s was Ezriel Szampan, and the manager in the 1930s was Michael Lipsker.

The bank was located on Zhava (Zhavia) Street, in the house of Bogoshavski (a Pole). Later the bank moved to the start of Plotzki Street, to the house of Ahron Lipka.

c. Shareholders' Bank

The second Jewish bank in Sierpc was the Shareholders' Bank (Bank *Odzialovi*) that was also called Merchants' Bank. The letter from the Aid Committee mentioned above, from 22 January 1939, states:

"The second cooperative bank was founded about 10 years ago (1929). A group of merchants (the wealthiest group in the Peoples' Bank) had left because of conflicts among the various groups in the bank. This group founded a new bank, also on a cooperative basis. The bank's capital is composed of a) Money from members' shares; b) Deposits. This bank did not get credit from the 'Joint' since it is difficult to obtain credit from the 'Joint' for two cooperative banks in the same town. The Shareholders' Bank has about 100 members. About 70% of the members are also members of People's Bank, and benefit from loans from both banks."

A letter from the same Aid Committee, written on 17 July 1939, states: "The chairman of Shareholders' Bank Shmuel Tatz."

The bank was located in the market, in the house of Ischia Shvitzer (previously the house of Moshe Tajtelbaum and Yakir Plato).

d. Credit Bank

The third Jewish bank in Sierpc was the Credit Bank (Bank *Craditovi*). The bank was founded by members of *Agudat Israel* and was called the *Aguda* Bank. *Aguda* Bank was the newest and smallest of the Jewish banks in Sierpc. Not only was it founded after People's Bank and Shareholders' Bank, it also stopped operating before they did.

The Credit Bank was also a cooperative bank. Its capital consisted of: a) Money from members' shares; b) Credit from the Banking Society of Agudat Israel; c) Deposits. The management and board members of the bank were, over the years: Mendel Gurfinkel, Moshe Grossman, Shimon Zapel, Mendel Melech Tajtelbaum, Nachum Tatz, Avraham Marantz, and others. The bank was located in the house of Nahum Tatz on the Jewish Street.

e. The Beneficial Fund

In addition to the three banks, a philanthropic Beneficial Fund (*Kupat Gmilat Hasadim*) was founded in Sierpc in 1927. The fund gave interest free loans with easy repayment conditions to small merchants and craftsmen. It was of great help to many families, allowing them maintain their meager existence under the terrible conditions in anti-Semitic Poland between the two world wars, and especially in the last years before the Second World War.

Important details about the fund are in a letter of 4 August 1938 from the Beneficial Fund committee to a group of Sierpcers living in America:

"A number of members have undertaken, by pledges and donations, to pay a monthly assessment. Registration for the Gold Book will be 100 zloty, and from time to time there are festive events whose income is dedicated to the fund. Thanks to these efforts, thirteen thousand zloty have been collected. Together with the credit extended by the "Joint" and the *Tchekaba Centrala Kas Bezprocentowych* (Center for Interest Free Funds the center for Beneficial Funds in Poland), the Fund has capital of twenty-six thousand zloty. (For each zloty that we collect, we receive an additional zloty from the "Joint.") 450 Families are now using this for credit with no interest."

The letter details who are the recipients: "57 tailors, 30 shoemakers, 2 carpenters, 4 butchers, 69 miscellaneous vocations, 13 notions sellers, 5 leather merchants, 35 grocery store shopkeepers, 35 stall owners in the market, 39 merchants in villages, 20 workers, 140 miscellaneous wage earners."

There are also interesting details about the Beneficial Fund in a letter of 22 January 1939 from the Sierpc Aid Committee to the Relief Committee of Sierpcers in America:

"The resources of the Beneficial Fund were limited in its first few years, and the maximum loan was 25 zloty. Because of this, the middle class did not turn to the fund for loans, and only the poorer class benefited from the fund. The maximum loan today is 200 zloty, and there are over 400 borrowers. The loans are made without interest, but there is a certain charge for administrative costs. The Beneficial Fund also has unpaid debts because of the difficult economic times."

The main founder of the Beneficial Fund was Elia Ber Czarnoczapka. For many years he was the most important advocate of the fund. He invested both his energy and his money in the fund, eased its monetary difficulties, and reduced deficits in the loan funds. He also gave, without any thought of compensation, a two-room apartment that the fund could use.

The only fact that we have about the Beneficial Fund committee at its founding is that its chairman was Nachman Horowitz. The committee in 1930 consisted of: Rabbi Yehoshua Heshel David Goldschlak honorary chairman, Elia Ber Czarnoczapka chairman, Mendel Shtinhoz treasurer, David Bergson secretary, Nachman Eichald, Moshe Berman, Baruch Mendel Gotlibowski, Ischia Meir Zilbersztajn, Mendel Lipszyc, David Maniamchevka, and Yakir Plato.

All the members of the Beneficial Fund committee signed a letter from August 1938: Menachem Bojmwol chairman, Hersh Pianca secretary, Matat (Matityahu) Przasnyszski treasurer, Yaakov Edelstein, Leibush Uszer, Elia (Eliyahu) Grossman, Moshe Grossman, Avraham Hersh Yurkevitz, Ahron Yosef (Yossel) Pukacz, and Moshe Aran (Ahron) Fetbrot. The active secretary of the fund was Neta Plonsker, a learned and enlightened young man.

*

Our respected townsman Ischia Lanter informs us that there was also a Beneficial Fund in Sierpc in the 1890s. The collectors were Akiva Glazer and Akiva Lanenter.

f. Local Aid Committee Rescue Committee

There was another financial institution in Sierpc. However, in terms of its extent, capabilities, activities, and duration, it was smaller and poorer than the other such Jewish institutions in the town. Formally, the institution was called Local Aid Committee for the Jews of Sierpc. Its official rubber stamp was inscribed (in Yiddish): "*Localer Hilft-Komitet Far Yiden in Sierpc*" ("Local Aid Committee for Jews in Sierpc"), but usually it was called the Rescue Committee. A letter from the institution to Sierpcers in America ends with the

Yiddish "*Retungs Komitat*" ("Rescue Committee"). The postal address for sending donations is of course in Polish "*Komitetu Ratunkowego*" (again "Rescue Committee").

In the letter mentioned above, the committee describes to the Sierpcers in America the bad financial situation of the Jews of Sierpc: Respected merchants and established craftsmen lost their properties and livelihoods; workers are unemployed, and yesterday's donors are today's recipients. With assets that are dwindling every week, the committee cannot help everyone that comes for aid. The fund is turning to the townspeople of Sierpc in America to send a substantial amount of money to help all those that have lost everything in this economic crisis.

If we judge on the basis of the two names of this institution, both official and unofficial, it seems that it is a charitable institution, whose purpose is to support the unemployed and the hungry. But we accept the words of Zvi Malewanczyk that this was an institution that distributed loans. According to him, it gave small loans (about 15 zloty) on easy terms, with no interest, no notes, and no guarantors, and with small weekly repayments. The customers of this institution were in very dire straits, and even this small loan helped them. There were also people who could not repay their loan to the Beneficial Fund, and used the money they received from the Rescue Committee to cover their debt, and then took out a bigger loan from the Beneficial Fund. The sources of the money for the Rescue Committee were charitable donations, both new and periodic, that were collected by Yechiel Greenberg (from Czerwinsk, son-in-law of Ischia Offenbach). There were also collections at weddings and in "bowls" left in prayer houses on Yom Kipper eve and on Purim. All the work in this institution, except for collecting donations, was voluntary.

The above letter was written in March, 1933, and apparently, the institution was founded at about this date. The letter was signed by Zvi Malewanczyk chairman, Yaakov Shimon Rosenfeld treasurer, Yehoshua Tajtelbaum secretary, Menachem Bojmwol, Isaac Grinbaum, Menachem Sloma, Moshe Pukacz (who was called *Der Blinder* Mata Blind Matte), Shimon Petrikus, Leibl Fleisher, and Eliyahu Meir Schleifer.

Because of their poverty, many borrowers did not pay their debts, and the institution closed after a few years. Its name does not appear in a March 1937 letter from the Aid Committee (a charitable institution in Sierpc in the years 1937-39) to the Sierpcer in America that lists the Jewish financial institutions in Sierpc.

B. Charitable Institutions

Two of the three attributes that characterize the people of Israel are pity and charity. Our wise men of blessed memory said: "And he said, there are three traits in this nation [Israel]: those who are compassionate, those who are timid and those who perform acts of loving-kindness" (*Yevamot* 79). Many of the Torah commandments are based on a feeling of pity and the obligation to help the poor and the weak, the widow and the orphan, and anyone who is despondent will be recognized. The attribute of mercy is deeply rooted in the character of the Jew, and from habit and persistence, it has penetrated deeply into his heart and soul. The Jews have, at all times and under all conditions, obeyed the commandment, "And if thy brother be waxen poor ... then thou shalt uphold him." The Jews established charity and aid institutions for their faltering brothers in all of the Diaspora of Israel, in every country and in every town and village. Every Jewish community had institutions and societies for housing poor travelers, providing dowries for poor brides, helping and lodging the sick. Every Jew was a member of one or more of these societies, and a donor to them.

Sierpc also had institutions that helped the poor and sick, men and women. These were:

- *Hachnasat Orchim* (Hospitality and lodging for poor travelers)
- *Bikur Holim* (Providing doctors and medicines for the poor)
- *Linat HaTzedek* (Lodging with the sick)
- *Malbish Arumim* (Clothes and shoes for poor children)
- *Hachnasat Kala* (Dowries for poor brides)
- *Beit Lehem* (Food for the poor)
- *Agudat Nashim* (Women's Society)

a. Hachnasat Orchim

Indigent travelers who would wander from town to town would present themselves at people's houses. In Sierpc, they would stay with the local poor (for a small fee), and also at the old *Beit Midrash*. This caused problems both for the poor travelers (who did not have a comfortable resting place) and for the worshippers (the lack of cleanliness in the prayer house, and the distractions during prayer). This problem was corrected when the *Hachnasat Orchim* institution was founded. A two-room (one for men, the other for women) apartment was rented, and furnished with good beds and clean sheets.

There was a *Hachnasat Orchim* (Bringing in Guests) society in Sierpc at the end of the 1880s and beginning of the 1890s. The *Gabaim* (collectors) were: Akivia Lanenter, Moshe Mintz, and others. The apartment was at the end the small street near the Kamnitza. It was shut down for various reasons at the end of the nineteenth century.

The society was renewed at the beginning of the twentieth century in the house of Shmuel Szampan (who was called Shmuel Nagid Shmuel the Philanthropist), near the *mikve*. This time the founders were Haskell (Yechezkel) Baszkes, Mendel Gorlitz (Lipszyc), Eliezer Sendrowicz, Yaakov Shimon Rosenfeld, and others. The caretaker of *Hachnasat Orchim* was *Der*

Geler Hershel (Yellow Hershel). The income of *Hachnasat Orchim* was from weekly dues of the members and various donations.

There was a *minyan* at the institution on Saturdays and holidays, and some of the members prayed there. (The building also housed a *shtibl* called the Second *shtibl* of Alexander.) The income from the *minyan* was dedicated to the institution.

There was a typhus epidemic in all of Poland in 1915, at the beginning of the German occupation of World War I. The German authorities in Sierpc prohibited the poor travelers coming to the town from going to people's houses or wandering in town, out of fear of spreading the disease. The community then rented a storeroom in the yard of Yashinski (a Pole), at the start of the road to Rypin. They renovated it and turned it into a *Hachnasat Orchim* house. All the poor that came to town were either directed there, or brought there by police. They would stay there one or two days, receive food and lodging and a little money, and be sent to another town. Mordechai Rosen managed the institution for the community.

The *Hachnasat Orchim* institution opened and closed a number of times, and wandered from one remote apartment to another, like its guests, until it found a permanent place at the beginning of the 1930s. The house was built for the institution on Gorna Street, behind the Kamnitza. It was a large one-story house with a basement.

The committee that was established to erect the building for two important institutions –*Hachnasat Orchim* and *Talmud Torah* devoted a great deal of effort to the task. Particularly devoted was the Town Rabbi, Rabbi Yehoshua Heshel David Goldschlak, who was the chairman of the committee. For many weeks, the Rabbi would pray each Saturday in a different synagogue (including the *shtibls*). The Rabbi would give a sermon before the Torah reading about the great importance and the great mitzvah in erecting this building that would house two such important institutions, both from the Jewish and the humane standpoints. During the reading of the Torah, the Rabbi would stand next to the table that held the Torah scroll. He would order the Torah reader not to assign more than three verses to each man called to the Torah. He would then make each of them pledge to the construction of the building and then dicker with anyone whose contribution did not satisfy him.

The dedication of the *Hachnasat Orchim* building was an occasion of great celebration. The Town Rabbi and rabbis of the surrounding towns participated, and gave speeches seasoned with Torah quotations about the great deed done by the Jews of Sierpc, in erecting a building for these two great institutions. The choir of *Agudat Israel* entertained the many spectators with their singing.

Among those that participated in the mitzvah of erecting the building were Yechezkel Baszkes, Hersh Motil, and others.

b. Other Aid Societies

The *Bikur Holim* (Visiting the Sick) Society helped poor sick people by providing doctors' visits and medicine at low cost, on the basis of a chit that the patient would receive from *Bikur Holim*. They would also receive medical instruments such as cupping glasses and thermometers.

The *Linat HaTzedek* (Lodging for the Righteous) Society sent its members, when their turn came up, to stay with a sick person (not necessarily poor). In cases where the illness lasted a long time, and the family members were weary, the help of *Linat HaTzedek* was very important. The members would bring "tasty foods" for the poorer patients.

The *Malbish Arumim* (Clothing the Naked) Society helped the poor, especially poor children, by donating clothes and shoes. This help was usually given just before the winter. The first recipients were the students at the *Talmud Torah.*

The *Hachnasat Kala* (Bringing in the Bride) Society helped poor brides, either by money for a dowry, or with clothes, underwear and bedding (it was called *Oysshteier*). Thanks to this help, poor families could also get their daughters married.

The income of all these societies, like the income of *Hachnasat Orchim* came mostly from the dues of their members. A paid collector every Thursday or Friday collected these dues. There were also collections at weddings and in "bowls" left in prayer houses on Yom Kipper eve and on Purim, and various donations.

All of the activists in these societies (they were called *Gabaim* collectors) were usually collectors for two or three societies. The collectors were: Kalman Arpa (called Kalman Yakiryehs), Yechezkel (Haskell) Baszkes, Mendel Gorlitz (Lipszyc), Nachman Horowitz, Akivia Lanenter, Benyamin Sobol, Yaakov Skornik, Avraham Fryd (Yerushalmi), Yaakov Shimon Rosenfeld, and others.

Women were also members of these societies. The women were especially active in the *Linat HaTzedek* and *Hachnasat Kala* Societies. These lady activists (they were called *Gabates* female collectors) were: Esther Baniet (Licht), Rachel Abbas (Weisgal), Rachel (*Di Shochetke* ritual slaughterer's wife) Bergson, Rellah Baszkes, Tovah Leah Migdal, Tzirel Lippies Naselski, Rosa Dina Klin, Rivkaia Tunbol, Yetta Sochaczewski, Sarah Grossman, and others.

c. Women's Association

The Women's Association (Froien Farein) was founded in Sierpc before the First World War. Its purpose was to provide help to the poor and sick, and to the weak and failing. The activists in the Women's Association were not called gabates. They belonged to a younger generation, and their aid society had a more modern character. The committee members of the Association were: Sarah Bluman, Leah Bergson, Rachel Zwikelski, Tzirel Lerer, Devorah Malkah

Malewanczyk, Hinda Kotcholak, and others. The committee meetings were held in the house of the Bergson (Yisachar) family.

The Women's Association was also active after the First World War. The committee members after the war were: Hana Atlas, Nasha Groda, Hinda Cohen (Rosen), Mindel Lipka, Hanna Frydman, and others.

d. Maot Hittin

The help called *maot hittin* [small coins] or *kimchee DePascha* [flour of Passover] that was given to families had a special character. It was seasonal, taking place once a year. Those that took part in this *mitzvah* were the most respected people in town. When the season for baking matzos approached, a few pairs of these respected people would visit the wealthy and the well to do, and collect money for matzos to be distributed to the poor. A similar undertaking was the distribution of wood, peat, and potatoes to poor families.

The participants in these undertakings were: Shmuel Asher Ostaszewer, Yosef Appelbaum, Avraham Chayim Graniewicz, Nachman Horowitz, Binem Wajsmel, Hershel Motil, Yehuda Baruch Skornik, Zalman Frydman (who was called Zalman Berias), Elia Czarnoczapka, Yosef Karpa, and others.

In addition to the money they collected in town, they also collected money for *maot hittin* from Jewish farms and manors near the town. These donations were especially significant at the beginning of the winter, when they were wood, peat, and potatoes.

The following are the names of some Jewish farm and manor owners near Sierpc: Bauman, Yehoshua Verona, Leib Yitzhak Szampan, (the three of them were killed by the Bolsheviks in the Russo-Polish War of 1920), Lavondzh, Mendel Lenczner, and others. Many praised the generosity of the sharia (landowner) Lavondzh. His property was in the town limits of Rypin, and of course he paid the Rypin community taxes and gave them donations, but he gave freely to the Sierpc community as well.

e. Beit Lehem

A new aid society called *Beit Lehem* [Bread House] was founded in Sierpc in the years before the Second World War, when the economic conditions of the Jews became worse and the numbers of the poor and unemployed increased. The members of the society would go in pairs from door to door, baskets in hand, and collect any food that was given to them: bread, challahs, fish, meat, potatoes, and the like, and give it to the poor. They would send meals to the homes of respectable townspeople who had become poor.

The main activist in the *Beit Lehem* society was Haskell (Yechezkel) Baszkes. He would invite others, pair them off, and send them to different areas for collection. His wife Rellah helped him in distributing the food portions.

f. Soup Kitchen

The first two years of the German occupation of Poland in the First World War were a very bad time economically for the Jews of Poland. The world was closed to them, and travel was limited. Most of the merchandise and crops were confiscated, and life came to a halt. If existence was still possible in the towns, because of their proximity to villages and farms and possibilities for surreptitious trading with the farmers, the large cities were impossible, with many starving for bread. Many people left the cities and settled in towns. Large numbers of poor people, men, women, and children, wandered between cities and towns, looking for a slice of bread and a warm meal.

During this period, about 1916, a soup kitchen opened in Sierpc. It served midday meals to the poor of the town and to the wandering poor at a cheap, token price. The income for this soup kitchen, besides the token payments for meals, came from monthly payments of townspeople and support from the community.

The soup kitchen was at first on the Vloki (Vlikes) Street on the road to Drobin (Drubnin), in the house of Sheiar (a Pole). Later, it was at the start of Plotzki Street, in the house of Moshe Elsztejn (later, the Lipszyc house, Maniamchevka).

Most of the members of the soup kitchen committee came from the intelligentsia of the Sierpc youth: Mendel Blum, David Bergson, Shmuel Glazer, Elia Rzeszotka, Zalman Yakobovitch, Chaska Lubaszka, Mindel Liebson, Selka Malewanczyk, Yechezkel Stari ("Hatzak" from the village Roshtchashovo), Andzha (Hana) Cipris, Zelig Rosen, Hinda Szampan, and Matilda Szerpherz.

The soup kitchen lasted for about two years. In the meantime, conditions changed. Life under the occupation became more orderly, trade (illegal, for the most part) and work developed, there were fewer waves of paupers, and so the soup kitchen closed.

g. Soup Kitchen for Children

At the end of the First World War, there was a great economic distress in newly independent Poland. The country, which had been impoverished by the German occupation for almost four years, battled Ukrainian gangs. A war broke out between Poland and Bolshevik Russia, which proved to be a great burden for the country and increased the suffering of its citizens.

In addition to the economic distress, an extreme anti-Semitic atmosphere was prevalent, that led to anti-Semitic outbursts in many cities. There were pogroms in some of them (Lwow, Pinsk, Kaltz, and others) that cost Jews their lives and much property.

The "Joint"]American Jewish Joint Distribution Committee[, organized by American Jews during the war to help Jews affected by the war, started its large scale activities and sent help in terms of money, food, and clothing to the

Jews of Eastern Europe. Thanks to this help, soup kitchens for children were opened all over Poland.

Such a soup kitchen was also opened in Sierpc, where children would get a midday meal for 10 "pennies" (the Polish coin was then called "mark"). About 50 children, (with the poorest parents) received their meals free of charge. In addition to the meal, each child received some cans of condensed milk every month. The soup kitchen was in the yard of Elsztejn's house. This soup kitchen was in place in the years 1920-1921.

The committee of the children's soup kitchen consisted of: Rivkah Gotlibowski, Leib Hiller (a dentist), Tzirel Lerer, Meir Malin, and others. In addition to the committee, a number of young ladies volunteered to come and serve the meals. The manager of the kitchen was Henyah Weingarten.

The report of the "Joint" representative for the Plotzki district from November 1920, states: "Sierpc has the following institutions: a kitchen for the needy, where 300 children receive their midday meal."

h. Supporters of Talmud Torah

A letter of 5 April 1939, from the Aid Committee in Sierpc to the Relief Committee of Sierpcer in America, states that Sierpc has a supporters of *Talmud Torah* society. Its goals are to support the students of *Talmud Torah.* The society gives breakfast rolls and milk every day during the winter to the students. The society distributes clothes and shoes to the students before the onset of winter.

Hershel Motil was the chairman of the society.

i. Nutrition Committees

The above letter also mentions nutrition committees that were auxiliaries of the *Tarbuth* School and the Government School for Jewish Children.

The letter states: "The money for children's nutrition is collected by Supporters of *Talmud Torah* and the nutrition committees from monthly dues paid by the supporters of these schools. In addition, Supporters of *Talmud Torah* receives backing from the community. The other two committees are supported by the *Tuz* Society (*Towarszystwo Ochrony Zdrowia* Society for Preserving Health)."

Nutrition for the children of the *Tarbuth* School was organized by the Women's Zionist Organization WIZO. The members would collect monthly donations of twenty pennies from each family. The WIZO members also prepared the meals, and came to the school every morning in pairs, in turn, to prepare the meals.

j. Aid Committee

The Aid Committee of Sierpc was formed at the initiative of Sierpc townspeople in America in 1937. Its purpose was the support of middle class Jews in Sierpc small shopkeepers, craftsmen, etc. These were foundering because of the anti-Semitic atmosphere and the anti-Semitic actions of the Polish population. There were also the various legal limitations and heavy taxes that were put in place by the Polish government, the purpose of which was to wreck the economic status of Polish Jews.

There were two avenues of support: small sums to families whose situation had deteriorated to the point where they were hungry (this did not include paupers who begged from door to door, who were not supported by the committee); and support with larger sums (which were also small, 30 to 40 zloty) of families who had some chance of rescue from their dire state.

After a while, a third, more constructive avenue was added, support by giving loans. Specific amounts were received from the Relief Committee in America and given to the Aid Committee for transfer to the Beneficial Fund.

The Sierpcer Relief Committee in America had representatives of four organizations: a) Sierpcer Young Men; b) Sierpcer Ladies Auxiliary; c) Sierpcer Beneficial Fund; and d) Sierpcer Branch 42 A.N.A.P. (Sierpc Branch 42 of *Yiddish Natzionale Arbiter Farband*" Jewish National Workers' Association.)

The members of the Aid Committee were Avraham Valuka chairman, Ber Charka secretary, Baruch Atlas, Baruch Mendel Gotlibowski, Moshe Gutsztat, Meir Rzeszotka, Hershel Motil, Binyamin Eliezer Sobol, Pesach Skornik, Eliyahu Meir Schleifer, and Yitzhak David Sznitzer.

C. Religious Leaders and Institutions

a. Rabbis

We have already presented a special chapter that relates all we have managed to find about the history of the Sierpc rabbinate. Below we will present just a list of those who served as rabbis of the town, with a few biographical details.

i. Rabbi Meirel Dabash

Rabbi Meirel Dabash is the first rabbi of Sierpc that we know about. He was called "Dabash" because it is an acronym in Hebrew for the three towns "Drobin, Biezun, Sheps" which he served simultaneously as rabbi. He was also a *rebbe* [leader of a Hasidic sect] of Hasidim. He was rabbi of Sierpc in the years 1790 to 1812 (approximate). He died in Sierpc.

ii. Rabbi Schrage Feibl Danziger

He was called Rabbi Fibili Gritzer," and was the father of the first Rabbi of Alexander, Rabbi Yechiel. He was a rabbi in Sierpc, Gombin, Gritze, and Makowa, where he died. He was rabbi of Sierpc in the years 1815 to 1820 (approximate).

iii. Rabbi Avraham

He was called Rabbi Avrahamel Charif. He was from Plonsk, where he taught Torah. He was rabbi of Sierpc in the years 1820 to 1830 (approximate).

iv. Rabbi Moshe Yehuda Leib Zilberberg

He was a rabbi in the towns of Kvuhal, Sierpc, Dobre, Lask, and Kutno. He made *aliyah* to Jerusalem in the year 5617 (1857). He was among the greatest of the wise men there, and died eight years later. He was rabbi of Sierpc in the years 1830 to 1840 (approximate).

v. Rabbi Mordechai Grinbaum

He was the grandfather of Yitzhak Grinbaum, and became rabbi of Sierpc in the year 5601 (1841). Before that, he was the rabbi in Nieshtat. He died in Sierpc on 15 Heshvon 5619 (1858).

vi. Rabbi Moshe Yosef Segal

He was the son-in-law of Rabbi Mordechai Grinbaum. Two days after the death of his father-in-law, on 17 Heshvon 5619 (1858), he was appointed as rabbi of the *mitnagdim* group by an Enlightenment group called *Kolhekot*. Previously he was the rabbi in the village of Kodzborg. He died in Sierpc.

vii. Rabbi Gedaliah

He was elected by the community to be the rabbi of Sierpc after the *Kolhekot* appointed Rabbi Moshe Yosef Segal as its rabbi. Previously he was the rabbi of the town of Zuromin. He served as rabbi of Sierpc in the years 5619-5624 (1859-1864).

viii. Rabbi Yehoshua Segal

He was the son of Rabbi Moshe Yosef Segal, and was appointed by the *Kolhekot* to take his father's place after his death. He left Sierpc for America In about the year 5644 (1884), and became a rabbi in Newark in the synagogue *Chevra Tehilim Anshel Vishkova*. He migrated to Jerusalem, but because of illness, was forced to return to Newark, where he passed away. The *Kolhekot* disbanded when Rabbi Yehoshua Segal left Sierpc.

ix. Rabbi Yechiel Michal Goldschlak

He was a rabbi in the towns of Kikol, Szreńsk, Poddębice, and Ostrołęka. In the year 5626 (1865), he was appointed as rabbi of Sierpc. He served in that position for 53 years, and passed away on 21 Shevat 5678 (3 February 1918), at the age of 88.

x. The Teacher Rabbi David Klajnman

He was called David *Chaver* (Our Friend David). He started to give rulings on matters of *kashrut* and *treife*, and what is permitted and forbidden, in the last years of Rabbi Yechiel Michal Goldschlak's life. He kept on with this work during the time of Rabbi Yehoshua Heshel Goldschlak's service as well.

xi. Rabbi Yehoshua Popowski

He was the son-in-law (from Nieshtat) of Rabbi David Klajnman. When his father-in-law became old, he took his place, and continued after his death. Rabbi Yehoshua did not get an official appointment as a teacher in Sierpc (nor did he receive a salary).

xii. Rabbi Yehoshua Heshel David Goldschlak

He was the grandson of Rabbi Yechiel Michal Goldschlak. He was elected rabbi of Sierpc in 1922, and started serving in that position in the month of Av 5683 (1923). He was the rabbi in the town of Przedecz prior to that. Rabbi Yehoshua Heshel David Goldschlak was the last rabbi of Sierpc. He was expelled from the town together with all the Jews of Sierpc by the bloodthirsty wild German animals, and perished.

b. Cantors (Hazan)

i. Reb Natan Meir

The earliest cantor in Sierpc that we know of is the cantor and *shochet* (ritual slaughterer) Reb Natan Meir ben Yona, who sang in the sacred places of our town in the 1860s.

ii. Reb Lazer Moshe Smolinski

He was the cantor and *shochet* in Sierpc after the death of Reb Natan Meir. (He was the grandfather of our townsman, Moshe Smolinski.) Before he came to Sierpc, Reb Lazer Moshe was cantor and *shochet* in Plonsk (Plinsk) and Grajewo. When he was appointed to serve in Sierpc (the exact year is unknown), it had no synagogue (the previous synagogue had burned down) and Reb Lazer Moshe prayed in the old *Beit Midrash*. After a synagogue was built (in about 1895) he prayed there.

When Reb Lazer Moshe Smolinski came to Sierpc, he lived on Zhava (Zhavia) Street, in the house of Binyamin Sobol. Later he lived on the Jewish Street, near the bridge, in the house of Yisraeltia Liebson (the father of Meiria and Naftali Liebson) which was later the house of Minchin. The cantor Reb Lazer Moshe Smolinski died in 1905 (approximate).

iii. Reb Daniel Shikas

After the death of the cantor Reb Lazer Moshe Smolinski, Reb Daniel Shikas became cantor and *shochet.* He came to our town in 1907 (approximate) from the town Nowa Wilejk, near Vilnius, where he was a cantor and *shochet.* He lived on the Jewish Street in the Kamnitza (the large walled house).

Reb Daniel Shikas performed the sacred tasks of cantor and *shochet* in Sierpc until the destruction of the community of Sierpc and its Jews.

c. Ritual Slaughterers

i. Reb Yoselitia

The earliest *shochet* (ritual slaughterer) in Sierpc that we know of is Reb Yosef Gatzal (who was called Reb Yoselitia, and was my mother's grandfather). He was a *shochet* in our town in the 1860s. When he became old, Reb Yoselitia stopped being a *shochet* and became the first caretaker of the new synagogue, which was built in about 1896. He passed away in the mid-1890s.

ii. Reb Chayim Bergson

Reb Chayim Bergson (who was called Reb Chayim Shochet) came to Sierpc as a *shochet* in about 1885, to take the place of Reb Yoselitia. He came from Ostrołęka, where he also served as a *shochet.* In about 1890, Reb Chayim *shochet* was removed as ritual slaughterer because of a plot against him.

iii. Reb Ischia Yossel Hanchovitch

Reb Ischia Yossel Hanchovitch was appointed as a *shochet* in Sierpc at the start of the 1890s, in place of Reb Chayim *shochet.* Reb Ischia Yossel came to Sierpc from Gustinin, where he had been a *shochet.* He left Sierpc in 1910 or 1911 when he became the *shochet* in Kalisz.

iv. Reb Yekel Ritzik

Reb Yekel Ritzik (who was called Reb Yekel Shochet) became a ritual slaughterer in Sierpc in 1912, in place of Reb Ischia Yossel. He came from the town of Sochocin, where he was the *shochet.* He passed away in 1919, along with others, as a result of the typhus epidemic that was raging then. He was 38 years old.

v. Reb Yossel Ajzensztadt

Reb Yossel Ajzensztadt (also called Reb Yossel Shochet) came to Sierpc as the ritual slaughterer in 1917, taking the place of Reb Yekel *shochet.* He came to Sierpc from the town of Czerwinsk, where he was the *shochet.* He performed his sacred tasks in Sierpc until the destruction of the community and the expulsion of its Jews.

vi. Reb Avraham Burgand

Reb Avraham Burgand (called Reb Avraham Shochet) was at first the ritual slaughterer for the *Kolhekot*. After the breakup of the *Kolhekot* (in the first half of the 1880s), Reb Avraham was appointed *shochet* in the village Skoilna. When after a few years it was necessary to find a new *shochet* for Sierpc, and he applied for the job, he ran into fierce resistance from the Gur Hasidim, who reminded him of his "youthful sin," when he was the *Kolhekot* ritual slaughterer. But Reb Avraham Shochet's backers would not yield, and the matter was brought to arbitration by rabbis from the vicinity. The arbitrators came up with a compromise decision. Reb Avraham *shochet* would be accepted as a slaughterer for fowl only. So that for all the time that he was a *shochet*, he would deal only with birds.

When he became older, Reb Avraham *shochet* stopped being a ritual slaughterer and lived off the pension that he received from the community. When he was in his old age and full of years, he was expelled with all the Jews of Sierpc by the evil Nazis in the Holocaust.

vii. Reb Shimon Petrikus

Reb Shimon Petrikus, from Drobin, the son-in-law of Reb Avraham *shochet* took his father-in-law's place when he retired. During the time of the Holocaust, Reb Shimon Petrikus was the *shochet* in the Sierpc ghetto. (Ritual slaughter was forbidden, and it was performed in secret.)

Ritual Slaughterers in the Region of Sierpc

In early days, when a good number of Jews lived in villages, there was a special kind of shochet: village *shochet*. He was responsible for a few villages, and would visit them by cart or by foot. He would come once a week, and lived in the largest village in the area, or in a nearby town.

The ritual slaughterers in the Region of Sierpc (called *Gulil* Sheps), composed of villages that belonged to the Jewish Community of Sierpc, were:

Reb Mordecai Yitzhak Karpa (my maternal grandfather) served at the beginning of the 1870s, before he became a ritual slaughterer and inspector in Zuromin.

Reb Avraham Tatz (father of Shmuel Yitzhak and Mendel Tatz). He served in the 1880s.

*

At the end of these paragraphs on *shochatim*, it is only proper to mention that the cantors also served as ritual slaughterers.

D. Prayer Houses

a. The Old Beit Midrash

The *old Beit Midrash* was the oldest prayer house in Sierpc. Unfortunately, we have not been able to determine when it was built. It was a popular prayer house in the full meaning of the words. The "whole town" would pray there during weekdays: *Mitnagdim* and Hasidim; simple Jews, scholars and learned men; rich and poor; young and old. They would pray in many *minyans*, one after another. The sound of the Torah emanated from this Beit Midrash for many hours every day, coming from both young men and mature worshippers, who arranged for sessions of the Torah.

The managers of the *old Beit Midrash*, at different times, were Avraham Yitzhak (called Itzik) Ostaszewer, Israel Barko, Yitzhak Graubart, Yaakov (called Yokev) Gorlitz, Yosef Vasolak, Moshe Vasolak, Shmuel Yitzhak Tatz, Michal Turkltaub, Akivia Lanenter, Binyamin Sobol, Yaakov Skornik (called "Yekel Shtrikmacher" rope maker), Yosef Pindek, Baruch Kanenbrand, Hersh Moshe Kanenbrand, Shlomo Richgut (called "Shlomo Chayayes," from his mother's name, Chaya), and others.

The prayer leaders in the *old Beit Midrash* during the ten High Holy Days were Yaakov Lemel Esikmacher (father-in-law of Meir Oved Balt), Yosef Divan (did not leave any sons in Sierpc), Israel Chayim Yeshaievitch, Yisraeltia Liebson (father of Meiria and Naftali Liebson), Lipaia Naselski (the first "Slichot," the special prayers recited in the weeks before the High Holy Days), Yaakov Skornik, Yechezkel Czarnoczapka (called Haskell Rieveshes son of Reuben; Yechezkel was the father of Dudia Czarnoczapka), Israel Karpa and others. All of the ritual slaughterers, each in his time, were prayer leaders in the *old Beit Midrash* during the High Holy Days. Before the synagogue was built in about 1895, the cantor Lazer (Eliezer) Moshe Smolinski prayed regularly in the *old Beit Midrash.*

The readers of the Torah in the *old Beit Midrash* were: Simchaia Licht (father-in-law of Yehoshua Goldman), Dudia Czarnoczapka, Israel Karpa (now in Uruguay), Yossel *shochet* (Ajzensztadt), and others.

The blowers of the *shofar* (ram's horn on the High Holy Days) in the *old Beit Midrash* were: Simchaia Licht, Leibl Licht, Yossel *shochet,* the leaseholder of the *mikve* Moshe Hendlisz (from Gombin), and others.

The caretakers of the *old Beit Midrash* were: Matityahu ("Mattes") Bornstein (until the synagogue was built), Shaul (Shoal) Karpa (the father of Mendel, Yitzhak, and Rivkah Karpa), Moshe Cohen (called Der Blinder Moishe Blind Moshe, who was blind in one eye, and died during the First World War), and the last caretaker, Israel Karp (came to Sierpc from Warsaw during the First World War; he was not related to the Karpa families in Sierpc). He served as caretaker of the *old Beit Midrash* as long as it served the Jews of Sierpc, and in one day the day of the expulsion - both of them completed their labors.

b. The New Beit Midrash

The *new Beit Midrash* was built in about 1886 (prior to that, there were a number of fixed *minyans* in various places. The worshippers in the *new Beit Midrash* were mainly survivors of the *Kolhekot*, Enlightened Jews, and *Hovevei Tzion*. There were few non-regular worshippers at this *Beit Midrash* and the students here were also from among the ranks of the regular worshippers.

The managers of the *new Beit Midrash* in various eras were: Eliezer Garfinkel (an attorney), Yitzhak Grappa, Nachman Horowitz, Avrahamia Valuka, Eliezer Vasolak (father-in-law of Avraham Yerushalmi), Leibl Malewanczyk, Azrieltia Podskocz, Kalman Fenster (father-in-law of Wolf Chazen), Metis (Matityahu) Prasnyski, Nachum Konitz, Leib Shvitzer, and others.

The prayer leaders in the *new Beit Midrash* during the High Holy Days were: Kalman Arpa (called Kalman Yakiryehs), Yosef Gatzal (called Reb Yoselitia the caretaker), Ephraim Yosef Valuka, his son Avrahamia Valuka, Baruchia Rzeszotka (the caretaker), Mendel Mai, Binyamin Marantz, and others. The ritual slaughterers, each in his time, were also prayer leaders during the High Holy Days in the *new Beit Midrash.*

The Torah readers at the *new Beit Midrash* were: Binem Gallant (the caretaker), Baruchia Rzeszotka (the caretaker), Azrieltia Podskocz, Yitzhak Charka, Leibush Rozenberg (the caretaker), and others.

The blowers of the *shofar* at the new *Beit Midrash* were: Menachem Bojmwol, Ephraim Yosef Valuka, Yitzhak Charka, Leibush Rozenberg (the caretaker), and others.

The caretakers who served at the new *Beit Midrash* were: Yosef Gatzal (Reb Yoselitia, the former *shochet*, who became caretaker in his old age), the first caretaker of the *new Beit Midrash* was Abba Hirsch Pomper (from Raciaz, called *leiferieh* the runner, later immigrated to America), Baruchia Rzeszotka, Leibush Rozenberg, and Binem Gallant (from Mlawa, called "*Binem Malach*" because of his father-in-law Chayim Yosef Gorlitz who was called *Der Hoicher Malach* –Tall Angel), the last caretaker in this post, until the Jews were expelled from the town of their birth.

c. The Synagogue

The synagogue was built in about 1895, in the same location as the previous synagogue that burned down. (Unfortunately, we have not been able to determine the year of the fire.) Most of the worshippers at the synagogue were "petite bourgeoisie." In later times, the worshippers were the generation of young Zionists and the young intelligentsia (who came to the synagogue only on holidays).

The managers of the synagogue in different eras were: Kalman Blum, Tzadok Bluman, Yaakov (Yokev) Valuka, Ischia Meir Motil, Zvi Malewanczyk, Meir Cipris, Yechezkel Kadecka (who was called Yehezkel Pasternak), and others.

The prayer leaders in the synagogue during the High Holy Days were the cantor, Yaakov Valuka, Yehezkel Kadecka, Israel Karpa, and others. The ritual slaughters, each in his time, were also prayer leaders during the Days of Awe in the synagogue.

The readers of the Torah were: Shimon Gelbard (the caretaker), Avraham Yitzhak Grodka, Baruchia Rzeszotka, Mordecai Hersh Mintz, Israel Karpa, Yitzhak Charka (the caretaker), and others.

The blowers of the shofar in the synagogue were Mordecai Hersh Mintz, Yitzhak Charka (the caretaker), and others.

The caretakers who served in the synagogue were: Matityahu ("Mattes") Bornstein the first caretaker, Mordechai David Turkltaub, Shimon Gelbard, and Yitzhak Charka the last caretaker to serve the synagogue and its worshippers until it was burned down by the accursed Nazis.

d. Houses of the Hasidim (Shtibls)

There were four Houses of Hasidim (*Shtibls*) in Sierpc, and these were:

- The *shtibl* of the Gur Hasidim this was the largest *shtibl* in numbers and quality (learning and zealousness) and also wealth.
- The *shtibl* of the Alexander Hasidim a *shtibl* of merry Hasidim, happy with their lot and worshipping God with joy.
- A second *shtibl* of Alexander Hasidim existed until the First World War.
- The *shtibl* of Plotzk Hasidim a *shtibl* in which a mixed crowd of Hasidim prayed: Plotzk and Otvotsk, Radzin and Gustinin. Their common denominator "cold" and "weak" Hasidim, and added to them were "exiles" and "troublemakers" that left other shtibls or were thrown out of them.

The *shtibls* were located in rented apartments, and therefore they would, from time to time, confirm the saying "they journeyed..., they pitched their tent," and move from apartment to apartment, and from street to street.

e. The Gur "Shtibl"

The managers of the Gur *shtibl* at different times were: Eliyahu Glazer, Moshe Grossman (son-in-law of Hanach Czarnobroda), Shimon Zapel, Mendel Melech Tajtelbaum, Ahron Lipka, Zalman Frydman (called "Zalma Bariyes"), Ischia Meir Rosek, and others.

The prayer leaders in the Gur *shtibl* during the High Holy Days were Avraham Ahron Burstein (the starting prayer leader), David Noach Zilberberg, Mendel Melech Tajtelbaum, Lipaia Naselski, Yossel Pukacz, Yossel Sznitzer, and others.

The Torah readers were Zalman Frydman, and others.

The shofar blowers in the Gur *shtibl* were Zalman Frydman, Yossel Sznitzer, and others.

Michal (son of Chayim) Sendrowicz took care of mending the holy books.

*

For a number of years there was a second Gur *shtibl* called the Rich Gur *shtibl* (*S'Reicher Gurer Shtibll*). The wealthier Gur Hasidim prayed in this shtibl; they were more progressive than the others, and most of them lived in the new market and its vicinity. It was on Zhava Street, in the yard of the house of Ezriel Yehuda Kotcholak. Later, it was in the house of Zalman Frydman, on the small street near the new market. The Rich Gur *shtibl* existed during the years 1912-1916 (approximately).

f. The Alexander Shtibl

The managers of the Alexander *shtibl* at different times, were: Yechiel Gallant (from Lodz, son-in-law of Beinam Wajsmel), Mendel Gorlitz (Lipszyc), Moshe Lidzbarski, Berish Sosnowska, Yehuda Baruch Skornik, Israel Karpa, Avraham *shochet* (Burgand), Eliyahu Meir Schleifer, and others.

The prayer leaders in the Alexander *shtibl* during the High Holy Days were: The First "Slichot" Avraham *shochet*, the starting prayer leader Mendel Lenczner, Morning Prayer Yakir Dobroszklanka, and later Wolf Nazemski, Midday Prayer Yaakov Meiria Kolas, Kol Nidre - Yakir Dobroszklanka, Closing Prayer Binyamin Szerpherz.

There were younger prayer leaders in later years, and these were Ischia Ash (from Mlawa (son-in-law of Binem Sendrowicz), Yechiel Gallant, Yosef Karpa, Israel Karpa, Eliyahu Meir Schleifer, and others.

The Torah readers were: Israel Karpa, Leibush Rozenberg, and Eliyahu Meir Schleifer.

The *shofar* blowers in the Alexander "shtibl" were Mendel Lenczner, and others.

*

A few organizations and societies that did not have their own facilities used the Alexander *shtibl* for their activities; these were The Small Merchants Association, The Rescue Committee, and others.

*

There was a *shtibl* called The Second Alexander *shtibl* before the First World War. The worshippers in this *shtibl* were a number of Alexander Hasidim that had once left the original *shtibl* because of a dispute, a few other Hasidim, and miscellaneous worshippers. Over time, this *shtibl* disappeared, and its worshippers joined the Plotzk shtibl.

The managers of the Second Alexander *shtibl* at different times were Avraham Burstein, Issachar Bergson, Yehoshua Goldman, and others.

The prayer leaders in this *shtibl* during the High Holy Days were Chayim *shochet* (Bergson), Yehoshua Goldman, Shlomia Tatz, Chayim Ber Klochavsky, and others.

The Torah reader was Yehoshua Goldman. The shofar blower was Chayim *shochet* (Bergson).

The Plotzk Shtibl The managers of the Plotzk *shtibl* at different times were Yechiel Meir Bergson, Shmuel Mendel Licht, Issachar Skorka, and others.

The prayer leaders in this *shtibl* during the High Holy Days were Chayim *shochet* (Bergson), Yechiel Meir Bergson, Shlomo Mordechai Fogel, Berel Czarnoczapka, Chayim Ber Klochavsky, and others.

The Torah reader was Yehoshua Czarnoczapka. The *shofar* blower was Chayim *shochet* (Bergson).

g. Minyans

In addition to fixed prayer houses, there were *minyans* [a *minyan* is the quorum of at least 10 Jewish men required for public prayer] that prayed in institutions or private dwellings. The number of *minyans* grew in town, especially in the years between the burning of the synagogue and construction of the new *Beit Midrash* (1886). During this time, except for the Hasidic *shtibls* there was only one fixed house of prayer, the old *Beit Midrash*. We will present below a short list of the *minyans* that existed at different times. However, we think that there were many *minyans* that we were not informed about, especially from the early years.

The *minyan* of *Kolhekot*: The group of Enlightened Mitnagdim that split off from the community appointed a rabbi and ritual slaughterer of their own. They prayed in a special *minyan*. It was located in the "Kamnitza" (the large, walled building on the Jewish street). The *minyan* existed until the new *Beit Midrash* was erected.

The *minyan* of the Psalms Society: There was a *minyan* of the Psalms Society in the 1880s and 1890s that prayed in the house of Avraham Hersh Lelonek (father of Ischia Meiria Lelonek), which was one of the small houses near the synagogue that were called Hornes Gitter (Horn's properties). The managers were Melech Berlinski, Avraham Hersh Lelonek, and others. The prayer leader was Hersh Leib Mai, and the Torah reader was Chayim Raphael Lipowecki (son-in-law of Wolf Ber Garber).

The *minyan* of the *Watchmen of the Morning*: The task of this *minyan* which existed in the 1880s and 1890s was, as its name implies, prayer in the early morning. It prayed in the house of Yehezkel Czarnoczapka (father of Dudia Czarnoczapka). The managers of the *minyan* were Israel Ahron Groda, Shimon David Szmiga, and others.

The *minyan* of *Talmud Torah*: During the 1890s, a *Talmud Torah* society took care of tuition payments of poor pupils. The *minyan* took place in the apartment of Moshe Mintz, one of the managers of the *minyan*. The income from the *minyan* was dedicated to the society, and its managers were the managers of the *minyan*.

The *minyan* of *Hachnasat Orchim*: Before the First World War, there was a *minyan* in the quarters of *Hachnasat Orchim* on *mikve* Street, in the house of Shmuel Szampan (called Shmuel Nagid; the same building housed the Second *shtibl* of Alexander). The income of the *minyan* was dedicated to *Hachnasat Orchim*. The manager of *Hachnasat Orchim* was the manager of the *minyan*.

The *minyan* of *Mizrachi*: In the first years of *Mizrachi* in Sierpc (founded in 1917), there was a *minyan* in the clubhouse of the party, in the house of Isaac Kutner, at the start of the Plotzki Street. The income from the *minyan* was dedicated to *Keren Kayemet*. The manager was Isaac Neiman.

The *minyan* of the *Craftsmen's Association*: There was a *minyan* of craftsmen in the 1920's in their association's quarters on the Jewish Street in the house of Luster (later, the Shvitzer house). The activists of the association were also managers of the *minyan*.

The *minyan* of *Poalei Agudat Israel*: In the last two years prior to the Holocaust, there was a *minyan* of *Poalei Agudat Israel* in their clubhouse in the house of Moshe Lidovarski, at the start of the Jewish Street. The party activists were also the managers of the *minyan*.

Only the *minyan* of the *Kolhekot* prayed every day. In the other *minyans* the prayers were only on the Sabbath and holidays.

E. Societies

a. The Ein Yaakov, Chayei Adam, Mishniot, Shas, and Other Societies

The *Batei Midrash* and *Batei Hasidim* (*shtibls*) served not only for prayer, but also for the study of Torah. In addition to the young men who studied Torah, usually in the old *Beit Midrash*, worshippers in all the prayer houses organized for the study of Torah. There were societies for the study of the weekly portion of Torah, with Talmudic exegesis, and societies that were named after the particular book that they studied: *Ein Yaakov*, *Chayei Adam*, *Mishniot*, and *Shas*. The members of the *Ein Yaakov* and *Chayei Adam* societies were usually simple Jews whose souls yearned for Torah, but could not study by themselves. They appointed one of the more learned as their *rebbe*, and he would teach them (some for compensation and others without compensation) and explain the legends in *Ein Yaakov* or the laws in *Chayei Adam*. Sometimes this would be every day, between midday and evening prayers, and sometimes once a week on the Sabbath. This way they studied both the portion of the week and the exegesis.

Jews with a higher level of learning studied in the *Mishniot* Society, and the participants of the *Shas* Society were scholars. There were two kinds of *Mishniot* and *Shas* societies. In one kind, one of the members, a recognized scholar would study in front of the members, and explain the issues to them. In the other kind, the members would divide the teaching between them; each one would study a different segment or tractate of the Mishna, and they would finish the Mishniot and Shas books together.

The *rebbes* that taught in these societies were: Moshe Asanter (son-in-law of Binyamin Lerer, from Mlawa, and he returned there), Yehoshua Goldman, Chayim Leib Wejs (a carter who was educated and taught Pentateuch and Rashi), Eliezer Vasolak (taught Bible and the portion of the week in the new *Beit Midrash*), Moshe Zomer (taught Bible in the new *Beit Midrash*), David Noach Zilberberg, Ephraim Zilberberg (son-in-law of Hersh Kanenbrand, from Warsaw), Yehoshua Popowski (son-in-law of David Klajnman), Shimon Petrikus, Leibl Kramarzh, Eliyahu Meir Schleifer (son-in-law of Chayim Shochet), and others. The "Daily Page" of the Talmud was taught in the Gur *shtibl* by Moshe Grossman (son-in-law of Hanach Czarnobroda), Yossel Pukacz, and others.

b. The Psalms Society

The purpose of the Psalms Society was not learning, but recitation of the Psalms. The society members would rise before dawn and go to the old *Beit Midrash* and together recite the Psalms until it was time for the Morning Prayer. They also publicly recited Psalms in the old *Beit Midrash* on Sabbath following the afternoon rest. The importance of the members of the Psalms" Society increased on the second day of Pentecost, the day of the death of the most dulcet of the singers of Israel, King David, may he rest in peace, the composer of the book of Psalms. On this day, they felt like bridegrooms at a wedding. After the holiday feast at the end of the day, they would assemble in the old *Beit Midrash*, light 150 candles for the 150 verses of the Psalms, and festively recite the Psalms from beginning to end. Later, they would go to the house of the Society manager, drink wine *lehaim*, and eat *leikach* (sponge cake).

c. The Book Repair Society (Tikun Sfarim)

Because of the ceaseless usage of the books in the old *Beit Midrash*, there was a constant need to mend them, and to buy new books. This was the reason for the existence of the Book Repair Society, whose members were the young men who studied in the *Beit Midrash*. Every Friday, two members of the society, in turn, would go from door to door and collect money for Book Repair. One of the older members would be the manager of Book Repair. He would keep the cash box, turn in books for repair, and would buy new books.

The managers of the Book Repair Society at different times were the young men: Yosef Appelbaum, Moshe Burgand, Moshe Ber Goldman, Avraham Chayim Granewicz, Mendel Lipszyc, Yosef Pastolski (called Der Meshuguner Yossel Crazy Yossel; from Dobrzyn, a relative of Yaakov Moshe Tajtelbaum, and grew up in his house), Leibush Zelig Plato, Gedaliah Plato, and others.

F. *The Mikve*

The *mikve* (ritual bathhouse) was an important institution in every Jewish community, and also in Sierpc. The importance of the *mikve* from the religious standpoint is well known. However, in later years, there were repairs and improvements to the *mikve* in Sierpc. In the second half of the 1920s, individual cubicles were built, with a bathtub in each cubicle. The *mikve* then became important from a hygienic standpoint as well.

Below is a list of "Lessees of the *mikve*" (the *mikve* belonged to the community, and the Community Council would lease it out), starting with the 1880s.

The first lessee of the *mikve* that we know of was Shmuel Chanales. Chanale, Shmuel's wife, was the granddaughter of Rabbi Meirel Dabash (see the chapter on "The History of the Rabbinate in Sierpc," and because of this pedigree, her husband was called by her name "Shmuel Chanales."

After her husband died, Chanale took a partner into the "business." The partner was Moshe Dudia Skorka (father of Hersh Skorka). After that, the *mikve* was leased by Shmuel Leib and his wife, Tona Yeshaievitch.

Following them, Leib Shvitzer leased the *mikve*. For a while, Madame Yetaia (called "Yetaia Yairs" daughter of Yair), the wife of Eliakim Rizh, was the ritual immerser (*tikern*). Because of this, the Rizh family lived in an apartment above the *mikve*, together with the Shvitzer family.

From 1935 until the destruction of the *mikve*, together with those who were purified and bathed in it, Moshe Hendlisz (brother-in-law of Moshe Lidovarski) from Gombin leased the *mikve*.

G. *Chevra Kadisha* (Burial Society)

The most ancient society, and the oldest of the societies, the one that leads the societies and observes their end, the first society of the diaspora, the source for the organization of the communities, the society that destroys all societies and expands the cemeteries that is *Chevra Kadisha*.

Chevra Kadisha is a society of grievous significance, segmented into "old" (the senior and distinguished) and the "young" (new and neophyte). A society with unpleasant tasks, performing the last rite, called "the true charity," for a human being, preparing and transporting him on his last journey, on the way to his final resting place.

The members of *Chevra Kadisha* were from all walks of life, Hasidim and *Mitnagdim*, scholars and simple Jews, merchants and craftsmen, rich and poor.

The managers of *Chevra Kadisha* at different times were: Yokev (Yaakov) Graubart (father of Yitzhak Graubart), Zalman Garlitz (called "Zalman Farber" Zalman the Painter), the father of Chayim Yosef, called "der Hoicher Malach," the Tall Angel, and of Yokev Garlitz, both of whom were managers in the 1880s, Mendel Gurfinkel, Eliyahu Glazer, Yokev (Yaakov) Gorlitz, Mendel Gorlitz (Lipszyc), Binem Wajsmel, Baruchia Rzeszotka, Yaakov Moshe Tajtelbaum, his son Mendel Melech Tajtelbaum, Michal Turkltaub, his son Mordechai David Turkltaub, Israel Chayim Yeshaievitch, Yaakov Hersh Yeshaievitch, Lipaia Naselski, Yehuda Baruch Skornik, Yossel Pukacz, Zalman Frydman (called Zalman Berias after his father-in-law in the town of Oberfeld), Meir Cipris, Yehezkel Kadecka (called Yehezkel Pasternak), Moshe Natan Klin, Eliakim Rizh, and others.

The *Chevra Kadisha* also had women members. They would sew the shrouds of all the deceased and also take care of the female departed. The same women who were active in charities that we mentioned previously were also the members of *Chevra Kadisha* (*Chevra Kadisha Veiber*). They were: Esther Baniet (wife of Simchaia Licht and mother-in-law of Yehoshua Goldman), Rachel Abbas (wife of Abba Weisgal and mother of Krusa Licht), Rachel who was called "di Shochetke" (wife of Chayim *shochet* (Bergson), Rellah (wife of Haskell Baszkes), Sara Grossman (wife of Moshe Grossman), Rivkaia (wife of Chayim Nachum Tunbol), Tovah Lea (wife of Mordechai Asher Migdal), Tzirel Lipias (wife of Lipa Naselski), Yetta (wife of David Sochaczewski), Roize Dina (wife of Zalman Klein), Sheina Blimah Karpa, and others.

*

Avraham Mlawa founded a new *Chevra Kadisha* at the beginning of the 1930s, in order to combat the discrimination of the old society, which assigned graves in one section of the cemetery to the "distinguished" and in another section to the less distinguished. The purpose of the new society was to bury the dead, next to each other, in the order of their passing, without consideration of their position in society.

The manager of the new *Chevra Kadisha* was Meir Rzeszotka (called "Meir Baruchias" son of Baruchia). The new *Chevra Kadisha* buried only a few deceased, because it lasted only a short time.

H. The Cemetery

The House of Life, The House of the World, The house of Eternity, Graveyard this institution has many different names, many pleasant and pretty for the unique institution that concludes and ends, the house of eternity for all the living. It was behind the synagogue and the town, between them and the river, the cemetery was a gathering ground. It gathered all those who had finished their service to the town.

The cemetery was two cemeteries an old and a new. The old cemetery was the resting place for the early generations of the Jews of Sierpc, and among them saints and sages. The Jews of the town would drop small notes (*pitkaot*) on their grave sites and request "long life and plentiful sustenance and aid from heaven and a healthy body with shining light and seed that is alive and hearty." In the new cemetery, the last generations lie in eternal sleep, fathers with sons. For many generations, over hundreds of years, hundreds and thousands of Jews from the town lay there: men, women, and children; young men and maidens, old men and youths, a great multitude, a complete city! That is how it always was, and how it will be all were sure of this, until the end of time.

And yet, there was a great and terrible storm, the like of which was unknown since man's foot trod on the earth. It hurled the sons from the town it destroyed most of them, and scattered the rest over the seven seas. The storm also ruined the dwellings of the town, also its prayer houses and its institutions. It exploded the wood and stone and ground them into a fine dust. There was no stone left upon stone, and no memory and no memorial in that place. Ruin and destruction everywhere, devastation and wilderness.

Thus was a venerable Jewish town exterminated and annihilated to its very foundations, with its fathers and sons, with the living and the dead and with the heart of its institutions, the cemetery.

"*Yit'gadal v'yit'kadash sh'mom*"
May their names be exalted and sanctified.

Zionism in Sierpc 60 Years Ago

by Shmuel Lanter

I was a young lad when it was proposed that I purchase a *shekel*[1] and become a member of the Zionist organization. This was at the end of the 1800s. I purchased a *shekel* and became active in selling *shekels*. This work had to be carried out in complete secrecy. Even my parents could not know about that "heretical" activity.

I used to visit Chaim Nachum Tanwel, where I became acquainted with Zionism, and with Reb Eliezer Wesselek, who was considered a "heretic" in Hassidic circles. He was knowledgeable in Talmud as well as general subjects.

It was not long before my father found out about the "terrible secret." He was not that fanatical, but he was afraid that my Zionist activity might damage my chances to find a marriage partner. He would tell me, "What will people say, you are a young lad, and we will have to discuss a match." This motive had no effect on me. Later, when the Mizrachi Organization was founded, my parents kept away from the subject and "looked away" from the Zionist heresy. I became a member of Mizrachi.

We organized a group for Bible study, and every day between *Mincha* and *Maariv*, we studied a portion of *Chumash* and a chapter of Bible with working youths. We rented a room from Feivel Boda for that purpose. The Hassidim fought against us. They attempted to interfere with our work, but they did not succeed.

Our organizational work strengthened. We founded a group for Talmud study, and we studied *Gemara* and commentaries every night in the new *beis midrash*. I recall the following names from that Mizrachi group: Eliezer Wesselek, Chaim Nachum Tanwel, Yehuda Leib Itzkowicz who was a military tailor, a great scholar, and a student of Reb Yehoshele Kutner of blessed memory, Eliezer Podskacz, Avraham Chaim Senk, Mordechai Hirsch Mintz, Shlomo Yehuda Belet, Moshe Belet, Yaakov Wluke, Avraham Wluke, my cousin Moshe Lastner, and others.

A library for the lending of books was founded in the home of Mordechai Hirsch Mintz.

*

My Mizrachi Zionist activity indeed impeded my marriage prospects... Even though this is a strictly private matter, it is important to mention this fact in order to understand how Orthodox householders related to Zionism at that time.

My parents wanted to arrange a marriage for me into the family of a wealthy *kulak*[2], Pasternak, an owner of a water mill. As was the custom, they came for a meeting at our house. My parents served a good snack, and we began to discuss household matters, and worldly affairs, until we came to the topic of the current heretics, the Zionists, who do not put on *tefillin* and dare to smoke a cigarette on the Sabbath... I, the potential groom, could not control myself, and I declared to my future father-in-law that this is a simple misunderstanding. I myself am a Zionist, and I go to pray in the *beis midrash* every day. We have a *Talmud* study group, and we study *Gemara* and commentaries every day...

After that declaration, it became silent at the table. The *kulak* and his family left, and we did not see them again. Nothing came of that match.

In later years, the Zionist idea penetrated to all strata of Sierpc Jews. A large Zionist organization was founded that helped greatly in the founding of the State of Israel.

Poale Zion Movement in the years 1904-1912

by Ch. L. Pukacz

The following memoirs of Ch. L. Pukacz, who died in the year[3], were published in the *Jewish Workers Ledger*, volume I, published in Warsaw in 1927. The memoirs are included here with certain abbreviations and editorial changes. The details of the Poale Zion activity at that time are presented unchanged. The subheadings were also added by the editor.

Among the Poale Zionists in the Polish Social Democracy

In the story year of 1905, I had three friends – Yitzchak Kone, Itche Karpe, and Yaakov Schnitzer. We four held together as a group and discussed socialist issues. Our group attracted the attention of the Sierpc student Lea Kahane, who studied in Warsaw. She would come back to our town from Warsaw with a mission from the S.D.K.P.L. (Social Democratic Krolestowa Polskiego in Litwa) which was shortened to P.S.D. (Polish Social Democratic). The student took it upon herself to set up a P.S.D. organization in our town. From all the Sierpc youth, she chose our group.

She communicated with Yitzchak Kone, and held a long, conspiratorial discussion with him, asking him to discuss with his friends about coming to a conference.

Yitzchak Kone came to us all worked up, and brought with him two brochures by Liebknecht[4], *The Spinning* and *Flying*.

We sat down in a separate room and literally thrashed through the words. Then, Ch. Kone told us that his friend Kahane had spoken to him very nicely and sincerely about the brochures... "We are eager for the time when we will meet up with the student in her home territory, in which we cannot speak even with our eyes" – that is what he had told Kahane, and his word must be sacred.

As we went through the mountains and valleys until we reached the Dolines, we crawled deeper into the bushes. There, we saw the slender, recognizable figure of the student with her good-natured, dreamy, blue eyes. We remained there a bit, afraid and speechless. However, she made us bolder with her good natured smile and warm greeting. With her own, nice, ringing voice, she painted for us one picture after another: "The great suffering of the proletariat, the liberation of mankind from pain and troubles, which could come only through a revolution, only through overthrowing Czar Nikolai II. Now, after the prelude war with Japan, the time has come where the proletariat can liberate itself from the Czarist yoke..."

Her fiery words had their effect on us. She understood what was inside us, and accepted us as youth who were fitting for the "holy work." She laid out a plan for future activity: creating conspiratorial groups of ten people, and bringing her an account of the activities from time to time.

We firmly became involved in the work. Within a period of four weeks, we had cobbled together an organization of over 60 members. Comrade Kahane was happy with our activity, and suggested calling a general meeting. Already by the next morning, we formed a committee and put together a plan on how to conduct a general meeting. However, there was an obstacle that brought the agitation of Comrade Kahane to a halt.

The student Beniek Niedzwiecz, who had already become involved with the Poale Zion idea, suddenly appeared in Sierpc. He detected that there was a Socialist movement in town. He found his way to us four friends, and found out from us in a very "diplomatic" fashion that we were conducting P.S.D. activities. We had a firm organization and were preparing for a general meeting.

Beniek also knew how to conduct discussions. He talked with us and broke down our muddled cosmopolitan ideas of that time. He demonstrated to us that the Jewish people have unique needs that can only find a resolution in a Jewish land. Comrade Beniek's words had their effect on us, and we accepted the program of Poale Zion.

We stopped going to Comrade Kahane as often, and stopped giving her reports. This became obvious to her, and she came to us wanting to know why we were not conducting any activity. We had expected such a visit and had prepared a response from the outset. We told her that we were planning to conduct the general meeting with a discussion in which Comrade Beniek would participate. The meeting was to take place in a few days in a secret location. Comrade Beniek held a discussion with Comrade Kahane, and we were on his side. Comrade Kahane left the meeting defeated, and, during the workers' songs, the organization took on the name of Poale Zion.

Comrade Beniek returned to his studies in Plock. We ordered a party insignia from him. At Sukkot, we waited for him together with the insignia. He indeed came for the holiday together with his brother, who was also a Poale Zionist. On the first day of Sukkot, we convened a general meeting with approximately 80 worker members. We were so amazed when Comrade Beniek showed us an insignia of the S.S. "Sionistn Socialistn" and declared that the S.S. is the only appropriate party for the current times.

Those gathered remained motionless and amazed. The glances turned to us, the leaders, as they wanted us to speak. We stood confused for a while, and could not orient ourselves as quickly as our Comrade Beniek was able to do so. Beniek's younger brother, Salomon Niedzwiecz, came to our aid.

"Comrades!" he shouted, "Down with such false saviors! Long live Poale Zionism!"

We immediately caught on and answered, “It lives!” This was supported by all those gathered. We all left the meeting singing workers' songs, and told the members that we will have a meeting with discussions on the latter days of Sukkot.

Comrade Salomon Niedzwiecz sent an urgent telegram to Comrade Yaakov Kowalski, a son of Rabbi Kowalski, in Włocławek, and Comrade Yaakov was already with us on the latter days of Sukkot. We conducted a discussion meeting in a grove in which Comrade Beniek and Comrade Kahane appeared as opponents. However, Comrade Yaakov defeated her, and we left in high spirits due to our victory.

From that time, we began to conduct Poale Zion activities. We conducted wage protests with tailors and shoemakers, and simultaneously conducted a large scale publicity effort regarding the Poale Zion program. To that end, we brought two “professionals” from Warsaw on our own account: Comrade Ish-Ivri (Sh. Landinski) and Comrade Perle.

Strikes and Wage Actions

At the head of the organization stood our four friends who always held together: Yitzchak Kone, Itche Karpe, Yaakov Schnitzer and the writer of these lines. We formed the committee that led the economic struggle in a systematic manner. We were immersed in the work for entire days, and everything was conducted in a strongly illegal fashion.

Our organizational activity resonated in the neighboring towns such as Raciaz, Żuromin, Bieżuń, and others, all of which joined our movement. We sent to them our members, and from time to time also our professionals, and set up Poale Zion organizations in the town. Even though there was already a regional committee in Włocławek to which we affiliated, Włocławek was unable to be satisfied with us. We conducted our party work entirely independently, and we established a contact with the Polish union of Poale Zion.

The surrounding towns caused us a great deal of work. The strikes that we conducted in those towns were very bitter, and were frequently accompanied by bloody battles. We conducted a strike against the leader shapers in Raciaz, and the factories declared a lockout. This was still not enough, and they organized and hired Polish hooligans who attacked the workers on a Friday night. The hired hooligans beat the workers with sticks, and badly wounded a large number of them. The committee leader barely escaped with his life. He was taken to the nearby hospital in serious condition, and was bandaged up by a medic. At night, he was brought to us, very ill, in Sierpc.

After hearing his report, we found no other way than to send to the town a “penal expedition” from our B.A. (*Bojowo Organizacia* – Combat Organization). Three “*Bojowces*” (Combat personnel) set out with the wounded comrade to go to the residence of the organizer of the attack against the workers.

The leader of the lockout was a Hassidic manufacturer with sons, daughters, and sons-in-law. We decided to settle scores with him on Friday night, at the time when he would be celebrating the Sabbath meal with the finest delicacies. This would be a revenge for the attack that was perpetrated against the workers also on a Friday night. Our wounded comrade was the first to open the door, and the three comrades shouted, “Do not move. Hands up.” The wounded comrade noted, “These are them!” Then, a few shots were fired. A large window was shattered by a shot. The bullet ricocheted off the glass and went through the foot of the manufacturer's son.

This was an unfortunate accident, for it was decided to avoid creating any victims, but rather to shoot as a demonstration. The “penal expedition” left and issued an order to not leave the house sooner than two hours from that time, and to pay a monetary fine to the chief who would be designated by our organization. After conducting this piece of work, the comrades set out for home very calmly in the fine summer night.

On Saturday morning, the “penal expedition” had already given us a report, and we were satisfied. First of all, on Sunday, all the workers showed up to work. All of their demands were met. We also received the monetary fine, which created great possibilities for our organization.

The Discussion with the Bundists

The Bundist press was unable to be silent about the fact that the Poale Zion organization, which called itself Social Democrat, had perpetrated a terrorist act. The Bund held the Central Committee of the Poale Zion party responsible for the actions of the Sierpc organization. The Central Committee was unable to offer any clarification to the public until it could ascertain what had taken place. To that end, the Central Committee sent Comrades Shmuel Warszewer and David Grün (today the Prime Minister and Defense Minister of Israel, David Ben-Gurion) from Plonsk to collect all the necessary materials at the location.

Mr. David Grün came to me, along with Comrade Sh. Warszewer on Friday morning, acting as a plenipotentiary of the Central Committee. I, the two delegates, and our permanent secretary Comrade Itche immediately set out in a carriage for Raciaz to clarify the entire matter.

At about 2:00 p.m., we were already in the large, fenced-in yard of the manufacturer. The manufacturer and his relatives came out with terror in their eyes, thinking that they were accused of something once again. We immediately calmed them and suggested that we go into a separate room, in which we could talk about several important issues. The representatives of the Central Committee heard all the details of the unfortunate incident. Our secretary, Comrade Itche, documented everything. The investigation lasted over four hours.

When we wanted to get back into the carriage, two policemen were close to us, as if they sprouted out of the earth. They asked us for our passports. We identified Comrade Shmuel, but instead of accepting the identification, they took hold of a revolver. However, I raised his hands in time, and whispered to the police that we could clarify the matter at an appropriate time.

The policemen took our documents. We turned to the manufacturer and asked him, for some price, to return the passports to us so that we could continue with our departure, and we would not hold him responsible for any outcome. The manufacturer was very afraid, and he immediately invited the policemen into a private room... Ten minutes later we received our passports. We left the town happily and traveled to Plonsk.

We arrived in town at about 10:00 p.m. and stopped by a friend. There, we ate something and found out that the Comrade Yitzchak Parizer, a student, had come to a "discussion" meeting to which Comrade Salomon (M. Jarblum) had incidentally come. We were very happy with that opportunity to hear the esteemed leaders of Poale Zion in discussion.

We fell asleep exhausted and woke up in the morning fresh, cheerful, full of life, and prepared to serve our party. Many guests from the surrounding towns came to the discussion that took place in the *beis midrash* at 2:00 p.m. on Saturday, and attracted the attention of the entire city. The police supervision completely disappeared. Due to this freedom, the meeting took place as a risk-free mass gathering with open doors.

Not only workers, but also older Jews, gathered around the *beis midrash.* The Bundists could not bring themselves to allow the Poale Zion to conduct the imposing free meeting without a sharp attack from the opposing parties, including the Bund. The members of the Bund therefore attempted to disrupt the meeting. Suddenly someone shouted: "Police are coming!" A tumult ensued. Order was restored through the efforts of all the forces. The meeting ended with a very exalted mood with the resonating sounds of the Poale Zion "oath."

Comrade David Grün remained at home. I returned to Sierpc. The secretary Comrade Itche with Comrade Shmuel Warszewer traveled to Warsaw via Włocławek, bringing along with them the clarification material from Raciaz to give over to the Central Committee. As they arrived in Włocławek, they were all arrested by home agents. After a stringent search, all the papers were found with them. Comrade Itche was immediately freed because he had a passport and did not let on that he knew Comrade Shmuel. I found out later that the Central Committee sent a female comrade to Włocławek to intervene with the police chief to free Comrade Shmuel together with the collected material. The comrade was Sabina Rafalkes.

We breathed freely. If I am not mistaken, the union committee then published a leaflet in which they answered the Bundist attack with regard the terrorist assault of the Sierpc Poale Zion in the town of Raciaz.

The union committee remained in contact with us the entire time. They began to discuss the question of transferring the regional committee in Włocławek to Sierpc. However, this did not take place for two reasons: first, Sierpc did not have an appropriate center, and second, our town did not have the appropriate intelligence forces that were needed for the activities for the work of a regional committee. At our request, Comrade Salomon (M. Jarblum) was appointed as a permanent professional of the regional committee in Włocławek.

It was decided to publish a weekly pamphlet in Włocławek under the editorship of Comrade Salomon. The appearance of the *Arbeiter Wort* (*Workers' Word*) was a celebration for us as well as for the surrounding towns. However, the newspaper did not last long. It ceased publication after a few editions. Despite the absence of the newspaper that would bind the members together, the party work was conducted in a wide arena.

Library Committee in 1916

Right to left

Seated: Rivka Karpe, Yisrael Yaakov Kohn, Esther Podskacz

Standing: Fishel Szampan, Avraham Fried (Yerushalmi), Leib Hiller, Leib Mintz, Yeshayahu Friedman, Zalman Goldsztejn.

Library Committee in 1917/1918

Right to left
Sitting: Yetta Feiga Cyna, Yisrael Yaakov Kohen, Mottel Grossman.
Standing: Moshe Cypris, Rasha Parkel, Avraham Fried (Yerushalmi)

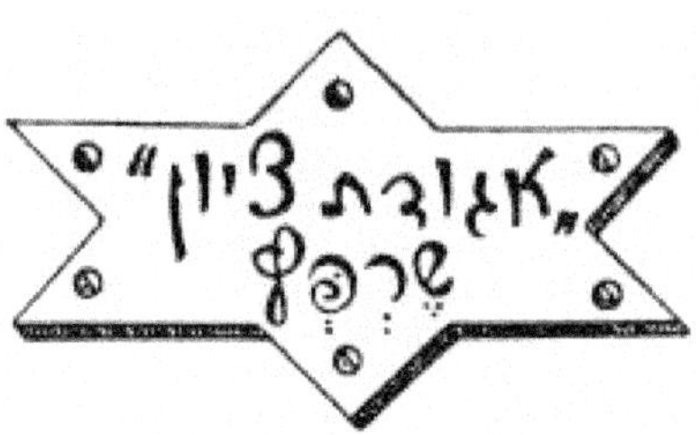

The committee of Agudat Zion in Sierpc in the year 5779 / 1919 at the departure of the committee member Yitzchak Zommer to army work.

Right to left

Sitting: Tzerl Bergzon, Avraham Fried (Yerushalmi), Yitzchak Zommer, Yeta Feiga Cyna.

Standing: Fishel Szampan, Hinda Roza Atlas, Mendel Blum, Yechiel Moshe Sendrowicz (Sidroni), Heja (Tzvi) Malowanczyk, Freida Ofenbach, Yeshayahu Friedman.

Agudat Zion in Sierpc

Our Sierpc professionals, comrade Ish-Ivri and comrade Perle, were sent out to the surrounding towns as lecturers. Comrade Salomon was a frequent guest lecturer for us. I wish to mention a few characteristic episodes from that time:

At that time, it was simply a holy duty that if a party invited an opposing group to a discussion meeting, nobody would be permitted to refuse.

Once, the Bund came and invited us to a discussion. At that time, our organization numbered over 150 male and female members. Even though we were a large organization, we had never refused a discussion. This time as well, even though we were concerned that the Bund might be able to convince the simple workers about their ideas, we did not refuse. In order to ensure our victory, we requested that the union committee provide us with responsible speakers. This time, we knew that a significant Bundist, named "Lasal the Second"[5], was coming.

Comrade Salomon had debated with "Lasal" and won in Kutno, Plock and Włocławek. Therefore, we asked the union to send Comrade Salomon (M. Jarblum) to us as well. The union office took our request into consideration and immediately informed us that Comrade Salomon was coming to the designated location.

We set up the discussion meeting in a private home. Over 50 members came. "Lasal" of the Bund did not come. A different speaker came, who talked about Marxism. After a 15-minute speech, he declared that he had finished speaking about the theory of Marxism, and now we could begin the discussion. In fact, there was nobody to oppose him. At the end, Comrade Salomon spoke about Marxism and the Jewish question. His performance was enthusiastically received by the entire audience with the shouts "Long live Poale Zion," and the meeting ended.

The following is a second characteristic episode: On the holiday of Passover, the students Beniek and Fetel Gorfinkel, Mietek Glazer, Rivche Tac and Esther Grobard came for their vacation. They were all Bundists and they made efforts to secretly win over several members of our ranks. The student Bundists had an influence on a certain number of our members who were unable themselves to give an answer to the contentious questions between Bund and Poale Zion.

We knew that the student Bundists were conducting their agitation with our members behind closed doors. The best members of Poale Zion who could knock down the Bundist claims were not let in.

We consulted about how to react, and decided to send two members of our committee accompanied by our "B.A."[6] to demand from the Bundists the possibility of participating in the discussion, as was the custom of all parties.

We issued that declaration on the spot, once we arrived. They responded through the door with a refusal. Within a few minutes, our "*bojowkas*"[7] succeeded in breaking through the door and taking control. Our two designated members entered and declared before the gathering that the Bundist students had conducted themselves in an improper manner by conducting their agitation behind closed doors. Our declaration had its effect, and the meeting was disbanded.

The student Bundists invited us to an open discussion. We accepted the invitation and asked the union committee to send us a good speaker for the latter days of Passover[8].

At 2:00 p.m. sharp, on the first day of the latter days of Passover, over 80 male and female members had already gathered in a grove behind the town. At the designated time, the speaker, Comrade Abosh, a 16-year-old youth with a sharp tongue, arrived via a side route with Comrade Pukacz. Comrade Pukacz opened the meeting and Comrade Abosh began his speech. Everyone, including the opponents, was enthused with the content-rich speech. Nobody spoke in opposition except for a young lad who asked, "What will be done with the Palestinian swamps and frogs which bring yellow fever with them?" Comrade Abosh gave a very succinct answer, and everyone remained still and rejoiced. After the meeting, we arranged ourselves in rows, and marched to the city and then through various alleyways singing workers' songs.

Persecutions, Searches and Arrests

That activity of the Poale Zion in Sierpc, who often demonstrated in the streets singing workers's songs, attracted the attention of the Czarist police, who began to conduct searches of our members. Once, during such a search, the Polish union committee of Poale Zion, which was located in Łodz at that time, almost failed. During the search, the entire correspondence that was conducted with the union office was captured. We received all the documents back from the police chief in return for two golden coins[9].

A second serious failure took place when we conducted an action in the town of Bieżun. Due to its proximity to the city of Sierpc (15 kilometers), we set out for a walk on a fine summer day. The four-member committee participated in the walk – Comrade Gross, a military tailor, and the two professionals Ish-Ivri and Perle. Together we were a group of seven members.

When we had finished our work in Bieżun and set out in a wagon to return to Sierpc, we encountered a mounted soldier near the village of Nadólnik. Immediately behind him was an entire military unit with police, which surrounded us. The soldiers pointed their guns at us, and waited for a command from the most senior police commissar. The commissar ascended our wagon and declared in the name of the highest authorities that they had been sent by the authorities to conduct a search. He first asked Comrade Ish-Ivri (Sh. Landinski) to come down. They found two Russian text books on him.

Simultaneously, a soldier searched through the straw on the wagon and found two revolvers that we had taken along with us, and some written material. Comrade Gross, an acquaintance of the soldier, promised to sew him a pair of soldier's trousers if he would be quiet about this. The soldier accepted. Comrade Gross pretended to have a stomach ache and asked the soldier to accompany him into the grove... There, Gross buried the two notebooks of written material in the sand. Thus, the search produced no results for the police.

Surrounded by the police and soldiers with pointed guns, we were taken through the city to the town hall. The entire city was in a state of agitation. Good friends were sorry and, on the other hand, those with whom we conducted a day-to-day struggle were happy that they were once and for all freed from the strikers.

The police commissar went to the town hall. The higher authorities were waiting there. They took the report of the search and immediately freed us, since they did not have any grounds for holding us. Only Comrade Landinski – Ish-Ivri – received an order to leave the city "on his own free will."

*

The dark clouds came over us more strongly and, as autumn came, we began to feel gloomy in our hearts when we received news on occasion that measures were taken against the revolutionaries in various places. The best leaders were hanged, sentenced to life in prison, or exiled to Siberia. Thus, the light of the workers' movement was weakened.

Our activity was also paralyzed on account of this situation. Our professionals, Comrade Ish-Ivri and Perle, left Sierpc, where arrests of Poale Zion activists were taking place. Comrade Bekman was arrested and sentenced to several years in prison, but he fortuitously ended up in Paris.

During that difficult and frightful time, the majority of our membership was made up of Orthodox youths. They would go to the *beis midrash* every day to pray and put on *tefillin.* Rumors came to us that a certain portion of our members, who had at one time blindly considered all the commands of our committee to be holy, were preparing to take revenge against those members who "seduced" them, and thereby atone for their sin against G-d. For a certain time, we had to protect ourselves and refrain from making ourselves overly conspicuous, until finally the matter was put to sleep in its entirety, and all the threads of party activity were torn up. From the four friends who stuck together and led the Poale Zion movement in Sierpc, Yitzchak Kone and Itche Karpe left for the Land of Israel, Yaakov Schnitzer left for America, and I remained alone.

Being alone for a long time, in 1910 I joined up with two other isolated individuals, a Bundist and an S.S. person. The three of us had the idea that, since the present time did not present a wide arena for party activity, we should form a culture center. We decided to take steps to create a library in Sierpc. We approached the authorities to obtain the appropriate permits. Within a few evenings, we had collected the necessary financial means. Later, we rented a premises, purchased books, and thereby created the first legal Jewish cultural institution in Sierpc.

I took upon myself almost the entire management of the library. By 1912, the library was established at such a level where it had a large number of Yiddish books, a respectable number of Polish books, a fine, orderly reading hall, and a superb inventory. This was the finest institution of the Jewish community in Sierpc. In 1912, I left Sierpc for private reasons and went to America.

The Activities of the Leftist *Poale Zion*

by Yosef David Wajsrore

The Leftist Poale Zion played an important role in Jewish societal life in Sierpc. Many youths, including those from religious and Hassidic homes, gathered at the premises of the Leftist Poale Zion every evening to spend time together after a hard day of work. From far away, one could hear their songs, which imbued strength and hope into hearts of the working youth, who were raised in poor homes and had to go to work in their early youth.

Friday nights were turned into major cultural evenings with discussions on various issues. Very often, there were exquisite evenings when every member was able to ask questions about issues that were on his mind, and receive answers.

The Poale Zion had a fine library and a dramatic club led by Moshe Gutstat and Itche Binem Rosenberg.

The two Poale Zionist activists were known not only within the circles of their party, but also within the broader Sierpc society. They conducted a struggle for their Poale Zionist principles within the city council and the Jewish community. The organization also maintained a sports club, where the working youth could stretch their shoulders after a hard day of work at the machine or the workbench.

Aside from the aforementioned members, Eliahu Grossman, Mendel Goldsztejn and others from all segments of the population who held the movement in esteem were active in Poalei Zion.

I will take the opportunity to mention a fact that shows how far the Sierpc youth went with helping each other:

We, a group of six friends: Aba Licht, Moshe Licht, Ber Flato, Moshe Meir Osteszewer, Berl Meir Najstadt and I, worked for Holender the gaiter maker. When he later became sick, traveled to Paris to convalesce, and died there during the operation, we six youths worked for a year without pay so that his wife and children would have what to live on.

The Bundist Movement in Sierpc

by Avraham Gordon, Brasilia

The Beginning of the Sierpc Bund

The organization of the Bundist movement in Sierpc had already begun by the year 1905. However, since the Czarist authorities suppressed the entire political life after the infamous October Manifesto of 1905, the Bundist organization was also liquidated.

First in 1916, at the time of the First World War when the city was occupied by the Germans, the first illegal meeting took place during Passover of that year in the home of A. Gordon, in which 22 workers took part, including tailors, shoemakers, and several members of the intelligentsia. At the meeting, the importance of organization into a political party was discussed, and it was decided to found a Bundist organization in the city of Sierpc. A committee of five members was selected, and the illegal work began.

Lectures and Cultural Activity

The first tasks of the newly founded Bundist organization were to: establish contact with the central committee in Warsaw, disseminate the party publication *Di Lebnsfragen,* set up a lecture club every Sabbath, illegally conduct educational clubs, bring in lecturers from the larger cities, conduct readings, and conduct cultural events.

A decision was made to participate in the regional Bundist conference in Włocławek that was to take place shortly.

The regional conference in Włocławek brought a great deal of life to our work. We began to disseminate more of *Di Lebnsfragen* as well as other illegal publications. Our influence in the city strengthened. We obtained new members and sympathizers.

The First Open Meeting Hall and Professional Union

When the German attacks on the battlefields began and we already felt that they were beginning to enter the city, we quickly decided to rent a meeting hall and to legalize ourselves. The first Bundist meeting hall was at Baruch Konenbrand's home opposite the old *beis midrash.*

The Germans left the city completely, and the Poles declared the independence of Poland and conducted themselves with anti-Semitism and hooliganistic attacks. A bit later, when life had already begun to normalize and the decree regarding electing city councils throughout Poland was issued, Sierpc also prepared for the city council elections.

The Bund turned to the Leftist Poale Zion and the Communists regarding an organizational conference that would deal with the question of electoral representatives and the possibility of presenting a united list. The conference took place but produced no results, and the Bund entered the city council elections independently with its own Bundist candidate list.

At the same time, the Bund turned to the Leftist Poale Zion, the Communists and the General Zionists regarding creating a general professional union. A conference took place in the Bund headquarters, at which a decision was taken to organize a large general meeting of all the trades. At the general meeting at the Bund headquarters, with the participation of 200 workers, a unanimous decision was taken to form the "General Professional Union." A committee of five members from all the directions was elected, under the chairmanship of A. Gordon. The secretary was the teacher Kohn.

The professional union developed well and was active during the city council elections.

Bundist Activity on the City Council and the Struggle Against Anti-Semitism

As in various other cities, the Bund had electoral list number four. We also took number four in the Bundist electoral list in Sierpc. At the elections, the Bund entered Sh. Gryn as a candidate for the city council, and A. Gordon as a deputy. Comrade Nathan Tac was elected on the general city list. He always voted with the Bundist councilor on the city council.

Immediately following the first sitting of the city council, the anti-Semitic Endeks[10] began their anti-Jewish activity that involved incitement and tearing Jews away from their businesses and livelihood. At a sitting in which several Jewish and P.P.S. (Polish Socialist Party) members were absent, they took the opportunity to push through an anti-Semitic decision to move the market days, which used to take place on Tuesdays and Fridays, to Saturday.

The decree caused a great commotion among the poor Jews, for they did not wish to desecrate the Sabbath, and the market days were their prime source of livelihood.

The law was soon to come into force. There were even some Jews who had come to terms with the idea, as long as not to stir up the anti-Semitism. The Bund, however, decided to call a large meeting, and turned to all the Jews of the city to conduct a battle against the anti-Semitic law.

The excitement in the city was so great that the chairman of the city council summoned a conference of all the Jewish parties at his home, and wanted to work something out so there would not be such a great tumult, and the law would be thrown out.

The representative of the Bund declared at the conference, "Despite the fact that we are not religious Jews, will fight with all our powers for the repeal of the law, so that Jews can continue to conduct their business."

The conference produced no results. However, the Bund joined with the P.P.S. to demonstrate the anti-Semitic character of the law and demand an extra sitting of the city council that would deal with the anti-Semitic law once again. The P.P.S. agreed.

It was arranged that all of the Jewish and P.P.S. councilors would be present at the sitting. The Endeks used all means at their disposal to cancel the sitting, but they did not succeed. The anti-Semitic decision was repealed with the votes from the P.P.S. and the Jewish councilors from all the parties. The large crowd in the gallery, members of all Jewish parties as well as the P.P.S., reacted with joy at the downfall of the anti-Semites. They applauded and manifested themselves against the Endeks.

The activity surrounding the repeal of the anti-Semitic decree imparted a great deal of importance to the Bund and to all the other political groups.

At the second city council vote, the Bund presented the city councilor Leibush Asher and Mendel Fetbroit as representatives.

Leibush Asher was a very good orator in both Yiddish and Polish. He earned love and recognition both from the city council and from the populist masses.

Cultural Work and the First of May

The Bund organized a dramatic club that conducted open literary and musical evenings. Some of the events took place in the Rudawskin movie hall on Plocker Street.

The first time we observed the First of May in a legal fashion was in 1918, when a First of May demonstration by the P.P.S., Bund, Peasants Party, and General Professional Union took place. Each party had its red flag and floats with various slogans.

Youth Organization

The Bund also had a large youth organization lead by Shimon and Chaim Jurkewicz and the Gornes brothers. The youth organization conducted literary and musical events, and brought in talented and good speakers.

*

From the 1930s until the outbreak of the Second World War, despite the great anti-Semitism of the Poles, a large-scale cultural and political movement among the Jewish folkist masses in Sierpc grew and developed. The youth were imbued with Socialist and nationalist ideals.

A battle against nationalist Polish anti-Semitism and chauvinism was conducted.

The outbreak of the Second World War and the entry of the German Nazi destroyers with the help of the local anti-Semitic Poles put an end to the vibrant Jewish life.

SKIF – The Socialist Children's Organization

by Chaim Jurkewicz, Santas Brazil

SKIF, the Socialist children's union of the Bundist organization in Sierpc, conducted fine cultural work that expressed itself in open events in the city theater. The song of the workers and populist songs, the march to the stage, the threefold declamation, the performance of various single act plays – elicited the admiration of everyone.

Once, after a SKIF performance in the city theater, Yitzchak Reichgot, a Zionist, came to me and said, “The conduct on the stage and the acting of those children from poor homes is amazing. It is truly a pleasure to see the children acting.”

The children were also the first and most punctual in participating in all organization activities – the first in the club, in the library, and in the circle.

The *Herzliya* Youth Organization

by Shmuel Cyna of Rechovot

I recall from the years of my early youth that the sole movement in our town of Sierpc was the General Zionist Organization, founded by Avraham Fried, Yeshayahu Frajdman, Tzvi Malowanczyk and others. This was the only expression of nationalist life within the Zionist movement.

During the 1920s, the Herzliya Youth Organization was founded by the Zionist organization. I had the honor of belonging to it and obtaining the appropriate education in the path of Zionism from it.

The activity of the Herzliya Youth Organization was conducted by the members; Shmuel Wluka, Efraim Wluka, Leibel Horn, Moshe Podskacz, Mordechai Reszatka, Ber Czarka, and Yossel Prasnicki. Later, the members David Dobroszklanka, Moshe Smolinski, Baruch Lielanek, Eliezer and Yeshaya Kurta, Dvora Skornuk, Rachel Lea Reszatka, Dvora Szapira, Eliezer Reszatka, Yisrael Sosnkowski, Pesach Skurka, Menachem Podskacz, Chanoch Podskacz and tens of other male and female members came aboard. They were active, and conducted the activity in which they were involved with dedication and wisdom.

Right to left
Seated: Moshe Belt, Henik Gorfinkel, David Manimczuwka
Standing: Yosef Potolski, Eliahu Jalonowski, Yitzchak Bergzon, Mula (Shmuel) Bluman

The Agudat Zion board in Sierpc, 5687 / 1927.

Right to left

Seated: Yitzchak Zylberberg (Simchoni), Tzvi Malowanczyk, Moshe Belt.

Standing: Feivush Kirsz, Noach Lesman, Yisraelik Smolinski

The Herzliya board in Sierpc, 5689 / 1929.

Right to left

Seated: Yuta Grefo, Shmuelik Wluka, Mordechai Jeszutka, Ber Czarka, Sara Skurka.

Standing: Shmuel Cyna, Zalman Najemski, Wolf Buda, Hena Uberfeld, Yitzchak Miranc, Eliezer Jasutka

On the *aliya* of Efraim Yosel Wluka to the land of Israel.

Right to left
First row: Ezriel Szampa, Chilik (Yechiel) Bachrach.
Second row: Elya Grossman, Yosel Mrasznicki, Moshe Podskacz, Efraim Yosel Wluka (Talmai), Yosel Myuncyn

On the *aliya* of Tova Lencner to the Land of Israel, Cheshvan 5686 / 1925.

Right to left
Sitting: Chana Gongola, Tzirel Czarka, Tova Lencner, Aidel Gorfinkel, Fradel Mac.
Standing: Sara Gotlwowski, Reizel Skurnik, Bluman, Golda Wluka, Gotza Flato, Sara Dvora Skurnik, Fradel Goldsztejn

The city committee of the Keren Kayemet LeYisrael (Jewish National Fund) in Sierpc, 5686 / 1926.

Right to left
First row: Ber Czarka, Mordechai Jaszutka, Yisrael Oszulk (Yizraeli)
Second row: Yaakov Shimon Rozenfeld, Yosef Apelbaum, Shmulik Wluka, Leib Horn, Hirsch Kristel (Elgabish)
Third row: Gershon Mintz, Naftali Czarnoczupka, Mina Konic, Gutking Rozinek, Noah Lesman

The Herzliya activity was expressed first and foremost through Zionist education, learning about general Jewish history and the history of Zionism beginning from the beginnings of Chovevei Zion[11], and following the happenings in the Zionist world. They also studied Yiddish and Hebrew literature, and some world classics. Special consideration was given to the workers of the Zionist funds: the Keren Kayemet LeYisrael (Jewish National Fund), and Keren Hayesod. The crown of the Herzliya organization was the library that numbered more than 2,000 books in Yiddish, Hebrew and Polish. It was directed by a special committee that had the task of purchasing newly published books from time to time, adding subscribers and conducting the day-to-day work.

The readings and lecturers in which the brothers Shmulik and Efraim Wluka appeared attracted a large crowd. For me, it was the greatest experience in those times to be present at a reading by the two brothers. Efraim Wluka was the first native of Sierpc who traveled with a certificate and made *aliya* to the Land of Israel. His place was filled by Leibel Horn, who was ebullient with Jewish and worldly knowledge. At the same time, he was also very familiar with the history of Zionism. Lectures by Mordechai Reszatka on Palestinian themes and by Ber Czarka took place every Friday night as well as Saturday.

Literary evenings and gala evenings also took place, at which actual questions were presented and discussed. The *Lebedike Zeitung*, in which our members were able to publish their activities and write articles and feuillitons, was very popular and aroused great interest. Zalman Narzemski excelled with his satirical feuillitons.

From time to time, we also conducted literary critiques that enjoyed great success. The consciousness of the youth increased, and time had its effect. There was pressure both from the right and from the left, and the Herzliya movement was split into two sections: Hashomer Haleumi from one side under the leadership of David Dobroszklanka and Moshe Smolinski, and Hashomer Hatzair on the other side under the leadership of Baruch Lielanek, Chanoch Podskacz and others.

The memories from my young days, when I participated in the Herzliya movement in our city, will accompany me forever. We, the surviving members in Israel as well as in the Diaspora must always carry in our hearts the holy memory of those idealistic members who imparted to us the Zionist ideal but themselves unfortunately did not witness the realization of their holy strivings. They are among the six million martyrs who were tortured by the Germans.

Personalities from the *Herzliya* Youth Organization

by Mordechai Reshatka

The meeting hall of the Herzliya youth organization was located in the yard of Melech Cyna, on the corner of the old market on Fara Street. The majority of the young people from that time are no longer here. They were murdered in a cruel fashion by the murderous hand of the German murderers... Only a few of that group have survived.

Permit me to recall in our Yizkor Book a few of those who were the leaders of that organization.

Leibel Horn

He was born in 1905 and soon became an orphan. His father died, and he grew up under the supervision of his mother Pese. They lived in poverty and want in a basement dwelling. Under such conditions, Leibel grew up physically weak and very nearsighted. Therefore, he became spiritually strong.

When he finished studying in *cheder*, he continued his studies in the *beis midrash*. Together with the *Gemara*, he also studied "external books" and delved into the content of Zionism. He quickly found his way to the Sierpc Zionist organization, and became one of its leaders and spokesmen. However, his demeanor was not that of a leader, but rather of a friend, like a son of the people.

After getting married with his chosen one, Tova Koplowicz, he tried to establish his family life in Sierpc, but without success. He had no luck, and he moved to Paris along with his wife and child. However, the matter of livelihood did not come easy for him there as well.

They lived in Paris until France was occupied by the Germans. As a Polish Jew, Leibel was sent to a concentration camp. He spent nine months there, and was freed by luck.

One night, when the Germans came to arrest his pregnant wife, he declared that he wanted to take the place of his wife. The Gestapo men agreed to the proposition, and took Leibel along with them...

We never heard from Leibel again... We, his friends as well as his relatives will always remember him.

Ber Czarka

As a young child, he came to Sierpc from the village in which his parents lived, so that he cold attend Sierpc *cheder* and study Torah. After concluding *cheder,* he studied in the *beis midrash.* However, the yoke of livelihood did not let him remain there for long. He had to become a "merchant" in order to help feed the family, who by then were living in the city.

The business consisted of street commerce. He also traveled to the fairs. His spiritual life found expression in Herzliya, where he was one of the teachers and leaders. Later, when he was older, he joined the Zionist party. He was a representative on the Jewish communal council, and he helped organize the institutions of the Jewish community. As a representative of the community, he also corresponded with the Sierpc Relief Committee in New York and described the difficult living conditions of the Jews in Poland during the years before the Second World War.

During the German extermination of the Jews, he suffered the same fate as the vast majority of the Sierpc Jews. Together with his wife, Sara Skurka, who herself was active in society; they fled to the part of Poland that was under Soviet occupation. After the Germans occupied those areas as well, Ber Czarka and his wife were murdered there.

Moshe and Menachem Podskacz

These were the two youngest of the wealthy Podskacz family. Moshe was a few years older than Menachem. From their wealthy home, they entered Herzliya, whereas for a girl or boy of lesser means, there was no other place in Sierpc to live one's societal life. As was the custom of children from wealthy homes, they received an appropriate education. They came to the youth of Sierpc in order to participate with them and their education. The youth held them in esteem and treated them with friendship and love.

The two Podskacz brothers were murdered together with the majority of Sierpc Jews.

There were other youths who served the Herzliya organization with heart and soul.

Let my lines be a memory to their young, snuffed out lives.

Translator's Footnotes:

1. A token of membership in the Zionist movement.
2. See http://en.wikipedia.org/wiki/Kulak
3. There is a blank space in the text here.
4. See http://en.wikipedia.org/wiki/Karl_Liebknecht
5. There is a footnote in the text as follows: At that time, the later Jewish-American Socialist and social activist B. Wladek, the brother of the well-known literary critic Shmuel Neiger, went by that name.
6. I am not sure what this abbreviation means – but it is evidently some leadership title within Poale Zion.

7. In Polish, "bojówka" means a fighting group or armed band.
8. The final two days of Passover are full festival days, as are the first two days.
9. *Finferlech* – literally five dollar bills, or coins denominated in fives.
10. The fascist, anti-Semitic National Democratic Party of Poland.

See http://en.wikipedia.org/wiki/Hovevei_Zion

Hashomer Hatzair in Sierpc

By Chanoch (Podskoc) Nachshon

This movement [*Hashomer Hatzair* –The Young Guard] was established in our town in 1928. It comprised about 200 boys and girls of all ages.

One day, a guest arrived from Mlawa, a neighboring town. This was Zev Yunish (now Chief of Pediatrics at Beilinson Hospital [in Petah-Tikva, Israel]), a member of the leadership of *Hashomer Hatzair* in the district. A few hundred people came to the meeting, and he started teaching them a pioneering song from Palestine, and thereby captured all their hearts. After the meeting, they all went outside and sang the well-known song "How Beautiful are the Nights in the Land of Canaan".

The town already had political and professional organizations that sponsored speeches, meetings, and discussions. But *Hashomer Hatzair* in our town, as in all of Poland at that time, gave the youth a distinct personal worldview, a feeling of fulfillment, and a readiness for *aliyah* [ascension – immigration to the Land of Israel].

The emissary left, and the next day, the activities had to begin – meetings, exercise drills, trips, and so forth. It is easy enough to say now, here in Israel, that we performed exercises, sat together with the young people, taught ideals, taught songs, etc. But then it was necessary to learn these things by doing, every day. The first "activity" was assigned to a group of young people under the leadership of Yeshayahu Korta (died in France in World War II) and the writer of this memoir. The meeting or "activity" (as a meeting is called to this day) was scheduled for seven in the morning. It was the season of school vacation, and everyone showed up.

Then the enlistment began of three age groups for activities – "the young lions" for young people of 10 to 12 years, the middle group whose name I already find it difficult to remember, and the senior group, starting at 16 to 18 years of age. This older group was of course expected to be ready to go to a training kibbutz, and then to go to the Land of Israel. It did not take too long for various politicians, who did not approve of the growth of a new movement with such a large number of members and influence, to start to undermine the *ken* [the local branch of *Hashomer Hatzair* was called a *ken* – nest] and cause a split.

One group followed Moshe Smolinski and left *Hashomer Hatzair* in order to start *Hashomer Haleumi*. It turned out later that not only did the split not hurt *Hashomer Hatzair*, but instead of one movement of 150 to 200 young people, the result was two movements with at least 100 to 150 members each.

Of course, at first there was a boycott on all dealings with the "traitors," and for years the members of *Hashomer Hatzair* and *Hashomer Haleumi* abstained from any contact, even not saying "hello" to each other. After a few years, everyone became fed up with the arguments, and they sort of petered out by themselves.

Hashomer Hatzair in Sierpc excelled in its quiet and serious daily activities. Tens of young boys and girls would sit and learn Hebrew and hold conversations three times a week. The group organized many trips. Once a year, dozens of young people would go to the "summer colonies" organized by the district council of the movement. These "colonies" were in the deep in the forests, or in the villages of Poland. Every summer, the various branches in the district would meet. There would be talks, moot courts, lectures, and trips with participation by emissaries from Palestine.

Action committees in various fields and the newspaper editorial board would be elected at these summer colonies. The seating place of a member of the editorial board was on a high branch of a tree, and each editor had to prove that he was suited to his exalted position by editing while sitting in a tree.

I am sure that these meetings of the editorial board in the treetops are etched in the minds of all those that sat in the trees and discussed very serious problems. One has to remember that this was a period of intense arguments about the future of the "seniors" group – those 18 and older. Hashomer Hatzair had 3000 to 4000 "seniors" and their numbers grew every year. However, the number of "certificates" [approval of visas for immigration to Palestine] was small – limited to 500. How then, would it be possible to hold on to the youth when there was no chance of *aliyah* soon?

This was a difficult and serious problem of thousands of young people that had been prepared for *aliyah* and absolutely rejected, in their youthful innocence, continuation of life in the diaspora. If there is no prospect of *aliyah* for most of them – what will they do?

There was also an ideological disagreement about this. This was the debate between Yehuda Gothilf (today a member of the editorial board of the newspaper *Davar*) and his comrade Mordechai Oren, the prisoner of Prague. [Oren, a leftist Israeli politician, was arrested and jailed in a cold war show trial in Czechoslovakia in 1951 when he visited Prague.] Gothilf supported democratic ideals while Oren espoused the Russian revolutionary orientation and its ideals.

The whole movement became involved in this debate, and it also enveloped the *ken* in Sierpc, which was very ideological. Unless you saw the youth in the towns during this period, without hope of *aliyah*, except for a small group, you cannot understand this debate. The youth in Hashomer Hatzair had been educated for pioneering, kibbutz life, self-fulfillment, and Socialism, but the great majority of them did not have a clear vision of their future. Therefore, it is not surprising that in 1931-32, after departures from the movement all over Poland, a group of counselors left the *ken* in Sierpc: Zelig Licht, Leib Minchin, and others.

I can still see that dramatic evening, when we were to have a moot trial and discussion of the play *The Weavers* by Gerhard Hauptman. The trial had been under preparation for months, about the transition period between a capitalist economy based on small manufacturing to industrial scale mechanization that drove the workers out and into starvation. There were workers riots in Western Europe then, with destruction of machinery. The trial had been arranged so that there was a prosecutor and defense attorney, as in any actual trial. However, that evening, the prosecutor closed his address with an emotional appeal to the young people to abandon Zionism and join the movement struggling for a new world – the Communist party. It should be noted that the number that left was not very large, but among them were some talented people who had embraced universal ideals. Some of those that left are now in the United States, doing "business," and forgetting all the ideals. The large majority of the *ken* remained faithful to Zionism, and continued their activities.

A second teacher of Hebrew came to the *ken* during this period, and a project was carried out that very few of the branches of Hashomer Hatzair in Poland would have dared to attempt. This was a "winter colony" at the estate of Lavandush. Tens of young men and women went for a week to a winter camp. The plans included trips, sports, talks, celebrations, and so forth. I remember one particular instance of a young boy, whose father had stopped him from coming because it was the tailors' busy season. He did not hesitate to walk 20 kilometers in the cold winter to get to the camp, and of course without his father's permission.

A number of factors led to feelings of depression. Some of the counselors went on *aliyah* to Palestine; there was a political hostility to Jews that was promoted by the Nazi propaganda in Poland; and especially the prohibition of any more Jewish immigration to Palestine.

The Period of Flight

With the outbreak of the Second World War in 1939, many fled from the town. Some of the members of Hashomer Hatzair escaped to the U.S.S.R.

Today, we know that only some of the members of Hashomer Hatzair survived. Leib Minchin died a natural death just before the war. Zelig Licht, Fibush Wilk and his wife Yedusha-Yocheved disappeared in the wide spaces of the Soviet Union. But some of the youth held fast and managed to stay alive.

Yeshayahu Lelonek returned to Poland with the Polish People's Army, and today he is in the United States. One of the two brothers Diogenes is now in Sweden, and the other is in the United States.

Many of the members of Hashomer Hatzair are now in Israel: Tovah Schwartz, Esther and Miriam Podskoc, Frieda Mlawa, Shlomo Charka (in Kibbutz Dan), Rivkah and Feina Minchin, and many others.

However, many of the young men and women, with whom for many years we dreamt of a free life in our homeland, did not make it.

All those that lived through that time in the *Hashomer Hatzair* youth movement in Sierpc will remember it as a turbulent period of dreams, experiences, personal hopes for a different life, a life of freedom and happiness in the homeland.

The Sierpc Zionist Organization Committee, 1934

Right to Left
Sitting: Itche David Schnitzler, Mira Leah Visroza (Konskowolski), Ber Charka, Hanna Oberfeld, Wolf Buda
Standing: Hershel Rotenberg (the Groom of Esther Rachel Szampan), Naftali Tcharnotchepka, Reuben Szampan, David Bergson, Yaakov Yosef Grodko

Hashomer Hatzair - Tel Hai 1930

Right to Left
Row 1, Sitting: Batya Gorlitz, Miriam Podskoc, Tula Green
Row 2, Sitting: Tova Lelonek, Fibush Wilk, Baltcha Shapiro, Mindel Neiman, Leib Minchin, Rivkah Plato, Gutkind Mlawa
Standing: Zelig Licht, Devorah Mlawa, Sheina Rivkah Valuka, Chanoch Podskoc (Chanoch Nachshon), Yocheved Gurfinkel, Malkah Tcharnotchepka, Pnina Fish, Yaakov Riezenshtat (From Warsaw. a teacher of Hebrew in the Hashomer Hatzair in Sierpc), Hanna (daughter of the "Shlisharken")

Official Rubber Stamp of the Sierpc Zionist Committee

Hashomer Hatzair, Sierpc, Akhava Group, 20 Tishrei 5680 (20 October 1919)

Right to Left
Row 1, Sitting: Tovah Lelonek, Tovah Horvitz, Baltcha Shapiro
Row 2, Sitting: Devorah Mlawa, Hanna (daughter of the "Shlisharken"), Rivkah Plato
Standing: Sheina Rivkah Valuka, Pnina Fish, Yocheved Gurfinkel, Bajlowicz, Chanoch Podskoc (Chanoch Nachshon)

[Hashomer Hatzair, "Laor" Company, Sierpc, 568? (192?)]

Right to Left
Row 1, Sitting: Esther Podskoc, Wilk, Henyah Lidak (Rypin), Tovah Schwartz
Row 2, Sitting: Gurna, Frieda Mlawa, Aryeh Kempner, Miriam Podskoc (the Company Instructor), Yaakov Hutnik, Leah Plachta
Standing: Gocha Zinaderka, Rivkah Minchin, Eliyahu Diogenes, Yaska Zemelman, Wolf Diogenes (Sweden), Clara Gongola, Rachel Sakowicz

Hanoar Hatzioni "Tel Hai" Battalion, 1930

Right to Left
Row 1, Sitting: Rosa Pukacz, ... Lewinski, Frimet Paperczyk, Hanna Bergson, Mattel Lelonek, Rivkah Finberg, Dina Lanter
Row 2: Sara Dorfman, Pinna Tchorek, Unknown, Malkah Podskoc, Huila Dobroszklanka, Rachel Finberg, Tovah Yeshaievitz
Row 3: Leah Atlas, Sara Rosen, Shoshana Korta, Avraham Bergson, Fela Lanter, Moshe Smolinski, Yeshayahu Korta

Hanoar Hatzioni, Group of Instructors, 1931

Right to Left
Row 1, Sitting: Heine Charka, Fela Lanter, Tziporah Sendrowicz, Yaakov Meir Grodka
Row 2, Sitting: Yitzhak Horvitz, Yosef Korta, Avrahamel Bergson, Gershon Bergson, Zina
Row 3, Sitting: Gananche Neman, Yeshayahu Korta, Naftali Tcharnotchepka, Moshe Smolinski, Zalman Gzhemski
Row 4, Standing: Yaakov Meir Pukacz, Sara Klein, Eliezer Rzeszotka

Hanoar Hatzioni, "Balfouria" Battalion,
Senior Members, For the Aliyah of Moshe Smolinski, 1932

Left to Right
Row 1, Sitting: Yosef Korta, Sara Klein, Moshe Smolinski, Fela Lanter, Yakov Meir Pukatch, Sara Lea (Saratche) Karpa
Row 2: Fishel Dobroszklanka, Avraham Meir Shultz, Tziporah Sendrowicz, Gershon Bergson, Yaakov Meir Grodka, Tovah Sendrowicz
Row 3: Ziskind Rajchholc, Hanna Charka, ... Rozinek, ... Juzelewski, Reuven Szampan, Yosef David Yeshaievitz

From the Life of *Hanoar Hatzioni*

By Moshe Smolinski

It was at the end of the 1920s. The public and Zionist life in the town, which in the past had experienced stormy waves that rose and fell, flowed very slowly, as if it were a slow-streaming brook. It seemed that the town's geographic location, a valley surrounded by hills, had begun to have an influence on the character of its people. Zionist activity went on quietly, without any great upheavals. Echoes of the outside world would pass by without leaving any marks. The youth of the town lived in a world of innocence and faith, receiving inspiration from within, and investing their energy in tools that were created and cultivated by this innocence.

An important chapter in the life of the town must be attributed to the school of Mordechai Hersh Mintz. His Improved *Heder* launched a whole generation of Hebrew speakers, devotees of Hebrew language and culture. These were also the Zionist leaders and activists in town, the spokesmen and advocates in all the public forums, starting with Yeshayahu Frydman of blessed memory, Shmuel Valuka of blessed memory, Zvi Malewanczyk, and many others. When the teacher Mintz left for the United States after the First World War, it left a void which was filled only years later by the *Tarbuth* School.

The students and graduates of the Mintz School were those that cast the organizational mold for all the Zionist activities of the youth of the town. One should remember the youth group *Herzlia*, which existed in the 1920s, an organization that was for most of its existence an independent Sierpcer creation. It was established with almost no counseling, and without any connection to a central national organization. It independently assembled the best of the town's young people and together with the *Biblioteque* [Library] directed exemplary cultural and organizational activities. I would like to mention some of the names that I remember of comrades that worked and stimulated others, and created a Zionist atmosphere among the youth, such as: Shmuel Valuka, Moshe Podskoc, Leibl Horn, and Ber Charka and, may they live a long life, Mordechai Rzeszotka, Latzcha Liebson, and Ephraim Yosef Valuka-Talmi, and many others. This was a glorious time for young people, who acted out of inner conviction and youthful innocence.

Life went on. A cohort born and educated during the First World War grew up, and the atmosphere at home became stifling, almost unbearable. They were detached, without values and with no future, and unable to take root. Then the first buds of individual immigration to Palestine sprouted, without an organizational pioneering framework. Others immigrated to countries beyond the sea. Young people looked for answers for themselves and for others. In 1928, a *ken* [nest] of *Hashomer Hatzair* [The Young Guard] was founded in Sierpc, under the influence of the milieu and prodded by the expansion of the pioneering youth movement. But most of the founders, in their Zionist innocence, could not accept its ideology. They left and founded a *ken* of *Hashomer Haleumi* [The National Guard] and after that *Hanoar Hatzioni* [Zionist Youth], which became the largest young people's organization in town. It included, in various periods, hundreds of young people from all classes, youth that were students and workers, from affluent homes and children of poverty. A pioneering educational framework was established that cultivated Zionist fulfillment, and provided release for the dormant youthful aspirations that were fermenting. The young people stood erect, and they had a Zionist spot which served for many of them as a substitute for home: a place where the main part of life was centered, whose contents were the meeting place and rendezvous at the *ken*, and the singing and dancing from the Land of Israel.

The *ken* was divided into age levels, and within them, battalions and groups with a staff of group leaders and counselors that strived to educate the young and to also increase their own knowledge. I remember the regular meetings of the counselors, with constant arguments about everything in the world, Judaism and Zionism, society and politics, etc. These would be transferred to discussions in the *ken* in general. The youth were ready for any Zionist activity and first and foremost, *Keren Kayemet*, which had a great educational basis; these were the traditional projects of every holiday and celebration, especially the penetration of the "Blue Box" [the small collection box of Keren Kayemet, with a coin slot on top and a blue Star of David on the front] into every home. The ceremony of emptying the box every month was an act of identification by the Jewish youth in the small town with every-day life in the Land of Israel.

The members of the *ken* did not rest on their laurels. They wanted to further their horizons and deepen their knowledge. Therefore they actively participated in the "Summer Colonies." These were organized together with other branches in the area and with the central management of the movement, and they were opportunities for both learning and vacation. In the bosom of nature, the trips and tours freed the hidden forces in the young people, and built character and initiative.

The leaders of the *ken* went beyond their local framework and actively participated in the organization of the movement in the district. They were involved in the neighboring towns, and later in the main leadership in Warsaw. It was a lively and effervescent seed that expected the maximum of everyone. It demanded that the individual compete and constantly advance and not be satisfied with their achievements.

With maturity, the time came for personal fulfillment. The founders of *ken* started to go to training camps and make *aliyah* [immigration to the Land of Israel]. There was a natural changing of the guard. Most of the first cadre went to Palestine. A new generation of counselors arose from the youth, and the chain went on until a cruel hand cut down the tree that had planted roots in Jewish Poland. The house of Israel in Europe was uprooted and destroyed, and with it, the splendor of Jewish youth vanished, its song terminated. Only some embers that were saved from the fire came to us after the tortures of hell, at the end of the Second World War.

I had the opportunity to meet these survivors, when I was an emissary in Germany in 1946-47. Among them were a few from the movement who had become refugees. I asked myself a number of times: should I go to visit our town, where I worked and spent the most beautiful years of my youth, where I left all that was near and dear to me? But I knew there was nowhere for me to go, that no one is waiting for me there. Because what was, is no longer, and never will be. Why should I wander through empty and hostile streets? I will find nothing! Only shadows will accompany me. I will not find the home of my father and mother, and not those delightful children of Israel that I left, with tears in my eyes, with the hope of seeing them again. Not my brother Shlomo, who knocked on the gates of the Land of Israel, and could not get in; not even a grave over which I could shed a tear. I am left with the memories and the echoes of days that have gone, whose sounds will always be with me. The sounds of vibrant young people searching for their way, full of hopes that have vanished, never to return.

May their memory be blessed.

Hehalutz Hamizrachi in Sierpc

By Yosef Appelbaum

With the help of God.

At the start of the Fourth *Aliyah* [immigration to the Land of Israel], when training groups were established all over Poland to prepare pioneers, our town of Sierpc did not hesitate. The organization *Hehalutz Hamizrachi* [The Mizrachi {Religious Zionist} Pioneer] was founded in Sierpc at the initiative of the comrades Gutkind Rozinek, Breine Neiman and Yosef Appelbaum to prepare our members for *aliyah*, physically and spiritually.

We receive a small room rent free from our friend Zvi Crystal. Many young people joined our group. Because of the religious nature of our organization, we couldn't accept everyone who wanted to join. The active members of the group, not including the founders, were Zalman Lenczner, and Wolf Boda, may he live a long life. We arranged twice-weekly sessions for studying the weekly Torah Portion, group singing, and lectures. In addition to local lecturers like the chairman of *Mizrachi* [the religious Zionist party] Reb Ezriel Podskoc, David Szerpherz, etc., we also invited outside lecturers like Rabbi Shmuel Haim Landau and Rabbi Hagar, may they rest in peace. The first practical activity of the organization was a trip to the training farm of *Hehalutz Hamizrachi* in Skoczkowa.

Skoczkowa was a Jewish estate on the road to Raciaz, about an hour from Sierpc with the “small train” (*kolika*). Skoczkowa was the main training farm of *Hehalutz Hamizrachi*, which hosted instructors' training, conferences, and various meetings. A well-known agronomist and agriculture teacher ran it. Instructors would complete a course every three months, and then leave to guide training groups.

This trip made a great impression on everyone, and left its mark on the Sierpc youth, and tens of young people started to join the organization. Crystal's room was too small to accommodate everyone, so we turned to the parents of one of the members, Kalman Kalmanowicz, and rented a large room from him. There we expanded our operations with daily meetings, lessons, lectures, and Zionist activities such as: selling *shekels*, *Keren Kayemet*, *Keren Hayesod*, and in addition, collecting for the *Hehalutz Hamizrachi* fund.

We also founded an agricultural training group that had five male and four female members in the village of Kopyczyńce, at an estate on the road to Rypin that was owned by our townsman Reb Mendel Lenczner, a simple Hasidic Jew who spent most of his time studying Torah. He had six sons and one daughter. Two of his sons made *aliyah* to the Land of Israel. His wife managed a big iron goods store, and some of the sons managed the estate at Kopyczyńce. One of the sons, Zalman, was active in our organization and even joined the group. This was the first training group in our area, and most of its members were able to make *aliyah.*

In addition to the training activity, our members were engaged in *Keren Kayemet,* at the initiative of Rabbi Hagar, may he rest in peace, the representative of *Keren Kayemet.* A non-partisan troop for *Keren Kayemet* was organized in our town with the aid of activists from the Zionist Organization. Members of all the youth organizations in town participated: *Tzeirei Tzion* [Zionist Youth], *Agudat Tzion* [Zionist Society], and *Hehalutz Hamizrachi.* The troop was tasked with emptying the *Keren Kayemet* boxes and collection of money at celebrations, in synagogues, at parties by distributing ribbons and selling stamps.

We once decided upon a day devoted to *Keren Kayemet.* This was before Passover, during the time of the baking of the matzos. As is well known, the baking of matzos in the small towns of Poland was very primitive. The matzos were made by hand and the women flattened the matzos by hand. This work was done by Gentile ladies from the area. We came to an agreement with the baker Jablonski from the small market that on Sunday, when the Gentile women did not come to work, he would not stop the effort. The boys and girls in the troop would do the work, and the wages would go to *Keren Kayemet.* The members also made deliveries, and brought the matzos to Jewish homes. The income from this project was substantial.

The Revisionist Movement in Sierpc

By Z. Appelbaum

The Revisionist Movement penetrated Sierpc relatively late, at a time when most of the youth were already organized in other movements, which had started a few years earlier. The organizers knew there were objective problems in establishing a strong movement in town.

I joined *Beitar* [the Revisionist Zionist youth movement] in Lodz in 1928-29. I examined the possibility of starting a branch of *Beitar* in Sierpc, which was the home of my mother, may she rest in Eden. After some inquiries and talks with friends, we decided to call a formative meeting during the Pentecost holiday in 1931. About ten young people participated in this first meeting, and

Shmuel Algavish was appointed as commander, and Gina Neiman and Chayim Lenczner were selected as members of the headquarters staff.

This founding meeting took place in the *Dolinki*, in the green and pleasant valley, the pride of the town, near the slow-streaming brook, beneath the rays of the late spring sun. A soft breeze caressed the body, but deep in the heart, there burned a desire to act to free the nation that lived without the hope of a better future. The assembled sat in a semi-circle, and the demands of membership in Beitar were explained to them. Most of them knew exactly what was expected of them. They knew that they were joining a group that that was fighting hard for its existence even within the Zionist movement. All of them made a firm decision to join Beitar and dedicate their energies to its flourishing and developing in our town. When we came back to town, our virtuous and innocent Jewish townspeople were already on their way to the evening prayer of the second day of the holiday.

When the Sierpc branch of *Beitar* was founded, there were already two other youth organizations in Sierpc, *Hashomer Hatzair* and *Hashomer Haleumi*, that were significant for most of the town's young people. Their clubhouses were already in existence, and their activities were well organized, while *Beitar* had to start everything from scratch. At first the meetings were held in the house of Gina Neiman, but after a while the movement purchased its own clubhouse, on the Warsaw Street, opposite the large Synagogue, in the house of Schweitzer.

The number of members increased steadily, and with time, there was also a group of senior members, which became a branch of *Brit Hatzahar* [Covenant of the Revisionist Zionists]. Menachem Podskoc was the main activist in this branch. In the final years before the Holocaust, Danziger was the main activist in the movement.

Beitar in Sierpc

By Shmuel Yitzhak Algavish (Krystal)

The newest youth group in Sierpc (in terms of when it was founded) was “Covenant of the Hebrew Youth named for Joseph Trumpledor” [known by its acronym in Hebrew] - *Beitar*. We say the newest, because it was founded in our town in 1929 in the month of *Elul*, 5689, after our town already had other Zionist youth groups.

The year of the founding of *Beitar* in Sierpc was a year that has become deeply etched in Zionist history in general and the Hebrew Yishuv [Jewish settlement in Palestine] in particular. That was the year of Meorot Tarpat [The Incidents of 5689 – the first organized Arab attacks on the Jewish settlement in Palestine].

Beitar in Sierpc did not have an easy path. Its members were all affiliated with Zionist youth organizations, but joined *Beitar.* They saw their way in Zionism and in the nation differently than others. The Zionist organization put obstacles in their way in spite of the fact that almost all the *Beitar* members were active Zionists, active in the Zionist library and also worked for *Keren Kayemet*, the *Tarbuth* School, and the Zionist athletic organization *Maccabee.*

Help for *Beitar* came from an unexpected source. The Association of Craftsmen and Small Tradesmen let *Beitar* use their office, initially without payment. It was on the Jewish Street opposite the town synagogue.

Once *Beitar* had a permanent clubhouse, it expanded its activities. In addition to the activities aimed at its members, *Beitar* had a broad publicity campaign. There would be lectures every Friday night on the topics that were in the news that week, and Jews of all classes and political circles started to come to these lectures. *Beitar* also organized public meetings with the participation of central figures from the movement, and these activities were welcomed and aroused enthusiasm among the public.

Beitar also organized Hebrew lessons at no cost. *Beitar* participated in general Zionist activity in town, and in the years 1932-34 was first, relative to its size, in collections for Keren Kayemet. This activity stopped after the Jewish Agency stopped distributing "certificates" [approvals for visas to Palestine] to *Beitar.*

Beitar continued in this way until the cruel woodcutter came and chopped everything down.

Few managed to make *aliyah* before the destruction of the Holocaust. And few of them, embers saved from the fire, managed to arrive in the state of Israel.

Agudat Yisrael in Sierpc

By A. I. Panfil

Every generation has its preachers; every generation has its leaders, and every generation has its conflicts. The great controversy between Hasidim and *Mitnagdim*, which took place in Russia and Poland and also in our town of Sierpc, was no exception. In our generation, this conflict subsided, but we were witness to a new one, a partisan split.

One could sense the continuation of the historic rift, because the sons of the *Mitnagdim* [Orthodox Jews who opposed the Hasidim] were attracted to Zionism, and the sons of the Hasidim went to the houses of Gur and Alexander and barricaded themselves to fight the war for the fortification of the original Judaism. The Rabi of Gur, of blessed memory, stated that the same tools that the enemy uses to take our children away from us, have to be used by us for defense.

The small *heder* that was in the house of the bookbinder Reb Ziskind Sapirsztajn, where thirty boys studied, or the *heder* of Reb Pinchas the Hunchback, was not enough for all those who had to be defended from the evil spirits in the streets.

Then the *Yesodai HaTorah* [Foundations of the Torah] School was founded in the house of the baker Litvinski, opposite the synagogue. It had large and spacious rooms, full of light and air, neat benches, teachers for every subject, and a principal to run the school. The principal was Reb Eli Meir Schleifer; the sacred subjects were taught by Reb Avraham Ahron Burstein, Reb Chayim Yosef, and others. The first teacher of Hebrew was Yerachmiel Weingarten, the writer for the newspaper *Nash Pszeglond* and son-in-law of Margel, now in America. Later the Hebrew teacher was Asher Watman.

Secular subjects were also taught there, because the school was subject to government supervision. Poland had a compulsory education law, and anyone studying at Y*esodai HaTorah* School was exempted from attending the public school. When the *Tarbuth* School became a serious competitor, educators were brought to *Yesodai HaTorah* who had finished the Teachers' Seminary, and they taught according to the latest pedagogical rules. The two educators were Shnipper and Kimchi. One of the Polish teachers was Turkltaub.

Among the members of the committee that were involved and helped with running the school, materially and spiritually, were Reb Shimon Wafel and Michal Koplowicz.

There was renewed concern about girls in the *Agudat Israel* seminary. It was accepted that the boys should study Torah. But what will the girls do? They were sent to the government schools, and later high school. What could come out of that? The boys that became scholars could not find girls to marry. We know of tragedies where girls from the families of Hasidim did not want to marry boys who were scholars. Then came a woman, Madame Sara Schneider, may she be at peace, and stated that girls must be educated in the spirit of the Torah as well. She founded the first *Beit Yaakov* School and later the Beit Yaakov seminary for female teachers in Cracow.

This message came to our town of Sierpc as well. Madame Sara Schneider visited Sierpc, and there was a women's meeting held at the *Yesodai HaTorah* School under the leadership of Brachah Goldschlak, the Rabbi's daughter. The visitor spoke of the values of *Beit Yaakov*, and a *Beit Yaakov* school for girls was founded in Sierpc.

The female teachers Wolf and Shidlowska were a spiritual influence not only on their pupils, but also on their parents, through a series of lectures they gave every Friday night and students' presentations throughout the year.

The members of the *Beit Yaakov* committee were: Reb Nachum Tatz, Leibl Piotrkowski, Menachem Bojmwol, Moshe Grossman, Mendel Melech Tajtelbaum, and Yitzhak Meir Rusak.

The concern began with the school, but when the children were out of school, it was necessary to organize the youth so that they would continue the ways they were taught at school. Then the organizations *Tzeirei Agudat Israel* [Youth of Agudat Israel] and *Pirchei Agudat Israel* [Cadets of Agudat Israel] were founded for boys; *Banot Agudat Israel* [Daughters of Agudat Israel] and *Beit Yaakov* were founded for girls.

Tzeirei Agudat Israel organized Torah lessons in the *Beit Hamidrash* [House of Torah Study] or in the Hasidic prayer houses, and lectures on Torah and scientific subjects in their clubhouse. The clubhouse was at first in the house of Mordechai Asher Migdal, and later in the house of Yosef Chayim Gutentag, where the members gathered for meetings and lectures. A library was also established that had about 300 books from the Haredi literature for the youth who were interested in it.

At the time when Rabbi Meir Shapiro of Lublin founded the Yeshiva of the Wise Men of Lublin, money was collected in all the towns of Poland for this cause, and collection boxes were distributed to homes. The members of *Tzeirei Agudat Israel* participated in this activity, and the member Yehuda Pukacz was the representative of the Yeshiva of the Wise Men of Lublin. A music club was part of *Tzeirei Agudat Israel* under the leadership of the member Yitzhak Leib Granewicz and there was a dramatic club under the leadership of the member Yisrael Sapirsztajn.

Among the activities of *Tzeirei Agudat Israel* members, as regular patrons of the *Beit Hamidrash*, was book repair, collection of money to fix or buy books for the old *Beit Hamidrash*, and to distribute notes for meals for the poor. There was then an increase in the number of unemployed poor people from all over Poland that came to beg. The members arranged for sleeping quarters for them in the old *Beit Hamidrash* or the Prayer House of the Alexander Hasidim which was in the house of Kalman Lidovarski, and later in *Hachnasat Orchim* [the public guest house]. They also received meals in various homes using the notes that were distributed to them. One of those who hosted these guests was the manager of the old *Beit Hamidrash*, Reb Yaakov Skornik, who achieved *aliyah* to the Land of Israel.

In the year 5690 [1929] *Agudat Israel* started a movement to settle in the Land of Israel. The *Keren Hayishuv* [Settlement Fund] was founded then by *Agudat Israel*. The members of *Tzeirei Agudat Israel* were mobilized for this sacred task. There were all sorts of activities – distributing *Keren Hayishuv* collection boxes, appeals, and fundraisers.

Among the activities was the baking of *matzo shmura* [matzos for ultra-orthodox Jews] on the eve of Passover, for the *Keren Hayishuv*. The members would do the work, sing the songs of praise, and distribute the matzos. During the month of *Elul* and on Yom Kippur eve, the members would stand in the cemetery and collect money for *Keren Hayishuv* from people who came to visit the graves of their ancestors.

When the first training camps of *Agudat Israel* were founded, our members participated in them, and some made *aliyah.* The members Yosef Eli Garbarczik and Alter Kempner were in the first group that left. Later, the members Ephraim Panfil, Yaakov Tcharnotchepka and Yosef Leib Tatz also went.

Members of *Banot Agudat Israel* also participated in the first kibbutz of *Banot Agudat Israel* that was organized by Reb Pinchas Mundari in Mlawa. The members Rachel Tatz and Hannah Lichtenstein made *aliyah.*

Together with the activities for the Land of Israel, the members started learning Hebrew. There were lessons in the *Tzeirei Agudat Israel* clubhouse, and the members conversed in Hebrew.

One of the most active and talented members of *Tzeirei Agudat Israel* was Neta Plonsker. He instructed the members in lessons and lectures. I remember his instructions on the book *Bechinat Olam* [An Examination of the World] by Yedaiah Hapnini, and his lessons on the Song of Songs. He spent all his income on the purchase of books. He was also a writer, and published a number of articles in the journals of the movement. He was also the secretary of *Kupat Gmilat Hasidim* [the Beneficial Fund] that was in the house of A.B. Tcharnotchepka. Our comrade Zev Grappa was also among the outstanding members, and shared his knowledge of the Torah with the other members. One of the members of *Tzeirei Agudat Israel* published a book of poems. This was the comrade Yisrael Sapirsztajn, the bookbinder.

One of the organizational activities of *Tzeirei Agudat Israel* was coordinating an annual meeting of members from all branches in the area in a specific town. At the initiative of our member Ephraim Ostaszewer there was a meeting in Sierpc in the year 5692 [1931] of tens of members from towns in the vicinity. Members of the central executive committee from Warsaw were also there. There was a midday dinner at the house of Yosef Chayim Gutentag, and a mass meeting in the afternoon in the *Stilova* movie house, which was on the New Market Street, attended by the many of the Jews of Sierpc.

At the end of the first cycle of *Hadaf Hayomi* [the tradition of reading and interpreting a specific page of the Talmud each day until the complete Talmud has been read], which is customary all over the world, and especially in Poland, *Agudat Israel* also joined in the festivities. It arranged a mass meeting in the firefighters' movie hall with the participation of the Secretary of *Agudat Israel* in Poland, Reb Zisha Frydman, the Lord Will Avenge his Blood, who spoke of the importance of *Hadaf Hayomi* and the Yeshiva of the Wise Men of Lublin, the grand project of Rabbi Meir Shapiro of Lublin. The meeting was attended by a great many of the Jews of Sierpc. Of the resentment that was expressed by many that the meeting was held in a movie theater, Reb Zisha Frydman replied that in the next world, when there will be a great denunciation of movie houses, where time is spent only on a life of debauchery, they will have credit that a mass meeting was held in a movie house to celebrate the study of Torah.

Agudat Israel in Poland also took an interest in the economic area. One of its activities was to establish banks. Bank *Kopitzki* was founded in Sierpc, in the house of Reb Nahum Tatz.

In the year 5696 [1935], at a time when the number of members in *Tzeirei Agudat Israel* decreased – some of the members got married and moved to other towns, some went to the Land of Israel – the comrade Mordechai Zimmerman, son-in-law of the Shlisharka [the owner of the Jewish Tavern in Sierpc], came to Sierpc from Gustinin. He organized the new generation of *Pirchei Agudat Israel,* who had grown up, into the organization "*Poalei Agudat Israel*" [Workers of Agudat Israel]. The members were Yitzhak Bergson, Avraham and Yaakov Sendrowicz, and others.

At that time, the *Yeshiva Beit Yosef* was founded in Sierpc, under the guidance of two young men from Novodruk. The great spiritual influence, by his regular lessons, was Reb Yehoshua Popowski, the son in law of the Teacher of the Law David Klajnman (a member), of blessed sainted memory.

The Gur way of Hasidim was exemplified in deeds and actions by the member Avraham Liebson. As a regular attendant of the *Beit Hamidrash,* who studied night and day in the Gur schools, he instructed the young members in lessons from the Torah and Hasidism.

The chairman of *Agudat Israel* in Sierpc was Reb Nahum Tatz of Blessed Memory, one of the outstanding people of Sierpc, and the head of the community for many years. He inherited this office from his father, Reb Yosef Leib, a community elder and public official of the old school and was devoted to all types of charity and neglected his own business in the public interest. Reb Nahum Tatz was the central figure in all the branches of *Agudat Israel* in Sierpc. All the activities of *Agudat Israel* were focused on his house.

If there was a *kiddush* of Gur Hasidim, it was at the home of Reb Nahum Tatz. When you walked through the Jewish Street during the holidays, the singing voices came from his house. The comrade Yaakov Sendrowicz, one of the survivors, told me that in the final *Simchat Torah* [the last day of the *Sukkot* holiday], Reb Nahum Tatz took all the wine from his cellars, and distributed it to the Jews of Sierpc, because he felt that the Holocaust was coming, and did not want to leave it to the Germans, may they be damned.

Aguda Youth Organizations and *Beis Yaakov* Schools

by Avraham Moshe Benczkowski

My grandfather Reb Michael was known as an upright, observant Jew and a great scholar. A large portion of the Sierpc Holocaust survivors still remember my grandfather, who had been their rabbi. Students who later became known for their scholarship came forth from him.

Reb Michael also had a great influence on the development of the Agudas Yisroel, Poale Agudas Yisroel, and Pirchei Aguda[1], which played a significant role in Jewish societal life in Sierpc.

As a member of Pirchei Aguda and later of Poale Aguda, I remember well the activity of those organizations. We were involved with religious-cultural work, with gatherings in a friendly atmosphere of camaraderie.

The multi-faceted work of the Beis Yaakov School was a strong expression of that religious-cultural activity. The girls received their religious education in that school. The educators were female teachers who had been sent by the Krakow Beis Yaakov Seminary. Nice girls, cherished, modest daughters, of whom the town was proud, graduated from that school.

Translator's Footnote:

1. Agudas Yisroel is a major organization of the non-Zionist stream of Orthodox Judaism. See http://en.wikipedia.org/wiki/World_Agudath_Israel Poale Agudas Yisroel is a workers branch of Agudas Yisroel, and Pirchei Agudas Yisroel is the children's branch of the movement.

Banot Agudat Israel and the *Beit Yaakov* School

by Hana Tzitrinbaum Lichtensztejn (Beit Hilkia)

The teachers in the public school in Sierpc were Jewish, but the culture that they taught us was foreign and estranged from the spirit of traditional Israel. Of course, we were taught to admire only the historic Polish culture. We did not know that "they made me keeper of the vineyards; but mine own vineyard have I not kept" [Song of Songs, 1, 6]. We can only imagine the results of this kind of education, and what the culture of a generation that was taught in this way would be. It would lead to complete assimilation. A few outstanding individuals stood up to stop this deterioration: the threesome of Leibl Piotrkowski, Nachum Tatz, and Brachah Fleisher the Rabbi's daughter, of blessed memory, and their helpers: the Tajtelbaum and Wafel families, of blessed memory.

The Beit Yaakov School [for girls] was opened in the year 5689 [1928] on Warshawska Street, in the house of Kasazh, with 30 pupils. The foundations for the "Banot Agudat Israel" [Daughters of Agudat Israel] movement were also laid in the two narrow rooms of this half-deserted house. We drew our handfuls of faith and confidence in our difficult path there. Beit Yaakov revealed our true treasures to us and we remained faithful daughters of Israel thanks to the school,. Our love for our resurrected country is a result of this movement that aroused in us a true desire for the land of our fathers.

The first teacher that succeeded in convincing us of this ideal was Ms. Wolfe, of blessed memory. The committee members who unstintingly helped her were the chairman Leibl Piotrkowski, Watman, Rusak, and Wafel, God will avenge their blood, and may he live a long life, Chayim Bojmwol, now in Israel. He influenced many people with his lessons that were full of substance and enthusiasm for our movement. The women's committee consisted of Tatz, Tajtelbaum, Pukacz, and Wafel, God will avenge their blood.

The "Banot Yaakov" society was founded one year after "Beit Yaakov" came into existence. There were 20 members at first, and the teacher Shidlowska was the chairlady. The committee members were Rachel Tatz, Tzirel Granewicz, Chayah Ostrich, and Hana Lichtenstein. "Banot Yaakov" members were able to use the library of "Tzeirei Agudat Israel". The books were interesting, and our members used the opportunity to expand their knowledge. There were lectures from time to time, and Watman, of blessed memory, was outstanding in that his lectures left an indelible impression on us. Bojmwol taught us the Bible. The "Batya" society, with 35 members, was founded during that time. The writer of these lines was their counselor, along with the teacher Burstein, of blessed memory.

Cheder Yesodei Hatorah

by Yosef David Wajsroze

The important educational institution, Cheder Yesodei Hatorah, was a modern religious school in Sierpc with bright rooms and teachers who felt the responsibility for the public.

The founder of Cheder Yesodei Hatorah was Michel Koplowicz. That activist placed much effort and work into the *cheder*, both in finding appropriate teachers as well as in ensuring the existence of the institution, for there were frequent threats that the school might close down. Thanks to the work and efforts of Reb Michel, Nachum Tac, and other Jews who were dedicated to this matter, the *cheder* blossomed and developed.

I recall how Reb Michel, as president of the cheder, organized the first public examination of the students. Rabbis and scholars from Sierpc and the region came and asked them about difficult discussions in the *Gemara* and *Tosafot*. Reb Michel glowed with joy and happiness because his hard work had paid off, and many children received awards from him. I was also among them. I will always remember that moment as the finest moment of my childhood.

A Battle with *Shkotzim*[1]

I will briefly describe here a characteristic event that demonstrates how we, the Jewish youth of Sierpc, did not display any fear when we had to defend all the Jews.

It took place during the First World War. The Polish youth went around proud and cheerful. At that time, they had their own legions in the Austrian Army and, from great joy, wanted to demonstrate their power over us Jewish youth. However, we did not let them do so, to the point were it came to a "war" between us and the *shkotzim*. Of course, the "war" was not with live ammunition but rather with stones. Despite this, the battle was very serious.

The Polish youth fortified themselves on the hill of the pig market in a stable full of stones. We, a group a Jewish youth, set up our fortress in the courtyard of Burstyn's restaurant and also at Yitzchak Grope's. We even prepared a "first aid" that turned out to be very important later on, during the height of the battle, for a few of us did get wounded.

The battle lasted a long time. There were times when we were stronger than them, and we even went to their "fortress" and took two *shkotzim* into captivity.

The war ended like all wars – with a peace treaty. However, the fact that we, a small group of youths, fearlessly conducted a battle with the wild *shkotzim*, made a great impression on the Jews of our city.

Footnotes:

1. A derogatory term for gentiles.

The Library in 1916

By Rivka (Karpa) Arpa

In the year 1916, the library was located in Szmigelski's house on Plocker Street. It occupied several rooms. The largest room served as the reading hall. In the middle of the room stood a long table, upon which lay various periodicals and daily newspapers that were available for everyone to read.

The library was located in the second room. There, one could borrow one or two books for a minimal monthly fee.

Reading sessions of the members were conducted in the library every Saturday. The members dealt with the works of the writers and conducted discussions about the theme. Literary evenings with lavish programs were held several times a year, which consisted of joint skits, declamations, singing, and the like.

We also had our own humorist, Zalman Goldstein. He evoked joy and laughter in his audience with his humorous monologues. Every person who had a bit of talent was able to contribute to the cultural activities of the library.

Dance evenings took place with various forms of entertainment. It was often a masquerade ball with prizes for the most original masks.

The youth were very interested in the existence of the library, which served as a spiritual corner for those who wished to know about cultural life. Therefore, everyone made efforts with their full energy, whether spiritual or financial, to help the library.

The Hebrew School *Tarbuth* in Sierpc

by Yitzhak Dichter

Principal of the School in Sierpc until the Holocaust and Destruction

The Building

The Hebrew school "Tarbuth" ["Culture"] in Sierpc was in a strange and hostile neighborhood, poisoned by hatred of the Jews, on a street without any other Jewish house.

The school was established with much toil and limitless devotion, without the help of the government or any outside support. The building served not only educational needs; all the Zionist activity in town was centered in the school.

The building had two floors. It was taller than all the houses in the neighborhood, and proudly stood in its stately majesty, observing the town of Sierpc. Children thronged to this house in the morning, and adults and youth in the evening. The Jews of Sierpc descended on this corner, on this house. Every Jew helped in building it, each one contributed his share, and all were attracted to it.

The "*Tarbuth*" School Building

Teachers at the "*Tarbuth*" School (the 4th and 6th Were Not Teachers)

Right to Left: Ahron Baumel (Ilan), Hadassah Goldberg (Kindergarten Teacher), Ahron Skoropa (Zhoromin), Ephraim Talmi (Valuka), Sheina Kleinerman, Moshe Podskoc

Rubber Stamps of the "*Tarbuth*" School

The Building Committee of the "*Tarbuth*" School, Sierpc 1933/34

Right to Left
Sitting: Avraham Groda, Yitzhak Klejnman, Yeshayahu Frydman, Yisraelik Smolinski, David Bergson, Shaul Rozenblum (the Principal)
Standing, Row 1: Moshe Balt, Tepper (a Teacher), Zina Bachrach (a Teacher), Nasha Groda, Hanna Atlas, Yaska Cohn (Konitz), Hanna Fleisher (Kindergarten Teacher), M. Handleman (a Teacher), Baruch Atlas
Standing, Row 2: Haza (Zvi) Malewanczyk, Hershel Rotenberg, Shlomo Kutner, Chayim Skorka, Avraham Zhabitsky, Yehuda Visroza

The Women of Sierpc For the School

Sunday. The Poles in the town are celebrating their day of rest, and we are beginning our workweek with joy and commotion. The bell rings, and heralds the first lesson. After 2 or 3 minutes, there is a hush in the whole building. Only the voice of a teacher or pupil can be heard in one of the classrooms. I wander the long corridor; listen breathlessly to the sounds of children studying, and my heart swells with delight at the hallowed efforts taking place in the school. Suddenly, a high note. Female voices reach my ears. I turn my head and I see three mothers hurrying to the school kitchen. They have left home for a few hours to prepare a hot meal for the ten o'clock break for students immersed in their studies. When I saw the children of Kasazh, the fishmonger, and others like them, who perhaps had not eaten anything until ten o'clock, leaving sated and warm, I always murmured a silent blessing. It is very, very hard to reconcile oneself to the thought that these dear women, the gentle wives of Sierpc, had such a horrible fate in store for them.

The End of the Week for Pupils and Adults

Friday we finish with *Kabalat Shabat* [welcoming the Sabbath]. The Sabbath songs escape the walls of the school and drift to the homes of the Jews of Sierpc. The boxes of Keren Kayemet tinkle with the children's contributions. Another song and the children leave the school for the Sabbath.

Sabbath eve. The whole neighborhood is quiet. Only our school is lit and pulsating with activity. Men, women and youth are flocking to it to listen to a lecture by one of the teachers, or a visiting lecturer. The Jews of Sierpc do not allow themselves any rest. After the weekday exertions, they want to learn. The Jews of Sierpc want to shake off the materialism that attached itself to them to them in the six days of doing things. They want to warm themselves in the light of the edifice. The auditorium is completely full. Our teacher Skoropa Aharon, of blessed memory, stands on the stage, his face is radiant and his words are gems. He is lecturing on the period of the destruction of the temple, on the reasons for the destruction, on the partisan quarrels, etc. The audience is completely prepared, completely attentive. Here and there, you see a tear glistening in someone's eye, a fist clenched. This whole audience is now living in its homeland, living the life of the people. As if all of this happened just yesterday. And surely resolving not to repeat the errors of the past.

A different Sabbath eve. The teacher Sheina (Yaffa) Kleinerman stands on the stage. She is discussing the subject of women in the bible and in Zionist literature. She talks about the matriarchs of the nation, about Devorah the prophet, Yael, Judith, and so forth. She speaks of the courage of the women of Israel and their wisdom, and their contribution to the freedom of the nation, and to its existence. The audience is listening with great interest. Sometimes – a literary trial. The culture committee selects a topic, a problem that is the subject of some book that is put on trial. Of course, then the auditorium cannot accommodate all of the spectators, and it is never over before eleven or twelve o'clock at night. Every one may be tired, but no one hurries to leave. Moreover, you feel that this audience will not tire of hearing an analysis of some topic or the chronicles of our people until the light of day.

The "*Tarbuth*" School Kindergarten - The Beginning of the "*Tarbuth*" School

Right to Left: the Kindergarten Teacher - Hana Fleisher, Her Aide - Gocha Zinaderka

The "*Tarbuth*" School - Teachers and Pupils

Right to Left: Yitzhak Klejnman, Menachem Avni (Mendel Shtinhoz), Tepper (a Teacher), Moshe Berman, Nasha Groda, Yeshayahu Frydman, Hanna Atlas, Shaul Rozenblum (School Principal), Yaska Cohn (Konitz), David Bergson, Hana Fleisher (Kindergarten Teacher), Unknown (a Teacher), Gocha (Gitel) Zinaderka (a Kindergarten Aide)

For the Aliyah of Avraham Bergson to Eretz Israel and the Departure of Noach Lesman for America

Right to Left
Row 1, Sitting: Yaakov Meir Pukacz, Gershon Bergson
Row 2, Sitting: Yaffa Yankelewicz (Papierczyk), Ber Charka, Noach Lesman (in America), Avraham Bergson, Fela Bergson
Row 3, Sitting: Yaakov Rabinowicz, Zalman Grodka, Hanna Levin (Oberfeld), Zev Aharonowicz, Libiah Danziger

Stamp of Keren Kayemet Committee in Sierpc

The Holidays of Israel in Sierpc

a. *Tu BeShvat* [15th day of the Month of Shevat]

It is cold outside. Snow covers everything, and the women of Sierpc who are members of "WIZO" [Women's International Zionist Organization] flock to the school to listen to a lecture by the teacher Hana Dichter on the values of the holiday, and on *Tu BeShvat* [Arbor Day] in Our Land.

It was on a Sabbath afternoon. We felt that the teacher was preparing something special, but we did not know what. The teacher came in – and the holiday spirit came with her. We open with a *Tu BeShvat* song, and then with the lecture. Today – the teacher says, is the first day of spring in Our Land, where they do not sit wrapped in furs or in a house that requires heating. There they do not celebrate as we do, at home. There they go outside and plant. They plant on the mountain and on the rocky hillside, and wherever possible. The teacher discussed the status of the tree in the homeland and its influence on the climate. She talked of the difference between desert and a settled country. On the desolation of the country because of the exile of its people, and the *mitzvah* [commandment] of planting trees, and more. In the room – silence and stillness. Apparently, everyone understood the great value of the trees, and why a certain day of the year was designated for planting them, and it was called the New Year of the Trees.

And then Madame Cipris, old but erect, stands up, walks over to the teacher, and says, "Now I shall say the blessing '*Shechechianu*' [the blessing when something new occurs] since I have heard the news of the blooming of our country. When I will prevail and live in our country, I will plant a tree with my own hands, and remember you forever, that you opened my eyes and taught me the importance of the tree to the homeland."

Now comes the surprise. The teacher opens a cabinet, distributes packages of fruit from the Land of Israel, and says, "*Beteavon*" [*bon apetit*]. But no one opens their package – "We will keep this as a memento". The evening arrives. The whole audience of women sits and sings together with the teacher "And when you will come to the land and plant every tree". They do not rush home. They do not want to return to the foreign country. They enjoy sitting here in the atmosphere of the Land of Israel. They feel good.

b. Passover

The joyousness of the holiday is everywhere. However, the Jews of Sierpc are busy preparing the bazaar for Keren Kayemet. Its place, of course, is at the school. As soon as the holiday begins, the school turns into a market. People bring all sorts of exhibits. All the rooms are occupied, each room has its own style. The opening is set for the intermediate days of the holiday. On the eve of the opening, the school is full of people, finishing the arrangements, appointing those responsible for each stall and for other tasks.

At eight o'clock, the teacher Hana Dichter stands on the stage. She opens the bazaar in the name of WIZO, the organizers of the event. She says, "Today the people of Israel celebrate the festival of freedom, the holiday that symbolizes our emancipation from the land of slavery, when we turned to the land of our origin, the Land of Israel. Today, we also turn only to the Land of Israel. This bazaar is dedicated to the redemption of the Land of Israel."

After her speech, the representatives of all the Zionist organizations and their supporters in Sierpc add their greetings. Everyone goes downstairs to open the bazaar, and she greets the chairman of the Zionist Organization, Dov Charka. A moment of anticipation and exaltation. Charka says the "*Shechechianu*" blessing and cuts the ribbon. The public flocks to the stalls. The school is full of visitors over the whole holiday. I looked at those around me, and saw a glow in their eyes. We achieved a great accomplishment, a good deed. Everyone is asking, "How much did this stall or that stall bring in? What kind of income is expected from this market?" Everyone helps, lends a hand, as if to say, "We are here, but our future, and the future of our children – is there."

The School and the Surroundings

a. Help for the Surroundings

The school in Sierpc was not just satisfied with its great accomplishments, and what it did for the town, but it offered its services to the whole area.

One Friday morning, market day in Sierpc, Yeshayahu Frydman, the parents' committee chairman, came to the school. We were dumbfounded to see him at this hour of the morning, and we understood that he had some news for us. He told us that he had received a phone call from the headquarters of Keren Kayemet in Warsaw. A bazaar for Keren Kayemet was going to open on Saturday night in Dobrzyn, a town 40 kilometers from Sierpc,. This will be the first activity of this sort in the town, and it has to succeed. The Keren Kayemet headquarters selected the principal of the school or his wife for this task. One of them must open the bazaar there for the headquarters.

The teacher leaves her work an hour early, in order to get there in time. In the town, they waited impatiently for the representative of headquarters, because everything was ready. On Sunday, the teacher returned full of impressions and told of the enthusiasm that she had sparked in the town, of their gratitude to the school in Sierpc that was ready to free the teacher from her work in order to open the bazaar. A week later, the school parents' committee and the school administration received a thank you letter for the help it provided in opening the bazaar. I can remember to this day that among the things they wrote was "The national spirit that pervaded the opening will stay with the Jews of our town for a long time."

b. Establishment of the Hebrew School in Plotzk

During the summer vacation, we went for a holiday to the forest near Gombin. There we met some Zionists from Plotzk, and after some discussions, I managed to convince them that it was possible to teach and educate in the Hebrew language. (They found this very difficult to believe.) Our proof was that there are Hebrew schools in Sierpc and in other towns. We called a public meeting in the Merchants' Bank of Plotzk. A Plotzk Hebrew School committee and a kindergarten parents' committee were elected. The school was to be established immediately after the vacation. The kindergarten parents signed promissory notes on the spot, and the school became a fact. At first, the "*Tarbuth*" center in Warsaw found it difficult to believe that I had managed to found a kindergarten in Plotzk because as hard as they had tried in the past, they had failed.

They appointed me the inspector of the kindergarten for the first year, and of the preparations for opening the school. I visited the kindergarten in Plotzk twice. The school committee found a beautiful apartment for the first grade, and the kindergarten children took great pride in the fact that they would be the first pupils of the Hebrew School in Plotzk. Regrettably, the war put an end to all our undertakings.

Inside the "*Tarbuth*" School in Sierpc

The school had 300 children in seven classes. All the children in town, with a few exceptions, visited the Hebrew School "*Tarbuth*". The level of education, as I assess it today, was high. Hebrew was the language used for all lessons, except the Polish subjects. There was a library for the pupils. Hebrew books predominated there as well. Once a month, there was a bulletin board newspaper. Students from all grades participated in the newspaper, each grade according to its capability.

A pioneering Zionist atmosphere suffused the school, an atmosphere of complete identification with the Land of Israel. We celebrated the accomplishments of the *Yishuv* [Jewish settlement in Palestine], and grieved for its suffering. Every event in Palestine immediately found its echo in the life of the school, in the lessons, and in the student newspaper.

The spiritual ties of the children to the land of Israel were demonstrated during a visit by the Polish inspector to the school.

During one visit by the inspector, he asked the following question (among other questions) of one of the pupils, "*gdzie mieszkaza*", ("where do you live?") The child answered "*w Polsce*" ("in Poland"). "*A gdzie twoja ojczyzna*?" ("And what is your homeland?") "Palestyna" ("The Land of Israel") the child answered.

The inspector recoiled as if bitten by a snake. He accused us of educating the children in an anti-government manner, and more. We had many problems because of the child's response.

The Keren Kayemet was a cornerstone of nationalist education. The ideal "And the land shall not be sold in perpetuity" [Leviticus 25, 23] found a willing resonance in the hearts of the children. Enthusiasm and larger contributions greeted each new purchase of land in the Land of Israel. We renewed the ancient custom of Rosh Chodesh [the beginning of every Jewish month]. We dedicated that day to the emptying of the boxes of Keren Kayemet. Each class participated with an appropriate declamation, dance, and a story from the life in the Land of Israel. The children would return to their homes happy and excited, and inspire their parents and neighbors with their joy. The happiest class in the school was the one that won the flag of Keren Kayemet for a month.

The School Graduation, and Where Next

The school year is over, and the seventh grade is celebrating its graduation. The joy is great. The tables are set. The mothers are preparing the refreshments. Many guests have arrived for the ceremony. Everyone is in his or her holiday clothes. The children are happy and joyful. Greetings, speeches, songs, declamations, and so forth.

As soon as the formal ceremony was over, one of the parents asked me, "What now, Principal? Where? What do we do with our child? The Polish High School does not accept our children. The nearest Hebrew High School is far away and I cannot afford it. There is no vocational school. What do we do?" And after him, a second and a third came with the same questions. The harsh reality of the diaspora cut off our happiness. Locked doors and impervious ears confront the Hebrew child. I knew, and the parents knew that there is no future for our children in exile. The youth will be redeemed only when the whole nation is redeemed.

Parents' Committee

These people were at the head of the school, and were concerned with it over the years:

Frydman Yeshayahu, of Blessed Memory, Chairman

Shnitzer, of Blessed Memory, Secretary

Bergson David, of Blessed Memory

Gutshtat Moshe, of Blessed Memory

Kleinman Yitzhak, of Blessed Memory

Smolinski Yisrael, of Blessed Memory

Visroza Yaakov Yosef of Blessed Memory

Florman, of Blessed Memory

Licht Abba, of Blessed Memory

Skornik Pesach, of Blessed Memory

*

These people took care of all the needs of the school: the budget, furniture, equipment, heating, cleaning, and more. I have not met people like them, so devoted to a school and Hebrew education, in my whole career. The difficulties that the committee ran into doing its work were immense. It was only the sublime ideal of Hebrew education that motivated them to make the sacrifices and super-human efforts that they did. “A handful cannot satisfy a lion” [Babylonian Talmud, Tractate Berakoth Folio 3, 72], and they could never balance the budget. The building debt was a huge burden to them, but nonetheless they managed.

They cared not only about the material side. The educational-pedagogical part was always their first concern. They were fastidious, and the best of the very best. A teacher who did not meet their standards would not remain for another year. Teachers and principals thought that it was difficult to meet the demands of the Parents' Committee of Sierpc, but it was not so. They had requirements, but they were fair requirements. Their first concern was for the educational and cultural quality of the school.

I bow my head in memory of these dear people. Blessed is the nation that had people like these! Blessed is the nation, whose “ordinary” people could erect and maintain schools by themselves, that could educate generations of pioneers and achievers. Your memory remains with us; you are the unknown heroes. You are the real builders of the fatherland. You are the anonymous ones who laid the foundations for the resurrection of the people and the land, in every town and village and in every remote corner of the diaspora. Their memory will remain blessed in our hearts forever.

WIZO in Sierpc

by Hana Dichter

In Memory of the Dear Women of Sierpc 1937/38

The Activities of the WIZO [Women's International Zionist Organization] in Sierpc

I came to Sierpc in 1937 to work as a teacher in the "Tarbuth" school. It took some time until I grew accustomed to the town and the school. The town was full of grace and charm. The Jews were a third of the population. The Polish language ruled everywhere. The Polish educational institution attracted the Jewish students, and they slowly became distant from their roots.

The parents were concerned because of the difficulties their children faced in the government schools. Also, that their children were not relating to the culture of Israel and the people of Israel. The questions of what do and how to act deprived them of their peace of mind.

During my first days in Sierpc, I made it my goal to get to know the women of Sierpc. I met Yehudit Malowanczyk, who was then head of WIZO in Sierpc. The conversation was short and very gloomy. She told me of the problems she faced. On paper, WIZO had many members. However, it was difficult to gather them in one place and start a significant activity. The only time that most of them were available was on Saturday afternoon, but few came, so that there was a problem in initiating a major project. We searched for a way to fix the problem. I said that we could reach our goal in two ways: a) To reorganize WIZO with a mass meeting; b) To prepare a detailed working strategy.

That Saturday, a general meeting was called on the subject of "The Woman's Contribution to the Revival of Israel". The auditorium was full of young women, mature women, and gray haired women. I spoke to them in Yiddish, and apologized for having to speak in Yiddish in a Hebrew school, but we should aspire to learn and speak only in Hebrew.

I lectured for over an hour on the bravery of the daughters of Israel, that sacrificed their time and energy, and some even their lives for the revitalization of the nation. I saw the exhilaration in their faces, and the joy that came over them. The room was silent when I finished. Then I heard the voice of Hana Frydman, "I am ready to be of service to the nation; show me what to do". All the other members then declared, "We are at your service." We elected a new committee, and I felt that a new spark had been lit in their hearts.

Activities of the Committee

After a week, the committee announced its list of undertakings.

- To organize a Hebrew course in the school in the evening, three times a week, at 8:30 PM. The teacher will be Hana Dichter, and the lessons will be without charge.
- The nutrition committee decided to give 10:00 o'clock meals to needy children. The resources for this will come from a levy of 20 *grush* [pennies] on every family in Sierpc. The collectors will be WIZO members.
- To help in activities of Keren Kayemet [Jewish National Fund] in the town. A bazaar would be held in the school in the intermediate days of Passover.
- The culture committee was tasked with organizing a series of lectures to educate the women and make the challenges of Zionism clear to them:
- There will be a meeting held every Saturday for lectures and news of the Jewish world and the Land of Israel.
- Increase the activities for educating the children in Hebrew institutions.
- To publicize the activities in order to attract all the women of Sierpc to WIZO.
- Every member should learn Hebrew.
- To mark each national holiday with a festive party.
- Expand the publicity campaign for the school, so that all Jewish children will attend.
- To hold a district conference, to implant the idea of redemption in the neighboring towns.

The activities of WIZO started with the beginning of the 1937 school year. More than 50 members participated in the Hebrew courses. In the dark and rainy nights of autumn in Poland, and in the winter's cold and snow, shadows would be moving towards the Hebrew school that was far from the Jewish neighborhood. The members were coming to learn Hebrew. Curious and glowing eyes would gaze at me during the lesson. They would swallow every Hebrew word that they heard. Late in the evening, at 10:30, they were still working diligently at their assignment. The next morning, they would meet refreshed at the market, and decide to purchase their goods in Hebrew.

At the end of the year, the course held a graduation party. The husbands and many other guests were invited. The members recited and spoke in Hebrew, like young girls. There was great joy. Each one felt that from now on, they would know how to bind their children's hearts to the culture of Israel.

The Children's Nutrition

At the beginning of the school year, the WIZO women went out to collect donations of 20 *grush* from each family. There were families that voluntarily increased their donations to 50 grush. The committee purchased the provisions directly from farmers in order to save a few pennies for this important project.

Two members would show up at the school every morning, each according to their turn, to prepare the meal. Everyone performed this task with a feeling of awe. They paid no attention to the cold, to the unsuitable time, but left their houses and children, and their work, and hurried to get there at 8 o'clock to perform their task.

I remember a Monday when Chavah Kopperman, nee Podskoc, stood next to the stovetop. The kitchen was full of suffocating smoke. The coal was no good, but she did not notice. Her face was shining, her eyes were swelling with tears, but she was preparing soup for the children.

At 10 o'clock, the children finished eating. Chavah is happy, and hurries home, because she left two infants at home. I accompanied her from afar, and my lips mouthed a silent prayer: may you prevail and arrive in the homeland to raise your children. However, she did not prevail. She died suddenly, still young. That morning, the children asked that there be no cooking, and to dedicate an hour in her memory. Everyone donated a few pennies to plant a memorial tree in the homeland.

Every member took her turn with the same devotion. However, Hana Frydman, who was in charge of nutrition, was the most devoted and cheerful. Hana was a simple and pleasant woman, kind hearted and always willing to help anyone who was weak and hungry. She was well off, and when her turn came, she would bring all the provisions from her home, and would put the best foods into the pot in order to please the children. I saw her radiant face after she had succeeded in feeding about 100 hungry mouths.

The Funds Committee

a. The activities for Keren Kayemet.

About a month after the Sukkoth holiday, Ms. Rozen invited the Keren Kayemet Committee for a meeting at her clean and tidy home. A bazaar was to be held on the intermediate days of Passover [the days between the first and seventh day of Passover which are considered part of the holiday, but when commerce is permitted]. She divided the work into various categories. On the following day, the WIZO members were already visiting the houses of the Jews of Sierpc to collect materials, and they came back satisfied. Every family responded generously, and Ms. Rozen did everything quietly and unpretentiously. In the last days before the bazaar, she was away from home most of the time, arranging all the stalls and emphasizing anything that could bring in more money for Keren Kayemet.

The atmosphere of the Land of Israel pervaded the bazaar. All the Jews of Sierpc forgot their exile and the distance between them and their country, and lived their life, if only for a brief moment, in Palestine. The enthusiasm and devotion inspired the younger generation that absorbed the ideals, and gave it a path to follow. They would go further than their parents would, until they reached the Promised Land.

I want especially to mention the work of Falcha Cipris. She was the oldest member, with white hair. She always had a look of concentration on her face, displaying energy, activity and willpower. She was not tall, but slender, quick, and wise. She was wholeheartedly devoted to the land of Israel. She left a great light in my heart, which I guarded during all the years of my wandering.

*

It happened on Passover eve, a few days before the opening of the bazaar. I was asked to contact some members that were going to visit houses and collect objects for the raffle. I went to Falcha Cipris. Her exhausted and elderly husband was alone in their store. She was preparing her home for the holiday. I was embarrassed, because as the younger person, I would not dare to ask her to leave her house at a time like this. Nevertheless, I went there. She heard my greeting, turned to me joyfully, and asked me what I needed. I very apologetically made my request that she go to certain houses with Ms. Boda to collect items for the raffle. Her answer was, “Whatever you want, my dear.” She took two baskets, left her house, and said “I don't need a partner; I'll do the job alone.” An hour later, she brought two full baskets to my house. Her flushed face astonished me and I asked, “Why did you carry such a heavy burden up the stairs?” She answered, “Holy works must be carried out to the end,” and hurried home to continue the holiday preparations.

*

The eve of *Tu Beshvat*, [the Jewish holiday that is equivalent to Arbor Day] was on a Saturday. All the WIZO members came to celebrate the spring holiday in the homeland. The culture committee prepared surprise packages of fruit from Palestine. The large room was too small for all the members. I spoke to them about the values of this holiday of the saplings, and on the importance of the tree in a desolate homeland. The committee members distributed the packages. The audience became as happy as little children. They opened the packages with great curiosity and tasted the fruit. But not Ms. Cipris! She came over to me, kissed me, and said very excitedly, “Thank you for this sacred moment that you have created for us. I will not open the package. I will keep it until I will go to the Land of Israel. And if I do not achieve that – it will come with me.”

We were both very excited, and at a loss for words. The tears in our eyes expressed everything. Our comrade Cipris never made it to the place of her heart's desire. Nevertheless, who knows, maybe the executioner did not steal the holy package from the land of her yearnings from her.

The Culture Committee and its Activities

The culture committee performed very important tasks. They arranged lecture series on various topics. These would entrance the listeners and enrich their knowledge. Thanks to their intensive activities, they persuaded many people, and brought women who were becoming assimilated to WIZO.

The WIZO Secretariat

Mindel Kociolek, the wife of Yosef Kociolek, was the secretary of WIZO in Sierpc. I speak of my memories of her, which are very dear to me, with the trembling brought on by something holy. She was an example to us all in her limitless energy, her methodical work, and punctiliousness. She was not just someone who knew how to talk. I will remember her until the day I die, and she is a remembrance of better times that will not return.

That is how they were. Twenty years have passed since I parted from them. I have maintained these dear memories for twenty years, and carried the Holy Ark inside my soul. Let us remember a few more of them.

The teacher Zina Smolinski contributed her talents to the school in Sierpc, where she worked for a number of years as a teacher and educator. She was the daughter of the shochet [ritual slaughterer] from Lithuania, in whose house she acquired her values. She also settled in Sierpc, and her husband was active in the parents committee of the school, even though they did not have children in the school. She was a member of the WIZO cultural committee. She was joyful at every accomplishment of her students, and disappointed by every setback. She was expelled together with the whole Sierpc community on that tragic day of November 8, 1939, and I never saw her again.

Our member Schwartz, nee Podskoc, was in poor health. She was thin and tired, the mother of two sickly children. In spite of this, she was the first to volunteer for every activity.

Her sister, Ms. Nedzwijed, single and lonely, always helped in WIZO activities. She always attended the Hebrew lessons, and studied diligently.

Our comrade Lipka always helped in every activity. I would often meet her, together with her 15-year-old daughter, on their way to the school where they both acquired a nationalist education.

Shifrah Loita was always among the first to volunteer. She was tall and graceful, with a tender and pleasant laugh that displayed all the emotions in her pure heart.

Poza Hodes was effervescent, quick, and active, always ready to help. She studied Hebrew diligently. I remember her pleasing smile when she came to receive her diploma.

School and Cultural Activity, the Zionist Movement

By Tzvi Malewanczyk

Already during my childhood years, I had heard my oldest brother Shlomo discussing that he studied with the teacher Alechnowicz. I did not even know whether the teacher was a Jew or a Christian. I recall only that parents of greater means let their children study "secular subjects" with Alechnowicz.

My brother Shimon already studied with Mordechai Tzvi Mintz, or, Mordechai Hirsch as they called him[1]. He was tall and slender, and very strict with the students. He was born in Sierpc. He was educated, and became an active and good pedagogue. In the school he was a teacher, and in the synagogue, he was a fine *shofar* blower and Torah reader. As one says, he was good to G-d and man. He educated a large portion of the Jewish youth of Sierpc, despite the fact that in those times there were other teachers such as Shmuel Pefer, Chaim Yosef, Moshe Sofer, Shmuel Wilk, Wolf Chazan known as the son-in-law of Kalman Fenster, and others.

Only 12 students studied in Mintz's school. He did not take more. However, the situation had changed when I began to study. The desire and striving for knowledge grew, and the school grew as well. Mordechai Tzvi took on a teacher by the name of Rosenbaum from Plock as an assistant. He was short and chubby. The school premises grew from one small room to two large rooms with a small room for *Gemara* study, where David Noach Silberberg and sometimes also Binem Weismel taught.

It is appropriate to note the form and program of that school, which was different from a *cheder*. The students did not call the teacher *rebbe*, but rather *lerer* [teacher].

Our teacher did not believe in vacations, so we indeed studied year round. We even attended school on the Sabbath when we learned laws from the *Shulchan Aruch* [Code of Jewish Law] and then sang Hebrew songs.

Friday was the only day that we studied only until 2:30 p.m. A half an hour was dedicated to reviewing the weekly Torah portion. One student recited the verses with the cantillation, and all the students responded as a choir in training. They concluded by singing the *haftorah.* It was no surprise that when a student of the school celebrated his Bar Mitzvah, he did not have to be taught the *haftorah.* For whatever *maftir* he was called up for, he would know how to recite the *haftorah* for that week. Mothers and other people would listen to the chanting of our Torah portion review.

Aside from holy studies, Hebrew literature, grammar, etc., secular studies and arithmetic were also taught in our school. Suffice it to say that the students who graduated from the school were able to enter the fourth grade of gymnasium with a brief preparation.

The school was also a location for Zionist preparation. The students maintained a "Hebrew Speakers Club," and their own "Post" in Hebrew. One wrote to the other, and in that way, they became experienced in writing, avoided mistakes, and found their style.

Already during their childhood, the students took part in the collections for the Jewish National Fund (Keren Kayemet), and national celebrations such as Chanukah, Tu Bishvat, Purim, and the like. Therefore, it was not surprising that the later Sierpc Zionist leaders were the former students of Mintz's school.

After the First World War, in 1920, Mordechai Tzvi Mintz immigrated to America. As I have found out, he was active in school leadership there as well.

Dedicated to the Zionist ideal, Hebrew Language and national education – in 1924-1925, with societal initiative, they organized the Tarbut School, and later built a Hebrew People's school with a Prevel School[2], in which 75% of the Jewish children of Sierpc studied. The Tarbut School was well established and was at a high level. The building, which stands to this day, became a Polish school.

The Jewish Library

The Jewish library, which was established thanks to a small group of volunteers and dedicated youth, contributed a great deal to the spiritual development of the youth. I wish to mention here a few names of the first idealistic disseminators of culture: my sister Sara known by the name Salka, Bronka Gorfinkel, Tzesha Lubaszka, and others. I only mention the girls, for at that time they were from other circles, revolutionary oriented by not Zionist. Each of them earned a "salary"[3] and they donated the book prizes that they received for excelling to the library. In this, the first group of books was obtained, which were used by a small group of readers. The book collecting expanded in a larger library, with all kinds of books in a variety of languages.

A *hachshara* group in Sierpc working in the lumber workshop of Mendel Gorfinkel. In the center of the photo: the owner of the warehouse, his wife (Fradel), their daughter (Chana Gitel Lenter), and their son (Simcha).

A *hachshara* group in Sierpc in 1930.
Some of those standing at the edges are Sierpc natives.

The final performance of the play "Azef" performed by the dramatic club of Poale Zion (united with Young Socialists).

Right to left: 1) … 2) Mlawa Gitkind, 3) … Dorfman, 4) …, 5) Wolf Aharonowicz, 6) Yaakov Pukacz, 7) Shlomo Reiczyk, -- the first and fourth were members of the *Hachshara* kibbutz of Sierpc.

The Freiheit Youth Movement in Sierpc, 1933.

The Bund committee from 1932

Right to left
Seated: Avraham Rybak, Leibish Uszer, Chaim Jurkowicz, Shmuel Alba.
Standing: Zalman Cudak, Avraham Hirsch Jurkowicz.

The organizing committee of the tradesmen on the occasion of the aliya of the chairman of the committee Avraham Mlawa in 1934.

הועד של קופת „גמילות־חסדים" בשרפץ, שנת תר״ץ

מימין לשמאל: יושבים: יצחק (איצ'ה) מאיר זילברשטין, נטע פלונסקר (המזכיר), אליהו דב (בר) צ'רנוצ'יפקה, הרב ר' יהושע השיל דוד גולדשלק, ברוך מנדל גוטליבובסקי, יקיר פלטו, מנדל ליפשיץ

עומדים: נחמן איכלר, דוד ברגזון, דוד מנימצ'ובקה, מנדל שטיינהוז (מנחם אבני), משה ברמן

על השולחן — ספר הזהב של הקופה

The committee of the Charitable Fund of Sierpc, 5690 (1930)

Right to left

Seated: Yitzchak (Itche) Meir Silbersztejn, Nota Plonsker (secretary), Eliahu Dov (Ber) Czronczipka, Rabbi Yehoshua Heshel David Goldszlak, Baruch Mendel Gotlibowski, Yakir Flatto, Mendel Lipszicz.

Standing: Nachman Eichler, David Bergzon, David Manimczuwka, Mendel Stejnhauz (Menachem Avni), Moshe Berman.

On the table: The Golden Book of the committee.

Charitable fund of Sierpc: *Gmilus-Chesed.* Stowarzyszenie Dobroczynne.[4])

The first premises that I recall was located on the old market. Sierpc did not yet have any electric lighting at that time. The library was lit with large flashlights. The keepers of order were volunteers. Their tasks included filling the lamps with kerosene, cleaning the tubes, sweeping, going to bring a flask of kerosene from Moshe Horowic, the wholesale merchant in the city at that time.

In 1913, at the time of the 300th anniversary of the Romanov Russian Czarist dynasty, the library was located in the house of Szmigelski on Plocker Street. At that time, all of the Zionist youth were invited to the library. Only a few individuals of the original founders participated. The walls of the reading room were decorated with pictures of Yiddish and Hebrew writers. Well attended reading events took place every Sabbath eve. At the time of the celebration of the Romanov Jubilee, the balcony of our library was illuminated with torches.

In the later years, the first library was given over to the Zionist organization. The Poale Zion and Bund parties created their own libraries. The Herzlia Zionist youth organization, which established its own library, united with the general library for a certain period of time. The library was indeed organized and running at a high level. It no longer ran through volunteers. They no longer had to burn kerosene and light cylinder lanterns, for electricity already existed in Sierpc. A paid librarian was employed.

The *"Agudat Zion Sierpc"* Zionist Organization

The "Agudat Zion Sierpc" Zionist organization was created precisely during the time of the First World War. The majority of its members were indeed graduates from Mordechai Tzvi Mintz's school. Then, at the time of the First World War, the organization was located in the anteroom of Mordechai Tzvi Mintz's school. People came there every evening in order to hear some news. Membership dues had to be paid once a month. The joy was great when they conducted a bit of Zionist work.

Zionist activity was taking place in Sierpc already before the First World War. In 1913, during my childhood years, I went out on Purim to collect for the Jewish National Fund together with my friend Tzvi, or Hershik Wluka as he was known. We were both 13-year-old lads.

We visited Avraham Yitzchak Lipsker the tinsmith. He was asked to give a full "*tzener*" (5 kopecks). After much negotiation, he put down another "*tzener*." My friend wrote a receipt for 10 kopecks. There were houses where in "principle" they would not support the Keren HaKayemet. Later, the number of donors grew. The children had an effect on those parents who thought that the Keren HaKayemet was not sufficiently kosher. The children influenced them, and they indeed began to pay through their sons or daughters who collected for Zionist funds.

The Maccabee Sports Organization

With the blossoming of Agudat Zion, the Maccabee Zionist Sports organization was also founded. Yaakov Bachrach, the son of the former owner of the food warehouse Zelig Bachrach, was its prime organizer. At that time, Yaakov was a young lad who had just returned from Belgium, where he went before the war to live at his aunt's home and to study. We utilized Hebrew commands during our formal ceremonies.

Boys and girls took part in Maccabee at that time. The training place for our sporting exercises was in the Monasz place near the Reitschul that had remained standing from Czarist times, when the 48th Dragon Regiment was stationed in Sierpc. When it was raining, we practiced in the Reitschul itself.

When Poland became independent, the Maccabee lost its building, which turned into a factory for agricultural machinery. After some time, the factory was liquidated and a grain storehouse was set up in the building, belonging to the Jews Binem and Azriel Dobroszklanka, the son of Yakir and Sara.

Maccabee had its own uniform: a velvet hat with a gleaming visor and a blue and white lace band. The uniform was worn at Maccabee practices. We exchanged greetings of "be strong and powerful"[5], while extending the right hand and placing three fingers on the visor.

We went out onto the street in our Maccabee uniforms for the first time on Lag BaOmer of 1916. We marched to the synagogue singing "Raise a banner and flag toward Zion – the flag of the camp of Judah." The blue and white flag that was carried by one of the older members fluttered in the wind.

A year later, in 1917, we made an excursion to the Jewish village of Chamsk that belonged to the Jewish magnate and forestry merchant Labendsz. We traveled with the "Kolejka" that crossed the Nasielsk-Lubicz route. That mini railway was built by the Germans who occupied Poland during the First World War, and connected us with the two large centers of Warsaw and Torún. We rented the railway and wrote our own tickets in Hebrew. We also took over the controls of the train ourselves. All of this led to good cheer. When we returned from the excursion, we marched through the city with our blue and white flag, in two rows, led by our commander. We went along singing *Hatikva*.

With the rise of independent Poland, our members were drafted into the army one by one, and Maccabee was liquidated. After some time, the Zionist organization moved to its own premises on Plocker Street. Mizrachi was headquartered in the new house of Izik Kutna across from Agudat Zion.

The Talmud Torah school was located in the yard of the Zionist organization, in the premises of the former low cost kitchen.

The Zionist Movement

The Zionist movement laid deep roots in our city already before the First World War. Orthodox, well-off householders were also taken by the Zionist idea. I recall a few people from the first Chovevei Zion[6] such as Eliezer Wesselik, a tall Jew with a pale, serious face, slender with wrinkles on his forehead; and Chaim Tanwel, who was short, with a proper belly, a black hat on his head, a fine semi-grey beard, known by the name Uncle Chaim Nachum. His wife, Aunt Rivka was a merchant who ran a haberdashery shop on the Jewish street. Chaim Nachum and his wife were childless. They raised my friend Moshe Belt, who later became the commander of the Maccabee in our city.

At that time, Chaim Nachum visited the land of Israel, but he did not settle there. He brought back a bag of soil from the Holy Land. That dedicated Zionist occupied himself with collecting money for the settlement of the Land of Israel, and also took part in other Zionist campaigns. Efraim Yosel Wluka (Efraim Talmai bears his first name) was also among the Zionist activists of that time.

As everywhere, Zionist activity was small-scale at that time. It began during the years of the First World War. Avraham Fried, currently the chairman of the Organization of Sierpc Natives and Avraham Yerushalmi, a brother-in-law of Eliezer Wesselik, headed the organization. Moshe Cyprys served as the secretary.

In 1918, after the rise of Poland, Moshe was drafted to the army and Fishel Szampan took his place. After some time, Fishel left the position, and I took the position of secretary. At the beginning of 1920, I went to the army, and the office of secretary was given over to Yerachmiel Wajngarten.

Zionist activity in the years 1919-1920 was especially difficult and serious. Anti-Semitism spread. Soldiers of General Haller, who had returned from France, began to beat Jews, cut their beards, and perpetrate other such acts. The Jewish National Committee of Poland was founded at that time under the leadership of the Zionist leader Yitzchak Grynbaum. A political committee, which had the role of defining protocols to counteract the excesses against the Jews, was active in every Zionist organization.

The writer of these lines, Yechiel Moshe Senderowicz (Sidroni – today in Israel), and Yitzchak Zumer worked in the Sierpc committee. We devised a protocol against the wild attacks of the Hallerczyks and also provided a certification from a doctor or a *feldscher* (medic) when a beaten Jew was wounded. Feigenman, a young man from Warsaw and a brother-in-law of Hirsch Krasner, worked as a *feldscher* at that time.

One morning, my mother had just gotten up when the milk carrier Roboto, or Biksel as he was called, a stout Jew, thickly built and also deaf, knocked and entered. Thinking that nobody heard, he shouted and woke up all the people in the house: "Where is your son?"

We were three brothers. My father was no longer alive at that time. My mother asked the milk carrier what he meant. He answered, "Those who are paying for the beard which the Hallerczyks cut off." "You know that the Jew did not allege anything. This is what the *feldscher* quipped after conducting the post mortem examination." To Roboto-Biksel's question about what will be, the *feldscher* responded," Malewanczyk is paying money for the beard."

We sent the protocols to the district office and the police, and sent a copy to the national committee in Warsaw. It is worthwhile to mention that we were once called to the police, and the district officer together with the police commander accused us. In fact, things later changed for the better in a positive way.

At one time, the three of us -- Senderowicz, Zomer, and I --were away in the army. After concluding our military service, we returned to Sierpc one by one. Each of us had our own worries, but we took upon ourselves the yoke of Zionist responsibility. In the meantime, Avraham Yerushalmi made *aliya* to the Land of Israel, and his role of chairman was taken over by Yeshayahu Frajdman. Unfortunately, like many faithful Zionist activists, he did not succeed in settling in Israel.

In the later years, the Zionist organization grew apart. When Yeshayahu Frajdman entered the city council, I became the chairman of Agudat Zion and Moshe Belt became the secretary. The following people were on the committee: Yitzchak Meir Silberberg – currently living in Israel as Yitzchak Simchoni, and Yechiel Moshe Sidroni.

After returning from the army, I made appropriate efforts to organize the work of the Keren Kayemet LeYisrael [Jewish National Fund]. We succeeded in enlisting representatives from all the Zionist parties into the Keren Kayemet Civic Committee, as well as in organizing a youth brigade of the Civic Committee, which carried out the money collection in a regular, diligent and serious manner, and distributed the Keren Kayemet LeYisrael charity boxes to the Jewish homes.

Later, my position was taken by Shmuel Wluka. Active workers included Feivush Lipka, Fishel Szampan, Yeshayahu Frajdman, Meir Cyprys, Tzvi Krystal – today Elgabish, Izik Najman, and others.

Maccabee renewed its activities in 1927-28.

Unfortunately, to our great sorrow, many of the Zionist activists did not succeed in witnessing the realization of their ideal. They were tortured along with the Jews of Sierpc.

Translator's Footnotes

1. Hirsch is the Yiddish form of the Hebrew name Tzvi.
2. I am unsure of the meaning of this term.
3. Probably here meaning a "scholarship."
4. The Polish term on the seal means "Charitable Association."
5. *Chazak Veamatz* – a traditional Hebrew greeting.
6. Lovers of Zion -- a precursor of the Zionist movement.

Beis Midrashes, Hassidic *Shtibels* and Political Organizations

by Menachem Beinwal of Kiryat Ono, Israel

Zionism and Religion

The new *beis midrash* with its patrician worshippers was a Zionist fortress in the city. The central figure of the house of worship was Avraham Wluka, a Torah oriented Jew, intelligent, with deep, wise eyes. He was stubbornly faithful to the so-called *Misnagdic* [non-Hassidic] prayer style.

The *beis midrash* engaged a prayer leader for the *Musaf* service on the High Holy Days. He was an original, folksy personality: Kalman Arpa – a tailor by trade who worked very hard for his livelihood, which did not come easily. However, he was a Jew from "head to toe," with his heart and soul. He poured his entire heart into leading the prayer services as the representative of the congregation. The sweetness of *Vechol Maaminim*, and the devotion of *Haben Yakir Li Efraim*[1] remain etched in my memory.

I wish to mention here a charming personality from that same *beis midrash* related to the long-time *parnas* [administrator] and Zionist activist, Yeshaya Frajdman, an intelligent man, respectable, and serious activist. By his side on Rosh Hashana services stood a fine, young, Hassidic lad, possessing a heavenly charm. In my imagination, I fantasized that he must be Joseph the Righteous... The lad was Yeshaya's nephew, a student of Yeshiva Chachmei Lublin, who came to Sierpc as a guest during the vacation time.

The old *beis midrash* was a house of prayer where everyone found a place and everyone felt good: hand workers, merchants, porters, wagon drivers, butchers, fisherman, wealthy people and poor people – everyone felt at home and Jewishly warm in the old *beis midrash*. Even such Jews and Yehoshua Goldman and Leibel Kramasz felt good there.

Yehoshua Goldman, my former neighbor, was full of expertise and scholarship in the Talmud and rabbinical decisors, chock full of scholarliness and sharpness. More than one rabbi would have loved to be at such a level in learning. He had the sharp head of a genius, an unusual memory, as if the angel of forgetfulness had no power over him.

Leibel Kramasz was a scholarly Jew who lacked livelihood throughout his life. How did this happen to him? His entire essence was invested in an entirely different world: the world of Torah and service of the Creator. Whenever one would enter the old *beis midrash* – ten in the morning or ten at night – one would find Reb Leibele with his *Gemara*.

It seemed that all Sierpc Jews knew Binyamin Sobol well. He was not scholarly and did not possess education. Words of Torah would circulate in his name in town, that would resonate like the "verses" of Tevia the Milkman[2]. Therefore, he was a man with a broken heart – none of the children would believe anything he said.

Despite this, nothing was lacking with him. He conducted large scale commerce, was very wealthy, and best of all, with him, "nobody would die over a penny". He was a philanthropist. He would give with an outstretched hand to whatever cause was brought to his attention. His wife was the same way.

The Gerrer Shtibel

The three-room Gerrer Shtibel played a large role in the religious life of the Jews of Sierpc. The holy place left its mark on everyone who came in contact with it. It was an educational institution in which religiously conscious youth were educated. The tall bookcases extended from floor to ceiling in the Gerrer Shtibel.

The Shtibel housed its own learning institutions, such as Cheder Yesod Hatorah for boys and a Beis Yaakov School for girls, in which even youths whose parents had nothing to do with the Gerrer Shtibel or Agudas Yisroel studied. The Pirchei, Tzeirim, Batya, and Bnos youth groups arose from the students.

The youth had their own premises with a library, replete with modern works of the Orthodox classics. This was not only a Gerrer Shtibel, but also simultaneously an organization that encompassed the Agudas Yisroel Orthodox movement that was represented in all institutions: in the community, the city council, the People's Bank, and the charitable fund.

The Gerrer Shtibel was also a repository of tunes – of melodies of various variants that were created by the Hassidic composers. There were heartwarming prayers, marches, dance hops – all creations were brought by the rabbi for the festivals and High Holy Days. From there, they were worked over by the active musicians, and then carried to all cities and towns where a Hassidic *shtibel* existed. The situation was entirely different with the popular Modzitzer melodies, which were composed by the Modzitzer Rebbe himself.

The *shtibel* had its dedicated activists who treated everyone properly without exception, whether friend or opponent. One of them was Nachum Tac, and activist in whom Torah and fear of Heaven, Hassidism and good character, activism with humility went hand in hand. His door was open wide for everyone. He went through various periods in his life, however there was nothing to hold against him – he was the same Nachum Tac in good times as in difficult times.

Shmuel Zainwil Dorembus, a young man from Plonsk who was Noach Silberberg's brother-in-law, was energetic and had a sense for societal activity. Due to these traits, he was elected on the Aguda list as a *parnas* (administrator) and became the president of the community. He led the community with a high hand. He did not take anyone into account, not even with the party whose representative he was. He always conducted business with his own hand and in accordance with his own opinion. This caused his term of rule to lack resonance. However, with time, he did succeed in bringing the community to a very high level.

Mendel Gorfinkel, the Aguda representative in the city council, was a patient man. At the meetings, he did not talk like a city councilor, but rather like an intercessor.

Yaakov Moshe Tajtelbaum, with his patriarchal countenance, had at one time been a wealthy man and an owner of a large leather enterprise in a large house, as well as a charitable philanthropist. Later, he suffered a downfall.

He suffered his downfall right after purchasing the large house. He had to deal with the tax office every Monday and Thursday[3]. However, he remained the same Yaakov Moshe, for whom people had great respect. He was an ardent Hassid. Even the gentiles did not call him by his family name, but rather "Mr. Hassid." He referred to the lads who had trimmed their beards (without a razor)[4] as "rebels."[5].

The following story characterizes Yaakov Moshe to a certain degree:

The Polish marshal Josef Pilsudski died in 1935. The government proclaimed a month of mourning. All government officials wore black armbands, and the red and white flag on every house was covered in black. That same decoration was not missing from the small wooden house where Yaakov Moshe lived. A flag was hanging to which he affixed a... *gartel*[6], which was no longer black but rather green from age.

The thick Hassidic *gartel* on the Polish national flag was the black emblem of mourning, and indeed remained in place for an entire month.

His son Mendel Melech had a weakness for serving as *gabbai* (he indeed served as the *gabbai* of the *shtibel*) and for the "*breitel*"[7]. He was able to sing nicely and all of his children were musically inclined and very successful.

Zalman Frajdman, the *shofar* blower of the *shtibel*, was a scholarly Jew who spent all his days studying and composing essays. In the introduction to his book *Ramzai Shlomo* [Hints of Shlomo], he expresses a special love for his wife Gittel, who took care of earning the livelihood, thanks to which he had the possibility of being involved in spiritual pursuits.

Binyamin Sochaczewski was a weeper. He would wail and weep during the services on the High Holidays. A broken skull, skin and bones, he would bang his fist against his chest and shout out and call out with a lament: *Ashamnu! Bagadnu! Gazalnu! Al Chet! VeAl Chet!*[8]. On my, what must that Binyamin have perpetrated, what type of bizarre deeds, such that he had to beg for a response from G-d?

Unfortunately, he had what to complain about. He did not have more than one child – Chaim Shamsha. He was handicapped, a freak [15], sickly, weak in intelligence and height. He was already thirty years old, but he had the emotional level of a seven year old child. On Simchat Torah, Chaim Shamsha went along with the six and seven year old children. On Yom Kippur, the freak[9] had to fast from before *Kol Nidre* until the following night. At 9:00 a.m., he already started to faint from the fast. He continued on fainting and fasting until night. He did not listen to his father who said that he should be taken home and given something to eat.

Chaim Shamsha stood before a military commission, which immediately dismissed him. Reb Binyamin joyously ran to the *shtibel* and told the Hassidim about what had happened: "My Chaim Shamsha stood before the Priziv today and was freed with G-d's help."

Yeshaya Papowski was a young man who served the city by answering questions about *kashruth*, about spoons and pots[10], as well as more difficult questions. He gave classes to boys of different groups at different times during the day, from morning until night, without interrupting at all except for the angry complaints of his own wife.

Michel Koplowicz was called "the Marok" [killjoy] because he never laughed and rarely spoke. He was, however, a wise Jew. When one came upon difficult times and could not decide what to do next in life, one would go to consult with "the Marok."

Nobody of the younger generation, as one called the youth in the *shtibel*, survived. I wish to mention here one young man who did not excel at anything in particular. His name was Shlomo Mordechai Kleczewski, and he was an ordinary lad. Simchat Torah was his greatest day. His excitement was indescribable. He held the entire *shtibel*, young and old, in suspense. His ecstasy reached an unusually high level. On the day of Simchat Torah, everyone heeded him and obeyed his orders so that they would not receive a blow...

The Aleksander Shtibel

The pillar of that *shtibel* was the activist Moshe Lidzworski, and the house of prayer was indeed located in his home. The *shtibel* was a place for all believers: Hassidim and half Hassidim, Torah scholars and half Torah scholars, Agudists and Mizrachists. It was also a place for those who were angry, who escaped from the Gerrer Shtibel, or who were asked to leave due to the "progressiveness" of their wives.

Among the worshippers of the Aleksander Shtibel, there were those who sent their children to Cheder Yeshod Hatorah, as well as those who sent their children to the Tarbut School, and also some who sent their children to the Polish Gymnasium.

Aguda activists such as Simcha Szulc and Eliahu Meir Szlajfer also worshipped in the *shtibel*. Despite the diversity of the worshippers, there were never any disputes or conflicts. There was more peace and calm than in the "uniform" Gerrer Shtibel.

The Aleksander Shtibel also served as the premises for various organizations that did not have their own place, such as the small business organization, and others. After various inter-party meetings to decide on common questions, they came to the Aleksander Shtibel.

Political Organizations

The Zionist Organization, which conducted vibrant activity, took first place. The Zionists established their own large house on Stadalek Street. There, the Tarbut School, which employed a staff of male and female teachers, was located. A large number of events took place in that house: meetings, presentations, dances with music, and sport. The youth were divided in all directions – from Tel Chai to Hashomer Hatzair. They were active in organizational life.

Committee of Agudas Yisroel Youth in Sierpc, 5690 / 1930

Right to left

Seated: Chaim Shlomo Licht, Efraim Osczeber, Ben-Zion Kamfner, Yehuda Pukacz.

Standing: Nota Plonsker, Yitzchak Meir Podskoc, Ezra Tac.

Committee of Agudas Yisroel Youth 5692 / 1932

Right to left
Hirsch Asz, Nota Plonsker, Yitzchak Meir Podskoc, Yaakov Grossman, Wolf Grafe, Yisrael Sapirsztejn, Yehuda Pukacz.

Agudas Yisroel Girls

Right to left

First row, sitting: Riva Czarnoczopka, Rivka Sochaczewski, unknown, Mirl Ostreich, Tzirl Grinewicz, Miriam Kramarsz, Chancha Tajtelbaum.

Second row, standing: Sara Plokowski, Rachel Tac, Ruchche Manpil, Gittel Plonsker, unknown (teacher), Sheina Dvora Sapirszejn.

Second row, standing: Hinda Rachelka, Breina Ryczyk, Sara Malka Grinewicz, Liba Czarnobroda, Sara Pasa.

Agudas Yisroel Girls

Right to left

First row sitting: Sara Plokowski, Miriam Kramarsz, Liba Czarnobroda, Feiga Polonsker.

Second row sitting: Sara Pasa, Sziedlowska (teacher), Rachel Tac, Tzirl Grinewicz.

Second row standing: Chana Lichtensztejn, Mirl Ostreich, Sheina Dvora Sapirsztejn, Gitel Plonsker, Rachel Carnoczopka, Hinda Rachelka, Y. Grabarczyk, Breina Ryczyk, Chana Grossman.

Committee members of the People's Bank (Bank Ludowy)

Right to left

Sitting: Avraham Gruda, Shlomo Przenycz, Ziskind Arbajter, Mordechai Lipa Atlas, Shmuel Pasa, Ezra Frankel (all members of the committee).

Standing: Yechezkel Pelka (bank employee), Michael Lipsker (official, bank director, from Lipna), Fela Rotman (official), Gitel Wesselik (cashier), Mala Rozen (official), Hersch Grajna (committee member), Baruch Atlas (committee member).

Haoved [Workers] Organization, Sierpc, 1933

Right to left

Front row, sitting: unknown, Radzanowski, Ezra Frankel, Shmuel Pasa, Yaakov Rabinowicz.

Second row, sitting: Yaakov (Jukob) Perl, Meri Zwirak, Baruch Lalunk, Tovia Pasa, Kasasz, unknown, Shmuel Leib Grodzanowski. Standing: Zamelman, unknown, Wolf (Zeev) Aharonowicz, Shlomo Reiczyk, Yoska (Yosef) Szikem, Yaakov Meir Pucacz. Yosef Manjenczowka.

Agudas Yisroel Youth committee in Sierpc, 5693 / 1933

Right to left
Wolf Wysroza, Ben-Zion Pukacz, Yitzchak Jesajawicz, Yehoshua Tajtelbaum, Hirsch Asz.

Group of members of Agudas Yisroel Youth

Right to left

Sitting: Yehoshua Tajtelbaum, Elia Moshe Czarnobroda, Yehuda Pukacz, Efram Manpil.

Sitting: Hirsch Asz, Yisrael David Burnszten, Shmuel Rajngewirc, Leib Grossman, Yehoshua Ostszewer, Yosef Leib Tac.

*

Leib Oszer was the head of the Bund. He was the representative of the Bund members. First and foremost, he was their representative. The Bundist councilor did not always stand with the Jewish circle in the city council, but rather with the P.P.S. Comrade Oszer was also the representative of the Bund in the bank. The Bundist had a fine premises in Loszinski's house. There, the member Leib Oszer conducted a "Welcoming of the Sabbath" every Friday night with a chapter from Peretz or Shefner's feuillitons from the *Folks Zeitung.*

*

The left leaning Poale Zion had is own idealistic activists, such as Itche Bunim Rozenerg, the son of the *shamash* of the New *Beis Midrash*; and Moshe Gotstat. The two leaders of Poale Zion were good speakers and shining polemicists. They used a sharp logic to clarify the complicated Poale Zion problems. They dealt with the Jewish societal organizations.

Assistance Committee

The Assistance Committee obtained income from the Sierpc natives in America, who sent large sums of money to help those in need. From the beginning of its activity, the Assistance Committee dealt only with philanthropy. Later, it moved over to rehabilitation activity via the issuing of loans for constructive purposes. The Assistance Committee invested more than 3,000 zloty in the Charitable Fund. Interest free loans were issued from those funds upon the recommendation of the committee.

Poor Jews who had no credit at all and who could not get appropriate guarantors were able to borrow specific sums upon the recommendation of the Assistance Committee, with the committee accepting responsibility. There was a cooperative partnership between the Assistance Committee and the Charitable Fund.

Handworkers' Unions

The handworkers were part of two organizations: A Bundist which was led by Leib Oszer and Avraham Hirsch Jurkewicz (Jurkewicz lives in Brazil); and a Zionist handworkers' union led by Avraham Mlawe. When he made *aliya* to the Land of Israel in 1934, the leadership was given over to Hirsch Grajna from the tailors section and Ezra Frenkel from the shoemakers section.

Small Business Organization

Its founder and leader for many years was Hershel Koplowicz. He bore the yoke of all the Jewish small businessmen in Sierpc. Anyone who had difficulty with the struggle for existence would come to Hershel Koplowicz.

He was tireless in opposing decrees against the Jewish small businessmen. If nobody could come, he would come. If nobody was able to open he door, he would push. If he could not get in through the door, he would go through the window... And if it did not succeed the first time, then by the second time he would able to hammer out various leniencies for his small businessmen or protest against a decree that could ruin their existence.

Hershel Koplowicz was always prepared to do favors for people. He would not only do favors for those people who supported him, but also for those who persecuted and denigrated him. There was no bureaucracy with him. People did not come to him with a bowed head. Everyone came to him boldly and even brazenly. People would even get him out of bed, and he would go if it was for the good of the public.

Original Sierpc Personalities

A Jew would sit in the new market near the butcher shop and sell a bit of green fabric. He wore a cloth robe summer and winter. In the summer, he wore it over his shirt, and in the winter, over a thick velvet coat. His name was Mota Pukacz. He was called the Blind Mota since he only had one eye. That impoverished cloth dealer had a warm Jewish heart. He was always concerned with other people's problems. He could not help with his own means, for he himself was poor. His foot was injured, but he would run in the rain, mud, snow or cold, through floors and steps -- and he was no longer a young man – in order to collect a few zlotys for himself, which he indeed needed.

Mota saw more with his one eye than others would with two. If he saw a child from a poor home going to school with torn shoes, and it was raining outside, Mota would run to find the child some shoes. If he saw a poor woman who had just given birth who needed something for her heart, he would make sure that the poor woman had what she needed.

*

David Bergzon was a joker. He knew how to laugh about anything, including himself. One could often find him near the benzene station in the market with a group of jokers engaged in their "work." They were not jealous of him, and when the "bit of work" was ready, the group would break out in hearty laughter.

*

Avraham Puter was a unique Sierpc personality. He did not have any special livelihood, and he never even dipped his hand in cold water in order to earn something. He would come to weddings uninvited, dressed in a large velvet hat, as he engaged in jesting and recited verses. He would sing along with *Mi Sheberach* prayers[11] that the cantor recited at circumcisions. If he did not have enough work from both "trades" he would collect donations.

He had a wife and children. His daughter was already a grown girl. She had the ability to earn money, but he would not let her go to work. He believed that it is a father's job to concern himself with livelihood.

Weekdays in the Town of Sierpc

In Sierpc, every day had its own manner of life. On Monday morning, there was a clamor and racket in town. Carriages hitched to horses arrived at the train with passengers who provided merchandise to the stores and merchants who were going to make purchases. Market travelers packed their merchandise on the racks of the wagons to travel to Zawidz.

Tuesday morning was the market day "*targ*" in town. Textile merchandise, haberdashery, boots, stockings and coats were placed on the racks of the wagons. Everyone was rushing, and nobody had time. There runs Leizer Pianka laden with boots. The fish sellers filled the barrels with herring. The purchasers of hens, eggs and butter were moving quickly. Farmers' wagons drove into the market place and stopped. The horses were unhitched, and the market day began.

The market day ended at night. The Jewish merchants and businessmen ran to the bank with their earnings to pay a promissory note with a date from a previous week, and requested that the promissory note that was due that day should be postponed until Friday, the second market day.

Thus did the days pass with the struggle for a difficult livelihood, until the week passed with the help of G-d, and one began to prepare for the holy Sabbath.

It was Friday afternoon. The aroma of cooked fish emanated from the Jewish houses. The older children carried the *cholent*[12] pots to the bakery. The men hastened to the *mikva* [ritual bath]. There was only a half an hour until candle lighting. Along the way, people stopped in the bank and made an accounting of the promissory note that had already been due three days earlier. They promised that they would pay the rest on Sunday at the time of the opening of the bank. At the end of the Sabbath, a farmer would bring a debt payment to the house.

After finishing with the *mikva* and, to differentiate[13], with the bank, the beloved Holy Sabbath would arrive along with the setting of the sun. The Sabbath candles which Jewish wives and mothers lit with such exalted feeling would already be twinkling through the windows. One would forget the difficulties in toiling for a living from the entire week.

Translator's Footnotes

1. Various segments of the High Holy Day services.
2. The Tevya of Fiddler on the Roof, who would frequently misquote or invent Biblical verses.
3. An expression meaning "frequently."
4. Cutting a beard with a razor is forbidden by the Torah, whereas trimming a beard, even closely, is not forbidden – but would be frowned upon in Hassidic circles. Note, in the modern era, shaving with an electric razor with a stationary button cutting head would not fall under the Torah prohibition.
5. There is a play on words here in the Hebrew with "shaving the chin."
6. A black belt wound around the waist during prayer, primarily used by Hassidim.
7. A colorful word, literally meaning "the piece of wood", referring to the prayer leader's podium. The term "loving the *breitel*" refers to someone who enjoys the role of conducting services.
8. Words from the Yom Kippur confessional, indeed accompanied by beating one's breast – although it seems that this man did such in an exaggerated fashion.
9. The terms used here are very old-fashioned and unacceptable in modern parlance – a cripple, a freak… I transferred the second term literally, but modernized the first term.
10. About kashruth mix ups of cutlery and dishes.
11. Prayers of blessing for the wellbeing of the baby and the mother.
12. Since cooking is forbidden on the Sabbath, a stew (called *cholent*) would be prepared for the Sabbath day meal. In order to avoid leaving the fire burning for the entire Sabbath, people would bring their *cholent* pots to the bakery to leave them heating all night until after services in the morning.
13. An interjection used when switching topic from the sacred to the mundane.

The Sierpc Handworkers Union in the Law of the Guilds

by Avraham Ben-David (Mlawa)

The law of the guilds, which was formulated during the Polish regime, stated that the right to engage in a trade would only be granted to those who completed a trade school. After three years of work as an associate and taking a master craftsman examination, the graduates of the trade school could receive a tradesman's card that gave the rights to conduct an independent workshop and hire employees. The entire procedure of going through the associate period, taking the master craftsman examination, and obtaining tradesmen's cards was given over to the Polish guilds, which were Jew-free and anti-Semitic.

That law with its penalties was directed against Jewish tradesmen who had no members in the Polish Catholic handworkers' guilds, and were not allowed in.

The examinations were also a difficult burden for Jews. Knowledge of Polish was a condition for taking the exams – and it was true that some of the older Jewish tradesmen did know Polish. The Jewish deputies of the Polish Sejm along with the Jewish handworkers' organizations conducted a fierce struggle against the anti-Semitic guild law. The struggle resulted in partial success. The rights of the Jewish handworkers' organization were recognized along with the Polish guilds in the trade examinations, and the Jewish handworkers' organizations were given the rights to issue tradesmen's cards independently. The Sierpc handworkers' organization also took part in this activity.

The first Jewish handworkers' organization was organized in Sierpc in 1916. The founders and future activists of the handworkers' union were Avraham Mlawa – chairman, Menachem Szapira, Mendel Lis, Baruch Atlas, Hirsch Grijna, Hutnyk, Shmuel Pasa, Yossel Pukacz, Ziskind Arbeiter and Itche Meir Lelonek.

The union proclaimed itself as a guild and thereby obtained the rights to issue tradesmen's cards and to send their representations to all the national institutions: the "*Izba Skarbowa*" [Treasury House], the city council committees, the leadership of the social security, etc. The handworkers' union represented the interests of Jewish tradesmen in all these institutions.

The Sierpc handworkers' union was Zionistically oriented and had its representatives in the civic Zionist committee. The tradesmen participated in the building of the Jewish-Polish People's School and later of the Tarbut School.

Once upon a time

My Town, Sierpc (Sheps)
By I.M. Sidroni

In this chapter of our memoirs, we will try to take a tour of our town, Sierpc, through its streets and alleyways. In this brief survey, we will recall and examine the people and places that we meet on our route, with stories of lives and happenings that that have remained in our memory. We hope that you receive these memories with understanding and forgiveness.

In this chapter, I also recall memories that are not my own, memories of events that happened before I "came" to Sierpc, and also after I left. Some of these memories I have taken from stories I heard.

1. A General Description

Sierpc – surrounded by mountains. Our pleasant and friendly town, Sierpc, nestled in the valley. There were hills everywhere around it. An approach from any direction – whether from Plocki [Plotzki] Street, from the cities of Bielsk (Balsk, 24 kilometers away) and Golub-Dobrzyn on the Drweca (Dobrin, 35 kilometers); or from the New Market, the direction to the cities of Lipno (37 kilometers) and Rypin (30 kilometers); or from the "Wloclavian" direction, from the cities of Biezun (Bazyun, 21 kilometers) .and Drobin (Drobnin, 26 kilometers) – was always a descent from the highlands down to the valley. Our Polish neighbors populated the hills that were at the edges of the town. The valley that was the center of town – the market and the streets around it – was almost completely Jewish. The Jews of Sierpc automatically affirmed the Psalm "Out of the depths have I called Thee, O Lord..."

* * *

There were a few garden spots in the vicinity, which were the joy of all the young people. Especially well known for natural beauty and charm was Dolinki ("The Valleys"). This was a beautiful place, peaceful and enchanting to all its visitors.

* * *

The Sierpianitza River (which was called the Zhika, from the Polish zhaka for river) brought freshness and charm to the town. The river cut through the town, and on its banks – but not in the town center – there was a cheerful and eye–filling vista of greenery and trees. The source of the river was in the Plock

District, east of Bielsk (Balsk). From there to the Sierpc District, and then – between the villages of Studzianitz and Vimishliny – flowing into the Skraba River, and into the Visla. The length of the Sierpianitza was over 42 kilometers.[1]

At the end of winter, when the snow melted, the river would rise. Then the Sierpc elders would remember the great flood of 1888. Our fellow townsman, S.I. Lanter, describes the great flood in this book. However, this author remembers a minor flood, in 1907 or 1908. There was a cold winter, and a lot of snow. At the end of the winter, around Passover, the weather suddenly turned warm, and all the snow started melting very quickly. The river rose by the hour, and flowed into the yards alongside it. Some of the houses that were near the river, like those of Rabbi David Klinman (Haber) and of Beria Oberfeld, were evacuated. The waters flowed mightily and quickly. They raged and clamored and swept large pieces of ice with them. A live cow was sighted floating on some wooden boards. A Polish girl was engulfed by the treacherous waves and drowned. Groups of Gentiles stood on the bridges throughout the day and night and broke up any chunks of ice that came near the bridges with long wooden poles, or they diverted them so they would pass between the columns that supported the bridges and not damage them. The high waters lasted for a few days.

There were four bridges over the Sierpianitza River, and they linked the two parts of the town. The bridge with the greatest traffic was the bridge on the Jewish Street. A second bridge was on Felka's property. (A rich German, who owned land and houses and a brewery.) This was a private bridge, and was called Felka's Bridge. A third bridge was at the end of Fara Street, behind the church. (These last two bridges carried very little traffic.) The fourth bridge was behind the New Market, on Third of May Street.

Both the young and the grown-ups would bathe in the river, outside of town, usually near the village of Boborova, about a kilometer from town. The children would play on the bank of the river, pulling small fish out of the water or skipping flat pebbles along the water. Women would wash their dishes in the river, and also their little children. On the first day of Rosh Hashana, after the mid-day prayer, the men would go to the river for Tashlich.

* * *

Sierpc received the dew from the heavens and the fat of the land. The surrounding countryside was well known for its fertile fields and the many orchards that provided quantities of tasty and juicy fruits. These orchards, which were owned by Gentiles, were leased to Jews, residents of Sierpc, who stayed there in summer, until the end of the fruit harvest. Then they would bring the fruit to town for sale.

2. The Market

The market was in the center of town. Its official name was The Old Market (*Stary Rynek*), but it was called just The Market, without an adjective (as opposed to the other market, which was called The New Market.) In the mid 1930s, the town council gave new names to the streets and markets, and the market became Pilsudski Place (*Pilsudskiego Plac*), in honor of the Polish leader, Josef Pilsudski.

The market formed a large plaza, with pavement of flat, large stones inlaid with simple, small ones. The houses around the plaza were, as in every town, usually wooden houses, with a few brick houses[2]. Most of the houses were two stories high: on the ground floor – stores, and on the upper floor – living quarters. There were a few small houses that had a sloping roof above the store level and, in the center of the roof, living quarters, a sort of half story. A few houses had cellars that were used for living quarters or as stores. In these houses there were three or four steps to the store level. In the front of the houses there were stairs made of cement. At the time of the First World War, the town council planted trees at the edges of the stairs around the market, and four trees around the pump in the center of the market. Jews did not take kindly to this improvement, and said, "They've turned the market into a village." Because nobody took care of them, the trees did not last long. They wilted and were uprooted, one by one, until none were left. Jews owned most of the stores in the market, as in every town. Just a few stores had Gentile proprietors. The women, both Jewish and Polish, sat on one side of the market – the north side – and sold fruits and vegetables.

* * *

The central building in the market was the Magistrat (Town Hall). This was a two-story building, with a police station on the bottom floor, and on the second floor – the town council offices. A tower with a large town clock was on the roof of the building, and the clock had four faces that displayed the correct time in four directions. The clock would ring every quarter of an hour. The clock would ring the quarter hours in a high tone, and the hour in a low tone. This clock was the recognized authority in its field; it determined the schedule of the town, and everyone would set their clocks by it. If it were to happen that the watch keeper forgot to set it, then either the clock or the watch keeper was sick, and the town was like a flock without a shepherd...

* * *

The clock tower was also the watchtower for the fire brigade, whose station was in the courtyard of the town hall. Their vehicles and equipment were in a large storehouse in the same courtyard, which also was used for parties and theatricals.

The fire brigade was very important to the children, especially those who lived near Town Hall. What child wouldn't be ecstatic when he saw the firemen in the beautiful uniforms, with polished and sparkling copper helmets, when they assembled every Sunday morning for roll call and training? And this is how the roll call proceeded: the call – an ornate blast of the trumpet, which a fireman blew as he passed through the town. The firemen gathered in the town hall courtyard. After the roll call, which took place in the courtyard, the fireman walked out in order, four abreast, with the band, led by Mr. Strigner in the lead, to Plotzki Street, and paraded to the outskirts of town, where they trained. They left at ten o'clock, and returned at twelve. All the children living in the street they passed through and nearby streets were thrilled. And if the truth be told, not only the children, but the adults too, were delighted with the firemen's parade and the band music. Sometimes they would take the fire pumpers, barrels of water, and the rest of their equipment to the market, and practice putting out a fire: put up the ladders, quickly climb them, and hose down the house that was "on fire." And out of the goodness of their hearts, by the way, they might moisten some of the curious Jews who watched their maneuvers.

And how we children rejoiced when a real fire broke out! The firemen were called, in case of a fire, by a trumpet call, a monotonic and sad call. (How sad and frightening it was when it came in the middle of the night...) But it took a long time until someone – of course, it was a Gentile – would find the trumpet (that was kept, in case of emergency, at the police station), and went to summon the firemen, who lived all around town, and especially near the outskirts. Because of this, there were bells in all the streets of the town. The first one who saw a fire would ring the nearest bell, and within a few minutes bells were ringing all over town, and all the firemen were alerted. Then the joy (of the children) started: the firemen came running, hurried and frightened, one in a fireman's helmet without a coat, and another in a fireman's jacket without a helmet, and a third with a fireman's belt with ax attached, and all running to the station in the courtyard of the Magistrat. Some of them swiftly took the fire pumpers and the water carriages from the storehouse, and others stopped the carriages in the market whose owners tried to get away (even though they were paid for every horse that participated in putting out the fire, the horses suffered, and the owners lost out), untied the horses, and ran with them to the station, tied them to the fire carriages, and all quickly galloped to the fire. If the fire was far away, they would open the taps of the water barrels, and they would ride with the water spilling into the street, just to get to the fire as quickly as possible. Most of the fires would break out in the villages, or at the town outskirts, in a hayloft, or a woodpile. There were also firemen who, during the fire, would first make sure that they were wearing neat and polished uniforms, and only then arrive at the station, too late, of course.

Right to left
Sitting: Yaffa Yankelevitch (Paoiratchik), Yosef Meir Forskotch, Hanna Levin (Oberfeld)
Second row, standing: Gutke Frankel, Dvora Shapira, Naftali Tchernotchepka, Shoshana Smolinski (Sandrovitch), Baruch Lalonk
Third row, standing: Marina (Miriam) Gurfinkel, Pesach Gros

And the spectacle of the fire was beautiful...how the children rejoiced – those who came from far away to watch the fire – when they saw the awe inspiring sight, the red flames rising and licking the walls of a building, like tongues of giant animals... There were also adults who enjoyed the spectacle, so that one Sierpc Jew said that he was ready to pay 10 groschen (groschen – the smallest coin) for a fire and a zloty (zloty – 30 groschen) for a flood...

Right to left
Sitting: Beria Plato
Standing: Meir Shtarkshtein, Moshe Fogel

The Town Committee of the Keren Kayemet in Sierpc, 5689 (1929)

Right to left
1st Row: Avraham Bergson, Shmuel Tzina, Yaakov Yosef Grodke
2nd row: Rachel Leah Zheshotka, Kar Charka, Noah Lasman, Hanna Oberfeld
3rd row: Wolf Boda, Israel Olshok (Yizraeli), Levi Tikolski, Smolinski, Naftali Tchernotchepka
Bergson and Grodke are in their "Zionist Youth" uniforms

A few Jews were firemen. These were: the brothers Avraham and Zadok Bluman, Yokev (Yaakov) Vloka, Azriel Waldenberg, Yosef Meir Koda, Shlomo Lubashki, Avraham Malawa, Yeshiayahu Friedman, and one of the band members, whose name was Ezra Frankel. It was not proper for Jews to dabble in such matters...

* * *

The building next to the Magistrat, a two story building, belonged to Modorsky. This building housed Tulatch's pastry shop. The Polish gentry patronized this shop. There was only one Jew among them: Meir Malin. Also some of the Jewish youth patronized Tulatch, played billiards, and enjoyed the food. But they did it on the sly. They would go in through the back and spend their time in the room behind the shop.

* * *

Yaakov Glazer lived on the second floor. Glazer had a record player that was loud and clear, and he would entertain an audience with the music. On Saturday nights he would put the record player on his balcony and play songs, tunes, and cantor's pieces at full volume, which could be heard throughout the market. A crowd would gather downstairs, to listen and enjoy. And of course, they voiced their opinions of the cantorial pieces and the cantors.

* * *

The second building, a one-story house with an apartment on the roof, belonged to Michael Koplovitch. This house contained two novelties. Novelty number 1: Yaakov Yischar (Yakov-Sugar) Greenbaum opened a shop that sold soda, ice cream, chocolates, candies and cakes. (Before that he had a soda water plant in Nachbin's yard in the New Market.) This was the first store of its kind in town. The store was neat and clean, with white walls and furniture, sparkling utensils, bright lights, and of course, the sweets. And not least, the smile and expressive face of the shopkeeper, Mrs. Gitele, attracted a lot of buyers to the store.

Novelty number two: The landlord, Michael Koplovitch, had a haberdashery store in the building. In addition, he put in a machine that made notebooks (the machine would cut the paper and bind the notebooks). This was considered very progressive, a spark of industry. In his shop widow (one of the few shop windows in town) he had the notebooks arranged one on top of the other in a giant spiral, with just their edges showing. This was considered a great novelty, novelty number three, by the children who stopped at the shop window and looked at it for a long time. Michael Koplovitch was a member of the town council for a while, representing Agudat Israel.

* * *

When I came home for a vacation from Polish Army service in December 1921, after an absence of 21 months, I went on Tuesday, market day, for a tour of the market. Instead of the few stalls that were in the market just a few years earlier, there was a sea of stalls, lined up in rows, with all sorts of merchandise: haberdashery, socks, underwear, textiles, etc. I was amazed at the large number of stalls. I spoke to some acquaintances and heard of the poor economic situation, and of the problems of making a living and the decline in opportunities, the cutthroat competition between merchants, the government inspections, and the hard and despised living to be made from a stall (*stragan* in Polish) and the hard life of going to neighboring towns for market days and fairs.

As I kept walking, I was stopped by someone who held out his hand, called my name, and looked very happy to see me. I couldn't remember who he was. He asked again and again, "Don't you know me?" I looked at him and looked again, and didn't recognize him. In front of me stood a grown-up person, with a dark brown beard, dressed in an oversized, shabby cloak, with an old belt and a large winter hat that covered his ears.

I cannot describe how astounded I was that this person was my schoolmate in the *heder* (one-room school), Hershel Koplovitch, who was all of 21 years old but looked at least 42, like an elderly Jew who had undergone much suffering and troubles. But he had already managed to become "settled" with a wife and "earning" a living...Gloomy reflections flooded my thoughts and dispirited me very much. I saw the future of the Jewish youth in the Polish town, and also my future; a poor future, bitter, and cold...

(In later years, Hershel Koplovitch was an important public figure. He had a number of respected positions: chairman of the Small Businessmen's Association, its representative in town and regional committees for assessing taxes, and was elected as a member of the town council and community council on the Association list.)

* * *

A third house, two stories high, belonged to two partners: Avraham Natan Rankel and Michael Smolinski. Avraham Natan Rankel had once been sentenced to death. It was in 1905, the year of the revolution. The revolutionary propaganda was very persuasive, and many of the Jewish youth joined the revolution. At different periods, the rebels (who were called strikers) were very strong, and instilled fear, not only in the Jews of the town (on matters of wages, working hours, working conditions; on strikes, impounding apartments for meetings and lectures, and collecting payments for the revolutionary fund), but also in the town authorities. There was an incident where a certain daring policeman who tended to harass the revolutionaries received a threat from revolutionary headquarters to resign from the force if he wanted to stay alive. And the policeman immediately quit. Therefore, everyone was careful about discussing the revolution, both pro and con.

Once, in a Sabbath conversation in the prayer house on the revolution and revolutionaries, on those "infidels" who were rebelling against the kingdom of the Lord and the kingdom of the Czar, and the catastrophe they would cause, heaven forbid, to all the Jews and especially those of Russia, Avraham Natan Rankel said, "It's a mitzvah to hand these heretics to the authorities so they get what they deserve." The revolutionary command heard of this (it was said that young spies would mix with the adults in the prayer house), and their court passed the death sentence. Only after much pleading was the sentence changed to a large fine.

* * *

We turn right, cross the street, and arrive at the houses of Yaakov Shlakman. Shlakman was considered one of the two richest men in town. (The other was Moshe Goldstein.) He had two brick houses, two stories each, next to each other, that extended over about one-half of one side of the market. In the larger one, which was on the corner of the market and Zhabia (Zhaba) Street, were two government institutions: on the first floor – the liquor store monopoly, and in contrast on the second floor – the courthouse. It was as if there was a connection between the two neighboring establishments: the yearning for the "monopoly" would in the end lead to the courthouse.

* * *

When Poland became independent, Shlakman sold the two houses. A Polish bank cooperative - Bank Spolddzhalechi - bought the corner house, and opened offices on the second floor (in place of the courthouse, which moved to Piastovska Street). Mario Livzhon, whose apartment and large textile store were in the second house, purchased it. Shlakman was a person who kept to himself. He lived far from the public eye and public life, and no one benefited from his wealth. After he sold the houses, he moved to Plock.

* * *

In the house behind Shlakman's houses, which was two stories high and belonged to Simcha Bonem Burstein (who was called "Beinam Esikmacher" [Vinegar Maker,] or "Der Heicher Binam" [Tall Binam] lived Avraham Shlomo Glazer, who had a bookstore, and later a printing shop. This family stood out in the traditional Jewish scene in Sierpc because they were assimilated. Except for the head of the family (who was involved with the community and public life, and was at the synagogue on holidays), all the rest of the family was distant from all aspects of Jewish life: in the religious sense, in the social sense, in the public activities, and in language (they spoke only Polish). In the end, one of the sons, Miazhek, converted. During the First World War, Avraham Shlomo Glazer was elected to the town council.

* * *

My parents lived on the second floor. My father (Eliezer) was an Alexander Hasid. In Sierpc, as in all Polish towns, the Alexander Hasidim were happier and more joyful than other Hasidim. They enjoyed company more than others, and on every holiday and feast day and rest day and sometimes also on ordinary Sabbaths, they would have a kiddush, a joint festive meal with a lot of singing, chanting, and dancing. Not all the worshippers in the Alexander *shtibl* (small prayer house) participated in all the parties and feasts. But there were a group of Hasidim that were naturally gay, and they were the "activists," the dancers who made everyone dance. Among them were: Avraham Shohet (Burgand), Yaakov Meiria (Kolas), Mendel Garlitz (Lifshitz)[3], Yankel David (Bornstein), and the younger men: Yehuda Baruch (Skornik), Moshe Falka, Yankel (Stahl)[4], who were joined by poor Anshel (Maash), who was used by the Hasidim for all sorts of errands and deliveries.

My father participated in all the kiddushim, the parties, and Sabbath eve feasts that the Alexander Hasidim held. Sometimes there would be a party at our place. In spite of the fact that there was only one room, the saying "Sitting jam-packed and dancing with a lot of space" applied.

My mother (Yochevet) would tell a story: once, during Simchat Torah, the Hasidim gathered at our place, drank, and sang. When the wine went to their heads, they started dancing. Avraham Shlomo Glazer's wife (Udel, whose apartment was below ours) yelled that the ceiling was shaking in her apartment and the hanging chandelier was going to fall! The Hasidim were not frightened by her screaming, but changed the character of their dancing a little: they took off their boots and continued to dance in their stockinged feet.

My father was one of the founders and leaders of the Hospitality Society. My mother tells the story: when he came back from army service, he brought with him the pillow he had slept on in the army. Since he had learned from experience the troubles of the wanderers, he decided to found a hospitality society in the town, and said, "This pillow will be the first property of the Society." And so it was.

I remember some of the other leaders, such as Mendel Garlitz, Yehezkel Bashkent, and Yaakov Shimon Rosenfeld. My father and Mendel Garlitz were the officers of the *koleles* in the Alexander *shtibl.* (This was the fund that collected money to support the Old Yishuv, religious Jews who emigrated to Palestine. They were organized in *kolelim* (communities): Polish Community, Galicianer Community, etc.) They would collect the money from Alexander Hasidim every month, and a Jew who would come from the Rebbe twice a year would take it to Alexander, and from there it was sent to Palestine.

* * *

A tailor called Zhabitsky lived in the apartment next to ours. I can remember two incidents that happened to our neighbor in the year of the revolution (1905). Zhabitsky then employed three or four workers. Once, on a winter's evening, two young men came to him and demanded that he let his workers go home, since they had already worked their full eight-hour day. The two young men would not leave until the workers stopped their work and went home.

I remember a second incident, when a lot of people gathered in our neighbor's apartment. One man, who was leaning on the back of a chair, spoke to all the people there. It was, as I understood later, an illegal meeting. Such meetings would take place in various apartments, whose owners would be notified of the meeting shortly before it took place, and without asking their permission. No one ever dared refuse, or notify the police, because the "strikers" (revolutionaries) intimidated the public.

* * *

There was a bakery for challahs and *cholent* in the basement that belonged to Avraham Moshe. There were a few bakeries like this in town that prepared challah and *cholent* for the Sabbath and matzos for Passover. A second bakery like this was (also in the market) in the basement of Pinchas Malave's house, and belonged to "Hanna Bekeren," (Hanna the Baker). A third bakery was on the Jewish Street in the Kamnitza (The large brick house near the New House of Prayer.) This belonged to "Malka di Bekeren" (Malka the Baker), and a fourth (also on the Jewish Street) in the basement of Avraham Valuka's house, and belonged to "Hava di Bekeren" (Hava the Baker). Besides these specialized bakeries, challahs and *cholent* were baked in some of the bread bakeries. The owners of the specialized bakeries were very poor, and led a very hand-to-mouth existence. This house later became the property of Avraham Aharon Burstein and David Noa Zilberberg, the son and son-in-law of Simcha Bonem Burstein.

***

The next house, a two story brick house, belonged to Itchier Klin. He had a unique means of making a living, other than the rent. He would broker between people who lent and borrowed money with interest, take from one and give to the other, and get a cut from both of them. Usually the lender and borrower did not know each other; they knew just the broker, and trusted him.

* * *

The same building also housed the *skaled aptchani* (a medical store, like a drugstore, except that it was permitted to sell only patent medicines) of Volkoviski. The Volkoviski family was assimilated, like no other in Sierpc. Both of them were far from Judaism, in both the religious and national sense. He would visit the synagogue only on Yom Kippur. And when the *gabbai* (synagogue leader) wanted to honor him with a mitzvah, it would be "*Tu tsu she nye movye*" (in Polish "that which you do not say the blessing aloud"), by which he meant raising and re-rolling the Torah scroll.

When Volkoviski's wife was about to give birth, and in labor, she yelled "*O bozhe!*"[5] (in Polish, as she was accustomed). Afterwards, she would yell in Yiddish "*Oy Got!*"[6]. Her neighbors said that apparently her pains had become worse, and she was close to giving birth. And that's what happened.

* * *

Yair Oberfeld's grocery store was in the basement of this house. The town jokesters would say, "*In Sheps ot a fraui geboiren 4 kinder un ain yar*" ("In Sierpc a woman gave birth to four children in the same year.") By this they meant four children and one Yair, since in Sierpc the word for "in" was pronounced like the word for "and", and the word for "year" was pronounced like "Yair."

* * *

The next house, a one story brick building, belonged to Lansky (a Pole). Pese Lubashka's haberdashery store, which was the largest of its kind in town, was in this building. The regular customers were the officers of the Russian battalion that was stationed in town, the Polish gentry, and the landowners that had large holdings outside of town. Mrs. Lubashka was an energetic woman, bold, with a lot of initiative, and she managed the business. (Her husband, Shlomo, was in America.) In spite of all the problems she had with the business, Mrs. Lubashka found the time, strength, and will to participate in charities and good deeds. She would collect money for, and give help to, respectable families that were hard up. She aided the sick and widows and orphans. Among her many customers were Russian and Polish officials, and she would use her influence to help one or another of the needy Jews.

* * *

Because of its location not far from the Russian-German border, Sierpc was used, like other cities adjacent to that boundary, as a base for smuggling people and goods. (The smuggling centers were in neighboring towns that were nearer the border, like Dobrzyn, Rypin, Zuromin, and Zielun. But some people in Sierpc were also active.) People who wanted to emigrate to America (draft dodgers or unemployed) with an exit permit from Russia (entry to America was not limited then) came to one of the border towns and the smugglers would take them into Germany, and from there they would sail to America. Using various scams, the smugglers would take the last pennies from the immigrants, and all their valuables. We used to call these emigrants "*neshumas*" (souls) and the smugglers "transporters of souls." You couldn't cross the border illegally every night. Sometimes there were problems on the Russian side or the German side of the border. The emigrants would wander the streets of the border towns, sometimes for weeks, and they suffered terribly. Sometimes they would be caught, with or without the smugglers, by the border guards. But usually they would be freed by the usual means – "a confidential gift."

* * *

I heard the following story from Zadok Lubashka: During the Russo-Japanese war (1904-1905), a lot of boys of draft age would come to Sierpc and would be smuggled, as usual, into Germany on their way to America. There were also army deserters among them. Once, four army deserters (Jews, of course) were captured by the border patrol, and when their status was determined, the authorities wouldn't free them at any price. The soldiers were brought to Sierpc and they were to be sent, by foot and under guard, to the district authorities in Plock, 42 km away, where they would be court-martialed. Mrs. Lubashka found out about this, and she arranged their rescue. She hired a horse-cart, and thanks to her intervention, the soldiers were sent to Plock in it, but in handcuffs, and with an armed guard. Like all the carts and carriages on their way from Sierpc to Plock, this one stopped in Bielsk (Balsk, a town 24 km from Sierpc), to rest and feed the horses, while the passengers went to the inn to drink some liquor, or tea, and relax. The handcuffed soldiers, with their guard, also went into the inn. Someone started a friendly conversation with the guard, treated him to a drink and good food and raised a toast to the guard. When the guard fell asleep, the soldiers left through the back door, boarded a cart with fresh horses, and disappeared...

* * *

Mrs. Lubashka would come, according to my mother's stories, to all the Sabbath gatherings in the new *beit midrash* (house of prayer), in spite of the fact that she was not religious. She would come in a *sheitl* (wig) and say all the prayers with heart-rending sincerity.

As I said, Shlomo Lubashka was in America. But even when he was in Sierpc (he returned a few years before World War I), he was not very interested in the store. He would stroll through the market, at a leisurely pace, talk to a group of the hangers-on (those whose main interest was market days) who stood beside one of the shops, or sat on the steps of a store, and start, in his slow voice, to spin yarns about the wonders of America, or jokes at the expense of devout Hasidim.

Once he told the following story, "One cold winter Sabbath day, I was walking in Brooklyn (I was unemployed then). A gray bearded Jew stood near one of the houses, wearing a long fur coat and a tall fur hat, his hands wrapped inside his coat sleeves, his right hand in his left sleeve and his left hand in the right sleeve. He was looking around, and when he saw me, he thought I was a Gentile and asked me in broken English if I would be willing to light his stove. I agreed and followed him into his house. Inside, I found everything near the stove that was necessary to light a fire (apparently prepared the previous afternoon). There were thin slivers of wood, chunks of coal, a bottle of kerosene, and matches. I put the wood and coal inside the stove, poured kerosene on them, lit a match, and threw it inside the stove. The Jew who was standing nearby and hadn't said a word till then, extended his hands towards the stove, and made sounds of pleasure, 'Aah, aah.' At this moment I stood up and said to him, "*Shma yisrael*, who would have thought that in the twentieth century in America there are still fools like this." And before the astounded Jew could say a word, I ran to the door and left."

According to a different version, the end of the story was this: when Lubashka finished his task, the Jew gave him a slice of challah. Lubashka took the challah, ran towards the door, and in a loud voice uttered the benediction, "Praise be O Lord, that you did not make me a Gentile," and left.

* * *

I heard the following story from Mr. Zadok Lubashka: At the beginning of World War I, Itchia Margel told his neighbor Shlomo Lubashka that he had found in one of the books a clear clue that this war was the war of Gog and Magog (the Apocalypse) and we would soon see the coming of the Messiah. Apparently the clue was not that clear to Lubashka, and an argument ensued. In the midst of the argument, Lubashka proposed to Itchia that he buy from Itchia, at a low price, his portion in the Next World, and Itchia agreed. He went home, brought a book, and let Lubashka write the bill of sale on the title page, and sign it. Lubashka signed, received compensation, and the transaction was done.

An hour later, Itchia returned and asked Lubashka to cancel the transaction. Because the Mishna says, said Itchia, "All of Israel has a part in the World To Come"; it is forbidden for a Jew to buy another Jew's portion, or for a Jew to sell it. Lubashka, however, stood his ground. He wrote and signed it, and the transaction was binding. But after Itchia's pleading, he agreed to nullify the sale, gave back the money, and had his portion of the Next World returned to him.

* * *

Lubashka returned to America a short time after the end of the First World War, and later his whole family joined him. Mrs. Lubashka continued her good works for the poor and sick in America. Both Lubashkas were especially active in helping the Jews of Sierpc. Both before the Holocaust, when the Jews of Sierpc were still living in their homes, and also after the catastrophe, when they were scattered in refugee camps in various countries, the couple worked hard to send help, in cash and clothing and food packages, to the suffering Jews of Sierpc. They visited the homes of former residents of Sierpc and collected money and clothing, helped pack aid parcels, and took them to the post office to send them to their destinations.

* * *

Usually, every house had a yard. In every yard there was a wooden shack that was divided into small storerooms, one storeroom for each tenant, where they would keep wood and peat for cooking and heating, potatoes, laundry utensils, and utensils of other kinds. In a large yard there might also be a dwelling. The yard would be between the houses. Some houses on this side of the market were exceptions: the houses of Shlakman, Burstein, Klein and Lansky, which stood side by side and were attached to each other. These houses also had yards, but the entrances to them were from a different street, Zhabia (Zhaba) Street. Only the entrance to Lansky's yard was from the market. This yard was common to Lansky's house and the next one, Malawa's house. It also fronted on Zhabia Street, and was used as an alleyway between the market and that street.

* * *

The next house belonged to Avraham (Ben-David) Malawa. Avraham Malawa was an active public figure, and very respected. He spent a lot of his time and energy working to benefit the artisans of the town. Avraham Malawa was one of the founders of the Artisan's Association, and was its chairman. He was also one of the founders of Bank Ludowi (a local bank) and was on its board of directors. He was member of the community ccouncil for 16 years, until he left Sierpc. He was also a member of the town council for 16 years, from the first council that was elected in independent Poland in 1916, until he left Sierpc.

I found two newspaper clippings in my archives that testify to the public activities of Avraham Malawe:

In *Das Yiddishe Folk* (The Jewish People), No. 160 of Av, 5679 (July 1919), there appeared the following item under the heading "Tolerance": "On Sunday, July 20, the speaker from Polaei-Tzion (Zionist Workers), Mr. Yorman, was to visit our town. When the Chairman of Polalei Zion, Mr. Cohen, requested permission for the meeting and speech, the police commissar told him that he could give him a permit for a speech in Polish, but not in Yiddish. The same thing happened to a member of the Artisans' Association, Avraham Malawe, who wanted to present a report from the first convention of the Artisans Association, and was denied permission on the same grounds."

In *Hatzfira* (The Siren) No. 1, of 11 Tevet, 5680 (January 2, 1920) there was a report of The Conference of Jewish City Councilmen in Poland. City councilmen from the Zionists, Mizrachi, and Artists participated in the conference. One hundred thirty representatives of about 600 Jewish city councilmen out of a total of about 1000 came to the conference. The proposal of the chairman of the organizing commission, Mr. Greenbaum, to found the Association of Jewish City Councilman, which would be a branch of the Interim National Commission of Polish Jews, was accepted. The list of the Central Committee included, among others, our friend, Avraham Malawe. (From the source, Malber, Sierpc).

Avraham Malawe defended the common man not only during his lifetime, but also after he died. To prevent the discrimination practiced by the *hevra kadisha* (Jewish burial society) between important and not-so-important people, he founded, in the early 1930's, a second burial society, whose members were all common folk. The chairman of this second burial society was my uncle, Meir Zashutke (who was called "Meir Baruchias," son of Baruchia). The second burial society existed for only a short time.

Avraham Malawe was among the founders of Poale Tzion in Sierpc, and he achieved his youthful ambition. In 1934, he left his business and activities in the diaspora and emigrated (*aliyah*) with his whole family to Eretz Yisrael (Palestine).In Israel, Avraham Malawe was active in the Organization of Sierpc Townspeople, and in the Polish Immigrants Association as a representative of the Irgun. He tried as much as possible to help survivors who came to Eretz Yisrael, by loans from the charity fund of the Irgun or from the funds of the Polish Immigrants Association. He managed, with great difficulty, to transfer money from the Irgun to the fund of the Polish Immigrants Association.

Avraham Malawe was especially active and interested in the preparation of a book memorializing the Sierpc martyrs. He was very active in the book publishing committee. Nothing was too much for him in this endeavor, and he was happy about every additional article and photograph, and anything that brought us closer to our cherished goal.In his final years, Avraham Malawe (Ben-David) was chairman of the Organization of Sierpc Townspeople and the charity fund of the Irgun. He was also chairman of the committee that published the Sierpc Notebook of the Irgun. On the first of Tamuz, 5716 (July 10, 1956) the Organization of Sierpc Townspeople held a gala banquet in honor of Avraham Ben-David on his 70th birthday. Many people from Sierpc came to this banquet, and in speeches full of affection and admiration, they talked about his activities and deeds for the benefit of the Jews of Sierpc. Avraham Malawe died on 7 Heshvon 5717 (October 11, 1956).

* * *

We turn right, cross the street, and we are standing in front of a large, two story house belonging to Elia (Eliyahu) Glazer. In the last decade of the nineteenth century and the first decade of the twentieth century, Elia Glazer was a member of the community council. Hanach Levin later owned the house.

* * *

The *tzhina*[7] of Elia (Eliyahu) Papieroshnik was in the cellar of that house. Elia Papieroshnik's family name was Fatbrot, so why was he called Papieroshnik? Because of his other occupation, selling cigarettes, without excise stamps, that he rolled himself.

* * *

There were four *tzhinas* for selling boiled water in town: 1) the one we just visited. 2) Moshe Natan Klin's: this *tzhina* was in his apartment, in his house on the Jewish Street before the bridge (on the market side). His wife, who was called “Di Hoiche Malka” (Tall Malke) or “Di Moshe Natanze,” (Moshe Natan's wife) was in charge there. 3) The Shlisharken's: This *tzhina* was in the tavern that she had in the Jewish Street, between the old *beit hamidrash* and Horowitz's house. 4) In the *mikveh*. The *tzhina* in the *mikveh* belonged to the *mikveh* caretaker (“the Mikvenik”). Once it was Shmuel Leib and his wife Tona Iszajewicz, and later, Leib Schweitzer.

The sugar cubes (used to pay for the boiled water on Sabbath), after the many reincarnations that they passed through, from the children who brought them there, through the owners of the *tzhina*, finally ended up in certain grocery stores, and from there, to the customers. These same grocery stores had another source of sugar: there were penny- pinchers in town, who instead of giving groschen (the smallest coin) to the poor people who begged at the door, gave them a sugar cube, which was worth only half a groschen. The sugar lumps, which would accumulate in the pockets of the poor, also finally came to the same grocery stores, and from there, to the customers.

* * *

Yakir Plato and Yaakov Moshe Teitlebaum jointly owned the next house. This house was a one story wooden one, and was torn down before the First World War, when a three-story brick house was put up in its place. The landlord, Yakir, was like his name, a dear man. He was a good man, generous, modest, and quiet. The landlady, Pesa, was a shrew. She ruled the house, the cash drawer, the property, and the business.

* * *

The same building housed Isaschar's (who was called "Sugar Bergson") store. Isachar Bergson was a wise Jew, was involved with the community, and was a very pleasant man. He was one of the modern Hasidim, very particular about his appearance, and always looked very neat, with a well-combed beard. Isaschar Bergson prayed in a *shtibl* (which had broken away from the Alexander *shtibl*) that was on Mikveh Street, in Shmuel (called "Shmuel Nagid") Shampan's house. His son, David, was banished from the *shtibl* for the "ultimate sin" – he wore a collar.

* * *

A tailor had his shop in the yard. A large young man worked for him as a laborer, and another boy was an apprentice (the boy was the son of Haim Gunsher, who lived next to the *mikveh*). It was customary in these shops that not only would the owner abuse the apprentice, but so too would the laborers, and they would make fun of him. Once the laborer stuck a needle, with its eye on top, in the apprentice's chair. The boy screamed; a doctor was called who did whatever he could, but he wasn't able to remove the needle. The laborer fled to America, and the boy suffered severe pains. He suffered for two years, and after an operation that was performed by a German Army doctor (during the German occupation in World War I; the incident took place before the war), he died.

* * *

David Kloch lived in a cellar in the same yard. He was a tailor who made simple fur clothes. He would say, "I prefer to make five furs, instead of making one kiddush in a sukkah on a holiday that occurs on the evening after a Sabbath." Some jokesters said that David Kloch's father died on the day of the first snow of that year. And since then, David Kloch observed the day of the first snow of the year as his father's *yahrzeit* (anniversary of his death.)

David Kloch had a nickname. He was called "Kloch mit di Kloitzkes" ("Kloch with Noodles"; apparently he liked noodles). Eventually, this house was sold to Itchia Shwitzer, a Jew from Raciaz, who went to America and came back. (He also bought the Lusmar house on the Jewish Street.)

* * *

The next house belonged to Yosef Haim Gutentag. This was also a one-story house, which was torn down during the First World War, and a three-story brick house was put up in its place.

I heard, from someone who knew Yosef Haim Gutentag's brother, Rabbi Gutentag of Suchatchin (Rabbi Tovyomi, who died in Tel-Aviv), that they were the fruit of the loins of the *Annotations of Yom-Tov* and that the family name Gutentag is a translation of Yom-Tov (Good Day or Holiday).

* * *

In both these houses, that of Plato and that of Gutentag, in their original versions, there were two grocery stores that belonged to two widows. The store in Plato's house belonged to Tchutcha Bilhe (Sara Baila, the sister of Shimshon Mordechai and Yehoshua Veisroze), and the store in Gutentag's house belonged to "Di Loite-Te" (the second wife and widow of Pinchas Loite). These two ladies were "women of valor" and bitter competitors. There was a constant battle between them. They would grab customers from in front of each other's store and draw them into their own store. There were rows and yelling there every day. Curses, juicy insults would pass back and forth and the town of Sierpc (or at least the nighborhood) would sit back and enjoy.

* * *

Loite's grocery store was passed on to her daughter, Shosha, after her death. Shosha was called "Shasha di Levitetas" ("Shosha, Daughter of the Loite-Te"). After her husband died, Shosha married Moshe David Mamalkin (from the province of Lomza). He was also a widower, and was called "Der Litvak."

Moshe David was an Alexander Hasid. During the "sale" of *aliyahs* (the honor of reciting the blessings during the reading of the Torah) on Sabbath and holidays, he would bid up to "*a gulden mit tzvei*" (A zloty and two groschen). He never made a higher bid. Therefore he was called "A Gulden mit Tzvei" (with the Litvak accent).

***

The next house, which had two stories, belonged to Moshe Zhalanovski. Unlike the other houses, the entrance to the yard was in the middle of the house (there were rooms above the entrance), and not at the side. The landlord had a textile store in this house. Later, he gave it to his son-in-law, Yosel Blachman. In the mid 1930's, Yosel Blachman was a member of the town council, representing Agudat Israel. He was also the Sierpc representative of Agudat Israel to the Great Congress of Agudat Israel in Vienna, in 1928. In 1934, he visited Palestine, and in 1935 he went on *aliyah*, together with his family, and settled in Haifa. He died in 5714 (1954).

* * *

Another store in this house was a small haberdashery, which belonged to Haskel (Yehezkel) Bashkes. He was a man with a kind heart and good deeds, who faithfully worked for the good of the community. He was a treasurer of the Welcome Guest Society, the Righteous Lodging Society, and the Sick Call Society. He would also give, for a deposit, various medical implements. Haskel Bashkes was called "Di Katzaftes Aidem" (Father-in-Law of Katzafte). He was called this because of his daughter-in-law, who was called “Di Katzafte,” and she was called this because of her husband, “Der Katzaf.” He was called this because he was a strong Jew, tall and broad, and looked like a *katzaf* (Russian peasant). Der Katzaf was a *melamed* (teacher) of little children, and the Katzafte had a haberdashery stall in the market. Haskel was just her father-in-law, but not his father-in-law.

***

We turn right, cross the street, and now we are standing in front of the large and pretty brick house of Radomski (a Pole). This was a corner house (the market on one side, and the Jewish Street on the other side), and it had – on the market side, the only pharmacy in town, and also a *sklad aptchani* (medicinal storehouse) and both of them belonged to the landlord.

One of the tenants of this house had very strange clothes. In all seasons, spring and autumn, winter and summer, he would wear a warm, long coat, galoshes over his shoes, a thick muffler wrapped around his throat, and carry an umbrella. He was a little touched in the head, but he was a quiet man. It was rumored around town that he had been a very learned man, who knew a number of languages, and spoke English fluently. Because of his constant studying, he lost his mind. The man's name was Zanbal Papiarchik. He lived with his sister, who was also not too rational. They had relatives in the United States who apparently supported Zanbal and his sister.

* * *

The small, low, wooden house of Pinchas Malawe was propped against the big brick house of Radomski, and it looked like a baby holding on to its mother's apron.... Later, Pinchas Malawe put up an apartment on top of the roof of his house, and it was also propped up on Radomski's house. Pinchas Malawe was a relative and protégé of Haim Nahum Tunbol, a scholar and an adherent of Hovev-Zion (predecessor of the Zionist movement); the prot?g? was also a scholar and knew his Bible.

* * *

Pinchas Malawa's shoe store was in this building during the 1890s. There was a tavern that belonged to the Malawe family. Here you could drink a glass of tea or sip a little liquor or a beer and have a simple cake, or stuffed meats, and other good things. Most of the customers at the inn were Jewish soldiers who served in the cavalry battalion stationed in Sierpc. In time, this became a club for the Jewish soldiers. Any soldier who received a few hours leave would come there, eat something, and have a pleasant time in Jewish company (since some of the young men from town would also come to talk with the soldiers). On holidays, when they had leave, the soldiers would make a minyan and pray there. The soldiers once scribed a Torah scroll there. The ceremony marking completion of the Torah scroll was held there, and it was done with great pomp, with the Rabbi and all the town elders in attendance.

The battalion officers were also invited, but because there was so little room, the officers had their party at the house of Mrs. Lubashka, whom they knew because they patronized her store.

I heard the following story from our townsman with the phenomenal memory, Shmuel Itchia Lanter: There were a few Jews among the soldiers of the cavalry battalion stationed in Sierpc. One of them, from the town of Lutzk, was short, thin, and weak and, in addition, a loser. When this "hero" went to serve in the cavalry battalion, it was obvious that he suffered a lot. He couldn't get on the horse or ride it or take care of it. And both the officers and other soldiers tormented and harassed him.

After a while, they exempted him from maneuvers and had him do odd jobs in the battalion. But there, too, he found no respite from his enemies, because he was weak and the work was too hard for him.

Once someone whispered to him that he would quickly be rid of his troubles if he converted to the Orthodox Church. Of course, at first he paid no attention to such talk. However, as his problems increased and his strength decreased and the whispers became stronger, the lad couldn't resist the temptation to "change his skin." In a splendid ceremony at the *tchrkava* (Russian Orthodox Church) in Sierpc, the Russians celebrated the addition of another soul to their church. This news caused a storm among the Jews of Sierpc, and especially among the Jewish soldiers, at the treachery of their comrade. But the deed had been done and there was no turning back.

For a while, the Russians treated their new co-religionist like a mascot and didn't bother him or harm him. But with time, his immunity wore off and the old times returned: torment, insults, and beatings. The soldier turned to his Jewish friends and pleaded and tried to justify his deed by saying he wanted to be rid of the persecution, and would return to being a pious Jew after he left the army. And he asked them to forgive his actions, which also shamed them, and he begged to be saved from his hell, or he would put an end to his life.

The Jewish soldiers started to discuss how they could help the fallen friend. They gathered, together with some of the town elders, in their "club," the Malawa family tavern, and talked of how to save the unlucky soldier. After a long discussion, it was decided to smuggle the unlucky soldier across the border into Germany. One of the participants in the discussion was a member of the community council, Israel Bluman, and he was appointed to perform the deed. According to plan, two soldiers brought this soldier late at night to Israel Bluman's house. They dressed him in girl's clothes (as we said, he was short and thin), put him on a horse cart and, with the help of professional smugglers, took him across the border into Germany.

* * *

Behind the next house, which was the hotel of Mrs. Lipchik (a Pole), stood the two-story house of Shmuel Grobard, who was called "Shmuel Lant". The name Lant was that of his wife, (who was called "Di Lenten"), Madame Esther

Lant, whom he married when she was a widow and owner of the house and of the tavern (*shenk* in Polish) in the house. Because of that, she was well known in town and her husband was called by her name. His son-in-law, Avraham Groda, later owned the house.

* * *

During the First World War, Shmuel Grobard was a *lavnik* (counselor to the mayor) in the Magistrat and also a member of the community council. The landlord and his wife went to America after the First World War, to visit their sons. Shmuel Grobard died there. His wife, who did not approve of the burial arrangements in America, returned to Sierpc to die.

* * *

The house had four stores: the tavern belonging to the landlady (afterwards owned by a Pole and, later, Shmuel Moshe Zabitski's cobbler's shop); my parents' haberdashery store (afterwards that of my brother-in-law, Yisrael Karpa, and still later, a shoemaker called Yeshiayahu Radzanovski Marchonz); the grocery store of Rehavia (who was called “Hevia”) Tzipris (afterwards, of her son, Meir Tzipris); and the flour store of Tuvia Lant (who emigrated to America).

* * *

This house was at the center of the market. Opposite was the parking area for the carriages, (*pawuz* in Polish, an enclosed stagecoach for six passengers), which took merchants, traveling salesman (*shpiliter* in Polish), ordinary travelers, and passers-by to Plock on their way to Warsaw. The tavern (*shenk*) in this house was used by the passengers from out of town and the wagon-drivers, a place to stop, rest, eat, and drink. The carriages would leave Sierpc at midnight, and after a stopover at Bielsk (Balsk), would get to Plock at six in the morning. From there the passengers would sail in a *statak* (steamship) on the Wisla (Veisel) to Warsaw. There would be tumult and lots of noise near the parking place and inn every evening, and especially on Saturday night and on Tuesday evening, after market day, when there were many passengers for Warsaw.

* * *

Our store was called Yehudit's Store. Each haberdashery shop, like every other store, had its own special clientele. The main customers of the haberdashery of Mrs. Lubashka, the largest of its kind, were the families of the officers of the Russian battalion stationed in Sierpc and the rich Polish gentry. The customers of Yokev (Yaakov) and Luka, the second largest haberdashery shop in town, were in part, the same type of customers as Mrs. Lubashka's, and in part, different. The main customers of the haberdashery shops of Naftali Liebson, Itcha Meir Sandrovitch, and some smaller stores were the farmers from the district, who came to town on the market days, Tuesday and Friday. Our store was Yehudit's Store. Our main customers were seamstresses (Jewish and Polish), and rich Jewish ladies who, more than just being rich, were "ladies" ("*Medames*" as they were called).

In that time - before the First World War – our shop excelled in the variety of ornamentation for ladies' dresses and hats, such as silk goods, velvet, and also buttons and pins of different kinds and a wide selection of lace for ladies underwear and bedding. The busy time in our store was in the evening. The ladies, who would stroll in the street in the evening, would wander into our store to see if there was something new that interested them. With great patience and politeness, we would answer all their requests, and they would turn the store over from top to bottom. In the end, they would leave, with a promise to return with someone else whom they could consult with. They promised, and kept their promise. And they would return not just once, and not just with one advisor. And after all the conferences, they would take the merchandise home to show to their mother, their daughter, sister, neighbor, or dressmaker. And more than once we had to go, after a few days, to the ladies' homes to get the goods back. Thus they would tire us out, and muddle us, every evening, especially on summer evenings, until ten or eleven o'clock or later. And in the end, when they finally bought the merchandise, it would be on credit. And we would have to go to their houses an endless number of times, to ask them to pay their debt, as if we were asking for charity. More than a small number of entries in our swollen "debt book" were never paid.

We were so enslaved to the store that we had to open it on Saturday night. And not only on the long evenings of winter, but also on the short evenings of summer. When I came back from the *shtibl* on Saturday night with my father, we went straight to the store, which my mother {Yochevet) and my sister (Gita Bila) had opened after saying the prayer "Gott fun Avraham" (God of Abraham). When we arrived at the store, our valued customers, who had been strolling in the vicinity and waiting for it to open, were already there. As usual, they were looking for new knick-knacks for underwear, bedding, dresses, or hats. Of course, they didn't buy anything. First of all, the "Sabbath was still in their pocket," and secondly, they had to come back with a mother, or sister, or dressmaker. Sometimes on Sarturday night, a Polish customer would come who needed something for Sunday. Then we would usually see "a live groschen" (actual cash) because it was "the beginning of the week."

When they went to open the store, my mother and sister would bring the wine, the wineglass, a candle, and the incense box for Havdalah (Saturday night prayer). When the right moment came, and the store was empty for a few minutes, we hurriedly shuttered the store; my sister would keep the doors closed, I would hold the twisted candle, and my father would quickly say the Havdalah blessing. We would eat the *Mlava Malka* (Saturday night feast) meal when it was very late at night, and finally get some sleep.

The haberdashery business was not like selling textiles. There was a resemblance, in that both used outside capital. However, in textile goods, the trade was based completely on I.O.U's, and bankruptcy was common; the haberdashery merchants would use money that had to be repaid with interest, or was loaned as a favor. Very few used I.O.U.'s, and bankruptcies were unknown in this business.

* * *

During the period when the Russians were in control, until the First World War, the stores had to be closed on Sundays for the Christian prayer times, between 10 and 12 in the morning. But Sunday mornings were good times for business, especially for the haberdashery stores. The Polish customers would come (like the Jewish customers on Friday afternoon) to buy items of clothing that they might be missing, or a Sunday ornament. On the one hand, it was a pity to close the store, on the other hand, the customers wouldn't stand for it, but it was the law. What did the storekeepers do? When the time came to close the store, they would shutter the doors, and serve the customers who remained inside. Or they would let new customers in, after making sure there were no policemen in sight. And they would let their customers out, also being very careful. And those storekeepers with stores with a rear entrance had nothing to worry about.

We had a lot of problems with this, because our store was opposite the Magistrat (town hall) and the police station. We wanted to close the store exactly at ten o'clock, but it was difficult, because the buyers tarried. Therefore, we were caught many times, but we were not brought to justice because we would give "small gifts." Once, a policeman gave us a summons, and my mother had to go to court. Those in the know told my mother to answer "yes" when the judge asks her if she admits to the crime. Then the judge would fine her one ruble, or sentence her to one day in jail. If she would try to justify her deed, she would receive a heavier penalty. And that is what happened. My mother confessed and was sentenced to a fine of one ruble, or one day in jail. Apparently, one ruble was a lot of money, and my mother selected a day in jail.

A day in jail was from 12 Noon until the same time the following day. So my mother entered the jail at 12 Noon. I accompanied her inside. The jail, which was called *koza*[8], was in the courtyard of the attorney Garfinkel, in an ordinary house with two large rooms, one for men and the other for women, and an entrance hall where the guard was stationed. Each room had a large, barred window, and the only furniture was a wooden cot.

After I had stayed awhile with mother, I went home. Afterwards, I brought her dinner, and sat some more with her. (Whoever wanted food from the jail, would get it. A guard would bring it from the *vanzhnia*[9] that was in the neighboring courtyard.) Because my mother was the only woman in prison that day, she asked the guard to let me sleep there, and he agreed. I went home to get supper and a blanket. In the morning, I went home again, and brought mother breakfast. At noon, we went home.

* * *

Rehavia Tzafris's grocery store was unique among the Jewish groceries: a large, clean store, with nice looking shelves on the walls, with goods neatly placed, large counters, and a display window. In the widow – samples of various kinds of goods: large candles and sweets wrapped in blue paper (or maybe just the wrappings of candles and sweets), and so forth. And at the bottom of the window, small cubicles, and in each cubicle, a different kind of ready-made noodle (something very new in our town): short ones and long ones (up to half a meter), thin and chunky, flat and round, solid noodles and hollow ones. Children would stop at the widow from time to time to stare at the strange noodles. The only customer for the noodles was the Russian Army battalion stationed in town. When Rehavia retired, his son, Meir Tzafris (who had been a grain merchant), took over. In the thirties, Meir Tzafris was elected to the community council as a member of Mizrachi.

* * *

The next two houses, two small one-story buildings, belonged to Shmuel Frank. When Frank became hard up, he sold the first house to Heet Kalman Bloom (who was called "Kalman Brenner"), who opened a ready-to-wear men's store there. The other store in the house, a textiles store, belonged to the brothers Nathan (he was not called "Nusan," as Nathan would be pronounced in Sierpc Yiddish, but "Natan," as it would be pronounced in Polish) and Wolf Tatz. Nathan Tatz was a member of the first town council that was elected during the German occupation in the First World War. He was a sympathizer of the Bund (the Jewish socialist anti-Zionist organization) and supported it financially. Nathan was a generous man, and helped many people with his charity.

Among the poor children who came to the soup kitchen during the First World War (it was in the yard where we lived, the yard of Moshe Elshtein) was a boy who would read a lot. He wouldn't take his eyes off the book even when mealtime came, not while he ate, and not when he finished eating. He also read while he walked. Nathan Tatz heard of him, and he took the boy into his house and brought him up as if he were his own son.

* * *

My grandfather, Avraham Sandrovitch, who was called "Avramie Zlochaver" lived in that courtyard. Zlochaver was my grandmother's (Rivka Feige) family name. Why was my grandfather called by my grandmother's name? It turns out that she was a "woman of valor" and was known all over town as a merchant. Because Grandpa would study the Torah all day and all night ("Work – is the study of the Torah") Grandma would sell things and support the family.

This is the source of the name "Partushkova," "Fartuch (apron)", or "Koshitzkova" (basket) as the Gentiles of the town and the surroundings called the Sandrovitch family. Our haberdashery shop (in the market, in Shmuel Grobard's house) was bought with my grandmother's money. She bought the store after there had been a fire there. Even in my days, there were packages of buttons in burnt cartons on the lowest shelf that had been saved from the fire. Before she bought the store, Grandmother would take her wares to the houses of rich Polish gentry, to the nuns (who were called *noness*) in the Catholic convent that was then in Sierpc[10], and to the houses of the Russian officials. (Grandmother would speak very delicately, and address every customer, even young girls, as *Pan*, *Pani*, or *Panienka* (Sir, Madam, Miss). And so, when Grandma would carry her wares in an apron, they would say to her "Pani Partushkova" (Madam with the apron) and when she carried her wares in a basket, they would say "Pani Koshitzkova" (Madam with the basket) and so her children and grandchildren were called by these two names (usually with the given names) by the Gentiles.

Grandma would say (my mother told this to me): when she was young, everyone would be addressed as "You." If someone wanted to show off and spoke in terms of zi (third person), people would make fun of him and say the following couplet: "*Heren zi, zehen zi, veissen zi vos? Sheyen zi, beysen zi, essen zi dos.*"

* * *

My Rabbi, Moshe Danziger (who was called "Moisheye Karmelkeies"), once told us, among his entertaining stories for his students: His (he meant my) grandfather never saw his grandmother. Grandfather would get up early and go to the *shtibl* to study. When he left the house, his wife was still asleep. Grandmother would rise at first light, wake up the children, clothe them, feed them, and send them to the heder. Then she would eat, clean the house, prepare food for her husband, and set out to find sustenance for the household.

At twelve Noon, after finishing his morning studies (a lesson in the Gemara, a Torah chapter with commentaries by Rashi) and prayer and the day's chapter in Psalms, Grandfather would come home. His wife wouldn't be home, but the table had been set. The tablecloth was spread; bread, utensils and salt were on it. He would remove the porridge from the stove, wash his hands, say the blessing, and eat his breakfast. After he finished eating, and had said grace, he would doze a little at the table, and then again go to the *shtibl* to study.

Before evening, after a long and trying day, Grandmother would return. She would prepare the evening meal (which was called *vietshere*), feed the children, and put them to sleep. Then she would eat, prepare food for her husband, and tired and exhausted from the day's labors, she would go to sleep.

In the evening, after the evening prayer, and after conversations with other yeshiva students like himself, Grandfather would come home. Grandmother was already asleep, and again Grandfather found the table set for a meal. He removed supper from the stove, sat and ate *vietshere*, scrutinized a book, and when he became sleepy, he would stand up, recite “Kriat Shma,” and go to sleep. This, said the rabbi, happened day after day and week after week, and Grandfather and Grandmother would not meet.

Another time, this rabbi told the following story: His (he meant my) grandfather would from time-to-time go to visit his Rebbe. (The Rebbe of Lublin, from the Iger dynasty. There were no Lublin Hasidim in Sierpc. Grandfather came to Sierpc from Lowicz.) He would arrive before “First Slichot” (before New Year) and stay until after Sabbath Bereishis (after Sukkoth). Once, his wife gave birth to a son, and the Sholom Zecher and circumcision took place when Grandfather was at the Rebbe.

* * *

There are no more houses in the market square. We turn to that most important and essential institution, the one that was used by all the tenants of the market and the surroundings, the one that was at the center of the market, and generously gave to everyone who came – the water-pump. The pump provided fresh water for all the neighborhood (hard water; soft water was brought from the well near the *mikveh*) in all seasons of the year. Jews and Gentiles, rich and poor, great and small, used the water. The great would take up the water by themselves, or use professional pumpers. The small would accompany the great, and benefit from their “aid” to the great, by pumping the water and carrying the buckets. The children would quench their thirst directly from the pump. Grown-ups would do the same thing when they didn't care about appearances. The peasants who came on market day would drink directly from the pump.

In the winter, the water that spilled near the pump would freeze, and a sort of iceberg would form around it, and the approach to the pump would become unsafe. The pumpers would bring sand and spread it over the ice to get to the pump. On especially cold days, the pump itself would be wrapped in straw, so that the pipe would not freeze. The children then had a double delight: seeing the pump and the surrounding ice, and also skating on the ice. There was also a children's riddle about the pump: “What stands in the middle of the market, and when you hold out your hand, begins to weep?”

The Old Market and market day were linked, not only because of the word “market,” but in many aspects. And in spite of the fact that there were a few markets in town, you could say that the heart of market day was in the Old Market. The income of most of the population of Sierpc, like that in most cities, was based on labor and commerce. The Polish population was mainly laborers and craftsmen, and the Jewish population (which was about 3500 out of a total of 10,000) was 40% merchants and 40% tradesmen and laborers (The rest were property owners, public officials, and miscellaneous). All of them looked forward to market days, which were the main factor in the economic life of the town.

Market days in Sierpc were twice a week, on Tuesdays and Fridays. The major market day was on Tuesday, and a minor market day on Friday. The peasants from the countryside would bring their produce for sale on market day. They would bring eggs, butter, cheese (the Jews didn't buy cheese made by Gentiles – they called it "Polish cheese" – and the sticklers wouldn't buy butter made by Gentiles – "Polish butter"), potatoes, grain, chickens, cattle, pigs, horses, and chopped wood for cooking and heating.[11] They would buy food, kerosene, ready-made clothing and shoes, tools, cattle, or horses. On market days, especially Tuesdays, the streets were crowded with people, cattle, horses, and carts--especially the Old Market. In the market, the tailors put up stalls with three walls and a roof made of posts that were wrapped in canvas, and showed off their wares (ready made men's clothing). The hatters would put up stalls with one wall and two narrow walls and a roof. Between the narrow walls were shelves with hats on display. The shoemakers would put up stalls with two pairs of high support legs with a rod between them, on which they would hang shoes and boots. Peddlers would show their merchandise on tables and stands: weaves, cloth, underwear, and all sorts of haberdashery. Trade in grains, furniture and rope was concentrated in the New Market. The lot behind the New Market was the pig market; on Plotzki Street, behind the German church, was the cattle and horse market.

There were fairs in Sierpc six times a year, before Christian holidays. The fairs would take place on Wednesday (there would not be a market day on Tuesday that week). Merchants, peddlers, and salesman from nearby and faraway towns would assemble for the fairs. Merchants (they were called *shachers*) who were more interested in fraud than in sales came even from Warsaw. Peasants came not only from the surrounding countryside, but also from farther away. During fair days, the streets and markets, the sidewalks and the roads, were filled to capacity. In addition to the stands and booths that were set up in the Old Market, as on ordinary market days, stalls were set up on the sidewalks around the market, and carts passed between the two rows of stalls and the crowds of people with great difficulty. The shouting, outcry, and patter of the merchants and peddlers would fill the air, and the din and commotion were deafening. The policemen of the entire district would be brought to town for the fair days. But also the thieves and swindlers from near and far, both from the tribe and not from the tribe, would be "recruited" for those days. A fair day never passed without robberies, frauds, quarrels, and fights. The police had plenty of work.

* * *

For as long as I can remember, there was a rumor that the authorities were going to move the Old Market to the New Market, and the Old Market would be turned into a park. And the anti-Semitic establishment plotted to deprive the shopkeepers in the market, who were almost all Jewish, of their livelihood. And they began the realization of their scheme, not by moving the market location, but by changing the market day. In 1927, the Town Council decided to move the market day from Tuesday to Wednesday and from Friday to Saturday. The anti-Semites argued that they should be able to eat fresh produce on Sunday, like the Jews were able to eat fresh produce on Saturday. And because they were shifting the market day from Friday to Saturday, they would also transfer the Tuesday market to Wednesday. But their real intention was that, since the Jews would not violate the Sabbath, more Polish owned stores would appear, and there would be more Polish merchants. The Jewish public, led by the Jewish town council members, opposed the edict, but to no avail, and the decree was published. A committee was formed whose members were representatives of the whole Jewish community, under the leadership of the Rabbi, against the desecration of the Sabbath. The committee sent patrols to market, to prevent defilers (if there were such) from shopping in the market. But the edict did not last for more than a few weeks. The Jews stood fast, and even the secular Jews didn't violate the Sabbath, neither by selling nor buying goods. When the peasants saw that there was no trade on Saturday and that they had to take their goods back home with them, they relented and, a few at a time, started coming to town on Friday. In time, the market day became legally Friday again. And Tuesday became market day again instead of Wednesday.

I found in my archives a newspaper called *Unzer Rayen Zeitung* (Our Regional Newspaper – a non-partisan weekly devoted to trade, the community, and culture of the Jews in Western Poland, Vlotzlabek, Plock, Kotana, Bydgoszcz) which was published in Vlotzlabek, No. (34) 9, from the 16 of MarHeshvon, 5688 (11 November, 1927) with an item from Sierpc on the shifting of the market days. The article was signed by Ben-Haver and a footnote: "Because of unforeseen circumstances, this article was late to print." This is what the article said:

"Our town is one of those whose previous town council decided to move the market days to Wednesday and Saturday from Tuesday and Friday, as was the usual practice. Jewish council members, with the backing of the whole Jewish population, vigorously opposed this proposition that could ruin all Jewish trade. But none of these activities had any effect, and the market days were set as Wednesday and Saturday.

"The people from the countryside, who immediately felt that the new law was against their interests, did not pay attention to the law, and continued coming to town on Friday, and not on Saturday. And so the market days became, in practice, Friday and Wednesday.

"The Christian merchants, the *endekim*[12] who campaigned ferociously for the new law in the previous Town Council, now felt the other end of the stick, that by trying to damage the Jewish businesses they also damaged their own, worked together with the Jewish representatives to return market days to Tuesday and Friday, because of the proximity of Wednesday and Friday. And starting with 20 September, 1927, Tuesday and Friday became the official market days."

3. Plotzki Street

We will continue our tour and our survey on the Plotzki [Plocki] Street. In the mid 1930s, when the town council gave the streets new names, this street was called Ridaz Shmigli after the Polish Marshall of that name.

* * *

At the beginning of the street there was a big two-story brick building, owned by Moshe Goldstein. The house was completely taken by the Russian authorities: the first floor, by the Post Office and the Government Bank, and the second floor, by regional offices and by the governor of the region (*natchelnik pivituvy*). In back of the house was a large yard that extended to the Zhika (the river). A one story wooden house with twelve rooms was in the center of the yard; it was occupied completely by the Goldstein family. (The only instance in town of such comfortable living quarters.) Between the two houses was a garden with trees and a green hedge and between the trees were benches. (The only garden in a Jewish yard in town.) There were large granaries in the other part of the yard.

Moshe Goldstein was considered one of the two wealthiest men in town (the other was Shlackman). He was a successful grain merchant, and was also the supplier of the Russian cavalry battalion stationed in town.

The House of Goldstein (both the building and the family) was very attractive. It was a rich house that was conspicuous in its wealth, but not in its haughtiness. The houses, the living conditions, the large and neat yard, the garden, and all the practices of the house were proof of the wealth of this family. But the whole town benefited from the wealth of the Goldstein family. The community, the town institutions, people of little means and poor people were supported by the Goldstein family's charity and volunteer efforts. The lady of the house, Mrs. Zvetel Goldstein, deserves special mention for these good works. She was a kind and generous woman, gentle and good-hearted.

"*Di Blinde Hene*" (Blind Hanna, she had one bleary eye) lived in the cellar of the front house, with her son, who was called "Dodia di Blinde Henes" (David son of Blind Hanna) and her daughter Nikhia (who was called "Nikhia di Blinde Henes" – Nikhia daughter of Blind Hanna). The mother and son made their living by selling milk from door to door and by selling wood for cooking and heating. Dudia would chop the wood every day after completing his milk rounds. Both mother and son would start conversations and tell all sorts of tales in every house they entered to sell milk.

* * *

After the First World War, the Goldstein family members who lived in Warsaw sold the house (the parents had passed away) to Aharon Lipke. Later, a second story was added to the house in the yard, and Shmuel Mendel Licht, who previously had a bakery, opened a hotel there. Part of the first story was used as the *shtibl* of the Gur Hasidim.

* * *

Moshe Shtarkshtein lived in the same house. (He came from Drobin before the First World War, and left Sierpc after the war.) He was not a very successful merchant. Moshe Shtarkshtein once came to the *shtibl* and said that he had just made 200 Marks. His listeners wondered – so early in the morning and such a large profit? And by who – Moshe Shtarkshtein? Then Shtarkshtein related how he came by this large sum:

Yesterday morning, someone offered to sell him a shipment of thread. He wanted to buy it, but somehow, he didn't. Today he heard that the contract had expired, and the value of the goods had gone down by 200 Marks. So it seems he saved 200 Marks...

* * *

Melobantchik's house was next to the Goldstein house. This was a small, one-story house. There was one store at the front of the house – Melobantchik's grocery and liquor store. The customers were mainly the large landowners from outside of town, who bought groceries and liquor in large quantities. The interior arrangements and furniture were a model of tidiness and order. It is doubtful that any other store in town, even among the Polish ones, could compare with this one in cleanliness and neatness. Because of its tidiness, and because of the many bottles on the shelves, the store looked like a pharmacy.

The Melobantchik family was a very respected one, and was considered one of the most intelligent in town. Mrs. Dvora Malka Melobantchik was a wise and generous woman, charitable, with many good deeds to her credit. At the beginning of the German conquest (in the First World War) Leib Melobantchik was appointed by the occupation authorities to the town council, and served as a *lavnik* (advisor to the mayor).

* * *

Moshe Gongola, the hatter, lived in the next house. His elderly father lived in the same house and helped out a little with the work. His father's name was Tzelelazer (Betzalel Lazer), and Rivka, Moshe Gongola's wife, used to say: "My father-in-law is *no ful Lazer* (half Lazer in Polish) but *tzali* Lazer" (complete Lazer in Polish.) If the elder Gongola's name had a Polish ring to it, so the name of the landlord, a Pole, had a Hebrew ring to it. His name was Shtandrmair.

* * *

A little bit further on there was an unpaved alley that extended to the Zhika (the Sierpianitza River). The alley didn't have an official name, but it was called Doli (*doles* – slope) because it inclined towards the Zhika. The alley ended with the *lava*, a low, narrow, wooden passage to ford the river that connected Plotzki Street with the Jewish Street (near the synagogue) and shortened the route between them.

There were few houses in the alley, and few Jewish families lived there. Among them were the Oberfeld (Mordecai) family and the Pshigoda family (Avraham, who was called "Penk" after his father-in-law, and Hirsh Rugza, who was called "Old Penk" – "*der Alter Penk*").

* * *

After the alley, there was a one-story house that was jointly used by Hershel Ishaiavetz and Mendel Lencher. The first had a grocery store, and the second, an ironworks shop, both in the same house.

* * *

Mendel Lencher was a quiet and unassuming man. His grown sons managed the ironworks store, and he spent most of his time studying the Gemara. During the First World War, he bought the Kovzanitz estate near Rypin. He died suddenly there in the year 5687 (1926) and was buried in Sierpc. Mendel Lencher was a reader of the Torah and blew the shofar in the Alexander *shtibl.*

* * *

Past the house of Lencher-Lencher, there was a narrow street that extended, like the alley, to the Zhika and the lava. This street was also called Doli, but its official name was Shvyenti Vazhinietz (Saint Vazhinietz) after one of the Catholic saints. In the mid 1930s, when the town council gave new names to the streets, this street was named "P.O.W." after the underground organization, a Polish military group that was organized at the end of the First World War and helped, according to the Polish version, to free Poland from the Germans.

This street too, like the alley, housed few Jewish families. Among them were the Lubianski (Mordecai) family, and the Shnitzer (Icha Itzhak David) family.

* * *

Mordecai Lubianski brought a matzo baking machine to Sierpc in the 1930s. The Rabbi, Yehoshua Heshel David Goldshlak, declared total war on the matzos baked by this machine, and declared them to be completely *chametz* (not kosher for Passover). Because of this, Lubianski had to bring the flour for the matzos from Plock. However, many people didn't pay attention to the Rabbi's prohibition, and ate these matzos. Every year, as the matzo-baking season approached, the Rabbi would renew his stubborn battle against the machine-made matzos, and every year, the number of people who ate them increased.

* * *

Icha David Shnitzer was one of a group of younger activists. He was an ardent Zionist, and was a leader at any Zionist, Hebrew, or cultural event. He was a member of committees of the Zionist Organization, of the Tarbut school, and of the library. He was also active in charitable works.

* * *

Zadok Bluman lived in the first house after Doli Street. This was a two-story brick house that belonged to Shich Lagrudnitski (a Pole). The Bluman family house was one of the few intelligent places in Sierpc. Zadok Bluman had a great deal of knowledge in matters of law and statutes. He was, as it was generally put, "half a lawyer." His occupation was writing applications to the court and other Russian government institutions, and giving advice on legal matters. During the German occupation in the First World War, Zadok Bluman was an official of the German court.

Icheia Papiarchik lived in the same house. Icheia was a clever Jew, a pleasant man to have a conversation with, with an agreeable smile. He would say, "I don't have to keep books in my business, the Jews in town do that for me."

* * *

In the next house, which belonged to Grabovski (a Pole), lived Azrieltia Podskotch, who was one of the senior Zionist intellectuals in town. He was a clever man, and respected by the whole town. His home was an intelligent and Zionist one. He was a member of the first town council that was elected during the German occupation in the First World War.

* * *

Shmulik Valuka lived in the same house. He was a teacher in the government elementary school for Jewish children. Shmulik Valuka was a faithful and devoted Zionist. He was active in all Zionist, Hebrew, and cultural activities, and one of the founders of the Zionist youth movement, Herzlia, and very active in it.

The school authorities did not look upon Shmulik Valuka's Zionist activities favorably. Only the fact that he had been a volunteer in a combat unit and had participated in Polish battles against the Bolsheviks (in 1920) prevented his dismissal from his job. But he was punished. It was an unofficial punishment, of "banishment"; for years, he was sent to teach in other towns.

* * *

The next house, one-story with a cellar, belonged to Shmuel Asher Ostashber. The landlord had a grocery store in the cellar, in addition to a textiles store in the yard.

In the first months of the First World War, Shmuel Asher Ostashber and his brother Itzik were sent to Siberia by the Russians on suspicion of spying for the Germans. They returned to Sierpc at the end of the war.

* * *

Above Shvyenti Vazhinietz Street, Plotzki Street split into two. A small park in the shape of a long triangle drove a wedge into the middle of the street. This park (which was called "*Der Kleiner List Garten*" – the Small Garden of Desire) was the only one in the streets of Sierpc. It had a few trees and a few benches, and the youth (of course, not the Hasidic young men) would stroll there in the evenings and on Sabbaths, or rest on a bench in the middle of their promenade. This park, which very likely brought couples together, any number of times was also responsible for splitting them up. Plotzki Street continued to the left of the park, to Bielsk (Balsk) and Plock. The road to Dobrzyn (Dobrzyn on the Drweca) began to the right of the park.

In later years, when the road to Dobrzyn (the start of the road, adjoining Sierpc) became busier and became a street, it was called Piastovska after Piast, the first king of Poland.

* * *

Beyond the park, both to the left and to the right, there were few Jewish tenants. Not far from here, the two streets became semi-rural, like a Polish suburb.

The first house beyond the park occupied all the space (together with its courtyard) between the road to Plock and the road to Dobrzyn. This house was a one-story house and belonged to a Jew, Moshe Kotzolk, who owned a grocery store (by the side of the road to Plock) and a lumber storeroom (in the yard behind his house, on the side of the road to Dobrzyn).

* * *

Beyond Kotzolk's house there were houses, empty lots, and tilled fields. On the road to Plock, on the left, not far away, was the *kirche* (the Evangelic Church; there were many Germans in the vicinity of Sierpc). After the *kirche* there was a large, fenced-in lot, with storerooms for agricultural equipment, that belonged to a Pole. He also had bicycles for sale and for rent, by the hour, to ride and for riding lessons. Obviously, children and boys from Hasidic houses didn't know how to ride bicycles, and also didn't take riding lessons (except for a few that dared, and folded up their pants' legs, and learned the ways of the "foreigners"). They would stand outside – if by chance they came to this Gentile neighborhood – and send jealous glances at the boys and young men inside riding bicycles and learning how to ride them.

Further on, in a large lot between the road to Plock and the road to Lublin, was the horse and cattle market. On market days, especially on Tuesdays, it was full of the sounds of men and cattle, with the yelling of the sellers and the brokers and sometimes with the sounds of shouts and fights of adversaries or drunks. A little bit further on, there was a large park (it was called "der Groiser Lis-Garten" – "the Large Garden of Desire"), and inside the park was the *tchrkava* (the Russian Orthodox Church, for the officials and the Russian Army). In the first days of Polish independence, the *tchrkava* was torn down, and in its place the *sarostva* (provincial authority) building was put up, and because of this, the area became developed, with more residents. Because it was in a Polish neighborhood, and far from the town center, the Jewish youth didn't tend to stroll or pass their time in the Large Park. But in quiet times, the Jewish youth would try to forget that they were among bitter enemies, and they would spend time in the park until late at night. But very often they would be chased out of the park by Polish youth. Beyond the Large Park there was the sawmill (together with a lumber warehouse) owned by Yisraelke Sherpherz.

* * *

Of the few Jews who lived in this neighborhood, I remember Binyamin Sochaczewski. His house was after the Kotzolk house, and before the German church, and he had a grocery store there. Binyamin Sochaczewski was an enthusiastic and fanatical Gur Hasid, and in addition, an idler.

* * *

Further on were the barracks of the 48th Russian Cavalry Battalion, which was stationed in Sierpc. The battalion came to Sierpc in 1888, and left it for Lolotzalbek in 1908. Also stationed in Sierpc was the 22nd Artillery Battery. The barracks had been built by Jews who rented them to the army.

We have arrived at the edge of town. We will go back by the other way, the road to Dobrzyn, which was called Piastovska Street.

* * *

We told the story of the small railroad (*kolaika*) that the Germans built from Lowicz to Nashlatz in the paragraph entitled "Traffic and Lighting" in the section "The First World War". [Of the chapter "Memoirs" in this book]. It passed through Sierpc and shortened the trip to Warsaw. The Polish authorities built a wide gauge railway from Sierpc to Nasielsk, which was completed in 1924 and permitted a direct journey, without transfers, and a quick trip from Sierpc to Warsaw in less than four hours (the distance – 144 kilometers). The railway station was on the road to Dobrzyn (Piastovska Street) and because of it the neighborhood developed further, and the number of inhabitants increased. New residences were built, and institutions moved their quarters to the area, including the court, the hospital, and the public elementary school for Jewish children. In 1937, the line was extended to Rypin, and instead of Sierpc-Warsaw, it became Rypin-Warsaw. In that year, another railway line was completed, Lipano-Sierpc-Plock.

* * *

We have already mentioned that this area, till the small park, was like a semi-rural Polish suburb, and only a few Jews lived here. I can remember only one Jew who lived in this area, and that was Mordecai Lupatka. He had a grocery store and was a grain merchant. In later years the lumberyard of Mendel Gurfinkel was situated here, and the photography shop of his daughters, and David Sherpherz lived here.[13]

Opposite the small park there was a lane with a rural atmosphere: small houses, barns, and no road. The name of this lane was part of the rural character – Studolna (barn in Polish). The lane extended until the fields of its inhabitants. In later years, large modern houses were built here, which outshone any in the rest of the town, and the lane became a street.

During the 1930s, when the town council changed the street names, this street was called Narutovitch after the first president of modern Poland, who was killed by a Polish nationalist.

* * *

A large, modern building for the Tarbut [Culture] School was built on the same street. The building was completed in 1935, and it was opened then. The Tarbut School began in 1931. A kindergarten named Tarbut was opened in the Jewish Street, in the yard of Yosef Valosk (the building was sold to Moshe Asman and Yisrael Barko). When the place became too small for the kindergarten and the lower grades, they moved to Plotzki Street, behind the Kotzolk house. The Tarbut School stayed there until it moved to its new quarters.

* * *

We return to Plotzki Street. The first house, a two story building, was owned by Mairkovski (a Pole), and Hanach Pepper lived there. For a certain length of time, Hanach Pepper was a member of the community council. He ran on the Zionist ticket.

* * *

A little further down was the house that belonged to the blacksmith Yitzhak Lipski (who was called "Der Geller Blachazsh" – Yellow Blacksmith). At the beginning of the 1930s, Lipski emigrated to America, stayed there for five years, and then returned to Sierpc. About a year before the start of the Second World War, Lipski tore down his small house and started to build a two-story brick house in its place. However, the war began before his house was finished, and he never had the privilege of seeing it completed.

* * *

David Noah Zilberberg lived in the same house, and his grocery store was in that house. David Noah was a learned man, one of the most popular educators in town, and one of the most important of the Gur Hasidim. His was a noble spirit. He liked the good and the beautiful, neatness, and order. His beard was well combed, and his clothes were always neat and tidy. He was a learned man who never had a speck on his clothes. He also appreciated books. He had a very large library in his house, and his books were not only rich in content, but also had very elaborate bindings, and among them were some very expensive editions. David Noah also was a talented artist. Like many other Jewish artists in previous generations, his artistic tendencies manifested themselves in drawings of the tablets of the commandments.

* * *

After he had married off his only daughter, Figa Rachel, David Noah moved to the market and lived in the house of his father-in-law, Beinam Burstein (who was called "Tall Beinam") and opened a kitchenware store there. He gave his old apartment, together with the grocery store, to his son-in-law, Zanvil Dormbus from Plonsk (Plinsk). With the passing years, Dormbus turned out to be an outstanding public figure. He was elected to the community council from the Agudat Israel list, and he was very active in it. In time he was elected chairman of the council, and he maintained this position until the destruction of the Sierpc community.

***

Leib Yitzhak Shafman lived in the next house; a two-story brick building that belonged to Frilinsky (a Pole). Shafman was a supplier of goods to the Russian Army stationed in Sierpc. After the army left town, Shafman became a rich grain merchant, with wide contacts among the landowners in the area. During the First World War, he bought an estate (*susk*) on the road to Plock.

The Bolsheviks captured Sierpc in August 1920 (the beginning of Elul) during the war between Poland and Bolshevik Russia, and held it for 10 days. During that short time they plundered many shops, especially shoe and liquor stores. The Bolsheviks would kill landowners in any of the places they captured, if even only one laborer complained about a bad attitude towards them by the landowner. Apparently, some of Shafman's complained, and the Bolsheviks executed him somewhere in the vicinity of Lipno.

The Bolsheviks also killed a second Jewish landowner from Sierpc, in addition to Leib Yitzhak Shafman – Yehoshua Verona. A third Jewish landowner, Bauman from Warsaw, was killed by the Bolsheviks in the vicinity of Sierpc.

* * *

The bakery of Yekel (Yaakov) David Bornstein (he used to be a grain merchant) was in the next house, a very small one (practically a shack) that belonged to Moshe Shperling. Yekel David was short, with broad shoulders, a wide beard, with a big smile on his face.

Yekel David was a prayer leader in the Alexander *shtibl.* He was called to the podium many times on Sabbaths. At the celebration of The Three Feasts he would always sing the chants "Yitzave." He suffered a lot because of the illnesses in his family, and from lack of income.

* * *

After Yekel David Bornstein's bakery went out of business, the brothers Natan and Wolfe Tatz bought the small house, tore it down, and built a two-story brick house in its place. The opened a textile store on the first floor, and lived on the upper floor.

* * *

The next house, a one-story brick house with an attic, belonged to the watchmaker Moshe Shperling. I heard a story about Moshe Shperling from my Rabbi, Moshia Carmelkias. One Tuesday, a market day, a peasant came to the watchmaker and showed him a pocket watch that had "stopped." The watchmaker took the watch, put the loup in his eye, examined the watch from every angle, opened it, and after a thorough inspection, told the peasant. "I see a lot of damage to your watch. The mainspring snapped, one jewel is missing and the second is worn, and in addition, it's full of dirt. If you want I can fix the watch so that it will be like new, but it will cost you one ruble."

The peasant didn't agree to the high price, and took the watch back, and left. By chance, he passed the shop of the watchmaker Michal Smolinski. He went in and showed him the watch. Smolinski also examined the watch carefully, and told the peasant that it would cost one gulden to fix it. (A gulden is thirty groschen. A ruble was worth 6 guldens and 20 groschen.) The Gentile agreed to the cost, and left the watch with Smolinski till the following Tuesday.

The peasant received the repaired watch back the following Tuesday. He paid one gulden and left, satisfied with the service and the price. From there he went straight to Shperling, showed him the working watch, and asked why he wanted one ruble for the repair, when another watchmaker did it for one gulden.

Shperling took the watch, opened it, examined it carefully, and burst out laughing. "Can't you see" he asked, "that the gears are moving backwards?" The Gentile was stunned, looked at the watch works like "a chicken looks at a man" and didn't understand what was happening. In spite of this, he summoned up the courage to ask "But the hands are still moving?" "Of course they're moving," answered the watchmaker, "but what good is it to you if the gears are moving backwards?"

The peasant took his watch and went to the market. He met some acquaintances there, and they went to the tavern for a drink. After they had emptied a few glasses, the peasant told them how the Zhidek (Jew-boy) had cheated him. He had seemingly fixed the watch, and the hands were moving, but the gears inside were going in reverse. He asked his friends to accompany him to the Zhid who had cheated him.

The peasant, at the head of this drunken group, entered Smolinski's store and said to him loudly "Zhidek, what did you do to my watch?" Smolinski took the watch, looked at the movement, checked the time against a large wall clock, and answered, "What's the matter? The watch is working fine."

"What's the matter, you ask?" the peasant answered Smolinski in a louder and more impudent voice, "Just don't try to look innocent, you cheating Zhidek. Don't you know and don't you see that the gears are turning in reverse?" Michal Smolinski understood that some watchmaker had told him this fairy story about gears turning in reverse. He tried to explain to him that the whole story about gears turning in reverse is a lie, and that one of his competitors wants to get at him by spreading this tale. But the peasant would not calm down, and together with his friends threatened to tear down the store if he didn't fix the watch properly. The only thing that prevented a dangerous outburst on the part of the watch owner and his friends was the timely arrival of the police from the nearby police station.

* * *

Fultia (Raphael) Klinhoz opened a furniture workshop and store in Moshe Shperling's house in about 1910. This was something new for our town, because not only was this the first furniture store in Sierpc, but he was also the first Jewish carpenter. The carpentry trade was considered a Gentile one in Sierpc, like masonry, for instance. There were Jewish craftsman in Sierpc, but they practiced specifically Jewish trades like tailors, shoemakers, dressmakers, hatters, and the like. There were also craftsmen who worked at specifically non-Jewish trades, like tinsmiths, locksmiths, blacksmiths, cobblers, and tanners. There was also a wood carver who worked for the Polish carpenters and even was a reader of the Torah in the Alexander shtibl during the High Holy Days. There was also one family that sold fish, and sometimes the father and two sons worked on road construction. But a Jewish carpenter had been unheard of in our town. Fultia brought the first Jewish carpenters to Sierpc. They came from Warsaw. Later on, a Jewish carpenter called Meshulam the Carpenter from Plonsk (Plinsk) settled in Sierpc, but he was only part carpenter.

Fultia Klinhoz's life was strange and extraordinary. His roots were in Ciechanow (Tchekhanova), from a family of Alexander Hasidim. When he came to Sierpc, after his wedding, he still wore Hasidic clothes – an Atlas *kapota* (long coat), and a *shtreimel* (fur hat) on the Sabbath. He prayed together with his father-in-law, Ashria (who was called "der Blinder Ashria" – "Blind Ashria") in the Gur *shtibl*, even though he had moved away from Hasidism. And suddenly he "reversed his *kapota*" and fell in with a bad crowd, and became such an extreme heretic that people said that he had sold his part of the next world and purchased the sins of others. Following this "conversion," Fultia left Sierpc for a few years. When he came back, he opened the furniture store and workshop, which didn't last very long. (His wife, Tubia, had a store that sold knick-knacks (buttons, pins, etc.) in the building that housed the pharmacy, on the side facing the Jewish Street.)

Fultia would stroll through the market, approach a group of Jews who were standing there talking to each other, and start expounding on matters of cosmic importance: on his travels through various countries, on the wonders of the world, on Jews and Gentiles, on domestic and foreign politics, on everything... When he happened to run into Hasidim, he would talk about Rebbes, and Hasidim, and schools of thought, and "miracles of Rebbes," sometimes in a mocking tone, and sometimes out of yearning and admiration. Anywhere that Fultia would be, he would become the center of a crowd and the main speaker. And whether his stories were truthful or imaginary, he knew how to fascinate his listeners. He would pepper his speech with the sayings of wise men, proverbs, quips, and jokes. And not only in Yiddish, but also in Polish, Russian, and German. In short, Fultia had a mouth that would produce gems, or as they used to say "His mouth moves on screws." ("*A fisk oif shroifen.*")

I remember that Fultia once came to the Alexander *shtibl* for First *Slichot* [pre-dawn prayers before the High Holy Days]. As is well known, in the *shtibl* they would say the First Slichot that were "Remember the Covenant" and "Thirteen Principles" after midnight. After the First Slichot there was a *Melave Malka* feast in the *shtibl.* During the feast, and for more than an hour afterwards, Fultia would talk about the world, about Berlin and Vienna where he had lived, according to him, for three years, and of the wonders and marvels he had seen there. And of his visits to Rebbes during his Hasidic period, and of the doctrines they had related to him, and so forth. We would get home very late, but they were interesting Slichot.

Dudi Beinam Sandrovitch lived in the same house as Shperling, in the attic. When his daughter, Sara Gitel, became engaged to Itcha Ash from Malawa, Dudi held a *Melave Malka* in his house, and invited his relatives, the Alexander Hasidim, and the neighbors. His neighbor Fultia was also among the guests. And he talked and told stories during the whole *Melave Malka.* Because all the guests were Hasidim, he related many Hasidic tales. I remember that he went into such a Hasidic ecstasy, that when a bowl of peach compote was put on the table at the end of the meal, Fultia stuck his hand inside the bowl (like Hasidim who grab remnants off the Rebbe's table), squeezed all the peaches in his hand, and put them directly into his mouth.

***

I heard the following stories about Fultia's pranks from our respected townsman, Icha Lanter. Once, during a meeting at the synagogue for the selection of community leaders (dozores), the congregation waited for the notables to arrive. They waited and waited, but they didn't come. Then Fultia announced, "I'm not waiting anymore. I don't care who is elected. They can pick Leib Shwitzer, Shaya Hitzer[14], and Meir Yitzer.[15]

***

A few days before Yom Kippur, Fultia sent his young son to Yokev Garlitz to ask him to lend his *kitel* [jacket] because "mother wants to make a *kitel* for father and she needs a sample." (This is what he told the boy to say.) He sent the same request to Simcha Licht, Michael Turkltaub, and a few other important people who prayed at the eastern wall of the old house of worship.

On the eve of Yom Kippur, before sundown, Fultia returned the *kitels* to everyone. Because of the lateness of the hour, none of them examined their *kitels*; they put them next to their Talith, and prepared to go to the house of worship. When they arrived at the prayer house and started to put on their *kitels*, all the worshippers at the eastern wall had their left hands raised, because Fultia had sewed together the ends of the left sleeves.

* * *

In the first few months of the First World War, when Sierpc was still under Russian domination, but the Germans would conquer it from time to time for a few days, there were rumors that the town was full of spies, both Jewish and Polish, some for the Russians, and some for the Germans. It was whispered about town that Fultia was a spy. Once the Germans arrested him, when they were in control, on charges of espionage, and released him after a few days. Another time he was arrested (together with Stringer, the chimney sweep and leader of the fire brigade band) by the Russians on charges of spying for the Germans. Using witnesses, he proved to the Russians that the Germans had arrested him for spying for the Russians, and was released (together with Stringer) after a few days.

Suddenly, "the boy isn't there." A short time after the second arrest and release, Fultia disappeared, and for over a year no one saw him or heard of him. In the summer of 1916, when the Germans occupied all of Poland, but travel between towns was restricted and allowed only with special permits, there were rumors that Fultia was in the vicinity of Sierpc. It was said that he had been seen near Rypin, dressed in a German officer's uniform, roving through the villages, investigating peasants who opposed the new regime, and handing them over to the Germans, who would send them to Germany. One day Fultia showed up in Sierpc. He was clean-shaven (until the day he left Sierpc, he had a handsome and thick black beard) and in uniform, with a light green military jacket, a green hunting cap, and yellow shoes. When the hem of the jacket lifted a little, a belt with a gun and holster was visible. During the first days after his return, Fultia would walk quickly through the market or some other street, without looking to the left or right. He would say "Good morning" or return a greeting to very few people. He didn't stop anywhere or talk to anyone. People would look at him, a little out of fear and a little out of respect. But in time, he became once again the popular Fultia from before the war. He removed his uniform, interrupted other people's conversations, and talked about all sorts of worldly matters. Only about himself or his exploits would he stay silent. And people were careful in his presence.

Fultia came back to Sierpc at a time when infectious diseases were spreading through Poland and in the town as a result of the war and, as in all wars, causing many deaths. In the week he came back, the two children of the Rabbi from Zielun, Rabbi Nachumtche, who lived in Sierpc, died. A meeting was held at the Old House of Prayer on the day of the funeral, after evening prayers, where Fultia was to speak. I was at this meeting, and it became so fixed in my memory that I remember it as if it happened yesterday.

The Old House of Prayer was completely lit, and full of Jews, great and small, old and young, and the women's section was also packed. The large congregation was in mourning because of the great tragedy of the family of the Rabbi from Zielun, and tensely awaited the speaker, the strange citizen-guest, and his speech. A murmur passed through the crowd – "Fultia is coming." The congregation squeezed together even more to let him pass through, and he went up to the platform, wearing the costume that has already been described. Silence gripped the whole Old House of Prayer, and all faces turned to him. Fultia stood straight for a minute, and then looked around. Then he bent over, leaned his elbows on the lectern, looked foreward with a slight smile, and started to talk in a quiet voice:

"*Ir vet dach avade fregen, tsuvas is der Fultia aher gekumen*" ("You will certainly ask – why has Fultia come here"). And he quickly straightened up, his face became very serious and red, and he roared with all his might, like a lion: "*Ich red mit mein blut*" ("My blood is speaking!")

I cannot describe the great fear that was felt by the audience as a result of this bellow. If the Kaiser Wilhelm himself had been standing there, he would not have inspired more dread. Fultia began his speech, which lasted more than an hour, and its gist was: The congregation must maintain sanitary conditions – a clean body, clean houses, and clean yards, because dirt and filth cause the kind of tragedies that occurred that day. He quoted verse from the Bible and the sayings of wise men that stressed the importance of cleanliness and purity, and he asked the congregation to keep these commands so that they would live a long life.

Because of the heat and lack of air in the packed prayer house, and a little because of a relaxation in the tension, people began to cough. And again, a huge bellow suddenly came out of Fultia. "*Ich farshik eich gleich kine Magdenberg*" ("I will send you straight to Magdenberg" – [a fort in Germany]). Terror and fear enveloped the audience; we were stunned and paralyzed. Not only did the coughing stop, but so did the breathing. And everyone felt as if the house of worship was surrounded by troops, and we would all be arrested when we left. This atmosphere of fear remained to the end of the meeting, and when I left I looked around me to make sure there were no soldiers or police waiting for us.

After this great and terrible speech, his premiere, Fultia began speaking there every once in a while. He talked about public affairs and various municipal problems. The number of listeners and their attention, as well as the speaker's prestige, became less and less each time he spoke--until he started to speak every Saturday afternoon. He would start with a quotation from the portion of the week, add clarifications from one of the commentaries, and go on to secular matters. In these speeches, the speaker became an orator, the speech became preaching, and respect for him diminished considerably.

When Poland became independent (at the end of The First World War, in November 1918), the authorities started investigating Fultia's activities during the German occupation. He had to appear in Plock a few times for questioning. His sister, Sarah Mendelson (a midwife in Sierpc, an educated and intelligent woman), accompanied him every time to these inquiries, to protect him from his enemies. Apparently, the Polish authorities could not find any hard proof against him, so they decided to get rid of him in another way. Once, when Fultia and his sister were walking in Plock, after they had left the office of the investigating magistrate, someone shot at them. The bullet, which was meant for the brother, hit his sister. A second bullet immediately hit the brother. Both of them died on the spot. Of course, the authorities began to investigate, but the gunman was never found...

Thus ended the strange and eventful life of Fultia (Raphael) Klinhoz. The whole town mourned the loss of the brother and sister. And especially the sister, a young and pretty woman, smart and learned, who was very necessary to the town. She was a mother of young children who were left orphans and without a provider, murdered through no fault of her own.

* * *

Yaakov Meiria Kulas lived in the attic of the same house, that of Shperling, next to Dudi Binam Sandrovitz. He was short and broad shouldered, with a short black beard with hints of silver whiskers starting to show up. He looked angry and annoyed. Yakov Meiria was an Alexander Hasid. He was the only one in the *shtibl* who worked, not at an ordinary trade, but a Gentile trade – wood carving. (Except for him, there were no Jewish woodcarvers or carpenters.)

Yakov Meiria would lead the Additional Prayer (Musaf) on High Holy Days in the Alexander shtibl. His praying was very warm, and he prayed with his whole body and with all of his strength, "All my bones will say the words" as the saying goes. He would begin the prayer "I am poor in deeds" (before the Musaf prayer) in a whisper. And then he would suddenly burst out in a great cry "God of Abraham, God of Isaac, and God of Jacob." The whole *shtibl* would be stunned. Then again he would pray in a whisper, and again a great roar would erupt "*Shadai*, the awful and terrible" and again the whole congregation would become alarmed. The children especially would be frightened when they heard the sudden yelling of Yakov Meiria.

In general, the boys and children in the Alexander *shtibl* were afraid of Yakov Meiria. When I saw him, I always pictured the Russian policeman Barchik, who resembled him in height, width, facial expression and beard. When I was a child and saw the policeman Barchik pass our store, I would be frightened to death, and I would hide deep inside the store. (During the year of the revolution, 1905, Barchik relentlessly pursued the rebellious workers, "strikers" as they were called. Until he received a threatening letter with a warning that if he valued his life he should leave the police force within three days, and that's what he did.)

As is well known, the best time for the mischievous kids in the *shtibl* was the hour of Bnei Hichla. At this time, the *shtibl* was dark, with the Hasidim at the dining table, eating the "three repasts" and singing; then the mischief makers would come out in strength. Ragging the Hasidim, helping to chant and sing, overturning the kettle with the water used for ritual washing of the hands, pouring out the contents of the bedpan, or throwing a towel at the head of one of the diners at the table. Neither persuasion nor threats were effective at this time in damping the high spirits and quieting the shouts of the gang of revelers. Then Yakov Meiria would get up and produce in a single roar, ""*Shkotzim, Lavuzes*" ("Infidels, rascals")! And all the mischief-makers would head for the door as fast as they could. And from fear, the quiet children would run too, because if Yakov Meiria got up from behind the table, he didn't make a distinction between quiet children and loud ones.

* * *

Moshe Falka, Yakov Meiria's son-in-law, was from Zdenska-Vola, and settled in Sierpc after marrying Yakov Meiria's daughter. Moshe Falka was a short, gaunt Jew, with a small, wispy beard, and on the Sabbath he could hardly be seen in the broad *kapota* (long coat) and large *shtreimel* (fur hat). He was a great scholar and enthusiastic Hasid. (He was a Strikov Hasid, but since there was no *shtibl* for Strikov Hasidim in Sierpc, and since the two courts, Strikov and Alexander, have common roots in the Byala court, he prayed together with his father-in-law in the Alexander *shtibl*.)

In his first years in Sierpc, Moshe Falka lived with his father-in-law and concentrated on Torah studies and Hasidism. When he struggled to become self-sufficient, he tried a number of ventures, but didn't succeed. For a few years he was a teacher in Mlawa, and his family continued to live in Sierpc. At the end of the 1920's, he moved with his family to Lodz.

* * *

Moshe Yehuda Karsh's small, low, house was behind the Shperling house. He was a member of the town council for many years. He was one of three *lavniks* from the Merchants Association. (*lavnik* – advisor to the mayor. The other two were Poles.) He was an active member of many committees in town.

* * *

The next house was a one-story brick house, and belonged to Moshe Elshtein. Elshtein would collect stones. Not precious stones or ancient stones, but simple rocks. When Moshe Elshtein saw a stone lying in the street, he would immediately take pity on it, bend down and collect it, put it behind the lapel of his coat, and take it back to his yard and add it to one of the piles of stones there...

* * *

During the First World War, about 1916, the Glazer sisters, Hanna and Poza, sold the house to Baruch Lifshitz and Shimon Maniamtzuvka. This was after the death of their Grandfather, Elshtein, and their parents, Akiva and Breina Yetta Glazer. After he acquired part ownership of the house, Baruch Lifshitz started living there. Baruch Lifshitz was a member of the community council for a while. He was selected from the non-partisan list. Baruch Lifshitz emigrated to Eretz-Israel with his family in 5693 (1933) and settled in Bnei-Brak. He passed away in the month of Av 5713 (1953).

* * *

Yakov Hollander lived in the yard of the house that we lived in. Hollander was from Plock. He owned a large shoe store there. After a year as a widower, following his first wife's death, he married the daughter of Yeshaya Kaliski (who had won the big prize of 3000 rubles in the lottery). At the beginning of the First World War, Hollander lost his fortune and came to Sierpc. He earned his living by stitching. For a time during the war, he fashioned soles for sandals by hand from wood blocks. He worked hard, and made very little money.

During the war between Poland and Bolshevik Russia, in the summer of 1920, in the moth of August (beginning of the month of Ellul in 5680) the Bolsheviks occupied Sierpc for 10 days. Our neighbor, Hollander, because he had a hard life, thought of himself as the “bridegroom” at this “wedding,” close to the Bolsheviks who brought salvation to the poor and oppressed. What did he do? He put on his dark Sabbath suit, which he still had from his Plock period. He put the gold watch and chain, which he still kept as a reminder of his glory days, in his vest pocket and went out to meet the liberators.

And what did the visitors do? The first Bolsheviks that he met took his gold watch and chain. And our neighbor returned home poorer, and humiliated...

* * *

A little further on was the house of the watchmaker Menachem Shapiro. It was a one-story dwelling that also housed his store. Menachem Shapiro was a member of the community ccouncil in the 1930s, representing the Artisans' Association. Shapiro had just one leg (he was called “Der Lemer Zeigermacher” – “the Lame Watchmaker”). In the yard adjacent to his (Shmiga's yard) lived

Ziskind Shpirstein, the bookbinder, who also had only one leg (he was called "Der Lemer Einbeinder" – "the Lame Bookmaker"). They both prayed in the Gur *shtibl.*

* * *

The second store in the same house, a grocery store, belonged to Yakov Hirsh Iszajewicz. He was called "Dem Meiden Machers Eidem" ("the Mead Maker's Son-in-Law"). He inherited the name from his father-in-law, who brewed mead. (Liquor made out of honey; it was called *meid* in Yiddish, from the Polish word *miud,* which means honey). He was called "Der Meiden Macher."

Translator's Footnotes

1. From the book *Slownik Geograficzny*, Krolestwa Polskiego, Warsaw, 1880
2. Everywhere on our tour, when we run into brick houses, we will refer to them as such. All other houses were made of wood.
3. Mendel Lipshitz was called by his family name. Apparently not to confuse him with Mendel Lancher, another Alexander Hasid, but a quiet and moderate Jew, who preferred to sit and study to participating in Hasidic parties.
4. Moshe Falka and Moshe Yenkl, very enthusiastic Hasidim, were Strikov Hasidim, a branch that was very close to Alexander (the two Hasidic groups descended from the Byala branch). Since there were no other Strikov Hasidim in Sierpc, they prayed in the Alexander *shtibl.*
5. ,
6. Calls to God
7. tzhina – from the Russian word "tzhi" – tea, i.e. there was a large stove in the cellar, with a large pot in it, where the owner of the "tzhina" would boil water, and sell it for making tea; on week days the transaction would be in cash, and on the Sabbath, for a sugar cube.
8. Jail for minor offenders
9. Jail for major criminals
10. The "Klashtor" that was on the street on the hill that was later called "3rd of May".
11. There were no gas or electric stoves (this applies to the countryside towns, since Warsaw already had gas and electricity for lighting and cooking). Kerosene stoves were not used much, and gasoline cookers were new and very rare.
12. "Endekim" – A nationalist, anti-Semitic party, whose name was "Narodova Demokratzia" (National Democracy) or N.D. for short, "En-De"
13. See further on, in the review of the streets Zhaba, the New Market, 3rd of May.
14. Family names
15. He meant Meir Rosen, who sold eggs, and was called "Meiria Yaishnik" or "Meir Yitzazh".

The Streets: Zhavia, New Market, Third of May

We will continue our stroll, and tour the streets of Zhavia, New Market, and Third of May. In the mid 1930s, when the Town Council changed the names of the streets, Zhavia Street became the First of May Street, in honor of the international workers day celebrated on that date.

* * *

The second house from the start of Zhavia Street was a one-story house that belonged to Biniatzki (a Pole). Yakov Shimon Rosenfeld's store was in this house. He sold flour and all kinds of grits there; he was called “Yakov Shimon Mel-shenker” (Yakov Shimon the Flour Store Owner). Yakov Shimon was a dedicated public figure and faithfully served the community. He was a treasurer in the Welcome Guests Society and the Funeral Society (*Hevra Kadisha*).

After the Biniatzki house there was a small street called Zhalona. This street extended to the New Market, and to the large lot that was used for the pig market.

* * *

At the end of this small street, near the pig market, was the small house of Zalman Friedman (who was called Zalman Berias, after his father-in-law Beria Oberfeld) and inside the house was his small grocery store.

Zalman Beria was a great scholar. His wife, Gitel, took care of the store, and he sat and studied Torah all the time. He wrote a book called *Rimzai Shlomo* (*Hints of Shlomo*) named after Shlomo Zalman (founder of Hasidism) that explains “many of the legends told by the wise men in all of the tractates by hints and implications” (as stated on the cover page). The first volume of the series is on the tractates Brachot, Shabat, Eiruvin, Pesachim, and Shekalim and was published in Bulgaria in the year 5695. The first part contained 239 pages, including a two-page summary and a nine-page introduction. Apparently, none of the other volumes ever appeared in print. The dedication that appeared opposite the cover page stated “And remember for her goodness my partner Madame Gitel, may she live a long life, who helped me with all her power to have this book printed, and her virtue will stand with her forever”.

Zalman Friedman initiated and carried out a great and important undertaking, an undertaking that had the elegance of truth, but not just the elegance of truth. Because, by this deed, he performed an act of charity for both the dead and the living. During the period that he was the treasurer of the Funeral Society, Zalman reformed the cemetery. He marked the rows of graves in alphabetical order, a different letter for each row, and numbered the graves in each row, and put up a sign next to every row with its letter and the grave numbers. He also prepared a notebook with the names of all those laid to rest in the cemetery listed alphabetically, with the row and grave number listed next to each name. In addition, he prepared a plan of the cemetery, with every lane and path, every row and grave noted, and on each grave, its letter and number. Using the notebook and the plan, it was simple to locate any grave. And the Jews of Sierpc who went to visit the graves of their ancestors were helped enormously and praised Zalman for this.

David Noah Zilberberg, who had an apt hand for these matters, did the laborious scripting of the notebook and drafting of the plan.

* * *

The house where Yisrael Vasolak lived, a two-story house, was on the other corner of this street. His textile store was in this house, with an entrance from the New Market. Yisrael was once a shochet (ritual slaughterer) in the village of Osvaka, and so was called Osveker Shoichet.

* * *

Yosef Karpa lived on the second floor of the same house. His origins were in Dobrzyn, and he settled in Sierpc when he married Hezkel (Yehezkel) Izikovitch's daughter, Nehama (who was called Hama), after he had lived for a few years in the nearby towns working as a clerk. Yosef Karpa was a handsome and pleasant man. He was a wise Jew and an interesting conversationalist. He was popular and well liked by his acquaintances. During the 1920s, Yosef Karpa was a member of the community council. (He was elected on the Aguda list as the representative of the Alexander *shtibl.*)

* * *

We return to Zhaba (Zhavia) Street. The restaurant and hotel of Lazer (Eliezer) Burstein was in the second house from the corner, a one-story house with an attic. For many years, until the 1930s, this was the only Jewish restaurant and hotel in town (not counting the inns of Zelig Richgut and the Shlisharken. During the 1930's, Mendel Licht opened his hotel.

* * *

Yeshaya Mordecaye Kaliski lived in the attic of that house. He taught little children, so obviously his heder (one-room school) was in his "large and spacious" apartment. In addition to his official occupation, teaching, Shaya Mordecaye had a side occupation, which was the sale of lottery tickets. More to the point, the sale of shares in tickets, quarters, or eighths of tickets, for what Jew in Sierpc would buy a complete, or half ticket? From his two callings combined, he lived a life of harsh poverty.

His second occupation didn't always bring in profits. Sometimes, when he could not sell all the parts of the ticket, he would have to cover the cost of the remainder from the "generous" income from his official occupation. This would occur from time to time, and each time, Shaya Mordecaye would regret the *shirim* (remainders) that he was left with. But Shaya was a Hasid (of Gur) and he believed that "remainders" held a special charm. But these were remainders from the table of the Rebbe, not heaven forbid, remainders of lottery tickets.

But once there was a miracle. A lottery ticket, three quarters of which had been sold by Shaya Mordecaye, and one quarter of which he was not able to get rid of, won the grand prize. The news that Sierpc had the grand prize hit the town like a bolt of lightning on a clear day. And who were the winners? Four Jews who were very poor. (One of them immediately returned money that had been collected for him a few days earlier.) And who was the agent? Shaya Mordecaye! And he was also among the winners! The winning of the lottery caused a great commotion in town, with joy and jealousy mixed together. People said that the Master of the Universe had performed a great mitzvah for these Jews by letting them win the grand prize. Many people saved from their pittance to buy a quarter or at least an eighth of a ticket.

Everyone talked about the "grand prize." Actually, the amount was only 12,000 rubles (the real grand prize was 75,000 rubles). This meant that they each won 3,000 rubles, but this was also a huge amount in those days.

After this event, Shaya Mordecaye left pedagogy, and developed his occupation as an "agent." He took on other businesses, married off his daughters, who had been of marriageable age for some time, and had a little satisfaction from life. The Gentiles called Shaya Mordecaye "*Stchaneshlivi Jid*" (the Happy Jew).

* * *

Zhaba Street (Zhavia ? First of May) extended to Pirogova Street. This street, Pirogova, went to Fara Street to the right, and to the New Market to the left. The town council changed the street names in the mid-1930s, and the name Pirogova was changed to Piaretzki, in honor of the Polish minister of the interior of the same name, who was assassinated by a political rival.

* * *

The house at the corner of Zhaba and Pirogova Streets (the house in which Yosef Meir Kuda lived) and the two houses next to it, all three of them two-story houses, belonged to Avraham Melave (Melave did not live in them himself).

In the first house (above Kuda's shoe store) lived Hershel Yosef Gotglas. The family name has an interesting story behind it. Hershel Yosef, who was usually called by the family name Gotglas, sometimes was called Dobroshklinka (the Polish translation of Gotglas ? good glass). His brother was called Yakir Dobroshklinka and his son was called Leibush Dobroshklinka, and his daughter ? Dvora Gotglas.

Hershel Yosef was one of the elders of the town, and one of the important Gur Hasidim. (In this too he differed from his brother, who prayed in the Alexander *shtibl.*)

Yisrael Yakov Cohen lived in the middle house, which was made of brick. Cohen was a partner of Volkoviski in the drugstore (*skaled aptchani*), and in the evening he tutored mathematics, languages, and other subjects. Cohen was a Zionist and a member of the committee of Agudat Tzion. Later he became a member of Poalei Tzion (before the schism). Cohen was not originally from Sierpc. He came to our town from Plonsk (Plinsk). After the war, he lived in Plock, where he was a teacher in the Jewish High School.

After the three houses of Melave, there stood the two-story brick house of Kabiatkovski (a Pole). This was the corner house of Pirogova and New Market streets. When the town council gave the streets new names, in the mid-1930s, the New Market was named The Plaza of the Sixth of Sharpian in honor of the date when Pilsudski's Polish Legion left Krakow for the front at the beginning of the First World War (6 August 1914) to fight the Russians.

* * *

The Butchers' House (*Di Yotkes*) was at the start of the New Market. This was a U-shaped red brick house, without plaster. The open side faced the market and was divided into cells. The building belonged to the town council, which rented the cells to the butchers. Almost all the cells (there were about 14 of them) were rented to Jews, and only about two or three to Gentiles.[16] At the front of the Butchers' House, facing the street, were two stores, Liechtenstein's grocery store and a store that sold eggs and butter run by Shepsel (Shabtai) Visroza. Between them was a passageway to the butcher stores.

* * *

Behind the Butchers' House lay the New Market. This was a large, paved square. On most days of the week, the New Market was empty, and you could, as the saying goes, "Sleep in the middle of the market." But on market days, especially on Tuesday, this market would be packed with carts full of grain, since the New Market was intended for grain sales. The carpenters also displayed their wares here: tables, chairs, cabinets, beds, and cradles. Rope was also sold here. It was hung in stalls that resembled those of the shoemakers: two tall posts, with a beam between them.

There were almost no stores in the New Market, and there were few houses there. One side, to the left, was occupied almost completely by lumberyards, and tall wooden fences, with gates, separated the yards from the New Market. The rear of the market was an open, unpaved lot, which was the pig market. Only at the rear were there two houses: one owned by a Pole, which had a tavern, and the second owned by Moshe Aharon Nachfin. The Poles lived on the right side of the New Market. Their houses were inside yards, and in the front were gardens and trees. Between these gardens there was a narrow, unpaved lane that reached the municipal slaughterhouse. From here on, lived the Jews.

* * *

One of the houses, a one-story house, belonged to Binyamin Neiman, and his lumberyard was in the yard. Avigdor Greenberg, from Mlawa, lived in the same house. He lived in town until the middle of the First World War.

In those days, the means of transportation between Sierpc and towns of the region were the cart, the *faubuz* (an enclosed carriage), and the omnibus, yoked to horses. A few years before the First World War, a bus line had a daily route Rypin-Sierpc-Plock. This was a huge innovation in the life of the town, and a sign of development and progress. Approximately at six o'clock, the bus would arrive in Sierpc on its way from Plock to Rypin, and stop for an hour at the Magistrats (town hall). For months, many people ? men, women, and children ? would gather in this part of the market, before the bus arrived, while it was parked, and after it left, amazed at this great wonder (such a large bus, and it moves without horses!), discussing and arguing about it, and about technology in general.

A few partners owned the bus, and Greenberg was one of them, the only partner from Sierpc. The ticket seller on the bus was Jewish, and he worked on Saturday as well. When he was asked why he rode on the Sabbath, he would answer "Why, is the Sabbath a bear?" (*Vos iz Shabos a ber?*) The answer would amaze and irritate all the listeners. Before the First World War, Avigdor Greenberg was a member of the community council.

* * *

A little further on stood the one-story house of Itzik Rosen, also with lumber stored in his yard. Itzik Rosen was one of the important Gur Hasidim. He was a wise and respected Jew, and was considered one of town's rich men. Before the First World War, Itzik Rosen was a member of the community council.

* * *

Itzik Rosen's son, Zelig, was an active Zionist. He was also an active library supporter. Zelig Rosen was a member of the first town council during the period of Polish independence, representing the Zionist party list.

* * *

After Itzik Rosen's death, the house was sold to Leibush Dobroshklinka and Yeshiayahu Friedman. In 1934, Leibush Dobroshklinka and all his family moved to Eretz-Israel. He passed away in 5716 (1955).

* * *

A little further on was the brick two-story house of Elkana Bukat. One of the daughters of the Bukat family, Rebcha (Rivka), was a teacher in the government elementary school for Jewish children.

Berish Loite lived in the same house, and his ironware store was there. Berish Loite, Shmualtia Vilk, and Avraham Fried (Yerushalmi) were a special group in the Alexander *shtibl*. They were considered a little heretical (actually, the first two were considered a little heretical, and the third, more than just a little). The Hasidim called them "The Trio" (*di Troike*). They always stood together, talked to each other, and left the *shtibl* after prayers together. For years, every Saturday, Avraham Fried would "buy" a *maftir* [the last blessing on the reading of the Torah) and honor one of the Trio members with it.

* * *

The *kleismer* (musician at weddings) Haim Liechtenstein lived on the second floor of the same house. In the yard lived Haim Yosef Garlitz (a tall, old Jew who was called "*Der Hoicher Malauch*" ? the Tall Angel) and his son Avraham the kleismer (also tall, who was called "*Malauch der Kleismer*" ? the Angel Musician).

* * *

Until the First World War, in the period of Russian rule in Poland, it was accepted in the Jewish communities that the candidates for army induction would get together in the prayer house every night for a few weeks before the date of induction. These gathering had two official purposes, and an unofficial one. The official purposes were: a) to say the Psalms and pray to be rescued from the Gentiles; and b) to inflict oneself with sleeplessness, to lose weight, and thereby, in combination with other torments, to become exempt from army service, or get a green card, i.e. deferment for a year. The unofficial purpose was the once-in-a-lifetime chance, on the eve of army service, for complete abandonment, boisterousness, and mischief.

In Sierpc, the candidates for induction would gather in the Old House of Prayer. The induction date was in the month of Heshvon, when the nights are already cold. In order to heat the prayer house, the group would pull up fences, take apart steps near stores, and confiscate wooden crates that it found. With this wood, they would heat the place, using the two big stoves in the prayer house, until they almost exploded from the heat. The pranksters among them would pull off various shenanigans. They would move items from one yard to another, and from one street to another. They would shut the door of a store, or an apartment, or a shutter, so that it would be very difficult to open in the morning. They would wake people up and inform them about burglaries or fires that happened to their relatives, and so forth.

Sometimes, there would be among the candidates for induction a pampered lad, the son of a wealthy family, or just plain lazy, who would not come to the house of prayer to "sing Psalms." When the group would hear of a shirker like this, a large delegation would go to wake him up and invite him to the house of prayer. The delegation would awaken not only him and his family, but all of his neighbors, and all the tenants of the nearby houses as well. When at last the slacker came out, after various excuses by his parents, that the lad wais not at home or in town, etc, the group would welcome him with great rejoicing, and accompany him with "all the honors" to the prayer house. After this "honor", the boy would not try to malinger any more.

Of course, there were boys who recited the Psalms. And there were boys, that didn't want to participate in all the mischief. But peer pressure forced them to take part in all the activities.

Before dawn, when the morning prayers were not yet required, they would go to a nearby bakery and buy fresh, hot rolls. They would also wake Zelig

Richgut or the *slisharkhe* and buy tea and salted herring, and dine as befits a night of sleeplessness and revelry.

I heard the following story from our respected townsman, Shmuel Itchia Lanter: His peer, Avraham Garlitz (the *kleismer* who was called Avraham Malauch or *Malauch der Kleismer*) did not come to the House of Prayer to "sing Psalms". Of course, the gang came to wake him up, and of course, the whole neighborhood woke up with him. Near the house of the Garlitz family there was a Catholic Church, with a Catholic priest who lived in the yard. The priest woke up in the "general awakening." He went out to the "revelers", scolded them, and lectured to them on morals. The words of the priest convinced the group, and they retreated without accomplishing their mission. After that, a saying became widespread "*Oz moves dem Malauch, kapt zich oif der galauch*" (When the Angel is aroused, so is the priest).

* * *

Sierpc had what many other towns of similar character and size did not ? it had a *kleismer group*. The group had four members: three Jews and a Gentile. And these are the members and their instruments: Avraham Garlitz ? fiddle, Haim Liechtenstein ? viola, Haim Krupiazh ? horn, and the Gentile Franek ? double bass. The group played at weddings in town, and also in neighboring towns that did not have their own group. Sometimes the group would play at a Polish wedding in town, or in the region. An inseparable member of the group was the comedian Avraham Futter (the brother in law of Yermia the bookseller), who would appear together with them at weddings (of course, not at Polish weddings). The "artistry" of the musicians was at a higher level than that of the comedian. And there were rich Jews who would invite a comedian from the big city to their children's weddings. But still, they would not withhold payment to the local comedian.

All the members of the *kleismer* group also had other jobs. The comedian also taught Torah to little children. And in spite of the two professions, he was a pauper. Garlitz, whose musical abilities were greater than that of his companions, would give music lessons. Krupiazh milled grits and sold them in a store on Zhaba Street (he was called *Kasha Macher* ? Maker of Grits). More characteristic was the second calling of Liechtenstein, which was the complete opposite of his main occupation. It was chiseling inscriptions on gravestones (he was called *Matzeva Kritzer* ? Gravestone Writer). I don't know anything about Franek's other job (if drinking can't be considered a job), but I do know of his second language. He spoke Yiddish almost like a Jew, with all the Hebrew expressions in Yiddish. When he was drunk ? and it happened fairly often ? Franek would say "*Ich Franek ehrlicher man*" (I, Franek, am an honest man). And possibly this hints at his other job?

* * *

A Catholic church called *Shabianti Duch* (Holy Spirit) stood next to the Bukat house (it was the smallest of the three Catholic churches in town), and next to it, the priest's residence. The church was built in 1519, destroyed in a fire in 1614, and rebuilt in 1850. (The dates are from the book *Slownik Geograficzny Krolestwa Polskiego*, Warsaw, 1880.)

Apparently, this spot was beyond the Jewish area in olden days, and the church was built here because of this. In our times, the church here, among Jewish houses, was like a baby held prisoner...

* * *

Beyond the church there was an unpaved lane. The lane was called Tzhalpin. When the town council, in the mid-1930s, changed the street names, this lane was called Zharomski after the Polish author, Stefan Zharomski.

There were few houses in this lane. At a certain time, starting in 1916 or 1917, the library was in one of the houses in this lane. (At the time, there was just one Jewish library in Sierpc, under Zionist management.) The lane continued to the village of Boborova, which was about one kilometer from town. The Sierpianitza River passed through the village, and many young people would go there to bathe in the river. There were Jews who knew how to swim, who on Friday, instead of going to the *mikveh*, would go to Boborova (in the summer of course) for a dip in the river.

* * *

We called New Market both the market square and the streets surrounding the market. The continuation of the street behind Tzhalpin Lane was called Klashturna, after the monastery (*klashtur*) that was there. In later years, this street was called Third of May, in honor of the Polish constitution, which was adopted on May 3, 1793.

* * *

The house that stood on the corner of Zharomski Lane and Third of May Street was a two-story brick house that belonged to Aharon Czernoczepka. Aharon

Czernoczepka, who owned a lumberyard, was considered one of the rich men in town. He was a respected Gur Hasid. At the start of the German conquest (during the First World War), Aharon Czernoczepka was appointed to the town council by the occupation authorities. He was a councilman after the war as well, and for a while, he was a *lavnik* (advisor to the mayor). Later on, the house was sold to Mendel Karpa.

The school of Mordecai Hertz Mintz was on the first floor. Previously, it had been on the small street near the Kamnitza (near the Jewish Street).

* * *

Czernoczepka house was near the bridge over the Sierpianitza. This part of the street had a rural air: gardens, trees, and houses in yards with greenery and flowers, and green fences at the front. Only Poles lived here.

* * *

There was a pavilion with three statues near the bridge, a Catholic holy place. When they passed, they would doff their hats and cross themselves. Jews called the place "*Menashe and His Three Sons*" (Menashe mit di 3 zihen) and when they passed by, they would try not to look at it.[17]

* * *

The bridge over the Zhika (the Sierpianitza River) was a link between the town and some busy roads, and therefore was built to last. It was also built high over the river, so that the light floods that would occur from time to time at the end of the winter wouldn't submerge it. The Zhika that flowed here was very deep, and its two banks were covered with a multitude of greenery: grass, flowers, and trees.

* * *

On the other side of the bridge there is a wonderful and charming vista: the street continues and climbs up, and to the right, a hill. Steps hewn into the side of the hill lead to a Catholic church at the top, and the hillside, tall and steep, separates the street from the church. To the left, a wide and beautiful valley unfolds, gladdening the heart with its colors and vegetation. These are the famous "valleys" (*Dolinki*) of the town and its surroundings. These are the valleys that, during the rule of the Tsar, were used for illegal meetings of the revolutionary parties of the Sierpc young people; these are the valleys where the Sierpc youth strolled on Saturdays and holidays, breathed their fresh air, lay on the soft grass, and bathed in the clean river, the Sierpc river, Sierpianitza, that flowed in those valleys.

* * *

The church, which stood on the summit of the hill, was put up in 1483 to house the picture of the Mother of God that had been miraculously discovered. The name of the church was The Ascension to Heaven of the Mother of God. In spite of modifications of the church building in 1787 and 1801, and a fire that broke out in 1794, the old building lines remained.

In 1620, a Benedictine convent was put up next to the church. When the wooden building of the convent burnt down in 1703, a brick building was put up in its place, and remains there to this day.

* * *

Beyond the church, there is a road with branches to the right and left. To the right, the road continues until the end of the Vloka (*Vlikes*), a suburb that was later incorporated into the town. From there it descends to the right, to the Jewish Street, or to travel, to the left, to Biezun (Bezvin). To the left the road continues to Rypin and to Lipno (it is called Rypin Road).

During the German occupation in the First World War, the Germans built a narrow gauge railway track for a small train (*kolaika*) that went between Lowicz and Nasielsk. This train also passed Sierpc, and the station was in this area, on the way to Lipano. Because of this, the area developed, some buildings were put up, and a few Jewish families lived here (the brothers Itcha Meir and Hershel Motil, Yosef Applebaum).

On the left side of this road were three adjacent Christian cemeteries (only brick walls separated them): Catholic, Orthodox, and Evangelical.

In the mid-1930's, when the town council changed the street names, the road to Lipano (the part close to town) was named Lipnovaska. The road from Lipnovaska Street to the right that goes to Rypin was called Rypinskaya. And the road that leads from the church to the right (and continues to the Vloka) was called Biazhonska. We have come to the end of town. We will go back on the other side of the street.

We mentioned the church that stood at the top of the hill. During the German occupation of the First World War, the Germans build a jail behind the church, and transferred the *koza* (prison for petty crimes) and the *vanzhnia* (prison for major crimes) from Pirogova Street, near Garfinkel's house.

* * *

There were a few houses in front of the bridge. Among the few Jewish families that lived there was the Mendel Gurfinkel family. He and his ancestors were men of the woods, expert workers who were clerks and cashiers in various forests. When the First World War broke out, Mendel Gurfinkel lived in the forests of Chomsk, 18 kilometers from Sierpc on the way to Rypin. A Gentile, who had been fired from his job by Mendel Gurfinkel because of theft, falsely informed on him to the Russians, saying that he had sold horses to the Germans. Cossacks arrested Mendel Gurfinkel, and took him into the forest in order to kill him. Peasants from the area came to his aid and pleaded with the Cossacks not to kill this Jew, that he was an honest and good man and helpful to the forestry workers and all the peasants of the area. The Cossacks heeded the importuning of the peasants and decided to bring Mendel Gurfinkel to their headquarters in Sierpc. When the Cossacks marched Mendel Gurfinkel through the streets of Sierpc, he managed to inform Meir Tzafris of his arrest. The report spread throughout the town, and Jews tried to save him. Aharon Tchernotchepka and Isaac Rosen testified to his honesty, and gave their houses as a guarantee for him. The *soltis* (village chief) of Chomsk testified for him, and proved, using the village ledgers, that the peasant who had been fired by Mendel had threatened to get even (at the time, Mendel Gurfinkel had made sure that the threat was recorded in the village ledger). Thanks to the efforts of Jews and Gentiles, Mendel Gurfinkel was saved from death.

Mendel Gurfinkel was a respected Gur Hasid, and he was the representative of the Aguda from Sierpc to the Great Assembly of Agudat Israel in Vienna in approximately 1928. For a certain period, Mendel Gurfinkel was a member of the town council and a member of the community council, representing Agudat Israel.

* * *

Across the bridge there were houses of Poles, surrounded by trees, flowers, and greenery.

A little further on, across from Tchernotchepka's house was a one-story house that belonged to the German, Fatlick. The teacher, Mordecai Hirsh Mintz, lived in this house (previously he lived in the narrow street near the Kamnitza). A small room in Mintz's apartment was the first office of Agudat Tzion, in the years 1916-1917.

* * *

After the Fatlick house there was a small street named Shkolna (School Street), because of the government school there. This street continued until Para (Farska) Street. In the mid-1930's the street was called Shpitalna (Hospital Street), after the hospital there. (The hospital was later moved to Piastovska Street.)

* * *

Binyamin Sherpherz lived on this street, and if my memory serves me correctly, he was the only Jew that lived on this street. Binyamin Sherpherz was not from Sierpc. He was clerk in a forest near Sierpc (he was also called "Binyamin Volyar" after his previous place of residence ? Volya) and from there he came to live in Sierpc. He was in the lumber business. He had a small cart and horse, and he would go every day to a village or to the woods, on business. But this business was not enough to maintain his household (he had a few intelligent daughters, Polish speaking, and well dressed) and he was supported by his son Yisrael (Yisraelke), a rich lumber merchant, who opened a sawmill (and next to it a lumberyard) at the edge of town, on the Vloka, on the road to Biezun, and later, at the end of Plotzki Street, behind the big park.

Binyamin Sherpherz was an Alexander Hasid. His younger son, David, studied at the Gur yeshiva, in one of the upper grades, and was one of the outstanding students there. He would come home only for the holidays. At the start of World War I, when the classes at the yeshiva were cancelled, David Sherpherz came back to Sierpc and remained in town.

David Sherpherz was an exception among the young men of Sierpc with regard to his Hasidic behavior. He grew a beard, and wore an Atlas *kapota* (long coat) on Sabbath. He prayed fervently, deliberately, and with a great many movements. In later years, when David Sherpherz entered the world of business ? the lumber business ? he shortened his beard and his clothes. In the end, he dressed in regular clothes, and the beard vanished entirely...

* * *

After Shkolna-Shpitalna Street, we again enter the New Market (Sixth of Sharpian Place). The first house, a one-story house, was that of Yakir Dobroshklinka. He was an Alexander Hasid. He would pray Kol Nidre and Neila in the Alexander *shtibl.*

* * *

Berish Sosnovski lived in the yard of the same house. He was from Lipno (37 kilometers from Sierpc) and he came to Sierpc as the son-in-law of Isaac Rosen. Berish Sosnovski was a quiet and serious man, and very particular about his appearance. His beard was always combed, and his clothes were clean. He was an Alexander Hasid, and he was always reading a book in the *shtibl.*

* * *

A little further on was the one-story house of Isaac Neiman, who owned the grocery store in the same house. Isaac Neiman was an enthusiastic Zionist, completely faithful and devoted. He was one of the founders of Mizrachi in Sierpc.

* * *

A bit further, opposite the Butchers' House, stood the house of Haim Itche Neiman (later sold to Avraham Lushinski). This was a big, handsome, two-story house. The owner was also a handsome Jew. Itche Neiman was a student of the Torah, a Hasid (Gur Hasid), and in spite of this, also a little Enlightened. He spoke Polish and Russian, knew how to prepare requests to the authorities and institutions, and knew some of the laws of the land.

I heard the following story from my Rabbi Moisheye Karmelkeies (Danziger). Haim Itche Neiman was known in the offices of the municipal authorities, the government, and the courts, where he would sometimes visit because of his own affairs, or representing others. Once a Polish clerk (this was during Russian rule, before the First World War) gave him an answer that was not to the point. I will tell you what Haim Itche said to him:

"During the Povstania (the Polish rebellion against the Russians in 1863), a *povstaniatz* (rebel) was looking for shelter after a defeat suffered by his regiment in a battle with the Cossacks. He came to the house of a Jew in a village, and asked to be hidden there. The Jew pointed to the baking oven as the safest hiding place. The soldier agreed, and with no other alternative, crawled in and lay there. A short time later, an officer of the rebels came running to the same house, with the same request: to hide him. He showed him the baking oven as well, and the officer crawled in and lay there also.

After he calmed down a little from the flight and the fear, he sensed that someone else was in the oven, and asked, ?Who are you?' The soldier identified himself, and then the officer said, ?What, you are a plain soldier, and don't show proper respect to an officer next to you?' And the soldier answered, ?But sir, now we are both in an oven.'"

The clerk took the hint and changed his answer.

* * *

All of Haim Itche Neiman's sons had an artistic bent. Their contemporaries said that when they were still students in the *heder*, Neiman's sons would be drawing pictures of the Rabbi and the students under the desk, during the lesson. The drawings were very good. One of the sons, Avraham Neiman, took up art, and became a famous painter in Poland and abroad. Most of his pictures are of the Carpathian Mountains.

Avraham Neiman visited Sierpc two or three times when he was already a famous artist. He had long hair, which came down to his shoulders, and the children would yell at him "*Galauch*" (priest). Once he went onto the bridge on Jewish Street dressed casually, with a satchel on his back, leggings on his feet, paint brushes in his hand, and started drawing the Zhika (river) and the surrounding scenery. Of course, all the passers by, and especially the children, stopped to stare at the strange person and his strange preoccupation.

I heard from our respected townsman, Shmuel Itcha Lanter, that he studied with a Gemara tutor called Itzhak Malchas (his family name was Prager). A few years earlier, Mendel Neiman studied with the same tutor. (His name was Avraham Mendel, and when he was a child he was called just Mendel.) The tutor told his pupils that Mendel once ran away from the *heder* in the middle of a lesson. When the children left the *heder* in the middle of the school day, they saw that a large picture of the Rabbi had been drawn in chalk on the outside door, with his beard hanging down and the *lulke* (pipe) in his mouth. They called the Rabbi and he saw it and liked the picture, which closely resembled him. That was the work of Avraham (Mendel) Neiman.

I also heard from Mr. Lanter (whose house was near the Neiman house) that Haim Itche Neiman greatly interfered with his son's attempts at drawing. He saw them as childish and mischievous acts that on the one hand lead to a disregard for the Torah, and on the other hand, have no practical outcome. It got to a point that once when he came home, after he had been out of town for a few months, the father demanded rent from his son for the room where he had left his pictures. But the sons of Lipa Cahana (the owner of the neighboring house) came to the artist's aid. Even then they were considered Enlightened, and saw artistic value in their young neighbor's pictures. They let him use a hut in their yard for his work. And Avraham Neiman stayed there and pursued his holy work during the time he lived in Sierpc, until he went abroad to study art.

Avraham Neiman was born in 1873. He studied painting at the Academy of Art in Krakow. During the First World War he was in Vienna (his wife was Viennese, the daughter of the famous publisher, Fisher) and in 1918 settled in New York. He came to Eretz-Israel from America, and then returned to Europe and lived in Krakow. During the Holocaust he was in the Krakow Ghetto, and was killed during the deportation of some of the Jews in the Ghetto, in 1942.

In the *General Encyclopedia* published by Masada, it states: "Neiman, Avraham: A Jewish landscape painter in Poland, born 1873. Became famous for his winter scenes of Zakopane and the Tatat Mountains. Visited Eretz-Israel at the beginning of this century, and also in the years 1925-27, and drew landscapes."

In *Davar* of 5 Sivan 5719 (2 February, 1949) there was an article by the poet Meir Busak titled "Avraham Neiman and Mordecai Gvirtik in Krakow Ghetto (Seven Years After their Death)." We include an excerpt from this article:

"In his search for a solution to the secrets of colors and their composition, to arrange them in harmonies and contrasts, his pursuit of the joy and splendor of the purified gold, green and white, Avraham Neiman wandered all over the world. He painted and exhibited in Poland, Germany, France, Italy, Belgium, Holland, England, America, and Eretz-Israel. When the Second World War broke out, he was in Krakow.

"With all the other ?lucky ones' who received residence permits in the Ghetto, he did not have to leave the city, and stayed in the new Jewish Quarter. He shaved his beard, and only when he started walking bare headed, a little humiliated, did his magnificent head of hair turn white. Tall and haggard, in a black suit, he was always in a hurry (God knows why), roaming through the Ghetto and giving the impression of a caged animal.

"He who was used to a life of luxury in Western Europe, a painter whose pictures were worth hundreds of dollars in America, lived in a damp, dark narrow room at the corner of Yanova and Vela, and starved.

(Here the article discusses Gvirtik)

"Avraham Neiman, when he was in the Ghetto, was absorbed in the world of art. He was rooted in nationhood and art. He always tied these two concepts together: nationhood (in terms of tens of thousands and millions) and art. Once, during an exhibition, he pointed at one of his pictures and said that it had received the First Prize ? the prize of the Jewish people. After a moment he added ?I saw that every Jew who came to my exhibition stood looking at this picture for a while. That is my prize.'

"He starved in the Ghetto. He had to make do with the spoon of sauce he received from the Judenrat, and his giant, strong, and healthy frame demanded food. He would earn a little money from drawing pictures for Ghetto dwellers. The hunger would leech his blood and nibble at his flesh, and he was immersed in a world of art. Once I met him in the street and his face was beaming with happiness. ?Some professors from the Art Academy visited me. They saw my new pictures and all of them said that Neiman is advancing with giant steps.' He was then 69.

"Everyone wondered where he got the money for paints and canvas. He hung his pictures in the display window of a tinsmith's workshop, above jugs and faucets. Since he had been accustomed to an environment of admirers and devotees of art, he couldn't get used to the fact that there had been changes in his life, that the struggle for existence had taken on a new, more brutal form. That the strong pushed away the weak, and that the despicable had taken over the supervision of the Ghetto and saw an artist as a superfluous being.

"Once, when he was refused support at some aid agency, Neiman threatened, ?You'll see what I'll do to you, you'll see!' he yelled, all rage and temper.

"What?" asked the agency official.

?I will stand at the entrance to the Judenrat and scream until the whole world will hear that the Krakow Judenrat stands by while the greatest of Jewish painters starves to death.'

"In spite of his ties to world painting, Neiman was all Jewish. He lived and painted for many years in Eretz-Israel, and his memories of that country filled his life in the Ghetto. Near his house there was a garden with a few trees. He would assemble the tenants of the house in this garden, and tell them:

'Do you see these trees? Well, listen to this. There, in that land, there is the greenery of spring; the trees are green like emeralds. And if you saw the heavens of that land... and the sun... There, it is not the glow of the sun that pours out, but the sun itself...'

"Very often he would read and interpret the Bible, which he kept reading, in an up-to-date way. There was a young man living in Neiman's house, a servant of the Gestapo (killed later by the Germans), who always tormented Neiman. From his second floor window he would yell out at the garden, ?Again that foolish old man is jabbering, a crazy man... I'll show you. I know people in Judenrat, and they'll throw you out of your apartment...'

"Neiman, with his temper, wouldn't back down. He would raise his clenched fists, spit out insults and curses, and finally turn to the tenants of the house:

"? ?I'm not afraid of him. I know the Bible.'

"Of course the tenants didn't understand the connection between knowledge of the Bible and fear of the Gestapo. But Neiman explained it to them:

"'What can he do to me? The principles of justice and integrity in our Bible will in the end be victorious. In any case, all the victories of these thieves amount to nothing. They will fail, and lose, even if they kill me. The ideals sown in the world are eternal, and they will win. What is this servant of the Gestapo compared to our Bible?'

"On June 4, 1942, when the rumor spread that among the 200 dead in the shipment from Krakow were both Neiman and Gvirtik, the words of the former came to mind: ?What can he do to me?' and the echo of the poem of the latter:

"'The scents of spring are in space, the world is in depression, and receding.'"

* * *

The grocery store and apartment of Beinam Veismal were in this house. He was one of the important and outstanding Gur Hasidim. He was the right hand man of Yakov Moshe Teitlebaum, but was not as strict as him. Beinam Veismal was a kind man, pleasant and easy in all his conversations with other people.

* * *

The ironworks store of Haim Mintz was in the same house. He had no sons, and brought up Yeshiayahu Friedman, whose parents died when he was a child. He brought him up and educated him as if he were his own son, and also had great fulfillment from him. With the passage of time, he let Yeshiayahu manage the store, and at the end of his life, signed it over to him. Yeshiayahu Friedman was a devoted and outstanding Zionist activist. He was active in all the Zionist institutions and funds, and also cultural and educational institutions. In the 1930s Yeshiayahu Friedman was a member of the town council and the community council. He visited Eretz-Israel in 1934, bought land in Yokenam, and returned to Poland.

* * *

We again find ourselves in Pirogova (Piaretzki) Street, which continues until Para (Parska) Street. The first house, a two-story house, belonged to Shimshon Mordecai Visroza (who was called "Shimshe Mortke").

Shimshon Mordecai's business was eggs, butter, and chickens. Before the market-days (which were on Tuesdays and Fridays), he would give money to poor people, and they would buy eggs, butter and chickens for him on market day. Shimshon Mordecai and his sons, Yakov Yosef, Shepsel (Shabtai) and Yehuda, would do the same. After the market days he would get the goods from his buyers, arrange the accounts with them, prepare the merchandise, and send it on to Warsaw.

Yehoshua (Shia) Visroza, Shimshon Mordecai's younger brother, who lived in the market in Pinchas Malave's house, traded in the same merchandise, but on a smaller scale. His main occupation was his grocery store, which was situated in the house in which he lived.

The two brothers were Alexander Hasidim, and not only were they not famous cantors, or much praised prayer leaders, but they also couldn't sing a single clear on-key note. As is well known, it is customary that someone who has a *yahrzeit* (the day of memorial for the death of a parent) stands in front of the Ark to lead the prayer. And as if it were the devil's work, the memorial days for their parents almost always were on the Sabbath. So what did Shimshon Mordecai and Yehoshua do? They would relinquish ahead of time those parts of the service that Hasidim would sing (the prayers of Sabbath eve with "Lecha Dodi" and the morning prayer with "El Adon"), and they would divide the rest of the prayers between themselves: Shimshon Mordecai would stand before the Ark on Sabbath Eve starting with "Barchu" and on Saturday morning with the Musaf, and Yehoshua would stand before the ark for the morning prayer until "Shochen Ad." But the brothers were unable even to reproduce the familiar melodies of these prayers. Shimshon Mordecai would pray in a tone that seemingly always became higher, and Yehoshua, in a tone that always went lower.

The Hasidim would make fun of them, "Shimshe Mortke asks, and Shia answers."

* * *

Meir Yisrael Iszajewicz (who was called "Shma Yisrael") lived in the same house. Meir Yisrael was a *shpiliter*[18] who brought merchandise from Lodz. There were a few *shpiliters* who brought merchandise from Warsaw: Yischar Bergson (and later, his son David), Shmuel Itzhak Tatz, Wolfe Nazhmaski, Elia Fish (a Jew from Warsaw who settled in Sierpc during the First World War), and others. But Lodz didn't have a *shpiliter*. Meir Yisrael was the first and only one who did this. He would bring from Lodz, usually on order, but sometimes without an order, one type of merchandise: stockings. Stockings of all kinds, types, and sizes. Previously, stockings had been brought, like other merchandise, from Warsaw, but because they were made in Lodz, it was cheaper to buy them in Lodz.

After a while, Meir Yisrael began to bring a new product of that type of merchandise, and this was *stoppes* (a kind of sole for a stocking) for repairing stockings. This product had a lot of buyers, because it made life easier for the housewives, and also saved money. Meir Yisrael's mother would sell the stoppes to store owners and to pushcart peddlers in the market.

Meir Yisrael Iszajewicz mother, Toona, was a simple and honest woman, good hearted, and innocent. When we once asked her (she would bring stoppes to our store, too) about the merchandise she sold on credit, Toona answered in a high and annoyed tone, with a quick motion of the hand. "*Ch'veis az z'machen mer an, nor zolen z'zech onessen gesinterheit*" ("I know that they're cheating me, but they should have a long life.") Toona was unable to utter anything more severe than that.

* * *

The second house, a two story building, was that of the lawyer Eliezer Garfinkel. A lawyer or doctor in a small town in those days was a great honor, and a Jewish lawyer or doctor then was usually assimilated, and distant from Jews and Judaism, but the Lawyer Garfinkel was not condescending, and not remote from the "people." He was a good Jew, and Jewish values were close to his heart. Garfinkel prayed in the New House of Prayer, and he came there every Saturday (except when he was occupied with a court case). He had a wide knowledge of the holy texts, and on occasion he would take time off to study a page of Gemara.

* * *

In those days, there were practically no Jewish natives of Sierpc who had a university education. Garfinkel came from Suvlak, and the dentist Lib Heler was also not from Sierpc. There were, however, Jewish doctors in Sierpc. There was Dr. Shapiro (he was in Sierpc a few years before the First World War); there was Dr. Kaddish Hirsh (he was in Sierpc for approximately the last half of the 1920s and the first half of the 1930s); there was Dr. Mintz Zigmund (he was in Sierpc from the beginning of the 1930s until the expulsion of the Jews from the town); and there was Dr. Komorovsky (he was in Sierpc in approximately the years 1936-39). There was also a Jewish lawyer named Dr. Tuch (for approximately the last two years before the war). But they were not natives of Sierpc. Only in Warsaw there was Dr. Zbikalski, and in New York, Dr. Etta (Esther) Grobard-Fox, a dentist, both of them born in Sierpc.

In the period between the two world wars, some Sierpc natives received a higher education, had academic degrees, and worked in various places at their profession. These were:

Dr Yoel (Yulik) Garfinkel (the son of the above mentioned lawyer, now in Israel); Dr. Azriel Shempan (lived before the war in Rypin, now in Israel); Dr. Yeshiayahu Kurte (studied in France, and died there shortly after finishing his studies); Dr. Eliezer Kurte, a dentist, (lived before World War I in Wierzbinik, near Radom, perished in the Holocaust); the lawyer Yehoshua Podskotch (lived in Warsaw before the war, and was active both before the war and in the Ghetto in the Tzentas society, an important group that took care of orphans, ejected from the Ghetto in the great expulsion of August 1942); the lawyer Yehoshua Tzafris (lived in Warsaw before the war, today in South America); the lawyer Yosel Farshnitzki (lived in Warsaw before the war, and perished in France during the Holocaust); Doctor of Chemistry Avraham Bluman (Kcholi) (lived in Warsaw before the war, today in Israel); and the Master of Liberal Arts Yitzhak Blachman (a graduate of the Hebrew University in Jerusalem).

* * *

The *koza* (prison for minor offenders) was in Garfinkel's yard. This was an ordinary house, with bars on the windows, and a guard at the entrance.

* * *

The *vanzhnia* (prison for major criminals) was behind Garfinkel's house. This was a low building with small windows barred with iron bars, surrounded by a large yard, and the yard was enclosed by a high fence, with a guard patrolling the yard.

We already mentioned that during the time of the German occupation in the First World War, the Germans moved both prisons, the *koza* and the *vanzhnia* to Third of May Street (Tzhechko Maya), to the hill behind the Catholic church.

In the large yard of the *vanzhnia* the Germans put up cylindrical corrugated tin huts and arranged them into a military hospital. Both the huts and the corrugated tin were novelties for Sierpc.

Before the Butchers' House was put up in the New Market, meat was sold in small stalls (*boodkes*) that stood on the wide sidewalk in front of the *vanzhnia.*

* * *

After the *vanzhnia* there stood a Catholic church that was called The Ascension to Heaven of the Mother of God. (See below, for a survey of Fara Street.)

We return to Zhavia Street (Zhavia ? First of May).

In the first house, a small one-story house that belonged to Lebogashavski (a Pole) there was a small store for textiles, that belonged to Dudi Beinam (Simcha Beinam) Sandrovitch. Before that, he had sold these goods from his apartment, which was in Plotzki Street, in Shperling's house.

It is interesting to note that in those days, when a trip to America was considered, especially among Hasidic families, a very strange act, and a relative who was in America was thought of as "unfit" for the family, Dudi Beinam went to America, stayed there for a few years, and came back--apparently, because of his business, which was not too successful there.

* * *

The second house, a long one-story home, was the house of Azriel Yehuda Kotcholk.

Some of the Gur Hasidim, the better-off ones, who were also more progressive, split from the rest of the Hasidim and founded their own *shtibl.* The new *shtibl*, which was called "*Shtibl* of the Rich Gur," (S'rache Gerer *Shtibl*) was in the yard of Azriel Yehuda Kotcholk (after a few years, the two *shtibls* united). The same room later housed the Alexander *shtibl.* Azriel would sit in the *shtibl* all day long, and study. Sometimes, when he found a worthy enough opponent, he would play chess in the *shtibl.* He was among the best chess players in town. Sometimes he would play with the Russian commissar, who was also an excellent chess player.

* * *

The ironworks store in that house belonged to Berish Poznanski.

The Jews of Sierpc suffered greatly under the oppressive enemy in the two months (8 September to 8 November, 1939) prior to the expulsion. The cruel foe tortured them physically and spiritually, and abused them. But the accursed Germans reached the peak of cruelty and violence in the tortures they inflicted on Berish Poznanski. He was jailed along with other Jews in the municipal prison house. They were tortured there with cruel and brutal torments. One day they were ordered to dig a trench in the yard, and when they finished digging, the accursed ones buried Berish Poznanski, in the presence of a doctor, up to his neck in the ground. Only when the doctor said he was in danger of dying, did they take him out. The Germans repeated this "game" several times.

During a period in the 1930s, Berish Poznanski was a member of the town council, representing Agudat Israel.

* * *

The second house, two stories high, belonged to Leib Mintz.

Leib Mintz both moved and talked slowly. He was a tailor by trade, and a little bit of a heretic in his outlook. He was among those of little faith, and looked skeptically at the world.

Leib Mintz would make fun of doctors and their knowledge. This is what he used to say: "When I don't feel well, I go to a doctor for advice. The doctor writes a prescription and I pay him. I don't believe him, or in his prescriptions, but he's a human being and needs to make a living. From the doctor, I go to the drugstore. I give them the prescription, receive the medicine, and pay, because the druggist is also a human being and needs to make a living. When I leave the drugstore, I pour out the medicine and throw away the bottle, because I'm also a human being, and I also have to live."

* * *

The next house, a brick one-story house, was that of Frilinski (a Pole). The only store in this house was the barbershop of Moshe Zomer, who was a medical aide. Behind the barbershop was a small apartment that was barely enough for Zomer's family. He would say, "The extent of my Hasidism is greater than that of all the Hasidim in town. It is the custom of Hasidim to put one bed next to one wall, and a second bed next to the second wall. And I put one bed in my room and the second one ? in the storeroom of Baruch Mendel Gotlibovski..."

Zomer was among the veterans of the Enlightenment in Sierpc, and well versed in the Bible.

* * *

Leibush Asher (who was called "Chaver Asher") lived in the yard of this house. He was from Plock, and he settled in Sierpc when he married Melech Tzina's daughter. The two of them, father-in-law and son-in-law, were tailors.

Asher was an outstanding Bundist activist, and was also a good public speaker. He was active in all the institutions of the Bund in town. For a time he was a member of the community council, and also a member of the town council.

Fara Street

We go on to our survey of Fara Street.

The first house, a big two-story house with a cellar belonging to Grabovski (a Pole) was the textile goods store of David Sochaczewski. His wife, Madam Yetta, took care of the store, doing both the buying and the selling. David himself worked in grains when he was younger, and when he was old, sat in the Gur shtibl, prayed, said the Psalms, and studied the Mishna or the Ein Yaakov. The jokesters call him "Radak," an acronym for Reb David Kraviatz (*kraviatz* in Polish is tailor).

* * *

The barbershop of Haim Kolski was in the same house. People would say about Kolski's work that, when many peasants entered his barbershop at the same time, on Sunday, or on market day, he would sit them all down and lather their beards, and explain that if the beard is lathered for a long time, it becomes softer and easier to shave. Once, when many lathered peasants sat in his store, the alarm bells rang because a fire had broken out in one of the villages. All the peasants dashed out of the barbershop, ran to their carts, and rushed to their villages with lather on their faces.

Kolski was also "half a medical aide." The medical fields in which he specialized were cupping glasses, leeches, and enemas.

* * *

The *shpiliter* Shmuel Yitzhak Tatz lived on the second floor of the house. His father, Avraham had been a *shochet* (ritual slaughterer) during the 1880s in the villages around Sierpc.

* * *

The next house, a small single-story one, was the house of the tailor Nuchia Pukatch. In the yard lived Mendel Tatz, who had a *povaz* (enclosed carriage) and a pair of horses, and would take travelers to Plock, on their way to Warsaw. After the railway reached Sierpc, Mendel Tatz traded in his *povaz* for a *droshky* (open carriage) and brought riders to and from the railway station.

Jokesters used to tell that once Mendel Tatz fell asleep in the middle of the seder. In his dream he saw his horse moving very slowly, and in order to speed him up he called "Vyo!" and gave hard pull to the reins. That's what was in his dream, but in reality he pulled the tablecloth off the table and sent everything on it crashing to the floor...

* * *

Anshel (Entzel) Mash lived in the same yard. He was short, with a short beard, and very lazy. In the Alexander *shtibl* (he was an Alexander Hasid), he was like an unofficial caretaker. Everyone used him and gave him orders (not for personal gain, perish the thought) and he did as everyone told him. Without Anshel, there couldn't be a kiddush or a Melave Malke feast, not a party, nor any gathering of Hasidim. He was the first and also the last in every festivity or Hasidic get-together. He helped to prepare every celebration, to bring and set up the tables, the benches, the bottles, glasses, and all kinds of utensils. If there was no water for the ritual washing of hands, a glass, a cup, a corkscrew, anything, someone would immediately yell, “Anshel, bring water! Bring a glass!” etc. And Anshel went to one neighbor, and then another neighbor, and brought it. And even when they overdid using him and it annoyed him, he still didn't refuse. He would grumble into his mustache, complain about the injustices being done to him, quietly, to himself, but he followed orders and brought whatever had been asked for.

Anshel was a *melamed* (teacher). He taught the alphabet to little boys. And his wife, Sara Dvora, was a *rabanit* (*rebetzin*) not just through her husband, but also by her own doing. She taught the alphabet to little girls. Apparently, Anshel's income was not enough to cover his “large” household expenses.

* * *

The nearby house, a single story one, belonged to Vova (Wolfe) Shlezinger. The paint store in the same house was also his, and it was the only store of its kind.

Vova had a kind heart, and he would dispense charity very generously and support everyone who asked it of him.

Vova Shlezinger was among the worshipers at the New Prayer House, and one of the veteran Hovevei-Tzion in town. He would say, “If every Jew would give a package of butter (*a asle puter*) a week, it would be possible to redeem Eretz-Israel.”

A little further on stood the small one-story house, of Yakov Moshe Teitlebaum. Inside his apartment in this house, Yakov Moshe had a large shop for leather and shoemakers' goods.

Yakov Moshe was a Gur Hasid, and not just a plain Hasid, but also an outstanding one, enthusiastic, a Hasid with a capital H. Even the Gentiles, the shoemakers who bought from him, called him “Husid.” Both in his own behavior and in his demands of others, Yakov Moshe was harsh, extreme, and strict, with no compromises. But because of his innocence and honesty, both in matters of Hasidism, and in trade, even the freethinkers would treat him with respect and politeness.

In the summer of 1910, there was an outbreak of typhus in Sierpc. Among the dead was the twelve-year-old daughter of Yakov Moshe Teitlebaum. In the summer of 1916, on the day his daughter would have been eighteen, Yakov Moshe and his wife Madam Rivka Toltza, held a grand and extravagant "wedding" for their daughter. They had a Torah scroll written in honor of the daughter, and on the day of the "wedding" they arranged for the ceremony of "the Completion of the Scroll" and the accompaniment of the scroll with great ceremony to the synagogue. For the "wedding" they invited all the Jews in town, and many from the neighboring towns. These were relatives, notables, and people who had ties of friendship or business with Yakov Moshe. Also invited (and they came) were the German authorities in town (this was during the German occupation during the First World War). The "father-in-law" Yakov Moshe carried the Torah scroll under the canopy, and sang and danced the whole time. With the accompaniment of a great congregation of Hasidim, and just plain Jews, and with *kleismerim*, the procession moved from the house of the "in-laws" to the synagogue with music and song and dancing. After the ceremony of bringing the scroll into the temple, there was the "wedding" feast. First a feast for the poor, with a generous gift for each pauper, as is customary at rich weddings, and then a feast for the invited and for "whoever is hungry" ? for the whole town. The feast was like the feast of Solomon in its time, everything that was wanted and good, generous and munificent. It went on until very late at night.

* * *

The wide part of Fara (Farska) Street ended at the square in front of the Catholic Church. There was then a narrow extension to the street to the right. Pirogova (Piaretzki) Street began to the left, and continued until the New Market.

* * *

The church that was situated here was the oldest, largest, and most important of the three Catholic churches in town. This church was named after the saints Vita, Modesta, and Kraschanchi. According to tradition, this church was put up in the eleventh century in place of a pagan temple on the spot. In 1569, the church was repaired, and apparently the steeple was added then. In 1630 and 1648 fires broke out there. The repairs made after the fires and repairs made in following years not only spoiled the earlier building lines, but also the later additions.

The church was enclosed by a brick fence, and near the fence, inside, were tall and wide chestnut trees. There was a widespread legend in town that the church and the fence were sinking at the rate of the size of one pea every day. Of course, we did not doubt, heaven forbid, the truth of this legend. But we, the children, still wanted visible proof of this wonder and miracle. We also wanted to see the downfall of the Gentiles, and the sinking of their "contamination." But we couldn't prove the sinking of the church, because we weren't allowed to enter the grounds and, because of its height, it was impossible to discern a change in height of one pea a day. But the sinking of the fence could be determined: we measured it with respect to our own heights, and made various marks. But to our disappointment, we could not prove the point, and we were not satisfied that we had actually seen with our own eyes and felt with our own hands this great miracle, and extracted pleasure from the sinking of the "contamination."

Jewish children came to the fence of the church for another reason, because of the chestnuts. In the fall, when the chestnuts fell, the children would come to gather the chestnuts and fill their pockets. At home we would crack open the green shell with a rock (this would blacken our hands such that they became very difficult to clean) and we would use the pits for various games, in place of nuts, or stones. Others would make a hole in the chestnut with a nail, thread a fine cord through them, and make a harness for a game of cart and horse for a little brother, or beads for a little sister.

* * *

As mentioned, there was a narrow extension to Fara Street between the church fence and the houses on the right of the street. Beyond the church was a street called Shkolna (School Street) after the only public school in town, which was on this street. As stated above, the street's name was changed in the mid-1930s to Shpitalna after the hospital that was there. The street continued from Fara Street to the left until the start of Third of May Street (Tazhchego Maia). Outside of school hours and prayer times at the church, the street was very quiet, because there were very few houses there. The church took up a large area on the left of the street; the school and the park next to it took up a large area to the right. And the remaining areas on both sides of the street were taken up by large gardens, with small houses in them. As mentioned previously, only one Jew lived on this street, and he was Binyamin Sherpherz.

* * *

In the book "Noach Prilotzkis Zamelbicher far Yidishen Folklor, Filologia un Kultur Geshichten" (A collection of Folklore, Philology, and Annals of the Culture of the Jews), Volume 1, page 72, the following phrase appears: "Shepser Rebetzin geit mit di soldaten, di kupke untern orem, in der shkole gas." (The Rabanit from Sierpc walks with the soldiers, her headdress under her arm, on the School Street.) I don't know the source of this saying.

* * *

Beyond the church, Fara Street continues downhill until the bridge over the Sierpianitza River. This was the lowest and weakest of the bridges in Sierpc, because it served only occasional light traffic. This was not an exit from town, and there was no road on the other side of the bridge, just a dirt path, that lay between wide fields of hay and vegetables. And only a few carts, loaded with hay or vegetables, passed over this bridge.

* * *

On the other side of the bridge there was a magnificent vista, with green fields producing perfumed scents, and good, clean air. There was also a small grove on the bank of the river. In the summer, the young people would stroll here in the evenings and on Saturdays. Also adults, the sick and the weak, would come here to spend a few hours during the day, in the shade of the grove, to breathe some fresh air. They would bring food and eat at this pleasant spot, in the fine air that would revive their poor appetite.

I was about five or six when the doctor decided that I needed convalescence. What did convalescence mean? It was to sit in the woods (*zitsen in veldie* as they used to say) and breath fresh air. And I remember that for a few Saturdays, my father woke up early, took provisions for me for the trip, and went to walk with me in the grove. After I sat, ate, played, and strolled there, we went home, and only then would father go the *shtibl* to pray (because of my weakness, I stayed at home).

Leib, the son of Dudi Moshe Sandrovitch, was already then among the boys who would get into trouble. He already had a trade (he sewed for Akiva Offenbach), visited the library, made friends with the "strikers" (revolutionaries), and instead of going to the afternoon and evening prayers, would go strolling in the evening. He would usually stroll with Avramie Horovitz, his neighbor and friend. On those evenings that they strolled in the grove and its vicinity, they would take me along. Thus I would convalesce, as per doctor's orders...

* * *

The path beyond the bridge continued until the foot of the hill. There stood a small, round pavilion (it was built like an octagon). There were narrow windows with colored glass all around the walls of the pavilion. Near the pavilion was a small, low well, that was called by the Jews the "conversion well" (*s'shmad*). It was said that the waters of the well were holy to the Christians, and were used to spray on babies during baptism.

The path stopped at the foot of the hill. From here there was a trail up the hill that met the road that I mentioned above, and continued to the right until the Vloka (Vlikes), and from the other side, until the Rypin Road.

* * *

We return to Fara Street. In 1916, during the German occupation, there was an outbreak of typhus in Sierpc (as in many other towns) that caused a high death toll. The German authorities opened a hospital on this street, opposite the church, in the house of Kulashinski (a Pole), and military doctors attended the sick. (There was also a branch of the hospital in Shkolna Street, behind the church, in the school building.) After a few years, the hospital was moved to Piastovska Street.

* * *

A little bit further was the one-story house of Elia Ber Tchernotchepka. A terrible tragedy occurred in the family of Elia Ber. Within a few years, his three children died. After the disasters happened, Elia Ber started to be active in public life, in the field of aid to the poor and suffering. In particular he did outstanding work in the Gmilut Hasidim Society(aid to the poor) fund. This fund loaned money to the general public: small merchants and tradesmen. He did not skimp on his efforts or money to maintain and strengthen this fund, and also gave a room in his apartment, with no compensation, as an office for the fund.

* * *

Further on was the single story house of Moshe Lerer. Moshe Gutshtat lived in this house. He was an enthusiastic supporter of Poalei-Tzion, and was a member of the town council from his party.

In 1925, the police searched Moshe Gutshtat's apartment and “found” illegal posters in the mattress in his bed. Gutshtat was arrested and was in jail in Plock for nine months. The concierge of the house, who was present during the search, testified at the trial, and said that he saw the policemen shaking the mattress, and the posters falling out of it. In answer to the judge's question, “In what state were the posters when they fell out of the mattress?” The concierge answered that they were rolled up and not folded or wrinkled. On the basis of this testimony (which showed that the posters had been inserted into the mattress on the spot), the judge freed Moshe Gutshtat. After a similar search on the same day, Gutshtat's party comrade, Abba Licht, was also arrested. He was in jail in Plock for six months. Later, Moshe Gutshtat changed his affiliation from Poalei Tzion Left to Poalei Tzion Right.

* * *

Further on was the small one-story brick house of Baruch Gotlibovski. Gotlibovski was a member of the community council in the 1930s, representing the Zionists.

* * *

Nahum Frankel lived in the same house. Nahum's original family name was Sochaczewski. But by changing his name, he “became” an only son, and according to Russian law, an only son was exempt from military service...

* * *

The house near the market, a small one-story brick house, belonged to the tailor, Melech Tzina. His store was in the same house. The store sold the ready-made underwear, vests, and tricot white goods of Shmuel Tatz (who was called "Shmeltia Beias," after his mother Baia). After his brother, Natan Wolfe Tatz, moved his store from Bloom's house to his new house, Shmuel Tatz moved his store to Bloom's house. Shmuel Tatz belonged to the Enlightened group in Sierpc. In the 1930s Shmuel Tatz was a member of the town council representing the Zionists. He also filled some other important public positions: he was chairman of the Merchants Association and chairman of the merchants' Bank Odzialovi (The Stock Bank).

* * *

Reb Eliezer Vasolak lived in the yard of this house. He owned the textile store in the drugstore building, (on the side of the Jewish street) which his wife managed. Reb Eliezer Vasolak was a great scholar of the Talmud and its interpreters, and an expert in the Bible and an exegesist. He was a leader of the Enlightened Group, and the Enlightened Mitnagdim (anti-Hasidism) that broke away from the community and was called Kolhekot (see the chapter "History of Sierpc"). He was also among the first Hovevei Tzion.

Reb Eliezer Vasolak left many manuscripts about Jewish religious law (Halacha) and legends, Bible research, and Judaism, and also wrote poetry. In accordance with his will, the manuscripts were sent to his sons in America for publication.

* * *

We have finished our stroll and review of Fara (Farska) Street.

Translator's Footnotes

1. Gentile butcher stores were in various parts of town, but Jewish butcher stores were only in the Butchers' House. In time the restriction was lifted and three Jewish butcher stores opened in different streets: a} In Zhaba Street in Vinitzky's (a Pole) house by Zalman Yakobovitch; b) On the Jewish Street, in Prashnitzki's house (used to be Tarkltov's house) by Haimel Kishilvitz; and c) On the Vloka (Vlikes) near the house of Baruchia Zashutke by the two partners, Zisia and David.
2. In the book "A Velt in Flamen" ("A Word in Flames") by our townsman, Y. Weingarten, in the chapter "Mein Charuv Shtetele Sierpc" (My Destroyed Village Sierpc) it is written that there was a legend in town that a rich Jew named Menashe who had three sons and wanted to be aloof from Jewish life, and away from their neighborhood, settled in this spot. Later on the sons converted, and all the Jews of Sierpc ripped their clothes and sat "Shiva". Before the end of the seven days of mourning, the three converts died, and the Gentiles put up the pavilion in their honor. But there are doubts about this legend. Neither I nor other people from Sierpc that I asked about this remember the legend. I think that this legend is the literary creation of this respected author. Two of the senior Sierpc townsman, Reb Shmuel Itcha and Mr. Yitzhak Yakov Boda, told me, each of them on his own, that the name "Menashe Mit di Drei Zihen" for the statues is from a different Menashe: Menashe Liechtenstein and his three sons who were all "Kleismer" (his fourth son was a tailor) and lived not far way. And I can think of a different explanation: In the book In the Forests of Poland, by Y. Opatoshu (translated by M. Lipson), page 27, there appears the following: " ? He won't go ? shouted Avraham. Hinted to the watchman not to wait, and turned to Mordecai: I told you, from the day that they put up "Menashe and his seven daughters" (a statue at a road intersection) at the base of

the forest, I will not go there. And you keep out of there too, do you understand me?" This quotation shows that the name of the statues "Menashe and his Three Sons" is not an original Sierpc name. But different statues in different places were called by similar names. Let me also ponder on another legend that Mr. Weingarten mentions in the same chapter of the same book, about the origin of the names "Sheps ? Sierpc". According to Mr. Weingarten, the town elders told a legend that the name of the town Sheps came from Jews who fled persecution in Germanic countries, like sheep fleeing from wolves, found a place to rest, and called it "Sheps" (sheep, in Yiddish sheps), and because of this there was picture of a sheep in the old great seal of the town. But out of shame that they were being compared to wolves, the Gentiles canceled this seal, and called the town "Sierpc". Neither I, nor any of the Sierpc natives that I talked to were familiar with this legend.

3. "Shpiliter" ? Small merchants, who were not able to who were not able to travel themselves to get merchandise, or bigger merchants, who needed, between trips, a small amount of goods, would place an order with the "Shpiliter" who would go to Warsaw once a week, for a percentage of the price of the merchandise. As, a joke, people would say instead of "Shpiliter", "Shpil mir Ae'er" (Play for me here).

The Jewish Street and the Vloka (Vlikes)

We continue our journey and review in the Jewish Street, and the Vloka (Vlikes).

The name, Jewish Street, was accepted by the people, both Jewish and Polish. But the official name of the street was Warsaw Street.

In the mid-1930s, when the Town Council gave new names to the streets, this street was called Dashinski after a leader of the P.P.P. (The Polish Socialist Party) of that name.

* * *

The first house on Jewish Street, a small one-story house, was that of Kalman Lidzbreski. At the front of the house was one store, which belonged to the owner, a wholesale establishment for grocery goods. Until the First World War, when the German occupation authorities controlled grocery goods, there were two wholesale grocery stores in Sierpc, and one of them was that of Kalman Lidzbreski.

The entrance to the Jewish Street from the market was narrow, and a bottleneck. Beyond Lidzbereski's house the building line moved back, and the street became wider. At the beginning of the 1930's when Kalman became older, and his son, Moshe, took care of the store, the small house was torn down and a two-story brick house was put up in its place. The new house was built along the same building line as the other houses on the street.

* * *

During a certain period, Moshe Lidzbreski was a member of the community council, elected on a non-partisan ticket.

* * *

The next house, a two-story house, belonged to Kalman Kalmanovitch (who was called "Kalman Schneider" ? Kalman the Tailor). The entrance to the yard was in the middle of the house, and not at its side, as was usually the case, and above the entrance there were rooms.

The teacher Atlas lived in this house. Atlas was one of the Enlightened group in town, knowledgeable in the Bible, and proficient in a number of languages. He also belonged to the Hovevei Tzion movement and was one of the first Zionists in town.

Atlas used a room in his apartment, a special room that was furnished for the purpose, as a school for girls to learn languages and arithmetic. After school hours, he also gave lessons to boys. The first Zionist meeting in Sierpc took place in Atlas's school.

* * *

The next house, a small one-story structure, was the home of Eliakim Ryz. Eliakim was one of the important Gur Hasidim, a quiet and unassuming Jew, well dressed and clean. He sold remnants of textile goods in his house. When he became older, he sold his house to his neighbor, Baruch Atlas. From then on Eliakim and his wife dealt in religious needs. He would sell chits for the ritual slaughter of chickens, and she was the *tikern* (performer of immersions) in the *mikveh* (ritual bathhouse), then leased by Leib Shwitzer. As a result, they received permission to live in an apartment in the *mikveh* building.

Eliakim's wife, Yetaia (who was called "Yetaia Yairs" ? Yair's Daughter) was a great expert in muttering against the "evil eye." People came from all parts of town to ask for treatments for children and adults, men and women, who were affected by *eina bisha* (evil eye), God help us. And she, a gentle and pious women, did not skimp with her favors, helped as much as she could, and would mutter a few words, and remove the evil eye from the victim.

In order to remove the evil eye it was necessary that the *kazhizhivka* (a triangular kerchief with long ends that mothers would use to wrap around a child's neck and tie in the back) of the sick child or the gown of the adult be brought to Yetaia. She would take the *kazhizhivka* or the gown into another room, and murmur whatever it was she murmured. Then she would bring the object back to whoever had given it to her and warn him to go straight home, not to speak to anyone on the way, and once home, place the object on the sick person...[19]

* * *

The next house, a two-story house, was the home of Moshe Grainbich, who had a textile store there. His son, Avraham Haim, was among the exceptional young men in town, an outstanding scholar. This house was near the bridge.

* * *

The bridge that was suspended here over the Sierpianitza was the central and chief bridge of the bridges in town. It was also the most useful one, because the river here passed through the center of town, and divided it into two densely populated parts. There was always heavy traffic over this bridge, both of pedestrians and of carriages. Because of this, the bridge was very strong. Because of the possibility of flooding, the bridge was built on top of tall pillars. The street on both sides of the bridge was in any case elevated, and the adjacent sidewalks at the four corners were lower than the street.

* * *

Across the bridge there was a small house with a store for textile goods. This was the store of Reb David Klinman (who was called "David Haver"). Reb David was a teacher in town, and his family took care of the store.

* * *

Beria Oberfeld lived in the small house in the yard. Beria was a wagon driver. Twice a week, he would take grain to Plock: on Sunday he would take the grain that merchants bought on Friday, and on Wednesday, the grain that they bought on Tuesday. (The market days were Friday and Tuesday.) He was an honest and reliable person, and the merchants had great confidence in him. He would bring large sums of money from Plock to Sierpc (for the grain), and also from Sierpc to Plock (to merchants, or to the banks) and he always carried out his responsibilities admirably.

Beria liked to drink a little, and would sleep during the trip, and his assistant would drive the horses. When he was asked, "Reb Ber, how is it that you allow yourself to drink and sleep during the trip, when you have large sums of other people's money in your pocket?" he would answer:

"When you get home, your wife serves you a bowl full of warm potatoes, tasty and steaming, and you fill your belly and enjoy. I also want this kind of food, but you can't get it in a carriage. So what do I do? It is well known that potatoes are used to make hard liquor. So I take some liquor, that's been made from a bowl full of potatoes, and I enjoy it as if I were eating the potatoes."

* * *

Beyond David Klinman's small house was the two-story house of David Turkltaub. Turkltaub was very opinionated. During the revolution, in 1905, he did not mince words, and spoke in public in opposition to the revolutionary Jewish youth, in opposition to their socialist aspirations and against their behavior and actions, which flouted both Jewish and universal morality. The revolutionary court sentenced him to three lashes for this. When the sentence was being executed and a young man was whipping him in a public street, Turkltaub shouted, "Nicholas was the Tsar, and Nicholas will be the Tsar."

* * *

Yosel Shochet (Isenshtat) lived in the same house. He was appointed as the ritual slaughterer (*shochet* ? *shub* ? slaughterer and examiner) in Sierpc after the death of Yankel Shochet (Richik). He came to our town from Szrensk in approximately the year 1917.

Yosel Shochet was an expert at his profession, and a fast worker. He was a good prayer leader, and an excellent hymn singer. He had a powerful voice, which shook the rafters of the prayer house. As part of his duties, Yosel would lead prayers in the synagogues and prayer houses on the High Holy Days (he was a Gur Hasid) and the Hasidim who enjoyed good music would go especially to the place where he was singing to hear certain parts of his prayers.

The conductor of the chorus in the Central Synagogue on Tlomatzka Street in Warsaw was Yosel Shochet's brother, David Isenshtat.

* * *

Matityahu Farshnitzki bought the Turkltaub house in the 1930s, tore it down, and built a brick house in its place.

* * *

The next house, also a two-story house, was the house of Zelig Bachrach. These two houses, that of Turkltaub and of Bachrach, were attached to each other, and they did not have a front yard on the Jewish Street (the yards were in the back, and they faced the street near the *mikveh.*) The narrow and dark foyers of the two houses had been taken over, for all intents and purposes, for passageways for those living on the other side of the bridge. They led to the small streets near the *mikveh* and to the *mikveh* itself. They were also used by the children who went to the two *heders* that were in these streets, that of Hershia Zlotzover and that of Haim Yosef Crystal.

Before the First World War, Zelig Bachrach had been a member of the community council.

Next to Bachrach's house stood the brick one-story house with a half-cellar of Nahum Tatz. His store, which was in the half-cellar, was the only store in town that sold only liquor.

Nahum Tatz was a Torah scholar, a goodhearted person with superior qualities: humble, generous, and a dedicated and outstanding public figure. He was an important Gur Hasid. Nahum Tatz was a member of the community council, and its chairman, representing Agudat Israel.

* * *

Nahum Tatz's piety was matched by the skepticism of his sister, Ika (Rivka) Tatz. Rivka ee field of education and the Bund schools in Warsaw. Before she left Poland she was a teacher in the above *pensia.*

In 1924 Rivka Tatz left Poland, and went to England. After a short stay in London, she moved to France and settled in Paris. In Paris, too, where she was known as Ika Richter (she had married Richter in London), she was active in the Bund. She was especially devoted to Colony Skolar (Settlements for Schoolchildren), a society that took care of Jewish children: sent children to summer camps, offered them medical care, and provided a cultured Jewish environment. (The society was under the patronage of the Bund.) In the Second World War, during the German occupation of France, the Colony Skolar Society established, in cooperation with other Jewish organizations, an underground movement to aid the Jews. The movement provided food for children, soup kitchens, and help for elderly Jews and Jews who had been detained. It hid children in convents and with Christian families. The movement was called Rue Amalo (Amalo Street) after the street where the offices of Colony Skolar were located.

Ika Richter was one of the main activists in this underground movement. She was one of those who risked their lives to help other Jews, until the oppressors, inhuman Germans, captured her, and she died the death of a martyr. Ika was arrested on May 29, 1941, and died in the prison in the city of Romanville on October 5, 1942. The Bund put up a holiday camp for workers' children, named Beit Ika, in her memory in Corvalle (60 kilometers from Paris).

Many letters twritten by Ika Richter (Rivka Tatz) during the German occupation about assistance to various people are in the Yivo archive in the United States. In the book *Yiddisher Umkum Un Vidershtand in Frankreich* written by P. Mintz, Ika Richter is mistakenly referred to as Esther.

* * *

This side of Jewish street does not continue in a straight line. After Nachum Tatz's house, the line of houses turned to the left until the Kamnitza (the large brick house). At the Kamnitza the building line turned to the right and continued until Niepomoshchik's house, and from there the two sides of the street were parallel to one another until the Vloka (vlikes).

The left turn of the left side of the street created a large plaza in the middle of the street. Part of this plaza had a house on it, and the rest, the larger part, which was unpaved, was used as a small, unofficial market. During market days, peasants' carts would be parked there, and they sold their wares there.

The house that stood in the plaza, a house with an attic, was the house of Meir Oved Balt. It was said that Meir Oved knew of the coming of rain three days before it arrived (he apparently had rheumatism). We children were very jealous of this knowledge of his.

The following saying was well known among the Jews of Jewish Street: "A daughter of Israel should know how to write a letter in Yiddish, and the address would be by Meir Oved." (Meir Oved would write messages to foreign countries for all of the Jewish Street)...

Later on, the house of Meir Oved was torn down.

* * *

Avraham Shochet (Burgand) lived in the attic of that house. He was tall and had a long gray beard. He was an excellent prayer leader. His words would be distinct and clear. His prayer was pleasant to the ear and touched the heart. The lines of the prayer "I Am Poor in Deeds" which said "Accept my prayer as an ordinary old man who has reached a becoming maturity and has grown a beard, with a pleasant voice and is concerned with his fellow beings" applied to him. Avraham Shochet was an Alexander Hasid, but as part of his duties, he would pray on the High Holy Days at the synagogue and the two houses of prayer, and many took pleasure in his prayer. He would say First Slichot in the Alexander *shtibl.*

Avraham Shochet was a ritual slaughterer of chickens. The slaughter of larger animals was forbidden to him because of the "sins of his youth." Elsewhere in this book, there is the story of the Kolhekot (a quarrelsome community, or a small group) in Sierpc. They were Enlightened Mitnagdim (anti-Hasidim) who had a dispute with the community and the Rabbi, and appointed a rabbi and ritual slaughterer just for their group. Avraham Shochet was the ritual slaughter for the Kolhekot, and after it disbanded (in the first half of the 1890s), Shochet lived in the village of Skvilna (18 kilometers from Sierpc, on the road to Rypin). Later, when there was a need for a ritual slaughterer in Sierpc, Avraham Shochet applied, but the Gur Hasidim strenuously objected. Their objections were three-fold: because he was the ritual slaughterer of the Kolhekot, because he was the ritual slaughter in a village, and because he was an Alexander Hasid. But Avraham Shochet's backers (the Alexander Hasidim and some of the Mitnagdim, especially those who were once part of the Kolhekot) were adamant. The matter was brought to arbitration by the rabbis of the area, and they declared a compromise judgment: Avraham Shochet will be a ritual slaughterer, but only of chickens. And he remained a chicken-slaughterer for the rest of his days.

* * *

When he became old, and was receiving a pension from the community, his son-in-law, Shimon Patrikus of Drobin (Drobnin) took his place. However, he was not an official ritual slaughterer of the community, because the Rabbi emphatically objected to it. But the public did not heed the Rabbi's objections, because it was well known that he was an "interested party" to the affair, since he wanted to give the job to his son-in-law, Leibl Flisher (from Pshitik; the Rabbi wanted his son-in-law to be appointed as a Torah teacher in town, and if not, as the ritual slaughterer). And all groups of the public ate food slaughtered by Shimon Patrikus, who was a Yeshiva student knowledgeable in the Torah, a public figure, and accepted by the community.

* * *

Beyond the house of Avraham Tatz there was a one-story house with a cellar that belonged to three partners: Itzik (Avraham Yitzhak) Ostshever,

Shlomo Reichgut who was called “Shlom Chayehies” (after his mother Chaya), and Baruch Konenbrand. The wives of these three were sisters, and they inherited the house from their parents. The three partners lived in this house, and also had their businesses there. The first one sold oil, the second had a grocery store, and the third had a bakery.

* * *

Itzik Ostshever had an oil-press, but it was not in his house, but in the Lusmer house, opposite the synagogue. He would sell the products from the store in his house. We, the children, used to buy halvah there.

* * *

The third house was the house of Isaac Charne. Leibl Horn lived in this house. He was an educated young man, dynamic, and a leader. He was among the founders of the Zionist youth group Herzlia and very active in it. He was active in all the Zionist and Zionist-culture activities in town. In 1932 or 1933 he emigrated to France, and there perished in the Holocaust.

* * *

Beyond Isaac Charne's house there was a small street. This small street housed some important institutions. At the end of the street, opposite to the entrance to the street, in the house of Shmuel Shampan (who was called “Shmuel Nagid”) was the Welcome Guests, where there was a minyan for prayer on Sabbaths and holidays. There was a *shtibl* in the same house whose worshipers were a “mixture” of a few Hasidic groups. Most of them were refugees from other *shtibls* that they had left after quarrels and angry words. On the same street were the *heder* of Dudi Hershia Zlochaver (in the house of the brothers Haim and Hirsh Gunsher) and the *heder* of Haim Yosef Crystal (in the house of Moshe Kasazh). An important person also lived on this street: Rabbi Haim Nachum Tunbol, one of the first of the Enlightened and Zionists in Sierpc. But the great importance of this small street was that the “whole town” passed through there on its way to the *mikveh*. It was not called Mikveh Street (S'mikve Gesel) for nothing.

* * *

The *mikveh* itself was on a very small street that began to the right of the small street we just mentioned, and continued to the fields of Falka (a rich German who owned a brewery). The *mikveh* was an old building, and so was everything inside. In approximately 1907, the building was repaired, and interior improvements were made during the First World War. Among other things, two enameled bathtubs were installed, and this was an enhancement that was discussed by the whole town.

A more fundamental repair job, almost a new construction of the *mikveh*, was undertaken in 1923 or 1924. The initiative for the reconstruction came from Mizrachi circles. A committee was set up, whose members were Meir

Tzafris, treasurer, Yosef Applebaum, Moshe Grossman, Beinam Veismal, and Yosef Karpa, and they supervised the construction work. Outside, around the *mikveh*, a brick wall was put up (the old wall had also been brick) to increase the available area, and new improvements to the interior were made as well. New individual cubicles with a bathtub in each cubicle were put in, along with other improvements. In order to pay for the work, the committee (which was called the Ritual Slaughter Committee) levied a payment of half a groschen on each chicken that was slaughtered. Eliakim Ryz, who sold the slaughter chits, collected the added payment for *mikveh* repair and turned the money over to the committee. In the meantime, a new community council was elected, and Yosef Karpa, who was the treasurer, demanded that Eliakim turn over the payments for the slaughtering together with the extra payment to the community fund. From then on there were problems in financing the construction, and it went on slowly and dragged out over a number of years.

On top of the *mikveh* building there was a small apartment, and the leaser (*mikvenik* ? operator of the *mikveh*) of the *mikveh* lived there. The holder of this office would change from time, whether because of old age or death. Once the leaser was Shmuel Leib and his wife Tuna Iszajewicz. After them came Leib Shwitzer.

There was a well near the *mikveh*. We did not know about "heavy water" then, but we knew about soft water and hard water (for cooking and laundry). The water from the well near the *mikveh* was the softest water in town, and many people used it.

There was just one house on this tiny street, and it was the one-story house that the tailor Uren (Aharon) Leib Yurkevitch lived in. His son, Avraham Hirsh (today in Brazil) was a member of the community council representing the Bund in the 1930s.

We return to the Jewish Street, and reach the Kamnitza (large brick house).

Before the Kamnitza, there were three small and short streets. One veered to the left and continued until opposite the *mikveh*. (Actually, this was not a street, but an alley or passageway between the rear walls of household sheds to the left, and the tall fence of a lot with parts of carriages and scrap iron to the right.) The second street was straight and continued until Felka's fields, and the third street (near the Kamnitza) went straight and up until the hill, where it turned right and continued behind the row of houses that were on the Jewish Street (this street was later called Gurna).

Most of the houses in the streets were low and small and meager (Mintz's house was the exception here in size) and most of the tenants were poor. This is probably the reason that this neighborhood was called "Kartofel mit Ferfel Geslach" (Potatoes and Crumbs Streets). Because this dish ? potatoes with barley flakes ? was the most popular food among poor people.

* * *

The house and school of the teacher Mordecai Hirsh Mintz was on the second of the above streets (before he moved the school to Tchernotchepka's house on the street that was later called Third of May and his living quarters across the street from there). Moshe Hirsh Mintz was one of the veteran Zionist and Enlightened figures in town. All by himself, thanks to his industriousness, diligence, and perseverance, Mintz became very knowledgeable in Judaic studies, especially in the Bible and the Hebrew language, and also in the sciences. In his modern school, which was very different from the traditional *heder*, both in the conditions of study and the subject content, the pupils were all sons of Zionist parents, Enlightened, and with Progressive tendencies. Mintz tried to give to the hundreds of pupils who learned in his school over the years some of the wide knowledge of Judaism and science that he had, and his Zionist philosophy. He contributed a great deal, both in his school, in evening school, and in private lessons to popularize the Hebrew language among the youth of Sierpc. Mordecai Hirsh Mintz was also a very capable public speaker and an excellent elucidator. He educated a whole generation, both in his school and in his lectures to Agudat-Tzion and in the synagogue, to be devoted and faithful Zionists.

In 1922, Mintz emigrated to America. There too, he engaged in teaching Jewish subjects, popularizing the Hebrew language, and spreading Zionist ideals. Mordecai Hirsh Mintz died on 21 Tevet 5699 (January 11, 1939).

* * *

The third small street near the Kamnitza and behind it, which continued up the hill, was almost empty and deserted. A few wretched and miserable houses were scattered, here and there, on the hill. In later years, when more houses, albeit poor ones, were put up here, the hill took on the look of a street. In the mid-1930s, when the town council named streets that previously had no names, this street was called Gurna (High Street). Gurna Street continued until the Vloka (vlikes) to the street that was then called Kolinsky.

* * *

One of the people who lived on the hill was Avraham Grushke (who was called "Olekia"). His house was opposite the New House of Prayer. There was a large cabin near his house, and he opened a "hotel" there for poor wanderers, musicians (*katarinarzes*) and street performers (*kintzen machers*). This "hotel" was called, in a mocking Polish verse "Hotel Nendzi, Bez Fieniendzi" (A destitute hotel, without payment).

* * *

Keila-Gitel, the water carrier, lived in this neighborhood ("Keila-Gitel di Vasser Tregeren"). When her husband (who was a porter) died, her son did not want to say Kaddish. What did Keila-Gitel do? She went to the *reshiran* (mayor) and complained about her son. With great difficulty she explained to the reshiran about the Kaddish and the usefulness to the dead man of saying

Kaddish. (He was the mayor, but still a Gentile.) But when the matter became clear to him, he decided to help the grieving widow. He called Sobolevsky the drummer (Sobolevsky was the town crier. When it was necessary to inform the townspeople of a proclamation or decree, Sobolevsky would go from street to street, gather a crowd with his drum, and announce the proclamation or decree of the town council or the government) and ordered him to bring Keila-Gitel's son.

When the boy was brought to the *reshiran*, he scolded him and asked him to obey his widowed mother and fulfill his father's wish and say Kaddish. But the boy still refused. The urging, and even the threats of the *reshiran* were of no use. He would not say Kaddish, no matter what.

Then the mayor ordered Sobolevsky to bring the boy, using force, to the prayer house, and not release him till he said Kaddish. And Sobolevsky faithfully carried out the mayor's orders. He dragged the boy to the prayer house and all along the way he yelled at him, "*Muv Kaddish! Muv Kaddish!*" (Muv in Polish is "say".) He brought him to the prayer house and didn't leave him until he said Kaddish.

From then on, the boy was called "Muv Kaddish"...

* * *

At the beginning of the 1930s, a large one-story brick building with a cellar was erected on Gurna Street behind the Kamnitza for public use. It was put up for two institutions: Welcome Guests and Talmud Torah. The first institution took up most of the building, and the second one (the smaller part) and the cellar were intended for the watchman. Because there was not enough money, the construction took a few years. A great celebration was held when it was opened, and many of the Jews of the town participated, along with the local rabbi and rabbis from the neighboring towns.

* * *

The accursed Germans put the Sierpc ghetto in Gurna Street and in the street where Mintz lived. According to the testimony of our fellow townswoman, Mrs. Isacovitch-Listopad (the only one who was in the Sierpc ghetto and survived), more than 500 people lived in the Ghetto. A few were not driven out on the bitter day of the expulsion (26 of Heshvon 5700, November 8, 1939) and most of them returned to Sierpc illegally after the expulsion, using circuitous and dangerous routes. Except for one family, Avraham Derbicher and his wife, from Zuromin, all the Ghetto dwellers were from Sierpc. The Ghetto was not fenced in, and German policemen guarded its entrances and exits. The members of the Judenrat were Yakov Pukatch, Mendel Lis, and Shmuel Kutner. Pukatch was the head of the Judenrat. The ghetto was put up, according to the same testimony, in March or April 1940. On January 6, 1940, the Sierpc ghetto dwellers were expelled to the Stezhgovo ghetto (a town near Malawa) that was a collection spot for the survivors of ghettos in the neighboring towns. The liquidation of the Stezhgovo ghetto was on November 24, 1942. All the Jews were brought to Malawa, and from there, to Auschwitz.

* * *

As was mentioned earlier, the building line turned right at the Kamnitza. All the buildings on this side of the street were on the slope of a hill. The sidewalk was much higher than street level up to Niepomoshchik's house, and much higher than the sidewalk on the other side of the street. Beyond Niepomoshchik's house, the street also sloped upwards, and was at the same height as the sidewalk.

* * *

The Kamnitza, a brick house, was a large house with many tenants. It had a live-in basement, two stories, with an attic above them. I don't know the history of this house. But its uniqueness in the area, its large proportions, and its solid construction bore witness to an unusual past.

According to our respected townsman Shmuel Itcha Lanter, the Kamnitza belonged to a priest called Adamski. (He was also the landlord of the building that housed the drugstore, and also owned the drugstore.) The house of Lieb Mintz on Zhavia Street was also his. This priest was an admirer of Israel. He was a great scholar, and knew many languages, among them Yiddish and the Holy Tongue. In his large library, among thousands of books in various languages, there were also some Gemaras. During the period that Avraham Yitzhak (who was called "der Bezoiner Melamed," the teacher from Biezun) lived in the Kamnitza, the priest would come to him from time to time about the rent, he would ask the students in Yiddish which portion of the Bible they were studying that week, and he would test them on their knowledge of the Pentateuch.

In the first years that the Russian Army was billeted in Sierpc (in the 1890s) the army offices and its workshops were in the Kamnitza. In later years, the Kamnitza belonged to Kashtalan (a Pole).

* * *

Moshe Grossman was one of the tenants of the Kamnitza. During a certain period before the First World War, Moshe Grossman was a member of the community council. In order to increase the income of the synagogue to pay for a review of its situation, Moshe Grossman (he himself prayed in the Gur *shtibl*, but he was not an enthusiastic Hasid), in his official capacity closed all the *shtibls*, using the official justification of unsanitary premises. A few of the Hasidim prayed in the prayer houses, together with the regular minyan, but most of them prayed in the synagogue at a special minyan, after the minyan of the regular worshipers. This gave the synagogue an added income. The situation caused great consternation among the Hasidim, and after a few weeks, the edict was withdrawn.

In 1905, the year of the revolution, when the word "revolutzia" was being uttered by everyone, a Hasid asked Moshe Grossman, "What is ?revolutzia'?" Moshe Grossman answered, "When a man fills his belly with potatoes and barley flakes, and then drinks soda water, and feels his stomach rumbling, that's ?revolutzia'."

* * *

The Cantor Daniel Shiakas lived in the same house, the Kamnitza. Daniel Shiakas was an important cantor in town. He came to Sierpc from the town of Novoshbentzian, which was near Vilna in about 1907. He was accepted as the cantor after the visits of many cantors to town, who demonstrated their talents as cantors on Saturdays at the synagogue. The connoisseurs said that he had a great aptitude for organizing a choir, and his prayers were best when accompanied by a choir.

Some of the Hasidim, the strictest of the strict, would not eat meat ritually slaughtered by the cantor during his first years in Sierpc. Not because, heaven forbid, they found any flaw in him. But just like that, because he was a Litvak and as is well know, you can't trust a Litvak... (This was not a public and organized opposition to the cantor, but in each of these houses, when a child was sent to the shochet to slaughter a chicken, he was warned not to give the chicken to the cantor.) The cantor tried to make himself accepted among the Hasidim. On Saturdays he would wear a Hasidic hat, and he would come to the *shtibl* from time to time. With time, the covert opposition disappeared, and the whole town ate food that he had slaughtered.

The Litvak cantor wanted his children to retain their Litvak accent. He paid the *melamed* (teacher) Shmualtia Vilk, who taught his eldest son, Liebke, an extra payment to teach him using the Litvak accent. But his efforts were of no use; his children's speech was completely absorbed into the Polish-Sierpc pronunciation.

* * *

Apparently, Hasidic opposition to cantors was very common. Rabbi Yehuda Abuda, in his series of articles "Worship for Generations", part 7, (*Hatzofe*, 1 Sivan, 5717, May 11, 1956) writes:

"However, in our times, there was no opposition to cantors as such. Because the Hasidim prayed in the *shtibl*, they didn't care if a cantor prayed in the synagogue with a choir of songsters. But the small communities could not appoint someone who was only a cantor, and therefore took a person who would serve also as a *shochet* (ritual slaughterer) and examiner. The Hasidim were not comfortable with this, because they didn't want to rely on someone for slaughtering and examination who was also a "songster." Therefore the controversies in the towns about a cantor-slaughterer-examiner were a regular occurrence. And the cantors, with the majority of the public on their side, became quite impertinent to the rabbis.

I have heard that in the town of Sheps, when there was a dispute between the cantor and the rabbi, and the cantor prayed in the synagogue on Sukkoth, when he came to the verse ?What will man do to me' he would repeat the word ?man' many times and shake the *lulav* (palm branch) in his hand in the direction of the rabbi's back. The public roared with laughter...

* * *

Kalman Arpa (who was called “Kalman Yakiryehs” after his father Yakir) lived in the same house, the Kamnitza. Kalman had a pleasing and soft voice, delicate and agreeable, and he was a good prayer leader. Every word, phrase, and verse that came out of him was clear and exact. And the worshippers at the New Prayer House greatly enjoyed his prayer.

It sometimes happened that the Alexander *shtibl* was closed for a few weeks time (either because of a debt to the landlord, or the hygienic requirements of the authorities). Because of this I sometimes prayed in the New Prayer House. On Sabbath eve, as usual, all the worshippers at the prayer house prayed in the same minyan. Because of this, I sometimes enjoyed the hearty prayer and sweet voice of Kalman Arpa.

Because of these instances, I became aware of two traditional melodies for “Lecha Dodi” of the Sabbaths between Passover and Pentecost and the Sabbaths of The Three Weeks, which I heard from Kalman Arpa.

* * *

A small one-story house that belonged to Fiboshia Rusak (a *melamed*) was beyond the Kamnitza.

Mendel Mai lived in this house. He was a sometimes tailor and complete pauper. He was very, very pious. Once, an impure incident occurred to him: he killed a mouse on the Sabbath. Mendel went to the Rabbi, told him what had happened, and asked that the Rabbi tell him how to atone for his great transgression. The Rabbi told him to fast for a total of forty days, every Monday and Thursday. Mendel accepted the Rabbi's judgment, and fasted as directed. He became very weak, but he atoned for his “great sin”...

The New Prayer House was next to this small house. The New Prayer House was built, as our townsman S.A. Lanter has told me, in 5646 (1886). The New Prayer House was, until the First World War, the center of the Enlightenment and Zionism in Sierpc. The earliest Enlightened persons and Hovevei-Zion in our town prayed here. This prayer house was also the center for the remnants of the Kolhekot. Before the New Prayer House was put up, the Kolhekot had their own minyan, in the Kamnitza.

The New Prayer House was an aristocratic one. Here there was order and discipline, not like in the old prayer house, where “everybody” worshipped. Only regular worshippers were here. It was the same with the Torah studies. A few of the worshippers would study here in the morning, and also between afternoon and evening prayers. Sometimes a few young men would study here also in the middle of the day, but this was not a communal place for studies during the day. It was quiet here, in any case, and the furnishings and equipment were, in comparison to the old prayer house, clean and unbroken. The books were also more intact and cleaner.

The entrance to the New Prayer House made a good impression. We mentioned that the sidewalk was higher than the street. Because of this there were a few steps here from the street to the sidewalk. There were additional stairs to go from the sidewalk to the prayer house. These were wide, and approached the prayer house from three sides. The high sidewalk and two sets of stairs served as an attractive entrance to the New Prayer House.

* * *

The next house, a single story house with an attic, belonged to Nahum Niapomoshchik. Nahum was a native of Russia. He served in the cavalry battalion stationed in Sierpc, and fell in love with the maiden Zisa Mirel. When he finished his service, he married her and lived in Sierpc. (There were some other similar cases, where soldiers who served in the battalion stationed in Sierpc married girls from the town and became residents. One of them was Shlomo Yuzhilevski.) Nahum Niapomoshchik died young, before the First World War, before he had finished building his house.

* * *

A Jew who was very essential to Jewish life in Sierpc lived in the same house. His normal occupation was as a porter, and because of this he was called Lazer Virevnik (*viravnik*, porter in Polish). But in addition to his regular work, he had a side job: he was the gravedigger of the Sierpc community.

* * *

A little further on was the two-story house of Haskel (Yehezkel) Lusmer. Very few people in town knew that his real name was Levkovitz. So why was he called "Lusmer"? His brother-in-law, our townsman Avraham Melave, told me. The name "Lusmer" came from his mother's ancestors (who lived in Dobrzyn), from the time when family names were determined. When the official responsible for family names came to his grandfather's grandfather, he didn't understand the request (because he couldn't speak Polish), and said "*Loz mir tzuria*" ("Leave me alone"). The official tried to explain his request, be he kept repeating "*Loz mir tzuria*". The official wrote down Lozmir as the family name. And "Lozmir" became "Lusmer"...

* * *

The *heder* (one-room school) of the *melamed* (teacher) Avraham Yitzhak, who was called "the Melamed from Biezun" ("der Bezoiner Melamed") was in this house. (Apparently, he was from Biezun, a town 21 kilometers from Sierpc.) He taught little children. He would tell many funny tall tales about himself. We will mention some of them here.

He would say: "There was a very hard winter. A lot of snow fell, and a bitter cold engulfed the universe. The snow that covered the ground didn't melt because of the cold, and became higher and higher, until it reached the level of the chimneys. I was riding in a sleigh, when all of a sudden ? trach! I fell into a chimney and straight into a pot that was on the stove with porridge cooking in it. When the lady of the house, a Gentile, who was an acquaintance of mine, wanted to taste the porridge to see if it was ready and took a little of it with a big wooden spoon, she pulled me up on the spoon, recognized me, and asked "*Pania Avram, tso pan tu roby?*" (Mr. Avraham, what are you doing here?)"

And when he was asked, "Avraham Yitzhak, how is this possible?" he would answer, "Well, you can see!"

* * *

He would also tell the story: "Once I went to the market to buy beets. I happened to see an exceptionally large beet and I bought it. The beet was very large and very heavy, and it took a lot of effort until I brought it to the door of my house. But the doorway was too narrow, and it was necessary to tear down the kitchen wall to bring it inside."

And when he was asked, "Avraham Yitzhak, how is this possible?" he would answer, "Well, you can see!"

* * *

He would say: "I am poor because of one word." When he was asked "Avraham Yitzhak, what happened?" he would answer: "I had to go to the bank. I saw there were packages on the table. Packages of bills of 10, 25, 50 and 100 rubles, so I asked the cashier, ?Sir, may I take these packages?' He answered ?No!' And because of this one word, I have been poor all my life..."

***

It was customary that when a Jew was to appear in court, the Rabbi would be called to swear him in, and the Rabbi would receive a payment for this. Once, when there was a court case between a Jew and a Gentile, the Jew had to be sworn in, and the Rabbi was called. The Rabbi was not feeling well, so he asked Avraham Yitzhak, "the Melamed from Biezun," who had an imposing presence with a long white beard, to take his place in court. Avraham Yitzhak consented and went to the court. When he started to swear in the Jew, the Gentile's wife yelled at him "*Chi to rabin? Pzhechezh to shklaz!*" ("Is this the rabbi? It's the glazier!") For a time Avraham Yitzhak had gone from village to village working as a glazier...

* * *

Once, on a cold winter night, the Melamed from Biezun entered the old prayer house. He went from spot to spot, held his right cheek in both hands, and had an angry look on his face. The young man Avraham Haim Greenivich came to him and asked him "Avraham Yitzhak, why does your face look so dreadful today?" "Don't ask," the Melamed from Biezun answered in a sad and hurt voice, "One of my teeth has become soft as butter and is causing me a lot of pain." "A tooth as soft as butter" wondered Avraham Haim, "I never heard of anything like that." "Touch it with your finger and you'll see" said "the Melamed from Biezun," who opened his mouth and pointed to the soft tooth. Avraham Haim wanted proof of this marvel, and stuck his finger into the mouth of "the Melamed of Biezun," who bit it robustly. Avraham Haim let out a yell that frightened the whole prayer house...

* * *

And a story about Dudi from Zuromin, a grain merchant, who came to Sierpc on business. "The Melamed from Biezun" came to him with a sample of pea, and offered him "a quarter pea.." ("*A fertel arbess.*" This is the manner of speech of grain merchants, "a quarter wheat", "a quarter rye", "a quarter barley", where the intent is a quarter of a quintal ? *kertz* ? 100 kilograms.) They agreed on a price and the seller was to bring the merchandise at a certain time to a certain place. At the given time "the Melamed from Biezun" arrived there, removed a folded handkerchief from his pocket, opened it, took a quarter of a pea grain out of it, and presented it to Dudi...

* * *

With the passage of time, Lusmar's house was sold to a Jew from Raciaz who had come back from America, and whose name was Itcha Shwitzer. The new landlord built a two-story house in the yard.

Itcha Shwitzer was a rich Jew. Because he had no business affairs to attend to, he would walk around the yard all day dressed in shabby clothes, holding a broom, shovel, hammer, or other tool, and would clean, fix, or arrange things. Once a pauper passed by, and he called him and gave him some money. The pauper left the yard and said to some people he met near the house, "Look at the difference between a rich man and a poor man. I went to rich people in the new house in the yard and got nothing. And this poor man, who was cleaning the yard, called me over and gave me a nice amount." And then he cursed the people living in the new house, and rich people in general...

* * *

One of the tenants in the new house was Itzia Bonem Rosenberg. Itzia Bonem (Beinam) Rosenberg was a smart man and pleasant conversationalist. He would sprinkle his speech with the adages of the sages and appropriate popular phrases, with a dash of humor. He was an outstanding and devoted activist of Poale-Tzion Left and a mainstay of the branch of the party in Sierpc.

For a certain period, Itzia Bonem Rosenberg was a member of the community council representing Poale-Tzion Left.

* * *

The next house, a new brick house, large and with two stories, was that of Litvinsky (a Pole). And consider the luck of a Gentile house, that it was full of Judaism. This building housed the respected religious-educational institution Yesodai Hatorah, which was founded during the First World War to take the place of the old *heders*. The last Rabbi of Sierpc, Rabbi Yehoshua Heshel David Goldshlak, lived in this house. The *shochet* (ritual slaughterer) Yekel Richik and the synagogue attendant Shimon Gelbard lived in this house. In addition, the house stood opposite the synagogue.

* * *

Rabbi Yehoshua Heshel David Goldshlak was the grandson and successor of the previous Rabbi, Yechiel Michal Goldshlak. Rabbi Yehoshua Heshel David was a great scholar, and good preacher. His sermons were interesting, full of appropriate adages of the sages. He had a large library of books on the Torah. Before he became the Rabbi of Sierpc, Rabbi Yehoshua Heshel David was the Rabbi of the town Przedecz. came to our town in 5683 (1923), in the month of Av, when he was about fifty years old. He served as the Rabbi of Sierpc until the day of the expulsion, until the extermination of the community of Sierpc.

* * *

Yekel Shochet (Richik) was appointed ritual slaughterer and examiner in Sierpc after the previous slaughterer, Itzia Yosel Chanakhovitch moved to Kalish [Kalisz]. He came to our town from Sochatchin [Sochocin] in the year 5672 (1912).

Yekel Shochet had an imposing figure, was an expert at his profession, had a good voice, and was a good prayer leader. He was a jolly man, pleasant to talk to, and interested in people.

But Yekel Shochet did not enjoy his position in the big city (compared to Sochatchin) for very long. He passed away in midlife during the typhus epidemic in the First World War. He died before Passover in 5676 (1916), when he was 38 years old.

* * *

The next house, a single story house, belonged to Akiva Offenbach, who did clothing alterations. This house was the last house on this side of the Jewish Street, and officially also the last house in town. This was the official boundary, until the 1920s, of the town of Sierpc. Between Offenbach's house and the next house (that of Shaletzki, a Pole) there was a barrier (called *shlagboim*) which was removed after a few years. Every cart that passed through here to town had to pay a toll.

* * *

In theory, the town ended near the bar cxzrier, but in practice, it continued on. There was no difference, either in the streets or in the houses, between the two sides of the barrier. Officially, the Vloka (Vlikes) began after the barrier, and though they were adjacent to the town, they were administratively attached to the village of Borkova, which was four kilometers from town, on the road to Drobin (Drobnin). For the convenience of the residents, there was a branch of the *gemina* (village hall) on the spot. The Vloka, most of whose residents were Polish, were annexed to the town in the 1920s, before the second town council elections, which took place in 1923, to increase the number of Polish voters in town. As a result, the number of Jewish council members decreased from eleven in the first to nine in the second council. (The number of town councilmen was 24.)

The Vloka were divided into two streets. One street continued on in a straight line, as if it were an extension of the Jewish Street, and the second street turned right. The town inhabitants called the first street Biezun (Bazyun) Road, and the second street, Drobin (Drobnin) Road. In the mid-1930s, when the town council named streets that previously had no names, the first street, the straight one, was called Kolinsky, after the Polish national hero of the Kosciusko uprising in 1794. The second street, which turned right, was called Raimont, after the Polish author who was a Nobel Prize winner for literature.

At the beginning of the first street of the Vloka, after the first house that belonged to Shaletzki (a Pole), there was a narrow street. This was the street on the hill, Gurna, which we previously mentioned.

The first few houses of the streets of the Vloka belonged both to Jews and to Poles. Most of the residents of the first few houses were Jewish. In the first street there lived: Yitzhak Charka, Avraham Zev (Wolfe) Laninter (emigrated to Palestine with his family in 1933), Yehuda Baruch Skornik, Yehezkel (Haskel) Izikovitch (all of them owned grocery stores), Avraham Mirantz (owned a lumber yard), Moshe Danziger (who was called "Msheye Karmelkeies," a *melamed*, and others. In the second street lived: the Zhabitsky family, Yischar Meir Skorka (who owned a lumberyard and a grocery store), the Charka family, Meir Zev Glasman, Leibl Kramarzh, Elia Fish, Bruchia Zheshotka, and others.

On the second street, to the right, there was a road that led to the cemetery. After the cemetery, the road continued until the water mill of Avraham Okart that was near the Zhika (the Sierpianitza River; the mill was sold to the Pole Gabronski, and he converted it to steam). This was the way people returned from the cemetery. (They took a different route to the cemetery.)

After the first few houses, only Poles lived in the two streets. Both streets acquired a rural look: small houses, barns, silos, and green fields. A little further on, there were no more houses and the town ended. The town streets became roads between towns. The first (the continuation of Kolinsky Street), to

Biezun (Bazyun), a town 21 kilometers away, and the second, the continuation of Raimont Street, to Drobin (Drobnin), a town that was 26 kilometers away.

* * *

In the first street, the straight one, Kolinsky Street, in the house of Daring (a German), lived Yehuda Baruch Skornik, and he had his grocery store there. His wife Mania (Miriam) and his children took care of the store, and he had another business, the coal and lime business. The storeroom for this business was in the house of his father-in-law, Mendel Garlitz (Lifshitz).

Yehuda Baruch was a tall man, dressed well and neatly, with polished shoes, a well-combed beard, and a wide smile always on his face. A good and pleasant man, who always tried to be kind to others.

Yehuda Baruch Skornik carried on an extensive business correspondence. He was one of the few people in town that rented a post-office box. He would go to the post-office every morning to take the mail out of his box. On his way back, he would walk slowly, his cane hanging on his arm, and would open letter after letter and glance at them, until he arrived at his store

* * *

Ber Charka lived in the second street of the Vloka (Vlikes), Raimont Street. Ber Charka was a faithful and devoted Zionist of the younger generation. He was one of the mainstays of the Zionist youth federation, Herzlia, and active in all facets of Zionism and culture in town.

During a certain period, Ber Charka was a member of the community council, representing the Zionists.

* * *

Leibl Kramarzh also lived in this street, and was known throughout the town as an outstanding scholar. He worshipped in the old prayer house, and studied there many hours every day. He studied, and also taught adults (Mishna) and young men (Gemara lessons).

* * *

The first house on this street (the second street of the Vlikes), the one-story house near the barrier, was that of Baruchias Zheshotka (who was called "Marekia" the nickname" Marek was apparently given to one of his forefathers named Meir by Gentiles.) Baruchia was a good and simple Jew, well liked and respected by everyone. He would take merchandise from Warsaw to Sierpc, and the merchants trusted him. When he became old, he was a caretaker in the New House of Prayer. Baruchia was a good prayer leader, and a pleasant prayer reader.

* * *

Going back to the Jewish Street, we see the small, one-story house of Mendel Garlitz, the last house on this side of the Jewish Street. Mendel Garlitz lived in this house and his grocery store was there. Mendel's family name was Lifshitz, and he was called "Garlitz because of his wife's name, Dinia Garlitz. The reason for this, in my opinion, is that Mendel married his wife when she was a widow. She was the landlady and she owned the store, and her name was well known in the neighborhood. Therefore, her new husband was called by her name.

Mendel Garlitz had a kind heart, and he would very willingly do favors for other people. He busied himself with good works and faith: he was a leader of the burial society, in the Welcome Guests Society, and other charitable groups. He was also a treasurer of the *kolelot* (funds that were collected by Alexander Hasidim for the *kolelim* --higher Tamudic academies in Eretz Israel, such as Kolel Polin and others). The money was sent to the Rebbe of Alexander, and from there, to Palestine.

* * *

There was an unpaved lane after Mendel Garliz's house. This lane did not have an official name, but it was called Przybozniczna (the lane near the synagogue). The lane's surface was much lower than the level of the street. There was a steep drop from the street, and not far from there was a rise, then again a drop, and then another rise. A few Jews lived at the beginning of the lane. The first was Finaia Makler. (He was a glazier. With time he changed from glazing to teaching little children, but that didn't change his poverty.) Further on there lived only Poles.

This lane led to the cemetery. The departed were carried through it on the way to their final resting place. (A horse-drawn cart was not used in Sierpc, but the dead were carried on the shoulders of the attendants.) It was customary that the attendants and mourners not return from the cemetery by the same route that they arrived. They went back through the Vloka (vlikes) by the road that went to Drobin (Drobnin). Under extraordinary conditions, in the winter, when walking through the lane would be difficult and sometimes dangerous, especially for the pallbearers, because of the descents and ascents, the same route was used coming and going, through the Vloka.

There were two cemeteries in Sierpc: a new one and an old one, and they were adjacent to each other. In the old cemetery, the early rabbis of Sierpc and some important *tzadikim* (righteous men) rested their eternal rest. One was Rabbi Meirl Dabash, who was Rabbi in Drobnin, Biezun, and Sierpc. Rabbi Meirl was also a rebbe of Hasidim. Rabbi Meirl was one of the giants of his generation, and Rabbi Levi Yitzhak of Berdichev would visit him in Sierpc from time to time. There was a tabernacle over his grave, and the townspeople would drop little notes with requests for him into it.

There was a second tabernacle nearby. This was the grave of Mordecai Greenbaum (the grandfather of Yitzhak Greenbaum) who had also been a rabbi in Sierpc.

My relative, I.D. Sandrovitch, told me about another *tzadik* who was buried in the old cemetery, whom he had read about in a book of stories and legends of Sierpc. There was the following legend:

A famous *tzadik* once traveled from Druvnin to Sierpc. When he came to the road between the village of Borkova and the town, near the cemetery, the *tzadik* said, "There is a good smell coming from this earth." Years passed, and the same *tzadik* again happened to be in Sierpc. He fell ill when he was in town, and after a few days returned his soul to its maker. A great mourning overcame the town with the death of the *tzadik*, and extensive preparations were made for his burial. The members of the *hevra kadisha* (burial society) dipped themselves in the *mikveh* for purification, and then prepared a special *mikveh* for immersion of the corpse of the *tzadik*. When the *hevra kadisha* brought the corpse of the *tzadik* to the *mikveh*, they couldn't immerse it because of the weight and rigidity of the body. Then there was a miracle and the body became light and flexible, as if the *tzadik* was helping the *hevra kadisha* to immerse his body in the *mikveh*.

The *tzadik* was buried in the old cemetery, in the same earth that had once smelled so good to him.

* * *

The watchman of the cemetery in the last years was a Jew called "Haskeltie fun Gitten-Ort" (Yehezkel from the Good Place). Haskeltie was a poor Jew and also ineffectual. He lived in a little house near the cemetery that was used by the watchman. In addition to guarding the cemetery, Haskeltie had some other occupations, all of them concerned with things sacred: on Sukkoth (Feast of Tabernacles) he would bring the palm branch and citron to many of the synagogue worshipers' houses (those that didn't have their own citron), for the women and girls to say the blessing; at the break of day on Hoshana Rabba (seventh day of Tabernacles) he would return to the houses and sell willow twigs for Hoshanot; on the eve of Pentecost he would sell cat's tail reeds (that were called *blishteshen*) to decorate the windows for the holiday, and other such jobs.

In earlier years the cemetery watchman had been a Gentile, a German (many Germans lived in the vicinity of Sierpc). His name was Schmidt, and because he was short, the Jews of Sierpc called him "Shmidtia." This watchman also had all sorts of odd jobs, also concerned with holy works. He was the official *shabos-goi* (the Gentile who would perform the tasks forbidden to Jews on the Sabbath) of the community. He would douse the candle, or a chandelier, in the synagogue or one of the houses of prayer, to prevent a fire. On Yom Kippur, at the start of the Neila service, he and his family would light the candles in all the prayer houses in town. The community would sell to him, on Passover eve, all the bread that was in all the Jewish houses and shops in town, and similar tasks.

In addition to all the tasks that I listed above, Schmidtia had one occupation that was completely secular, and this was the sale of white sand.

There was a time in the community of Israel, before the arrival of the fashion for laying down carpets (long and narrow, that were called *hudnik*), housewives would spread white sand on the floor on Sabbath eve after it had been washed, to keep it clean. Schmidtia, the cemetery watchman, sold the sand to the housewives. Schmidtia would bring the sand, which had been dug up from the hills outside of town, in a small, narrow cart hitched to a haggard (and also white) horse. He stopped the cart at every house and sold the sand to the waiting housewives in bulk. The bulk was measured in an old bucket, and the price was two groschen for a bucket.

* * *

Not only the living Jews suffered from the blows of the accursed Germans, but also the dead. In their cruelty and savagery, these vandals did not overlook the cemetery. They pulled the gravestones from the graves and used them (with the inscriptions facing downwards) to pave the sidewalks in the Jewish Street. The few Jews who returned to town at the end of the war and after the Holocaust, took the gravestones from the sidewalks, with the permission of the authorities, and returned them to the cemetery. Of course, they didn't know how to, and could not, return them to their original places.

Our neighbors, the Poles, also participated in the desecration of the holy place and the degradation of the dignity of the dead. They ploughed the cemetery and planted grains and vegetables. The same Jews, those who returned to town, obtained a pledge from the authorities, that after the removal of the grains and vegetables, the spot would not be planted again, and that the municipality would put a fence up around the cemetery.

After the gravestones had been returned to the cemetery, the Jews put up a memorial to the martyrs of Sierpc who had perished in the Holocaust.

* * *

Beyond the alley was the synagogue. The synagogue was in a special place, an isolated spot that seemed to have been made for it at the time of the Creation. On one side, to the north, the street rose to the height of a few meters, and on the other side, to the south, there was a wide green valley that extended to a line of trees, and behind them flowed the Sierpianitza River. And so the synagogue stood on a spot that was between "a soaring tower and a deep well."

The synagogue was built, according to our townsman S.A. Lanter, in about 5655 (1895) in place of the previous synagogue, which had stood on the same spot and had burnt down. (Unfortunately, we have not been able to determine the year of the fire.) The new synagogue was also built of wood.

Both the exterior and the interior of the synagogue were impressive. The building style, with three domes on the roof, stained glass windows, a foyer, and the unique location gave the synagogue an air of majesty and splendor, grandeur and reverence. The fittings and furnishings inside the synagogue were also beautiful. There was a splendid Torah Ark of carved wood, with striking pictures surrounding it: two landscapes, of winter and summer, and paintings of musical instruments, and on top of it, a stunning curtain with the heavens and the hosts of heaven. (The paintings were by the Jewish artist Stshalko from Plock. The synagogue was renovated in about 1907, and the paintings were added then.)

The majority of the worshippers at the synagogue were simple family people. A minority was of the intelligentsia of the younger generation (the Enlightened and the Zionists of the older generation prayed in the New House of Prayer), some of whom came only on holidays.

* * *

During the horrible time of the Holocaust that fell on the Jews of Sierpc, the synagogue was a loyal agent of the community, and devoted to its flock. It was the first to go up in flames to the heavens, as if it wanted to hasten to the Throne of Glory and beseech mercy for the congregation of the flock of Israel that was in Sierpc. (The synagogue was burnt by the Nazi savages on the second night of Sukkoth, 5700 (1939).

That same night, the second victim among the Jews of Sierpc was killed. (The first victim, Arie Zhitalni, died in an air raid on September 4, 1939.) This was Pinchas Valtsman (called "Pinie dem Farbers" ? the Son of the Housepainter) who was 21 years old. When all the Jews in the area began to run to the synagogue to save whatever could be saved, the evil Germans blocked their way, and would not let them approach the site of the fire. This boy succeeded in passing the barrier, but the murderers shot him, and he fell dead.

* * *

The street continued here in a downhill slope, and there was a railing made of wooden beams on the side (like the railing on a bridge). To the side of the street, in an area below the level of the street, there was something like an unpaved lane that extended from the synagogue to the house of Dudia Tchernotchepka (and the railing also extended till this spot). Along this lane were some small and pitiful houses.

* * *

One of the landlords here was Horn. For some reason, the whole neighborhood was called by his name: "Horns Giter" (Horn's Properties).

My Rabbi, Moshia Karmelkeies (Danziger), told me:

"Horn always wore, both on sunny and on rainy days, a *chalatia* (thin coat). The only difference was what he wore beneath the *chalatia*. On sunny days, he wore a shirt and trousers, and on rainy days, a peasant's fur coat."

* * *

Avraham Yitzhakie Mai (called "the *shihl-kleperie*") lived in one of the small houses. Avraham Yitzhakie was a community-attendant, and his job was to wake the congregation every morning by tapping on the widow shutters for the Service to the Creator. Usually he would tap three times, and when he died, God help us, somebody in the town tapped twice.[20] He would also proclaim every Friday, before sundown, in all the streets of the town, "*In shihl aran!*" (To the synagogue!)

Once, the *gubernator* (district governor) from Plock visited Sierpc, and as he walked in the street, he heard the call of the *shihl-kleperie*. He told one of the policemen accompanying him to call the *shihl-kleperie* over. When he came over, the *gubernator* slapped him in the face, reprimanded him for yelling in the street, and ordered him arrested. Avraham Yitzhakie tried to apologize to the *gubernator* in his broken Russian, and explained why he was shouting, and then he was released.

* * *

There was an unpaved lane after the row of little houses. The lane continued to the Zhika (river), till the *lava* (a narrow crossing about half a meter wide, made up of wooden boards laid on wooden columns sunk into the riverbed and jutting out of the river by about a half a meter.) The *lava* crossed over the river and reached the other side opposite the lane and street called Doli (Dole) that extended from the Plotzki Street. The lava shortened the distance between the Jewish and Plotzki Streets considerably. There were a few small houses in this lane. There was also a well, which had soft water, and many people from the neighborhood, and also from outside the neighborhood, used it.

* * *

After the lane was the one-story house of Dudia Tchernotchepka. It was possible to revive one's soul with a glass of brandy in his store, or a glass of beer, and have a desert of cake, roll, herring, fried liver, or other delicious foods. The adults, of course, enjoyed these delicious foods, and we children enjoyed the cooked, salted and peppered chickpeas (*gezotene arbess*), which we bought there for a groschen (half a Russian kopek, the smallest coin there was) a cup.

* * *

The next house, a two story house, belonged to Yukov (Yaakov) Garlitz. Yukov Garlitz was the chairman of the community council before the war, and a very respected man in town.

* * *

Immediately after the Garlitz house was the small, one-story house of Reb Ephraim Yosel Valuka. The only store at the front of the house belonged to the landlord.

Reb Ephraim Yosel Valuka was an outstanding scholar, Enlightened, and one of the first Hovevei Tzion in Sierpc. He was one of the survivors of the Kolhekot (the group of enlightened Mitnagdim that broke away from the community and set up a separate congregation). Reb Yosel was a student of the Torah, well versed in the Bible and proficient in the Talmud.

* * *

In our time, the house and store belonged to Avrahamia Valuka, the son of Reb Ephraim Yosel. Avrahamia Valuka was one of the second generation of the Enlightened and Zionists in Sierpc, and was one of the important worshippers in the New House of Prayer. He was a clever man and an interesting conversationalist. He was concerned for his fellow men and admired by them, as the phrase goes "a friendly man with whom to make friends." His speech was full of quips, good jokes, and deft proverbs. Anywhere that Avrahamia Valuka would go, people would gather around him to listen to his opinions and enjoy his witticisms.

* * *

Next to Avrahamia Valuka's house was the one-story house of Dudi Moshe (Moshe Mordecai) Sandrovitch (who was called "Moisheye Rudes")[21] the owner of the haberdashery and shoemaker's supplies store in the same house.

Moisheye Sadrovitch's shop was unique. It had two kinds of merchandise, haberdashery and shoemaker's supplies, and the customers were different. There were men, women and children, Jews and Gentiles, tailors and shoemaker, artisans and apprentices, paying in cash and buying on credit (there were not a few buyers of the latter kind, also among our brethren, the children of Israel), who came from all parts of town to this shop. The store was open from six in the morning till midnight, and was always full of buyers, noisy, and boisterous. They closed their store with great difficulty on Friday nights when dusk fell. On Saturday night, even before the first candle, people were already pounding on the door of their apartment (which was near the store), asking to open the shop. Many of the customers were Polish shoemakers' apprentices, wild and unkempt ruffians, who offended both the shopkeepers and the customers. There was neither order nor civility there, and all addressed each other as "you."

It was hard labor for the whole family, and they worked eighteen hours a day. My Aunt Ruda, who managed the store, was sick in bed every Saturday. But as soon as three stars were seen in the sky and the first candle was lit, she became like a lion, got up from her sickbed, and went to her night shift. She stood all week in the store, with one foot on the floor and the other, which was ailing, on a stool. For seven days after a trip to Warsaw (there were frequent trips, because the store bought and sold great quantities of merchandise), Uncle Moshe would work day and night auditing the merchandise he had brought and balancing the accounts (*oprifen di schoira*). The jokesters said that he numbered each needle... From all this hard work, they never earned more than a very modest living, because of their "partners" (the credit customers that I mentioned).

* * *

Because of his advanced years, Moshe Sandrovitch was not exiled with the group that was expelled from Sierpc by the German murderers. He stayed in the town, and moved, along with the others who remained in town, to the Ghetto. He died in the Ghetto at the end of 5700 (end of the summer of 1940), at the age of eighty-seven.

* * *

Shimon Yakobovitch, who had a horse and cart, used the second store in the same house as living quarters. He would use his small cart, with a gaunt horse harnessed to it, for delivering light cargo in town. He was called "Shmia mitn Veigltia" or "Shmia mit di Kotsh" (Shimon with the Cart or Shimon with the Carriage).

Shimon and his horse and cart prospered during the German occupation of the First World War. They were almost officials of the Royal German Mail. Shmia would take the mailbags every day from the post-office (that was in Goldstein's house, at the beginning of the Plotzki Street) to the *kolaika* (small railway), and from the *kolaika* to the post-office.

* * *

The son of the landlord, Hirsh Michal (Michael) Sandrovitch, had his "chemistry lab" in the cellar of the same house. He started and developed a thriving industry of chemistry products here. He produced various kinds and colors of inks (for writing, for shoemaking, and more), wax for different purposes and of different colors (for shoemakers, for seals, and so forth), and shoe polish of various colors.

Hirsh Michal Sandrovitch was an expert in his field. He was inquisitive by nature, and he came by his expertise through his inquisitiveness. At first he learned his trade from other "industrialists" by paying tuition fees. But he did not accept what he was taught as if it were the Torah from Mount Sinai. He experimented with every product before he would start selling it. He would add to one ingredient, and reduce the amount of another ingredient. He would mix and cook, spoil and fix, until he achieved the ideal product, and only then would he put it on the market. His creations were such an improvement that there were cases where his former teachers wanted to return his tuition fees and add to them, just so that he would teach them his new methods.

But the trouble was that Hirsh Michal Sandrovitch was a man of "many labors but few blessings." For many years he could not afford to order bottles and boxes with the name of his company on them. Because of this he would sell his wares in used bottles and boxes of various companies that he would buy from junk dealers, and thereby publicize their products.

* * *

The next house, a narrow two-story one attached to the Horovitz house, was that of Lipaia Nasielsky. The Yiddish proverb "*Ver s'hot a sach techter, dem geit nisht an kine gelechter*" (He who has many daughters does not have a lot to laugh about) did not fit Lipaia. He was blessed with many daughters, but he was always happy. He was a bright Jew, and full of fun. He was always full of pithy sayings and wisecracks that he would come out with on the spot, during the course of a conversation. Here are some of Lipaia's utterances.

There are some prayer leaders (*bal koras*) that can read only the first part of the weekly portion of the Torah. These prayer leaders read the Torah during the Saturday afternoon prayer or the morning prayers of Monday and Thursday, when only the first part is read.

Lipaia would call a prayer leader of that sort *pershivi bal koreh.* (A prayer leader who can only read one verse; "*pershiv*" in Polish ? afflicted with boils)...

Lipaia would say, "I will never let any of my daughters marry a young man who trades in, or has an occupation that begins with the letter "f". He justified this by stating that any trade or occupation that begins with an "f" is "feh" (a Yiddish expression for something ugly or despicable) like *fisher, fleisher, furman, ferds-hendler, farber, frizirer, fotografist* (fish monger, butcher, horse trader, housepainter, barber [transgresses on the prohibition against shaving], photographer [deals with women])..."

When he was an old man, Lipaia once sat at a feast, and emptied glass after glass. Somebody told him, "Slow down Reb Lipa, the liquor is ninety proof (*ninetziker*)." Lipaia answered, "I'm eighty (an *achtziker*) and the liquor is 90 proof (*ninetziker*), and when an eighty year old drinks 90 proof liquor, he becomes 100." (?'*Oz an achtziker trinky ninetziker vert er a hunderter*')..."

He would say, "*htarben yak shtarben, nor di dira iz in drerd.*" (It's not so terrible to die, but the apartment is in the ground. The phrase in drerd has a double meaning: literally "in the ground," and "something bad." Here the meaning is two-fold: both a bad apartment, and the apartment is in the ground.)

* * *

As mentioned, Lipaia's house was attached to that of Horovitz. Aharon Moshe Horovitz's house was a new, two story brick house. The front of the first floor was the wholesale grocery store that belonged to the landlord. We have already mentioned that, until the First World War, there were two wholesale grocery stores in Sierpc. One was that of Lidovski, and the other one belonged to Horovitz. There was an interesting innovation in this store. It was shut, not by doors, but with a shutter made of corrugated tin, that could be raised and folded. Everybody went to look at this novelty. Possibly the adults knew that the shutter folded, but we, the children, were sure that there was a space in the wall that the shutter would disappear into when it was raised.

* * *

Beyond the Horovitz house there was a narrow, unpaved lane that led to the Zhika (river), where there was a path to the *lava* (a crossing over the river) that was a short cut to the Plotzki Street. There were a few small houses in this lane, and some poor families lived there. Among them was the melamed (teacher) Haim Yosef Crystal (he used to live on the small street near the *mikveh*).

The *melamed* Haim Yosef was quick-tempered (he was called "the soldier" because in his youth he had served in the Russian army, and there was something military about him till old age) and any misbehavior, whether trivial or serious, by his students would warrant a severe beating. This was well known to the students' parents, and most of them, especially the fathers, consented to it. There is a story that Moshe Yehuda Karsh came to Haim Yosef and offered to send his Fibush to the *heder*, on condition that he wouldn't be beaten. Haim Yosef answered, "If so, it's better that he stays at home." And Fibush didn't stay at home, but in the *heder* of Haim Yosef.

My Rabbi, Nosheie Karmelkeies (Danziger) told a story.

"One of Haim Yosef's students was Yosek (Yosef) Kotcholk. The Kotcholk family was rich and intelligent, and in contrast to most of the parents, they did not agree, especially his mother and sister, to Yosek being beaten by the *melamed*. But Haim Yosef did not discriminate between students, and from time to time Yosek would also receive his share of blows.

"Once when Yosek received an especially harsh beating from Haim Yosef, he ran home and didn't return to the *heder*. After a couple of days had passed, and the boy still did not return, Haim Yosef went to the trouble of going to Moshe Hirsh Kotcholk (because it's a pity to lose a student, especially a rich one) to ask him to send Yosek to the *heder*. There he had to listen to the strenuous protests of the student's mother, Mrs. Hinda Kotcholk, about her son's beating. After he justified himself to the mother and promised not to beat him again, the mother told Yosek to return to the *heder* with the Rabbi. Yosek did not have any great desire to return, but he recognized his mother's authority, and went with the Rabbi.

"The same thing happened a few more times. The Rabbi, out of habit, beat the student, the student ran away from the *heder*, the Rabbi went to the student's house, received a tongue-lashing from the mother, promised not to repeat his "transgression" and Yosek returned with the Rabbi to the *heder*.

"Once, after the above scene had repeated itself, when the Rabbi and the student were returning to the *heder* and crossing the *lava*, the Rabbi in front, with the student behind him, the student pushed the Rabbi into the Zhika (river). The river was shallow, and there was no danger, heaven forbid, to Haim

Yosef, but he was soaked to the skin, from head to foot. He got up and went home, sad and wet, as the saying goes ?humiliated and embarrassed.'

"When Haim Yosef came home, because of his helpless anger, he broke down the door of his room, threw himself on the floor, and lay there, silent with his face down. The students became frightened, the *rabanit* started screaming, the neighbors arrived, and they all tried to revive Haim Yosef, to get him to stand up, to turn him over. He wouldn't move and lay there like a corpse. All of a sudden, he got up, and let out a roar, ?That *sheigetz* (abomination)! That criminal! That destroyer of Israel!' He smashed his head with his fist, pulled out his hair, and continued yelling. The *rabanit* and the neighbors tried to calm him down, but Haim Yosef continued his terrible and wild screaming. Finally, he calmed down, and related what the *sheigetz* had done to him.

"Haim Yosef never went back to the Kotcholk residence, and Yosek never returned to the *heder* of Haim Yosef."

* * *

The house behind the lane, a one-story house, belonged to the Shlisharken, and the tavern was there. One could drink a glass of brandy there and have some fried liver with it. One could eat a piece of pickled or smoked herring, with a biscuit or a stuffed roll. One could also get a full meal: a large portion of fish and a quarter of fried goose. The name of the Shlisharken was Rosa Zind, but the whole town called her "Shlisharken." She was a widow (her husband was a locksmith (*shlosser*, and in the Sierpc accent, *shlisharz*), and because of this she was called "Shlisharken." Her two daughters helped her with the business.

As we previously mentioned, the Shlisharken had a *tzhina* in the store, and she sold boiling water for tea.

* * *

Behind the Shlisharken house stood the Old House of Prayer. (Unfortunately, we have not been able to determine when it was built.) This small temple was a popular place of worship, and "simple folk" prayed here. The regular worshipers at the Old House of Prayer were mostly small property-owners, artisans, tailors, shoemakers, butchers and fish mongers, many of whom were not overly familiar with the fine points of the Scriptures. This applied to most of the worshippers at the Old House of Prayer who worshipped there on Saturdays as well. But on weekdays, the worshippers were from all classes, and of all ages: Mitnagdim and Hasidim, artisans and merchants, rich and poor, young and old. The first worshippers would come to the house of prayer at dawn, and would start by repeating Psalms and Maamadot until the time that prayers would begin. When the prayers would start ? "Time to read the Shma of morning prayers" ? many minyans would pray, one after another. The morning prayers would last for many hours. The same happened for the afternoon and evening prayers: one minyan would end, and another minyan would start.

The Old House of Prayer was not only used for worship, but also for Torah study. From the break of dawn till late at night, the sounds of Torah would be heard in the House of Prayer from young men, youths that had just left the heder, and from adults who were studying alone, or in groups, or *Ein Ya'akov* [reading collections of ethical teachings]. The Old House of Prayer hummed for eighteen hours every day with the sounds of Torah and prayer, voiced by young and old men who were occupied with Torah for its own sake, and who pleaded to their fathers in heaven.

* * *

The Old House of Prayer escaped the great destruction of the Jews of Sierpc. It was not destroyed when its worshippers and students were annihilated, and was not demolished along with its fellows ? the other places of worship in Sierpc. The accursed Germans set up a concentration camp for offenders in that holy place, with its cruel and criminal inquisitors. The "offenders," Jewish and Polish, were kept there, and taken out daily to perform hard and humiliating labors. And like they left certain Jews alive (for a limited time) who were denoted by the letters "W.W.J." (*Virtshaftes Vertike Yuden*, Jews with an Economic Value), so they left the building of the Old House of Prayer, which had some economic value for them.

* * *

The house after the Old House of Prayer was a two-story house that belonged to Zelig Richgut.

Rabbi Yechiel Michal Goldshlak of the Righteous of Blessed Memory, who was a Rabbi of the Sierpc congregation, lived here for 53 years. Rabbi Goldshlak was known as a great Torah scholar, and for his good works. He also wrote many books, of which only a few were published. Rabbi Goldshlak was born in the town of Szrensk in 5591 (1831). When he was 17, he was appointed the Rabbi of the town of Kikol, and was afterwards the Rabbi in Szrensk, Podembitza, and Ostrolanka. He became the Rabbi of Sierpc 5625 (1865), when he was 34 years old. The Rabbi died on 21 Shevat 5678 (February 3, 1918) when he was 87 years old.

* * *

Zelig Richgut, the landlord, had a tavern in the same building. One could get tasty provisions there, sweet and strong: glasses or bottles of brandy, 45 or 90 proof; regular herring, or pickled herring, or smoked herring; a generous portion of fish; boiled or fried meat, and all sorts of desserts.

* * *

We heard from our distinguished townsman, Shmuel Itchia Lanter, about a terrible tragedy that occurred there in the 1870s. In a fire that engulfed the house, Icheia Tatz (the father of Shmualtia, Natan, Wolfe and Ella Tatz), who lived there, was burned alive.

* * *

The two-story house of Yosef Vasolak was attached to the Richgut house. Next to the house and behind it was a large yard, and at the end of the yard was a two-story house whose first floor was a grain storeroom. (In 1931, a kindergarten called Tarbuth was opened here. This was the beginning of the Tarbuth School in Sierpc.) Avraham Fried (Yerushalmi) lived on the second floor.

This building was later sold to Moshe Lasman and Yisrael Barjo.

Avraham Fried was profoundly involved in Zionist and communal activities. Because of his concern with public activities, he neglected his businesses, and ruined them, one after the other. He had a kitchen utensils store (in the market, in Eliyahu Glazer's house), and he put an end to it. He had horses and a carriage to transport merchandise from Warsaw to Sierpc, and he got rid of that. The same thing happened to his other businesses. Later, Avraham Fried did something quite different, pioneering: he bought two cows and wanted to live by selling milk. There were Jewish milkmen in town, but they bought the milk from Gentiles, but Avraham Fried wanted to set an example as a pioneer, as a productive, Zionist Jew. He would take care of the cows, he would milk them, and he would earn his keep by selling their milk. But in the end, this business shared the fate of his other ones. His other activities prevented him from properly taking care of the cows. And without proper care, there was no milk and no bread.

In 1921, Avraham Fried took another pioneering step. He emigrated with his family to Eretz-Israel.

* * *

Eliyahu Grossman (who was called "Alia") lived in the same house. Alia Grossman was an active member of Poalei-Tzion Left. In the 1930s, he represented that party in the community council.

* * *

The next house, a two-story house, belonged to Wolfe Chazzan. (He was called "Wolfe Kalmias" after his father-in-law, Kalman Fenster, who was the landlord.) Wolfe Hazan was a *melamed* of little children and sold books by rabbis and wise men at his home. His outward appearance was that of an idler-*melamed* of the old school, but actually he was an Enlightened Jew, knowledgeable in grammar, and very inquisitive.

Moshe Yaakov Shtahl lived in the same house, and had a store there. Moshe Yaakov was an enthusiastic Hasid, but he lived off the sweat of his brow. He worked hard, baking muffins and selling them wholesale to store owners and to retail customers in his own store. He also sold chocolates, candies, and other delicacies in his store.

Moshe Yaakov Shtahl was not from Sierpc, but came to our town from Pabianice (a town near Lodz) and he left Sierpc in about 1924. He visited Sierpc once or twice as an agent for a manufacturer of curtains.

During the Fourth Aliya, some rebbes emigrated to Israel. Among them were: the *rebbe* from Yablonana with a group of Hasidim who founded Moshav Kfar Hasidim; the rebbe from Kozienice with a group of Hasidim who founded Moshav Avodat Yisrael. The rebbe from Strikov also emigrated with a group of Hasidim. (The rebbe stayed in Palestine for a short time and returned to Poland.) Moshe Yaakov, who was a fervent Strikov Hasid, decided to follow his rebbe, and left without any passports or money, and of course was caught and arrested. He drifted through various prisons in various countries, until he was finally sent back to Poland.

* * *

Moshe Lasman's shoemaker's shop was the other store in the same building. Later, he bought the house.

* * *

The next two-story house belonged to Zelig Mionchin. The small haberdashery store of Reb Haim Nachum Tunbol was there. Reb Haim Nachum Tunbol was one of the first Enlightened Zionists in Sierpc. He was the only one in town who had then, in about 1908, visited Eretz-Israel. He was one of the residue of the Kolhekot. Reb Haim Nachum was a student of the Torah, knowledgeable in the Bible and the Talmud.

* * *

There was a shack attached to this house, which was the locksmith shop of Yisrael Barko (called "Yisrael Shlisharz," *shlosser*, locksmith).

The son of Yisrael Barko, Avraham Leib, became engaged at an early age to Hanna Rozink, the daughter of the baker Natan Rozink. After a time, the groom fell ill with typhus, and his condition was critical. When neither the doctors with their medicines nor repeating Psalms were of any use, or adding a name, nor other remedies, they tried a very special remedy. The bride-to-be and her mother entered the sickroom and tore up the *tnaim* (the written conditions and vows of the engagement), as a sign that the engagement was annulled. (The intent being that if her groom-to-be was destined to die, then after ripping the vows, he was no longer her groom-to-be.) And this remedy worked. A "miracle" occurred, and the condition of the patient improved. And he slowly recuperated, and regained his full strength.

* * *

Because we have mentioned a Jewish remedy that "saved" a man from death, we are reminded of a Gentile remedy that "saved" a man from death.

The “miracle” occurred in our house. A three-year-old child, the son of our relative Mendel Karpa, who was the *shochet* (ritual slaughterer) in the village of Tlochova, came down with diphtheria. When his condition became worse, he was brought to town, and the child and his mother stayed at our house. His condition deteriorated. Nothing helped, not medications, not Psalms, not adding the name Alter to his previous name. Until one day Dr. Gomovski announced that there was nothing to be done, and only God could come to his aid.

Then the Gentile woman who brought us water offered to try the following remedy: to rip open a live pigeon above the patient's head (apparently, a Gentile version of *kaparah* [the custom of swinging a live chicken over one's head on Yom Kippur eve]) and she volunteered to do it. Because we had no other choice, we agreed. The Gentile woman performed the remedy as described, and a “miracle” occurred, and the child got well.

* * *

Yisrael Karp lived in the yard of this house. The Karp family was new to Sierpc. They came from Warsaw during the First World War, when hunger and want were rampant in the large cities. Israel Karp was penniless when he came to Sierpc. The only fortune that he brought with him was some daughters of marriageable age. Not only did Reb Yisrael not have dowries for his daughters, he also did not have any work. At that time, (after the death of Moshe the attendant, who was called “der Blinder Moishe,” Blind Moishe) there was no attendant in the Old House of Prayer, and Yisrael Karp was given the position of attendant.

It is well known that many people believe in the superstition, that *aliyah* to the Torah (reading the Torah in front of the congregation) for the weekly Portion containing the section “Tochecha” (Warning) is a bad sign for the reader. Different congregations have different customs concerning this particular *aliyah*. In the House of Prayer in Sierpc, it was customary to “honor” the attendant with this particular *aliyah*. And Yisrael Karp, who liked to joke, used to say, “After every ?Tochecha', I marry off another daughter.”[22]

The sidewalk in front of Mionchin's house was used for selling fish. On Thursdays and Fridays, and sometimes on other days, fishmongers would stand there with their cartons, scales, and the rest of their equipment, and sell their merchandise. Of course, there was no shortage here of cries and swearing, greeting and insults. Later, the fish sales were moved to the wide area in the middle of the street, near Balt's house.

* * *

We have arrived at the Zhika (Sierpianitza River) and the bridge across it, which was described above.

All the houses that were on the other side of the bridge, between the bridge and the market, were narrow two-story houses that were attached to each other, without a yard or space between them.

* * *

The first house was jointly owned by Avush Liberman (later he moved to Plock) and to Fivel Buda. The two stores in that house belonged to the two landlords. The first had a textile store, and the second had a leather and shoemaker's goods store. During the time when Poland was independent, this house was torn down by order of the authorities, because of the hazard of it collapsing.

* * *

The second house belonged to Krusa Licht. Madame Krusa was a shrewd and bold woman, who new how to run a business. She had a haberdashery store in the same house. When she was widowed, Mrs. Licht married Yisrael Haim Iszajewicz, who was an important Gur Hasid.

* * *

The third house belonged to Leibush Rosenberg. Leibush Rosenberg was a kind and sensitive man, who suffered greatly because of his family troubles and the problems of making a living. He was the owner of a small and meager shoemaker's goods shop that was in the same house. He was a teacher of Bible and Gemara to children between the ages of eight and ten for many years. Later he was an attendant at the New House of Prayer, and he died there unexpectedly one day.

* * *

The fourth house belonged to Moshe Natan Klein, who had a *tzhina* (he would sell boiling water for tea). His wife, Madame Malka, had many names: "di Moshe-Natante" (Moshe Natan's wife); "di Hoiche Malke" (Tall Malka, because of her height); and also "Malke Kozak" (Malka the Cossack, because she was "a woman of valor" and had a sharp tongue).

I heard the following story about Malka Kozak from Avraham Ben-David (Melave).

* * *

Lazer the tailor (who was called "der Blinder Lazer," Blind Lazer) lived in the same house. In the year of the revolution, 1905, the Poale Tzion committee would meet in Laser's apartment. The neighbors found out about these meetings, which were, of course, secret. And the neighbor, Madame Malka, talked about them in public, with very pointed comments about the "heretics" and "abominations" who violated the Sabbath and ignored the bounds of morality and order.

The revolutionary committee tribunal decided to punish Malka, so that she would stop her chattering. The punishment was planned meticulously, and the comrades Mordecai Tchaslak and Haim Tzudek (who was called “Papush”) were appointed to carry out the verdict. This is what happened:

Haim Tzudek, who was short, entered Moshe Natan's house one evening, carrying a teakettle, and asked for tea (boiling water) for two groschen. Moshe Natan was sitting, as usual, at his table reading a book by the light of a small kerosene lamp. Malka took the teakettle from Haim Tzudek, went over to the pot, and bent over it to pour the boiling water. At this point, Mordecai Tchaslak, who was tall, came in holding a sack with tar. He quickly put out the kerosene lamp, put the bag on Malka's head, smoothed it over her hair and face so that it would stick well, and swiftly got out of there together with Haim Tzudek. Malka and Moshe Natan started screaming, neighbors and passers-by came in, and when they turned on the light, found Malka lying ion the floor, her head covered in a sack, screaming. When they tried to remove the sack, they found out that it was stuck to her head and face.

From then on, Malka Kozak learned how to hold her tongue.

* * *

Later, this house belonged to Fivel Buda, who moved his store (leather and shoemaker's goods) there from his house near the bridge, which was in danger of collapsing.

Fivel Buda was one of the worshippers at the New House of Prayer, which was the center for the Enlightened group, Hovevei Tzion, and the Kolhekot. The Polish shoemakers who came to his store to buy goods would sometimes ask, “Mister Buda, what is Kolhekotnik?” When they were asked, “Where did you hear of this word?” they would answer, “Sometimes when we go to the Hasid Mister Teitlebaum to buy goods,” (as is well known, Yakov Moshe Teitlebaum carried on a big business selling leather and shoemaker's goods in his house) “he tells us, ?why do you buy at Buda's, he's a Kolhekotnik'...”

* * *

The fifth house, which was brick, belonged to Yazef (Yosef) Nishat, and he had an iron works store in the same house.

The landlord's grandfather, Reb Avrahamka Nishat, was one of the town elders, and an enthusiastic and outstanding Gur Hasid.

* * *

The large and handsome brick house of Radomski (a Pole) stood at the corner of the Jewish Street and the market. The side facing the market had a drugstore, and the side facing the Jewish Street had three stores: the ironworks store of Yehoshua Goldman, the haberdashery store of Elia Meir Shlifer, and the textiles store of Tobieie Klinhoz. Yehoshua Goldman's wife, Roiza, ran the store, and Yehoshua spent most of his time in the house of prayer (sometimes the old one, sometimes the new one) studying either by himself or with others. And if by some chance he were in the store, he would be looking at a book there too.

Yehoshua Goldman was a distinguished scholar, acute, and well versed. He liked to study complex problems, which required applying the brain, wrinkling the forehead and diving into the sea of the Talmud and its commentators: the Tosefot, the Maharsha, the Maharshal, the Maharam, and similar commentators. He would rejoice in arguments about problems of this sort, and when he found a worthy adversary, he would display his perception and insight.

* * *

When we were writing about the houses in this section of the Jewish Street, the section between the bridge and the market, we started to wonder. None of these houses had yards, because behind them and attached to them was the yard of Radomski, the drugstore owner, which extended until the Zhika (river). And if there is no yard ? then there is no outhouse. So the question must be asked: what did all these residents do ? men, women, and children, boys and girls, young and old ? all those “under the bridge” who did not have “an ideal place” like we had, the students of the heder of Rabbi Leibush Rosenberg.

We turned to someone who had been very close to this situation, and from his answer we learned of the great distress of the residents of these houses. A distress that lasted for years, something that the residents of other streets, even of the other side of the same street, neither felt nor were aware of. A few of the residents had agreements with one of the landlords of the houses across the street, to use the outhouse in his yard. But most of them had to use a chamber pot that was kept in the attic and would be emptied late at night into the *Zhika*. Sometimes, one of the residents would be caught in the act by a policeman, and fined for polluting the river. What could these miserable people do? They paid the fine, and in the evening went again to Tashlich [the ceremony of tossing one's sins into a body of water on the first day of Rosh Hashana].

The Germans solved this problem during their occupation in the First World War, by building a public bathroom on the other side of the street, on the large, empty lot that was used as a yard for the houses of Eliakim Ryz and Moshe Greenbich. First the Germans proposed to the suffering residents that they build the outhouse in that lot. But when they explained that they couldn't build it on someone else's property, the Germans built it themselves, and charged the expenses to the owners of these houses.

* * *

We have finished our stroll and review of the Jewish Street and the Vloka (Vlikes) and the nearby streets.

* * *

To our great sorrow and heartbreak, all that we have related and described above, was and is no more. The wild Germans, with the active collaboration of our Polish neighbors, uprooted not only the Jews of Sierpc, but also their houses. All the wooden houses of the Jews (and most of them were of wood; the few brick houses were specifically mentioned as such) were burnt to the ground. Our townsmen who visited Sierpc after the Holocaust said that when they stood on the Vloka (Vlikes) they saw that all of the Jewish Street, until the house with the drugstore at the corner of the market and the Jewish Street, was bare of houses. The houses that were left on this street (including the adjoining small streets) were: The Old House of Prayer (that was used by the Germans as concentration camp, work camp, and torture center); the Shaletzki House; the Litvinski House; the Kamnitza (a Polish brick house); the Niapomoshchik House; the Horovitz House, the Prashnitzki House (Jewish brick houses); and by chance also the Kasazh House (a small, wooden, Jewish house). There remained one or two houses between the bridge and the market, on the right side. Most of the wooden Jewish houses on the other streets were destroyed as well. (The destruction of Jewish houses made of wood was a general phenomenon in all the Polish cities. The accepted view is that the main contributors to this destruction were Poles who were searching for gold and silver in the walls and floors.)

The "Wise Men" of Sierpc

There is a folk saying that goes, "Each town has its own village fool." Sierpc was blessed with a few of these types, the village fools. But they were not of one kind; they were of different degrees of absurdity and foolishness. But they had something in common: they were all foolish, and they were all a part of the community of Sierpc. When we remember the Jews of Sierpc, we must also remember these ill-fated ones.

* * *

We will begin with Zanvil, because he was the wisest fool in town. Zanvil (his family name was Papiarchik) was tall, with a clipped black beard. Throughout the year, in all seasons, he wore a warm, long and black coat, galoshes on top of boots, carried an umbrella, and had a scarf wrapped around his neck. If we judge by the saying of the Elders of Blessed Memory, "Silence indicates wisdom," then Zanvil was the wisest of all men, because he was silent all the time, and hardly ever uttered a word. It was said that he was a very learned man who knew many languages and especially English, and because of his great desire for knowledge, had turned into a fool...

* * *

In contrast to the silent Zanvil, Mordecai Yudel was very noisy. Mordecai Yudel (family name ? Rosenfeld) was of medium height with a short yellow beard. He was always in motion and doing things, always with other people, walking quickly, talking to himself and answering in a loud voice. He would do various odd jobs for a fee: run errands, carry parcels, pump water, and so forth. Mordecai Yudel was a prototype of the "village fool."

In the summer of 1910, approximately, two Circassian Jews who spoke only Russian and the holy tongue came to Sierpc. They sold summer hats for girls. Mordecai Yudel wanted to tell them to go to the house across the street, and said in the holy tongue, "*Halach yelech dort ahin*" [an unintelligible mixture of Yiddish and Hebrew].

At the beginning of the First World War, the Russians banished Mordecai Yudel to Siberia, on suspicion of spying for the Germans, and he never returned.

* * *

Aviomye was a different type (Avrahamia; his family name ? Pearl). He was older, with a clipped black beard with the first inkling of gray, short with a slight stoop, leaning on his cane, and dragging himself around slowly and wearily. His clothes, shoes, and cap were shabby, the peak of his cap was always turned to one side, and his pockets were full of papers and breadcrumbs. He was a *melamed*, teaching poor children the alphabet in their homes, and receiving in return food and a few pennies. His brother, Ahzhe, was a fur tailor (as he called it "*putzen macher*") and Aviomye was also a little acquainted with this trade. He sometimes worked for his brother, or for Kaliuch. Aviomye would visit many houses (he was always welcome at our house) and everywhere he was very cordially received. He could recite by heart some chapters of the Psalms, the Song of Songs, and some verses from Isaiah. On request, he would repeat them with the intonation of a preacher.

Aviomye wanted to get married. His ideal was a bride wearing a wide apron. When he was shown a girl with a wide apron, he would dissolve with pleasure. And in a good-hearted way, he would permit himself a swift gentle touch of her sleeve with the tips of his fingers. He couldn't pronounce the "R" sound correctly (because of that he was called Aviomye, which was his pronunciation of his name), and also the other sounds formed with the palate ? "Z," "S," "Tz," and "T." In his lisping pronunciation, he would say: "*Hoshene Uven izsh nish ashtie biveit oftsheshen*" (To wed is not to eat a slice of bread)...

* * *

Yosha, the son of Zelig Reichgut, was different from the others. Yosha was a young man, happy and quick. He was kind, liked other people, especially of the opposite sex, and would cheer them up. He called every girl "Tchutcha" ("Auntie" in Polish), and in special cases would add some doggerel, "*Tchutcha, diene eugen hobn miech tzigatzoigen*" (Auntie, your eyes have dragged me behind you). He was ready to do all sorts of odd jobs in any dwelling that included a young lady. Many housewives, or their daughters, exploited this weakness. Yosha was an "in-law" at all the weddings in town. He helped arrange the tables and chairs, and performed all sorts of tasks. He would entertain the bride and groom, and dance when they went to and returned from the bridal canopy, and of course, he did not refrain from eating the good food.

Once Yosha broke the mirror in his house. When he saw the his face reflected from every one of the pieces of glass on the floor, he ran to his mother and joyfully told her, "Mother, I have made many *yosha'yer*"...

* * *

The women of Sierpc also had a representative in this group of fools. Our Elders of Blessed Memory have said, "Women are feather-brained." But there was only one lady fool in our town, and her name was Malka-Lea, the daughter of Shlomo Richgut (who was called "Shlomo Chayehies"). Malka-Lea was not outdoors very often, because she helped to take care of her parents' house. When she walked in the street, she was always in a rush, and she would answer every question with "*Nimam sasa.*" (*Niemam tchasso* in Polish, "I don't have time.")

And wonder of wonders, a young man was located, a poor young man called Goldak, absolutely normal, from a respected family in the neighboring town of Kuczbork who married Malka-Lea. This was a topic of conversation around town for a long time. (After a few years, he left her and sent her a divorce decree.)

* * *

All the characters that we described above could be considered fools. But Sierpc also had its village idiot. This was Bereshie (his family name was Pearl), who had the honor of being the only village idiot in Sierpc. In addition to this singular quality, Bereshie also had a distinguished relation: he was Avyomie's brother. Bereshie was a quiet type of madman. He would walk around with worn out clothes in tatters, didn't harm anyone, didn't speak, and didn't ask for anything. When he was given a slice of bread, he would take it and smile at the benefactor. Sometimes he would help Yosef Wolfe Plonsker (who was called "Der Ata Macher," the Maker of Cotton Wool; he lived at the start of the Vlikes in Baruchia Zhashotke's house) making cotton wool. He worked and slept in a storage shed. He froze to death one cold winter night.

* * *

As if its own fools were not enough, Sierpc received reinforcement from a nearby town. This was "Yosha Hazurominai" or "Yosha the Water-Carrier" (to distinguish him from "Yosha the Sierpcer"). The two designations testified to his hometown and to his trade. He was a native of Zuromin and he lived by bringing water to people's houses. He came to Sierpc before the First World

War, when he was called to appear before the draft board. From then on, he became a citizen of Sierpc.

Yosha had broad shoulders and a scraggly blond beard. He was heavy and clumsy. When he walked, even when the heavy yoke was not on his shoulders, and the full buckets weren't pulling him to and fro, he would move left and right, in rhythm with his pace. He had a slight stutter and a screeching voice, a slow walk, and his clothes and shoes were torn, filthy, and wet. Yosha was the only one of these (male) unfortunates who was married.

Yosha had not always been a water-carrier. In his youth, in his native town of Zuromin, he had made ropes. He would turn the wheel of the twisting machine. Avraham Yerushalmi, who comes from Zuromin, tells the following story.

When he was in charge of informing the workers of Zuromin during the revolutionary year of 1905 not to work more than eight hours, he talked to Yosha as well, and told him to quit work at four o'clock, even if he was in the middle of a rope. Yosha caught only the end of his statement, and when he came to work the next day, he kept asking his boss if they were at the middle of the rope. When the boss answered yes, Yosha abandoned the wheel, and said that he wasn't going to work anymore. When his employer asked him, "Yosha, what's happened to you?" he answered, "Black Zalman's son (*Dem schvartzen Zalmens ying*) told me to stop working in the middle of the rope..."

* * *

And last but not least, we shall honor "His Honor."

The eldest of the company of fools was "His Honor." His Honor was an old Jew. His name was Lazerie and he was the father of Meir Rosen (who was called "Meiria Yaishnik"). Apparently, when he grew older, he became senile. His "madness" was that he believed he was a great cantor. He would tell everyone about his strong, mellifluous voice, his excellent and hearty prayer, and the large audience that came to listen to his prayers in the past. He would very willingly respond to any request for a demonstration of his cantorial abilities. He would start singing, "His Honor Fills the World" from the Kedusha. And from this came his name, His Honor.

Translator's Footnotes

1. Compare this to Kings II, Chapter 4, Verse 29: "Then he said to Gehazi: 'Gird up thy loins, and take my staff in thy hand, and go thy way; if thou meet any man, salute him not; and if any salute thee, answer him not; and lay my staff upon the face of the child."
2. This custom is mentioned in Yeda Am Book 2-3, (Volume 3) Tishrei 5716 (1955), p. 117: "Tap of a mallet. In places when the attendant would call the congregation to prayer in the morning by tapping with a mallet, they would tap every day three times, and on the day he died, only two taps. (Mkorei Minhagim Sign 90, 62)" An explanation of this is in the same issue, p.112: "The attendant taps three times on the window, and rouses the community of the God-fearing in the middle of the night for services to the Creator. If someone in the community passes away, God forbid, the attendant taps only twice, to inform you that of the three partners to a man ? the Most Holy Blessed He Be, the

father, and the mother - one of them, the first one, has dissolved the partnership…"

3. My aunt Ruda was "a women of valor", and she ruled the household and the pocketbook, and apparently because of this her husband was called by her name, "Moshe Rudes". We have mentioned a number of instances where husbands were called by their wives' names (Avrahamia Zlotzover, Shmuel Lant, Mendel Garlitz). These were identified by their wives' family names. This case is different, in that the husband was identified with his wife's given name, using the possessive case, as if he were her son. There were two more cases like this in Sierpc: The attendant at the mikveh in the 1880s was called "Shmuel Chanales." The reason for this seems to be that his wife, Chanale, came from a distinguished background. She was the granddaughter of Rabbi Meirl Dabash, who was a rabbi, and the Rabbi of Sierpc. The Gemara melamed in the 1880s and 1890s, Yitzhak Prager, was called "Yitzhak Malkes" apparently because his wife, Malka, was the saleslady in the grocery store (which was in a small house that was behind the shlisharken). I heard about these two cases from our townsman Shmuel Itchia Lanter.
4. It is interesting to consider the customs in different places concerning the *aliyah* to the Torah in the Portion containing the "Tochecha" section. In the Alexander Shtibl in Sierpc and Zoromin, the "honor" would go to the Prayer Leader. But to protect him from the curses, it was customary that the prayer leader on that Sabbath would call the purchasers of the *aliyahs* to come to the Torah. (The *aliyahs* would be sold every Saturday before the reading of the Torah, and usually the treasurer would call the purchasers to come to the Torah.) The section containing the "Tochecha", which had not been sold, would be taken by the Prayer Leader himself, without anyone inviting him or calling his name (so that the curses could not be addressed to him). In addition, he would be greeted twice after he had finished reading the section with the blessing "Mie Sh'borach" (He who blessed). And after all this, he would, as an additional substantial compensation, be honored by being called for the "Maftir" (last Torah section that is read that day) of the second day of Shavuot (Pentecost) for the "Tochecha" of the Portion "B'Hukotai" (My Statutes), and the "Maftir" of the second day of Rosh-Hashana (New Year) for the "Tochecha" of the Portion "Ki Tavoe" (When Thou Art Come). In the synagogue in Sierpc, there was a regular "Tochecha" reader, who would receive money for doing this. In the Gur Shtibl of Zhoromin, the prayer leader would be "honored" for the *aliyah* of "Tochecha", and he would not receive any compensation. The reason for this is that the prayer leader reads "for you", "to you", with you", etc. (in the "Tochecha" of the Portion "B'Hukotai") or "on you", "in you" "you", etc (in the "Tochecha" of the Portion "Ki Tavoe"), so that the curses are not intended for him. But if the prayer leader is a "cohen" or "Levi" (descended from those who performed the rituals in the ancient temple), then one of the worshippers is "honored" with this aliyah", and he is greeted twice after the aliyah" with "Mie Sh'borach". The custom of "honoring" the Prayer Leader with the aliyah" of "Tochecha" because he addresses the congregation with "to you" and "on you" so that the curses are not directed at him was also mentioned to me by a Jew from Budapest. The same Jew also described two other customs to me:
5. The person who distributes the *aliyahs* says, "Stand up, whoever wants to" and someone from the congregation (by agreement in advance) goes up for the *aliyah* and receives monetary compensation for this.
6. Someone in the congregation is called in the usual manner, and in the "Mie Sh'borach", after the Portion, a sentence is added to turn the curses into blessings.
7. In various towns in Poland, it was customary (and is now customary in various synagogues in Israel) that the executor of the *aliyah* with "Tochecha" (third section in the Portion of "B'Hukotai" or fifth section when the portions "B'Har" and B'Hukotai are combined, and sixth section in the Portion "Ki Tavoe") says the second benediction when the Prayer Leader reaches the "Tochecha" (since the Portion starts before the "Tochecha"). After saying the benediction, the *aliyah* executor remains on the podium near the Torah scroll. And the prayer leader reads the "Tochecha" without a person responsible for the *aliyah* and without a benediction before or after the reading.

Street Names in Sierpc

No	Popular Name	Official Name	Street Name in mid 1930's	Comments & Clarifications
1	The Market	Stari Rink (the Old Market)	Platz Pilsutskigo	Named after the Polish leader
2	Plotzki Street	Plotzka	Ridz-Shmigli	
3	Dols (Doli)			After the Polish Marshall Descent. An alley that leads down to the river and the "Lava"[1]
4	Dols (Doli)	Shvintago Vazhnitza[2]	P.O.W.	"Polska Organizatzia Waiskovo" – Polish Military Organization[3]
5	Dobrin Road		Piastovska	After Piast – the first Polish king
6	The street opposite the small park	Studolana (Barn Street)	Narotovitcha	After the first Polish president, Narutovitch, who was assassinated by a Polish Nationalist
7	Zhava Street	Zhavia	Pirwashago Maya	May Day, for the international workers' holiday
8	The street near Zelma Beries	Zhelona (Green)		
9	The street near the New Market (or: near the "Vanzhnia" – Prison)	Pirogova	Piratzkigo	After the Polish Interior Minister, who was killed by a political opponent
10	The New Market	Novi Rink	Platz Shostego Shrepnia	Sixth of August Place[4]
11	Boborova Road	Tchalpine	Zheromskigo	After the Polish writer Stefan Zharomski
12	The street near the monastery	Klashturna	Tazhchego Maya	Third of May. In honor of the Polish Constitution, which was signed on May 3, 1793
13	Rypin Road		Lipnovaska	The road to Lipno
14	Rypin Road		Ripinskaya	The road to Rypin
15	"Vloka" Road		Biazhonska	The road to Biezun
16	School Street	Shkolna[5]	Shpitalna	Hospital Street, after the hospital on this street
17	Fara Street	Farska		
18	The Jewish Street	Varshavska	Dashinskigo	After the leader of the P.P.S, Party, Dashinski[6]
19	"Mikve" Street			
20	"Kartofel mit Ferfel Geslach"			Streets of potatoes with barley flakes[7]
21	The street near the "Kamnitza" (the large brick building)		Gurna	An elevated street (spread out on the hill)
22	The street near the synagogue			A small street that led to the cemetery
23	The lane near the house of Dudia Tchernotchepka			A lane that led to the river and the "Lava"[8]
24	The near Horovitz's house			A lane that led to the river and the "Lava"
Vlikes (Vloka) – a (former) suburb that was incorporated into the town and had the following two streets:				
25	Bezhiun (Bizhun) Road		Kilinskigo	After the Polish national hero in the Kosciusko uprising of 1794, Kilinskigo
26	Drubnin (Drubin) Road		Raimont	After the Polish author Vladislav Raimont, winner of the Nobel Prize for literature

Translator's Footnotes

1. The crossing over the "Zhika" (Sierpianitza River) between Plotzki Street and the Jewish Street.
2. St. Vazhinietz, a Catholic saint.
3. An underground organization formed at the end of the First World War.
4. The day the Polish Legion, under Pilsudski's command, left Krakow for the front and the war against Russia, August 6, 1914.
5. After the school that was on this street.
6. "Polska Partia Sotzialistichna" – Socialist Workers' Party.
7. Two small streets, made up of poor people, which were called after the most popular food there.
8. The crossing over the "Sierpianitza" between the Jewish Street and Plotzki Street.

The Jewish Community of Sierpc between 1892-1907

by Y. A. Libsohn of Detroit, Michigan

The Sierpc Jewish community was similar to all other Eastern European communities. It had various groups, organizations, groups of *Hassidim*, *Misnagdim*, non-partisan householders, and regular Jewish women. In the community, there were parties, individualists, believers, holy people, *kabbalists*, hidden righteous people, *tzadikim*, scholars, honorable simple folk, various merchants, tradesmen, small-scale manufacturers, and regular people.

The groups in Sierpc included the philanthropic organization, the clergy, school teachers, and charitable funds that were maintained with a small amount of credit from a few individuals of means. Sierpc was not a wealthy city. Among the population of 4,000-5,000 there were only about ten very wealthy people. Approximately 50-60 Jews were mid-range businessmen and employers. The rest were poor businessmen, tradesmen, and brokers. Everyone had credit with the charitable organization. Nobody was sent to prison, Heaven forbid, for failing to pay on time.

Bikur Cholim took care of the sick. One did not need a special nurse to tend to the sick. Every Jew considered it to be a great mitzvah to visit the sick and to help them, for they believed that visiting the sick removed one sixtieth of the illness.

Hachnasat Kallah ensured that there would be no poor girl who would be unable to go to the marriage canopy without an appropriate outfit and a modest dowry. The good Jewish women of Sierpc made a top secret accounting of what type of help a marriageable girl required, so as not to shame such girls. Thus did they fulfill the commandment of tending to a bride.

Poor children studied in the *Talmud Torah* for free, without tuition. The *Chevra Kadisha* performed the last rights for the deceased. At a time when a funeral took place in the city, the businesses closed in honor of the deceased. During the funeral, a charity box was shaken with calls of "Charity saves from death," and charity was collected.

There was *Chevra Mishanyot,* in which scholarly Jews studied *Mishna* with simple Jews.

*

Religious and cultural life in the city centered around the rabbi, rabbinical judges, *halachic* decisors, *cheders*, teachers, schools, houses of worship, cantors and fine prayer leaders.

The rabbi of the city, Rabbi Yechiel Michel Goldszlag was the rabbi in Sierpc for 53 years. He was known as a great expert in Judaic wisdom. He worshipped in the Great Synagogue every Sabbath, *Rosh Chodesh,* and festival. On the other days, he worshipped in the old *beis midrash.* He would respond to queries on *kashruth,* conduct Torah litigation cases, deliver a sermon on the issues of the day every Sabbath and festival, and deliver moral admonition to the congregation.

After his death, his grandson Reb Hershke became the rabbi. Reb Hershke was my first rabbi in the *beis midrash.* I studied Torah with him.

The rabbinical teacher and judge, Reb Yehoshua Segal, later immigrated to America.

His son is currently a major lawyer in New York.

There were ten *cheders* in Sierpc. The Jews of Sierpc fulfilled the commandment of "Thou shall teach them to your children"[1] - teaching Torah to children. Even the poorest studied in the *talmud torah.* The teachers were Shmuel Pefer (the Bezwiner[2]), Wolf Chazan, Reb Michael, Reb Avraham Aharon, the Zloczewer, and others. Aside from the *cheders*, the city had two modern schools: Atlas' school and the *Maskil* school of Mr. Mordechai Hirsch Mintz

The Sierpc community had cantors and prayer leaders.

Cantor Moshe Leizer Smolinski used to lead the services in the Great Synagogue along with a choir on the festivals and *Shabbat Mevorchim*[3]. He would also be asked to come to weddings to entertain the guests with his singing. He blessed the Czar and sang the Russian National Anthem very nicely at national ceremonies.

Yechezkel Czarnoczopka was among the finest prayer leaders. He had a fine, holy voice. When he would intone *Hamelech*[4] on Yom Kippur in the Old *Beis Midrash,* it resonated in the market place. Reb Itche Yossel, the Gostyniner *Shochet* [ritual slaughter from Gostynin], was known for conducting services on Yom Kippur. He was assisted by his four sons with their resonant voices. People would come from everywhere specially to hear his *Avoda*[5]. His *Hakohahim* resonated and lifted the spirits.

Reb Baruch Reszatke was a sweet prayer leader. He recited the words with such devotion that the meaning of the words would become clear to everyone, even to those weak in the Holy Tongue.

There was a constant bustle in the Old *Beis Midrash.* The lads, supported sons-in-law[6], and householders would study. Regular householders who would only come to pray would also snatch a bit of *Mishna.* Others would recite a chapter of Psalms or just peer into a book.

Two or three different services would take place in the *beis midrash* every day. In the back area near the heating oven, people discussed politics and repeated news from various newspapers to which people subscribed in partnership. The worshippers would bring that news from the primary source home from the *beis midrash.*

After eating breakfast, the older students of means would return to the *beis midrash* and learn with the younger, poorer students without payment. They studied *Gemara* and *Tosafot*[7]. Some conducted a class for themselves. Various political discussions would take place among those studiers, especially during the time of the Russo-Japan war.

The worshippers would return for *Mincha.* Most of them worshipped in the congregation daily. Between *Mincha* and *Maariv,* they would again talk about the latest news. An emissary of a *yeshiva,* a preacher, a morality sermonizer, or a regular teller of stories or miracles would often be present in the *beis midrash.* Such a person would address the congregation and everyone would listen.

The average householders from the Old *Beis Midrash* were simple, G-d fearing Jews. They worshipped with devotion, with a melancholy tune, suffused with sadness that expressed the weariness of a persecuted people, who suffered and hoped with full faith for the redemption - that G-d will once again perform miracles and help the People of Israel as He had done in the old, good times...

The worshippers would revel in the chapters of Psalms, in which King David had pleaded, loved G-d more than anything else, and expressed his love for the Creator and his fellow men. They would study Torah, give charity, and perform commandments and charitable deeds in order to hasten the coming of the Messiah and to get to the Garden of Eden after 120 years[8]... In the meantime, they bore the yoke and the suffering of exile in the world.

I wish to mention here a few householders and charitable donors of the Old *Beis Midrash*:

Yisrael Libsohn, Michel Turkeltaub, the Gerlic brothers, Yitzchak Grobart, Wessalek, Glazer, Golibawski, Zwikelski, Goldsztejn, Glazer, Rozen, Tinske, Smolinski, Lelonik, Szweicer, Nemczupke, Karpe, Cyprys, Hartbrat, Bursztejn, Lopotke, Czarke, Krasner, Licht, Koniec, Malinowski, Lichtensztejn, Ostaszawer, Rozinek, Gongola, Baruch Beker, Rosenberg, Kadecki, Cyna, Szabicki, Grijna, Nachbyn, Galant, Zytelnia, Okart, Przygode, Czykes.

The *New Beis Midrash* and the *Misnagdim*

Jewish scholars and known *Misnagdim*, who did not believe in the mystical-philosophical actions of the *Hassidic rebbes*, worshipped in the New *Beis Midrash*. The leader of those *Misnagdim* was Rabbi Moshe Yehoshua Segal. The students Efraim Wloke, Hirsch Lolenter, Chaim Nachum Tanwel and Eliezer Wessalek understood the Bible and the *Talmud* in a straightforward and logical manner, with an emphasis on the straightforward meaning. They also studied the *Guide for the Perplexed of Maimonides*.

The new methodology of studying divided the Jewish community. The observant people called the initiators of the new methodology "*kolokotnikes*." The young students: Ezriel Podskoc, Shimshon Bude, Avraham Wloke, Gotlibowski, Bluman, Yosef Pindek and Mordechai Hirsch Mintz were *maskilim*, and the future leaders of the Zionist movement. They exerted a spiritual influence on us, the younger generation.

A few of the distinguished householders of the New *Beis Midrash* were Lubaszke, Gorfinkel, Feivel Bude, Lehrer, Maliwanczyk, Sarne, Grude, Kaleski, Waldenberg, Bluman, Dorfman, Szlokman, and Szmige.

Hassidim

During my time, *Hassidic shtibels* of Aleksander, Otwocker, and Gerrer *rebbes* existed in Sierpc. The Gerrer *Hassidim* were the majority. From time to time, the *Hassidim* traveled to their *rebbes* in order to warm themselves with the *Hassidic* ambience, bring their personal problems to the *rebbe*, ask advice and obtain blessings. The *Hassidim* served G-d with joy and enthusiasm. They even performed physical matters with devotion: they would eat in order to have the energy to serve the Master of the World and worship with devotion, enthusiasm, and song. Like all G-d fearing Jews, the Jews of Sierpc believed that in a short time the great day, the eternal holiday, where "the righteous would be sitting with the crowns on their head basking in the light of the Divine Presence"[9] would come. The *Hassidic* melodies that resonated like heavenly symphonies were brought to Sierpc from the table celebrations of the *Hassidic rebbes*, and the Jewish homes were filled with enthusiasm and joy. Most of the *rebbes* were against Zionism, since one must wait until the Messiah and one must not force and hasten the coming of the redemption. The *Hassidim* and *kabbalists* studied little Bible. They rather studied *Talmud* and *Zohar*. The delved deeply and concentrated on the spiritual mystical belief and joyous hymns.

The well-known *Hassidim* from my time were: Yisrael Najstadt, Moshe David Jeszajewicz, Note Margel and Avraham Senderowicz - who were known as pure *tzadikim* who studied Torah day and night, Kahana, Sznicer, Krul, Tac - who were *Hassidim* who were devoted to Torah, Divine service and good deeds; Grosman, Tajtelbaum, Goldman - who were among those who believed in "worshipping G-d with joy." There were also modern progressive and liberal charity donors such as: Glazer, Szperling, Silberberg, Horowicz, Rozen, Libsohn, Najman, Lidzbarski, Czarnoczopka, Kaczalek, Grobart, Lent, Grynbaum, Bachrach, Lipke, Tuchendler, Lipske, Plate, Lenczner, Jeszajawicz, Licht, Reichgot, Osonte, Dobraszklanka, Grynberg, Zelinowski, Silbersztejn, V. Margel, and Itche Margel.

Sabbath in the Town

People were busy with preparations for the Sabbath throughout the entire Friday. Wives baked *challas*, cooked fish and meat, and took their *cholent* to the bakery oven. The shops finished their work in the afternoon, and the tradesmen left their work to hasten to the *mikva*. Close to the time of sunset, the *shamash* went through the streets and called out, "Go to the synagogue!" Those who were late ran home. Everyone dressed in their Sabbath clothes. The house was cleaned, and the table was covered with a white tablecloth. The sparkling, fine Sabbath candelabrum was placed down. The mother lit one candle for every member of the family. She covered her head with a Sabbath kerchief and recited the blessing over the candles. From all the streets, Jews in their Sabbath clothing streamed to the Jewish street, where all the synagogues, *shtibels*, and *beis midrashes* were preparing to welcome the Sabbath.

The *Hassidim* were wearing *streimels*, which looked like crowns on their heads. Thus did they go to welcome the Sabbath Queen and the extra soul that comes to every Jew on the Sabbath.

The singing of "Come my beloved to greet the bride, let us greet the Sabbath," could be heard from all the houses of worship. After the services, people invited home a guest, if one was present, and then they went home to the bright Sabbath house. At home, they would sing "Peace unto you, angels of Heaven," praise G-d who gave the Sabbath to the world; make *kiddush*, eat the Sabbath delicacies, and sing hymns between each course. After eating, they recited the Grace After Meals with devotion, thanking the Master of the World for the Sabbath and for all good things that the Sabbath brings.

The older people peered into a book until they fell asleep from weariness and the plentiful Sabbath food. Then, the Sabbath gentile came to extinguish the light, and everything was quiet in the Jewish home.

The younger people went out for a stroll or for covert meetings. The streets were dark, for most businesses were Jewish and were closed on the Sabbath. Indeed, it was more joyous on the streets than on all other nights. The youth, bedecked in their best clothing, met with their beloved and friends on their stroll, and everything was cheerful and joyous.

The *Hassidim* wore their *streimels* for the entire Sabbath. They studied *Zohar*, the *kabbala* book that many of them did not understand. They hoped for the day that would be a complete Sabbath[10], uttering their own prayer, "Let our lot be with them."

Everyone rested on the Sabbath. Nobody worked. The businesses and workshops were all closed. The law of the land did not promote Sabbath rest, and certainly did not prevent working on the Sabbath, but the Sabbath rest was upheld with holiness by all the Sierpc Jews.

All of the Jews in Sierpc would "make" the Sabbath. Guests from other cities, who had come to town for a certain purpose, such as raising money for a poor bride, or other such a holy endeavor, most of them poor, would be invited by the householders to their table on the Sabbath. Everyone was taken care of, and nobody was left behind, for Jews are merciful people, descended from merciful people.

On the Sabbath morning, everyone went to worship in the synagogue. Women were dressed in their finest clothing and were adorned with jewelry. When people returned from the synagogue, they recited *kiddush* over liquor. They fetched the *cholent* from the bakery, ate, and sang hymns. The songs were of the Sabbath, reminiscent of the additional soul, and satisfying. Then they would recite the Grace After Meals, and lie down for the Sabbath rest.

Older people would take a nap after the *cholent*, and would go to the Old *Beis Midrash* around the time of *Mincha* to listen to a lecture from a sermonizer, or to listen to Chaim Leib Furman, with his fine, grey beard, teach *Pirke Avot* [Chapters of the Fathers][11]. The more modern Orthodox Jews, already members of Mizrachi, gathered together with Chaim Nachum Tanwel, studied *Pirke Avot* and *Talmudic* lore, and sang "Hatikva" and "Shoshana" or other Hebrew songs. People studied *Talmud* and *Pirke Avot* in the shtibels, recited Psalms, or reviewed the weekly Torah portion. Women went to visit friends. Older women would study *Tzena Urena*[12]. After eating the *cholent*, the younger people would go out to the gardens, the forests, the roads and to the "Dolinkes." Around the year 1905, some people would go to clandestine meetings where they would sing revolutionary or Jewish nationalist songs.

After *Mincha*, the *Hassidim* would return home for the third Sabbath meal, and then return back to their *shtibels* and *kloizes* to conclude the meal, recite the Grace After Meals with a quorum, and sing hymns and *Hassidic* songs together. The singing continued in this manner until it got dark. They extended the Sabbath and therefore held on to the additional soul, thereby also delaying *Gehinnom*, for as is known, it does not burn on the Sabbath, and the wicked are not sent to *Gehinnom*[13]...

They recited the *Maariv* service, made *Havdallah* [ceremony to conclude the Sabbath],and it was once again the weekday. Many of the *Hassidim* observed a *Melave Malka* meal until late Saturday night.

The Jewish Holidays

b. Passover

Immediately after Purim, the Jews of Sierpc began to prepare for the festival of Passover. The Purim family meal with the Purim players and the giving of gifts to friends [*shalach manos*] was still fresh in the memory. Everyone was concerned that they not forget to whom they sent *shalach manos* or a gift. Then, they were already involved with preparations for Passover.

The fear of excision [*karet*][14], which the Torah prescribed for those who do not observe the festival of Passover, drove the people to *kasher* and to clean, and to make preparations for the great festival of the Exodus from Egypt. People would whitewash the house, air out the clothing and the books, wash, clean, *kasher* all the dishes, make new clothing for the festival, and prepare the matzos, eggs, onions, borscht, etc.

The *Hassidim* baked their matzos - *matzo shmura* - themselves. The wheat was guarded from the time of cutting to ensure that it made no contact with water so that there would be no chance of it becoming *chometz*. They went to the river to draw water, using a new pail and new drawing ladle. The water was filtered through a new sheet of linen. Everyone performed a *mitzvah* by drawing a ladle-full of water. *Hallel* was sung during this procedure. A special oven was *kashered* for the baking of the matzos, and the baking of the *matzo shmura* was accompanied by special devotion and reverential awe.

In the morning of the eve of Passover, the firstborn would go to worship at the *beis midrash* and remain for the *siyum*[15] They would all gather together to complete the tractate so that they would not have to fast during the day, and they would be able to celebrate the conclusion of the tractate with cake and liquor.

Then people went home to burn the *chometz* that was collected the night before, and to partake of the final *chometz* meal. They would then go to the rabbi to sell the *chometz* from the businesses. The "grave gentile"[16] was already present, who the rabbi paid to say "Yes" - i.e. that he would purchase the key...

In the meantime, it became late afternoon. People ran quickly to the *mikva*, and returned from the *mikva* dressed in new clothing. In the meantime, the *shamash* began to call "Go to the synagogue!" People went to services. The would bring home a guest for the festival from the *beis midrash*, and go home to conduct the *seder*.

Everything was ready at home. People sat around the table. The youngest child asked the questions. The father responded with the old answers -"We were slaves." It was joyous and lively. The children searched for the *afikoman* that the father had hidden, and they would not give over the *afikoman*, without which they could not conclude the observance of the *seder*, unless the father promised to fulfill their requests. Late at night, they concluded with the recital of *Song of Songs* and the greeting "Next year in Jerusalem."

Passover in the town was very intimate. The town was suffused with festive joy and newness. Aside from the new clothes that were worn by the young and the old, specially made for the festival, students and workers from the larger cities would come home for the festival and bring a fresh, vibrant Jewish life to Sierpc.

c. Shavuot

Shavuot was an exceptionally interesting holiday. At the celebration of the Season of the Giving of Our Torah, the Jews of Sierpc sincerely believed that their souls were together with the Jews of that time, standing beneath Mount Sinai. They taught that it was the aromatic trees that encouraged them to first say "We will do" and then "We will listen" at Mount Sinai - therefore, the *bima* in the synagogue in Sierpc was adorned with tree branches. The windows and the Holy Ark were also adorned with greenery. They did the same in the *beis midrashes* and other houses of worship, which took on the aroma of a forest.

First and foremost, the tasty egg *kichels*, cheesecakes filled with raisins and nuts, and the other dairy delicacies specially prepared to celebrate the festival of Shavuot, made everyone happy. The joy of the festival of Shavuot was especially great because it fell out at the conclusion of the *Sefira* days, when one is not permitted to be happy. One is not allowed to celebrate weddings due to the loss of Bar Kochba and Rabbi Akiva during the time of the uprising against the Romans. Therefore, when the festival of Shavuot arrived with the recital of *Akdamus*[17], people began to feel a bit happier.

d. Tisha BeAv

When the Jews of Sierpc sat down in the synagogues and *beis midrashes* in their stockings and recited the dirges - "How does it sit in desolation, the city..."[18], and thereby lamented the destruction of the Holy Temple, many Jews of Sierpc would be unable to wait until the coming of the Messiah, when Tisha BeAv would turn into a festival. They already began to joke and throw barbs, so that it would be "joyous." I do not know from where they got that custom. It seems as if they had a different intention, namely to cause anguish through the barbs in order to feel the destruction of Jerusalem in a stronger manner.

e. The Fearsome Month of Elul

When the month of Elul arrived, the Sierpcers felt an extraordinary sense of awe. People felt a special sense of responsibility - the Day of Judgment was rapidly approaching, when one would make an accounting with G-d. Therefore, they were very serious and G-d fearing. They guarded themselves against carelessness, exaggeration, and excesses. They became more friendly one to the other, gave more charity, and the shopkeepers were extremely careful about exacting measures.

During that month, people also worshipped with greater devotion. They did not recite the prayers in haste, and added chapter of Psalms and other prayers to the daily services. They also recited Psalms publicly.

A week before Rosh Hashanah, they got up very early to recite *Selichot* [penitential prayers] prior to services. The *Hassidim* would recite the first *Selichot* at midnight after the *Melave Malka*. The *Selichot* of the eve of Rosh Hashanah, known as "*Zechor Brit*"[19], were also recited at midnight. In the half dark Jewish street, shadows appeared running to the *beis midrash* for *Selichot*. Soon, the weeping voice of the prayer leader could be heard on the silent streets, "The soul is Yours and the body is Yours, have mercy on your handiwork..."

f. Rosh Hashanah, Yom Kippur, and Sukkot

On the eve of Rosh Hashanah, everyone was occupied with the special preparations for the holiday. Aside from fish and meat, people purchased honey, grapes, and pomegranates for Rosh Hashanah, as a portent for a sweet year. They would also purchase a new fruit for the *Shehechayanu* benediction[20]. People also obtained new clothes.

As in all towns, people in Sierpc went to the cemeteries in order to visit the graves of friends to recite the "*Kel Maleh Rachamim*"[21] for their souls. They would also visit the graves of tzadikim who were buried in the cemetery. The women wept over the graves and begged the souls of their dead to intercede in Heaven for them and their loved ones.

Later, people went to the *mikva*, and then came home and dressed up in their festive clothing. The sun began to set, and the *shamash* of the synagogue went through the Jewish streets, calling out with all his might, "Go to the synagogue!" The businesses closed, and the women lit the candles in the houses. The men went quickly to the synagogue... and they recited *Mincha* with the congregation.

*

The cantor began to recite the *Maariv* service with the special, lovely Rosh Hashanah melodies that were suffused with a mood of supplication. The entire congregation joined in. Soon, the silent *Shmone Esrei* was recited, which was recited silently an entire year, but recited out loud by the congregation on Rosh Hashanah night due to the special prayers such as: "Remember us for life, inscribe us in the book of life, inscribe for a good life..."

Y. A. Libsohn and his wife

Mordechai Hirsch Mintz

Max Sina

From top right to lower left: Yosef Blachman, Moshe Gotstat, Mendel Gorfinkel

From top right to lower left: Nachum Tac, Natan Tac, Baruch Lipszyc

From top right to lower left: Avraham Ben-David Mlawe, Yehuda (Leib) Malowanczyk, Henech Pefer

From top right to lower left: Ezriel Podskoc, Yeshayahu Frajdman, Dov (Ber) Czarka

From top right to lower left: Aharon Czarnoczopka, Moshe Yehuda Kirsz, Yosef Karpe

From top right to lower left: Izik Rozen, Zelig Rozen, Itche-Binem Rozenberg

Avraham Yerushalmi (Frajd)

The cantor concluded with Kiddush and sang the section "And You gave us with love this Day of Remembrance, a day of *shofar* sounding." They sang *Anim Zmirot* and *Adon Olam*. After the services, everyone shook hands with each other and wished one another: "May you be written and sealed immediately for a good life." On the way home from the synagogue, people stopped in to visit parents and older brothers and sisters to wish them a good year.

When the man came home, he would kiss his wife and children and wish them a good year. At home, the table was already covered with a fine tablecloth, and the lovely silver candelabrum was glowing with candles. He made *kiddush*, and then *Shehechayanu* over a new fruit - grapes or pomegranates. They washed their hands and recited *Hamotzie* over a high *challah*, and then a blessing for a good and sweet year over an apple spread with honey. Then they ate the rest of the festival meal: fish, meat, and tzimmes. After the meal, the Grace After Meals would be recited, and a request for a good year would also be made during the grace.

Thus was the custom of the Sierpc Jews year in and year out.

Activists of Hanoar Hatzioni in Sierpc at the beginning of the 20th century

From right to left
First row: Yitzchak Uren (Aharon) Libsohn, Shmuel Szampan, and Feivish Lipka.
Second row: Shmuel Tac, Chaim Pindek, Avraham Gerlic, Yeshayahu Frajdman

g. *Shacharit* and *Musaf* on Rosh Hashanah

Still today, a religious tremble goes through my heart when I recall the Rosh Hashanah services in the Sierpc synagogue and houses of worship.

Everyone went to the synagogue early in the morning: men, women and children, for everyone had to hear the blowing of the *shofar*. Two prayer leaders conducted the services: one for *Shacharit* and the second one for *Musaf*.

The leader of the *Shacharit* services would go to the *mikva* early in the morning, before ascending to the prayer leader's podium dressed in a white *kittel*. He had a difficult task to sing the *yotzros*[22]. Even though most of them were fine poems, designed as an alphabetic acrostic and ending with a rhyme, the *yotzros* had many words which were rarely used and were not understandable by many of the worshippers. Those non-understandable *yotzros*, however, fit very well to the fine tunes that the cantor sang, and everyone helped him. When the cantor began to recite the repetition of the *Shmone Esrei*, everyone sang along, especially the *kedusha*. When they came to the prayer “Our Father our King, open the gates of heaven to our prayers,” they became very serious, as they supplicated with their full heart.

Immediately after *Shacharit*, two Torah scrolls were taken out, and the important members were called up to the Torah reading: the rabbi, the cantor for *Shacharit*, the cantor for *Musaf*, and the Torah reader.

The *shofar* blower and the cantor for *Musaf* then went to the *mikva*, returned all neatened up, and donned their white *kittels*. The *Shacharit* cantor and Torah reader took the Torah scrolls, and went around the podium together with the rabbi of the city and the *shofar* blower, all dressed in white *kittels*. After reciting the chapter *Lamnatzeach Livnei Korach Mizmor*[23] seven times in a voice full of dread, and after reciting a silent prayer, came the *shofar* blasts, which the Sierpc worshippers received with a pious, holy shudder in their hearts. The congregation recited a prayer after every *shofar* blast, and called out to a specific angel that was appointed to each sound, asking that he bring the sounds to the Throne of Glory and beg for mercy for the people of Israel, and help drive away the Satan.

The cantor for *Musaf*, dressed in his *kittel*, standing by the podium with the choir, began to sing *Yisgadal*[24] with the tune of *Musaf*. Everyone sang along with the fine, melancholy melody that left a special imprint upon all.

After the silent *Shmone Esrei*, the cantor began to sing the repetition of the *Shmone Esrei* with the lovely, Rosh Hashanah melodies. The *Musaf* cantor reached the poetry and rhymes composed in alphabetic acrostic by the liturgical poets of Spain. At *Unetane Tokef Kedushat Hayom*[25], which the cantor recited with a heartrending voice, and at “Who shall live, and who shall die, who will become rich and who will become poor...” most of the worshippers wept. They reminded themselves of the dead, the ill, and the poor, and they comforted themselves with “Repentance, prayer, and charity remove the evil of the decree.”

After the services, when the congregation finished their Rosh Hashanah prayers, everyone went home calmly. Every Sierpc Jew was certain that he had supplicated for a good year and that he would be inscribed for the good.

Throughout the entire week until Yom Kippur, the Sierpc Jews got up very early and went to the synagogue for *Selichot.* This period was the Ten Days of Penitence, when one could regret one's sins and could request through prayer a good inscription.

On the eve of Yom Kippur, people performed the *Kapores*[26] ceremony and went to make up with people that they had disputes with, for Yom Kippur does not forgive sins between one's fellow man. In the afternoon, they went to the synagogue for *Mincha* service. When they arrived, the table was covered with charity plates for various Sierpc charitable institutions, and everyone put charity donations into the plates. After *Mincha,* they went home, partook of the final meal quickly, and returned to the synagogue for *Kol Nidre.* The next day they sat in the synagogue all day, wearing their socks, banging their hearts for *Al Chet,* and weeping during various prayers. Thus, they prayed a whole day until *Neila.* After *Neila* and *Maariv,* they wished each other that they might be sealed positively, and "Next year in Jerusalem," and went home to eat something after the fast.

After eating, they immediately started to build the *sukka,* for Sukkot comes five days later, and one must already become involved with a *mitzvah* immediately after Yom Kippur.

*

The Jews of Sierpc ate in the *sukka* for the entire eight days. Even if it rained or was cold, no Jew skipped eating in the *sukka.* A *Simchat Beis Shoeva*[27] was celebrated by the *Hassidim* on the second day of Sukkot, as in the time of the Second Temple. However, the Sierpc Jews drew wine instead of water, and rejoiced until late at night with *Hassidic* melodies, etc.

When Simchat Torah came, the *Hassidim* began to conduct the *hakafot*[28] ceremony one night earlier, on the eve of Shemini Atzeret. The regular Jews would conduct *hakafot* only on the night and morning of Simchat Torah.

There was a custom in Sierpc that before going to *hakafot,* a Torah scroll would be carried in a great parade from the *beis midrash* to the synagogue and back. People would carry burning candles and sing along the way. As they returned to their *shtibels,* the *Hassidim* began to enjoy fresh liquor and mead. They danced on the tables and the benches until late at night.

The songs *Sisu Vesimchu Besimchat Torah* [Rejoice and be glad on Simchat Torah], and *Agil Veesmach Besimchat Torah* [I will be happy and rejoice on Simchat Torah] resonated far through the surrounding streets. Among the *Hassidic* songs that were sung in the *shtibels,* they also sang a number of Yiddish folk songs, such as "Torah is the best merchandise," "Thus did we study with the rabbi," and others. They also sang various prayers, such as "And purify our heart," "Blessed is our G-d," and others.

Thus did the Jews of Sierpc rejoice on Simchat Torah.

Jewish Weddings and Jewish Bands in Sierpc

At Jewish weddings, there was a custom that the groom would sit around the table in a special room, surrounded by unmarried boys, and all the guests would be treated to cake and liquor. The groom did not taste anything, as he would fast until after the wedding ceremony. The bride would sit in a different room with her friends, and rejoice by dancing with the accompaniment of music played by the Jewish musicians.

The Jewish musicians in Sierpc were Menashe and his sons, (Malach) Gerlic and Chaim Krupiasz (Keler). They would also play at Jewish weddings and other Jewish joyous occasions, as they would entertain the Jews of the town.

The veiling of the bride took place in the following manner: the parents of the bride and groom would enter the house where the bride was sitting, and they would veil the bride, for married women were not allowed to go around with uncovered hair. The jester recited a rhyming speech of admonition to the bride, warning her of her fate, as the women wept... After the veiling, the wedding ceremony took place.

The wedding ceremony took place in the *beis midrash* on the Jewish Street. First, they led in the groom, accompanied by musicians who played joyous songs. Relatives and friends accompanied them holding candles. At the wedding ceremony, the cantor welcomed the groom with "Blessed is he that comes." The groom stood and waited under the wedding canopy, and then the bride was brought in. The bride may have lived in the other end of the city, and they accompanied her in with musicians. She was led with music and candles to the *beis midrash*, where the wedding canopy was standing. The bride was also greeted with "Blessed is she that comes." At a wedding of wealthy people, the cantor and the choir would sing special pieces. The rabbi of the city conducted the wedding ceremony.

The bride and groom left the wedding ceremony together. The in-laws danced and the musicians played joyous music. At the wedding feast, the cantor sang, the musicians played, and the jester recited witty verses. The musicians broke out in a joyous medley, and everyone danced.

In my time, men and women did not dance together. Only at the mitzvah dance[29] would men and women dance together, but not touching. The *mitzvah* dance was conducted in the following manner: the men would hold one end of a napkin, and the woman would hold the other end, and thus they would dance. After the *mitzvah* dance, the mother-in-law would cut the bride's hair so that she could put on a wig.

This is the manner in which Jewish weddings took place in Sierpc. Joy was blended with spiritual piety.

The Modern Jewish Way of Life

As in other towns, the modern Jewish way of life began with the Jewish theater.

When Chaim Leib Pukac, a former member of the cantor's choir, and Zalman Goldsztejn, returned from America in 1905, and Leib Krupasz (today Keller in America) returned from London, they organized an amateur group to perform Jewish theater.

This was the time of Goldfaden's[30] and other operettas, such as: *Shulamit, Bar Kochba, Dos Pintele Yid* [The essence of the Jew], and the dramatic plays such as Yaakov Gordon's "*Der Vilder Mench*" [The Wild Person], and the very popular monologue "*Der Meshugener in Shpital*" [The Crazy Person in the Hospital]. All the theatrical pieces were novel and popular in the Jewish cities and towns in Poland. The following people performed: Chaim Leib Pukac, Leib Krupiasz, and Tzadok Lubaszka. The amateur troupe consisted only of men. Men also performed the female roles, dressed up as women. The theatrical performances took place in the firefighter's hall, near the magistrate.

Thanks to the amateur troupe, the following songs from the operettas became popular among the tradesmen, tailors and shoemakers associations: *Rozhinkes Mit Mandlen* [Raisins and Nuts], *Men Shikt mich in Gasse Arain Epis Koipfn* [I was sent out to the street to buy something], *Azoi Zogt Gott Atzind* [This is What G-d Says Now], and others. One could hear these songs being sung everywhere, day and night.

The Zionist Organization, The Pogrom in Kishinev and its Effect on the Jews of Sierpc, The Influence of the Maskilim

The young *misnagdim*: Ezriel Podskoc, Avraham Wloke, Mordechai Hirsch Mintz, S. Tac, Yosef Pindek, and other successors of Efraim Yosel Wloke, Eliezer Wessalek, and Chaim Nachum Tanwel were the first to found a Zionist organization. The first meeting of that Zionist organization took place in Atlas' school. The Zionist organization later attracted a large following. In town, they proclaimed the Basle program of political Zionism that demanded an open, just, and secure home for all Jews in the Land of Israel.

With the founding of the Zionist organization, discussions and disputes began in town with the fanatical *Hassidim*, Reb Itchele Margel and others, who claimed that Zionism is contrary to Judaism, and that Jews must wait for the Messiah to come for the redemption and must not go to the Land of Israel before that. The discussions, disputes and battles were very stormy.

We must mention the following from among the active Sierpc Zionists: Gotlibowski, Mlawe, Blum, Malinowski, Koniec, Senk, Zabietski, Lopatke,

Shimshon Buda and others. Thanks to those Zionist activisits, the "Hatikva" song of the Jewish national awakening and other Jewish nationalist songs were heard in town.

The terrible news of the pogrom against the Jews of Kishinev in 1903 left a frightening impression upon the Jews of Sierpc, as in all other cities. Aside from the deep sorrow for the tortured and afflicted Jews, they also were afraid for the security of their own lives. Jewish villagers were afraid to live in the villages, and started coming to the cities. The gentiles wished to repeat the events of Kishinev and said so openly - the terror in the villages was very great.

*

In 1904, I returned home from the Novominsk Yeshiva, where I had been studying. From the secular books, I was convinced that Jewish life must forge new, more worldly paths. I organized the *beis midrash* youths and gave them new books to read: *Ayit Tzavua* [Hypocrite Eagle] by Mapu, *Chatat Neurim* [Sins of Youth] by Moshe Leib Lilienblum, and the works of Shulman, Smolinskin, and others. All these books brought a new spirit to the youth.

The following people joined me: Szampan, Gerlic, Avraham Podskoc, Chaim Pindek, Glazer, S. Tac, Yeshayahu Frajdman, and others. Together we began to disseminate books to read among the *yeshiva* and *beis midrash* youths. Many of the books were uncensored, and forbidden to read. I purchased most of the books myself. My father also surprised me with secular books that he hid in the closet between the *Talmud*, Bible, *Midrashim* and other holy books. With those books, and together with the library of Mordechai Hirsch Mintz that consisted of many uncensored publications, we founded a group called *Chovevei Sfat Ever* [Lovers of the Hebrew Language]. The members talked Hebrew amongst themselves. We also sang Hebrew such as "*Yah Ha Li Li,*" "*Seu Tziona,*" "*Chushu Achim,*" "*Yona Homia,*" "*Bimkom Shem Arazim,*" "*Shechav Hardom,*" "*Shamash Aviv Nata Yama,*" and others. In the *beis midrash*, on the street , and also in the Dolinkes, one could hear Hebrew songs. The leadership in the *beis midrash* was transferred over from Avraham Chaim Granewicz and Sperling to Libsohn and Szampan.

*

In the year 1905, when a wave of terrible pogroms spread through Jewish cities and towns, and the Czarist regime helped the hooligans, the idea to create a self defense organization was hatched among the Jews of Sierpc.

Chaim Nachman Bialik, in "The Destruction of Nemirov, in the City of Murder," where he prophetically and sharply expressed his anguish that Jews did not stand up against the pogrom perpetrators and let themselves be slaughtered, was frequently a factor in the creation of self defense organizations.

The Jews began to see the shame, and began to create secret, clandestine self-defense organizations.

Such a clandestine, self-defense organization was also set up in Sierpc. Its leaders, who were chosen covertly, included: Shmuel Szampan, Eliezer Szampan, Avraham Gerlic, Yeshayahu Frajdman, and the writer of these lines. Our leaders were Chaim Leib Pukac and Yaakov Sznicer. My task was to collect weapons and lead to produce *knouts* [a type of whip].

The Illegal Movement of Bund and Poale Zion

In the years of the first Russian Revolution, around 1905, the Bund started to become active among the Jewish workers in Sierpc. The following people took part in organizing the Bund: Yitzchak Karpe, Yitzchak Kone, Chaim Leib Pukac, Yaakov Sznicer, Nathan Tac, and Ethel Grobard (today Dr. Fuchs, who lives in America). Yitzchak Karpe had some Jewish books and enlightenment literature. He secretly brought them to the Jewish workers to read. The intelligentsia all read Hebrew books and newspapers.

The *Der Freind* and Der Veg Yiddish newspapers began to be published at that time. The Jewish masses began to read. People read Mendele Mocher Seforim, Shalom Aleichem, Peretz, Asch, Reisin, Spector, and Digenson. The literary Yiddish sprang up from "jargon," as the Yiddish language was once called.

The Poale Zion Jewish workers party was also founded at that time. Sharp discussions took place between the Bund and Poale Zion. David Grün (today David Ben Gurion) came to Sierpc from Plonsk and conducted a strong agitation against Bund.

Thanks to the strong discussions, many *beis midrash* youths and former Bundists moved over to Poale Zion. The Poale Zion committee consisted of: Kone, Karpe, Pukac, Sznicer, Lubaszke, Gorfinkel, Malowanczyk, and the youths: Czarnoczopka, Yitzchak Yaakov Buda, A. Mlawe, A. Podskoc, Ch. L. Pukac. Rich and poor, scholars and less scholarly all united to struggle for a better life for the Jewish people.

*

The revolutionary movement of 1905 forced the Czarist regime to grant the population certain freedoms and a parliament (Duma).

Simultaneously, a wave of anti-Jewish pogroms afflicted Russia. The Schwartzmenikes and the regime stirred up the peasants to rob and kill Jews.

The fear of pogroms also existed in Sierpc, and every market day passed in fear, for the pogrom agitators spread rumors that the farmers would attack the Jews on the market day. Fortunately, our underground self-defense organization was in place, and no pogrom took place.

The Czarist manifesto of October 17, 1905 also granted the rights to organize legal cultural organizations. In Sierpc, we utilized those rights to organize an open library. I gave over my books; Karpe brought his Yiddish books; Mordechai Hirsch Mintz brought Hebrew books; and Manya Sznicer brought her Polish books. Among those books, there were many that had previously been illegal, and there was a fear of owning them. Now, those books together with the legal ones were used to build up the first Jewish library in Sierpc.

The first committee of the Jewish library in Sierpc consisted of the following members: Karpe, Libsohn, Szampan, Goldsztejn, Chaim Pindek, Lubaszka, and Keler.

Szampan and I rented a fine hall and gave it over to the library committee.

We traveled to Yitzchak Leibush Peretz of blessed memory in Warsaw, where all young people were welcome, and asked for his advice about which books to purchase for the library. Peretz received us very nicely and invited us to the opening showing of Osip Dymow's drama *Shema Yisrael* that was being performed then in the Yiddish theater. In the theater, we met Dymow[31], the author of the play. We also met Shalom Asz, Nachum Sokolow, Avraham Reisin, Mordechai Spector, Hillel Zeitlin, Nomberg, and Dinezon. Peretz introduced us to them. I recall very clearly everything that took place.

We purchased the books that Peretz recommended to us. We also subscribed to the Yiddish and Hebrew newspapers and periodicals of that era.

Our library obtained the best news publications that were available, and it was very popular in Sierpc. All of the Jews in the city who had registered - whether wearing short jackets or long jackets, whether being Yiddish speakers or Polish speakers - all participated in the activity of the library and were its readers.

After the Czarist regime broke up the first Duma and did not prevent the arrests and pogroms against the Jews, emigration overseas increased. Many people also left Sierpc, including Ethel Grobard (today Dr. Fuchs).

Following the elections for the second Duma, the ideological differences between the parties within the Jewish communities increased, especially among the P.P.S. that had a Jewish section, the Bund and Poale Zion. In Sierpc, that struggle overtook many, even while out for a stroll. It was also expressed through various songs.

When the Bundists sang the Bundist “Oath,” Poale Zion responded with the Poale Zion Oath. The Bundists - “When you plow and you sow”... the Poale Zion - “With the hook plow comes luck and blessing.”

That same year, 1906, Ben Gurion came to town once again. This time, it was to take leave before traveling to the Land of Israel. His small, young face, the long black hair and the black, French cape gave him an air of honor. His fiery arguments and discussions with the internationalist assimilationists who delighted in “First help other people to obtain their freedom, and that will help our people,” and his arguments against them were all very effective. At that time, about 80% of the Bundists and assimilationists transferred to Poale Zion.

Sierpc then gave an impressive farewell to Ben Gurion, and led him out on his journey to the Land of Israel with great love and honor.

*

It was now 1907. Chaim Czarnoczopka was arrested for issuing proclamations among soldiers. A pall fell upon the town, and every opportunity was taken to accuse someone or another of being a revolutionary. The fanatic bourgeoisie Jewish householders of Sierpc took every opportunity to take vengeance upon the youth and revolutionary elements.

Once, a *Hassid* overheard in the *beis midrash* that Libsohn, who was studying Bible with Moshe Yakir, was translating the verse from Isaiah, "If you come to see my face, who asked this from you, to trample in my courtyards"[32] in a modern fashion. The fanatical Itche Margel heard this and would not let the Sabbath services proceed on Friday night. He shouted out that Libsohn and his friends were heretics and revolutionaries. (Such a case, where the services were interrupted, had taken place once before. This was when the tall Motel demanded that they should force Yehuda Licht to be given *chalitza* without payment[33].)

[Page 272]

The accusation of Libsohn being a revolutionary reached the gendarmes, who wanted to know whether he believed in G-d and in the Czar. Libsohn realized that it was impossible to remain in Sierpc, and he decided to travel to the Land of Israel.

The committee and the members of the library decided to make a farewell evening for Libsohn before his departure. During the evening, they gave him a bust of Herzl, which he gave back to the library.

The farewell evening was conducted by the chairman of the library, Shmuel Tac. The following members took part in the special farewell program:

Chaim Pindek recited Bialik's "The Final Word." Leib Krupiasz conducted "The Crazy Person in the Hospital." Pukac recited fragments of *Shulamit*. Goldsztejn recited sections of Bar Kochba. Gerlic, Szampan and Frajdman sang "There, there are Cedars." The farewell evening was concluded with the singing of "Hatikva" and "Techezakna."

I left on a Friday night. The following people helped me on that secret journey: Rivka Tac, Mania Sznicer, and Gorfinkel. In order to avoid any suspicion by the gendarmes, I traveled without a passport and under the bench. That is how I arrived in Odessa. In Odessa, Ussishkin[34] created a passport for me and introduced me to the gentle Mendele Mocher Seforim, Achad Ha'am, Klausner, Bialik, and others.

After spending some time in Odessa, I traveled to the Land of Israel. Shalom Asz and Ahad Ha'am traveled on the same ship.

Translator's Footnotes

1. Deuteronomy 6:7
2. From Bierzwienna.
3. The Sabbath prior to *Rosh Chodesh* when a special prayer is recited to bless the upcoming month.
4. The phrase that marks the beginning of the *Shacharit* service on Rosh Hashanah and Yom Kippur.
5. A portion of the Yom Kippur *Musaf* service that reenacts the Yom Kippur service of the Holy Temple. *Hakohanim*, mentioned in the next sentence, is part of the *Avoda* service.
6. Sons-in-law receiving support from their fathers in law so that they could continue studying Torah.
7. *Tosafot* is a Talmudic commentary.
8. A number used to express the maximum lifespan.
9. A reference to the World to Come. This quote is from the Grace After Meals of the Passover Seder.
10. A reference to the World to Come.
11. A *mishnaic* tractate dealing with ethical issues - commonly studied on summer Sabbath afternoons.
12. See http://jwa.org/encyclopedia/article/zeenah-u-reenah
13. There is a tradition that the wicked people are not punished in Hell (*Gehinnom*) on the Sabbath.
14. See http://en.wikipedia.org/wiki/Kareth
15. A *siyum* is conclusion of a tractate of *Talmud.* There is a custom for firstborns to fast on the eve of Passover, but they may exempt themselves from this obligation by attending a festive meal that would follow a conclusion of a tractate of *Talmud.*
16. I assume that this means the gentile who worked as the gravedigger in the Jewish cemetery.
17. A hymn recited on the first day of Shavuot prior to the reading of the Torah.
18. Lamentations 1:1.
19. "Remember the covenant" - named for one of the prayers of the *Selichot* of the eve of Rosh Hashanah.
20. The *Shehecheyahu* benediction, thanking G-d for keeping us alive to reach this season, is recited on every festival, as well as on other special occasions. Since there is a doubt whether *Shehechayanu* should be recited on the second night of Rosh Hashanah as well, the custom arose to have a new fruit at the table, which would warrant a *Shehechayanu* in its own right, and thereby obviate the doubt.
21. G-d full of mercy - the Jewish prayer for the dead.
22. The poetic additions to the regular services recited on Rosh Hashanah and Yom Kippur, and in some congregations on other occasions.
23. Psalm 47.
24. The first word of *kaddish.*
25. See http://en.wikipedia.org/wiki/Unetanneh_Tokef
26. See http://en.wikipedia.org/wiki/Kapparot
27. See http://en.wikipedia.org/wiki/Simchat_Beit_HaShoeivah
28. *Hakafot* is the ceremony of processions around the synagogue with the Torah scrolls, conducted on Simchat Torah. In synagogues that worship according to the Sephardic rite, including Hassidic synagogues, *Hakafot* would also be conducted on Shemini Atzeret night.
29. See http://en.wikipedia.org/wiki/Mitzvah_tantz
30. See http://en.wikipedia.org/wiki/Abraham_Goldfaden
31. See http://www.yivoencyclopedia.org/article.aspx/Dymov_Osip
32. Isaiah 1:12.
33. A ceremony of release from Levirate marriage. See https://en.wikipedia.org/wiki/Halizah
34. See http://en.wikipedia.org/wiki/Menachem_Ussishkin

The Great Flood of Sierpc

by Shmuel Yitzchak Lenter

This took place 67 years ago, in 1888. I was then a 9 year old child, and I remember it like today. That year, there was a difficult winter with great cold and even greater snow that continued until before Passover. A few days before Passover, it suddenly became warm. The sun came out with its rays, and the snow began to melt very rapidly.

We did not go to *cheder* on the eve of Passover. I and a few other friends went to play in the Wlokes. I had no idea of what was coming to the city. The sun was doing its job. The snow and ice turned to water, which increased from minute to minute. The lower places in town were flooded.

In the meantime, it was noticed that I was not at home. At that time, we lived on Szaba Street. To this day, I do not know how my parents found out that I was in the Wlokes. Suddenly, my brother came running with a warning, "What are you doing here? The entire city is drowning." He grabbed me and dragged me away. We came to the bridge as it was coming apart, and we could not cross it. With difficulty, and with the protection of the mayor who was at the bridge at that time, my brother took me on his shoulder, and we crossed the bridge.

The destruction caused by the flood in Sierpc at that time was exceptionally great. I will write about one incident, to give you a bit of a concept of the destruction. At that time, there were two rows of shops on both sides of the bridge. The large stream with even larger pieces of ice, as large as houses, covered over all the shops. There was insufficient time to save the merchandise. The owners were left impoverished and destitute.

There was a wealthy Jew named Moshe Meir Aberfeld, Moshe Graniewic's brother-in-law. His house was next to the bridge and he built a hut next to the house, in which he used to sit and study. He had silver, gold and precious stones in the hut. He was an expert in those matters and used to collect them. The large stream and pieces of ice came and swept everything away, as if it never existed.

Houses, stables with cattle and horses, and pens with fowl were floating. It was impossible to save them, however, for there was no opportunity to do so. Also, there were few people who were able to take a risk to save them in the storming water.

The Jewish Street was cut off from the city, and pieces of ice were flowing along. I remember how a large piece of ice was lying by the Old *Beis Midrash*. One can imagine how large it was, for it remained until Shavuot.

We could not go to worship in the *beis midrashes* on the first days of Passover. Everything was cut off. We worshiped with Moshe Mintz, where the

Talmud Torah Society was located in the house of Leib Zhelinoski. The neighbors on Plocker Street also made a *minyan* at the home of Yisrael Bluman. A *minyan* took place in the new marketplace at the home of Elkana Buket. The Torah scrolls from the Old *Beis Midrash* were rescued and brought to the New *Beis Midrash.*

I recall that Michael Bentkwoska the teacher ran to save them with his two daughters. They were carried off by the stream and floated some distance. It was only with the risk of their lives that some people managed to save them. Manisia the tailor lived with his wife in the house of the wealthy Shmuel Szampan. They were very old, and they were unable to escape. They lived on the first floor. The water reached the window. Everything that they prepared for Passover was ruined. On the first day of the festival, they were saved with the help of a boat. The flood lasted for three days and nights, after which the water began to recede. People talked about the incident for many years.

Sierpc Was My Spiritual Home

by Meir Weisgal[1]

My birthplace is the village of Kikol, and not Sierpc, but Sierpc is etched in my memories of the first ten years of my life. They are as close to me as Rehovoth is to Sha'arayim[2]. I feel that I am inseparable from the town of Sierpc, as if I was born there, and the town is very important in my family's history. Sierpc is where my family and my relatives lived. My grandfather and grandmother, my father and mother, my uncle and aunt and cousins - all lived in Sierpc. I remember those far off days, before my father immigrated to the United States, when I was ten years old.

Sierpc and Kikol were part of my being; there I absorbed the Jewish way of life, traditions, and customs - everything that's called "*heimkeit*". These two places were more than a geographic unit; they were the essence of Judaism, an inseparable part of "*Yiddishkeit*" that united and sustained our people in Poland and in the rest of the diaspora, and is the main reason for their existence as Jews.

Like other towns and villages in the diaspora, Sierpc was one of the strongholds of the enlightenment and the Zionist tradition. My childhood memories of the town of Sierpc became stronger and clearer when I visited in 1925. I was about thirty years old then, and this was my first trip to Europe since I came to America as a child. First I went to Poland and Sierpc, and then I went to the land of Israel.

I found that Sierpc had changed a lot in the twenty years since I had left. But there can be no doubt that Poland went through many transformations after the First World War; places changed, there were new people. One figure did not change - that was my grandmother. I found her exactly the same as when we left her to go to America. An elderly women, wise and sharp, but still ready to reprimand a "*sheigetz*"[3] like me. She sat on the sidewalk with a copy of "*Tzeina VeReina*"[4] in her hands, a pair of glasses perched on her nose, with a look of devotion and piety on her face. She was engrossed in her reading and would stop only to serve the occasional customer.

I was in Kikol and Sierpc for only three days, because I was in a rush to get back. I reviewed my childhood days hastily, and now, after thirty-five years, I see that the real culture of our times and our forefather's' times was there, both visible and hidden to the naked eye. It was rooted deep within the spiritual life of the Jews of Sierpc and Kikol.

Everything is finished and gone, blown away by the malicious waves of an indifferent history. But we, the natives of those small towns in Poland will not forget. We will remember and understand that this was the true significance of our existence as Jews; the heart of a philosophical outlook that is a vision of the true Judaism.

Translator's Footnotes

1. Meir Weisgal (1894-1977) was a president of the Weizmann Institute of Science in Rehovoth, Israel.
2. Sha'arayim is a neighborhood in the southern part of the city of Rehovoth, Israel.
3. non-Jew, assimilated Jew
4. A book of homilies in Yiddish for Jewish women

A Pious Jew from the Old Generation

(From my grandfather's memoirs)

by Elisheva Rabinowich

Many years ago, on the banks of the Sierpienica River, on both sides of the bridge that led from the Jewish street to the market, houses stood atop pylons. In the summer, the Jewish children would bathe behind the houses, showing off their tricks and swimming. In the winter, they would skate on the ice, and their joyous shouts and laughter would spread through the Jewish street.

In one of the houses, atop the posts in the river, lived my uncle Yaakov with his wife, Aunt Miriam. They had an only child, Michel, who was good-looking, intelligent, and a good student, but a big brat. The parents loved their only child very much, and tended to him with great care. However, it was inevitable, and protecting him did not help. Michel would often escape from *cheder* or run from the house to the river - to skate in the winter or to bathe in the summer.

Once, after Passover, when the parents were busy with their fashion business, the child drowned while bathing in the river. The parents no longer had a child, and their sorrow was deep and terrible. Uncle Yaakov filled his house with other children. He would learn with them, not requesting any wages. Aunt Miriam would stuff them with goodies. They loved them all, and knew each one's weaknesses and tastes. They gave them everything, and would sneak each one the snack that they preferred the most. Thus did she express her warm motherly feelings by bringing joy to the children's hearts, while her husband tended to their souls and minds by the clear and polished learning.

A poor, lonely, fisherwoman widow lived in the city. She had a six year old son Velvel. He was a fine child with black curls and moist, deep, cherry-like eyes. He would sit with Aunt Miriam for the entire day. She took him to *cheder* and brought him home. Very often, when his mother the fisherwoman was away in the river to catch the fish for the Sabbath, Velvel would spend the night with Aunt Miriam.

At one point, the fisherwoman became very ill. The doctor that Uncle Yaakov brought for her did not help, and the unfortunate woman died after a few days. Before her death, the child confided with Miriam. In this manner, Velvel remained with Aunt Miriam, as if he were her own child. Uncle Yaakov learned with him, and they treated him like their own child. When Velvel became older, he studied in the *beis midrash*, where he became acquainted with enlightened youths. He secretly acquired books, and placed them beneath the *Gemara*. He studied and read them, and became a completely different person. He would then often stroll behind the city. He would walk around immersed in his thoughts and sit at the table silently, without uttering a word. He grew older and more mature, and when he was twelve, he appeared as a full-grown, serious young man.

The first to notice this was Aunt Miriam. She asked him questions, felt his head and examined his tongue. However, she found out nothing. Finally she and her husband determined Velvel's situation. He finally told the truth to my uncle: he, Velvel, sees no purpose here at this point. He wants to go to the capital city to study Torah there.

At first, my uncle did not approve; but, not wanting to hinder him, he finally said that he would send him to the capital city right after Passover. As they shook hands, Velvel agreed that he would observe all of the religious laws, and remain a serious, observant Jew.

My aunt took this like a thunderbolt. She begged Velvel not to leave. She wept bitterly for him and wracked her hands, but he only hugged her, comforted her, wiped the tears from her face, and stood his ground. He told her that he would write often, and let her know everything that was happening. Velvel left shortly after Passover.

Velvel kept his word. Letters from him arrived very often, and Aunt Miriam sent him packages with underwear and food. She packed her longing, motherly feelings in those packages. She dreamed about him day and night. She counted the days until Sukkot, eagerly awaiting the time when he would come home.

However, Velvel did not come home for Sukkot. He wrote some sort of excuse to my uncle in a letter. My aunt was not very pleased. Something was not proper. My uncle was sad, but the letter was clear and succinct, for some reason he could not come.

The holiday at my uncle's and aunt's home passed in a lonesome fashion. The cloudy, rainy days were even gloomier, as the melancholy imbued a bad feeling, and their hearts were depressed and upset. Until finally, it happened...

A neighbor from the capital city came and said, "Velvel left the yeshiva long ago, and has fallen into bad paths." Uncle Yaakov traveled to the capital city that same day. My aunt did not close her eyes for the entire night. She hoped, above all, that this was not true. She even prepared a package for Velvel, as she did every week. When her husband returned from the capital city after two days, she did not ask him anything. He entered the house in silence, kissed the *mezuzah*, slowly removed his fur coat, washed up, and immediately, without words, put on his coat again. He went to the door and quietly told his wife, "I am going to the *beis midrash*."

She knew him well. This had always been his manner. When he bore some resentment, he immediately went to the *beis midrash*.

When Yaakov returned, he said:

"Miriam, to us, Velvel is dead. His name should not be mentioned in the house anymore."

She stood still in the middle of the room, without even asking the reason. In her heart, she had a harsh dilemma, and she fell, half dead, onto the nearby bench. From that time on, Miriam, had a weak heart.

She lay down with open eyes on the harsh, dark, winter nights. In the thick darkness, she saw him, Velvel, so clearly and vividly. She had to exert effort to refrain from calling out to him. She knew that there, in the second bed, her husband was lying, awake like her, also thinking about him, about their Velvel.

Yaakov went around in darkness. The slight smile that had formerly lit up his face when he would sit and learn with Velvel, or later when he would read his very intelligent letters, had now disappeared forever. They both went around like silent shadows. They did not look directly into each other's eyes, and they seldom uttered a word.

Miriam loved Velvel very much. However, she loved her husband even more strongly and deeply and was in awe of him. The letters that continued to come from Velvel for a long time, exasperated her husband. She had to watch as he ripped them into pieces, unread. To her, this was like ripping her heart from her chest into pieces. She only thought:

"Perhaps he was asking for help. Perhaps he is hungry. Perhaps he has repented." However, she could not do anything to help him. Her heart grieved even more, and her eyes shed tears during the long, dark nights.

*

Thus passed summers and winters. The world, which died during the winter, blossomed in the summer and again became joyous. For Uncle Yaakov, it was the same routine of life. The couple never complained. Velvel's name was never mentioned. They both became older and greyer, she in the shop and he in the *beis midrash*, as they forgot their discomfort.

There were better and worse times. Of course, more worse times than better. Often, things became so bad that one doubted whether there indeed ever were good times.

Then, the Polish revolt against the Russians broke out. As usual, the Jews were the first to be persecuted. The Poles imposed a large contribution upon the Jews of the city. Since the Jews could not pay such a large sum, they put three of the most important householders in jail. Uncle Yaakov was among those arrested. They were all sentenced to hanging if the Jewish community would not pay the money within three days.

People ran to the city commandant, begging him and weeping; but nothing helped. People fasted, prayed to G-d, and cast desperate glances at the hanging event which was taking place in the middle of the market. Dark shadows fluttered around at the hanging, and everyone was overtaken by a death pall. However, the Jews did not lose their hope. People knew that the Russians were not far from the city and, sooner or later, the Poles would have to leave the city. In the meantime, they bought off the guards, reached the captives, hid them in safe places, and waited for G-d's help.

The Poles flooded the Jewish street. They entered all the houses, searching for the escapees, and stealing Jewish property in the process. They found some Jew who looked similar to Uncle Yaakov, and sentenced him to hanging without any trial. Fortunately, the rumor that the Russians were close spread further, and the Poles left the city hastily. The Russian military indeed arrived on the second day. The hidden Jews still had fear about being seen openly. Above all, they were afraid of the return of the Polish revolutionaries.

*

On a wintery Sabbath afternoon, Miriam had already recited Grace After Meals after their lonely and melancholy midday meal, and she was sitting by the window. On account of the Sabbath, she wanted to forget her pain and discomfort. She chased away her sad thoughts and stared at the street. The lane was covered with white and silver snow. The faded, old houses of the Jewish street with their arched roofs were covered with a white, fluffy covering and appeared magical and dreamlike. In the winter windows that had been placed in the walls, white pieces of cotton were placed, decorated with colored thread and smartly cut pieces of paper. People were seldom seen on the street. Sometimes a man with a thick fur coat or a woman with a thick kerchief slinked along with silent steps. A group of children with fur or cotton coats and hats covering the ears came out from a nearby house. They came out to the street, looked at the frozen streams, and thought about skating. Today is the Sabbath, and one is not allowed to skate. However, they could run, throw snow, laugh loudly and shout. Miriam looked at them. The laughter of the children penetrated through the double windows. She recalled how, once, she would watch Velvel play through the same window. Her husband would often call the six-year-old child into the house and lecture him:

"It is not appropriate for a child of your age to throw snow."

So clearly, so plainly could she see the child near to her with his red cheeks and bright eyes, that she barely noticed that a sleigh had quietly stopped beside her door. Suddenly, she heard a knock on her door, and she jumped up in a fright. A man with an expensive fur coat then entered the house after a knock. Under the fur, several gold medals sparkled on the lapel of a red uniform. The man remained at the door for a moment and looked at her with happy, moist eyes, which seemed to her like a blend of Velvel's red cheeks and his sparkling, velvet-black eyes. She collapsed on her armchair and stared carefully at the guest. He then ran to her and bent down at her knee. "Mother, mother," he shouted, placing his face against her chest, "do you not recognize me? Mother. Your Velvel?"

She took his face between her hands, looked sharply at his face, and then pushed him away from her.

"Yes, I recognize you," she whispered with pale, trembling lips, "Yes, I recognize you."

Then, a gentle joy overtook her. She forgot who he was today. She forgot that he is no longer someone's lovely child, her Velvel. Today, he arrived on a sleigh in the middle of the holy Sabbath and showed up at her door. As in a sweet dream, she caressed his face, placed his head at her chest, and whispered with a sweet ecstasy:

"My Velvel, my sweet, beautiful child, my little son..."

She woke her up from her dream.

"Where is Father?" he asked her.

She closed her eyes as if a terror fell upon her. She sat down drained of energy and put down her hands like two dead wings. Velvel noticed this and nestled her closer. He smothered her old, wrinkled hands with hot kisses. She felt his tears between her fingers. He began to tell his life story:

He pursued knowledge, studied and explored, and stirred up the world with his knowledge and wisdom. He suffered greatly until he entered university, studied medicine, and became a well-known physician. He had become the physician and darling of the archduke, the Czar's uncle. He remained in town for a total of two or three hours. His only dream had always been - to see them both, to see Mother and Father, to see them and beg their forgiveness. He always thought about them. He had to hide his Jewishness. He did so, but he was not able to remove his longing for his parents from his heart, and he always sent his regards to them, if he could at least have a glance at them. Now, the opportunity came. He is here. He had inquired about them and knew everything. He had already sent for Father, who would soon be here. He, Velvel, would now look after them and do everything so that their old age would be fortunate and peaceful.

He rose up, stood at his full height, and with a happy, radiant face began to pace through the room. He opened the doors, looked into the kitchen, the den in which his bed used to be. He caressed the furniture with his finger, and it moved slightly. He looked at the furniture, looking for the chair where he used to sit by the table. He stopped at the place where his father used to sit, and caressed the chair gently.

"Everything is as it was. Everything as it was in my yearning and in my dreams. Only you are older," he said to Miriam, who was still sitting, overcome by her dreams, staring with her eyes at all his movements.

"There is a deep discomfort in your eyes. I know, Mother, that I am responsible for this," he said with a sigh.

Suddenly, Uncle Yaakov appeared at the open door. He saw the stranger in the house, and looked at him acutely.

"Father," Velvel uttered to the old man.

Yaakov extended his right hand, and the guest, as if through a secret force, stiffened himself and remained standing in his place. Both men silently stared at each other, Velvel with fear and longing in his eyes; Yaakov with stern, cold glances from beneath his gloomy, grey eyebrows. Velvel was the first to shift his glance to the ground. Yaakov turned to Miriam and calmly said:

"Miriam, I am going to the *beis midrash.*"

The door was already long closed behind the old man, and Miriam was still sitting tight in her chair. Now, she was looking at her guest with fear. He was standing in the middle of the room, with his strong, bright, open eyes turned toward the door.

The Sabbath twilight had already long ago turned to darkness when the guest left Yaakov's house. He went to the sleigh with a bowed head. The children who had surrounded the sleigh made way for him. He waved toward the window where Miriam's pale face could be seen through the frozen windowpanes. The sleigh started to move away with haste and disappeared as if a dream.

Miriam looked outside through the window for a long time. She forgot "*Nachalat Tzvi.*" She did not recite "G-d of Abraham"[1] and when the maid entered the house frozen from the street, she saw Miriam standing by the window, alone, in the darkness.

Years again passed by. Every year, the winter spread its cold upon the earth and covered it with white snow. After the winter, spring again came. The earth was kissed with dainty rays of sun, spreading over the snow-white dead covering and reawakening the earth to life with their warmth. The earth woke up again, filled with fresh, youthful sap. Flowers and plants of various colors sprouted up, as if for a joyous festival.

A person, however, becomes a year older with the passing of each summer and winter, and no spring can return him to his youth and freshness as before. Yaakov and Miriam grew older and weaker. They no longer awaited and dreamed of a joyous spring. Miriam grew smaller and thinner. Yaakov's face became paler, and deep wrinkles covered his high, white brow. Only Yaakov's eyes remained eternally young. There was some sort of undiminished luster in them. It was an eternal flame, a holy fire that the years, suffering and worries could not extinguish.

The times took a turn for the worse. The businesses became difficult. Uncle Yaakov even had to pawn his seat in the synagogue. He would have to spend his senior years without a roof over his head.

It was close to Passover. They needed money, and there was nobody from whom to obtain it. The old man sat on a cold evening near the oven, in which Miriam had lit a few twigs to warm up their old bones. It was quiet in the house. Only the wood in the oven was crackling, and Yaakov was staring at the fire. He stroked his grey beard and swayed gently. A long, dark shadow swayed on the walls, and the clock, with its brass weights and long chains, stroked rhythmically.

Miriam sat by the table, with heavy, brass glasses on her eyes. She darned a sock by the glow of the small lamp, glancing from time to time at the old man, as heavy sighs emanated from her old, collapsed chest. She finished her work and got up from her chair. She walked slowly to the clock, took out a paper from behind it, and approached the old man.

"Yaakov," she said with a request in her voice, "see, Yaakov, he left me this and said that any time that we need something, we should put this letter in the mail and he would quickly help us. We can ask him for thousands of rubles. Everything that we need he will do for us. He will give us good fortune. So, take it, take it, Yaakov."

The old man took the letter. He slowly folded it up in his palm, and without even looking at it, tossed it into the fire.

Miriam uttered a quiet groan and looked at her husband with fear. She instinctively stuck her hand in the fire where the letter was rolling around, half burnt. Yaakov took her by the hand, moved it away from the fire, stood firmly on the ground, calmed her, and quickly said:

"Miriam, give me my fur coat, I am going to the *beis midrash.*"

Translator's Footnote

Recitations at the end of the Sabbath.

Chapters of Memories

by I.M. Sidroni (Sendrowicz)

A. I Learned Something From All My Melameds

a. My First Melamed [1]

I can't remember the name of my first *melamed* because he was never called by his real name, but only by his nickname. He was called “the hunchback of Bielsk” (*der Bielsker hoiker*). He lived in the house of Reb Zalman Berias (Friedman; so called because his father-in-law was Beria Oberfeld), near the new market. This was a *heder*for the first stage of learning: alphabet, *ivri* (recognizing words from their letters), and prayer (reading the prayer book). The pupils were four or five years old; the implements of learning were a board with letters of the Hebrew alphabet on it, a rod, and a prayer book, and the “miracle” that would happen in every primary *heder*, and happened in mine too: every now and then, an '”angel” would drop a *groschen* (penny) on the alphabet board for the child who knew how to read.

All the “virtues” that writers and poets ascribed to the *heder*were also in this one, as the poet says: “a small room, narrow and warm, with a flame on the stove top” with the Rabbi's wife with her kitchen utensils and domestic labor, and a few sticks of furniture and some sparse belongings, and the children (of the Rabbi, his only assets) with their shouts and tears. All this in the small and narrow room, but as for the rest of the poem “hear and remember my lessons, my sweet little boy; whoever reads Hebrew quickly, I will give him a prize” and similar comforting words, we never heard them from that Rabbi. He was strict and very bad-tempered. His scolding and yelling, at his pupils, at his wife and children, could be heard in the high heavens, and he would very often apply the thongs of a lash (it was called *kantshik*) to the bodies of the little children. There were not a few outbursts of real cruelty, incidents engraved deeply into the soul of a tender child and retained in memory until today. The Rabbi used the same lash with the leather thongs to beat his baby who was lying in his crib...

b. Rabbi Hershia Zlociower

My second *melamed* was my uncle, Rabbi Hershia Zlociower. He lived in the Gunsher house, near the *mikve*[2]. This was a *heder*for the second phase of learning: the Pentateuch with comments by Rashi[3], the early prophets, and the beginnings of the Gemara[4] (the Tractate *Baba Mezia*). The pupils were six to eight years old.

The Rabbi was a good and even-tempered man. However, he too had a lash, with which he would “honor” one of his pupils from time to time. But he did it tenderly, and out of pity. He used a warm-hearted tone to explain the

Pentateuch to us, and especially the biblical stories. He had a special melody, a sentimental and cordial inflection, whose echo has lasted in my memory to this day, which he used to recount to us, and sing with us, various parts of the Torah. This included the legend about the verse "And as for me, when I came from Paddan, Rachel died unto me in the land of Canaan" [Genesis 48, 7] (which he would begin with the words "When Nebuzaradan exiled the Jews, they passed by Rachel's grave"). Also the last testament of our patriarch Jacob (both in the Torah portion "And Jacob lived in the land of Egypt") or "The Song of the Sea" [Exodus 15] (in the portion "And it Came to Pass") and the song "Give ear, ye heavens" [Deuteronomy 23]. Similarly, the Rabbi would teach us, and sing with us the song *Akdamut*[5] and the scrolls of "The Song of Songs," "Ruth," "Ecclesiastes," and "Esther." We would learn and sing each scroll [*megilla*], together with its legends before the holiday with which it was associated, with a melody so beautiful and delicate and captivating, that its sweetness remains in the student's heart to this day.

When we began studying the Torah portion "they take for Me an offering" [Exodus 25], the Rabbi would use chalk to draw a menorah, the altar, and the other implements of the tabernacle on the blackboard. During the lesson on a particular implement, he would show us a drawing, whose form was not to be questioned. Similarly, the following week, during the Portion "And thou shalt command," he would draw the ephod and *hoshen*[6] on the blackboard to make it easier for us to understand.

*

During the short winter days, it was customary to learn in the *heder* in the evenings as well. Evening lessons began two weeks after the Sukkoth holiday, with the Torah portion of "Get thee out of thy country" [Genesis 12] ("Get thee out" to the *heder* also in the evening), and lasted until the portion "They take for Me an offering" [Exodus 25] (the "offering" being stopping learning at night). There would be a special feast for the children to mark the end of the evening lessons. Of all the *heders* I studied in, I remember only the feast that was held in the *heder* of my uncle, Rabbi Hershia Zlociower (apparently, in the *heders* for older children, they did not have feasts). The feast was held on the last evening of lessons, that is, on Thursday evening of the Torah portion "They take for Me an offering." There was no learning that evening, and it was completely dedicated to the meal.

And this is the account of the feast: On the first day of the week of the portion "They take for Me an offering," the children started bringing money for the feast; one would bring 10 *groschen* (pennies), and another would bring 20 *groschen* . There were also children who brought a full *guilden* (30 *groschen*). They gave the money to the Rabbi, and he bought wine, fruits, and nuts. On the day of the feast, each child would bring some baked goods and sweets from home, and give them to the Rabbi. The Rabanit [Rabbi's wife], with help from her neighbors, prepared servings of "tasty things" that the children had brought and the Rabbi had purchased, and set the table. In the evening, when the children came back to the *heder*, the table was brimming with all the good food. They sat down, and the feast began. The atmosphere was joyful, and the children's faces shone with happiness and bliss, and the Rabbi and Rabanit were also happy at the joy of "their" children. The children would repeat the blessings for all the "tasty things," and ate everything that was set before them. The Rabbi and Rabanit would serve them, and also taste the good food. The Rabbi would relate tales and also sing, together with the children "The Rock from Whom we have eaten." The feast would keep going, with laughter and song, and the children would stop studying in the evenings.

*

There was also a meal on *Lag B'Omer*[7] in my uncle's *heder*, but this meal was less festive. On that day, we would come to the *heder* later than usual. Every boy came armed with a rifle or sword (of wood) and in addition, a cap pistol. Every boy would also bring a roll with butter, cheese, eggs, and scallions, and a bottle of milk or coffee, and we ate breakfast together. Later we went out with our full pack, accompanied by the Rabbi, for a hike outside the town. We went through the alleys[8] near the *mikve*and up the hill behind the "Kamnitza" (a large walled house) up to the boundary of the fields of the German called Falka. There we ran, jumped, fired our pistols, fooled around a little, and then sat down to eat the remnants of our breakfast. Then we returned to the *heder*. We didn't learn that day, and after we came back to the *heder*, we immediately went home.

*

In addition to the regular holidays that were in all the *heders* , we had special vacation days in this *heder*. Rabbi Hershia Zlociower would travel to see his Rabbi, the Rabbi from Radzin, before Rosh Hashanah and return after Yom Kippur, so that all the Days of Atonement were like a long vacation.

*

Rabbi Hershia Zlociower was a Hasid of the Rabbi Gershon Henich of Radzin. This Rabbi did a great deed that was quite extraordinary. He would make blue threads and his followers would put them on their *tziztiot*[9]. And this is the story:

The Talmud (Tractate Sanhedrin 91) says that once every seventy years a snail called *hilazon* comes from the sea. The temple priests, who knew how to predict the time and place of the appearance of the *hilazon*, would trap it, and make a pale blue dye from its blood. This was used to color the clothes that were worn in the temple. The followers of Rabbi Gershon Henich of Radzin said that their Rabbi had caught the *hilazon*, and made a blue dye from its blood. In order to be certain that the dye was authentic, the Rabbi traveled to Rome - so said his followers - to compare his blue with the blue of the curtain of the Holy Ark that was brought by Titus to Rome after the destruction of the temple, together with all the holy artifacts, and is now in the Papal archives.

He found that his blue was identical to that blue. The Rabbi then prepared blue threads for all his followers to put in their *tziztiot*, as is written "and that they put with the fringe of each corner a thread of blue" [Numbers 15, 38]. I can remember very well that on one of the front fringes of the *tallit*[10] that my uncle, Rabbi Hershia Zlociower, wore, there was a blue thread.

*

Apparently, the income from teaching was not enough to maintain even the impoverished life of the Rabbi. Because of this he had two other unique sources of income. He made and sold wine from raisins for the *kiddush*[11], and baking and selling *matzo shmura*[12]. The students would help the Rabbi in this work. In the "wine industry" we would help in dicing the raisins. It was done in the following way: the raisins were spread over the bottom of a wide tub, and we would beat them with a large pole that had a sharp S-shaped piece of iron at the end. In preparing the *matzo shmura*, we would help by cleaning the wheat, and sorting the split seeds from the rest of the seeds. These tasks would be done by two students, while the rest of the class studied. Every now and then, the "workers" would be replaced. It is not necessary to state that we obeyed this commandment, "thou shalt surely release it with him" [Exodus 23 5], with all our heart and soul.

I have previously mentioned that the *heder* was close to the *mikve*. Once, during the winter, when we returned home in the evening, the rumor spread among us that in the evenings, especially on Thursdays, women bathe in the *mikve*, and when they leave, they abduct children... This rumor caused fear and terror among us. The dreaded thought pervaded us every evening that we had to cross this dangerous passage, through dark alleys and yards (we would go through a dark alley and then through the yard and entrance, also dark, of Mordechai David Turkeltaub, or of Yosef Pindek), until we reached the Jewish Street.

But we quickly recovered, and decided not to give in to feelings of fear, but to go home with head held high. We made the brave decision to fight if necessary with all the means at our command (sticks, stones, etc.) for our lives and honor. (Because, in addition to the danger, there was also the indignity - to be kidnapped by a woman.) So this is what happened: every evening we would walk home together in high spirits and ready for battle. Apparently the women became aware of our decision to fight and defend ourselves, and therefore abandoned the idea of abduction...

*

Once someone left some iron rails near the *mikve*. The rumor spread among us that Russia was preparing for war, and therefore they were beginning to lay a railroad track. Later, it turned out that the rails were brought to repair the roof of the *mikve*...

c. Rabbi Leibush Rozenberg

I was seven and a half years old when I went to a higher *heder*, that of Rabbi Leibush Rosenberg. He lived on the Jewish Street, the third house from the bridge (on the market side). In this *heder* we studied the Pentateuch, the other books of the Bible (*Pasuk*) and *Gemara*, but at a higher level. The Rabbi was a gentle soul, mild tempered, well-liked by everyone, including his pupils. But he had poor fortune. Many troubles were visited on him during his lifetime; family problems, very little income. These caused bitterness and depression.

I started learning in the *heder* of Rabbi Leibush Rosenberg almost by chance. This is how it happened: On the morning of the Friday after Passover, in the year 5668 (1908), I was at home with my mother. I was not going to the old *heder* anymore, and was not yet attending a new *heder*, because my father had not decided whether to send me to the *heder* of Rabbi Leibush Rosenberg or that of Rabbi Chayim Yosef Crystal. Suddenly, the door opened, and a boy came in and said, "The Rabbi said that Yechiel Moshe should come to the *heder.*"

"Which Rabbi?" my mother asked.

"The Rabbi Leibush Rosenberg," the boy answered.

My mother thought that my father had decided to send me to the *heder* of Rabbi Leibush Rosenberg, and had told the Rabbi, who had sent the boy to get me. So she said "Go with the boy to the *heder.*" So I went.

Every Friday was very busy in our store, like in all stores. Friday was market day. Until about midday, customers would come from the surrounding villages, and after that, customers from town: Polish seamstresses who would want sewing notions for Saturday (there were no haberdashery shops in Sierpc yet), and Jewish men and women who needed a button, a pin, a shoelace, or a ribbon, or other item that was "required" for the Sabbath. And all of them were in a rush, and all of them pressing the shopkeeper: "Me first! Me first!" In addition to the proceeds, there was crowding, chaos, and noise. When my father finally closed the store and came home, it was late. Then he would quickly put on his Sabbath clothes, rush to the *mikve*, and then to the *shtibl.*[13]

At the evening feast, when father started talking about me and my next *heder*, my mother told him that I had already gone today the *heder* of Rabbi Leibush Rosenberg. She told him how it happened, and what she had thought. My father heard her out, thought about it for a moment, and said, "Oh well, let it be." And so I remained the pupil of Rabbi Leibush Rosenberg.

The truth of the matter is that neither this Rabbi nor the *heder* were "genuine" or "natural," but rather were "artificial." In fact, Rabbi Leibush Rosenberg had a store that sold shoe leather and other cobbler's essentials. But the store was small, the stock limited, and his needs were large, both for sustenance, and for tending to the sick in his family (that after all his efforts were not cured, but died young). Rabbi Leibush Rosenberg opened a *heder* and became a Rabbi only because of his desperate condition. Even the room containing the *heder* was not "natural." It was separated from the kitchen, and from the other residents of the house. They spent the day downstairs in the room near the store, and the *heder* was upstairs. The work did not suit the mild temper of the gentle Rabbi Leibush Rosenberg. Although the Rabbi had some pieces of leather (instead of a lash) with which he sometimes punished his pupils, but if truth be told, he did not know how to use them properly...

The house containing the *heder* had a tiny yard (shared with Madame Krosa Licht), but it lacked the most important amenity. Instead of this, we had an alternative, which we wouldn't have traded even for a palace - a place beneath the bridge (which was, as we said, nearby). Imagine for yourselves this wonderful place, this pleasure, this spaciousness, a river and a riverbank, a paradise on earth, all for us. An ideal place for games and passing the time, very difficult to part from and return to the *heder*. A number of times some pupils would forget to return to the *heder*, and the Rabbi sent an emissary to return the lost boys, and the emissary would also forget, until a second emissary came to get the first, and a third to get the second... In these instances, the Rabbi would apply his pieces of leather, but as I have said, he didn't know how to use them properly.

The biggest and oldest pupil among us was Avraham Licht (son of Shmuel Mendel Licht, the baker, and now in Argentina; because of his size he was called "Avraham Malech" [Avraham the angel]). Understandably, he was also the biggest mischief maker. Once, "Avraham Malech" took the Rabbi's leather strip and hid it under the bridge. Some of the pupils, including the author of these words, knew who the culprit was and where it was hidden, but no one revealed the secret, both because of solidarity, and because of fear of the culprit, who was the strongest boy among us. After a few days, "Avraham Malech" returned the leather strip to its place, and the secret was never revealed.

*

I remember two instances of rebellion in this *heder*. This is what happened: One of the pupils was Gutkind Grina (son of Zalman Grina, the butcher). He resembled the rest of us in just about everything: age, studies, behavior, and so forth. For a short time, his older brother Toviah also learned with us, and he was different from us in just about everything: he was bigger (in age and size), and a big *sheigetz*[14]. His friends included not only Jewish *shkotzim*, but real *shkotzim*, Gentiles. The day of the fair was considered a vacation day, and there were no studies in the *heder* (because of the danger in walking to the *heder*). The older Grina convinced us not to go to the *heder* also in the evening before the fair (this was winter, when we studied in the *heder* in the evenings as well). We liked the idea, and agreed to meet in the evening in the market. So that we left our houses after the afternoon meal, as if to go to the *heder*, but we really went to the market.

It was a pleasant, wintry evening. The moon was wandering in the sky, and lit up the market, the water pump at its center, and everything else. The stars twinkled at us, as if to say, "We know the secret, but won't tell anyone." The white surface beneath our feet, the snow, added to the loveliness of the evening and its congeniality. Some of the peddlers' stalls were already set up, and in another section, the owners were busy erecting them. There were many people in the market: some were working, and some wandering around; some laughing and some throwing snowballs and it felt carefree. We, with Grina in the lead, ran, jumped, threw snowballs, and generally fooled around. Grina reveled in his capabilities and his might. With every jump he would topple the upper rafter of a grain stall (apparently, they weren't fastened yet). We ran and jumped after him, but couldn't compete with his achievements.

Thus passed a good, pleasant, and happy evening. As far as I can remember, the aftermath of the evening was not terrible, either. At home, nobody knew about it. And the punishment we received from the Rabbi wasn't great, because the legal vacation day of the fair that separated the crime from the punishment lessened the crime and weakened the punishment.

*

The second rebellion did not have a specific ringleader: As is well known, study is forbidden on the evening before *Nittel*[15], and there were no lessons then in the *heder*. But the next day, the day of *Nittel*, studies were as usual. And so we, the students of Rabbi Leibush Rosenberg, had to go to *heder*. But if on the evening of Nittel, before it even began, it was forbidden to study, then shouldn't it be obvious that it should be forbidden on the day of *Nittel* as well? We decided not to go to *heder* the next day and instead to meet on the riverbank, on the slope behind the yard of Reb Wolfe Hazan.

The next morning, we left home as usual, as if on our way to *heder*. But we went straight to the riverbank to our agreed upon meeting spot. We were just a few (I can remember only Baruch Burgand, the son of Reb Avraham Shochet) and we didn't know what happened to the rest of our friends. Where were they? The riverbank was covered with snow, and the edge of the river had any icy crust on top. We explored, played around, ate the meal we took with us to the *heder*, but we did not feel very happy. First, we were just a few, and second, we didn't know what happened to the rest of our friends, and were worried in case they had gone to the *heder*. Also, we didn't have much room for playing games, since we were afraid that some acquaintances would see us, either from the bridge, or from the yards that looked out on the river. So we wandered around until three in the afternoon, and then went home, as usual, for dinner.

As soon as I got to my house, my mother asked me, "Where were you all day?" "In the *heder*," I answered. "What *heder*?" my mother raised her voice. "The Rabbi sent someone to look for you."

I tried to justify myself, adding a sin to the crime, and said that I hadn't gone straight to the *heder*, but came a little late, and in the meantime the Rabbi sent someone to search for me. This was like adding fuel to the fire, and my mother started to yell at me: not only had I become a *sheigetz*, I had also become a liar. They made their own holiday, these shkotzim, a new holiday, *Nittel.* (I wondered, who told my mother, who revealed the secret?) From shouting, she went to weeping, crying about her bitter fate, left alone, with no one to watch me, to educate me (my father was no longer alive). I stood there, rooted to my spot, mortified, and didn't know what to say. If the earth had opened up at that moment, I would have willingly jumped into the pit, in order to save myself from my mother's screams and wails, and from my own guilty conscience, because in my heart I knew she was right. But what could I do now, after the fact? How could I take back the wrong I had done?

The lady who brought us water was sitting in our house at that moment. Of course, she backed my mother in her complaints. Not only that, but she would recite to me from time to time, a bit of doggerel (I don't know if she already knew it, or she composed it on the spot): "*Nittel, farech interen hittell*" ("*Nittel, boils under your hat*"). This little jingle irritated and humiliated me more than my mother's crying and shouting.

Finally, my mother gave me my dinner. I sat down to eat as if on hot coals. The food tasted to me as bitter as wormwood. I finished eating, and went to the *heder*. Going to the *heder* this time was like walking to the gallows. I was filled with feelings of fear and shame, and so, full of melancholy thoughts, I came to the *heder.*

Feeling weak in the knees, and with a bowed head, I went up to the stairs that led to the *heder*. Here began a new saga. Where were you? What did you do? Who incited you? I kept quiet, and didn't answer, for what could I say? I received my "portion" and sat down in my place. My friends received the same dose. Thus ended the second rebellion.

*

Rabbi Leibush Rosenberg initiated an important reform in his *heder*: writing. We would write in Yiddish for an hour a day from a lexicon (*briefenshteler*). We also wrote a little in Polish. I remember that I left a few partially empty lines in my notebook at the beginning and end of each paragraph, as I saw in the lexicon. The Rabbi told me not to use the lexicon as an example: the author left partial lines empty, because he profited from it. If you leave partial empty lines, you lose from it...

d. Rabbi Michalitia

I went from the *heder* of Rabbi Leibush Rosenberg to that of Rabbi Michael Bendkowski (who was called "Rabbi Michalitia") when I was nine years old. At first he lived in the house of Binyamin Sobol, and later in the house of Yehuda Tcholk on Zhava (Zhavia) Street.

This was a typical *heder* for the study of *Gemara*. We learned the Bible there as well, but the main subject of study was the Gemara. We studied it in a number of ways: the “simple” *Gemara* (*Pushet Gemara*), *Gemara* with commentaries (*Sheur*), and independent study of the *Gemara* (*Leinen*, without the help of the Rabbi; this name evidently came from the word *alein*, alone). Rabbi Michalitia fulfilled for us the saying of our sages of blessed memory “Before the age of six do not accept pupils; from that age you can accept them, and stuff them with Torah like an ox” (Tractate Baba Bathra, Folio 21a, which Rashi interpreted as “until the age of six, do not oppose the child, and from then on, feed and irrigate him against his will, like an ox that has a yoke put upon it”). Rabbi Michalitia was very strict, and there was a firm discipline in his *heder*. Instead of a lash, the Rabbi had a rubber belt from a sewing machine (*zeit* in Yiddish; his daughter, Chayah, was a seamstress). But he usually used a more “natural” form of punishment, and generously applied smacks above the table and boots beneath the table to his pupils. (And if the smacks always hit their target, the boots would often hit the boy sitting next to the target.) Rabbi Michalitia was old and completely gray, but he was quick and agile. He was short (because of this he was called “Michalitia”). Some comedian said that when his wife Yetta (who was tall) went to buy fabric for pants for her husband, she said “*Far Michaltien oif a por heizier.*”[16]

*

During that period, the authorities issued a ruling that Jewish children learning in a *heder* must spend two hours each day in the government school. Jews viewed this ruling as a punitive edict, which would lead to ignorance of the Torah, and they alleviated its harshness by paying bribes. But there was a period when bribery didn't work and the children of the *heders* had to spend every day between four and six in the afternoon in the government school that was on Schools Street, behind the church.

This obviously took a couple of hours a day away from the Torah. But to tell the truth, we did not regret it at all. We considered it as bliss that we had never dreamed of; like a prize that was suddenly dropped on us from heaven. How much running, jumping, pushing, fighting and making up did we have every day going to and from the school? How much did we shout, yell, whistle and laugh on the way. Who would have thought that we would have great times like these!

The school itself was not bad at all; in everyone's opinion, it was better than the *heder*. First of all it took some time until all the pupils were in their seats and the deafening noise quieted down (the older ones among us felt themselves “responsible,” and calmed us down). Then the teacher came in (his name was Dembski, and all the children rose when he came in) and he started to read from a Russian text book, line by line. Avraham Licht (Avraham Malech, whom I mentioned earlier, who knew a little Russian) would translate into Yiddish. (There was another translator, and the two would take turns, translating every other day.) He would translate only a few words correctly (because the teacher understood the meaning of those words in Yiddish, according to the translator). The rest of his text was a mixture of silliness and nonsense. The children sat and tried not to burst out in laughter, out of fear of the teacher (he would hit them with a ruler) and also out of fear of the translator. After a while, the "edict" was withdrawn (apparently again by the payment of bribes), and we stopped going to the school.

I gained very little pleasure from going to the school. I went there for only a few days, and when it was over, the Rabbi told his grandson Hershel Yosef (who was also the grandson of my uncle Reb Moshe Sendrowicz) and me, "it would be a shame if your time would be wasted; better to stay here and we'll have a special lesson." And so it was.

*

Nittel is apparently a day made especially for getting into trouble. I have already described the "incident" that we experienced on *Nittel* in the *heder* of Rabbi Leibush Rosenberg. Well, this is an "incident," similar but not completely so, that happened to us in the *heder* of Rabbi Michalitia.

The Russian Orthodox community in Sierpc held a festive and splendid procession on *Nittel*. The procession included many icons (it was said that the glittering icons were made of gold), statues, and pictures of saints. The army regiment and military band also participated in the procession. The procession started at the *Tcherkva* (the Orthodox church) passed Plotzki Street, the market, Zhava Street (Zhavia, where our *heder* was located), the new market, and through the alley near the house of Reb Ahron Tcharnotchepka, went to the village of Bovorowa, and there they immersed the statue of Jesus in the river (that is what Jews said) in commemoration of the baptism of Jesus in the Jordan River.

When the procession passed on the street in front of the *heder*, we heard the sound of singing and the music of the band, and of course we could not remain in our seats. Using the excuse that we had to go to the bathroom, we went out one by one to watch the parade. The splendor of the procession and the music of the band enthralled us, until we completely forgot who and where we were and started following the procession. We kept going until we entered the above alley (that was at the edge of town). Only then, as if we had become sober and opened our eyes, did we realize our strange situation and the double sin we had committed: we had left the *heder* for an extended time and followed the "ceremony," with its priests, icons, and the rest of the profaneness.

Depressed and full of remorse we started back to the *heder*, full of fear of the heavy hand of the Rabbi. Embarrassed and fearful, we entered the *heder*. The Rabbi didn't even bother to ask, "Where were you?" Without saying a word, he pounced on us and distributed smacks in every direction, until our cheeks and ears were red as if on fire.

Like I said, *Nittel* is a day for getting into trouble...

*

We were treated to a slight relaxation in the severity of our studies in the winter of the year 5672 (1911-1912). The community of Sierpc had to find a new *shochet* [ritual slaughterer] and inspector, in place of the previous one, Reb Ischia Yossel Hanchovitch, who had left to become the *shochet* in Kalisz. A number of *shochatim* from different towns (of course smaller than Sierpc) proposed their candidacy. Among them was the son of the Rabbi, Reb Henich, who was the shochet and inspector in Lubitsch. Of course, the Rabbi wanted his son to be the shochet in Sierpc (a town considerably larger than Lubitsch) and he tried to influence various people who could be helpful in the matter. Because of this, the Rabbi would leave his house frequently, and people would come to visit him frequently, and talked, consulted, and whispered secrets. In the end, the Rabbi's son did not get the office of *shochet* and inspector (it went to Reb Yekel Ritzik of Sochocin), but we received many hours of freedom.

*

The longest period that I ever attended any *heder* was that which I spent in the *heder* of Rabbi Michalitia. I studied for five "semesters" in this *heder.* (This included an interval of three months because of illness and vacation. When it came to school and work, the term "semester" was considered to be six months - from Sukkoth to Passover, or from Passover to Sukkoth.)

e. Rabbi Ischia Margel

During the summer of the year 5672 (1912), I studied with Rabbi Ischia Margel (who was called *Der Kleiner Itchia* - the short Ischia). I purposely didn't say "in the *heder* of Rabbi Ischia" because he didn't have a *heder* at all. He had a small store with readymade goods in the small house of Frilanski (at the beginning of Fara Street; the house later belonged to Avraham Mlawa). The saleslady who did most of the work was his wife, Devorah (who was called Devorah Ischia's). He was very old, short, but a great scholar and a great Hasid. He studied the Torah and worked and behaved modestly and charitably all day long, and was indifferent to the problems and experiences of everyday life. Because of his poverty, he tried to open a *heder*, and a few parents (very few; there were six or seven students in this *heder*)[17] sent their sons there to study. But this *heder* was like "Jonah's gourd vine," which came one night, and then was gone. The *heder* didn't last more than a "semester," and parents left their children there only out of pity, because we hardly learned anything during that "semester."

The *heder* was in two rooms: at times we would learn in a room next to the store, and at other times in the Rabbi's apartment, which was in Lieberman's house on the Jewish Street near the bridge (on the market side). Our daily schedule was as follows: we would first learn for less than an hour, and then the Rabbi would begin preparations for the Morning Prayer. The preparations for prayer were no small thing for him. When he left the room to "prepare himself," he would remove his capote and put on a different one. He would say that it is forbidden to learn or pray in an article of clothing that was worn in the bathroom. The preparation took a long time. At ten o'clock when we went home for breakfast, the Rabbi went to pray. At twelve o'clock, when the Rabbi came back, we were already in the *heder* for some time, pretending to study. Actually, we were playing various games (I remember that we once played the game called *shechelech*[18] and continued it for many days until someone scored a thousand). Then the Rabbi would start doing three tasks at once: eat breakfast, teach, and doze off. This combination, which resulted in no eating, no learning and no sleeping, kept up until three o'clock, when we went home for dinner. When we came back, we again learned for less than an hour, and again the Rabbi would start preparing himself for the afternoon and evening prayers.

This was how the day passed, and how the weeks passed. That "semester" was like a long vacation.

f. Rabbi Moshia Karmelkeies

And finally, my last *melamed* was Rabbi Moshe Danziger (who was called "Moshia Karmelkeies") who lived at first at the edge of town, in the *Vlokt*[19] near Yehuda Baruch Skornik, and later in the house he (and his sister, the wife of Avraham Dikan the tailor) inherited from his father on Fara Street, near the church.

This Rabbi was different from his professional colleagues in two characteristics: physical and spiritual. Physically, he was a young man, thirty-six years old, but handicapped by a bent spine, who had difficulty walking around the room while leaning on his cane. Spiritually, he would "peek" at books about the Enlightenment. He was not really "spoiled" by this, as he was a strictly religious Jew, but he did have advanced ideas about the world and Judaism. The difference between this *heder* and other *heders* was a result of these two differences between this Rabbi and other Rabbis. The dissimilarities were evident in many aspects, but mainly in the number of pupils. All the other *heders* with children of this age had twelve pupils, but this *heder* had only six. Therefore, the tuition for this *heder* was almost twice that of other *heders* (6 rubles a month, compared to 4 rubles in other *heders*). And another difference: in all the other *heders* the pupils would come at eight o'clock in the morning, pray, eat something, study till ten, and then go home for breakfast. In this *heder*, the pupils would arrive at nine o'clock, after praying and eating breakfast at home. The Rabbi settled on this arrangement because of his frailty, since he couldn't get up at an early hour.

Before starting to teach, the Rabbi would talk to us for about an hour in a friendly manner, about the news, or tell us a story, or a joke. He would say that such small talk would bring the pupils closer to the Rabbi and because of this they would learn not by coercion, but willingly. He brought a proof of this from the Gemara (Tractate Pesachim 117a): "Even as Rabbah used to say something humorous to his scholars before he commenced [his discourse], in order to amuse them; after that he sat in awe and commenced the lecture." But the Rabbi did not have just a pleasant side; in times of need he also had a tool of fury. He had a lash with a few thongs whose handle was made of elegant braided leather. It was always by his side on the table or in his hand. But it was used more for entertainment than punishment. (We were already "big boys," after bar mitzvah... and we also didn't cause much need to use a lash.)

After the initial short conversation, we started the lesson. The first hour was dedicated to the Pentateuch, the Torah portion of the week with interpretation by Rashi. After that we started to study the Gemara by ourselves (called *leinen*) with the Rabbi sitting on the side and listening. He would help us only in special cases, when we encountered "obstacles" that we couldn't handle by ourselves. (At the end of the week we repeated for the Rabbi the leinen of the whole week.) We studied till twelve o'clock, when had a half hour recess for eating and play. After the recess we started to learn *sheur* (Gemara with commentaries). We studied until three, and then went home for dinner. We came back at five o'clock.[20] From five to seven we studied "simple Gemara" (Gemara without commentaries). Here too the Rabbi did something different. We studied the "simple Gemara" like we did the *leinen* - alone, with almost no help from the Rabbi.

In "simple Gemara" we studied the Tractate *Sabbath* from the beginning till page 90, the end of the chapter "Rabbi Akiva Said." From there, the beginning of the chapter "If one lays aside" to the end of the tractate we studied as "sheur." In this way we completed all of Tractate *Sabbath.* For *leinen* we studied Tractate *Sanhedrin.*

The last hour - it usually lasted an hour and a half, and sometimes more - was dedicated to the study *Nach*[21]. The study of *Nach* in this *heder* had a completely different nature than in other *heders* . All the other *heders* treated study of *Nach* as a less important topic, as if just to satisfy an obligation. But in this *heder*, learning of *Nach* was an essential study, scholarship for its own sake, equal in value to the study of the Gemara. I remember that during the winter we studied the Book of Kings, so that at the end we could confidently answer such questions as: "How many kings ruled in Judea and how many in Israel, and what were their names? How many years did each king rule? Which of them died a natural death and which were killed, and by whom? How old was each king when he died? Who inherited his throne?" We could also answer compounded questions easily, such as: "How many kings of Judea and how many of Israel ruled for five years, what were their names, and what did they do? How many kings of Judea and how many of Israel died a natural death and how many were murdered, their names and stories? Similarly, we knew the important events that occurred in Judea and Israel during the life of each king. The Rabbi was very proud of our expertise, and if one of the parents visited the *heder*, he would show off our knowledge. It was like a small Bible quiz each time.

The six students who studied in this *heder* were divided into two groups, in accordance with their knowledge and capabilities. The first group consisted of Moshia Niapomoshzyk (who had an exceptional grasp of the material), Moshe Aaron Richgut, and the author of these lines. The second group consisted of Yisrael Osiolek (Yizraeli), Binyamin Burstein, Yechiel Meir Berman, Yisrael Wilk, Shepsel Visroza, Nissan Richgut, Gutkind Rankle, Ischia David Schnitzer - those who did not attend for all the three "semesters" that I studied in this *heder*. The two groups learned everything together, except for the self-study (*leinen*) of the Gemara. Here there was a difference, since each group studied a different tractate.

*

I mentioned above that only six students were in this *heder*. Once, a seventh pupil was added in the middle of the semester. This was Yisrael, the son of Shmuel Wilk (called "Shmualtia"). Shmuel Wilk was himself a *melamed* (for children, for "ivri" and Pentateuch). In addition he had a store that sold some haberdashery and some readymade underwear, and a stall in the market where he also sold these goods (he never made much money from all three enterprises put together). One of the pupils in the *heder* was Binyamin Burstein. His mother (Toviah) and brother (Avraham, his father was not among the living) also had a stall in the market that sold the same merchandise as Shmuel Wilk, and near his stall. They heartily hated each other and would quarrel every Tuesday and Friday (market days in Sierpc). After Shmuel's son started attending, Binyamin's brother once came to our *heder*, angry and agitated, pounded on the table, and yelled, "*Voss teet do Shmualtia yung? Der mdubar iedech geven oif zex!*" ("What's Shmualtia's boy doing here? We talked about only six!") The Rabbi talked with him for over an hour (he sent us, the pupils, outside in the meantime), and apparently, they reconciled. The new pupil stayed with us until the end of the semester.

*

It seems that being a *melamed* was not enough to support the Rabbi's family, and so the Rabbi's wife took up commerce. For as long as they lived in the *Vloki*, she would buy butter and eggs on market days from the farmers for Shimshon Mordechai Visroza (the butter and egg merchants would give money on the eve of market days to many people who would buy merchandise for them, and settle accounts the day after market day). After they moved to Fara Street, she opened a stall in the market that sold readymade underwear.

*

The *heder* of Rabbi Moshia Karmelkeies was the leading *heder* in Sierpc. There were none in Sierpc that were better. The continuation of this *heder* was the *Beit Hamidrash*.[22]

g. In the Beit Hamidrash

On the holiday of freedom, in Passover of the year 5674 [1914], I became a free man. I stopped learning in a *heder*, and started studying in the (old) *beit midrash.*

This transition - from studying in a *heder*, where the boy has to be present all day, from morning till evening, and even later, imprisoned within the four walls of a small and stuffy room, confined to his seat under the constant watchful eye and strict discipline of the Rabbi - to studying in the *beit midrash* where the boy is in a large and roomy hall all day, among different people, young and old, studying and praying, and enjoying the freedom and independence -- is a great event in the life of the youth. It is an event that places a mark on the youth's development, and has a great influence on the future course of his life. To be sure, the freedom that the youth enjoys studying in the *beit midrash* is not absolute. There are enough elders and worriers - like uncles, friends, neighbors, and ordinary acquaintances - that come to the *beit midrash* to pray and incidentally follow the actions and deeds of the youth and pass detailed reports to his parents. But even the relative freedom that the youth enjoys has a bad influence, whether on the continuation of his studies, or his behavior in general. Also his sudden entrance into the company of grownups can have a negative influence. In previous times, when the *beit midrash* was full of studious youths, two or three “new boys” would study with one of the youths, who would be a sort of guardian of the “new boys,” keeping an eye on them. But during this period, because of our many sins, the glory and splendor of the *beit midrash* had diminished, and also of the youths attending it. Only a few remained in the *beit midrash* and they were there only a few hours of the day. The events that happened around that time almost completely silenced the sound of Torah in the *beit midrash.*

*

I studied there for a short time with Motel Ritzik (now in the United States) and Yossel Goldman overseen by Yossel's brother, Moshe Ber Goldman (now a rabbi in the city of Cleveland, United States). He was a learned and enlightened youth. There was gossip about him that he strayed a little from the “straight path” and also read “outside books.” His outward appearance suggested, in fact, that he had “glanced and been smitten.” His face was fringed with a beard that was trimmed short, he wore a white collar, his clothes were spotless, and his shoes were brightly polished. Our one hour lesson was in the morning, between nine and ten o'clock. We sat at the small table that was next to the stove opposite the door that looked out onto the courtyard. Sometimes, after a lesson, Moshe Ber would teach Yossel and Motel a new melody that he had composed.

Yossel Goldman had a short and turbulent life. From a zealously religious youth, he turned into a passionate communist. The extreme communism of the son clashed with the extreme piety of the father. The father, Reb Yehoshua Goldman, was an outstanding scholar and devout and strict *hasid*, and the son left his father's house, together with Hanna Leah, the daughter of Wolfe Hazan (called "Wolfe Kalmaias" after his father-in-law Kalman Fenster) and her bridegroom (a young man from Lodz who worked in Sierpc as a tailor). They illegally crossed the Polish-Russian border, and the three of them were arrested by a Russian border patrol, and charged with desertion of the cause of communist activity and propaganda (according to their view, a loyal communist must remain outside of a communist country so that he can participate in communist propaganda and activity there). After they were released - thanks to the efforts of another communist, a Jew from Lodz who was a friend of the bridegroom - the three of them studied at the Teachers' Seminary [in Warsaw]. Yossel Goldman would sometimes publish poetry in the Yiddish newspapers in Poland or Russia. During that time he died tragically, and his brief and stormy life came to an end.

h. Secular Education

At the end of this chapter - "I Learned Something From All My *Melameds*" - I want to mention my two teachers of secular subjects (Russian, Polish, and arithmetic) with whom I studied during that period. (I talk about my teachers from a different period, Mintz and Cohen, in another chapter.) During a short period of the summer of 1914, Shlomo Finberg (called *Der Lutvak* who lived in a house near the *mikve*,) and Shimon Gelbart (lived in Litvinski's house, near the synagogue), were, in succession, my teachers. They were both good and honest people, who lived lives of poverty and distress, but concealed their hardship. Shimon Gelbart was an enlightened man on Jewish subjects who was knowledgeable both in secular matters and medical topics. Later, Finberg was a clerk in the town hall, and Gelbart was a caretaker of the synagogue.

B. World War I

a. The First Period - The Russians

i. The First Days

War between Russia and Germany was declared on August 1, 1914. Within a short time, most of the European countries were involved, and when the United States joined in (in April 1917), it was honored with the name "The First World War." August 1 was on the ninth day of the Month of Av[23], and Jews saw this as more proof that this day is marked for calamities.

I still have the picture in my mind: it was Thursday, June 30, just before evening. I left the *beit midrash* after the afternoon prayer, and I saw a large gathering at the entrance. The caretaker of the *magistrat* (town hall) pushed his way through the crowd with a *Bund*le of papers in his hand. All the people who had gathered there, and all those coming there forced their way to the wall to read the large notice just put up by the caretaker. The notice states, in large letters, that military mobilization has been declared in all of Russia and every man who is subject to conscription will be notified of the place to which he must report. The notice was signed by the Minister of War, Sokhomligov. The shocking news immediately penetrated the *beit midrash*, and all the worshipers poured outside to look at the depressing news for themselves. A mantle of gloom descended over the whole town, accompanied by fear and panic, especially in families where the husband, son, or sons were subject to the draft. Everywhere there were groups of people talking about the great event and the disaster that was about to take place. Everyone showed off his knowledge of politics and strategy, and everyone agreed that this war would not last long and at the most for three months. This was because no country could withstand the effects of the advanced tools of destruction that both sides had prepared for a longer period than that.

The conscription of the Sierpcers subject to the draft never took place. From time to time, the would-be conscripts were called to come to Plotzk on a certain day, and they traveled to Plotzk, but they didn't report. The Germans, who in the meantime had conquered the other bank of the Visla River, apparently knew the date of the coming conscription every time, and they attacked the area with artillery and prevented the recruitment.

On the day that war broke out (it was Saturday), the "Greens" (they border patrol were called "Greens" because of the color of their uniforms) could be seen in town. They had retreated from the border near Rypin. There were also a few carts that brought Jewish refugees from Rypin. The stopped at the market, opposite the *magistrat*, and the people living in the area gave them food and drink, and after a short stop they continued to Plotzk. It should be noted that these refugees were an exception. Usually, the residents of the border towns in our region stayed put.

On Sunday, a small panic started, with food hoarding. People bought two or three loaves of bread and a few more staples in quantities a bit larger than usual, and thought that would be enough to get by during the days of rage.

On that day, just before evening, the first plane flew over Sierpc. It was during the afternoon prayer, and all the worshippers came out of the *shtibl* of Gur that was in our courtyard (we lived in the house of Moshe Elsztejn at the beginning of Plotzki Street), wrapped in their ritual shawls and adorned with their phylacteries (it was the Fast of the Ninth of Av that had been postponed [because of the Sabbath]) to look at this great wonder. The airplane flew at a very high altitude, and looked like a bird to us, but we could hear its engine. If it was "ours" or the enemy's - we did not know.[24]

*

With the outbreak of the war came a shortage of small change. Small coins, whether of copper or silver, disappeared. One conjecture was that the Russian

Bank was stockpiling silver coins, collecting them but not issuing them. A second conjecture was that people, especially the peasants were hoarding the metal coins (both silver and copper) because they had no faith in paper money. But either way (or maybe both), the lack of small coins caused big problems for the shopkeepers. It was hard enough to cope with the Jewish shoppers who bought for a few *groschen* (pennies) or kopeks (two pennies) and paid with a two ruble bill. (It should be noted than one ruble bills were not in circulation before the war; they were issued only at the start of the war.) It was harder to deal with the Gentile shoppers who were acquaintances and honest. And it was still harder to handle unfamiliar Gentiles. They would shout, threaten, and act outraged. And the worst were the *shkotzim*, criminals, and soldiers. They would simply grab merchandise and run.

Relief from the shortage of coins and a reprieve for the shopkeepers came from paper vouchers issued by the *magistrat*. Vouchers for one, three, and five kopeks were issued with the notation "Kop. towar " (kopeks for merchandise) written on them. The first vouchers were hand-written with the rubber stamp "*Kasa pomocy bratniej w Sierpcu*" (fund to aid our brothers of Sierpc) with a drawing of two linked hands at the center of the stamp. After a short time, the rumor spread that vouchers were being forged. New vouchers were then issued, printed this time. In addition to the previous rubber stamp, the other side had an indecipherable Latin phrase stamped in sealing wax. The colors of the vouchers were: for one kopek - purple; three kopeks -green; and five kopeks - pink.

ii. Troubles, Suffering, and Insults

It was the second day of Rosh Hashanah of the year 5675 [1914]. As everyone knows, it's forbidden to interrupt the *Mussaf* [additional prayer for the holiday] prayer (with conversation) on Rosh Hashanah, starting with the blessings prior to blowing the *shofar* [ram's horn]. This prohibition extends during all the time that the prayer of the *Shmone Esrei* [Eighteen Benedictions] is said in a whisper, the *t'kiot* [sounds of the shofar], when the prayer of the *Shmone Esrei* is said aloud (repeated by the prayer leader) with the *t'kiot*, until the final *t'kiot* that are in the middle of the *Kadish* that comes after the *Shmone Esrei* prayer. All this lasts for about two hours, but when we had just started whispering the *Shmone Esrei* prayer, Pultiah (Raphael Klinhoz) entered the *shtibl* (the *shtibl* of Alexander, which was then in the courtyard of Ezriel Yehuda Kotcholak on Zhava Street). The young men and those older worshippers who stood near the entrance and saw Pultiah understood that something was wrong in town. They were struck with foreboding and wanted to know what happened with all their souls, but - it was forbidden to stop praying. A soft, mute murmur passed through the congregation and reached the Eastern Wall. All the worshippers turned towards the entrance and peeked through their prayer shawls. Whether or not they saw Pultiah, they all felt the fear that was hanging over the *shtibl*. They very much wanted to know what happened in town, but - it was forbidden to stop praying. Only two youths (Ber Lanczner and Ezriel Dobroszklanka, who were not among the most pious, during the pause after *Malchuyot* when the congregation is waiting for the *t'kiot*), dared to ask Pultiah, "What happened in town?" But Pultiah remained silent and didn't answer. In spite of the apprehension and anxiety of the worshippers about what was happening in town, the prayers and *t'kiot* continued as usual. Pultiah also stood and waited patiently, without uttering a word, until the prayer ended.

At the end of the whispered *Shmone Esrei*, Pultiah approached the podium, banged it with his hand, and said, "Gentlemen, you should be aware that a cavalry company has entered town. The company commander went to the Rabbi and told him that he demands that the Jews provide all that is necessary for his men and their horses during their stay in Sierpc. In addition, he warns the Jews not to walk in the streets and to glance out of their windows, especially in the market. Whoever looks out of a window will be shot. The Rabbi is now consulting with the *dozors* (community leaders) about supplying the company. He sent me to inform all the prayer houses about this."

Fear grabbed every one of us. Everybody wanted to ask what was happening in town. Had, God forbid, some disaster occurred? And what do Jews in other prayer houses say? What should we do after the prayer - go home, or maybe it's preferable to remain in the *shtibl*? Everyone wanted to ask these and similar questions, but - it was forbidden to stop praying. And Pultiah, when he had finished talking, left.

The prayer leader for the *Mussaf* starts the service with the words "Agitated and terrified" (Reb Yaakov Meiria {Kolas} was the regular *Mussaf* prayer leader of the Alexander *shtibl*) and said the *Shmone Esrei* prayer aloud (repetition of the prayer leader), and the worshippers were agitated and terrified as they went through the liturgy and heard the *t'kiot*.

At the end of the *Shmone Esrei* prayer, the last *t'kiot*, and *Kaddish*, a torrent of words, questions, fears, and guesses broke out in the congregation. Everyone expressed his worries and qualms; everyone asked questions, without anyone being able to calm people down and answer the questions.

Slowly, those worshippers that lived near the *shtibl* or in the new market dispersed to their houses. But those that lived in the (old) market or had to pass through it stayed a while at the *shtibl*. Since there was nothing suspicious in sight, and no noise was heard, the people who lived around the market began to try and get home. In small groups of two or three we started towards the market, and when we were near the market, we separated and went one by one. We saw nothing unusual in the market, just a few soldiers standing next to their horses near the *magistrat*.

Many Russian army regiments passed through Sierpc on their way to the German border[25]. They came day and night, coming from the road to Plotzk, and going to the road to Rypin. Thus went company after company and battalion after battalion, tired and dusty, and sometimes hungry, with just one question on their lips, "*Daloko du Berlina*?" ("Is it far to Berlin?")

The Polish Jews suffered many tribulations and insults during this period, and the Jews of Sierpc experienced the bitterness as well. Beatings, name-calling, snatching merchandise from stores were everyday occurrences. The suffering was especially bad on days when just a small group of soldiers were in town, and few officers were seen on the streets. On those days, the Jews and their property were defenseless. Blows to the heads of Jews were regular occurrences. The soldiers took anything they wanted from the stores, not only for themselves, but also for their companions, the local *shkotzim*. The more "honest" soldiers would try to pay with a bill, and because there were no coins available for change, they would take the merchandise and go. On those days, the Jews would refrain from going outdoors as much as possible. When the day turned into evening, the Jews, and especially Jewish girls, totally avoided the market. The Jews would stay in their apartments in the evening, with locked doors, shades drawn, lights lowered, walking slowly and talking quietly. They were very fearful, with ears attentive to the slightest sounds from outside.

After the great and shameful Russian defeat in East Prussia, a few of the survivors again passed through our town on their way back. Individual soldiers or small groups from various regiments and companies would drag their feet through the streets with no order or discipline. Coming on the road from Rypin, and disappearing into the road to Plotzk, they were tired and depressed, filthy and full of dust, in tattered and worn out clothes, one without a hat and another without shoes, one slightly lame or in shabby vehicle or on a haggard horse (sometimes two on one horse). There were no officers to be seen among them. Apparently, because of the disgrace, they didn't accompany them. This mournful procession came through the town day after day.

In order to appease the soldiers, the Jews set up tables in the streets that the soldiers passed through and gave them food, fruits, sweets, and cigarettes. A thin stream of soldiers also came through the Jewish Street. They came from the *Vloki*, passed the Jewish Street and the market and turned to Plotzki Street. There was a table near the house of Dudia Tcharnotchepka from which the offerings were distributed to the soldiers. A friend and I were on the sidewalk across the street when two soldiers received some gifts. One of the soldiers, after he had distanced himself by a few steps from the table, aimed and threw the apple that he had just received from the Jews, and hit me in the face. The blow hurt, but more than the physical pain, I felt an inner ache. I thought about this villain, "Were you also such a hero there, and hit your target with the same accuracy? At the front you had a terrible and disgraceful defeat and now you show your bravery against a Jewish boy? And for this you use a gift that you just received from Jews, you despicable coward."

*

Most of the Jews were happy about the failure of Russia. They had suffered many ordeals over the years because of this evil and corrupt empire. The cruel and savage Russian soldiers had shed a lot of Jewish blood in the few months since the start of the war.[26] But the Jews were careful about voicing their opinions, because there were rumors that the streets were full of spies. Not only those not from the covenant (who understand Yiddish), but also members of the covenant. But among friends, they could talk about their hopes for the defeat of the villains and ridicule their heroism.

iii. Changings of the Guard

Sierpc changed hands a few times. Sometimes the Germans would come into the town and stay for a while - from a few hours to a couple of weeks - and then leave as quickly as they came. Every time that the Germans came into the town, the Jews could lift their heads and breathe easier. The fear left their hearts and the gloom departed. The German soldiers were nice and very polite in their behavior towards the Jews, since they knew that the Jews were friends. (What a difference between the Germans of the First World War and the Germans of the Second World War! Who can understand the heart of man and the reversals of men and nations?) It was the opposite with the Poles. The Germans did not harm them, but they knew that the Poles were allied with the Russians and therefore treated them with suspicion. There was also the matter of language that separated them.[27] However, the Jews kept their feelings to themselves, and did not get too close to the Germans, so as not to give any food for thought to informers or excuses for spies.

Once, when the Russians came back to Sierpc after the Germans had been there for a few days, they found a picture in the show case of the photographer Esther Podskocz. It was of Mordecai-Yudel (Rosenfeld, the village idiot) standing between two German officers. The Russians saw this as proof that Mordecai-Yudel was a German spy and, in spite of all the entreaties and intercessions, banished him to Siberia, from where he never returned.

The brothers Shmuel-Asher and Itzik Ostaszewer were also exiled to Siberia. They had gone to Rypin on business during a period when the Germans were in Sierpc, and didn't get back in time before the Russians returned. On their way back to Sierpc they were captured by the Russians and sent to Siberia. After the war they came back to Sierpc in good health.

There were a number of cases when, without a shot or any noise whatsoever, a policeman would rush into the *magistrat* (the town hall; our store was opposite the *magistrat*), which had the police station on the first floor, and immediately policemen would come out carrying rifles and packages and head towards Plotzki Street. Then we knew that the Germans were getting close to town. Sometimes they would enter the town hall for a short time, and sometimes they wouldn't, and after a few hours the policemen would return to their station.

Once we woke up at night because of a loud noise. When we looked outside, we saw red skies in all directions. It turned out that the Russians left the town, blew up the bridges, and set fire to the lumberyards at the edges of town. This happened on Wednesday, the fifteenth of Heshvon, in the year 5674 (November 4, 1914). There was little damage to the town. The fires were immediately put out, and the bridges, which had hardly been damaged, were soon fixed.

*

One time, during the first weeks of the war, in midday, there was a panic in the market. The people went into their stores and shut the doors halfway. A cart hitched to two horses appeared from the direction of Zhava Street. It was driven by a peasant and surrounded by mounted Russian soldiers, armed, about ten in number, holding bayonets. The procession passed the market, and went to Plotzki Street. It turned out that the Russians had captured two German soldiers. So what did they do? They confiscated a peasant's cart along with its owner, padded the cart with hay, made the two prisoners lie inside face down, covered them with blankets, and took them wherever they took them.

Usually, news of something that happened in the market reached the Jewish Street within half an hour and the *Vloki* within an hour. That is what happened this time as well. A long time after the alarm subsided and the people dispersed and the conversations stopped and the normal course of affairs returned to the market, there was a panicked rush of people from the Jewish Street to the market. At first there were children and a few young people, and then a multitude of adults. The people in the market became frightened and peppered them with questions. "What happened?" "What happened in your neighborhood?" The people from the Jewish Street answered that there was a lot of panic because something had happened in the market, the doors were shut, and the people went into hiding. Only after an hour did they work up the nerve to leave the street and go to the market to find out what happened.

At a later time, ten German prisoners passed through town surrounded by twenty mounted and armed Russian soldiers.

iv. Battles

There were no pitched battles in the vicinity of Sierpc. However, there were days when we heard gunshots, machine gun fire and artillery all day. Sometimes the window panes rattled after every cannon shot. A few times, as the firing grew louder, we would go into the shelter. Of course, the shelter then was not an "essential common necessity" found in every house. But by chance, our courtyard had a good shelter. Beneath the house at the front of the courtyard (which was the sales room for Berish Poznanski's ironworks) there was a half cellar (it was a cellar only on the street side) with very thick walls and an arched ceiling. The cellar served as the storeroom for the iron goods of the shop owner, but there was enough room for the residents of the house and nearby houses, as well as a few passersby.

There was a heavy engagement near Sierpc on Yom Kippur eve. We shut the windows and rushed to the shelter. After quite a long time, the firing died down and we left the shelter. I went to the grocery store run by "Shasha di Levitetes" to buy a large candle for Yom Kippur. When I was in the store, the gunshots resumed. The people in the street rushed into the stores and shut the doors after them. After a while, the guns went silent, the doors of the stores opened, and people went home.

There were also air raids. German planes dropped bombs on Sierpc a few times. One bomb fell in the yard of Toviah Bluman. It hit the corner of the roof of the house without causing any appreciable damage. Some shrapnel from this bomb hit a Polish man who was walking on the sidewalk across the street, near the bakery of Yehuda Licht, and killed him immediately. Another bomb fell in the fields behind the houses on Plotzki Street (on Licht's side), and did not cause any damage.

*

A very fierce battle - the only one that was not only heard in town but also caused damage and was momentous for the town - took place on Thursday, the 27th day of Shevat in the year 5675 (November 2, 1915). We were in the shelter for many hours, from around three in the afternoon till late at night. We sat in fear and silence and listened to the muffled echoes of the thunder of cannons. Sometimes we heard the sound of galloping horses in the street. (We thought: are those soldiers rushing into battle, or running away from it?) Sometimes there were sounds of men walking fast on the sidewalk. Once we heard a women crying. Terror came over us when we heard this sound. Listening to it, we understood that a calamity had occurred. Later we found out that it was the voice of Leahle Kotcholak, who was hurrying to get the medic Vlotzkovski for her brother, Abba, who was hit by shell shrapnel. (He had been in the shelter but went out to bring food to their horse. He died of his wounds. People said that some soldiers in the street had also been hit by shell shrapnel.)

There were many people in the shelter then - men, women, and children, residents of the house and of nearby houses. They had come at the beginning of the attack, or while it was going on, taking advantage of a lull in the fighting. There were also passersby who were nearby when the fighting started. As the sounds of the battle get louder, the fear increases, and the silence and attentiveness inside grows. When the sounds die down a little, there is less tension, and conversations about strategy begin. One of the people in the shelter proposes that we recite the Psalms, but another answers him that under these conditions it is impossible even to say the Psalms. (The proposer was Noach Zilberberg and the responder was Shmuel Frank.) One of those who happened by chance to be in the shelter was Bronka Garfinkel, daughter of the lawyer Garfinkel. She sat in a corner all the time, and wrote in a diary. Everybody was amazed at her calmness and restraint, that she was capable at such a time to busy herself with writing in a diary.

In the evening the attack quieted down and the sounds of gunfire lessened. But we all stayed in the shelter for another long hour. It was very late when we left. There was absolute silence outside. We strode the few steps between the shelter and our house in awe and fright, and went inside. The other residents of the house and neighboring houses did the same. But those that lived far away stayed in the shelter until morning.

That was a sleepless night for many of the townspeople. They waited for the light of day with anxiety and expectations. In the morning, there were groups of German soldiers streaming into town through all the streets and entrances. (The first Germans had entered the town at 10:30 in the evening.)

b. The Second Period - The German Occupation

i. Nit Kosse, Nit Kosse

The front did not move far from Sierpc. The German army halted its advance somewhere between Sierpc and Drobin, and stayed there for a few months. It seems that battles took place there from time to time, and then we could hear the muffled sounds of artillery fire in the town.

After fierce battles in Lodz and Sochaczew, the Germans conquered these cities in the month of July. Then the German army advanced along the entire front, conquered Warsaw (on August 6, 1915), and all of Poland was captured.

The front near Sierpc also moved. In a battle that took place between Sierpc and Drobin, the Germans took about a thousand Russian prisoners, and moved them through Sierpc. That morning, the Germans ordered every landlord in the market to prepare food for twenty prisoners. Before evening, the prisoners were brought to the market and divided into groups of twenty accompanied by two German soldiers, and each group went to one of the houses in the market. The prisoners sat down on the edge of the pavement and the residents served them bread and cooked food in large pots. There were many Jews among the prisoners, and they were served special food. Among the group of prisoners near our house there were two Jews. With the permission of the German guards, we took these two Jews from the group, sat them down on the steps of the store, and the neighbors brought them food. Two German soldiers, who were not among the guards, approached the prisoners and asked if any of them spoke German. We pointed at the two Jews and said that they spoke German. The two Germans went over to the Jews and asked, "*Shmekt iIhnen das essen*?" ("How does the food taste?") The Jews, who were apparently very hungry and also didn't understand the question, did not pay attention to the inquiry and kept on eating. Then we turned to the

Jews and said, "The gentlemen are asking if the food is tasty?" One of them lifted his head to the Germans while he was holding a spoonful next to his mouth, and said in his Litvak [Lithuanian accented] Yiddish, "*Nit kosse, nit kosse*" ("Not hard, not bad.") and quickly put the spoon to his mouth and continued to eat. The Germans marveled at the sound of this "German" that they could not understand. We explained the answer of the Jews to them, and they left.

ii. New Times, New Melodies

All the time that the front was near Sierpc, we felt that we were trapped inside a small circle, from which we could not move in any direction. Obviously, this situation had a bad effect of trade and on life in general. Because of this, people started working at dangerous and deceitful occupations. On the one hand, smuggling of all sorts of merchandise developed. On the other hand, there were families - even decent ones - that opened cafes in their houses for the soldiers, and thanks to the girls in the family, these business flourished.

Even after all of Poland was conquered, life did not return to normal quickly. It would be more correct to say that it never went back to the previous state. The way of life that we had been used to changed entirely. First, civil rights increased, with freedom of speech and political activity. All types of political parties were established, educational and cultural organizations were founded, and newspapers appeared with all sorts of opinions and ideas. In general, social and cultural life thrived. However, in contrast, economic and trade activity was limited. The decrees that barred free trade in all sorts of necessities and merchandise sprouted like mushrooms after a storm. All sorts of grains, wheat, bread, sugar, oil and other staples were regulated by the occupying authorities. Necessary food products were rationed using ration cards. Free trade decreased, and in its place an underground traffic developed. Smuggling and black market, activities that can bring large profits, but also danger and large losses, flourished. At first the underground operators had a lot of problems, because unlike the Russians, the Germans didn't know about bribery. But slowly, the Jews started teaching them, and because they had tasted the fruit, they took without limit. The businesses grew in spite of the large expenses for bribing the Germans and money to silence the Jewish informers. As in the whole world during the war, and also in all Polish cities, there emerged a class, albeit thin, of war profiteers in Sierpc.

In about 1917, when the shortage of goods and materials in Germany became very noticeable, the German occupation authority in Poland issued a confiscation decree for items made of copper and brass. (The Germans also removed the copper bells from the church towers and hung metal bells in their place.) With great sadness and longing people parted from their dishes and pots, some very old and costly, with artistic value, heirlooms from a grandmother or great-great-grandmother. Some of them had adorned the

Sabbath table and evoked an aura of family warmth, and some had decorated the walls of kitchens for generations. Chandeliers, candlestick holders, large pots, pans, mortars and pestles, basins, and all kinds of tools were handed over to the authorities. They were paid using the German price list, measly pennies.

iii. Transportation and Lighting

The transportation and lighting in Sierpc and vicinity improved considerably during the German occupation. New roads were paved and old roads were fixed inside and outside of Sierpc. But the most important achievement of the Germans was to lay down a track (*kolieika*) for a light railway line that went through the towns of Lubitsch, Kikol, Lipno, Skempe, Sierpc, Racionz, Plonsk, and Nasielsk. The railway cut the travel time between Sierpc and Warsaw significantly. Before the war, the journey from Sierpc to Warsaw took a long time. This was how we traveled then:

The travelers would leave Sierpc in a *povoz* (a closed horse drawn carriage for six people) or an omnibus. At midnight, after about a two and a half hour ride, they would get to Bielsk. The coach stopped there, and the travelers would go to an inn and drink a cup of tea, and in the winter, a shot of liquor to warm themselves, eat something from the hamper in their luggage or that they bought in the inn, and talked and joked with each other. The horses also dined, and rested a bit. After three on the morning, they continued on their way to Plotzk. If the road was in order, they would get to Plotzk at six in the morning. But the road wasn't always in order. In the winter, after a heavy snow, the travelers would have to get off the *povoz* or omnibus, and push it to get it out of the snow. When they arrived in Plotzk, they would go to the Visla River (Visel, or in the Sierpc accent, " *Waassel*") and buy tickets and board the statek (steamboat) that sailed to Warsaw. The ride on the *statek* was pleasant and took a day, from about 7 in the morning until seven in the evening. The travelers (most of them were Jewish merchants) had plenty of time to pray, recite a few chapters of Psalms, eat, study, rest, doze a little, organize their lists, orders, and bills, talk about business, listen to and tell tales and jokes. Also, for the more sensitive among them, time to look around and enjoy the beautiful views of the river and nature, and the towns on either bank of the Visla. That is how it was during the summer. In the winter, when it became cold and the Visla froze (though this did not happen every year), they had to travel on roundabout routes, something that caused more expenses and much discomfort.

When the light railway line came, the whole journey from Sierpc to Warsaw would take one night. Travelers would leave Sierpc at ten in the evening and arrive in Nasielsk. There they would transfer to the regular railway, and they would be in Warsaw by seven in the morning. Then they had the whole day before them to buy merchandise and arrange other matters.

*

Lighting also was improved during the occupation. Both the streets and the houses had electric lights. Before the war, it never occurred to anyone that it was possible to bring electricity to small towns. Many small towns in Poland were connected to electricity during the war. The owner of the flour mill in Sierpc, Rudovski, brought a generator to power the mill, and this machine provided electricity at first for street lights and then for the houses. The generator was really too small for the needs, and there were blackouts, but in spite of that, it was an advance and achievement for the town.

*

Because the owner of the flour mill had a generator, he bought a movie projector, put it in an auditorium, and showed movies twice a week, on Saturday evening and on Sunday. This was also an achievement that the residents of Sierpc and the surrounding villages had not dreamt about before the war, and attained during the German occupation.

Once, they showed pictures from the Land of Israel. It showed holy places, cities, settlements, youth, *Shomrim*[28], street festivals for Passover, riders on horses, and so forth. I can still see the galloping noble horses on the screen, with their young riders from the settlements. The horses get larger and larger, and come closer every fraction of a second, and I instinctively flinch out of fear that in another moment they will run over me. These pictures, especially those of the new settlements, the youth, and the *Shomrim*, excited the audience, and particularly the young people, and brought about a wave of enthusiasm for the Zionist movement. These pictures were shown for a week, and the movie theater was full every night. In order for *hasidim* to see this show, one evening it was restricted to men only.

iv. Pressed Into Work

I stated above "New roads were paved and old roads were fixed inside and outside of Sierpc." Residents of the town were used every day for roadwork in the vicinity. One day (in the spring of 1916) the Germans announced that the residents were expected to volunteer every day for work, and bring a basket or a sack with them. I was among the first volunteers that presented themselves to a place near the magistrat (I can only remember one other volunteer - Avrahamia Valuka). But since the volunteers were few in number, the German soldiers went through the streets and seized young men and added them to the volunteers. The soldiers took us to the road that leads to Rypin and ordered us to pick up rocks from the field and set them up in piles. That was the day that the episodes of pressing people into work began, and was repeated day after day.

One morning, about a week after my volunteer day, when I was in the (old) *beit midrash*, some German soldiers barged in and began seizing young men from among the students and worshippers for work. Some of the men (those near the entrance) were captured, and some ran out the back door and scattered in all directions. I and two others (one was Libia Serena, son of Shmualtia the Glazier, another one, I think, was Gutkind Renkel, son of Avraham Natan) did something daring. We jumped into the river and ran across it, with the water coming to above our knees, to the other bank, where the garden of Mashrowski was located. The Germans, who had in the meantime reached the courtyard of the *beit midrash*, didn't chase us, and went back into the *beit midrash*. We were happy about our victory, and the beautiful spot, full of wildlife, flowers, and trees where we had found ourselves by chance. We wandered back and forth, talked, and said the Morning Prayer for which we had not yet had time (we had managed to take our phylacteries with us before we ran out). Meanwhile, our clothes were drying out, when suddenly, like they had popped up out of the earth, we were confronted with two German soldiers. They were delighted at the prey they had just captured, and asked, amid loud laughter, "*Zind zi gegangen smecken Mai-luft*?" ("Have you gone out to smell the air of May?"). From there they took us to work. (This upset me no end. After I volunteered on the first day, they come now and snatch me. This is my reward for volunteering?)

We worked in the same fields and at the same tasks as on my volunteer day. Some of us gathered stones and piled them up in the field, and some took the stones from the piles and carried them to the road and stacked them nearby. Apparently, people had informed our families that we had been pressed into work, and they sent us food. At the midday break, we ate and prayed.

The forced labor caused a lot of suffering to the residents in general and to the Jews in particular, because most of the abducted laborers were Jews. This is the place to note that the idyll between the German soldiers and the Jews that happened at the beginning of the occupation did not last long. When the Germans and the Poles started getting friendly and learned a bit of each other's language, the attitude of the Germans changed immediately. They were still far from expressing hatred, or any open enmity. Also all through the occupation the Jews felt themselves to be far freer than before the war. But here and there, in isolated cases, the Germans would show anti-Semitic tendencies, and there were anti-Semitic incidents. Also in finding forced labor, there was pronounced anti-Semitic bias. They would look only in Jewish streets, even in the *beit midrash*, so that only, or almost only, Jews were abducted.

But in the end, there was an arrangement. A quota of people was established that the magistrat had to supply each day for work. The town hall drafted people from a list of households in town, so that each household, in turn, would supply someone for work. However, even with this arrangement, the Jews were the majority of the laborers. This was because the town clerks, using various pretexts, removed many Poles from the lists. But even then, this arrangement, while flawed, was better than the abductions.

The labor could be done by the member of the household, or by an agent. There were people who made a living from this labor, working every day in place of someone else.

In addition to the workers sent by the town hall, there were also permanent laborers. Among these were the brothers Leibush and Moshe-Meir Ostaszewer, whose father had been banished to Siberia by the Russians (as mentioned above). Moshe-Meir, who was still a young man, but tall and alert, was liked by the Germans, who appointed him to be an interpreter. He had a white ribbon on his sleeve and rode with the foreman in a handsome carriage, and everyone envied him.

v. A "War" Within a War

It is worthwhile describing here the "war" within the war that took place in all the towns of Poland between the "Germans" and the "Russians."

The "war' was between Jewish children (who called themselves "Germans") and Polish children (who called themselves "Russians"). It occurred during the summer months of 1915 and 1916. The combatants at the "front" were boys between the ages of twelve and fifteen, and sometimes older. Younger boys contributed by supplying ammunition from the hinterland. The weapons were right hands, and the ammunition - stones. The sharp-shooters used a slingshot made of a strip of leather with two strings tied to its ends.

In Sierpc, the battles took place in the pig market and the field behind it, up to the foot of the hill. The top of the hill was the bastion of the "Russians." When they were in trouble they would flee up the hill. The "Germans," who gave chase, would get to the middle of the hill, but didn't dare to go any higher. The "German" fortress was in one of the lumberyards in the new market. When the "Russians" gained the upper hand, the "Germans" fled there and closed the gate. The "Russians" could not, and would not dare to enter the closed fortress. The "battles" took place every day, in the late afternoon.

On some days, a certain *sheigetz*, about eighteen years old, would decide to play a practical joke. He would join the Jews, and at their head, he would chase the Poles up the hill. But sometimes he set a trap for the Jews. In the middle of chasing the Poles, he would turn around and start beating the Jews. The Poles in an instant would become attackers instead of attacked, and the Jews would retreat with loss of face and under heavy blows.

Sometimes a German soldier would pass through the battlefield during a "skirmish." The "Germans" explained the "war" to the soldier, and the names and allegiances of the combatting sides. The German soldier would immediately join the "Germans" and at their head would chase the "Russians." The defeat of the "Russians" was then complete, and without showing any opposition, they fled to their fortress. The "Germans" then scored an easy victory.

Sometimes, a combatant would be seriously hurt by a stone to the head or eye. One of the Jewish boys died after he was hit by a stone to his head. Once one of the warriors, a Polish boy, received a very serious blow to the head and died as a result. The Jews were fearful of revenge by the Poles, but the incident passed quietly. The "battles" then stopped for a few days until everything calmed down, and then broke out again.

vi. Doctors, Medics, Midwives, Pharmacists, and "Doctors"

Medicine in Sierpc was born under the sign of the twins [Gemini]. Every one of the medical professions had two representatives, sort of "there went in two and two unto Noah into the ark"[29].

There were two doctors in Sierpc before the war. One of them, Dr. Gizler, was considered a "righteous Gentile." He was a kind and pleasant man, esteemed by the public in general, and by the Jews in particular. His agreeable and comforting manner won over his patients, and they trusted him completely. The other doctor was Dr. Gumewski, and he was known to be an anti-Semite. But he did not show his dislike when he treated his patients, and only their recovery was important to him then.

Dr. Gizler died a few years before the outbreak of the war. Then, for the first time in the history of Sierpc, a Jewish doctor, Dr. Shapiro, came to town. Again, there were two doctors, and the twins principal was not violated. Dr. Shapiro was considered to be a good doctor in the town. He was a nationalistic Jew who was friendly with other Jews, and spoke only in Yiddish with them. He stayed in Sierpc for only a few years. He left the town shortly before the beginning of the war.

There were also two medics (*placherim* - doctors' assistants) in Sierpc. One, Vlotchkowski, was a specialist medic, "half a doctor," and with respect to children, the women said he was a "complete doctor." He was not an anti-Semite, but he was not a lover of Israel either. During the "boycott" that came after the election of Yagalalo[30], he opened a stationery and book store, which his family managed. (It was said that his daughters were open anti-Semites.) The second medic was a Jew, Moshe Zomer. His expertise was not great, but in spite of this, people would turn to him when Vlotchkowski was busy.

Sierpc also had two midwives. One of them, Zelda, was very famous as the "grandma" of most of the children in town, or more correctly, "grandma" of fathers and sons in the town. The second midwife, Sarah, was the mother of Zomer the medic, and was less famous than the first.

Near the start of the war, there came to Sierpc two more midwives, "modern" and educated. One was Madame Sarah Mendelsohn (the sister of Pultiah {Raphael} Klinhoz, she was murdered in Plotzk in 1919 together with her brother). She came from Ciechanów and had a lot of work (because the two midwives mentioned previously were old and frail) and because the women of the town liked her. The second midwife was the wife of the medic Moshe Zomer, Madam Makhala-Tirtza, who was not as busy as the first one.

There were also two pharmacies in Sierpc. One was the well-known drugstore of Radomiski, at the corner of the market and the Jewish Street. The second pharmacy was in the house of Ischia Klein and was owned by Wolkowiski, a Jew from Warsaw. Officially, it was not a pharmacy (a Jew could not get a permit for a pharmacy in Czarist Russia) but a *sklad aptachni* (a medical warehouse, which can only sell patent medicines), but Wolkowiski also prepared prescriptions there. For a time, the teacher Yaakov Cohen (from Plonsk, later a teacher in the *gymnasia* [high school] in Plotzk was a partner in the *sklad aptachni.*

Dentistry was an exception to the rule of "twins." There was only one dentist in town. This was Leib (Leon) Hiller.

*

Epidemics are a common phenomenon during a war, and a direct result of it. We did not escape this misfortune during the World War. In 1916, typhus broke out in Sierpc and the surrounding towns, and many people died. There were no local doctors in town. Dr. Gizler was already dead, Dr. Shapiro had already left, and Dr. Gumewski had been drafted into the army by the Russian authorities at the beginning of the war. The Germans then established a hospital in town[31], and army doctors treated the patients. These same doctors also made house calls.

I said "There were no local doctors in town." This is not completely correct, because we did have two local "doctors." Not just local, but native Sierpcer, and in addition - Jewish.

One "doctor" was the wife of Moshe Zomer, Makhala-Tirtza. She apparently acquired her "expertise" by inheritance. Her husband was a medic, her mother-in-law was a midwife, and she was a "modern" midwife herself, so that she in any case had familiarity with medicine. (Here we must defer to the saying in Yiddish "*mimaila haut zi gekent a krenk*" [anyway, she knew someone who was sick].) She was called when there was a mild illness, a suspicion of a contagious disease and people were afraid of calling a German doctor or the medic Vlotchkowski, because the patient might be taken to the hospital. She also brought the medicines.

The second "doctor" was the shoemaker Hershieh Brutigam (called "Hershieh Shister" or "Hershieh Dudek"). Hershieh became friendly with one of the German doctors, and would accompany him everywhere, both in the street and in the hospital. Because of this, people stopped calling him "Hershieh Shister" or "Hershieh Dudek" and started calling him "Hershieh Doctor." Because of his friendship with the German doctor, "Hershieh Doctor" became intimate with the powers that be. He knew the occupation authorities well and became "*a macher*" [wheeler-dealer]. He would pass discreet gifts to officials and do favors for Jews. Understandably, he himself no longer worked as a shoemaker, but opened a workshop with laborers who worked for him. He always walked around with a leather briefcase. Some pranksters said that once they had opened the briefcase, and found - a shoetree. In the end (after the war) he became sick both physically and mentally, and died.

vii. "Independent" Poland

The war became more extensive (in area) and ferocious (with time). The Germans went on to greater victories, and with them their economic problems also grew. As a result, it placed greater burdens on the conquered countries, including Poland. They confiscated grain, cattle, the little machinery that was there, and anything else that they thought they needed. Of course, the confiscations made the residents hostile to the German authorities.

In order to win over the population and gain its willing cooperation, the two conquering powers, Germany and Austria, decided to declare Polish independence. This was announced on November 5, 1916, with the independence to occur in stages. A provisional national government was formed, whose members were appointed by the occupying authorities. Decisions were to be made by two governor-generals, the rulers of the two occupied zones of Poland. These were the German governor-general Von Beizeler, the Governor of Warsaw, and the Austrian governor-general Von Cook, the Governor of Lublin. There was a call for volunteers for the Polish Legion. (The Polish Legion was founded in Galicia[32] by Pilsudski, and together with the Austrians, fought the Russians.)

The enthusiasm of the Poles for this "independence" was very restrained. Over time, as the irrelevance of the declaration became obvious, the enthusiasm died down completely. The following joke, widespread in Poland at the time, demonstrates the extent of this "independence." A German soldier sees a Polish peasant carrying some flour. The soldier, as usual, confiscates the flour. The Pole says to him, " *P'shechezh Polska nasha*" ("But Poland is ours"). The German answers " *Polska washa, aleh munka nasha*" ("Poland is yours, but the flour is ours").

The enlistments in the Polish Legion were a disappointment for the occupying authorities, but their disappointment was even greater when they wanted them to swear allegiance to the conquering power. (The Germans wanted to send them to fight on the front in France.) The Poles, to a man, refused. The leaders of the Legion, with Pilsudski at their head, were imprisoned in the fortress of Magdenberg, and remained there until German defeat and the retreat of its army from Poland.

If the recruitment of the Poles was unsatisfactory, then understandably the recruitment of the Jews was non-existent. But there is no rule without an exception, and there were exceptions here too. Even in Sierpc, one Jew volunteered for the Polish Legion (he was called " *der legionist*" - the legionnaire).

viii. The Underground

The war dragged on and spread. In spite of its great victories and extensive conquests, the situation in Germany became worse every day. A lack of materials, a lack of food, and also a lack of manpower affected the German war machine. In April 1917, after Germany declared an expansion of its submarine warfare, and the sinking of the hospital ship Lusitania, the United States joined the Allied Powers (Russia, England, France, and eighteen other nations) in the war against the Central Powers (Germany, Austria, Turkey, and Bulgaria). With its defeat on the horizon, with its defeat in the battles of the spring of 1918, the German army started pulling back from the front in France.

The weakening of Germany at the front had an influence on the mood in the occupied countries. The fear of the German policeman, gendarme, and soldier faded a little. Underground resistance groups were established to sabotage the German war machine. An underground Polish organization called P.O.W. was established, (*Polska Organizacja Wojskowa* - Polish Army Organization) whose members were supporters of P.P.S. (*Polska Partja Socjalistyczna* - Polish Socialist Party). The resistance went from talk to action, and in a number of places, German policemen and soldiers were killed.

At the beginning of August 1918, four German soldiers were killed in the vicinity of Sierpc. The Germans imposed harsh punishments on the villages of the area, and Sierpc was also punished: a strict curfew from six in the evening till sunrise.

ix. The End of the War - Independent Poland

The situation of Germany became worse and worse, both inside the country and at the front, until the country collapsed entirely. On November 9 1918, Kaiser Wilhelm resigned, and on the eleventh of the month, Germany surrendered to the Allied powers. This was the end of the First World War.

With the German defeat, its armies left the many occupied countries. The exit from Poland was a funeral procession for the Germans. Their respect had faded and their spirit was broken. The Poles mocked them, laughed at them openly, took their weapons and equipment, tore off their insignias of rank and unit, and also spit in their faces. And they, yesterday's strong and proud men, turned into base cowards who saw, heard, and felt their disgrace, and would not respond.

The Germans left Sierpc on November 11. It was on a Tuesday, market day. Only some of the stalls were set up in the market (out of fear of disturbances, not all the merchants had set up their stalls) and not very many peasants came either (from the same fears). The members of the fire department kept order, and prevented the mob from harming the passing German soldiers. They came by in small groups, on foot and by vehicle, from Plotzki Street and through the market to the new market and the road to Rypin. In spite of the presence of the firefighters, there were a few minor incidents of rabble attacking the Germans that led to small disturbances in the market, and caused panic among the Jewish traders. Small groups of German soldiers passed through the streets of Sierpc the next day as well, coming from Plotzk.

This brought an end to the First World War and the period of occupation by the Germans of Sierpc and all of Poland. It also began a new era - that of independent Poland.

x. Defense *("Haganah")*

Towards the end of the First World War, there was apprehension (that turned out to be correct in a number of towns) that following the exit of the Germans, the Poles would initiate pogroms against the Jews. In order to prepare for the hard times, defense groups [*Haganah*] were organized in many towns, composed of the best members of the "Maccabee" athletic organization.

Sierpc also had a defense group organized by a delegate from Warsaw, also of members of "Maccabee." The group was divided into cells of five members each, and each member knew only the colleagues in his cell. Every member had to pledge allegiance to the *Haganah* when he joined and to a strict discipline. The swearing in took place in a dark room, in the courtyard of Aaron Tcharnotchepka. The group managed to obtain some weapons (pistols), purchased from German soldiers. (Because of the retreat of the German army, the famous discipline of the German soldier crumbled.) The town was divided into zones, and during tense days, especially between the departure of the Germans and the establishment of Polish rule in town, the members of *Haganah* would "wander" in pairs through the streets, each pair in its zone, when one of the pair would carry a pistol.

The *Haganah* groups existed for only a few months. To the delight of the members, and of the Jews of Sierpc, there was no need for the use of force.

The members of the *Haganah* committee were Natan Metz, Maiorek (Meir) Cohen, Avraham Fried (Yerushalmi), David Rosen, and Shmuel Szampan. In the district council of the *Haganah* group that met in Włocławek - where the Rabbi of Włocławek, Rabbi Kowalski, also participated - the representative of Sierpc was Avraham Fried.

The members of the *Haganah* were Yitzhak Bergson, Hanik Garfinkel, Salak Garfinkel, Mendel Tatz, Leib Mintz, Fishel Szampan, Yitzhak Rosen, and others.

C. Zionism, Education, and Culture

a. Zionism

i. Development and Progress

For all of Polish Jewry, including the community of Sierpc, all the aspects of public life, and especially Zionism, flourished during the German occupation of the First World War. I have already mentioned that during the occupation, various political parties were formed. Newspapers were published, and new ideas appeared. Of course the government was that of the occupation authorities, and there was military censorship, but internal Jewish life was not adversely affected. And if there were some limitations, they were negligible compared to the restrictions at every step during the Russian government period.

During this time, the Zionist Organization, *Mizrachi* [Religious Zionists], *Poalei-Tzion* [Socialist Zionists] (before the split), and *Bund* [Yiddish Socialists] came out from the underground. These parties had been illegal under the Russians and therefore of limited extent and few activities. They now expanded and spread all over Poland. They opened branches in every city and town, and their ideas and spokesmen reached all these branches. At the same time, the religious party *Aguda*t Ortodoxim [Orthodox Union] was formed. (Most of its members were Gur Hasidim.) It was later called *Agudat Israel* or *Aguda* for short. It was founded at the initiative of Dr. Kahan and Dr. Karlbach. The "Popular Party" was also founded at that time by Noach Prilotzki. It was a party with few members and few supporters. Each party published its own newspaper, either daily or weekly, as well as propaganda pamphlets. In addition, each party held meeting and lectures, so that its ideas and aspirations were spread both in print and by word of mouth.

In addition to the political parties, national organizations of workers and employers were formed. Among these were workers' unions that tended to favor the *Bund*, with a minority for *Poalei-Tzion*, craftsmen's unions, merchants' societies, and small tradesmen's organizations. The organizations also supported professional activities, cultural endeavors, and disseminated information and propaganda, including bulletins and newspapers.

The Zionist Organization developed the most during this period. The Zionist ideal excited many people, both among the youth and adults. Many joined the Zionist Organization and the majority of Polish Jews supported it. The Zionist Organization did not only engage in strictly Zionist activity such as encouraging a return to Zion, the sale of *shekalim*, collections for the Jewish National Fund, and spreading the Hebrew language. It also was concerned with, possibly primarily concerned with (in the spirit of the decisions made at the Helsingfors Congress of 1906 on "Tasks for the Present"), the everyday problems of Polish Jewry, such as the civil rights of Jews, protection of their economic interests, community matters, education, elections, and so forth. It was from such activities, especially elections, that it was possible to determine the sympathies of the public in favor of the Zionist Organization.

Branches of all the above mentioned parties were founded in Sierpc as well during the German occupation, except for the "Popular Party." They held meetings, arranged lectures, and carried out various partisan and cultural activities. Unions with branches for every vocation were founded, alongside a craftsmen's union and a merchants' society.

The largest branch of a political party in Sierpc, as well as the most active and well-known, was the branch of the Zionist Party, known as *Agudat Tzion* .

ii. Hovevei Tzion - Bnei Tzion

There were a number of *Hovevei Tzion* [Lovers of Zion] and Zionists in the previous generation in Sierpc: Ephraim Yossel Valuka, Eliezer Vasolak, Chayim Nachum Tunbol (who visited the Land of Israel in 1908); and some younger Zionists: Azrieltia Podskocz, Mordechai Hirsch Mintz, Avrahamia Valuka (son of Reb Ephraim Yossel), and others. They were also known as students of the Torah, enlightened, and tolerant in religious matters. They prayed in the new *beit midrash*[33] and were considered the remnants of the "Kolhekot."[34]

The active Zionists in Sierpc during the period between the beginning of the twentieth century and the start of the First World War were Yitzhak Karpa, Yitzhak Aaron Liebson, Shmuel Szampan, Avraham Podskocz, Avraham Gorlitz, Yeshayahu Friedman, and others, and after he came to Sierpc in 1910, Avraham Yerushalmi (Fried). Some of them were just plain Zionists ("General Zionists" did not exist yet as a party), and some were *Poalei Tzion* [Zionist Workers party]. Many of the youth in Sierpc belonged to this new party, and they made an important contribution to the Second *Aliyah*[35]. Six young men from Sierpc went to the Land of Israel then, in about 1907. They were David Bornstein, Akiva Glazer, Yitzhak Kahana (Kana), Yitzhak Aaron Liebson, Yitzhak Karpa (Itche Karp), and Shmuel Szampan. Regrettably, most of them followed the path of the majority of the Second Aliyah, and left Palestine. (Only Bornstein stayed, and Karp returned to Israel a few years ago.)

Agudat Tzion, which we have previously mentioned, was not the first Zionist Society in Sierpc. It was preceded by *Bnei Tzion*. There was a certificate of registration in the Gold Book of the Jewish National Fund on the wall of the office of *Agudat Tzion* of Sierpc. I have heard from Avraham Yerushalmi (Fried) that when he came to Sierpc he found some money held by Zionist functionaries that was collected for the Jewish National Fund, and some documents belonging to the *Bnei Tzion* Society. (He was born in Zuromin, near Sierpc. In 1910 he married Sarah Vasolak, daughter of one of the *Hovevei Tzion*, the enlightened Eliezer Vasolak of Sierpc, and settled there.) He took the money, sent it to the Jewish National Fund, which in return registered the Bnei Tzion Society in its Golden Book.

iii. Agudat Tzion

Agudat Tzion was founded, according to the same Yerushalmi, in 1911. But its unrestricted emergence and public activity only began in 1916, during the

German occupation. The offices of the society, from its beginnings to the middle of 1917, were in a small room in the apartment of the teacher Mordechai Hirsch Mintz, in the house of Patlick (a German), near his school, which was in the house of Aaron Tcharnotchepka. Later it moved to two small rooms in the courtyard of the house of Moshe Elsztejn. The steering committee of the Society (in 1918-1920) was made up of Frieda Offenbach, Hinda Rosa Atlas, Mendel Bloom, Tzirel Bergson, Yitzhak Zomer, Zvi (Hezhe) Malowanczyk, Yechiel Moshe Sendrowicz (Sidroni), Avraham Fried (Yerushalmi), Yeshayahu Friedman, Yetta Feiga Tzina, and Fishel Szampan. The chairman of the society and its driving force was Avraham Fried (Yerushalmi). He dedicated all his energy and thoughts to *Agudat Tzion* and its communal activities. He was the initiator and the executor, the activist and the operator, and thanks to him, *Agudat Tzion* became accepted as an important public institution in Sierpc. The secretary of the society was at first Fishel Szampan (who died tragically in Paris in 1933 or 1934), and from the beginning of 1920, Zvi Malowanczyk.

Some of the younger members of the committee would take turns serving in the office of *Agudat Tzion* . Each one in turn would be in the office for a week, two hours every evening, during which he was available to answer members' questions, collect the monthly dues and arrange various activities.

*

In accordance with the wishes of the chairman, Avraham Yerushalmi (Fried), the steering committee had a number of subcommittees, each with its chairman and secretary. There were five such subcommittees: culture, Jewish National Fund, political, housekeeping, and correspondence. The chairperson of the culture subcommittee was Tzirel Bergson, and the secretary was the author of these lines; Yeshayahu Friedman was chairman of the Jewish National Fund subcommittee and Zvi Malowanczyk was its secretary; the political subcommittee was chaired by Avraham Yerushalmi and its secretary was Zvi Malowanczyk; the housekeeping subcommittee was chaired by Hinda Rosa Atlas and your author served as its secretary; the chairman of the correspondence committee was Fishel Szampan, and your author was its secretary. It should be noted that the society chairman, Avraham Fried (Yerushalmi) was the guiding force behind all the subcommittees, and especially the culture committee.[36]

*

The culture subcommittee organized a meeting every Saturday (Saturday night during the winter, or Saturday afternoon in the summer). This would be a political lecture, a literary reading (reading a story and interpreting it), or a question and answer evening (*kestel ovent*). The lecturers and readers were the members Avraham Yerushalmi (Fried), Yeshayahu Friedman, Hinda Rosa Atlas, Fishel Szampan, and Leib Mintz. On vacation days, or for a festive occasion, the teacher Mordecai Hirsch Mintz would give a lecture. Avraham Yerushalmi (Fried) also had many roles in these Saturday meetings. In addition to those Saturdays where he was scheduled to give a lecture or to read, he would substitute for any lecturer who for some reason could not make it to the meeting. The meetings took place in the building of *Talmud Torah*, which was in the same courtyard as the offices of *Agudat Tzion* , that of Elsztejn.

The subcommittee would also hold a memorial evening on the twentieth day of the month of Tammuz[37], or a show an exhibit on the holidays: the intermediate days of Sukkoth, the intermediate days of Passover, Hanukah, Purim, and Lag B'Omer. The arrival of a lecturer sent by the central committee, an author or artist who came from Warsaw, would be managed by the culture subcommittee. It would prepare and arrange the lecture or the festivity, and order pamphlets from the central committee and distribute them (for a fee) among the members.

The Balfour Declaration[38] was announced on November 2, 1917. This news was announced in Poland, under German occupation, without the enthusiasm and publicity that accompanied it in the countries that were allied with England. In spite of this, the news of the Balfour Declaration brought joy and exhilaration to all the Jews of Poland, and especially the Zionists. *Agudat Tzion* held two festive meetings in Sierpc in honor of the event: in the synagogue and in the movie theater. The speakers in the synagogue were Azrieltia Podskocz, Mordecai Hirsch Mintz and Avraham Yerushalmi (Fried). The speakers in the movie theater were: Mordecai Hirsch Mintz, Avraham Yerushalmi (Fried) and Yeshayahu Friedman. In both meetings, the speakers talked about the historical importance of the event: the announcement by a great power of a Jewish homeland in the Land of Israel, a declaration that was made because of the political activity and actions of the Zionist movement, and which will become, if we know how to take advantage of it, the beginning of our liberation. Both meetings were held in a festive atmosphere, with a large audience, and ended with the singing of *HaTikvah.*[39]

*

The Jewish National Fund (JNF [or *Keren Kayemet*]) committee would collect money for the fund at every suitable occasion. They would collect money in pairs (two boys or two girls) from stores during school holidays, at weddings, distributing and emptying the blue *Keren Kayemet* boxes, selling *Keren Kayemet* stamps, placing collection bowls in prayer houses on Yom Kippur eve, Purim, and other occasions. In order that not even a penny of Jewish National Fund moneys would be spent for anything other than their intended purpose, the expenses of sending the money to the Warsaw center (there were no collection expenses) were paid for by *Agudat Tzion* . The JNF committee also sold shekalim[40] during the month of Nissan. Members, in pairs, would fan out all over town, visiting stores and apartments, trying to convince all the Jews to buy shekalim.

My partner in selling shekalim was Shmerel (Shmaryahu) Hazan of blessed memory (drowned in the month of Tammuz 5686 {1926} in the sea near Tel-Aviv, when trying to save some people from drowning). Our area was a section of the Jewish Street. Beryl "Shmatcharz" (a rag dealer) lived on the top floor of the house of Zisa Mirel Nipomoscz. The way up to the top floor was very difficult, the stairs being more like a ladder than stairs. When we saw the state that the house was in, we were sure that there was no chance of selling a shekel, and wanted to go on to the next house. But the landlady said to come up, so we did, and we weren't sorry. The "Schmatzerkan" (her name was Devorah Rechel), when she heard we had come to sell her a shekel, welcomed us joyfully. She gave us an enthusiastic "speech" about how Zionism will liberate the Jews from exile and from all their problems and make the Jewish nation equal to all the nations, and the shortsightedness and foolishness of those Jews that do not support Zionism. Surprised and deeply gratified, we stood and listened to her "speech." We gave her the shekel and took the money, and very carefully went down the stairs, with the "Schmatzerkan" accompanying us with blessings and compliments for us and for the whole Zionist movement. Encouraged by her enthusiastic words, we continued with our task with greater determination and energy.

*

The political subcommittee was a sort of "foreign office" of *Agudat Tzion* . Its functions were dealings with other parties in town, relations with the Jewish community, contacts with the authorities (concerning permits for meetings, festivities, and exhibits), election matters, and so forth.

In those days, there was no defined authority for the Sierpc community. Of the prewar community board, some members had resigned, some left town, and only the chairman, Nahum Tatz, was left. The occupation authorities established a community council and appointed two members to it from each party, society, and house of worship. The council only had advisory status; the decision making power was exercised solely by its elected chairman Nahum Tatz. The representatives of *Agudat Tzion* in the council were the chairman of the political subcommittee Avraham Yerushalmi (Fried) and the subcommittee member Yeshayahu Friedman.

*

It was customary in the Diaspora for the leaders and elders of the town to collect money before Passover to provide the means for the poor people to celebrate the holiday. This appeal was called *maot hittin* [small coins] or *kimchee DePascha* [flour of Passover]. And in spite of our brothers, the children of Israel, being the most compassionate and generous contributors to charities and all causes, the collection of money was always tough and unpleasant work. So the appeal for *maot hittin* would run into problems every year.

Avraham Fried (Yerushalmi) once suggested, as a member of the community council, to cancel the *maot hittin* appeal. In its place, he proposed that the community council should bake matzos for all the Jews of the town. It would then sell the matzos from the community center to everyone according to his capability to pay. The rich will pay the most, the less fortunate will pay little, and the poorest will receive the matzos at no cost. The profits from the sale of matzos will go to *maot hittin*. The proposal was accepted. The community baked the matzos, and sold them from the community center at progressive rates. The member Yerushalmi was designated as the seller of the matzos. He established order and discipline in the matzo sales. He would not allow anyone to touch them in order to choose better-looking matzos. Only his assistants could handle them: weigh them, wrap them, and give them to each buyer in turn.

Among those who bought matzos was Avraham Glazer, a well-respected Jew and member of the community council. He didn't ask any questions, but went to the head of the line and started picking matzos for himself, nice ones and bright ones, thin and without any creases. Comrade Yerushalmi did not interfere, waited until he had finished and then took them and handed them over to a poor Jew who was waiting in line. Obviously this greatly annoyed Avraham Glazer, and he left without taking any matzos, after giving Yerushalmi a piece of his mind.

The next morning, the chairman of the council, Nahum Tatz, reproached Yerushalmi for his abrupt manner towards a respected Jew and a member of the council. Yerushalmi replied that Avraham Glazer had readied enough wine, eggs, oil, fish, meat potatoes, and sweets for Passover, and he and his family would not need matzos. On the other hand, the poor Jew who received the matzos cannot afford to buy all of those staples, so that he and his family will need the matzos more than the Glazer family. So why shouldn't he get good, nice and thin matzos?

One winter, there was a lot of snow, which melted in the spring. The rivers overflowed, and it was impossible to get to the flour mill in the village of Bovorowa, where the flour intended for matzos was stored. The access to the mill became passable only a few days before Passover, so that they managed to mill only part of the wheat. The community baked the matzos, stored them in the community center, and distributed just a portion of its matzo needs to each family. The poor, who received their matzos from *maot hittin* also received only a part of their needs. On the intermediate days of Passover they milled the rest of the wheat, baked the matzos, and distributed the rest of the matzos to each family. The poor also received the rest of their needs.

*

The political subcommittee accomplished a great deal after Poland was liberated. As is known, the independence started with persecutions of the Jews. In some towns such as Lwow, Kielce, and others, there were very serious pogroms, resulting in loss of Jewish lives and property. But there were minor pogroms in almost every town in Poland. During that time, the Zionist Organization proposed to all the [Jewish] parties to establish a National Jewish Council which would be the sovereign and legal representative of Polish Jewry, and would protect its interests. According to the proposal, there would be elections in all of Poland for a committee of all Polish Jews, and the committee would choose a national council. As usual, there were negotiations between the parties, along with debates and arguments. This went on and on and the problems increased, and the need for representation and protection became greater. Therefore a provisional committee was set up, without elections, composed of the Zionist Organization, *Tzeirei Tzion*, *Mizrachi*, and the communities. (Understandably, the communities that participated were only those which had a majority of Zionist parties.) It chose a "Temporary National Jewish Council. (The Sierpc delegate to the provisional committee was Avraham Shlomo Glazer, the representative of the community.) The council was headed by Y. Grinbaum and A. Hertglas. They handled all the complaints and requests for aid that came to the Temporary Council from all cities and towns. These came from Jews that suffered from large and small pogroms perpetrated by hooligans from the rabble or from the army. They would pass all these painful topics on to the higher authorities, and demanded protection for the Jews and their property,

In addition to protecting the Jews and their property, the Temporary Council also defended the rights of the Jews as a national minority in Poland. This included community rights, the situation of the Jewish schools, the right of Jews to keep their stores open on Sundays, etc.[41]

Sierpc too experienced outbreaks and attacks on a few Jews and the snatching of goods from their stores. These were not pogroms in the accepted sense of the word, but the misery of the Jews never stopped for even a day. Complaints to the police on these matters were of no use. A Jew who protested to the police about these matters would be met with ridicule, and would leave the police station disappointed and humiliated. The Jews knew that in place of the police there was an association that handled these matters and maintained respect for the Jews and for their belongings. This was *Agudat Tzion* . The political subcommittee documented all the incidents that occurred. They would record the words of the complainants (the note takers were: the secretary of the subcommittee, Zvi Malowanczyk, and a member, the author of these lines) with all details of the incident, and send the minutes, with their signatures to the Temporary Jewish National Council. These were handed over to the Interior Ministry and from there they arrived, through a number of conduits, to the Sierpc police with instructions to investigate the matter. When the investigation was begun a number of months after the incident, there were no results. However they caused no end of headaches and unpleasantness for the police, and to prevent this they were forced to keep the peace in town more effectively.

*

The political subcommittee of *Agudat Tzion* carried out an important activity during the elections for the first Polish *sejm* (parliament) in September 1919. There was an energetic campaign for the Temporary National Jewish Council. The representatives of the subcommittee spoke in all the prayer houses for this list.

There was a lot to get done in the office of *Agudat Tzion* on the evening before the elections. All the members were called to the office that evening. The town was divided into districts, and a pair of members (two boys or two girls) was assigned a district. The task of each pair was to go next day from house to house in the district, visit every apartment, basement and attic to remind everyone that today is "a day of destiny," election day. The occupants would be asked to get to the polling place early and given a slip of paper with the symbol of the National Council on it, and to beware of using a different symbol when voting.

My partner was Shmerel (Shmaryahu) Hazan of blessed memory, and our district consisted of the "Kamnitza" (a large walled house), the streets called *Kartoffel mit Ferfel Gesselech* ("Potatoes and Dough Crumbs Alleys"), an area of very poor people. We reached our district very early since our instruction was to reach the voters at an early hour to find them when they were still at home. We knocked on the first doors and woke up the occupants. They opened their doors, and when they found out why we were there they welcomed us and invited us in.

I still remember the conditions in many of the apartments. Small and stuffy rooms with low ceilings, no circulation of air inside. The rooms were crammed with old beds and shabby furniture. Almost all the floor was covered with raggedy bedding, with disheveled heads of hair peeping out curiously and sleepily from under piles of old clothes and raggedy blankets. The darkness of the room, because of the early hour, added to the general gloom and completed this picture of extreme poverty. Those pictures of destitution that I saw then left a deep impression on me and were imprinted in my mind and my heart.

*

I mentioned earlier that the same courtyard that contained the office of *Agudat Tzion* , that of Moshe Elsztejn, also contained the *Talmud Torah* school. The school was in the long building in the middle of the courtyard[42]. The *Talmud Torah* in Sierpc, as in all towns, was a community institution. But because the institution was founded at the initiative of Avraham Fried (Yerushalmi) and because of his devoted efforts for the school, it was effectively under the supervision of *Agudat Tzion* . Therefore, *Agudat Tzion* was able to use the *Talmud Torah* auditorium when necessary.

Agudat Tzion once showed a movie, the proceeds of which were dedicated to providing clothing and shoes for the children of the *Talmud Torah.* The author of these lines paid the suppliers for the merchandise, according to instructions from Avraham Fried (Yerushalmi). I pasted a Jewish National

Fund stamp on every receipt, and deducted its cost from the payment. It should be noted that no supplier protested.

As part of the aid given to the *Talmud Torah* by *Agudat Tzion* , Zvi Malowanczyk provided the students there with exercise lessons.

*

Yaakov Bachrach, the secretary of *Agudat Tzion* , was among the few in town, and almost the only one among the youth who had ever been to a foreign country. He returned to Sierpc after having lived in France for a few years. He had been touring with Shmuel Szampan, who had also been to Belgium and Palestine and returned to Sierpc. The young people admired them and were jealous of them, and considered them authorities on any matters concerning far away countries, other peoples, and social problems. In the end, they both returned to France, where Szampan died a few years later.

iv. "The Breachers of the Fence"

My friend Itzik Zilberberg (Y. M. Simchoni) and the author of these lines were the first of the boys from the *shtibl* and *beit midrash* to join *Agudat Tzion* . Being a Zionist then was considered heresy, so despite that in our hearts we were enthusiastic Zionists, it was difficult for us to make it public and become members of *Agudat Tzion* . We knew that when this step became common knowledge, it would cause a severe reaction, and we wanted to avoid this. Therefore, we looked for a way to register as members of *Agudat Tzion* when there would be no superfluous people in the office. To do this, we hung around for many nights near the window to the office and across the street, on the sidewalk in front of Aaron Tcharnotchepka's house. Unfortunately, the curtain along the lower half of the window hid the inside of the office from us, so we tried to get a peek from above and from the sides. We wanted to see what was going on in the little room that seemed like a mysterious and holy place to us. It was a place where things were happening that would fulfill our highest aspirations, to redeem the Land of Israel and liberate the people of Israel.

One evening, when we thought there were no extra people in the office, we plucked up our courage, and went in. As soon as we opened the door, we knew we were mistaken. In addition to the secretary Yaakov Bachrach, the chairman Avraham Fried (Yerushalmi) and the committee member Yisrael Yaakov Cohen were sitting in the corner. Since it was impossible to just leave, we entered, walked over to the table, and stated our request. Our appearance apparently surprised those present, so they asked us some questions about the status of Zionism in our circles and about the steps we were about to take. We answered that for the time being we were alone among our crowd, and we were sure that this move would cause consternation among the youth of the *shtibl* and *beit midrash*, and cause us some unpleasantness, but that were firm in wanting to do this. In the meantime, the secretary registered us in the membership book, and gave us the "membership card." This was a small, thin, and good looking notebook, with a nice looking rubber stamp in the shape of a Star of David as if attached to the page by six rivets. Inside were the words "Certificate Number 118," signed by the chairman Avraham Fried and the secretary Yaakov Bachrach. A nice, pleasant, and cherished notebook. This happened on the 27th of Nissan 5677 (19 April 1917). The chairman asked us if we would also participate in the procession that *Agudat Tzion* was planning for Lag B'Omer together with Maccabee. We answered that two such revolutionary steps within such a short time were too much for us. We left the office happy and recognizing that we had started on a new path in life, the right one. The road for every young Jew who is loyal to his people and his land.

They say that the walls have ears. The rumor about the "evil deed" that these two boys had done, the "breaching of the fence," started a series of denunciations of us. Neither I nor my friend was studying then in the *beit midrash*, but we came there every day to pray. We had to stand there every day, near the bookshelves between the stove and the door to the courtyard. We were the few against the many, and had to stand up to the bitter attacks and arguments about the "Zionist religion" that were aimed at us by many boys our age. We argued for many hours every day until we were hoarse, and even though we were a minority, we manage to repulse the attacks and leave the battlefield each day in one piece.

Obviously, the matter became known at home instantly. The informer added his own personal touch and stated that we had also joined Maccabee. But there was no opposition at home to our act. On the contrary, it was apparent that my mother and sister were proud that I was a Zionist.

v. Mizrachi

Reb Sander Tkorzh, the shochet [kosher ritual slaughterer and inspector] from Vlotzlabek (and father of Rabbi Tkorzh) came to Sierpc in the summer of 5677 (1917). He came for the express purpose of founding a branch of the *Mizrachi* [Religious Zionist] Organization. We saw him as a marvel and an innovator: a very religious Jew in all his manners and customs, and in addition a *shochet*, and not just a member of *Mizrachi*, but an organizer and proselytizer for the movement! If there weren't yet any *Mizrachi* in Sierpc, we all knew who the candidates for membership were. Most of them were people who had strayed a little from tradition, whether by a change in their garments, or by shaving their beards, or both, and by their general behavior. The *shochet* Tkorzh gave an enthusiastic speech on Zionism and religion in the new *beit midrash*, and *Mizrachi* was established in Sierpc.

The chief founder of *Mizrachi* in Sierpc and only activist was Isaac Neiman. He prayed in the Alexander *shtibl*, but he was not a fervent Hasid. However, he was a fervent *Mizrachi* member. He was the chairman and the only one who bore the yoke. The members who signed onto *Mizrachi* were the veteran Zionists such as Mordechai Hirsch Mintz, Azrieltia Podskocz, and others who were not comfortable with *Agudat Tzion* , and various men of means who prayed in the *beit midrash* or synagogue. Among the worshippers in the *shtibls*, the only one who joined, if I remember correctly, was the chairman, Isaac Neiman.

Mizrachi did not display an excess of activity. For an office, it rented a room in Isaac Kutner's new house, and arranged for a *minyan*[43] there on Saturdays. Those called to read the Torah would pledge money to the Jewish National Fund, and after the prayers they would sing *Adon Olam*[44] to the melody of *HaTikvah*. This was almost all of their Zionist activities. The *minyan* too assembled with difficulty until they started sending invitations to members to come pray next Saturday at *Mizrachi*. (Meir Malin, who was a member, came frequently, because he liked to lead the prayer - he had a nice voice - and there he could always find an opportunity.) *Mizrachi* had a few younger members, and on the appropriate occasions they would collect small sums for the Jewish National Fund.

At the urging of Mordechai Hirsch Mintz, the young members of *Mizrachi* founded a group called Sons of the Prophets. The purpose of the group was to practice giving speeches. We would assemble every Saturday in the *Mizrachi* office and a member of the group would give a speech on a Zionist, social, or historic topic. The members of the group that I remember were Itzik Zilberberg, Livieh Serena, Avraham Kutner, Gutkind Renkel, and I. Because we were embarrassed and didn't want our practice sessions to be public, we locked the door. At the end of the speech, before people came for the afternoon service, we unlocked it. Once, while someone was speaking, we heard a knock on the door. We made believe we hadn't heard a thing, and didn't open it. When the knocking resumed, we opened the door, and found Shlomo Lubaszka standing in front of us. He came in and said in his mild tone, "You're probably smoking cigarettes here, and that's why you locked the door." I must admit that no famous orator ever emerged from this group.

*

A short time after *Mizrachi* was founded, a "preacher" (a "modern" interpreter of text) came to Sierpc. The local branch arranged for his sermon to be given at the new *beit midrash*. (Usually, the visitors would speak at the old beit midrash.) The substance of the sermon was religion and Zionism. By using references in the Bible and in the maxims of our sages of blessed memory, he proved not only that Zionism and settlement of the land of Israel were permitted, but that their enactment was a great commandment and an obligation for every Jew.

vi. Hebrew

As the Zionist ideal deepened and Zionist organizations were established in all the cities and towns, the ambition to learn the Hebrew language became keener. Hebrew lessons were instituted everywhere, either by the local Zionist organization, or at the initiative of the students themselves. The young people studied the language in groups or in private lessons.

The aspiration to learn Hebrew came to Sierpc, and became a fashion that encompassed almost all the youth. There were evening lessons given by the teacher Mordechai Hirsch Mintz. Many young people took private lessons from the teachers Mintz and Cohen.

*

We were a group of four students who learned Hebrew and general subjects with Mordechai Hirsch Mintz. We would learn three days a week, two hours a day. The others in our group were Shepsel Visroza, Binem Lanczner, and Moshia Nipomoszcz. The pupils who went to the school of the teacher Mintz and were educated by him are better equipped to talk about him, but I must recount the great marvel that I witnessed. I personally heard the teacher Mintz talking to his son Shimon (now in America) only in Hebrew! (Remember, this was in Sierpc in 1916!) There was a story that there was an agreement between father and son that for every word that the son would say to his father that was not in Hebrew, he would have to pay a fine.

There was one more father in Sierpc who spoke to his son only in Hebrew, and that was Shmuel Yehudah Balt, the son of Meir Oved. Also the two friends, Shimon Mintz and Naftali Balt, spoke only Hebrew between themselves.

After a while, our group went to Yisrael Yaakov Cohen to learn Hebrew, and Itzik Zilberberg joined us. Teacher Cohen's style was lively and quick, appropriate for older students, whereas Mintz's teaching style was more gradual, better suited to younger pupils.

vii. Maccabee

At that same time, the idea of a new activity infiltrated minds of the Jewish youth - that of athletics. Exercise and sports, which were as far from Jewish life as east is from west, became a preoccupation of Jewish youth all over Poland. There was an athletic association founded in almost every town and village. All of them were called “Maccabee” and they were distinctly Zionist organizations. The Maccabee organizations, with their double purpose, sports and Zionism, inspired young Jewish people. It strengthened and invigorated them and gained them respect from the Gentiles. Sport then was limited to gymnastics and soccer but was still unknown in Jewish circles. The coaches and trainers in all the towns were German soldiers.

The Society for Exercise and Sport Maccabee was founded in Sierpc in the month of Nissan 5677 (1917). In Sierpc too, the coach was a German soldier, and the practice field was the *Manazh* (the field used by the Russian cavalry battalion once assigned to Sierpc, at the end of Plotzki Street). The first public appearance of Maccabee (as it was called for short) was about a month after its founding, on Lag B'Omer, before it really had a chance to practice and train sufficiently. *Agudat Tzion* and Maccabee staged a joint procession through town and a hike outside of town for the whole day. The hatter Moshe Gongola had hardly enough time to prepare hats for Maccabee (a gray hat with a blue and white hatband and a shiny black visor) and the female members of the *Agudat Tzion* committee barely finished preparing the Maccabee flag (blue and white with the Star of David, and the word "Maccabee" inside).

The men of Maccabee strode in straight lines, four to a row, with the flag carrier at the front holding the big, new, beautiful flag. After them came the members of *Agudat Tzion* , also in straight lines, four to a row. Beside them strode the chairman, Avraham Fried (Yerushalmi) wearing his Sabbath coat, and on its lapel was a large streamer with two ribbons, one white and one blue, that reached to his knees and fluttered in the wind. Fried was the commander and inspector of the procession. The parade passed the Jewish Street, the market, and Plotzki Street, and then continued out of town. From there they went to the woods of Lavondzh, where they spent the day playing games, singing, and dancing.

Maccabee may have been a new and untrained creature, but it made a great impression on the youth and on every Jew that had any nationalist feelings in his heart. The Gentiles too watched the procession, with the flag and the muscular young men marching, with awe. The parade was exactly one week after the 3rd of May, the Polish national holiday, when there was a grandiose procession in Sierpc, with many participants, and accompanied by the firefighters' band. The Jews then looked on with envy at that parade, at the freedom of the Poles and their nationalistic feelings and unity. Our procession, though it was small and meager compared to the 3rd of May parade, nonetheless compensated somewhat for the longing of the Jews for a crumb of freedom and a public appearance of the national identity.

Maccabee also made a great impression on the twentieth day of the month of Tammuz at the memorial service for Herzl at the synagogue. They came to the synagogue in a procession with the flag in the lead. They arranged themselves in the synagogue in two lines, on both sides of the platform, from the entrance to the Holy Ark, with the flag carrier and his partners standing between the Ark and the platform, facing the platform. During the speeches by Avraham Fried (who opened the service), Azrieltia Podskocz, and the teacher Mordechai Hirsch Mintz, and during the prayer *El Malei Rachamim* ["God Full of Pity"], the Maccabee members stood quietly and listened. When the time came to sing *HaTikvah*, they stood at attention. Their quiet and orderly demeanor and the presence of the national flag added color to the memorial service for Dr. Herzl, the national leader.

Also impressive were the ceremonies connected with bringing out and putting away the flag. (The flag was kept at the Mintz School.) The Maccabee members, standing in two rows, would stand at attention and sing *HaTikvah.* The flag carrier and his partner would leave the line, take the flag out of the school or take it into the school, come back to their places, finish singing, and then the procession would disperse.

*

The Maccabee of Lipno came to visit Sierpc that summer. The visit turned into a great holiday for the Jewish youth of Sierpc. The local Maccabee went to the outskirts of town to receive the guest Maccabee. The two groups went back through town with their flags and a small brass band with a group of motorcycle riders with sidecars carrying the equipment (" *ovoz*") of the visiting society. They passed the new market, Zhava (Zhavia) Street, the market, and Plotzki Street, to the courtyard of Moshe Hirsch Kotcholak, which had been designated as the encampment place of the guest society (the guests were lodged in private homes). It was a wonderful sight that lifted the spirits of the young people, and not just the young people.

The next day, the visitors displayed their achievements in gymnastics. In the afternoon, some of the motorcyclists rode through town, with small national flags on the handlebars, and bugles hung around their necks. They would blow short blasts on their bugles to muster their members. They lined up at the encampment and from there they went to the exhibition place, which was in one of the lumberyards of the new market. All the young people and many of their elders streamed there to see the show of gymnastics. And it was worthwhile watching. The guests showed us some very nice exercises. They displayed very good training, with a great deal of agility and precision. A number of groups showed off their accomplishments, and all of them played their parts well. But the best exercises were performed by the select team. This group showed us drills that we thought were miraculous. The show ended with a huge and beautiful pyramid.

The next day the guests returned to their town. Again the two societies passed through the town with their flags and all the equipment of the visiting society. The local Maccabee accompanied the guests to the outskirts of town, and there they parted.

It is difficult to describe the great impression that the visitors from Lipno made on the residents of the town, young and old, Jew and Gentile. Their proud and pleasing appearance, their gallant and orderly stride, and their sublime and splendid exercises stirred all of us. Both the young people and a great many of the grownups - that part that looked forward to the rebirth and renewal of the nation - were delighted with these young men, men who realized and could display their promise. The Gentiles also observed them with regard and respect, and called them " *Zydowski wojsko*" (the Jewish Army). The term " *der Lipner Maccabee*" (the Maccabee from Lipno) became a household expression among us, signifying beauty, order, courage and capability. We remembered their performance for a long time.

When they marched through the streets of the town, the visitors sang various songs, and between songs, the small band would display its capabilities. One of the songs that they played was *Nes Tziona*[45] with a melody different from the one we used when we sang it in Sierpc. The new melody quickly spread throughout the town, and was called " *der Lipner Nes Tziona*" (the Lipno *Nes Tziona*).

viii. *Aliyah, Hehalutz,* Training

For weeks and months after the end of the First World War, insecurity and disarray were widespread all over the world, and travelling by road was dangerous. Gangs of deserters, ex-soldiers, and plain robbers would lie in wait in forests and roads to rob and kill travelers. In spite of this, an undertaking for *aliyah*[46] to the Land of Israel began, the start of the Third *Aliyah*. Groups of young people from Ukraine and Russia immigrated using chaotic and dangerous roads, and by sea. Not a few of them were lost on these harsh voyages.

There was a restlessness and desire for *aliyah* among the young people in Poland as well. The Zionist youth in Rypin sent a representative to the Zionist youth in Sierpc about *aliyah*. A restricted meeting was arranged in the Mintz School. The representative gave a talk and told us about groups of young people in various towns that were planning *aliyah*. He told us that a group from Będzin had already left (incidentally, the Będzin group was among the first of the Third *Aliyah*) and a group from Rypin that was ready to go but was delayed because of rumors of strikes on the Polish and Czechoslovak railways. He talked about an emissary that that would be sent to scout the way to the Czechoslovak border, and after his return, a decision would be made on what to do next. His purpose in coming to us was: a) organize a youth group for *aliyah*; b) get our participation in scouting the border with our emissary; and c) general cooperation between our two groups to ease somewhat the many difficult problems involved in accomplishing our aims.

Those present decided on the spot to organize an *aliyah* group and cooperate with the Rypin group. Participation in scouting the way to the border was also agreed upon. Also discussed was the necessity of getting assurances from the emissaries that when they reached the border, they would not cross it, but return and report on road conditions. To pay for the expenses of the joint operation, everyone contributed two Marks.

In order to prepare the way for this revolutionary step, I informed my family slowly and with half-truths, until the entire secret was revealed: that I was a member of a group planning to go to Palestine. The news caused agitation and sorrow at home. My mother and sister tried to persuade me to change my mind, because of my young age, my lack of experience at working and earning a living, and the suffering that I might cause.

In the meantime, the situation on the roads got worse. The railway strikes increased and spread and nothing came of our grand plans.

The meeting took place one or two months after the end of the war (December 1918 or January 1919). There were about fifteen participants. I can remember the following: Avraham Fried (Yerushalmi), Yeshayahu Friedman, Leib Mintz, Y. M. Zilberberg (Simchoni), and the author of these lines.

*

A short time later, the *Hehalutz* [The Pioneer] organization was founded in Poland. The main office was in Warsaw, and branches were opened in various cities. The purpose of *Hehalutz* was not immediate *aliyah*, but *aliyah* after a training period. All members of *Hehalutz* were supposed to prepare themselves for working at one of the vocations that were required in the Land of Israel, usually in agriculture. It was also necessary to get a working knowledge of the Hebrew language. Only then could the member obtain permission for *aliyah* from the main office.

A branch of *Hehalutz* was founded in Sierpc as well. At a restricted meeting of about twenty members at the offices of *Agudat Tzion*, the chairman, Avraham Fried (Yerushalmi), read a letter from the main office of *Hehalutz* in Warsaw. The letter contained the first directives for founding a branch in Sierpc, and especially for filling out a questionnaire that should be sent back to Warsaw. The questions were about the name of the member, gender, age, education, occupation, and which training vocation would be chosen. On the choice of vocation, almost everyone answered agriculture, the most necessary occupation in Palestine.

Only two of those present did not choose agriculture. One of them, Yitzhak Zomer (was in Palestine for a few years, then went to America in 1933) said that agricultural training is a very difficult proposition: one has to leave the town for the countryside. Leave your parents' home for a house or barn on a Polish farm. It means changing all your habits and way of life, along with problems in supporting yourself that you won't know how to solve. His opinion was that it's better to learn metalworking. This is a very necessary occupation in a country that's starting to be built. And this vocation can be learned in town, with a Polish blacksmith, and the products made can be used to pay for tuition without any difficulty.

But we decided to start agricultural training. However, there was no one among us with the initiative to find a place to train, so nothing came of our grand plan. The Sierpc branch of *Hehalutz* died before it had a chance to live. The participants of that meeting that I can still remember are Avraham Fried (Yerushalmi), Yitzhak Zomer, Hezhe (Zvi) Malowanczyk, and I.

*

There was an attempt at agricultural training, without any connection to the above decision, by a small group of members.

About five kilometers from Sierpc, on the road to Drobin (Drubnin) there was a Jewish farm that belonged to four brothers and a sister, all single and well into marriageable age. One of the brothers had been to Palestine and had returned before the war. Itzik Zilberberg (Y. M. Simchoni), Shmerel Hazan, Moshe Fogel, Gutkind Renkel, and I went to this farm on the first day after the Passover holiday in the year 5679 (1919). We wanted to learn farming. We told the owners of our objective, and they agreed to our proposal and promised to teach us all the tasks so that we would be expert at them. We agreed among ourselves to return home to prepare work clothes for farming (during the war and afterwards, it became customary to use work clothes made out of the material of burlap bags) and then return to the village to work. They showed us around the farm and explained various things about farm work, and then invited us in for a midday meal. We ate a tasty and excellent meal of potatoes and sour sorrel soup. After spending a few hours at the farm, we went home.

But this attempt did not lead to anything either. Whether because we lacked the nerve, or for some other reason, this plan ended like the other ones. At least Shmerel Hazan and Moshe Fogel worked for two or three days at the farm, but they never continued.

b. Education and Culture

i. Education

When the Germans came to Poland during the First World War, it was as if a new spirit had come to the country, a taste of Western Europe. A spirit of enlightenment and education entered the dwelling places of Israel. This spirit brought about deviations, if small ones, from the accepted customs and truths, and brought about changes in values in many fields.

There was a great change in the field of education. (We are talking about the *Haredi* [extremely pious] education that was learned by ninety per cent of Jewish children.) The *heder*, that ancient and widespread institution that educated millions of Jewish children, that instilled in them Torah and morality, and brought them up to live the traditional Jewish life, almost entirely disappeared. Because of the requirements of the authorities for improvements in the hygienic conditions at places of learning, and the "new spirit" that encompassed the Jewish community, *Haredi* educational institutions called " *Yesodai HaTorah*" [Foundations of the Torah] were founded in all the towns' of Poland. Out of habit and because of a wish to maintain the traditional name, they were popularly called "*hederYesodai HaTorah*." But in actuality, these were an obvious copy of modern schools, with classes, a principal, a secretary, an office, exams, and grades. In addition to Gemara, exegesis by Rashi, and commentaries, a number of hours a day were devoted to secular subjects. There were also Poles among the teachers.

Sierpc also had a *Yesodai HaTorah* school. It was in Litvinski's house, across from the synagogue. Perhaps one or two *heders* , small and illegal, were left in town in their former condition. Except for these, they were all swallowed up by *Yesodai HaTorah* and the *melameds* of the *heders* became *melameds* in the classes of *Yesodai HaTorah*. The institution was run by a committee, which decided on the curriculum, and accepted the pupils. It collected tuition and paid wages to the principal, the secretary, the *melameds* and the teachers, and was responsible for all the expenses of the institution.

The principal of *Yesodai HaTorah* of Sierpc was Eliyahu Meir Schleifer, the son-in-law of Chayim Shochet (Bergson, formerly a ritual slaughterer). Schleifer, who came from Drobin, was a learned Yeshiva student, and had been ordained as a ritual slaughterer. It was generally accepted that a ritual slaughterer in town should also be a cantor, but this Yeshiva student had a wooden voice, unpleasant, that grated on the ears. He tried, from time to time, to stand before the ark in the *shtibl* of Alexander, and pray, perhaps thinking that maybe this time a clear and pleasant tone might emerge from his throat? But it never happened, and the worshippers laughed when he sat down. Some jokers said that he had a stick jammed in his throat, and because he couldn't succeed as a cantor he never tried to apply as a ritual slaughterer and inspector in any town or village. He remained in Sierpc with the "ordination" in his pocket and made his living from a store that sold readymade items which was at the start of the Jewish Street, in the same house as the drugstore.

The *Yesodai HaTorah* institutions were under the influence of *Agudat Israel*, which was associated with the courtyard of the Rabbi of Gur. The Alexander Hasidim sent their children to the school, since there was no other alternative, but they were unhappy about the arrangement, which increased the stature of Gur.

One of the most active functionaries of *Yesodai HaTorah* in Sierpc was Yudel Rabbinowicz, who was the secretary of the institution. He was a native of Sierpc, but he had lived for many years in Lodz, and during the war, when there was hardship and hunger in the big cities, he returned to Sierpc. He had many relatives in town (the families Sendrowicz and Yeshaievitz). He was a Hasid of Alexander, and the other Hasidim in the *shtibl* were offended by his activities for *Yesodai HaTorah*.

*

All the changes and transformations brought something new to town. A Polish progymnasium was opened and a few parents (Tzadok Bluman, the brothers Yaakov (Yukev) and Avraham Valuka, Zelig Minchin, Mordechai Hirsch Mintz, Yaakov Maniamchevka, Avraham Podskocz, Matityahu (Matat) Przasnyszski, Esther Rachel Szampan, and others) sent their sons to study there, even though they were obliged to attend on Saturday (though they were exempt from writing on Saturday). Something like that would not have happened in Sierpc before the war.[47]

A number of the "bourgeoisie" (not Hasidim; worshippers in the *beit midrash* and the synagogue) started during that time to clip their beards and shorten their coats and also replace their traditional hats with flat European hats. (I remember Avraham Bluman, Kalman Brenner, Nachman Horowitz, Kalman Kalmanowicz, and others.) One time Lipaia (Lipa Naselski, a Jew who enjoyed telling jokes and entertaining people) asked Nachman Horowitz "Tell me Nachman, how much did you pay for that frying pan?" (He was referring to the flat hat.)

Many of the young people then started walking around outside bareheaded. The change came gradually, in two stages. First they went bareheaded, but held a hat in their hands. After they had grown accustomed to the first stage, they went on to the next step: they went outside without any hat at all.

ii. Culture

There were also immense developments in the area of culture in Poland during that period, that of the First World War. Libraries were opened in all the cities and towns, or already existing libraries were renewed or expanded. In the small towns there was a single general library that served all the young people, without any association with political parties. In the cities each party had its own library. During that period, when political parties developed, many general libraries split up into political libraries. Obviously, these schisms caused great cultural damage. A library that had great significance as a single institution lost all value when it was turned into a few tiny libraries.

A drama club that was associated with the library was founded in every town. From time to time, the club would present a play, either all on its own, or with the help of an actor (understandably, of the second or third rank) that was invited from a large city. The income from the presentation would be for the benefit of the library. A successful show would be presented in the surrounding towns as well, and if the income did not increase appreciably, at least the prestige did. A play with visiting actors would make the local youth envious, and such envy increased the number of times the play was presented. Sometimes the town would host a visiting troupe of professional actors that would present a number of plays. Like the libraries, the drama clubs would be united in the towns and divided, according to political parties, in the cities.

The libraries or the parties would from time to time invite lecturers from the large cities. They would talk about various subjects: literary, historical, social, or partisan.

There was a library in Sierpc before the war. Then, there were no official political parties or societies in town, and the library served as the single center of cultural and social life. All the progressive youth in town were there, of all classes and persuasions.

During the period of the German occupation, the library was in the alley behind the house of Aaron Tcharnotchepka (Chalpin Street). There were already political parties in town, but just one library. Because most of its members were Zionist, the committee was composed of Zionists. From time to time, the library would hold question and answer evenings (*kestel ovent*), parties, and exhibitions, and the income was dedicated to buying books.

Young men from Hasidic homes also started reading secular books then. Most of them didn't come to the library themselves, or join as members. They took books to read from their sisters, or from their friends' sisters, or from others. Few had the nerve to come to the library, register as members, and take out books for themselves.

This book contains a photograph of a library card, made out to the author of these lines, and signed by Yossel Goldman, who was then the regular librarian. A previous library card was signed by Rasha Farkal (grew up in the house of Binyamin Sobol, now in America), a volunteer librarian.

The library also served as a meeting place for friends. It was said that one girl, who wanted to meet with Yeshayahu Friedman, who was the librarian for a time (before the war), would come to the library every day to exchange books. Some clowns noticed this, and started to ask her about the contents of the book she was returning. Of course, she couldn't answer, and with that her daily visits to the library stopped, as well as her daily meetings.

Among the young men that came to the library were those that out of respect for their father would go the *shtibl* on Saturday to pray. The Hasidim did not care for this very much, and once, before the reading of the Torah, Yehonatan Lipchitz (in the Gur *shtibl*) pounded on the table and announced, " *Di Iden vos geien in di lebetik aran, zoln nisht geien shtibl aran; in di Iden vos geien in shtibl aran zoln nisht geien in di lebetik aran*" ("Those going to the library, don't come to the *shtibl*, and those coming to the shtibl, don't go to the library").

From time to time lecturers visited Sierpc, invited by the library or one of the political parties in town, or were sent by one of party offices in Warsaw. Not just literary talks, but political speeches. Youth from different circles would attend. Members of the rival parties would ask questions, argue, and try to contradict the lecturer. He would answer his hecklers, and try of course to prove his points. Sometimes the discussions would be conducted quietly, and sometimes with interruptions, shouts, and very lively spirits. These were always interesting and instructive evenings,

*

In this section "Chapters of Memories" I have recorded my memoirs of Sierpc (Sheps), until the end of the First World War. This was also the end of the Russian and German occupation of Poland, and the start of a new era - independent Poland.

With the beginning of the revival of Poland, skirmishes began between the Polish army and Ukrainian irregular forces and revolutionaries. These skirmishes became a war between Poland and Bolshevik Russia. The draft of youth for the army and war then began. With my conscription into the army, the period of Sierpc (Sheps) in my life ended.

Translator's Footnotes

1. A *melamed* was the teacher of little children in the *heder*, the one room school. As a courtesy he was called "Rabbi" but he was not necessarily an ordained rabbi.
2. The *Mikve* was the ritual bathhouse.
3. Rashi - the acronym used for Rabbi Shlomo Yitzhaki, an eleventh century Jewish sage.
4. The Gemara is that part of the Talmud that is analysis and commentary on the Mishna, which is itself a review and analysis of biblical commandments.
5. *Akdamut* is a song written in the eleventh century and is an introduction to the 10 commandments, sung in the synagogue on the first day of the Shavuot (Pentecost) holiday.
6. *Ephod* - vest; *Hoshen* - breastplate. Vestments worn by the high priest in the temple.
7. 33rd day of the Omer, the 49 days between the Passover and Shavuot holidays, a traditional day for picnics and camping outdoors.
8. These alleyways were called " *Kartoffel mit Ferfel Gesselech*" ("Potatoes and Dough Crumbs Alleys"). Most of the residents of these alleys were the poorest of the poor, and so was their food, from which these alleys got their name.
9. The ritual fringes that Orthodox Jews wear with their underwear.
10. Ritual prayer shawl.
11. The prayer recited on Saturday and holiday eves, or on festive occasions at the prayer house, sanctified with the blessing over a glass of wine.
12. Specially prepared matzo, in accordance with the very strictest ultra-orthodox standards.
13. A small prayer room of a Hasidic sect.
14. A Yiddish term, usually derogatory, which literally meant non-Jewish boy, but also applied in a more genial way to Jewish boys who were considered mischief makers. The plural is shkotzim.
15. *Nittel* is the 25th of December, the date of the birth of Jesus. (The origin of the word is the Latin " *Natale*" meaning birth.) The prohibition of studies is to prevent mentioning to his credit "that man" who studied Torah. Because of this prohibition, Hasidim and others would play cards on that evening. Yeshiva students and *beit midrash* students would play games with scraps of paper. The Jews in Russia and Russian Poland preferred the *Nittel* according to the Julian (Russian Orthodox) calendar over the Gregorian (Catholic) calendar. The preference of the Julian calendar was undoubtedly due to the influence of Russian rule. This night is called " *Bozche Narodziny*" (the birth of God) in Polish. In Yiddish we called it " *Baiz Gvoiren*" (the birth of bad). Probably called so in Yiddish because of the play of words *Bozche - Baiz.*
16. "For Michalitia, for a pair of houses"; a pun in Yiddish: " *heizier*" (houses) sounds like " *hoizen*" (pants).
17. Usually, a *heder* of little children had about 20 pupils, and a *heder* of older children (called "Gemara boys") had about 12 pupils.
18. " *Shechelech*" [jacks] is a game played with five stones (also with five nuts or five links from a chicken's throat), where you throw one or more up into the air, pick up the ones on the ground and then catch the ones in the air. The name " *shechelach*" probably comes from the word *sharelech* (graden - scratching, since some people pronounce the "r" sound as "ch"), since the stones on the ground are dragged one after another in order to pick them up all at once.
19. A neighborhood on the edge of Sierpc which was once a separate town, but later annexed to Sierpc.
20. In other *heders* the afternoon break was only one hour, but in this heder it was two hours, because the pupils went home only once a day.
21. " *Nach*" is the Hebrew acronym for the books of the Bible not including the Pentateuch - the books of the prophets ("Nvi'im") and the other writings (" *Ketuvim*"). The complete Old Testament is referred to in Hebrew as " *Tanach,*" the acronym for " *Torah, Nevi'im, Ketuvim.*"
22. In addition to the *heders* that I have mentioned above, there were other *heders* in Sierpc. The most important were: the *heder* of Rabbi Chayim Yosef (Crystal) that was at a level similar to that of Rabbi Michalitia, and the *heder* of Rabbi Avraham Aaron (Burstyn) that was at the same level as the

heder of Rabbi Moshia Karmelkeies.

23. Called *Tisha B'Av*, the day is a fast day in the Jewish calendar, to commemorate the destruction of the first and second temples.
24. About two years before the war, a German airplane made a forced landing near Sierpc. Many people went to see it, and the rumor spread that the plane had flown on a spy mission. The pilots were arrested for a while by the police, and then released.
25. It is now known that the Germans set a trap for the Russians. They allowed them to enter a region of Prussia that was heavily mined. After the army of General Samsonov went in there, one hundred thousand troops with all their equipment, they were all blown up by pressing one button. Only a few survivors were saved from this hell.
26. The bodies of two Jews were found in the vicinity of Sierpc, murdered by Russian soldiers. (We did not know who they were or where they came from, and they were buried in the cemetery near the fence.)
27. The Jews spoke Yiddish, which is a dialect of German with additions of Hebrew and other languages.
28. *Shomrim* (Guards in Hebrew) - an early quasi-military Zionist organization in Palestine set up to guard Jewish settlements.
29. Genesis, 7: 9
30. In 1912 there were elections in all of Russia for the Fourth Duma (Russian Parliament). The Polish right wing put up Kochaczewski as their candidate, and the left wing put up Yagalalo. The left wing won, with the help of the Jewish vote. The Poles declared a boycott of the Jews and opened private cooperative stores (*spulki*) in all the towns and villages. (I said "the Poles declared" because in the matter of anti-Semitism, they were all, both the right and the left, of the same opinion. In many places, especially the villages, there were physical attacks on the Jews. In one village, the Poles set fire to a house along with the eight members of the Jewish family who were inside.
31. The hospital was on Farah Street, opposite the church, in Kulashinski's house (one house after the Falka house). There was also a branch of the hospital on Shkolna Street, behind the church, in the school.
32. The region between Poland and Ukraine, not the one in Spain.
33. The people who prayed in the old *beit midrash* were simple men of means and the poor. The worshippers in the new *beit midrash* were "bourgeoisie" who knew the Torah well, *Hovevei Tzion*, and enlightened and advanced people. The worshipers in the synagogue were simple men of means, and in later years, also "bourgeoisie," Zionists, and intellectuals (these came to the synagogue only on holidays).
34. *Kolhekot* - small community. They were a group of enlightened *Mitnagdim* [opposed to *Hasidim*] that had a controversy (schism) with the rest of the community and the rabbi, and appointed their own rabbi.
35. The Zionist immigration to Palestine between 1904 and 1914.
36. I will mention an interesting fact here. A few months after the steering committee had been divided into subcommittees, there was a national congress of the Zionist Organization in Warsaw, which elected a new central committee. At the suggestion of its chairman, Yitzhak Grinbaum, it was divided into subcommittees, similar to those of *Agudat Tzion* in Sierpc. The members of the society were very pleased with this result, and called Avraham Fried "the little Grinbaum."
37. The day of Herzl's death.
38. The declaration by the government of Great Britain that it considers Palestine to be the homeland of the Jewish people.
39. The Zionist (and Israeli) national anthem.
40. Vouchers in lieu of a currency to be issued by a future Jewish state; Shekel - the plural is Shekalim - is the present Israeli currency.
41. We should mention here the outstanding work of the great scientist and activist Noach Perlotzki who, on his own, dealt with complaints of many communities and of individual Jews who turned to him.

His efforts were an immense help to the suffering Polish Jews.

42. This same long building was used as a soup kitchen during the years 1916-1918 for the poor of the town, as well as the poverty stricken from other cities, especially from Lodz and Warsaw. Economic conditions and the supply of food were terrible there. The volunteers at the soup kitchen were Shmuel Glazer, Zalman Jakubowicz, Czeshka Lubaszka, Falka Malowanczyk, Yehezkel Stari ("Hatchek" from the village of Rozcheshuwo), Hinda Szampan, and others.
43. The minimum of ten men required for a public prayer.
44. The hymn that closes the service.
45. An anthem of the first Zionist flag, from "Set up a standard toward Zion" - Jeremiah 4,6
46. The Hebrew word and Zionist term for immigration ("ascent") to the Land of Israel. It is usually identified by consecutive numbers, which then refer to the periods in which these immigrations occurred: thus "First *Aliyah*" was 1880-1904, "Second *Aliyah*" was 1904-1914, " *Third Aliyah*" was 1919-1923, etc.
47. An interesting curio: One of the teachers at the progymnasium, a Polish professor called Maievski, would buy a Zionist Shekel every year, not from love of Israel, but from enmity. "Maybe in this way" he said, "I will help to rid Poland of the Jews."

Memories from my Childhood Years

by Moshe B. Goldman, Cleveland Ohio

My First *"Cheder"*

Religion in my father's home, as in other Hassidic homes in Sierpc in those times, was not superficial and arbitrary. Faith was not bounded by a few dogmas and by celebrating holiday ceremonies, such as observing the Passover seder and going to the synagogue on Rosh Hashanah and Yom Kippur. In my father's home, religion was deeply rooted. It was felt above everything. Pious Judaism was observed in a practical manner under all conditions.

When I was three years old, my father decided that the time had come to send me to *cheder*. My mother was more progressive than Father. She strongly protested, "Yehoshua, it is cruel to send a three year old child to *cheder*!"

In matters related to religion, my father did his own thing. When something came to his mind, nobody could change his decision. It must be as he wished. He was the ruler over the home. His word was the verdict that one could not question.

After a discussion between Father and Mother, my father concluded calmly, "A person is compared to a tree in the field, which the gardener prepares for planting: water, manure, and nurturing - thus we must begin to teach our children the holy Torah as soon as they begin to talk."

Father wrapped me in a *tallis*, placed his hands on my head, and recited the Priestly Blessing: "May G-d bless and keep you, may G-d shine His countenance upon you and be gracious unto you, may G-d raise His face toward you and grant you peace." Then he added, "May G-d make you like Ephraim and Manasseh." He then took me from my weeping mother to learn Torah in *cheder* from Noach the Hunchback on the Jewish Street.

Noach's *cheder* was located in a damp basement. Two long benches stood lengthwise along the walls, and Noach's small chair with his table was in the center of the room. A sack of tobacco with rectangular pieces of newspaper to roll his cigarettes were on Noach's table, along with a *siddur* [prayer book] and a leather whip.

As soon as we entered, Noach, with his dirty yarmulke and a burning cigarette in his mouth, greeted us. There was a smile on his lips. I badly wanted to laugh when I looked at him, but I controlled my laughter, for I was afraid of my father.

Noach's wife, Yenta Breina, was a short, stout woman. Her wig went down to her eyes. She stopped plucking feathers and greeted us with the words, "the kitten is coming."

Even though I had been calm the entire way from home to *cheder*, I began to complain bitterly when Noach attempted to seat me down among the children. The teacher used various tricks to try to win me over. Among other things, he dramatically tossed coins into the *siddur*. He told me that they were coming from heaven for children who study Torah diligently. I, however, did not believe a single word he said. I held on to my mother's apron, and my mother pushed toward the door. Right after that, when my mother sat down with me on the bench among the children, I began to cry, and looked into the *siddur* that Noach had opened. He began with a tune from Song of Songs, "Woe unto me, tell me oh child, what is it? It seems like a small man, with a small head, hands, a reciter with a sheaf. Oh say, what is it, what?"

A child was sitting near me. He was a lot older than I. Noach called him "Fishel Ox." Fishel responded instead of me, "This is Noach the Hunchback."

The children broke out in laughter. Noach became upset. His face turned red. He looked at Fishel with an angry glance and hauled him to the whip. It seemed as if he was about to tell Fishel to lower his pants so that he could whip him. I was also afraid, and I almost cried. However, Noach did not do anything to Fishel. As I later heard from my father, when my mother told him about Noach's *cheder*, Fishel Ox was a well-pedigreed child. His father was a veterinarian in the Russian army, and his grandfather was Reb Lipa Podriadczyk.

With great difficulty, my teacher calmed things down and pretended that he had not noticed anything. Once again, he showed me in the *siddur*, "This is an *aleph*, say child, an *aleph*."

I had already known the *aleph beit* well by then. My father had already taught me to recognize the letters. However, the fear of the *rebbe* took away my speech. I repeated after Noach, "*Aleph*." He believed that I had a good head, and again showed me, "You see child, it is closed on three sides and open on the left side. Say, child '*Beit*'."

As soon as I succeeded in saying "*Beit*," Fishel Ox again uttered a crude, funny, statement. The children laughed, which brought me to a cheerful mood. I was freed from my fear of the *cheder*, and began to smile.

My rebbe showed me the third letter, "See child, what is this, a little line, yes, say child?"

I leaned over the *siddur* and began to point to the letters, saying, "*Dalet, he, vav,*" and onward until the end.

Reb Noach smiled good-naturedly and asked my mother, "Mrs. Roiza, why did you not tell me that Moshe Ber already knows the *aleph beit*?"

My mother responded apologetically, "Believe me, Reb Noach, I myself knew nothing of this."

My *rebbe* turned to me with a smile, "Earlier, I said that you have a good head. You need to learn how to pray when you are six years old. It takes only one year for a good head to learn how to pray. You must be five years old."

"I am only three years old!" I shouted brazenly.

"Oh, oh, Yente Breina, come here!'" the *rebbe* called to his wife, "A genius, ha, ha, he is only three years old and he already knows the entire *aleph beit*."

"Yes, Reb Noach," my mother said, "Moshe Berele is indeed three years old. I was against sending him to *cheder* so early. However, my Yehoshua was in favor."

"What is the wonder," Yenta Beila[1] stated, "The son takes after the father. Who does not know what a great scholar Reb Yehoshua is..."

The *rebbe's* wife brought some candies and said to me tenderly:

"You are an exceptional child. You will bring a great deal of pleasure to your parents."

I took the candies and treated my new friend Fishel. Before I put the sweets in my mouth, I recited the "*shehakol*" blessing which aroused the wonder of my *rebbe*. I already knew all the blessings that are to be recited over various foods: "*hamotzie*" over bread, "*mezonot*" over cakes, "*hagafen*" over wine, "*haeitz*" over fruit, "*adama*" over potatoes. My father had taught me all that.

Reb Noach pinched me lovingly on the cheek and asked, "What else do you know?"

In a non-bold, embarrassed voice, I answered him, "I know the names of all the Jewish holidays. I can ask the four questions of Passover."

Reb Noach interrupted my speech and said to my mother, "He is indeed a good child. Take him home. You do not have to come with him tomorrow to *cheder*. I will send my assistant Yoshe Chush, who will fetch him from the house every morning. You do not have to worry. My Yente Breina and I will take care of him. I want to place him in a higher class, and will soon begin to teach him Hebrew. He will not have to remain here for long, for he will soon have to begin learning *chumash.*

We left the *cheder.* The rest of the students looked at us with jealousy.

When we came home, my mother told my father about my success with the teacher of children Reb Noach. My father said with joy, “See Roiza, I told you that he is growing into a genius. Tell him something once, and he already knows it. You will see that he will grow up as a great scholar.”

Then my mother answered with a worried voice, “Yes, Yehoshua, he has a sharp head. Perhaps too sharp for his age. This indeed causes me worry. He is too serious for a three year old child. He is always pensive...”

Yoshe the *Cheder* Assistant and My Friend Fishel

There was no need to use ruses to get me to go to Reb Noach's *cheder.* Yoshe the assistant came for me the next morning and took me by the hand, along with my breakfast that consisted of a bagel with butter, an egg, and a flask of milk, and we set off to *cheder.* This was repeated every morning. Yoshe would take me to *cheder* and bring me back home in the afternoon. Every morning, I waited impatiently for Yoshe's call. I was worried if he was late. In such cases, I climbed into a corner, looked through the window and, with childlike fear, wondered whether something bad happened to Yoshe. A happy shout emanated from my throat when I saw him coming. He would pass by our window and greet me in a friendly manner as always.

Thanks to my feelings for Yoshe, I also began to love my rebbe, Yenta Breina his wife, and even her cat and hen. I thought about the day when I would have to leave Reb Noach's *cheder* and leave Yoshe. I wished to remain there always.

All of Noach's students felt a strong connection to Yoshe. He had an exceptionally warm relationship to children and had wonderful ideas and tricks to delight the hearts of children. He could make small paper boats in which he placed candles. They would float at night in the Sierpienica River, which cut through the city. We children loved to look from above at the small floating boats with burning candles that ignited the boats as they floated along.

Yoshe was a gifted woodcutter. With his small, five groszy, Gypsy knife, he carved all types of playthings and would give them to us children to play with. Furthermore, he was a husky lad. He would save us from the gentile thugs who enjoyed attacking Jewish children.

One morning, Yoshe was leading us to *cheder.* We encountered a group of gentiles who were on their way to their school. The thugs attacked us by calling us names and throwing stones at us. Yoshe, however, gave them such a “lecture” that they no longer were so bold as to attacks us. It seemed then that if we were merely to mention Yoshe's name to the scoundrels, they would flee in terror.

Yoshe was only twelve years old at the time. He had been orphaned from both parents at the age of five. His aunt, Rachel the widow, took him into her home to educate him. However, she could barely educate her own five orphaned children, and when Yoshe was a bit older he left his aunt and tried to prove his "independence." It is a wonder how that orphan child, educated on the street, did not leave the straight path. On the contrary, he found employment, and was full of love for children and adults.

Reb Noach took Yoshe out of the old *beis midrash*, where he used to sleep on the hard benches. "Come out, Yoshe, be my assistant. I will give you food, a corner to sleep on the floor of the *cheder*, a pair of shoes, and a pair of pants every year." Thus did Noach approach the orphan, whom he would educate along with us children.

Noach gave Yoshe a difficult task: to bring the children from their homes in the morning and to take them home in the afternoon; to ensure that the children ate their breakfast; to help them take care of their natural needs; to play with the children; to help teach the *aleph beit* to the children who were slower to pick it up[2].

The rebbe's wife gave Yoshe other tasks: to sweep the floor every day and wash it once a week; to feed the cat, the hen and clean the hen cage every Friday afternoon; to take wood from the shed and light the oven. Aside from this, Yoshe had to carry water and empty the slop pail every morning.

Yoshe was never bitter with any of these tasks. He was always good to us children. We shared everything that we brought form home with him - both food and sweets. We even gave him a bit of the pocket money that we received. Aside from the weekly payment, he received something from the parents for protecting us. The weekly payment was ten groszy per child. Some of the parents took pity on him and paid him more, for he was an orphan.

It was pleasant to go to *cheder* under the leadership of Yoshe. He led us as one leads soldiers: the oldest and largest children in the front lines. Yoshe himself was in the rear. As he led us, he held a leather whip that Noach had given him for his position as an assistant. However, he never used the whip. Instead of prodding us, he played a mouth harmonica.

At the same time, Bazimowski, the town shepherd, prodded his cows with the whistle of a pipe and with a whip in his hand.

Yoshe never forgot to stop by the pump in the old marketplace to pump water. We helped each other drink. We trudged in the mud and got splattered from head to toe. At home Mother would become angry and yell. However, I, and I believe the other students as well, never blamed Yoshe.

*

Aside from the assistant, I also became close with Reb Noach's well-pedigreed student Fishele.

Reb Noach used to insult Fishel and call him names in front of the entire *cheder*. He would say to him, "Fishel, you are nothing more than an ox, a donkey, an unintelligent animal. I have already had various students, and during my twenty years of teaching, nobody was as foolish as you. I cannot stuff even one Hebrew word in your foolish head." Indeed, Fishel was not as foolish as the rebbe made him out to be. He spoke Russian and Polish, and knew how to write with fine handwriting, as if it was printed. The *cheder* studies did not interest him at all. Later, when I got older and no longer studied in the same *cheder* as Fishel, I met up with him, and he told me about his studies with a children's teacher at that time, when he was already more than eight years old.

"I wanted to go to a Russian school, just like the gentile children. I do not want to be a rabbi, nor a teacher like our former rebbe, Reb Noach. I want to go to a gymnasium and after completing the eighth grade, to study for four years in a polytechnium in order to become an engineer.

My parents are also not strong proponents of *cheder*. My father is the veterinarian of the 27th Calvary Regiment. He works also on the Sabbath. My mother is also not observant. She does not even keep a kosher kitchen. I went to *cheder* in order to make my observant grandfather Reb Lipa happy. He demanded that I study Hebrew and know something about Judaism. If not, he threatened to disinherit my parents.

Reb Lipa's wish could not be ignored and his threat had to be taken into consideration since he was a millionaire. His influence within government circles was great. "*Gospidin*[3] Lipa" the Czar's contractor, was known everywhere. From Warsaw through Petrograd until Kiev and Omsk, Fishel's sole hope was to be accepted in a Russian polytechnium, into which it was impossible for a Jew to be accepted. It was, however, open for his grandfather, who was duty bound to support his studies so long as he would first learn Judaism.

For this reason, Fishel began to go to *cheder* so late, when he was already eight years old. The religious studies did not penetrate his head.

Fishel grew tall and

had a strong build. He appeared much older than he truly was. At Reb Noach's *cheder*, he felt his pedigree and treated the teacher with exceptional brazenness.

If Reb Noach would lift up his leather whip to beat Fishel, Fishel would grab the whip from Noach's hand, look at him in the eyes, and say, "*Ti sukin sin!*[4] Try it and you will get it instead of me!" He also had a sense of responsibility for his fellow students in *cheder*. Anytime that Noach would attack a child, Fishel placed himself between the rebbe and the student. With the blink of an eye, Noach became afraid, and sat down again without saying a word. I often wondered why Noach still kept him in *cheder* after such outbursts. Reb Lipa, however, used to pay good tuition for his grandson.

Fishel's parents lived outside the city. They were the only Jews who lived in that area.

*

When I completed my fifth year, my father took me out of Reb Noach's *cheder* to bring me to Reb Yisrael the *chumash* and Rashi teacher.

One Sabbath afternoon, I was looking out the window as Reb Yisrael with his thin goatee and hairless cheeks approached our house. I was bewildered and ran into the bedroom to hide behind the door. I did not want to go to Reb Yisrael's *cheder.* I did not want to leave Yoshe and his cheerfulness. Reb Yisrael did not have an assistant who would protect me from the gentiles who would lay hiding in the old market square to attack Jewish children and trip them. Even worse, I would lose my best friend Fishel, with whom I had become bonded.

Reb Yisrael entered the house, and said "Good Sabbath" with his hoarse voice. He took off his *kapote,* placed it on the sofa, and sat down at the table. My mother served hot tea with sugar, lemon, jam, and cakes.

Reb Yisraelke was by nature an easygoing man. He never hurried. He was always in a good mood. After tasting his snack, he began speaking in his peculiar, easygoing manner: "As you know, I am not an excitable man. I never lay a finger upon my students. Yet, they all learn well. You will see, this is the accomplishment. I never hurry. I present to you that he will praise my good name, which is designated for me, and nobody will take it from me."

As he talked thus, Reb Yisraelke put sugar in his tea, put in the lemon, and began to sip it slowly without interruption. When he finished the first glass of tea, he praised my mother for preparing good cakes and asked for another glass of tea. He drank five glasses one after the other.

From behind the door, I looked at my new *rebbe* with bitterness. I begged G-d to make a miracle and disrupt the plan to transfer me to his *cheder.*

I heard my father's voice. He called me to introduce me to the new *rebbe.* At first I did not answer, but my father did not stop calling me. I entered the room and said, "I do not want to go to his *cheder.* I want to remain with Noach!"

My father responded to me, "Nobody is going to force you. Reb Yisrael did not come only to take you to *cheder.* He had heard from Noach how smart a child you are. He wanted to find out if this was indeed the truth."

My father felt that he would not succeed in making a fool of me, so he said smiling, "In truth, you must begin to study *chumash.* Later you will go to Chaim Yosef to study *gemara,* so that you can become a rabbi."

"However, I still want to remain with Noach, together with Fishel," I said with a crying voice.

Reb Yisrael, hearing that name, turned to me with a begging voice, "Don't say Fishel, say Reb Lipa's grandson."

I shook my head, and thought, "Yes, that is him. Fishel is my best friend. If he could come with me, I would not refuse to go to your *cheder*."

Yisrael began to pinch my cheek and said, "First thing next week, Reb Lipa will register Fishel in my *cheder*. First of all, Reb Lipa wants me to teach him a bit of *chumash*. Then I will have to prepare him for his Bar Mitzvah. He will not go on to study *gemara*. That 'gentile' does not want to learn."

Reb Yisrael smiled at my father and said, "If I would have several such Fishels in the following year, I will be finished through and through."

The news of Fishel's transfer to the new *cheder* worked magic on me. I began to dance and shout with joy, "I will have my Fishel, I will have my Fishel!" Then I sat at the table waiting for the examination.

Stroking his beard and wrinkling his brow, Reb Yisraelke asked me several questions about the *chumash* portions that Reb Noach had studied with me. He asked me to recite a passage from a *siddur* with small letters. A happy gaze came across Reb Yisrael's face.

He asked for another glass of tea, which my mother prepared for him. After drinking up the tea, he said happily to my father, "Reb Yehoshua, I am very happy to accept your son as a student." Then he left.

I studied in Reb Yisrael's *cheder* for several terms. When I was nine, I transferred to the *gemara* teacher Reb Chaim Yosef. I studied there for two years. Then my father decided to take me out from Reb Chaim Yosef and study with me himself, for he felt that there was no *cheder* in town where he could send me.

Thus ended the summer term. The joyous Sukkot festival came. My joy was especially great for I knew that I would no longer be going to *cheder*. I had a wonderful festival, which is deeply etched in my memory. I felt grown up and participated in the festivities like a grown up. I was with the entire crowd for the Simchat Torah celebrations. I marched through the Jewish street with a burning *havdalah* candle, and torches, and carried Torah scrolls at the *hakafot* [processions] in the synagogue. We sang, danced, and celebrated, and I danced along with everyone.

I danced with the old rabbi, Rabbi Yechiel Michael under the canopy that was carried along, and, on the other hand, with the official Konstantinov Strazemski, who was dressed in a uniform adorned with gold, and with shiny silver epaulets. His long, snow-white beard appeared splendid. If it were not for his red nose that came from drinking too much liquor, and for his words of profanity that he used frequently, one could have mistaken him for a rabbi rather than a Russian police officer. Konstantinov walked at the right side of Rabbi Yechiel Michael during the march. Every time that the rabbi said, "*Anah Hashem Hoshia Na*"[5], Konstantinov repeated in Russian "*A Bog Pomagai Nas*," which means "G-d help us."

Many other army officers from the 37th Cavalry Regiment, in their shiny red and snow-white uniforms, were present. The never missed the formal Simchat Torah celebrations, and felt as if it was their own festival. They danced Cossack dances and drank liquor like water. They even gave me a taste of their bitter drink.

I met Fishel, my friend from Noach's *cheder*, at the Simchat Torah celebration. We laughed heartily when we recalled how the rebbe, Reb Noach, used to call Fishel "Ox" because he did not grasp the studies at *cheder*. On the other hand, Fishel learned very well in the gymnasium. He looked very snazzy in his uniform with the shiny silk knot and tidy silver hat. Oh, how I was jealous of him on account of his uniform.

On Simchat Torah morning, my father took me along to *hakafot* in the Aleksander Hassidic *shtibel*. I was very tired. Even Yaakov Meir Toker's acrobatic dances could not change my mood. I was happy when the services were over and we went home.

The next day, my *rebbe* Chaim Yosef, in his usual manner at the beginning of a new term, came to us to be present when my father tested me.

Chaim Yosef made the teaching of *gemara* his life's goal, and not just a means of earning a livelihood because he was not successful at business. His *cheder* was one of the best in the city. He used to study constantly. He did not smoke in the *cheder*, nor did he administer beatings or even insults. He was known for his knowledge of Talmud, and was the top *gemara* teacher in town. He also knew Yiddish, Hebrew, and Russian well. He learnt Russian in the army when he served for five years in the Czar's Cavalry. Reb Chaim Yosef had taken part in the Russo-Japanese War and was wounded during a battle. He returned from the war with decorations for heroism, and attained the rank of Chief Sergeant.

Reb Chaim Yosef told my father, "Yehoshua, I want to test your child to see how diligent he was during the last term." My father answered with a smile,

"On the contrary, Simchat Torah is the most appropriate time to be involved with Torah."

My father asked me to take out a *gemara* from the book closet. He opened a tractate, pointed to a place with his finger, and told me to start learning. I began a *gemara* didactic discussion and finished properly. My *rebbe's* eyes glowed from contentment. He was certain that he would get the student for his *cheder*, but my father quickly pointed out his mistake. He told him:

"Reb Chaim Yosef, I found no fault in your learning with my son. You have done a great deal to bring Jewish children to the path of Torah, but my son needs special supervision, because I want him to already receive ordination at the age of 18, and this cannot happen at your *cheder*.

My *rebbe* attempted to convince my father that he, Reb Chaim Yosef, as a *gemara* teacher, was able to bring him to such a level in *Talmud*. However, my father stood his own.

After Reb Chaim Yosef left, my father said to me, "The *gemara* says that a father is obligated in five things toward a son: circumcision, redemption of the firstborn, teaching him Torah, teaching him a trade, and ensuring that he will get married. Some say, also to teach him to swim so that he would be able to save himself in the event of danger. Next week, at the beginning of the new term, we will begin to learn."

I was not overly happy with my father's decision to be my *rebbe*. I knew about his stringency and his ambition to make me into rabbi. Therefore, I told him that I would prefer to go to *cheder*.

After a long discussion with my father, in which he repeated his wish that I obtain ordination by the age of 18 in order to become a great rabbi, I finally told my Father that I would prefer to study to be an engineer like my friend Fishel. My father responded, "Indeed, an engineer would not be bad, but I am not Reb Lipa the millionaire. I have no money or influence to get you into the polytechnium." He thought for a minute and said, "Even if I had the money and influence, I would not allow my son to turn into a gentile."

My father told me that he wanted me to learn with him. When I would already become an expert in *Talmud*, he would study the commentators, *Yoreh Deah, Choshen Mishpat*[6], the *Yad Chazaka* of Maimonides, and other books that a scholarly Jew must know. The teacher Zeinwil would teach me Russian, Polish and other secular subjects twice I week. I considered him to be crazy, since in July he dressed up in a fur cap, gloves and galoshes. On the other hand, my father felt that Zeinwil was a completely normal person, and if he wishes to wear his winter clothes in the summer, that is his private business. He was very erudite and G-d fearing.

My father began to learn with me for the new term. Every morning at dawn, he woke me up with the well-known verse of Proverbs, "For how long will a lazy person sleep, when will you get up from your sleep!" He took me out of my warm bed in the winter and led me through the length of the snow and ice covered streets to study Torah in the old *beis midrash* by the light of a tallow candle.

My father believed that the morning hours were the best time for the most difficult sections of the Talmud, which require a clear mind. My eyes were closed. I was still half asleep, the *beis midrash* was cold, but my father used to say, "The Torah is compared to a flame. It lights and it warms."

No children's games or days off existed for my pious father. Even on Chanukah, Tu B'Shvat, Purim and Lag BaOmer, when all the children used to be off from *cheder* having fun and playing, my father sat with me and learned. My father had his view regarding all of our festivals. According to his interpretation, they are all connected with the Torah. Chanukah was the time of the purification of the Holy Temple and the rekindling of the menorah. "Torah is light," therefore one must occupy oneself with the study of Torah on Chanukah. The fifteenth[7], says the Talmud, is the New Year for trees. The Torah is called a "Tree of Life." On Purim, the Jews were saved from Haman.

The Megilla says, "The Jews had light." Once again, that means the Torah. Lag BaOmer is dedicated to the memory of thousands of students of Rabbi Akiva who fell under Bar Kochva's leadership at the hands of the Romans. What better memorial can there be for the scholars and brave men than to study Torah on that day?

I remember how my father used to take me on his walks to the bridge and to the workshop in Babiec, in which he had a financial interest. On those walks, he also spoke words of Torah to me. As soon as we reached the Rypin Highway that led to Babiec, he began, "And you should speak of them when you sit in your house, walk along the journey, lie down, and rise." That was the beginning. Then he reviewed the *gemara* and *Yoreh Deah* sections that we had studied during the week.

My head was not on learning. I enjoyed strolling. The blue sky, the sun soaked fields and forests filled my entire being with joy, and made my blood sizzle. My father noticed my preoccupation cased by the beauty of nature. He mentioned that the*Mishna* states, "Rabbi Yaakov says: one who walks along the way, stops his learning and says: How nice is this tree, how nice is this field, the scripture considers as if he has forfeited his life."[8].

No other thing in the world other than Torah existed for my father. This was his life, his feelings, his thoughts. Every other thing was merely a waste of time and energy, "Vanity of vanity... all is vanity."[9].

Translator's Footnotes

1.
2. I believe this is a typo, and Breina was intended.
3. Literally - who have dense heads.
4. A formal term for a gentleman or a mister.
5. I am not sure what these words are intended to mean.
6. Please G-d, save now - the refrain of the Simchat Torah processions.
7. Two of the four section of the Code of Jewish Law.
8. Tu Bishvat.
9. Pirke Avot 3:9.
10. Kohelet (Ecclesiastes) 1:2.

The Jewish Self Defense in Sierpc

by Avraham Mlawa

The first attempt to organize a Jewish armed force in Sierpc took place in 1906.

The members of the self defense met in the fields. There, they conducted exercises with weapons, with iron "gloves." Publicity to join the self-defense was carried out among the Jews. The Polish hooligans knew that the Jews were prepared with weapons to defend themselves against an attack. That succeeded in evading excesses against the Jews of Sierpc.

In neighboring Drobin, a "small" pogrom took place against the local Jews. On an annual market day, the farmers suddenly overturned the table with merchandise of the Jewish businessmen and began to rob and beat Jews, causing a great tumult. There was a large tannery in the town that employed Jewish workers. They went out with the large, long tanning knives and began to beat off the attack upon the Jews. The hooligans fled and the Jews were saved.

The heroic attitude of the Jewish workers had an effect on the entire region. The farmers knew that Jews would not let anything happen in Sierpc, for there was an armed Jewish self-defense organization there.

In 1918, after the Germans left Poland and there was no regular Polish regime yet in Sierpc, a Jewish self-defense organization was organized, in which a large number of youth joined. The heads of the self-defense were Yeshayahu Frydman, Nathan Tac, Avraham Mlawa, Yaakov Gross, and Salek Gurfinkel. The office of the self-defense was located in the office of Agudat Zion at the home of Moshe Elsztajnen on Plocker Street.

A third self-defense organization was organized in 1920 during the war between Poland and the Soviets. After the Soviet army left the city, a joint, voluntary Jewish-Polish civic self-defense organization was set up under the leadership of the firefighters.

The following Jews participated in the leadership of the self-defense. Tzadok Bluman, Yeshayahu Frydman, Avraham Mlawa, and Frenkel. At that time, plans were made in the underworld to rob the Jews, but the civic joint self-defense organization prevented this.

Even during the time of the Hallerczyks, no pogroms took place in Sierpc. Sierpc had good luck: the Hallerczyks did not station themselves in the town.

Special mention must be made of the Sierpc priests who restrained the population from hooligan style attacks on the Jews. Everyone was familiar with the old Prowocz, who the Jewish town must thank for holding the peace during that time.

My Town Sierpc

by Ephraim Talmi (Wluka)

Sierpc, the town of my birth. Little Sierpc, squeezed between hills and valleys, with the Sierpienica River dividing it lengthwise and leaving its imprint. Sierpc, a city in the Polish exile at the crossroads of Warsaw, Plonsk, and Danzig. At the junction of an entire district of towns and villages, farms and estates of Gentiles. And among them and within them - toiling Jews occupied with bargaining, Torah, and work, with commerce and peddling, with skills and small manufacturing. Sierpc - the bells of memory toll and shake the depths of the soul. Forgotten sights, from far away, return and shake off the dust of obliviousness, take on a clear, certain form, which the hand tries to transform into script.

Sierpc, a town of ten or eleven thousand, about a third of whom were Jews. It served as a center for all the towns in the area; Sierpc is mentioned in a book by Joseph Opatoshu, *In Polish Forests*[1]; it was the regional seat, with all the requisite government offices. There were roads and highways, paths and streets from all the corners of the heavens that led to Sierpc. It was situated between green hills and emerald valleys, a landscape of beauty and color. The land was not flat. If you came from the direction of Plotzk, you had to go down the steep Plotzki Street to get to the center of town. If from Drobin or Biezun, you would glide down the Jewish street to the central market square. But if you came from the direction of Prussia, from Rypin-Dobrzyn-Golub, you would find yourself tossed around in the carriage or cart or in later years in the bus, as you rapidly traveled down the street leading from the towering Catholic Church, erect on a high mountain with a marvelous vista for miles around.

The town was surrounded by vast fields of wildflowers that in the summer looked like an ocean of stalks of grain drifting in the wind, bending and bowing and becoming upright again. And the spacious gardens added their accompaniment of magic to the undulating shoots. All the fruits that Poland was blessed with grew in the orchards in and around the town. With the long and winding, narrow Sierpienica River dominating it all. The river that every boy in town remembers, and will recollect to the end of his days. The source of the river was undoubtedly unknown to any Jewish boy in Sierpc, because who would try to trace its path, to find its beginning and its end? There, in the Diaspora, we did not investigate the wonders of nature very much. From the time we were old enough to think for ourselves we saw the river as part of the town, something that was always there, a part of the way of life, for our entertainment and our dreams. The river was frozen in many places during the winter, covered with a layer of ice and snow. In the spring - the snow would melt. The cracking of the armor of ice that had constrained the water let it rush in from all the brooks and creeks and rivulets into this one river. A mighty swelling and the joy of spring, a storm of wild movement, sweeping away everything in its course, its strength finally liberated. The first rays of a warm sun dazzled the waters, and aroused them to unaccustomed life. The river swelled and waxed and widened and occupied new banks and the water poured into the yards that bordered it. There was a multitude of trees, planks, and small utensils whirling in the furious and turbid water. This lasted for a brief time, until the river returned to its boundaries, its power enfeebled, and became the steady river again. But in years of torrential rain and much snow, a flood followed the thaw, a flood that does not fade from memory and people do not stop talking about. There were mild floods that damaged only the lowest areas, where the poor lived. But every few years there was a greater flood, whose effects were visible for a long time because of the damage they caused. But when townspeople mentioned "The Great Flood" they meant the frightful flood that occurred at the end of the nineteenth century, which destroyed almost half the town, and whose damage was unprecedented, with lives lost. That flood, or as it was called with anguish in Yiddish, "*Das Gevister*" was a nightmare that could not be erased or forgotten.

But when summer came, the river would shrink and flow peacefully. We were acquainted with the length of river between the flour mill of Mr. Frilanski and the Bovorowa dam. There were shallow spots in the river, where you could cross by foot during the warm days of summer. And there were deep places with whirlpools that sucked you in and deep, dark pits. There were other places, usually in the Gentile neighborhoods, where the riverbanks were green and pleasant, and the land near them would astonish you with the vegetable gardens and fruit orchards. However, many sections of the river which passed through the Jewish areas were for the most part rundown and neglected. They were filthy and polluted with the debris of pots and pans. There were places, during the summer, in years with little rain, where the river would shrivel so much that a foul smelling green slime would climb its dry banks. Fragments of casks, hoops, and all types of discarded tools would stick out of the standing, moldy water, as if thrown into a sewer.

I can remember very well when the river was cleaned; the picture remains clear to me. It was during the German occupation, in 1915 or 1916. The conquerors, devotees of order and neatness, introduced new attitudes to the town. They decided to rid the river of its pollution, something that had not been done for generations. They dammed up the river outside of town, and diverted it to a different channel, until the stream in town dried up. Those were good times for the kids in town. All of a sudden, there was no water and no river, and you could walk on dry land. Barefoot, we plodded through the mud searching for treasures. And what riches we found! Broken pots and pans of generations past!

After the cleanup, and boosting and bolstering the soil of the riverbanks, the water was once again allowed to flow through the river, as in the old days. The searching and the scratching and the wonder of finding antiques were over.

A river provides a lot of activity for the boys in town; endless entertainment and satisfaction. In the winter, you could skate on the ice. To feel the cold air that cuts into your very soul! To fear and tremble that the ice will open up at some spot and to yell like a wild man when you finish skating with no mishaps. The body is warm; the cheeks are enflamed. Your face is flushed from the wind and the cold and the effort, and your eyes are flashing sparks of delight, and your mouth is a trumpet full of joy!

And in the summer, you could go fishing with a big sieve or colander filched from father's store, where it was used for straining flour or grain. Sometimes we would use a fishing rod, like real fishermen. We would sit for hours on the bank of the river, waiting for a bite which rarely came. Or we would walk with the old sieve through the clear water that reflected the sun, chasing the minnows that hurried away. Sometimes we were successful, and from their hiding places between the river weeds the fish would rush into the large sieve. Then there would be no end to our joy, but these were exceptional circumstances. But in spite of this, our enthusiasm and eagerness never abated.

It was a river for sailing in boats. This was a popular sport during the summer. The young people would go down to the boat station near the bridge, by the statues of "Menashe and his Sons."[2] They would row the boats till the Bovorowa dam. Usually they would sail in the afternoon or before evening. But there were also moonlit nights, and the young blood pulsed in their veins. Bands of rowers would swarm over the river with its pale silver light, punctuated with shadows of the tall trees with wide branches that grew by the side of the river. There was youthful singing, full of tenderness and longings of the heart that broke the stillness of the night. From time to time there were shouts of joy that would frighten the birds that nested in the tall trees. And there were secret whispers of young lovers. It was a rich web of life that flowed like the waves of the river.

But these excursions were not always quiet and idyllic. There were times that *shkotzim*[3] would attack the Jewish rowers, throw rocks and try to sink the boats. The rowers would be beaten and injured, and then their hearts would be full of pain and anger. To be a Jew in the Diaspora....

People would swim in the river all summer long, beginning right after *Sukkoth*. As soon as it became known that a *sheigetz* had drowned in the river, and it had received its sacrifice, the Jews began to bathe there as well. There were a few swimming places in town: near Frilanski's flour mill; near the *Lunka* not far from where the *Valker* lived; near the Bovorowa dam, and a few other places.

There were more than a few Sierpc townspeople who knew how to swim, and there were some that were excellent at it. People spoke with great admiration about the expert swimming styles of Motel Tikolski, Leibl Kashe-Makher, Avraham Wluka, and others. They spoke with awe especially about their *vasser-strit*; as if they were "walking on water."

The swimming in the river also had peaceful periods and periods of troubles and harassment. If there was a black cloud hanging over the *shkotzim*, they would find pretexts to beat the Jewish swimmers. They would hit them until they drew blood, steal their clothes, and abuse the defenseless younger swimmers. There were times when we counter-attacked and paid them back in full, or more. But I remember one incident where we were swimming in Bovorowa, and a large gang of *shkotzim* pounced on us. We managed to get out of there with great difficulty, carrying our clothes, and naked as jaybirds we ran for two kilometers until we reached the first Jewish houses.

During the winter, we had other pastimes, skating on the frozen lake near the railway station. As soon as the ice was thick enough, we came out to skate on the lake. Some of the Jewish skaters showed great artistry. Until they learned, they would tumble seven times, but they would get up and continue. There were many sprained knees and injured hands. Sometimes the ice was not thick enough in places, and a skater who wandered to a weak spot like that would find that his leg had broken through.... But generally they were careful and the pleasure of skating was complete.

In addition to the pleasures connected with the river and the lake, there were other special events in town, the big fairs and market days. Because Sierpc was the largest town in the area, it would hold large fairs, where thousands of peasants from the whole region would come to sell their produce and purchase supplies. It was a vibrant exhibit of all the kinds of fruit of the earth and different types of commercial goods. There were thousands of horses, cows, sheep, grocery stalls, and peddlers. An enormous crowd in colorful clothes rambling through a great festival, with loud and piercing noises. A huge symphony of shouts, braying and whinnying horses, snorting of bulls and lowing of cows, squealing of wheels and lashing of whips, cackling of hens and quacking of ducks, the honking of geese; a commotion that did not stop from the morning until closing time at ten at night. When the town emptied of the great throng, the markets and squares and malls became quiet, like an abandoned battlefield....

Life went on in all of its variety in the small town. Sometimes the tide would crest with fairs, special gatherings, festivals, state holidays, the international workers' holiday on the first of May, Polish independence on the third of May, and in contrast, the second of November, the anniversary of the Balfour Declaration[4]. When the tide ebbed, life would go on as before, quietly and sedately. The Jews would finish their weeklong struggle to begin preparing for the Sabbath. The nimble ones would rush to Schweitzer's *Mikve*[5] on Mikve Street to get a proper immersion in steam. They would leave there bathed, with mist rising from their bodies, wet haired and beards dripping, red faced and refreshed, hurrying home to put on their Sabbath clothes and go to public prayer, to greet the Sabbath queen. Not much earlier and the same Jews were busy earning their living, encrusted with oil and flour and kerosene, and smelling of all kinds of groceries, and now they had turned into different people. They had removed their worldly garments and become the sons of kings. The sounds of prayer filled the village spaces, an accompaniment of grace and glory to the light of the candles and radiance of the chandeliers that came from the prayer houses and homes. The Sabbath queen was everywhere in the dwelling places of Israel.

On Saturday, the fervent Jew would study *Mishna* and *Gemara*[6] and the layman would read the Psalms and chapters of *Ein Yaakov*[7]. Fathers would quiz their children about their knowledge, to see if they had properly learned their lessons during the week. The women would pore over a Pentateuch with a Yiddish translation, the *Tzeina VeReina*[8], and stories of wise and pious men. The political parties would hold literary sessions, question and answer evenings. There would be discussions of the important topics facing the world, both Jewish and secular. There were visits with relatives, friends, and acquaintances. When the Sabbath came to an end, the wheels of the quotidian life would again start turning - until the next Sabbath. The merchants returned to their stores, the craftsmen to their labors, the peddlers to their stalls, the *melameds* to teach the Torah. In the rooms of the very fervent, a return to the six books of the *Mishna* and the tractates of the Talmud. In the improved *heder* of Mordecai Zvi Mintz, Hebrew studies in Hebrew. Every man to his own needs and traditions.

Jewish life was rich and full of substance. If from the outside it looked like a forlorn and declining town, sleepy and sluggish, without spirit and ambitions, inside it was bursting with life, stormy and restless, a life of the spirit and the mind. There was Torah study and there was nationalism. The pious were preparing themselves for God, all their deeds directed towards the creator and eternal life. The nationalists were doing their utmost to revive the feelings of patriotism and national glory among the youth and the rest of the population, the aspiration to be a free people in the transformed fatherland. And there were workers' organizations, laboring to improve their economic status, their prestige, and their intellectual experience. There were appearances by emissaries from headquarters in Warsaw, and representatives sent to conferences in the capitol. There were arguments and turbulent meetings, and attempts at convincing someone to switch from one political party to another. There were many cultural events, amateur drama productions, and artists' appearances. Libraries were founded that disseminated knowledge and enlightenment. Schools appeared, such as *Tarbuth*[9]and *Tzisha*[10]. And there was *aliyah*[11] to the land of Israel and constant contact with the immigrants. As the economic conditions worsened and the persecutions and the spitefulness increased, the desire to leave the valley of tears of the Diaspora became stronger. But only a few hundred went to Palestine over the years, and others went to the lands in America. But most of the Jews of Sierpc remained in town, troubled and fearful, busy and preoccupied, worried and hopeful.

So thus the wheel of life revolved, a cycle of happiness and grief, pain and trouble. Contentment and longing, disappointment and despair would follow each other and then repeat themselves. Generations came and went, until the awful catastrophe, until the Holocaust came for Polish Jewry, and everything descended into the din of desolation. The town was destroyed and crumbled into the depths of devastation. Sierpc was no longer Jewish. The song of life was interrupted for thousands of our sisters and brothers, our mothers and fathers, our relatives and acquaintances, friends and companions. We shall remember them forever.

Translator's Footnotes

1. See the Chapter on "Chronicles of the Sheps Rabbinate" in this Yizkor book.
2. Small statues near a Christian shrine just outside of town; see the chapter "My Little Shtetl of Sierpc, Now Destroyed" in this Yizkor book.
3. A Yiddish term, usually derogatory, which literally meant Gentile boy. *Shkotzim* is plural; sheigetz is singular.
4. The declaration by the government of Great Britain in 1917 that it considers Palestine to be the homeland of the Jewish people.
5. Ritual bathhouse.
6. *Mishna* and *Gemara* are the parts of the Talmud.
7. A book of legends and sayings of the ancient wise men.
8. A book of homilies in Yiddish for Jewish women
9. A modern Hebrew school, see the chapter "The Hebrew School *Tarbuth* in Sierpc" in this Yizkor book.
10. The acronym for an organization of Yiddish schools, *Centrale Yiddisher Shul-Orgenazatzie in der Poilisher Republik* (Central Yiddish School Organization of the Republic of Poland).
11. Immigration to Palestine, literally "ascent" to the land of Israel.

My Little *Shtetl* of Sierpc, Now Destroyed

by Yerachmiel Weingarten

(A Chapter from the book, *A World in Flames*)

Translated by Dr. Jacob Solomon Berger

It is a cold autumn day. A cold wind blows through the streets that drives everyone indoors. However, my wife and I must go into the city, because this is the day we are supposed to travel to Vilna, and we have to visit a number of friends from Bialystok, in order to take our leave of them, and to thank them for their extraordinary generosity to us.

We come out into the plaza where the municipal building is, and we remain standing there, as if turned into stone... what is this? Have the wandering groups from Hirschbein's "*Galut*" come to life, and broken out of the confines of the novel?

Here go young men. They are wearing long *Hasidic kapotes*, and are dressed in European clothing. Their faces are long, unwashed, with overgrown beards, sunken eyes sunken (from tears, or from beatings?) and heads bowed to the ground – the mark of two thousand years of exile lies in their eyes and in their demeanor, pressing down on their backs, and bending them to the earth. They go in one group, holding on tightly one to another, as if they did not trust anyone around them... Master of the Universe! From where do I know these people, if not from the picture portrayed by Hirschbein?

My wife suddenly runs over to this band of wanderers. She leaves her basket, with her purchased "treasures" standing on the ground, and calls out:

– Baruch! Dear Baruch!

The group of wanderers halts. Their state of paralysis is broken. They ring around my wife, and heartily take joy in her presence, because with her arrival, a breath of their memories of their home, family, and town where they were born, was infused into them.

*

My wife's little *shtetl*, Sierpc... now I finally recognize all of you. I may not remember everyone's name, but I remember you all exactly: part of you once studied in my school, when many years ago I was a teacher in Sierpc, others I recall as listeners to my speeches, as members of the Sierpc library, Zionist Organization... Whose hand has so cruelly concentrated you together in this way, and brought you here to unfamiliar Bialystok?

Sierpc, the little *shtetl* where my wife was born... The little *shtetl* of my own early youth... You were a symbol of the Jewish Ideal for me, in Poland. How beautiful were your small houses, in which a community of God-fearing Jewish people lived; with an unwavering faith, they believed in God, as it were, and lived in the best possible state of amity with the peasant of the village, who would come to the market twice a week, Tuesday and Friday, in order to earn a living from the Children of Israel. How handsome and how good-natured were your unusually idealistic youth.

My little *shtetl* of Sierpc! I will never forget that small town Zionist leader who, on that great sunny fall November day, when the telegram about the Balfour Declaration arrived, ran from house to house, with his small sack of potato peels (he would by this to feed his two cows), knocking on all of the shutters, on all the doors, while calling out: "Jews, come to the synagogue, and let us praise God; the Messiah is coming," and days afterwards – the mass meetings, when the faces of all the young people were inflamed, their eyes drawn wide open, and, in pathos said: "somewhere a great thing is being built, but we want our share!"

Or can those "bench evenings" ever be forgotten, when with the greatest fidelity, philosophized and ruminated about the cosmos: "Did God create Man, or did Man create God?"

*

My little *shtetl* Sierpc...you are one of the oldest Jewish settlements in Poland, but your pedigree – the old folios of the town records – was taken away by the fire a number of times, and all that remains is a remnant of your old bricks, which the Polish authorities prohibited anyone to use. This old brick of Sierpc was a symbol like a sheep, that Jews were like “a muted sheep before its shearers”... and this situation aligns with the old legend: that Jews, fleeing German funeral pyres, created a new place in which to live in an alien and desolate land, which they called “*Poy-Lin*”—“Lodge Here”– and it was from this that Polish Poland later arose.

This is what the legend tells about the settlement of the Jews in Sierpc: they had fled oppression, like a sheep fleeing the teeth of a wolf, finding an unencumbered and separate place between two valleys, and there they put up the tents of Jacob, there they planted Torah, and the practice of good deeds, built a formidable synagogue there, and called the place Szeps [sic: sheep]. The gentiles then arrived, who did not grasp the reference, that they were the “wolves,” and they altered the name of the little *shtetl* to Sierpc.

*

My little *shtetl* of Sierpc, hills surround it... Over the quiet streets, in the evening, the sound of Torah [study] was carried, and on your Rabbinical seat, shepherds of your people sat, who nourished the folk in an enlightened God-fearing manner. The Jewish street was always suffused with *Yiddishkeit*. In the morning, the beadles would lead their “sacred flock” with a sacred melody. The four year-old lambs – leading them into the *Heder*. After the noon hour, happy young boys from the *Heder* would run through the streets to a reading of the *Shema* – many, many “*Shema* Readers,” would, no evil-eye intended, fill up that tiny, small little street.

Occasionally a long, substantial funeral cortege would make its way to the old, distant cemetery: all the stores would be closed, because all the Jews of the little shtetl rendered their final respects , when one of their own – and everyone was considered to be one’s own – had been torn out from among the living, and was transiting into the Better World. Out in front of the coffin carrying the deceased, a host of young Heder boys stretches out, and intones: “May justice go before him...”

My little *shtetl* of Sierpc... each hillock and each vale within you, is suffused with Jewish history. Wondrous tales from ancient times are told in Sierpc, in every little hut, and across each threshold, every little byway, and even every little bridge over the small bit of water, that flows through the little *shtetl*, in order to avoid needing to cross the Vistula at Plock, or the Drw.ca [River] in [Golub-] Dobrzyn, or to the creek in nearby Rypin, if, God Forbid, it becomes necessary to write out a Get for a Jewish daughter.

*

Near one of these small bridges, a distance from the Jewish street, there stood a small "*Kapelitsa*"[1], and in it, there were several sacred Christian figurines. Jewish boys would ran past that location, with their hearts pounding, in order that they not, God forbid, be forced to doff their head wear. This small hallowed structure was given the name, "Menashe with the three sons."

Elderly grandmothers, heaving a sigh, would tell of a certain Menashe, a rich Jewish man with three sons, whom it didn't suit to live among Jews – and the end of this was that they "turned their coats inside out..."

The Szeps community suffered much shame and abuse from this, in which all of the Jews in the Jewish street sat *Shiva*, and tore their garments in mourning [sic: *K'riah*], and before this seven day period of mourning was over, they came to their violent end... and so the gentiles built a small shrine to them, and demanded that Jewish children [walking by] show them respect...

"This is how it starts" – the elderly grandmothers would sigh, using a moralizing tone of voice – first you abandon the Jewish street, later on *Yiddishkeit*, until, God forbid... and then they spit out three times, so that it not be said at an inauspicious hour.

But the Jewish street, God forbid, did not become emptied of Jews, rather the opposite – in the last years, this little Jewish street spread out, and absorbed all the streets that circumscribe the old marketplace, and the large municipal pump. A little at a time, Jews began to relocate into gentile neighborhoods, but they did not sunder the thread of *Yiddishkeit*, and did not forget the way to the synagogue.

"Pamphlets" and "Magazines" began to appear in Jewish homes. Those, who were Enlightened, told of a broader larger world, but Sierpc was a world unto itself, practically a Jewish nation, with its own community house, its own synagogues, houses of study, Heders, an inn for transients, a mikva for ablutions, and a funeral facility for after one hundred twenty years...True, the poverty was great, and the Jews of Sierpc left to go out into the larger world – to America, sending money back from there, and taking over their relatives there... Cracks began to manifest themselves in the solidarity of the community, but it remained rock-solid.

*

A World War broke out in 1914: the Russian r?gime abandoned Sierpc, and three German soldiers began to guard the mills, the bakeries and eating places... But in the larger cities, the hunger was more widespread and intense. Accordingly, refugees from those locations began to stream in, to take advantage of the wheat fields around Sierpc, and to benefit from the better air of the hills and dales around Sierpc. Among those who came, was an elderly Jew, wearing a hat, and sporting a small gray beard. An elderly Jew – in a hat – this alone was an extraordinary occurrence in Sierpc, and today, he walks through the streets and in a loud voice, speaks in Hebrew?! He became a teacher [for children in] the wealthier homes. It was said that, before the war, he was a wealthy merchant, and he possessed property in the Land of Israel. This very elderly Jew, who wore a hat, brought with him a young son, who goes through the streets bare-headed, having a head of thick, black hair, surrounded by a claque of little boys and girls, who only want to reconstruct the world, and all they do is read pamphlets, they "take courses," and use libraries, dedicating their time to long promenades, over the "*dolinkas*" (dales) that are around the *shtetl*, from which they return home in late at night, with ruddy countenances and inflamed imaginations...

And so, the sorrow and fear if the God-fearing fathers grew larger, when the young man with the mass of black hair on his head, Lord save us, "cast his eye on the *Hasidic* daughter of R' Wolf..."

You can easily understand that this young man, "with the mass of black hair," is, in fact, me, and the "*Hasidic* daughter" (like all "*Hasidic* daughters" of that time, could not even speak a proper Yiddish) – this is my wife.

*

And here comes The Second World War. We wandered off to Bialystok and other Sierpc refugees came after we did.

My wife is now standing, ringed by hapless itinerants, the remnant of her birthplace, Sierpc. Like in a kaleidoscope, pictures run by my eyes, starting from the origins of Szeps, to the modern city of Sierpc, in the year 1939...

When a person feels that death is imminent – an old folk expression says – he sees everything he has experienced in life, in a split second... it appears that instinctively, I sensed the extermination of this old, deeply rooted Jewish community, as if its entire history, with a sudden clarity, roused my thought processes, and with such pitiless speed, summoned the sight of these images, of types of people, and personalities, that had lived, breathed and suffered, and now, an uncivilized bestialized horde of people has descended [on it], and the community is to be destroyed.

Immediately, I am surrounded by this group of escapees from Sierpc.

– How is it that all of you come together here? – I ask them.

Chaotically, they begin to tell, with one interrupting the other, but from their interrupted words, sighing, and choked back tears, I obtain a confirmation of my tragic, instinctive premonition, that an old Jewish community has been wiped out.

Translator's Footnote

1. A roadside miniature chapel, or sacristy.

Memories of Chanukah from my Town of Sierpc

by Matel Rajczyk

a.

From my early childhood and onward, I remember Chanukah as the lovely "weekday festival." Businesses were open. I did not get any new clothes. I had to attend *cheder* and look at the face of my *rebbe* Chaim Yosef. Still, I felt the festivity. Something mysterious hung in the air. The white snow covered the holes and the mud on the Jewish streets. One could not make out the mountain around the Vlokes, or the area from the mountain to the synagogue and Mendel Gerlic's workshop. All the windowpanes were covered with snow and the frost covered flowers sparkled in the cold.

The most important part of that Chanukah festivity was that I did not have to return to *cheder* after supper. My heart used to pound when I used to go to *cheder* in the dark nights with my homemade paper lantern. Precisely at the moment when the lantern was needed due to a vicious dog, a drunk who was sleeping on the streets and was ready to beat a Jewish child who was in his way, or just an ordinary gentile who threw snowballs and shouted "Jew to Palestine" – exactly at that critical moment, the paper lantern went out. I threw down the burning paper, which went out, and I remained standing in the darkness.

The heart pounded like a drum. Like stones, my feet did not lift themselves off the ground, and the street had been dark for some time. That is why I felt so festive on the week of Chanukah, because for a full eight days I did not need to endure these tribulations. I used to beg G-d that more miracles would take place, and it would be Chanukah for the entire winter.

As the eldest son, on the eve of Chanukah, I had the good deed of cleaning the Chanukah menorah. I removed every speck and cleaned it. The two lions engraved on the menorah sparkled strongly. When the candles burned, one could see the red tongues that hung from their mouths. When my father and I returned home from the old *beis midrash* after *maariv*, the house was lit up. Light shone from every corner. My father held the lit *shamash* high up as he recited the blessings. As he lit the first candle, we children put our hands on his hand so that we could take part in the commandment of lighting the Chanukah candle. We all sang together *Haneirot Halalu*, *Maoz Tzur*, and *Mizmor Shir Chanukat*. Mother looked on and quietly wiped away a tear.

The Chanukah dinner was tastier than all others dinners of the year, for mother was preparing the animal fat for Passover and for the winter. At this time, the animal fat was more plentiful. Every spoonful of food was accompanied by *grivn*[1] with large or small fat globules. After the meat, we would have a course of latkes. Throughout the day, my mother with the help of my sisters would peel and grind the largest potatoes. My mother sifted off the white starch, collected it for a week, and put it in a Passover vessel so that it could be used for cakes on Passover. The amount of latkes that mother brought to the table was not enough. We sprinkled white sugar on the latkes, and ate them along with tea.

After dinner, Father gave us children Chanukah *gelt* [money], and we sat on the floor with the neighboring children to play lotteries, dominoes and *dreidel.* The men sat in the dining room and played "Oko" (a card game). The following men were sitting there: Yosef Koperman (Lipie's brother-in-law), the Cantor Danielke (Sheike's), and Avraham Shochet, the bird *shochet* [ritual slaughterer] (Burgand). Yehoshua Goldman sat at the side and constantly shouted "*Oy vey*, a waste of time!" The kibitzer was Lipia (the"Hershele Ostropoler"[2] of Sierpc). When the cantor played a "stake" and was angry, Lipie would sing to the tune of *Tal*[3], "Cantor, cantor, if you cannot, do not undertake."

At that time, the house became very hot from the frying latkes and from the clouds of smoke from the cigarettes, cigars, and pipes. My father smoked the pipe that he had inherited from his father, Shlomo Meir Shu"b, the Nasielsker *shochet.* When my father was occupied with "*Tehiliml*" (cards in the vernacular)[4], I snuck a puff of the pipe. We children, tired and choking from the stinky, smoky air, fell asleep one after the other on the floor.

b.

When the Agudas Yisroel set up the Tvuna youth organization in our town, all of the bar mitzvah aged lads who studied in the *shtibel* or the *beis midrash* became members. The organization set up evening courses where we studied Hebrew grammar and Jewish history. The teacher was Mr. Kohn. His helper, if I am not mistaken, was Mendel Yonatan's (Lifschitz). David, Avraham Aharon Melamed's, also helped.

Yossel Blachman, one of the chief organizers of Tvuna, a lover of song, organized a concert in honor of Chanukah with a choir performance. I remember only a few names of the choir members: Itche David Sznitzer, Moshe Aharon and Nisan Rajchgot, Moshe Nipomoszcz, Menachem Grosman, the lame Yossel, Yossel Goldman, Aba Licht, and the writer of these lines. Berl Pliata played the fiddle.

Rehearsals took place between *mincha* and *maariv*, and on the Sabbath during the third meal [*shalosh seudos*] at the Gerrer Shtibel that was located in the courtyard of Aharon Lipka. The Chanukah concert took place in the Gerrer Shtibel. Yossel Blachman held his left hand over his ear and used his tuning fork and directed with his left hand. We sang cantorial compositions, *Hanerot Halalu*, *Mizmor Shir Chanukat*, and a few Hebrew songs.

After the concert when all the guests went home, we singers received some refreshments. Zelig Rajchgot sent sufficient marinated herring. Moshe Grosman sent soda water and kvass, and Nachum Tac sent several flasks of wine. We brought kichels from home. The concert was successful, and the evening will never be forgotten.

c.

When I got older and already studied myself in the old *beis midrash*, I still felt the festivity of Chanukah. The Gerrer Hassid Binyamin Yehuda's (Yehuda Beker's brother-in-law) would always reprove us youths when we were sitting with open *gemaras* and chatting about worldly matters. However, in the week of Chanukah, he turned his head and looked away.

In the evenings, instead of sitting at the class, we played chess and a card game called Twenty One. Binyamin looked away and did not reprove us. Even the two large, tiled ovens in the old *beis midrash* knew that it was Chanukah.

Throughout the entire winter when the frost was biting in the street, the ovens were cold. They were almost like a piece of ice. However, in the week of Chanukah, they were hot. Indeed, this was a Chanukah miracle. The wood was dry and the flames were crackling higher and higher toward the chimney.

On the side of the oven, near the copper sink, a few old Jews were sitting and playing cards. I recall only one name of the players: Itzik Kvetcher. The kibitzer on the side, or as we used to call him, Shcaria with the Pipe, smoked the tobacco that he purchased from Shlomo Chaya's and snatched glances at the cards.

The Chanukah candles burnt festively in the windows on all the streets where Jews lived. The warmth of the candles melted the snow with the frost flowers on the window panes. The clear flames told about the legends of generations ago, the heroism of the Maccabees.

Translator's Footnote

1. Cracklings made out of skin of fowl.
2. See http://en.wikipedia.org/wiki/Hershele_Ostropoler
3. The Prayer for Dew recited with a unique melody on the first day of Passover.
4. I suspect that this is a euphemism, referring to a card game by a holy term.

Images and Memories from my Hometown

by Gershon Bergson

From my earliest childhood years, I recall Wolf Chazan's *cheder* with the broken steps and dark corridor. It was located behind the bridge. My heart pounded from terror when I went to *cheder* alone for the first time, and had to go up the broken steps in the dark.

The place of Torah of Avraham Aharon, a *cheder* in the middle of the market, was the opposite of that *cheder*. Avraham Aharon was a *gemara* teacher, a scholarly Jew and a fearer of Heaven. I mention his name with trembling and respectful awe. He served as the example of faith and belief for me and for tens of other children in town.

Later came Mintz's modern *cheder* with "*lawkes*"[1] instead of tables. The teacher wore a short jacket, was partly shaved, and wore pince-nez glasses like a professor. Only the progressive *maskilim* allowed themselves to give their children over to his hands. To Nachum Tac, Mendel Tajtelbaum and other Orthodox Jews, he was like a gentile[2].

In a later period, Litwinski's *cheder* modernized with a "principal," Eliahu Meir, who taught secular subjects for an hour a day. Turkeltaub was a teacher there. A clean-shaven person, may G-d protect us, Asher Watman taught Hebrew.

The modern *cheder* had to represent the striving for knowledge and education that tore through the town, and simultaneously protected the Jewish children from entering the "Szabaszowka"[3] with the director Eichel, a complete gentile[2], and even worse, with female teachers. There, one sits with a bare head... and girls learn together with boys. A Jew does not send his children to the "schools." A Jew is a Jew.

However, the striving for Jewish worldly education grew and now I can see before my eyes the first classes of the Tarbut School. It was two rooms, and neighbored the gristmill that belonged to Licht, close to the riverbank. "Woe unto us, what will be, if, Heaven forbid, suddenly a flood comes and the children cannot go home. They will then say that the ' ;gentiles' are guilty, the teacher of the Tarbut School." This is what the school activists frequently thought.

Fortunately, no flood came, and the first kindergarten teacher, the "aunt" as one called her, and the first principal Rubel laid the foundation of the exemplary school in Sierpc where today's citizens of Israel received their education.

The Tarbut School grew high, wide and deep. It was already located in the building opposite the Polish government gymnasium. The Jewish children specifically learned in their own language in that Polish region. Later the Tarbut School building came with its nice classrooms and a hall for performances – for spite, specifically in a Polish area.

The dedicated activists invested energy and thought in order to set up the building. Yeshayahu Frydman, David Bergson, Feivush Lipka, Wajsroza, Berl Czarka, and a great many others – some with money, some with energy – all of them did everything possible in order to establish the Jewish culture center in Sierpc, that served as an example for the towns in the district: Rypin, Lipno, Raciaz, and others, which were jealous of Sierpc on account of its fine Jewish school.

Sabbath in the Town

The synagogue, the new *beis midrash*, the old *beis midrash*, and the *shtibels* were all full of worshippers. Jews worshipped one G-d in many places.

People went to services. Here goes Yaakov Moshe Tajtelbaum. He walks step by step, majestically, with his *tallis* laying atop his coat. Women stood in the windows and watched where the crowds were going for *kiddush*. Everything was quiet in the town. For Jews in general the Sabbath was infused with holiness. The shopkeepers, the large and small businessmen, who were seeking an endorsement for a promissory note, the entire weekday tumult and brouhaha, the concerns of livelihood – everything stopped. It was the Sabbath in Sierpc.

When I went to *cheder*, a ban was put on me because... my brother went out with girls on the Sabbath. I was embarrassed. I put down my eyes and was quiet... I then gave my word that when I will grow up, I will not do so... I must admit – I broke my promise...

When I became an older lad, people were no longer placed under a ban for going out with girls on the Sabbath in Sierpc. We would walk on Plocker Street from here to there. Groups of boys and groups of girls, one group opposite the other – they glanced at each other, with a smile on their lips, passing by embarrassed and quickly, in order to repeat the same pattern five minutes later.

Later, a bit later when the sun set and the holy Sabbath ended as it got dark – we walked in the same direction. The girls were in front of us, and we were behind them. We simply walked back and forth, when suddenly we were walking in pairs – two boys, two girls, and so on until we reached the "Fundeven Ice creams." One of us would purchase ice creams and bring them to the girls, still silent. Then we would continue walking back and forth.

Those restrained, awkward meetings between boys and girls continued until the youth movements were established, where the boys and girls joined together in the ideals of societal activity, feelings and striving, which throughout the generations had been concealed in the hearts of the Jewish youth, and now were spurting forth and coming to normal human expression.

The Beginning of Societal and Cultural Activity

Michel Kopolowicz lived in the old market not far from the magistrate building. There was a large yard there, which bordered on other yards and places until Niemciewsko's yard. There, there were all sorts of things for the Jewish boys and girls who were growing up: stables with horses, carriages, wagons, and most important – Kaminski the mechanic had his workshop there.

We saw the fire that sizzled as he blew the air sack, the red hot iron, large hammers and various wheels. We heard the banging on the anvil and the squeaking of the file. My brother worked with the gentile locksmith as a journeyman. My grandmother cried before Father – can it be, a tradesman in the family?

The most important things in the yard were the bicycles that could be borrowed. One could borrow a bicycle from Kaminski for a half an hour or an hour. Who would not want to learn how to ride a bicycle? Everyone, the entire town: children, *cheder* youths, school gentiles, and *beis midrash* youths. I recall that Chaim Shlomo Licht with his *kapote* [Hassidic cloak] and Jewish hat came there to learn how to ride.

Thus, the yard turned into a club for culture and sport. Youth played cops and robbers, tennis, buttons, chess, and they ran around and made noise. People "conducted business," acted foolishly, requested a ride from the bicycle riders, played games such as football with hats stuffed with rags, and when we were tired, we went up to an attic of a barn and spent pleasant time there.

Slowly, we got tired of the barn attic. I do not know how the word "club" came to us – we began to think about a place. A club... where could we get it? We searched and we found... A widow with two children lived inn Shlomo Glazer's courtyard. She and her family began to make cigarettes, that is, they used to purchase tobacco and paper, rolled the cigarettes and sold them, ten in a package. This house was an illegal factory. The widow tricked the Polish regime and did not pay any "banderole"[4]. She had two rooms. The "factory" was in the kitchen, and the "warehouse" for the merchandise was under the pillows.

We looked for a place, and the widow looked for a livelihood – we negotiated, and this became the "club." We went to the club every evening and played dominoes or chess. We had to pay monthly dues, and that is how we obtained our own premises. This was in the year 1924-25.

We secretly spent time at the club for approximately a year and a half. Aside from our group of youths, nobody knew. However, the club at the widow's house soon became too crowded for us. It did not satisfy our cultural needs and did not calm the fermenting striving of the maturing youth to meet with the opposite sex. We again began to think and search for ways of bringing a change to our lives.

The town slowly began to come under the influence of the new aspirations of the Zionist movement. The youth slowly began to understand the need for freedom from the foreign yoke and began to aspire toward an independent life in their own homeland.

The first bold steps toward *Aliya* had already begun in Sierpc. The following people went to the Land of Israel: Avraham Frid, my brother Yitzchak, Efraim Wloke, and Mordechai Rozen. Youth began to study Hebrew and founded libraries. Two libraries already existed: a large library and a second one for the Herzliya youth organization. Hersh Malowanczyk, Leibel Horn and Mordechai Rzejsotko were the popular Hebrew teachers.

We decided to emulate the adults and found our own library. It was indeed simple; we purchased a few books, put together a box, and exchanged the books. We talked and we acted.

Our member Fishel Dobroszklanka had parents who already at that time displayed great understanding for the modern aspirations of their children. Dobroszklana had a home with two entrances. The small room with its own entrance was placed at our disposal. There, we opened our library under the name of the Hatechiya youth library. My brother David provided books on credit. We had up to 30 subscribers, including several girls.

With time, the library became a cultural club. On Friday nights, we would gather together in the little room to chat and sing.

We sung hymns as well as small pieces, which we used to sing with Yosel Shochet. The girls taught us Polish songs from school. Thus, a choir was formed, thereby expressing our aspirations and strivings through song.

Zionist and Cultural Activity

In the years 1927-1928, the Hashomer Haleumi youth organization (Later Hanoar Hatzioni) was formed. This entirely changed the way of life of our youth group, and also had its effect upon the wider circles of Jewish youth of Sierpc. Our activities grew broader. The evening hours were no longer sufficient for us. At six in the morning, they knocked at the doors – Yaakov Meir, Yosel, Shoshana... a “Zwiurke”[5]. We had to gather together, also in the early hours of the day, to study, read, and conduct practices.

We read everything that was new for us: Zionist writers: Herzl, Pinsker, Nordau, etc.; world literature: Tolstoi, Dostoyevski, Shenkevitch, Reimont, Kelerman, Mafason; Jewish writers: Asch, Peretz, Sholom Aleichem, Mendele, Tshernikovsky, Bistricki, and scores of others. Of course, “The hands were full of work”: cleaning the clubhouse, the sports place, sports practices, the library, collecting money for the funds, performances, excursions, demonstrations, elections. We were everywhere.

For the most part, our gatherings took place in the meadows, in open nature. We would go there on Friday nights, even on frosty evenings. On the hot days in the summer, we would go to the river. There we would have meetings of the groups and the brigades, marches, listening to reports, singing, dancing, and playing.

Gentiles often attacked and threw stones, but we courageously held our stand. We felt secure when Yosel David Jaszwicz accompanied us. At that time, he was the strongest of us, and even the gentiles were careful about beating him. The gentiles finally came to the conclusion that it did not pay to start up with us. The Jews occupied the meadows, and there was a truce. We would sit there and study, have discussions, sing and dance the hora.

Our cultural work was expressed in various forms. We conducted "trials" at our headquarters. We "tried" "Bonche Shweig" and the fire guardian from Y. L. Peretz' allegories, Josephus Flavius and the Bund. Nobody left our hands without a proper verdict. Our national celebrations were celebrations for the town. First of all, we distributed pictures from the Jewish National Fund and pasted them to the windows. Then we marched through the streets with blue and white flags, dressed in festive uniforms: white shirts, green pants with drums and trumpets, with the Maccabee orchestra in the front.

The procession departed: Moshe Smolenski with the shining barrels over the wheels, and following him were the group leaders A. Bergson, Y. Kurta, N. Czarnoczapka. The heads of the sections were at the sides: Y. Kurta, P. Lanenter, Tz. Sendrowicz, Sh. Klajn, and others. The Hebrew language resonated through the streets. Songs and commands were in Hebrew. The Zionists were proud. The mothers, the pious mothers who were not so happy with the gentile demeanor of their children, blessed them nevertheless – "Let your walking be in peace" – a mother is a mother.

We traveled to conventions – at first with wagons. Meir Klajn had a pair of horses. We rented the wagon and traveled to Żuromin and Raciaz. The trip took three or four hours, from 4:00 a.m. until 7:00 or 8:00 a.m. When we arrived in the town, we arranged ourselves in rows and marched along with songs, which aroused everyone's admiration.

We also went on excursions by foot for a day or two in duration to Studzieniec, Susk, and other villages. It was not so easy for us to arrange transportation for the excursions. We had to wage a "war" with our parents. The parents did not give any money, and they did not permit the trips at all. We battled with tears, we threatened to escape from the home – "I will go out to *hachsharah* and will never come back." Father was angry, mother became soft, the child was crying, "The child may indeed run away – how can I remain without him?" – a mother would think.

There are six children in the house – if one of them is missing, the house will be empty...

At the end, they permitted us to travel. Having endured the battle, we were victorious. We traveled to Skwilna, Masczisk and other places, in the forests and the fields. We breathed the air of the field and the manure, as we sang the song "and the smell of the manure." We dreamed at night about our own country in the Land of Israel.

The Dream of the Land of Israel Took on Wings

Avraham Schultz, Yaakov Meir Pukacz, Zalman Nazemski, S. Sendrowicz, and Tzipora Rozinek – sons and daughters of Aguda members – went to hachshara. The exile was difficult: in town it was crowded, the taxes were higher, the boycott of the Falangist anti-Semites was stronger, there was nothing to look forward to. "One must go to the Land of Israel. At first the children, and then later we too will follow after them ." the parents were already saying.

In the meantime, Jews had to remain in the town. We could not travel to the desired Land. The British did not let people in. Jews must wait for a good market; perhaps one could earn a few zlotys. Then tomorrow and the day after, we would travel to fairs in the surrounding towns or in far-off Pomerania, where one could load up a wagon and earn a few zlotys. It did not always succeed. Often, the fair was called off, or a heavy rain fell – one packed up the merchandise, turned the wagon shaft, and set out for home.

However, Jews are not pessimists. The following week we again traveled. We tried our luck, as we must indeed live. The town does indeed live: one lights candles on Friday night, on Chanukah one places Chanukah candles on the windows and fries *grivn* [cracklings] with festive animal fat, one builds houses, one erects *sukkot* [tabernacles] in the yards and on the balconies in front of the houses on Sukkot. One is not afraid of the gentiles.

Zelda the midwife wakes up at night and runs to a woman in childbirth. She "takes" out children. One purchases "*shir hamaaloses*"[6] and children run to study how to read the *Shema*. Jews run to exorcise the evil eye, to recite psalms, to supplicate at graves. People make weddings in town – Gerlitz-Malach with the fiddle and Kropasz with the trumpet – were busy, very busy – for they were the only musicians in town. On Passover one was a king, on Lag Baomer one marched to the fields, and on Shavuot, one brought the aroma of the forest and the field into the house.

Thus did Jews live in Sierpc, as in all the towns in Poland, as they awaited the speedy final redemption. Instead, the great destruction came.

In the autumn of 1932, the thought of leaving the town was ripe with me. My destination was Vilna, the Jerusalem of Lithuania. I left my home on a frosty pre-dawn. My mother kissed me and shed a tear. My beloved father accompanied me to the "Darozhka" and parted from me with two words "Be successful."

His blessing, the blessing from a sincere father, came true, and I was indeed successful in the path that I had set out. My inner desire to meet my beloved parents once again, borne in my heart but not expressed on my lips – unfortunately never came true. I never saw my warm home again, and never again met my dearests.

Let these lines of mine serve as a monument for the unknown grave of my parents and for the martyrs of Sierpc who were tortured by the Germans.

Translator's Footnotes

1. I
2.
3. could not find a definition, but I believe it means student desks.
4. The word here '*goy*' is not literal, and refers to a Jew that 7;comports himself like a gentile.
5. A state run Polish school for Jewish children where the language of instruction was Polish and there were minimal Jewish studies, but which was closed on the Sabbath and Jewish holidays.
6. The tax for the official paper stamps to be placed on such packages.
7. I am unsure what this means.
8. The *Shir Hamaalot* psalms are a series of 15 psalms (120-134) beginning with "A song of ascents." In this context it is used as an amulet or sign of good fortune.

My Girlhood Years in Sierpc

by Hena Oberfeld Lewin

Today, after I have already swum to shore after many difficult wanderings through the world, I will attempt to bring to memory the life in my hometown of Sierpc.

I return with memories to the days of my childhood. I see a small girl. I run quickly in the morning to my first teacher Anshel Mesz, who taught me the *aleph beit*. All the girls from the surrounding streets learned with him. There, we played under the tables with his own Zundele, who passed away very early, while still a child.

I still remember the smell of tobacco that emanated from my *rebbe* as he frequently stuffed tobacco in his nose. His wife Sara Devora, a tall, slender woman, was the director of the *cheder*. The tuition arrangements and payments went through her. She was strict with us, and the rebbe Anshel at times grabbed our faces to scold us or hit us.

While still a young girl, happy and carefree, I was sent to the "Pension" of Mrs. Reich, who was called in Polish Reichowna. There, I took part in excursions to the two mills and the Dolinkes (valleys) -- the seven lovely Dolinkes with the Kakasza Mountain. This made us seem so grown up next to our friends from the surrounding towns, who were unable to do so. There, we spent time, went to the beach with the white sand, and took pictures.

My mother bore the entire burden of livelihood and raising the children. My beloved father, a quiet, honest, pious Jew, was not involved in our upbringing. He had other businesses, such as: on Purim he would gather all the neighbors and read the *megilla* with his lovely voice, as all the children banged for Haman with what was permitted – with *graggers* [noisemakers], rolling pins, and other such things. On Rosh Hashanah and Yom Kippur, my father conducted services. He started to prepare and rehearse the prayers and *shofar* blowing a few weeks before the High Holy Days.

As we got older, our home became a club for discussions. I – a Zionist; my two brothers – left leaning Poale Zion; and my younger sister Dvora – a pious Beis Yaakov student. She always reported to my parents that my brothers had eaten on Yom Kippur. My parents held me responsible for the missing food, and I was silent... All four of us participated in various performances that were conducted by the drama circles of the parties to which we belonged. In general, all four of us, my brothers and my sister, lived in peace.

The town of Sierpc was a typical Jewish town. On Friday afternoon, when the market with all of the business being conducted with the gentiles ended, and the *cholent*[1] pots were already placed in the bakeries, Yaakov Moshe Teitelbaum would appear, washing his silk cloak that covered his wide *tallis kattan*. He already came all combed out and steamed up from the hot *mikva* [ritual bath], and went to the *shtibel* for services. Then, the iron shutters of his block of stores on the market place were shut. Shortly thereafter, all of the shops, other than the gentile pharmacy, were locked. The Sabbath asserted its power.

In the market, as well as in other Jewish streets, only guards were Polish. In the Jewish quarter, they had important tasks, such as: putting out the candles and putting away the candelabrums on Friday nights, lighting the ovens during the winter, and purchasing the *chometz* on the eve of Passover.

When my male and female friends and I ended school, we simply had nothing to accomplish. Youths from our group such as Yosef Meir Podskoc , Naftali Czarnoczapka, Pesach Grosman and others became independent because their fathers had died early and they had to take upon themselves the yoke of livelihood for their homes. Others became involved in Zionist party work, which was a tolerable livelihood, just as it is here in Israel. My girlfriends and I began to study hand embroidery with Beila Ajzenstat. However, this was no solution for us, and did not give us a livelihood.

In the evenings, we would get together at Marina Gurfinkel's photography shop, where we spent good times. We often danced, flirted, discussed, and played cards to the light of the moon that came through the glass roof. Mendel Gurfinkel, the observant Jew with the fine, black beard, who traveled to the *rebbe* for every festival, at times took the camera in his hands and photographed us, so that his Miriam[2] would be included in the photograph.

On Sabbath afternoons we would get together at Gutka Frenkel's when the old Yaakov Ber was asleep in the second room. However, our situation was sad when he suddenly woke up and heard combined voices of boys and girls. He then chased us away in all directions.

I began to go to the Herzliya society where I was chosen for the management committee, and was active in the library in which I invested a great deal of energy and effort. I worked together with Naftali Czarnoczapka. He was the president of the small library. I was the secretary and cashier.

I always had troubles with the cash. I lent all the money from my neighbors Rachele Brin and Shmuel Henech Dragon. A few times a week, they traveled to fairs in the surrounding towns, and always were free with money. When the time came to pay a debt, I really did not want to make demands on them, and I was embarrassed to remind them. My father always threatened that I would end up in jail on account of the library.

On one occasion, the electric company took me to court for stealing current for the library. We did not have money to pay for the electricity, and the electric company cut off the power. We set things in order. I came out just barely exonerated due to the assistance of a lawyer who was engaged by the library committee.

When I was already in Warsaw, I still underwrote promissory notes and sent books to the library.

I was also active in the Keren Kayemet [Jewish National Fund] committee in the city. The following people belonged to that committee: Yeshaya Frydman, Hershel Kristal, Mordechai Rzejsotko, Tzvi Malowanczyk, Ber Czarka, Izak Najman, Leibel Horn, and others. We collected money for the Land of Israel.

My parents and my friends' parents did not have the means to meet the growing needs of already grown girls. We had to concern ourselves with setting ourselves up in life. In 1934, my best friend Reizel Sendrowicz and I decided to travel to the Land of Israel. We presented our requests to the Palestine Office, and received our confirmations a few months later that we were accepted as candidates to travel. My friend then traveled. Unfortunately, I did not possess the material means to do so.

A year later, I went out on *hachshara* in Warsaw under the auspices of WIZO [Women's International Zionist Organization]. I concluded *hachshara* a year later and was registered on the list to obtain a certificate. The number of certificates was minimal, however, and I was not able to travel.

When the war broke out, I went to Russia. My sole goal was to survive the war at any price and begin anew.

After my return from Russia, my first desire was to look at my town of Sierpc, which still appeared as before in my memory. I traveled to Sierpc after spending a brief time in Stettin. I got off the train with a palpitating heart, and saw what the cruel Germans had perpetrated. I saw a strange, unrecognizable town. When I arrived at the market, I stood still like a stone. Later, I ran like a crazy person to the house where we lived and to other houses in which Jews lived. A field with grass occupied the place of the Jewish houses, and horses were grazing. I did not say a word to anybody, nor was there anyone to whom to ask questions. I stood for a while next to the shop which used to belong to my father Wolf Margel the clockmaker, and I wept bitterly.

Translator's Footnotes

1. The *cholent* [stew for the Sabbath daytime meal] would be left cooking from Friday afternoon. To avoid the oven having to be left on in every house, the bakeries would often leave on their ovens so that everyone could put their *cholent* pots into the common oven.
2. Miriam would be the Hebrew name of Marina.

Jewish Livelihoods in Sierpc

by Tzvi Malowanczyk

Fishermen and Butchers

The fish business in Sierpc was entirely in Jewish hands. The fish merchants who were called "fishers" in fact had no connection with the fish catchers. They went to the true, gentile fishermen in the villages, purchased their merchandise and sold it to the Jewish people.

Let us recall one of those fish merchants: Moshe Kszarsz, a short man with a thin beard, who was only a little involved in the fish business.

[Page 353]

He was a cobblestone layer, who placed stones on the roads. His wife Chana Golda, a woman with red cheeks, round, black, burning eyes, and a healthy high voice, was the true fisherwoman. She conducted the fish business.

Moshe's brother Zelik Kszarsz was involved in the fish business together with his wife and some of his children. The business was given over to them by their father Meir, who was known by his nickname Meir Moreinu (Meir our Teacher).

Another family of fishermen was the Berlinski family who earned their livelihood from the fish business. In general, the fish business in Sierpc was transferred from parents to children.

The Jewish butcher trade was also in the hands of specific families. The four brothers Yitzchak (Itche), Yechezkel, Meir and Mendel Dorfman were separate butchers. They were four brothers with their own families who worked in the butcher shops with the assistance of their wives.

The Grajna family was another family of butchers. I do not recall their first names. They were also a considerable number of brothers with wives and children, each of whom had their own butcher shop. The Brodacz family and others were also butchers.

The Jewish butcher shops were located in a civic building in the new market. There were also non-kosher, Christian butcher shops there. In general, the butchers in Sierpc did not live badly. They were generous and had an appreciation for Jewish cultural and Zionistic activity. Like the fishermen, the meat business was passed down as an inheritance to the children.

Fruit and Vegetable Dealers

The fruit and vegetable business also held a place in the spectrum of Jewish sources of livelihood in Sierpc. There were pomiculturalists who in early spring leased orchards from the landowners, agriculturalists, farmers, and the like. In the summertime when the fruit ripened, the pomiculturalists left the city and went out to the orchards with their families to harvest the apples, pears, and plums from the trees and sell them in the city.

The vegetable business consisted of the professional occupiers of stalls in the market, who stood in the market for the entire year and sold potatoes, carrots, beets, chickpeas, horseradish, radishes, parsley, apples, pears, plums, raspberries, strawberries, etc. The market sitters were involved in their business throughout the entire year. In summer they sat with their merchandise under an umbrella to protect against the sun and the rain, and in the winter with a pot of live coals to warm their hands during the time of intense cold.

The fruit and vegetable dealers did not earn their livelihood in abundance. They lived under meager circumstances.

Glassmakers and Clockmakers

Several Jewish families earned their livelihoods from glassmaking. This trade was easy, and did not require any physical exertion or special learning. It was sufficient to purchase a diamond to cut glass, and the livelihood was already assured. The following glassmakeres were known to us in town: Yisrael Yitzchak, Shmuel Sarna – a witty Jew and a joker, Pinchas Mekler and others. Glassmakers earned a good livelihood. On Tuesday and Fridays, the farmers from the villages would come and bring the windows to the glassmaker to fix the glass and cement it. They would invite the glassmaker to come to the village for larger jobs.

On ordinary days, the glassmakers would go out to the streets. Anyone who needed them would summon them for various jobs that were taking place. Later on, Christian glassmakers came on the scene, taking away a portion of the livelihood of the Jews.

The clockmaking trade was entirely in Jewish hands. The following Jews were involved in that trade: Moshe Szperling – a tall Jew with a hoary, grey, fine long beard, Menachem Szpido, Wolf Margel – an enlightened Jew, and Michael Smolenski – the son of the cantor of Sierpc who had a sense of music and song.

Aside from repairs, the clockmakers were also involved with the sale of new clocks, wall and standing clocks, wedding canopy hoops as they were called in the trade lingo, ordinary bracelets, tie hooks, and other silver and gold jewelry. For the most part, they had their own houses, and were of reasonable means or even wealthy. Aside from their work in earning a livelihood, they were also involved in societal activity in the bank, charitable fund, *beis midrash*, and the like. Until 1939, this trade was given over from parents to children, and was exclusively in Jewish hands.

Tailors and Shoemakers

In Sierpc as everywhere, the primary sources of livelihood of the Jews were the tailoring and shoemaking trades. The tailors manufactured men's and women's clothing including overcoats, pants, men's jackets, women's dresses, etc. There were two categories of tailors: those who purchased merchandise and sewed clothing to sell to the purchasers; and confectioners who conducted business with ready-made clothing which they sold in their stores. The primary confectioners were Nachum Koniec, Kalman Blum, Elimelech Cyna, Kalman Kalmanowicz, and others. The merchants were of significant means, even wealthy. For the most part, they purchased ready-made clothing and resold them. However, each one of them knew their work, and even had a small tailoring workshop next to their business.

Aside from the public businesses, there were many home businesses where people worked in their homes. On the market days of Tuesday and Friday, they would stand on the street with a covered wagon and sell their manufactured merchandise to the farmers who came to the city.

The confectioners also sold their wares in the markets in other cities and towns, such as Wednesday in Skepe – 24 kilometers from Sierpc, Thursday in Srwilno – 18 kilometers from Sierpc, and the like. Such trips were made in the following manner: three or four tailors hired a farmer with a wagon. They loaded the merchandise before dawn and traveled to the fair. They came home late in the evening. The livelihood was tight, but Jews continued on until 1939, when the Germans annihilated everything.

The shoemaking trade was set up along the same lines, and had the same categories. Some of the shoemakers manufactured boots and footware, whereas others were professional shoe merchants with their own shops. There were also home workers who went out onto the streets on the market days of Tuesdays and Fridays to sell their merchandise, or traveled to the market in other cities and towns. The merchants of ready-made shoes also were not badly off materially. Some of them even owned their own houses, such as, for example: Pinchas Mlawa, Avraham Mlawa, Baruch Atlas, and others.

The stitchers were a different branch of the shoemakers trade: Yosef Pundek, a Jew from the world of *maskilim*, a prayer leader in the synagogue, who took part in societal institutions; Avraham Yitzchak Grodka – a Torah leader, a regular donor to Keren Hayesod, Keren Kayemet (Jewish national fund) and other Zionist funds, an owner of a small, wooden house; Yechezkel Kadecki who was active in the *chevra kadisha* [burial society], a *gabbai* [trustee] in the synagogue, and a prayer leader. The stitchers' trade later spread among the former *beis midrash* youths who wished to learn a trade.

The hat makers trade was also considered to be one of the honorable professions. The following people were involved in that trade: Betzalel Eliezer Gongola, a *maskil*, a shofar blower, a Torah reader and a prayer leader not for reasons of livelihood. He was a jolly Jew who enjoyed telling a joke. He gave over his profession to his children, especially to his oldest son Moshe Gongola, who partly inherited his father's humor. The younger Gongola was active in the Handworkers' Union, and, despite his difficult situation, he was active in volunteer institutions. When his children grew up, his material situation improved and he did not live badly. Aside from hats, which Moshe manufactured himself with the assistance of his brother Shlomo, he also imported ready-made merchandise such as fancy hats, fur hats, and other such items, and resold them. This trade as well was especially Jewish until 1939.

The Germans put an end to all the Jews and their workshops, warehouses, and shops.

May their memories be a blessing.

Memories

by Yaakov David Sendrowicz

In memory of my beloved father, mother, brothers and sisters:
Yitzchak Meir, Miriam Rachel, Chana Tova,
Avraham Yosef, Eliezer, Aharon – of blessed memory.

A. The Pure and Straightforward Reb Moshe

He was a small, shriveled Jew with a large, wrinkled forehead. His eyes under the grayish blond brows peered toward the sky. His long, patriarchal beard covered three quarters of his face, which always had a thin, thin smile that would not lead, Heaven forbid, to frivolity.

At the table in the side of his semi–warped shop from which he earned his livelihood, one could always find books into which Reb Moshe would glance between customers. It was difficult for him to go with the orderly daily flow. He was always a bit short on time. He cast a glance at the Book of Psalms. He had barely recited one chapter when a customer appeared – a tailor looking for pant buttons, or a shoemaker looking for a few nails and metal horseshoes that were threaded over the wire.

In his little shop, Reb Moshe had a special item for the tailors of the town: "velvet collars" in three colors – brown, black and garnet. The following people purchased most of the collars: Kalman the tailor, Shlomke the tailor, and the mute tailor from Ferfl Street. When someone came to ask about the merchandise, Reb Moshe would lift up his pants, pucker all his wrinkles, fix his belt, and sigh deeply. He took a package stuffed with many papers down from the shelf, blew away the dust, opened it, got the merchandise, and discussed the price that must be paid. They quickly found out from Reb Moshe how much it had cost him, and they realized immediately that the pious shopkeeper was more afraid of overcharging than they were of overpaying.

Aside from collars, Reb Moshe had in his store a bit of haberdashery that would be purchased by village Gentiles. Reb Moshe treated them the same as his Jewish customers. He was very careful to never overcharge for the picayune merchandise such as buttons, collars and new yarn. He was always careful not to trick the purchaser. Reb Moshe would say, "In business, one must always withstand the test." And tests are unfortunately common for sinful humans. The tailor girl comes to the store. She purchases buttons, yarn, and other such items. She sticks out her bare hand to Reb Moshe. With a worried face Reb Moshe quickly leaves the room through a door and goes into the workshop. His wife, Grandmother Rachel, deals with the business with the girl. She concludes the great "transaction" with the customer. Thus, in a very delicate fashion, he let the girl know about what had taken place[1]. One must retain a customer.

The home manufacturers who primarily sewed pants for the city tailors in the market and who made their purchases from Reb Moshe's shop all knew to put on a hat when they passed over the doorstep of the pious businessman. But one is only human, and one forgets oneself and comes to Reb Moshe in a frivolous mood. He sizes up the customer with a gruff glance and a clear smile. The tailor immediately understood what was going on here. He apologized several times: "Reb Moshe, forgive me, I forgot completely what was happening. The family members are urging me to finish the pants. I have not seen one coin from them, but my wife does not want to know about this. The children are driving me crazy. Reb Moshe, you will not have to bear more of this."

This is the way everyone had respect for the small, thin, merchant, on account of his simplicity and honorableness. Everyone realized that he was G–d fearing with his whole heart.

Reb Moshe would also enjoy a bit of liquor, especially early every morning. As soon as he had washed his hands after getting out of bed, he would cast a glance at his bookshelf that stood at the head of his bed. There, on the side, one could find a small flask with a bit of liquor, to warm up the withered body a bit so that it could continue to serve its longtime master, the Master of the World. As long as he remains Reb Moshe, he must put his entire effort into maintaining and upholding the soul in the sinful body. Books were indeed housed in the bookshelf: the Bible, the *gemara, halachic* works, *mishnas*, and Hassidic works, which warm the Jewish soul; as well as liquor, which warms the body a bit to impart energy to serve the Creator with fervor and enthusiasm during his old age.

After tasting a bit of liquor, Reb Moshe's day began. He would return from the morning services, put his *tallis* and two pairs of *tefillin* (Rashi's and Rabbeinu Tam's) in the closet, and then take out the little flask with his beloved cup. He would pour a bit, recite the *shehakol* blessing, and enjoy it with two good *kichels*[2] that his wife had baked. His pale face took on a rosy color; his heart warmed up; his eyes became somewhat radiant. Now he had energy to serve the Master of the World. His wife soon called Reb Moshe to breakfast. That is how he spent day after day, in an honest fashion, with the same order of the day.

On Sunday afternoon, Reb Moshe would go to visit the teachers, while checking on how his grandchildren's studies were progressing. He would ask them some questions, to see what type of contentment he could have from his grandchildren. The teachers would treat him in a cordial fashion on account of his innocence, and say little. He never had a complaint against the teacher regarding a grandchild whose knowledge was weak. He would always blame the children for the weak learning, and not the teacher.

Reb Moshe was a good grandfather. The grandchildren would wait for the Sabbath to come, when their grandfather would test them about what they had studied. They would enjoy the Sabbath fruit and the *kichels* with tea that the grandmother prepared.

Reb Moshe had a special fondness for the *mikva* [ritual bath]. He would immerse himself for so long that he would faint. They would have to quickly pull him out by the arms and wash his face with cold water until he revived. Then they led him home. I would come to tend to Reb Moshe and take him home after a fainting spell at the *mikva.*

Reb Moshe's wife Rachel brought three sons and a daughter into the world. They grew up, and just as the pious father was the symbol of honesty, restraint, and simplicity in words and in deeds, they too displayed all the traits of their father. Itche Meir had his famous long beard and wide eyebrows. Hirsch Mechel was very similar to his younger brother, but somewhat more wide–boned. Chaim was the youngest and the tallest, with a fine, white, wide face, bedecked with a wide, combed beard. The only daughter, Beila, wore glasses with gilt rims. One would never meet her in an agitated frame of mind. She was always goodhearted. The poor people already knew that they would receive a 5 groszy donation from Beila, along with a few "*nagrapkes*"[3] in addition.

On the Sabbath, the elder son Hirsch Mechel would often come to sit with his father a bit, and drink a glass of Sabbath tea brought from the "*Shlisharkn*"[4]. They would sit there, looking at each other in silence. Both did not like to talk much. The silence continued until the mother finished reading "*Tzena Urena*"[5]. Then, she began to ask, as usual, how the children were doing and about the grandchildren, thereby creating a theme for discussion. However, what can one talk about so much on the Sabbath? One must not mention secular matters. Therefore, Reb Moshe slept a great deal in order to avoid, Heaven forbid, falling into the trap of uttering a weekday word.

The grandchildren loved their grandfather very much. He would give them a weekly allowance of 10 groszy and *kichels*. Everything was prepared for when they came. Grandmother prepared the fine, clear Sabbath tea as if for important guests. The most important thing was testing the grandchildren on what they had learned throughout the week. However, Reb Moshe could not spend a long time with the grandchildren. As he began to recite the *mishna* along with his grandchildren from his little *gemara*, the Sabbath sleep overtook him, as his eyes closed. He struggled with sleep as he hummed the *gemara* tune with his grandchild. The grandmother prepared the bedding on the side, and Reb Moshe spread himself out.

*

On the festivals, the grandchildren knew that they would be going to their grandfather. All of the sons with their children gathered there. The son–in–law Binyamin rarely came to Reb Moshe. There were rumors that good relations did not exist between the father–in–law and the son–in–law. Something was kept in check under the beard. Like a German, he did not worship in the *shtibel*, but rather in the new *beis midrash*[6] – showing himself as spoiled. This caused Reb Moshe to look askance at his grandson – his daughter's son – especially because he did not have *peyos* or wear a long frock. The grandmother, however, overlooked the iniquity of her grandson, and delivered sweet *kichels* to him. Whenever he would come over, she would immediately take him into the dark kitchen and stuff his pockets with fruit. She would give a bit of fresh strawberries with sugar, give him a heartfelt kiss, and tell him that he should come again.

All of the sons with their children came for festivals. They sat around the table. The elderly father, facing Hirsch Mechel, was at the head of the table. All four of them had long beards; and, with their serious faces, had almost the same appearance. All three sons were wearing black beaver pelts, still from their weddings; black velvet collars, and black velvet Sabbath hats. The grandchildren received nuts from their grandmother, and everything felt homey. They sipped hot tea. After every sip, one could hear a loud "ah ah ah." They dried their sweaty brows with the napkins.

The grandchildren were very busy in the yard playing with the nuts. The sons were engaged in a conversation about everything and anything other than business. They also did not directly talk about the holiday. Hirsch Mechel spoke a bit from the heart, saying that the children are not obedient. They do not want to go to *cheder* anymore. Chaim the youngest casts a compassionate glance toward his unfortunate elder brother. His heart is overflowing with contentment as he mentions his only son Mechel, who studies in the *yeshiva*, and of whom he is very proud. The middle son Itche Meir also has contentment from his four children, all with Jewish hats, *kapotes*, and *peyos*. They obeyed the *rebbe* cheerfully. Everyone in the *shtibel* was jealous of him due to his calm children.

In truth, the children were completely unruly and acted as brats in the house, but the teachers always boasted about them. The three girls were different: already not as religious as the boys. In truth, they did not read any Polish books at the table on the Sabbath. They recited the *Shema* every day, but not enough for Itche Meir. In their minds they had Zionist thoughts, which were completely non–kosher and invalid for Itche Meir.

Thus did they sit around the table and discuss the children and a bit about politics. Reb Moshe heard everything and said nothing. He cast a glance at a Hassidic book that was lying on the side, or in the *Midrash Tanchuma*[7]. He uttered brief sighs, mixed with hidden festive joy. He looked paternalistically in a heartfelt manner at his sons with his serious, patriarchal face. The old, hoary, grey father wants to say something, and asks what is going on in the world. Before a response comes from his sons, the old father nods off with a faint smile on his lips.

Dark clouds hovered over world Jewry. Sierpc Jews felt the hatred that came through from the Gentile streets. Reb Moshe began to feel the hands of the devil. Gentiles, who would never have previously dared to bully the "*stara zakonni*"[8] – as they would refer in polite Polish to a Jew who was a long–time resident of the city, and an honest businessman – recently began to greet Reb Moshe with an ironic smile, as they mocked him behind his back. The pious shopkeeper, whose head was always occupied with Torah thoughts, began to think about things that were transpiring in the world, about bad times for Jews. Doctrines from the righteous men of the generation who had already gone to the World of Truth, about the End of Days, began to go through his mind. He attempted to make sense of the current times.

Then, the news arrived about the passing of the great giants of the generations. The author of the "Chofetz Chaim" of blessed memory[9] passed away.

Reb Chaim Ozer Grodzinski of blessed memory also passed away[10]. They were the two greatest Lithuanian *gaonim* and *tzadikim*[11]. The following people also passed away: Rabbi Chaim Sonnenfeld of Jerusalem of blessed memory, the Czortkower Rebbe of holy blessed memory, Rabbi Meir Shapira of blessed memory, Reb Yosha Dvinsker (the Rogotchover Genius) of blessed memory – rabbis, *rebbes* from all parts of the world were needed in Heaven. Something was summoning our protectors of the generation home. What was happening?

We remain like sheep without a shepherd, thought Reb Moshe, as his eyes literally saw the dark clouds spreading over the Jewish skies.

Hassidim sent emissaries to their *rebbes*, searching for comfort, but alas, no clear responses came. The ground began to burn under the feet. The righteous of the generation were taken to Heaven. The earth was flowing with clouds of anti–Semitism and terrible decrees, with nobody realizing where things were leading.

Pickets were placed by the Jewish shops to prevent the Gentiles from purchasing, Heaven forbid, from Jewish shopkeepers. They also came to Reb Moshe, the epitome of honesty, to prevent him from bringing guilt upon the Gentile who purchased pant buttons or shoelaces. The Angel of Death was already located in Europe. The newspapers brought news of a new war that was about to come. This was nothing other than the "footsteps of the Messiah," but must the birth pangs of the Messiah come to that village? What was going on?

The elderly Reb Moshe suspected everything that younger people did not want to believe. Nevertheless, he did not despair. One must always have hope. With the Master of the World, everything is possible. The Chofetz Chaim of blessed memory was a great lover of Israel. He will stir up the souls of the great *tzadikim* in the Garden of Eden, and all would intercede positively for the People of Israel. However, it seemed that the prosecutor was defeating the defender before the Throne of Glory, and therefore the great ones of the generation were taken away so they would not witness the birth pangs of the Messiah – this is what Reb Moshe thought when the Germans began to destroy the town of Sierpc.

The Great Synagogue had already been turned into a heap of coal. The vibrant Jewish life was paralyzed. Terror was present as people got up in the morning and went to sleep in the evening. Reb Moshe did not go out on the street so as to avoid being captured by the Germans, who cut off beards. The joy of the family was thwarted – from the grandchildren and sons, and from the old father. One was cut off from the other. The bandits wandered around all corners of the cities. Death hovered overhead. Uneasy thoughts fluttered through the mind of the old Reb Moshe, "Dear Father, and great God! Who knows if I will merit burial in a Jewish grave?" thought the pious Jew.

What could one think about when everything was already clear before everyone's eyes? Germans were driving people out of the houses. One must part forever from the town, from Sierpc, with which one was bound with thousands of strands. Every stone had a story to tell about Sierpc Jews. Every gravestone was a piece of history. And now, everything was lost. Everyone – young and old – had to go to the old marketplace.

Reb Moshe was standing immersed in his thoughts when his grandson brought him the sad news. Reb Moshe then recited *Shema*. It was 6:00 a.m., but the grandson asked that they set out already. The Germans were shooting. As he was going, Reb Moshe donned his *tallis* and *tefillin*. Meanwhile, the grandmother had prepared something to eat for the way. They put the Sabbath knife, the *techina* book[12], his *tallis* and *tefillin* in a basket. The elderly couple held each other by the arms, like young children who were afraid that the wind might blow them down, as they set out for the old marketplace with slow steps.

The Gentiles watched as Reb Moshe cast sad glances at the burnt synagogue and the lonely *eis midrash*, as their eyes moistened. His old Polish female security guard, who served him for decades, found it difficult to endure the experience.

Thus began the Jewish death march. Reb Moshe and his wife were behind the crowd. The German murderer had already taken hold of his gun, when suddenly Reb Moshe's only daughter, Beila, let out a pathetic cry and begged that they let her old father and mother return home. Something must have "moved" the stone heart. The German ordered the old couple to return. Reb Moshe turned his face toward the "train of sorrow" in order to part from his near ones. Unfortunately, however, they did not see anyone. Thus did they, the children and grandchildren part from their very beloved, honest and straightforward father and their dedicated mother – by glancing from afar.

G–d fulfilled her request. G–d heard the weeping of his elderly servant. Reb Moshe merited receiving a Jewish burial in Sierpc. He lies together with those near and dear to him, and waits until the birth pangs of the Messiah will end and the great day of complete redemption will arrive.

May his merit protect us!

B. Three Brothers–In–Law

A small house stood on the right side of Plocker Street, a bit in from the street, near the house of the head of the community, Shmuel Zeinwil. The little house contained two shops: On the left side there was a Gentile pork business. A porcelain piglet looked out the window. When we *cheder* youths ran by, we would spit three times and say, "You shall surely hold it detestable"[13]. In the grocery store on the right side, one could see the splendid face of Yosel Sznicer. He wished a hearty good morning to everyone who passed by his grocery store. Yosel's wife and their son, Itche David, who helped a bit with the business, were also always standing in the store.

Yosel Sznicer was from Plonsk. His father was Yitzchak Aharon Sznicer, and he was indeed a carver[14]. One could find various carved objects among his children's and grandchildren's jewelry. He earned his livelihood by carving various ornaments. He engaged in his craft during his free time between one customer and the next. The elderly Yitzchak Aharon was a very wealthy man, but he did not spend more than two hours a day in the store. For the rest of the time, in the morning and the evening, he studied with Jews in the *beis midrash*.

The Sznicers were a large and wide–branched family. They were well–known even in far–off Siberia. The following is an anecdote from my personal experience, which seems a bit fantastic.

I was in the Siberian taigas in the winter of 1940. The homesickness, the loneliness, and the hunger tormented me and reminded me of home. Coming home alone after a hard workday of wood chopping, I met two elderly people sitting on a cut down tree, whispering to each other in the ear. Broken, tired, homesick, and full of worry, I sat down beside them. We struck up a conversation, and one old man asked me, "From where do you come, young man?" "From Sheps," I responded. When he figured out that Sheps meant Sierpc, a city in Poland, he began to speak Polish and said that he comes from Plonsk, and had already been in Russia for 30 years.

I told him that my family also came from Plonsk, and he asked me, "Do you come from the Sznicers... from the family of Chilek Sznicer, who was in the wheat business?" "Yes," I responded.

It turned out that the old man, the camp doctor Nawicky, who had been sentenced to eight years in Siberia, knew the Sznicers.

Several branches from that extended family were in Sierpc. Among them were the three Sznicers: Yosel Sznicer, Meir Libson, and Yisrael Chaim.

Reb Yosel was a modest, honest, straightforward Jew who was pleasant to his fellowman. He was loved by both Jews and Gentiles on account of his modesty and honesty in business. He belonged to the "old guard" of the Kock Hassidim, who would tell over their old Torah thoughts and various stories. He was one of the rare people who avoided commotions, and it was this modesty that evoked the greatest honor and respect. Every year, Yosel served as the prayer leader for *Shacharit* on the High Holidays. He earned his livelihood from a small store, run mainly by his wife.

His son Itche David was not similar to his father in all ways. In his private life, he was completely like his father - honorable and refined. One would seldom hear a loud word from him. He loved communal work for the benefit of the community in various social institutions. He was a member of various organizations and charitable funds - the Bank Lodawy and the Zionist organization. He was a pillar of the Sierpc Tarbut School. He demanded something from the world as well as himself - everything was supposed to be exceptional.

I recall that in 1936, when the well–known tragic unrest broke out in the Land of Israel. A protest meeting was organized in the Great Synagogue. Various activists of the Zionist organization, including Itche David, spoke. During his speech, his voice turned into a powerful protest shout to the world. The entire gathering was bound to their seats and overcome with deep outrage against the murder of Jews in the Land of Israel.

In the old market, near Yonatan Lipszyc's house, there was a fine brick building (still standing today) with a balcony. The house belonged to Meir

Libson, Yosel's brother–in–law. He lived a patrician life, and was considered as one of the wealthy Sierpc merchants. He ran a fine manufacturing business.

Meir Libson never forgot anyone – he was generous in every detail. An honorable poor person could always be found at his table at lunchtime. He was a typical Hassidic merchant. His wife Sara was the protector of everyone who was suffering or tormented. There was always a sensation of guilt in her eyes, as if she owed the world a debt. She felt that she had not fulfilled her obligation no matter how much charity she gave. She suffered from the pain of many orphans, widows, and poor people. Many honorable families discreetly received her goodhearted donations. No poor person ever left her house ashamed. Charity was the content of her day–to–day life.

Yisrael Chaim Szajewicz was almost always sitting on a bench near the entrance to his somewhat rickety shop near the bridge. From time to time, he coughed from all the cigarette smoking. In the springtime, when the snow melted causing an overflow of the Sierpc brook, Yisrael Chaim was the first victim. His shop literally floated. The canals were clogged up. Then, the entire street came out with buckets and iron implements to clear out the water from his shop.

Yisrael Chaim, with his tall, broad bones and his figure that was already stooped, gave off the impression of an elderly aristocrat who was already weary and weakened from his many years of communal activity. Yisrael Chaim was a member of the *Chevra Kadisha* [burial society] from his childhood on. This was a directive from the Gerrer Rebbe of blessed memory, who called upon Yisrael Chaim's father Avrahamele to register his five year old child in the *Chevra Kadisha*, as a omen for a long life. In his old age, he was the veteran man of the *Chevra Kadisha*.

Reb Zalman, the *gabbai* [trustee] of the *Chevra Kadisha*, was happy when Yisrael Chaim arrived at the feast on the 7th of Adar, the *yahrzeit* of Moses[15]. Zalman and Yisrael Chaim, both old men, had what to talk about – things that the younger people had never known. They sat next to each other and shared memories of decades past.

On Rosh Hashanah, we grandchildren knew that we had to run to the old *beis midrash* to hear our grandfather Yisrael Chaim lead the services. However, when it was difficult for the old man to conduct services, he resigned from that holy mission. The congregants and the *gabbaim* did not want to forego his fine voice and sweet prayers. Two *gabbaim*, Hirsch Moshe Kanebrand and Shmuel Yitzchak Tac came to beg Yisrael Chaim, in the name of the entire congregation, to lead the *Shacharit* service and not give up his customary role. Yisrael Chaim, already weak, elderly, and in his eighties, after a while agreed to do what the gabbaim requested. With awe, they took Yisrael Chaim by his arms and led the old prayer leader to the beis midrash. The congregation was already waiting outside, and greeted Yisrael Chaim with a hearty Shana Tova.

His lovely prayers still ring in my ears. Despite his age, his voice was very young. Strongly etched in my mind is the "*Ashrei Haam*" recited after the *shofar* blowing, as he leaned against the podium on the Torah reading table. The cheerful *shamash* Yisraelke stood on one side of him, and Yosel the *shochet* stood on the other side, with his *shofar* under his *kittel*. The hoary, grey Yisrael Chaim stood in the middle.

I saw my grandfather in great splendor at the Purim feast, when all the children and grandchildren arrived with *mishloach manot* [Purim food gifts] to grace the old father's table and to partake of the feast together with him. Grandmother acted as if it was a wedding. She nimbly took out the two brass candlesticks from the meat shelf, lit the candles, and set things up like a festival. Everyone behaved with deep respect toward the old father. The father, sitting on his plush "father's stool," was radiant with joy.

When our neighbor Asher Lewin came on the eve of Yom Kippur after the meal to extend good wishes to my father and mother, Mother reminded us that we must go to Grandfather for him to bless us. We four brothers set out to my grandfather's. As we went through the door, we immediately felt the dread and fear of the Day of Judgment. The large, wax candles were standing in an old pot filled with sand. We heard Grandmother weeping as she recited the *techina* at candle lighting before Yom Kippur. Grandfather put on his glasses, stood with his hands over his grandchild's head, and whispered a prayer.

With a wink from Grandfather, we approached him. He asked us to arrange ourselves in a semicircle. He placed his trembling hands over our heads and recited a silent prayer. We also trembled without knowing why. A solemn spirit overtook us. We stood there with bowed heads under his hands until tears began to fall from Grandfather's eyes. Then, our eyes moistened as well. When he concluded his prayer with the word Amen, we extended our hands to Grandfather and wished him that he be sealed in the Book of Life for the good. We ran quickly to *Kol Nidre*, and we ran well and spryly after the blessings from our good, pious grandfather.

The three brothers–in–law Yosel Sznicer, Meir Libson, and Yisrael Chaim, with their lives suffused with honesty and love of their fellow Jew, merited death before the destruction, and burial in a Jewish grave – this was a great merit in our times.

C. The Sabbath During My Childhood Years

The entire Friday was dedicated to preparing for the upcoming Sabbath. The mothers were rushing: to the bakery to knead the challahs and the strudels, to the fish seller so as not to be late for the fish, to the store to purchase something, and then to the stall to lay out the merchandise on the tables. The mothers helped earn the livelihoods. When it was a short Friday, one literally lived in fear of, Heaven Forbid, being late for the Sabbath, being late in cooking the fish and meat, and, most important, being late in making the *cholent* and *kigel* and taking it to the baker before he smeared the oven with lime.

The fathers and grandfathers prepared for the Sabbath in their own manner. They went to immerse in the *mikva* and took a steam bath in the bathhouse. Everyone loved the hot *mikva.* When the red Efraim came to immerse himself, we children immediately knew that we had nothing to do there, for it was going to be like fire – that is in the boiling *mikva.* Therefore, we nicknamed him "The brave man of the *mikva.*"

As the sun dropped lower, Yaakov Moshe ran back from the *mikva.* He was dressed in a long coat, and he lifted up the collar so as not to catch a cold, and held his underwear under the hem. All of the shopkeepers and passers–by immediately understood the purpose of his quick pace – the Holy Sabbath was arriving in Sierpc and one must lock the stores. His white, patriarchal beard and good deeds in daily life evoked the greatest respect from all circles of the population, even from the Gentiles, who called him Hassid. When Yaakov Moshe ordered someone to close the door of a shop, the owner immediately understood that there was no point in appealing. When Yaakov Moshe returned from the *mikva*, it was a sign that it was late and one must lock the store.

Ordinarily, the Satan knew what he had to do on late Friday afternoon. For an entire week, one remains in the store and asks the Master of the World to send a few good Gentiles, and one does not see them. However, just before candle lighting, as if in spite, they appear. This was indeed a great test for the shopkeeper. Yaakov Moshe, however, with his patriarchal, sharp voice, warned the shopkeeper that he must not make any compromises with the Torah. One should give away the merchandise to the customer at the base price, so as to avoid desecrating the Sabbath.

In our *shtibel*, we had a custom to not recite "*Barchu*" unless the poor guests had been taken care of for the meal by the householders. If the poor people were ever late and came at the end, they would remain in the *beis midrash* without food. The many efforts of the *gabbai* Mendel Elimelech did not help at all. Then, we children took the initiative and organized the dividing up of the guests in the following manner: each of the lads would take a guest and take him to the householder just when he was at the fish course and eating with gusto. He would then announce that the *gabbai* had sent a guest for the Sabbath.

We tricksters conducted this task in its entirety. We had a great victory. The next day, the guests came to services happy... Mendel Elimelech the *gabbai* was especially happy that a Jew did not miss the Sabbath.

Mendel Elimelech was our dedicated *gabbai* in the Gerrer *shtibel.* He turned, cleaned, and lit the ovens tens of times with a special love and dedication, so that Reb Avraham Aharon and his students who learned there would not freeze.

Concern for the Gerrer *shtibel* took a major place in the day to day concerns of the *gabbai*. His presence pervaded everywhere. In all corners it was happy and joyous in accordance with the adage: worship G–d in joy. The sound of a melody and of practicing a recent tune was never missing from the *shtibel*.

It was Saturday morning. Everyone was running to the Great Synagogue, the old *beis midrash* and the new *beis midrash*. The city was in a Sabbath spirit.

I go quickly to the services in the *shtibel*. The gentle youth with their thick *gartels* [ritual belts] and fine silk cloaks were sitting by open *midrash* books on the weekly Torah portion. The older Jews, with boxes of tobacco in their hands, were peering into the Holy *Zohar*. The elderly Chaim Yosef was sitting at a corner of the table with his poplar cane by his side (for he limped a bit) peering into a book with his sleepy eyes, more dozing than awake. This was because when everyone else was lying in their warm beds dreaming their sweet dreams, it was the most peaceful time for Chaim Yosef as he united himself with the Creator by reciting his daily Psalms.

In Chaim Yosef's low house, located in the area of *mikva*, it was already light at 3:00 a.m. Chaim Yosef sat by the weak light of a lamp and conducted his daily Divine Service, for when the students arrived to learn, he must be finished with his service of the Master of the World.

In the same building of the Gerrer *shtibel*, there was a hotel that belonged to Mrs. Licht. The owners of the hotel had a certain connection with the *shtibel*. Throughout the entire week, Avraham Aharon, the tall, hoary, grey teacher, studied *gemara* with several youths. His place was in the last bookroom. The students sat at one side of the long table, and Avraham Aharon sat opposite them with his large *gemara*. Thus did he study with his students until 8:00 or 9:00 in the evening.

A few times a week, one of the students came up from the hotel to bring a glass of tea to the *rebbe*. Mrs. Licht served the *rebbe* with great contentment and good heartedness. Often, she did not wait for the maid, but rather brought the clear glass of tea herself with the warm feeling of helping the pious Avraham Aharon, who was known in the city as a *tzadik*. Mrs. Licht would often send the *rebbe* a bit of chicken soup, and a good chicken wing for his sickly daughter, Chana, who suffered from a lung illness.

After a sweet glass of tea, the *rebbe* would utter a deep "ahhh," as he wiped with his large, red handkerchief his forehead, nose, and face, and especially the wrinkles yellowed from many years of smoking tobacco. He would then tell us children, "I guarantee Mrs. Licht the World to Come, for she refreshed me with tea. I wish her all the best wishes in my name, and wish her that she should be well."

We worshipped the service and then prepared for the reading of the Torah. It was a strong custom in the Gerrer *shtibel* that people would purchase honors during the Sabbath services[16]. When would this be, if not for the Torah reading? There was always something to purchase: one must pay rent. The *gabbai* had a complaint – people did not pay their pledges, and there was no order in the room. As always with Jews, there were forthright youths who believed that one must always state exactly the opposite. Then, they began to act with frivolity. The voices ascended to the heavens. For us children, we never understood how there could be a Sabbath without shouting and without raising a ruckus.

The final arbiter was always Yosel Pukacz. With his perpetually wise brow and smiling face, he would find a compromise, and a way out of the difficult problems. The *shtibel* was the second home for Yosel Pukacz. In his free moments, he would take a glance at the *Yad Chazaka*[17], his beloved book of study. The book of Maimonides always lay on the table at his seat. We students had the task of protecting the books. From time to time, we would collect the books from the tables, and put them in their correct places in the book room. In that manner, we knew which book each person was studying from.

After *Musaf*, the congregation prepared to go home. Every guest was already standing with his host, waiting to be taken to the host's home. I fulfilled my duty of helping my father put away his *tallis* after services. My older brother Avraham Yosef was already ready with Father's coat. This small act was a special expression of thanks from us brothers toward our beloved father Itche Meir for the education that he gave us and for the warm home that he created for us.

We went home. The old market was bustling with Jews returning from the synagogues and *shtibels*. Wishes of "Good Sabbath" could be heard from all sides. The mothers and grandmothers with their long, lace shawls wrapped around their necks, with the *Korban Mincha* prayer book and *techina* books in their hands, were hurrying home. Young women with children in carriages were walking along the street, near the Christian church, the old market and out onto Plocker Street. An idyllic Sabbath spirit pervaded the town. People were free from the weekday concerns about livelihood.

We came home. To our astonishment, our beloved mother was not yet home. We waited for *Kiddush*. Perhaps, Yosel Shochet conducted the services in the old *beis midrash* that day. We already knew that if the old shochet conducts the services on *Shabbat Mevorchim* in the *beis midrash*, our mother, along with all the women, would be in the women's section of the synagogue for longer than usual. She derived special enjoyment from his high and sincere prayers. With such prayers, one could cry out from the heart somewhat. And where is it more appropriate to cry than during petitions at the synagogue?

Finally, Mother arrives with her joyous Good Sabbath greeting. She then called to us with enthusiasm, "Children, since food has already been prepared for the entire Sabbath, I did not leave before the end of Yosel Shochet's prayers. In his blessing of *Rosh Chodesh*, one can sense that it is the Sabbath."

We ate the first course of the Sabbath lunch, until the *cholent*. Father tested the children about what they had learned through the week. My brother Leizer, with his lovely blue eyes and constant smile on his face, was already standing near Father with his *gemara* in his hands, telling him what he knew. He was the top *gemara* student in *cheder*. Father derived enjoyment from his learning, and waited with great pride and perseverance for his son to be recognized as a genius and a scholar. Our youngest brother Aharele also had something to show – he already knew *chumash*. Father has brought him a new *chumash* from Warsaw to mark the beginning of his study of *chumash*.

One hurried to the baker for the *cholent*. Almost all of Jewish Sierpc was running: the mothers, the children, the school girls – all were running with hand towels to the basement of Malka, the baker woman. They went down to the cellar via the half broken and rotting steps. One had to be an acrobat in order to come back up with the hot *cholent* with all of one's limbs intact. However, in the merit of the holy Sabbath, Jewish children were not injured. In rare cases, one may have merely been burned a bit by the *cholent* pot. After coming home with the Sabbath food, the second course of the Sabbath meal proceeded with joy and enthusiasm. The *kugel* was prepared. Father and the children joyously sang the Sabbath hymns.

The songs from Mendel Elimelch's house resonated from the neighboring courtyard. The joyous Sabbath songs could be heard in the streets.

On Saturday afternoons, one began to see the first couples strolling along Plocker Street. The youth were making haste – some to the sporting match and others the party headquarters. The older Jews enjoyed the pleasures of the Sabbath. After drinking the Sabbath tea, they were overtaken by weariness, and they took a nap. In the winter they did so near the oven, with their hands lying underneath, and in the summer, at the table. We children also enjoyed the Sabbath calm. We told stories. We were free from the yoke of Torah and from the spankings that we would get from the teachers.

For the third Sabbath meal in the *shtibel*, Jews sat around the set tables. People discussed world politics a bit, mentioning old history and applying it to the current situation. Zalman Frajdman, the elder of the *Chevra Kadisha*, sat at the long table opposite the Holy Ark, looking into Tractate *Chullin*[18]. From time to time, he uttered a word about his *Chevra Kadisha* matters and told stories about American Jews who had come to visit their ancestral graves. It would take a great deal of effort to find the grave that had become overgrown with vegetation over many years. He, Zalman, had put together a map of the graves, which eased his work. However, he did not come out of this dry. The tourist had to pay a certain sum to the *Chevra Kadisha* for honey cake and liquor.

The shadows grew as the conversation continued. The sun set behind the houses of the town. Sierpc parted from the Sabbath. The streets bustled with the happily strolling Jewish crowd. Youth ran toward the sport place. People wanted to hold onto the Sabbath with all their power, they did not want to part from the pleasant day.

In the dark rooms of the *shtibel*, people set the table and partook of the third Sabbath meal. We children sat in a corner and conducted our quiet discussions in the dark. Menashe told fascinating stories that he had read in various Hassidic books. The adults at the table sang *Bnei Heichala*. We ran quickly to the table to sing together with Mendel Malach and his choir.

This is how we observed the Sabbath in Sierpc.

D. Noach Pukacz and his *Mangel*[19]

Sierpc was a provincial town like all provincial towns. There were Jewish scholars, simple Jews, merchants, porters, and teachers. There were very important personalities, such as the *mikva* [ritual bath] attendant, and the guard of the cemetery, etc. There was another personality, who was called "*Mangel*." This all formed the character of a homey town. People knew what was going on with their neighbors; they whispered secrets in the ears about everything that took place between the four walls of the family nest of Sierpc residents. This I discovered after seeing as a child when I went with my late mother to the *mangel* of Noachya Pukacz.

The small house of Noachya Pukacz was located on Foreh Street not far from our house. It was said that he was not far from being a centenarian, but when one asked him his age, he would have an immediate answer on his tongue: "What does it mean how old I am? Over 60." His small house also did not appear all that young. It was a bit crooked on the side. The roof already had one patch atop another. The walls were already bent from rain, snow, and frost. Noachya's general appearance was appropriate for him. He was a short Jew, with a short cut beard, neat and tidy. He would walk on the patio between the *mangel* and his house. He would cast a glance through the door to see who had come with a package of freshly washed, starched, stiff clothes. However, the payment was meager throughout the day, because the main source of income was from the Jewish mothers who did not have the time because they had to help in the store or go to the fair in Skwylna–Skempa to purchase some merchandise, as well as conduct the housework. Is this a small thing? They would have to peel potatoes, roll blintzes, or knead dough for noodles. The latter was not one of the easy tasks. Not everyone's child was as fortunate as I, with my mother. She was an artist when it came to cutting the noodles very thin. They also had to wait for the precise moment when everyone's child arrived home from *cheder*, where he studied "*chumash* and verses" with Lomen Ajnbinder, *aleph beit* and Hebrew with Pinchas Hoiker or, if he was fortunate, a page of *gemara* with Avraham Aharon. The weak children had to eat something warm, to warm up their insides and have energy to study in *cheder*.

This is how all Sierpc mothers spent their days. Where would they have time to go iron the laundry that the Gentile woman had washed three days ago, which was now all washed, soaked in clear blue starch, and dried? The matter of the laundry and drying the laundry was no simple matter. To truly describe it, one must provide a special chapter, for example, about how the house appeared on the days that one did the laundry, about boiling the water in the middle of the day, about the righteous women, about the vapor that was created by boiling the water with non–kosher soap, about looking for attics of the neighbors to hang the laundry; about how in the winter, it would take one week to dry the wash; and then, with good fortune, everything was back in the house. Then one had to stretch out the large sheets to remove their stiffness, or prepare the Sabbath tablecloths to be pressed. Then there would still be time on the fine summer evenings or the long, cool winter nights to dedicate to the iron.

Now I wish to try to go back with the help of my memory to the town workshops, and go a bit to the iron, to where I had certainly been taken tens of time with my beloved mother or grandmother Krose of blessed memory.

This was in a long, wooden building. The old character sighed. The rain pelted down during the cloudy days and nights. During the winter, one had to push away the thick snow cover, until spring came and the pleasant sun melted the snow, and all sides were clear. However, the poor walls were weary from age and from bearing the heavy load of white snow. I was sometimes sent with cold drops on the neck[20] to put out the candle that lit up the iron, as I stood on the sill of the small window.

Inside, there were two long, shiny tables along both walls in order to prepare the laundry for ironing. Two round meter sticks stood on the sides, that were called *valtzes* in "iron terminology," which were used to spin the laundry for ironing. When everything was ready, it was carried to the long machine and placed under it. The two machines were filled with large, heavy stones, to press upon the *valtzes*. As a child, I believed that the reason they were so heavy was because they were special ironing stones. It seemed that the sweat of our weary mothers and grandmothers from many decades was perhaps mixed with a few tears, as they wet the stones and placed them upon the heavy *valtzes*, forming a considerable portion of their weight. At the same time, the tears that moistened the aprons of the Jewish mothers came from the heavy burdens locked in their soft, warm, hearts.

Of course, when the calf turned around, the iron got mangled and the hand got scalded, the tongues also did their thing. One had to talk a bit, and one indeed did so – about nothing in particular, about weddings and divorces, about fights between husband and wife and who made peace between them until the next fight. What lunch was cooked today, and what would be cooked tomorrow. Whose daughter was set up with a boy, and whether it was appropriate or not based on family pedigree, and whose wife, may we not hear of such, purchased non–kosher cheese at the market. During such serious discussions, my grandmother Krose forgot that her hand was under the machine, and that her grandchild was playing near the calf. Fortunately, only the little finger of her right hand got burnt by the iron. What happens when a finger got ironed? It was bound up for a few months, and one spot remained on the finger as a souvenir.

Regarding these secrets that one whispered in the ear, I should not hear – it was only the stones of the iron that calmly heard year in and year out, and thereby added to their weight. Was it therefore a wonder that they seemed heavy?

This is how one spent the evenings at the iron. From time to time, one would eat a bit of a piece of bread with *schmaltz* and *grivn* [cracklings] that one took along. Then one would go play with the calf again.

I never heard any discussions about the price when Noachye's son came to collect. There was a long term connection between them, and the owner was content to obtain any payment, as long as they would come to use his dedicated, trustworthy iron that served the residents of Foreh Street in the old market for many years.

Thanks to the fact that the candles did what they customarily do, and went out one by one, one would be reminded that one had to shorten the iron–secrets somewhat and conclude them at the bakery, where the baker was smearing the challahs on Friday at dawn, or coming home from the synagogue on the Sabbath. They arranged towel after towel, blanket cover after blanket cover, tablecloth after tablecloth, wrapped them in a bed sheet and carried them home.

E. Yosha with the "*Shandes*"[21] and Yosha Zelik's the Perpetual In–Law

Yosha the water carrier was never short of work. Summer or winter, he was never unemployed. He served his customers faithfully. He would even bring two pails of water up to the second story, hanging on his *shandes*. He was so dedicated to his *shandes*, that on the Sabbath when he did not work, he did not want to give a rest to his shoulders. The *shandes* had to rest on them.

His shoulders were made especially for water carrying, like a camel that was created with two humps with a ridge between in which to place the load. He did not always receive an invitation to be treated with a bit of barley soup in the kitchen near the smokestack. He already knew which women cooked tasty food. He could be seen on the street every morning, with round cheeks, red like fine apples, a rope tied around his belly, always prepared for work. Unfortunately, in the winter it was not so easy to carry.

In the winter, Yosha had to fetch water from the pump that was located in the middle of the market opposite the courthouse. He had to take care not to break his hips on the ice that the young "*labuzes*" – Simchale, Yankel and

Meir – had made especially near the pump. They would pump a bit of water onto the frozen ice. They did this two or three times on the ice, and it was ready. When Yosha came to take water and saw the wedding, the "*labuzes*" made the true "*Misheberach*"[22].

Yosha could not pronounce the letters gimel but rather daled. He would tell us children: "I will report to your father that you are not going to cheder"[23]. For the group of children, this was a great joy. To his good fortune, the Sierpc policeman Pasterunek was standing beside the pump. At Yosha's call for help, the policeman started staring at us. Of course, we left.

Yosha charged five groszy for a "*parl*", that is two pails, of water from the pump. The wealthy people ordered "*mikva* water" from Yosha – that is, water from the well near the *mikva*, which was considered very good water. That water was colder and tastier – so thought the most important householders of Sierpc. It also seems that this was some sort of secret. Perhaps the old women of the city indeed knew the secret of the *mikva* water, but they never told it. Therefore, Yosha charged a double fee, 10 groszy to bring water one time from that well.

Yosha had a fellow–tradeswoman, Zishete from Ferfl Street. She wore a pair of large man's shoes, bound with wire so that they would not fall off. She had a rope around her belly, like all the water carriers. Yosha got along peacefully with his fellow–tradeswoman. She was ahead of Yosha with one thing – with curses. She always had a ready lexicon of curses, as if ready on order. It was possible that this was the reason that Yosha never fought with Zishete. Most of the time one could find her wandering around with her pail and turning the long rope with the bucket of water near the *mikva*. She never went to the pump, so as not to encroach on his territory.

Yosha with the *shandes* aroused the pity of everyone. He had a tough life. In the summer, he was thoroughly soaked with sweat, as if he had just come out of the water. In the winter, he was like a complete stick of ice. His clothes were as stiff as a window from ice. He himself was rigid. From the moisture of his nose, little frozen "candles" hung down. His eyebrows were white from the frozen vapor, and his hands were stiff with cracked skin. He did not worry about this, and felt that he was going to go quickly to the Creator. And who had it as good as Yosha? He had a perpetual source of livelihood, one must only beg for years.

On the long winter nights, Yosha would come to Sheina Leah in the cellar to drink tea. Sheina Lea lived in the old market in the cellar of Nachum Lewin's home. She had a food store in the front. A large kettle with brewed tea was always available at one side of her shop, for the Gentiles who would come to the city for purchases, and for Sabbath tea for the Jews. Yosha could be found there every evening. He would enter, sit at a bench, untie the string, and melt away the frost. There was always a puddle of water around him from the melted snow.

Sheina Lea knew well that Yosha would not drink from a glass. What was a glass of tea for Yosha? He could not hold it in his hands, which were swollen from cold. He was served the pot of tea, Yosha took out a piece of hard sugar from his pocket. It smelled like onions, because it was kept together with onions in his pocket. He sipped and sipped, until the children decided to have a bit of fun with him. Then he gathered up all the rags with a rope, tied them together, and went home to rest his tired bones. He was an important guest for Sheina Lea – and why not? If not for Yosha, from where would she get water to cook tea?

There was another Yosha in the city – Yosha Zelig's. Everyone knew him as well. Anyone who attended a joyous occasion in the city or who hosted a joyous occasion such as a *bris*, bar mitzvah, or a wedding must have met Yosha. He was considered as one of the members of the clergy in the city. He then arranged for the jester [*badchan*], and considered himself a relative. Both of them waited for weddings in the city. The jester, who lived under a roof near the slaughterhouse, awaited a few groszy for his services. Unfortunately, he was a poor man. He was blessed with several daughters and one son.

Yosha Zelig's was the first person in the city to know when a wedding was coming. He then immediately announced it to Avraham the jester. Without Yosha, there could not be a wedding in Sierpc. He ran to fetch benches from the *beis midrash*, and he summoned the waiters and cooks. He helped bring the water and looked for places where they could do some baking.

Yosha was the first to wish *mazel tov* to the bride and groom. He did so with great joy, as if they were his children. All of the in-laws called him Uncle. He dressed festively for all the weddings and rejoiced as if the occasion was his own. When the bride was ready for the *chupa*, he did everything to ensure that he would be the first to see her in the bridal gown. In the middle of the wedding, he whispered to everyone about what he had seen.

Yosha was also close with the musicians and with the tall Malach and his choir. When they began to lead the bride to the *chupa*, Yosha was the first to announce to the tall Malach that it was time to go.

Yosha was employed for several days after every wedding. He did not conclude until he had collected the last money from the uncles and the aunts. They knew that they could deposit the gifts with Yosha Zelig's.

He lived near the old *beis midrash*. He had lost his mother, and often came to services to recite *Kaddish*. He was unable to understand the small letters[24], so Yisraelke the Shamash always helped him with Jewish things. He helped him put on the *tefillin* and recited *Shema* with him. Yisraelke Shamash would recite a word, and Yosha would repeat after him, thereby reciting the *Kaddish*.

On account of his success with weddings in Sierpc, Yosha expanded his activity and went to weddings in the entire Sierpc region. Once, he was away from Sierpc for an entire week. His father went to search for him, and found him at weddings in Zuromin–Badzyn and Drobin.

How did one know that he was in the towns? They found out from Avraham the jester when he returned from the weddings in those places. Yosha had to remain a bit longer, for was there no shortage of work there? He accompanied the in–laws, received the last money, and brought the benches back from where he had taken them. Of course, there was no shortage of food at a Jewish wedding. Yosha was certainly eating well for eight days[25].

Translator's Footnotes

1. I believe this means that he had religious compunctions about touching a woman. Instead of telling her outright, he transferred the transaction over to his wife.
2. See http://en.wikipedia.org/wiki/Kichel
3. *Nagrapkes* is likely a type of food.
4. The name of a teahouse in Sierpc. See page 185.
5. A Torah commentary in Yiddish customarily studied by women on the Sabbath.
6. A hint that he may have had a more modern outlook than his father–in–law. German Jews would be more modern in outlook than Polish Jews.
7. See http://en.wikipedia.org/wiki/Tanhuma
8. Literally, "the old religious order."
9. This was in 1933. See http://en.wikipedia.org/wiki/Israel_Meir_Kagan
10. This was in 1940. See http://en.wikipedia.org/wiki/Chaim_Ozer_Grodzinski
11. *Gaon* (plural *Gaonim*) – religious geniuses. *Tzadik* (plural *Tzadikim*) – Righteous people.
12. A book of Yiddish petitions recited by women at candle lighting time.
13. Deuteronomy 7:26.
14. *Schnitzer* in Yiddish.
15. One of the traditional dates for the annual *Chevra Kadisha* feast.
16. Not with immediate payment, but rather with pledges.
17. Maimonides' summary of Talmudic law.
18. A Talmudic tractate dealing with the laws of *kashruth* and ritual slaughter [*shechita*].
19. An iron or clothing press.
20. An obscure phrase. It likely means that he broke out in a cold sweat.
21. I suspect that the term here refers to the water carrier's pole.
22. This sentence is full of nuances, implying that the pranksters waited around to see the results of their prank, which would be Yosha slipping on the ice.
23. The Yiddish version of this quote has the 'g' sound interchanged with 'd'.
24. I.e., he was not overly literate Jewishly.
25. Referring to the feasts during the *Sheva Brachot* week following a wedding.

Rabbi Zalman Hasid

by I.M. Sidroni (Sendrowicz)

In this chapter, we would like to pay tribute to an exalted and famous *Hasid*, Rabbi Zalman Hasid, who lived in Sierpc at the beginning of the nineteenth century.[1]

We quote below an excerpt from the book *Ramathaim-Zophim*, a commentary on the book *Tana Rabi Eliyahu*, by Rabbi Shmuel Zilhah[2] from

Sinyava, who was the Presiding Judge of the Community Courts of Wlodawa, Brok, Siedlce, Łowiczm, and in his later years, Presiding Judge of the Community Court of Nasielsk. In the book, published in Warsaw without any notation of date, he writes on page 210:

"When I was in Przysucha, one of the students told me about the charitable acts of the *Admor* of blessed memory[3], of how he once traveled to Danzig, through the town of Sheps. An exalted personage, Rabbi Zalman Hasid, who was very poor, lived in Sheps. When he arrived at his lodgings, he sent for Rabbi Zalman Hasid, and said that he wanted to make a feast for him in the style of the *Hasidim*. He gave him a fistful of silver coins, and Rabbi Zalman took the coins home and purchased fish and poultry and all that would be necessary for the guests, and he still had coins left.

"After Rabbi Zalman had gone, Rabi Simchah Bunim asked the landlord's servant to bring a furrier, and bought a warm coat and hat for Rabbi Zalman, and also purchased shoes and boots. He also bought some linen, and had a shirt made for Rabbi Zalman, as well as other clothes. When it was time for the feast, he told the servant to wrap everything, and bring it to Rabbi Zalman. They went to Rabbi Zalman's house and he told the family to dress Rabbi Zalman warmly, because it was winter. He saw that the family was very poorly dressed, and he immediately gave some coins for the servant to bring clothes, and they brought the merchandise to the house and there was great rejoicing.

"After they had eaten he ordered some drinks, and gave the family many coins. After the feast he went to his lodgings accompanied by Rabbi Zalman. When they parted, the *Admor* took some RT[4] and gave them to Rabbi Zalman as a parting gift. The latter did not want to accept it, since he still had coins remaining from the first two times, as well as the clothes. The *Admor* replied that 'The Torah says 'Thou shalt surely give him, and thy heart shall not be grieved when thou givest unto him' [Deuteronomy 16, 10]. There may be controversy about the particulars of the saying, but the simple explanation is that he who gives out of pity is not giving charity, but is restoring his own good health because his body cannot withstand more pity and distress. For this, one must give a number of times, until his 'heart shall not be grieved when thou givest unto him' when there is no more pity for the poor recipient, and only after that can he realize the commandment of charity. And now that I have given you everything, my heart no longer grieves for you, and I can fulfill the charity commandment as directed by the holy Torah. All my efforts were to achieve this level, and if you do not accept it from me, all my labors will be for naught, God forbid. ' When Rabbi Zalman heard this, he immediately accepted it cordially, and they parted amicably. See how a person like this has the spirit of God within him."

*

In the newspaper *HaModia* that was published in Tel-Aviv on the 17th of the month of Kislev 5715 (4 December 1954), in the column "Tales of *Hasidim*" by Yehudah Leib Levin, there is a different version of the same incident:

"Wounds of Compassion"

"When he was a lumber merchant, Rabi Simchah Bunim would travel every year from Przysucha to Danzig, and would stop to rest in the town of Sheps, at the house of Rabi Zalman, a learned *Hasid*, a poor and beleaguered man.

"Rabi Simchah Bunim bought utensils and sheets, and even brought food to the house, and dressed Rabi Zalman in new clothes against his will, and did the same for his family. On Saturday night, as he was about to leave, he placed a large sum of money in Rabi Zalman's hand.

"Rabi Zalman refused to accept it, and said, 'You have already given me a great honor, sir. Much too much. '

"'All that I gave you was to cure my wounds of compassion,' answered Rabi Simchah Bunim, 'Not to you, but I gave it to myself, because your troubles distressed me. Only now can I fulfill the commandment of charity. Why would you stop me from doing this?'"

*

We heard the same story from Rabbi David Hamburger of Żuromin of blessed memory, who heard it in his youth (more than sixty years ago) from Rabbi Avrahamke Nishat of blessed memory (one of the most outstanding and honored Gur Hasidim in Sheps).

Translator's Footnotes

1. Rabi Simchah Bunim of Przysucha was a lumber trader, and would travel to Danzig on business. He was ordained a Rabbi in the year 5575 (1815), and ceased trading and traveling. This is our proof that the event described here happened at the beginning of the nineteenth century.
2. May his memory be blessed in the next world.
3. Rabi Simchah Bunim of Przysucha
4. Reich Toller – a German coin

Uncle Chaim Nachum

by Chaim Pundek

As in all Jewish communities in Poland throughout the long period of exile, various groups and hues arose in Sierpc. There was a Hassidic and Kabblistic outlook, the *Haskalah* outlook, and the realist Galician consciousness. Among others, there was also a "collective" leaning, a revolutionary attitude against fanatical beliefs and the ideas of the pious.

When Dr. Herzl shook up the Jewish world with his visionary striving for Zion, the dream enchanted almost all of the communities of Polish Jewry.

Chaim Nachum Tanwel, known as Uncle Chaim Nachum, was one of the first in our town to become enthused with Herzl's dream of the concept of the return to Zion. Uncle Chaim Nachum, filled with the spiritual inheritance of the Jewish people, fought strongly for a Jewish national consciousness amongst the Jewish people of Sierpc. He gathered the workers and tradesmen together every Sabbath afternoon to study *Pirke Avot* [Chapters of the Fathers], *Shulchan Aruch* [Code of Jewish Law] and *Agadot* [Jewish lore], and infuse them with national consciousness. At those times, the situation of the workers, tradesmen, and small–scale businessmen was very low, both materially and spiritually. The poor strata of the Jewish community toiled hard and lived in a meager fashion, in poverty as well as in a low status. Those hours that they spent with Chaim Nachum were precious to them – radiating light in the darkness.

From time to time, emissaries would come to the city to collect money for their institutions. A *magid* [preacher] or an emissary from a yeshiva would deliver a lecture about the Jewish faith, Jewish customs and traditions on the Sabbath afternoon or between *Mincha* and *Maariv* during the week. Uncle Chaim Nachum always came to their assistance, hosted them, and helped them raise money. My uncle's wife, Aunt Rivka, a woman of valor who also worked very hard at business to earn livelihood, cooked and provided food for the guest.

However, Uncle Chaim Nachum was not only a first class communal activist. He was not only the first in the *Haskalah* stream or in Chibbat Zion. His house was a center for all meetings, including for various communal purposes, charitable committees, and the like. My uncle was also a *mohel* [circumcisor] who donated his services to all the children in Sierpc.

My uncle also functioned as an arbitrator who mediated between people. He was the trustee of charitable monies for the communal funds. At his home there were pledges left by people, various documents and confidential papers. I remember once on a fine day when a fair was taking place, when Uncle Chaim Nachum and Aunt Rivka were occupied in their shop, thieves broke into their house and took everything that belonged to the community and to other people. When he found out about the theft, my uncle became very sick and the entire city worried about his health and life.

My uncle summoned the well–known city thief (a Jew who used to worship with two pairs of *tefillin* when he was not in jail) to his sickbed, and begged him to return the stolen goods. After a long and hot discussion, the thief returned everything. He pointed out the place where the stolen objects were located, under a stone near Felke's Lodownia [ice cream parlor].

Before his death, my uncle, who had visited the Land of Israel years earlier, left a will stating that his *Talmud*, Bible and other books should be transferred to a *yeshiva* in Meah Shearim in Jerusalem.

Uncle Chaim Nachum died in 1915, during the First World War. He did not merit hearing about the Balfour Declaration in 1917 and witnessing the upbuilding of political Zionism and the great phenomenon of the Jewish Legion that helped the English Army liberate the Land of Israel.

May his memory be a blessing!

From my childhood, I often visited Uncle Chaim Nachum's house. I loved him and held him in esteem. When I registered in the Jewish Legion shortly after the Balfour Declaration in 1918, to serve in the English Army to help liberate the Land of Israel from the Turks, I registered under the name Tanwel. I fulfilled a vow that I had made that if I were to fight for the liberation of our Land, I would do it under the name of the beloved lover of Zion, Uncle Chaim Nachum Tanwel.

Avraham Fried Yerushalmi – Zionist No. 1

by Ephraim Talmi

Avraham Fried Yerushalmi, our revered activist, deserves an honored place as the number one Zionist in the history of Zionism and public affairs in our town. If in the previous generation of *Hovevei Tzion*[1] in our town, the name of Reb Chayim Nachum Tunbol was on everyone's lips, in the era of *Agudat Tzion* and widespread Zionist activity, Avraham was the leader, the patron, the mentor, the counselor, the propagandist, and the implementer.

He came to us from the neighboring town of Zhoromin, after he married Sarah, the daughter of the well-known Reb Eliezer Vasolak, a scholar and among the first *Hovevei Tzion* in our town. Avraham was the son of an eminent and scholarly *Hasid*, who was zealous and sharp. He was raised in the *Hasidic* tradition, but his religious beliefs lapsed, and with all of his youthful enthusiasm he became wholeheartedly inspired by *Hovevei Tzion*. He was fervent and passionate, agitated and an agitator, active and motivating others. He leapt into the sea of communal Zionist involvement and swam in it with a *Hasidic* exuberance, with the devotion of a fanatical believer. He was the foremost of the speakers and the foremost of the doers. He did not just politely ask; he also consistently implemented. He lectured, explained, and preached, and achieved. He labored and persevered in his Zionist activity.

He was not like some Yeshiva students in town whose public activity served as a launching board for a political career. Their activism was for them like the pleasures of the Sabbath, a light burden because it came with the wages of honorable acts. Avraham paid dearly for his agitated activism; he neglected his family and his livelihood. He had many detractors whom he had exasperated in disputes that had upset their complacency and the slow drift of their lives. But he had many admirers, followers, supporters, and friends. He was not a man to be deterred by difficulties or terrified by any sacrifice. He knew how to defend his convictions and stubbornly persist in achieving his goal. But everyone, even his most voluble opponents, recognized his integrity and honesty.

Avraham Fried Yerushalmi, who preached Zionism and *Aliyah* to the Land of Israel did not rest on his laurels, and he wanted wholeheartedly to realize his principal hope, his life's yearning, and be one of the builders of the new fatherland. He set up a barn like one of the peasants. He may have been the chief activist and leader of the Zionists in our town, but he saw no loss in dignity in this simple and dirty labor. He went from house to house to collect potato peels and other vegetables, food for his cows, and would then sell milk to his customers, and barely eke out a living from his manual labor.

Avraham realized his Zionist dream one day at the beginning of 1921, when he packed his few belongings and went to the Land of Israel with his wife and three small children. This was a daring "Leap of Nachshon"[2] that surprised many and enhanced his reputation. This was a Zionist leader who shows by example that which he has been preaching. He was the first immigrant from Sierpc before there were certificates[3] and the first after the Balfour Declaration.[4]

His beginnings in the Land of Israel were not strewn with roses. When he arrived at the Port of Jaffa, he was housed along with young immigrant pioneers in the *Beit Olim*[5] in Jaffa, just as the bloody riots broke out in May, 1921. Arabs attacked the *Beit Olim* as well and cruelly murdered many Jews as the Arab policemen looked on or aided them.

This was the baptism of fire for the Zionist leader and enthusiastic pioneer. He went with his family to the sands of Nordia, which today is a bustling urban center, but was then a dangerous wilderness, where jackals howled at night. He set up a tent there, and worked at transporting gravel from the nearby beaches that was used for the building of Tel-Aviv, which was then proceeding at a fast pace. This was very brutal labor for a family man his age, but a man like Avraham did not flinch at hardships, suffering, or difficult work. He followed his camels laden with boxes of gravel with love and joy, and would accompany the tinkling of their bells with bursts of an exuberant new Hebrew song, "Camel, my camel, you are like a brother to me with your gravel."

Sarah, who stood by Avraham's side, suffered greatly as a mother and housekeeper in the new land. The tent was their living quarters, kitchen, bedroom and guest room.

But people like Avraham and Sarah were not satisfied with just providing for their own family. Very quickly they became known to every pioneer and immigrant from Sierpc and the surroundings. Their tent, and later their house on Bograshov Street, was open to everyone in need. Every pioneer from Sierpc and Zhoromin, from Rypin and Raciaz, and all the towns in the district would initially come to the house of Avraham and Sarah. They came for a first meal, for a warm greeting, for a guarantor for their first loan, and even to borrow some cash (to be returned or not...). From his few pennies he would give to the destitute, and the one loaf of bread that the family had he would share with the hungry. He would offer a piece of his red watermelon to the visitor, and never said to anyone "I have been deserted, I am alone."

It was a home in the fatherland, a fortress for everyone, and many of the pioneering immigrants would credit Avraham with convincing them to remain in the Land of Israel when he supported them and nurtured them. And many of the women, whose privation and resentment at their new way of life was getting the better of them, found comfort and aid with Sarah, who was the good mother to them all.

Avraham is a man of the people, devoted and diligent in activities as a Zionist, public servant, and humanist. He was a father to all, and Sarah was the mother of all of us. This will be forever to the credit of the Yerushalmi family.

Translator's Footnotes

1. [*Hovevei Tzion* – the precursor of the Zionist Movement]
2. [A leap of faith – according to rabbinical tradition, when the Children of Israel were fleeing the Egyptian Pharaoh's army and arrived at the Red Sea, they hesitated. But Nachshon ben Aminadav jumped in to lead the way, before the Red Sea had even parted.]
3. ["Certificates" (*sertifikaten* in Yiddish) was the name given to the visa and documentation required by the British Mandatory Government in Palestine for permission to settle in Palestine.]
4. [The declaration by the British Government in 1917 that Palestine would become a Jewish homeland.]
5. *Beit Olim* – house for immigrants to the Land of Israel

Natan Tatz

by Rivka Eshajwicz (Alter)

Natan Tatz was born in the city of Sierpc. He stemmed from an important Hassidic household.

He was tall and slender, with a fine head of grey hair, a thick moustache in the style of Polish landlords, trustworthy eyes, and an aristocratic bearing. Natan Tatz made an exceptionally good impression upon people.

He was a man with a resolute character and physical vigor. He had a wide open heart to everyone. He was well-known and recognized in the city and the region, both by Jews and by the Polish population. He knew how to overlook trivia, and always demonstrated simplicity, folksiness and a love for truth in his interpersonal relations. He was always prepared privately to go to others and assist anyone who was in need.

The Jewish societal and cultural life in Sierpc had to thank Natan to a great extent.

He was a founder of the Jewish Public Library, a city councilor, a financial supporter of the Culture League, and supported all cultural as well as Bundist activities and undertakings.

He helped publish various publications and proclamations. Thanks to him, it was possible to conduct the evening courses where one could learn to read and write. He played a great role in the work for the Yiddish School.

Natan Tatz himself set up a private charitable fund which gave loans to poor people. If someone could not repay the loan on time, he would not refuse to lend to him again. When giving financial assistance, he never investigated to which party the needy person belonged. Bundists, Zionists, Orthodox people and Hassidim – if someone turned to him, the loan would be granted.

Natan was respected by everyone, and everyone displayed great politeness and esteem toward him. He was a spiritual and cultural leader in Sierpc.

A the outbreak of the Second World War, when Tatz was forced to leave the city, he gave over the manufacturing enterprise to his employee Chaim Buda, so that he could distribute all the merchandise gratis to whoever came.

Natan Tatz was in the Warsaw Ghetto during the time of the German annihilation of the Jews. He was murdered during the time of the ghetto uprising.

*

Chaim Jurkewicz writes the following about Natan Tatz.

Comrade Tatz was not involved in technical work in the Jewish Bundist organization of Sierpc, but he always remained in tight contact with the party. He felt obliged to find out about everything that took place with the organization. Representatives of the central committee or lecturers who came to Sierpc had to stay with Natan Tatz.

I recall the 1927 city council elections. The Bund obtained a victory and elected two councilors. The party members requested that Comrade Ehrlich of blessed memory come to the accounting meeting. The central committee responded that Comrade Ehrlich was occupied. We found out that he was in Plock, not far from Sierpc. A delegation of the Sierpc Bund went to Plock and lobbied Comrade Ehrlich to come to us as well.

Our joy was great when Comrade Ehrlich arrived to us in the city. Every member wished that Ehrlich would stay at their place. Finally, Comrade Natan Tatz arrived and declared, “Comrade Ehrlich will be at my home, and all the members must gather at my home. If I cannot conduct the day-to-day party work, I wish at least to have the merit of hosting our party leaders.”

*

During the time of a financial campaign for the party or for the cultural activities, Comrade Tatz always made his own generous contribution. Once, the female Comrade Ika Tatz came to Sierpc from Warsaw. We met at the home of Comrade Natan, and discussed party matters: the organization was growing apart. The headquarters was too small. What should they do?

Comrade Natan Tatz listened to everything and finally declared, “If I will give you a half of the sum, things will be good.” Indeed, with Natan's help, the fine headquarters in “Dom Lodowy” was rented. It was sufficient for Natan Tatz to receive a letter from the Bund central headquarters about dues to the party or to the school organization to save the schools – for him to pay the required sum with the greatest punctiliousness. Immediately thereafter, as if he felt that he was coming with a complaint, “Comrades, what have you done recently for the action?”

Thus was Comrade Natan Tatz, who was tormented by the Germans along with the six million Jews.

Reb Nachum the Head of the Community

by Yaakov David Sendrowicz)

He was of average height, with a small, black beard, strands of grey hair, and two deep and thoughtful eyes that exuded his pious Jewish good heartedness and demonstrated that the person feels the pain of those that suffer, and rejoices with others' joy. He was always clothed in a cut-off *kapote* and short sleeves in accordance with the Gerrer manner. The always open door and the spacious, friendly, Jewish home of the Tatz family was always open to guests and activists, as well as to poor people, who were given something to eat as well as something to wear. For such people, or for a young child that a poor woman held in her bosom or by the hand, the large kitchen that was active from morning until late at night was available – for the frequent guests, an emissary from a yeshiva, a collector from Kupat Ramban”[1], a collector from Yeshivat Chachmei Lublin, general activists, Hassidim who had come from afar – all knew that Reb Nachum's house was open for them.

Now, after a hiatus of 20 years, when I think about the interesting personality of Reb Nachum, I am faced with a riddle: how could so many fine traits have been concentrated in one person? He was the head of the community, a position that demanded pride, stubbornness, and intelligence.

Simultaneously, he was a man of the people and a populist Hassid. When he was involved in a communal matter, he was enveloped in stubbornness and wisdom, pride and refinement, as he struggled with persistence and patience until he accomplished what he intended. He was completely different when a broken person with a pained heart stood before him. Someone's horse had died, and he had to be lent a few zlotys from the communal coffers to purchase a "new" horse so that he could earn a livelihood for his household. Someone else had a sick person in the house, and had to purchase medicine to save a life, but unfortunately there was no money in his pockets. A third person required a bit of wood and coal to heat the house so that the children would not, Heaven forbid, freeze on the cold winter days. There were many other similar problems. At such a moment, one could see two broken people, one opposite the other. Reb Nachum stood deep in thought, as he wrinkled his forehead. His words sounded like they emanated from a prayer leader with an anguished heart, whose duty was to help Sierpc Jews. Thus did the people approach their communal leader and relate to him with trust for many long years.

Hassidic Jews or Aguda activists would come to take council with Reb Nachum or to have a discussion with his son-in-law, Leibel Pietrikowski, who directed the Aguda Bank, which was headquartered in his house.

*

Just like yesterday, I see Reb Nachum dressed in his silk *kapote* with his silk *gartel* [ritual belt], with a velvet Sabbath hat on his head, sitting Friday night at the Gerrer *shtibel* at the corner of the long table during the break between the service of the welcoming of the Sabbath and *maariv*, as was the custom in the *shtibel*. Reb Nachum held a Holy Zohar and studied the weekly Torah portion from it. His face was beaming, his forehead was full of wrinkles, and his glasses jutted out high on his forehead.

*

The air was full of anti-Semitic incitement. The fundamentals of the long-time homey town life were breaking down. It felt as if things were becoming uncomfortable. People were lost in thoughts about the old Jewish home of the Land of Israel. The old homeland was casting off the sorrowful garments and clothing itself in new garments of freedom. Even with Reb Nachman, the intercessor, the Jewish intermediary with the government offices, things were becoming somewhat divided. He sent two children (a son and a daughter) away on *hachshara*, and later to the Land of Israel.

The terrible war broke out. I met Reb Nachum in Warsaw, in a small room in a multi-story house. He was sitting *shiva* for his son Henech (Chanoch) who fell while walking on the street. A wall was damaged by bombs, and fell down, covering over many people including my friend Henech (Chanoch) Tatz.

Our Sierpc acquaintances came together through various routes, in order to avoid being captured for work by the accursed Germans. They came from cellars or attic rooms, or from temporary lodgings that they requested from people so that they could set themselves up with their children until one found another temporary location, or until they would succeed in escaping across the border. We all came together in a small room in order to comfort the mourner, Reb Nachum.

That good natured man had no more energy. He was without the luster, completely broken. He was silent, and the wrinkles on his forehead were much larger. Reb Nachum's wife, the former princess of the Tatz home, the former Jewish mother with a wide apron and a good heart, the typical merciful Jewish woman from whose house nobody was left hungry, sat on a low bench on the side. Now she herself was in a strange house, mourning for her fallen son. With tears in her eyes, she silently whispered chapters of Psalms from the Korban Mincha Siddur, with her head lowered, covered in a kerchief, appearing to be mute and powerless.

With heavy hearts and mute lips, we left Reb Nachum's home forever.

His merit should protect us.

Translator's Footnote

1. See http://en.wikipedia.org/wiki/Kupath_Rabbi_Meir_Baal_Haness

My Girlfriend Ika

by David Meir

Ika (her proper name was Esther Rivka Richter, nee Tatz) was born on January 20, 1887 in the town of Sierpc, Poland. Her father, Yosef Leib Tatz, was a wealthy wine merchant and a Gerrer Hassid. She was given an Orthodox Jewish education in her childhood. At the same time, she was sent to a private Polish pension school where they taught the curriculum of a Russian gymnasium (middle school) of that time.

In her youth, she was exceptionally pious. Her very close childhood friend, Dr. Esther Grobard (Fuchs) tells that one Sabbath afternoon, when they both went walking behind the city engaged in conversation, they did not notice that it was getting dark. Ika suddenly stopped in the middle of the sentence, and went under a tree to recite the *mincha* service, like a pious Jew.

From her early childhood, Ika was noted for her warm, humane heart, which was constantly ready to help a poor, weak, or needy person. Under the influence of the *haskalah* tendencies, she, along with other girls, began educational activities for the poor girls in town. They taught them to read and write Yiddish and Polish, as well as other subjects. They agitated the maid girls that they should demand more free time from their employers so that they could study. The activity took on a philanthropic character. The girls did not know about Socialism.

At the age of 15, Rivka traveled to Warsaw to complete her education. There, she became indoctrinated into the Bundist movement, which opened up a new world with new ideas to her. Her burning striving to justice and uprightness and her desire to help her fellow found their proper expression.

At the end of 1915, when Warsaw was taken by the German armies of Wilhem II, creating the possibility for open activity among the Jewish working masses, Ika became one of the first and most active doers in the "Large Children's Homes" [*Grosser Kinder Heimen*] set up by the Bundist organization.

Normal Yiddish day schools that were later organized into the well-known "Our Children" [*Unzere Kinder*] sprouted from the children's homes. Ika was active for the entire time in that society, in which she was a central figure – the soul and driving force.

As the administrator of the first "*Grosser Kinder Heimen*," she did a great deal to build up that Jewish pedagogical workers' institution in an exemplary fashion.

For clearly personal reasons, she left Poland for London, England in 1924. There, she survived a difficult personal tragedy. Shortly thereafter, she settled in Paris.

In France, she was always closely connected with the Bundist Movement, and was especially very active in the Skif Children's Organization of Paris, where the children were veritably improved.

When the Workers' Circle in Paris founded the Workers's Kitchen at the outbreak of the Second World War in September, 1939 for the refugees from Germany and Belgium who began to stream into Paris, the Bundist Organization designated Ika as the administrator of the kitchen. One could not have made a better selection. Ika immediately became the soul of the new institution. She threw herself into that work with all her energy. Nothing was too difficult for her.

When the Nazi Army approached Paris, her friends begged her to use her American visa and leave France. She categorically refused to do so. She knew what was awaiting her when the Germans entered. However, she remained at her post and continued to extend assistance as long as she was free.

The Hitlerists entered the Workers' Kitchen (110 Rue Vielle Du Temple, Paris) on May 29, 1941 and arrested Ika. She was taken to Fort de Romaninville.

Even in prison, she conducted herself as a holy person. She did not reveal the names of the remaining members of the kitchen administration, and took everything upon herself. Even the murderous Hitlerists had to bend their thick skulls at the inner light of a soul that radiated from the holy martyr.

As the Germans reported, she died on October 5, 1942 of a heart attack.

The Bundists of Paris honored her by building an institution in Corvol (about 60 kilometers from Paris) in a large, beautiful house with a lovely garden, where workers' children would come to rest during the summer months and winter vacations. The place bears her name "Ika Home"[1], thanks to her, who lived and was murdered like a holy one.

Translator's Footnote

1. See http://dlib.nyu.edu/findingaids/html/tamwag/photos_048/dscref181.html

Riva Alter (Rivka Iszajewic)

by M. Alter

Rivka Isziewicz, the youngest daughter of Reb Shmuel Leib and Lipsha-Tane, was born in 1894 in the city of Sierpc. Her unassuming parents were very beloved in the city.

The Iszajewic family consisted of seven people: the parents and five children – two brothers Yaakov Hersch and Meir Yisrael, and three sisters Nicha, Shifra, and Rivka. Everyone in the family was Hassidic and religious except for the youngest daughter, Rivka, who moved out of her surroundings and branched out into modern Jewish societal life. In order to be independent, Rivka became an undergarment seamstress.

During the first years of her societal activity, she affiliated with Zionism. At that time, we were a group of friends who began studying the Hebrew Language.

Together with the group of friends, she helped found the "Jewish General Library," which was the meeting point of the progressive youth of the city.

Later, Rivka became involved in cooperating with the future martyrs Ika (Rivka) Tatz and Mania Glazer (Wasser) in the Bundist movement. During its first years, she was one of the active doers in the Bundist Organization of Sierpc.

A few years before the First World War, she worked in Lodz, where she was active with the General Bundist movement.

Later, during the time of the First World War, she often visited her Iszajewic family (Oved Iszajewic) in Wloclawek. In Wloclawek, she soon became active in societal life and in the Bundist Movement.

In the Bundist circles of Wloclawek, she met her husband Meir David Alter at the Zukunft cultural society. They were together for 37 years.

They went to New York in 1921. There, her only son, Shmuel (named after her father) was born.

Even there in the large city of New York, she always took a strong interest in societal and political life. Even though she had been away from her hometown of Sierpc for 36 years, she constantly pined for her hometown the entire time she was in New York.

During the time of the German annihilation of the Jews, she often regretted that she was not there, to go along the martyr route together with all the Jews.

Always healthy, happy and joyful, she suddenly became ill on October 30, 1956. As she lay on her sickbed, she left her husband an oral will providing that, after her death, he should give $500 dollars in her name to the Bundist and cultural organization and $100 to the Sierpc charitable fund in Tel Aviv in memory of her eldest brother Yaakov Hirsch of blessed memory, who was occupied a great deal with charitable deeds in Sierpc during his lifetime.

Let these lines in the Sierpc yizkor book, in which Rivka took great interest and unfortunately was not able to see during her lifetime, serve as a dedication to her.

In honor of her memory!

Types and Personalities of the Bundist Movement

by Chaim Jurkewicz of Santos [1]

When I recall my hometown of Sierpc, a lovely visage spreads before me, surrounding the tall mountains and valleys that were called the Dolinkes (dales) in Polish. We often went on excursions there. Who of us at that time, in the days of our youth, did not stroll in the Dolinkes and swim in the river that cut through the town? We always conducted our circles there in the green meadows during the summer.

Together with the beautiful nature, the flowers and trees, the Jewish youth also lived and carried the finest dreams of freedom and brotherhood, of a bond between the Poles and Jews. I will mention here some of those youths, who were the leaders of the Bundist Movement in Sierpc.

Comrade Leibish Oszer

I will recall here our beloved comrade Leibish Oszer. Who in the city did not know Comrade Oszer? He was a working man who possessed an innate intelligence and acquired worldly knowledge. His steps in the city council were conducted with the greatest attention. Even his opponents were more than once forced to swallow the bitter feelings due to the way in which Comrade Oszer treated them. His oratory talent was amazing. He was fluent in several languages.

The Polish workers' representatives in the city council were very respectful and held the responsible activity of Comrade Oszer in great esteem. When they had to select various committees in the city council, such as for social assistance for the poor, for hygiene, and the like, the Polish workers' representatives voted for Comrade Oszer.

Comrade Oszer was not afraid of the most difficult societal work. He neglected his family life and his private job as a tailor. Therefore, he earned a meager livelihood, but he was always in first place in societal endeavors. Comrade Oszer was a known person in Sierpc. Even the opponents of the Bund, the bourgeois people, would summon none other than Comrade Oszer when they had to speak with a representative of the Bund.

I recall the First of May celebrations. All of the preparations were made so that the May Demonstration would be fine and imposing. Jewish and Christian workers would march together. The red flags of the Bund-Zukunft fluttered with their Yiddish writing and slogans and left the greatest impression in the city. The committee delegates walked in the first row, with Comrade Oszer at the head. The delegates of the Polish workers spoke, and the Jewish masses waited for the words of Comrade Oszer. He appeared at the podium, and was greeted with stormy applause. He spoke briefly, sharply, with feeling and in spurts.

We forgot that we were surrounded by enemies. We marched further and sang Jewish workers' songs. At night, we came together again at the traditional First of May banquet. Comrade Oszer again addressed the members. His words brought into the hearts strength and belief in Socialism.

The Leaders of the Zukunft Youth Organization

I wish to mention here our beloved members of the Jewish Youth Zukunft. The young members were divided into three circles that bore the name of Bundist leaders: Medem, Michaelewicz, Grosser. A self-educational circle was active to prepare the young members to lead the cultural activities, as was a press committee to distribute the "Yugent-Veker" and other publications. There was also a dramatic club that conducted various regular events.

In the self-educational circle, one could find the writer of these lines and the beloved martyred comrades such as Yitzhak Gurna, Yissachar Sakowicz, David Gurna, Hersch Tikalski (later went to Argentina where he died), the female comrade Masha Arfa, and others. All of the members belonged to the Zukunft organization from their youngest years.

The comrade Yitzchak Gurna was a quiet, unassuming working youth. He worked during the day and studied at night. He grew up and became one of the leaders of the Bundist youth movement in Sierpc. He was sent as a delegate to the youth conferences. His lectures, performances and discussions caught everyone's attention.

During the war, he went off to the Soviet Union, where he was mobilized in the Red Army and was killed on the front.

Yissachar Sakowicz conducted the work of the press committee with great responsibility. He read a great deal and had a sharp memory. When friends mentioned a writer or something about articles that were published a long time before, it was sufficient to ask Comrade Sakowicz, and the answer was already given on the spot with the greatest detail. Comrade Sakowicz was a young worker, a tailor from a poor family. He was murdered together with thousands of brothers, sisters, fathers, and mothers from Sierpc.

David Gurna, a young worker, led the drama club of Zukunft. He was at the helm of all cultural undertakings, which were performed very impressively under him. Everyone was captivated by the workers' songs and folksongs that the choir performed in the dramatic presentations of the drama club.

Mention should be made of the female members who played an active part in all undertakings: Paula Krida, and Yenta Tatz; as well as the male comrades: M. Zabicki (today in Mexico, an active doer in the local Bund), Nota Fasa (today in Brazil), and the bakery worker Comrade Elbe, who was the head of the superb chapter of the Culture League that was created despite all the financial difficulties. The library and all the party institutions were located there. Elbe and his wife ensured that the culture hall was kept tidy, as appropriate for a Socialist institution. The keys were indeed found in their hands. Comrade Avraham Rybak was the overseer of the library.

With great dedication, the simple workers and common folk worked in the cultural institutions, giving over all of their free time.

Translator's Footnote

1. On the coast near Sao Paolo, Brazil.

Attorney Yehoshua Podskocz

by Chanoch Nachshon

This man deserves recognition because of his character and his courage during the period of the Warsaw Ghetto.

After he finished high school, he went on to Warsaw University, where he studied law. During this period, he had already made his mark as a public activist who was self-effacing and not one trying to build his career. During those days, he was the chairman of the students' election committee.

He was active during the "Jablonna" period – a name that is unknown today, but in its time was well-known among Polish Jews, as the camp for Jewish students who volunteered for the Polish army during the war between Poland and the U.S.S.R. after the First World War. But the Poles did not want to give these students any responsibility, or to conscript them at all, so they shut them up in an army camp and kept them there with nothing to do. In protest, a famous song "Jablonna" (the name of the place) was written during that period that expressed their frustration.

Yehoshua was active in the camp, and reportedly one of the composers of the song. He was not directly involved in politics, but was active in the protection and nourishment of children in Poland. He was a member of the "Centus" group that erected enterprises and institutions for children. During the Warsaw Ghetto period, the Jewish mutual aid group Z.O.O.S. was founded, and encompassed the most dedicated activists of all the parties. (This was an organization that over time included about 3000 workers and volunteers.) Yehoshua was the head of the legal department along with the attorney Mieczysław Warem. Jonas Turkow says in his famous book "The Destruction of Warsaw," that this mutual aid organization, "ZOS" as it was called for short, became in time the illegal but recognized representative of the Jews in the Ghetto, until the command group of the militia organization was established.

The Ghetto also had a vibrant intellectual life. The underground leaders made sure that the spirit of the Ghetto inhabitants would not be crushed. Jonas Turkow relates (in the above book, on page 230) that among his closest supporters in the special committee that was set up for this purpose were Dr. Emanuel Ringleblum, Elhanan Zeitlin, and also Attorney Yehoshua Podskocz. Yehoshua was also the head of the committee (see page 240) that took care of hundreds of artists in the Ghetto.

On the tenth of August, 1942, according to Jonas Turkow, there occurred the "liquidation" of the "Little Ghetto" and thousands of Jews were banished to the *Umschlagplatz* (collection point). Turkow states, "The quiet procession of thousands of people made a horrifying impression... I stand and look through the windows and see familiar faces, Professor Balaban, Yanusz Korczak at the head of his children, Dr, Lichtenbaum Shpiel-Fagel, Attorney Y. Podskocz, the wife of Dr. Shmuskewyz, ... Dr. Braude-Heller and so on – a complete legion of activists and people of note."

That was the end of a brave, good, honest and modest man, who did not seek honors and was involved in public affairs for the good of all, courageous and a shining example.

I can still see him standing in front of me. In one of his letters to us, before the outbreak of the Second World War, he wrote that he was thinking of *Aliyah* to the Land of Israel. Everyone who knew him will not forget him, and is proud to have known him.

The Holocaust

I Will Not Cry...

by Ephraim Talmi (Wluka)

I will not cry, I will not sigh,
Because there is no tear in my eye;
Nor will I send
My scream to nowhere.
Silently my pain will part
From the hiding places of my heart
Until it forms a pile
Full of bitter bile,
Until it rises like a watery pillar
A scalding fire, ablaze
The memento of sin, blame,
The mark of Cain and shame
For a generation evil and vile
Standing in the blood of mine...
I will not cry and will not shout,
Their blood will only wait out
My silent fury
For my day of vengeance, to come.

5703 [1943]

Publication and Pamphlets about Sierpc:

"United Sherpser Relief Committee", "A Collection of Sierpc Survivors of the Holocaust", "The Destruction of Sierpc 1939-1945"

The Tombstones that the despicable Nazis used to pave the Jewish Street were removed from the street and prepared for restoration

The Kamnitza (Great House) is visible on the hill; the houses to the right of the Kamnitza including the New Beit Hamidrash (School and Prayer Center) - were destroyed. The small houses that are visible there are on Gurna Street

The "Tabernacle" (where the bodies of the deceased were purified) remained standing in the destroyed cemetery

The tombstones being transported back to the cemetery

Sherptzer Cemetery; Tombstones Restored to their Places; the Sherptzer Committee; Year 1946?

The Monument That Was Erected by the Surviving Remnants in the Sierpc Cemetery, and Inscribed: *"In Memorium to the Sierpc Jews That Were Overcome by the Hitlerist Murderers in the Years 1939/45"*

The Jewish Street, where most of the houses were destroyed.

On the right is the Old *Beit Hamidrash* (School and Prayer House) and Horowitz's house. To the left - the houses of Nipomoszcz, Rozynek, Litvinski, and Shaletski. (With the exception of the *Beit Hamidrash*, they were all large houses)

RABIN
Gminy Wyznaniowej Żydowskiej
w Sierpcu.

Sierpc, dn. ________ 19__r

№ ________

Rabbinate of the Jewish Religious Community in Sierpc

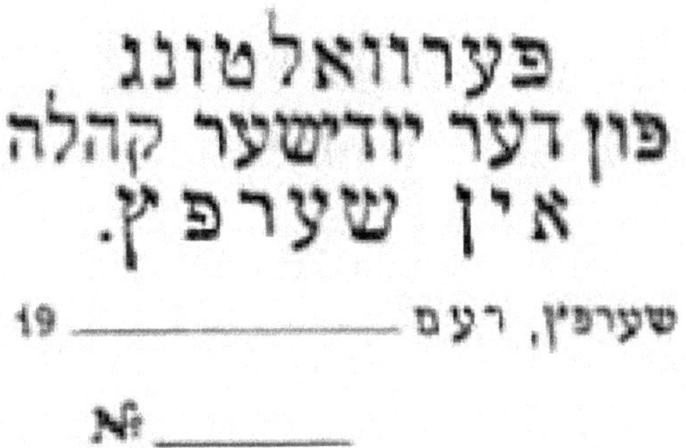

פערוואלטונג
פון דער יודישער קהלה
אין שערפץ.

שערפץ, דעם ______________ 19

№ ________

Administration of the Jewish Community in Sierpc

Heshel David the *Gaon* (Genius) Goldschlak
Head of the Rabbinical Court of Sheps and the District (Rubber Stamp)

Administration of the Jewish Community in Sierpc (Rubber Stamp)

In the Valley of Tears

by I.M. Sidroni (Sendrowicz)

I have called this chapter, which describes the economic and security conditions of the Jews of Sierpc in the last years before the Second World War, before the horrible days of the Holocaust, “In the Valley of Tears.” This is because before the evil, wild and cruel Germans turned Poland into a hell for the Jews of Europe in general and the Jews of Poland in particular, their Polish neighbors turned the country into a valley of tears for them, a place of troubles and calamity, of poverty and neediness, of threats and fear.

* * *

I have before me a bundle of letters that includes correspondence between the “Aid Committee” in Sierpc and the “Relief Committee” of Sierpc townspeople in America. They are about sending monetary assistance, both in the form of support and in the form of constructive help to the poor Jews of Sierpc. (Those that became poor recently, and those that were already poor; those whose poverty was well known and those who tried to keep it a secret.) These letters were written near the outbreak of the Second World War, that is, in the “good days” before the wild animals came out of their lairs, and before they burst into the dwellings of Israel and destroyed and tortured and killed men, women, and children, six million Jews, one third of our people. I do not have the complete correspondence before me. Many of the letters from the “Aid Committee” in Sierpc to the “Relief Committee” in America are missing, and only two that were written from America have survived.

In spite of this, with just part of the correspondence still in existence, and written before the deluge, the picture of the lives of the Jews in Poland and in Sierpc in particular is desolate and depressing. The cries for help that are present in the lines and between the lines of these letters is proof of the state of the Jews in the Polish valley of tears before the Holocaust that uprooted all of Polish Jewry; the conditions worsened with time both in terms of personal safety and of economic circumstances.

A cold and dispirited odor emanates from the letters in front of me; all of them relate tales of sadness and poverty, depression and wretchedness. But some of them, the most “interesting” among them, excel in expressing these conditions. Some of them exhibit a chill that is enough to freeze the blood in one's veins and deprive the reader of any will to live. The most “challenging” of the letters are those that include a list of recipients of aid. One is shocked to read names, many names, of persons that are remembered as people of means, with secure positions. They were collectors of donations and contributors to charity, yet here their names appear as recipients of support. There are more “interesting” letters that describe in detail the security and economic state of the Jews of Sierpc as it degenerates and collapses with each passing day. You watch your brothers, the Jews of Sierpc, in the downward spiral of their living conditions, as their livelihoods disappear and their powerlessness when their personal safety is placed in the hands of hooligans, with no savior in sight.

The last letter is especially shocking. It was written on August 15, 1939, fifteen days before the outbreak of the Second World War, which brought the great and awful destruction, the almost absolute end of Polish Jewry and the extermination of the Jews of Sierpc. It uprooted them, dispersed them, and abandoned them to starvation, disease, and death. You can see the deep abyss opening beneath their feet, as they are troubled by their mundane problems, not feeling the coming catastrophe that will completely consume them and all their families, that is coming towards them so swiftly. The feeling while reading this letter is terrible, a letter written at the brink of disaster.

As I mentioned earlier, I do not have all the letters in this correspondence. I have 24 letters from the "Aid Committee" of Sierpc to the "Relief Committee" of Sierpc townspeople in America, with five lists of aid recipients including names enclosed, and one list without names (but with amounts and occupations listed). There are also two letters from the American "Relief Committee" to the Sierpc "Aid Committee." The first of the letters from Sierpc was written on March 1, 1937, and the last on August 15, 1939. The letters from America were written on January 4 and March 17, 1938. The letters from Sierpc were written by the secretary of the "Aid Committee," Dov Czerka (except for one letter written by the committee member Moshe Gutsztat and parts of two letters written by committee member Meir Zashutke). Mordecai Rzejsotko, the secretary of the "Relief Committee," wrote the letters from America.

The "Relief Committee" was composed of representatives of four organizations of Sierpc townspeople in America: *G'milut Hasadim* [Beneficial Fund], *Yung Mans* (the young auxiliary), the "Ladies' Auxiliary", and *Agudat Poalim* (branch 42 of the "National Hebrew Workers' Union"). The heads of the "Aid Committee" were appointed by the "Relief Committee", and added the rest of the Sierpc members to the committee.

* * *

Among the letters that I have before me, there are also letters some that came from other institutions in Sierpc, and by individuals. Their content is similar to the other letters – requests for help from the brothers across the ocean. These also reflect the depressing state of Jewish life in Sierpc, forlorn and threatened, lives of poverty and waste. The two letters from individuals are especially shocking, detailing their private problems – which are typical of the troubles in general – where every line and word cries out to heaven about distress, helplessness, and impossibility of escape from the awful reality.

* * *

I have translated below [into Hebrew] short summaries of these letters. The more important letters are presented with almost a complete translation and sometimes fully translated.

A. Letters from the "Aid Committee"

I am presenting the full text of the first letter in this correspondence. It is the basis and the badge of honor for the institution that the townspeople of Sierpc in America built to help their poor brethren in Sierpc. These were suffering from the financial crisis and anti-Semitism, and had seen their livelihoods collapse as a result. Their numbers grew in Sierpc, as they did all over Poland. As can be understood from the letter, the initiative for an aid fund came from our brothers in America, and they named the first committee members in Sierpc. These members asked the rest to join them. Avrahamia Wluka was appointed chairman and Dov (Be'er) Czarka was the secretary.

This letter also contains a brief description of the anti-Semitic atmosphere and the beleaguered state of the Jews of Poland, including those of Sierpc. It was written by Czarka on March 1, 1937:

"To the provisional committee for 'The Relief of Sierpc Jews' of America.

"Very Honorable Gentlemen:

"After we received your letter about the aid organization you want to establish for the distressed Jews of Sierpc, the persons named in your letter met. We discussed the importance of such an organization at this time, and expressed gratitude for your initiative. We want to convey our hope that this organization will be formed with our mutual agreement. We feel that the aid should be constructive, and with a shared will we can introduce new values into the help we will provide. The reputation of the people who want to establish your organization are the assurance that it will be successful, forward looking, and built on practical principles.

"At this opportunity, we would like to inform you in brief on the situation in Poland in general, and in Sierpc in particular.

"The influence of the reactionaries on the Polish people and political affairs is increasing. We are seeing an increasing collaboration between the *Andatzia*[1] and government circles. They are easy to understand in their attitude towards the Jewish question: they all feel that the Jews are a foreign constituent, and should leave Poland as quickly as possible. They are constantly occupied by this problem, with the old formula of 'Let's get the better of them,' meaning how can we remove the Jews from their positions in the economy, that they gained over hundreds of years. The government ignores the terrible incitement against the Jews in the reactionary newspapers. A result of these constant provocations is that every day there are cruel attacks on Jews, and in many cases, Jewish blood is spilled. They cannot forgive our great sin that we are alive and exist. The boycott is applied very strictly, the economic situation of the Jews is becoming worse, and we, the Jews of Sierpc, are no exception. It is enough if we inform you that over 200 families are receiving the meager support that the community can allow itself. It is not an exaggeration to state that another 200 families are starving because they do not want to reveal the extent of their hardship. We all have an obligation to try and ease, even if only a little, their terrible distress. Let us hope that together we can do something about this matter.

"We have decided to add five more people to our committee. The composition of the committee is now as follows:

1. Avraham Wluka, 34 Warshawska Street
2. Moshe Gutsztat, 6 Basharpian Place[2]
3. Hirsh Mottle, Lipnovska Street[3]
4. Ber Czarka, Wloky Male 7
5. Eliyahu Meir Schleifer, Farska Street
6. Yitzhak David Schnitzer, P.O.W. Street[4]
7. Pesach Skornik. 8 Warshawska Street
8. Baruch Mendel Gotlibowski, Farska Street
9. Baruch Atlas, Warshawska Street

"We would like to ask you to send the money to Avraham Wluka and the correspondence to Ber Czarka. It is best to send Polish Zlotys from America.

"We have no other news. We wish you well in your efforts.

"In the name of the committee:

- Ber Czarka
- Hirsch Mottle
- Avraham Wluka
- Moshe Gutsztat

Sierpc, 1.3.1937"

Apparently, the four signatories of this letter are the committee members appointed by the "Relief Committee" in America.

* * *

The letter from April 19, 1937 starts with an accounting of the money that was distributed. Two hundred and eleven families received a total of 1,574 Zlotys. These were:

2 families each received 25 Zlotys
3 families each received 20 Zlotys
21 families each received 15 Zlotys
41 families each received 10 Zlotys
4 families each received 12 Zlotys
18 families each received 8 Zlotys
8 families each received 7 Zlotys
12 families each received 6 Zlotys
53 families each received 5 Zlotys;
31 families each received 4 Zlotys
18 families each received 3 Zlotys
4 families each received 2 Zlotys

This letter is also worthwhile translating almost completely, because of its descriptions of the bitter life and hardships of the Jews of Sierpc that it contains. We present a translation below of large parts of the letter.

"As you can see from our report, the committee distributed support to 211 families, that is, to 40% of the Jewish population of Sierpc. If we take into consideration that there are many people who do not want to reveal the extent of their poverty and distress, we come to the conclusion that half of the Jews in Sierpc are going hungry.

"You are probably wondering about the great difference between the largest and smallest amounts of support. We want to inform you that in distributing the money, we had to consider the following factors.

"Among the recipients, there were people who were receiving support for the first time. These are people who are still known to the public as merchants who are making a living at their trade, who were reduced to such a state that their neighbors turned to us, without their knowledge, and asked us to provide for them. We gave these people large amounts, between 15 and 25 Zlotys. We gave 10 Zlotys to those not supported by other institutions such as the community or *Beit Lehem.* 5 to 8 Zlotys were given to those who receive aid from various charitable institutions, and do not hide their poverty anymore. People who do not pass up any opportunities to receive money were given 2 to 4 Zlotys. Some of them go from door to door in the town, and others beg in other towns. Of course, we took into consideration the size of the family, and their real conditions.

"Mordecai Rzejsotko asks in his letter, 'What do we mean by constructive aid? We must clarify this. All the people who received the aid, with few exceptions, had to spend the money on their Passover expenses. This means that the support was a temporary solution, for only a week...Otherwise, it would have been constructive aid that decreases the privation and reduces the number of recipients. There were a number of recipients who could have become independent if they were each given 100 Zlotys. Such an amount would have allowed a poverty stricken craftsman to renew his workshop, or a depressed merchant to revive his store or stall, or a peddler in the villages to renew his stock or rent a fruit orchard to earn some money. We should point our aid in this direction...But we will never accomplish this with gifts of ten Zlotys...We must be ready to support every economic undertaking that is apt to fail because of the boycott and the whims of the ant-Semites. That, we feel, should be the purpose of this committee.'

"...We have not listed the recipients in our report because we did not want some of their names to become public. There is an apprehension that because of the sensational nature of the issue, that formerly wealthy people of Sierpc are now in need of support, their identities will become known through private letters sent from there to here. We hope that you agree with us in this matter. Please write and give us your opinion,

"You have requested that we let you know the occupations of the recipients. The present status of Polish Jews is such that it is difficult to find the dividing line between the laborer and the craftsman, and the craftsman and the merchant, because many of them are willing to accept any work they can find, and they still do not have enough to feed their families. In spite of this, we can inform you that the situation is as follows: 75 merchants, 25 craftsmen, 10 peddlers, 60 laborers and unemployed, and 41 that are not capable of working,"

The letter is signed by the members of the committee:

1. Ber Czarka
2. Avraham Wluka
3. Yitzhak David Schnitzer Eliyahu Meir Schleifer
4. Hirsh Mottle
5. Baruch Atlas
6. B. M. Gotlibowski
7. Pesach Skornik
8. Moshe Gutsztat

* * *

Apparently, the "Relief Committee" did not accept the explanation in the previous letter, that there is a fear that the names of the recipients will become public knowledge, and demanded to know their names. Of course the "Aid Committee" acceded to the request, and following the receipt and distribution of every dispatch of money, it sent the list of recipients. The first list in this correspondence is from May 30, 1937 (the accompanying letter is missing). The heart breaks looking at the names in this list. Many of the names are those of established bourgeoisie, known as good providers and generous contributors to charity. Some of them are remembered as the wealthy people in town, and here they have been reduced to begging for a few measly Zlotys. And even if we know that the troubles that came later were much worse, and ended with destruction and annihilation, we are still shocked today by the names of the recipients, and instinctively, a shriek bursts out, "Woe to the eyes that are reading this."

The sum that was distributed according to this list was 1,574 Zlotys, which was divided among 212 families. The signatories of this list: Dov Czarka, Pesach Skornik, B. Atlas, B. M. Gotlibowski, Moshe Gutsztat, Eli Meir Schleifer, Yitzhak David Schnitzer, Avraham Wluka, and Hirsh Mottle.

* * *

In the letter dated August 9, 1937, the "Aid Committee" writes to the "Relief Committee" that they distributed the received money, between 1 and 40 Zlotys per family. Some families were given larger amounts than usual because they wanted to re-establish them, but there is a feeling that they may need more help. They could not carry out the "Relief Committee" recommendation to give ten families 50 Zlotys each because of the many needy families. In addition to the signers of the previous letters, this one had two more signatories: Meir Zashutke and Binyamin Eliezer Sabel.

According to the list of recipients enclosed with this letter, the sum of 1,581 Zlotys was divided between 177 families. (1,575 Zlotys had been received and 6 Zlotys were lent by committee members.)

* * *

Czarka, the only signer of a letter from November 11, 1937 states that the committee received 200 dollars and distributed them immediately, and will send the list of recipients in a few days.

The following is a translation of a long passage from this letter that describes the forlorn situation of all the Jews of Poland, including the Jews of Sierpc, in the Polish valley of tears:

"You have probably read the latest news from Poland in the newspapers. Unfortunately, we have to tell you that the situation is becoming worse every day. The reactionaries in Poland are advancing in giant steps. We here in Sierpc can feel the anti-Semitic provocation in all of its brutality. Because you want to know what is happening to us in our daily lives, we can send you the following news.

"The anti-Semitic hooligans have lately come up with a new innovation. This is called *picketen* (inspectors). Their method is very simple: They stand in front of the Jewish stores and do not let the Polish customers inside. This activity began in Sierpc on the day of the fair, on Wednesday, the third of this month. They stood outside some Jewish stores, and would not let buyers enter. On market day, Tuesday, the ninth of this month, some tens of hooligans came from out of town, and 'inspected' not only the stores, but also the pitiful stalls in the market, and dragged the buyers away. This had a shocking effect on us. Our fear is great, because we don't know what the next day will bring. We turned to the authorities without any success. They said that the 'inspection' activities are permitted. As is well known, this is the position of the central government in Warsaw, especially of the prime minister, that the economic struggle against the Jews is welcome.[5] This is our situation in Poland in the twentieth year of its independence. We are searching for ways to deal with this vulgar hooliganism. Safety on the roads has disappeared a long time ago, and the peddlers in the villages who travel to fairs suffer insults and beatings. The situation is getting worse, there is complete lawlessness. The anti-Semitic craze has infected everyone, from the rectors at the universities to the pupils at the elementary schools. If this anti-Semitic war of eradication continues, the poorer classes face total financial ruin."

Signed, Ber Czarka.

* * *

In a letter from December 13, 1937, which has a list of recipients enclosed, the "Aid Committee" informs the "Relief Committee" that it is sending a list of the people who received parts of the 200 dollars that were received six weeks earlier. The list was not sent promptly because some of the committee members were involved with the activities of the self-defense committee set up for protection from the *picketen*. The past two weeks in Sierpc have been quiet.

They write that only small sums have been distributed, as can be seen from the list, the largest being 10 Zlotys. This is only a minor relief. The committee feels very uncomfortable about constantly asking for money, each time saying, “Give! Give!” but it has no choice. Money is being collected every day in Sierpc as well, but it is all only a drop in the ocean.

As mentioned, a list of recipients is attached to the letter. There is a summary at the end of the list which states that 202 families received 1050 Zlotys:

17 families each received 10 Zlotys	37 families each received 5 Zlotys
6 families each received 9 Zlotys	31 families each received 4 Zlotys
23 families each received 8 Zlotys	48 families each received 3 Zlotys
14 families each received 7 Zlotys	15 families each received 2 Zlotys
10 families each received 12 Zlotys	1 families each received 1 Zlotys

Signed were Dov Czarka, Yitzhak David Schnitzer, Pesach Skornik, Baruch Atlas, Avraham Wluka, Moshe Gutsztat, B. M. Gotlibowski, Eli Meir Schleifer, Binyamin Eliezer Sabel, and Meir Zashutke. A comment states that committee member Hirsch Motil was ill and thus is not among the signatories, but he had participated in distributing the money.

* * *

There are two letters sent by the “Relief Committee” in America among this correspondence. The letters were written by Mordecai Rzejsotko, the secretary of the “Relief Committee,” on January 4 and 17 March 1938. The gist of these letters is that the “Relief Committee” had decided to change the form of the aid – at least most of it – from donations to loans. The committee had contacted the “Organization of Polish Jews in America” (that also sent monetary aid to the Jews in Poland). They had agreed to set up a fund of 1000 dollars for no interest loans with easy terms to those Jews in Sierpc for whom a loan like this – not large but significant – would prevent total financial collapse. The two parties would be equal partners in this fund. The money would be sent to the agent of the organization in Warsaw who will send a representative to Sierpc to determine, together with the “Aid Committee” the procedures for granting loans. Because the “Relief Committee” knew that there is a similar charitable institution in Sierpc, *Gmilat Hasadim* [Beneficial Fund], it asked the “Aid Committee” in Sierpc to explain to the emissary as clearly as possible what is *Gmilat Hasadim*, its goals, activities, the kind of people to whom it lends money, on what terms, the size of the loans, etc.

We see the reverberations of this proposal in many letters written from Sierpc to America following these two letters from the “Relief Committee.” But we do not have a clear understanding of them, not only because we don't have more letters written from America to Sierpc, but because we do not have some of the letters written from Sierpc to America. The matter dragged on for some time, and in the end, the “Relief Committee” cut its ties to the “Organization of Polish Jews in America” and sent the money through the “Cooperative Banking Union” in Warsaw.

* * *

In the letter of January 12 1938, the "Aid Committee" writes to the "Relief Committee:"

"The *Gmilat Hasadim Fund* received a letter today from Warsaw from the "Committee for the Distribution of Funds Sent by Organizations of Polish Jews Abroad." They write that they have sent, through the People's Bank in Sierpc, the sum of 3,960 Zlotys, which is 750 dollars. The *Gmilat Hasadim Fund* is supposed to use this money to give loans, but has to consult with the "Aid Committee." The "Aid Committee" is supposed to approve receipt of the money.

"The committee convened a meeting, at which it was decided not to accept the money, for the following reasons: a) according to your correspondence, we were supposed to have receive 1500 dollars, not 750 dollars; b) they want promissory notes from *Gmilat Hasadim* for the money received; and c) the committee in Warsaw has not contacted us about the plans and conditions for granting loans. We await your instructions on whether to accept the 750 dollars. Till then, it will remain deposited in the People's Bank. We hope that you will respond to the fact that the 'Organization of Polish Jews in America' is not acting in accordance with the agreement you made with them.

"The demand for money by our suffering brethren is great; their distress has increased this winter because of the expansion of the boycott by the local anti-Semites."

Signed: Dov Czarka, Eli Meir Schleifer, Baruch Atlas, Moshe Gutsztat, and Yitzhak David Schnitzer.

* * *

In a letter dated March 24 1938, the "Aid Committee" writes to the "Relief Committee:"

"We have not yet received the 250 dollars that the 'Organization of Polish Jews in America' was supposed to send us as per your last letter. Additionally, the emissary that the Organization was supposed to send here according to your arrangement has not come. In the meantime, Passover approaches, and the hardships of the Jews of Sierpc increase.

"As for your question, about our plan if you would send us for instance 500 dollars, then our plan is: deposit part of the money, depending on the amount sent, with the *Gmilat Hasadim* Fund. Possibly enough money will accumulate there so that we can grant loans. We will distribute the rest of the money, a somewhat larger sum, as you requested, to the poorest people.

"Please write about how everything is with you and your plans for the future. Let us know how the impression that the events in Austria[6] made on American Jews. Tomorrow is Judgment Day for Kosher slaughtering. Tomorrow the *Sejm* (Polish parliament) will discuss the edict on prohibition of Jewish ritual slaughtering. The Jewish counter attack is very weak. The 'Rabbinical Union' has decreed the reading of Psalms tomorrow."

Signed by Dov Czarka.

* * *

The “Aid Committee” wrote to the “Relief Committee” on May 16, 1938:

“The money was received on the last week before Passover, and we managed to distribute it among the needy. We will send the list of recipients in a second letter. The emissary of the “Organization of Polish Jews” who was supposed to visit us so that we could prepare a plan for future aid together has not come yet. Perhaps you can speed up his coming?”

Signed: Dov Czarka, Meir Zashutke, and Yitzhak David Schnitzer.

* * *

In a letter from May 31, 1938, the “Aid Committee” of Sierpc writes that it is sending the list of recipients that received support before Passover. (The list is not among the correspondence that we have.) The committee takes note of the recommendation of the “Relief Committee” and will add the person recommended and invite him to the next committee meeting. (The name of the person is not given.) At the end of the letter, the committee mentions the increase in anti-Semitism as a result of what happened in Brześć[7]. All the Polish newspapers justify the savage acts against the Jews, and government circles also exhort against the economic positions of the Jews. It is very difficult to live in this atmosphere saturated with hate.

Signed were Dov Czarka, Pesach Skornik, B. Atlas, Yitzhak David Schnitzer, B. M. Gotlibowski, Avraham Wluka, Moshe Gutsztat, Hirsch Mottle, and Eli Meir Schleifer.

* * *

In a letter dated June 23, 1938, the “Aid Committee” turns to the “Relief Committee” about a personal matter. This concerns a public figure that has lost most of his assets, and in addition he has (and not just him) a new problem. The cities and towns of Poland have been engaged in municipal improvements. Because of this, the authorities order that old houses that are in the center of town be torn down. These edicts usually affect Jews, and many families face the prospect of being without a roof over their heads. This Jew was affected by this edict. He may be able to defer the implementation for a year or two, but he needs money for this. He wrote to his brother in America about this, but did not receive a positive reply. Apparently they find it difficult to believe that their brother's situation has become so bad. Therefore the “Aid Committee” requests that the “Relief Committee” contact his brother about this urgent matter.

Signed by Dov Czarka.

* * *

A list of recipients is enclosed with the letter of August 20, 1938. This states that 2,023 Zlotys were shared by 233 people. In addition, 77 Zlotys were deposited with the *Gmilat Hasadim* Fund.

The committee apologizes for the delay in sending the list, and promises to select a more active secretariat in the next few days, that will take care of the correspondence more expediently. The committee writes:

"This list will convince our brethren in America that the poverty and misery have grown among our brothers in Sierpc. In contrast with 211 recipients a year ago, there are now 233 recipients. If some of the Sierpc townspeople in America tend to believe that the aid is not very necessary, let us explain the gravity of the situation. At the end of the list, we state that we deposited 77 Zlotys in the *Gmilat Hasadim* Fund. But do not think that there was no one to whom to give the money. The actual case is that when you informed us that you are sending 400 dollars we thought we would put at least 300 Zlotys in the *Gmilat Hasadim* Fund, as a start to a project that would deal with constructive aid. This would be either by way of loans, or another way to be determined in consultation with the emissary of the 'Organization of Polish Jews in America' who is supposed to visit us. But the pressure of the needy was so great that we were able to deposit only 77 Zlotys in the fund, and that with great difficulty. We ask you to talk to the 'Organization' to expedite the emissary's visit.

"We agree with you that there is a need to set up a credit institution for the very poor, but this arrangement must be based on feelings of compassion and not on legalities. This means that it must be clear that some of the debtors, in spite of the pressure from the institution, will not repay the loans, and your help for this institution will still be necessary in the future,

"The anti-Semitic propaganda is increasing, and now the edict about municipal improvements and tearing down old houses has been added. This edict is a heavy blow to part of the Jewish population."

Signed were Meir Zashutke, Hirsch Mottle, Pesach Skornik, Binyamin Eliezer Sabel, Yitzhak David Schnitzer, Eli Meir Schleifer, Moshe Gutsztat, Atlas Baruch, Avraham Wluka, and Dov Czarka.

* * *

The "Aid Committee" wrote on September 24, 1938:

"We have received your letter. We have not yet received the money. The emissary from Warsaw has not visited us yet. The *Gmilat Hasadim* Fund has received a letter from the Warsaw representatives of the 'Organization of Polish Jews in America' that they have 750 dollars for them.

"The 'Aid Committee' requests that the 'Relief Committee,' if it has not already sent the money, to send 200 dollars to the enclosed address. If it has already been sent, perhaps you can send part of the 750 dollars to the same address."

Signed by Dov Czarka.

* * *

In a letter dated December 3, 1938, the "Aid Committee" writes to the "Relief Committee:"

"We have not yet distributed the 200 dollars; so that in any case we are unable to send the list of recipients to you. We have written that the 200 dollars has been deposited in our name, but we will be able to use it only after we receive a letter from you that you want the money forwarded to the address that we sent you.

"The visit of the emissary from Warsaw concerning the 1,500 dollars has still not taken place. This matter has been up in the air for over a year, with no sign of a conclusion. In the meantime, the poverty is getting worse and the distress is increasing and expanding. Please do something about this problem at the 'Organization of Polish Jews in America' so that they will hurry up and put an end to the affair.

"About our correspondence, we are at fault for the delay in writing, but not purposefully or because of negligence of our duties. The few people who are active in the "Aid Committee" are occupied in various fields of public service. With the increase in misery, the efforts for rescue become greater. Secondly, we were in a state of anticipation: we were waiting every day for the 200 dollars and for the arrival of the emissary. And so, time passed.

"If only we had enough talent to describe the hardship that is prevalent among our brethren in Sierpc, it would undoubtedly shock our brothers in America. But we do not have the talent for this. Therefore, we are writing in brief. The economic situation here gets worse every day: eviction from apartments and the hunger of families are an everyday occurrence. We collect charity every day to ease the lives of those in misery. But it is all a drop in the ocean. It is not an exaggeration to state that the number of recipients exceeds the number of donors."

Then the letter talks about the distress of the Jewish refugees from Germany who are floundering on the border between Poland and Germany.[8] Over 10,000 Jews were ejected from their houses, naked and barefoot, rotting in horse stables and suffering from cold and hunger.

The letter ends: "This is the life of the Jews in our country, and the example set by our neighbor to the west."

Signed by Dov Czarka.

* * *

An undated letter to the "Relief Committee" written by "Aid Committee" member Moshe Gutsztat belongs, in our opinion, in this place in this series of letters.

The author of the letter apologizes (as in previous letters) on the sluggishness in the exchange of correspondence, and promises to submit a proposal about this at the next committee meeting. He gives a reason for the scarcity of letters: because most of the other members are busy with other public service... A letter with a list of recipients was sent some time ago. The letter continues:

"Concerning the complaint received by the 'Relief Committee,' please review the list of recipients, and give us your opinion of the distribution. In the view of almost all the members of the 'Aid Committee,' – the judgment of the people who are on the spot – the distribution is excellent. Certainly, there is no reason to doubt the integrity of the committee. It is unfortunate that someone feels that he needs to send complaints. The complaints are apparently due to the fact that the ability of the committee to help is less than the extent of the misery. Unfortunately, we do not have a solution for this problem."

Signed by Moshe Gutsztat.

* * *

We are translating the letter of January 22, 1939 almost in its entirety, because of its great value in describing the three financial institutions in Jewish Sierpc. These are the financial institutions that assisted the Jews of Sierpc – a lot, or a little – in the period between the two world wars. This was help in their struggle for existence with their Polish neighbors, who plotted to steal their daily bread from them. These were the financial institutions that helped the Jews – a lot or a little – to subsist, inadequate as it was.

"To the Committee for 'The Relief of Sierpc Jews' of America.

"Very Honorable Gentlemen:

"We have received your letter of December 26, 1938. We want to inform you that the allotment of 1500 dollars between the three financial institutions will not result in any benefits. So that you can understand our opinion, we will explain the nature of these institutions.

"There are two banking cooperatives in Sierpc. The first is Bank Ludowi (People's Bank), which was founded 25 years ago[9]. This bank serves most of the Jewish population of Sierpc by giving loans. It has more than 300 members. The bank receives long term credit from the 'Joint' [American Jewish Joint Distribution Committee]. It receives the rest of its money from the share holders' fees that members are obliged to pay, from savings, and from deposits. The bank went through a serious crisis ten years ago (caused by the severe economic depression). But because of the efforts of its members, who covered the deficit, the crisis was overcome. The bank does not have any profits because of debts caused by the present financial crisis - the number of victims of the crisis is increasing. But the bank is well managed and is also growing. The maximum credit has reached 1,200 Zlotys, depending of course, on the financial situation of the borrower. It is the largest bank in (Jewish) Sierpc.

"The second cooperative bank was founded about ten years ago[10]. This second bank was established because of disputes between different groups in the first bank. A group of the more affluent merchants left the first bank to start the second one, also a cooperative. This bank has about a hundred members. Its capital is composed of share holders' fees and deposits. It does not receive credit from the 'Joint' because the 'Joint' refuses to extend credit to two cooperative banks in the same town. About 70% of the members of the second bank are members of the first bank as well, and receive credit from both institutions. This leads to the conclusion that both banks are useful to the Jewish population.

"When we write 'Jewish population,' our implication is people who can get credit and find good guarantors. But those affected by the economic crisis cannot get credit from the banks. You cannot find even five people among our list of recipients that have a credit line at the banks. About one hundred of our recipients never benefited from the banks at all. Another hundred or so were once members of the bank, but now can no longer receive credit. Some of them owed money to the bank and their guarantors paid off their debts (these are everyday occurrences) and some of them still owe money. In brief, these two banks do not serve these people. If each bank receives 2000 dollars, the poorest classes of the Jewish population will not benefit from it. None of them will receive credit and the list of recipients will not be any shorter. Even if they wanted to, the banks could not change their relationship with the poverty stricken population, since they are based on business principles... We have, therefore, decided to ask you not to send the money to these two banks. This is the opinion of all the Jewish population that is concerned with the fate of the poor and those that have become impoverished.

"Now we will describe the nature and status of the *Gmilat Hasadim* Fund. It was founded fifteen years ago[11], with very limited resources. In its early days, the fund would grant loans of 25 Zlotys. Only the most impoverished segment of the population benefited then, because the middle class had no need for such small loans. The capital of the fund is composed of monthly payments, fund-raising events (in the early days), bequests, and support from the 'Joint.' The loans officially are given at no interest, as is shown by its name, *Gmilat Hasadim* ['Giving out of Loving Kindness']. However, every borrower must participate in the administrative costs (secretary, office, office supplies). Over 400 borrowers now benefit from loans of the *Gmilat Hasadim* Fund. The maximum loan is 200 Zlotys. The fund also has old loans that have not been repaid, and some of our recipients that had credit with the fund still owe money, and cannot get any more credit.

"Because it is not possible to found a new credit institution, since then we would have to maintain a special administrative structure, we have decided that the best option is to send the full sum, 1500 dollars, to the *Gmilat Hasadim* Fund. It will be distributed as loans in consultation with our 'Aid Committee.' Then we will be able to extend credit to poor borrowers, taking each one's situation into consideration, without being unduly restrictive. Obviously, deficits must be expected under such conditions, since not all the money will be returned, and from time to time we will have to give additional money to the fund to cover the deficits. To make sure that the total amount available is not reduced, we will take the money from the remittances you send for distribution to the poorest. Of course, we will take only small amounts from this money, to make sure that we have not harmed the poorest, for whom the money was intended..."

Signed by Ber Czarka, Pesach Skornik, Binyamin Eliezer Sabel, Moshe Gutsztat, Baruch Atlas, Eli Meir Schleifer, Yitzhak David Schnitzer, Meir Zashutke, Avraham Wluka, and Hirsch Mottle.

* * *

The letter of February 20, 1939 begins by tendering the sympathies of the Sierpc "Aid Committee" to the "Relief Committee" in America for the passing of its honorary chairman, Mordechai Hirsch Mintz of blessed memory. His former students had held a memorial service for him at the *Tarbuth* School. The speakers were Avraham Podskoc, Eliezer Rozinek, Fibush Lipka and others.

Next there came a loud and bitter cry, the likes of which had not been heard in previous letters, to their beloved brothers in America that starts with "Out of my straits."[12] It describes the terrible predicament of the Jews of Sierpc, the poverty and distress that scream for immediate help, for the sufferers and the tortured. The letter reads:

"Out of My Straits...

"Beloved Brothers.

"In our previous letter we wrote about the wave of anti-Semitism that is spreading in our surroundings. We wrote that the peddlers cannot show themselves in the villages. Unfortunately, today we have more news for you. On Tuesday, the 14th of this month, a new anti-Semitic drive started here. The anti-Semites placed drunken men near the Jewish stores, and would not let customers enter. The situation in the market was worse: they surrounded the stalls, overturned them, and the merchants were forced to flee from the market. These acts were in broad daylight and in sight of the keepers of order. We have been assured that these acts will continue till the Passover holiday... This means that the stall owners and the travelers to fairs are facing complete financial ruin. Not only are they prevented from going to fairs, but they cannot make a living in town. Worse, we have nowhere to turn. The authorities promise us that there will be no *ekscasijm* (pogroms). That means that they will not beat or kill people. But in fact, there were many instances of assaults. The mood of the Jewish population is very dejected.

"The acts described took place on Tuesday, February 14. When we woke up in the morning on the 17th, we found that all the Jewish signs had been defaced with tar. This 'cleanup' work was done by the hooligans at night, and the keepers of order did not see anything or hear anything... Today, Monday the 20th, the police ordered that all the signs are to be cleaned or replaced.

"Today, Monday, all the Jews are worried about what to expect tomorrow. There are terrible rumors going around. This is the state we are in in the twentieth century. There is no one that is capable of describing the material, physical and spiritual situation that is such a torment at this terrible time. We must remind you that it is primarily the poorer classes that suffer from this, who face actual starvation.

"Beloved brothers, it is possible that there are some unemployed among you as well. It is possible that every penny that you collect is collected with difficulty, both by those asking (we know how hard it is to collect money) and by the donors. But considering the deep misery of the Jewish population of Sierpc, nothing should be too difficult. We are doing everything we can here, and we turn to you, merciful brethren, to also do everything you can.

"Beloved brothers, listen to the pleading of the tormented Jews of Sierpc, and answer it with the merciful and warm Jewish heart. Perhaps it was fate that at this time you would be far away, and could help your brethren in time of need. We hope that our supplication will reach you, and you will listen and reply as brothers. The Jews of Sierpc will be grateful for it."

The letter states that the "Aid Committee" has yet to receive the 200 dollars. The 750 dollars received by the *Gmilat Hasadim* Fund was distributed, in consultation with the "Aid Committee" as loans. The list of people who received the loans will be sent in two weeks.

The letter is signed by Ber Czarka and Meir Zashutke.

* * *

In a postcard from March 28, 1939, the "Aid Committee" states that the money sent by the "Organization of Polish Jews in America" was received and already distributed. The list of recipients will be sent during the intermediate days of Passover. Because of the bad situation, the list is not small, but has increased by about 20%. The money for the banks has not yet been received.

Signed by Dov Czarka.

* * *

The letter of May 4, 1939 contains a list of recipients. 245 families received a sum of 2588 Zlotys. These were distributed as follows:

3 families each received 50 Zlotys
1 families each received 30 Zlotys
4 families each received 25 Zlotys
18 families each received 20 Zlotys
34 families each received 15 Zlotys
12 families each received 12 Zlotys
59 families each received 10 Zlotys
5 families each received 9 Zlotys
34 families each received 8 Zlotys
13 families each received 7 Zlotys
12 families each received 6 Zlotys
1 families each received 5.5 Zlotys
29 families each received 5 Zlotys
14 families each received 4 Zlotys
5 families each received 3 Zlotys
1 families each received 2.5 Zlotys

The amount received was 2776 Zlotys. The amount distributed was 2588 Zlotys, so that 188 Zlotys remained.

In the letter, the "Aid Committee" apologizes that in spite of the fact that the loans were granted by the *Gmilat Hasadim* Fund, the number of recipients did not decrease, but grew by some tens of families. The reason for this is the bad state of affairs lately. Problems with the *picktenikim*[13] began two weeks before Passover, and lasted until the panic caused by the international situation[14]. The state of the bank cooperatives and the *Gmilat Hasadim* Fund has also become worse, because loan repayments have decreased due to the crisis. The money for the bank cooperatives has not yet been received; please find out about this matter at the "Organization of Polish Jews in America."

The 188 Zlotys that were not distributed were deposited with the *Gmilat Hasadim* Fund on account of unpaid loans. The loan grants trial did not succeed because of the terrible crisis in Sierpc.

Signed by Dov Czarka, Hirsch Mottle, Baruch Atlas, Avraham Wluka, Meir Zashutke, Schleifer, Yitzhak David Schnitzer, Moshe Gutsztat, Binyamin Sabel, and Skornik

* * *

The next letter has the date "5.IV.39." Its content however, indicates that is a reply to a letter written by the "Relief Committee" in answer to the letter above dated May 4. Apparently, there was an error in the Roman numeral of the month, and "IV" was written instead of "VI." Therefore, the correct date of the letter is June 5, 1939.

The beginning of the letter contains significant materials on the nutrition of children in the Sierpc schools. Because of the importance of this information, the complete letter has been translated:

"...About the feeding of poor children, we would like to send you some facts about conditions in the schools in Sierpc.

"We have a *Talmud Torah*[15] that is maintained by the community. There is a 'Benefactors of the *Talmud Torah* Committee' whose purpose is to support the children learning there. The chairman, Hirsch Mottle, who is a member of the committee, tells us that from time to time, the children receive clothes, winter shoes, etc. In addition, the children receive breakfast during the winter – rolls and milk.

"The *Tarbuth* School[16] also has a nutrition committee which serves breakfast for the children daily during the five winter months. The *Tarbuth* School is maintained by tuition fees. Of the 220 students in this school, sixty come from poor families who do not pay tuition. The committee serves them a daily breakfast as well.

"In addition to the above committees, there is a similar committee attached to the 'Government School for Jewish Children' that serves breakfast in the winter months to the poorer children, comparable to what the *Tarbuth* School does. About fifty children receive breakfasts in this school.

"As you can see, there are nutrition committees attached to each of these schools, but the activity takes place only during the winter months. It may be that the committees should extend their activities to the summer as well, because the poor children are hungry in school then also, but the fact is that it is done only in the winter.

"The above committees are maintained by monthly payments made by the patrons of each of these schools. In addition, 'Benefactors of the *Talmud Torah* Committee' receives support from the community, and the other two committees receive assistance from TOZ[17]. (An institution dedicated to the support of poor children, supported by the American Jewish Joint Distribution Committee.)

"Therefore, it is our opinion that we should keep the money you sent us in the *Gmilat Hasadim* Fund until the above committees resume their activities, and then we will divide it in accordance with the number of pupils in each school. We will send you a detailed report on the nutrition committees shortly: the status of their budgets, how many children they feed, what are the sources of their support, and also which activities are not carried out at all because of a lack of money. When we both have this report, we will be able to distribute the money with complete objectivity, for all the hungry school children. In the meantime, we have not yet received the 320 Zlotys."

The "Aid Committee" next asked the "Relief Committee" to thoroughly investigate the matter of the 750 dollars with the "Organization of Polish Jews in America." This money, that the Organization states has already been transferred, has not reached the banks in Sierpc. Three or four Zlotys are given to people who are constantly asking for money and cannot be turned away empty handed. 188 Zlotys were not handed over to the *Gmilat Hasadim* Fund, but kept back to cover bad loans. 70 of these Zlotys have been spent in the meantime. 50 Zlotys were given to a sick person who had an operation and 20 Zlotys to two other sick people. The "Aid Committee" did not write that loans were not being returned, but that was a real possibility, since the loans were given to extremely poor people, and the situation is getting worse. People who yesterday stood on their own two feet are now collapsing. The reasons for this – pressure of the anti-Semites, the tense international situation, and the financial crisis. Last Friday the *picktenikim* again stood in front of Jewish stores. This made a disheartening impression on the Jews. Even when the foreign enemy wants to swallow the whole country, our neighbors think of how to wage war against peaceful Jewish citizens.

Signed by Dov Czarka.

* * *

The letter of July 2, 1939 was written by two members of the "Aid Committee;" the first half by Meir Zashutke, and the concluding portion by Dov Czarka. The writer of the first part of the letter again justifies the 180 Zlotys that were not distributed for upkeep (according to the previous letter,

188 Zlotys were left over) and the very small amounts used for support. The probable reason for the change in authorship was to placate the "Relief Committee," and so that it would feel that the "Aid Committee" was trustworthy.

The writer states that the small amounts were given to persons who are constantly in need of money. The remaining 180 Zlotys have been almost completely spent already on very urgent cases: 50 Zlotys were given to a respected person who has always earned his own living, who needed an operation; 50 Zlotys were given to another respected person who has a very sick son; another 40 Zlotys were distributed to four people, ten Zlotys each. 320 Zlotys that were received for food for children have been deposited in the *Gmilat Hasadim* Fund until the month of Heshvon, when the children's nutritional activities begin. A telegram about the money for the cooperative banks was received on June 22. Representatives of the committee went to the bank and by chance met the emissary from Warsaw, the supervisor of cooperative banks, Dr. Salman. When he was asked about the money, he gave all sorts of excuses. When he was shown the telegram, he said to tell the "Relief Committee" that the money had been received. The emissary went back to Warsaw the same day, and one bank received part of the money the next day.

That was the first part of the letter, written as mentioned previously by committee member Meir Zashutke.

The second part of the letter states that one bank received 500 dollars and the other bank received 250 dollars. The allocation was made by the comptroller committee in Warsaw according to the size of the banks[18]. The money was given to the banks as a loan with a 3% annual interest rate, to be returned in ten monthly payments. The first payment is to be made six months after receipt of the loan. If the "Relief Committee" has any objections to these terms, it should present them to the "Organization of Polish Jews in America." The situation here is grave and the reasons for this cannot be described. Please continue your noble work for the Jews of Sierpc.

Signed by Dov Czarka.

* * *

The letter of July 17, 1939 again mentions the 320 Zlotys for children's food that was deposited with the *Gmilat Hasadim* Fund until winter, when nutritional activities for children begin.

Then, the letter discusses the matter of the 750 dollars. The committee states that the day before the letter was written, Dr. Shoskes[19] stopped off in Sierpc on his way back from America. According to him, and also from the letter sent by the "Relief Committee" from America, the "Relief Committee" had broken off its relationship with the "Organization of Polish Jews in America." It is not up to the "Aid Committee" to tell the "Relief Committee" which of the two institutions, the "Organization of Polish Jews in America" or the "Joint" it should link up with, and which one will be better. Both have good and bad points. According to Dr. Shoskes, the "Union of Cooperative Banks" is not responsible for the delay in receiving the money. The "Organization of Polish Jews in America" did not have money to send, and therefore the matter took almost a year. He says that recently, just a few days before he left for America, he received the money and informed the banks in Sierpc, but the "Aid Committee" did not know about it.

Dr. Shoskes consulted with the management of the banks. He advised them to ask the "Relief Committee" that all the money be sent to them. The "Aid Committee" wants the "Relief Committee" to note that all the people who benefit from the cooperative banks are well-to-do, people from whom payment is assured and whose guarantors are reliable. However, the poor people in town, who are suffering and miserable, do not benefit from the banks. The people will benefit from the aid only if it is sent to the *Gmilat Hasadim* Fund (apart from the support that needs to be sent from time to time before the holidays). This is stated with complete objectivity, because the "Aid Committee" is looking after the good of the banks; a number of committee members are also members of the bank and receive loans from them. The comrades Czarka, Schnitzer, and others are also part of the bank management.

In conclusion, the letter states that the chairman of *Bank Ludowi* is now Leib Usher; the chairman of *Bank Udzialowi* is Shmuel Tatz; and the chairman of the *Gmilat Hasadim* Fund is Menachem Baumel.

* * *

The letter dated 28 July 1939 contain the answer of the "Aid Committee" to the "Relief Committee's" question about the terms for the repayment of the money that the cooperative banks in Sierpc received from the "Union of Cooperative Banks" in Warsaw as a loan:

"The 'Union of Cooperative Banks' states (Dr. Shoskes said the same thing) that it does not give money as support, but as loans. The loan was granted with an annual interest rate of 3% with the condition that it is returned in six consecutive equal monthly payments. The first payment will be ten months from the date of the loan, in May 1940[20]. The 'Union' deducts the interest when giving the loan, which is not 750 dollars but 750 dollars less 3½ %. (The rate for each dollar was 5.20 Zloty.) In addition, another forty or so Zlotys were deducted (by *Bank Ludowi*, it is not yet known how much *Bank Udzialowi* will charge). We mentioned this to Dr. Shoskes and he promised to return the money as 'miscellaneous expenses.' The 'Union' says (and so does Dr. Shoskes) that after the banks have returned all the money, he will give them the same loans with the same conditions."

Signed by Dov Czarka.

* * *

The letter of August 15, 1939 – like the letter of July 2 – was written by two members of the "Aid Committee" - Meir Zashutke, and Dov Czarka. The end of the letter contains a note: the letter was written unintentionally by two secretaries, but it does not matter – they complement each other.

The "Aid Committee" member Meir Zashutke begins the letter by thanking the "Relief Committee" members for their efforts on behalf of their poor brothers in Sierpc and for their promise to send money for distribution to the needy before the holidays.

Next come the particulars of the 1500 dollars sent in the past few months[21]. On February 28 of this year[22] the *Gmilat Hasadim* Fund received 3,960 Zlotys, and signed promissory notes for this amount. *Bank Ludowi* received 2,600 Zlotys on June 28 of this year. After an interest deduction of 78 Zloty, the bank was left with 2,522 Zlotys. On the 24th of July of this year, *Bank Udzialowi* received 1,350 Zlotys; after deducting 48 Zlotys for interest the bank was left with 1,302 Zlotys. The two cooperative banks received in total 3,824 Zlotys. This money has to be returned over a period of eighteen months.

The letter writer adds that the money received by the *Gmilat Hasadim* Fund was distributed as loans with the participation of the "Aid Committee." The committee takes part in all meetings of the fund's management, which are held once a week. It adds to the sum given to each borrower an amount equal to that received from the *Gmilat Hasadim* Fund. The "Aid Committee" does not participate in the activities of the cooperative banks. The people who receive loans from the banks are well off, and money that the "Relief Committee" wants to continue sending should go to the *Gmilat Hasadim* Fund. The impoverished of the town will benefit only from this fund. But first, please send money so that we can distribute support before the holidays.

The first writer ends his part of the letter with greetings for a good new year.

The second writer of this letter states that the cooperative banks received 5.27 Zlotys for each dollar. Then he writes that they are sending the letter five weeks before the holidays, and hopes that it will be received at the proper time. He then describes the financial situation, the crisis, and the distress in town.

The financial situation is very bad. The reasons for this are those of which it has been said "Tell it not in Gath, publish it not in the streets of Ashkelon" [Samuel 2, 1:20]... We do not know what will come next. The well to do can cope, even if the situation lasts a few more months. But the poor do not have enough to exist from day to day. They can anticipate famine. The pressure of the needy on the "Aid Committee" is great, but what can the committee do to help? People are going around town every day collecting charity but "the scraps cannot satisfy the lion" [Babylonian Talmud, Tractate *Berakoth*]. The writer concludes "I hope that you, beloved brothers, will understand us and reply to our desperate pleas."

Signed: Dov Czarka

*

The letter dated August 15, 1939 is the last in the correspondence that I have before me. It is also probably the last letter that was written by the "Aid Committee" of Sierpc to the "Relief Committee" in America. Very soon after it was written – just half a month later – the Second World War broke out. The war brought destruction and extinction to European Jewry in general, to Polish Jews in particular, and the Jews of Sierpc were among the first sacrifices to be burned at the stake. They felt that something sinister was coming, and there was a reason for them writing "We don't know what the future will bring." But could anyone anticipate such a complete devastation, annihilation, eradication? Did anyone think that they were approaching – and very, very, soon – a Holocaust the likes of which, in its cruelty, extent, and planning, was unknown in the history of the world, and in the history of the Jewish people so well versed in disasters? No! Not even the most doom prophesying prophet could predict this devastation.

I was shocked while going through this correspondence when I reached this letter, the last one, as its date gives evidence that the Jews of Sierpc, on that date, already stood at the edge of the precipice. In my imagination, I saw them, obviously under impact of their daily distress and fear of the future, going about doing their regular chores with their everyday problems. Life, disturbed by the events of the day and the worries about tomorrow, nevertheless goes on as usual; the well to do here and the impoverished there, celebrations one day and troubles the next day. And beside the personal difficulties, there are communal problems. They turn to the brethren in America to hasten sending aid to the poor, and especially support for the upcoming holidays. Funds are collected in town for the same purpose – granting loans by the *Gmilat Hasadim* Fund and by the cooperative banks for merchants or craftsman; worrying that the promissory notes that the *Gmilat Hasadim* Fund had signed and the payments that the cooperative banks would have to make starting May, 1940. All of them together and each one separately do not realize that they are at the brink of the abyss. In another few days the ground will open up beneath them and swallow them and everything they have, without leaving almost any trace or survivor. What a terrible thing this is and what a horrible feeling!

B. A Letter from the "Rescue Committee"

As stated in the introduction, the bundle of letters that I have includes some from other institutions (other than the "Aid Committee"), and also two letters from individuals. All the letters contain requests for financial help from the townspeople of Sierpc in America. These letters, just like the previous ones, tell of the great misery of the Jews of Sierpc, their diminished position and their impoverished state.

*

The letter that I am looking at was sent by the "Rescue Committee" in Sierpc to the Sierpc immigrants in America on March 3, 1933. (The previous letters were sent by the "Aid Committee" on and following March 1, 1937.) The name "Rescue Committee" is mentioned at the beginning of the letter but the rubber stamp at the end of the letter contains the name "Aid Committee." According to Zvi Malowanczyk, who was the chairman of the committee, the accepted name was *Retungs-Comitat* ("Rescue Committee"). This is the letter:

"To our brothers from Sierpc in America:

"Our town has a 'Rescue Committee' whose purpose is to provide substantial financial support to merchants and craftsmen that have lost their livelihoods and without immediate support face the possibility of complete ruin. We provide aid to these people so that they can hold out and not become a burden to the community. Because of the crisis in Poland in general and in Sierpc in particular, a crisis that undermines the status of affluent merchants and craftsmen, wage earners and donors to charity and transforms them into the recipients of charity. Our meager resources and small incomes are not enough to help all those that ask for and need aid.

"Therefore we are turning to you, dear brethren, who have always remembered your comrades in Sierpc and helped them on various occasions. So please gird yourselves this time for an extra effort, and collect a substantial amount from the Sierpc immigrants in America, so that we can help all those that turn to us. All those that ask us for help are humble people, who only a year ago were people of status, earning a livelihood, and philanthropists. They do not want their economic problems and material distress known in public. They and their families may become hungry without our help. These families, who suffer from their hunger in private, are exposed to various diseases that can lead to great tragedies. We have an obligation to save them from their terrible misery and the disasters that lie in wait.

"In the name of the many suffering families we ask you, our brothers, to do as much as possible to gather a significant sum of money and send it to us as quickly as possible, so that we can really help these families to stand on their own two feet, and to be able to earn their daily bread.

"Please send the money to our chairman, Malowanczyk, in the name of the 'Rescue Committee.'

"Signed: Chairman - Zvi Malowanczyk; secretary – Yehoshua Tajtelbaum."

The rubber stamp imprinted at the end of the letter contains the address *Localer Hilft-Comitet far Yuden in Sierpc* ("Local Aid Committee for the Jews of Sierpc").

*

At the end of the letter there is a letter of endorsement from Rabbi Goldschlak, the Rabbi of Sierpc. He writes:

"Because of the terrible economic conditions in Sierpc, I cannot remain silent, and turn to you, the immigrants from Sierpc in America. I want to encourage the feeling of Jewish mercy that is in your hearts, and tells you that as fellow townsmen you have a sacred duty find ways and resources to ease the plight of your brothers and sisters. They hold out their hands in a cry for help in the misery in which they find themselves. By virtue of this, God will send salvation to all of Israel."

Following this, the Rabbi writes that if it were not for the strenuous labors of the "Rescue Committee," many families would have collapsed. But there is a terrible heartache that because of a lack of resources, many families are turned away empty handed. The Rabbi concludes "I hope that you will understand how great a *mitzvah* this is and send your help quickly and generously."

Signed with blessings of charity, the younger Yehoshua Hashil David, son of the Gaon Yaakov Chayim Zelig, here in the community of Sierpc.

The rubber stamp imprinted on the letter has the notation: Hashil David, son of the *Gaon* Yaakov Chayim Zelig Goldschlak, chief of the Rabbinical Court of Sierpc and the district.

The rubber stamp imprinted at the beginning of the letter contains the following notation in Polish: *Rabin Gminy Wyznaniowej Zydowskiej w Sierpcu, Sierpc, dn. 5.III.1933 r. Nr. 30/33* (Rabbi of the Jewish Community of Sierpc, Sierpc, 5th day of the third month of the year 1933, no. 30/33)

C. A Letter from the Gmilat Hasadim Fund

Another letter from the same bundle of letters was written by the committee of the *Gmilat Hasadim* Fund to the Sierpc townspeople in America on August 4, 1938. The letter describes the worthy activities of the fund which help hundreds of families of poor small merchants and craftsmen. The letter also describes the intensive efforts of the fund to collect money locally so as not to require outside charity. But because of the economic crisis and the terrible anti-Semitism, the fund has been forced to ask for aid from Sierpc immigrants abroad. The following is an abbreviated version of the letter. We present the most important parts in full, those that present statistics on the activities of the fund.

"To our brothers across the sea, greetings and a blessing.

"The *Gmilat Hasadim* Fund has been in existence in Sierpc for over ten years,[23] performing its tasks quietly and confidentially; helping tens of families to survive and earn their living. This is well known, and we are not revealing any secrets, but only reminding you of what is common knowledge in order to ask for your help. Thus this important institution will be able to continue its essential activities.

"The fund committee is opposed to lifting the burden from itself and placing it on others, so we have never turned to you before for help.

"We have increased our efforts in collecting money among ourselves for the fund. We have undertaken a number of projects: recruiting new members who pay a monthly fee; organizing pledges and contributions; opened a 'Gold Book' that contains a special page of 'everlasting memory' to memorialize whoever contributes 100 Zlotys to the fund. Thanks to these efforts we have managed to accumulate an equity of 13,000 Zlotys.

"13,000 Zlotys is a significant sum. You can all understand that this amount was not gathered easily or quickly.

"Together with the credit from the 'Joint' and the *Cekabe*[24] – the center for *Gmilat Hasadim* Funds in Poland – we have a working capital of 26,000 Zlotys used by 450 families in our town for credit at no interest. Among them are tens of families whose existence depends on this money. For instance, about 30 gardeners receive loans of 100 or 150 Zlotys so they can rent an orchard, work hard and guard it day and night against robbers and other mishaps. In the end, they earn three or four times the amount they invested. There are peddlers in the villages that receive loans of 100 Zlotys, and return to the villages and buy everything they can and so earn their livelihood. There are about 35 owners of stalls in the market who receive loans of 150 or 200 Zlotys so that they can order goods from Warsaw or Lodz and sell them in the market in town or in another town on market day and earn their living. These groups' existences are dependent on the *Gmilat Hasadim* Fund.

"The people who receive loans from us have various occupations: 57 tailors, 30 shoemakers, 2 carpenters, 4 butchers, 69 miscellaneous craftsmen, 13 haberdashers, 5 leather merchants, 35 grocery store owners, 39 market stall owners, 20 laborers, and 140 various types of occupations.

"In previous years we gave loans for repayment over ten weeks; the borrower would have to return 10% of the loan each week. But experience has taught us that the loans have to be made for four, five, or even six months. This means that because of the lack of capital in the fund, it is often impossible to respond to requests of members waiting for a loan. In addition the number of people wanting to borrow money is increasing, and the sources of local income have shrunk because of the bad state of affairs."

The letter goes on: "You must know of the conditions in the towns of Poland. Yesterday's 'donors' have become today's 'recipients.' That is the situation in Sierpc as well. Polish stores are opened, and they ruin the Jewish stores. The Polish stores are helped and supported by large long term loans given by government financial institutions and Polish society and by two Polish '*Gmilat Hasadim* Funds' that have been established in our town. We, with our meager resources, are forced to compete with these forces.

"Therefore we are forced against our will to ask you for help. You are the only asset we have that can help to maintain our important and very necessary institution. Call a meeting of the immigrants from Sierpc immediately, explain to our brothers the gloomy situation of the Jews of Sierpc, and collect a substantial sum of money and send it to us. Then we can distribute loans for seasonal undertakings before the holidays. Consider that we have distributed loans for leasing orchards in the amount of 1,500 Zlotys. The borrowers will start returning the loans only after the holidays when they begin returning to town from the orchards to sell the fruit. Meanwhile, there is no money in the fund for loans to other borrowers.

"Brothers and dear friends! He who provides for the *Gmilat Hasadim* Fund provides for the existence of the Jews of Sierpc. Remember that for every Zloty that we collect, we receive a Zloty from the 'Joint.' Thus, any amount that you collect will be doubled. Remember also that your help, in addition to the material benefit that it brings, encourages us and strengthens our resolve in the bitter struggle for existence of our brothers and sisters."

Signed by the members of the committee of the Gmilat Hasadim Fund of Sierpc: Chairman – Menachem Baumel, Secretary – Hirsch Pianca, Treasurer – Matat Farshnitzki, Yaakov Edelshein, Alia (Eliyahu) Grosman, L. (Leib) Usher, A.H. (Avraham Hirsch) Yurkevitz, Ahron Yosef Pukacz, Moshe Aran (Ahron) Fetbrot, Moshe Grosman (son-in-law of Hanach Tzcernobroda).

The rubber stamp imprinted at the beginning of the letter contains the text: *St. Dobr. Gmilus Chesed w Sierpcu Nr. 1133/38* (*St. Dobre – Stowarzyszenie Dobroczynne* - A Charitable Association).

The rubber stamp imprinted at the end of the letter contains the text *Gmilut Hesed* Sierpc – *Stowarzyszenie Dobroczynne Gmilus Hesed Sierpc.*

*

There were three letters of endorsement enclosed with the letter of the *Gmilat Hasadim* Fund that testify to the importance of the Fund to the poorest Jews of Sierpc, and recommend that it be urgently given aid. The letters are from the Jewish Community, the Craftsmen's Organization, and the Small Merchants Association.

The letter from the Jewish Community states: "We hereby verify that the institution *Gmilat Hasadim* in our town is one of the most important Jewish social organizations we have. In its efforts for the support of tens of families and its practical and constructive activities it performs a vital task at this time for the impoverished Jewish population that is in distress. It deserves to be aided in an appropriate manner."

Signed by the chairman, Nahum Tatza.

The rubber stamp imprinted at the beginning of the letter contains the text: *Fervaltung fun der Yiddisher Kehille in Sierpc. Sierpc dem 2 Sherpien 1938. No VIII/38* ("Management Committee of the Jewish Community of Sierpc. Sierpc,

August 2, 1938.") The rubber stamp at the end of the letter contains the text: "Authority of the Jewish Community of Sierpc. *Fervaltung fun der Yiddisher Kehille.* Sierpc."

*

The letter of the Craftsmen's Organization states: "We are also turning to you, our far away brothers, to ask that you pay attention to the request of the *Gmilat Hasadim* Fund and help it significantly. This is our most important financial institution, one that poor craftsman can depend upon, as well as the throng of destitute Jews."

Signed with greetings from the members of the Craftsmen's Organization, Ezra Frankel, Chairman.

The imprinted rubber stamp contains the text: *Centralny Zwiazek Rzemieslnikow Zydow w Polsce. Oddzzial w Sierpcu.* ("Central Organization of Jewish Craftsmen in Poland, Sierpc Branch.)

*

The letter from the Small Merchants Association states: "To our townsmen across the sea – a plea for help. We, the small merchants, ask you to heed the request of the *Gmilat Hasadim* Fund. Its task is to render help to the small merchants who are fighting for their lives. Urgent help from you in these times is the order of the day in order to strengthen the economic situation of the Jews."

Signed by the chairman of the Small Merchants Association, Zvi Koplowicz.

The imprinted rubber stamp at the beginning of the letter contains the text: *Centrale fun Detalisten un Kleinhendler Farband in Poilin. Avteilung in Sierpc.* ("Center of the Association of Retailers and Small Merchants in Poland, Sierpc Branch.") The rubber stamp at the end of the letter contains the text: *Centr. Detalicznych i Drobnych Kupcow w Polsce, Oddzzial w Sierpcu.* ("The Retailers and Small Merchants Center, Sierpc Branch.")

D. Letters from the *Tarbuth* School

The bundle of letters also contains two that were written by the committee of the *Tarbuth* School in Sierpc. These letters are similar but different from the other letters sent from "The Valley of Tears" to the Sierpc immigrants in America. Similar, because they also ask for financial help. But different because unlike the other letters quoted in this chapter, that ask for material aid for a material purpose, these two letters are requests for material help for spiritual needs.

Another difference between these two letters and the others: all the other letters are addressed to all the Sierpc immigrants in America, whereas the two letters of *Tarbuth* School are for only one ex-Sierpcer, Mordecai Rzejsotko. They ask him to become active in, and convince others to help the educational institution *Tarbuth* in Sierpc.

The two letters that I have are apparently part of a wider correspondence between the townspeople of Sierpc and the immigrants concerning aid to the *Tarbuth* School. In spite of the fact that both letters came from the same institution, the writers are different, the heads of the school are different, their dates are far apart (more than two years), and the purposes of the aid requested are different. In the first letter, help is asked for finishing construction of the school building, and in the second letter, aid in meeting the budget and the debts owed by the school.

The first letter was written using the official letterhead of *Tarbuth*, which contains the following text in Polish and Hebrew: *Hebrajska Skola Powszechna Tarbut w Scierpcu, ul. Stodolna.* "The General Hebrew School *Tarbuth* in Sierpc, Stodolna Street."

The letter was written on September 13, 1935 (the number "335" appears erroneously instead of "935"), Number 63.

We mentioned above that the two letters were not addressed to the immigrants from Sierpc in general, but to one of them in particular, Mordecai Rzejsotko. Even though the letter is directed to two recipients, "To our Honorable Fellow Townsmen in America" followed by "To Our Honorable Comrade Mr. Rzejsotko," the body of the letter is meant for M. Rzejsotko.

The following is the content of the letter:

"We turn to you, our honorable townsman, as someone who is tied to the town of his birth and feels its joys and its tragedies. You know of the repression and poverty in which the Jews of Sierpc are mired. The crisis has destroyed the economic status of the Jews. The 'landlords' are on the edge of financial ruin, and the chances for improvement in the situation are nil.

"In spite of the terrible conditions, we have the opportunity to do something great and important that is our consolation, hope, and pride. We opened the *Tarbuth* School, with great efforts, four years ago. This is a school that gives its pupils a nationalistic education in their national language. This idea seemed like a dream, opening a school all of whose costs would be borne by the poor Jewish population. But the lofty goal of giving a new generation a nationalistic education inspired the committee and the teaching staff. After prodigious struggles we managed to build a wonderful school, where almost 200 pupils are being educated.

"In the past two years, we have had many hardships finding a location for the school. It has been impossible to discover a location in town suitable for the school from the standpoint of pedagogy and hygiene that meets the requirements of the government. Therefore we were forced to erect a building for the school. This required great sacrifices from the parents, the committee, and the whole Jewish population. We were able to build this structure, which cost close to 25,000 Zlotys, in time for the beginning of this school year.

"But this is not the end of the matter. We may have been able to finish a few classrooms for the children but the complete building is not finished, and the educational authorities are threatening to close the school if we do not finish construction this school year. We find ourselves in a desperate situation. We have a deficit of 10,000 Zlotys because of the construction. We do not have an income because we have already used all our resources. Now we find ourselves facing closure of the school by the court, and abandoning hundreds of children without Torah and without education.

"Therefore, all our hopes are with you, honorable sir; through you, and with the help of our brothers, former townspeople of Sierpc, you can help us finish this building on time. We hope that you, as someone who was active in the cultural life of Sierpc, will understand our dire situation and do everything you can to help us complete this structure.

"Remember, our honorable townsman, that the fate of hundreds of Jewish children, our only solace in our dark and severe lives, is in your hands. Help us finish our holy work!

"In the name of the Construction Committee of the Tarbuth School in Sierpc

Chairman, Yesha Friedman Secretary, Moshe Balt

Committee of the Tarbuth School in Sierpc Chairman, Yisrael Smolinski

Administration of the Tarbuth School in Sierpc Principal, Shaul Rozenblum[25]

"Our Address for correspondence: Bank Ludowy Sierpc dla szkoly 'Tarbut' Poland"

The rubber stamp imprinted at the end of the letter bears the text: *Stowarzsyszenie Kulturalno-oswiatowe: Tarbut w Polsce, Oddzial w Sierpcu* "Culture Organization in Poland, Sierpc Branch."

* * *

The second letter of the Tarbuth School contains, as mentioned, an appeal for financial help in lessening the burden of the budget and the load of debt weighing down the school committee. Its content shows that a similar letter had already been sent, and a reply had been received. The letter in front of us repeats the request, emphasizes the need for help and prods the recipient into activity.

This letter was written on November 11, 1937, and is directed to "the comrade and friend, M. Rzejsotko." This is its content:

"We have received your letter and thank you for starting the efforts for our school. Despite your statement that it is not possible to do great things, we still hope that with good will you will be able to do something significant. There are more than a few Sierpc townspeople in America, and if there will be just a few advocates who will understand the urgency of our appeal for help and apply themselves to it, donors will not be lacking. Therefore we reiterate and ask you to fully explain the importance and seriousness of the predicament that faces us, at a meeting of immigrants from Sierpc.

"I must add that because of the hard-pressed conditions of the Jewish population, the situation of our cultural-educational institution worsens every day. The percentage of students that pay nothing and those that pay only a little is increasing, and we manage to balance our budget only with great effort. In addition we are faced with a large debt that threatens to force us to transfer ownership of the building to foreign hands. Therefore we again ask you to speak at a meeting of our townspeople about our serious problem and encourage them to extend substantial help. We are confident of the feelings of solidarity of our townsfolk in America.

"In the name of the committee, Yitzhak David Schnitzer."

The rubber stamp imprinted at the end of the letter bears the text: *Powszechna Szkola Hebrajska Tarbut w Sierpcu.* "The General Hebrew School *Tarbuth* in Sierpc."

The following two addresses appear at the end: *I.D. Sznyzer Sierpc ul. Mr. Sz. Rydza 18; A, Dichter Sierpc ul. Narutowizca 17, Skola Tarbut.*[26]

E. Letters from Individuals

I mentioned earlier that the bundle of letters in front of me also contains letters written by individuals. I have three such private letters, written by two Jews from Sierpc, who sent their letters to their townsman, Mordecai Rzejsotko. They spread their troubles before him and ask him to convince the committee[27] to send them financial help to get them out of their plight.

I do not know if Rzejsotko received other, similar personal letters. But reading the letters from institutions published here, it is certain that many Sierpc Jews were living in conditions comparable to those of the two letter writers – lives of despair and misery, poverty and want. These letters present an instructive example of their state and their lives.

These three letters are very depressing. A bleak plea cries out from the lines and from in between the lines of these letters.

*

In one letter dated November 9, 1937, a father asks and then repeats his request in an undated second letter, for money for a dowry for his eldest daughter, who had reached marriageable age some years ago. He reveals his many problems, opens up his heart, and says that two years ago, when his daughter became engaged, he had a dowry for her. But in the meantime he had become so seriously ill that he was not expected to recover. When he did recover, thanks to his daughters, his wife became ill, and had to be operated on and hospitalized. With the grace of God, his wife also recovered, but the dowry money was spent on doctors and medicine. Because of her anguish, his daughter, the bride, fell ill. She is now feeling a little better, and the doctors say that after the wedding she will mend. The bridegroom does not know about her sickness and wants to get married. He asked the rabbi in his town to tell the rabbi in Sierpc to notify the bride's father that he wants the wedding to take place soon; otherwise he will abandon the match. The father asks and begs the committee to have pity for him and his wife, and send him the money for the dowry, so that he will not be shamed and disgraced by the groom's desertion. His plea is shocking: "Save me in my old age and save my daughter in her youth!"

* * *

A second father states in a letter from December 12, 1938, that his daughter had married and he had promised her a dowry of 1,000 Zlotys in addition to linens, lingerie, and so forth. Around this time, his son became engaged, and he wants his father to pay for the wedding. His second son, who had spent six years in a training camp for *Aliyah*[28], had received permission [from the British mandate government] to immigrate to Palestine, and he asked his father to give him 500 Zlotys for travel expenses, because if he cannot go to the Land of Israel, his life won't be worth a penny. But the father does not have the resources to fulfill his promise to his daughter and satisfy the demands of his sons. He had written a number of times to his relatives in America, but they did not answer. He asked for help from his brothers in town and they said that they cannot help him. Therefore, in his desperation, he asks the committee members to be his brothers and help him and save him from his great suffering and distress. Because how can he watch the suffering of his sons and daughters? He ends his letter with the cry, "My house is burning, save me!"

* * *

The reader of these letters – those written by institutions ("Aid Committee," Rescue Committee," *Gmilat Hasadim* Fund, *Tarbuth* School) and those written by individuals in Sierpc, and sent to former Sierpcer in America asking for financial help – does not need commentaries and singular clarifications. The letters speak for themselves and describe very well the situation of the Jews in "The Valley of Tears" of Poland in general and Sierpc in particular in the thirties before the coming of the great and horrible Holocaust. The anti-Semitic regime in Poland with the help of the whole Polish population and all of the political parties persecuted and oppressed Polish Jews. It robbed them of their bread, of their rights, and their freedom. Polish Jews were hounded to the brink and pushed into poverty, distress, and despair. Following the infamous statement of the Polish Prime Minister, Skladkowski to the Sejm[29], "An economic boycott of the Jews – *Ovsem*!"[30] the central and local authorities issued various edicts against Jewish craftsmen, large and small merchants, and stall owners in the market. (The anti-Semitic movement put up competitors even for this "lucky" group.) The economic and safety situation of the Jews became worse every day. There was no one to complain to about the everyday attacks of hooligans and mischief makers and ask for protection.

The life of a Jew and his property were forfeit to hoodlums and ruffians who could do anything they wanted. The situation went from bad to worse and they became second class citizens, without opportunities for livelihood and no rights to defend themselves. And worst of all – with no possibility of improvement in sight.

Thus the Jews lived in poverty and despair, fear and terror, until the Nazi predators came and finished what the Poles had started and turned "The Valley of Tears" into hell.

Translator's Footnotes:

1. *Andatzia – Partia Naradova Demokratitzhna* (National Democratic Party) whose initials were N.D. It was a blatantly anti-Semitic party.
2. A new name for the new market.
3. The beginning of the road to Lipno.
4. A new name for the narrow street called "Doly" ("Dales")
5. This is a reference to the famous statement of Prime Minister Skladkowski in the Sejm (Parliament): *Ovsem* (of course!).
6. Meaning the *Anschluss* – the Nazi conquest of Austria.
7. A policeman was killed in Brześć in a melee between Jews and Poles.
8. Jewish citizens of Poland who lived in Germany were suddenly expelled to Poland in October 1938. Poland refused them entry, and they remained on the border, in the village of Zbąszyń, in great misery, without anything.
9. The author of the letters considers "People's Bank" to be a continuation of the "Savings and Loan Fund" that was in Sierpc before World War 1.
10. The name of the second bank was *Bank Udzialowi* ("Mutual Bank")
11. According to the letter the *Gmilat Hasadim* Fund was founded 15 years earlier, in 1924. But the letter writer exaggerated the age of the fund slightly, because it was established in 1927. We have read an article written in the newspaper *Unser Rayan Zeitung* ("Our Regional Newspaper") Number (26) 1 dated September 19, 1927: "Thanks to the initiative of our local rabbis, the institution *Gmilat Hasadim* Fund was created."
12. [Psalms 118:5. "Out of my straits I called upon the Lord"]
13. Hooligans who stood at the entrances of Jewish stores and turned away Polish customers.

1. The tense situation in Europe, and especially on the Polish-German border, before the outbreak of the Second World War.
2. [A religious school for young children from poor families.]
3. [A modern Hebrew day school.]
4. TOZ – Towarzystwo Ochrony Zdrowia – the Society for Preservation of Health
5. According to a previous letter, the larger bank is *Bank Ludowi* (People's Bank), and the smaller bank, which was founded later, is *Bank Udzialowi* ("Mutual Bank").
6. Dr. Shoskes – Supervisor of cooperative banks.
7. The letter from July 2 states that the loan will be returned in 10 monthly payments beginning six months from the date of the loan.

14. Reference to the letter of January 23, 1939.
15. There is an error in the date here. See the end of the letter of February 20 of that year.
16. The *Gmilat Hasadim* Fund was founded in 1927.
17. *Cekabe – Centrala kas bezprocentowych*
18. The principal Shaul Rozenblum was from Warsaw
19. Mr. Dichter was the principal of the *Tarbuth* School in the final two years of its existence, before the Holocaust.

20. The intent is the "Relief Committee" of Sierpc Jews in America.
21. [Immigration to a *kibbutz* in Palestine.]
22. The Polish Parliament
23. Of Course

When I Came to Sierpc from the Land of Israel

(Excerpt)

by Ephraim Talmi (Wluka)

...I am at the railroad station in the town of my birth. I am on my way to my parents' home in a carriage. A tall, thin horse is harnessed to it, and an old Jewish man is driving it. The wheels clatter against the rickety stone pavement. Echoes and loud counter echoes reverberate in the spaces of the old town and draw the attention of the few passersby. The eyes of many Jews, standing in the entrances to their stores, follow me. The same old sights, the same hunched, rundown houses. Only their color has faded more, and it is as if they have shrunk and sunk further into the ground. Here is the ancient bridge, planted over the river, a river of the days of my childhood. As for the river, it's as if its waist has become narrower and its current has slowed down over time. There are scattered spots with green grass. Here is the special Jewish Street with its synagogues, all concentrated in one area. Here are the gloomy houses with the peaked roofs, sticking to one another. A dark fear comes over me in the middle of the day. My heart aches with a sharp pain, and my eyes silently fill with tears. I see it all as a bleak and dismal symphony. A town where the houses are piled one on top of the other, as if ready to collapse, but left standing by some miracle. The tops of the many trees planted on the bank of the river that divides the Jewish quarter jut out over the houses. They sway over them and glisten in the light of the sun, like a greeting from a foreign world, tranquil, blessed with ample fields and abundant trees that surround the narrow, dark Jewish street that helplessly awaits its slow and inevitable extinction... And here are the Jews! My God! Here are the Mark Chagall archetypes. Like then, but here and now. The unique round Jewish hat, with its pointed, faded visor and a crown full of many wrinkles. The sorrowful smile drenched in tears and the eyes - God! What depths of grief are perceived there! How great is the fear and powerlessness! But what is even more visible is the will to live that flashes through the veil of annihilation so vividly. Here in the same long coat, split from the back down to the ground, just more archaic and more faded, with a gait that has become more slipshod. But in spite of everything our Jewish brothers stubbornly maintain their peculiar life and characteristic dress.

Grabbing on to any ray of light, any protrusion that seems to be an opportunity, just to carry on. The roots may be slowly rotting, but the branches in their vitality can still bear outstanding fruit. The lust for life is great and cannot be comprehended.

There was one question asked by all those who came to greet and visit with me after so many years: "What is over there? How do you feel in the Land of Israel? " The eyes implore with a silent prayer: please, a little reassurance! With simple words I talk about the Land of Israel, the hardships, the troubles and the suffering, and of the hopes and gratification we feel with the progress and the development. I can see the relief in the deep gloom of their eyes, the spark of life that is ignited beneath the mound of ashes that covers them...

Before the Holocaust - the Town in 1938

by Shlomo Czarka, Kibbutz Dan

In 1934, I went to the training camp of *Hashomer Hatzair*[1] at Grodno, in Lithuania. Before I immigrated to the Land Of Israel, I went back to the town where I had lived and grown up. There I spent my evenings in conversations, in lectures, and in activities at the local *ken.*[2]

When I left for training in 1934, I remembered the town as vibrant and full of life. When I came back after four years of training in order to arrange all the documents for my trip, I felt a huge change in the life of the town. The young people were almost all gone. Many had gone to Warsaw searching for jobs and livelihood. The girls became nannies in well-to-do families; the boys worked as tailors, clerks in merchant houses, or assistants in stores, etc. Public life in Sierpc was almost at a standstill. In the evenings, there were no Jews in the streets. I could not find even a *minyan* of young people on the promenade, in the part between Hiller and Grodka.

How different were the Sabbath and Friday from what I remembered before I left for training. Near the old *beit midrash*, on Saturday night, I saw just two people - the custodian and a bystander, talking to each other.

The Jews refrained from showing themselves in the streets. A heavy aura of concern, fear of the future, lay over the town. Every face looked worried.

In a conversation with some young people, I asked who put up the new and attractive stores that I saw. They told me that these belong to Gentiles. There are already Gentile watchmakers, and so forth.

The faces of these young people showed sadness and apathy about the future. No love of life and no hope.

Translator's Footnotes:

1. A Zionist Socialist youth movement
2. [A local chapter house of the *Hashomer Hatzair* is called a *ken* - literally, nest.

Of the Blood

by Ephraim Talmi (Wluka)

Do not forget the fury!
Do not forgo the mutiny!
Reverberate like thunder,
Shatter like a gunshot,

Of the blood that was splattered
And flowed for nothing,
Thickened and simmered,
They will not get my blood...

The First Months Under Bloody German Rule

by Tzvi Malowanczyk

A few months before the war broke out, at around Purim time, our calm town of Sierpc suddenly bustled with military people. As we understood at that time, this was a test mobilization. There were strong Jewish men in Sierpc at the time who had been sent by the army from the eastern areas: reservists from Baranovich, Vilna, Bialystok, Brest Litovsk, Lomza, etc. At that time, I went along with representatives of the Jewish community to General Anders[1], who today is sadly well-known, and in that time was the chief commander of the Mlawer Front with his headquarters with us in Sierpc. We made efforts to ensure that the Jewish soldiers would be granted leave for the holiday, and be provided with kosher food for Passover. The Jews of Sierpc had a very warm relationship with the Jewish soldiers from outside. The interest in taking a Jewish soldier home for the holiday was so great that there was a shortage of Jewish soldiers, and I was left without a guest for the Seder.

With time, the situation normalized. The people grew accustomed to seeing groups of armed soldiers. Jewish girls already became well acquainted with them, and everything went properly for some time... until the great confusion.

It was Wednesday, August 30, 1939. It was the market day, and the sun was shining brightly. At around 1:00 p.m., wild voices could suddenly be heard shouting. People ran lamented, and wept. The farmers whipped their horses to go faster, and everyone escaped in great haste. This was the announcement of the mobilization. Large placards stated that Thursday,

August 31 would be the first day of the mobilization. People quickly began to run, pack up, and set out for the trains, in order to fulfill their civic duty and report to the appropriate military formation. My cohort and category had not yet been called up.

On Friday, September 1 at around 8:00 a.m., as I was in the new *Beis Midrash* (at that time I was saying *kaddish* for my mother of blessed memory) I suddenly heard the howl of the firefighter's siren. Then the police came in helmets and drove out the civilian population. This was the beginning of the Nazi assault. This time, however, they were only passing through in order to destroy other cities. However we no longer had any rest.

It was the first dark Friday night. It was still warm outside, and the moon could be seen in the clear sky, but the moods were already overcast and devastated. Parents prayed for their children, and wives for their husbands. The first refugees from Zuromin appeared on Saturday afternoon – naturally the wealthy – "saving of life overrides the Sabbath."

The days were long, and the nights were sleepless. Our town had not been bombarded yet. We already knew from the radio, however, that a considerable number of towns had been severely attacked, including our neighboring city of Plock, where the barracks had already been destroyed on the first Friday of the war. The weather, as if to taunt us, was fine. On Monday, the fourth day of the war, our city was suddenly bombarded. There were no specific human casualties, but the confusion was great. People began to run.

Together with my family, my brother, sister, and my brother-in-law Ezriel Dobraszklanka, we set out for Dobrzyń with 85 people. These people included men, Jews and Christians, postal workers, district officers, police and others.

We traveled during the night and rested during the day. We already felt the exile. Just as we had hosted the refugees from Zuromin on Saturday, the people of Dobrzyń hosted us on Tuesday. However, in the evening, when we set out along the Wisla on our way to Gostinin, a considerable number of young people from Dobrzyń joined us.

We continued along slowly and with extreme caution until we finally reached Gostinin. We spent the night there after having traveled for two nights. On Thursday night we set out again on our way to Gąbin. That large district city was so overcrowded that we literally could not find a place for ourselves. Water and bread were also lacking. We ate plums (Gąbin was the chief source of plums).

Relatives, acquaintances and regular young people had all gone along the way. I met my two sisters, my brother-in-law, and a young niece, who had set out from Plock. We wandered around for the entire day and finally set out to return to Plock. We arrived in Plock once again at about 10:00 p.m. The open pipes provided water for those who were thirsty from the journey. Christian neighbors gave bread – it seemed like the relationships had improved. We lay down and quickly fell asleep.

Suddenly, at around 1:00 a.m., we were startled by an explosion. My brother-in-law ran outside into the street, and immediately returned with an order, "Get up! The bridges have been broken." We can still travel to the other side for five zloty. And what will be after? We went back to Gąbin, and decided to remain there.

On Saturday morning, around dawn, we saw the first German officials. By around midday the high officials set themselves up in Bodzanów. The military arrived from the direction of Sierpc, where they had entered on Friday at about 10:00 a.m.

We wandered through the streets of Plock. We met acquaintances and discussed returning to Sierpc. Zalman Atlas took the initiative to rent a wagon, and on Sunday, the first day of *Selichot*[2], after services, we set out on the route back to Sierpc. We set out crowded onto the wagon like geese filled with fear and trepidation. We had already passed through Bielsk thank G-d and were approaching Lelice (a large town, 14 kilometers from Sierpc), when the demons saw us and greeted us with a shout, "Halt! Jews?" We were all silent. "Who speaks German?" There was a good friend there, who advised me. My heart fluttered. They examined me, and asked me inane questions which I answered. Finally they shouted, "Let them go!"

Our heart lightened up, and we traveled on until we came to Manesz, just before Sierpc, where the Maccabee Sports organization used to hold its practices. There, we separated and snuck into the city one by one. The town was "excited" about us. It was a joy that the first group of "brave ones" had returned. "What have you heard?" We were peppered with questions from all sides. We asked as well, and they asked.

In the meantime it was calm in the city. There were barely any groups of German soldiers. They let us know, "When we leave and the S.S. men arrive things will be much worse." Unfortunately they spoke the truth.

On Monday, the Gestapo men arrived, wearing black uniforms but dressed very civilly. On Wednesday, the eve of *Rosh Hashanah,* the entire Jewish population of Dobzryń was expelled to Sierpc, and they spread out in "Manesz." Merciful Jews sent bread. There were many people who performed good deeds. My neighbor Rachel Lerer, the wife of Zecharia the butcher, played a large, lively role in this effort. On Friday, the second day of Rosh Hashanah, all the men were asked to register.

The Dobzryń Jews were freed on *Shabbat Shuva.* However, immediately after *Rosh Hashanah,* a series of one decree after another was issued. Public prayer was absolutely forbidden, and we had to worship like the hidden Jews[3]. *Minyanim* [prayer quorums] were formed I the homes of Gershon Mintz, and David Horowicz the son of Moshe Horowicz. Some of the Gerrer Hassidim gathered for prayer in the old manner in their *shtibel,* in the yard of Moshe Goldsztajn's home. Some of the ruffians took them out in their *kittels*[4] and made them sweep the old marketplace.

Nobody was allowed to appear on the street between 6:00 p.m. and 6:00 a.m. Every Jew, even a child, had to wear the inscription "Jude" on the left side, and was not permitted to walk on the sidewalk. Rather, they had to walk in the middle of the street. They would capture Jewish passers-by, over and above the quota of people whom the Jewish community had to provide for work every day. The Germans murdered several Jews for various pretexts. They shot the following people under such circumstances: the American citizen Wesolek, the son of the *shochet* of Osówko who lay in his house, sick in bed; and Yechezkel Czarnoczapka, the son of Yeshaya Czarnoczapka, who was mentally ill. Thefts and beatings became normal occurrences.

On Wednesday, the eve of *Sukkot*, young people were captured from Sierpc, Bierzwienna and Zuromin, put them in prison, and drove them in automobiles throughout the entire next day. Later we found out that they were thrown over to the Soviets via Pultusk. The young people were left there and did not return across the border, and they survived.

On the second night of *Sukkot*, Thursday going on Friday, we were all suddenly frightened by a bright light in all the rooms. We understood everything; however, where could we run? We were forbidden from appearing in the streets, and here, unfortunately, the synagogue was burning... Our Torah scrolls were burning in a bloody fire... We, the Jews of Sierpc, were left bereft of our fine, gorgeous, holy, old-time synagogue.

As a supplement to the terrible tragedy, the Germans sent the Jewish community a notice as follows: "Last night, a Jewish young man set the Jewish temple on fire. The German police captured the person who set the fire and shot him on the spot. Of course, the Jewish community must take responsibility for the damages caused by the fire. We are imposing a contribution of 70,000 zloty upon the Jews. The money must be paid within three hours. If not, you Jews already know what will happen."

We understood that failure to pay meant death for tends of Jews, so of course, we paid the contribution.

The persecution and cruelty grew from day to day. Every day brought fresh decrees and fresh cruelty. As we were driven to and from work, we had to remove our hats and sing. The Jews sang various tunes. Their favorite song to sing was, "When will the redemption come already." The elderly Lopatka would sing the song, clap his hands, and end with a rhyme, like a jester, with a curse on Hitler. Reb Avraham Wluka, the long-time *gabbai* [trustee] of the *Beis Midrash,* had to appear at the police station every day with the keys to the new *Beis Midrash.*

At the same time, various contributions were imposed. Until the payment would be delivered, they would take hostages, including the following well-known householders: Yeshaya Frydman, Dr. Mintz, Leib Hiller, Shimon Malowanczyk, Meir Cyprys, Moshe Hirsch Kocalek, and Berish Poznanski. They placed crowbars (chopped, sharpened stones) in the prison courtyard, and ordered the hostages to roll up their pants and crawl on their naked knees. The Jews would quickly pay the contribution, but this did not impede the punishment. After they freed the people, they would arrest them again under various pretexts.

The Jews, who were taken as hostage by the Germans for the most trivial of reasons, endured difficult torture. Berish Poznanski, who attempted to evoke feelings of fairness from the hooligans by using his impeccable German dialect, was buried in the ground up to his neck. Due to the heavy weight, or perhaps the terror, he exhibited symptoms of death. This alarmed Dr. Mintz, and he ordered them to save Poznanski. When the wives, sisters, or children of the unfortunate hostages brought them food, the murderers opened the door at once and said, with their sadistic friendliness, "They are already dead, they are buried over there; they no longer need food any more." They showed them specially dug graves which were dug by the hostages themselves. After the wailing, screams and weeping of the relatives, they led the live hostages into the prison courtyard.

Thus did the Germans bully our unfortunate brothers and sisters. We stopped believing that we would continue to survive.

The situation became more difficult and serious from day to day. Some of the young people crossed over the Green Border to Bialystok on bicycle. There were even cases where the Germans expelled wanderers, but the governing authorities did not always carry this out.

On one occasion, an edict was issued that all the Jewish merchants must present written lists to the magistrate outlining three examples of the merchandise in their shops. This took place at the beginning of November. Once again, they put the entirely innocent hostages in prison. On Monday, November 8, they issued an order that all of the Jews, even women with suckling babes, must appear in the old market with their suitcases within 30 minutes. Not knowing what was coming, people left their possessions behind. Some of them, still believing in the humanity of the Germans, did not even take their necessities with them as they carried out the order.

A wind orchestra was waiting at the market, and all of the sheep-to-slaughter were marched to the train, urged on by the German bayonets and the wind orchestra. They were loaded onto the wagons, and sent off.

I succeeded in remaining in the city because I lived in a Christian quarter. Meir Czarek and Dvora Fajnberg lived together with me in the house. Together, we purchased two horses and a wagon, and escaped from Sierpc on Thursday together with the Fajnberg and Szmiga families. We went through Dobrzyń, Raciaz, Ciechanow, Makow, and Ostrołęka. There, we snuck across the order. As we passed through Raciaz, the Germans were perpetrating wild orgies against the local Jewish population, who were forced to gather in the synagogue. The scoundrels separated the men from the women. They forced them to strip stark naked, beat them with rods, and forced them to dance around the *bima*. Meanwhile, the women had to toss away their gold rings, clocks, earrings, and the like.

On Thursday, November 15, we were already in Bialystok.

Translator's Footnotes

1. See http://en.wikipedia.org/wiki/W%C5%82adys%C5%82aw_Anders
2. Penitential services held early each weekday morning during the period leading up to *Rosh Hashanah*, as well as between *Rosh Hashanah* and *Yom Kippur*. The first *Selichot* service is conducted on a Saturday night in the middle of the night, on the week prior to *Rosh Hashanah*, or two weeks before if *Rosh Hashanah* falls early in the week.
3. A reference to the Marranos during the time of the Spanish Inquisition.
4. The white robes worn by the worshippers on *Yom Kippur*.

The First Days of German Cruelty in Sierpc

by N. Frenkel

At the outbreak of the war, a mass flight of the Jewish population of Sierpc took place. Men and women, children and old people, all escaped on foot, by car, by wagon and by whatever means they could. Everyone believed that they would succeed in escaping from the city, into which the German Army had already entered. A small group, I among them, went to the city of Dobrzyń. We crossed the river on small boats and arrived in the city on the second day of *Rosh Hashanah*.

At around 2:00 p.m. that same day the Germans arrived in the city. Their first task was to drive the Jews out of their houses. They went from house to house looking for the Jews, and forced them out onto the street. We stood that way for the entire day. A heavy rain was falling. In the evening, we were ordered to return to the cities from which we had come. We set out on our return journey after being under the Germans for a week. They beat us murderously for the entire day. Many Jews, especially the weak and elderly, could not withstand the beatings and difficult journey, and died along the way.

When we arrived in Sierpc, we saw a horrifying scene. The Jewish businesses had been robbed by the Germans and the local population, the Jews were in hiding, and nobody even dared to appear on the street. Every day, they were searching for men for work. However, instead of being sent to work, they were tortured. For entertainment, they had ripped off the breads of Cantor D. Szykes and Sh. Kadecki, and beat them murderously. However, this was merely the beginning.

After sealing the synagogue and *Beis Midrash*, and arresting the president of the community Nachum Taks, they put up placards ordering the Jews to register. The Jews understood what this meant, and nobody went to the registration depot. The next morning, the Germans went from house to house, driving the Jews out of the houses.

Zalman Kanenbrand and I hid in an attic. The Polish neighbors discovered us and showed our hiding place to the Germans. They broke down the door. Zalman Kanenbrand attempted to escape, jumping over the first story. I remained. I was beaten with a whip, expelled from the city, and taken to a collection point where they were gathering the remaining Jews of the city.

From there, we were taken to the head of the region, where we were lined up in rows of two. The merchants and handworkers were registered separately. After the registration, they took merchants to a secluded location and began to torture them terribly. The horrifying images of the torture are etched in my mind to this day.

The terribly beaten Avraham Wluka, Yisrael Karpa, Yitzchak Asz ,and Moshe Podskocz stand before my eyes to this day. They were allowed to go home in the evening.

A few days later, they captured Jewish young people and sent them to "work" in the horse marketplace. There, they were terribly beaten again. I was also among those tortured at that time. I recall that they beat Lichtensztejn, Tarparcz' son-in-law, particularly harshly. In the evening, they put us in jail. A group of S.S. men stood at the entrance, each holding a stick in his hand, with which they beat everyone as they entered.

In the morning, we were forced onto vehicles under a volley of beatings. We did not know where we were going. They first let us get off the vehicles in Pultusk, and ordered us to escape. We thought that they would shoot after us; however, they did not do so, and immediately drove away. A few hours later, we realized that we were on the Soviet side. Thanks to that fortunate event, I survived.

The Last Night in Prison

by Y. Shurek

A few days before *Sukkot*, immediately after I woke up in the morning, I heard people going up the steps. My brother barely had time to hide when two Germans entered the house and asked my mother about the whereabouts of her husband. When they saw me, they ordered me to go out, and they brought me to the market under a hail of beatings.

I saw a few hundred Jewish men already standing in the market. They were standing in two rows under a heavy guard of armed Germans. They then put us into rows of four, and led us to the train station under heavy guard, where several wagons laden with grain were standing. The Germans put down their guns, and took up a stick or a whip. We were given sacks and ordered to fill them up with wheat, and then run to deposit them in a nearby storehouse. The beatings during the work were indescribable. Whoever stood still for a bit or could not run so fast received murderous beatings.

A short time after the work, other Germans came who wanted to "play" a bit.

They separated the married people from the unmarried people, whom they placed four in a row.

They then led us to the Gestapo headquarters, where we once again had to work. For the most part, this was torture rather than work. We hauled rocks from one place to another, and then hauled the same stones back. They gave us full pails of water, and we had to run with the pail. We were beaten terribly if we spilled a bit of water. The cries of the tortured people pierced the heavens, but this did not stop the German sadists from continuing with their torture.

Late at night, when we no longer had the energy to stand on our feet, the murderers got tired of "amusing" themselves with the Jews who were tormented to death. Two more vehicles of Jews arrived from Zuromin, and they began to torture them as they had tortured us. Immediately after getting off the vehicle, each of them received a blow over the head with a stick. They arranged us four in a row and ordered us to sing as we were driven back to the jail in the city.

There, we were forced into a large room. As we entered, every one received a blow over the head with a stick. Tired and hungry from an entire day without food, and we lay down immediately. We had just succeeded in lying down, when another pair of Germans bandits entered and warned us that if anyone dared to cough or sneeze during the night, every fourth Jew would be shot. In order to drive the point home, they beat some of us harshly. It is clear that one could not even talk of sleep. Everyone was terrified and did not know what tomorrow would have in store for us.

As soon as it got light, they led us out of the jail. Several transport trucks were standing in the prison yard. They loaded us onto the trucks and drove us out of the city. We did not know where they were driving us, and we were afraid that our final hour was at hand. After passing through Pultusk, we were tossed out onto a field not far from a forest.

There, they put us into two groups and ordered us to run. They warned us that any person attempting to return would be shot.

We wandered through the forests and fields for two weeks until we arrived in Bialystok. We had no means of existence in Bialystok, so we were registered to be sent to work in Soviet Russia.

The High Holy Days Under German Rule

[lit. "the Days of Awe"]

by Yaakov Sendarowicz

They had already blessed the new month of *Elul* in the *Beis Midrash* and the *shtibels*. The anticipation toward the Day of Judgment awakened in the community. One could already hear the sounds of the *shofar* while walking in the streets in the morning. The town took on a completely different appearance, anticipating the upcoming holiday. Thus did things go in Jewish Sierpc until the autumn of 1939. *Rosh Hashanah* of that year appeared entirely different. Everyone was uncomfortable and was waiting for some terrible thing. They even conducted themselves differently in the Gerrer Shtibel that they did every year. They had the fine custom of traveling to the Gerrer Rebbe, may he live long[1], where the Hassidic youth would attempt to learn good character traits, listen to Torah, and learn new melodies. That custom of traveling to the Rebbe on festivals was thwarted that year.

The first bombs that fell on our town instilled the Jews with a terrible fear of the German murderers, even though they had no premonition of the atrocities that were to begin later. My brother Avraham, our friends from the Gerrer Shtibel, and I packed our *tallises* and *tefillin* and some underwear, and set out into the world. We did not know where we were headed. The fear of the unknown urged us on. As we were on the way to Dobrzyń during the night, we met my cousin Yitzhak Szajewicz and his wife, mother, and both children. We had to go about 35 kilometers on foot to Dobrzyń. When we arrived there, we were taken the *Beis Midrash* where the *shamash* made sure to provide food for our group.

We rested a bit and discussed what we would do further. My aunt Leah and Yitzchak Szajewicz asked what they would do with the two young children, who could not be taken on such a difficult journey. My older brother and I advised them to remain there until they would get some news about what happened with the remaining Sierpcers. My brother, my cousin Yerachmiel Michel, the remaining friends and I decided to travel to Gostinin on the other side of the Wisla. We succeeded in swimming across the river and reaching Gostinin despite the great number of German airplanes that shot at the civilians on the way

The town was already filled with refugees from the entire district. There, we received our first greeting from Sierpc. Not one of them was happy. I found out then that my cousin Yechiel Ozer Kraut was killed by a grenade and was buried in Sierpc.

In the meantime, the High Holy Days were approaching. *Rosh Hashanah* was already on the threshold. We collected money in order to purchase food. It was a cheerless holiday – a true day of judgment. We found ourselves in a veritable exile. We were sleeping on plain boards, eating at strange tables – hungry and in a strange place. And who knows what tomorrow will bring? The prophecy of my grandfather Moshe Mordechai, who constantly discussed and warned of the difficult times that were coming for the Jews, was coming true. At that time, we did not want to believe him, but today we were living in the horrible times.

Rosh Hashanah in the synagogue left a fearful impression. The weeping and wailing of those who had been driven out of them homes broke through the heavens. The rabbi delivered a sermon before the *shofar* blowing. He consoled us and encouraged us not to lose hope and faith. However, it was difficult to console the oppressed Jews. The elderly rabbi choked on his tears.

The prayers were accompanied by strong weeping. Everyone poured themselves out to their Father in Heaven and begged mercy for themselves and for their entire people. After the services, the worshippers dispersed. I went to the grandson of the Gostininer Rebbe, who wished to fulfill the commandment of hosting guests, despite the fact that he himself was a very poor man. This was my first *Rosh Hashanah* in a strange place, without my parents, and lonesome. The day of the attribute of justice was full of pressure and pain. To this day, I recall the words of the rabbi of Gostinin regarding the sharp sword and the sanctification of the Divine Name, which served as a harbinger to the upcoming destruction.

Translator's Footnotes

1. The Gerrer Rebbe was headquartered in Gora Kalwaria.

The Synagogue is Burning
by Yaakov Skurnik

My father and I lay awake in the beds in the house opposite the synagogue, in which Pineh Mekler once lived. I fell asleep due to weariness. My father suddenly woke me, "Get up – a vehicle is driving by." We both went out to the street.

I quickly got dressed and cautiously went out into the thick darkness, where we heard metal barrels rolling by. We understood. We snuck across the street, and peered through the darkness toward the eastern wall of the synagogue. We watched the Germans cover the walls with a fluid. We realized that they were preparing to set our synagogue on fire. My father ordered me to awaken the neighbors. He crossed the street to where my mother and brother were sleeping, in order to awaken them. After I came back from the neighbors, I went to Grandmother Dina. My sister Sara Dvora and her husband Eliahu Grossman were already up and about. The synagogue was already burning. Grandmother Dina's arms and legs froze from terror. I took Grandmother by her hands and led her to Szalecki, who was a Christian. Our house and Litwinski's house were already burning, and the fire was threatening the entire town. The murderers carried out their desires in a bestial fashion. The stood on the street with cameras and photographed the burning synagogue.

In the meantime, Jews from the entire town set out to the burning synagogue with pails of water. At that moment, a chain of soldiers stopped the running Jews. A young *Yeshiva* student, the painter's son, broke through the Germans and ran in the direction of the synagogue in order to rescue a Torah scroll. The *Yeshiva* student did not run for long. A bullet hit him, and he fell dead at the fence of the new *Beis Midrash*.

A wind started up. The fire was fanned, and threatened to burn the entire town. Then, the Germans shouted wildly at the gathered Jews to wet the neighboring houses with water. The murderers ran from house to house and drove all the Jews out, including women, children, and the elderly. As they did this, they stole whatever they wanted.

The Jews fought the fire until dawn. Next morning, fresh tribulations afflicted us.

God's Temple Went Up in Flames
by Yaakov ben Shlomo Juzelewski

Tongues of flame devoured what was left of the foundations. The smoke thickened and covered everything, as if to hide the great crime from the sun beginning its rise in the east. The offense was perpetrated with cunning arrogance by the scum of the earth. There was a dull sound of a collapsing building and the panicked scurrying of people carrying buckets of water to douse the fire, goaded by their oppressors. This happened at dawn on Monday, the second day of Sukkoth, in the year 5700 [1939].

But the synagogue still stood. As if with a hidden and secret pride, it remained, spreading its radiance everywhere. As if the engravings and adornments of prideful lions supporting the tabernacle were guarding it against the malicious crowd. But suddenly, it collapsed, disintegrated. It could not withstand the fury of the tongues of fire that surrounded it, that subdued it. The Torah ark of the main synagogue in Sierpc went up in flames, illuminating with its crimson blaze the dismal clouds that foreshadowed the evil to come. When the flames were extinguished, so was a pure soul. The soul of a young Jewish boy, God fearing, martyred when he rushed in to put out the flames.

It had stood in its magnificence, that large, spacious structure. Its roof was three domes, bearing the Star of David to the skies. It had broad and high stained glass windows; in front of the wide entrance there was a green lawn, proudly overlooking the valley full of foliage spread out beneath it. On three sides there were houses, bustling Jewish houses that for generations had contained serene lives full of bliss and rejoicing, longing and hope, of deep spiritual inspiration.

I can remember the feelings of otherworldliness that enveloped me as I stepped over the threshold. Full of admiration and respect and pride at the sight of the splendor and the beauty, at the great columns that supported the high, curving roof. At the sight of the exalted platform in the center of the temple and the Holy Ark situated at the eastern side.

The building may have been old, but it appeared proud. When you came in and looked away from the entrance, above was the women's gallery, handsomely arranged; pleasant seating and appropriate prayer books for the worshippers. (How many pure tears were shed there!) Downstairs, in front of you, rows of benches for the male worshippers were arranged neatly. These were wide and comfortable benches with receptacles for storing the prayer shawls and books. In the center was the platform from which the Torah was read, and sermons were delivered on matters of the day. The Torah ark was directly in sight from the entrance, at the eastern wall.

The ark was large and spacious, and on its sides were outspread wings (as if to provide shelter) with etchings that were masterpieces of art. I still recall with wonder the colorful wind and other types of musical instruments. Above that were the tablets with the Ten Commandments, and to its sides were the erect lions, with their flowing manes.

The other decorations in the building were beautiful as well, the handiwork of meticulous artisans who drew landscapes inspired by a divine spirit to apply idyllic scenes to the eastern wall. On either side of the ark were the violet curtains, leaving an impression of weighty silken drapes, hanging from above.

It had glorified the Jewish Street for generations by its appearance and its sanctity. For generations it had drawn its audiences to prayer and sermons, to unburden themselves of the longing, to listen to exhortations and tales of the renewed Zion. And now...

We stood silent and frightened in the dark of that night where an evil hand tossed a torch and set God's temple on fire. (An unknown automobile came by at the start of night. Two men jumped out of it and approached the building. They stayed in the area for a few minutes, then turned around and returned from where they came.)

Silent - because there was no possibility of putting out the fire.

Frightened - because we knew and understood that the cruel and malicious enemy had declared a war of extermination on us. And its beginning was the destruction of the chief strength of the eternal nation - its spiritual strength.

The flames died down with the light of day. The smoke still rose above the ruins. The sacrificial martyr had not yet found peace. And the wicked evildoers were not yet satiated. Mad dogs had descended on their prey to tear him and finish him.

Setting the Synagogue on Fire

by A. Majeranc

This took place on the second night of *Sukkot*, after the Germans had entered Sierpc. As I was laying in an uncomfortable sleep, full of terrifying images, I was suddenly awakened by terrifying shout, "The synagogue is burning!"

My parents and I quickly got dressed. When I looked out the rear window in the direction of the synagogue, a terrible picture unfolded before my eyes: The entire area was covered in flames that had overtaken the synagogue. The shouts of the people who were running around, not knowing what to do, reached to the heavens. The neighbors of the synagogue were removing their belongings from their houses in order to save them from the fire.

I ran out to the street together with Naszelski in order to help extinguish the fire. In the meantime, the fire worsened and spread to the neighboring wooden houses, in which Seroka's family lived. Young and old people were running with pails of water to help save the holy place by extinguishing the fire. I felt as if bullets were flying around my head. The Germans were shouting about, and I suddenly saw Farber's son, who was running with a pail of water, get hit by a bullet and fall down like a fallen tree. He was running to save a Torah scroll. His dead body lay there until the next morning. The Germans in the area shouted and searched for the people who set the synagogue on fire. However, we knew very well who had perpetrated the fire. The Germans could not fool us.

In the morning, the Polish guard confirmed our suspicions. He said that at about 2:00 a.m., Gestapo agents drove to the synagogue with a cargo truck, spread benzene on the interior and exterior, and set it on fire.

The Deportation from Sierpc

by Golda Goldman

A short time after Poland was occupied by the Nazis, the areas near the German border, Sierpc included, were declared as "holy" German territory, where no Jew may live any more. Jews were forced deeper into Poland. Such a fate also overtook the Jews of Sierpc.

It took place on November 8, 1939. We were awakened from an uncomfortable sleep, filled with terrible images, by a brutal knocking and pounding at the door by the heavy boots of soldiers. Before we realized what was happening, the door was broken down. We heard wild shouting, "*Raus, Raus, Zufurt, Juden, Raus!*[1]"

Gestapo men with the so called "*Volksdeutschen*"[2] broke into the dwelling. They drove us all out to the market. The news that all the Jews would be expelled from the city spread like lightning. From all sides, Germans were dragging men, women, and children, pallid from deathly fear. We were arranged in long lines. We were close to 4,000 people. A deep, heavy silence pervaded. We could literally hear the beating of the human hearts. Children did not cry or beg for anything. We awaited the worst.

We were arranged in rows of six, and forced to move. The wind orchestra of the local firefighters led the procession, followed by a pipe orchestra. In front of us, behind us, and at the side were the local representatives of the civic organization, such as the local authorities, the mayor and his entourage, the Gestapo and the S.S.

Thus were we led out of the city, accompanied by the wind orchestra, the pipe orchestra, the beating of drums, and the lashes of whips delivered from their clumsy hands onto our backs and heads. Photographers stood along the streets and paths, working industriously, radiant with pleasure and joy; as well as German Samaritan women (Barmherzig Sisters)[3]. We did not walk, but rather ran. We made frequent stops so that the spectacle would not end quickly. We stopped and then ran again. If anyone had luggage, he would have to abandon it if he did not want to be beaten to death for failing to maintain the pace of the run. We heard the incessant salvos of gunshots. We would hear, "Na Wiat," and the sounds of thee beatings of their guns over our bodies.

Three or four kilometers behind the city, they packed us into hermetically sealed train wagons, without food or water, and sent us off. The train moved very slowly and stopped from time to time. We were choking for lack of air, and burning up from thirst. What took place in the wagons that were traveling along for so man hours, and the manner in which people took care of their physical needs is literally beyond description. Finally, about five or six kilometers past Nowy Dwór, the wagons were opened and we were ordered to descend. It was already dark.

It was a dark, rainy, autumn evening. We could not even see each other. We were once again chased in a crowded, uncoordinated mass of several thousand individuals. There were ill and handicapped people, women in labor with their infants and children. Laden with luggage and children, everyone pushed, shoved, and stumbled over each other's feet.

Suddenly, we were given an order, "Run!" They urged us into a gallop, under a hail of whip lashes and gun shots. It was a dark night, and the way was unknown. The situation was indescribable. I recall that I thought about Dante's "Inferno" at that time, and came to the conclusion that Dante could not have a proper notion of terror if he had not endured such a nightmare. People were walking over each other, crowded and choking. Wild, frightening screams could be heard, that curdled the blood in the veins. Mothers lost their children, and children lost their mothers. We were forced up a hill. Suddenly, the hangmen asked an innocent question, 'Can you swim?" A shudder overtook us like the blade of a knife. We understood that we were standing close to some body of water, and the murderers had the intention of drowning us.

We were at the banks of the Narew River, and they were forcing us into the river. In the rush and congestion, children as well as adults fell into the river. Then, they forced us through a barbed wire fence. Terrifying, nightmarish scenes played out before us again. The number of people who died during the diabolical march will remain a secret for eternity.

We arrived in the city of Nowy Dwór. The city was enveloped in the darkness of Egypt[4]. The darkness from the houses stared at us through windowpanes covered by blinds. There, the murderers again perpetrated a bloodbath and left us behind. We found ourselves in the Jewish quarter of the city. We could not remain in the street for even a minute, due to the wartime condition. We threw ourselves at the doors and gates like madmen, and shouted with a lament: "Jews, merciful people, take us in, let us in, brothers!"

One after another, like the wave of a magic wand, the doors and gates of the impoverished Jews opened and the unfortunate, tortured masses were brought in to the dark interiors of their houses.

Very early the next morning, we were again startled, and summoned to the marketplace, from where a large number of us were sent off to Warsaw.

Translator's Footnotes

1. Out, out, get going Jews, out!

2. A term used for ethnic Germans in a different county (here, Poland).
3. Literally: Sisters of Mercy
4. A reference to the biblical plague of darkness.

The Deportation

by Yaakov ben Shlomo Juzelewski

Dedicated to:
My father, Shlomo ben Yaakov, of blessed memory
My mother, Sarah bat Rizel, of blessed memory
And my sisters, Malkah, Miriam, and Tzirel, of blessed memory

The train moved. Slowly, slowly, the station disappeared, and behind it, the streets and houses of the town to which we had been so attached disappeared as well. We sat fearfully in the railroad cars on our fateful trip into the unknown. A chapter in our lives, in our wanderings, had come to an end. We found ourselves in the middle of broad fields, in a freight train, terribly crowded. I could still hear the music of the marching songs played by the fire department band that escorted us on our way to the station - such a jolly ending! Our "friends" were accompanying us with drums and bugles on the way to the unknown tragedy. Slowly, like scenes in a movie, the events that occurred since the German boot had crossed the country's border passed before my eyes.

It's a clear Friday morning. The boastful declarations of the Polish government calling for general conscription. The increasing tension with every announcement that the front is getting closer. The barbaric bombings of the enemy airplanes. That very Friday, the enemy troops first came to the outskirts of the town. How great was the fear in our hearts. I remembered the thousands that were cruelly and inhumanly expelled from filthy Germany. And now it was our turn. The enemy came and took control, and this was what the fifth column was waiting for so that it could take revenge. Restrictions were put in place. A curfew starting in the evening and wearing a yellow patch on the front and the back. Walking on the sidewalk was prohibited, onerous taxes were levied, and the community leaders were tortured in prison. Apprehending people for menial and humiliating labor, and abuse in the town square of religious Jews who were wearing their prayer shawls on the Day of Atonement. The burning of the main synagogue, imposition of a public fine, and the despicable libels. The confiscation of Jewish businesses and the collection of all Jewish registries. All this on that bitter morning.

Hesitantly, as I did every day, I peeked at the street through the narrow crack left after the black curtain had been drawn. The effects of the curfew were still apparent. There was not a soul visible in the neighborhood. The sun had started to rise in the east, spreading its light over the universe. The bridge in front of the house was empty and unguarded, with just the sounds of burbling water beneath it breaking the stillness. I silently began to dress, and my heart was full of dread of what was to come. Slowly, the rest of the family arose.

It was still very early in the morning. My mother, of blessed memory, had left a few minutes earlier when people started moving about outside, to do her daily shopping, and my father, of blessed memory, had begun saying the morning prayers. And I (as usual in those disorderly days, with no school to go to) stood by the window and gazed outside. To see and hear what was going on.

Suddenly, everything changed. Like an earthquake that made the earth tremble, traffic began to move, followed by terrified running and wild yells. People were searching in terror for refuge from the blackshirts.

Swiftly, the street emptied, and the silence ruled again, and we all felt the doubt and the questioning inside of us. Quickly the adults found places of refuge. I was left alone at home awaiting whatever was to come. From time to time, I would go to peek outside. From time to time, uniformed thugs would pass by, carrying clubs which they waved threateningly in the direction of the houses while shouting wild yells which I could not understand. And slowly neighbors came out of their houses with their families, carrying bundles.

I remained standing in place, trying to clarify in my mind what was taking place. And suddenly, a blow from a cudgel. I felt a strong shaking, opened my eyes, and recognized him. The *volksedeutsche*, the loathsome face, the caretaker from our neighbors' courtyard. He stood there, frenzied, like a wild animal about to pounce on its prey, and shouted, "Outside, miserable Jews. This is the day we have waited for. Ten more minutes to get to the town square." He slapped my face and left.

I considered the situation. I informed the ones who were hiding, and went out to look for my mother. Pushing my way through the crowds and forcing myself through openings in fences, I got to the bakery of Kanenbrand of blessed memory. There was great commotion. A group of thugs who served the enemy raged wildly. It was hard getting inside since the door was closed, with only a small opening for the people who were leaving, and anyone who left received blows. I managed to sneak inside, but I didn't find my mother.

I pushed my way out, carried on a wave of people shoving and getting beaten. When I passed the bridge, I joined my family - without mother. We carried a few bundles and went to the square.

The town square was spacious, paved with cobblestones. It was surrounded on all sides with tall buildings. The homes of Jews who only yesterday had led peaceful lives there. Many of the Jews were already gathered there. Silent and afraid, trying to guess what was to come, the thousands stood there, and more came from every direction, egged on by blows and shouting.

The time passed slowly. The town hall clock showed nine. The project of the gathering of the wretched came to an end. The rows were arranged, and the long and awful parade in the direction of Plotzk Street began to move. You could hear sighs and wailing with every step. With every step you could hear terrible screams that were swallowed up by the sounds of the orchestra that marched in front. Indeed, our enemies had honored us with the "great privilege" of a merry accompaniment on our final way - the orchestra. The fire department band made up of our "former friends." They had not managed to play their march tunes as victors at the head of the parade of their army. Now they showed their mettle by leading the victims of our enemies - and theirs.

Guarded on every side, humiliated and beaten, we marched in a procession along the long boulevard to the railway station, accompanied by the scornful looks of our neighbors. Behind us, the streets and houses of our town are disappearing.

The route the train took was strange to us. We could not recognize the places and the direction. At first it went through familiar places, but then it changed direction. Tense, tired, and shattered, we sat quietly and stared at our surroundings. The sun declined into evening, and the train stopped. Before we could find out where we were, we were again surrounded by savage animals. These uniformed hoodlums went wild as they took us off the train and into a clearing in a thick forest.

Fear and trembling went through the encampment of deportees. From now on we were at the mercy of our guards with their rifles and machine guns in the middle of a dark forest. Here, we thought, is the end to our fateful journey.

Again we were arranged in rows, and our wanderings continued. As we left the clearing, we saw a road sign. "Punihovk," a way station in the expulsion. Yes! The same place in the region of the famous fortified triangle - Warsaw, Modlin, Kutno - of our "friends" of yesterday was now a transit stop in our fateful journey. As we got to the road, we noticed the signs to Nowy Dwór.

Night came. In the shadows, people were moving in the faint moonlight, everyone with a bundle on his back, each with his groans. From time to time, the night is disturbed by a muffled gunshot. A gunshot that marked the end of the life of a straggler in the journey.

It was nearly midnight when we reached Nowy Dwór. This town, which had not yet experienced our fate, served as our lodgings for the night. It is hard to describe the impression we made on the Jews of the town, and the warmth and help they provided for their unfortunate brethren. After a day full of unfortunate events, we had a little respite, since we were with our brothers with their warm Jewish hearts. They tried to lessen our sorrow a bit, but at the same time started to fear for their own fate.

We were invited into their houses. The children and the adults dined with their hosts. No one was left outside. The night passed in a tense silence, with everyone trying to get a little sleep. Because we all knew that our journey had not yet ended.

Daybreak again, and the autumn sun shone brightly. The refugees were made to walk along the wide road from Nowy Dwor to Jabłonna. The procession walked fifteen kilometers, children, women, old people, accompanied by their guards, until they reached Jabłonna.

The main square of the small town did not have enough room for all the people. We were still guarded by our oppressors. Suddenly, there was an announcement for the deportees: here you are free; do not dare to return to your town; anyone who does and is caught will be executed.

Silently, we stayed in place, alone and abandoned in a strange town, without means and with no security in our place of shelter. Shattered, people dispersed to look for a solution, to find shelter for themselves and their families.

Late in the evening of Thursday, the twelfth of November, 1939, the narrow-gauge railway dumped thousands of helpless people into Praga, the western borough of Warsaw. The Jewish refugees from Sierpc were the first in a series of mass deportations that our enemies carried out from the occupied territories to achieve their awful objective - the extermination of the Jews...

The Day After I Arrived

by Yoel Pas

When I arrived in Sierpc, the Germans were everywhere. My friend told me, "Don't go!! The Germans are lying in wait all over the place. It's dangerous; there is no one at your home." But I did not pay any attention and went home. When I got there, I found the house locked, with a German seal on it. I broke in.

After about an hour, the cemetery caretaker walked in. He was German and a declared Jew hater. He talked to me as if I were his slave, and asked: "Who gave you permission to enter the house?" Interesting, he asks me what right do I have to be in my own home.

He took a pistol out of his pocket. I had no choice but to draw the knife that I had hidden on me just for such an occasion. I stabbed him and he fell down, dead.

I went to some good neighbors, who lived near me. But they pleaded with me to leave their house, frightened of the Germans and their fury. I wandered the streets in fear and could not find my parents, but everywhere there were Germans. In every house, there were Germans.

Even now, I don't know how I got out of there. And I often ask myself: Is all this real? Was everyone killed and I managed to come out alive?

My parents were killed. Burnt alive in the gas chambers. My father, my mother, and my two sisters. The synagogue on our street was totally incinerated. The books. The dear Torah that gave us faith and energy for living over the millennia, all the people who were there. The murderers destroyed everything.

I crossed the border in spite of the great dangers. I came to the homeland, to Zion.

After the Expulsion

by A. Majeranc

It was already ten days since we were expelled from Sierpc, when I found myself in Warsaw. The situation was terrible. Nobody knew what the next day would bring. The wildest rumors were circulating. People were talking about murder and liquidation. The economic situation was also dreadful. Hunger and want were rampant in the ghetto. It was only through happenstance that my father managed to put somewhat of a roof over our heads. An old acquaintance with whom my father had done business prior to the war took us in.

Unable to continue to bear the need and loneliness of my parents, I asked them if I should return to Sierpc, where our sacks of money lay hidden. Perhaps that would help us somewhat. At first, they did not even want to hear about my trip. However, later, when the hunger and cold worsened in the ghetto, they had no choice but to agree to let me travel to Sierpc.

I set out from the ghetto in the morning. The route was full of danger. Gestapo men were lurking at every step. Falling into their hands would mean immediate death. Another week of torment and hiding, another week of traveling at night – and I reached Sierpc in the middle of the night. My first stop was to the person who guarded our house. He received me in a friendly manner and warned me that if any of the Germans noticed me in town, it would mean death.

I set out to our house and saw that the door had been sealed by the Gestapo. I abandoned the door and entered through a window. It looked like a pogrom had struck. I was unable, however, to remain long in thought.

Someone could enter at any moment. I quickly filled up a bag of items and left the city that same day.

My return trip to Warsaw with the sack on my shoulders lasted nine days. I went by foot the entire way because Jews were forbidden to travel by train, and it was dangerous to travel by wagon.

The items that I brought enabled our family to live for a certain time and not die from hunger. However, the items ran out. I then decided to go once again to Sierpc in order to dig up the money that we had hidden. My mother, having a premonition that the trip would not have a good ending, would not even allow us to discuss it. She did not even want to talk to me about traveling. However, the lack that was rampant in the house forced me. I did not listen to my mother, and I set out.

The way to Sierpc passed uneventfully. In Sierpc, I went to the cellar of my uncle Hersh Michel's house, where the money had been buried; however I was unable to find the money. Tired and edgy from my unsuccessful work, I exited the cellar.

A Polish acquaintance ran into me on the street.

He had become a *Volksdeutsche* when the Germans entered. He grabbed his revolver and shouted, “Halt, from where you came, accursed Jew?” I tried to escape, but to my misfortune, a Gestapo agent was passing by at that that moment, and they both arrested me.

A friend of mine was also among the prisoners whom they captured. When they brought us to the depot, we heard a shout: “Damn it! From where did these accursed Jews come?” Not understanding what they were saying, and seeing the disarray, I again attempted to escape from their hands. However, they began to beat me so fiercely that my head turned into a bloody mess within a few moments. I fainted. They revived me with a pail of water and continued to beat me.

They took Ch. Mintz and me to work. We both had to clear out the Jewish businesses. However, the work was not so straightforward. Every 15-20 minutes, they stood us against the wall and loaded their guns to shoot. They actually shot a few times. We then had to load the wagons with merchandise and hitch the horses to drive the wagons to the S. S. warehouses, from where the merchandise was shipped to Germany.

We found a *tallis* and *tefillin* in one of the warehouses. The S. S. men were so happy with the find, and they commanded me to put them on. I went through the streets of Sierpc dressed in the *tallis* and *tefillin*, shouting “*Shema Yisrael*!” I also had to dance and perform gymnastics during that procession.

In the evening, I thankfully found an opportunity to escape, and I arrived in Warsaw after another perilous journey. A short time later, I escaped to Russia and enlisted in the Red Army.

The Sick Mother

by Asher Mlawa

Our house was located in the marketplace, which was the collection point for Jews who were sentenced to be deported. Jews were gathered together from the entire city, from all streets and alleyways.

What would we do? We had a sick mother, who had already being lying in bed for ten years. How could we leave her alone?

My wife had advice. We decided that the men would go out to the street, and my wife and child would prepare in the meantime. When the bandits would enter, my wife would attempt to state that she could not leave the sick woman alone.

Immediately, two S.S. officers burst in with whips and weapons in their hands. They beat everyone in the house

and drove everyone out. When my wife attempted to state that my mother was sick and helpless and could not be left alone, they responded with their whips over her head and drove her out into the street along with our child. My sick mother begged the murderers, "Please shoot me, I beg of you." In the meantime, the Germans took the key, locked the dwelling, and posted a placard, "This house is requisitioned – here there is a live Jewish woman with a live goose." (Indeed, at that time, we were raising a goose.)

Her daughter Dvora, who was living in Drobnin at that time, came a few days later and took Mother, still alive, to her. A short time later, our mother Sheina Mlawa, died in Drobnin.

My Town Sierpc

by B. Fejnberg

In the beauty of clusters of gray clouds
When green gardens writhe from cold,
What will the next day bring?
The fine autumn pervades the world.
With tremendous suffering, blood flowing everywhere,
With ghettos, prisons, very many hangings,
With torture, Jewish pogroms
Perpetrated by the Nazi regime.

My town Sierpc
Enduring the torment

You suffer in pain
I feel like weeping.
Oh, town of Sierpc,
I recall your splendor
Your springtime beauty
And gentle nights…

The synagogue lit up the night with red flames
The Nazis rampaged with savage hate
Piniele went out to extinguish it[1] –
A gunshot pierced the silence.
When I will go on broad, long paths
I will perpetuate the terrible image:
The synagogue burning, a corpse lying.
The youth, Pinia, calm and gentle.

Refrain: My town Sierpc…

Never in my life will I forget you
You are enmeshed in my struggles, my heart, my dreams…
On your green bosom, the Germans
Bloodily murdered 5,000 Jews
With guns, knives, and their whips
The night ruled in your streets.
After seven years of pining and wandering
I have come to see my city, my street, my house
Over Pinie's grave and other graves
I placed a white rose.
Refrain: My town Sierpc…

Never in my life will I forget you
You are enmeshed in my struggles, my heart, my dreams.

Translator's Footnote

1. Piniele, a diminutive of Pinchas, may be Farber's son mentioned on page 430.

Old Man and Child on the Route of Torment

by Yaakov Skornik

The train stopped. The murderers opened the doors, and again there were wild shouts, "Get out." The exiting of the trains was accompanied by lashes of the whips. A blow fell upon the year-and-a-half old child of my sister, whom I nestled under my overcoat, and bloodied the child's face. There was no possibility of stopping.

We were four kilometers from Nowy Dwór. They were prodding us on by foot. Old and sick people had no more strength to continue. The murderers beat, pushed, and threatened with guns anyone who could not keep up with the "march."

Reb Avraham Shochet, 78 years old, with his splendid face and long, white beard, his face pallid from terror and weariness, was prodded along together with us. Having exhausted his energy, he stood still and did not continue further. My father and brother took him from behind and helped him, so that he would not remain behind, Heaven forbid. We all knew what that would have meant. In this manner did we arrive in Nowy Dwór late in the evening, afflicted and tormented.

Experiences of a Thirteen Year Old Boy

From a letter from Elia Grynberg from Antwerp to his grandchild Leo Grobert.

In 1939, the Germans expelled us from Sierpc. They chased us and made us weary, as they prodded us by foot all the way to Warsaw. We arrived in Warsaw weary and exhausted, without even one groszy of money.

A few days before the expulsion from Sierpc, I had earned 200 zloty, which my parents did not know about. At that time, the Germans issued an edict that all Jews must give over their money and valuables. I did not give over mine.

I plastered into a wall in the kitchen of our house a bit of money, as well as the golden watch that I once sent you, dear grandchild, as a gift. Seeing the hunger and thirst in the Warsaw Ghetto, I thought about going to my mother and telling her that I intended to return to Sierpc to fetch the bit of money and other belongings. When my mother heard about my plans, she wept and begged me not to go, for the Germans would capture me, which would spell my certain end. However, I decided to carry out my plan and return to Sierpc.

My mother could not be calmed down, and decided to accompany me. Very early the next morning, we set out for the railway station, from where we travelled to Plonsk. The train stopped along the way. Gestapo men came aboard and searched for Jews among the passengers. However, to our fortune, they did not notice us.

At that time, Itka Izraelweicz, my mother's younger sister and her family, were still in Plonsk. When we arrived at her home, she was very surprised to see us and wondered how we could have done such a thing - for we risked our lives. My mother begged me once again with tears in her weak eyes to not go on further, but rather to wait until we heard something from Sierpc.

In the meantime, night fell. It was dark on the street, and one was afraid to be seen outside, since the Germans captured Jews and deported them. I conducted an internal battle: should we travel or not? After a lengthy debate, we decided to travel to Sierpc. We concealed ourselves in various side alleyways until we arrived at the train station from which we set out.

We arrived in Sierpc at about 1:00 a.m. It was dark and empty, and a deathly silence prevailed. We hid ourselves as far off as possible and proceeded into the city slowly. Our hearts beat quickly from fear - slowly, slowly, for who knows what they could do with us. Thus did we arrive at our house in the Jewish street near the old *Beis Midrash.* We noticed a large placard on the door with a warning that anyone who would enter the house would be immediately killed. Mother talked to me again with a stressed voice and begged me not to enter. However, come what might, I ripped off the placard and entered the house.

Tired and weary from the journey and from fear, my mother fell onto the divan and fell asleep. I proceeded on, quickly covered the window and lit a candle. With a hammer, I broke the wall in which the objects were plastered. Each bang let out a loud echo into the silent night, and I was terrified that someone might hear. I proceeded on, and controlled my fear. I finished my terrifying mission. I quickly woke up Mother and we ran through the crooked, dark alleyways to the train station. We straight away caught the train and returned to Plonsk. The train stopped along the way, and the Gestapo men searched and screened everyone to see if they could capture a Jew. We sat among the Poles and looked out the windows to avoid any suspicion. By luck, we were saved from the talons of death, and we returned to the house of my aunt Itka.

A difficult question arose once again: how to go back to Warsaw. It was impossible to travel through Nowy Dwór, for the surveillance there was extraordinarily severe. That was currently the border between the Third Reich and Poland. I looked for ways to travel through there. I advised my mother to travel to Nowy Dwór. I took all the belongings along with her, and set out to Nasielsk. In Nasielsk, I found in the dark, far beyond the city, an abandoned cottage in which a light was shining. I went in and found out that people were going to be traveling to Nowy Dwór by boat at night via the Narew. I paid them, and at 5:00 a.m. we already found ourselves on the other side of the Narew, from where we dragged ourselves into the city.

We again met up with my family in Nowy Dwór. We were together: Mother, Father, a sister, and also many other Sierpcers were there, waiting to travel to the Warsaw Ghetto. At the same time, they were again perpetrating an attack on the Jews of Nowy Dwór. Again, as usual, we were suffering murderous blows, and they were searching us for money. Miraculously, I managed to save a large part of our means of livelihood.

Then, the Jews received a command to leave Nowy Dwór and run for three hours. We decided to divide ourselves up. In the event that something happened in one place, perhaps the others would be safe in another place.

My father and my sister Chana traveled back to Warsaw, while my mother and I went to Father's parents in Sochocin. It was still calm there. The Angel of Death had not yet arrived at that town.

Unfortunately, this did not last long. The terrible news reached us that they shot to death my beloved father and dear sister.

From Nowy Dwór to Auschwitz

by Meir Teitelbaum

On December 12, 1942, the Germans from Nowy Dwór sent a transport of Jews to Auschwitz, among which were Jews from Sierpc.

The deportation took place while we were still at work.

"*Laus, Schneller, Laus*,"[1] shouted the German overseer, and we worked quickly. With superhuman strength, tired, and downtrodden, and with broken hearts, we loaded the barbed wire onto the wagons.

When our torturers led us home from work, they issued an order, "Sing." Thus, arriving with song, we saw that the ghetto had been surrounded with German soldiers. This did not foreshadow anything good. Helpless and downtrodden, we protested against this with sighs and groans.

The ghetto was guarded by soldiers... Indeed, they were deporting us... It was winter... Oh, oh. With my young children... my wife is pregnant... My mother is ill... Oh, oh!... Woe unto us!

In the ghetto, confusion pervaded. Weeping women and children were getting dressed to leave. The men were calm, but they were also desperate. With tears of desperation, Mother blessed the candles on that Friday night. The services did not last long that day, and we went home devoid of courage, as if ashamed before G-d. Thick, dark clouds spread over the heavens.

It was a sleepless night... The hours were endlessly long... The minutes were full of fear and terror. We did not sleep, but rather listened and waited to see upon whom would fall the fate of being a victim of the German extermination.

It was the Sabbath morning. It was gloomy on the streets. There was noise, and it was seething like a kettle. The alleyways were guarded by Germans. The clang of the soldiers' boots and the gunshots mixed with the voices of those being expelled. The orders of the murderers were reaching us, "*Laus, laus*, everyone out of the houses!"

Holding hands tightly, we left the crowded ghetto house with a lament, and looked behind us like dogs driven from their doghouse. We were prodded toward the ghetto market, placed in rows of five, and led toward the train under a heavy guard, with beatings and torture.

We were loaded into the wagons like cattle, with up to sixty people in each wagon, healthy and sick people together. With sealed doors, without water, air and the possibility to attend to one's bodily needs, we were taken to a place unknown to us. There was not even any talk of water. We got a very small amount of air through a narrow window. After a few hours, there was also a lack of air.

We found ourselves in a terrible situation. The groaning and lamenting of the ill people and the children mixed in like a nightmare with thoughts of the German murders in the eastern regions about which we had heard but had not been able to believe until this point. Only a few of us, who were strong in faith, consoled and strengthened the rest of us.

The farther we went, the more serious our situation became. Parents wished for death, being unable to witness the pain of their children. The hours passed like years.

On the morning of Monday, December 14, as we were laying semi-comatose in the wagons, immersed in dark dreams, we were suddenly awakened by the sounds of gunshots. The doors opened with a noise, and a stream of cold winter air penetrated the wagons.

At first, we were intoxicated by the air, and we did not understand what was taking place. The murderers did not let us dream for long. They awakened us with the butts of their rifles and kicked us off the wagons with their feet. When we had arranged ourselves somewhat, we heard a command, "Leave the packs, and arrange yourselves - men separately, and women and children separately." We did not hear anything further. The wailing was so loud that no human mind could imagine, and no human hand could describe it in writing. Everyone understood that they were with their dear ones for the last time.

My mother wept. She wept her eyes out until the last tear, and blessed us all, "Remain healthy, my children." She lamented bitterly, "I am together with you today perhaps for the last time. With you, for whom I have sacrificed myself for my entire life and for whom I am prepared to sacrifice myself today."

We kissed, hugged, and parted without words. Beatings from the butts of rifles forced us apart.

A *selektion* of the men took place. S. S. officers looked over each person, asked how old they were and whether they were healthy. My brother told me to say that I was 18 years old. I saw that those younger than 18 and old men whom they did not approve of were sent back to the women and children.

When they came to us, they asked me how old I was. "Eighteen years," I responded. They looked me over and sent me to the selected men. My brother was also quickly sent over. When they asked my father how old he was, he answered, "Forty-nine years old." They looked him over and sent him to the women and children. I looked at him with my eyes, not knowing who was better off - we the selected ones, or they, the doomed ones.

When the selection ended, we were led away under a group of S.S. men with dogs. As we, a few hundred men, went away from the train, we saw barracks surrounded by electrified barbed wire, upon which placards were posted, "High voltage - danger of death." Among the barracks, we saw emaciated, weak men dressed in camp uniforms.

In the camp, they greeted us with music from several dozen instruments. The camp inmates begged us to throw them a bit of bread. Many of them, who bent down for a morsel of bread, fell down and could not get up. They led us, terrorized and beaten, to a barrack. We had to give over all of our valuables such as money, gold and the like. Then, they registered all of us and tattooed numbers on our arms. This lasted for half the night. Then they led us to a bath, where they took our clothes, cut the hair from our head and our bodies, and gave us camp uniforms. As we left the so-called bath, we could no longer recognize each other, to the point where I could not even recognize my brother as I was standing next to him.

We stood under a cold rain for the entire night. They placed us, soaked, tired, thirsty, and hungry, in the allotted barracks.

The entire time, we were preoccupied with the thought: in which camp are our parents. Various terrible thoughts ran through our heads, which we could not believe at all. Later, we met some acquaintances who had already been in the camp for a week. We had a conversation with them about the fate of our parents. At first, they answered with half words, but after a long conversation and many requests, they led us to understand that our parents were no longer alive, that they were already gassed and burnt. A general weeping broke out amongst us. In our hearts, we recited *Kaddish* for their souls. Pouring out our bitter hearts, we prepared ourselves for the same end as our dear relatives had suffered.

Translator's Footnote

1. Parasites, quickly, parasites!

In the Sierpc Ghetto and in the Camps

by Hela Listapad-Izakowicz

Sierpc was occupied by the German soldiers on September 8, 1939. They beat the Jews in a bestial matter and robbed their goods. On the second night of *Sukkot* they burnt our sanctuary - the Great Synagogue. This depressed my father. He was lying in bed, sick and with broken morale. However, he strengthened himself, got out of bed, and ran with a pail of water to help put out the fire in our fine sanctuary. The goodwill of the Jews to save the synagogue from the flames surrounding it was fruitless. A certain yeshiva student, the son of Farber, who forced his way into the synagogue with self-sacrifice, was shot by the Germans.

After the terrible fire, my father's state of health took a strong turn for the worse, and he died in his own home after great suffering on October 15, 1939, prior to the expulsion from Sierpc. He was buried in the Sierpc cemetery, accompanied by his children, sons-in-law, grandchildren, relatives, neighbors and acquaintances. The Jews were jealous of my father, who had still merited to be brought appropriately to a Jewish burial.

On Wednesday, November 8, 1939, the Germans gathered the Jewish population in the old marketplace opposite the city hall. Under the chords of a wind orchestra and being mocked by those deporting them, they were loaded onto cargo wagons and sent to Warsaw.

In Sierpc, the murderers only left behind the craftsmen they needed. They were housed in a special place in the city and a ghetto was created.

The Jews of Sierpc, who lived in Warsaw after the deportation without a home and without livelihood, realized that there were still Jews remaining in Sierpc. They sneaked across the borders and returned to their hometown. My family and I did the same.

The German mayor appointed a Judenrat consisting of the following people: Yaakov Pukacz, Mendel Lis and Shlomo Kutner. These three people were given the responsibility for the remaining Jews in the ghetto in accordance with German instruction. There were no Jewish policemen in the Sierpc ghetto. Every day, the Judenrat had to give people over for various jobs, such as sweeping the streets, collecting the trash and other menial, dirty tasks.

On the way to the train, there was a rivulet which was known to us Sierpcers as "Jeziorki." We would skate on the rivulet in the winter when it was frozen over. The celebrations of the sea holiday would take place there in the winter. The rivulet was neglected and full of dirt. The Germans decided to drain the rivulet, and employed some of the remaining Jews of Sierpc for that task, including my brother-in-law Yosef Karpa and his son, and my second brother-in-law Moshe Moszkowicz and his three sons. They all stood half naked in the mud and cleared the river.

Risking my life, I often sneaked from Sierpc to Warsaw, to my cousin Binyamin and his wife Sara Sobel, who at one time had been wealthy people and were known for their kindheartedness. I provided them with bread, meat, various baked goods and other necessities. During my smuggling trips, I was searched by Germans, but they did not recognize that I was Jewish on account of my blond hair, and I fortunately came out clean from the search each time. Each time my cousin saw me, she wept bitterly and lamented, "What are we living on?" I often brought my nephew Yosef Moszkowicz on my risky trips.

After a certain time, it became forbidden to travel to Warsaw. Even Poles were not allowed to travel. At that time, I decided to send my cousin money in a letter, without knowing the name of the place to send it. The prices in Warsaw were so high that the money was insufficient for the necessary expenses. In the interim, I received a letter from my cousin stating that her husband Binyamin had died from a disease of the nerves. With that news, the true tragedy in everyone's life began.

The Expulsion from Sierpc

At 5:00 a.m. on January 6, 1942, when the stars were still sparkling in the sky and the frost burnt the face, the Germans woke up the Jews of the ghetto. The confusion was great. Everyone took along what they could. All the property was carried to the "Ludowy" (People's House) in the New Market, where Nazi police took it. Everyone, men and women, was arranged separately, stripped naked, and searched in a bestial manner. They were searching for money, gold jewelry, foreign currency, etc. Every person was permitted to carry up to 20 German marks. Any person with whom was found valuables or currency was murderously tortured and beaten.

After the search that lasted for several hours, 50 people were loaded on the cargo truck, under Gestapo guard. Together with Jews from the Sierpc region, they were sent to Strzegowo in the Mlawa region. We arrived there in the evening, tired, hungry and half frozen. Many people who were left behind along the way were shot on the spot. I recall that Rivka Lipski and Noach Pukacz were among those shot.

A Judenrat was functioning in Strzegowo, consisting of B. Bojgen, Sh. Stawicki, and Rybak. They received us very well, and made every effort to provide us with housing, food and drink. When we were there, we received a very bad letter from my Sobol cousin, who was in Warsaw. She wanted to come to us. I discussed this with Mrs. Nijemczewko and decided to travel to Warsaw to bring our relatives and Mrs. Nijemczewko's relatives, who were in Warsaw, to us.

The border guard in Ciechanów arrested us, and took our money and food that we had with us. After 24 hours of arrest, they took us out to shoot us. We fell at the feet of the police, begged them and wept until their hearts softened and they permitted us to return home. After a long journey on foot, we arrived in Strzegowo tired, hungry and half frozen, and lay sick in bed for a few days.

A short time later, they captured Jews and sent them to Masajewo. There was a hard labor camp and an ammunition factory there. During such a hunt in the month of March they captured 20 men, including 3 Sierpcers: Efraim Yosef Lelionek, Yechezkel Pessa, Tovia Zeelni from Bieżuń, as well as others. The arrested people were placed in cellars. One of them, Moshe Gutsztat, escaped. They captured him and shot him on the spot.

After we sat in the cellars for six weeks, policemen came from the surrounding region and ordered the Jewish population to prepare gallows so that they could perpetrate the atrocity of hanging the Jews. All the Jews - old, sick, women following childbirth - were hauled out of their houses to witness the act of German bestiality. The Germans ordered that a father should hang his son, or on the other hand, a brother would hang a brother.

The Liquidation of the Camp and My Life Among the Farmers

On September 1 1942, the Germans began to liquidate the ghettos, as well as the Jews in the camps. From our camp, they sent off the elderly and the sick to the gas chambers. My mother was among them. I realized that the end of everybody was approaching and I decided to escape and return to Sierpc. I left the ghetto together with the Alterowicz sisters from the village of Jeżewo in the Sierpc district. We were successful, and we fortunately reached the suburbs of our former Sierpc. I was taken in by Mrs. Celina Kokowski, a very poor woman. Her husband was in captivity. I remained there for 16 months.

Of course I would have liked to remain with that honorable woman, but the village population knew that she was hiding a Jewish woman. Since everyone would suffer on account of this, I decided to leave there and seek a new home.

I left without the agreement of Mrs. Celina Kokowski. She would have never permitted me to leave her house. We lived together very well. That very evening when I left her home, the police came to search for me at Mrs. Kokowski's home. The Germans beat the woman soundly and demanded that she give me over. The woman claimed that she did not know me. The Germans noticed a piece of fresh pork, which they immediately demanded, and then they arrested the woman.

The information about the arrest on my account spread like lightning among the farmers. Therefore it was difficult for me to find a shelter. I wandered for many days. I could not spend the day at the places where I spent the night. I often spent the night in the field, in cement pipes and in other places where I could hide.

In the winter months of 1944, the police often conducted raids and searched for Jews who were hiding. An announcement was issued stating that every citizen who knew of a Jew would receive a prize of more than 500 Marks and other benefits, such as being permitted to slaughter animals, which at that time was forbidden. There were many volunteers for such rewards, and it was impossible to hide. During the night, I often had to sneak from one place to another where they did not know me.

I felt that my energy was leaving me, and therefore I became weary of life. My hope was that I would die a quick death and would not fall into the hands of the German murderers. I had no stable place to live. The farmers were afraid to take in a strange person.

During the ensuing months, I saw partisans, among whom there were also Jews. Then, my situation improved. I was able to work in a place for a long time. Thus did the situation maintain itself until January 20, 1945.

The war had ended. I returned to my hometown of Sierpc. A shudder went through me as I saw the ruins left behind by the German murderers. The town was empty of Jews. I could no longer meet with my relatives, neighbors and acquaintances.

My former Christian neighbor Mrs. Pataszinsko took me in and comforted me. However, I did not want to be dependent on anyone, and, wearing my wooden shoes and linen dress, I went out to look for acquaintances.

I met up with the sisters Celia Izakowicz and Eva Dygola, who had been hidden by Christians and survived by a miracle. The three of us began to do business to earn a livelihood. After a short time, we rented a dwelling in partnership and lived together, out of fear of being separate, for there were terrible attacks against the Jews by wild Polish anti-Semitic gangs.

One day, the mailman came to me, the same one from before the war, and brought me the news that a letter from America was awaiting me. I went with him to the post office, and to my great surprise, I saw a letter from my cousin Rashe Mintz from America. Tears of joy poured from my eyes.

Additional Declarations from Mrs. Listapad-Izakowicz

There were three Sierpc natives among the 20 hanged Jews in the Strzegowo Ghetto. I was a witness to the terrible murders and I remember well how they were carried out. Lipski and Levi Grossman were not hanged. Lipski was deported from the Strzegowo Ghetto to Auschwitz along with all the old people.

When they were snatching people in the Strzegowo Ghetto to send them away, Levi Grossman and Moshe Gutsztat escaped together. They hid in the wheat fields. *Shkotzim*[1] began to shout "Jude" and show the Germans where the two Jews were. Two Germans who were conducting searches took the Jews and quickly shot them.

The following people were shot as they were deported from the Sierpc Ghetto: Noahke Pukacz, the Yellow Fleiszer's wife and 11-year-old son, and the son of Mulia Czarny. The child was ill. The father carried him on his shoulders. The Germans shot him in that position.

The Sierpc Ghetto was created in March or April 1940. Only those who were going out to work could leave the ghetto. Many people sneaked out. This primarily took place at noontime when the Germans were eating. Movement in the ghetto was permitted until 10:00 p.m.

Qualified tradesmen worked at their trades in the ghetto. Other ghetto residents were employed at sweeping the streets, cleaning the latrines and working in the fields for the *Volksdeutschen* (native Germans) in the vicinity who had become officers, policemen and merchants in the Jewish enterprises. For a day's work, the *Volksdeutschen* paid 80 pfennig, which was insufficient to live on. Requisitions for workers came to Yaakov Pukacz, and he sent them to work. He also received the money from the city hall and paid the workers.

Worshipping with a *minyan* [prayer quorum] was forbidden. Avraham Shochet's[2] son Shimon Petriks performed *shechita* [ritual slaughter] secretly. His mother and sister lived in Drobnyn. With the help of Yaakov Pukacz, from time to time the *shochet* received permission to travel to Drobnyn, where he also performed *shechita* in secret.

Translator's Footnotes

1. A derogative term for gentiles.
2. Here it means Avraham the ritual slaughterer.

Sierpcer Jews in the Warsaw Ghetto

by Yechiel Nemlech of New York

It was after the deportation from Sierpc. We had already been in Warsaw for over a year. Hunger was rampant in the streets of the ghetto and caused the deaths of thousands of Jews. The Germans took the younger people to labor camps. In our region around Sierpc and Plonsk, the situation was better. The hunger was not quite as severe.

In our home, we were still able to purchase necessities for survival. The question arose - what next? We decided to risk our lives and sneak out of the ghetto, where death from hunger was threatening. Someone would remain behind. I would go with my sister and my mother, and in the event that we did not succeed along the way, we would have a place to which to return and where to lay down our heads.

Therefore, my brother Shmuel and my father remained in the Warsaw Ghetto. They agreed to remain since my brother worked for a Jew who commissioned apprentices for sheet metal work for the Germans. Therefore, it was certain that he would not be taken to the camp, and would have a morsel of bread. My father felt too weak to go on the journey.

We set out - my only sister Adela who was older than me, my mother, and I. With great tribulation and terror, we broke out of the Warsaw Ghetto and smuggled our way to Plonsk. There were still Jews there, and we were together with acquaintances.

There was also a ghetto in Plonsk, but the situation was far better than in Warsaw. They were still not hungry, for it was easier to smuggle in food. That part of Poland was also designated as part of the Third Reich. They treated us well, but not for long.

At that time, it was perilous to host a person who was not registered by the city council, and registering was impossible. We succeeded in obtaining work with a farmer in a village in exchange for a bit of food. We indeed did so. By chance, we succeeded in obtaining positions not far from each other. This was the beginning of the summer, and we tended to grazing animals in return for a bit of food. We were content with the work. We hoped to bring the rest of the family to us soon, so we could all be together.

Sunday was a day off for us, when the employers did not force us to work, so I went to visit my beloved sister and dear mother. Jews sneaked into the Plonsk Ghetto in great numbers. Whoever had the energy would risk his life and escape from the Warsaw Ghetto. This was noticed by the German authorities of Plonsk, and they conducted a search for Jews in the entire district of Plonsk. Whoever could not show the appropriate papers was sent away.

After some time, a Sierpcer told me that they had sent these people off to a camp in Pomiechówek. My beloved mother and sister were also among those sent away.

I was 18 years old at that time. I felt lonesome and alone. As I was following the cattle in the broad fields and meadows on summer days, I would usually think about everything that transpired. I was taken by a desire to somehow memorialize the deportation of Sierpc and the subsequent suffering of the deportees. I wrote in verse everything that took place with us[1].

On a fine bright early morning
When nobody had yet
Begun to think
About the fresh statutes,
Suddenly - to us
Who were sitting by the door and the window;
Like thieves in the forest
They ordered us to leave our homes immediately

Naked, barefoot, without clothing, we had to go
Along the path of hunger and pain
Trusted fathers and mothers
Where should we go?
They ordered us to go to the marketplace.
All Jews had to gather there.
They issued further commands to us,
And prodded us to the train with music.
We had to go into the trains
As if we were going into stables.
They beat us and plagued us with sticks -
And we went to Nowy Dwór.
In Nowy Dwór, they shouted at us again:
"Jews, arrange yourselves in rows!"
As a sign that we must go.
They began to shoot at us
A lament, a plea from Jews to Jews:
"Jews, let us in,
We are deathly tired,
From a journey of an entire day
Open the doors and gates
And then we will tell you
About our suffering and pain.
And after spending only one night,
They issued a new order:
In the early morning, there was a cry and a lament,
The Nowy Dwór police
Had taken over the government
And we moved again toward suffering,
For they sent us to Warsaw,
In Warsaw, in the large synagogue –
And in every synagogue, there was new death,
A new victim every minute,
That is how they behaved toward us.
Jews of Sierpc, do not be discouraged
For you will not be bloodied forever.
A new time will come,

When we will all be free!
A time will come,
When we all together
Will be joyous and glad
In our own homes!

My dream did not come true... European Jewry was destroyed... Including the community of Sierpc and my own dear family.

I went through the hell of Auschwitz and Dachau, and survived miraculously. After spending a few years in liberated Germany, I, along with a few other fellow natives, succeeded in coming to America with the help of our important and beloved fellow native and friend Sineh, where we began a new life.

Translator's Footnote

1. There is a footnote: We bring these verses as a memorial to the survival of the author (editor).

Life in the Ghetto and the Activity of the Partisans

by Hela Listapad-Izakowicz

The Sierpc Ghetto consisted of Kilinskiego Street, or as it was called earlier, the Wlokes or the Gurno.

We were not hungry in the ghetto. Everyone had their own farmers they knew in the villages. People sneaked out of the ghetto and arranged for food. Everyone had to go to work: men, women, and young girls. Children between the ages of ten and twelve wandered in the streets, assembled cigarettes and did various similar jobs.

During the evening, it was forbidden to venture beyond the borders of the ghetto. Police guarded us. There were more than 500 of us in the ghetto, of whom 200 had a permit to cross into the Aryan side. These were the tradesmen, tailors, shoemakers, and others who worked at their trades. Those who did not have a trade had to engage in menial work such clearing garbage, cleaning the streets, etc.

Eighteen-year-old Yisca Zemelman, the daughter of Rachel and Hirsch Zemelman, caught a cold during the course of her work and died within a few days.

The ghetto was not closed, but rather guarded. We found hiding places with Poles.

At the beginning of the German occupation, we had to wear a yellow patch on the right side with the word "Jude." Later, these were replaced with larger yellow patches with a black, 12 centimeter, Magen David. Every Jew had to wear such patches - one in the front and one in the back. Whoever was caught without the Jewish designation was warned or sent to concentration camps.

We lived under very crowded circumstances in the ghetto. The dwellings were small. Many people would be housed in a large dwelling.

The old *Beis Midrash* was turned into a concentration camp. Poles caught conducting illegal business were also imprisoned there.

We were taken to Strzegowo in January 1942. The Jews of Plock had been sent there earlier than we were. They were led through Sierpc. They begged us for bread. Meir Zemelman, collecting garbage that day, went into a bakery in order to obtain bread for the Plock Jews. The Gestapo men captured him, led him to Dzialdowo, and murdered him there.

In general, the Poles did not behave badly toward the Jews. The more intellectual Poles were also persecuted by the Germans - of course, not to the same degree as the Jews. However, they were expelled from their fine houses.

The two Kiszelewski brothers, grandchildren of the elder Kiszelewskis, belonged to the partisans. One of them was called Zelik, and the name of the other I do not recall. They survived the occupation, but unfortunately, after the liberation, they were murdered by the "A. K." (Armie Krajowo). Heniek Pszenica as well as the young Brorocz youth from Janczowo also met the same death.

Many people hid in the Plock forests or in the so-called "Tzelinsker Velder." The situation of the Jews improved when the partisan groups were organized. If the partisans found out that someone had turned in a Jew, that person would be killed the next morning on his own bed. The farmers were afraid, and began to help the hidden Jews.

In the city, the Germans took the houses of the Jews: Koplowicz from the old market, Tzina Lewin, Gotlibowski, Czarnoczapka from the Fareh Street in which there was a charitable fund, Pianke's house, as well as the houses of: Noach Pukacz from Ząbie, Katszalki, Mintz, the tailor's, Jedwabnik, and Grodka. On Warsaw Street, the hut where the Rosenbergs lived, Mianczin's where Leib Krysztal lived, Pundek', Nachum Tatz, Joszelewski', and Zemelman's. On the Jewish Street, aside from Glazman's and the old *Beis Midrash*, all the houses were together. There were the houses of Chodower, Grona, Karmilski, Wluka, Rozenek, and Sakowicz in which Shia "Koze" lived. Further, there were the houses of Reszatka, Lelonek, Czarnabrades, and Gonsior whose house housed the Jewish *mikva* [ritual bath], and Szampan's house in which Kasiarz lived. Szwaczer's large house remained standing. There were also the houses of Myranc, Kramarsz, Skurki, old Szapira the watchmaker, Lea Panfil, Kutner, Blum, as well as many other Jewish houses that were also taken.

German Murders in the Strzegowo Camp

There were no Jewish police in the Sierpc Ghetto. On the other hand, in the Strzegowo Camp, there were Jewish police under the supervision of the Judenrat, consisting of the following people: Yossel Nijemczewko, the Kiselewski brothers, Feldman the butcher from Rudzienice, and Lederman.

Feldman was shot in Strzegowo. The Germans noticed that he paid too much attention to a loaf of bread that his wife held in her hands. During the role call, Feldman was ordered to prepare the Jews to travel. The Gestapo men grabbed the bread and pierced it with a spear. Foreign currency and gold fell from it.

It seemed that Feldman had obtained the holdings as ransom from various people who were to be sent to concentration camps. In their place, he sent others who did not have the means to pay. That is how the business went until the Germans shot him before everyone's eyes.

In Strzegowo, the Germans paid 80 pfennig a day for work. It was impossible to live from this money. The Jews found ways to manage. Whoever was a tradesman would quietly work in his home, even for Christians. Others would sneak to the villages and bring back from there whatever was possible. I belonged to the latter group. There were many Poles among the village dwellers who sent us potatoes and bread. There were also some Germans who helped. However, most of them would rob from us what they could, and beat us murderously.

The Germans especially tortured elderly women who were unable to take on any work. The last elderly women sneaked out of the ghetto, which was not closed off, and helped the farmers work the ground. They hid in the villages.

There were only Sierpcers in the ghetto, aside from one family - Avraham Derewiczer and his wife from Żuromin. Everybody thought about how to survive. Many went out to the town at night, and returned to their work in the early morning. Nobody thought about clothing.

Once Mrs. Nedzwijedz (nee Podskocz), wrote a letter in German to the Starosta [district head] on behalf of a Christian, requesting that the Christian's son be freed from the concentration camp. The Germans summoned the Christian and asked her who wrote the fine letter for her. She gave over the address, and the Gestapo dragged Mrs. Nedzwijedz out of bed at night and sent her to a penal camp in Wymyślin, where the German commandant chopped her up with a sword. The unfortunate victim begged the murderer to kill her with one blow, but this was to no avail. He quartered her body in a wild, bestial manner until she died. The bloodied body was placed on a wagon and driven to the Jewish cemetery. Four Sierpc Jews were summoned to the funeral, including my brother-in-law Moshe Moszkowicz. Throughout the entire journey, the boards of the wagon trickled with the blood of the deceased victim.

Moshe Lidzbarski's 16-year-old daughter met a similar death.

In the Camps

by Y. Ch. Grinberg

Stalag[1], Auschwitz, and Mauthausen

In 1914, the German authorities set up a Stalag Camp near Konigsberg for the Jewish war captives. All the Jewish war captives from the Polish army were concentrated in that camp. My friend Yechiel Borensztajn and I were also brought there.

After a short time, an order was issued to take all of the Jewish war captives to Lublin. Already then, we became familiar with the concept of a death march, for that is what the Germans perpetrated in Lublin. They demanded 300,000 zloty from the Judenrat in order to call off the *aktion*. As soon as they received the money, they broke their word and the *aktion* was perpetrated. A transport was prepared and

dispatched. It went in an unknown direction. Later, we found out that they murdered everyone.

With the belief that we would not avoid death when we would come to Lublin, my friend Bornsztajn and I decided to escape from the transport. When we arrived at the Gdanska Station in Warsaw, we both jumped out and started to run. The German guards noticed us and began to shoot after us with automatic weapons. We succeeded in hiding among the bunkers. We remained there for a few hours, until the train departed.

We came out of our hiding place and set out for the city. After a short time in Warsaw, I set out for Plonsk, where my family lived. I remained there until 1942, when the Germans liquidated the local ghetto and sent everyone to Auschwitz. That time, I did not succeed in fleeing, and I had to be a witness of my entire family being murdered in the camp. I was in Auschwitz until 1944, when the evacuation began. Then, they sent us to the Mauthausen Camp in Germany[2], where hundreds of people died daily from hunger or were shot and murdered by the S.S.

I lived through the terrible situation until May 4, 1945, when the American Army liberated me.

Translator's Footnotes

1. See http://en.wikipedia.org/wiki/Stalag
2. Mauthausen is actually in Austria.

In Auschwitz

by Yechiel Nemlich

It took place on December 5, 1942. It was a cold day. It snowed fiercely, and it seemed that nature was the only thing that sympathized with the fate of the Jews and was infuriated with the injustice being perpetrated against us.

We had already been travelling for a number of days, and we did not know the direction. Suddenly, our train stopped. We did not know where we were located, but we instinctively felt that this was the place were the fate of many of us would be sealed. After remaining on the ramp for12 hours in sealed wagons packed with people who had no place to sit or even to stand, and where one could literally choke from the air, they opened the wagons. S.S. men were waiting for us, who raised a commotion just like a bunch of hungry wolves would do when they saw a pack of sheep.

Frightful scenes, which I do not have the power to describe, took place as we exited the wagons.

With the help of dogs and beatings from the butts of rifles, the terrified masses, who were nestled against each other, were placed five in a row, and the young Oberscharführer began to conduct the *selektion.* The number of those to be sent to death increased by the minute. Transport trucks ready to transport the victims were filled up with people, who were loaded up like herring in a barrel. Most of them were women, children and elderly men. The line became smaller, and as my row approached, I felt that the coming minute would determine my fate. I was the only one left from the entire family. Images of my parents and our house passed before my eyes as if in a film...

Suddenly I heard that the S.S. man asked me my name, age and trade. I answered him mechanically, and I heard him say to me, "To the left." I went to the group who was waiting for the vehicles, and then I heard the voice of the S.S. man again, "Return, to the right!"

I returned as if in a dream. At first I looked around and saw that I was in the company of only young, sturdy men who were guarded severely by the S.S. men. They put us in rows of five, and we marched.

A deathly silence pervaded in the rows. Nobody talked. We heard only the orders of the officers who chased us and urged us to go faster. Each of us was immersed in our own thoughts. It is not hard to imagine what each person was thinking about. Everyone's thoughts were focused on those who were driven away by the vehicles. Almost every one of us had someone who was among them. Each person was thinking only, "Will I see them again?"

However, the officers did not even let us think. They chased us and prodded us to go faster. The way was difficult. The ground was soft in places, and our legs would sink up to the knee in the mud. The only thing that we wished for was to come to the camp, lie down and go to sleep. However, the shouts of the officers, the mud on the feet, and the broken hearts kept us awake.

We suddenly saw the light of electric lamps in the terrible darkness. We were approaching the camp. The yellow light of the electric lamps unfolded before our eyes.

I was assigned to live in block 14. Despite the fact that we were occupied with the various camp formalities for the entire night, they sent us to work in the morning. In the commando unit to which I was assigned, I met several of my friends who had arrived in Auschwitz in earlier transports. They knew the camp very well. Most of them had become weakened and tired. When we went to work they asked us, the neophytes, to go slowly, for they had no energy. However, we had to be careful of going slowly, for the kapo would beat us for that.

The workday in the camp went as follows. In the morning, the inmates [*häftlinge*] would search for a commando where the work was easy. A commotion would break out, and the kapos and S.S. men would instill order via beatings and torture. After organizing the commando units, we would go out to work to the accompaniment of the camp band. The return from work was even worse. The men, tired from work and beatings by the S.S. men, could barely drag their feet. A certain number of them could not walk at all, and the other inmates had to help them. People also died during the return from work. And the same dismal train, as it arrived to the camp tower, had to go slowly, cheerfully, as if on an excursion, as it entered the camp to the accompaniment of the same band.

When we returned from work after an entire day of difficult labor, we had no rest. In the block, we were tormented by the block elder and the house elder.

That is how the days and weeks went by, filled with need and pain, until, one day a registration of a new commando took place in the camp. They only took those who were in good shape and of sturdy build. Immediately following the registration, the *arbeitsdienst* leaders of the camp ordered all the men between the ages of 21 and 32 to report in. Younger and older people also registered, for the registration would free them from a day of work, which was the greatest holiday for the inmates of Auschwitz. Shortly thereafter, we found out that they sterilized all the men.

At the same time, that is around the New Year of 1943, they began to organize transports for "Buna"[1] in Auschwitz I. I registered for such a transport and arrived in Auschwitz I.

In Buna, we were almost given the possibility of surviving the terrible time. They put me in a school for the brick trade, which prepared us for various building roles. We went to work during the severe cold, and this helped me extraordinarily. On the other hand, I suffered greatly from the block elder and especially from the Polish kapo who was known by the name Kacmarek. That man displayed great sadism to the Jews, and he tortured us throughout the entire winter.

When spring came, they sent us to various building jobs. At first, we were not content with the work. Later, however, after we had already worked for a certain time, we began to feel that this was the best place to have a hope of surviving the war. Civilian workers worked together wish us, and we often obtained something to eat from them, or we bought something if we had money. We were, however, strongly warned by the S.S. to refrain from talking with civilians. For such a “crime” we would be punished with a “bunk stay.”

That same year, I was sent back to Birkenau, for they needed bricklayers there. I found most of my friends in that camp. They were tortured, and I felt their loneliness. They housed me in Block 7, Camp D. The number of inmates had greatly increased at the time. They had started to bring in Jews from all the countries that the Germans had occupied. *Selektions* took place every day, and the crematoria operated day and night.

They brought Hungarian Jews to us in 1944. At the end of that year, on account of the approach of the Red Army, they evacuated “our” camp and sent us deep into Germany. I myself was sent to Dachau, where I was enlisted in the Kaufering subcamp[2], Camp II. Sick and broken, I was liberated from there on April 30, 1945 by the American Army.

Translator's Footnotes

1. Buna was a subcamp of Auschwitz.
2. Kaufering camps were a series of subcamps of Dachau.
3. These two sentences are a bit convoluted, and I cannot parse the exact meaning. But it seems that there was some storehouse for animal fodder which may have been somewhat edible, or perhaps some person who distributed animal feed. They exchanged some of the cotton seed for some food that was edible by humans.

German Cruelty and the Tormented Life as a Refugee in the Soviet Union

by Beila Rabinowicz

My father was a cantor and *shochet* [ritual slaughterer] in Sierpc. He studied the cantorial arts from the famous cantor Gershon Sirota[1]. My father practiced as a cantor in Sierpc from 1907 until 1939, the time of the misfortune of the German annihilation of the Jews. My childhood was spent in the Beis Yaakov School and ended in a public school. I eventually found my societal place in the Hashomer Hatzair educational youth movement.

I will never forget the great fire that spread through the Jewish street when the Germans set the synagogue on fire. We ran to a neighbor. From there, we looked out the window. Suddenly, my father shouted, “Children, look. The Holy Ark is tumbling down.”

We heard a shot. Victims who ran to save the Torah scrolls fell. All the neighbors, including us, went out to our neighbor Yechezkel Kadecki, where we sat in fear for the entire night.

The next morning, the murderers imposed a contribution upon the Jews as a fine upon us for burning down the synagogue...

I recall other details from the first sadistic murderous deeds of the Germans. The Gestapo ran into the slaughterhouse and found my father slaughtering a hen. One of the robbers ran around and ripped away the knife, pushed him away and shouted out, “Do you not know that slaughtering is forbidden?” Then the murderer ripped off my father's beard together with some flesh. Blood spurted, and the murderer laughed out loud with wild enjoyment.

My father came home bloodied and called out, “Blessed is He who revives the dead, and saved me from their hands.”

I recall another incident. It was Rosh Hashanah. A considerable group of householders, including my father and my neighbor Yechezkel Kadecki, were gathered together and brought to the market to clean the buses. The Germans mocked the Jews and beat them sadistically. They only let them go toward evening.

My father once again came home beaten and with bloodied clothing. His beard had been shorn, and he had two black eyes from the beatings. That is how our holy days as well as our weekdays passed until the expulsion.

The expulsion day began with alarms and shots from the Gestapo. All the Jews had to assemble themselves in the market near the Magistrate. We had to stand there for a second day. We put some jewelry into a pouch and took it with us as a means of salvation in case of need. When we arrived at the market, we were no longer among those in a good station of life. Jews were already waiting with packages, sacks, pouches, and cloaks. There were younger and older children, old and sick people. It was a dire picture that makes me shudder even today as I remember it.

The sorrowful procession was prodded to the train. There, we waited for neighboring towns: Zuromin and Biezun. Together we travelled on the way to torment. As we traveled, we heard shots and alarms over the wagons. The shots were from the Gestapo murderers. I remember the heartrending scenes at each shot from the murderers. My father and other Jews called out each time "*Shema Yisrael.*" People were speaking with each other.

They let us off in a field and ordered us to strip naked. They robbed all of our possessions, beat us murderously, and prodded us on further to Jablonna, Nowy Dwór and onward to Warsaw with beatings.

We did not remain in Warsaw for long. My older brother took us over to Ciechanow. The deportation had not occurred in that town. From Ciechanow, my brother and I moved over to Soviet territory. There we met up with our younger brother.

We attempted to bring our parents over, but it was already too late. The borders were already closed. The Russians took my brother and me to Archangelsk. We no longer heard anything about our other brother. A year and a half passed in that manner. Then, we were sent to Central Asia to "warm up" in a cotton-growing kolkhoz [collective farm].

Forty evacuated people lived with us. We worked very hard. We were nourished by a food called "*Makvicha*" for animals and with a sort of grit that we called *libeda*. At work, when we picked flax from the field, we "nourished" ourselves a bit with the kernels that we removed from the flax. They had a bit of oil in them. The number of people ill with dysentery increased by the day. Many people's lives ended because of the illness. My brother Yisraelik was among those whose lives ended with that same death from hunger. After his death, the true tribulations began for me: loneliness, homelessness, hunger, and general epidemics. A person who could hold up through all this was indeed stronger than iron.

Translator's Footnote

1. See http://en.wikipedia.org/wiki/Gershon_Sirota

One Occurrence from Among Many

by Chava Digala

I recall the day, the tragic day. It was on January 16, 1942, when the remaining Jews from the surrounding towns were gathered together. They sent us to the Strzegowo Ghetto.

After a year in the ghetto, we heard the dismal news that they were going to kill us all. I decided to escape from the ghetto with my two children, my sister, and three orphaned children of another sister who had perished in the ghetto, and whose husband had been killed in a concentration camp.

We escaped in the middle of the night of November 1, 1942. Hela Izakowicz also fled with us. We arrived in the Sierpc district. There, we all separated. Each of us had to save ourselves separately. I cannot describe the pain that I suffered when I had to part from my two young children. Each set out on a different path. I did not see my children for several months, and they were not together with each other.

Fate had it that I and my elder son survived, whereas my younger son Shmuel was killed by the hand of the murderous Germans four months before liberation. My sister Lea became ill, and there was nothing with which to save her from the arms of death. My sister's son was murdered like the others. We were liberated in the Sierpc district, and we met up with each other after the liberation. We came to Sierpc, where we found a few more Jews. Around us it was a ruin and a cemetery. After a few months, we decided to go to Germany in order to travel from there to our homeland.

On the Verge of Extermination

by Yaakov ben Shlomo Juzelewski

The terminal, the last station of life. This is the station that is “honorably” situated at the foot of the snowy Carpathian Mountains, glistening white from great distances. A station that contains within it a complete history, a tragic history of a people led to slaughter, a history etched in blood and torment. The station that had not yet recovered from the horror scene of the previous night, but was roused again by the same feverish activity that augurs only evil. The prey dash madly as if accompanied by the shadow of the Angel of Death. It was not easy to dispel the strange and awful impression that every corner heralded the coming of death. From every side, lustful eyes that “looked and didn't see” watched with revenge, a pathetic revenge against enemies that only yesterday were friends that fought shoulder to shoulder against a common foe.

That same town at the foot of the Carpathians, Auschwitz, was again awakened to the sound of the wheels of the passing train with its living cargo going to extermination. The citizens of the town knew, from the registry of those living in their country, the number of “Kikes” that had been sentenced to annihilation. Again and again they smiled at the calamitous end of the innocent victims. Again and again, that “noble” nation revealed its true face. Not the slightest pangs of conscience about the enormous offense committed in their motherland or the eternal stain that covers their hands because of this crime.

The train slowed down. Gray freight cars, full of people who had just been deprived of any power to resist and any will to live. Shut off and surrounded, detached from any means of existence, destroyed both spiritually and physically. People who had left nothing behind, except for anonymous graves where their loved ones were buried, victims of torment and suffering, victims of plagues and murders who, in spite of all the horrors, at least received a burial. These poor souls stand, squeezed against each other, pressing their young ones to their breasts, as if to protect them from wild beasts. Terror and fear are in their eyes, and on their lips, a prayer.

Prayer - no! It was a silent scream, the scream of a human being about to die. The silent scream of the victim in the hands of his killer. A silent scream that, even if it were voiced, would not have been heard by the rulers of the world.

The squeal of the brakes and a sudden shift: horrendous yelling of uniformed men accompanied by barking dogs brought the victims face to face with the grim reality. Blows to the head and bites by hungry dogs, like "masters who declared themselves the superior race, the bearers and representatives of world culture," these added to the fright and panic in the hearts of the oppressed and shocked travelers; screams; howling and cries for help. The voices of infants calling for their parents when they were in the hands of those who had torn them away; severed heads everywhere. The place was like a slaughter house for human beings.

Knocks and kicks, blows to the heads of children and elderly, rending of children from their parents, shots to the heads of old men along with screams, contempt, and curses. This is what those thousands faced on that morning, shadows of human beings, lost and cut off from the rest of the world.

The Angel of Death reaped his harvest. They passed in front of him like a flock of sheep, and received their sentence. And he, with his furious eyes and thunderous voice, raised his sickle and brought it down pitilessly on young and old, man and woman. With one stroke, families were separated, children from parents, husbands from wives. One by one, they passed in their final parade, with their terrified eyes, searching and yearning, looking at the groups arranged in files, testing and examining the surroundings. Maybe, perhaps, they will meet someone. To gaze for a final time at the most loved one. To take leave with a silent glance forever.

The marchers disappeared in the dense thickets (as if planted to hide the great terror and horrors) on their way to eternity. Silent and mourning, their eyes weeping and their lips trembling, their legs walked down the narrow path as they surveyed their surroundings. On every side they met the glances of their enemies and murderers.

The gates opened wide, and the large yard swallowed the sacrifices.

Above the treetops, the tall smokestacks stood out, belching tongues of flame and smoke. The tongues of flame were there all day and all night. All day and all night, the pure souls of the holy martyrs who were suffocated in the gas chambers ascended skyward.

The portals of the world didn't tremble, and the day was not darkened by the smoke and fire that rose, carrying the souls of children and elders, men and women, who wait up high for their salvation.

The final station, Auschwitz - the place where our nation tragically lost a third of its sons, and where our parents and brothers and sisters from the community of Sierpc also died. The place will be cursed forever. The nation that raised sons who could perform such horrendous crimes will be cursed, and the nation that aided them will also be cursed.

Wartime Memories

by Binem Maj

My parents -- my father Moshe Aharon, my mother Freida -- my brother Shmuel and I lived in Sierpc prior to the war, in a small wooden house near the synagogue. The house was an inheritance from generation to generation. My Uncle Berman, who also lived there in that house in good health, was also a partner in that inheritance.

My father, Jew for all seasons, worshipped in the old *Beis Midrash* during the week, and in his usual place in the synagogue on the Sabbath. He earned his livelihood from his business by selling fancy goods on the street. My mother also assisted with the livelihood. We lived on meager means. From my childhood, I recall that my father was always occupied with Torah and books, and my mother would often ask, "What will be the end of sitting and learning in the house if there is no livelihood?" My father would answer that learning is also a "livelihood," for one can see from the Torah how little a person needs to have.

Aside from religious books, my father also read newspapers and books. He had premonitions of the Second World War and also predicted the terrible suffering that the Jews would endure during the war years. When I was in the midst of Hitler's tortures and the extermination camps, I recalled my father's speech.

As I have already mentioned, we were two brothers in the house, in whom our parents placed great hope that we would grow up, and whose earnings would help ease the very difficult situation. Unfortunately, things turned out entirely differently. We did not bring them any joy, and did not ease the livelihood. On the contrary, they had to worry about us.

I, the elder son Binem, went out at age 13 to learn a trade. I joined the left leaning Poale Zion Party[1]. My parents did not like this at all. However, I must tell the truth. I received an entirely different education in Poale Zion, which served me well during the time of torment in the German extermination camps.

My spiritual mentors in Poale Zion were Itshe Binem Rosenberg, Eliahu Grossman, Pesach Grossman, the Feinberg brothers, and other members whose names I no longer recall. Unfortunately, none of them survived the onslaught of Hitler's Germany. There were murdered in the Warsaw Ghetto along with the thousands of other Jews. Honor to their memory!

My brother Shmuel joined the same group. Our thoughts began to turn toward the future. Anti-Semitism, from which we suffered greatly as children, was rampant in Poland. Therefore, we began to think about going to the Land of Israel.

Within a period of time, we decided at home that one of us would go to a kibbutz and go through the *Hachshara* [formal *aliya* preparations], so that he could go to the Land of Israel. I, the older brother, would work in the meantime to earn the amount necessary for a certificate[2].

Shmuel indeed went out to “Hechalutz Haklal Hatzioni” [General Zionist Poineers]. After several months, he was sent to Lomza, and was one of the first founders of that *Hachshara* depot. He worked hard physically; however his ideal became even stronger. I helped him from time to time with my earnings. However, unfortunately, he became overly vital to the party. They saw him as a person full of energy, love and life, dedicated to the Zionist ideal. They appointed him as the organizer of other kibbutz *Hachshara* depots in the district of Łodz, Zgierz, and Zduńska Wola.

That is how his youth passed. He spent six years in the kibbutzim. In the interim, others went to the Land of Israel, while he remained behind forging a path for us. Time marched on. The war between Poland and Germany began. I then saw him and was together with him for the last time. He had already obtained a certificate, but it was unfortunately too late. I received a draft notice from the Polish Army to be prepared to enlist and be ready for the war against Germany. They did not let my brother leave Poland.

The war broke out with lightning speed. I fought at the Modlin Fortress[3]. However, after one month of fighting, I was taken into captivity with all the others. I remained in captivity until 1940. At that time, a command was issued that all Jewish soldiers are to be freed. We understood that they were going to kill all the Jews together.

They did indeed free us, but I no longer had a home, for our town Sierpc had already been *Judenrein*[4] for a long time. In Lublin, I found out that all the Jews from the towns of the Warsaw region were now residing in Warsaw. I sneaked into Warsaw, and after a great deal of searching, I found my parents -- my father, my mother, my aunt Berman and her son Yisraelik, my daughter-in-law and her child, my daughter Dina and her husband, as well as many other people from our city.

My father had so greatly changed throughout the entire time that I could barely recognize him. He was broken from tribulations, hunger, and the living conditions of twenty people in one house. He no longer wore the black Jewish cap out of fear that he beard might be cut off. My mother held up somehow. Unfortunately, I could not help my parents.

I learnt about the fate of my brother from my parents. When the Germans entered Sierpc, they arrested my brother and a certain number of other youths as Zionists. After several weeks in prison, they were sent to Białystok. He jumped out of a window of the moving train and fled to Vilna in a manner that I do not know.

In Vilna, he again founded a kibbutz, set up contact with fellow natives in America, with my Berman cousins, and also with Zionist circles who helped him. From time to time, he sent packages of food and money to my parents.

I realized that Warsaw was not for me, and I decided, with the knowledge of my parents, that I must get out of there. Since I was still dressed in military garb, I set out by foot pretending to be an invalid, to whom the Germans behaved properly. Thus did I arrive in Plock, but I did not have energy to go further.

A short time later, I received the news that my father Moshe Aharon had died in the hospital. This was in 1940, two weeks before Passover. The reason for his death was understandable: he could not withstand the tribulations, hunger and weakness. All of this precipitated his premature death. I received no news about what was happening with my mother. Apparently, she was killed along with many thousands of other Jews in the Warsaw Ghetto. I also found out that my only brother was also killed in the Vilna Kibbutz when Hitler's soldiers took over the city.

Translator's Footnotes

1. Poale Zion had split into left leaning and right leaning factions.
2. Certificates were issued by the Zionist authorities to authorize *aliya*. At times, there were restricted quantities of certificates available.
3. See http://en.wikipedia.org/wiki/Modlin_Fortress
4. Nazi terminology for an area emptied of Jews.

My Experiences in the Soviet Union

by Avraham Majerance (Meron)

My parents arrived in Warsaw after the expulsion from Sierpc. My father Binyamin arranged accommodations with his Warsaw merchants on Franczyskan Street, and worked a bit with Uncle Chaim Senderowicz at collecting nails that were scattered around after the German bombardment of Warsaw.

My mother Beila and young sister Rivka Feiga were put up with a distant relative on Brony Platz. My lot was to be the go–between. At that time, I was 16 years old, healthy, and nimble. I fearlessly set out by foot from Sierpc. I endured many difficulties in obtaining some clothing, underwear, and money for my suffering family. After a two week arrest in the Gestapo dungeon on Stadolna Street, I succeeded by chance in escaping to Płock by foot.

My father's family in Płock took interest in my fate. Since they were still in their place and had money, they gave me several hundred zloty. After a few difficult days and nights walking by foot and avoiding the German patrols along the way, I arrived in Warsaw to my father. Above all, I was under the impression that the Germans were chasing me with dogs and shots. Along the way, I encountered large groups of Jewish youth who set out toward the German–Russian border that was located at the Bug at that time, and waited for a miracle to happen that would enable them to cross the river. I too thought of setting out along the same route.

In Warsaw, the Germans were snatching people for work and shooting at those who were fleeing. Various rumors were circulating among the refugees: they were going to starve all the Jews of Warsaw; all the provincial Jews would be concentrated in a ghetto.

I turned to my father with a request that he give me only 10 zloty and I would go to the Russian border.

"What, to the Bolsheviks!" my father shouted with a severe glance, "They are the same as the Germans.

Furthermore, as an illegal refugee, they will treat you worse than a spy."

I answered my father that this was the only way to save their lives.

"Good," Father said, "I will give you 20 zloty. Part of it will be for the Polish border directors and the other part for the journey. Perhaps you are correct. Prepare for the journey and be successful. G–d should protect you." He said this with tears in his eyes.

I set out on the journey immediately the next morning. I took a bit of underwear, food, and money. Father accompanied me to the Gdanska Station. We parted with great weeping. I entered the train that was full of Poles and Volksdeutchen. All of them were traveling to villages along the Bug that bordered Russia.

After a trip of a few hours, I arrived in Malkinia, the final station near the border. It was evening. Gestapo agents with armed agents met the passengers, and shone flashlights on all the people coming off the train.

"Jew or Pole," the Gestapo men shouted loudly.

Tens of Jews were led away by the murderers, accompanied by a hail of blows over the head from whips, as well as shots. One Gestapo agent flashed the light into my face and asked, "Jew?"

"No, Pole," I boldly answered.

This allowed me to blend myself amongst the farmers who lived along the Bug and follow them. I confided in one of the Polish smugglers and gave him 5 zloty to show me the way to cross the water border. The smuggler led me to the natural pass where thousands of people waited day and night, and he left me to cross alone.

Suddenly, there were shots from a German patrol. The reflectors lit up the area and bullets flew over the people. After lying on the ground for 15 minutes, I attempted to lift up my head, and a volley of bullets once again flew over me.

I wandered around further and did not know where the border was. I noticed a group who were going in the direction of the forest. I followed after the group step by step. Finally they were lost from my sight, and I remained in the field alone. I was afraid of making a step further. I lay down and slid on my stomach with my last strength, thereby approaching the forest.

Suddenly, I heard a shout, "Halt, hands up!" Two Russian solders with pointed guns and bayonets approached me. They led me into a small house and ordered me to turn toward the wall. After searching my knapsack, they ordered me to "go back." They loaded the guns and threatened to shoot if I would not go back. I fell before the soldiers and, with a hysterical cry, begged them in Polish, "Let me live, or else shoot me, but do not send me back to the German murderers."

"No," shouted the soldier and poked me in the calf with the gun, "Go back."

I went back about 100 meters, and after three times of not succeeding to steal across the Soviet border, that same night, I succeeded in crossing the border on the fourth attempt, before dawn. This was possible thanks to the Polish border guards whom I noticed coming after me.

"You want to cross over into Russia?" he asked me, "Go along the way and be successful."

I thanked him and crawled further on my stomach. That is how I succeeded in going along the way without anyone noticing me. I was bold and began to run. I went onto a side path and went boldly, with joy. After a few hours of walking, I found many refugees who were going along the way to Bialystock.

The next day, I arrived by train in Bialystock, the Jewish center of Polish refugees. I knew that all the Sierpc refugees were gathered in a certain synagogue. I went to the synagogue, where I was joyfully greeted by my fellow natives. I found tens of my friends from Sierpc. These were friends with whom I had studied in the Tarbut School.

Days and weeks passed. The Sierpc group grew with fresh refugees. In the interim, I learned to speak a bit of Russian and got to know some Russian officers. They invited me into their homes and helped me with various necessities. I often went to a certain Russian family. They treated me warmly. I knew that the head of the family was a high officer in the N.K.V.D.

"You are a good lad. It is better for you to go deep into Russia. There you will be a free citizen, and will certainly survive," the N.K.V.D. officer told me with goodwill.

I understood the hint. It meant that something could happen to the refugees in the cities near the border. The authorities might deport the non-secure elements.

Working Deep Inside Russia

At the beginning of 1940, I voluntary registered to travel to work deep into Russia. I signed a contract for a year of work with the Ministry of Construction. I traveled to the city of Zlatoust in the Ural region deep in Russia with a transport of several thousand people.

The long journey from Bialystock to Ural, a distance of approximately 4,000 kilometers, lasted for over a month. Forty to fifty of us were crowded into a single wagon. We travelled in lamentable sanitary conditions. We received food rations from the echelon leaders. I had the impression that we were like a flock of sheep being led from Europe to Asia.

Approximately 3,000 young workers of various nationalities – Jews, Poles, White Russians and Ukrainians – were occupied with building a new strategic point for the "24th Construction Trust," ten kilometers from Zlatoust. The barracks and general kitchen were already built. I was assigned living quarters with ten "cavalry" in one room. We had our meals at the general kitchen (*stolovka*) three times a day.

The aim of the Soviet Construction Ministry was that the newly arrived workers would build tens of ammunition factories within the next three years. My work during the first three days of the "*Ploshtshtake*" was very difficult: digging pits deep in the ground. Digging a cubic meter of rocky soil took from five to six hours. After ending the work, I was able to purchase from the general kitchen a soup with 200 grams of bread three times a day.

The Russian overseer would always shout, "Work quickly." The cold in the winter was 40 degrees. The clothing that I received there was too light for the climate. One had to get up very early for work and certainly one could not be late. Lateness could result in a trial with a prison sentence.

I went to work hungry and without energy day by day. When I went home to the wooden barrack, a cold wind penetrated the wooden walls and rafters. The nights were much worse. We slept on wooden beds stacked two cots high, and we were often so frozen that we could not feel some parts of our body. I fell asleep weeping, dreaming of my former home and my beloved parents who were under the hand of the German murderers.

I survived the "*Ploshtshtake*" for several months. The hunger prodded me to seek ways to improve the situation. Through various connections with the kitchen officials I received a side serving of noodles or buckwheat with my soup. I received recognition from the administrative directors and obtained a pledge from them to free me from work. It remained a pledge. I worked at many workplaces throughout the year.

A terrifying occurrence gave me the possibility of leaving the workplace. Early one morning, I was standing alone on the high scaffolding of the work site. Suddenly I could no longer feel my ears, hands and feet. I shouted to my overseer to take me down. I came down, with my frozen body parts covered in snow. All of my toes were frozen.

I was sent to the hospital, and was discharged after several weeks of recovery. I then asked the authorities to release me from the hard labor.

The local authorities sent my request to the N.K.V.D. office with an appeal to grant me a Soviet five–year pass. After receiving the Soviet pass, I was freed from the work camp and I set out on my way to Ukraine, where the largest concentration of Russian Jews was located. I arrive in Kharkov and met many good Jews there who helped me get myself set up and live normally and freely. I spent four good months in the large city of Kharkov. I did not imagine that here too, the danger of the destruction of Russian Jewry was approaching.

On July 22, 1941, Moscow radio announced that the German air force had bombarded Kiev, and Hitler had declared war on Russia. At the same time, the German army had crossed the borders, destroyed the fortresses and marched into White Russia and Ukraine. The Kharkov population was overtaken by a great panic. They were saying that the Red Army would mount a decisive resistance against the enemy in Kharkov.

I wandered through the city streets and noticed that life had become paralyzed. I was saved by death through a "miracle" when the German aviators bombarded the main Kharkov railway station. During the bombardment, military vehicles evacuated the families of high army rank. All of the regime offices and everything else were transported deep into Russia.

My Kharkov acquaintances prepared to set out on a journey to Central Asia. They asked me whether I was prepared to flee. "Unfortunately no, "I answered, "I must first sell my belongings in order to obtain the several thousand rubles that I would need for the journey."

My friends advised me to leave Kharkov immediately, for the Germans were 30 kilometers from the city.

I finally decided to leave Kharkov and sat on the steps on the last wagon of the last train that was to leave the city. German airplanes bombarded the last train. A few wagons were crushed. However, the rear part of the train, where I was sitting on the steps, did not suffer. After various difficulties fraught with mortal danger, I arrived at the central gathering place, about 200 kilometers from Kharkov. From there, I set out on the long journey to Central Asia. I went from one train to another, traveling in uncovered wagons under the open sky, through wind and cold. I ate a bit of warm soup and dry, black bread that the Russian workers gave me.

My difficult journey lasted for two months until I arrived at Alma Ata. Life was normal there, in the large city. The local authorities had not been informed about me, and I had to leave the city within three days. The only way was to register in a kolkhoz.

I spent time in several kolkhozes for three months. It was difficult me to get accustomed to the Uzbek primitive life. The military commissars recommended that I travel back to the former place of Zlatoust, where I had received the five–year pass. I had to follow their advice. I was now back in the Ural region. I tried my luck once again in Sverdlosk and succeeded in setting myself up there. I encountered great difficulties, and set out to Zlatoust, where a Russian photographer who was an acquaintance helped me get set up in the city.

The Difficult Life in the Work Unit

At the beginning of 1942, when the Russian Army endured a difficult crisis, the military authorities mobilized all active and not active people to military service in work units. Tradesmen were enlisted into the military factories. I too, one of the military undesirables, was mobilized into the "Stroy Battalion." I was affiliated with the large "Military Metallurgical and Copper Plant," and was designated as a "*stolivar.*" I had to stand by a 2000 degree oven and mold iron.

I worked 14 hours every day. The authorities demanded a 120 percent quota, as Stalin had ordered. Fifty percent of the workers were Russian woman in men's work clothes. Many workers suffered a loss of energy due to the poor food. The "*stakhanovches*"[1] who produced more than 150% of the quota received a glass of milk with 100 grams of bread above the normal rations, and sometimes also a "goulash." I would help out the waitresses and canteen administrators in various ways.

All the workers received soup with buckwheat and 800 grams of bread three times a day. Everyone lived together in a wooden barrack. Almost every day at the roll call, when the lieutenant called out the names of the camp list of those who were going to work, a few people were missing. Finally, the control would find dead, swollen, Russians lying on the cots.

In the Red Army

For me, 1942 was the worst time. I was suffering physically and my morale was low. The latest news from Poland regarding the liquidation of the ghettos by the Germans strengthened my desire for revenge. My goal was to enlist in the Red Army and go immediately to the front in order to fight against the Germans. At that time, a voluntary Ural tank corps was formed. I presented a request to be taken along with all the volunteers, but received a denial due to two reasons: I was a Polish immigrant and I was needed by the factory, which was working for the front.

At the end of 1942, I along with other Polish Jews from the factory succeeded in enlisting in the Red Army. To that end, we turned to the Ministry of War in Moscow and received the following response from Stalin's secretariat: "We have compassion on you, and we are prepared to grant you the opportunity to take revenge for the spilled Jewish blood."

My first military reserve point was in the city of Sumy (Ukraine). Thousands of volunteer Poles were formed there into the First Polish Division, which was organized by Wanda Wasilewska and Colonel Berling[2]. I was later sent back to Russia to a military school in the city of Volsk near Saratov.

After eight months of military education, I served as an under–officer commander in the Second Polish Division that was already at the Bug at that time.

Lublin had been taken by the Russian forces and I arrived in Włodawa, a town near Lublin, with my division. From time to time, I traveled to Lublin, where the headquarters of the Polish military was located.

One fine day as I was walking along the main street, I encountered a familiar face. I ran closer and recognized my cousin David Senderowicz. We kissed each other with joy and wept as we recalled our near death.

"Avraham," my cousin said to me, "Take off your uniform and let us escape to Romania, and from there to the Land of Israel."

"No," I responded, "my conscience does not permit me to desert the military. I owe a debt to the murderers: Revenge!"

At that time, the Germans mounted a strong resistance in Poland. All of the Polish military forces were concentrated around Warsaw to help the Red Army. We prepared ourselves and set out for the German front. Our division received an order from the general headquarters to march to the First "Byelorussian" Front.

I followed the orders of my officers. Every step was accompanied by fire. The main battles took place at night. We were already fighting on German soil. I went through German villages and cities, and I looked at the burning houses and automobiles with a gleeful feeling of revenge. Instead of streets, there were hills with stones. Instead of Germans, hungry dogs and cats were roaming around. We destroyed tens of villages. We went from one battle to the next. I got accustomed to life on the front.

One of the most difficult military experiences came behind the Niesse (Oder Niesse). The Germans sent storm units into battle – the well-known Russian "*Vlasovches*"[3]. I was surrounded by them, without water or bread, several times. After a heroic assault battle, we broke through and realized that the final victory of the enemy was near. I found murdered Jews in a few places from which we pushed out the Germans. They had been taken captive by the Germans and had poked-out eyes, and cut -off noses and ears.

The general victory over the Germans approached. Hundreds of German officers and soldiers fell captive to us. We found out from them that the Germans were retreating with great panic and fear of the Red Army. Many of them ran over to the Americans. The situation was similar to 1939 with the difference that at that time, the Polish soldiers were fleeing on the highways of Poland. Finally, we received the joyous news that the German general command had surrendered.

After the War, In Destroyed Jewish Sierpc

In April 1945, I returned to the city of Kalusz in Poland with my division. The Polish population greeted us enthusiastically. I became affiliated with the political division. The command was in Ostrów Wielkopolski. I received a two week furlough after three months of service, so that I could visit my native city. At the same time, the Polish anti-Semites raised their heads and began to murder Jews. The epidemic of anti-Semitism also spread in the military divisions. There was a hatred of Jewish officers who had received medals. Attacks against Jewish military personnel began. One night, I was shot with an automatic weapon by the fascist AKA personnel (AKA – Armia Krajowa[4] – the underground Polish army). This forced me to end my relationship with my office in the Polish military and to find a new path for the future.

During my furlough in July 1945, I visited my town of Sierpc, to see with my own eyes what had been described. When I arrived at the Sierpc railway station, I was surrounded by many Poles. They were impressed by my Polish uniform decorated with medals. Many of them accompanied me to the Jewish committee, which consisted of eight Jews.

I found several Jews in Sierpc, among them several customers of our shop. We wept over the great destruction. I arrived at Daszinski Street, where I was born and had lived for 16 years. The street was empty. There were no Jews there. My heart wept inside. I raised my revolver and shot three shots in memory of the martyrs. Tens of Poles gathered together at the sound of the shots. I declared to them that I was born right there on the Jewish Street in 32 Daszinski, and had lived there for 16 years until the destruction. Give honor to our holy martyrs!

A silence overcame everyone. They removed their hats from their heads.

After a two day visit, I left my unforgettable city of Sierpc forever. My only thought and aim when leaving Sierpc was – to search for a home. All of my thoughts concentrated on the primary point: to be among our brethren and among Jewish military people fighting for a Jewish homeland. I left the Polish army after the end of my two week furlough.

I went to Wrocław, and then went to the Russian–America border as a civilian. I was arrested by the Russian border patrol and held under strict guard in a penal bunker. The Russian officers interrogated me and freed me after several weeks of arrest. The Russian guard led me to the American guard. That same night, I found myself in the American Zone. I immediately traveled to Munich by train.

I lived in the large German museum where the Nazi leader used to conduct his hateful speeches against Jews. I received assistance from the Zionist institutions.

In August 1945, I was sent to the Fernwald Jewish D.P. Camp near Munich. The aim of most of the survivors was to immigrate across the ocean to their relatives in America.

In 1946–1947, I tried to sneak across the Austrian–Italian border several times in order to immigrate illegally to the Land of Israel. All of my attempts failed. My material situation worsened. I often fell into despair. I felt superfluous to the world. I could not do business with others, because I had nothing with which to do so. I returned illegally to Munich and met other Sierpc natives. We connected mutually and singularly with the Assistance and Relief organization of America, from which we received great support. I will never forget our brothers in America for their material help that the Sierpc survivors received, and for the enthusiastic and encouraging letters from Mordechai Reshatka, Max Tzina, and Leib Mintz.

The illegal immigration from Europe to the Land of Israel became more prominent at the beginning of 1948. I was among the voluntarily mobilized Hagana personnel who made *Aliya* prepared to fight for the Jewish State.

I left Marseilles in April 1948. After four months of military exercises, I arrived at the shores of my homeland, the Land of Israel, with a Hagana transport.

We were let out near Akko with small boats. We arrived in Haifa. After a medical examination, I was sent to a military camp with the rest of the mobilized comrades. I was sent to the Latrun military point, on the way to Jerusalem, after being in the Land for three days. The Arab Legion threw its best energies on Al–Kabab and along the way to Hulda. My unit mounted a decisive resistance that brought many victims. I hovered between death and life for a long time, until the armistice.

After a year of serving in the Israel Defense Forces, I was discharged from the military on May 15, 1949. I settled in Tel Aviv – the final stop of my long journey. Here, in the liberated State of Israel, I laid down the foundations of my family home.

Translator's Footnotes

1. See http://en.wikipedia.org/wiki/Stakhanovite_movement
2. See http://en.wikipedia.org/wiki/First_Polish_Army_(1944%E2%80%931945) , http://en.wikipedia.org/wiki/Wanda_Wasilewska and http://en.wikipedia.org/wiki/Zygmunt_Berling
3. The Russian Liberation Army, an anti–Communist group of Russians aligned with the Nazis. See http://en.wikipedia.org/wiki/Russian_Liberation_Army
4. See http://en.wikipedia.org/wiki/Armia_Krajowa

On The Ruins of Sierpc

by Y. Frenkel

I left the town in 1937. After that, I was called up to the army. In 1938, I received a furlough. Much had changed in the town during the year that I had been away. The impending war was already sensed. Anti–Semitism strengthened. The "*Awszem–Politik*" of Premier Składkowski[1] left difficult marks on the life in the town. The ban on Jewish *shechita* by Madame Prystor[2] also did not pass over our town. The only theme under discussion was "war." Everyone felt that something was going to happen, and everyone knew that no good would come from the entire uncomfortable situation.

I returned to the army after the furlough. Our military unit was sent to the front immediately on the first day. In a small grove near Garwolin, I met my acquaintances Yaakov Waldenberg and Shmuel Czarna. I spent some time together with Czarna because he became ill, but my duty in the military called, and we parted.

I fell into Soviet captivity, and was sent to Russia as a Polish soldier. There, I found out by chance that they had expelled the Jews from Sierpc and sent them to Warsaw. I immediately contacted my family by mail and received a response that they were suffering from hunger. I sent a packet of food with my last money; however, I received no response.

The war between the Soviet Union and Germany broke out on July 21. I had not heard anything for two years and did not know what was going on with the Jews in Poland. The first terrible news about the mass annihilation of Polish Jewry reached us in 1943. I enlisted as a volunteer in the army together with hundreds of other Jewish men. Unfortunately, I was not accepted in the army, and remained in Ural.

One fine day, I heard on the radio that Warsaw had been liberated. A few days later, I heard that my native town of Sierpc had also been cleansed of the

German military. Joy blended with endless pain overtook me. I already had detailed information that the Jews of Sierpc had been annihilated, and nobody survived. I could not conceive of and could not believe that they could poison people and then burn them. Since I was unable to travel to Poland, I wrote a letter to the Sierpc city hall with a question about my family. I did not receive any response. I continued to live and wait for the day when I could travel to Poland and find out precisely what happened with my family.

The war ended. The long awaited day came. I arrived in Poland on March 22, 1946. My first destination was Sierpc. When the train approached my town, I felt my heart turn to stone. Who knows what I would find there? I saw many carriages at the railway station. It seemed to me that I saw the old, well-known carriages of Mendele Tac, Shmuel Paseh, and others. However, as I came nearer, I saw that they were only Christians. There was not one Jew among them.

I went into town on foot. Every Christian looked at me as if I had horns. The Christian districts of the city were whole. Only the Jewish quarter was completely destroyed. Christians lived in every Jewish house, and they utilized the Jewish property. Every Jewish business had been turned over to Christian hands.

The destruction of Jewish Sierpc was evident at every step. The destruction was most poignant for me when I found the few surviving Jews, such as Yaakov Skornik, Dr. Szampan, Roza Motil Lofka from Żuromin, and Hela Izikowicz. All together, we were not even ten. The stories of the survivors were horrifying. Dr. Szampan told me how Yosel Prosznicki committed suicide, and how Dvora Rizowa died. Their stories were terrifying.

The next morning, the three of us, Dr. Szampan, Yaakov Skornik, and I, went through the town. We passed by the shop of Nathan Tac, who had done so many favors for Jews and Gentiles, and who was tragically murdered in the ghetto. Yechiel Meir Bergson, Yisachar Bergson, Aharon Lipka Lidzbarski and others came to mind.

At the bridge, everyone recalled his family. We silently walked through the Jewish lane, which was once bustling with Jewish life and Jewish creativity, and was so cruelly cut off. A shudder went through all of us as we thought about what happened with a Jewish town. We only found the old *beis midrash*, which the Poles and turned into a location for other purposes. We witnessed the destruction of Sierpc, and from every corner, an agonized voice shouted out, "Take revenge for our blood!"

Translator's Footnotes

1. There is a footnote in the text here, as follows: The politics of economic exclusion of the Jews, whose founder was the Polish Prime Minister of that time, General Sławoj Sładkowski.
2. See http://www.jta.org/1936/03/06/archive/sejm–body–adopts–anti–shechita–bill–mme–prystor–assails–jews

After Everything, I Have Arrived...

by Avraham Tac

Dedicated – to my father Shmuel Yitzchak
My mother Esther
My young brother Velvel —
Of Blessed memory

In Sierpc After the Destruction

The train travelled quickly and got closer and closer to the small railway station of Sierpc.

A dream of years, of long years of travelling and loneliness. During those years, the town always stood in my imagination and enticed me with its inaccessibility, with its fantastic distance in time and geographic location... And now the train was racing along on that hot June day and carrying me closer and closer to my dream. It is no wonder that my heart was beating loudly, and that my breast was heaving so strongly that my breath was taken away.

Engrossed in my thoughts and mood, I did not notice that we were slowly sliding into the station, and that the terminal appeared before my eyes with the same inscription, the same spaciousness, the same ideal peacefulness, as it once was... as it once was...

However, why was I alone in the crowd of people, who were moving around with valises, baskets, and bags? Where were the Jews who were supposed to arrive on the same train? Tomorrow is Tuesday, and nobody would miss the market day. I looked around, and I did not see anyone. However, I felt their shadows and heard their steps as if they were returning from Warsaw and Łodz with valises, bags moving along, faster... faster...

The long street from the train to the city rolled away before me. It was once so strange to me, and remains so today. I was indifferent and cold toward it. My city - Jewish Sierpc - was further on. However, from nowhere, a building with a red, gothic roof pierced through my heart. The redness and the pointy roofs protruding skyward reminded one of the former householders to whose tastes those red, pointy roofs were built.

The city was nearing. There is Płocker Street with its houses as in former times. The old market looked to me like a mourner.

It was silent around.

A lonely automobile ran by with a loud screech that resounded and fell away somewhere. Then a farmer's wagon squeaked by. Then again, silence, silence...

I remember well every shop in the market as well as their former owners. There was the store of Noach Zilberberg. He knew how to draw and paint very well. I recall that during my childhood, I admired his factory painted tables. There was the shop of Naftali Libsohn. His son Avraham practiced Hassidism, traveled to the *rebbe*, and constantly studied.

From afar, I cast a glance at the Jewish Street. There, not far from the intersection, lived Shia Goldman, the man with the iron–clad, scholarly logic. There, on Fareh Lane, at the threshold of the low hut, Rivka Gotlibowski used to stand and discuss things with my mother opposite the balcony. A bit farther, deeper into the lane, lived Yaakov Moshe Tajtelbaum, the stringent Hassid. His little house had also disappeared like the neighboring ones. Only the house in which we lived remained. It stood somber and sad. New neighbors whispered something on the steps and cast curious, bold glances at me.

Nothing blocked the silent sunset, but the past still lives with me. I am a mourner, and my heart is filled with deep sorrow. My Sierpc Jews were murdered. They are no longer in Sierpc...

*

Morning came. The sun was already playing with the curtains of my window, and I thought above all of the former Jewish life that once flowed here.

I was close to the brook at the Jewish Street. The brook was possibly somewhat more beautiful on the other side, where it is surrounded by fine orchards and soft, green meadows.

However, it was near and etched in my heart on the Jewish Street. That was where I went to *cheder* three times a day. There once was the small house of the rabbi, old and inclined, reflecting in the water. There, everything was crowded together. There was another row of houses on the right side, not leading to the bridge, where there would be a danger of slipping in the water. Once, this all was. Today, nothing is there. Everywhere there is empty space, which seems somewhat smaller, as if it is writhing in pain.

Only the old *beis midrash* stands.

It is faded, as if it grayed from so many Jewish tragedies. The boarded–up windows look blind and obscured. One can no longer hear voices from inside. There is no singing, no worshipping, no life. A deathly silence pervades the ruined, weakened four walls.

Perhaps only at night, when sleep covers the world with a veil of dreams, the holy congregation of Sierpc comes together in the old *beis midrash* and worships once again as it once was, as it once was...

This is one of the new Sierpc legends.

The Jewish Street, starting from the old *beis midrash*, sported a new sidewalk that led over the hills. However, this was not an ordinary sidewalk. Oh, no! Gravestones from our cemetery were used to pave the sidewalk. The holy stones of course had their letters facing downward – the square letters that for hundreds of years noted honorable Sierpc Jews and their modest wives after their passing.

I turned my gaze to the left and saw that the new *beis midrash* was missing. All that remained were the pyramid shaped, tall steps that led to the entrance from three sides.

In a night that will never be extinguished, my memory was full of all the Sierpc Jews in the world, Pinie the painter lay on the steps with a shot in the chest. He ran to save the burning synagogue and was running to the new *beis midrash* when he was felled by a German bullet. Pinie was a child of poor parents. His pale, sickly mother educated him as a scholar in Lithuanian *yeshivas*, so he was able to hold his own in learning with the best youths of the city... Pinie no longer lived when his synagogue burnt down.

Instead of the thin walls, the broad roof, and the majestic domes of our synagogue, I now see a blue horizon in the sunshine. Low grass now grows n the place of the Holy Ark, where there used to be wonderful carvings of people raising their hands heavenward in eternal prayer.

Looking this way, the synagogue flickered in my memory, as it flickered on that dark night together with its Torah scrolls.

*

Long, long, I tarried at the Jewish Street. I cannot shield myself from it. Jews lived there and flourished there during the centuries of Jewish existence. I left as if from a recent, dear grave.

The Mikva Lane could be seen clearly from there. No houses, no courtyards, no fences marked the place, as they once did. From the *mikva*, only the spring remained.

*

Long shadows already spread from one side of the street to the other when I secluded myself in my Holy of Holies – in my Fareh Lane. There I was born; from there the Germans chased me out. The panes of our windows peered at me mutely, as if they wanted to tell me something but could not. The linden trees on our lane had grown so tall that one could barely recognize them. They stand still and motionless. Even the ancient tall chestnut trees stand congealed with their green, majestic, crowns. I slink around my Fareh Lane. I enter a known house. With awe and respect, I listen to the whisper of generations emanating from the walls. My dreams turn over to the question of the new residents. Who are they? Where did they go? Do they remain here?

Slowly, night falls.

Dear, nearby shadows descend from every corner, from every alleyway. They peer at me mute and strange... I close my eyes and also become a shadow, just like them.

One Who Survived

by B. Dorfman

After a few days with the Germans, I, together with a group of youths, crossed to the other side of the border. From there, I went to Białystok, and then went deeper into Russia, to Ural, together with the family of Hershel Glasman. However, I could not get myself acclimatized there or accustom myself to the new circumstances. I returned to Białystok. After a few months, I was arrested by the Russians and sent to a camp where I remained for two years.

I returned to Poland on June 20, 1946. I enlisted in the Hanoar Hatzioni Kibbutz in the city of Kielce.

Two weeks later, on July 4, 1946, the well–known, terrible Kielce Pogrom broke out. I was badly wounded.

I want to paint here a small picture of the pogrom, along with a few words about myself personally.

It was Wednesday at 10:00 a.m. The house where we lived was surrounded by the police. A crowd of approximately 10,000 people had gathered.

When the first military unit broke into the kibbutz, they led us all to the crowd that was shouting terrifying slogans before my eyes. In the first minutes, we attempted to mix into the crowd. However, I quickly received my first blow and lost consciousness. When I regained consciousness a bit, I again received sharp blows in the head, teeth, and eyes, with a gun, stones, and metal rods. I heard one of the pogromchiks saying to the other that they should shoot me. The other answered that it would be a waste of a bullet, for he will die in any case...

After regaining consciousness again, I went to the hospital in Kielce after three days. I remained there for a year. I endured two difficult operations and several smaller ones, and left as an invalid. I had lost an eye, and my vision in the other one is only 10%. I lost my teeth, and had broken three vertebrae, my nose, and my head.

I returned to the Hanoar Hatzioni Kibbutz in Lodz. After some time, I set out for France. On July 6, 1948, I arrived in the Land of Israel, in the middle of the battle with the Arabs.

Henryk Przenice

by Golda Goldman

The struggler for the freedom of Poland, murdered by Polish hooligans. The 23 year-old Chaim Nachum (Henryk) Przenice, the son of Shlomek and Dvora, was an officer in the Polish Army that was created in the Soviet Union (the Kosciuszko Army). Przenice took part in all of the victorious battles of that military formation against the Germans, and went all the way to Berlin.

The Jewish hero, decorated with awards, returned to Poland. There he was murdered by a band of "Chłopci z liaso"[1].

A dry, laconic, newspaper notice.

Henryk Przenice!

All of a sudden, there is a lightning bolt through my consciousness that evokes a sharp, prickly pain in my heart.

Heniek – the small, vivacious, pleasant Heniek. I remember his mischievous, urchin-like pranks when he would play in our yard, and our windowpanes were in peril. Later, I also knew him as a student in our local gymnasium, with his student cap pushed to one side, with battle ready flashes in his black, expressive, eyes. There, the thread of my experiences was interrupted, for Heniek disappeared from me, along with hundreds and thousands of other Henieks, Chaimels, Davids, Mosheles, Shlomoles, and many other names – through mother's tender darlings[2].

However, I did indeed run into Heniek by coincidence. I unfortunately saw him for the last time. I met Heniek as an officer in the victorious anti-Fascist Polish Army. He excelled boundlessly in the battles against the Nazi monster. Prior to his heroic death, he was decorated with high military honors.

Heniek came from beyond the legendary Stalingrad and arrived all the way to Berlin through a hellish fire. From there, a gnawing nostalgic feeling brought him back to his native Polish soil. However, there, he saw in despair that his work was far from over. The Nazi beast was not dead. It survived in the hearts of the Polish underground, the fascist anti-Semitic bands who licked one's fingers with the blood of six million murdered Jews, and were still not satisfied. They grit their teeth and lay in ambush in every corner.

Chaim Nachum Przenice went to a Jewish area, but he could not find his way back. His Polish environment was full of hatred and venom toward Jews. The 23-year-old Jewish hero paced through a city that celebrated the murder of all the Jews – not one remained in the city of Jewish murder – he was the one and only Jew there. He heard the steps of his murderer, but he could not leave his position. Torn away from his relatives and friends, he dragged himself alone on the Polish soil until the Polish underground bandits murdered him.

His Final Letter

Kałuszyn, June 28, 1946:

My dear and beloved ones!

Your letter that I received yesterday gave me partial contentment and enthusiasm, but did not calm me completely. In a certain way, the letter caused me some disconcertment. You must be wondering why? This is the reason. It seems that I, a sole Jew – am able to live calmly in an atmosphere of the anti–Semitic "Pale of Settlement" where I find myself now. I present before you such a city as Kałuszyn: before the war, Jews numbered 70% of the population here. Today, I am the only Jew in Kałuszyn and its region. Furthermore, I am the commandant of the entire province.

I must admit to you that I am very jealous of you who live amongst your own, amongst Jews, while I am like a miserable orphan amongst hate–filled pogromchiks. Here I am considered as an unusual phenomenon – a Jew who is still alive.

I generally find myself in dangerous and frightful situations, always in action against the Jew haters as well as against the progressive regime. I write to you to tell you that you should attempt to escape from such a danger – but I must tell you with an open heart that I do not have the possibility to do so in the situation that I find myself today. "One does not get a furlough!" And I am in such a strange state of embarrassment that I cannot extricate myself from this. My situation is even more complex in that against my will, I was suddenly summoned to a medical committee, and I was immediately placed, without any questions, into a military fleet.

I do not know what I should do now. I have no possibility of freeing myself from my difficult situation. Therefore, I will wait... Perhaps a miracle will occur... However, my dear ones, I do not have faith in miracles... I feel... That when your next letter arrives I will no longer read it... Unfortunately, this is the bitter truth about my situation...

... So ... Possibly it is not so tragic! I have lived through so many terrifying moments during my short life – I have gone through the seven levels of hell and emerged whole: I will, so I hope, also survive now... "Everything is in the hands of Heaven."

Believe me, I want to see you all so much – not only to see you as relatives, but also to have the possibility of again living as a Jew amongst Jews.

(signed)

Chaim Nachum (Heniek) Przenice

Translator's Footnotes

1. First two words are "Boys with". I am not sure about *liaso*.
2. Seems to be an extremely ironic phrase, referring to the murderers (who facilitated the disappearance of all these people) as mother's tender darlings.

Autumn in Poland

by Ephraim Talmi (Wluka)

In Memoriam for my Parents, My Teachers
My mother Mindel And my father Avraham,
Their souls are in Eden

A

The paths we played on grew silent
The mound of grass paled and yellowed
Trees were standing bereft
With sadness that knows no rest...

The rustle of the leaves in fall
Only that can be heard
A loss, abandoned reigns here
Forlorn is the universe and tearful...

B
In the Fall

Weary of walking
In the midst of the leaves
I was tired
Sitting on a milestone
The fields greening and yellowing to infinity
Caress the boundaries of the sky...
The pale blue becalms like after a storm...

On the horizon - the wood...
Quiet surrounds me, and serenity.
The peace of fall reigns...
The world sprawls like an open book
Tilled, sowed.
Come, I will fall to my knees
I will kiss that rim...

Sierpc 1938, 5699

Before the Storm

by Zvi Arpa

Introduction

The blood freezes in my veins, and my lips tremble as I sit down to write these chapters.

Again I see those terrible years of the Holocaust, those terrifying and depressing war years that I will remember forever. They appear to me as if they were still alive, all the dear friends whom I lived with, worked with, and together with them hoped and aspired for better lives... Everything sank into that pit of forgetfulness, everything very cruelly stopped. My soul rebels; it is difficult to put those terrible days on paper.

But a holy obligation commands the hand to write, and to declare everything cherished that was lost, so I sit and fulfill my duty. I made an oath to be carried out anywhere I would find myself, on the day that I was freed from the camps.

I cannot put everything on paper. The Holocaust is too big to bear description. What I will recount in the following chapters is a drop in the sea of suffering and the torment in general, and that of our townspeople in particular, who were among its first victims in Poland.

Even before the outbreak of the Second World War, the Jews of Sierpc started to feel the winds of Nazism that came from Hitler's Germany. The Poles were greatly influenced by Hitler's ideology and prepared themselves for it. Long before the German conquest, they sharpened their swords on the Jewish communities, including that of Sierpc, to destroy them and eliminate them and their property.

The beginning came from the *Sejm*[1] where the Minister of the Interior Skladkowski said "*Bojkotowac owszem*" meaning that a commercial boycott by the Gentiles of stores and workshops was permitted. This meant not to buy in Jewish stores or give work to Jewish artisans. This caused a large drop in the income of Polish Jews. I remember that in November 1938, groups of Poles from the OZN[2] Party stood in front of every Jewish store in Sierpc and wouldn't let Gentile customers enter to buy goods. They moved around in pairs near every store and handed out fliers to passersby. These contained slanders, curses, and pictures: how a Jew sits at home, feasting on fish and meat and all sorts of good foods; on the other side was a picture showing the poverty of the Gentiles. Beneath the pictures, a caption: how the Jews suck our blood. Or another picture: a Jew is standing next to some food and scratching his beard so that lice will fall into the food, which is to be sold to Gentiles. Whatever was not in the flyers, the *picketen*[3] would add verbally. The police did not interfere in any of these provocations, because this was the official policy of the Polish government. They would stand in shifts twice a week, on Tuesday and Friday, the market days in Sierpc.

In January 1939, the Jews of Sierpc woke up in the morning to find all the signs on their stores and workshops covered with tar. This was the work of the *picketen* who came from Plotzk and Rypin to help the local hooligans spread their anti-Semitic propaganda in our town. They were not satisfied with their day's work on Friday, but stayed till Saturday night. They lay in wait near the synagogue and *beit midrash*[4] to finish the job. The worshippers, smelling what awaited them outside, decided to remain inside their places of worship until they left.

Two Jews managed to sneak into the new *beit midrash* where Rabbi Goldschlak was praying to inform him of what was happening outside: Poles carrying clubs and knives were waiting near every Jewish place of worship.

The Rabbi left the *beit midrash* through a back door and went home and contacted the *Staroste*[5] by phone to inform him of the situation. The *Staroste* promised to send police to the houses of worship to safeguard the Jews so that no harm would come to them. The police came, but could not control the situation. That evening, a number of Jews were injured by these hooligans.

This rabble ruled in Sierpc for few months before the outbreak of the war. It was simply too dangerous for Jews to go outside in the evenings. The organizers of these incidents were from the Polish intelligentsia: Dr. Malewitz, Witschalkowski, and others. They decided to intensify the economic boycott, continue the terror in the streets against the Jews, to provoke a loud propaganda campaign, and destroy the Jews of Sierpc economically, physically, and spiritually.

The Jewish community of Sierpc was depressed and in despair because of the situation in town, more than any other group in Sierpc. Because there was a hooligan network in Sierpc: the hub of the organization was the new political party called OZN that was organized following the venomous anti-Semitic speech in the *Sejm* by the interior minister, Skladkowski. The community sent a delegation to Warsaw to meet with Jewish representatives in the Sejm. These individuals would contact the Polish authorities who would try to improve our situation, to protect us, and stop the stream of hatred in our town. But nothing came of this. All Polish lips repeated the same words: "Hitler is coming to destroy you." Every Gentile in Sierpc had already decided which Jewish property he would plunder when the German army entered Sierpc; which store and which apartment would be his...

The Jews of Sierpc stood up to this with conscience, spirit, and religion. They maintained their brotherly mutual aid, helped the poor willingly and sincerely. They founded the beneficial fund that supported the needy, the artisans, the small merchants that needed interest free loans; to maintain the other banks like Bank Ludowi, Bank Kopitzki, Bank Kreditowi, that sustained all the Jews in Sierpc without exception. The Jews also contributed to all types of funds, such as Keren Kayemet, Keren Yesod, Keren Hayishuv, and in addition – many yeshivas.

Boys' education was of a very high level. Religious Jews invested mighty efforts in the *Heder Beit Yosef* and *Beit Yaakov* to bring up the younger generation in the spirit of the Torah and tradition.

An impressive building was erected by the Zionist party in Sierpc for the Tarbuth School, where the students received both a nationalistic and traditional education. The schools were the pride of Sierpc Jewry. The sounds of the Torah never ceased in the new and old *beit midrash*, and the houses of the Gur and Alexander Hasidim.

The public guest house (*hachnasat orchim*) that was built with pennies collected from the town residents was a *talmud torah* during the day, where poor children whose parents could not afford to pay tuition could learn. This *heder* was supported by the Sierpc community.

The political parties[6] were active: *Agudat Israel, Poalei Agudat Israel, Tzeirei Agudat Israel, Mizrachi, the Zionist Party, Poalei Tzion, Bund, Hashomer Haleumi,* and *Hashomer Hatzair* The youth of Sierpc spent its evenings and its spare time in the party headquarters that had well stocked libraries, athletic equipment, and so forth.

I remember that during the Passover before the war, a Polish army battalion came to our town. They stayed for a few months and there were disturbances initiated by the soldiers. The Jewish community persevered in its efforts to have the authorities intercede, but without success. The Gentiles were saturated with wild anti-Semitism.

And then came the day of the destruction of the community of Sierpc. On Friday, September 1, 1939, the war between Poland and Germany broke out. This is a terrible date for the Jews of Poland, including those of Sierpc.

The next day, Saturday, the first refugees from Mlawa and Żuromin arrived. They were fleeing the Germans that had penetrated into Polish territory. These towns were bombed by the German Air force. The fugitives came for shelter in Sierpc, but before they had a chance to settle down, the German planes reached our town as well. The municipal hospital on Plotzki Street was bombed, and four patients were hurt. This was on Monday, September 4, 1939. That same day, an edict was issued by the *Staroste*: the youth must leave town and go towards Drobin or Warsaw, because the German army is approaching.

The fear and despair are difficult to describe, or the separation of the sons from their parents. Where? For how long? What will happen to those left behind? What will the Germans do to our parents and dear ones, with their cruel system of governing that is about to take over the town in a few hours? Everyone felt that whatever would happen to their dear ones would happen to them too. The streets were full of confused Jews, seeking advice from one another. No one could decide what to do, and time was short and the danger was coming closer.

In the end, many young people left the town. Few were left. These were people who did not have the strength to wander the roads, and said: "Whatever will be, will be," because in any case they would collapse by the roadside. There was no transportation, and they were not capable of moving on foot. My parents, of blessed memory, also remained. How great was the pain, as if we were separated forever. The community of Sierpc was wrapped in wailing and tears.

I left the house accompanied by my parents, with tears streaming down their faces. As I walked down the stairs, I could still hear the blessing of my father, of blessed memory: “Come back safely!”

Those leaving town walked toward Plotzki Street carrying small packages, their gear for the trip. I met David Bergson on Alter Park Street. He had decided not to leave town because there was no point to this flight. In any case, the whole country would be overrun by the Germans in a short time. In spite of this, we left the town, without knowing where to go. We went with thousands of Jew from other towns. During the day the roads were bombed, and at night there was nowhere to sleep. Most of the people from Sierpc remained in the town of Gostynin because they could not walk any further. Some continued in the direction of Warsaw.

In the meantime, between the retreats of the Poles and the German occupation, Sierpc was without any authorities whatsoever. A few citizens, Gentiles and Jews, got together, among them David Bergson and Berish Poznanski, to try and bring some order to the town. There was a shortage of small coins, and they printed notes signed by the town governors, David Bergson and Berish Poznanski. The stores, bakeries and workshops operated according to their instructions, and the town functioned well until the Hitlerist occupier came.

*

After about a week of wandering, we arrived at the outskirts of Warsaw. We traveled together, and as best I remember the names, we were: the brothers Natan, Shmuel, Wolf, Tatz, Yehudah and Moshe Pukacz, the attorney Toch, a Jew who settled in Sierpc together with his family before the war. (It is fitting that we mention his name. He should be remembered as an exemplary man: he was kind hearted and a philanthropist, an expert at his profession, who brought honor to the Jews of Sierpc among the Gentiles because of his talent and wisdom.) I came with all of them to Warsaw. When we entered the city, we were caught by the Polish Guard for labor duty: to dig ditches and break up the roads so that enemy tanks would not pass. We were tired and weary from our journey, but worked for the Polish military for twenty-four hours without rest or food. What we did receive were many heavy blows from the Polish soldiers who guarded us constantly, using their shovels and hoes. They let out all their frustration with their situation on us. We accepted our condition silently, for what could we say or do? To whom could we complain or ask for consideration?

In Warsaw, our contact with our relatives was cut off entirely. We did not hear or know what happened there. We worried and feared the worst, in spite of the fact that we had our own problems in Warsaw – bombing and conflagrations day and night – because Warsaw became the second Madrid[7] in the annals of war.

We did not leave the shelters during all those days, except when we moved from one shelter to another when the previous one had been bombed and destroyed entirely. It was a miracle that we stayed alive. All passageways between streets were barricaded, because the Poles planned to fight from house to house. We were in the Jewish quarter, and we saw how Jewish property was lost. Large stores full of consumer goods on Nalewki, Franciszkańska, and Jensha Streets went up in smoke from the bombs dropped by German aircraft. We ran from place to place looking for shelter. We were without electricity or water. But in Warsaw you could get candies, pickles, and preserves that were strewn in the streets because a large factory for pickles and preserves had been bombed. The acting president, Stazhinowski, promised victory, and comforted the citizens of Warsaw by saying that England was coming to the rescue. But in the third week of the bombing, Warsaw surrendered, in a state of ruin and without any resources. This was on the eve of Sukkoth. On the first day of the holiday, the German army already marched through the streets of Warsaw. With their entry, they started to destroy and kill Jews and loot their property. Jews were thrown into the ditches full of mud, injured and covered with blood. The Germans were helped by Polish soldiers and civilians. On Bonifraterska Street, the Germans distributed warm soup to the starved citizens, who waited in a queue thousands of people long. The German soldiers walked along the line, searching for Jews. Every Jew who was discovered was removed from the line and badly beaten. Jews walking in the streets were arrested and made to do hard labor.

On Nalewki Street I saw two Germans holding a Jew with a long beard. They brought a young woman who was passing by, and forced them to kiss. The Germans photographed them in the act.

When we Sierpcer saw what was going on in Warsaw, we could only imagine the state of affairs in Sierpc. In spite of this, we decided to return to our town, even if the roads were still dangerous, especially for Jews. We left Warsaw.

After two days of wandering, we were captured by Germans and sent to a labor camp. Our task was to make order out of the Polish weapons that had become German booty. After a few days we were let go, and continued on our way to Sierpc. We passed through Plotzk and spoke to the local Jews, and they told us what had happened in our town. About the synagogue that had been burned, and about 40 young men who had been sent to an unknown destination. We were overcome with fear and trembling. We hired a horse and carriage and rode home, each one of us with his own thoughts and terrible suspicions.

In Sierpc

The streets were empty. Everyone was confined to his own house. The streets where the Jews lived: Warshawska, Alter Mark, Neier Mark, looked like graveyards. Only we, the guests, dared disturb the quiet with our footsteps in the city streets. Each of us went to his own house. I entered mine and found my dear parents, my brother, and my sisters. I began to weep out of joy and sadness. I almost did not recognize my father when I saw him, without a beard, wearing a hat and crying bitterly. My mother, her eyes full of tears because of the family's desperate fate, rejoiced at seeing me alive. She never expected to see me again.

The Nazis rampaged in the town, every day grabbing people for labor, young and old, weak and strong, sick and healthy. This was simply to harass them, for the work was without any purpose, loathsome labor, such as: cleaning toilets without any cleaning tools, or emptying cesspools. My father told me what had happened to the Jews of Sierpc during this brief time. On Kol Nidre night the Jews were taken to the Staroste building on Plotzki Street for labor. The Germans knew that this was the holiest night for the Jews and purposely wanted to humiliate and degrade them. While they worked, the Germans had a "performance" of Jews with beards. They cruelly pulled at the beards with scissors, and beat those who couldn't run with full pails of filthy water. He choked with tears when he talked about the synagogue:

There was martial law: going outside was forbidden after four in the afternoon. At ten o'clock at night, we see flames coming from the direction of the synagogue. We hear an order in German: "Jews, get out of your houses and put out the fire in your synagogue!" The voices reached all the Jewish sections. Everybody left his house with full buckets to save their dear and holy place, or at least to remove the Torahs from the tabernacle. Jews came running from all directions. They knew that this was the work of the Nazis. But maybe they will succeed in putting out the fire? But the Nazis did not call the Jews from their homes to douse the flames, but to cause panic and chaos among them. German soldiers surrounded the conflagration. When the Jews approached with water to put out the fire, they were beaten. The murderers yelled, "Why did you come here? Go home!" When the Jews turned to go home, they shouted, "Who told you to go home? Go put out the fire." Warshawska Street was full of Gestapo men, who came to see the show. They constantly fired shots into the air. That evening, there was one young victim, 20 years old. It was Pinchas Walcman, the son of the painter. When he was running, carrying buckets to put out the flames, he was shot by a Nazi. He was wounded and bleeding when he fell at the boots of the German murderer pleading for his life and to be allowed to live. The murderer's response was another bullet. He was a quiet boy, a fellow student in the *Heder Yesodai HaTorah*, a fellow member of *Pirchei Agudat Israel* and *Tzeirei Agudat Israel*, and he studied for two years in the Lubavitch Yeshiva. Lately he had been studying Torah day and night with the group led by Avraham Liebson of blessed memory, who spent their days in the Gur prayer house and were called the ten loafers, staying all the time in the Gur prayer house occupied with the Torah and the commandments. Let him be remembered forever by the townspeople of Sierpc.

The fire spread to the nearby houses, and the Jews there removed their belongings. No Jew slept that night. It was a terrible vigil.

One day – I'm continuing my father's story – the Germans went into Jewish houses and removed 40 boys between the ages of 16 and 20, kept them under arrest for a few days and then sent them to someplace unknown.

I also saw our other neighbors. Danielka the cantor and Kadetzki, without their beards. It was difficult to recognize them. The German commander would issue new edicts from time to time. Among them was an edict with eight clauses:

a) Jews are forbidden to walk on the pavement, only in the middle of the street.
b) A Jew, upon seeing a German, must remove his hat.
c) Every Jew must sew a yellow patch of material, 3 x 5 centimeters in size, on which the word "JUDE" is written.
d) Every Jew must submit a detailed report about his property: his money, his jewelry, his inventory, etc.
e) The Jews are forbidden to use electricity.
f) The Jewish community must pay 50,000 Zloty ransom.
g) In addition to the general 50,000 Zloty payment many families will receive notification to make individual payments.
h) The Jews must send 80 people every day for labor.
i) As for the first clause, how humiliated we were walking in the middle of the street. The Gentiles mocked us, and considered us beasts. Who walked in the middle of the street – horses, dogs, animals…

For the second, if a German passed on the pavement and the Jew didn't notice and take off his hat, or if he did take off his hat, in both cases he would be beaten. In the first case, the German would say "Why didn't you take off your hat?" In the second case the German would say, "What am I, your friend, that you doff your hat to me?"

Clause c): the piece of material could be obtained from the Jewish Community Center. The municipality supplied them at 10 pennies apiece. This was inspected by the *Volksdeutsch.*[8] Everyone above the age of 16 had to wear one.

Clause d): the Jews worked diligently: they tried to present detailed and accurate reports on all their properties, such as consumer goods and stores; they measured each piece of material to the last centimeter; they weighed every bit of food and made an exact count of every button. This was done out of fear that a German inspector would come and find an erroneous report, and they would be killed. But in the end, the Germans took everything without any inspection.

Because of Clause e), every Jewish house was dark. All the windows were covered with thick blankets, so that no sign of light could be seen outside. Inside, only a candle would be lit, because Jews were forbidden to use electricity, and there was no kerosene available.

As for Clause f), the Jewish community received a letter from the *Landrat*[9] that the Jews of Sierpc must collectively pay a ransom of 50,000 Zlotys. The community elders started collecting this amount. Everyone gave what he could, and within two days the amount was available. Nachum Tatz and Shmuel Zeinvil Dormbus went to pay the ransom. The clerks at the *Landrat* accepted receipt of the money in their way: kicking and shoving them out the door.

The community received reminders about Clause g) a few days after paying the above sum to the *Landrat.* That day, they had to pay huge individual ransoms. Each reminder had the exact amount, and the minimum was 200 Zlotys, with many reaching 1000 Zlotys. For the most part, they had no money at home, and could not pay on the stated date. Only a few managed to pay, so as not to fall into the hands of the accursed oppressors. The arrests began that evening; all those who didn't pay the required sums were put in jail. The jail was full of men from the Gestapo, experts at extorting money, who threatened everyone with hanging or the firing squad. It became like a market place: they asked everyone, "How much can you pay? No more than that?" In between blows, they would squeeze out the last penny. But there were Jews who did not have any money to give, and they remained in jail at night. Among them was Berish Poznanski. He was especially cruelly tortured; the Germans forced him to dig a pit in front of his house as deep as he was tall. When he finished digging, they threw him in there and filled it with dirt up to his neck, so that only his head was visible. They beat him so badly that it was impossible to distinguish between his face and the dirt. He was half dead when they took him out and released him.

Why did the Germans select Berish Poznanski in particular? Because he had signed the notes for the small coins that had been issued a few days before the German conquest.

As for Clause h), the stated number of workers who should show up for work, according to the agreement with the Gestapo, was 80. In spite of this, the *Volksdeutsch* went from house to house to get people for that labor, and also for other tasks, to load firewood, chop trees, clean rooms, and bring water, so that no one would get any rest. They would go through Jewish houses every day, opening closets and removing clothes, bedding, anything of value, also good furniture. They said that all this was for the Germans and their families who had come to live in Sierpc.

To them we were like animals, and they could do anything they wanted to us. Not only did they not expect any punishment for acts of cruelty against Jews, but the opposite: when they had a get-together, whoever could show that he had done something exceptionally bad to a Jew, which delighted the rest of them, would be promoted.

It is impossible to describe the suffering of the Jews of Sierpc. It was frightening to go outside to buy a loaf of bread or other provisions.

On market days, when the Gentiles would gather with their carts on Warshawska Street, or in Neier Mark, the Jews would try to sneak in between the carts and quickly buy potatoes, carrots, and other groceries that the peasants would bring to town for sale. But woe to the Jew who was caught performing such a "crime."

The Jews lived under these conditions for six weeks, without any income, in fear of torture, doing humiliating labor, among frightening rumors of what was happening in the nearby towns. We heard the story about Lipno. All the Jews there were removed from their homes and put into a large empty lot. The Germans told them that they were going on a long journey, to take their money and jewelry, to put on their best clothes (holiday apparel). Because they would not be returning, it would not be worthwhile leaving these things at home.

The Jews of Lipno listened and did as they were told. They went home and took out everything valuable, packed what they could, put on their best clothes, took their money and jewels with them, and went back to the same empty lot. But as soon as they were all ready for the journey, the Germans issued their order: to take off their clothes, shoes, boots, and furs, and put them all in one pile, and to put the money and jewelry into the box that had been placed in the lot. Whoever would not do that would be killed on the spot. Of course no one wanted to take any chances, and everyone obeyed. When they were all left in their underwear, they were sent home. This was in the winter, November, 1939.

Something similar happened in the town of Drobin. Jews who were walking in the street in nice clothes or shoes would have them removed by the Germans and would have to return home barefoot and in their underwear.

The Jews of Sierpc heard these rumors which, along with the conditions in town that became worse every day, reinforced the wish to run away, to find a sanctuary. But where? The youth started to consider the towns of Bialystok and Grodno, which the Russian army had taken over from the Poles[10]. These towns were the closest to the Polish border, and at that time it was possible to cross the border, since peace and amity reigned between Germany and Russia then.

But it was forbidden to be on a train without a special permit, especially for Jews. This permit could be obtained only at the *Landrat (Staroste)*. And the permit was only for travel to some town just inside the Russian-German border. After that, it was necessary to sneak across the border. In spite of the difficulties in getting such permits, there were some that managed to do it. Tens of young men and women packed their belongings in back packs, parted from their families, and started on their way. I also had a permit like that, but I didn't manage to use it. Apparently, Fate wanted me to be with my family and my townsmen on the day of deportation. Not many managed to get away, since the idea of finding sanctuary first occurred to people just a few days before the deportation.

We had heard about deportation, but we could not imagine it happening to us. Nobody believed in such a possibility. How could you, in the middle of winter, eject people, children, babies from their houses? Old people, women, invalids? Would a cultured German nation perform such an act? And what would the rest of the nations of the world say? Would the whole world remain silent? And not one nation would react to such an action? The Jews of Sierpc went to sleep on Tuesday evening, the last night before the deportation, with these thoughts on their minds.

On the morning of Wednesday, November 8, 1939, at six o'clock, the *Volksdeutsch* came, and woke us up with their loud screaming and yelling. "Every Jew must go outside to *Alter Mark Street*, and assemble near the *Magistrat*[11]. Everyone, without exception, dressed or not." When we asked where they were taking us, they answered, "To the land that you love, to the Land of Israel. The train is waiting for you. Hurry up before you miss this great opportunity!"

I can hear the crying and the wailing of the children and babies to this day, as they were awakened abruptly by their parents to take part in this procession. My ears are still full of the groans of the sick and elderly... The streets were full of Jews walking in the direction of *Alter Mark*. Many were in pajamas, because they hadn't had a chance to get dressed. There were those who had managed to get dressed, but wore old or torn clothes because they thought that the Germans were doing to us what they had done in the town of Lipno.

Torn and worn out, we left our houses for that place. We were arranged in rows of five according to families. At the head of the procession were the Poles of the Fire Department band, who were ready with their instruments. The parade started off to the railway station, accompanied by the band music: children, women, old people, and youths. Naked and destitute, depressed, broken, torn and worn, without a penny in their pockets, with dark faces and downcast eyes – because the Gentiles, our neighbors, accompanied us, laughing all the way, until the railway station. We were considered lambs going to the slaughter. If at that moment the earth had opened up and swallowed us all, we would have been grateful.

Those were our last steps in the streets of Sierpc. We abandoned our homes, our work, our places of worship, our schools. A few days before the deportation, many had deposited all their assets and belongings with Gentiles. They thought that this way they would be more secure, because the Germans never plundered anything from the Gentiles. They would hold onto it until the wrath had passed, that is until after the war or until German policies changed. So that at this moment of our departure from Sierpc, the Gentiles doubly rejoiced: first, that the Jews were being ejected from their homes; and second, because of the deposits that they would be able to hold onto forever.

*

We approached the train station. The band stopped at the entrance to the waiting-room, and did not stop playing until the last Jew had entered the railroad cars. These were freight cars. The doors closed, and we started to move.

The freight cars were tightly packed. We were over 100 people in cars that had standing room for 50, crowded like fish in a barrel of herring. People and children had to defecate in the cars, because the doors were closed, with seals on them. I cannot describe what we went through in these cars. We passed the towns of Racionz, Plonsk, and reached Punihovk, seven kilometers before Nowy Dwor. It was already 2:30 in the afternoon. We left the railway cars hungry and weary. Once again, they arranged us in rows of five, and we started on foot. We crossed a temporary bridge over the Narew River, and we thought that the Germans had brought us there to drown us. Because why should they bring us here if not for that purpose? We crossed the bridge in the dark. The *Volksdeutsch* searched our pockets and said that whoever would not give them all their cash and jewelry would be killed on the spot.

We walked the seven kilometers to Nowy Dwor because the train could not reach this village, since the railroad tracks had been destroyed by the bombings. We got to the village after dark, and the German guards left us. We were free for the night.

We spread out in the town to look for Jewish houses, because everyone was still at home. We were not chased out of there. The Jews took us in as brothers in misery. They did for us above and beyond what was necessary. They gave their beds and bed sheets to our children. They kept the tea boiling all night, and took the Sierpcer into their houses. They heated their stoves to make us warm and brought bread to all of us. But many remained sitting on the floors...and others in the cold or in the stairwells, because there was not enough room for all of us in their apartments. No one slept that night. Everyone was preoccupied with his own thoughts, what to do without a roof over one's head, without clothes, and without any money? Little children, babies, invalids, old people, what will become of them? --- The Germans had said specifically at the train station in Sierpc that whoever returned would be shot or hanged, and none of us dared to think about going back. That whole night I sat on the floor in the room together with my parents and thought about how to get out of this situation. In the end I decided to go back to Sierpc, enter our house, and take out whatever I could. My parents tried to convince me that I was endangering myself, but I insisted and explained to my father that in any case we were lost. Maybe I could, in spite of everything, save something from the house: clothing, winter garments, or a blanket, so that we would not freeze. When my father saw that he could not change my mind, he agreed, and said, "Son! I have one request of you. Do not forget to take my prayer shawl and phylacteries. They were all my life to me, and they will remain all my life until the day I die. Otherwise, I would never agree that you should return to Sierpc, and because of them you will be protected on your way and will be safe from the murderers. When you get to our house – the first items to take are my prayer shawl and phylacteries." Those were my father's words before I left him in Nowy Dwor on Thursday morning, November 9, 1939, as I parted from my parents for the second time, not knowing if we would ever see each other again.

I passed through the Jewish quarter and I saw the poverty and hardship of the Jews of Sierpc, sitting in courtyards, freezing, crying and moaning. The mothers held their children very close in order to warm them. The men were looking around helplessly. And I was walking nervously back towards Sierpc; I didn't want to think about what was to come. I had no other option. All of the Rozynek family was walking with me, and they were: Leib Rozynek, his wife and his daughters, Sara of blessed memory, and Miriam, today my wife, may she live a long life. They agreed with me and we walked together until we reached a German guard post near the bridge over the Narew River. We passed with difficulty after we managed to bribe them. Because this was the border. The area up until the Narew, on the Sierpc side, belonged to the Reich, and from the other side up to Warsaw it was part of the *Generalgouvernement*[12]. If we succeeded in crossing this border, we became residents of the Reich. There were some other towns that still had Jews, such as Neustadt, Nasielsk, Plonsk, Mlawa, and Ciechanów, and where it was possible to find places to stay and somehow manage to get along. The cost of living was less here than in the *Generalgouvernement*.

We came to Neustadt. The daughter of the Rozynek family of blessed memory, Tzirel, lived there. The parents stayed with their daughter, and Sarah, Miriam, and I went on and arrived in Sierpc on a horse cart. On the way, we heard that Sierpcer who were in Nowy Dwor had been sent to Warsaw.

We got to Sierpc through Vloki Street. There was no one to be seen on Warshawska and Vloki Streets. The Jewish quarter was completely empty. The houses were empty and the doors locked as we had locked them when we left. Every lock had a German seal on it.

Two or three *gendarmes* patrolled the streets to make sure that no one entered the houses. The Jewish property already belonged to the Nazi state.

Without too much hesitation we removed the seals with swastikas on them and entered our houses. I started to stuff everything I could find into sacks. I fulfilled my father's request the moment I started my labors. I took the prayer shawl and phylacteries, and did not think of the possible danger, because in any case I had nothing to lose. We were the first to take this step. While I was packing, the landlady, a Gentile, Kashtaln, came in and told me that the Gestapo was coming. My wife Miriam also saw that the Gestapo was coming towards our house through the window in her house, and ran to tell me. I quickly left our apartment and hid in the attic, and Miriam locked me in there from the outside. She had just managed to leave, and the Gestapo men came, searched the house, saw that the seal was missing, put on a new seal, and left.

I managed to take out three sacks full of clothes and other items, and sent them with a Gentile woman acquaintance to Warsaw, to my parents who were staying with my brother Aaron, who had been living in Warsaw since before the war. This was a great salvation for my parents: they had something to sell so that they could buy food.

After my great "crime," "stealing" from our own home, the three of us discussed what to do next, and how we could stay, in spite of everything, in our town. We decided that Sarah Rozynek would go to the *Landrat*, to try and get a permit for her father and his family to return to Sierpc as a professional, since they had a buckwheat mill. This was an essential resource, since buckwheat flour was necessary for the butchers to make sausages. They asked her many questions about how she had returned to Sierpc and gave her many beatings, but in the end she got a permit from the *Landrat*: the Rozynek family could come back to Sierpc to work in the mill, on the condition that they not leave their home, so they would not be seen wandering around town. Otherwise, they would come to a bitter end. Leib Rozynek and his family returned to Sierpc and did their work there for a few weeks without leaving their house, because a) It was forbidden for them to go out and b) There was no one to go and visit. There was no other Jew in town. All you could see on Warshawska Street were two Gestapo guards walking around. The new *beit midrash* was closed. The Torah scrolls and other holy books were strewn about, on the floor. The curtain of the Holy Ark was ripped: total ruin had befallen the new *beit midrash*! Yehoshua Goldman no longer sat there studying the daily Talmud page. Avraham Wluka no longer stood there praying the *Shmone Esrei* [Eighteen Benedictions] longer than any other worshipper. (That was Avraham Wluka's custom.) And Avraham Wluka no longer studied the *Ein Yaakov*[13] every day between the afternoon and evening prayers with a *minyan*[14] of worshippers, who would sit on the wooden benches near the stove in winter.

So we sat in the house and looked out at the empty building and remembered old times, and our hearts shrank; the sanctity, the radiance, the magnificence, lost forever. Everything destroyed.

We decided that there was no place for Jews anymore in this town, and we left for Neustadt, to the Rozynek daughter Tzirel, who had lived there since before the war.

During the time that we stayed in Sierpc, a few families returned from the deportation. They had no other choice even if they were risking their lives. Slowly their number climbed to about 150 souls. The Germans knew about this, but pretended not to care. Because they needed servants and artisans.

In this way, the returnees managed to stay in their houses, worked at all sorts of odd tasks and simple labors, and stayed legally in the town – they received identity cards up to a certain date. But any more Jews who would arrive after that date were liable for the death penalty. The Germans conducted a census, and found that there were 150 Jewish souls. Thus the Jews lived in the town; they were only allowed to live in the Ghetto, which was defined as the area between the Great Walled House (Kamnitza) and the houses of Tcharnobrodna, Dentus, Zhitalni, and a few other houses which were on the street of the Tcharnobrodna house on the way to the Lankes. The Jews went to work every day, swept the streets, worked at gardening, and at all sorts of menial tasks. There was a yellow Star of David with "Jew" written on it on the front and back of their clothes. Theirs was a difficult situation since they didn't earn much from their work, but existed by selling items such as their clothes, and so forth. Food was not expensive, so they were able to get along somehow. A "*Judenrat*," a committee of Sierpc Jews was set up to represent the Jews. There was also someone that was responsible to the German authorities to ensure that no more Jews would come to town. The members of the committee were: Mendel Lis and Yaakov Pukacz. These Jews could help their families that were in Warsaw, where there was great famine. They sent them food packages by mail, and with all sorts of opportunities that arose. But the Jews of Sierpc did not remain in the town for very long. In 1942 the Jews of Sierpc were banished by the Nazis to the town of Stezhgovo (where there was an enclosed and very crowded ghetto; my brother Avraham Chayim of blessed memory and his family were also among those expelled to Stezhgovo.)

The Sierpcers in Warsaw

The refugees from Sierpc arrived in Warsaw on November 9, 1939, two days after the deportation from Sierpc, by rail from Nowy Dwor. The journey was under German supervision on a special train for the Jews of Sierpc that left Nowy Dwor guarded by the *Volksdeutsch*. When they arrived at the train station in Warsaw, the Germans told them that they were free, and could go anywhere they wanted, but not to return to Sierpc. The few refugees that had relatives or acquaintances in Warsaw moved in with them that very same day. The majority stayed on the streets of Warsaw, outdoors, in the bitter cold of that winter. Thanks to the Joint[15] which was active in Warsaw at the time, the Sierpc refugees were housed in *batei midrash*, schools, warehouses, and the like. Conditions were very bad. There were no beds or minimal furniture. But at least they were not outdoors in the snow that covered their clothes and the dampness that permeated their flesh. Their worry now was: Where could you lie down? What could you cover yourself with at night? Where to find some warm food for the hungry children? Within two days, the Joint set up a communal kitchen and prepared hot soup for all the Sierpc refugees. Every person received coupons for meals and bread. A committee of three Sierpcers was appointed by the Joint and they received some old clothes and warm bedding to distribute to the neediest. And who didn't need these things at this time? All those in Warsaw were equal in wealth and condition. All were in the same despairing and gloomy circumstances. It goes without saying that the food rations of the Joint were not enough. Also the little clothing that they received was not enough to keep the hungry and sleepless warm. The famine spread among the refugees from Sierpc, and everyone asked, "From where will our salvation come?" Everyone tried very hard to recall if they had friends or acquaintances in Warsaw who could help them. A few found some, and managed. The rest remained in their place. We called this place *punkt* – the spot. As best as I can remember, remaining in these spots were Meir Zashutke and his family, Binyamin Sobol and his wife Sarah, Shaul Grappa and his family, Avraham Groda and his family, and others. Binyamin and Sarah Sobol became confused because of the hunger. They wandered the streets and begged. Binyamin would tell everyone: "Whoever will lend me one Zloty, I will pay him back one dollar after the war."

It was impossible to recognize these people anymore. They had changed terribly. Who doesn't remember Binyamin Sobol, a Jew who always contributed generously and willingly to anyone who asked him, and to all kinds of institutions and funds without thought of politics? Even before the fund raisers arrived, Binyamin already had his hand in his pocket, ready to take out a coin, and his wife Sarah always kept an open house for the poor. The needy would be found every day, sitting at her table and dining. How many poor brides she married off! She used her own money to have wedding feasts for them, and sewed the bridal clothes, and arranged a place for them to live after the wedding, with kitchen utensils and other necessities.

Reb Yossel Shochet[16] Eisenstat, was also in Warsaw with his daughter Coca, his son-in-law, and his grandson. They lived with his brother David Eisenstat, the *dirigant* – conductor – at the great Synagogue Tlumaczka. It is good that they had a place to rest. But where could a Jew like that earn some money? There was no need for ritual slaughtering. I saw him often on the streets of Warsaw, depressed, despairing, and hungry. He told me that he prayed as a cantor and received a pittance. Sometime later, Shmuel Yitzhak Tac told me that Yossel Shochet went to pray on Rosh Hashanah carrying his prayer shawl and collapsed and died on Mornovska Street.

Reb Yossel Shochet was a Jew who was liked by everyone. He was a learned scholar and an excellent prayer leader. He had a sweet and pleasant voice. When he was praying in front of the Holy Ark in the old *beit midrash*, his voice could be heard in all of Warshawska Street (the Jewish Street). During the High Holy Days, the old *beit midrash* was very crowded, because many people came to hear Rev Yossel pray with his choir – his two sons, Ezriel and Leibush, Henich Lopatka, Aaron Kanenbrand, and others.

I also saw Nahum Tatz of blessed memory and his family in Warsaw. His son Henich lost his life when a building on Graniczna Street collapsed. The building had been destroyed by bombs, and Henich, who could not find any other place to stay, found some shelter there. But one day the walls buckled and Henich was buried beneath the ruins. He was a young man, and he used to sit day and night in the prayer house of the Gur Hasidim studying Torah for its own sake. He died a few days after the refugees from Sierpc came to Warsaw.

His son Yaakov did not remain in Warsaw. He walked in the direction of Russia, and crossed the German-Russian border. The rest of his family went to the town of Grójec, where his son Ezra lived.

The second victim was Eli Moshe Tzcernobroda, the son of Henich. A typhus epidemic broke out soon after he arrived in Warsaw. The disease spread because of the crowding, bad hygienic conditions, and poor nutrition. Eli Moshe was a religious youth, twenty-five years old. He came down with typhus, and died after a few days. (His sisters Libe and Fraidel were with him, together with their husbands.)

The typhus epidemic spread through the Jewish quarter in general and, in particular, among the Sierpc townspeople, who lived under the worst conditions. Yehoshua Goldman and Meir Zashutke died at that time. Yehoshua Goldman died in his apartment in Warsaw on 42 Mornovska Street. He was already feeling very bad at the time of the deportation from Sierpc. I can remember that I saw him getting on the train in the Sierpc station with his face covered by a bandana to hide the beard that he had managed to save from the savage Nazi barbers who would pull out the hair of the beards of our townspeople. Leibl Kremzh also died. Reb Leibl used to spend long days in the old *beit midrash*, winter and summer, studying Torah.

Death took away Meir Zashutke who lived in the synagogue on Mila Street together with his family and his son Yosef. The cold and hunger vanquished him as well.

The Sierpc community in Warsaw was shrinking from day to day. Every day we heard about a new victim. Old and young, weak and strong, all were equal. It was difficult to recognize people, some of whom were swollen from hunger. Their clothes were torn because the good clothes had been sold to buy a little bread or a bowl of thin warm soup that was sold in the streets of the Jewish quarter of Warsaw. Among the unfortunate were the rabbi of Sierpc, Yehoshua Heshel David Goldschlak and his family. They arrived in Warsaw from Lodz, where they had stayed with their son Eliyahu. When the Germans closed the Lodz Ghetto, they managed to flee to Warsaw. There was a rumor that the tabbi's wife had lost her mind because on the way from Lodz the Germans had searched their clothes and taken everything, not even leaving them a loaf of bread. The rabbi worked for the Joint; he was the representative of the Sierpc refugees and did a great deal for his townsmen. He would rush every day to various institutions trying to improve the conditions of the refugees. He took off the clothes of office that he had worn in Sierpc and visited almost every place where there were Sierpcers to comfort them. He also visited my father a few times to console him. He said, "In a little while the war will be over, and we will be rid of these hateful Germans."

The Rabbi was well known in Warsaw as an important and honored personage. When my father died in 1941 on the first day of Tammuz, the Rabbi came and said that he would try to get the *Hevra Kadisha*[17] to provide a separate grave for him. They were burying 50 to 100 corpses together in the cemetery on Ganesha Street. They would place them one on top of the other and close the grave immediately, to prevent epidemics. The Rabbi said that Reb Kalman deserved his own grave because of his piety and complete faith all his life. And the Rabbi succeeded in finding a separate grave for my father of blessed memory.

The young men were afraid to walk in the streets because the Germans would take them and send them to work camps. I was caught one day by a Gestapo man while walking on Mila Street near Nalewki Street. I felt a sudden kick from behind, and when I turned around, I saw a German murderer with a dog. He ordered me to climb onto the truck that had stopped nearby. The dog started to leap at me, and I, as if carried by the wind, jumped onto the vehicle. Tens of victims who had been captured before me were sitting there. The truck was moving and I was full of worries – how would my family know where I was and what happened to me? Like a miracle from heaven, I saw the daughter of the attorney Tzadok Bluman passing by. I managed to shout to her, "Blumanova! Shirkowska 4, Maishkania 25." She heard my address and informed my parents where I was being taken. Because it was well known in Warsaw that whoever was caught in the truck with the dog would be brought to the Palanti Gestapo camp. This camp would release only those who became sick.

There were a few hundred young Jews in this camp. We did not do any productive work there, and it brought no benefits to the Germans. It was there only to harass and occupy young Jews. For half the day we cleaned the disgustingly filthy toilets in the camp. We would go down to the pit in our clothes and shoes and take out the feces with our hands. One would hand it to the next... A chain of people stood there for half a day doing this work. For the second half of the day, a few Gestapo men would come to look for victims they could beat. They looked for sick people to release, but before releasing them they would give them a horrendous thrashing. Here I found Ephraim Zilberberg. He had come to Sierpc from Warsaw in 1929 and had married the daughter of Hirsh Moshe Kanenbrand of blessed memory. He was a very learned Jew and for the ten years that he lived in Sierpc, he would sit in the old *beit midrash* studying Torah. On Saturdays before the afternoon prayer, he would study Pirkei Avot[18] or a *midrash*[19]. On Saturdays he would quiz pupils from Yesodai HaTorah on the Bible and Rashi[20] and Gemara[21]. He was loved by the people of Sierpc. One Saturday evening in the camp, I saw a group of people in the courtyard of the camp, and in the center was a man whose face was covered with a handkerchief to hide his beard, holding a cup of tea and saying the *Havdala*[22] benediction. I came closer, and I recognized him: Ephraim Zilberberg, who had seriously endangered himself by this act. I went up to him and asked him why he imperiled himself in this way. He answered that he didn't care! They could do with him what they wanted, in any case we were lost, and whatever was needed to live – let it be.

We were this way for six weeks, with a feeling that at least we were with one townsman in this time of troubles. Our relatives did not know anything about us. They would go from place to place trying to find out where we were, and what had happened to us. They had heard that I was in Palanti, but there was no way they could get there.

One day the Germans brought 25 bearded Yeshiva students. They had taken them out in the middle of their studies. For the whole day, they did that revolting work: cleaning the toilets.

But the boys bravely accepted their bitter fate. They sang as they worked, in spite of the fact that half their clothes were covered with feces, and their hands were filthy up to their upper arms. They lived on dry bread and water, but would not give in to the conditions in the camp. They were joyful and happy, and their behavior comforted us a little.

*

We were jailed for six weeks in that camp, until we became sick and were released. The situation in Warsaw became worse every day, and the cost of living rose. A kilo loaf of black bread cost eight Zloty (the price during normal times had been twenty pennies). A kilogram of potatoes was four to six Zloty (usually four pennies). A kilogram of coal was a Zloty (usually five pennies). All the other food prices had increased a hundred fold, and people could not afford them because they did not earn any money. There was not enough cash, even at the lower prices, to buy foodstuffs. The ghetto was extremely crowded. There were a million Jews in the Warsaw Ghetto. People would fall in the streets like flies. Dead bodies would be lying on the sidewalk, covered with sheets of paper because the carts carrying the corpses could not manage to collect them. There were people whose job it was to roam the streets and cover the dead bodies. It was difficult to identify many of the dead because there were refugees from many towns who had no relatives. Nobody searched for them or asked after them. They were buried without names and without count, 40 to 100 in a grave, and covered with lime.

There was a lot of food for sale in the streets, but it was very expensive. How did the food get to the ghetto? In all sorts of ways. The Jews who left the ghetto to work outside (under guard) would leave with all sorts of items for sale. The Gentiles who would come to their workplace would bring food for barter. Or Jews would leave the ghetto, bribe the guard at the gate, buy food, pack it in bags or suitcases, get on the trolley, and when it passed through the ghetto would jump off because it was forbidden for passengers to get off in the ghetto. The policeman and conductor were bribed. The policeman always stood at the exit to prevent any Jew from going into the ghetto, but if a Jew with packages had to get off, the policeman would move aside and look the other way. The conductor also slowed the trolley at this moment. This was how commerce was carried on all the time that the ghetto existed. It's not surprising that the goods were very expensive, since many people had to profit on each item that was brought into the ghetto. There were other ways of sneaking food into the ghetto. Like over the roofs of houses that bordered Gentile houses. Or through the cellars of houses that were near Gentile houses. They dug tunnels which were wide enough to even allow passage of carts. Whoever had a cellar like this was assured an income and food as well. Or Jews would leave the ghetto and arrange with Gentiles that at a certain time, on a certain street, to toss some bags of food from a trolley passing through the ghetto. Their fees would be paid ahead of time, and the Jews would wait for the trolley at the designated time and place. However, many times the Germans would confiscate these goods.

There were many temporary kitchens in the streets, where soup, tea, and coffee would be boiled. A few pennies would be enough to buy a bowl of soup or tea, but most people didn't even have a few pennies. My father, of blessed memory, never bought from these kitchens, because he didn't think they were kosher. People ridiculed him, saying that in these times there was no point in keeping kosher. But he insisted on it; it was preferable that he die of hunger rather than defile his body with food whose *kashrut* was in doubt. My mother, of blessed memory, did the same.

The Germans did not prevent the Jews from listening to news of the world. They hung loudspeakers on lampposts and broadcast the news in German a few times a day – about their victories. The loudspeakers were also used to announce new edicts and laws.

Everything in the ghetto was run by Jewish policemen, in accordance with the German orders to the head of the Jewish police. The second authority was the Polish police. Near every gate there were three policemen: one Jew, one Pole, and one German. At many places there were just a Jew and a Pole. The height of the brick wall of the ghetto was three meters. There was a gate at those places where the trolley went through. But there were places where the whole width of the street was blocked by a fence with broken glass and all kinds of obstacles strewn along the top of the wall, which made it impassable. Many Gentiles wandered around on the other side of the wall and made a living out of catching Jews who left the ghetto: they would hold them and say, "Either pay me a ransom or I will take you to the *gendarmes*." The Poles were responsible for the death of three million Jews in Poland. They caused us much more harm than the Germans. All the ovens and crematoriums were built in their country. Only the Poles agreed to this.

The Poles, from the smallest to the biggest, from the intellectual to the simple peasant, from the politically right to the left, brought destruction to the Jews. Young Polish men, who could recognize who was a Jew better than the Germans, would shout, "That's a Jew." Jews that escaped the ghetto and looked for shelter would be caught by boys and turned over to the Germans.

There were those that wanted to escape the ghetto in order to save their lives, but they hesitated and stayed in the ghetto because of the fear that they would be caught by the Gentiles and turned over to the Gestapo. I left the ghetto in 1941 with my wife, and sensed this very well. As soon as we managed to go through the gate at four in the morning, there were many Gentiles around us. But the dark and the cold hampered them in recognizing us as Jews. They chased us until the train station (Gdańska), but we were not wearing the blue and white ribbon, and we managed to evade them, to our good fortune. The Sierpcer Yehezkel Stari took us out of the ghetto. He would take Jews from the ghetto to small towns: Plonsk, Nowy Dwor, and Mlawa. He would cross the Narew River twice a week with people. He knew the roads, and how to bribe the policemen at the gates of the ghetto. He took people out of Warsaw over a long period of time, and on the way back he would bring groceries, meat, and butter. In the end, he was captured by the Germans. I heard that a Pole informed on him. He was arrested and sent to a concentration camp,

*

It took about two years to set up the camps and crematoriums for the mass destruction of the Jews.

The Germans even laid railway tracks to these places, which until then had been forests. They paved roads for automobiles, so they would have easy access to the places of destruction. And I want to emphasize again that the Poles were complicit in every way in this mass destruction in their country and their houses. Many Poles stole money from the Jews, robbed them of everything and killed them. They slaughtered them with knives and murdered them with axes. Polish houses were decorated with carpets and filled with furniture that belonged to Jews; many wore their clothes.

I will mention one fact here out of many: At Auschwitz we started to organize an underground before the revolt. Because the camp had prisoners from all nations, we had to have an underground meeting of Russians, Poles, and Jews. I remember that the Poles were against having the Jews participate in this meeting, and didn't come to it. The Russians said that in this sort of camp you could not discriminate because of religion and race, and insisted that the Jews participate. The Poles couldn't rid themselves of their hatred of the Jews even in the death camp. (I could fill a book about how the Poles treated the Jews in the concentration camps.) That is why so few were left out of a population of three and a half million. The Jews were flushed out of holes and cracks and all sorts of hiding places where the Germans wouldn't have thought of looking. But the Poles collaborated with the murderers.

*

Jews from all over Poland were forced to construct the death camps, without knowing why they were doing it. The Jewish laborers were held in enclosed camps near their work place. They would go to work every day, and no one thought that the quarters they were building would be places of annihilation, that they themselves would be put inside the electrified fences they were erecting, and never leave.

The Jewish laborers did not have much time for thought. They were busy working at a fast pace from morning till evening. There was little food, and punishment was harsh, the discipline of concentration camps. No one thought, in those two years, that the Germans would implement the mass extermination that they did. We presumed that they would disperse the Jews to all the conquered countries. We would be forced to do hard labor, locked up in concentration camps, tortured, separated from our families, and so forth. But no one could imagine what actually happened. And I, who passed through all the gates of hell, until today sometimes think it must have been a horrible nightmare, and not the terrible reality.

*

During this period, the Germans set up ghettos in a few towns in Poland in the vicinity of Sierpc, such as (Mlawa) Strzegowo, Plonsk, Ciechanów, Nowy Dwor, and Neustadt. All these towns belonged to the German Reich, including Lodz, Warsaw, Piotrków, and Czestochowa. In other towns where there were Jewish communities, they were wiped out and the Jews deported to these towns, where there were ghettos. The Germans did this to make their secret plan easier, and so that the Jews would be living under such conditions that they would be depressed and broken in body and spirit, so that there l would be no rebellion during the "operation." Not a hair would be mussed on any German when the victims would be taken to the crematoriums. Their leaders did not have to be brave or seasoned and experienced fighters. They just had to wear S.S. or Gestapo uniforms, even without weapons, as the Jewish hordes were hastened to the railway cars. The main thing was to put an end to these lives, lives of fear and panic, starvation, humiliation, and depression.

The Sierpcer Jews in Warsaw became fewer every day. The last Jews of Sierpc that remained until the expulsion of the Jews from Warsaw were the family of Mendel Lipchitz of blessed memory, the son of Yehonatan Lipchitz of blessed memory and his family, and his sister-in-law, Sarah Rozynek of blessed memory. About two thousand Sierpc Jews, of blessed memory, lost their lives in the Warsaw Ghetto between November 9, 1939 and the end of 1942.

Now something about the ghettos in the vicinity of Sierpc: On September 1, 1942, the Jews who remained in Sierpc were expelled to the Strzegowo Ghetto. The ghetto was very small, with few residences, but with many people, about 3,000 souls. There were no sources of income. Sanitary conditions were bad, and the crowding was great, and a typhus epidemic raged. Every house had a patient. The Jews had no medicines; the Angel of Death cut people down left and right, victims on top of each other. The Sierpcers, who lived under worse conditions than the Strzegowons, fell like flies. These were the remnants of the Sierpcers, who stayed put after the general deportation in November, 1939.

They did forced labor every day, without receiving any compensation. Their living conditions were terrible. They had no income, and were despondent and depressed. No complete family was left. They were all scattered and isolated, without any contact among them. They were despised by Gentile neighbors, living in fear of tomorrow, of the future, in a state of shock from news of the other ghettos about the state of Jews there, hanged and killed by the Nazis. But you could not compare their conditions to those here in the Strzegowo Ghetto, where they didn't have a place to rest their heads, without a penny to buy a slice of bread, and nowhere to heat a little water for their children. If it was difficult for them in Sierpc before the expulsion, it was now far worse. Despair in the full sense of the word.

I will mention here Avraham Wluka of blessed memory, his daughter Sheine Rivkah and her husband Moshe Kadecka of blessed memory, who were also in the Strzegowo Ghetto. Avraham Wluka, who was known affectionately in Sierpc as Reb Avrahmel, was liked by all the Jews of Sierpc. He was a very wise Jew, and many would come to consult with him, both Jews and Gentiles. He was a learned man, studied Torah by himself and with others in the new *beit midrash*, where he was a treasurer and a prayer leader during the High Holy Days and holidays. He was the standard bearer of the new *beit midrash*, a philanthropist, and he gave encouragement to all those who came to him with aching hearts. Many of the townspeople who came to pour their hearts out to Reb Avrahmel left comforted after talking to him. He was a religious Jew, enlightened, modest and moderate, with very many good qualities, and good-hearted. I never saw him become annoyed or angry. When the Nazis burned down the great synagogue in town, they grabbed Reb Avrahmel and told him to sign a detailed statement, that he had set fire to the synagogue with his own hands. They destroyed him by doing this, mortally wounding him, with no chance of recovery. The Nazis deliberately chose him to sign such a declaration. From then on, it was impossible to recognize him. He would walk around despondent and apathetic. He who all his life had rejoiced in the joy of his townsmen, and who sympathized with all their troubles, saw their suffering in the Strzegowo Ghetto and wanted to help, but could do nothing since he and his family were living under the same conditions. Those were the last years of Reb Avrahmel. May his memory be blessed forever.

Avraham Chayim, my oldest brother, was also in the Strzegowo Ghetto with his family. His wife died of typhus and left four small children. Eli Leib, a small child and the son of my sister Sarah, also died of typhus.

There were new edicts every day in the Strzegowo Ghetto. One day they took 20 young Jews and imprisoned them (there was a jail in the ghetto), and held them without food until they themselves asked to be put to death. After a few days, they gathered all the Jews in an empty lot, prepared gallows for the twenty youths, and the whole community was forced to be present at their hanging. Among them were five from Sierpc, and these were: Toviah Zhitalni, Ephraim Yosef Lelonek, Leib Grosman, Yehezkel Fasa, and M. Lipski.

There were also a few Sierpc Jews in the town of Mlawa, but living under conditions slightly better than those in the Strzegowo Ghetto. This town also had a ghetto, and here too they hanged Jews in the presence of all the ghetto residents. There was gunfire into the assembled onlookers, and they had to wear a patch on their clothes, a yellow Star of David on the back and on the chest, and do hard labor every day. In addition to the Jews of Mlawa, there were also Jews from many other towns that had been expelled from their dwellings and found shelter with relatives and acquaintances in this ghetto.

In comparison with other ghettos, conditions here were good. The chairman of the *Judenrat* was Ramek, and he knew very well how to bribe the *Landrat* and all the German institutions in town. The Jews lived in the ghetto, but it was tolerable. The ghetto had Jews from Sierpc, Lipno, Rypin, Racionz, Dobrzyń, and other towns. Wolf Visroza, Yitzhak Meir Rusak, the daughters of Mendel Gurfinkel, Motil Garbarczik, Zalman Beria (Friedman), the daughter of Reb Naftali Liebson, and Shmuel Wluka and his family, the son of Reb Avrahmel. He worked as a clerk in the *Judenrat.* His job was *arbeitsdienst* – he would take care of allocating the labor. People wanted a day's labor, because they would be paid for it. He helped many Sierpcers to find work.

I met Fogel, the son-in-law of Naftali Liebson, in February, 1941. He told me that the wife of Yitzchak Meir Sendrowicz left the Warsaw Ghetto on her way to Plonsk and froze to death between Legionowo and Jablonna. He obtained a travel permit from the *Landrat* to go there and arrange the burial of his aunt in a Jewish grave.

A short time later, Fogel was sent to a concentration camp, to Auschwitz, because he became engaged in public affairs. He sent a letter to America and wrote about what was happening in Poland in general and in the towns in the region. The letter was intercepted by the Germans and for this he was sent to Auschwitz. His wife, the daughter of Naftali Liebson, received a box of ashes a few days later, together with the clothes of her husband of blessed memory.

I heard of something that happened in Plonsk in October, 1939. A Gestapo officer, who always rode on horseback, once entered the synagogue on his horse, took out his pistol, and fired into the Holy Ark, and said, "Here I am, shooting your God!" Immediately after this, he went out to the Plonsk-Neustadt Road. A German army truck struck him head-on and killed him.

*

The Plonsk Ghetto was fenced in: in some places with wooden slats and in others with barbed wire. It was forbidden to leave the ghetto, but in spite of this people came and went, and everyone was more or less able to make a living. The ghetto had a Jewish administration including police, a court, a jail, a hospital, and Jewish doctors. The aforementioned Ramek was called *der Judenkenig*[23]. All the small towns such as Neustadt, Sochocin, Nowy Dwor, that had ghettos belonged to Plonsk, to *der Judenkenig.* Ramek had an armband on his right sleeve that said *Judenälteste*[24]. As far as I know, he treated the Jews humanely.

There were Sierpcers in Neustadt – Nowe Miasto – before there was a ghetto there. The names of the Sierpcer that were in Neustadt: Popowski and his family, Hersh Asch and his sister, Yaakov Grosman, Leib Rozynek and his wife, my wife and I. We left the town every day to do forced labor, without any pay. But food stuffs were cheap. All the Sierpcers in all the towns I have mentioned were illegals, without identity cards from those places, because we were all already assigned to the city of Warsaw, to the *Generalgouvernement*, where we had been deported. All the residents of the above towns had German documents with fingerprints, and we, the Sierpcers, were there like uninvited guests. The Germans knew very well that there were illegals in these towns, but they waited patiently and prepared the following operation: one morning in May 1941, at six in the morning, they took all the Jews out of their homes, in all the towns. All those without identification cards stood on one side, and all those with identification cards on the other. Murderous blows rained down on everyone; practically no one missed getting his "portion." Horse carts of farmers from neighboring villages were waiting outside of town, conscripted for this purpose, to take the illegal Jews to an unknown place, and again deported. But this time it was even worse than the first deportation. All the Sierpcers in these places that I have mentioned were among the deportees. My wife and I managed to evade this deportation. We had heard that the deportees had been assembled in a lot outside of Plonsk that was enclosed by a barbed wire fence. Entry was through a gate, and at the entrance stood two Gestapo men with big clubs who hit everyone who entered in the head. Blood flowed, and there were puddles of blood in the lot. The prisoners remained that way, in the open, for two days, without food and water, and no one was allowed to approach them. Many died from the murderous blows they received, covered in blood, without any medical help.

On the third day they took all the prisoners to the Modlin Fortresses, which are near Nasielsk. There were about 3,000 of them. The guards were *Volksdeutsch* and they did whatever they wanted with the Jews. They searched everyone, removed watches, rings, and so forth. During the day, they went through the rooms, singled out young women and ordered them to sleep on a certain side of the room so that they would be able to take them out at night without searching for them (it was dark at night). At midnight, the *Volksdeutsch* entered and took them to hill of the fortresses, and raped them. After that, they shot and killed them. This went on every night. Their excuse was that the girls wanted to escape from the camp, so they had to shoot them...

The prisoners lived that way for a few days, without food or drink. It was very hot, and they slept on the floors, crowded together, next to each other. They were all filthy. They couldn't even wash their faces because there was no water, until a typhus epidemic broke out, and people fell like flies. The guards wouldn't let them lie down. Everyone had to get up at six in the morning, and lying down was forbidden during the day, so our brethren walked around with high fever like drunkards. There was no one to take care of them; they were isolated from the whole world. No one could get to this camp. Even *Judenälteste* Ramek did not know where the wretched souls were.

Only a few days later did we learn that all the deportees were in the Modlin Fortresses, and their situation was awful. A few of us gathered in the town of Neustadt and decided that three men would travel there with food for our brothers. I and two others received a travel permit from the *burgermeister*[25], and hired a horse and carriage. We took about one hundred loaves of bread, and went to see if we could succeed in distributing them to the hungry for the first time, after a fast of six days. We were not allowed to enter the camp, and were stopped just outside of it. The first to recognize me was Wolf Grappa, and he yelled, "Arpa, give bread, I'm starving to death!" The rest of the people there, when they heard the name Arpa, even if they didn't know me, shouted as if in one voice, "Arpa, give bread!" They all rushed to the gate, shouting, yelling, an inhuman wailing: "Bread, bread, we are dying of hunger and thirst."

The three of us stood there as if glued to the ground. We didn't know what to do. And we said to one another, is this reality, or are we dreaming a nightmare?

We went to the gate to distribute the bread, but this was impossible. One was pushing the other. A whirlpool of people, the guards hitting them on the head with their rifles, blood flowing like water. We very much regretted having caused this situation. But the Germans, who enjoyed seeing panic and quarrels among the prisoners, took the loaves of bread from us, and said, "We will distribute the bread." And what did they do? They threw the bread into the crowd. Anyone who succeeded in catching a loaf was jumped upon by a mob, and everyone pinched a piece off the loaf. That was how the distribution ended. After that, we were ordered to get out of there.

We went home to Neustadt and called an emergency meeting of some of the townspeople, and we decided to bring a few hundred more loaves of bread the next day. These would be wrapped in paper with a name on each package, and we would call people by name to the gate, so that everyone could come and receive a package. And if the bread was already inside the camp, the people would share it among themselves. We did this, and succeeded in getting a few hundred loaves of bread into the camp.

On the third day, we collected about thirty barrels in the town. Every Jewish home boiled some dry potatoes. A few families cooked cherry soup. They brought the dishes at the appointed time, and put them into the barrels. We hired carts and horses, and brought them to the camp. This time there was more order to the food distribution, also because they weren't as hungry. We did this for a few days, and there wasn't a need to bring more food, just tea, because the people were sick, and they couldn't eat. So we brought more tea in the same barrels.

As I mentioned above, there was a wakeup call at six in the morning, and no lying on the floor during the day. Everybody had to walk around. Whoever lay down and couldn't get up was shot. Many were killed in this way. My brother-in-law, Lemel Zashutke was also shot there. The situation became worse from day to day. Everyone was sick with typhus. About a thousand people died in two weeks. There was no one to turn to. When we spoke to the *Burgermeister*, he would send a note to the *Landrat*, and the *Landrat* would send it to the commandant of the Gestapo. Everyone answered that they didn't know of any such camp, and it wasn't his business. This was how the people stayed there for six weeks!

We were in constant contact with *der Judenkenig* Ramek, and looked for ways to get the people out of their troubles. We also contacted the *Judenälteste* of the town of Mlawa. His name was Perlmutter, and he had some influence with the *Landrat* of his town.

First we managed to get one Jew out of the camp. His name was Melech from the town of Nowy Dwor. He helped the Germans and informed on Jews who had silver or gold. He also helped the Germans to select young women, and so forth. We took him out of the camp, brought him to the Plonsk Ghetto, and locked him in the jail. He came to a bitter end. Every Jew would go into the jail, and hit him with a rock, until he begged to be killed. When Gestapo men came to visit him, Melech told them that if the Gestapo rescued him from the Jews, he would tell them many secrets about the Jews. But they ignored him, because they had been bribed. In the end they injected him with a fatal injection, and buried him standing up with his head down and feet up.

He was the only Jew in these ghettos that acted that way.

After six weeks, the people who were still alive in this camp were sent to the Warsaw Ghetto. They numbered 1,200 out of the original 3,000 souls. There were many Sierpcers among them. Some had died in that place and the rest were stuck in the hell of the Warsaw Ghetto. That was in the summer of 1941. But not all remained in the Warsaw Ghetto, but returned to the towns from which they had been expelled, where they had family or friends. Hungry people do not think of the consequences of acting illegally. The hunger overcomes the fear, and even a death sentence does not deter. But they succeeded this time. The Germans did not carry out any more searches in the above towns. Apparently, the plan for mass extermination was already complete in the German government offices, and they pretended not to see or know anything. In general, many restrictions were eased, such as: providing more food rations; if a Jew was caught outside the Ghetto, he would be turned over to the Jewish police, and so forth. But we never forgot that we were inside the vise of Nazi rule.

That was what life was like in these ghettos until September, 1942, and we thought it would stay that way until the end of the World War. But one day we started to feel as if there were a fire burning beneath us. We heard rumors that the Germans were taking ten thousand people a day out of the Warsaw Ghetto, putting them on trains, and sending them to an unknown destination.

There were a million Jews in the Warsaw Ghetto from various towns. Their terrible living conditions were already well known. One day, the head of the Jewish community in Warsaw, Czerniaków, was summoned to the Governor-General Franco, who was based in Krakow. It was said that the two knew each other, having studied together at schools of higher learning for a few years before the war. Franco, an S.S. man, demanded that Engineer Czerniaków bring ten thousand people from the ghetto every day to a gathering place near the railway station to Gdansk, *zum Umschlagplatz*[26], and they were not to take much baggage, up to a maximum of ten kilograms. Engineer Czerniaków asked, "Where are you taking them?" The answer was "To workplaces." But he understood what their purpose was from the answer. Czerniaków answered that he could not agree to this on his own, because there were other community leaders. He would go back to Warsaw, arrange a meeting and tell them of the order he was given. When he came back to Warsaw, he met with all the community leaders and told them why he had been summoned to Governor-General Franco. He also gave them his opinion that he had no doubt that the Germans were starting a mass slaughter of the Jews of Warsaw, and that he would never agree to hand over even one Jew to the Germans. After he finished, he asked for a glass of water, swallowed some poison pills, and died on the spot. He chose death over sending Jews to the gas chambers or other places of extermination.

But the Germans were not frightened or influenced very much by the suicide of the head of the community. They gave an order to the Jewish police in the ghetto to bring the above number of Jews to the above mentioned location, and the operation started to be carried out by the Jewish police. Without being forced to, people started to arrive at the *Umschlagplatz* early in the morning because the loudspeakers in the streets announced that every passenger would receive a kilogram of bread, jam, and half a kilogram of sugar. How delighted these people were upon hearing that they would receive such a generous ration! These miserable people ran to that train station, and didn't care what would happen to them after they filled their stomachs with that meal. Every day, tens of thousands of people, swollen with hunger, who didn't believe that they would ever again hold a loaf of bread, would come to that station. There were also Sierpcers in this multitude. I don't remember their names, except for Mendel Lipchitz and his family, my sister-in-law Sarah Rozynek, and my sisters Chayah and Esther Sarah Zashutke of blessed memory. (Bronka Mlawa and her husband Pepper are now in the Land of Israel.)

The trains went in all directions: to Treblinka, Majdanek, and more. The passengers forgot all their fears of being transported to their death; they were being taken to work places because they had just received food so that they would have the strength to work. In this way the Germans succeeded in removing the Jews from Warsaw without one casualty during the operation. On the one hand, the people were too weak for any resistance; on the other hand, people who were capable of reacting were influenced by the food provisions that they received. In the end, perhaps the will to live remains because there is a one percent chance of remaining alive. This is what brought the masses to the incinerators. And this is how the story of the Sierpc Jews in Warsaw ended.

The Warsaw Ghetto was empty, and in the meantime the Jews in the other ghettos had to be kept busy so they wouldn't have time to think about the Jews of Warsaw. And so the expulsions started. All the Jews in Drobin were deported to the Neustadt Ghetto. A few hundred from Ciechanów were also sent to Neustadt. At the same time, Sierpc Jews were deported to the Stezhgovo Ghetto. The following families came to the Neustadt Ghetto from Ciechanów: the Cantor Daniel Scheikes, his wife and two daughters, Chayaleh and Miriam, and the son of Yechiel Meir Bergson, Chayim, of blessed memory. Their absorption into the Neustadt Ghetto was very difficult. The stairwells were occupied by refugees. I took the Sierpcers in in spite of the fact that I was living in a tiny place with four other families. The crowding was terrible. The number of people in the Neustadt Ghetto reached 3,500. The place was fit for 100 families at the most. Sanitary conditions were very bad, and the result was immediate. A typhus epidemic broke out in the Neustadt Ghetto. There was no house without a sick person. A few of the people in town came together, and we decided to put up some sort of hospital. There was a public room that was not very big that was used by the refugees, who slept on the floor. We found room for them in attics, fixed the roofs, built brick ovens, and housed them in the attics. We also provided beds for the sick. In the small towns in Poland, there were wooden fences between the houses. We took down those that were in the ghetto, and made beds out of the boards. We went from house to house collecting blankets, pillows, and sheets, and we improvised a hospital, that could at least take the sick that were living in the stairwells, I was one of the organizers of this hospital, and I was its head until I too came down with typhus.

Conditions in the hospital were as they were in the ghetto: four people in one bed. Once a week, the doctor from the Plonsk Ghetto, Dr. Bar, came with a nurse from that hospital. The nurse taught me how to make injections, and I injected the patients according to the instructions I received from the doctor. The Cantor Scheikes was seriously ill with typhus. We sent him to the hospital in Plonsk and he died there. His wife and his daughter Miriam also died in Plonsk.

Our situation in the Neustadt Ghetto became worse every day. We received a lot of bad news. On the evening of the first day of Rosh Hashanah, a Jew approached the fence of the Ghetto and asked to enter, because he had a lot to tell us. The Jewish police let him come in for a few hours, something that was usually strictly forbidden. This Jew, whose name was Gurfinkel, from the town of Ciechanów, told us that he had been among the transport[27] of Jews from the Warsaw Ghetto to Treblinka. He was picked together with a few hundred men to work packing the clothes of those who had been burned in the crematoriums. He had managed to escape in a railway car, by hiding among the packages of clothes. He saw with his own eyes how Jews went into the incinerators, and only their clothes were taken out. We broke into a cold sweat when we heard this. Now everything was clear; we had no more doubts. We would also be facing the same situation, in a very short time. But we were being choked – what could we do? We also read in the German newspaper *Völkischer Beobachter* that Hitler had said: "The Jews are laughing at me, that I will lose the war. Well, many Jews are not laughing anymore! And those that are still laughing – very shortly their smiles will be wiped from their faces. And if in Europe, in the lands that I have conquered, in 1943 there will still be a living Jew – bring him to me, and I will give him all the honors. I will bow to him, and take off my hat to him..." In other words, in 1943, there would be no Jews left in the countries under German occupation. This was the Germans' complete plan. This was why they wiped out all the small ghettos and concentrated the Jews in a few places, so that it would be easier to send them to the extermination camps. The Jews of Ghetto Neustadt panicked after this. We started wailing, trying to get advice from each other like wild people. The religious Jews gathered in the prayer house, read the Psalms, said the *Selichot*[28], blew the shofar, fasted, went to the cemetery and measured its length and width, vowed to give charity to the poor and warm clothing to orphans – perhaps the fury would pass. The town elders decided to convene a "Heavenly Court."[29] There was an empty lot in the middle of the ghetto, and everyone gathered there, from young to old, women and children. In the middle of the congregation sat a lesser *Sanhedrin*[30], 23 wise men and town elders. Among them was Yehoshua Popowski of blessed memory, the son-in-law of the teacher of religion in Sierpc. Yehoshua Popowski was the defense attorney in this trial, and opposing him was a prosecutor. The first to speak was the defense attorney. His questions to the heavenly court were as follows: "Why have you become so fed up with us so as to bring the complete extinction of your children, the nation of Israel? Even if we have sinned so much, why are the babes and small children who haven't sinned to blame? For three years we have been wandering from place to place. Our bodies have been scalded like raw materials for a smith. We do not look like human beings anymore. Our families are scattered all over the earth. There is not one good tiding for our future. We are all paupers, and in any case we are considered dead." Thus he spilled out his guts and cried, and everyone cried with him: "Enough! Lord of the world! Save us in our time of trouble, take us out of the lion's mouth, because he plans to tear us to pieces soon."

And this is how the prosecutor started. "There are desecrators of the Sabbath among us, people who eat forbidden foods, are stingy with charity, the orphans do not have warm clothes on freezing days," and so forth. After these speeches, the *Sanhedrin* issued a verdict: "From this moment, candles must be lit in the prayer house, and Psalms must be said day and night, without stopping for a moment. On the next Sabbath, no flame is to be lit by any Jew, and keepers of the Sabbath will go from house to house to make certain of this. The rations of meat that we receive from the Germans are to be accepted, but the butcher will not sell it, and it will be buried in the ghetto. An extensive campaign will be carried out in the ghetto to collect clothes, shoes, boots, and underwear for orphans, and then we will certainly be redeemed and saved from the cruel ones. The evil edicts will become benign decrees that rescue and comfort us and we will be granted the defeat of the German nation."

The meeting of the *Sanhedrin* ended, and we started to carry out the verdict that was imposed on us. We did not spare anything, Sabbath was Sabbath, we did not eat non-kosher food, gave to charity, clothed the orphans, and so forth; the keepers of the Sabbath went to visit in the houses. We truly fully repented, according to all the laws and commandments that we are ordered to keep. But the gates of heaven were closed to us, and our prayers were not answered. We shed our tears for nothing; our eyes became weak from anger, but to no avail. The chanting of Psalms by our children was not heard on high. A command was issued by the Germans on the first of November, 1942 to deliver all the Jews of the ghetto who were not capable of working, *unproduktive*, to the *burgermeister.* This command was issued simultaneously in all the ghettos. These people were allowed to take with them a small package of not more than five kilograms. This included men and women. Twenty men from the Ghetto would be hanged if one person remained in the Ghetto belonging to the group that was incapable of working. This transport had to be ready within twelve hours of the time of issuance of the command. The people had to be brought to the *burgermeister's* office, and handed over to him.

The edict spread immediately throughout the whole Neustadt Ghetto. The old people started to hide in cellars, attics, behind false walls, in all sorts of hiding places. A terrible panic descended on the ghetto. Today they were taking the old people and tomorrow they would take all of us. A spirit of revolt was felt; perhaps now was the time to say the word, "No!" and "Whatever happens will happen. After all, you only die once. In any case, we are lost. We will shut the gate of the ghetto! We will not let one German enter, and whatever they want to do to us somewhere, let them do it here, in the ghetto. How can we send our beloved parents to their certain death with our own hands? Even if we remain alive, what point will there be to living after we committed such offenses to our relatives and dear ones?"

People wandered here and there in the ghetto, harboring these ideas. There were discussions at every corner. The *Judenrat* also held a meeting, and decided to send two of its people, who knew the *burgermeister* well – maybe the edict could be cancelled. “Shlomke” Friedman, the chairman of the *Judenrat*, and the *burgermeister's* tailor, Chayim Kotcholak, went. They brought with them a gold pocket watch with a long gold chain, to bribe the burgermeister. He greeted them civilly, and explained the command that he had received from the *Landrat* (Staroste). But if in addition to the watch, they would add a fur coat for his wife (a lynx coat), he would be satisfied with just fifty-five old people, and he would send a report to the *Landrat* that this was the number of *unproduktive* that were found in the Neustadt Ghetto. The rest were strong young people capable of working. And that is how it was. The *Judenrat* handed over 55 men and women to the *burgermeister'*. The daughter of Yekel David Bornstein and her husband were among them. She had not been chosen to go with this transport, because she was young. But her husband was older and was chosen as a scapegoat, so she went along, saying that whatever would happen to her husband would happen to her as well. She did not want to be separated from her husband. I remember standing near the exit gate, and seeing them go through. He was holding his prayer shawl and phylacteries. He turned towards the ghetto and said, “If only we could be the last atonement for all the Jews of the ghetto. Maybe the Germans will be satisfied with us, and will not annihilate all the Jews. Whoever said enough, then enough to all our troubles?” The wailing and shouting of those escorting them tore at the fabric of the heavens.

We heard later that these people were brought to the Auschwitz camp, together with a large transport of Jews who were like them from all the other ghettos, and they were suffocated in the gas chambers.

We knew that our end was approaching. Another day or two, and it would be our turn. But the will to live had its hold on us. I know this from bitter experience over the years that I spent in ghettos and concentration camps. The flame of life and the will to live burn in everyone's heart. This flame is stronger than anything, and overcomes all distresses and tortures, both physical and spiritual. I want to state here what my thoughts were: “Maybe in spite of everything we will stay alive, when we will work and be productive? We have already reconciled ourselves to our fate, to be exiled someplace and do all sorts of hard labor, but we will live! And a living person still has hope. There could be a change in the German people, or other changes.” But our conjectures and imagination were useless. The die was cast on the fourteenth of November, 1942. all Jews, without exception, had to be ready at four in the morning, with luggage of not more than ten kilograms. To arrange themselves in groups of ten, according to their choice; there would be a cart for every 10 people. There was a mobilization of all the peasants in the vicinity of the town. They all had to show up at four in the morning on November 14 with a cart and two horses. To be ready near the ghettos. The decree was issued a few days before that date.

On the 10th of November, the Germans surrounded the ghettos day and night with a heavy guard of *Volksdeutsch*. There was an order not to approach the fences. There were instances in all the ghettos where *Volksdeutsch* fired into the ghettos and killed people. They were allowed to do anything. Who would say anything to them?

For three years, we only heard, "You are dogs." ("*Ier drekishe Juden. Ier zoy zoy zoy vek. Ferfluchte hunt.*") And similar phrases.

What could we do? Sit patiently and wait. There was nowhere to escape to, and it was also impossible after the German guards had surrounded the ghetto. The Jews inside the ghettos made ready for their trip. It was forbidden to take more than 10 kilograms. Whoever had any money or jewelry left found hiding places for it.

The bakeries received flour without limit for baking bread day and night, to sell as much as they wanted to their customers. The grocers received jams, sugar and other foodstuffs, to supply their customers with as much as they wanted, and the Jews bought a lot. Everyone said, "If we live, we will need it all. And if we die, what's the use of money?"

The 14th of November was a long vigil, a sleepless night in all the ghettos. Groups gathered in the streets. Each group of ten sat with their packages and waited for the opening of the gate, listening for the order to board the cart! Outside of the ghetto there were already hundreds of carts with horses. There was a lot of noise both inside and outside the ghetto. At four in the morning the *burgermeister* of Neustadt came with some Gestapo men and *gendarmes* and gave the order to leave the ghetto without making any noise. If there was any weeping or yelling, they would fire into the crowd. Nobody was to make a sound! And that is how it was. The groups went quietly, boarded the carts, and sat down holding their packages. One more glance at the ghetto houses, a last look. The peasant pulled on the reins, and the cart moved. The first question to the peasant was, "Where have you been ordered to go?" He shrugged his shoulders, "I don't know."

The column of hundreds of carts covered the whole road from Neustadt to Plonsk. The residents of all the ghettos were assembled in Plonsk, for moving to towns that had railway stations. The Jews of Neustadt, among them many Sierpcers, were placed in the Plonsk Ghetto. This was on Friday morning.

There were many living places available in Plonsk after the Germans had removed the *unproduktive*, that is, the old people, a few days earlier. The new refugees that came on Friday from Neustadt were put in there. They opened their luggage and prepared themselves for the holy Sabbath, the day of rest. We said to ourselves, "They won't take us out on a Saturday!" The women prepared the Sabbath candles, the men got ready to go to some place of prayer to greet the Sabbath. We accepted the situation for what it was. When the Sabbath comes, rest comes, and maybe we will stay here until the end...

But that Friday night, the ghetto police spread out in all directions, went into every house, and ejected all the people of Neustadt together with their packages to specific gathering places. Some were sent to the synagogue, some to other places that were meant to be concentration points for those who were leaving by train on Sabbath morning.

Again on the road, and this would be the last trip... But to our great misfortune, this was not just the last trip. This was a trip accompanied by cruel demons, murderers, bloodsuckers, wild animals who only had human shapes.

And again we sat on our packages, because there was no place to lie down because of the overcrowding. We sat and waited all day and all night, until five in the morning. And then we heard announcements: Everyone to go outside and arrange themselves in groups of five. We did not see even one German. Everything was taken care of by Jewish policemen from the ghetto. Everyone got into his place and we started our procession to the railway station. My wife and I managed to hide, and we didn't leave with this transport. We were of the opinion that we wouldn't miss anything if we left with a later transport.

The train with the people from Neustadt left. No one knew in which direction it was heading and where they were taking the wretched victims... There was a group of Gestapo people waiting near the train, and they accepted delivery of three thousand souls. It was not their first transport. These were Gestapo personnel who were specifically assigned to the places of extermination, because not all Germans were allowed entry to such places.

These transports went from the above towns every day. The people of the Stezhgovo Ghetto were brought to Mlawa, and from there to the Auschwitz extermination camp.

Each transport carried 3,000 souls. It took the train two days to get to its destination. The trip took such a long time not because of the great distance, but to confuse the people, who wouldn't know where they were headed, and also to weaken them and torture them with the horrible crowding and asphyxiation. Every railroad car had room for 30 to 40 people, but 150 were pushed inside. The travelers stood next to each other for the whole time. When a man has been in such conditions for two days, when he gets off he begs to be taken to wherever they want, even if it means suffocation and immolation. The people who arrived were not human anymore; they had lost the will to live.

I have to note that the Sierpcers did not have the "luck" of dying an easy death. In 1942, the modern crematoriums had not yet been built at Auschwitz. The gas chambers were primitive, as I will describe below.

Two sheds, each 30 meters long, were situated in a grove, among the trees. They were separated by about 20 meters. One shed was for disrobing and had a sign on it – *auskleidungsraum.* Men, women and children, all together, entered this shed and received an order to quickly take their clothes off. The Nazis hit them on the head as soon as they entered. The people became confused and disrobed hurriedly and waited for a new order. It was November and cold outside, and they were told to leave this shed and go to the other shed. The Gestapo men sent attack dogs into the shed to chase the miserable people into the second shed. The dogs bit the naked people terribly. The screams could be heard in the heavens. The women who held their babes in their arms embraced them with eternal love until their final moments. They all parted from each other with kisses, with weeping and confessions.

When everyone had entered the empty shed, which then became completely full, the door was shut. There was a small hatch in the middle of the shed. An S.S. man poured a canister of Zyklon B gas into it, and closed it. He himself wore a gas mask. Within half an hour the people inside had suffocated – poisoned by the deadly gas.

Then the *sonderkommandos*[31] started their work: opened the shed door to let air in, took the corpses out and put them into a trolley (*lorca* in German), and brought them to a deep ditch, where they burned them. After that, the *sonderkommando* men cleaned the ditch, the sheds, and the plot, to make everything ready for the next transport...

Among these transports were all the refugees of Sierpc from the following ghettos: Stezhgovo, Neustadt, Ciechanów, Mlawa, Plonsk, etc.

The trains would arrive at twilight, so that the people would not be able to determine where they were. The train would stop not far from the incinerators. Two S.S. men stood next to the train, along with some men from the *kommando*[32], who were called *Kanada Kommando*[33], each one with his own function. At the sound of the order "Out of the cars," everyone gets out. Everyone holds on to his own package and makes sure he is not parted from his family. Everyone is outside, and a new command comes from the S.S. men: "Put all the bundles in one pile." Then the *Kanada* men started their work: to gather all the packages and valuables. Then came the order: "Men separately and women separately." It was not easy to separate families. But the S.S. men were ready for this too. They used clubs to beat women, children, and babies. The screaming and weeping was awful. When the two groups had been separated, a group of men and a group of women, an army doctor with the rank of *Sturmbannführer* came. He carried an order from the Political Department of the Auschwitz camp, with the sentence: how many people to send to the work camp, that is, how many will be left alive, with the rest to go to the gas chambers.

The doctor approached the women's group. Every woman was marched in front of him, and he asked them their age and profession, very gently and politely. He did the same with the men's group.

The two groups were divided into four groups, young people separately, and adults and children separately. A young man or woman who was accompanied by a child was sent to the group of adults and old people.

Some S.S. men stood next to the doctor, to separate the people according to the doctor's orders – one to the left and one to the right. Many did not want to be parted; like the son or daughter that did not want to be separated from their parents, in spite of the fact that the doctor had told them, "Right!" In most cases, the doctor did not interfere, and said, ""Go with your father," or "Go with your mother." When the doctor saw that he had the number of people that were in the order, he said, "I'm finished; I already have 250 men and 50 women. The rest – get on the trucks. You are going to work camps. The work there is easier because you are adults, children and old people. You will be able to correspond with your relatives, get a special diet, and be well taken care of."

But we knew very well that the two groups who were being taken in cars were being brought to the nearby gas chambers. The S.S. men piled the people into the cars using blows, slaps, and kicks. As each car became full, it drove off and returned within ten minutes, then filled up again. Shouting erupted from the cars: "Take revenge for us on these murderers. We are going to die, to be burned in the gas chambers. Avenge us!" There were two groups left in the empty field: 250 men, and 50 women.

We reached the men's camp at eleven at night. We saw a flame and a large column of smoke not far away. When we asked the veteran inmates what was the smoke and fire that we saw, they answered, "Your parents, children, and wives have just been burned." It was difficult to believe, but we didn't have much time for thought. Our supervisors, the *bockältester*[34] and the *stubenälteste*[35], told us to hand over all valuables, money and so forth. In any case we wouldn't need them anymore, and they pointed in the direction of the incinerators, so that we could see the smoke and fire. We realized that all this was not a nightmare. It was the frightful truth. Everyone emptied their pockets of all they had: money, watches, valuables, and gave it to the *bockältester*. We used our legs to dig holes and we hid money in the ground, as much as we could, since there was no floor in the shed. We ripped up paper money, and threw it away.

The *Aufnahmeschreiber*[36], along with twenty inmates, came at two o'clock at night. These were the special *kommandos* for registering new transports. They prepared cards for everyone. There were some Jews among them. Two of them tattoed a number on the left hand of every inmate who came to Auschwitz. This was very painful, but no one thought of his own pain because we were in such despair that we didn't care what they did to us.

I Will Now Describe the Stezhgovo Transport

We know that most of the Sierpcers who were in the Stezhgovo Ghetto ended up in Auschwitz. Not one woman was sent to a work camp from this transport. All the women went directly to the crematorium. That was the order of the political department in Auschwitz. Two hundred fifty men were chosen for the work camp; that is, to live. Of this number, one hundred men were stood to one side. This was when they were still near the train, before they entered the camp.

No one knew why he had been chosen, and where he was going. These 100 men were picked to work in the incinerators, and there were 20 Sierpcers among them. Of course, they did not know why they had been separated from the rest of the 250 men selected from the transport, and for what kind of work they had been chosen. They were given showers, received haircuts, clothed in camp uniforms, and taken by S.S. men who formed a strong guard, to a shed surrounded by barbed wire inside the Birkenau camp[37]. It was a camp inside a camp. They were isolated from everyone else, because they carried out all the tasks inside the crematoriums. That same night they went out to do their work, after having received instructions on what to do.

When they entered the shed with the corpses that had been suffocated by the gas, they felt sick. They fainted, ran outside, wept and screamed. Here were their wives, children, parents, and relatives lying in front of them choked by gas. Only a few hours ago they had been together in the train. But they were not given time to think. The S.S. men beat them, and they were forced to remove their own flesh and blood from the shed, to a deep and wide ditch, where a fire was burning. They worked all night, until all the corpses had been burned.

The people who did this work, who were called *sonderkommando*, did not have any way of changing their job. They were forbidden to talk with other inmates in the camp. They were always locked inside their shed. If they went somewhere else in the camp, like the showers or the kitchen to get their food rations, there were always S.S. guards with them to make sure that they weren't in contact with other prisoners and talk about their work. The Germans thought that no one knew what was happening in the camp, in spite of the fact that the crematoriums were nearby, and we saw the flames and the smoke. If one of the *sonderkommando* became sick, they didn't send him to the hospital together with other prisoners, but gave him a fatal injection...

In spite of this I was able to come into contact with them, spoke to them, and they told me everything. I especially saw the Sierpcers almost every day. (I will mention their names later.)

They received special food, because they worked hard in three shifts. Twelve hundred people worked in these *kommando* units in the years 1942-43. Every shift consisted of four hundred men. The transports came day and night, without any respites, and the *sonderkommando* were not unemployed... There were also professional people among the *sonderkommando*, such as dentists, barbers, and goldsmiths. Every professional man had his job: the barbers cut off the hair; the dentists pulled out gold teeth; the goldsmiths melted and cast the gold teeth. All this was done after the people had been suffocated by gas. They weren't burned until after these professional people had done their work. They even found a use for the hair. After all these activities the bodies were burned by the "firemen." This kommando consisted only of Jews. They knew that they didn't have much time because they would be exterminated in some manner. But they still thought that maybe there might be a miracle. The war would end, or there would be some other change. So they kept on with their work. They were also in the chamber where the people took their clothes off before going into the death-chamber and kept order there. They also watched the victims to make sure that all went into the gas chamber. Everything was done according to the orders of their superiors, the S.S. men.

The gas was poured into the chamber by the camp doctor, a German who was a high ranking officer (*Lager-Arzt*), whom I have mentioned earlier.

The *sonderkommando* were more or less free during the time that they were working. The S.S. men did not pay attention to them. They wore good clothes and good shoes; they got food from the transports, took what they wanted, and nobody stopped them. They helped their friends in the camp. There were always many inmates standing around their shed, and they would throw food, clothes, underwear and shoes to them. Of course if a prisoner was caught committing this kind of transgression, he came to a bitter end, but for a hungry and naked person there is no fence, no door, or fear of any punishment. If they were caught on one side of the shed, they were beaten, and then went to the other side, until they had achieved their goal. When the *sonderkommando* men went to the showers, many prisoners waited for them on the road inside the camp, and the *sonderkommando* men would throw whatever they had to them. They knew that their friends or just plain hungry people were waiting for them. So in spite of the fact that they were under strict S.S. guard, they took things with them. They were usually not punished, because their work was punishment enough for anyone.

When I met with them, they complained to me and said, “It has become our horrible fate to carry out this tragic work; there is no more left to live for.”

That is how they worked for ten months, until the transports became fewer, and there was not enough work for all the men of the *sonderkommando.* Then they chose 100 of them for a different line of work, paving roads. Almost all the Sierpcers who had been in the *sonderkommando* were transferred to this job. They were happy to be free of working in the crematoriums, despite the worsening of their conditions in terms of food and so forth. But these 100 men were still isolated from the other prisoners, as if only they knew what was being done to the Jews, and all the other inmates in the camp were completely ignorant.

It is worthwhile mentioning some details about the Sierpcers who were employed in this work. For instance, Moshe Grossman, the son-in-law of Henich Tcharnobrodna. On the eve of Passover, 1943, he brought me a small piece of matzo that he had baked in the oven of the crematorium. He had found a little flour in some clothes from one of the transports, and wanted me to have the honor of eating matzo.

He told me that they say *Kadish*[38] when the bodies are being burned, outside of the watchful eye of the S.S.

Yaakov Pukacz also had this job. He came down with typhus in February, 1943. As I have mentioned, they didn't take the men of the *sonderkommando* to the hospital. They took him in a car of the "Red Cross" and he never came back. They undoubtedly finished him with a fatal injection, as they did to the rest of the *sonderkommando* who became sick.

*

These hundred men did not work for very long at paving roads. The policy of the Germans was not to leave any man of the *sonderkommando* alive.

In January 1944 they were told that they were being sent to work in the crematorium in Majdanek. There were 17 Sierpcers among them, and these are their names:

Moshe Grosman
Israel Meir Bornstein
Yaakov Bukat
Pinchas Schwartz
Beno Schwartz
Zeidman
Chayim Bergson
Pesach Skornik
Elia Grosman
Henich Brodacz
Ben-Zion Mai
Hirsch Lazer Sakowicz
Zalman Lelonek
Chayim Lanczner
Yosef Nemczewko
Meir Konskowolski
Elkana Kasazh

Before they left the camp, they took a shower and received clothes for the trip. I had the opportunity to say goodbye to them because I worked in the showers (*entlassungskemer*) and it was my shift that night. Our *kapo*[39] received an order from the *Lagerführer*[40] to give them the following clothes: a short summer coat, pants, and wooden shoes. This is what they had to wear in the January weather of Europe.

It is no wonder that they understood that they were sending them outside of the camp to be exterminated. There were those that understood this from the clothes they received, which would prevent them from escaping. In spite of the fact that I could have been severely punished, including death, I gave these Sierpcers sweaters, underwear, socks, and hats, and they hid them beneath their coats. I was certain that none of them would inform on me in case of an inspection.

They left on the train at three in the morning. According to reports I received, they went to Majdanek near Lublin, to a place that is called Auschwitz Number 2. There they cunningly sent them into the gas chambers. The few Sierpcers who were in the *sonderkommando* in the Auschwitz Birkenau camp continued their work in the crematoriums until the rebellion in the Birkenau camp, which I will describe below.

Until March 1943, all the extermination activities were carried out in Brzezinka (Birkenau), as I have described above. At the end of that month, the construction of four large, modern buildings was completed, and all these activities were transferred to these structures; that is, suffocation by gas, incineration – everything was done inside the building. We couldn't see anything from the outside. Two of the buildings were very large, and the other two were slightly smaller.

This is how the building looked from the outside: it was a two story building, about 30 meters long, with five or six steps at the entrance. There were a few windows on the second floor, and the roof had fifteen chimneys. The wall of the lower floor had three small windows that faced the death chamber, which jutted out from the exterior of the building. A poured concrete roof that covered the basement where the people were suffocated protruded from the ground. There were four openings on the roof, each 50 x 50 centimeters which were used to pour the poison (gas) into the columns made of a steel mesh that went down to floor level. These columns were also square, and the same size as the outside openings. There was a large yard of about 1000 square meters around the building, with a fence of concrete columns and barbed wire. The fence was electrified at a high voltage. There was a large sign on the entrance gate that said *zum baderaum* in German, meaning "to the showers." There was a guard tower manned by the S.S. every 30 meters just outside the fence. A gravel road led to the crematorium.

A description of the inside of the building: the transports would enter the building, and go through a small corridor to the cellar. As they went downstairs, they saw arrows and signs, "to the disrobing rooms, to the showers" (*Auskleidunsraum, baderaum*). First they went into the disrobing room. Inside there were benches along the entire length of the room. The walls had hooks with numbers on them. Everyone went into this room together, men and women. When the room was full, an S.S. man stood at the entrance and ordered, "Take off your clothes!" Everyone took his clothes, made a package of them, hung them on a hook, and was supposed to remember the number where he had hung his clothes.

Next to this room was the death chamber (*gas kamer*). The entrance was a wide, thick and heavy door which could be hermetically shut with iron rods. In the middle of the room were four square columns of steel mesh, 50 x 50 centimeters. The distance between the columns was about 4 meters.

There were shower heads in the ceiling, like in a regular shower room. All this was in the cellar. There was a long marble table in the first room of the ground floor, with two water faucets at the side. The table was used for "scientific" experiments on live people (Jews). They would remove their blood and send it to the German blood bank. They also amputated live organs and sent them to German hospitals. They cut off ears, breasts, noses, cheeks, without anesthetics, and the people would die on the spot.

Not far from this room there was a big, long hall with 15 ovens along its length. The oven doors were the width of 4 people. There was a small stairwell near each oven. The fire stoker (*der heirtzer*) who made sure that the flame was not extinguished sat there. The fire was fed by coal. The other side of the oven was flush with the floor, with an opening through which the bodies were put in. There was no floor, but three concrete pillars, 20 centimeters apart, and the flames came from downstairs between the pillars, so that the bodies were burned. They were not really burned, but sort of melted from the great heat. Inside the oven there were metal rails and a cart shaped like a stretcher that went inside with four corpses. The incineration lasted for 20 minutes. A calculation will show that it took 20 minutes to incinerate 60 corpses. Each oven was fed with 2 men and 2 women. Because the flesh of the women had more fat, the bodies melted more quickly.

The bodies were taken by an elevator from the gas chamber in the cellar to the ovens on the first floor. There was a procedure for taking a corpse from the gas chamber to the elevator: they would tie a belt to a hand of the corpse, and drag it on the floor after pouring some water on the floor to make it slide more easily. About twenty corpses at a time were loaded onto the elevator.

All this took place in the two crematorium buildings, Building No. 1 and Building No. 2. The other two crematorium buildings were more primitive and smaller. They were used only for transports of fewer people, of about a hundred.

All these tasks were performed by the Jewish *sonderkommando*. But as I mentioned earlier, the *sonder* men did not live long. They knew this and talked about it every day. They made themselves ready, as best they could, by collecting ammunition, hand grenades, and explosives. Not in great quantities, because this was impossible. There was endless surveillance of everyone in Auschwitz by the S.S.. There were searches every day at the entrance gate and when returning from work. The pockets and the whole body were searched.

But in spite of this the men succeeded in organizing, in gathering some things for the day when they would have to defend themselves. They agreed among themselves that if they sensed something suspicious, such as the Germans wanting to send them somewhere else – not to go! To actively resist! They knew this from experience. They decided that if they heard gunfire from any crematorium, this would be a sign that the rebellion had started, and for all the crematorium workers to proceed with their plan.

The day came. On a summer day in 1944, the *sonder* men in Crematorium Number 3 received an order from the S.S. man who was their superior to leave the building and line up in the yard. When they asked him why, he told them that they wanted to send 200 people to work somewhere else. Everything was clear. They decided to resist. They burned the straw mats they slept on, and threw rocks at the S.S. men. Crematorium Number 3 went up in flames, but the sonder men didn't leave; they wanted to be immolated inside. The S.S. men fired into the building, and a reinforcement of S.S. men arrived within a few minutes that succeeded in putting out the fire. The *sonder* men who survived were caught, stripped of their clothes, and made to lie on the ground naked with their faces down.

The *sonder* men in the other buildings, who saw that Crematorium Number 3 was burning and heard shots from that direction, went into action. They captured their kapo, a German inmate, and put him inside an oven. The S.S. men became frightened and hid. The *sonder* men hurried out of the building, took the ammunition and grenades out of their hiding places, cut the electrified barbed wire fence and ran, shouting the signal to the other prisoners: "Freedom! (*Wolnosc*) Escape together with us." But they managed to run only a few tens of meters, when they were already being chased by the S.S., who had come with many men and dogs and were firing at them with machine guns. None of the *sonder* men managed to do much. From what I heard, 5 Germans were killed in this action, and 450 *sonderkommando* were killed. None of the resisters remained alive; among them was one Sierpcer, Avraham Wilk.

All prisoners who were working outside the camp were rushed back. The 200 people from the *sonder* that the Germans wanted to send someplace were sent not far from Birkenau and were shot. That same day, before nightfall, the *Lagerführer* assembled the *sonder* men, and warned them that this incident was not to be repeated. If it was – he would exterminate them on the spot.

I was on the night shift then, so I slept during the day. But the S.S. men woke us up and assembled the whole camp in one place, under guard. We were certain that they would shoot us right there, because there were machine guns aimed at us from all directions.

That is how that rebellion in Birkenau ended.

*

The transports came without end in 1943; from Greece, France, Belgium, Holland and Poland. They also brought the last transport from Warsaw. These were Jews who were American citizens. In Warsaw they had lived outside the Ghetto, did not have to wear an armband, and they had all the privileges of American citizens.

One day the Germans gathered them in one place in Warsaw, and told them that they were being sent home, to America. But instead of home, they were brought to the death camp Auschwitz and straight to the crematorium, without picking one man or woman for labor, as was customary with the transports. There were about 1,000 people in this transport: men, women, children, and old people. They arrived at Crematorium Number 1, went down the cellar, and were put into the disrobing room.

An S.S. man called Shillinger stood at the entrance. He was a cruel sadist, more so than anyone else in the camp. He received all the transports that came to Auschwitz, and brought the people to the crematoriums. He was also responsible for the destruction of the transport. During the day, he visited all the camps, and would find all sorts of infractions: this one was not working hard enough, that one was eating on the job, etc. He would kick, slap, and hit people with a stick. He would ride around on a motorcycle all day, hitting and yelling, until his end came. From a Jewish woman who was an American citizen, part of the latest transport.

He stood at the entrance of the disrobing room and gave the order for everyone to take their clothes off. A young woman approached him and said, "Sir, how can we get undressed, men and women together, in the same room?" But he slapped her face and kicked her a few times, drew his pistol, and shouted, "Whoever does not get undressed will be killed on the spot!" Everyone started taking their clothes off, the young woman as well, but she threw her brassiere in his face and said to him, "Here's a gift for your wife!" He became very angry. This was the first time that anyone had dared do something like that to him. He went inside the room a few meters, and slapped the woman until she fell to the floor. The woman's husband went behind Shillinger and hit him on the hand that was holding the pistol, which dropped out of his hand and fell near where the woman was lying. She took advantage of this and shot him a number of times. He managed to shout "Help!" and died. The prisoners saw that Shillinger was dead and started to demolish everything inside. They broke the doors and destroyed the columns of steel mesh, and ran out of the crematorium room. This was the first time that a transport had rebelled. But no one in this transport was left alive. They were all transferred to Crematorium Number 2 and suffocated there.

I heard that the woman and her husband were theater actors from New York.

In order to avenge the death of Shillinger, 1,500 people were taken the next day from the work camp and put to death. They were all healthy and capable of doing hard labor, but were taken to the gas chambers and suffocated. They all knew what was going on in the camp. Everyone saw the mass extermination. The Germans hid almost nothing from the camp inmates, because they were considered as good as dead. "No one will leave this place alive," as the camp commander (*Lagerführer*) put it.

We could not do anything. There was a very heavy guard in the camp, and nobody dared to resist. Not only the Jews, who were the weakest prisoners, but also the rest: Poles, Russians, Frenchmen, and others. All went along the path of suffering and extermination. Many tried to escape, but they were all caught.

A young Jewish woman tried to escape in 1944. She was fluent in a number of languages, so she worked as a translator for the S.S. She was from Poland, and had lived in Belgium. Her name was Mala.

Since she was always with S.S. women, she managed to get a female S.S. uniform. She put on the S.S. uniform and simply walked out of the gate. But after a few days she was captured in the city of Krakow and brought back to Auschwitz. She said she would not go to the crematorium alive, and committed suicide by slitting her wrists with a razor blade as she was marched there.

There were other escape attempts, but I cannot remember any that succeeded. The camp was surrounded by a few rings of guard posts. Even if someone managed to penetrate some of the rings, he would be caught at the last one.

And the prisoners in the camp underwent much suffering in the event of an escape. We would be assembled in a formation and stood many hours in the cold, after a day of work, without food, sometimes until midnight.

There were also times when they deliberately announced that two or three prisoners were missing in the camp, so that we would stand in formation for many hours. But it was all a put-on. Nobody had escaped,

There were no attempts of escape from the women's camp during all those years, except for the instance above.

We talked about partisans that were operating in the vicinity of the camp, but we never felt their presence, nor did they do anything for the camp inmates.

Whenever someone was caught trying to escape from the camp, he was hanged in the center of the camp, in front of all the prisoners. Before the hanging, the *Lagerführer* read the sentence, and then it was carried out by a hangman, an inmate specializing in this task.

Usually the hangings took place on Sunday, because then we worked only until twelve noon, and it was more public. The victim would be left hanging there until twilight.

There was another punishment for attempted escape: the culprit was shot, and the body was placed upright near the gate so that it could be seen by prisoners returning from work. The victims stood erect (and dead) with two spades under their armpits.

There were a few punishment methods in the camp, such as: isolation, a narrow room with no possibility of turning around. There was also hanging by the ankles with the head down for 15 minutes. Most died on the spot. There was a room full of water up to a half meter in height. There was also a table with a hole in it for inserting the head and receiving lashes, in accordance with the verdict of the *Lagerführer.* Once I received a punishment of 45 lashes. This is what happened:

On the third day that I was in Birkenau (Auschwitz), I found out that my eldest brother Avraham Chayim and his son Mordechai were in the camp. I looked for them and found them. They were difficult to recognize because they did not look like human beings. They had come from Stezhgovo Ghetto and were freezing, without clothing, tired from working, and injured from the blows they received while working. My brother told me that he had seen my wife Miriam in the women's camp, since he worked there. I was overjoyed to hear this, since I did not know what happened to her after we were separated from each other at the railway station when we arrived at the camp.

The next morning, when my brother went to work, I gave him half my ration of bread for my wife. How did he give her the bread? When he passed the road of the women's camp and they saw each other, he threw the bread into a ditch and she picked it up, because it was forbidden to talk to a woman in the camp. I did this for a few days.

A week later I recognized my wife, who was about fifty meters away, on the road that separated the two camps. I called out, "Miriam." At that moment an S.S. man noticed me, arrested me, and took me to the S.S. rooms (*block-führer-stuba*). I received 45 lashes, and my torturers wanted to know who I was talking to, so she could also receive her helping of lashes. I said I didn't know her. I saw her on the train, but I didn't know who she was. They gave me a notification report (*maldung*). Whoever received a *maldung* (judgment) was placed with the *straf kommando* (s.k.). A Jew would not live for more than two days with this *kommando*. The *kapos* killed them with work. But to my good fortune, the S.S. man who recorded my number came down with typhus the next day, and the piece of paper disappeared from his pocket. Apparently, my time had not yet come.

A German *kapo* (an inmate) in the *kommando* s.k. killed a young Sierpcer, Moshe Dobroszklanka, the son of Binem Dobroszklanka. This happened in February 1943 when he went through the gate to work. They searched his clothes and found that he was wearing two shirts. They recorded his number, and in the evening, during the assembly, they took him to the *kommando* s.k. They killed him with overwork in two days.

He stood next to me when he was called from the assembly, because we were in the same block.

What is s.k.? The letters stand for *straf kommando*, meaning punishment unit. They worked and did everything while running. Their food rations were half of those of the other camp prisoners. Since the other inmates did not receive enough food, it was even worse for the s.k. people. In addition, the *kapos* in the *kommando* were German criminals who were brought from jails in Germany. They had spent half their lives in prisons in Germany and Austria. The more people they killed, the more food rations were left for them.

One day at eleven in the morning, as I worked in the *entlassungskemer*[41], they brought the clothes of the dead from the above unit to be disinfected. A kapo told me that until now, that is, until eleven o'clock, there were already 65 dead. They would be finished when the number reached 100 for the day. There were always about 400 prisoners in the s.k. who were sent there for all kinds of violations.

I managed to evade this "charming" *kommando* a few times.

"Selection" in the Camp

"Selection"[42] took place once a month in both the men's and women's camps. All the inmates went out to work and only Jews were left in the camp. The camp doctor (*Lager-Arzt*) examined all of us while we were naked. A camp clerk stood next to the doctor.

If the doctor said to the clerk, "Number!" this meant that the clerk would write down the number and this prisoner would be sent to the crematorium. If he didn't say anything - that was good, the prisoner stayed in the camp. He examined by looking at the bodily appearance. If there was a bit more flesh on the body, it was good; if not, he would say, "This is a *Muselman*[43]. He's not capable of working." And if there was a sore or wound on the body, it could be contagious, and the number was also noted.

The examination of a few thousand people took him two hours, at the most..

Before evening, during the assembly, all the people whose numbers were written down during the "selection" were called and gathered in one shed. These were destined for the crematorium.

When they were brought there, they refused to take their clothes off, and the S.S. men had to make an effort to get them into the gas chamber. What did they do? They were all shouting, "I'm healthy, strong, and capable of working, why am I being sent to the crematorium?" So the S.S. men said, "That's right, you really are healthy, stand on the sideline." They assembled about 50 prisoners in this way, and told them, "You are going back to the camp, to work, but first you have to help us in getting all the others into the gas chamber." The deception worked. These 50 prisoners did the work. In a few minutes they were all inside. It was not difficult to manage just the 50 prisoners. The S.S. men used their clubs and hit them all so hard that they ran into the gas chamber.

A victim from Sierpc, Yehezkel Frankel, son of Nahum Frankel, was chosen in a "selection" in February 1944. He had a number of sores on his body but the Sierpcers of the *sonderkommando* asked their supervisor, an S.S. man, to send him back to the camp, and he was sent back. But his sores didn't heal, and there was a "selection" the following month, and this time Yehezkel was taken to the crematorium. Not always could the *sonder* men influence the S.S.

There were a few Sierpcer women in Birkenau who were sent to the crematoriums because they had scabies: Mania Lipka, the daughter of Aaron Lipka, the wife of Fibush Kirsch, and Lily Eichald.

We managed to arrange some relatively light work for Rivkah Sosnowska, a job in which she would never have to undergo "selection." We knew that if she had to go through "selection," the doctor would immediately choose her, because one of her hands was paralyzed. We were able to hide her for half a year, and took care of her as much as we could. But one day she slipped and broke her leg. They took her to the hospital and from there to the crematorium.

We tried to take care of all the Sierpcer women as much as we could, so they wouldn't go hungry, have easy work, clothes, and so forth. We were already veteran inmates, with "good" jobs. I worked as a disinfector. Kaufman Kasiarz also had a "good" job, working in the sewage, so that we could help, but we could not save someone from death. We accepted our fate. We knew that there was nothing that would help us. From here, from Auschwitz, we would never leave. Everyone according to his fate and in his time.

*

Once, a transport left Auschwitz for a different work camp. I shoved my way into this transport because I also wanted to go to another place so that I wouldn't see the extermination of the Jews from up close. But a S.S. man saw me, pulled me out, and beat me, and said, "Stupid Jew! I want to save you from death, and you thrust yourself into the arms of the Angel of Death!"

Two weeks later, they brought this whole transport back to Auschwitz, straight to the crematorium. The Germans asserted that they had found a contagious disease there, and they had to burn everyone.

Once I underwent a "selection": the doctor examined me for five minutes, which was unusual, and said that I had fever. I was very frightened. Then he said, "Alright, go to work. I'll see you next time."

At the end of 1944, a movie theater was arranged for the prisoners. Once a week we could watch films from the Russian front, but only German victories. Attendance at the movie was compulsory. There was also a bordello in Auschwitz for the Christians. There were only Christian girls in it. Jews were forbidden to enter because of the "racial purity" laws...

When the Red Cross came from Geneva to visit the camp, they showed them the movie theater and the bordello, so what more could the prisoners want? They had everything, more than they would have outside the camp during wartime. They would take them for a visit to the hospital. But before that they would decorate the rooms, put white sheets on the beds with wool blankets and white pillows. Doctors and nurses in white coats would wander around among the patients. The patients received good food on those days: diet, white bread, milk, and all sorts of good food.

The general camp kitchen also cooked better food when the international delegation visited: there would be meat with noodles, a double ration of bread, sausage, margarine, jam, and more.

They also showed them the crematorium buildings, but told the committee that they were used only for those who died in the camps. First, there was no place to bury the bodies, and second, it was more hygienic to burn them in time of war to prevent epidemics. The committee members left the camp satisfied with what they had seen, and reported accordingly to the Red Cross in Geneva. They didn't talk to the prisoners, and didn't hear of what was going on inside the camp. They did not see how millions of Jews were slaughtered. The committee also declared that there was no need to send food parcels to the prisoners, because the Germans provided good food for these concentration camps. They themselves went into the kitchen and tasted the food. This was how the Germans fooled the world, and everyone believed them. And the furnaces burned day and night...

When they brought the Hungarian Jews, about three-quarters of a million Jews within two months, they burned thirty thousand Jews in twenty-for hours. This went on every day, and they did it in great haste, and we didn't know why. It was said in the camp that after the Hungarian Jews, they would have to bring Rumanian Jews. We knew that they were bringing Hungarians, because they looked for people who knew Hungarian. After that, they asked for people who could speak Rumanian. And Italian Jews also came.

At the end of 1943, they brought Czech Jews from Theresienstadt. The Germans put them in a special camp, and families were kept together. They didn't cut their hair, they didn't get special clothes, and they didn't take their money and jewelry from them. They received good food, and did not go out to work. This camp was called "The Family Camp from Czechoslovakia." They gave them postcards so that they could write that they were being treated well. They were photographed many times as they wandered idly about the camp. They had an athletic field where they played, and they did whatever they wanted. They gave special food to the children; the sick received a special diet, double rations, etc.

One day they were all sent to the crematorium. It was the same for Gypsies, who were brought from all countries. The Germans treated them the same way that they had treated the Czech Jews and then took them to the crematoriums.

In the months of June and July of 1944, they brought the last Jews from Poland. They came from the city of Lodz, and from Płaszów, which is near Krakow.

There were also Sierpcers in the transport from Lodz: Yehoshua Ostaszewer and his wife Tovah Yeshaievitz, with a child. Tovah and the child went to the crematorium, but Yehoshua Ostaszewer was chosen to work in the camp. I met him because he came to wash and have his hair cut, and he found out that his family, who came with him, was no longer alive. I made sure that he was dressed well enough for work, and that he had everything he needed. (Yehoshua Ostaszewer is now in the United States.)

I worked in the shower room.

This was a huge building, and all the camp inmates came there once or twice a week, where they showered and their clothes underwent disinfection from lice. Everyone had his hair cut and all the hair from his body was shaved with a shaving machine or a razor. After that they went into the showers.

At the entrance to the shower room there was a small tub filled with Lysol. Everyone had to dip their feet in the Lysol, and then to shower.

At the shower exit, everyone was smeared with a liquid which was made from a gas (Zyklon) that was used for suffocating people in the crematoriums. Then they went into another room to dry out and get dressed.

The workers at the above two sides of the shower were forbidden to have contact with the bathers during work hours, so that the lice would not spread. Following the drying out room there was a big chamber – for getting dressed.

It was the same for new transports that came from outside. Those who had been picked to live went into this building, but the procedure was different. When they entered the big room on the "unclean side" they underwent a search by the S.S. and prisoners who were called *Fils-Kommando*. There was a closed box with a small opening in the middle of the room, where people would put the money and valuables that they had brought with them. Then the number was tattooed on their arm. Then they went through the process described above. When the large number of transports came from Hungary and Lodz, all this work was done by men, that is, hair cutting and showering of the women as well, in spite of the fact that women barbers worked in the women's showers. Sometimes the men and women barbers worked together. All the workers here were Jews.

This building also had a special *kommando* unit that worked at sorting clothes. They sorted the clothes and distributed them to the new transport arrivals that went through the showers. This *kommando* was called "dressing room." They were also Jews.

There was another method of disinfecting the people and clothes. Three large tubs were placed on the road in the middle of the camp. Each tub contained 2,000 liters of water. The inmates from the same block came together, took their clothes off in the street, and put their clothes inside a tub, which was full of a liquid made from Zyklon gas. The clothes would remain in this liquid for about a quarter of an hour, after which they would be taken out. The people who did this work were called *entlassungs-kommando*, and worked while wearing gas masks. I also worked in this *kommando*. The sheds, mattresses, and blankets were also sprayed with the same liquid.

The prisoners would put on the wet clothes, in spite of the fact that it was winter. Many people caught cold and came down with pneumonia. The also wore the wet clothes to work. But what did the Germans care? Cleanliness –

that was the main thing! The women could not hold on. The crowding in the blocks was very great; they were starving for food while working at the same tasks as the men. Therefore the women's quarters were less clean than the men's. Also the "selections" were more frequent in the women's camp than in the men's camp. They also went willingly to the crematoriums. They asked to be gassed; they couldn't take the torture. Their *kapos* were mainly German women, prostitutes who were brought to the concentration camp so they wouldn't be free. The prostitutes were *bockä ltester* and *kapos*, and had various jobs in the hospital, kitchen, and so forth.

*

The situation in Auschwitz improved a little at the end of 1944. The kapos received instructions not to beat prisoners while working. The food was better and so were the clothes. We did not stand in formation for extended periods of time. We felt a marked change. We also heard that people would no longer be suffocated by gas and wouldn't be burned in the crematoriums.

The crematoriums were supposed to be used only for people who died in the camp. But despite all this, they still kept bringing transports and suffocating more hundreds of thousands of Jews. In this sense, we saw no change, regardless of the announcements and promises.

When they brought Jews from Lodz, the *Reichsführer* Himmler visited the camp. He went into the crematorium, put on gloves, and put a body into an oven, and said, "Here, with my own hands, I am burning a Jew." One of the *sonderkommando*, who had heard Himmler himself say this, told this to me.

The *Reichsführer* Himmler visited our camp as well, and entered the sauna building. I was then on the night shift, spreading Covarex, a disinfectant, on people. And suddenly I heard the command to stand to attention.

First a tall fat man entered, dressed in civilian clothes; then came the camp commander, Kramer, who was well known, and more high ranking officers from the S.S. The first man approached me, and asked me in a gentle voice, "What do you do here?"

I answered, "Disinfection! Decontamination of the body after shaving." "What are you?" "A Jew," I answered. "What?" he said in wonder, "How long have you been here in the camp, sir?" "Twenty-two months," I answered him. "What? Such a long time and you are still alive?" I answered him simply, "Yes, I'm still alive."

I didn't know who he was, and I didn't care.

He wandered around the whole building, curious about everything, and asked the prisoners a few times if they were all Jews. After they all left, the S.S. man responsible for our *kommando* came to me and laughed. I asked him what was so funny. He told me, "Do you know who you were talking to? That was the *Reichsführer* Himmler!"

*

It should be noted that all the Sierpcers in Auschwitz were devoted to each other, heart and soul. No Sierpcer ever informed to the German authorities. The Sierpcer went through many trials during the war years.

The names of the Sierpcer who stayed alive in Auschwitz:

- David Sochaczewski
- Meir Tajtelbaum
- Isaac Tajtelbaum
- Kaufman Kasiarz
- Yosef Rajchold
- Avraham Robota
- Meir Tuchendler
- Meir Nemlich
- Chayim Yorish
- Shimon Roemer
- Leib Yorish
- Chayim Berkowitz
- Yaakov Juzelewski
- .... Gongola
- Binem Mai
- Yehoshua Ostaszewer
- Zvi Arpa
- Miriam Arpa
- Bronka Mlawa
- Bina Gorna
- Lutka Friedlander
- Frieda Juzelewska
- .... Przygoda
- Yaakov Sakowicz

They are all now in different countries. The majority settled in Israel. They go on with their daily lives, but I am sure that none of us forgot for a moment what we went through.

We haven't forgotten, and we will never forget! We will remember!

We will remember forever what the German *Amalek*[44] did to us. We will tell the story of what we went through. We will follow the commandment, "And you shall tell your children," and the appeal of our dear ones of blessed memory, before they died, "Take revenge on the Germans!"

*

As the Russian army neared Krakow, 55 kilometers from Auschwitz, the Germans began preparing us for the road: to distance us from the front, to concentrate all the camps in Germany and Austria. Not to hand us over alive to the Russians or other foreign armies.

We received an order on January 17, 1945, an announcement that we were leaving the camp. They didn't stop us from putting on clothes that were intended to be sent to Germany (the good clothes). On the contrary, they were apparently interested that we wear as much as possible, because they didn't have any transportation. Everything was already cut off.

We went on the road. About a quarter of a million prisoners, from all the camps in the vicinity of Auschwitz, men and women. We walked for about a week. Some arrived at the Mauthausen camp in Austria, some in Gross-Rosen and in other camps. Most of the women went to Bergen-Belsen and Ravensbruck in Germany. Thousand were killed along the way by the S.S. on the pretext that they were trying to escape, and many died of exhaustion.

I got to Mauthausen together with Shimon Roemer, a Sierpcer. We were there for about a week. After that they sent us to the camp at Melk about 80 kilometers from Vienna. We worked very hard, and the cold affected us badly. We didn't have any clothes because they took what we brought with us at Mauthausen during the *antlauzung*.[45]

We were in the Melk camp for three months. They didn't bring transports here for suffocation. There was only one small crematorium for burning the dead bodies. Many died of the beatings they received at work, and many did not last very long under the harsh conditions. The *Lagerführer* was an evil man, like all the S.S. men. We despaired of life, and had only one question, "Till when?" There were no women in this camp, and I had not heard about my wife since we left Auschwitz. There were rumors that all the women were exterminated on the way.

I managed to get work in the kitchen in this camp, peeling potatoes. I was overjoyed that I could stay inside the building, and not have to work outside. I could also help our townsman, Shimon Roemer. I brought him a few uncooked potatoes every day, which was strictly forbidden.

This small incident can testify to the cruelty and evil of the S.S. men. A Russian prisoner sneaked into the kitchen in the middle of the day, with a 10 liter pail. He managed to dip the pail into the large cauldron, and take it out full of soup (noodles and potatoes). To his misfortune, he was caught near the door by the S.S. man who was in charge of the kitchen.

He didn't do anything to him. He just said, "Sit there and eat everything you took." The prisoner started eating and finished three or four liters, but the S.S. man wouldn't leave him alone. He was forced to finish everything. The prisoner was contorted with pain, and the S.S. man stood above him with a pistol in his hand and yelled, "Either you finish, or I finish you."

The Russian collapsed. They took him to the hospital, and a few hours later he was dead.

*

The Melk camp was near the city, and I, together with other prisoners, went to town a few times under S.S. guard to get provisions from the storehouses. The pain we felt in our hearts! A great longing for freedom hit us. We saw people walking freely in the town, and we – already in prison for many years. We were always in pain, without hope and without purpose.

At the beginning of April, 1945, the allied armies of Americans, English and Russians started massive attacks in the air and on land against the German army.

We could see flights of about 70 American aircraft bombing German troop concentrations, railway stations, and other strategic targets about 5 or 6 times a day. We started to feel that the end was coming near.

The S.S. men walked around with their heads bowed low. They were getting bad news from home, about bombings and about family problems.

An order came on April 15 to leave the camp. We crossed the Danube in motorboats and came to Salzburg. From there we walked to a new camp called Ebensee. On the way from Salzburg to Ebensee we crossed the Alps, which were covered with snow. We managed to gorge ourselves on the snow. But many were shot by our guards when they stuck out their hands to take this blessed manna. But the hunger and thirst were so strong that we didn't pay attention to the shots. Whoever was killed – was killed, and the rest continued to extend their hands and grab the snow to replenish our broken souls.

We started new jobs in Ebensee under new conditions, different than those in all the other camps. We all had swollen bodies.

The clothing was a short jacket, pants without underwear, and wooden shoes without socks. In general, it was the most unusual camp of all those we passed through. Inmates were walking around with a bone or a piece of charcoal in their hand. They would suck at this, and then drink a lot of water, of which there was no shortage in camp.

When we asked, "What are you sucking on?" They answered, "This is our food until we die!" We didn't have to ask much more. That same day we felt it ourselves.

We were 18,000 men, 5,000 of them Jews, in 29 wooden sheds. Of these, one was used as a kitchen, three for washing, and three for bathrooms. One shed housed 1,200 people. The beds were one on top of another in bunks. The beds were 60 centimeters wide. Four prisoners slept in one bed,

If someone wanted to turn around, he would have to waken his bedmates, and the four of them would turn around together.

We slept like pickled fish in a barrel.

When we had to go to the toilet, we would do it in a bucket in our shed because the doors were shut all night from seven in the evening to three in the morning. Then we were awakened by water being poured onto our beds. We tried to wake up before this, and were immediately herded into the yard.

There was a very cold rain outside. It rains every day in the Alps during April, and our clothes were suitable for summertime in Asia.

The prisoners would bring the tea from the kitchen. Once I also went to bring tea, and I saw a prisoner hanging, with a sign on him, "He stole one potato." We brought the tea to the courtyard of our shed. Our supervisors would distribute the tea in two liter bowls, one bowl for every four people.

We would stand in the courtyard for about three hours, and each one would rub the back of the next person, in order to warm up a little. Our clothes were wet, because at six in the morning we went to the main courtyard, where we would be sent for work outside.

We worked at removing the iron rails from the railway stations that had been bombed by the Americans, and other very hard labor. We would travel every day for thirty kilometers in freight cars. To our good fortune, we could warm up a little bit inside, and we managed to nap a little on the way, which took about an hour. By the sides of the road, we could see the great changes in the war situation. There were German families on the roads, carrying parcels and luggage, running to and fro without any order, dirty and unshaven. We also saw soldiers, disorganized, handicapped, riding in carts with horses. Like it was on the first days when the war broke out in 1939, in the vicinity of our Sierpc.

The S.S. men who were guarding us started to confess to us and to justify themselves: "Why are we to blame? It's all him, the Führer! He gave the orders! Look, we don't have anything to eat either. We just got one sandwich today, and it's supposed to last the whole day."

But they were talking to dead people, not to living ones. Instead of working, every one of us looked for a little grass. To revive the soul. Under the grass we would find live worms. That was our food: grass and worms. Once we found the hide of a cow stored in salt inside a ruined barn. We cut it up and shared it. Everyone received a tiny piece, and we sucked on it all day...

At three in the afternoon we would return to the camp and go to the market in the camp. What was the market? You could buy tiny pieces of meat from corpses. There were inmates who managed to sneak into the morgue and cut pieces of flesh from the bodies – if they had any flesh left on them. Because knives were forbidden in the camp, they sharpened spoon handles, and these served as knives.

The pieces of meat would be traded for the bread ration that was handed out the previous night. Also for the cigarette that each one of us got once a week.

The trade went on until it became known to the S.S. and they shot some of those who sneaked into the morgue. And so the commerce in meat was ended...

The situation became worse. The inmates walked around like shadows on the accursed earth. Each inmate weighed about 40 kilograms. At six in the evening we received our rations: 100 grams of bread that was like plaster.. But not everyone even managed to get that. Every day there were a lot of rations missing. And if I managed to get my hands on the ration, often I would feel a strong blow on my arm, usually from a Russian prisoner, and the bread fell, and was stolen from me.

We also received half a liter of soup. The soup was very thin, water boiled with the peels of potatoes that were cooked for the S.S. men. And who was the lucky man who found a peel in his portion? Usually there was not enough soup, especially for the Jews; because the other prisoners would stand in line twice or three times and the barrel quickly became empty, and we would go back with empty bowls.

I and a friend of mine, Bezalel Jakubowicz from Zakroczym in Poland, decided to commit suicide, instead of dying of blows or starvation. But apparently, the Angel of Death didn't want us...

One morning, the *bockältester*, a German inmate and a very malicious man, came in and told us: "Today, you will get your bread ration in the morning. The ration will be 250 grams. From today, the soup will be thick, so much so that you can stick your spoon into it, and it will not fall over..."

"Today you won't go out to work, and if you do go out, you won't be beaten anymore."

We didn't know what was happening. A new transport arrived within an hour, and on it were 150 Jews. I looked at them and recognized them. In 1943 they were in Auschwitz, and now they arrived from Germany. They had worked there for about a year and a half, printing all sorts of money, foreign currency like dollars, pounds sterling and identification cards used for espionage. They were specialists at this kind of work, and they lived in a camp with underground barracks; that was where they worked and lived.

The S.S. men that had brought them to Ebensee had received an order to liquidate them in the forest, but their officer abandoned his troops in the middle of the way, and the order was not carried out. A surprising event.

At eight in the morning we heard shouting: "Everyone to the main assembly point." We thought that they were going to transfer us again to another camp. But the camp commander got up on a chair so that everyone could see and hear him, and said: "Honorable sirs! I am asking for translators, because I have to tell you something important." The translators went up to him – a Spaniard, a Polish man, a Russian, and a Frenchman and the camp commander began his speech.

Because the American Army had already arrived in town, and certainly intended to shell the Ebensee Camp, he advised us to go into the tunnels that had been dug under the Alps. There we would be safe from the American shells, and we would stay alive.

As if automatically, there were cries from all sides.

"We're not going!!!"

The first ones to yell this were German inmates, *kapos* and *bockältester*. It turns out that on the previous day they had seen S.S. men digging in the ground in the tunnels, and planting explosives and mines there. That was meant for us. To put us in there and exterminate us in the last hour before freedom. But the murderers did not succeed in accomplishing their satanic plan.

After an hour, the explosions started inside the tunnels and went on for about twelve hours.

This was the first time that prisoners dared oppose the S.S. men, and the first time in six years that we heard the word "Sirs!" from the S.S. men. The phrases we always heard were "Dogs," "Filth," and similar words.

That same day, in the afternoon, two American tanks broke through the camp gate. The tanks were manned by black soldiers. They threw candy bars, biscuits, and food to us, and shouted, "You are free! The barbed wire fences have been torn down! Go out to freedom!"

We could not believe our eyes. It was like a dream. The blood froze in our veins. But we recovered quickly, grabbed the weapons that the S.S. men had tossed away, and we shot those who were running away. The revenge started with the *kapos* and *bockältester*. We paid back anyone we could catch.

But not all those who were freed stayed alive. Many died after they started to eat too enthusiastically after the extended starvation. Because the Americans had brought fatty nourishments and others types of foodstuffs that harmed the unlucky people. The cemetery at Ebensee became fully occupied after a few days...

General Eisenhower, today[46] the President of the United States, came to the camp the day after the liberation. When he saw the prisoners, and the piles of corpses in the courtyard, his eyes filled with tears. He issued an order that all the German men in the town of Ebensee had to come to the camp and take care of the corpses. And the Mayor would be responsible that everything be done correctly.

Within half an hour, all the German men from the town were in the camp and started to look after the dead. They started to justify themselves, that they never knew about this camp. They had heard that there were workers in the camp, who received wages and food...The bastards! They immediately tried to pretend that they were innocent...

The problem was that the Americans wouldn't let us take our revenge out on them. They even punished us for any act of revenge that we took out on the Germans. We would walk around town, and we turned over any S.S. man that we recognized from the camp to the American Military Police.

I rested for two weeks to gain a little strength and went off to search for my wife and my relatives; maybe someone was left alive. I went through Austria and Germany. I looked through lists of survivors but, to my great anguish, I could find neither relatives, acquaintances, nor townspeople.

After three months of wandering, I came to Sierpc, and there I found my wife. At the outbreak of the Holocaust, we agreed if something unusual happened, and we stayed alive, we would meet in Sierpc, and that is what happened.

There were four Jews in Sierpc then. When I was walking down a street, I met a Gentile who recognized me and was surprised that I was still alive. He asked me, "You're still alive? This jolly group will never be lost." He was simply sick at heart that he saw another Jew left alive.

We could not stay in Sierpc. I saw Warshawska Street paved over with headstones from the cemetery. As long as I was far away from the town, I did not feel the pain of the great calamity that we had undergone. Everything was lost. No parents, no brothers or sisters, no acquaintances or neighbors or friends. All we saw were empty lots where there once were Jewish houses. The Gentiles had taken over the stores, standing there and selling things, as if it all were theirs; as if there had never been a Jewish community here...

We stayed in the town for four days. From there we returned to West Germany, which was under American occupation, and then we came to Palestine in 1946. We have put down roots in Israel, but we will never be able to forget what we went through in those terrible years of the war, what the German *Amalek* did to us. May it be cursed forever!

פנחס ואַלטסמן

(„פיניה דעם פאַרבערס")

נרצח בחושו להצלת בית־הכנסת מהדליקה

[Notice –]
Pinchas Walcman ("Pinia the Painter")
Murdered when he Rushed to Save the Synagogue from the Conflagration

Rivkah Tatz (Ika Richter)

Active in the Underground Resistance Who Aided Children and Adults in France

Attorney Yehoshua Podskoc

Active in the Underground Resistance
Who aided children in the Warsaw Ghetto

Hanna Kaufman

Murdered While Bringing Weapons into the Warsaw Ghetto

איסר צ׳אֶשלק

(אשר בן־מרדכי)

נפל במלחמת־העצמאות בצפון הארץ

Isser Czeslak
(Asher Ben-Mordecai)
Fell in Battle in the War of Independence in Northern Israel

A Partisan
Drawing by Avraham Meiron (Marantz)

A Group of Illegal Immigrants from the Sierpc Survivors in Cyprus[47]

Right to Left:
First Row: Zvi Lehrer, -- --, -- --, Filinger
Standing: Birnbaum, Binem Mai, -- --, -- --, David Frank, the wife of S.L., Shlomo Lewinsky

Translator's Footnotes

The list of translator's endnotes (inside of square [ ] brackets) to indicate that they are not part of the original text.:

1. [Polish Parliament]
2. [*Obóz Zjednoczenia Narodowego* (Camp of National Unity) – a Polish right-wing Anti-Semitic party.]
3. [So called "inspectors" who enforced the boycott.]
4. [A house of study and worship]
5. [The chief administrator of the county]
6. [See "Institutions and Activists" (page 61) in this Yizkor Book.]
7. [Madrid had been the first city ever to undergo sustained aerial bombardment, by the Germans during the Spanish Civil War.]
8. [Ethnic Germans living in Poland who formed an armed militia at the beginning of the German occupation.]
9. [The German district occupation authority.]
10. [Under the terms of a non-aggression treaty signed between the U.S.S.R. and Nazi Germany shortly before the war (The Molotov–Ribbentrop Pact), Poland was divided between the two countries.]
11. [Town hall]
12. [The "General Government" was what the Germans called those sections of Poland that were not annexed to the German Reich, but under German occupation.]
13. [A book of legends and sayings of the ancient wise men.]
14. [The minimum number of 10 men required for a Jewish prayer service.]
15. [American Jewish Joint Distribution Committee]
16. [A man who was a ritual slaughterer of kosher meat]
17. [Burial Society]
18. ["Chapters of the Fathers" - a compilation of the ethical teachings and maxims of the Rabbis of the Mishnaic period.]
19. [Homiletic stories told by Jewish rabbinical sages to explain passages in the Bible]
20. [The acronym for Rabbi Shlomo Itzhaki, an 11th century sage who wrote an extensive commentary on the Talmud and Bible.]
21. [The parts of the Talmud that are the rabbinical commentaries on the earlier sections of the Talmud which are called Mishna.]
22. [The ceremony that marks the end of the Sabbath day.]
23. [The king of the Jews]
24. [Leader of the Jews]
25. [Head of the town council]
26. [The departure point for the camps in the Warsaw Ghetto]
27. [The term "transport" is used throughout this chapter by the author as a noun referring to groups of Jews who were sent together to camps by the Germans; it was the accepted term in Yiddish and Hebrew. The office responsible for getting the Jews from one place to another was the German Ministry of Transport.]
28. [Penitential poems and prayers usually said before the High Holidays.]
29. [A Jewish concept of a supreme rabbinical court that can influence the decisions of the heavenly court presided over by God himself.]
30. [A court convened in ancient Israel to determine religious laws and edicts. The reference here is to the judges. The lesser *Sanhedrin* had 23 Judges, and there was such a court in every town in ancient Israel]
31. [The Jewish units in the death camps that were forced to do the work of disposing of the corpses.]

32. [The German term for a military type unit; it was the basic unit of organization for slave laborers in the camps.]
33. [This was a unit that collected the belongings of the victims and took them to a warehouse facility for sorting and shipping back to Germany.]
34. [Block leader – a prisoner]
35. [Room leader – a prisoner]
36. [The Political Unit for the Registration of Arrivals]
37. [Birkenau was the death camp inside of Auschwitz.]
38. [The Jewish prayer for the dead.]
39. [A work supervisor who was a prisoner.]
40. [Chief S.S. officer in the camp.]
41. [Delousing room]
42. [The term used in the original Hebrew text is *selektsia*, which is obviously not originally a Hebrew word, but comes from English or German. In Hebrew, it is used almost exclusively to denote the process by which individual Jews were chosen by the Germans to live or die. In the English translation here, "selection" always appears inside double quotation marks.]
43. [The word means Muslim in Yiddish and German, but was used in the camps as a derogatory term for those who looked like living skeletons.]
44. [The Amalekites were the chief ancient nemesis of the Hebrew tribes, known in the Bible for their viciousness, ruthlessness, and tyranny.]
45. [Delousing]
46. [This *Yizkor* book was published in 1960.]

[After World War II and prior to the establishment of the State of Israel, the British government forbade Jewish emigration to Palestine. Jews who were captured on ships trying to run the British blockade were interned in camps in Cyprus.]

Excerpts about the Holocaust

by I.M. Sidroni (Sendrowicz)

It is impossible to comprehend the extent of the huge and terrible Holocaust that was perpetrated upon the Jews of Europe in general and the Jews of Poland in particular, by the German murderers and their allies during the Second World War. Neither the heart nor the mind can understand it or encompass it. The Holocaust has not yet penetrated the hearts and minds of the peoples of the world, but also not the hearts and minds of the Jewish world, in its full significance and terror. We know, from extensively reading the newspapers and the literature of the Holocaust, and from hearing eye-witnesses – people who went through the seven circles of hell and survived thanks to thousands of miracles – that they themselves have not yet grasped all the events that happened around them and all the tragedies that affected them. It is not surprising then that others, on whom the Holocaust did not leave its terrible mark directly, have not been able to comprehend that awful period.

This chapter describes the effect of the Holocaust on the Jews of Sierpc. We want to present to the readers, both our townbspeople and others, excerpts from newspapers and books that discuss events in the town itself, before the deportation, and outside of the town, after the deportation. We also present some excerpts from the "Ringelblum Archives"[1] of the Warsaw Ghetto.

The Jews of Sierpc were not mentioned much in the press and literature in all the years of their existence, just small citations here and there. This was not the case during the period of the Holocaust and afterwards. During this time they achieved "fame" prior to their destruction.

Below are passages that were found in the literature and the press, as they were written, and in their original language.[2]

A. Before the Deportation

c. Intense Battles on the Sierpc-Plonsk Line

The newspaper *Davar*, published in Tel-Aviv on 23 Elul 5699 (September 7, 1939) contained the following dispatch:

[H] "Warsaw, 7 (Reuters). An official Polish announcement states: 20 German aircraft were shot down yesterday (the day before yesterday) and 15 more aircraft today (yesterday). Only six of our Polish aircraft were intercepted and destroyed. There are intense battles going on north of the Torun Sierpc-Plonsk line. The enemy did not advance at all yesterday.

"Their aircraft were heard a few times over our positions and over Warsaw."

d. The Burning of the Synagogue and other Misfortunes

The newspaper *HaTsfira* published in Tel-Aviv on 19 Kislev 5700 (December 1, 1939) had the following item:

[H] "The Horrors of the Nazi Occupation

"The synagogue in Sierpc went up in flames, and the man who tried to extinguish them was killed on the spot.

"A postcard from Orsha, Russia that was sent on the sixth of November reached here on 29 November, to a family in the Ahuza [neighborhood] on the Carmel.[3] The writer tells (in Polish) that he escaped from the Nazis only by a miracle. After a trip of 200 kilometers on roads full of troops and refugees, he arrived in Orsha, where he wrote this postcard.

"Among the other atrocities and insanity of the Nazis, he says that the synagogue in the town of Sierpc, that was built 100 years ago[4] and was among the most magnificent in Poland, had been set ablaze. A young Jewish man, who tried to put out the fire, was shot and killed on the spot by German soldiers.[5]

"When the Hitlerist army entered the town, 53 Jews were abducted and their whereabouts are unknown. Residents and leaders of the town were among them. The writer lists three names, and they are: Selik Nemczewko, Yaakov Waldenberg, and Avraham Tac.[6]

"The mercantile house of the 'Tac Brothers' was plundered and entirely destroyed."

e. The Suffering of the Jews of Sierpc

The newspaper *Morgen Freiheit* that appeared in New York on January 3, 1940 contained a lengthy letter written by Beryl Feinberg (the writer of the above postcard) on November 12, 1939 to his uncle Shlomo Feinberg in Brooklyn. We are presenting the sections that pertain to Sierpc below:

[Y] "A Moving Letter from Jews who Fled the Shtetl Sierpc, Poland

"I will write to you of what happened to us in Sierpc when we found out that the Germans are coming to our town. All the men between 14 and 60 and older were told to flee. We were told that if we succeeded in getting to the other side of the Vistula River, we would be saved.

"I took to the road by foot together with Israelken, Yehudan, and Chaiman. You can imagine what they thought about this at home. It was very hard for mother to let four sons go out into the world. Rachel, Rivkah, and Biella were crying. Mother was devastated, and only we did not feel any tears.

"We started on our way and traveled to Dobrzyn and from there made our way to the Vistula and crossed it in boats. We had to wait a long time for them,

"...It turned out that the on the other side of the Vistula it was exactly the same as on our side, and that we had to go home.

"...Mother and the others at home thought that we were already not among the living. You can imagine their joy when we returned home, when many others were killed on the road. But don't think that home had become the Garden of Eden. So listen to what the Hitlerists did to us:

"They went from house to house and took out Jews for all sorts of labor. For instance, the old man Yehoshua Goldman had to sweep up the market square in front of the town hall, and on top of this, they lashed him with whips. The old Cantor Scheikes had to sing while sweeping in the middle of the market and afterwards they put a straw on his shoulder and told him to jump. And when the straw fell off, they beat him mercilessly.

"A policeman came to Moniak Podskoc's house and when he noticed that he was trying to hide, he beat him so badly that they had to take him to the hospital. He is still confined to his bed.

"Three weeks ago the Hitlerists set the synagogue on fire. When a Jewish boy came running with a bucket of water to put out the fire, they killed him on the spot. Afterwards, they stood the Jews in the street and forced them to say that they themselves had set fire to the synagogue. They shot at David Bergson, but they didn't hit him.

"They completely emptied out Shmuel Tac's store. Lately they have been taking Jewish girls and women to clean the toilets in the jail. Among others there were Golda Goldman, Rocha Tac, and Rosina.

"One time I was in the store selling things, and two soldiers came in and told me to put on my coat and come with them. One of the soldiers went outside, and the other whispered into my ear that I'm going to be sent together with a large group to a place from which I will never return. I immediately caught on, cut off a piece of material and gave it to him, and I immediately left by the back door. Since that day, I have not gone to the store. I have been hiding with all of my brothers in a pantry which is concealed by a closet.

"Israel, Chayim, and I have decided to go to the Soviet area[7]. We wanted to go to Ostrołęka, where we had heard that there was a unit of the Red Army. We bought three bicycles, packed a little laundry, and with many tears we left our town for the land of all the workers.

"We were the first from Sierpc to leave, and we were very lucky because of that. Others had their bicycles, clothes, and money taken away from them, and they crossed the border confused and naked. They didn't take anything from us, and almost without any incidents we managed to cross to the Soviet side, near łomazy.

"It was already evening. The town, in ruins and burned down, was covered with the first snow. A very nice girl invited us into her home, gave us something to eat, and let us sleep over.

"...I am now in a town in White Russia, Orsha. My two brothers, Israel and Chayim, stayed in Bialystok.

"...I forgot to write to you about something else: When the soldiers came for me in my store, and I managed to get away, they took 53 youths out of the town. Their parents did not know where they were. That day, the Jewish population of Sierpc underwent an indescribable tragedy. Among those that were taken away were: Sallek Nemczewki, Avraham Tac, Lichtenstein, Baruch Nemczewko, Yaakov Rotman, Zhitalni, Granewicz, the Greener brothers, and others. When we got to Bialystok, we met them all..."

f. In the Warsaw Ghetto

I have in front of me five eye witness testimonies by deportees from Sierpc in the Warsaw Ghetto. They are part of the Ringelblum Archives that are now located in the Jewish Historical Institute in Warsaw, after they had been extracted from underground hiding places beneath the ruins of the ghetto, where they had been concealed.. One of the testimonies has the initials of the witness, P.K., and another has a date, May13, 1941. The testimony of P.K. briefly mentions the ghetto in Sierpc, and says: "At this moment, there is not even one Jew left in Sierpc, because half of them died, and half were sent to Stezhgovo." This proves that this testimony was taken after January 6, 1942, the day that the residents of the Sierpc Ghetto were banished to Stezhgovo. Three of the testimonies are in Yiddish, and two are in Polish. We quote here excerpts from these statements about events and tribulations that were not noted by other Sierpc survivors, or described in general, without details.

[Y]"On September 11, a security police force was formed, composed of *Volksdeutsch*[8]. Their first job was to take the keys of all Jewish businesses. They used the opportunity to beat Jews. They gave the keys back the next day, and used the opportunity to renew the beatings.

"...We started to do forced labor. It was very hard work and we were mercilessly beaten while doing it, so Jews started hiding all day and night in attics and closets, under stairwells and beds. This gave the Germans the opportunity for making searches and inspections, and beating the people there while they were at it. The Poles played not a small role in this. Not only did they show where the Jews lived, but they actively helped in the police raids and searches.

"...An edict was issued that merchandise can be sold only by showing ration cards. Jews were not given such cards.

"...On the 15th (of September), registration was required of everyone between 16 and 60, under penalty of death. There was a great panic in town; people did not know what this will lead to. Mothers became very distressed, because they thought that they would all be sent away immediately.

"The S.S. came to town on the 18th. Their first visits were to the leaders of the community and the sextons of the prayer houses. They immediately sealed the houses of worship and the community center and made the leaders and sextons responsible for collecting the signatures. They had to show up twice a day to declare themselves, in the morning and in the evening. Understand that each time they had to wash and clean the toilets. And when [the Germans felt like it, they took them to a stable and ordered them to face the wall and took out their weapons to frighten them into thinking they were going to shoot them.

"...That is when the grief and sorrow began, with the forced labor, beatings, and the taking of merchandise. In order to find forced labor, they would take a few Polish underworld types who would show them who is Jewish.

"...That is how the synagogue was burned down to its foundation, without a drop of water allowed inside. Only when the fire came close to the Polish houses did they allow the firemen to start extinguishing it, and then they took the Jews for forced labor. That was on the second night of Sukkoth. The next day, when the Jews came to work, they were told to turn over the person who had set the synagogue on fire. And they immediately stationed military units next to other places of worship to prevent them from being burned down[9].

"...On the 12th of October a regulation was issued that Jews must wear a yellow patch which had "Jude" written on it. We cannot walk on the sidewalk and must doff our hats to Christians. These regulations were released by the town hall.

"On the 14th all Jewish stores were closed, and everyone had to declare how much the business earned.

"Since there were a lot of *Volksdeutsch* in our neighborhood, they allowed themselves a really good time. They took furniture from the Jews, merchandise, whatever any one of them felt like taking. They caused many problems for the Jews.

"...After we returned to Sierpc, the Gestapo came, and immediately terrible times began for the Sierpc Jews. All Jewish institutions were closed and their books were confiscated. The *batei midrash*[10] were sealed shut. They took the tools away from the ritual slaughterers.

"...On the 18th of October, the civil administration of Sierpc was shut down. New edicts were issued against the Jews: Jews cannot manage their own workshops, cannot use electricity, and everyone must relinquish his properties.

"...On the 22nd, they sent a letter to the Jewish Community that within three days they have to pay 50,000 zloty. This meant taking a lot of money from many people. Understand that wealthy Jews did not especially want to reveal how much money they had. Some of them fled from Sierpc. But all their efforts were not enough to reduce the sum. A delegation went to the *burgermeister*[11] with 40,000 zlotys, and they were given a postponement until the 27th. After a lot of hard work, we finally succeeded in collecting the 10,000 zloty.

"Together with meeting that deadline, on the 29th, sums from individuals that totaled half a million zloty were demanded. The smallest amount was 800 zloty, and the largest was 40,000, which had to be given within 48 hours. The whole world started chasing after as much money as they had, but in the *magistrat*[12] they ordered that it be brought on Monday. That same evening, as soon as it became dark, gendarmes went through the town to certain addresses of individual contributors, and arrested them all, a total of 100 men. They harassed them for the whole night and beat them until they bled. They broke one young man's hand. That is how they treated them until nine in the morning. One of their officers came in the morning and said that whoever gave a thousand zloty would be set free. Some rich men gave 800 zloty or 600 zloty, and the last there gave 20 zloty. One of them was released without even giving a penny.

"Two days later, they took over all the Jewish businesses. They came with trucks and removed all the merchandise. This took several days.

"At the end of October, baking by Jewish bakers was forbidden."

g. About the Expulsion and the Ghetto

[Y]"...From among all the Jews (who were assembled in the marketplace for deportation) they chose 50 families, most of them artisans: shoemakers and tailors, who were allowed to stay. Also left behind were a few old people, whose because of age and physical condition were not able to walk.

"With time, a ghetto was formed there."

B. A Minor Deportation

h. The Deportation of About 50 Young Men

The newspaper *Davar* of 14 Tevet 5700 (December 12, 1939) published the following letter:[13]

[H]"They Took Us for Work, but Really for Torture"

"Someone who was deported from Sierpc by the Gestapo and who is now in Vilnius[14], wrote a letter to his siblings in Tel-Aviv:

"Ever since the Germans conquered Sierpc, the conditions of the Jews there have become insufferable. When they came, the gangs of the Gestapo and Storm Troopers took the Jews from their homes every day and forced them to do any sort of labor. Age didn't matter to them. The abuse during this labor cannot be put into words. Some Jews needed a doctor after finishing work, those that were still alive. They took our father from our house on the morning of Yom Kippur, shaved his beard, and forced him to sweep the street while wearing his prayer shawl. To his good fortune, they didn't keep him there for very long. You can only imagine our Yom Kippur... Some Jews were cruelly tortured that day while working. Thanks be to God on high, they didn't find anyone else in our house except on Yom Kippur. The days passed in this way until the eve of Sukkoth.

"That day, the Gestapo men went from house to house and took over fifty young men. I was one of them. They took us for work, but really for torture. But what can we do? We waited for it to end and a chance to go home. Suddenly, a Gestapo man appeared with a piece of paper in his hand and started to read a declaration which said that we have to leave the territory conquered by the Germans, without ever returning. If anyone returns here, he will be stoned and shot. We were forced to sign this declaration. None of us were allowed to go home, not even to get a parting blessing from parents and relatives and take something for the road. They kept us in the jail overnight.

"The next morning, the first day of Sukkoth, they took us with buses to Plonsk, and told us to run. We didn't manage to take anything with us. Mothers who apparently heard that we were being deported came in the morning and stood at a distance from the jail. (Men didn't dare to come.) But they didn't let them approach us or talk, or give us a package or something for the road. Wearing just light clothes and without a penny, we went on our way. As we passed through the villages, the peasants took pity on us and from time to time gave us pieces of bread. This is how we wandered until we arrived at the area occupied by the Russians. About twenty of us reached Vilnius."

i. A Letter from the Refugees in Vilnius

The following letter appeared in the newspaper *Forward*, published in New York on December 26, 1939:

[Y]"Jews who fled the shtetl Sierpc (Plotzk Administrative District, Poland) write to the Forward.

"To the worthy Editor of the Forward:

"We are a group of refugees from the town of Sierpc (Poland), and we turn to you with a request that you publish this letter in your important newspaper, for which we thank you in advance. In this way, you can save us from ruin.

"With great respect, the undersigned refugees.

"An urgent appeal to our Sierpc compatriots who are in America!

"We are a group of refugees from the town of Sierpc, Plotzk District (Poland), with the following request: If you are acquainted with the miserable situation of the Polish Jews, then we can inform you that, unfortunately, we are still among them. It happened in the following way. The Germans occupied our town Sierpc eight days after the war broke out. That is when the suffering of the Jews in the town started. Every day they would drag the Jews out of their houses and take them for the hardest labor without considering their age, and beat them until they drew blood. They cut the beards of all the adult Jews with dull knives and tried to carve swastikas in them. On Rosh Hashanah the *batei midrash* were shut by the Gestapo and the Torah scrolls were tossed on the ground and ripped apart by the filthy hands of the Nazis. Then all the Jews hid in the cellars, where we stealthily said the Rosh Hashanah prayers, so that they would not be heard in the street. Very early in the morning of Yom Kippur, all elderly Jews were dragged from their beds, and under the watchful eye of the storm troopers, had to sweep the streets with their bare hands while wearing their prayer shawls. All Jewish businesses were immediately confiscated, and the ritual slaughterers were forbidden to work, and their tools were taken away. On the eve of Sukkoth, without being told anything, they took us for forced labor, which was actually like a living hell, so that we wished for death instead of this persistent brutality. After this inhuman treatment, we were forced to sign a declaration that we will leave the German territory, never to return home, under penalty of death. Then they took us to a prison, where we spent the whole night. The next morning, the first day of Sukkoth, they took us by bus to the not yet finally determined German side of the border, not allowing us to take anything with us except what we wore on our backs. We had to walk for a few weeks under horrible conditions, suffering from hunger and cold. As much as was possible, we didn't stay the night anywhere until we reached Vilnius. We realize that our parents do not know what happened to us, and that we do not know our parents' fate. When we were on the road, we heard the tearful news that the Sierpc synagogue was burned down by the Gestapo, and that a Jewish boy was shot trying to rescue the Torah scrolls. In Vilnius all we have is a room where we sleep on the floor and one meal a day. We are suffering from the cold and hunger, and walk around without clothes and barefoot, and have no way of earning our living. We are all ready to work, and we don't want to be a burden to anyone. Therefore we are sending you this urgent appeal to quickly send us material help, and to also get immigration permits to America for us. We believe that you will fulfill our request, considering our current tragic state. We thank you in advance, and send you regards from all our hearts, from far away.

"With respect,

The Sierpcer Refugees who find themselves in Vilnius: Yitzhak Bergson, Fibush Grainne, Yaakov Grainne, Yitzchak Gedaliah Danziger, Yehoshua Tcharnotchepka, Eliezer Tcharnobrodna, Avraham Sendrowicz, Michal Sendrowicz, David Sendrowicz, Zalman Grodka, David Aaronson, Pesach Friedman, Avraham Sendrowicz, Shmuel Mai"

j. A Letter from the Refugee Committee in Vilnius

The following letter, though it did not appear in a newspaper, deserves to be in this book and in this chapter.[15]

[Y]"Vilnius, January 28, 1940.

"To the Relief Committee of Sierpc Townsmen in America.

"We have the honor of telling you that we received your letter of the 2nd of this month, wherein you sent through HIAS[16] three hundred (300) lita[17], for which we are very grateful.

"We can inform you that we have called a meeting of all the Sierpcer who are now in Vilnius - 33 people who came on the 25th of this month. We chose a committee of five who will work with you on the matters of concern to the Sierpcers in exile in Vilnius. This committee is composed of the following people: David Nemczewki – a teacher, Michal Lipsker – a director of the Folks-Bank in Sierpc, Eliezer Zashutke, Yitzhak Bergson, Avraham Sendrowicz

At the meeting it was decided that your grant of 300 lita would be distributed equally to the Sierpcer in amounts of eight lita and eighty cents each. (We decided to withhold 10 lita for necessary expenses.) We are sending a receipt from the Sierpcer in Vilnius.

"You should realize that beginning with the deportation from Sierpc, all the Jews in our town were driven out, and they were not allowed to take anything with them. Many found themselves in Warsaw in tragic circumstances, many were in Bialystok and other towns occupied by the Soviets, and their situation was not very good either. They are all trying, with all their resources, to come to Vilnius. From here they have an opportunity to get in touch with the outside world, to try and emigrate.

"The Lithuanians are now registering all refugees. A large part of them immediately get residence orders to settle in small towns or villages in Lithuania. The situation is very unclear. This makes it imperative that the outside world should take an interest in the refugees. And it would be very helpful if our dear compatriots in America could actively concern themselves with our situation.

"During the above-mentioned meeting, the question came up of how we could support our dear ones in the German occupied areas monetarily, because their situation is critical. We believe that there is a way that we can successfully manage to transfer money to our families.

"We can inform you that the following families are in Bialystok: Szmiga, Jurkewicz, Fabian, Rotman, Malowanczyk Zvi, and other individuals. In our town, Sierpc, there are a few Jews whom the Germans allowed to stay: Moshe Yehuda Kirsch and his wife, Henich Tcharnobrodna and his wife, Yaakov Rabinowicz (who managed an iron business together with the Friedmans), and Leibl Gotlibowski, his wife, child, and mother.

"We thank you for the sum you sent and ask you to reply to us soon.

"Write to us and tell us if it is possible to get residence papers for us in America. This would be the only help in our present critical situation.

"We await your answer and remain, with respect: David Nemczewki, Michal Lipsker, Eliezer Zashutke, Yitzhak Bergson, A.I, Sendrowicz

"We can be reached at the following address: Care of HIAS, D. Niemczewko, Vilnius, Konsca q-ve 26-13, Lietuva"

A receipt for the money received from the "Relief" (Aid Fund) of Sierpc townbspeople in America is enclosed with this letter. It is signed by 33 Sierpc exiles in Vilnius, and reads as follows:[18]

k. [Y]"Receipt"

We the undersigned hereby acknowledge the receipt of eight lita and 80 cent (8.80) from the Refugee Committee of Sierpc Townbspeople in Vilnius.

1. Eliezer Zashutke
2. David Nemczewki
3. Yitzhak Bergson
4. Shlomo Rajczyk
5. Zalman Niemczewko
6. Baruch Niemczewko (son of Ita)
7. Wolfe Lichtenstein
8. Yitzhak Danziger
9. Avraham Yosef Sendrowicz (son of Yitzhak Meir)
10. Avraham Yosef Sendrowicz (son of Hirsch Michal)
11. David Sendrowicz
12. David Aronson
13. Michal Sendrowicz
14. Pesach Friedman
15. Yaakov Shultz
16. Avraham Zhabitsky
17. Shlomo Grajewan
18. Israel Zhabitsky
19. Fibush Grina
20. Yaakov Grina
21. Lazier Tcharnobrodna
22. Avraham Lipchitz
23. Sara Graniewicz-Lipchitz
24. Menachem Graniewicz
25. Avraham Podskoc
26. Mendel Podskoc
27. Yosef Leib Zomerowicz
28. Shmuel Mai
29. Motel Wafel
30. Shimshon Engelmann
31. Yehoshua Tcharnotchepka
32. Zalman Grodka
33. Michal Lipsker"

C. The Deportation

In the book *Yon-Metzula HeHadash*[19] by Moshe Prager that was published in Tel-Aviv in 5711 [1950], page 44 has the following passage:

[H]"On the 7th of November[20] a sentence of deportation was issued to the Jewish residents of the region of Sierpc, who numbered almost 20,000 souls. In one day, the Jewish settlements in Sierpc, Racionz, Zhuromin, Biezun, and the neighboring villages were wiped out."

l. [H]From the Horrors of These Days

The newspaper *Davar* of 2 Tevet 5700 (December 14, 1939) writes, among other reports under the above headline, the following:

[H]"All the Jews of the town of Chęciny received an order to leave town. The Jewish residents of the towns of Sierpc and Zhuromin and some towns in the region of Plotzk were also expelled."

m. [Y]"Terrible Information from Wojsławice, Plotzk, Chelm, Hrubieszów, Sierpc and other Towns in Nazi Poland"

In the *Forward* newspaper in January, 1940, the following is written under the above headline:

[Y]"Jews are being driven out of their living quarters every day in Wojsławice, Plotzk, Sierpc, Drobin, Lipno, and other towns.

"All the Jews have already been expelled from many streets there.

"In Sierpc, the Jews were taken to the train station accompanied by band music. They were forced to form three separate columns, and not allowed to take even a shirt.

"In all of Poland, husbands, wives and children were separated, one not knowing where the other was headed.

"In Plotzk the Jews were once forced to run in the streets chasing after ducks. When they couldn't catch a duck, they would be beaten.

"In Sierpc and Plotzk, the Jews were made to wear their prayer shawls and forced to walk through the streets singing Jewish songs."

The same news item appeared in the newspaper *HaTzofe* of the 9th of Adar A, 5700 (February 18, 1940).

n. [H]"Bloody Incidents in the Towns of Poland"

The newspaper *Davar*, on the 6th of Adar A, 5700 (February 15, 1940) wrote as follows beneath the above headline, among other items:

[H]"Our Jewish brethren were expelled from the towns of Sierpc and Zhuromin. Some children got lost on the way, and their parents were not allowed to look for them."

o. [H]"From Eminent People Who Fled Poland:

Jews are Being Driven from Town to Town"

In the newspaper *HaBoker* of 11 Adar A, 5700 (February 20, 1940), under the above headline, the following is written, among other items.

[H]"The Nazis are responsible for conditions that have caused the outbreak of diseases among the Jews: they are being driven out, from place to place. Thus 7000 Jews were expelled from Sierpc, Plonsk, Rypin, etc. to Warsaw, and each was allowed to take only a small valise. There was no room for them in

Warsaw, and they were forced to sleep in the streets or in synagogues, hungry and dying from the cold"

p. [H]"The Handiwork of Eradication in Nazi Poland"

The newspaper *Davar* of 17 Adar A, 5700 (February 26, 1940) contained the following under the above headline:

[H]"London (Jewish Telegraphic Agency). Polish officials[21] have received information from the German occupied territory that the Nazi authorities have started deporting the Polish and Jewish populations from the Plotzk district. The Jews have already been expelled from the towns of Wojsławice, Drobin, Sierpc, Lipno, and Plotzk.

q. [Y]"Jewish Life in Nazi Poland"

In the newspaper *Neiveldt,* Tel-Aviv, of April 4 and 18, 1941, Z. Arthur wrote an article with the above headline, which contained, among the rest:

[Y]"One day, as I was sitting with another member of the community leadership, we were told that a delegation of displaced Jews from the shtetl Sierpc had come.

"We asked the delegation to come in. Two young Jewish laborers were standing in front of us. They looked depressed, with frightened eyes darting from side to side. They did not feel safe even in the office of the Jewish Community. Their clothes and shoes were torn and wrinkled. It took them a long time until they felt enough at ease to say what they wanted to say.

"And this is what they told us:

"A *Volksdeutsch* militia group was stationed in their shtetl for some time. These were German peasants who lived in the villages in the area, and were Polish citizens. On the first day they declared that Jewish property was forfeited. They then decreed that the Jewish community must pay a very large amount of money. In this way, the held the Jewish population hostage, since they would be shot if the money was not paid on time.

"Then they ordered all Jews to shut their stores. A day later they ordered them to open the stores and went inside by themselves. The Jewish stores were completely plundered. After this they brought wagons with horses to all Jewish homes and thoroughly searched and emptied them, taking everything they could find. Also furniture, and even dishes and brooms. They divided it among the German peasants in the surrounding German villages. In a few cases, the Polish neighbors also took something. They answered when asked about this, "You see, they are taking everything; let a little bit stay with 'your own.'

"After that came an order that all Jews, without exception, young and old, should gather in the marketplace. When all the Jews were in the marketplace, the Volksdeutsch militia searched all Jewish houses to make sure there wasn't a Jew squirreled away somewhere.--- They ordered them to stand in rows. The

German militia surrounded the crowd, a German orchestra[22] started playing, and that is how they led them to the railroad station. There, they stuffed them into freight cars. The cars were sealed, and the Jews were suddenly robbed of all their possessions, and shipped out of their town.

"---[23] The two boys stole away from the group after Nowy Dwor and made it quickly to Warsaw. The group of Jews that were expelled from Sierpc was still on its way. More than 1700[24] men, women, and children were deported.

"The Jews driven out of Sierpc did not arrive in Warsaw together. Near Warsaw, they were released, and ordered to go there. They were told that anyone who dared return to his shtetl would be shot.

"Three days after the two boys came, there were already 1200 Sierpc Jews in Warsaw. More came in the following days. The Jewish Community registered 1600 Sierpc Jews who came to Warsaw.

"What would people do back in the destroyed town? We talked it over among ourselves, we went to the head of the Joint,[25] we put the Jews up in synagogues and Hasidic prayer rooms.

"In one Hasidic prayer room, on Grzybowska Street, where there was, at the most, room for 40 people, there were 300 Jewish refugees from Sierpc. The people had come sick and broken. They fell on the floors, and they couldn't move for a few days. There was already an abdominal typhus epidemic raging among the Jews of Warsaw. Almost from the first day they were there, it started to break out among the Sierpc Jews. Every day we had to take tens of them from the places they were staying to the hospital, and many of them to the cemetery."

D. In Exile

r. In the Synagogue in Warsaw

In the newspaper *Di Voch* that appeared in Paris on December 22, 1939, the journalist S.L. Schneiderman published an article with the heading [Y]"This Is How the Jews in Warsaw Live," a conversation with Dr. H. Shoskes, who relates, among other things:

[Y]"The last Saturday before I left Warsaw, I prayed in a synagogue on Rinkowa Street near the Iron Gate Square. We prayed in the women's section, while beneath us, in the men's section, there were Jews from Sierpc lying there. They were hungry, abandoned, without any change of clothes."

s. [H]"Exiles from Kalisz, Sierpc, Racionz, and Others"

In the book *Yon-Metzula HeHadash* by Moshe Prager, Tel-Aviv, 5711, page 96, there is the following passage:

[H]"On 5 Rinkowa Street, in the little building of a small synagogue, 350 souls found shelter. They were the most miserable and unluckiest of the refugees from Kalisz, Sierpc, Racionz, and other places. Within just a few weeks, there were 35 cases of typhus here."

t. In Mlawa

In the book *Mlawa Notebook*, published in New York in 1950, on page 400:

[Y]"There were then in the city (Kislev 5701, December 1940) 6000 Jews, many of them from Sheps, Rypin, Zhuromin."

E. The Ghetto In Sierpc

The book *One From Town and Two From the Family* edited by Binyamin Tanenbaum, Merhavia, 1947 contains the following excerpt"

[H]"Yitzhak Dygola, 16, (nine years old at the outbreak of the war), relates:

"---We had relatives in Sierpc, so we went to that town and lived there for a year. I would go to work until we were deported to a ghetto of 200 Jews,[26] where we were crowded together, 15 or 20 to a room. There were many diseases, and many died of hunger. There too, I worked hard to earn my living."

F. The Stezhgovo Ghetto

The above book, *Mlawa Notebook*, says on page 405:

[Y]"Again after much pleading, the authorities consented to leave the Stezhgovo Jews where they were, and to bring there the Jews from Sheps, Racionz, and Biezun."

*

In the *Stezhgovo Yizkor Book*, that was published in New York in 1951, on pages 93-94 of the article by Ben-Zion Bagen:

[Y]"This time we again were successful in bribing the authorities and it was decided that the ghetto in Stezhgovo would be enlarged. We would take the Jews from Sierpc and Biezun, who were previously supposed to be expelled to Warsaw. On the sixth of January, 1942, military vehicles brought over a thousand souls from Sierpc and Biezun, with their meager belongings, to the gates of the ghetto.

"It is hard to describe the terrible suffering of the newcomers, frightfully beaten and bloody. They had managed to drag themselves out using their last ounces of strength. Our Stezhgovo Ghetto keepers of order went outside of the ghetto, and under a rain of beatings with clubs by the S.S., managed as quickly as possible to bring in the people and their parcels.

"The Schutzstaffel (S.S.) did not come into the ghetto because they were afraid of contracting diseases. We had told them that they were rampant among the Jews.

"It is hard to imagine the great compassion and devotion that the Stezhgovo Jews showed under these circumstances. During that night, living quarters were found for all the newcomers. A public kitchen was set up that served 400 dinners every day. The crowding was unbearable. There were on the average more than 10 people in a room. Everyone accepted this with love, knowing that they were fulfilling a humanitarian duty of the first order.

u. Jewish Policemen

In the same book, in the article by Fishel Marantz on page 98, it says:

[Y]"The majority of the Jewish police consisted of youthful deportees from Sierpc. The police commissioner was also a Jew from Sierpc, who was shot by the Germans in the Mlawa train station during the deportation of the Stezhgovo Jews. Unfortunately, I cannot remember his name."[27]

v. The Hanging of 20 Jews Including 3 from Sierpc

The same article in the same book relates the following:

[Y]"The sixth of August was a dreadful day for all the Jews in the Stezhgovo Ghetto. On that day, the Judenrat[28] received an order to assemble all the Jews. When all the Jews had gathered, a Gestapo man, apparently an officer, stood up and read out a prepared list of 20 people who must immediately be arrested and executed. He read out the following: Leib Finklestein (age 65), Avigdor Goldstein (age 38), Gedaliah Tyk (age 30), Reuven Ozarowidz (age 43), Eliezer Ozarowidz (age 48), Yaakov Goldstein (age 25), Avraham Binem Margolin (age 60), Yechiel Platt (age 28), Simchah Rybek (age 30), Nachman Grynbaum (age 25), Feibl Brieftreger (age 19), Chayim Chodek (age 30), Hersh Gurfinkel (age 27), Yehezkel Zochlinski (from Mlawa, age 60), Yehezkel Pas (Pesa) (from Sierpc), Ephraim Yosef Lelonek (from Sierpc), Toviah Zhitalni (from Sierpc), Malewiak (from Bieżuń), and two more Jews who are anonymous.

Altogether twenty people.

"All the Jews were shut up in a small and dark tomb. The Jewish police received a firm order to guard those arrested and not permit any relatives to contact them. It is hard to understand how they were able to hold on there without food or water. All 20 Jews were sentenced to death by the Germans in the basement of the prison. They assumed that none of the victims would be capable of any resistance during the execution. The Germans stood guard along with the Jewish police. But there was a moment when the Germans were not paying attention, and it was possible to approach the prison. It was not possible to throw them any food; they could only sing the Psalms. Others recited prayers for the dead. Heartbreaking scenes took place near the prison.

Mothers slit their veins. The victims suffered in that basement for four weeks. From time to time, Hitlerists from Mlawa would go down to the basement and see if the Jews were still breathing, because for the hanging – so say the hangmen – they must be alive.

"A day before the execution, they put barbed wire around the prison, and let the Jews out of the basement. Standing behind the barbed wire, they could see them building a gallows about five meters from the prison. The Jews in the ghetto were forced to bring wood and stones for the gallows. Some Jews were beaten and made to rehearse how to pull the stool out from underneath the hanging man. When they were given a special order, they had to put the stool in its place, and when given another order, they had to very quickly pull the stool out from beneath the feet.

"On September 2, 1942, while it was still dark, all the Jews – men, women, and children – had to come to the gallows site. The Jews were also forced to set up benches for the Volksdeutsch, who came cheerfully and brought their wives and children. The Germans laughed loudly, as if they were at a show, and told their children that when they grow up, they will also be able to order the destruction of Jews. At about eleven o'clock, three Gestapo men came from Mlawa to carry out the execution. Each Jew that had been arrested had his hands and feet bound, and a noose was placed around his neck. One Gestapo man gave a speech where he explained why they were hanging 20 Jews. For one Jew, it was because he had sneaked out of the ghetto. A second one, because he had smuggled food. About Yaakov Goldstein, he said that he had played a Polish song that called for freedom.

"---The souls of the 20 martyrs departed from their bodies in just a few minutes. They had all been hanged by six in the evening. Later they took them to Calvin's Wood, where a large pit had already been prepared.

"(January 22, 1948, Thursday Shevat 11, 5708, the bodies of the 20 martyrs were exhumed, and were taken for a proper Jewish burial)"

w. The Destruction of the Ghetto

The same book and the same article states on pages 102-103:

[Y]"From that miserable day onward, no Jew in the ghetto had any doubt that all the Jews would perish. Everyone's nerves were frayed, so nobody could fall asleep. Everybody waited, since the worst could happen at any moment.

"On November 20, 1942, the Jews received an order at night to assemble in the ghetto. The Germans separated the older men and women and brought peasants with carts to take them to the Mlawa Ghetto. When they came to Mlawa, Gestapo men were waiting for the victims and started beating them. They added a tranbsport of Mlawa Jews to the Stezhgovo Jews, and took them all to the railway station. With the wild yells of the Hitlerists mixed together with the screaming of little children, they were hastily driven to the train. Anyone who fell would not get up anymore. They immediately shot him. The peasants said that the whole way from Mlawa to Wieliczka was covered with dead Jews. That tranbsport of the 20th of November was taken to the most horrible of all the death camps, to Belzec, and brought to the gas chambers there.

"Four days later, on November 24, 1942, the final liquidation of the Stezhgovo Ghetto occurred. This time all the Jews in the ghetto were assembled, and were taken in peasants' carts straight to the Mlawa train station. They were forced into the freight wagons under a hail of blows and bullets. These cars had been sprayed with chloroform, which tore at their eyes.

"Up to 240 people were packed into a wagon. The crush was so great that people were pushed out of the moving train. There were wild Germans in the station who 'for the fun of it' fired into the wagons. The train came to Auschwitz, but only a small number of those in the wagons were still alive. The greater part suffocated from the crowding and lack of air. There were also some, the lucky ones, who had a little poison with them and put an end to their lives quickly."

*

Ben-Zion Bagen writes on page 99 of the above article, about the liquidation of the Stezhgovo Ghetto:

[Y]"When the Stezhgovo Jews arrived in Auschwitz; I was already a senior resident there. I already had a lot of experience. I had an inkling of which day the Stezhgovo Jews were coming because the tranbsports arrived in a certain order: from Ciechanów, Mlawa, Plonsk, and so on. I hoped with all my heart to see the Stezhgovo Jews just once before I died. But the dark destiny would not allow it. The Stezhgovo tranbsport of women, men and children were almost all shipped directly to the gas bunkers. Only four or five people made it to the camp.

"All the others were immediately gassed, and their souls left them with the most frightful and terrible suffering. 'May their souls be bound in the bundle of life.'"

G. Miscellaneous

The newspaper *Davar* of 26 Heshvon 5702 (November 16, 1941) contained the following item:

x. [H]"Germanizing the Names of Towns in Poland"

[H]"The Germans changed the names of quite a few of the towns in the occupied areas of Poland. For instance: Brodnica (Pomeran) – *Strasburg*; Ciechanów – *Zichenau*; Przasnysz – *Praschnitz*. For these names, the Germans at least attempted a phonetic resemblance. But here are some more changes: Maków – *Makheim*; Plonsk – *Plöhnen*; Ostrołęka - *Scharpenoiza*; Mlawa – *Milau*; Plotzk – *Dettersburg*; Pułtusk – *Ostenburg*; Sierpc – *Zichelberg*; Rypin – *Ripan*; Lipno – *Lipa*."

*

The following announcement appeared In the newspaper *Des Neie Leiben*, No. 43 (68), that was published in Lodz, on 27 Heshvan, 5707 (November 21, 1946:

[Y]"The Jewish Committee in Sierpc extends its heartfelt thanks to The Sierpc Relief Committee of America for its unfailing help to the Sierpcer Jews in Poland.

"The Jewish Committee in Sierpc: Y. Sakowicz, M. Skornik, Moshe Grapa"

*

In the newspaper *Der Amerikaner*, that was published in New York in 1947, there appeared a series of articles by the singer Emma Scheiber titled *Mir Zeinen Doh* ("We Are Here") about *HaBreicha* or *Aliyah B* (["The Escape Movement"] the illegal immigration of the Holocaust survivors [to Palestine]). In the issue No. 43, 29 Av, 5707 (August 15, 1947) of that newspaper, the following excerpt appears:

[Y]"We came to a town. There "Mr. Escape" awaited us, a certain Ephraim, from Sierpc, Poland.[29] We immediately knew that we could totally rely on this youth, that he has everything well in hand. He organized the groups, and gave the group leaders their orders."

*

In the newspaper *Unzer Veldt* that appeared in Paris on 26 Adar B, 5708 (April 6, 1948), there was an article titled;

y. [Y]"A Stroll Through Ten Once-Jewish Towns Which Do Not Have a *Minyan*[30] of Jews."

This discusses the towns of Plonsk, Zakroczym, Wyszegrod, Ciechanów, Sochocin, Mlawa, Rypin, Dobrzyń on the Drwęca River, Plotzk, and Sierpc. About Sierpc, it states:

[Y]"There are now a total of eight Jewish families inn Sierpc, or Sheps as the Jews called it, including two greengrocers and two shoemakers. "

In the newspaper *Davar* of 11 Tishrei 5709 (October 14, 1948), there appeared the following item:

z. [H]"German Prisoners of War Will Return Gravestones to Jewish Cemeteries

"Warsaw (P.A.P. [Polish Press Agency]). A new order issued by the Polish Justice Ministry requires German prisoners of war to collect all the gravestones in the town of Sierpc, and return them to the Jewish cemetery. During the German occupation, the gravestones were removed from the Jewish cemetery and used for paving the sidewalks.

"In addition, the Polish government acceded to the demand of the Jewish Committee of Lublin, and ordered the return of the tombstone that was removed from the Jewish cemetery in Zamschatz."

[The banner states: "Remember the Souls of the 5000 Martyred Jews of Sierpc that were Destroyed by the German Murderers 1940-1943]

Holocaust Survivors of Sierpc at a Memorial Meeting in Munich, Germany, on the Anniversary of the Expulsion of the Jews of Sierpc – 8 November 1947"

[The tombstone shaped sign states:" In Memory of the Souls of the 5000 Martyrs of the Town of Sierpc that were Killed by Various Means by the German Murderers in the Years 1940-1943. God Will Avenge their Blood."]

Holocaust Survivors in Sierpc - with Lewis Segal, Secretary of the National Jewish Workers' Organization of America (*Yiddishe Natsionale Arbeiter Farband*) - Visited Poland and Brought $200 for the Holocaust Survivors in Sierpc from the Sierpcer Relief Fund of America.

Because of the Dangers in the Period Immediately After the War, He was Accompanied by Bodyguards.

Right to Left:

Row 1, Sitting: Tula Rapatzki (Biezun), Yaakov Skornik, Mintcha Kirshenbaum (Bieżuń), Malewiak (Bieżuń)

Row 2, Sitting: Legel (Lipno), A Guide from Mlawa Accompanying Lewis Segal, Yetta Rapatzki (Bieżuń), Lewis Segal, Raizke Motil, Hanna Tcharnotchepka (Koźmin, a Village Near Sierpc)

Standing: Driver and Bodyguard of Lewis Segal, Shlomo Portaifian (Osieck, a Village Near Sierpc), a Bodyguard of L.S., Yetta Moskowicz, Leon (Lipno), Shimon Listofer (Mlawa, husband of Chayah Izikovitz), Chayah Izikovitz (Listofer), Baruch Lipka (Zhoromin, Husband of Ruska Motil), Hirsch Koral

A Group of Sierpc Townspeople [in Palestine] with their Guest Yeshayahu Friedman, in the Year 5694 (1933)

Right to Left

Row 1, Sitting: Avraham Bergson, Pnina Bergson, Batya Ben Ari, David Ben Ari (Dobroszklanka)

Row 2, Sitting: Avraham Ben David (Mlawa), Tovah Valuka, Avraham Yerushalmi (Fried), Yeshayahu Friedman, Yitzhak Bergson, Sara Bergson

Standing: Gustah Berman, Moshe Berman, Ephraim Talmi (Valuka), Menachem Avni (Shtinhoz), Mordechai Rosen, Yechiel Moshe Sidroni (Sendrowicz), Mnucha Ben David (Niza Mlawa)

[The Sierpc Townspeople Organization – Land of Israel]

Grade 6 of the Elementary School

The Names of the Teachers from Right to Left:
Row 1: Kratuszinska
Row 2: Mizails, Reich, Feigel

[The handwritten note in the lower left hand corner states: "=Class V=Polish School No. 2 in Sierpc – 1924"]

Right to Left

Row 1, Sitting: Esther Kadecka, Chibka Dobroszklanka, Sara Gorna, Frania Papierczyk, Mania Podskoc, Golda Skovitz, Esther Leah Pukacz, Zaltzer

Row 2: Tziporah Rozynek, the Teacher Revtcha Bukat, the Teacher David Maniamchevka, the Teacher Broniah Laska, the Teacher Shinvitz, the Teacher Nachman Eichler, the Teacher Altman, the Teacher Shmulik Valuka, Roza Lelonek, Helena Kasiarz

Row 3: Simtchak, Tovah Lelionek, Esther Leah Schlachter, Gongola, Sara Klin, Fela Lanter, Avraham Meir Dorfman, Ganiah Bukat, Mendzha Podskocz, Yaska Arpa

Row 4: Tzippa Bukat, Blumah Nejszaten, Sheina Openchaim, Hanna Atlas, Juzelewski, Tovah Szmiga, Bizel Gunsher, Malkah Tcharnotchepka, Esther Frankel, Yetta Grappa

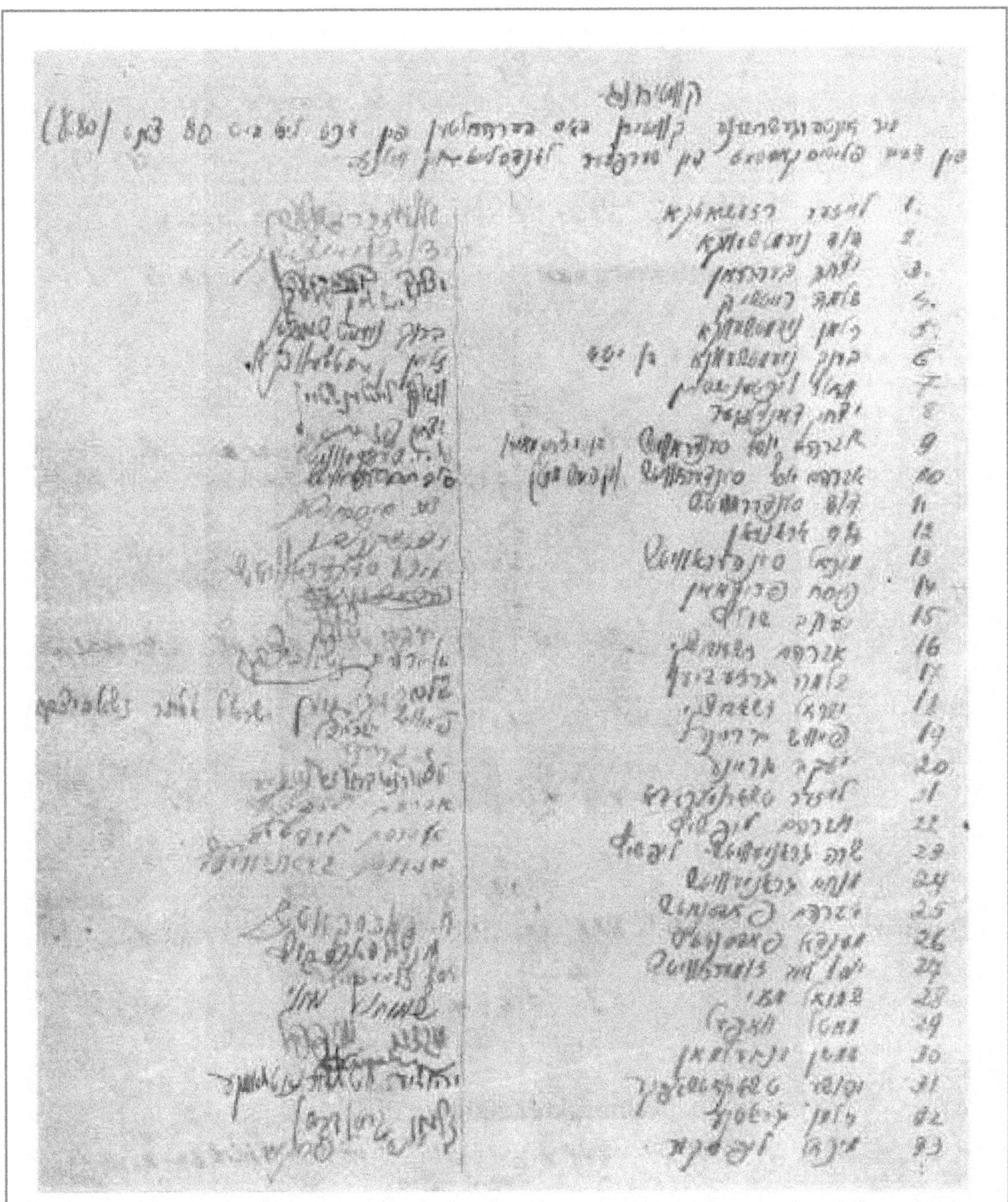

[Handwritten List of Names]

[A photocopy of the receipt for eight lita and 80 cent from the Refugee Committee of Sierpc Townbspeople in Vilnius described in this chapter in Section B – "A Minor Deportation, A Letter from the Refugee Committee in Vilnius"]

Avihamia Melamed

Translator's Footnotes

(The following is a list of endnotes. The translator's endnotes are inside of square [ ] brackets to indicate that they are not part of the original text; the footnotes that were part of the original text are listed here as endnotes, without the square brackets.)

1. [The Ringelblum Archives were (partially) found hidden among the ruins of the Warsaw Ghetto after the war. They were objects and documents assembled and written by Dr. Emanuel Ringelblum, a Polish-Jewish historian and his associates in the Ghetto to chronicle what was happening there. Ringelblum and his associates were all exterminated by the Germans.]
2. [These excerpts were written either in Hebrew or Yiddish, and are marked with "[H]" or "[Y]" accordingly.]
3. The postcard was received by the Blachman family [in Haifa]; it was written by Beryl Feinberg.
4. The synagogue was built in about 1895, that is, 44 years ago.
5. The young man who was killed was Pinchas Walcman (who was called *Pinia dem farbers* [Pinia the painter])
6. This refers to fifty plus young men that were taken for hard labor on the eve of Sukkoth, and were expelled the next day to the territory under Russian occupation.
7. [Under the terms of a non-aggression treaty signed between the U.S.S.R. and Nazi Germany shortly before the war (The Molotov–Ribbentrop Pact), Poland was divided between the two countries.]
8. [Ethnic Germans living in Poland who formed an armed militia at the beginning of the German occupation.]
9. The satanic cynicism of these criminals should be noted.
10. [Houses of study and prayer]
11. [Head of the town council]
12. Town Hall
13. The letter was written by Avraham Yosef Sendrowicz (son of Yitzhak Meir) to his two sisters in Tel-Aviv. The writer died in Vilnius.
14. [In Lithuania, then still an independent state.]
15. The letter was written by Lipsker.
16. [Hebrew Immigrant Aid Society, an American aid institution.]
17. [The Lithuanian currency.]
18. [A photocopy of this receipt is among the pictures at the end of this chapter.]
19. ["The New Deep Mire", where "Deep Mire" (the title is a quotation from Psalms 69; 3) is a Hebrew chronicle of Pogroms against the Jews during the 17th century.]
20. The deportation was on the 8th of November.
21. [A Polish Government-in-Exile was established in London after the Polish surrender.]
22. The orchestra was that of the local Polish firemen.
23. There is a description here that does not match reality. The deportation continued as follows: they rode in closed cars, without any air, without food, without water, or any place for their most basic necessities for the whole day, until they came within five or six kilometers of the town of Nowy Dwor. There they were chased out of the cars and walked in the dark while receiving cruel beatings until they reached Nowy Dwor. Then the guards took off and left the deportees there. These poor people, who were hungry and thirsty, broken and shattered and tired, scattered among the Jewish houses. The Jews of the town took them in, revived them with food and drink, and gave them a place to stay. The next morning the accursed guards went through the town and collected the deportees (some had managed to hide) and expelled them, on foot, to Warsaw.
24. The number of people deported from Sierpc was almost 3000.
25. [American Jewish Joint Distribution Committee, an aid organization]
26. The Stezhgovo Ghetto.
27. "According to our townswoman Cheila Isaacovitz-Listopad, the policemen were: Yossel Maniamchevka, the brothers Kiszlewski (one of them was called Zelig), Lederman, and Feldman (a

butcher from Racionz). The Germans found foreign currency and gold in a loaf of bread of Feldman's, and killed him. The same testimony states that the brothers Kiszlewski were later partisans in the Cetlinski forests near Plotzk. They were killed after the war by the A.K. (Armia Krajowa – Home Army – a right wing Polish underground)"

28. [The local committee that represented the Jews.]
29. We assume that this Ephraim was Ephraim Ostaszewer, who served in the Jewish Brigade [a Jewish unit from Palestine in the British Army in World War II] and was active in "The Escape Movement."
30. [The minimum number of 10 men required for a Jewish prayer service.]

Vision of the Dry Bones

- Ezekiel 37:1-14

הַיְבֵשׁוֹת הָעֲצָמוֹת חֲזוֹן

The Vision of the Dry B

א ,וְהִיא ;וַיְנִיחֵנִי בְּתוֹךְ הַבִּקְעָה ,וַיּוֹצִאֵנִי בְרוּחַ יְהוָה ,יַד־יְהוָה ,הָיְתָה עָלַי
.מְלֵאָה עֲצָמוֹת

ב ,סָבִיב סָבִיב וְהִנֵּה רַבּוֹת מְאֹד עַל־פְּנֵי הַבִּקְעָה ,וְהֶעֱבִירַנִי עֲלֵיהֶם
.וְהִנֵּה יְבֵשׁוֹת מְאֹד

ג אֲדֹנָי יְהוִה ,וָאֹמַר ;הֲתִחְיֶינָה הָעֲצָמוֹת הָאֵלֶּה ,וַיֹּאמֶר אֵלַי־־בֶּן־אָדָם
.אַתָּה יָדָעְתָּ

ד וְאָמַרְתָּ אֲלֵיהֶם־־הָעֲצָמוֹת ;הִנָּבֵא עַל־הָעֲצָמוֹת הָאֵלֶּה ,וַיֹּאמֶר אֵלַי
.שִׁמְעוּ דְּבַר־יְהוָה ,הַיְבֵשׁוֹת

ה רוּחַ־־ ,הִנֵּה אֲנִי מֵבִיא בָכֶם :לָעֲצָמוֹת הָאֵלֶּה ,כֹּה אָמַר אֲדֹנָי יְהוִה
.וִחְיִיתֶם

ו ,וְקָרַמְתִּי עֲלֵיכֶם עוֹר ,וְנָתַתִּי עֲלֵיכֶם גִּידִים וְהַעֲלֵתִי עֲלֵיכֶם עוֹר בָּשָׂר
.כִּי־אֲנִי יְהוָה ,וִידַעְתֶּם ;וִחְיִיתֶם ,וְנָתַתִּי בָכֶם רוּחַ

ז ,וַתִּקְרְבוּ עֲצָמוֹת ,וְהִנֵּה־רַעַשׁ ,וַיְהִי־קוֹל כְּהִנָּבְאִי ;כַּאֲשֶׁר צֻוֵּיתִי ,וְנִבֵּאתִי
.עֶצֶם אֶל־עַצְמוֹ

ח ;מִלְמָעְלָה ,וַיִּקְרַם עֲלֵיהֶם עוֹר ,וּבָשָׂר עָלָה ,וְרָאִיתִי וְהִנֵּה־עֲלֵיהֶם גִּדִים
.אֵין בָּהֶם ,וְרוּחַ

ט {ס}הִנָּבֵא בֶן־אָדָם וְאָמַרְתָּ אֶל־הָרוּחַ ;הִנָּבֵא אֶל־הָרוּחַ ,וַיֹּאמֶר אֵלַי
,וּפְחִי בַּהֲרוּגִים הָאֵלֶּה ,מֵאַרְבַּע רוּחוֹת בֹּאִי הָרוּחַ ,כֹּה־אָמַר אֲדֹנָי יְהוִה
.וְיִחְיוּ

י וַיַּעַמְדוּ עַל־רַגְלֵיהֶם־־ ,וַתָּבוֹא בָהֶם הָרוּחַ וַיִּחְיוּ ;כַּאֲשֶׁר צִוָּנִי ,וְהִנַּבֵּאתִי
.גָּדוֹל מְאֹד־מְאֹד ,חַיִל

יא הִנֵּה ;הָעֲצָמוֹת הָאֵלֶּה כָּל־בֵּית יִשְׂרָאֵל הֵמָּה ,בֶּן־אָדָם ,אֵלַי ,וַיֹּאמֶר
.יָבְשׁוּ עַצְמוֹתֵינוּ וְאָבְדָה תִקְוָתֵנוּ־־נִגְזַרְנוּ לָנוּ ,אֹמְרִים

יב הִנֵּה אֲנִי פֹתֵחַ אֶת־ ,כֹּה־אָמַר אֲדֹנָי יְהוִה ,לָכֵן הִנָּבֵא וְאָמַרְתָּ אֲלֵיהֶם
אֶל־אַדְמַת ,וְהֵבֵאתִי אֶתְכֶם ;עַמִּי ,קִבְרוֹתֵיכֶם וְהַעֲלֵיתִי אֶתְכֶם מִקִּבְרוֹתֵיכֶם
.יִשְׂרָאֵל

יג וּבְהַעֲלוֹתִי אֶתְכֶם ,בְּפִתְחִי אֶת־קִבְרוֹתֵיכֶם :כִּי־אֲנִי יְהוָה ,וִידַעְתֶּם
.מִקִּבְרוֹתֵיכֶם־־עַמִּי

יד וִידַעְתֶּם כִּי־ ;וְהִנַּחְתִּי אֶתְכֶם עַל־אַדְמַתְכֶם ,וְנָתַתִּי רוּחִי בָכֶם וִחְיִיתֶם
{פ} .דִּבַּרְתִּי וְעָשִׂיתִי־־נְאֻם־יְהוָה ,אֲנִי יְהוָה

1 The hand of the LORD was upon me, and the LORD carried me out in a spirit, and set me down in the midst of the valley, and it

2 and He caused me to pass by them round about, and, behold, there were very many in the open valley; and, lo, they were very dry.

3 And He said unto me: 'Son of man, can these bones live?' And I answered: 'O Lord GOD, Thou knowest.'

4 Then He said unto me: 'Prophesy over these bones, and say unto them: O ye dry bones, hear the word of the LORD:

5 Thus saith the Lord GOD unto these bones: Behold, I will cause breath to enter into you, and ye shall live.

6 And I will lay sinews upon you, and will bring up flesh upon you, and cover you with skin, and put breath in you, and ye shall live; and ye shall know that I am the LORD.'

7 So I prophesied as I was commanded; and as I prophesied, there was a noise, and behold a commotion, and the bones came together, bone to its bone.

8 And I beheld, and, lo, there were sinews upon them, and flesh came up, and skin covered them above; but there was no breath in them.

9 Then said He unto me: 'Prophesy unto the breath, prophesy, son of man, and say to the breath: {S} Thus saith the Lord GOD: Come from the four winds, O breath, and breathe upon these slain, that they may live.'

10 So I prophesied as He commanded me, and the breath came into them, and they lived, and stood up upon their feet, an exceeding great host.

11 Then He said unto me: 'Son of man, these bones are the whole house of Israel; behold, they say: Our bones are dried up, and our hope is lost; we are clean cut off.

12 Therefore prophesy, and say unto them: Thus saith the Lord GOD: Behold, I will open your graves, and cause you to come up out of your graves, O My people; and I will bring you into the land of Israel.

13 And ye shall know that I am the LORD, when I have opened your graves, and caused you to come up out of your graves, O My people.

14 And I will put My spirit in you, and ye shall live, and I will place you in your own land; and ye shall know that I the LORD have spoken, and performed it, saith the LORD.' {P}

Appendix

Former Residents of Sierpc in Israel

by I.M. Sidroni (Sendrowicz)

A. The Earliest

Sierpc Jews took part in all the *Aliyot*[1] to the Land of Israel, except for the First Aliyah.

The following young men from Sierpc came with the Second Aliyah (1904-1914): David Bornstein, Akiva Glazer, Yitzhak Kahana (who was called "Kana," originally from Plonsk), Yitzhak Oren (Aaron) Liebson, Yitzhak Karpa (Itche Karp), and Shmuel Szampan

However, the Land of Israel was then desolate and wilderness, and it was a constant battle to attain the minimum conditions for existence. Most of the immigrants of the Second Aliyah did not make it, and left the country. Among those that left were five of the six immigrants from Sierpc. The only one that remained was David Bornstein. (Itche Karp returned a few years ago.)

David Bornstein (1870-1944) was one of the founders of the first *moshav*[2] in the land, Ein-Ganim (1907-08). He was an advocate of Jewish labor and of Hebrew as an everyday language for all of his life. He championed manual labor and farming, and was contemptuous of all those who, in that period, abandoned the land and looked for easier occupations, or left the country. He himself was a model of the "new Jew" in the renewed homeland. He was the first and a leader everywhere, whether in guarding the *moshav*, or on its council. He never asked anyone to do anything that he would not do himself. Even when he was more than 70, he worked his land by himself; he tilled the earth with his hoe and irrigated his orchard. Until his last day, he did the same things that he asked of others.

One morning, when he was 74, he was found unconscious in his barn, on his milking stool. His head was resting on the cow's stomach, and the milk was overflowing from the milking pail. He never recovered consciousness and died in his house in Ein-Ganim... May his memory be blessed.

In 1908, during the period of the Second Aliyah, Chayim Nachum Tobol visited the land of Israel. He was among the first of the *Hovevei Zion*[3] in Sierpc.

*

Between the Second Aliyah and the Third Aliyah, during World War One, the following four young men from Sierpc immigrated to the Land of Israel: David Lieberman, Noatak Lerer, Chayim Pindek and Shmuel Rosen. They emigrated from America as volunteers in the Jewish Legion[4] at the beginning of 1918. Their unit, the volunteer unit from America, was called "the 39th King's Sharpshooters." It fought alongside other units of the English army, and freed Palestine from the Turks.

Some of the soldiers of the Jewish Legion left Palestine at the end of the war. Some others, Zionists that wanted to remain to protect the Jewish settlement, left after the disbandment of the Jewish Legion by the English government. This was a punishment for their participation in the defense of the Jews of Jaffa in the bloody clashes with the Arabs on May 1, 1921. Only a few of the volunteers remained in the country, and among them was the Sierpc volunteer, David Lieberman.

*

The first of the immigrants from Sierpc during the Third Aliyah (1919-1923) was Avraham Freed (Yerushalmi), who came, together with his wife Sarah (daughter of Eliezer Wesolek) and their three children at the beginning of 1921. They "managed" to get a taste, soon after they arrived, of the bloody clashes of the first of May in that year. The others that came during the Third Aliyah were Avraham Zajdemark and Yaakov Meir Neiman (the latter returned to Sierpc).

*

Thus the links from *Aliyah* to *Aliyah* continued and grew longer and stronger, until the day when the number of former residents of Sierpc in Israel grew to 215 families; thus may they multiply.

In those days there was no organization of Sierpcers, nor was there need for one. The modest home of Avraham and Sarah Yerushalmi was open to all the people of our town and also to the former residents of the surrounding towns (who were almost all bachelors), and they shared their meager pieces of bread with all their guests. If someone needed a reference, he would get it from Avraham Yerushalmi; if someone needed a guarantor for a loan, Avraham Yerushalmi would be it (and in many instances, also the payer).

In a few cases, there were organized activities by all or some of the Sierpcers. In the intermediate days of Sukkoth in the year 5695 (1934) there was a meeting of all the Sierpcers in Avraham Yerushalmi's house in honor of two guests from Sierpc, Yossel Blachman and Yeshayahu Friedman, who were visiting the Land of Israel.

To mark Avraham Yerushalmi's 60th birthday and 25 years since his *aliyah*, in the year 5705 (1945), he was registered in the Gold Book of the *Keren Kayemet*.[5]

The newspaper *Davar* that appeared on 23 Sivan 5705 (June 4, 1945) wrote: "The certificate of registry in the Gold Book of *Keren Kayemet* was presented by a group of friends and admirers to Avraham Yerushalmi, a dedicated veteran Zionist activist from Sierpc, Poland, upon his reaching the age of 60 and 25 years since his *aliyah* to the Land of Israel."

***

A tragedy overtook the Sierpcers in Palestine when Shmerel (Shmaryahu) Hazan drowned in the sea near Tel-Aviv.

Shmerel Hazan left Sierpc in 1919. He stayed for a time in Danzig and Berlin, and later traveled to America. He arrived in Palestine in 1925. He worked in various places at various jobs (for a while he worked together with a partner as a carter) and often he was unemployed. He heard of an opportunity to find work in Haifa, and he went to the "Office" (the employment office of the Histadrut[6] was in the "Red House" on the seashore of Tel-Aviv) to ask for two or three days work to pay his expenses for the trip. When he was in the "Office," he heard screaming that people were drowning in the sea. Shmerel ran to rescue those that were drowning. This happened on the 25>sup>th of Tamuz, 5686 (1926).

In Sivan, 5702 (1942), a headstone was erected over his grave in the old cemetery by the "Zion" committee (a Histadrut committee for erecting headstones on the graves of workers and anonymous *shomrim*[7]). This was done with the participation of the community council and some of the former residents of Sierpc, and in their presence.

B. "The Sierpc Townspeople in Israel Organization"

There were no organizations of townspeople (*landsmanshaften*) in Israel until World War Two. There were associations of expatriates from different countries, but the well-organized *Yishuv*[8], which gloried in its Zionist ideology, did not especially approve of these associations. The organized *Yishuv* considered these associations a diaspora phenomenon, something that reinforced the differences within the Jewish people and prevented a union of the exiles.

During the War, when details of the horrible Holocaust of the European Jews became known, groups of townspeople from various towns started to organize. The purpose was to be ready to render aid, when the war would hopefully end, to the survivors. The former residents of Sierpc in Palestine, who were few in number, also became organized.

The activities leading to the organization of the Sierpc townspeople began in the year 5704 (1944).

The meeting of the Sierpcers in Palestine took place on the second intermediate day of Sukkot in 5705 (October 5, 1944). The meeting confirmed the resolutions of a preliminary meeting and elected the members of the interim committee as members of the executive committee of "Association of Sierpc Townspeople in the Land of Israel." In addition it was decided that all those present would each contribute one [Palestine] pound, in addition to the six pounds to be contributed by each member during the course of the year. This would go to the "Aid Fund of Sierpc Townspeople in the Land of Israel" that would be used to assist Sierpc refugees anywhere in the world.

In the first meeting of the committee, Avraham Yerushalmi and Zvi Algavish (Crystal) were elected chairman and secretary respectively.

*

The Second World War ended on May 8, 1945. New immigrants started coming to Palestine, the survivors who had been saved from the great destruction. They came in a number of ways - both "kosher" and "non-kosher" (according to the laws of the [British] Mandatory Government). Many were captured and interned in Cyprus. There were residents of Sierpc among both those that managed to get into Palestine and those that didn't. It was necessary to help them to become accustomed to the life in the new land.

The activities of the *Gmilat Hasidim*[9] fund of the "Association of Sierpc Townspeople in the Land of Israel" began during this period. The fund's capital was composed of money received from Sierpc townspeople in America (the major portion), and money collected from Sierpc townspeople in Palestine (the smaller portion). The aid was distributed as loans (without interest, of course) with easy conditions for repayment.

But the loans were considered grants by many of the immigrants, and the money was never repaid. The state of the fund worsened, until its activities were stopped altogether.

After many misgivings and much hesitation, the activities of the fund were renewed. The new committee started to collect money from the association members in Palestine.

During a visit by Sierpc townspeople from Mexico, various sums were contributed to the Gmilat Hasidim fund, thereby allowing it to continue with its undertakings.

***

At the end of the war, the townspeople's organizations started to arrange for memorial meetings for the martyrs on the anniversaries of the destruction of their communities. The large organizations started first, and the smaller, less active ones, followed suit.

This custom became accepted in the country, and the organizations held memorial meetings every year for their martyrs.

Before the memorial service, there was an open meeting of the townspeople, who had not seen each other for a year, or for years. After the memorial service, there was usually a regular meeting of the organization. The agenda consisted of a report of the activities, discussions, and election of the committee.

The first memorial meeting for the martyrs of our town was held by the "Association of Sierpc Townspeople" on Monday, 26th of Heshvan 5711 (November 6, 1950), the anniversary of the day of deportation of the Jews of Sierpc, the 26th of Heshvan. Since then, the memorial meeting is held every year on the anniversary of the deportation. (The date of the deportation was selected as the day for the memorial service by the Sierpc survivors when they were in the refugee camps in Germany.) The members meet prior to the memorial service, and afterwards hold a regular meeting, and elect the committee.

*

In addition to the above meetings, a number of meetings were held in honor of former residents of Sierpc from the United States, Argentina, and Mexico, who were visiting Israel.

*

In addition, the "Association" held two meetings in honor of two important members, who were dedicated activists in Israel and abroad, upon their reaching 70 years of age. These were Avraham Yerushalmi Fried, on the 20th of Tammuz, 5715 (July 10, 1955), and Avraham Ben-David Mlawa of blessed memory, on the 1st of Tammuz, 5716 (June 10, 1956).

***

Many Jews living in Israel and the diaspora, including the survivors, have felt that the various annual memorial meetings were not enough to remember the millions who were lost. The nation looked for a way to commemorate the millions of sacrifices that would be appropriate to the enormity of the extent of disaster and the loss.

Thus was born the idea to erect a monument that is fitting for the People of the Book - a monument in the form of a book. There would be a book for each city and town whose Jews were tortured and destroyed by the oppressor. The book would be written by the Jews of the town, about their lives in the past, their struggles in the years before the Holocaust, their torments during the Holocaust, up to the moments of their death. The idea spread to all of the Diaspora, and found enthusiastic support among all classes of people. Intense activity began, gathering historical material, writing memoirs, descriptions of ways of life, and collecting testimony about the Holocaust. Considering all the difficulties in realizing this mission - from both the cultural-spiritual and technical and financial perspectives - about 150 "Yizkor" books have already been published in Israel, the United States, and Argentina.

The "Sierpc Townspeople in Israel Organization" began its work on a Yizkor Book for the martyrs of our town. The first circular on this topic appeared in the month of Nisan, 5712 (April 1952).[10]

The comrades who were preparing the book ran into many difficulties. It turned out that it was not simple to create something where there was nothing, to publish a book by people who were not writers, without sources and historical records about Jewish life in the town in the past, and without documents and data about Jewish life in the town more recently. The book was written with the hard work and devotion of a number of friends in Israel, with the help of a number of comrades who are Sierpc townspeople living in the United States. We are also very thankful to three friends, who to their great credit, contributed to the financing of the book. These are Avraham Ben-David (Mlawa), Yitzhak Oren (Ahron) Liebson, and Mordecai (Max) Sina.

The preparation of this book took seven years full of great effort, persistence, and patience.

*

At the end of this article on the townspeople of Sierpc in Israel, we must remember our townsman Isser Czeslak (Asher Ben-Mordecai). He fell in battle in the Israeli War of Independence, in the north of the country, near Kibbutz Daphne, on the 10th day of Tamuz, 5708 (July 17, 1948). He was 28 years old.

In the "Yizkor" Book published by the Israeli Ministry of Defense, page 117, it states:

"Asher Ben-Mordecai was born in 1920 in the town of Sierpc, in Poland. His father was Mordecai, and he called himself by his father's name after he survived the desolation of the diaspora. He was the son of pious parents who were merchants. He was at first schooled at home, and then continued his education in the Hebrew school, "Tarbuth," and joined *Poale Zion*, Left[11] when he became older. When World War Two broke out, he went with other refugees to Russia. He joined the Polish Army in Exile when it was formed, and with it reached Palestine in 1944. He lived for a while in Kibbutz Beit HaArava, and later moved to Tel-Aviv, and was a construction worker.

"When the War of Independence broke out, he enlisted immediately. In July, 1948, he came with his company to Tel-Aziziat, which is near Daphne in the Upper Galilee. He was slightly wounded, and was sent to recuperate. But he would not rest until he was returned to his place on the Northern Front, where he fell on July 17, 1948. He was buried in She'ar Yashuv - Dan. On March 3, 1950, he was reburied in the military cemetery in Haifa. He was the last surviving member of a family of seven souls who were exterminated in the great Holocaust. He sanctified the name of his people in the homeland."

Translator's Footnotes

[The following is a list of endnotes. The translator's endnotes are inside of square [ ] brackets to indicate that they are not part of the original text; the footnotes that were part of the original text are listed here as endnotes, without the square brackets.]

1. [Aliyah (pl. Aliyot) is the Hebrew term for the various cycles of Zionist immigration to Palestine. These are denoted as First Aliyah, Second Aliyah, etc.]
2. [A *moshav* is a cooperative agricultural community where the members own and work their own land.]
3. [*Hovevei Zion* - literally "Lovers of Zion" was a forerunner of the Zionist movement.]
4. [A Jewish volunteer group that fought in the British army during the First World War.]
5. [Jewish National Fund, an organization dedicated to purchasing land and planting trees in Palestine.]
6. [The Jewish labor union]
7. [Members (literally - guards) of the first Jewish self-defense groups in Palestine.]
8. [Literally - settlement; the term applied to the unofficial authority of the well-organized Jewish population living under the British Mandate government in Palestine.]
9. [Beneficial Fund]
10. In the years 1947-1948, there were four pamphlets published to the memory of the martyrs of Sierpc. Two pamphlets were issued by the Sierpc Holocaust survivors in Germany. One was called "The Destruction of Sierpc" (printed in Latin letters), and the second was titled "An Anthology of Sierpcer Survivors." Two pamphlets were issued by the Sierpc townspeople in America. One was called "Yizkor;" the second did not have a name. These pamphlets give an account of the suffering of the Jews in Sierpc until the deportation, a description of the expulsion, and the torments in the death and labor camps.
11. [A Zionist-Socialist Organization.]

"Mister United Sierpc Relief"[1]

by Yehuda Leib Mintz

When one discusses or writes about Sierpcer Jews, their life and economic creativity, their societal and cultural activities, the four Sierpc Landsmanschaft organizations in New York play a very important role. These are the old Sierpcer Gemilut Chasadim, the Independent Sierpc Young Men, its ladies' division called the Sierpcer Ladies Auxiliary, and the Sierpc Branch 42 of the Jewish National Workers Union.

Each of those organizations had its own role in various realms of Jewish societal life in America, as well as in Europe, the Land of Israel, and, of late, the State of Israel.

The most noble of their activities, as well as the most prominent, was the founding of the United Sierpc Relief - the Sierpc help organization that was created by all four organizations with the goal of assisting Sierpc natives wherever they are found, whether in Sierpc itself (before the great misfortune of Hitler, may his name be blotted out), in the countries where the bitter fate had brought them, or in their new home in the Land of Israel.

It is natural that in a book about Sierpc, mention must be made of that united organization - the United Sierpc Relief Organization. Its founders included Mordechai Tzvi Mintz of blessed memory - the Sierpc teacher who educated a generation of Zionists and Hebraists in the town and continued his teaching work in America; Shlomo Loeb (Lobashka) of blessed memory, who belonged to the Zionist workers' camp both in Sierpc and in New York, and, together with his late wife Pesha, spent all of his years involved in charitable activities; and Yaakov Sand of blessed memory a long-time member and leader of the Sierpc Young Men's Organization.

It is obvious that in order to function properly, an organization must have workers - people who are willing to dedicate their time and energy to the goals of raising the necessary financial means, maintaining contact with the needy people and distributing the assistance to those in need. To move forward, the activists required the driving force that would propel the organization forward. That driving force was no longer a physical driving force alone - let us say an electric motor that would be set in motion once and continue to go. The driving force that was needed for this type of relief work must be spiritual - a driving force that springs forth from the depths of the soul of the individual personalities who possessed warm hearts and fine senses of sensitivity to the ideal goal for which the help organization was created.

The United Sierpc Relief Committee had the fortune of having that very internal drive embodied in the personality of Mr. Max Sina - a long time member and activist in the Sierpc Young Men's Organization. A book about Sierpc and its Jews would simply be imperfect if it failed to mention Max Sina and his good deeds amongst us. Standing near to him in our joint work - I as the financial secretary and my wife Rashe and Mordechai Rzejszokto as corresponding secretaries of the Sierpc Relief, of which Max Sina was the president - we often admired his singular deep dedication to the work for the Sierpcers. For him, the word "Sierpcer" was a magic word that instilled a life spirit - a soul - in him, an inspiration that reflected off of him and influenced those with whom he worked together.

When a Sierpcer requested assistance, or if he merely heard that there was someone who required assistance, Mr. Sina would immediately feel a great sense of responsibility and would strive to help without any additional clarification of qualifications - the word "Sierpcer" was already a sufficient qualification. This was just like the word "Jew" to Rabbi Levi Yitzchak Berditchever[2] of blessed memory, for whom he would always serve a righteous intercessor before the Master of the Universe. Can one ask a mother about the qualifications, or positive and negative traits of her child? It is her child - she loves him - and that is all. That was the very relationship that Max Sina had with his dispersed Sierpc fellow natives, wherever they might be found. With him, there was no cause for doubts. If he took something on, if he set off on a designated path to help his fellow natives, there would never be a case of "return us back" - always forward, forward, and never back.

It seems that Max Sina himself had for a long time not been vigorous and healthy. However, he displayed exceptional strength when it came to his beloved relief work for Sierpcers. I can never forget the warm evenings and nights that we spent in the basement of my house in Brooklyn sorting the clothing and food to make packages to send to the Sierpcer refugees in France, Italy, France, the Land of Israel, and Africa. He himself was a capable man who could have permitted himself some personal comforts after a hard workday in New York. Instead of traveling for a weekend to his summer home by the sea to cool off and rest, he came to our house where everything was collected and undertook the work that was holy to him. If it was too late to go home, he would spend the night with us and wake up very early in the morning to catch the train to go home. He never complained about others who were not as willing as he was to work. He carried out his holy duty that certainly brought him spiritual enjoyment.

When it was decided to undertake the activity for the Sierpcer Relief, for various reasons of which here is not the place to write, Max Sina was conducting a "Sierpcer Relief" on a small scale by himself. He obtained money, of course putting in no small amount of his own cash, and sent it to where he thought there was the need.

When the first refugees from Germany began to arrive in America, he himself conducted the individual assistance activity for them. He found work for those he could, and if it there was the need, he would take them into his own shop. They learned the trade of sewing on the machine, and then they were employed by him or by someone else. On many occasions, he spent entire evenings with the students in the shop, in order to avoid a meeting with his partner or with the Workers Union. When it was possible, one of the new arrivals would find a paternal accommodation at Mr. Sina's house during his first days in New York, and receive warm maternal treatment from his prominent wife.

When at last the undertaking of creating a Yizkor Book to perpetuate the memories of the martyrs of Sierpc came to the fore though the initiative of our fellow natives in Israel, and a leading hand was needed in order to turn to the fellow natives in America for financial assistance as well as to collect written material and documents or data from historical works, Max Sina took upon himself the mission to conduct this work and to do everything that was needed, to make it possible for our fellow natives in Tel Aviv to do their work. Due to his poor state of health, he had already retired from his private business. On account of his weakness on his feet and his poor vision, and after several serious operations including on the eyes, he suffered from several serious accidents that caused him no small amount of additional physical suffering. However, none of this held him back from continuing with the work. He continued to connect with everyone by telephone, to call meetings at his home, and to do everything that he could do to help actualize the Sierpc Yizkor Book, which had lately become his purpose in life.

That intensive dedication to his work to help the Sierpcers had its influence upon those surrounding him, so that it was almost impossible to refuse his requests to become involved and do work, even in cases where one was not in complete agreement with him. There was something about the dedication of Max Sina that stood higher than any cold reckoning and accounting.

That characteristic of Max Sina shone like a ray of light through all the years of our mutual work for the Sierpcer Relief until his final undertaking to create the Sierpc Yizkor Book - and from that stems our respect for Mr. Max Sina, "Mr. United Sierpc Relief."

Unfortunately, he did not merit in seeing the Sierpc Yizkor Book. He passed away on May 20, 1959, corresponding to the 12th of Iyar, 5719. May his memory be a blessing!

Translator's Footnotes

1. The title of this article is slightly different than the title as listed in the table of contents.
2. See http://en.wikipedia.org/wiki/Levi_Yitzchok_of_Berditchev.

Independent Sierpcer Young Men's Benevolent Association

(Sierpcer Society)

The Sierpcer Society, whose official name is the Independent Sierpcer Young Men's Benevolent Association, has now celebrated the 50th year jubilee of its existence. This is certainly an appropriate opportunity to tell – albeit in a restricted manner – the important details of its founding and development.

It is obvious that the founding of the society dates back to the epoch of Jewish immigration during the early years of the 20th century, when large masses of Jewish immigrants from Eastern Europe built a new home for themselves. The largest number of arrivals to the New York harbor arrived alone, without relatives, and with a haunting longing for familiar surroundings. The downtrodden, lonely people in a wild, strange city, among strange people, with a strange language, without assurances for the next day, searched for a homey corner with familiar people with whom they could talk from the heart and seek advice. People who came from the same city would seek out one another, and would become close to each other with joy in their hearts. That is how groups of people from a single city were created and later grew into organized associations known as *landsmanschaft* societies.

During that time, many Sierpcers left their hometown due to economic or political reasons, arriving here in the new, free America.

The homey corner for the Sierpcer natives was the house of a fellow townsman, Yitzchak Nathan Sina of blessed memory. In that homey corner, the idea of founding a Sierpcer Association was born. There, the Sierpcers discussed together and decided that it was already time for the Siercper natives to organize into an association.

They talked and they carried it out. On a fine day, May 13, 1906, the group of Siercper natives gathered at the home of their comrade, Simon Rosenfeld, and organized an association. The association was given the name: Independent Sierpcer Young Men's Benevolent Association.

The organizers and founders consisted of the following people: the two brothers David and Joe (Yosef) Shlakman; the two brother Nathan and Philip (Nasan and Pesach) Leit, David Cohen, Moe (Moshe) Lerer, Kalman Zabitsky, Simon Rosenfeld, Julius Rosen, Abe Rosen, Victor Waldstein and Max Sina.

The goals of the founding of the association were as follows:

- To relieve the need of its members in the event of illness.
- To ensure cemetery facilities after 120 years[1].
- In general, to help a comrade in a time of need.

Over and above all else, benevolence at all times – brotherly dedication and love.

That is how at the first, small meeting on May 13, 1906, in the home of the comrade Simon Rosenfeld, the cornerstone of the Independent Sierpcer Young Men's Benevolent Association was laid, and its growth and development began.

From that time on, regular meetings were held with regular dues of ten cents a week.

At the meetings, they mainly discussed how to solicit new members and how to create a treasury. Indeed, the first steps of the builders of the society were difficult. Only those people who are more or less familiar with the conditions of those years can properly appreciate the work of our pioneers.

A little later, with the arrival of more immigrants, the society grew much larger and stronger, both in terms of number of members and finances. It also increased its activities in the area of timely help for the members and by supporting certain social institutions within the Jewish community. The latter brought it recognition and visibility in Jewish societal life.

The society enhanced its activity between the years 1908 and 1912. In 1908, the society introduced its charter, which turned it into an organization recognized on a civic level. During that year, several active members joined, such as Hymie Silverman, Emanuel Rosenberg, Harry Kaplan, and Max Rosen – people with a great deal of experience and a broad view on life. They soon became very involved with the work of the society. Also that year, the society signed up as a member of the United Hebrew Charities and of the Russian-Polish Union, with specific annual payments.

The financial situation improved somewhat, and in 1909, the society began paying weekly benefits to its ill members. In that year, the society also purchased a cemetery area for the sum of 3,000 dollars.

During those years, a loan relief fund (Gemilat Chasadim Fund) was founded to lend a specific sum of money to a member in the case of need. During those years (1900-1910) the society also broadened its support for many external organizations. It should also be noted that during those years, many strikes took place in the various trades. Not only did the society not demand membership dues from the members who were on strike, but it even helped such members with weekly support until the end of the strike. With more incoming activists who had a strong and positive effect on the functioning of the society, it also became involved with impulsive activity – until the outbreak of the First World War in 1914.

During the war years, the society excelled with great vitality and efforts to send relief assistance to the suffering brothers and sisters in the native town of Sierpc. The leaders of the society set up a Sierpc assistance fund (Relief) from among their fellow townsfolk, and through their initiatives, they also involved many Sierpc natives from outside the society. The chairman of Relief was brother Victor Waldstein and the treasurer was Yaakov Zand of blessed memory. The Relief collected large sums of money, from which the society paid out significant sums on several occasions. In this manner, several thousands of dollars were collected, which were sent to Sierpc immediately after the war. The various institutions in Sierpc, including the fund, the Talmud Torah, the Bikur Cholim, and others were helped from this money. A *maot chittin* committee [2] was also formed through the initiative of the leaders of the society. Before Passover every year, the committee collected money for Sierpc. The society members Yaakov and Chana Zand of blessed memory, and for many years Fishel Wallerstein, Hennie Rachel Fer, and the Kamer brothers and their wives were active in the committee. Tzvia Wallerstein of blessed memory was also active in the committee.

The year 1921 was also an important time in the activities of the society. In that year, the wives of our members, with the help of several active members of the society, founded the Sierpcer Ladies Auxiliary. Quickly after its founding, the Sierpcer women's organization displayed great energy in its good and necessary work. It helped our society a great deal in its important undertakings and helped greatly with the Sierpc relief effort. It was very active in the *maot chittin* committee and in other important assistance efforts. In this manner, the society, with the help of the Ladies Auxiliary, continued with its activities until the outbreak of the Second World War in 1939.

Naturally, with the outbreak of the Second World War, the entire assistance work for Sierpc was temporarily interrupted. At the same time, they did not sit with folded arms, but rather planned, and they collected money for a major assistance fund in order to be ready for the fortunate day when normal contact with our beloved and dear ones in Sierpc could be restored. When the war ended, and the great misfortune of our people was revealed, and we found out what the bestial Germans did to our dear ones, we began, with weeping hearts, to concentrate our efforts on those few who miraculously survived the great misfortune. The Sierpc Relief was quickly reorganized thanks to the initiative of the active members of the society together with the Ladies Auxiliary and the Sierpc branch of the Jewish National Workers Farband. This quickly enabled us to send help in the form of cash, food packages, clothing and other assistance to the survivors who were spread out in many countries in Europe and Israel. From the society, the members Max Sina, Philip Walerstein, Max Apelbaum, and Morris Kamer were very active. From the Ladies Auxiliary, Mrs. Kamer and Mrs. Rivka Arpa were very active in the Sierpc relief effort.

At the time of the establishment of the State of Israel, the society, with the help of the women's organization, collected and sent several thousands of dollars for the building of houses for the newly arrived immigrants. Also, since the establishment of the State, it purchased many thousands of dollars of Israel bonds and also supported the Histadrut with several thousand dollars. It also supported annually the Histadrut, the Jewish National Fund, and the United Jewish Appeal.

Since its founding, the society always stood at a high level in the realm of charitable assistance, despite the fact that it was established on the foundation of mutual benefit and was responsible for assisting its own members. It always supported various charitable causes and Jewish institutions. The society joined and supported with an annual stipend such organizations as the United Jewish Appeal, HIAS (Hebrew Immigrant Aid Society), the Jewish Congress, the Denver Sanatorium, the Deborah Sanatorium[3], ORT, the Federation of Jewish Charities, nurseries, orphanages, and many other social organizations.

The record of the Sierpc society during its 50 years of existence was very rich and active. We have celebrated the jubilee of the organization with joy. Unfortunately, many of the founders and active members are no longer with us, and we remember them with honor. Let us hope that all the members and their families will be with us for many long years.

The Sierpc Branch of the 42nd Jewish National Workers Farband [Union]

Its Founding and Activities

By Levi Kalisky

Perhaps it is not always necessary to repeat the generally known fact that the history of the past 40 years cannot be compared to other 40-year periods. The last 40 years are equivalent to many hundreds of years in light of the political and social changes. It is very true that reading or writing in the spirit of our times about the activities of an organization that lived and persevered over the last 40 years should serve as a guidepost for the evaluation of our organization, its goals and its founding.

What is the purpose for which a group of Sierpc natives organized themselves under the name of the Sierpc Branch of the Jewish National Workers Farband? What were their ideals?

When the branch was founded, the Sierpc landsmanschaft in New York already consisted of two established organizations or, as we call them here in America, societies. The older one was the Sierpc Charitable Organization [Sierpc Chevra Gemilut Chasadim] and the younger, larger, and more progressive one was the Independent Sierpcer Young Men's Benevolent Association. Like all such societies or unions organized by the *landsmanschafts* of every city and town from the old home, it concerned itself with providing its members with assistance in the event of illness or other cases of need, as well as cemetery plots after 120 years[1]. For the most part, the members were newly arrived immigrants who got together frequently and lived as an intimate family.

Despite the fact that those societies did not claim to have any ideas of a more general scope, but rather were involved solely with their own local interests, they had a great moral influence upon their members, as many of the newly arrived immigrants gathered together at their meeting places. At the meetings, the new arrivals from the old home found their relatives and previous friends and felt the warmth that they so greatly needed. During those years, those *landsmanschaft* organizations served as warm nests, and often as sources of direction for the "green" nostalgic natives of the towns. The intellectual lives of the members were marked by hot discussions at the assemblies, and by joyous events at various occasions. The discussions, which were mainly focused on the question of mutual assistance for a sick or needy "brother," were conducted in accordance with the strict principles of the constitution of the society. If the chairman of the meeting was not expert on all the opinions, he must at least be knowledgeable in parliamentary procedure and clear about the constitution of the society. The meetings of the Sierpc Young Men's Society often included discussions on trade unionism or heated civic or national election campaigns. It was the good fortune of the Sierpc society that some of its leaders were active in their union locals and members in the Socialist Party. Incidentally, not all of the leaders were Sierpc natives. The so-called "intellectual atmosphere of the meetings of the Sierpc Young Men's Society was strongly influenced by the Socialist cosmopolitan motives of the celebrations and recreational activities. The annual ball was conducted in the fashion of all the societies. The annual ball of the Sierpc Young Men's Society was a major event for all the natives of Sierpc and the surrounding area. The Sierpc ball was conducted with great pomp and circumstance. For the natives, it served as a manifestation of the glorious existence of the Sierpc Independent Young Men's Benevolent Association.

However, not all of the newly arrived town natives remained under the tent of the societies. Some of them, who had already become a bit "*oysgegrint*" [4], became lost and left for the broader circles that were involved with different types of "Americanisms." Many of those who left became completely estranged from the groups of fellow townsfolk. As well, many left the societies, because they had already raised their levels of factional awareness above that of the old country, where they did not find sufficient spiritual freedom. Even though the Sierpcer Young Men's Society was one of the strongest and most enthusiastic of the societies in those years, with a membership solely of young, energetic people, there too, a group of their young members were no longer satisfied.

This was a group of newly arrived young people, the majority of whom were in their early twenties. A few who were older had already been influenced by the Poale Zion ideology already in the old country, whereas the younger ones had not yet experienced programs of a political Socialist orientation. With youthful curiosity, they searched for "ways" to live in a more charming manner than could be found in the meetings of the Sierpcer Young Men's Society. The discussions about the general problems of the society did not interest the new, young members at all. They regarded as obnoxious the long, elaborate debates over the often repeated questions that were typically important at the society meetings such as cemeteries. In order to live in a cultural fashion more appropriate to their spiritual needs, they founded a club, while simultaneously maintaining membership in the Sierpcer Young Men's Society. The club was named the Sierpcer Social and Educational Club.

The founding of a separate club by the young "rebels" aroused a strong discontent within the society. In truth, there was already strong tension between the leaders of the Young Men's and the "group" from before. The youthful stubbornness of the young group who refused to adapt to the leadership of the society often provoked debates at meetings, and embittered the mood of the officers and leaders. In this manner, the "group" had already obtained a nickname – "the new generation." The nickname would be pronounced with no small amount of derision. The strong tension grew even stronger with the founding of the club. Those who set themselves up in a separate organization eventually established the houses of the two separate camps, each with different tendencies, under a single roof. The signs of a full scale rift were evident, and within a short time from the founding of the club, the "group" separated from the Sierpc Young Mens'.

The members of the club, now without a connection to the Sierpcer Young Mens', intensified their activities, and increased the number of members. They arranged lectures and entertainment events with greater frequency than previously. They carried on with their activities until the sounds of the relatively new national Jewish organization reached their ears and found its way into their hearts.

With the appeal of the Jewish National Workers Farband, a new spirit penetrated the Jewish street in America. In those days, it was new and revolutionary. It indeed demanded might and spiritual energy to spread and defend such a slogan. The Jewish workers' organizations, at the pinnacle of their blossoming and development in those years, were not interested in the message of Jewish national consciousness. Their founders and leaders, who were Socialists and revolutionaries from the old home, were with a small exception thoroughly assimilated. They were aggressively inimical to any thought and impression that was involved with the ideal of Jewish national consciousness. Those leaders owned or controlled pretty much the majority of the Jewish press. Their influence on the Jewish immigrants was strong and effective. It was therefore natural that in such an inimical atmosphere toward Jewish national strivings, the rise of the new organization which took on the program of Labor Zionism evoked a negative reaction. Despite this, the call of the Jewish National Workers Farband received a warm answer from a significant portion of the Zionist oriented Jewish workers. The young members of the Sierpcer social club, the working element who had a warm relationship to the Zionist ideal, responded to the call of the Farband. Through the initiative of a few older members who were already affiliated with the Poale Zion ideology, they organized the club as a branch of the Jewish National Workers Farband.

The founding and installation of the branch took place in February 1916. A considerable number of the members were from the town of Żuromin. The new branch was given the name: Sierpcer-Zurominer Branch 42 of the Jewish National Workers Farband. The following names were among those inscribed in the charter: Comrades Shlomo Peretz Fefer, Meir Lichtenstein, Nachman Lichtenstein, Shmuel Yaakov Horowitz, Yaakov Graubard, Noach Lerer, Mendel Reichgot, Shual Munter, Hirsch Binyamin Lisobitzky, Chaim Greenberg, Shepsl Tik, Tobi Tik, Avraham Zabitsky, Mordechai Segal, Chaim Zabitsky, Hirsch Chazan. The first secretary was David Liberman.

When one casts a backward glance to the long range of activities of the branch since its founding, one sees among other things an endless, broad canvas of world events, and of horrific events that plagued our people during the course of a mere four decades. Despite the fact that our branch had a limited number of members, never more than 80, it nevertheless became involved with heart and soul in almost every important Jewish happening. The activities of the branch excelled during the era that was filled with Jewish pain and also Jewish murder.

The mood becomes a bit lighter when one casts a backward glance to the first years of the branch and its activities. The world and Jewish situation were very different then – much, much better than in the later years. Like all Jewish organizations, the activities of the branch were not so burdensome. In truth, the world was not then as free and open as it was two years prior, when the First World War broke out. America was not yet at war, but the Jews here were very worried about the situation of the Jewish war victims in Europe. They took action to help through the relief organizations that were founded then. Nevertheless, one cannot compare the mood and the duties of the Jews in America from that time to the later years.

These were the honeymoon months, when the newly established branch began functioning. The first members of the club lifted their hands and became involved in the work with great enthusiasm. The meetings were ebullient with life. The young officers willingly undertook the duties and tasks of the organization. With their youthful energy, they inspired the members to perform their tasks. The leaders and officers of the Farband were frequent guests at the meetings, and with their speeches, they succeeded in educating the new family of members to the spirit and direction that the Jewish National Workers Farband stood for. These were the first stages of education in the direction of Labor Zionism that the young members received. It did not take long for the Sierpcer-Zurominer Branch 42 to become one of the favorite branches of the Farband. The members of the branch took part successfully in all of the fundraising campaigns undertaken by the Farband, whether for the national fund, agricultural machinery for Palestine, or for schools in America. As Sierpc natives, the members played a strong role in the assistance work for the victims of the war from Sierpc by the Sierpc Relief led by the Sierpcer Young Mens' Society, in the branch itself and in the Chevra Gemilat Chasadim.

The young members led a rich societal life. They often got together, celebrated joyous occasions, went on excursions, and engaged in other societal undertakings.

The following were among the leaders who stood at the cradle and the helm of the branch:

Members: Meir Lichtenstein, Nachman Lichtenstein, Shaya Rosen, Shlomo Peretz Fefer, Shual Munter, Hirsch Chazan, Shmuel Yaakov Horowitz, Hirsch Binyamin Lisowitzky, Mendel Reichgot, Tobi May, Noach Lerer, Shmuel Lopotika, Yaakov Graubard, Avraham Zabitsky, Zecharya Zlochower, Chaim Pundek, and Shmuel Green.

This was the so called romantic period in the existence of the branch.

The temperature of the branch activities fell a bit with America's entry into the First World War. A considerable number of the members went off to war with the American Army, and a smaller number went with the Jewish Legion[5]. With the establishment of normal communication between America and the outside world, the society activities in general shrank. The situation played itself out in the activities of the Farband, and naturally also in the branch. The members were involved with their work, held meetings as always, and conducted activities that met the demands of the time. Where possible, they maintained correspondence with the members who were soldiers. This is how things went until the end of the war.

The following are the members who fought with the Jewish Legion: Noach Lerer, Chaim Pundek, David Liberman, Shmuel Rosen, and comrade Hart (from Żuromin – he died on his way to the war).

Shortly after the war, new life streamed into the branch. The various activities were conducted under weakened circumstances, but this did not last for long. In the meantime, the members were involved with celebratory banquets in honor of the returning soldiers and with other various other pastimes.

The frequent gatherings on festive occasions bound the members into a large, intimate family.

However, after the festival come the weekdays. American Jews returned and established contact with Jews from around the world, and lifted up their hands to help.

The requirement to alleviate the need of the Jews who had suffered in the war took first place in the order of the day of the American Jewish assistance organization. The activists of the organizations expected and demanded the assistance of every Jew, including a financial contribution to the extent possible. The work on behalf of the Land of Israel also recommenced with a much broader scope. The *aliya* from Poland and other Eastern European lands, and assisting the pioneers in the Land of Israel became very pressing, as did the demanding problems in every area of American Zionism.

The demands upon the Farband at the branch meetings became heavier. Two strong fundraising campaigns were undertaken by the Farband – for funds for the Land of Israel and for Jewish schools in America. Incidentally, the Jewish National Workers Farband was the first Jewish organization to found Yiddish-worldly schools in America – or as they were called Yiddish Radical Farband Schools. The new, difficult tasks demanded a strong level of activity from our branch members – and this indeed took place.

Thanks to the already developed feeling of the branch leaders toward Jewish national needs, accompanied by fresh energy from a number of newly arrived active members, the activity was at a strong level. The meetings had better attendance, and were full of enthusiasm. The business and discussions regarding the various goals of the Farband, as well as from other Jewish assistance organizations, helped strengthen the Jewish national consciousness of the members, who were stimulated with the appropriate enthusiasm toward the work. The fundraising campaigns for the various funds took on a strong tempo and encouraged the majority of the members to agree to their duties.

The branch was also greatly involved in cultural activities. The leaders of the Farband would frequently visit the meetings and deliver enlightening lectures. In the literary realm, the branch also sponsored lectures from well-known speakers and writers. They also conducted gatherings and friendly discussions from within "their own powers." The members would participate readily in the friendly discussions that primarily dealt with practical Jewish themes. From time to time, concerts took place with the participation of well-known artists. There were celebrations of the national festivals and also festive occasions of the local branch. In this manner, the members lived with culture and festivity along with the undertakings and lessons of Labor Zionism, and the new Jewish national consciousness in general. The branch continued with that tempo of societal and cultural activity from the end of the 1910s until the economic depression in America.

The following people especially excelled from among the newly arrived active members: Mordechai Reshatka, Yosef Judkow, Mordechai Goldstein, L. Kalisky, Leib Mintz, Tzadok Lisovitsky, and Yosef Mendel Dwornik. The following people remained strongly active from among the older leaders of the branch: Leib Rosen, Shlomo Peretz Fefer, Hirsch Chazan, Mendel Reichgot, Noach Lerer, and Shmuel Lapotka.

However, the famous "American Depression" came, and lasted for a decade. It weakened the powers of all the Jewish organizations, and naturally, our branch suffered.

In order to concentrate the energies of the smaller, weaker branches, the Jewish Natoinal Workers Farband merged smaller branches into larger ones. Thus, our branch was united for about two years with the Farband of the Zelichower natives. During that time, the branch was called the Sierpcer-Zelichower Branch. The name Zurominer was no longer used because very few of the Żuromin natives remained in the branch. Apparently, however, the leaders of our branch were not particularly satisfied with letting "foreign" leaders lead, so the merger broke up. With the return of its own independence, our members re-adopted the name Sierpcer Branch 42 with great enthusiasm.

The reorganization involved with returning to our own independence had a great moral influence upon the members and leaders of the branch. The desire to lift the branch out of its weakened state was great. A bit later, a few active members joined, including: Yitzchak Wrona, his cousins the two brothers Yitzchak and Nathan Horowitz, and Wolf Buda. The leaders seized the opportunity and, despite the general decline in societal activities on the Jewish street due to the economic pressure, they brought back a great deal of liveliness and vigor to the branch, with the help of the new active members. The various activities strengthened one by one, and in March 1941, the celebration of the 25th anniversary of its existence took place with a fine banquet and a rich artistic program. We should note here that the guest speaker and representative of the Farband at the banquet was the renown activist and pedagogue Pinchas Gingold, may he rest in peace, who was also the installer of the branch at its founding. He imparted a great deal of joy and spiritual satisfaction to the celebrants of the banquet.

A new chapter of activity was inscribed in the history of our branch with the outbreak of the Second World War, the Hitlerist destruction, and the greatly awaited establishment of the State of Israel.

During the time of the war, there was only one concern. The members who were too old to serve in the army (with the exception of the two young members Nathan Horowitz and Wolfe Buda who were at war in the American Army) had their children on the battlefields. The concern now was for the Jewish people as a whole.

The meetings of the branch were marked by unrest and agony. The business and activities at that time played out in common with the entire organization of Jewry in America, with the firm decision to be prepared with everything – time, energy and money – for the awaited day when help could be given to the surviving victims of the destruction. When that day came, the branch displayed great energy in carrying out its duties.

As Sierpc natives, the members of the branch played a large role in the work of the Sierpc Relief, a united body of all the Sierpc organizations. One of the active doers and founders of the Relief was a member of ours, the chairman of the branch at the time, Yitzchak Wrona. Our members Mordechai Reshatka, Leib and Rashe Mintz, and Mr. and Mrs. Shlomo Lyubashka especially excelled with a great deal of strenuous work.

Following the war, the shocking Hitlerist destruction, and with the realization of the Jewish dream of the establishment of the State of Israel, the Farband became very active like all other active Jewish organizations and grew to some degree. This means that our branch also had the duty of carrying out a much greater quantity of work.

The efforts that took place during the forty difficult years of the existence of the branch did not weaken. On the contrary, under the influence of the extraordinary worldly and specifically Jewish events, the branch remained ripe and hearty. It was full of a lively desire to take on the work of its ideals and mottoes, and to help with everything involved in the upbuilding of the State of Israel, improving Jewish culture, ensuring the Jewish existence and future, and being constantly active partners with the builders of social justice and propriety.

Translator's Footnotes

1. The expression for a full lifetime.
2. Maot Chittin is a fund to provide the needy with Passover supplies.
3. See http://en.wikipedia.org/wiki/Deborah_Heart_and_Lung_Center
4. There is no great way to translate this colorful term. It means – who have passed the stage of being "greeners."
5. See http://en.wikipedia.org/wiki/Jewish_Legion

In Eternal Praise for the Martyrs of Sierpc

Shmaryahu (Shmerl) the son of Reb Avraham Zeev (Wolf) Chazan

Drowned in the sea of Tel Aviv on the 25th of Tammuz 5686 [1926], in his 25th year of life, through his desire to save people from drowning.

May his soul be bound in the bonds of eternal life

Pinchas Waltsman

Murdered in sanctification of the Divine Name by the Nazis, on the second night of Sukkot, 5700 [1939] in his 23rd year of life, through his desire to save the synagogue of Sierpc from the fire ignited by the Nazis.

May his soul be bound in the bonds of eternal life

Chana the daughter of Reb Yosef Koperman

Active in the underground of the Warsaw ghetto. Murdered as she attempted to bring weapons into the ghetto.

May her soul be bound in the bonds of eternal life

Rivka the daughter of Reb Yosef Leib Tac

(Ika Richter)

A teacher and educator who had concern for children. Active in the underground in offering assistance of children and adults in France.

May her soul be bound in the bonds of eternal life

The lawyer Yehoshua the son of Reb Ezriel Podskoc

One of the activists of "Centas" (orphanage). Active in the underground in offering assistance to children in the Warsaw Ghetto.

May his soul be bound in the bonds of eternal life

Isser (Asher the son of Mordechai) the son of Reb Mordechai Czeslak

Fell in the War of Independence in the north of the Land, in the area of Dafna on the 10th of Tammuz, 5708 [1948] in his 28th year of life.

May his soul be bound in the bonds of eternal life

In eternal memory

The important activist of many deeds in the Diaspora and in the Land: Avraham the son of David (Mlawa), a member of the town council and communal council of Sierpc, and Chairman of the Organization of Sierpc Natives in Israel.

The Mourners: the Organization of Sierpc natives in Israel, and the organizations of Sierpc Natives in the United States

In eternal memory

The important activist of many deeds on behalf of his fellow townsfolk and others

Max Sina (Mordechai Czina), chairman of the Young Mens' (the youth), and chairman of the United Relief Committee of the Sierpc natives in the United States.

The mourners: The organizations of Sierpc Natives in the United States, and the Organization of Sierpc Natives in Israel

My parents Meir and Sara Liebson

My brother Avraham Baruch Liebson and his family

My sister Mindel, her husband Feivish Lipka, and their daughters Dina and Hadassah

My sister Beila Rachel, her husband Menachem Sloma, their daughter Dina and son Yisrael

My sister Pesa, her husband Yechiel Ozer Krol and their daughter Dina

My relatives:

Moshe and Kuka Wesolek, their daughters Mindel and Gitel and son Zalman

Naftali and Sheina Mindel Liebson, their daughters Reizel and Rachel and son Avraham

Pese Eibeshitz and family

Bracha Gotlibowska and family

Wolf Sznicer and family

Yosef Sznicer and family

Yisrael and Dina Liebson

Yisrael Chaim and Reizel Jeszajewicz

In sorrow: Yitzchak Aharon Liebson, Detroit, Michigan

My sister Chana

My brother-in-law Yeshaya Horowitz and children

My sister-in-law Miriam Karpa and children

Freidel Bril and children

Yitzchak Karpa, wife and children

Malka, Sara, and children

In sorrow: Rivka Arpa (Karpa), Brooklyn, N.Y.

My parents: Menachem Mendel and Chaya Sara Bendkowski

My sister: Perl

My brothers: Meir and Yechezkel

In sorrow: Morris Bendkowski, Bronx, N.Y.

Children of Yaakov David Bornstein

Miriam, Beila, Rachel, Menucha, Yechezkel, Yisrael Meir

In sorrow: Anna Aler, Brooklyn, N.Y.

My parents: Mordechai Leib and Rachel Bryn

My brothers and sisters: Yaakov Zeev, Yitzchak Meir, Asher, Gittel, Aryeh, Sara

In sorrow: Binyamin Bryn, Bronx, N.Y.

Our parents: Shmuel Asher and Pese Malka Ostoszower

Sara and her children Rechl

Tova and her son Shmuel Asher

Sister Rivka and her husband Wolf

Sister Rachel Lea and her husband Hirsch

Brother Leibish, his wife Mindel

Brother Berl, his wife Sara

And their children

In sorrow: Morris, Mordechai and Yehoshua Ostoszower, Brooklyn, N.Y.

My parents: Baruch Mendel and Rivka Gotlibowski

My sister Feiba Gotlibowski

My brother Leml Gotlibowski and family

My sister Sara, her husband Zalman Atlas, and children

My sister Elka, her husband Moshe Niepamacz, and their child Neshe

In sorrow: Nathan Gotlieb, Bronx, N.Y.

Ester Sara Buda

Yeshaya Buda

Chava Leah Liebson

Yehudit Liebson

Neshe Niemczowka

Freidel Folda

In sorrow: Willy and Dina Buda, Yonkers, N.Y.

Our parents Reb Yehoshua and Rozia Goldman

Our sister Yocheved and her husband Yitzchak Kleinman

Their son David, and daughter Leah

The mourners: Rabbi Moshe Dov Goldman, Cleveland Ohio; Golda Goldman, Brooklyn, N.Y.

My parents: Shlomo and Chava Gongola

My sisters: Malka and Tzirel

In sorrow: Leibel Gongola, Bronx, New York

Mordechai Leib Neznokani

In sorrow: Joe Harris, Chicago, Illinois

My sister Nisel, her husband and children

My sister Reizel, her husband Meir Zemelman and children

In sorrow: Meir Gancher

Baruch Burgand and wife

Pesa Burgand, Moshe Reichgot, Hinda, Pesa, Chana

In sorrow: Yitzchak Horowitz, Brooklyn, N.Y.

My parents Yitzchak and Chaya Sara Glasman

My sister Pnina Glasman

My brother Meir

Tzvi Rotenberg and family

Ben Zion Szampon and family

Nechama and Manya Benkelsdorf

Esther Rachel Szampon

In sorrow: Tovia Glasman, New York

Shimon Petrikus, Sara, Pesa, Moshe, Avraham Czarnoczopka, Beila

In sorrow: Nathan Horowitz, Jackson Heights, N.Y.

My parents: Feivish and Rivka Diagenes

My brother: Feivel

My sister Hene

My step-father Chaim Moshe Rubinstein

My brother: Mendel Rubinstein

My brother: Henech

In sorrow: Alex Diagenes, Bronx, N.Y.

My parents: David Tuchendler, Sara Tuchendler

In sorrow: Meir Tuchendler

Rachel Leah Lerer, Moshe Aharon, Bronia, and two children

Meir and Gutsha Czarek, Gutkind Renkel, Ita Lazenska, Hirsch Lazensky and two children, Masha and Meir Konskowolski

In sorrow: Nachman and Milia Czarek, Brooklyn, N.Y.

My brother Hershel, his wife Freda

My brother Chaim, his wife Esther and daughter

My brother Aharon

My sister Rivka and her husband David Altman and children

My sister Zisa Lesman

My step-mother Chaya Sara Lesman

In sorrow: Noach Lesman, New York

My parents Shmuel and Sara Krida

My brother David

My sister Malka and her fiancé Yehuda Cudek

My sister Bluma Gitel

My sister Masha Chaskelowicz and family

Moshe, Mendel, Chaim Tzudek Czarslif and families

Sara Zumerowicz and children

Avidgor Konskowolski and family

In sorrow: Fela Czarnow, Bronx, N. Y.

My father Avraham Burgand (ritual slaughterer)

My brother Moshe, his wife Dvora, and their children Dina, Leah, Nathan

In sorrow: Rikl Moskowich, Brooklyn, N. Y.

Pesa Buchalter and family

Yaakov Antkowicz, wife Tzirel and children

In sorrow: Saul Jurish, New York

Binyamin and Sara Sobol

Gershon Mintz and his family

Avraham and Breina Kriger and family

In sorrow: Leib and Rasha Mintz, Brooklyn, N.Y.

My parents: Avraham Yitzchak and Rivka Lipsky

My sister Mindel

My sister Leah

My sister Yeta

Their husbands and children

In sorrow: Julius (Gedalia) Lipsky, Hewlett, New York

My parents: Abish and Rachel Nemlich

My sister Adela

My brother Shmuel

Pinchas and Adela Gut and their two children

In sorrow: Harold Nemlich, New York

David and Rikl Lea Rozen

Sara Rozen, Malka Szurik, Sara

In sorrow: Max Sina, Brooklyn, New York

My parents: Yosef and Yeta Pindek

My brother Moshe

My sister Mindel

My sister Chana

Their husbands and children

In sorrow: Chaim Pindek, Brooklyn, N.Y.

My parents: Michel and Mirel Smolenski

Rachel, Yisrael, Sara Dvora, Beila

In sorrow: Leon Smolen, New Jersey

Esther Holender and two daughters

Sara Rozen, her husband and children

Melech Koliski's four daughters

In sorrow: Levi Koliski, New York

Shmuel Elba, his wife and children

Eliahu Elba, his wife and children

Tzirel Nogrodzka and family

In sorrow: Reuven Elba

Hirsch Kutna, his wife and children

Zisa Malka Kutna, Shlomo Kutna

In sorrow: Morris and Roiza Kamer, Brooklyn, N.Y.

My mother Rachel Podskoc

My wife Rivka

My daughter Chana

My mother-in-law Beila Sperling

In sorrow: Yaakov Podskotch, Brooklyn, New York.

My parents; Shmuel Yitzchak and Esther Tac

My brother: Velvel Tac

In sorrow: B. Kuyovsky, Montreal, Canada

In eternal memory

My brother Yaakov Hirsch Jeszajewicz and his wife Chaya Sara

Murdered by the Nazi murderers

In sorrow: Rivka Alter (Jeszajewicz) New York

Meir David Alter

My parents: Meir and Malka Rzeszotka

My brother Yosef, his wife Tzipora

My sister Rachel Leah, her husband and their children

My brother Hirsch Michael (died in Buenos Aires)

My grandfather and grandmother Baruch and Chana, their children and grandchildren

In sorrow: Mordechai Reshotka, New York

My parents Leib and Sara Szweicer

In sorrow: Ben Schweitzer, Brooklyn, N.Y.

Dvora Szampon, Reuven Szampon, Rachel Szampon

In sorrow: Aharon Shampon, Long Island, N.Y.

My parents: Lipa and Tzirel Nasielski

My sisters, brothers, brothers-in-law, sisters-in-law and their children

In sorrow: Keidi Schweitzer, Brooklyn, N.Y.

The Jeszajewicz family of Sierpc

In holy memory of my beloved, unforgettable wife Reva Alter (Rivka Jeszajewicz)

Born in Sierpc, died on October 30 1956 in New York

Her father Shmuel Leib, her mother Lipsha Tona (died before the Second World War)

Her brothers Yaakov Hirsch, his wife Chaya Sara; Meir Yisrael, his wife Chana

Her sisters Nicha and husband Henech; Shifra and husband Yidel

And all their children, uncles and aunts, with the large, wide-branched family who were murdered along with the entire Jewish community by the German Hitlerist murderers.

May these lines serve as a monument for those who were murdered and died

Honor to their memory: Meir David Alter, New York

In eternal memory

Our dear parents Reb Shmuel Asher and Pesa Malka Osczewer

Our sister Rivka, her husband Wolf Osczewer, and their children Shifra Yiska, Zisa, Rachel (Rachcha), Avraham Yitzchak

Our sister Rachel Leah, her husband Hirsch Kamin, and children Shmuel Asher, Moshe.

Our brother Leibush, his wife Mindel Osczewer and their son Yosef

Our brother Berel, his wife Sara, and their children Shmuel Asher and three other children

Our brother Efraim (who died in Israel)

Sara Osczewer (Gothelf) and her daughter Rechel

Tova Osczewer (Jeszajewicz) and son Shmuel Asher

The mourners: Moshe Meir Oschever (United States), Mordechai Oschever (Israel), Yehoshua Oschever (United States)

Avraham Yitzchak (Itzik) Osczewer and his wife Sara The mourner: Bennet Zaman (Berlin)

Leibush and his wife Reizel Osczewer and their daughter Trana and her husband

---

Yehoshua and his wife Hena Osczewer, and their children Avraham Yitzchak and Berl

---

Moshe and Solek and his wife, and their children: Zalman and his wife, Gitel and her husband Klopfisz, Yitzchak and his wife Meir and his wife Tova Rivka Gothelf, and their children Yosel, Frimet, Berl, Feiga The mourners: Mordechai and Rela Osczewer

Leib and his wife Nechama (Chuma) Rozenthal

Shlomo Zalman and wife Gitel Freidman

Mordechai and his wife Rivka Lopatka, and their children Hirsch and his wife Fradel and their children; Esther and her husband Moshe Juan; Henech *{translator's note, this is a composite memorial, and the dedication below apparently applies to the entire bottom part of this page.}* Remaining in grief: Moshe Meir (United States), Mordechai (in Israel), and Yehoshua (United States) Oschever

For eternal memory

Our beloved parents: Yechezkel and Tova Leah Eizikowicz

Our beloved sisters and brothers-in-law: Nechama Chana and Yosef Karpa, Sara Rachel and Moshe Moszkowicz, Esther and Fishel Bramzon, and their children

In sorrow: Chaya Listopad (Eizikovich), Fishel Eizikovich

My relatives: Binyamin and Sara Sobol

My aunt Esther and uncle Feivush Zabicky and their children

In sorrow: Chaya Listopad (Eizikovich)

In memory of our parents, sisters and brothers of blessed memory who perished in the Holocaust, may G-d avenge their blood

Arpa Kalman, Tova Leah, Aharon and his family Chaya, Zerach, Yakir

The mourners: Miriam and Tzvi Arpa and their families; Yiska and Yitzchak Modzivsky and their families

---

In memory of our sister and her family of blessed memory who perished in the Holocaust, may G-d avenge their blood

Yaakov Lemil Jotko, Esther-Sara (nee Arpa) Jotko, Eliahu Leib, and Yakor Jotko

The mourners: Miriam and Tzvi Arpa and their families. Yiska and Yitzchak Modzifsky and their families

---

Gedalyahu Friedman, Tzirel (nee Rozinek) Friedman, Hershel and Rachel Leah Friedman, Rivka and Manya Friedman

The mourners: Miriam and Tzvi Arpa and their families. Tzipora and Yisrael Korotkin and their families

---

In memory of our brother and his family of blessed memory who perished in the Holocaust, may G-d avenge their blood

Avraham Chaim, Rachel, Eliahu-Leib, Yakir, and Esther Arpa

The mourners: Miriam and Tzvi Arpa and their families; Yiska and Yitzchak Modzivsky and their families

---

In memory of our sister and her son of blessed memory who perished in the Holocaust, may G-d avenge their blood

Nicha Gonski (nee Arpa) and her son

The mourners: Miriam and Tzvi Arpa and their family; Yiska and Yitzchak Modzivsky and their family

---

In memory of our parents, brothers, and sisters of blessed memory who perished in the Holocaust, may G-d avenge their blood

Leib, Esther, Tzadok, and Sara Rozinek

The mourners: Miriam and Tzvi Arpa and their family; Tzipora and Yisrael Kortkin and their family

In memory of our dear parents of blessed memory who perished in the Holocaust

Yair and Sara Oberfeld

And in memory of our sister who died in Russia: Dvora Oberfeld

The mourners: Henia Lewin (Oberfed); Nathan Oberfeld (Mexico), Yaakov Oberfeld (Mexico)

In eternal memory

Our grandfather: Chaim Bergson, who died in 5676 (1916)

Our grandmother Rachel (nee Segal) Bergson who died in 5700 (1940)

Holocaust victims:

Our uncle: Yaakov David Bergson and his family

Our aunt: Chana (nee Bergson) and her husband

Our uncle: Yechiel Meir and his family

Our aunt: Liba (nee Bergson) and her family

Our aunt: Tzirel (nee Bergson) and her husband

May their souls be bound in the bonds of eternal life

The mourners: Yitzchak Bergson and family, Avraham Bergson and family, Gershon Bergson and family

These are the names of our dear ones, victims of the Holocaust

Yisachar Dov Bergson – our father and grandfather

Leah (nee Zeligman) – our mother and grandmother

Chana and Chava – our sisters and aunts

David Bergson – our brother, father and grandfather

Rozia (nee Berman) – our sister-in-law, mother, and grandmother

Avraham, Hena, and Fishel – the children of our brother and nephew

Menachem Mendel Blum – our brother-in-law and uncle

Tova (nee Bergson) – our sister and aunt

Hena, Chaim, and Avraham – children of our sister

David Winer – our brother-in-law and uncle

Tzirel (Czesia) nee Bergson – our sister and aunt

Tamar – daughter of our aunt

For the song of their lives that was cut off in the middle

The mourners who refuse to be comforted

Yitzchak and Sara Bergson and their family of Givatayim; Avraham and Penina Bergson and family of Givatayim; Gershon and Manya Bergson and family of Oprider; Shmuel and Ela Bergson and family of Rishon Letzion.

And my heart is a container of tears

In memory of my father, mother, brother, sisters, brothers-in-law, sisters-in-law and their children

Mother Mindel (died in 5697 / 1937)

Father Avraham Wloka

Brother Shmuel Leib

Sister-in-law Genia nee Niemczowka

Their daughter Malia

Sister Dvora Feiga

Brother-in-law Avraham Lenet

Their two children Shmuel David and Rachel Leah

Sister Sheina Rivka

Brother-in-law Moshe Kadecki

Who perished in the Holocaust

In eternal Agony, Efraim Talmai (Wloka)

In eternal memory

Grandfather and grandmother: Baruch and Chana Zaszotka

Our dear parents: Meir and Malka Zaszotka

Our brother: Yosef and his wife Tzipora Zaszotka, and their children Chana, Yisrael, and Mordechai Yitzchak

Our sister: Rachel Leah, her husband Yosef Skjocznowski and their daughter Chana

Our brother Hirsch Michael who died in Buenos Aires on the 9th of Tammuz 5719 / 1959

The mourners: Sara Tova Kadecki (Argentina), Mordechai Reshotka (United States), Eliezer Meiri (Israel)

In eternal memory of our dear ones who perished in the Holocaust

Grandfather and grandmother Reb Yaakov Moshe and Rivka Tulcha Teitelbaum

Uncle Meir Henech Teitelbaum and family

Our dear parents: Mendel Melech and Shrpintza Teitelbaum

Our brothers and sisters: Yehoshua and family, Chana Sara and family, Ester, Freidel, Tulcha, Leib, Ber, Chaim Aharon, and Tova

The mourners: Yitzchak (Izik) Teitelbaum (London), Meir Teitelbaum (Buenos Aires)

In memory of our father, mother, and sisters, may G-d avenge their blood

Shlomo the son of Avraham Jozilovski of blessed memory

And his wife Sara the daughter of Baruch Leib

Their daughters: Malka, her husband Aharon, and their children Moshe and Tzirel

Miriam and her husband Moshe Dragon

Tzirel

Their daughter-in-law Yenta nee Dragon

May their souls be bound in the bonds of eternal life

[Dedicated by] their sons and daughters: Yona, Batya, Freda, Avraham Moshe, and Yaakov

In memory of my parents, brother, sisters, and their families of blessed memory

Father: Shmuel Mendel Licht
Mother: Hinda (perished in the Holocaust)
Brother: Fishel
Sister: Tula "
Sister: Dvora Feiga Lubinicki "
Brother-in-law Mordechai "
Their daughter Manya "
Their sons Shmuel and Meir "

The mourners: Yaakov and Tula Uri (Licht)

In memory of our parents, brothers, sisters, and their families

Our dear father Reb Mendel Lenczner

Our dear mother Beila – perished in the Holocaust

Our brothers Shmuel Yitzchak and family, Ber and family, Yosef and family, Zalman and family, Chaim – all perished in the Holocaust

Our sister Tova who died in Israel

The mourners: Bunim and Meir Lenczner

We weep bitterly for our dear ones who were murdered by the bloodthirsty murderers

Our father Yitzchak Meir and our mother Feiga Motil

Our sister Fela, her son Sender and husband Menachem Grosman

My wife Yocheved and my son Sender Motil

Our aunt Chaya, her sons Moshe and Sender, and her husband Reuven Ruda

Our uncle Binyamin and his son Shimon Sochaczewski

The mourners; Shabtai and Avraham Parpari (Motil) and families, Rishon Letzion and Holon

---

In memory of our dear parents of blessed memory who perished in the Holocaust

Hirsch and Chana Motil

The mourners: Rechavya Parpari (Motil), Shoshana Lapka (Motil, United States), Shmuel Motil (United States)

In eternal memory

My father's paternal grandfather Reb Yehuda Senderowicz
My father's paternal grandmother Freda
My father's maternal grandmother Reb Moshe Zlocower
My father's maternal grandmother Miriam Beila
My mother's paternal grandfather Reb Yosef Karpa
My mother's paternal grandmother Gitel
My mother's maternal grandfather Reb Yosef Getzel, a *shochet* in Sierpc
My mother's maternal grandmother Chana Tova
My paternal grandfather Reb Avraham Senderowicz, who died on the 20th of Tammuz 5670 / 1910 at the age of 80
My paternal grandmother Rivka Feiga who died on the 6th of Kislev 5670 / 1909 at the age of 82
My maternal grandfather Reb Mordechai Karpa, a *shochet* in the region of Sierpc and Żuromin, died on the 4th of Kislev 5676 / 1915 at the age of 66
My maternal grandmother Sara Leah, who died on the 24th of Tishrei 5668 / 1907 at the age of 57
My father Reb Eliezer Senderowicz who died on the 19th of Tammuz 5668 / 1908 at the age of 37
My mother Yocheved who died in Żuromin on the 12 of Adar II 5698 / 1938 at the age of 66
My sister Gitel Beila Karpa who died on the 17 of Cheshvan 5683 / 1922 at the age of 32
The daughter of my sister, Rivka Feiga, died on the 9th of Nisan 5696 / 1926 at the age of 11
The daughter of my sister, Sara Leah who died during the Holocaust in Łodz, in 5710 / 1950 {translator's note, something seems incorrect about this date as the Holocaust was over by then} at the age of 28
The son of my sister, Eliezer, who perished during the Holocaust, born in 5678 / 1918

The mourner: Yechiel Moshe Sidroni (Senderowicz)

In eternal memory

My dear parents Reb Avraham (perished in the Holocaust) and Lipcha Karpa

My dear sisters Rachel and Freda (perished in the Holocaust)

Our dear children Beila and Mordechai Yitzchak

The mourners; Tova Sidroni (Gitel Karpa) and Yechiel Moshe Sidroni (Senderowicz)

In memory of our parents, sisters and brothers who perished in the Holocaust

Our dear parents Hirsh Michael and Pesa Senderowicz

Our sisters: Gela and her husband Meir Konskowolski; Chana

Our brothers: Avraham,Yehuda, and Shimon

The mourners: David and Eliezer Senderowicz

In memory of our parents, brothers, sister and her family who perished in the Holocaust

Our dear parents Yitzchak Meir and Miriam Rachel Senderowicz

Our sister: Chana Tova and her husband Reuven Szampon, and their daughter Sara

Our brothers: Avraham Yosef, Eliezer, and Aharon Senderowicz

The mourners: Shoshana Stolinsky (Senderowicz), Tzipora Zucker (Senderowicz), Yaakov Senderowicz

---

In memory of our dearly beloved who perished in the Holocaust (except for grandfather)

We will never forget them

Grandfather and grandmother: Reb Mendel and Dina Gerlic (Lipszyc)

Our dear parents: Reb Yehuda Baruch and Miriam Skornik

Our sister Sara and her husband Eliahu Grosman and their children

Our sister Rasha and her husband Aharon Szapira and their children

Our brother: Yochanan, Zalman, Chaim, and Moshe Skornik

The mourners: Pnina (Skornik) and Menachem Avni (Steinhaus) and their children; Hirsch Mordechai Skornik and his family (United States), Yaakov Skornik and family

---

In eternal memory

Our parents Yisachar Meir Skurka, Yiska nee Zabicki; Tzvi (Hershel) Czarka, Yetta nee Zeligman

Avraham Zabicki, our brother-in-law; Ester Miriam nee Skurka; my sister and my sister-in-law; David and Pesach, their children

Sara nee Skurka, my sister and my sister-in-law; Dov Czarka – my brother and my brother-in-law; Meir and Hena, their children

Yosef Skurka, my brother and my brother-in-law; his wife Sara

My brother and my brother-in-law Pesach Skurka (perished in an accident in 1930)

My sisters and sisters-in-law: Tova (nee Czarka) Przygoda (died in 5717 / 1957 in Brazil); Elka Czarka (died in 1932); Esther and Breina Czarka

Our uncles: Zelig Czarka, Yisrael Przygoda, Shmuel Czarka, Yitzchak Czarka, Yaakov Zabicki, Yitzchak Zabicki, and their families

Those bitterly mourning: Chaim and Hena Skurka of Givatayim, and their daughter Avia

In eternal memory

Our father Aharon Czarnoczopka and our mother Esther Leah

Our sisters: Chaya and Freidel; our brother-in-law Avraham Mirnac, and their three children.

Our sister Tamara, our brother-in-law Gedalyahu Markowic, and their three children

Our sister: Karola our brother-in-law Gurko and their daughter.

Our sister Fela, and our brother-in-law Burnsztejn

Our brother Avraham; our sister-in-law Bina, and their three daughters

Our brother Hirsh Wolf; our sister-in-law Roziya, and their son

Our brother-in-law Moshe Yitzchak (Szyzek) Grynberg and his daughter

Honor to their memory

Mourning bitterly: Hyman (Chaim) Schwartz (Czarnoczopka), United States; Anka and David Tauman and family; Sara and Yitzchak Bergson and family; Mania Horowitz, United States.

In eternal memory

Our dear parents: Yaakov the son of Reb Yehuda Penfil, died on the 14th of Iyar 5680 / 1920

Leah the daughter of Reb Shimon David Szmiga, died on the 25 of Adar II, 5711 / 1951 in Tel Aviv

Our sister Rivka Mitgang and their daughter Tova who perished in the Holocaust in Stalinabad Russia {translator's note: now Dushanbe, Tajikstan}

The mourners: Efraim and Yosef Penfil; Rachel Magenishevski (Penfil); Dvora Feiga Jeszajawicz (Penfil)

In eternal memory

Our parents, brothers, sisters, and their families

Our dear mother Chaya Sara Frankel the daughter of Reb Eliahu Glezer, died in Sierpc in 1917

Our dear father Yaakov Dov Frankel

Our sister Esther Rotensztejn, her husband Yisrael, and their child

Our brother Asher Frankel, his wife Roza

Our brother Aharon Frankel and his wife

Our brother Nachum Frankel and his wife Dora

Our sister Gutka Zylbersztejn and her husband

Our brother Moshe Frankel, died in Tel Aviv in 1936, his wife Roza, and two children

Our brother Avraham Frankel his wife Malka, and their two children

Who perished in the Holocaust

The mourners: Aryeh and Yitzchak Frankel; Rivka Burnstein (Frankel)

In eternal memory

Dr. Yeshayahu (Salek) Kurta the son of Shmuel and Chana

Died in his prime in 1937 in Montpellier, France from a malignant disease at the end of his university studies

The mourners: His parents, brothers, sisters, and their families

---

In memory of my dear parents

Avraham and Breina Kriger

My sister Rachel

My brother Tovia

My relatives Shimon and Manya Haberberg; Gershon and Leah Mintz, and their children; Falek, Masha, and Marek Junisz

Who perished in the Holocaust

The mourner: Moshe Kriger

With great sorrow and endless agony

We weep bitterly for our dear family members who were murdered by the impure murderers of our people during the Holocaust in Poland

My father, the dearest of people, modest and upright, Reb Moshe David of blessed memory Kempner

M mother, righteous and a doer of good deeds Ita Tzvia of blessed memory

My sister, a refined soul, Chaya Yehudit of blessed memory and her son Yerachmiel of blessed memory

My young and pleasant brother Aryeh Leib of blessed memory

Our dear grandfather Reb Yisrael Juan of blessed memory

Uncles and aunts and their families of blessed memory

May G-d avenge their pure blood. May their souls be bound in the bonds of eternal life. Their memories are etched in our hearts forever

Mourning bitterly: Alter Ben-Zion Kempner and family, Bnei Brak, Israel

Baruch Kempner and family, Chicago United States

With deep grief and sadness, we weep over the tragic death of our beloved parents, sisters and brothers, and their families

Our beloved father Yitzchak of blessed memory Grapa

Our beloved mother Yocheved of blessed memory

Our beloved brother Shual of blessed memory, his wife Rivka and three children

Our beloved sister Leah, her husband Moshe Aharon Grapa, and two children

Our beloved brother Wolf Grapa, his wife Pesa, and two children

Our beloved sister Dvora (Grapa) Fenster, her husband Yosef, and one child

Our beloved brother Yehoshua Meir, his wife Breina of blessed memory

Our unforgettable beloved youngest sister Rachel Grapa of blessed memory

Our uncles Feivish Grapa, and David Grapa and his wife Michla

Our aunt Chana Horowitz (Karpa), her husband Shaya, and two children

Our uncle Tanchum Grapa and his entire family

Our aunt Breina Grapa and her entire family

Our aunt Miriam Karpa and family

Their bright memory will remain etched in our hearts until the end of our lives

Son Moshe Grapa and family, daughter Yiska Grapa (Kempner) and family

---

"And every heart will weep, and every eye will drop tears"

"These I remember and my soul will pour out"

Our dear parents who perished in the Holocaust: Reb Menachem Aryeh (Leibel) and Ruda Kramarz of blessed memory

The mourners: their daughters and families: Miriam Kramarz – Dorfman, and Leah Kramarz – Topor

---

Our dear father Yitzchak (Itcha) Papirczyk

(died on the 23rd of Nisan 598 / 1938)

Our dear mother Udel (perished in the Holocaust)

Our dear sisters: Esther Gitel, Rachel, and Dvora, who perished in the Holocaust

The mourners: their daughters and sisters: Frania, Hasa, Fruma, Yafa and families

In memory of our dear parents, sisters, and brother of blessed memory who perished in the Holocaust, may G-d avenge their blood

Simcha Szulz, Chaya Szulz, Chana Szulz, Yitzchak Szulz, Bina Szulz, Sara Sulz, Yehudit Szulz

The mourners: Dvora and Baruch Bachin and family; Ida and Avraham Szulz and family; Yedidya and Efraim Szulz and family; Yaakov Szulz

---

The dentist, Dr. Eliezer Mendel (Leon) Kurta the son of Shmuel and Chana

Perished in his prime on a death train on the way from the Wiarzbnik-Starachowice Camp to the Auschwitz Camp in 1944

The mourners: his parents, brothers, sisters, and their families

For the untimely deaths of our dear ones:

Aharon Yehoshua Weisroza and family

Yitzchak Meir Rusak and family

Yaakov Weisroza and family

Mirle, Leah, and Sara

Yenta Weisroza and family

Sara Beila Weisroza and family

Shimshon Mordechai Weisroza and family

Yaakov Yosef Weisroza and family

Shepsl (Shabtai) Weisroza and family

Yehuda Weisroza and family

Avigdor Konskowolski and family

Baruch Atlas and family

Zalman Atlas and family

Mordechai Lipa Atlas and family

Leib Danczyk and family

The mourners: Yosef David and Henia Weisroza

In memory of my dear parents, sister, brother and family

My father Reb Yosef the son of Reb Yitzchak Aharon Sznicer of blessed memory, died on 20 Tishrei 5696 / 1935

My mother Tova Silka the daughter of Reb Moshe of blessed memory, died on the 22nd of Shvat 5700 / 1940

My sister Sheina Hendel Sznicer, her husband Yitzchak Aharon, and their children Moshe, Leah, Beila, and Chava

My brother Yitzchak David Sznicer, his wife Chana, and their children Leah, Beila, and Tova

Perished in the Holocaust

The mourner: Aharon Leib Sznicer

My dear family who were tortured and murdered by the Nazi wild men

My dear mother Esther Rachel Szampon

My sisters Pesa Steinhaus and family; Chaya Sara Glasman and family; Chana Rivka Rotenberg and family; Nechama Bengelsdorf and family

My brother Ben-Zion Szampon and family

I will never forget them

The mourner: Dr. Ezriel Szampon and family

Necrology from "The Community of Sierpc" (Poland)

Transliterated by Al Silberman

Note: for the purposes of the publication of the physical book, several columns of this Necrology had to be deleted: Age, Sex, Names of Submitters, remarks and Page. Please refer to the on-line version at http://www.jewishgen.org/Yizkor/Sierpc/sie559.html for the full version; on that web site, there is a column lableled "Pages," which refers to the pages of the original Yiddish and Hebrew Yizkor Book and NOT the pages in this translation. The original Yiddish and Hebrew Yizkor Book can be viewed at http://yizkor.nypl.org/index.php?id=2590, and please note that the page numbers referred to are on the bottom of the pages.

Family name(s)	First name(s)	Maiden name	Age	Father's name	Mother's name	Name of spouse	Additional family members
	Ahron					Malkah	
	Gurka					Krule	and daughter
	Chanah	PINDEK		Yosef	Yitte		and her family
	Chanah	BERGSON		Chayim	Rachel		her husband
	Yitte	LIPSKI		Avraham Yitzchak	Rivkah		her husband
	Leah	LIPSKI		Avraham Yitzchak	Rivkah		her husband
	Mindel	LIPSKI		Avraham Yitzchak	Rivkah		her husband
	Mindel	PINDEK		Yosef	Yitte		and her family
	Malkah	JUZIELEWSKI		Shlomo	Sarah	Ahron	
	Moshe			Ahron	Malkah		
	Nisel	GANSZER					her husband
	Tzirel			Ahron	Malkah		
	Krule	CZARNACZAPKA		Ahron	Esther Leah	Gurko	and daughter
	Rachel Leah	RZEJSOTKO		Meir	Malkah		her husband
EDELSZTAJN	Avraham			Yaakov	Chayah		
EDELSZTAJN	Hersh Wolf			Yaakov	Chayah		
EDELSZTAJN	Chayah		48			Yaakov	
EDELSZTAJN	Yaakov		50			Chayah	
EDELSZTAJN	Malkah			Yaakov	Chayah		

EDELSZTAJN	Roize Beile			Yaakov	Chayah		
AHARONOWICZ	Feiga						and her family
OBERFELD	Devorah		22	Yair	Sarah		
OBERFELD	Yair		56			Sarah	
OBERFELD	Mordechai						and his family
OBERFELD	Sarah		55			Yair	
OSTASZEWER	Avraham Yitzchak			Wolf	Rivkah		
OSTASZEWER	Avraham Yitzchak			Yehoshua	Henyah		
OSTASZEWER	Avraham Yitzchak					Sarah	
OSTASZEWER	Berel		30	Shmuel Asher	Pesa Malkah	Sarah	and 3 children
OSTASZEWER	Berel			Yehoshua	Henyah		
OSTASZEWER	Henyah	NASZELSKI	44			Yehoshua	
OSTASZEWER	Wolf		47			Rivkah	
OSTASZEWER	Zisa			Wolf	Rivkah		
OSTASZEWER	Tovah	ISZAJEWICZ	27				
OSTASZEWER	Tranah		24	Leibush	Reizel		
OSTASZEWER	Yehoshua		47			Henyah	
OSTASZEWER	Yosef		6	Leibush	Mindel		
OSTASZEWER	Leibush		39	Shmuel Asher	Pesa Malkah	Mindel	
OSTASZEWER	Leibush		49	Yitzchak		Reizel	
OSTASZEWER	Mindel	WESOLEK	46			Leibush	
OSTASZEWER	Pesa Malkah		63			Shmuel Asher	
OSTASZEWER	Rivkah			Shmuel Asher	Pesa Malkah	Wolf	
OSTASZEWER	Rachel / R?zia			Wolf	Rivkah		
OSTASZEWER	Reizel		43			Leibush	
OSTASZEWER	Rechel		3		Sarah		
OSTASZEWER	Shmuel Asher		3	Berel	Sarah		
OSTASZEWER	Shmuel Asher		3		Tovah		
OSTASZEWER	Reb Shmuel Asher					Pesa Malkah	
OSTASZEWER	Shifrah			Wolf	Rivkah		

	Yiskah						
OSTASZEWER	Sarah		26			Berel	and 3 children
OSTASZEWER	Sarah	GOTHILF	32				
OSTASZEWER	Sarah					Avraham Yitzchak	
UKERT	Avraham			Eliezer			
UKERT	Eliyahu						and his family
UKERT	Eliezer		69				
UKERT	Asher Leib			Eliezer			
UKERT	Zev			Eliezer			
UKERT	Miriam			Eliezer			
ATLAS	Baruch		50			Henyah	
ATLAS	Henyeh		45			Baruch	
ATLAS	Zalman		48			Pesa Sarah	
ATLAS	Chayim		22	Baruch	Henyah		
ATLAS	Leah	ATLAS	28			Mordechai Lipa	
ATLAS	Mordechai Lipa		40			Leah	
ATLAS	Pesa Sarah	GOTLIBOWSKI	40	Baruch Mendel	Rivkah	Zalmen	
AIBESZYC	Pesa						and her family
AIZIKOWICZ	Tovah Leah					Yechezkel	
AIZIKOWICZ	Yechezkel					Tovah Leah	
AJZENBERG	Avraham					Chanah	
AJZENBERG	Chanah	PRASZNICKI				Avraham	
AJZENBERG				Avraham	Chanah		and his family
AJZENSZTADT	Yosef						
ELBA	Eliyahu						and his family
ELBA	Shmuel						and his family
ELBA						Shmuel	
ELBA						Eliyahu	
ALTMAN	David					Rivkah	and child
ALTMAN	Rivkah	LASMAN				David	and child
ALTEROWICZ	Avraham						

ALTEROWICZ	Avraham			Yosef	Rashah		
ALTEROWICZ	Esther			Yosef	Roize		and 2 children
ALTEROWICZ	Yosef					Rashah	
ALTEROWICZ	Yosef					Roize	
ALTEROWICZ	Pola			Yosef	Rashah		
ALTEROWICZ	Rashah					Yosef	
ALTEROWICZ	Rozia					Yosef	
ALTEROWICZ						Avraham	
ENGEL							and his family
ANTKIEWICZ	Yaakov					Tzirel	and child
ANTKIEWICZ	Tzirel					Yaakov	and child
ESTEREICH	Mendel						and his family
ARBEITER	Ziskind						and his family
ARBEITER	Chayim David						and his family
ARONSON	Itsha						and his family
ARFA	Avraham Chayim		38	Kalmen	Tovah Leah	Rachel	
ARFA	Avraham Mordechai			Avraham Chayim	Rachel		
ARFA	Ahron			Kalmen	Tovah Leah		and his family
ARFA	Eliyahu Leib			Avraham Chayim	Rachel		
ARFA	Esther			Avraham Chayim	Rachel		
ARFA	Zerach			Kalmen	Tovah Leah		
ARFA	Chayah			Kalmen	Tovah Leah		
ARFA	Tovah Leah		55			Kalmen	
ARFA	Yakir			Kalmen	Tovah Leah		
ARFA	Yakir			Avraham Chayim	Rachel		
ARFA	Kalman		57			Tovah Leah	
ARFA	Rachel	RZEJSZOTKO	38			Avraham Chayim	
ASCH	Hersh		27			Miriam	and child

ASCH	Yitzchak		52			Sarah Gittel	
ASCH	Miriam		27			Hersh	and child
ASCH	Rivkah		2	Yitzchak	Sarah Gittel		
ASCH	Sarah Gitel		52			Yitzchak	
BASZKES	Yechezkel		60			Rella	
BASZKES	Rellah		60			Yechezkel	
BUDO	Yeshaye						
BUDA	Esther Sarah		60				
BUDA	Belcza			Yehoshua	Fraidel		
BUDA	Yehoshua					Fraidel	
BUDA	Fraidel					Yehoshua	
BUDA	Tzvi Zev			Yehoshua	Fraidel		
BOJMWOL	Pesa						and her family
BUCHHALTER	Pesa						and her family
BAUMSON	Lipa						and his family
BUKI	Feiga	ISZAJEWICZ	32				and child
BUKART	Yaakov						and his family
BURG	Avraham						and his family
BURGAND	Avraham		65				
BURGAND	Baruch						
BURGAND	Devorah		45			Moshe	
BURGAND	Dinah			Moshe	Devorah		
BURGAND	Leah			Moshe	Devorah		
BURGAND	Moshe		45	Avraham		Devorah	
BURGAND	Nathan			Moshe	Devorah		
BURGAND	Pesa			Baruch			
BURGAND						Baruch	
BORNSZTAJN	Beile Miriam			Yaakov David			
BORNSZTAJN	Yechezkel			Yaakov David			
BORNSZTAJN	Yisrael Meir		32	Yaakov David		Malle	
BORNSZTAJN	Meir Yechiel						and his family

BORNSZTAJN	Malle	GARNIVICZ	32			Yisrael Meir	
BORNSZTAJN	Niche / Menucha			Yaakov David			
BORNSZTAJN	Fela	CZARNACZAPKA		Ahron	Esther Leah		
BORNSZTAJN	Rachel			Yaakov David			
BORNSZTAJN						Fellah	
BURSZTAJN	Adam			Henich / Henik	Natze		
BURSZTAJN	David		45				
BURSZTAJN	Henich / Heniek					Natze	
BURSZTAJN	Chanah		35				
BURSZTAJN	Natze	CZIFRIS				Henich	
BURSZTAJN	Pesa						
BURSZTAJN						David	
BIALOSKORNIK	Hena					Hersh	
BIALOSKORNIK	Hersh					Henna	
BIALOSKORNIK				Hersh	Henna		
BAJMAN	Wolf						and his family
BAJMAN	Meir						and his family
BLUM	Avraham			Menachem Mendel	Tovah		
BLUM	Hena			Menachem Mendel	Tovah		
BLUM	Chayim			Menachem Mendel	Tovah		
BLUM	Tovah	BERGSON	42			Menachem Mendel	
BLUM	Menachem Mendel		45			Tovah	
BLUM	Rachel	SZAPIRO	40			Shmuel	
BLUM	Shmuel		42			Rachel	
BLUMAN	Leib						and his family
BLUMAN	Tzadok						and his family
BLUMAN	Rivkah						and her family
BLAT	Moshe		40				
BLACHMAN	Yaakov						and his family

BENGELSDORF	Manye				Nechamah		
BENGELSDORF	Nechamah	SZAFMAN			Esther Rachel		
BENDKOWSKI	Chayah Sarah		55			Menachem Mendel	
BENDKOWSKI	Yechezkel			Menachem Mendel	Chayah Sarah		
BENDKOWSKI	Meir			Menachem Mendel	Chayah Sarah		
BENDKOWSKI	Menachem Mendel		55			Chayah Sarah	
BENDKOWSKI	Perel			Menachem Mendel	Chayah Sarah		
BEHMAN	Hersh Wolf					Leah	
BEHMAN	Leah					Hersh Wolf	
BEHMAN	Leib			Hersh Wolf	Leah		
BECKERMAN	Chanah						and her family
BERGSON	Avraham			David	Rachel Roize		
BERGSON	Devorah					Yechiel Meir	
BERGSON	David		44			Rachel Rozyah	
BERGSON	Henyeh			Yisachar Dov	Leah		
BERGSON	Henyeh			David	Rachel Roize		
BERGSON	Chavah			Yisachar Dov	Leah		
BERGSON	Chayim			Yechiel Meir	Devorah		
BERGSON	Yechiel Meir			Chayim	Rachel Segal	Devorah	and his family
BERGSON	Yaakov David			Chayim	Rachel		and his family
BERGSON	Yitzchak			Yechiel Meir	Devorah		
BERGSON	Yisachar Dov		60			Leah	
BERGSON	Leah	ZELIGMAN	60			Yisachar Dov	
BERGSON	Fishel			David	Rachel Roize		
BERGSON	Rachel	BERMAN	43			David	
BERGSON	Rachel	SEGAL				Chayim	

BERGSON	Shmuel			Yechiel Meir	Devorah		
BRODACZ	Avraham						and his family
BRODACZ	Ahron			Shlomo	Rachel		
BRODACZ	Henich						
BRODACZ	Wolf						
BRODACZ	Rachel					Shlomo	
BRODACZ	Shlomo					Rachel	
BROMBERG	Mordechai						and his family
BARON	Chayim						and his family
BRONA	Moshe						and his family
BRAJTGANZ	Zisha						and his family
BRAJTSZTAJN	David						
BRIN	Aryeh			Mordechai Leib	Rachel		
BRIN	Asher			Mordechai Leib	Rachel		
BRIN	Gitel			Mordechai Leib	Rachel		
BRIN	Yaakov Zev			Mordechai Leib	Rachel		
BRIN	Yitzchak Meir			Mordechai Leib	Rachel		
BRIN	Mordechai Leib		60			Rachel	
BRIN	Rachel		55			Mordechai Leib	
BRIN	Sarah			Mordechai Leib	Rachel		
BERLINSKI	Sarah Malkah						and her family
BRAMZON	Esther	AIZIKOWICZ		Yechezkel	Tovah Leah	Fishel	
BRAMZON	Yaakov Moshe			Fishel	Esther		
BRAMZON	Fishel					Esther	
BRAMZON	Rashah			Fishel	Esther		
BRAMZON	Rachel			Fishel	Esther		
BRAMZON	Shmuel			Fishel	Esther		
BERMAN	Dinah						and her family

BERMAN	Chayah Sarah		55				
BERMAN	Yisrael						and his family
BERMAN	Rivkah		28		Chayah Sarah		
BERKO	Chanah Golde	LICHT				Shmuel Leib	
BERKO	Yisrael						and his family
BERKO	Shmuel Leib					Chanah Golde	
BERKOWICZ	Ahron						and his family
BERKOWICZ	Zisa		43			Shlomo Melech	
BERKOWICZ	Chanoch			Shlomo Melech	Zisah		
BERKOWICZ	Yosef			Shlomo Melech	Zisah		
BERKOWICZ	Mordechai			Shlomo Melech	Zisah		
BERKOWICZ	Feiga			Shlomo Melech	Zisah		
BERKOWICZ	Rachel			Shlomo Melech	Zisah		
BERKOWICZ	Shlomo Melech		45			Zisah	

Family name(s)	**First name(s)**	**Maiden name**	**Age**	**Father's name**	**Mother's name**	**Name of spouse**	**Additional family members**	**Pages**
GABINCZ	Gedaliahu						and his family	
GUT	Adele	NEMLICH		Abish	Rachel	Pinchas		
GUT	Esther			Pinchas	Adel			
GUT	Moshe			Pinchas	Adel			
GUT	Pinchas					Adele		
GOTHILF	Berel			Meir	Tovah Rivkah			
GOTHILF	Tovah Rivkah		54			Meir		
GOTHILF	Yossel			Meir	Tovah Rivkah			
GOTHILF	Meir		57			Tovah Rivkah		

GOTHILF	Feiga			Meir	Tovah Rivkah		
GOTHILF	Frimet			Meir	Tovah Rivkah		
GOTLIBOWSKA	Berachah						and her family
GOTLIBOWSKI	Pesa						and her family
GOTLIBOWSKI	Eliyahu					Chanah	
GOTLIBOWSKI	Baruch Mendel		60			Rivkah	
GOTLIBOWSKI	Chanah	CZIFRIS				Eliyahu	
GOTLIBOWSKI	Yaakov			Eliyahu	Chanah		
GOTLIBOWSKI	Lemel			Baruch Mendel	Rivkah		and his family
GOTLIBOWSKI	Feiga		25	Baruch Mendel	Rivkah		
GOTLIBOWSKI	Rivkah		60			Baruch Mendel	
GUTENTAG	Avraham						and his family
GUTSZTAT	Eidel			Moshe	Manyah		
GUTSZTAT	Isser						and his family
GUTSZTAT	Chayim Yosef					Feige	
GUTSZTAT	Yehudah			Moshe	Manyah		
GUTSZTAT	Manye	KUNIEC	38			Moshe	
GUTSZTAT	Moshe		43			Manyah	
GUTSZTAT	Feiga						
GOLDMAN	Yehoshua		60				
GOLDMAN	Yehoshua					Roize	
GOLDMAN	Rozia					Yehoshua	
GOLDMAN	Shifrah Feiga	FLATO	50				
GOLDSZTAJN	Avraham						
GOLDSZTAJN	Esther						
GOLDSZTAJN	Herzel						
GOLDSZTAJN	Herschel						
GOLDSZTAJN	Yaakov Wolf						
GOLDSZTAJN	Yisrael						
GOLDSZTAJN	Minel						
GOLDSZTAJN	Zalman						and his family

GOLDSZTAJN	Mendel						and his family
GOLDSCHLAK	Chavah			Yehoshua Heschel David			
GOLDSCHLAK	Rabbi Yehoshua Heschel						
GOLDSCHLAK	Leibl			Yehoshua Heschel David			
GOLDSCHLAK	Rabbi's wife					Yehoshua Heshel David	
GOLOMB							and his family
GONGOLA	Hersh						and his family
GONGOLA	Chavah					Shlomo	
GONGOLA	Malkah			Shlomo	Chavah		
GONGOLA	Moshe						and his family
GONGOLA	Tzirel			Shlomo	Chavah		
GONGOLA	Shlomo					Chavah	
GONSKA / GONSKI	Niche	ARFA	34	Kalmen	Tovah Leah		
GONSKA / GONSKI					Nicha		
GORNA	Chayim Yosef						and his family
GORNA	Yosef						and his family
GORNA	Feigel						and her family
GORNA	Shulem						and his family
GORNA	Shmuel Ahron						and his family
GURFINKEL	Eidel			Mendel	Fraidel		
GURFINKEL	Esther				Yocheved		
GURFINKEL	Zehavah			Mendel	Fraidel		
GURFINKEL	Chayah			Mendel	Fraidel		
GURFINKEL	Yocheved						
GURFINKEL	Mendel		55			Fraidel	
GURFINKEL	Miriam			Mendel	Fraidel		
GURFINKEL	Fraidel		55			Mendel	

GURFINKEL	Simchah			Mendel	Fraidel		
GURFINKEL	Shifrah			Mendel	Fraidel		
GURFINKEL	Sarah			Mendel	Fraidel		
GZIEBIEN	Avraham Yosef		60				
GZIEBIEN	Shlomo			Avraham Yosef			
GLAZER	Shmuel						and his family
GALANT	Yechiel						and his family
GLASMAN	Chayah Sarah	SZAMPAN	38		Esther Rachel	Yitzchak	
GLASMAN	Yitzchak		40			Chayah Sarah	
GLASMAN	Meir			Yitzchak	Chayah Sarah		
GLASMAN	Peninah			Yitzchak	Chayah Sarah		
GARBARCZIK	Golde		37				
GARBARCZIK	Herschel			Shlomo Leib	Tzirel		
GARBARCZIK	Yoel		40			Golde	
GARBARCZIK	Yoel			Shlomo Leib	Tzirel		
GARBARCZIK	Yechiel			Yoel	Golde		
GARBARCZIK	Matiel			Shlomo Leib	Tzirel		
GARBARCZIK	Pinchas			Shlomo Leib	Tzirel		
GARBARCZIK	Frimet			Shlomo Leib	Tzirel		
GARBARCZIK	Tzirel						
GARBARCZIK	Tzirel		44				
GARBARCZIK	Shlomo			Yoel	Golde		
GARBARCZIK	Shlomo Leib		47			Tzirel	
GARBARCZIK	Sarah			Yoel	Golde		
GARBARCZIK	Sarah			Shlomo Leib	Tzirel		
GRADZANOWSKI							and his family
GRODA	Avraham		50			Nesha	
GRODA	Neshe		50			Avraham	
GRODA	Shmuel		16	Avraham	Nesha		

GRODKA	Avraham		62			Dobrish	
GRODKA	Avraham		4	Moshe Ahron	Esther		
GRODKA	Esther		32			Moshe Ahron	
GRODKA	Dobrish		58			Avraham	
GRODKA	Zalman			Avraham	Dobrish		
GRODKA	Yaakov Yosef			Avraham	Dobrish		
GRODKA	Miriam			Avraham	Dobrish		
GRODKA	Moshe Ahron		35			Esther	
GRUZA	Yisrael						and his family
GROSMAN	Avraham		50				and child
GROSMAN	Avraham Chayim			Moshe	Fraidel		
GROSMAN	Eliyahu		36			Sarah	
GROSMAN	Devorah	SZAPIRO	34			Pesach	
GROSMAN	Hinde			Moshe	Fraidel		
GROSMAN	Hersh		35				
GROSMAN	Yaakov Meir						and his family
GROSMAN	Yaakov		30			Frimet	
GROSMAN	Leib						and his family
GROSMAN	Mendel						and his family
GROSMAN	Menachem		38			Fellah	
GROSMAN	Moshe		30			Fraidel	
GROSMAN	Sender			Menachem	Pella		
GROSMAN	Fela	MOTIL	35	Yitzchak Meir	Feige	Menachem	
GROSMAN	Pesach		34			Devorah	and child
GROSMAN	Fraidel	CZERNOVRODA	28			Moshe	
GROSMAN	Frimet		30			Yaakov	
GROSMAN	Sarah		70				
GROSMAN	Sarah	SKORNIK	35	Yehudah Baruch	Miriam	Eliyahu	and child
GROSMAN		GUTENTAG				Avraham	and child
GROSMAN		LICHT	33			Hersh	
GROSMAN			4	Hersh			
GROSMAN			4	Yaakov	Frimet		

GRUSZKA	Avraham						and his family
GRAJNA	Gutkind						and his family
GRAJNA	Hersh					Yehudis	
GRAJNA	Yehudit					Hersh	
GRAJNA	Manye			Hersh	Yehudis		
GRAJNA	Moshe Ahron						and his family
GRINBAUM	Eizik						and his family
GRANIEWICZ	Menashe			Avraham Chayim	Leah		
GRINBERG	Moshe Yitzchak						
GRINBERG	Salim Shlomo			Moshe Yitzchak			
GERLIC / LIPSZYC	Dinah					Mendel	
GRANIEWICZ	Avraham Chayim		53			Leah	
GRANIEWICZ	Esther			Avraham Chayim	Leah		
GRANIEWICZ	Yitzchak Leib		31				and his family
GRANIEWICZ	Leah		48			Avraham Chayim	
GRANIEWICZ	Menachem			Avraham Chayim	Leah		
GRANIEWICZ	Miriam			Avraham Chayim	Leah		
GRANIEWICZ	Rivkah			Avraham Chayim	Leah		
GARNIECZ	Yaakov						and his family
GARNIECZ	Meir						and his family
GRAPA	Breine						and her family
GARPA	Breine					Yehoshua	
GRAPA	Devorah				Breine		
GRAPA	Devorah			Yitzchak	Yocheved		
GRAPA	David					Michlah	
GRAPA	Wolf		30	Yitzchak	Yocheved	Pesa	and 2 children
GRAPA	Chayim Yaakov				Breine		

GRAPA	Tovah			Shaul	Rivkah		
GRAPA	Yehudah			Moshe Ahron	Leah		
GARPA	Yehoshua Meir			Yitzchak	Yocheved	Breine	
GRAPA	Yocheved		60			Yitzchak	
GRAPA	Yiskah			Tanchum	Reizel	Chanah	
GRAPA	Yitzchak		60			Yocheved	
GRAPA	Leah			Yitzchak	Yocheved	Moshe Ahron	and 2 children
GRAPA	Meir			Yitzchak	Yocheved		
GRAPA	Michla					David	
GRAPA	Mordechai Mendel			Moshe Ahron	Leah		
GRAPA	Moshe Ahron					Leah	and 2 children
GRAPA	Feivish						
GRAPA	Fela				Breine		
GRAPA	Pesa		30			Wolf	and 2 children
GRAPA	Rivkah	KLEINHAUS	40			Shaul	and 3 children
GRAPA	Rachel			Yitzchak	Yocheved		
GRAPA	Reizel					Tanchum	
GRAPA	Refa'el			Shaul	Rivkah		
GRAPA	Shaul		40	Yitzchak	Yocheved	Rivkah	and 3 children
GRAPA	Sheine Chayah			Wolf	Pesa		
GRAPA	Sarah			Wolf	Pesa		
GRAPA	Tanchum					Reizel	
GERCENSZTAJN	Pesa	GLASMAN				Tzvi	and child
GERCENSZTAJN	Tzvi					? Pesach	and children and family
DOBROSZKLANKA	Eliyahu Yaakov		27				
DOBROSZKLANKA	Billa	MALOVENCZIK	45			Ezriel	
DOBROSZKLANKA	Binem					Chanah	
DOBROSZKLANKA	Binem						and his family
DOBROSZKLANKA	David						and his family
DOBROSZKLANKA	Chanah	SZARFHARC				Binem	
DOBROSZKLANKA	Motel			Binem	Chanah		

DOBROSZKLANKA	Ezriel		45			Billa	
DOBROSZKLANKA	Tzvi Herschel		77			Rachel Leah	
DOBROSZKLANKA	Rachel Leah		75			Tzvi / Herschel Yosef	
DOBROSZKLANKA	Rinah			Binem	Chanah		
DORMBUS	Yehudah Binem			Shmuel Zanvil	Feige Rachel		
DORMBUS	Nechemiah			Shmuel Zanvil	Feige Rachel		
DORMBUS	Feiga Rachel	ZILBERBERG	40			Shmuel Zanvil	
DORMBUS	Shmuel Zanvil		40			Feige Rachel	
DORMBUS	Sarah Miriam			Shmuel Zanvil	Feige Rachel		
DORFMAN	Avraham Meir			Yechezkel			and his family
DORFMAN	Esther			Yechezkel	CWETL		
DORFMAN	Berak			Yechezkel	CWETL		
DORFMAN	Meir						and his family
DORFMAN	Mendel						and his family
DORFMAN	Rivkah			Yechezkel	CWETL		
DZIALDOWSKI	Hinde			Meir	Rachel		
DZIALDOWSKI	Chayah			Meir	Rachel		
DZIALDOWSKI	Leah			Meir	Rachel		
DZIALDOWSKI	Meir		50			Rachel	
DZIALDOWSKI	Miriam			Meir	Rachel		and his family
DZIALDOWSKI	Moshe David			Meir	Rachel		and his family
DZIALDOWSKI	Rachel		47			Meir	
DIOGENES	Avraham David						and his family
DIOGENES	Henna			Feivish	Rivkah		
DIOGENES	Feivel			Feivish	Rivkah		
DIOGENES	Feivish						
DIOGENES	Rivkah						
DIMKOVSKY	Hersh						and his family
DIMKOVSKY	Leib						and his

							family
DIKAN	Yosef						and his family
DIKAN	Moshe						and his family
DENTUS	Yaakov Meir						and his family
DANCYGER	Avraham Hersh						and his family
DANCYGER	Chayah Feiga	RADZINOVER	34			Leib	
DANCYGER	Chayim			Leib	Chayah Feige		
DANCYGER	Libe			Leib	Chayah Feige		
DANCYGER	Leib		34			Chayah Feige	
DANZIG	Leib						
DRAGON	Hinde					Shmuel Henich	
DRAGON	Chayim			Shmuel Henich			
DRAGON	Yente			Shmuel Henich	Hinde		
DRAGON	Miriam	JUZIELEWSKI		Shlomo	Sarah	Moshe	
DRAGON	Moshe			Shmuel Henich	Hinde	Miriam	
DRAGON	Feiga			Shmuel Henich	Hinde		
DRAGON	Shmuel Henich					Hinde	

Family name(s)	First name(s)	Maiden name	Age	Father's name	Mother's name	Name of spouse	Additional family members
HONA	David		55				
HONA	Niche		45				
HONA			75				
HABERBERG	Manye	MINC				Shimon	
HABERBERG	Shimon					Manyah	
HODES	Yisrael					Poza	
HODES	Moshe			Yisrael		Poza	
HODES	Akiva			Yisrael		Poza	
HODES	Poza	GLAZER				Yisrael	

HODESMAN							and his family
HUTNIK	Moshe						and his family
HOLENDER	Esther						and her 2 children and family
HOROWICZ	David						and his family
HOROWICZ	Chanah	KARPA				Yeshayahu	
HOROWICZ	Yeshayahu					Chanah	
HOROWICZ	Moshe			Yeshayahu / Shaie	Chanah		
HOROWICZ	Sarah Feiga			Yeshayahu / Shaie	Chanah		
HOROWICZ	Sarah						and her family
HELER	Leib						and his family
HENDLISZ	Moshe		48			Rivkah	
HENDLISZ	Rivkah		46			Moshe	
HARTBROT	Hinde						and her family
HARTBROT	Hersh						and his family
HARTBROT	Michael						and his family
HARTBROT	Moshe Yitzchak						and his family
WOBIK	Libe	BERGSON		Chayim	Rachel		
WOBIK						Libe	
WAFEL	Meir						and her family
WAFEL	Mordechai						
WAFEL		GLAZER	50				
WALDENBERG	Rivtza / Rivkah	WALUKA					and her family
WLUKA	Avraham		64			Mindel	
WLUKA	Genya	NIMCZEVKY	38			Shmuel Leib	
WLUKA	Devorah	SZAMPAN				Hersh	
WLUKA	Hersh		39			Devorah	
WLUKA	Lutak Eliezer			Hersh	Devorah		
WLUKA	Malle			Shmuel Leib	Genyah		

WLUKA	Shmuel Leib		40	Avraham	Mindel	Genyah	
WLUKA				Shmuel Leib	Genyah		
WALCMAN	Pinchas Pinye		21				
WESOLEK	Gitel			Moshe	Kuke		
WESOLEK	Mindel			Moshe	Kuke		
WATMAN	Avraham		41			Rachel	
WATMAN	Asher		40			Tzirel	
WATMAN	Gitel		4	Avraham	Rachel		
WATMAN	Mordechai		16	Asher	Tzirel		
WATMAN	Tzirel	BERGSON	40	Chayim	Rachel	Asher	
WATMAN	Rachel	MALOVENCZIK	41			Avraham	
WIGDOROWICZ	Blumah		12	Levi	Devorah		
WIGDOROWICZ	Devorah		35			Levi	
WIGDOROWICZ	Levi		38			Devorah	
WILDOK	Shlomo						and his family
WILK	Avraham			Shmuel			and his family
WILK	Feivish			Shmuel			
WILK	Shmuel						
WINER	David		35			Tzirel	
WINER	Tzirel Tzasyah	BERGSON	35			David	
WINER	Tamar		3	David	Tzirel		
WAJNSTOK	Freide						and her family
WAJS	Yosef						and his family
WAJSMEL	Binem						and his family
WAJSROZA	Ahron Yehoshua		63			Hadassah	
WAJSROZA	Hadassah		60			Ahron Yehoshua	
WAJSROZA	Wolf			Ahron Yehoshua	Hadassah		
WAJSROZA	Chanah Perel		28			Yaakov	
WAJSROZA	Yehudah		36			Miriam	
WAJSROZA	Yaakov Yosef		42			Frimet	

WAJSROZA	Yaakov		30			Chanah Perel	
WAJSROZA	Mirel Leah	KUNSKOVLAVSKY	36				
WAJSROZA	Miriam		33			Yehudah	
WAJSROZA	Pesa		40			Shepsel	
WAJSROZA	Frimet		38			Yaakov Yosef	
WAJSROZA	Tzirel		65			Shimshon Mordechai	
WAJSROZA	Reizel			Ahron Yehoshua	Hadassah		
WAJSROZA	Shimshon Mordechai		66			Tzirel	
WAJSROZA	Shepsel		41			Pesa	
WAJSROZA	Sarah Billa		67				
WAJSROZA	Sarah Yente		6		Mirel Leah		
WAJSROZA				Yehudah	Miriam		
WISZOGRODSKI	David						and his family
WESOLEK	Zalman		44	Moshe	Kuke		
WESOLEK	Chanah						and her family
WESOLEK	Yitzchak		42	Moshe			and his family
WESOLEK	Moshe		67			Kuke	
WESOLEK	Kuke					Moshe	
WESOLEK						Zalmen	
WESOLEK						Yitzchak	
WRONA	Yonah						and his family
WRONA	Moshe						and his family
ZATOK	Beile						and her family
ZATOK	Yaakov						and his family
ZABICKI	Avraham		39			Esther Miriam	
ZABICKI	Eliyahu Ber						
ZABICKI	Esther Miriam	SKORKA	37			Avraham	
ZABICKI	David			Avraham	Esther Miriam		

ZABICKI	Pesach			Avraham	Esther Miriam		
ZABICKI	Avraham					Esther Miriam	
ZABICKI	Esther Miriam	SKORKA		Yisachar Meir	Yiskah	Avraham	
ZABICKI	David			Avraham	Esther Miriam		
ZABICKI	Zlata					Shaul	
ZABICKI	Chayah						
ZABICKI	Yaakov						
ZABICKI	Yitzchak		50			Rachel Leah	
ZABICKI	Feiga						
ZABICKI	Pesach			Avraham	Esther Miriam		
ZABICKI	Rachel Leah		50			Yitzchak	
ZABICKI	Shaul		30			Zlata	
ZABICKI							and his family
ZULTY	Rachel						and her family
ZULEK	David						and his family
ZOMEROWICZ	Sarah						and her child and family
ZURKIEWICZ	Hersh						and his family
ZURKIEWICZ	Wolf						and his family
ZURKIEWICZ	Chayim						and his family
ZURKIEWICZ	Leib						and his family
ZETELNI	Avraham						and his family
ZETELNI	Hersh Yosef						and his family
ZETELNI	Toviah						
ZETELNI	Yitzchak						and his family
ZIGFRID	Breine						and her family
ZAJDNER							

ZAJDNER		CZARNACZAPKA					
ZILBERBERG	Binah Rechel		57			David Noach	
ZILBERBERG	David Noach		62			Binah Rechel	
ZILBERBERG	Chayim		30			Rivkah	
ZILBERBERG	Rivkah	LIDZABERSKY	28			Chayim	
ZILBERBERG	Tamarah		5	Chayim	Rivkah		
ZILBERSZTAJN	Gutke	FRENKEL		Yaakov Dov	Chayah Sarah		
ZILBERSZTAJN	Libe	CZERNOVRODA	26			Moshe	
ZILBERSZTAJN	Moshe		28			Libe	
ZILBERSZTAJN						Guttke	
ZELAZNAGORA	Gitel Leah						and her family
ZELAZNAGORA	Gamliel			Yaakov	Zisah		
ZELAZNAGORA	Henyeh			Yaakov	Zisah		
ZELAZNAGORA	Herschel			Yaakov	Zisah		
ZELAZNAGORA	Zisa		43			Yaakov	
ZELAZNAGORA	Yaakov		50			Zisse	
ZELAZNAGORA	Yitzchak						and his family
ZELAZNAGORA	Malkah						and her family
ZELAZNAGORA	Miriam			Yaakov	Zisah		
ZELAZNAGORA	Feivel			Yaakov	Zisah		
ZALCMAN	Hindel		64			Chayim	
ZALCMAN	Chayim		65			Hindel	
ZALCER	Pesach						and his family
SEMELMAN	Broncia		28			Yitzchak	
SEMELMAN	Hindel Feiga					Hersh	
SEMELMAN	Hersh					Hindel Feige	
SEMELMAN	Yitzchak		30			Bruntzyah	
SEMELMAN	Meir					Reizel	
SEMELMAN	Reizel					Meir	
ZABICKI	Esther					Feivish	
ZABICKI	Feivish					Esther	
CHUDI	Yosef Meir						and his family
CHOMONT	Beile						and her

							family
CHOMONT	David						and his family
CHOMONT	Moshe						and his family
CHOMONT	Shmuel						and his family
CHESKELEWICZ	Mashe						and her family
TAUB	Berel						and his family
TAKS	Yehudit Chayah	KEMPFNER	32	Moshe David	Itte Tzivyah		
TAKS	Yerachmiel		8		Yehudis		
TAKS							and his family
TUCHHENDLER	Eliyahu Ber						and his family
TUCHHENDLER	Esther		38			Mordechai Leib	
TUCHHENDLER	David					Sarah	
TUCHHENDLER	Mordechai Leib		40			Esther	
TUCHHENDLER	Moshe Yosef						and his family
TUCHHENDLER	Sarah					David	
TAJTELBAUM	Meir Henoch			Yaakov Moshe	Rivkah Tultza		and his family
TAJTELBAUM	Esther			Mendel Melech	Schprintze		
TAJTELBAUM	Chayim Ahron			Mendel Melech	Schprintze		
TAJTELBAUM	Chanah Sarah			Mendel Melech	Schprintze		and her family
TAJTELBAUM	Tovah			Mendel Melech	Schprintze		
TAJTELBAUM	Tulcza Rivkah		70			Yaakov Moshe	
TAJTELBAUM	Tulcza			Mendel Melech	Schprintze		
TAJTELBAUM	Yehoshua			Mendel Melech	Schprintze		and his family
TAJTELBAUM	Yaakov Moshe		70			Tultza Rivkah	
TAJTELBAUM	Leib Ber			Mendel Melech	Schprintze		
TAJTELBAUM	Mendel Melech		50	Yaakov Moshe	Rivkah Tultza	Schprintze	

TAJTELBAUM	Fraidel			Mendel Melech	Schprintze		
TAJTELBAUM	Szprynca		50			Mendel Melech	
TCHOREK	Gucia			Meir			
TCHOREK	Meir		60				
TANGRUS	Avraham						and his family
TAC	Alah						
TAC	Esther		55			Shmuel Yitzchak	
TAC	Henich			Nachum			
TAC	Wolf		16	Shmuel Yitzchak	Esther		
TAC	Wolf		48				
TAC	Velvel			Shmuel Yitzchak	Esther		
TAC	Yaakov			Nachum			
TAC	Mendel						and his family
TAC	Matiel			Nachum			
TAC	Moshe						and his family
TAC	Nachum		60				
TAC	Nathan		55				
TAC	Shmuel			Nachum			
TAC	Shmuel Yitzchak		60			Esther	
TAC			58			Nachum	
TAC						Wolf	
JABLONSKI	Esther					Shia	
JABLONSKI	Hersh			Shia	Esther		
JABLONSKI	Chanah			Shia	Esther		
JABLONSKI	Reuven			Shia	Esther		
JABLONSKI	Shia					Esther	
JABLONKA	Baruch Leib			? Yaakov	Malkah		
JABLONKA	Yaakov		37			Malkah	
JABLONKA	Malkah	RAJCZYK	37			Yaakov	
JABLONKA	Shimshon			? Yaakov	Malkah		
IWAN	Esther	LOFTKA	42	Mordechai	Rivkah	Moshe	
IWAN	Yisrael / Yisraeltche		100				

IWAN	Moshe		42			Esther	
JUZIELEWSKI	Tzirel			Shlomo	Sarah		
JUZELEWSKI	Manye		23	Shlomo	Sarah		
JUZELEWSKI	Shlomo		60	Avraham		Sarah	
JUZELEWSKI	Sarah		55	Baruch Leib		Shlomo	
JONISZ	Mashe	MINC	35			Fallek	
JONISZ	Mark		6	Fallek	Mashe		
JONISZ	Fallek		36			Masha	
YORISH	Hersh Leib						and his family
JURISZ	Melech						
JAKUBOWICZ	Zalman						and his family
JAKUBOWICZ	Yente					Shimon	
JAKUBOWICZ	Shimon					Yenta	
ISZAJEWICZ	Yisrael Chayim					Reizel	
ISZAJEWICZ	Lifshe Tanne					Shmuel Leib	
ISZAJEWICZ	Niche			Shmuel Leib	Lipshe Tane	Henoch	
ISZAJEWICZ	Reizel					Yisrael Chayim	
ISZAJEWICZ	Shmuel Leib					Lifsha Tanna	
ISZAJEWICZ	Shifrah			Shmuel Leib	Lipshe Tane	Yidel	
JASZWICZ	Herschel		60			Leah	
JASZWICZ	Chayah Sarah		54			Yaakov Hersh	
JASZWICZ	Chanah		50			Meir Yisrael	
JASZWICZ	Yaakov Hersh		55	Shmuel Leib	Lipshe Tane	Chayah Sarah	
JASZWICZ	Yitzchak						and his family
JASZWICZ	Leah		60			Herschel	
JASZWICZ	Meir Yisrael		53	Shmuel Leib	Lipshe Tane	Chanah	
CHASKELEWICZ	Mashe	KRAJDE		Shmuel	Sarah		and her family
KOHN	Hinde	ROZEN				Yehoshua	
KOHN	Yehoshua					Hinde	

KAHANA	Moshe						and his family
KAC	Eliezer					Chavah	
KAC	Chavah					Eliezer	
CARMEL	Beile					Yechezkel	
CARMEL	Yechezkel					Beile	

Family name(s)	First name(s)	Maiden name	Age	Father's name	Mother's name	Name of spouse	Additional family members
LEW	Hersh						and his family
LEWKOWICZ	Devorah				Chayah		
LEWKOWICZ	Chayah		58				
LEWKOWICZ	Leibl				Chayah		
LUBINIECKI	Devorah Feiga	LICHT	48			Mordechai	
LUBINIECKI	Meir			Mordechai	Devorah Feige		
LUBINIECKI	Mordechai		50			Devorah Feige	
LUBINIECKI	Miriam			Mordechai	Devorah Feige		
LUBINIECKI	Shmuel			Mordechai	Devorah Feige		
LUBRANICKA	Broniah	FRYDMAN					
LUBRANECKI	Yosef						and his family
LEWITA							and his family
LEWIN	Eliyahu			Asher	Doba		
LEWIN	Asher					Doba	
LEWIN	Dobah					Asher	
LEWIN	Sheina			Asher	Doba		
LEWIN	Shmuel			Asher	Doba		
LOPATKA	Mordechai					Rivkah	
LOPATKA	Hersh		39	Mordechai	Rivkah	Fraidel	
LOPATKA	Henich		28	Mordechai	Rivkah		
LOPATKA	Fraidel	KALMANOWICZ	35			Hersh	
LOPATKA	Rivkah		63			Mordechai	
LUSZINSKI	Avraham						and his family
LAZANSKI	Itte	RANKEL				Hersh	and 2 children

LAZANSKI	Hersh					Itta	and 2 children
LIBSON	Avraham		23	Naftali	Sheine Mindel		
LIBSON	Chavah Leah		40				
LIBSON	Yehudit				Chavah Leah		
LIBSON	Naftali		55			Sheine Mindel	
LIBSON	Rachel	NAFTALI	28				
LIBSON	Sheine Mindel		55			Naftali	
LIBSON			28			Rachel	
LIBERMAN	Chayah			Chayim	CIPRE		
LIBERMAN	Tziporah					Chayim	
LIBERMAN	Shifrah			Chayim	CIPRE		
LIDZBARSKI	Esther Leah			Moshe Yosef	Gittel		
LIDZBARSKI	Gedaliah			Moshe Yosef	Gittel		
LIDZBARSKI	Gitel		49			Moshe Yosef	
LIDZBARSKI	Mordechai Simchah			Moshe Yosef	Gittel		
LIDZBARSKI	Moshe Yosef		52			Gittel	
LIDZBARSKI	Kalmen Meir		73				
LAJZEROWICZ	Eliyahu						and his family
LAJZEROWICZ	Chanah Gitel			Eliyahu			
LAJZEROWICZ	Feiga			Eliyahu			
LAJZEROWICZ	Reuven						
LAJZEROWICZ	Rozia			Eliyahu			
LICHT	Abba		42				
LICHT	Hinde		45			Shmuel Mendel	
LICHT	Chayim Shlomo						and his family
LICHT	Tulla		18	Shmuel Mendel	Hinde		
LICHT	Leibl					Sarah	
LICHT	Krusse		72				
LICHT	Rivkah			Leibl	Sarah		

LICHT	Shlomo						and his family
LICHT	Sarah					Leibl	
LICHTENSZTAJN	Wolf						and his family
LICHTENSZTAJN	Yehoshua						and his family
LICHTENSZTAJN	Yaakov						and his family
LICHTENSZTAJN	-						and his family
LIMCEWKA	Yitte						and her family
LIMKOWICZ	Yaakov						and his family
LINDE	-						and his family
LIS	Mendel						and his family
LIBSON	Avraham Baruch			Meir	Sarah		and his family
LIBSON	Dinah					Yisrael	
LIBSON	Yisrael					Dinah	
LIBSON	Meir					Sarah	
LIBSON	Rachel			Naftali	Sheine Mindel		
LIBSON	Reizel			Naftali	Sheine Mindel		
LIBSON	Sarah					Meir	
LIPMAN	Herschel					Frida	
LIPMAN	Frida					Herschel	
LIPSKA	David						and his family
LIPSKA	Yitte						and her family
LIPSKA	Leah						and her family
LIPSKA	Mindel						and her family
LIPSKI	Avraham Yitzchak					Rivkah	
LIPSKI	Rivkah					Avraham Yitzchak	
LIPKA	Ahron						and his family
LIPKA	Dinah			Feivish	Mindel		

LIPKA	Hadassah			Feivish	Mindel		
LIPKA	Meir						and his family
LIPKA	Mindel	LIBSON	45	Meir	Sarah	Feivish	
LIPKA	Feivish		48			Mindel	
LIPSZYC	Avraham		30			Sarah Malkah	
LIPSZYC	Eliezer		60			Feige	
LIPSZYC	Dobah		40			Mendel	
LIPSZYC	Chanah Gitel			Eliezer	Feige		
LIPSZYC	Chanah			Mendel	Doba		
LIPSZYC	Yitte			Eliezer	Feige		
LIPSZYC	Yitzchak			Eliezer	Feige		
LIPSZYC	Leibl			Mendel	Doba		
LIPSZYC	Mendel		44			Doba	
LIPSZYC	Feiga		55			Eliezer	
LIPSZYC	Sarah Malkah	GARNIVICZ	29			Avraham	
LIPSZYC	Sarah			Eliezer	Feige		
LELONEK	Esther	ROZENFELD				Zalmen	
LELONEK	Efrayim Yossel						
LELONEK	Billa					Yitzchak	
LELONEK	Gitel						and her family
LELONEK	Zalman					Esther	
LELONEK	Yitzchak					Billa	
LELONEK	Mendel						and his family
LELONEK	Miriam						and her family
LENT	Avraham		45			Devorah Feige	
LENT	Devorah Feiga	WALUKA	39	Avraham	Mindel	Avraham	
LENT	Rachel Leah				Devorah Feige		
LENT	Shlomo David				Devorah Feige		
LANENTER	Hinde			Hersh	Manyah		
LANENTER	Hersh					Manyah	
LANENTER	Yisrael			Hersh	Manyah		
LANENTER	Manye					Hersh	

LANENTER	Sarah			Hersh	Manyah		
LANCZNER	Beile		70			Mendel	
LANCZNER	Ber		44	Mendel	Beile		and his family
LANCZNER	Hersh						and his family
LANCZNER	Zalman		38	Mendel	Beile		and his family
LANCZNER	Chayim		35	Mendel	Beile		
LANCZNER	Yosef		42	Mendel	Beile		and his family
LANCZNER	Shmuel Yitzchak		46	Mendel	Beile		and his family
LASMAN	Ahron						
LASMAN	Esther					Chayim	
LASMAN	Herschel					Freide	and his family
LASMAN	Zisa						
LASMAN	Chayim					Esther	
LASMAN	Freide					Herschel	
LASMAN				Chayim	Esther		
LESMAN	Chayah Sarah						
LERER	Broniyah	KLINSKY				Moshe Ahron	and 2 children
LERER	Yeshayahu						and his family
LERER	Moshe Ahron					Bronyah	and 2 children
LERER	Tzirel	GREENVITZ	33			Moshe	
LERER	Rachel Leah						
LERER	Moshe		35			Tzirel	
MAY	Esther		55				
MAY	Ben-Zion				Esther		
MAY	Hudis				Esther		
MAY	Hersh Leib				Esther		
MAY	Moshe Ahron					Freide	
MAY	Freide					Moshe Ahron	
MAY	Shmuel			Moshe Ahron	Freide		
MAJEROWICZ	Mendel						and his

							family
MARGEL	Hencze					Menachem	
MARGEL	Menachem					Hentza	
MARGEL	Tzirele			Menachem	Hentza		
MARGEL							
MIGDAL	Avraham			Moshe	Mindel		
MIGDAL	Dov Binyamin			Moshe	Mindel		
MIGDAL	Hersh Wolf			Moshe	Mindel		
MIGDAL	Yisrael			Moshe	Mindel		
MIGDAL	Mindel					Moshe	
MIGDAL	Moshe		40			Mindel	
MIGDAL	Roize Billa			Moshe	Mindel		
MIGDAL	Shifrah			Moshe	Mindel		
MIGNOSZEWER	Golde			Herschel	Mindel		
MIGNOSZEWER	Herschel		45			Mindel	
MIGNOSZEWER	Mindel	PINDEK	42				
MIGNOSZEWER	Sarah			Herschel	Mindel		
MOTIL	Hersh		60			Chanah	
MOTIL	Chanah		60			Hersh	
MOTIL	Yocheved	MLAWA	30				
MOTIL	Yitzchak Meir					Feige	
MOTIL	Sender				Yocheved		
MOTIL	Feiga					Yitzchak Meir	
MOSZKOWICZ	Yosef Meir			Moshe	Sarah Rachel		
MOSZKOWICZ	Mendel			Moshe	Sarah Rachel		
MOSZKOWICZ	Moshe					Sarah Rachel	
MOSZKOWICZ	Pesa			Moshe	Sarah Rachel		
MOSZKOWICZ	Shmuel Hersh			Moshe	Sarah Rachel		
MOSZKOWICZ	Sarah Rachel	AIZIKOWICZ		Yechezkel	Tovah Leah	Moshe	
MITGANG	Tovah		4		Rivkah		
MITGANG	Rivkah	FANFIL	32	Yaakov	Leah		
MICHALOWICZ	Wolf						and his family

MICHALOWICZ	Mordechai						and his family
MINC	Gershon		44			Leah	and his family
MINC	Leah					Gershon	
MINC	Dr. Leib		50				
MINC	Malkah		38				
MINC	Sheina						
MINC			45				
MINC			10	Leib			
MAJERANC	Avraham					Chayah Fraidel	
MAJERANC	Billa	SENDEROWICZ	44			Benyamin	
MAJERANC	Benyamin		44			Billa	
MAJERANC	Zlatke			Avraham	Chayah Fraidel		
MAJERANC	Chayah Fraidel	CZARNACZAPKA		Ahron	Esther Leah	Avraham	
MAJERANC	Yaakov			Avraham	Chayah Fraidel		
MAJERANC	Yitzchak			Avraham	Chayah Fraidel		
MAJERANC	Rivkah Feiga		12	Benyamin	Billa		
MLAWA	Avraham		1	Gutkind Alexander	Chayah		
MLAWA	Gutta		35				
MLAWA	Gutkind Alexander		28			Chayah	
MLAWA	Chayah		25			Gutkind Alexander	
MLAWA	Pinchas Tzadok		64			Sheine Yehudis	
MLAWA	Tzarna		6		Gutta		
MLAWA	Sheine Yehudit		61			Pinchas Tzadok	
MLAWSKI	Yitzchak						and his family
MALOWANCZYK	Hindel	LEVIN	52			Chaymin Shlomo	
MALOWANCZYK	Chayim Shlomo		52			Hindel	
MALOWANCZYK	Yehudit		39			Shimon	
MALOWANCZYK	Libe			Chayim Shlomo	Hindel		
MALOWANCZYK	Simchah			Chayim	Hindel		

	Yehudah			Shlomo			
MALOWANCZYK	Shimon		48			Yehudis	
MALOWANCZYK	Sarah		50				
MLYN	Meir						and his family
MEKLER	Moshe Leib						and his family
MARGALIT	Tovah	BORNSZTAJN	43				
MARGALIT			43			Tovah	
MARKOWICZ	Arthur			Gedalyahu	Tamrah		
MARKOWICZ	Gedaliahu					Tamrah	
MARKOWICZ	Gutta			Gedalyahu	Tamrah		
MARKOWICZ	Krusse			Gedalyahu	Tamrah		
MARKOWICZ	Tamrah	CZARNACZAPKA		Ahron	Esther Leah	Gedalyahu	
NAGRODSKA	Tzirel						and her family
NADULAK							and his family
NORDEN	Avraham Hersh						and his family
NAZEMSKI	Moshe						and his family
NIEDZWIEDZ							and his family
NAJMAN	Avraham						and his family
NAJMAN	Bunim						and his family
NAJMAN	Benyamin		60				
NAJMAN	Berta		60			Yaakov	
NAJMAN	Chanah			Yaakov	Berta		
NAJMAN	Yosef			Benyamin			
NAJMAN	Yaakov			Benyamin			
NAJMAN	Yaakov		62			Berta	
NAJMAN	Luniah			Yaakov	Berta		
NAJMAN	Leon			Yaakov	Berta		
NIEMCIEWSKO	Ber						and his family
NIEMCIEWSKO	David						and his family
NIEMCIEWSKO	Yosef						and his family
NIEMCIEWSKO	Moshe			Shimon	Nashe		

NIEMCIEWSKO	Nashe	BUDA				Shimon	
NIEMCIEWSKO	Salisha			Shimon	Nashe		
NIEMCIEWSKO	Shimon					Nashe	
NIPOMOSZCZ	Elke	GOTTLIEBOVSKY		Baruch Mendel	Rivkah	Moshe	
NIPOMOSZCZ	Moshe					Elke	
NIPOMOSCZ	Nashe / Neshe			Moshe	Elke		
NAISZATEN	Billa						and his family
NAISZATEN	Rachel						and his family
NACHPIN	Moshe Ahron						and his family
NEMLICH	Abish					Rachel	
NEMLICH	Adel			Abish	Rachel		
NEMLICH	Rachel					Abish	
NEMLICH	Shmuel			Abish	Rachel		
NEZNOKONI	Mordechai Leib						
NASZELSKI	Lipa					Tzirel	and his family
NASZELSKI	Moshe						and his family
NASZELSKI	Tzirel					Lipe	and her family

Family name(s)	First name(s)	Maiden name	Age	Father's name	Mother's name	Name of spouse	Additional family members
SOBOL	Benyamin					Sarah	
SOBOL	Sarah					Benyamin	
SOCHACZEWSKI	Chayah Libe		55				
SOCHACZEWSKI	Benyamin		65	Yitzchak Meir	Feige		
SOCHACZEWSKI	Chayim Shamsha		35	Benyamin			
SOSNOWSKA	Rivkah						and her family
SURGAL	Yosef						and his family
SURGAL							and his family
SOROKA	Esther					Yosef	
SOROKA	Yosef					Esther	

STARI	Henich						and his family
STARI	Yechezkel						and his family
STAWICKA	Yitte						and her family
STAWICKI	Hersh			Shlomo	Liftzah		
STAWICKI	Liftshe					Shlomo	
STAWICKI	Pulah(?)			Shlomo	Liftzah		
STAWICKI	Shlomo					Liftza	
STAWICKI	Shmuel			Shlomo	Liftzah		
SLOMA	Beile Rachel	LIBSON		Meir	Sarah	Menachem	
SLOMA	Dinah			Menachem	Beile Rachel		
SLOMA	Yisrael			Menachem	Beile Rachel		
SLOMA	Menachem					Beile Rachel	
SMOLENSKI	Beile			Mirel	Michal		
SMOLENSKI	Michel					Mirel	
SMOLENSKI	Mirel					Mechel	
SMOLENSKI	Rachel			Mirel	Michal		
SMOLENSKI	Sarah Devorah			Mirel	Michal		
SMOLENSKI	Beinisch		55			Chanah	
SMOLENSKI	Zeine		36			Yisrael	
SMOLENSKI	Chanah		53			Beinish	
SMOLENSKI	Yisrael		41	Mirel	Michal	Zeine	
SMOLENSKI	Shlomo		22	Beinisch	Chanah		
SMOLENSKI	Sarah		33				
SMOLENSKI			3	Yisrael	Zeine		
SMOLENSKI			33			Sarah	
SENDEROWICZ	Avraham			Hersh Micha'el	Pesa		
SENDEROWICZ	Avraham Yosef			Yitzchak Meir	Miriam Rachel		
SENDEROWICZ	Ahron			Yitzchak Meir	Miriam Rachel		
SENDEROWICZ	Eliezer			Yitzchak Meir	Miriam Rachel		
SENDEROWICZ	Hersh Micha'el		55			Pesa	
SENDEROWICZ	Chayah			Chayim	Yehudis		

SENDEROWICZ	Chayim		48	Moshe	Rachel	Yehudis	and his family
SENDEROWICZ	Chanah			Hersh Micha'el	Pesa		
SENDEROWICZ	Yehudah			Hersh Micha'el	Pesa		
SENDEROWICZ	Yehudit		48			Chayim	
SENDEROWICZ	Yitzchak Meir		52			Miriam Rachel	
SENDEROWICZ	Micha'el			Chayim	Yehudis		
SENDEROWICZ	Miriam Rachel		49			Yitzchak Meir	
SENDEROWICZ	Moshe Mordechai		80			Rachel	
SENDEROWICZ	Pesa		55			Hersh Mechel	
SENDEROWICZ	Rachel		75			Moshe Mordechai	
SENDEROWICZ	Shimon			Hersh Micha'el	Pesa		
SAPIRSZTAJN	Ahron						and his family
SAKOWICZ	Hersh						and his family
SAKOWICZ	Zalman						and his family
SAKOWICZ	Pesa						and 3 children
SAKODELS							and his family
SKORNIK	Zeine					Pesach	
SKORNIK	Zalman			Yehudah Baruch	Miriam		
SKORNIK	Chayim			Yehudah Baruch	Miriam		
SKORNIK	Yehudah Baruch					Miriam	
SKORNIK	Yochanan			Yehudah Baruch	Miriam		
SKORNIK	Miriam					Yehudah Baruch	
SKORNIK	Moshe			Yehudah Baruch	Miriam		
SKORNIK	Pesach					Zeine	
SKORNIK							and his family
SKORKA	Yosef		32	Yisachar	Yiskah	Sarah	

				Meir	ZABICKI		
SKORKA	Yiskah	ZABICKI	55			Yisachar Meir	
SEKORKA	Yisachar Meir					Yiskah	
SKORKA	Sarah					Yosef	
SKRZECZANOWSKI	Chanah			Yosef	Rachel Leah		
SKRZECZANOWSKI	Yosef		31			Rachel Leah	
SKRZECZANOWSKI	Rachel Leah	ZHOTKA	30	Meir	Malkah	Yosef	
FALKA	Yechezkel						and his family
FASA	Ben-Zion						and his family
FASA	Chavah Rachel						and her family
FASA	Yechezkel						
FASA	Yisrael						and his family
FASA	Leah						and her family
FASA	Leib						and his family
FASA	Shmuel						and his family
FOGEL	Hersh		35			Reizel	
FOGEL	Reizel	LIBSON	30			Hersh	
PODSKOC	Avraham						and his family
PODSKOC	Eliezer						and his family
PODSKOC	Hinde						and her family
PODSKOC	Chanah Feiga						
PODSKOC	Chanah		8	? Yaakov	Rivkah		
PODSKOC	Yehoshua			Ezriel			and his family
PODSKOC	Yosef Meir				Chanah Feige		
PODSKOC	Mindel				Chanah Feige		
PODSKOC	Menachem						and his family
PODSKOC	Miriam				Chanah		

					Feige		
PODSKOC	Moshe						and his family
PODSKOC	Rivkah	SZPERLING	40		Beile	Yaakov	
PODSKOC	Rachel						and her family
PODSKOC	Sarah						and her family
POZNANSKI	Berish						and his family
POTER	Avraham						and his family
PULWER	Meir						and his family
FOLDA	Hinde			Meir	Fraidel		
FOLDA	Meir					Fraidel	
FOLDA	Fraidel	BUDA				Meir	
POPOWSKI	Yehoshua						and his family
PUKACZ	Benyamin					Chanah	
PUKACZ	Berachah					Yosef	
PUKACZ	Chanah					Benyamin	
PUKACZ	Yehudah			Yosef	Brachah		
PUKACZ	Yosef					Berachah	
PUKACZ	Moshe			Yosef	Brachah		
PUKACZ	Noach						and his family
PETRIKUS	Moshe			Shimon	Sarah		
PETRIKUS	Pesa			Shimon	Sarah		
PETRIKUS	Shimon		40			Sarah	
PETRIKUS	Sarah	BURGAND	40			Shimon	
FIALKO	Esther			Tzvi	Yocheved		
FIALKO	Yocheved	GURFINKEL				Tzvi	
FIALKO	Tzvi					Yocheved	
FIANKO	Eliezer						and his family
FIGELMAN	Efrayim		32			Chayah	
FIGELMAN	Chayah	MAY	30				
FIGELMAN	Sarah						and her family
PIOTRKOWSKI	Leibl						and his family
FAJNBERG	Baruch		33			Genyah	

FAJNBERG	Genya		31			Baruch	
FAJNBERG	Yehudah		33				
FAJNBERG	Rachel		27				
FAJNBERG	Shoshana		7	Baruch	Genyah		
PINDEK	Yosef					Yitte	
PINDEK	Yitte		68			Yosef	
PINDEK	Moshe		43	Yosef	Yitte		and his family
PISASZ	Motel						and his family
FLATO	Gedaliah						and his family
FLATO	Leibish Zelig						and his family
PLONSKER	Zeldah				Feige		
PLONSKER	Yechezkel				Feige		
PLONSKER	Yitzchak				Feige		
PLONSKER	Feiga		65				
FLURMAN	Moshe Ahron						and his family
FLATO	Ber		40			Chanah	
FLATO	Chanah	GONGOLA	38			Ber	
FENSTER	Devorah	GRAPA		Yitzchak	Yocheved	Yosef	
FENSTER	Yosef					Devorah	
FENSTER				Yosef	Devorah		
PANFIL	Moshe		40				and his family
PANFIL	Shlomo						and his family
PANFIL	Sarah Rivkah						and her family
PEREL	Eizik		60				
PEREL	Dinah						and her family
PEREL	Moshe						and his family
PEREL	Rachel Leah		25	Eizik			
PAPIRCZYK	Udel					Yitzchak / Itsha	
PAPIRCZYK	Esther Gitel			Yitzchak / Itsha	Adel		
PAPIRCZYK	Devorah			Yitzchak	Adel		
PAPIRCZYK	Rachel			Yitzchak	Adel		

PFEFER	Sarah	FANFIL					
FRID	Golde	WALUKA				Moshe	and her family
FRID	Moshe					Golde	and his family
FRIDLENDER	David			Chayim	Yocheved		
FRIDLENDER	Chavah						and her family
FRIDLENDER	Chayim		55			Yocheved	
FRIDLENDER	Chanah			Chayim	Yocheved		
FRIDLENDER	Tovah			Chayim	Yocheved		
FRIDLENDER	Yocheved		49			Chayim	
FRIDLENDER	Yitzchak			Chayim	Yocheved		
FRIDLENDER	Frimet			Chayim	Yocheved		
FRYDMAN	Bronka			Yeshayahu	Chanah		
FRYDMAN	Gedaliah		38			Tzirel	
FRYDMAN	Gitel		58			Shlomo Zalmen	
FRYDMAN	Herschel			Gedalyahu	Tzirel		
FRYDMAN	Chayim			Yeshayahu	Chanah		
FRYDMAN	Chanah	GLAZER	45			Yeshayahu	
FRYDMAN	Yeshayahu		45			Chanah	
FRYDMAN	Miriam Manye			Gedalyahu	Tzirel		
FRYDMAN	Fela			Yeshayahu	Chanah		
FRYDMAN	Tzirel	ROZENEK	36			Gedalyahu	
FRYDMAN	Rivkah			Gedalyahu	Tzirel		
FRYDMAN	Rachel Leah			Gedalyahu	Tzirel		
FRYDMAN	Shlomo Zalman		60			Gittel	
PERMUTER	Hersh						and his family
FRANK	Shmuel						and his family
FRENKEL	Avraham			Yaaov Dov	Chayah Sarah	Malkah	and 2 children
FRENKEL	Avraham			Ezra	Hindel		
FRENKEL	Ahron			Yaakov Dov	Chayah Sarah		
FRENKEL	Asher			Yaakov Dov	Chayah Sarah	Roza	
FRENKEL	Dora					Nachum	
FRENKEL	Hindel					Ezra	

FRENKEL	Chayim Meir						and his family
FRENKEL	Yechezkel						and his family
FRENKEL	Yaakov Dov					Chayah Sarah	
FRENKEL	Malkah					Avraham	and 2 children
FRENKEL	Moshe						and his family
FRENKEL	Nachum			Yaakov Dov	Chayah Sarah	Dora	
FRENKEL	Ezra					Hindel	
FRENKEL	Roza					Asher	
FRENKEL	Roza					Moshe	and 2 children
FRENKEL						Ahron	
PRZYGODA	Avraham		36			Feige	
PRZYGODA	Elke			Yisrael	Sarah		
PRZYGODA	Esther			Yisrael	Sarah		
PRZYGODA	Ber						and his family
PRZYGODA	David			Avraham	Feige		
PRZYGODA	David		28			Yehudis	
PRZYGODA	Hinde						and his family
PRZYGODA	Chanah			Yisrael	Sarah		
PRZYGODA	Yehudit	MLAWSKI				David	
PRZYGODA	Yitzchak						and his family
PRZYGODA	Yisrael		62			Sarah	
PRZYGODA	Yisrael					Tovah Tzerke	
PRZYGODA	Yisachar						and his family
PRZYGODA	Motel			Yisrael	Sarah		
PRZYGODA	Feiga		35			Avraham	
PRZYGODA	Sarah		60			Yisrael	
PRZENICA	Devorah		40			Shlomo	
PRZENICA	Chayim Nachum			Shlomo	Devorah		
PRZENICA	Shlomo		49			Devorah	
PRZENICA	Shimon			Shlomo	Devorah		
CZEBICZERCZIK							and his

							family
CUDEK	Yehudah						and his family
CUDEK	Yisrael						and his family
CUDEK / CZERSZLIF	Chayim						and his family
CUDEK / CZERSZLIF	Mendel						and his family
CUDEK / CZERSZLIF	Moshe						and his family
CZITAG	Benyamin						and his family
CYLIK	Shmuel Mordechai						and his family
CYNADARKA	Ahron					Fogel	
CYNADARKA	Tovah			Ahron	Fogel		
CYNADARKA	Yitzchak			Ahron	Fogel		
CYNADARKA	Fogel					Ahron	
CYNADARKO	Toviah						and his family
CYNA	Elimelech					Yiskah	
CYNA	Chanah Rivkah				Yiskah		
CYNA	Yitte Feiga				Yiskah		
CYNA	Yiskah					Elimelech	
CYNA	Pesa				Yiskah		
CYNA	Perel Esther				Yiskah		
CIPRIS	Avraham						and his family
CIPRIS	Efrayim						and his family
CIPRIS	Meir		60			Paltza Bila	
CIPRIS	Paltza Beile		55			Meir	
CZARNOBRODA	Eliyahu Moshe			Henich	Rivkah		
CZARNOBRODA	Eliezer			Henich	Rivkah		
CZARNOBRODA	Henich		60			Rivkah	
CZARNOBRODA	Rivkah		60			Henich	
CZARNACZAPKA	Avraham			Yeshayahu		Beile	
CZARNACZAPKA	Avraham			Ahron	Esther Leah	Binah	
CZARNACZAPKA	Ahron					Esther	

						Leah	
CZARNACZAPKA	Esther Leah					Ahron	
CZARNACZAPKA	Beile					Avraham	
CZARNACZAPKA	Binah					Avraham	
CZARNACZAPKA	Berel					Gittel Miriam	
CZARNACZAPKA	Gitel Miriam					Berel	
CZARNACZAPKA	Hersh Wolf		42	Ahron	Esther Leah	Rachel Rozyah	
CZARNACZAPKA	Hersh Wolf			Berel	Gittel Miriam		
CZARNACZAPKA	Chayah			Berel	Gittel Miriam		
CZARNACZAPKA	Yehoshua			Berel	Gittel Miriam		
CZARNACZAPKA	Yitte						and her family
CZARNACZAPKA	Yaakov						and his family
CZARNACZAPKA	Moshe Eliezer		12	Hersh Wolf	Rachel		
CZARNACZAPKA	Reuven			Berel	Gittel Miriam		
CZARNACZAPKA	Rachel Roze		42			Hersh Wolf	
CZARNACZAPKA	Shimon						and his family
CZARNACZAPKA				Avraham	Binah		
CZARNACZAPKA				Avraham	Binah		
CZARNACZAPKA				Avraham	Binah		
CZARNESZLIP	Mendel						and his family
CZARNESZLIP	Moshe						and his family
CZARNI	Avraham						and his family
CZARNI	Pinchas						and his family
CZARNI	Shmuel						and his family
CZARKA	Itte / Yitte		57			Tzvi Herschel	
CZARKA	Anshel			Chayim	Miriam		
CZARKA	Esther			Tzvi	Itte		

				Herschel			
CZARKA	Breine			Tzvi Herschel	Itte		
CZARKA	Dov		35			Sarah	
CZARKA	Henyeh			Dov	Sarah		
CZARKA	Zelig					Tzipporah	
CZARKA	Chavah	GOLDSZTAJN	50			Yitzchak	
CZARKA	Chayim					Miriam	
CZARKA	Yitzchak		60			Chavah	
CZARKA	Meir			Dov	Sarah		
CZARKA	Miriam					Chayim	
CZARKA	Feiga			Zelig	Tzipporah		
CZERKA	Tzvi Herschel					Yitte	
CZARKA	Tziporah					Zelig	
CZARKA	Reizel			Zelig	Tzipporah		
CZARKA	Reine			Chayim	Miriam		
CZERKA	Shmuel						
CZARKA	Sarah		35	Yisachar Meir	Yiskah	Dov	
CZESLAK	Disha						and family
CZESLAK	Chanah Gitel			Mordechai	Sarah		
CZESLAK	Mordechai		55			Sarah	
CZESLAK	Simchah Bunim			Mordechai	Sarah		
CZESLAK	Sarah		54			Mordechai	

Family name(s)	**First name(s)**	**Maiden name**	**Age**	**Father's name**	**Mother's name**	**Name of spouse**	**Additional family members**
KALMAN	Shlomo						and his family
KANO							and his family
KONSKOWOLSKI	Meir						
KONSKOWOLSKI	Mashe						
KOPPERMAN							and his family
KAROL	David						and his family
KARPA	Eliezer		21		Gittel Billa		
KARPA	Esther			Yitzchak	Tzirel		

KARPA	Gitel			Yosef	Chanah		
KARPA	Devorah			Yitzchak	Manyah		
KARPA	Chayim Yaakov				Rivkah		
KARPA	Chanah Nechamah		48	Yechezkel	Tovah Leah	Yosef	
KARPA	Yosef		50			Chanah	
KARPA	Yechiel			Yitzchak	Tzirel		
KARPA	Yitzchak		40			Manyah	
KARPA	Yitzchak		34			Tzirel	
KARPA	Yisrael Shimon			Yosef	Chanah		
KARPA	Manye		40			Yitzchak	
KARPA	Tzirel		30			Yitzchak	
KARPA	Rashah			Yosef	Chanah		
KARPA	Rivkah		48				
KARPA	Rachel				Rivkah		
KARPA	Sarah			Yosef	Chanah		
KARPA	Sarah Leah		28		Gittel Billa		
KADECKI	Yechezkel		60			Rivkah	
KADECKI	Mashe			Yechezkel	Rivkah		
KADECKI	Moshe		38			Sheine Rivkah	
KADECKI	Rivkah		60			Yechezkel	
KADECKI	Rachel Leah			Yechezkel	Rivkah		
KADECKI	Sheine Rivkah		35	Avraham	Mindel	Moshe	
KOTNOWSKI	Zalman						and his family
KUTNER / KUTNA	Hersh						and his family
KUTNER / KUTNA	Zisah Malkah						and her family
KUTNER / KUTNA	Shlomo						and his family
KOCHEN	Devorah					Nachman	
KOCHEN	Chanah			Nachman	Devorah		
KOCHEN	Yonah			Nachman	Devorah		
KOCHEN	Menachem			Nachman	Devorah		
KOCHEN	Nachman					Devorah	
KOLCZYN	Nissan						and his family

KUNIEC	Leib						and his family
KUNIEC	Nachum						and his family
KONSKOWOLSKI	Avigdor		65			Pola	
KONSKOWOLSKI	Gela	SENDEROWICZ		Hersh Micha'el	Pesa	Meir	
KONSKOWOLSKI	Meir		33			Roize	
KONSKOWOLSKI	Meir					Gela	
KONSKOWOLSKI	Pulah(?)		65			Avigdor	
KONSKOWOLSKI	Rozia					Meir	
KOPOLOWICZ	Herschel		40			Sarah	
KOPOLOWICZ	Chayah	KANENBRAND				Mordechai	
KOPOLOWICZ	Mechel		65				
KOPOLOWICZ	Mordechai					Chayah	
KOPOLOWICZ	Moshe		32	Mechel			
KOPOLOWICZ	Sarah		40			Herschel	
KOPOLOWICZ			65			Mechel	
KOCIOLEK	Chayim						and his family
KORAL	Alah			Chayim Yaakov	Sheine		
KORAL	Esther			David	Yuris		
KORAL	Gitte			David	Yuris		
KORAL	David		45			Yuris	
KORAL	Zeldah			Chayim Yaakov	Sheine		
KORAL	Zelig			Chayim Yaakov	Sheine		
KORAL	Chayim Yaakov					Sheine	
KORAL	Yaris		44			David	
KORAL	Feiga						
KORAL	Perel			David	Yuris		
KORAL	Rachel			David	Yuris		
KORAL	Sheina					Chayim Yaakov	
KORTA	Dr. Eliezer Mendel			Shmuel	Chanah		
KORCZAK	Mordechai						and his family
KRZYWANOWSKI	Devorah		29			Yisrael	
KRZYWANOWSKI	Chanah			Yitzchak	Roize		

KRZYWANOWSKI	Yitzchak		47			Roize	
KRZYWANOWSKI	Yisrael		31	Yitzchak	Roize	Devorah	and his family
KRZYWANOWSKI	Tzivyah			Yitzchak	Roize		
KRZYWANOWSKI	Rozia		44			Yitzchak	
KIRSZ	Hena						and her family
KIRSZ	Moshe Yehudah						and his family
KIRSZ	Feivish						and his family
KISZLEWSKI	Chayim						and his family
KLAJN	Esther		42				
KLAJN	Yisrael						and his family
KLAJN	Meir				Roize Dinah		
KLAJN	Moshe Mordechai		17		Esther		
KLAJN	Sallek		15		Reitze		
KLAJN	Perel				Roize Dinah		
KLAJN	Roize Dinah		65				
KLAJN	Reitze		42				
KLAJN	Simchah Bunim				Roize Dinah		
KLAJNHAUS							and her family
KLAJNMAN	David			Yitzchak	Yocheved		
KLAJNMAN	Yocheved			Yehoshua	Roize	Yitzchak	
KLAJNMAN	Yitzchak					Yocheved	
KLAJNMAN	Leah			Yitzchak	Yocheved		
KLAJNMAN							and his family
KALINSKI	Ahron						and his family
KALINSKI	Berish						and his family
KALINSKI / KRALISKIS	Melech						and four daughters and family
KALINSKI	Reuven						and his family
KALMANOWICZ	Hersh		40			Chanah	

KALMANOWICZ	Chanah		38			Yurish	
KALMANOWICZ	Malkah						
KALMANOWICZ	Rivkah		10	Hersh	Chanah		
KLAPFISZ	Gitel		43	Moshe			
KLAPFISZ			43			Gittel	
KLECZEWSKI	Poza		60				
KLECZEWSKI	Shlomo Mordechai		32				
KLECZEWSKI			30			Shlomo Mordechai	
KLECZEWSKI			4	Shlomo Mordechai			
KAMIN	Hersh		34			Rachel Leah	
KAMIN	Moshe			Hersh	Rachel Leah		
KAMIN	Rachel Leah		32	Shmuel Asher	Pesa Malkah	Hersh	
KAMIN	Shmuel Asher			Hersh	Rachel Leah		
KEMPNER	Itte Czivyah		50			Moshe David	
KEMPNER	Aryeh Leib		23	Moshe David	Itte Tzivyah		
KEMPNER	Moshe David		50			Itta Tzivyah	
KANENBRAND	Brachah			Zalmen	Chayah		
KANENBRAND	Hersh Moshe						
KANENBRAND	Zisa			Hersh Moshe			
KANENBRAND	Zalman					Chayah	
KANENBRAND	Chayah					Zalmen	
KANENBRAND	Maniah						and her family
KANENBRAND	Masha			Zalmen	Chayah		
KANENBRAND	Shmuel Yaakov			Zalmen	Chayah		
KANENBRAND						Hersh Moshe	
KAPERMAN	Chanah			Yosef			
KAROL	Dinah			Yechiel Meir	Pesa		
KAROL	Yechiel Ozer		40			Pesa	
KAROL	Pesa		38	Meir	Sarah	Yechiel	

						Ozer	
KAROL	Sheina						and her family
KRIGER	Avraham		62			Breine	and his family
KRIGER	Breine		42			Avraham	and her family
KRIGER	Toviah			Avraham	Breine		
KRIGER	Rachel			Avraham	Breine		
KRIDA	Blimah Gitel			Shmuel	Sarah		
KRIDA	David			Shmuel	Sarah		
KRIDA	Malkah			Shmuel	Sarah	Yehudah Tzadok	
KRIDA	Shmuel					Sarah	
KRIDA	Sarah					Shmuel	
KRISTAL	Esther			Leib	Sarah		
KRISTAL	Chayim Yosef		70				
KRISTAL	Leib		50			Sarah	
KRISTAL	Moshe			Leib	Sarah		
KRISTAL	Tzivyah			Leib	Sarah		
KRISTAL	Sarah		48			Leibl	
KARMEZESZ	Leibl Menachem Aryeh		65			Roda	
KARMEZESZ	Roda		60			Leibl / Menachem Aryeh	
KRASNER	Yeshayahu					Malkah	
KRASNER	Meir Yisrael						and her family
KRASNER	Malkah					Yeshayahu	
KARP	Yisrael						and her family
KARP	Simchah						and her family
KARPA	Avraham					Liftza	
KARPA	Billa						
KARPA	Chayah Gitel		14	Chayim	Chanah		
KARPA	Chayim		55			Chanah	
KARPA	Chanah		51			Chayim	
KARPA	Malkah						
KARPA	Mordechai						

	Yitzchak						
KARPA	Miriam						and her family
KARPA	Frida			Avraham	Liftzah		
KARPA	Rachel			Avraham			
KRESZNIEWSKI	Yechiel Meir						and his family
KRESZNIEWSKI	Yisrael						and his family
KRESZNIEWSKI	Manye						
KRESZNIEWSKI	Moshe					Manyah	
KZARZ	Chanah Golde					Moshe	
KZARZ	Moshe					Chanah Golde	
KSZARSZ	A.						and his family
KSZARSZ	David						and his family
KSZARSZ	Zelig					Rachel	
KSZARSZ	Mendel						and his family
KSZARSZ	Rachel					Zelig	
RABINOWICZ	Yaakov						and his family
RABINOWICZ	Sarah						and her family
ROBOTA	Herschel						and his family
ROBOTA	Yaakov						and his family
ROBOTA	Feivel						and his family
ROBOTA	Simchah						and his family
RUBINSZTAJN	Henoch			Chayim Moshe			
RUBINSZTAJN	Chayim Moshe						
RUBINSZTAJN	Mendel			Chayim Moshe			
RUBINSZTAJN	Henoch			Chayim Moshe	Rivkah		
RUBINSZTAJN	Chayim Moshe					Rivkah	
RUBINSZTAJN	Mendel			Chayim	Rivkah		

				Moshe			
RUBINSZTAJN	Rivkah					Chayim Moshe	
RODA	Itsha						and his family
RODA	Chayah			Yitzchak Meir	Feige	Reuven	
RODA	Mashe						and her family
RODA	Moshe			Reuven	Chayah		
RODA	Sender			Reuven	Chayah		
RODA	Reuven					Chayah	
RUZGA	Yosef						and his family
RUZGA	Yisrael						and his family
RUZGA	Moshe						and his family
ROZENEK	Ahron			Eliezer	Chayah		
ROZENEK	Eliezer		55			Chayah	
ROZENEK	Esther		55			Leib	
ROZENEK	Chayah		55			Eliezer	
ROZENEK	Leib		56			Esther	
ROZENEK	Tzadok			Leib	Esther		
ROZENEK	Sarah			Leib	Esther		
ROZEN	David					Rikel Leah	
ROZEN	Malkah Shurik						
ROZEN	Rikkel Leah					David	
ROZEN	Sarah			David	Rikel Leah		
ROZEN	Sarah						her husband
ROZENBERG	Beile		42			Yitzchak Binem	
ROZENBERG	Yitzchak Binem		42			Beile	
ROZENBERG	Manye			Yitzchak Binem	Beile		
ROZENBERG	Moshe			Yitzchak Binem	Beile		
ROZENTAL	Leib		44			Nechamah	
ROZENTAL	Nechamah / Chomah		44			Leib	
ROZENFELD	Yaakov						and his

	Shimon						family
ROTMAN	Avraham						and his family
ROTENBERG	Devorah			Herschel	Chanah Rivkah		
ROTENBERG	Chanah Rivkah				Esther Rachel	Tzvi Herschel	
ROTENBERG	Yehudit			Herschel	Chanah Rivkah		
ROTENBERG	Tzvi Herschel					Chanah Rivkah	
ROTENSZTAJN	Esther			Yaakov Dov	Chayah Sarah	Yisrael	
ROTENSZTAJN	Yisrael					Esther	
ROTENSZTAJN				Yisrael	Esther		
ROSEK	Avraham Menachem			Yitzchak Meir	Chanah Pesa		
ROSEK	Chayim			Yitzchak Meir	Chanah Pesa		
ROSEK	Chanah Pesa		37			Yitzchak Meir	
ROSEK	Yitzchak Meir		37			Chanah Pesa	
ROSEK	Sarah			Yitzchak Meir	Chanah Pesa		
RZEJSOTKO	Baruch					Chanah	his grandchildren
RZEJSOTKO	Chanah					Baruch	her grandchildren
RZEJSOTKO	Yosef			Meir	Malkah	Tzipporah	
RZEJSOTKO	Meir					Malke	
RZEJSOTKO	Malkah					Meir	
RZEJSOTKO	Tziporah					Yosef	
RATMAN	Avraham						and his family
RYBEK	Avraham						and his family
RIBKA	Tulcza						and her family
RIBKA	Yaakov						and his family
RIBKA	Mashe						and her family
RIBKA	Shepsel						and his family
RYZOWY	Yehudah					Nicha	

RYZOWY	Niche					Yehudah	
RYZOWY	Yehudah						
RAJCH	Yitzchak						and his family
RAJCH	Shimshon						and his family
RAJCHGOT	Hinde					Moshe	
RAJCHGOT	Zelig						and his family
RAJCHGOT	Chanah			Moshe	Hinde		
RAJCHGOT	Yitzchak						and his family
RAJCHGOT	Moshe					Hinde	
RAJCHGOT	Pesa			Moshe	Hinde		
RAJCHHOLC	Wolf						and his family
RAJCHHOLC	Meir						and his family
RAJCHHOLC	Moshe						and his family
RAJCZYK	Breine		27		Manyah		
RAJCZYK	Chanah		30			Shlomo	
RAJCZYK	Manye		62				
RAJCZYK	Shlomo		30			Chanah	
RAJCZYK			2	Shlomo	Chanah		
RICHTER	Rivkah Ikke	TAC		Yosef Leib			
RAJCHENBERG	Zisia						and his family
RAJNGEWIRC	Bezalel			Wolf			
RAJNGEWIRC	Wolf						
RAJNGEWIRC	Shmuel			Wolf			
RACHELKA	Benyamin		60				
RACHELKA	Lemel			Benyamin			
RACHELKA	Rachel			Benyamin			
RACHELKA			55			Benyamin	
RENKEL	Gutkind		40				
RAK	Beile		31				
RAK			32			Beile	
RAK					Beile		
RZEJSZOTKO	Eliyahu Leib			Yaakov Lemel	Esther Sarah		
RZEJSZOTKO	Esther	ARFA	36	Kalmen	Tovah	Yaakov	

	Sarah				Leah	Lemel	
RZEJSZOTKO	Baruch		90			Chanah	
RZEJSZOTKO	Chanah			Yosef	Tzipporah		
RZEJSZOTKO	Chanah					Baruch	
RZEJSZOTKO	Yosef		41	Meir	Malkah	Tzipporah	
RZEJSZOTKO	Yaakov Lemel		36			Esther Sarah	
RZEJSZOTKO	Yakir			Yaakov Lemel	Esther Sarah		
RZEJSZOTKO	Yisrael			Yosef	Tzipporah		
RZEJSZOTKO	Meir		63	Baruch	Chanah	Malkah	
RZEJSZOTKO	Malkah		60			Meir	
RZEJSZOTKO	Mordechai Yitzchak			Yosef	Tzipporah		
RZEJSZOTKO	Tziporah		40			Yosef	
SZWAJCER	Yitzchak						and his family
SZWAJCER	Leib					Sarah	
SZWAJCER	Sarah					Leib	
SCHULTZ	Binah			Simchah	Chayah		
SCHULTZ	Chayah		54			Simchah	
SCHULTZ	Chanah			Simchah	Chayah		
SCHULTZ	Yehudit			Simchah	Chayah		
SCHULTZ	Yitzchak			Simchah	Chayah		
SCHULTZ	Simchah		55			Chayah	
SCHULTZ	Sarah			Simchah	Chayah		
SZWARC	Leib						and his family
SZWARC	Pinchas Eliyahu		40			Rivkah	
SZWARC	Rivkah		40			Pinchas Eliyahu	
SZWARC				Pinchas Eliyahu	Rivkah		
SZUREK	Malkah		55				
SZUREK	Sarah				Malkah		
SZUREK							and his family
STEINHAUS	Pesa	SZAMPAN			Esther Rachel		and her family
SCHEIKES	Cantor Daniel		60			Sarah	
SCHEIKES	Chayah			Daniel	Sarah		

SCHEIKES	Yoska						and his family
SCHEIKES	Yaakov			Daniel	Sarah		
SCHEIKES	Yitzchak						and his family
SCHEIKES	Yisrael						and his family
SCHEIKES	Leib		40				and his family
SCHEIKES	Miriam			Daniel	Sarah		
SCHEIKES	Sarah		55			Daniel	
SZLECHTER	Gitel Leah						and her family
SCHLEIFER	Eliyahu Meir		54			Chanah	
SCHLEIFER	Chanah	BERGSON	50			Eliyahu Meir	
SZMIGA							and his family
SZAMPAN	Esther Rachel						and her family
SZAMPAN	Ben-Zion				Esther Rachel		and his family
SZAMPAN	Devorah						
SZAMPAN	Chanah Taube	SENDEROWICZ	24	Yitzchak Meir	Miriam Rachel	Reuven	
SZAMPAN	Reuven		28			Chanah Tovah	
SZAMPAN	Rachel				Devorah		
SZAMPAN	Sheike						and his family
SZAMPAN	Sarah		2	Reuven SZAMPAN	Chanah Taube		
SZAMPAN		LICHT				Ben-Zion	
SZAMPAN				Ben-Zion			
SZNIFER	Eliezer					Chanah Beile	
SZNIFER	Chanah Beile	LICHT				Eliezer	
SZNITZER	Wolf						and his family
SZNITZER	Yosef						and his family
SZNITZER	Chavah			Yitzchak Ahron	Sheine Hindel		
SZNITZER	Chanah		29			Yitzchak David	

SZNITZER	Tovah			Yitzchak David	Chanah		
SZNITZER	Yitzchak Ahron		50			Sheine Hindel	
SZNITZER	Yitzchak David		34	Yosef	Tovah Silka	Chanah	
SZNITZER	Leah Beile			Yitzchak Ahron	Sheine Hindel		
SZNITZER	Leah Beile			Yitzchak David	Chanah		
SZNITZER	Moshe			Yitzchak Ahron	Sheine Hindel		
SZNITZER	Sheine Hindel	SZNITZER	46	Yosef	Tovah Silka	Yitzchak Ahron	
SZAPIRO	Ahron					Rasha	
SZAPIRO	Rasha	SKORNIK		Yehudah Baruch	Miriam	Ahron	
SZAPIRO	Shimon						and his family
SZAPIRO	Shimshon		34			Tezyah	
SZAPIRO	Tetzyah	NAJMAN	32			Shimshon	
SZPERLING	Beile						
SREDNI	Mendel						and his family
SZARFHARC	David						and his family
SZARFHARC	Yisrael						and his family

INDEX FOR THE MAIN BODY OF THIS BOOK.
Please note that the Necrology is NOT contained in this index

A

B

C

D

E

F

G

H

I

J

K

L

N

O

P

R

S

T

U

V

W

Y

Z

www.ingramcontent.com/pod-product-compliance
Lightning Source LLC
Chambersburg PA
CBHW061832260326
41914CB00005B/970
* 9 7 8 1 9 3 9 5 6 1 2 4 4 *